BATTLES WITH THE NACHTJAGD: THE NIGHT AIR WAR OVER EUROPE 1939-1945

BATTLES WITH THE NACHTJAGD

THE NIGHT AIR WAR OVER EUROPE 1939-1945

Theo E.W. Boiten & Martin W. Bowman

Schiffer Military History
Atglen, PA

Acknowledgements
Gebhard Aders; John Aldridge; Mike Allen DFC**; Harry Andrews DFC; Theo 'Bluey' Arthurs; Frau Anneliese Autenrieth; Mrs. Dorothy Bain; Günther Bahr; Charlie 'Jock' Baird; Harry Barker; Raymond V. Base; Don Bateman; A. D. 'Don' Beatty; Jack Bennett; Alfons Borgmeier; Jack Bosomworth; Len Browning; Don Bruce; George Burton; Jim Burtt-Smith; Maurice Butt; Philip J. Camp DFM; Jack Cannon; City of Norwich Aviation Museum (CONAM); Bob Collis; Jim Coman; B. G. Cook; John Cook DFM; Dennis Cooper; Coen Cornelissen; Leslie Cromarty DFM; Tom Cushing; Hans-Peter Dabrowski; W/C S. P. Daniels; Arnold Döring; Dr. Karl Dörscheln; Richard 'Ricky' Dyson GM; J. Alan Edwards; Ronnie H. 'Squiggle' Eeles; Wolfgang Falck; David G. Fellowes; Elwyn D. Fieldson DFC; Karl Fischer; Stephen M. Fochuk; John Foreman; Vitek Formanek; Stanley Freestone; Ian Frimston; Prof. Dr. Ing. Otto H. Fries; Ken Gaulton; Jim George; Group Captain J. R. 'Benny' Goodman DFC* AFC AE; Alex H. Gould DFC; Hans Grohmann; Charles Hall; Steve Hall; Brian 'Darkie' Hallows DFC; Roland A. Hammersley DFM; Jack F. Hamilton; Eric Hammel; Trevor A. 'Happy' Hampton; Erich Handke; James Harding; Frank Harper; Leslie Hay; Maurice 'Frank' Hemming DFM; Bob Hillard; Peter C. Hinchliffe; Neville Hockaday RNZAF; Werner 'Red' Hoffmann; Ted Howes DFC; Air Cdre Peter Hughes DFC; John Anderson Hurst; Zdenek Hurt; Ab A. Jansen; Alfred Jenner; Mick Jennings MBE; Karl-Ludwig Johanssen; Wilhelm 'Wim' Johnen; Arthur 'Johnnie' Johnson; John B. Johnson; Graham B. Jones; Hans-Jürgen Jürgens; Erich Kayser; George Kelsey DFC; Les King; W/C Rollo Kingsford-Smith RAAF; Christian Kirsch; Hans Krause; Reg Lawton; J. R. Lisgo; Chas Lockyer; Günther Lomberg; Peter Loncke; George Luke; Ian McLachlan; Nigel McTeer; Brian Maidment; B. L. Eric Mallett RCAF; The Honourable Terence Mansfield; Eric Masters; Larry Melling; Bernard 'Max' Meyer DFC; Cyril Miles; Colin Moir; Frank Mouritz Friedrich Ostheimer; Maurice S. Paff; Simon Parry; Pathfinder Association; W/C David Penman DSO OBE DFC; Richard Perkins; Peter Petrick; Karl-Georg Pfeiffer; Eric Phillips; Bob Pierson; Norbert Pietrek; Vic Poppa; John Price; Frank Pringle; Ron Read DFC; Stan Reed; Ernie Reynolds; Peter Richard; Albert E. Robinson; Ernie Rodley; Heinz Rökker; S/L Geoff Rothwell DFC; Fritz Rumpelhardt; David M. Russell; Kees Rijken; Eric Sanderson; Klaus J. Scheer; Dr. Dieter Schmidt-Barbo; Karl-Heinz Schoenemann; Jerry Scutts; Johan Schuurman; G/C Jack Short; Leslie R. Sidwell; Wilhelm Simonsohn; Don L. Simpkin; Derek Smith DFC*; Leicester G. Smith; SAAF Assn; E. N. M. Sparks; Albert Spelthahn; Dr. Ing. Klaus Th. Spies; Peter Spoden; Bob Stainton; Dick Starkey; S/L Hughie Stiles; Mike 'Taff' Stimson; Ted Strange DFC; Maurice Stoneman; Ken Sweatman; Arthur R. 'Spud' Taylor; Paul Todd; Fred Tunstall DFC; Hille van Dieren; George Vantilt; Rob de Visser; Andreas Wachtel; Georg Walser; David Waters; Edwin Wheeler; H. Wilde; John Williams; H. J. Wilson; Henk Wilson; Dennis Wiltshire; S. T. 'Tom' Wingham DFC; Louis Patrick Wooldridge DFC; Cees Wind; Harry Wubs (Nieuwsblad van het Noorden); Johnny Wynne DFC; Fred Young DFM; Cal Younger.

Book design by Robert Biondi.

Library of Congress Catalog Number: 2006928271.

Printed in China.
ISBN: 0-7643-2524-8

We are always looking for people to write books on new and related subjects. If you have an idea for a book, please contact us at the address below.

Published by Schiffer Publishing Ltd.
4880 Lower Valley Road
Atglen, PA 19310
Phone: (610) 593-1777
FAX: (610) 593-2002
E-mail: Info@schifferbooks.com.
Visit our web site at: www.schifferbooks.com
Please write for a free catalog.
This book may be purchased from the publisher.
Please include $3.95 postage.
Try your bookstore first.

In Europe, Schiffer books are distributed by:
Bushwood Books
6 Marksbury Ave.
Kew Gardens, Surrey TW9 4JF
England
Phone: 44 (0)20 8392-8585
FAX: 44 (0)20 8392-9876
E-mail: info@bushwoodbooks.co.uk
www.bushwoodbooks.co.uk
Free postage in the UK. Europe: air mail at cost.
Try your bookstore first.

CONTENTS

PREFACE

Battles of the Nachtjagd traces the parallel developments in RAF night-bombing and night-fighting in the Luftwaffe, from the pioneering efforts on both sides in this new form of airwar up to the climax of the strategic bombing offensive in 1945 and the simultaneous introduction of the Me 262 jet in the German night fighter arm.

After the fall of France in May 1940, only RAF Bomber Command had the ability to carry the war to the enemy. Early attacks on Germany met with heavy losses but under the leadership of Sir Arthur Harris; Bomber Command grew into an enormous force, capable of launching 1,000-bomber raids. After the war, Harris was denied the peerage awarded to other service chiefs and the men of Bomber Command were denied a campaign medal. Theirs was the glory but in recent years Bomber Command's glorious campaign has been widely criticized in the media and the unveiling of a statue of Harris in London provoked renewed controversy. But if Bomber Command raids on German cities had not taken place in 1940 Hitler would never have diverted his legion of Luftwaffe bombers from pulverizing Britain's fighter airfields and radar sites to target London. It was a decision that cost Germany the initiative at the very time Fighter Command was exhausted and close to collapse. In time the ever-increasing number of attacks on German cities by growing numbers of "heavies" forced Hitler to withdraw hundreds of thousands of personnel, fighter aircraft and heavy guns from other fronts to defend his industrial heartland. Did the sacrifice of 55,000 British, Commonwealth and Allied airmen shorten the war? Of the 7,953 Bomber Command aircraft lost on night operations, an estimated 5,833 fell victim to Luftwaffe night fighters while *Nachtjagd* aircraft destroyed 200 American heavy bombers by day during 1943-1944.

The authors – both leading experts in their field – have traced surviving aircrew from both sides and have succeeded in matching many Bomber Command losses to German night fighter claims. Above all this book is the gripping story of the German night fighter versus bomber war over the Third Reich 1941-1945. There are contributions from scores of veteran RAF and Commonwealth aircrew and their German adversaries, which shed new light on many aspects of the giant and deadly nocturnal battle over northwestern Europe. In order to understand the emotions of the Commonwealth, RAF and German nightfighter crews the authors have carefully selected personal stories from the airmen who confronted each other in the night skies of the Third Reich, combatants in the longest and most intensive airwar campaign the world has ever witnessed. These stories were recorded during the authors, combined period of research stretching back more than thirty years of countless interviews and extensive correspondence with both allied and German aircrew and their personal operational experiences. Their compelling first-hand narratives are moving descriptions of the defining experience of a generation of airmen and describe their hopes, fears and their successes; their failures and defeats in combat and their incredible feats of airmanship. They describe their comradeship and loneliness, dedication to duty, patriotism, heroism and sacrifice and we hear their tales of survival, injury and violent, sudden or slow deaths.

The narrative is extensively illustrated with more than 400 rare and mostly unpublished photographs from the personal collections of the veterans, wartime albums, which grippingly illustrate the strategic and tactical developments in this most deadly struggle. Combined, they present a vivid picture of this savage and impersonal battle and permit the reader to reach a better understanding of the personal experiences of the tens of thousands of young men who flew, fought and often died a violent death in the fierce battle for air supremacy in the night skies of Hitler's Third Reich.

CHAPTER ONE

'NIGHT FIGHTING! IT WILL NEVER COME TO THAT!'

In the late 1930s the RAF considered that bombers like the twin-engined Hampden, Wellington, Whitley and Blenheim with machine-gun turrets and flying in close formation to maximize defensive fire power against attacking fighter aircraft were unbeatable: It was even assumed that these aircraft did not need any form of fighter escort to reach and destroy their assigned targets. Events would soon shatter this illusion but in the 1930s for anyone who wanted to fly, the RAF was considered to be the best 'Flying Club' in which to do just that. When war with Germany began in September 1939 young RAF bomber pilots were enthusiastic and confident in their aircraft and equipment. The RAF believed that modern aircraft like the twin-engined Hampden, Wellington, Whitley and Blenheims with machine-gun turrets and flying in close formation to maximise defensive firepower against attacking fighter aircraft were unbeatable. The strategy was that these aircraft did not need fighter escort to reach and destroy targets but as the Luftwaffe would discover in the Battle of Britain (and much later the Americans from 1942 onward), this was all wishful thinking. The Handley Page Hampden and the Vickers Armstrong Wellington, Armstrong Whitworth Whitley, and Bristol Blenheim, all twin engined bombers, were the mainstay of Bomber Command early in the war. The Wellington, affectionately known as the Wimpy[1], which had carried out the first RAF bombing raid of the war and suffered high losses by day had been conceived by the brilliant British scientist, Dr. Barnes Wallis using geodetic or lattice work structure. Like many of its *genre,* the Wellington was weakly armed but quite often it was this bomber's exploits, which featured in the headlines in the British press and sometimes in German papers as well. Wellington and Blenheim operations against elements of the German fleet at Brunsbüttel and Wilhelmshaven on 4 September 1939 met with stiff opposition from fighters and Flak and two Wellingtons and five Blenheims were lost. The 3 Group Wellingtons and 5 Group Hampdens kept searching for the German navy in daylight during the remainder of September 1939 but the serious losses inflicted on 29 September, when a complete formation of five 144 Squadron Hampdens were destroyed over the German Bight between Heligoland and Wangerooge Island by Bf 109s of I./ZG 26, soon convinced the Air Staff that a profound change of its daylight policy was necessary.[2] Following heavy Wellington and Blenheim losses in daylight the elderly Whitley squadrons in 4 Group were immediately employed in night leaflet dropping operations and made no apprearance in daylight at all.

When Bomber Command took the decision in May 1940 to start strategic bombing of Germany by night, there was little the Luftwaffe could do to counter these early raids. The subject of night fighting was raised at a conference of German service chiefs just before the war and according to *Kommodore* Josef Kammhuber, who was present at the conference, it was dismissed out of hand with the words, 'Night fighting! It will never come to that!' Up until May 1940 the night air defence of the *Reich* was almost entirely the province of the *Flak* arm of the Luftwaffe. No specialised night fighting arm existed though one fighter *Gruppe* (IV./(N)JG 2) was undertaking experimental *Helle Nachtjagd* (illuminated night fighting) sorties with the aid of searchlights in northern Germany and in the Rhineland. IV./(N)JG 2 flew the Bf 109D with the cockpit hood removed as a precaution against the pilots being blinded by the glare of the searchlights. On the night of 25/26 April *Ofw* Hermann Förster of the 11th *Staffel* shot down a Hampden on a minelaying operation near Sylt, the first Bomber Command aircraft to be shot down by a fighter at night.[3] The *Helle Nachtjagd* technique used in 1940 (and early 1941) was entirely dependent on weather conditions and radar-guided searchlights simply could not penetrate thick layers of cloud or industrial haze over the Ruhr and other industrial centres in the *Reich*. Kammhuber realised that *Helle Nachtjagd* was only a short-term solution and soon concentrated all his energies in developing an efficient radar-controlled air defence system.

Despite early heavy losses in daylight RAF Bomber pilots were enthusiastic and confident. Bernard 'Max' Meyer, who had been posted to 144 Squadron at RAF Hemswell in Lincolnshire at the beginning of October 1939, recalls[4]:

'144 Squadron was equipped with the fairly new Handley Page Hampden, a twin engined medium to heavy bomber which, having taken part in several daylight sorties over the North Sea searching for enemy naval units, had suffered heavy losses in engagements with enemy fighters. I was one of several replacements and a fairly junior officer with about 500 flying hours, which was average for someone with my length of service in the RAF. From the pilot's point of view perhaps the Hampden's biggest drawback was the narrow fuselage. It was impossible to have side-by-side seating in the cockpit as in other aircraft, which meant that you sat there entirely alone and once strapped in on your seat type parachute, remained there for the duration of the flight. On one flight I sat there for 9 1/2 hours and was so stiff when I got back that I had to be lifted out of the cockpit by the groundcrew. However, despite these problems and until the really heavy bombers came into service later on, the Hampden proved to be a very efficient and successful bomber much liked by its crews for its responsiveness and versatility. It was also solidly constructed and capable of taking a lot of punishment. The engines were especially reliable and economical to run. One occasion later when we were hit by *Flak* in one engine over Hanover, the other engine, working very hard, I must admit, brought us home safely.

'After the Airspeed Oxford and the Avro Anson during training the Hampden was something quite different. The greater performance of the two Bristol Pegasus XVIII engines with propellers in fine pitch at full take-off boost was quite startling. You felt a massive punch in your back as you opened up the throttles. Once off the ground with wheels and flaps up, it handled beautifully. With its two 1000-hp engines, it became a fast, powerful and highly maneuverable flying machine. The pilot's field of view was excellent. From a high seating position the outlook forward and on both beams was much better than that of most other operational aircraft at that time, a most useful characteristic particularly when low flying was to become very important for Hampden operations in the future. However, you certainly couldn't take liberties with the Hampden. As with most powerful aircraft on take-off, especially with a full bomb-load, it would, given the chance, swing viciously to starboard and if action was not taken immediately to correct the swing, you would find yourself hurtling along at right angles to your intended take-off path. Another rather more unpleasant trick of the Hampden could occur if you made a very flat turn, for example, on a bombing run up to the target. There was a tendency for the twin rudders to slam right over and lock in that position. I think it was called a stabilized yaw. Unless you took immediate corrective action, which was to push the nose down and build up a high speed, it was impossible to centralize the rudders and you would remain in a sort of flat spin until you hit the ground. If you had insufficient height in which to recover control, it was of course, usually fatal, as quite a number of Hampden Pilots found to their cost.

'It was decided that the losses suffered in daylight raids were becoming unacceptable and in future we would operate under cover of darkness. It was therefore rather a disappointment for me to be told by my Flight Commander that I would have to gain considerably more night flying experience before I could go on my first night operation over enemy territory. It was mid-April 1940 before I was considered to be sufficiently qualified to take part in operations at night. My first night operation was a minelaying sortie to the mouth of the River Elbe. You were usually detailed for several easy 'trips' to start with, until you had gained sufficient experience to undertake the more difficult ones later. Our flight to the mouth of the Elbe was fairly uneventful. We crossed the North Sea to Terschelling and then followed the Friesian Islands until we reached our target area. It was a moonlight night – we saw a few searchlights on the mainland and encountered some light *Flak* in the target area. The round trip took just on fivehours flying time.

'My next three operations were all on minelaying, in the Baltic, necessitating flights of around seven hours' duration. During this period the weather was never very good and on one occasion I was diverted on return to an airfield in Scotland because the weather in Lincolnshire was unfit for landing. Minelaying was carried out at low altitude and with great care, to ensure accurate positioning of the mine. Because the sophisticated navigational aids were not available in these early days of the war, we navigated by dead reckoning[5], and map reading in the final stages. We usually had to spend quite some time flying around in the target area to establish our correct positioning of the mines. This made us extremely vulnerable to attack from ground defences and *Flak* ships. A small parachute attached to the mine to retard its entry into the water separated on entry and floated on the top for a short time. The German navy used fast, armed boats to search for the parachutes and buoy the spot for sweeping later. In an attempt to stop the patrol boats doing this, we used to remain in the area as long as fuel permitted and shoot them up, if they appeared. I can well remember an occasion when we spotted a smallish vessel just ahead of us. It looked like one of these boats so I put the nose of the aircraft down and gave it a good long burst from my fixed forward firing gun and at the same time told my rear gunners to also have a go. However, the stream of tracer from my gun completely dazzled me and reduced my night vision to almost nil.

'Unfortunately for me, the armorers who had prepared the aircraft had not changed the ammunition to that for nighttime use, which has much less tracer in its makeup. Just as I pulled up and away from the boat I felt a distinct shudder run through our aircraft. At the same time I wished I had been less adventurous and given the vessel a wide berth because it suddenly replied to our attack in a very hostile manner with a barrage of multi pom-pom and cannon fire as we passed over it. Fortunately we were diving at high speed and quickly drew away down at sea level. We had, of course, picked on a *Flak*-ship, which the Germans used to guard likely minelaying areas. The following day my ground crew had to fit new bomb-bay doors to replace the old ones which were not only badly damaged, but, also had lengths of aerial wire imbedded in them which we must have removed from the mast of that ship.

'By now, and having successfully carried out several quite difficult minelaying operations, we as a crew were considered to be competent to attack targets on the mainland. So, on 11 May we were detailed to bomb the railway yards at Mönchengladbach in an attempt to slow up the German advance. These were really pioneering days for the RAF. Few people had much experience of flying long distances at night, sometimes in appalling weather conditions let alone against highly efficient enemy defences. To find our way, we flew by dead-reckoning navigation and by map reading if we could see the ground. The sophisticated navigational aids did not become available until much later in the war.'

P/O (later S/L) Geoff Rothwell recalls:

'My first tour of operations commenced at Newmarket in May 1940 with 99 Squadron. I had logged a grand total of about 240 hours flying time at the controls, about one hundred of these being on the Vickers Wellingtons. I was allotted as second pilot to P/O Thallon. At the time I joined the squadron the German Wehrmacht was advancing through the Low Countries and the allied armies were in retreat. The targets for our Whitley, Hampden and Wellington bombers were roads, bridges and railways by night, whilst Battles and Blenheims attacked the German armored columns and troop concentrations by day. Our attacks were very primitive as we had limited navigational aids to establish our position and had to rely on wireless fixes, pinpoints on the ground and by dropping illuminating flares and dead reckoning. We had to cope with equipment failure frequently and there were always a number of aborted sorties in the squadron. Losses were fairly light but many aircraft were damaged from light *Flak* because most of our operations were carried out at heights of 3000-5000-ft and, at times, as low as 1000-ft. Despite the difficulties morale on the squadron was high and there was always a jolly atmosphere in the Mess. However, a very sobering occasion was when, after the evacuation of the Allied Forces from Dunkirk, we were ordered to parade late at night. Our CO addressed us in the moonlight. He sent cold shivers up our spines when he announced that a German invasion was anticipated and that we were to be prepared to fly at short notice to Northern Ireland for refueling and then on to Canada from where the fight would continue. When it was apparent that there was no stopping the German army the offensive was directed against the *Fatherland* and strategic bombing of oil refineries and storage depots in the Ruhr Valley began. A favourite target was the railway marshalling yards at Hamm. Schiphol airfield was bombed on a number of occasions. Target identification was extremely difficult and it was often only the light *Flak* and searchlights in the target area that led us to our objective. Throughout the summer of 1940 attacks were made on targets in Frankfurt, Wilhelmshaven, Berlin, Kiel, Hamburg, Düsseldorf, Munich and many towns in the Ruhr Valley. The defenses, which at the outset, had been rather haphazard and not particularly effective, showed a marked improvement and our losses mounted.'[6]

1940 was a very bad year for Britain's military hopes. France fell and Italy entered the war on Germany's side. On 11/12 June 1940 Turin, a distance of 1350 miles there and back was bombed by Bomber Command. The leader of the raid wrote later:

'We were warned that over Italy fighter opposition would probably be encountered. The Italian fighters – CR.42s, it was pointed out, were biplanes, with considerable powers of maneuver and probably better suited to the task of night interception than the Me 109 or 110. We must be on the look out for them. Nothing much happened till we were over France after refueling in the Channel Islands. Then we ran into electrical storms of great severity. There was a good deal of lightning. When we emerged from these into a clear patch somewhere near Bourges the lightning continued. This time it was produced by French *Flak* through which we flew till we ran into heavy weather again and began to climb in order to get over the Alps. I got my heavily laden Whitley to 17,500 ft flying blind on my instruments but before the climb started in earnest I got a perfect 'fix of my position from Lac Léman. The town of Geneva at its western end showed bright with many lights. It was 10/10th cloud over the Alps but we knew we were crossing them because of the bumps, which the aircraft felt every time it crossed a peak. Down we went through the murk till I altered course 15 degrees to starboard so as to find the River Po. I reached it in darkness but I could make it out by the patches of cultivation along its banks, which showed a deeper shade against the prevailing black. I could not see the waters of the river. On we went till I judged we were over Turin. Then I let go a flare, which lit up the middle of the city. I turned back at once and climbed to 5000 ft. When I got to that height I loosed another flare into a cloud which began to glow and shed a soft light over the whole town including the target. I ran in, dropped two bombs, one of which burst on the Fiat building, the other in the railway sidings beside it.

'The bursting of the bombs seemed to be the signal for the enemy to switch on his searchlights. These could not find us but innumerable flashes of light, constantly renewed, appeared beneath us. It seemed as though the whole of Turin was firing at us. I have never seen anything like it before or since. But no shells could be seen bursting anywhere. We were still at 5000 ft but the air about us remained unlit by anything except our flare, though the flashes below winked at us with unabated zeal. I did my second run and hit the north end of the works. There was a large green flash, which meant that the bombs had certainly fallen on the annealing plant. I knew that, if I hit that, the flash would be a green one. Having no more bombs I dropped more flares to guide other attacking aircraft and drew off a little to watch the show. The flares lit up everything. I climbed to 10,000 ft, keeping a smart look out for the CR.42s. I did not see any and no one else did; but we did run into a heavy A/A barrage. The shell-bursts made a squeaky, gritty noise. It was only then that I realized what had happened. The Italian gunners, who had been producing all those flashes I had seen below, had evidently decided that we were flying at 10,000 ft when we bombed. As we were only at 5000, naturally we saw nothing of the bursts, which were about a mile above our heads.'

Valuable experience was gained as the result of this raid and two months later, on the night of 13/14 August 32 Whitleys, nearly all of which reached the target area, bombed objectives in the Plain of Lombardy. The Fiat aircraft factory at Turin was hit repeatedly, for by good chance a parachute flare fell on the roof, burning slowly and lighting up the target. Many fires and heavy explosions were caused, both at these works and at the Caproni works in Milan. The attack was repeated on the next night, in very unfavourable weather, by four Whitleys and a fortnight later Genoa and Alessandria were amongst the objectives bombed.

On 22 June 1940 *Hptm* Wolfgang Falck, *Kommandeur*, I./ZG 1 who had some experience with radar-directed night-fighting sorties in the Bf 110 flying from Aalborg, Denmark during April 1940, was ordered to form the basis of a *Nachtjagd*, or night fighting arm, by establishing the first night fighter *Gruppe*, I./NJG 1. Four days later Falck was appointed *Kommodore* of NJG 1 and IV./(N)JG 2 was incorporated into the first *Nachtjagd Geschwader* as III./NJG 1. From Düsseldorf airfield NJG 1's Bf 110s and Do 17Zs undertook experimental night-fighting sorties in defense of the Ruhr with the aid of one *Flak* searchlight regiment. In July the creation of a true night air defense for the Third *Reich* was dramatically accelerated when Göring ordered Kammhuber to set up of a full-scale night fighting arm. Within three months, Kammhuber's organisation was remodeled into *Fliegerkorps* XII and by the end of 1940 the infant *Nachtjagd* had matured into three searchlight batallions and five night fighter *Gruppen*.[7] *Nachtjagd*'s first official victory over the Reich was credited to *Ofw* Paul Förster of 8./NJG 1 when off Heligoland he destroyed a Whitley of 10 Squadron on 9 July.[8] F/L D.A. French-Mullen and his four-man crew, who were on a bombing operation to Kiel, survived and were taken prisoner.[9] In July 1940 *Oblt* Werner Streib, *Staffelkapitän*, 2./NJG 1 scored the first two of his 67 kills including the first 'official' victory of the nightfighter force on 19/20 July.[10] By the end of the month I./NJG 1 had destroyed six bombers in the *Helle Nachtjagd* system.[11] I./NJG 1, at this time operating from Gütersloh airfield near Münster had a fortunate spell of operations. At midnight on 1/2 October *Lt* Hans-Georg Mangelsdorf of the 2nd *Staffel* shot down a Whitley over Holland.[12] Two weeks later, on the 14/15th, the *Gruppe* claimed five *Helle Nachtjagd* kills.[13] Three of I./NJG 1's victories were credited to *Oblt* Streib, a feat which earned him the award of the *Ritterkreuz*.

Lt Ludwig Becker of 4./NJG 1 and his *Bordfunker Uffz* Josef Staub claimed *Nachtjagd*'s first ground radar-directed kill on the evening of 16 October at Oosterwolde. Flying a Dornier Do 17Z-10 equipped with the experimental 'Spanner' night-vision device,[14] they were guided onto the tail of a Wellington[15] by *Jägerleitoffizier*[16] *Lt* Hermann Diehl of the experimental *Freya* station at Nunspeet, Holland. After obtaining visual contact and without the aid of the 'Spanner', Becker shot the Wellington down with a five-second burst from a distance of 100 ft.[17]

Wellington observer Albert E. Robinson in 115 Squadron recalls that:

> 'Bombing by night presented a formidable barrier to the young crews of Bomber Command in 1940-41. If groping blindly through the curtain of darkness that had descended over Europe was to be overcome, it was crystal clear that in the initial stages an awful lot was going to depend on the crews themselves. Trial and error mostly only resulted in a high casualty rate. Unfortunately, it was with little result for so great an effort, a potpourri of calculated risk, personal skills and circumstances that favoured the more successful crews. The 'X' factor, a quality difficult to define but one that enabled them to take advantage of more than a full share of luck lifted them high above average. Whatever the mixture, a fierce determination to succeed in spite of the numerous setbacks was a common denominator and it united the crews almost without exception. With such resolution, the crews attempted to face up to their task. It was not made any easier by briefing officers who spoke at length about the necessity for precision bombing. It would not be too critical to suggest that some of these briefings were out of touch with reality. Truthful crews considered it a reasonable effort if the city itself was found, let alone a specific aiming point.
>
> 'There were many reasons for this but the principal culprit was night navigation. This was based almost entirely on the age-old theory of dead reckoning. There was no problem if all the links in the chain were known but if not, it could turn out to be a hit-or-miss affair, especially with little or no radio assistance to help with the calculations. The basic requirement for success was to establish the wind speed and direction but in order to assess these it was necessary at various times during the flight to define the position of the aircraft in relation to the ground – obtain a 'fix', as it was known to the navigator. Under variable conditions this was not always possible. The flight could be blown well off course, sometimes miles away if there were adverse winds and with it went little chance of finding out the true position of the aircraft. This in turn usually added up to wasted effort, with bombs being brought back or jettisoned in the sea.
>
> 'Inexperienced crews could end up on the slopes of a mountain or in the gray wastes of the sea. The North Sea in particular was a big enemy to Bomber Command; a heaving predator, menacing in its vastness to any crippled bomber struggling to maintain height over its darkened wilderness. The enemy coast to the hoped-for landfall in England offered little hope if a crippled bomber had to force-land and most certainly so if contact had been lost with any listening post as a result of a damaged radio. A bomber aircraft then was a lonely and desolate figure, struggling against the odds and with the chilling thought that no matter how expertly the aircraft was set down on the sea – turbulent or calm – the bomber would sink within minutes. There was the rubber dinghy, of course. It could be paddled but when exhaustion came and effort faded it would just drift along with the wind and tide, aimlessly and without hope, to a tortured end, unless providence took a hand. God knows how long this would take. Perhaps better not to have taken the dinghy at all.
>
> 'That's how it went. Such possibilities could only be accepted by crews with a philosophical shrug of the shoulders. It came with a host of other things but even so most crews were optimistic and they set their sights on completing the mandatory, magical number of 30 operations before being taken off for a rest at some training squadron. In comparison to the numbers involved, very few managed to achieve this; the average could have been as low as five missions before the Grim Reaper called the tune. Given the conditions, the chances of survival on any one operation, whether it was the first or 30th were not good. Any discerning bookmaker would rate the betting odds low. All aircrew were volunteers to a man but in saying this they needed to be. Each raid was equivalent to 'going over the top' in the 1914-18 war. However, if one were to put the clock back to the briefing room in 1940-41 and peer through the haze of cigarette smoke that hung in swirling clouds no one would have guessed it. It was more like a gathering at any sports club. We were boisterous, outgoing and extrovert but underneath this cloak there was a quiet confidence and rugged determination. Such an outlook was essential. The effort

needed to penetrate Germany, certainly with the out-dated aircraft at the crews' disposal in 1940-41, required a deep-seated motivation and a special quality.

'The Wellington was probably the best of the bunch when compared to the other bombers. A good old war-horse, it was as loyal and forgiving as the crews were to the bomber. But the fact remains that it was outdated, unable to reach much height over the target, poorly armed, had no internal heat and when carrying a full bomb load of 4000lb had a speed of less than half that of an enemy fighter. Freezing temperatures often coated surfaces with ice and frost, froze controls and radio sets and brought instant ice-burn should metal surfaces be touched without a glove. Engines were often suspect. (They invariably coughed and spluttered) and the dials on the instrument panel were constantly watched with anxious eyes, hoping that the readings would not give reasons for concern. Should one engine fail, as they often did, it was a heart-stopping moment with the certain knowledge that the Wellington would not be able to maintain height over a sustainable period. Its flying range would then be determined by irreversible factors such as the state of the aircraft, height at the time, angle and speed of descent and the skill of the pilot to nurse the aircraft along. They were always apprehensive lest the extra workload would cause the remaining engine to overheat – not the least of the problems was the possibility that it too could fail.

'If all this sounds gloomy, then add for good measure the fact that from take-off to return the Wellington would be flying in isolation. In many respects the raid would be one of individual effort and self-planning by the crews. Often the route to the target would be varied by crew preference. They normally took into account the known *Flak* areas but defenses could alter their tactics or geographical position, so even the most carefully thought-out plans could go astray and bring the sting of the serpent at an unexpected moment. Strict radio silence did not help but this was essential because of the enemy's rapidly increasing radar detection. To break this silence was to invite trouble, the equivalent to sending a telegram to the Luftwaffe notifying them of intent!

'But all these shortcomings were shrugged off with an unflagging optimism. Metaphorically speaking we were all in the same boat and in any case anything bad happened to the other fellow – or at least so said the mind's defense mechanism. The more missions that were flown, the easier it became to believe this. It could also induce a state of mind dubbed by the crews as '*Flak* happy'. This could loosely be interpreted as over-confidence, a mistake for which many usually paid dearly, joining the list of doomed aircraft. These unfortunate souls just took off and literally vanished, never to be seen again -just like a conjuror's rabbit. The toll under this category became harder to stomach as the casualty list mounted.'[18]

On 17 September 1940 F/Sgt Edwin Wheeler, WOP-AG in the crew of F/L Harry 'Rocky' de Belleroche in 214 Squadron, learned that they would be making their first 'Wimpy' operation that night. Having made a last flight in the Fairey Battle on 25 August, just as far as Stradishall in Suffolk to join 214 Squadron in 3 Group for a conversion course to Wellington Ics, cross-country exercises were the order of the day for the next two weeks. Not having flown in a Wimpy at night the brief to fly in a Wellington[19], take off at 2340 hrs and attack invasion barge concentrations at Ostend came as a surprise. Wheeler recalls:

> 'After the discomfort of flying in Fairey Battles the 'Wimpy' was luxury indeed. I had a reasonable seat and warmth to operate the TR1154/55 radio receiver/ transmitter. The security of having two pilots and armament at front and rear and armor plate behind my seat gave me much more confidence than I had felt before. Ginger Thomas, the observer had the luxury of a seat and table to consult his maps and at last his log was glycol-free! We reached the target and sighted the rows of barges but Rocky must have had a lapse of memory as he put the Wimpy into a dive – must have thought he was still in Battles. The reaction from the crew was immediate! 'What the bloody hell!' was yelled from each crew position. It is a wonder that the wings were not torn off – such was the angle of dive! However, we survived and there were fewer barges when we left. The operation was repeated on the nights of 23/24 and 24/25 September against Calais and Le Havre with great success. P/O Paul Carlyon, the second pilot, was proving to be a pilot of great ability and quickly gained the confidence of the crew. It was obvious that he would receive captaincy of his own aircraft in the very near future. Paul was a genial giant of a man and he had actually gone the full distance; ten rounds with that great American Heavyweight Boxing Champion Jack Sharkey. With Rocky and Paul, we considered we had the best two pilots in the Squadron.'

While Rocky de Belleroche and his crew were inexperienced others in RAF Bomber Command like P/O David Penman, pilot of a 44 Squadron Hampden at Waddington had peacetime experience to call upon. He recalls:

'I was fortunate to have gained experience of the Hampden before the war started, including flights of up to six hours and as far as Bordeaux as well as a good deal of low and high level bombing with practice bombs. However, weather forecasts were far from accurate and on many occasions very badly out. On one occasion after a weather briefing giving good weather over the Channel we flew into severe storms and it was all I could do to keep the aircraft from turning upside down. When I questioned the forecaster back at Waddington he said that the Station Commander had rubbed out certain lines on the weather chart before the briefing as he thought it would be best if the aircrew were not worried about bad weather! Nevertheless there were times when the forecasts were well out and one of them was on my first trip to Berlin, on 24/25 September carrying 4 500lb bombs. We got there more quickly than expected and the bombs were dropped on B56, an area of Berlin. Apart from heavy gunfire over Berlin and searchlights we had little opposition. However on heading home we found we were not making good progress and then realized that a very strong tail wind had helped us reach Berlin and now as a head wind was cutting our ground speed for home. We had no warning of strong winds against us on return from Berlin that night. I did my best to control the fuel consumption and when well out over the North Sea we threw out everything we could, including the machine guns and ammunition. Reducing height to get below the strongest winds saved us from landing in the sea. 'We were unable to make radio contact but our selected course heading was good and with the dawn breaking we crossed the English coast at Cromer with engines spluttering from lack of fuel. We crept over the coast only to find all possible landing areas spiked with long poles against the threat of invasion. After nine hours 20 minutes in the air I had no option but to do my best with a small, unspiked area. We touched down alright but with brakes locking the wheels skidded into a mound at the end of the area and bounced over it breaking one leg of the undercarriage before coming to rest a bit lopsided but otherwise intact. The aircraft was not badly damaged and was soon flying again.'[20]

Sgt Alf Jenner, a Wellington WOP-AG fresh from OTU arrived at the famous horseracing town of Newmarket. His war began on 16 November when he flew with Sgt Fletcher's crew and flew a 6 hour 10 minute round trip to bomb Mannheim 'in retribution for the destruction of Coventry a month before'. He recalls:

'Incendiary bombs were exploding in 99 Squadron's sleeping quarters when I arrived on a cold, foggy November evening. They were going off in the open fireplace of the room under the grandstand on Newmarket Racecourse, which then served as NCO aircrew billets. Fortunately, the bombs were British incendiaries, or pieces of them, which bored airmen were throwing into the fire to enliven their lives after the previous night's raid on Gelsenkirchen. The talk was all of earlier raids, old comrades on other stations and those who had already 'gone for a Burton' (killed).'I soon found out that every other aspect of life on an operational squadron was different from that at disciplined training establishments. You were not for instance expected to parade at 6 am or to worry about kit inspections, nor even to be particular about dress unless you were in Newmarket where Army Police never could understand the camaraderie of the air. You were expected to be meticulous in the performance of the job you had been trained to do and when in the air to obey commands without question. Discipline was vital we soon discovered, not the least because of the primitive conditions in which we had to live and fight. Newmarket is a racecourse, not a sophisticated permanent station like other squadrons enjoyed. Our mess was just another room under the grandstand. Our ablutions were a makeshift building outside. Our armory, the erstwhile harness room. Our aircraft were dispersed all over the racecourse, wherever there were trees to provide cover.

'Casualties were light for my first two months at Newmarket. Then it began, first with a loud bang while we were at lunch one day. We rushed outside and there at the racecourse winning post was the twisted remains of a Wellington. All inside were dead, including a young pilot who only the night before had been proudly displaying the small revolver given to him by his father 'in case he ever needed it in an emergency'. Worst of all was the loss of the so-called Broughton bomber, bought by the good citizens of the English town of that name. We knew every member in the crew of that machine and were therefore devastated when it crashed on take-off at the end of the runway and burst into flames. There were only two survivors, badly injured. The others burned to death as we watched helplessly. The rest of us then had to take off over the still burning funeral pyre of our comrades.'

Nachtjagd's final kills over the Continent during 1940 went to 4./NJG 1[21]: At least 19 Bomber Command aircraft were destroyed July-December 1940 in the 'Kammhuber Line', as the continuous belt of searchlights and radar positions between Schleswig-Holstein and northern France was christened by the

British bomber crews. About 30 bombers were brought down by *Flak* during the same period. Apart from organising an effective short-range defensive *Nachtjagd*, Kammhuber also appreciated the value and effectiveness of long range night intruding (*Fernachtjagd*) over Britain but the intruder force was never raised beyond one single *Gruppe* (I./NJG 2) which operated the Ju 88C-6 and Do 17 from Gilze-Rijen in the Netherlands. It never exceeded 21 aircraft but despite this and severe operational losses (21 aircraft alone during 1940) *Fernachtjagd* made a promising start. The *Gruppe*'s first intruder victories were two Wellingtons destroyed by *Fw*'s Otto Wiese 100 km west of Texel and Georg Schramm over the North Sea on the night of 22/23 July and by December claims for another 16 bombers followed. By October 1941 the handful of crews in I./NJG 2 had claimed more aircraft destroyed than all other *Nachtjagd* units combined but Hitler personally put a stop to these highly efficient intruder operations. He told Kammhuber:

> 'If the long-range night-fighting really had results, the British would have copied it a long time ago, as they imitate anything good that I do.' 'And' he added, 'The German citizen, whose house has been destroyed by a British bomber, would prefer it if the British aircraft were shot down by a German night-fighter to crash next to his burning house.'

This decision allowed Bomber Command (and later the 8th AF) to build up and launch a crushing strategic bombing offensive against Germany virtually undisturbed over the British Isles and it undoubtedly was a decisive factor in the outcome of the war. Victory claims submitted by night-fighter crews in the *Reichsverteidigung* (Air Defense of Germany), coupled by the long-range intruder operations over the UK and the North Sea grew steadily. During January 1941 eight bombers were destroyed by *Nachtjagd*.[22]

F/Sgt Edwin Wheeler in 214 Squadron meanwhile, was once again re-united with Paul Carlyon with Freddy Savage as 'second dickey' on 7 January. Wheeler, delighted with this move, recalls:

> 'Two nights later on 9/10 January in Wellington IC R1042 we recommenced operations, this time against Rotterdam, a return flight of 3 hrs 15 minutes. An uneventful trip, during which Paul Carlyon gained the confidence of the crew by his unflappable attitude. His ability was proven a week later when on 15/16 January we set off to attack naval installations at Wilhelmshaven and found ourselves in cu-nim cloud conditions with huge formations of ice building up on the wings forcing us to descend rapidly. It was not unexpected when we were compelled to abandon the mission and return to base. Of the 96 aircraft operating that night, only one was lost. The heating system in our aircraft failed and the cold was intense and numbing. We were to learn from later missions that the heater system was likely only to work to the extremes. I.e. nothing at all, giving freezing conditions or the other extreme – baking almost to melting point! I don't know which of these extremes I preferred. Weather conditions precluded our flying operationally again until 10/11 February when in *C for Charlie* we made our longest flight yet, to Hanover.'

Sir Richard Peirse committed a total of 222 aircraft to oil targets in Hanover on 10/11 February, which fell during the February new moon. The previous highest Bomber Command sortie rate was 135, to Gelsenkirchen in the January 1941 moon period. The bulk of the Hanover force was made up once again of Wellingtons, of which 112 took part.[23] Sgt pilot Bill Garrioch and his crew of 15 Squadron in 3 Group took off from RAF Wyton near Huntingdon in Wellington IC T2702 *H-Harry* for their 16th operation of the war as he recalls:

> 'The briefing officer announced the target, the route in and out and the bomb load – 4000lb made up of seven 500lb bombs and the balance in incendiaries. The Met Office forecast clear skies, strong westerly winds, a full moon and very cold. The CO, G/C Forster said that this was to be the biggest show of the war to date, wished us all the usual good luck and told us to beware of moving stars (night fighters)! This great man, a First World War pilot, still wore a steel brace on his back caused by spinal injuries received in a crash. Even so, he flew with us occasionally. Take-off was timed for 1730 hours and the flight duration expected to be about seven hours. Then followed the usual pre-flight planning between pilot, navigator and crews. We then went to the mess for our tea of bacon and eggs, back to our quarters to change into warmer clothing and of course to empty our pockets. The ritual of this act always gave me a momentary feeling of apprehension until I put some small change back into my pocket in case we had to land away from base on return. The funny thing is I had only half a crown in small change, which I put into my pocket, that being the only article carried on my person.
>
> 'We boarded the Bedford crew bus for the six-mile journey to Alconbury our satellite airfield. Generally during these bus journeys there was the usual chatter, pocket chess or cards but on this occasion everyone seemed quiet and preoccupied with their thoughts, so

much so that our navigator Sgt Bob Beioley remarked on it. Bob and Sgt G. 'Taffy' Rearden, WOP/AG had completed 12 operations with me on Blenheims prior to converting to the 'Wimpy'). Prior to air test in the morning Taffy expressed the wish to be front gunner that night as a change from being cooped up inside the cabin. I agreed, as WOp/AG Sgt George Hedge RNZAF was also a fully qualified WOp/AG. Soon we arrived at our dispersal. I signed the Form 700 and as I climbed the ladder into the aircraft Chiefy Wright said to me, 'If you break this one, don't bring it back!' (*H-Harry* was F/L Morris's aircraft but my *D-Dog* was being repaired after I had accidentally hit my wingtip on the control caravan during a previous take-off). I laughed and said that I would be a good boy and nurse his precious 'Wimpy'. I glanced at my watch and at the other aircraft around the dispersal area.

'Time to start up. Fuel on, first port and the starboard engines coughed, burst into life, and warmed up at 1000 rpm. Soon we ran each engine up to take-off rpm (2650), tested the magnetos, oil pressure and temperature and cylinder head temperature and checked and set the gyro, cooling gills, flaps, etc. All the crew reported ready. The time was now 1725 hours. I gave the signal and with a final wave to our much-appreciated ground crew, we moved out towards our take-off position near the end of the runway. We were No.2 to go. At precisely 1730 hours No.1 started his take-off run and as he reached the end of the runway I lined up and got my green light from the caravan. Brakes off, I opened the throttle slowly to maximum power as we started rolling. As we gathered speed the noise was deafening and seemed to reach a crescendo that vibrated throughout the loaded aircraft. I kept the nose down until the last bit of the all-too-short runway loomed up, then, pulling up; she lifted clear, a light kiss on the concrete and off. Wheels up and nose kept down to increase flying speed. I throttled back to climbing rpm to reach operating height and the engine noise now changed to a welcome hum. All was well.

'Bob gave me the course, which I confirmed from my kneepad. As the snow-covered countryside receded far below in the darkness, Sgt Bill Jordan, the 2nd pilot who was on his second trip with me for familiarization, flew the aircraft and the gunners entered their turrets while I visited each member of the crew to ensure that all was in order. Soon we reached the coast at Orfordness and levelled off at 11,000 ft. The navigator and the wireless operator were at their stations and the lighting was very subdued, creating an eerie yet efficient atmosphere tinged with the smell of dope and fuel, amid the roar of the smooth-sounding Pegasus engines. When we were over the sea Taffy and Sgt Jock Hall, rear gunner, a Scotsman with many trips in Coastal Command, test-fired their guns. From now on we were on the alert for night fighters. It was cold and clear. The patches of white cumulus would make us an easily identified target seen from above. I took over before we reached the Dutch coast, which we crossed at 1850 hours – another 213 miles and 65 minutes to the target. We had a very strong tail wind and ground speed was nearly 200mph. Bob got a pinpoint. We were almost dead on track – a slight course alteration and all was well. We were lucky so far.

'It was unbelievably quiet. We flew towards the target and still there was no *flak*. We were very much alert but it was the easiest run-in so far and the ground was easily identifiable. Only five minutes to the target. Then we saw it. Bob was a good navigator – we were almost spot on. On the eastern horizon the rising moon assisted target identification. With bomb doors opened and bombs fused Bob went down to the bombsights. He saw the target nestled in the crook of the 'Y'-section of a big road junction. We had a following wind so I throttled back a little and kept the aircraft steady. Right a little ... I did not see any activity at all, not even a little *flak*. The first Wimpy's bombs burst. Then suddenly there was a series of flashes close to Gilmore's aircraft. Bob called, 'Left ... left ... left ... a bit more ... steady now ... steady.' *Flak* now curled lazily up towards us, then there was heavy ack-ack to our left. It was accurate for height but was not near us. Must be the other aircraft in trouble. Bob called 'Bombs gone!' and I immediately turned steeply to port. Jock in the rear turret watched our bombs burst. There were only six flashes. Where was the seventh? Gilmore's aircraft started a fire and our incendiaries were well alight. Ack-Ack was almost non-existent with us but as we flew away we saw other aircraft getting a hot reception and the sky was full of *flak*. All this time the fires seemed to grow in intensity – Hanover was visible 40 miles away. The moon was up and it was like daylight. We watched for enemy fighters but all was quiet and we could not even see other aircraft.

'Against a strong head wind our ground speed was now only 85 knots; it was going to be a long haul home. Large white cumulus clouds were building up below. As we crossed the eastern coast of the Zuider Zee at Kempen, Jock suddenly called out, 'Fighter below and behind!' I put the engines to cruising revs and steep turned to starboard to face him. As I turned I saw a Me 110, which was turning to meet me. I turned violently to port to avoid him. Jock gave him a long burst but he still attacked, hitting the aircraft in the fuselage and port engine. I put the flaps down and soon the shooting stopped. He had overshot.

'I heard the cannon fire hit the aircraft somewhere behind me. Jock said that he had been hit. Could we get him out of the turret? The port engine was on fire. I turned off the fuel and full throttle. Bob called, 'Are we on fire?' Bob's sudden announcement on the intercom must have paralyzed my senses if only for a fleeting instant because as I was looking through the cockpit window, superimposed in space, just outside the windscreen was a very clear picture of my grandfather and a great uncle looking directly at me. It was so clear that I even recognized my uncle's old tweed jacket! Then it was gone and I was back to reality. It frightened me because these two much-loved relatives had been dead for about seven years. Much later George told me that cannon shells came through the fuselage and exploded in his radio equipment. How he and Bob were not hit I'll never know. I was saved by the armor plate behind my head. At that moment I knew we had to survive and I seemed to find added strength and courage to risk anything that would bring us out of this alive. I looked back and the fuselage was full of smoke. I could not see anyone. Perhaps a flare was burning. Taffy moaned faintly saying, 'Get me out' and I saw the fighter turn to port over our port wingtip. Bill Jordan went forward to open the escape hatch and to get Taffy out of the turret. I told the crew to prepare to bale out and raised the flaps.

'We were diving now. The fighter came in again and once more I put the flaps down and the aircraft yawed violently to port while I throttled back and side slipped to almost stalling speed. Cannon and machine-gun tracer went just over the top of us but miraculously we were not hit. This time, as the fighter went over the top of us I raised the flaps and control was easier. I think only the starboard flap worked. I told Taffy to shoot the fighter down, position 10 o'clock. He did not answer. Bill Jordan tried desperately to operate the turret door release and get him out. George Hedge was standing beside me ready to help when Bill opened the floor escape hatch. Bob and Jock were still back in the smoke-filled fuselage. Were they alive? I did not know. I decided that unless we baled out or landed quickly we would all die. We were blazing very badly now. I signalled to George not to jump as I had not given the order and I dived for the ground in the hope that a crash landing might save some of us. The aircraft persisted in turning to port. We were diving very steeply and fast, over 300 knots. Through the cockpit window I saw the port engine and that the inner wing was now on fire. Off all fuel and full throttle starboard engine. The frozen expanse of the Zuider Zee was hurtling towards us. I tried to level off but the elevators were sluggish and we hit the ice slightly nose down and skidded for what seemed to be miles. Then, suddenly, she broke through the ice and the nose filled up with water and ice through the open escape hatch. Then the aircraft stopped. We must have crashed at about 2230.'[24]

By now Sgt Alf Jenner, Wellington WOP-AG had flown nine operations in 99 Squadron and was still alive to tell the tale:

'By early 1941 the war at sea was taking a disastrous toll of our shipping lifeline across the Atlantic so we were not exactly living like fighting cocks. Flying supper before a raid, for instance, could be as frugal as beans on toast. Fried eggs seemed to be reserved for the cooks. On 24 February 99 Squadron were briefed to attack the *Von Hipper* in Brest Harbour. Brest was very clear. From about two miles away I could see two ships when the Sgt Pilot ordered, 'Bomb bay doors open'. The bomb aimer, surprised, said, 'But we're too far away'. We dropped them anyway. Our pilot, who was only one short of his tour, was determined to survive. It was the only case of 'sugaring' I recall during my operations. On 14/15 March [when 101 aircraft were dispatched to Gelsenkirchen] the raid ended with me firing 1000 rounds from my twin Browning machine guns at targets on the former Dutch airfield at Haamstede. I was flying front gunner in a Wellington captained by Sgt Kiteley, a tough Australian who was determined not to waste any opportunity of hitting the Germans hard. As was often the case in those days, we could not find Gelsenkirchen, shrouded as it was in industrial haze but as we were flying back to England Kiteley noticed German aircraft practicing night flying from Haamstede. He first bombed the airfield at 0200 hrs and then ordered his gunners to fire at any lighted target as he dived the aircraft across the drome at less than 1000 ft. So, the Germans were on the receiving end of eight 250-lb bombs and at least 2000 rounds of ammunition that night. Shooting up Haamstede was my most exhilarating episode of the war because for the first time I could actually see the enemy. As we roared down I saw the German trainees inside the cabin and could imagine their moment of terror. As we came out of the dive we shot off unharmed across the one hundred miles of the North Sea, excited and eager to get back to Newmarket to tell our story.

'Soon after we were moved to Waterbeach, a brand-new, purpose built station with concrete runways, a few miles away. In mid-March 1941 Britain could not have been more obviously losing the war, yet when we were briefed for the move we were told the War Cabinet had decided that we must prepare to go on to mobile offensive after we had invaded the Continent! This meant developing the ability to move lock, stock and barrel to a new location and then to operate against the enemy. To our surprise we did in fact succeed in operating that night and to make the discovery that the village cemetery was the last thing to be seen as we took off and the first when we came in to land, sometimes in need of the gravedigger.'

On 12/13 March F/Sgt Edwin Wheeler in 214 Squadron flew his next op, to the Blohm und Voss U-boat yards in Hamburg. The force of 88 aircraft included Avro Manchesters and Handley Page Halifaxes for the first time on a German territorial target.[25] Two nights later it was the turn of Gelsenkirchen to be attacked by 101 aircraft of which 100 returned safely. In each of these raids on German territory the anti-aircraft and searchlight defenses were superb and caused much consternation among the aircrews – incredulous of their accuracy – and no doubt were responsible for many bombs being scattered.

On 27/28 March 38 Wellingtons and a Short Stirling I set out to attack Cologne and 39 aircraft[26] set out for Düsseldorf. One of the Manchesters[27] of 207 Squadron at Waddington was piloted by F/L Johnnie A. Siebert RAAF with Sergeants Robson, second pilot, George Fominson, navigator/bomb aimer/front gunner, J.A. 'Jim' Taylor, 1st W/Op, McDougal, 2nd WOpAG in the mid-upper-turret and Peter Gurnell, rear gunner. The crew had recently recommenced operations following a tour with 44 Squadron on Hampdens and had already visited Cologne, Brest, Lorient and La Rochelle. G/C J.N. Boothman the station CO saw the crews off at around 1930 hrs.[28] His parting words, as the crews climbed into the lorry, which took them to their dispersed aircraft, were to the navigator, who was wryly advised to be sure to "pick out a nice, fat maternity hospital" in Düsseldorf as his aiming-point. This was a sarcastic jibe at 'Lord Haw Haw' who was claiming in propaganda broadcasts at that time that the RAF only bombed hospitals and non-military targets. Their route took them over Holland again. In Eindhoven, which was situated on the bombers' route to and from the Ruhr. Kees Rijken, who was 12 when the Germans attacked his country and thus about 14 when the air war really started was an avid watcher:

'Almost every day and night the allied bombers came over Eindhoven, Most nights my father and I stood in the garden, watching, listening and sometimes sheltering from the shell splinters of the German ack ack with a pan on our heads. When the ack ack stopped we knew that the German fighters were airborne. From our house we could see the sky in the direction of Germany start to light up and eventually turn red. When we were standing in the garden my father had the habit of signalling the *V for Victory* sign to the overflying aircraft with his pocket lantern. The impact of the great numbers of bombs that were dropped upon targets in the Ruhr was so great that sometimes the doors in our house started clattering.'

Düsseldorf was bombed at around 2230 hrs in two approaches, dropping eight bombs of 500 lbs on each run over the target area. Very intense *Flak* was encountered and one shell burst beneath L7303 and buffeted the starboard wing up in the air. Level flight was resumed and as they set course for England the crew speculated as to whether they had experienced a near miss or whether any damage had occurred on the starboard side. Approaching the searchlight belt on the Dutch border the *Flak* died down and fighter attacks were expected. At this moment the starboard engine began to smoke, lost power and had to be stopped. Immediately the Manchester began to lose height and the port engine started to lose power too. The notorious Vulture engines were proving inadequate to the task. Johnnie Siebert called that he couldn't hold them up any longer and the aircraft fell into a sideslip to port, nose down but still under some semblance of control. Taylor in the wireless operator's position slammed the switch of his W/T set over to transmit and without waiting for the 15 seconds necessary for the set to warm up began transmitting their position to base. As he did this he suddenly noticed tracer passing on their port side. The Manchester had been intercepted by a Bf 110 nightfighter piloted by *Ofw* Gerhard Herzog of 2/NJG 1. The time was 2330 hrs.[29]

Taylor was temporarily cut off from the intercom as he transmitted and missed the captain's first order to abandon the aircraft. The starboard engine had by now caught fire and a hydraulic failure was experienced in the aircraft. Neither of these were unusual experiences in Manchesters at this time and it is not absolute certain that Fenske's fire actually hit the crippled Manchester. Taylor was then slapped firmly on the shoulder as the second WOP-AG, Sgt McDougal, hastened forward to the escape hatch beneath the nose, struggling into his parachute as he went. Taylor slipped the clip over his Morse key to clamp it on 'transmit', ripped out his intercom lead and oxygen tube and followed McDougal. By this time the aircraft was sideslipping viciously, diving steeply and one engine was racing. The hydraulic failure had severed power to the rear turret and the main undercarriage had flopped down. As Taylor dived through the hatch Pete Curnell, the rear gunner, who had been unable to rotate his turret by hand, closely followed him. The starboard main wheel narrowly missed Taylor and Curnell as the aircraft sideslipped over them. They were the last crewmembers out alive. It is likely that Siebert escaped the same way but was hit by the main wheel. The Australian's body was located next day some distance from the wreckage of his aircraft in a depression, which testified to the force of the impact. His parachute had not fully opened and it was surmised that he might have been stunned as he left the aircraft or did not get out soon enough.

Herzog had attacked the Manchester from below and as he broke away he observed the parachutes of the five remaining aircrew in the glow of the searchlights. The aircraft dived away beneath them, an engine still racing and crashed on a farmhouse at Bakel, northeast of Helmond, near Eindhoven, killing some cows. None of the family of nine was killed or injured. Herzog then dropped a flare, which burst beneath the descending airmen. In its glow they could see that they were falling into an area of open water. Taylor and Curnell were feverishly blowing up their Mae Wests when they splashed down into four inches of water overlying a further two feet of mud. Taylor sprained an ankle in the landing and after disposing of his 'chute waded for about an hour before reaching firm ground and discovering a pub in the village. He was given first aid and fed, before being sent on his way with the 'name' of a contact in the underground movement in Eindhoven. Early next morning he was spotted and arrested by a German patrol who took him to the airfield of Eindhoven nearby, where he was reunited with the survivors of his own crew and that of one of the Wellingtons shot down. By a strange coincidence one of the two pigeons carried in L7303 arrived back in its loft in the early hours of 28 March in the very street in Lincoln, where Taylor's' girlfriend of the time, later his wife, then lived. How the pigeon managed to escape may never be known.

At the airfield the surviving RAF crewmembers met *Ofw* Gerhard Herzog, who described to them his combat with their 'Wellington'. Many glances were exchanged among the crew, as they knew that no Manchester had previously fallen in occupied territory. Following this meeting Taylor and Curnell had the tragic task of identifying the body of their pilot, brought in by the Germans and were later kept in solitary confinement, deprived of cigarettes and interrogated for almost three days. The Germans must by then have inspected the wreckage of the aircraft and in the absence of any of the distinctive geodetic structure must have suspected that they had not shot down another Wellington.

Kees Rijken concludes:

> On 29 *March* 1941 a staff member of the *Ortskommandantur* asked my father to see that a grave be dug in the '*Ehrenfriedhof*' (military part) of the municipal cemetery. A RAF flight lieutenant would be buried at 1500 hrs. The German official showed my father the identity-disc of the fallen airman, who appeared to be John Siebert RAAF and RC, No.36155. At the town hall the officials did not know what the second 'A' in RAAF meant but the letters 'RC' were understood. Though the Germans had forbidden any public gathering the rumour that an 'English' airman would be buried that afternoon had spread quickly and thousands of inhabitants assembled around the cemetery. A German chaplain, a military band, a firing squad and a Roman Catholic Dutch priest were present. Luftwaffe personnel carried the coffin, covered with the British flag, to the grave. The German military band played *'Ich hatte einen Kameradan'* ('I had a comrade') and a salute of honor was fired. After the funeral the Dutch people crowded round the grave and clearly showed their sympathy with the fallen airman and their antipathy to the Germans by wearing red, white and blue or orange knots. Many flowers were laid on John Siebert's grave.'

On 30/31 March 109 aircraft including 50 Wellingtons were ordered to attack the two German battle cruisers, *Scharnhorst* and *Gneisenau* – nicknamed 'Salmon & Glukstein' (a famous London department store) lying in dock at Brest on the French coast. WOP-AG F/Sgt Edwin Wheeler flew his 14th operation in one of six 214 Squadron Wellingtons and received a close shave:

> 'Intense *Flak* and searchlights were encountered in clear conditions but the attack was pressed home. When we returned to base a 'red' warning was on with a suspected enemy intruder in the circuit and once again we were circling the 'drome awaiting clearance. Sgt Vic Coleman attempted to land and was attacked by cannon and machine gun fire and sustained damage to a landing wheel and petrol tank. He promptly opened up the taps and weaving violently to ward off further attack, he diverted to Waddington and landed satisfactorily. We too went to Waddington, not wishing to risk being shot down over our own base.'

Wheeler flew his next operation on 8/9 April when Bomber Command returned to Rotterdam to attack oil storage tanks:

> 'Only five of our squadron aircraft were involved. One of these, captained by F/L Frank took a heavy *Flak* battering over the target, lost all of his hydraulics but got back safely to base with bomb doors still open, no undercarriage or flaps but to our delight he made a safe belly landing. Boy, did that crew beat the record in evacuating the wreck! We had for the first time Sgt Sam

Huggett as our second pilot. Sam was such a shy reserved person, not reading to all our usual crew banter but he was a good pilot.'

Meanwhile, some Wellington crews in 99 Squadron were having mixed emotions. One of the pilots, Sgt Eric Masters, was becoming desperate to get the first op 'under his belt, to discover for himself whether he would make it – to find out just how scared he would be:

'Whilst I knew I had a super crew, I also knew they would be watching me very closely to see if I had any of the faults of their previous skipper. Finally, the day arrived and we set off to bomb Cologne. I was very nervous, not at the prospect of enemy action but having S/L Stanley Black, the CO along as my second pilot! It was in fact quite enjoyable and the ack-ack fire was nothing more than a nuisance. At times the Germans seemed keen on playing possum rather than give away the locality of a town by defending it too vigorously. One felt sorry for the crew of the other aircraft, coned in ten searchlights, weaving this way and that, trying to get away but we were glad they were taking the attention of the enemy. My landing back at Newmarket was my one 'black'. I dropped the Wimpy on the deck from about 25ft instead of the normal 5-10ft and she bounced quite violently. I had to give her quick burst on the throttles to keep her flying and let down again more gently. Black suggested that it was because I had been used to concrete runways which reflected what little light there was and enabled one to judge 'hold-off' more accurately. Grass was comparatively non-reflective and one had to judge height entirely by the flares. I was feeling rather miserable about it myself. However, no harm was done. I did my second trip a night later, with the CO coming along, to Cologne again.'

Sgt Alf Jenner meanwhile, was crewed up with S/L David Torrens, a new flight commander who had flown fighters in the Battle of Britain. 'As he was new to Bomber Command it was decided to give him the most experienced crew. I was by now something of a veteran with 12 ops and I became Torrens' front gunner. First WOP was Arthur Smith, a splendid wireless operator who had served in the pre-war RAF in Iraq. The second pilot was Eric Berry, who came from a well-off Yorkshire family and who had flown private aircraft before the war. His wartime training had been short, converting straight from a Tiger Moth to a Wellington. Although he had only flown two or three ops he was well thought of and was about to skipper his own crew. Our rear gunner was P/O Palmer and our observer, F/O Goodwyn, was from Ipswich:

'At Waterbeach we played a guessing game. If there was a 'breeze' that an op was on that night we would watch the petrol bowsers refuelling the Wimpys and note the number of gallons. If it was about 400 gallons that meant a trip to the Ruhr; if it was over 650, it must mean Berlin! Everyone was worried but did not show it. We had things to do to pass the rest of the afternoon. The wireless had to be checked and guns cleaned. At five o'clock on the afternoon of 9 April we entered the briefing room and sat down.[30] At the end of the room was a large map, covered with a curtain. The Briefing Officer dramatically pulled the curtain aside and we were startled to see a red ribbon that seemed to go on forever! It was Berlin, then the longest trip in the RAF repertoire. The RAF hadn't been to the Big City since the previous September. We all thought, 'Jesus Christ! Why me?' The trip would take the clumsy, overladen Wellington nearly five hours just to get there and each machine followed the other at intervals of about five minutes. The theory presumably was that the German civilians would be scared out of their wits by the thought that the RAF had unlimited supplies of heavy bombers. In fact there were 90 aircraft from several stations that night.

'After briefing finished we ate our flying supper in the mess. It was rather poor fare, usually corned beef and chips, bread pudding and tea. Everyone was in a high state of nervousness and excited hysteria, although no one showed any sign of despondency. We were quite well trained and highly motivated. It was really dark, cold and clear. A bomber's-moon shone overhead. I climbed into the astrodome area of *M for Mother* and stowed my parachute. Our pilots wore theirs in flight. As we taxied out and lined up on the new tarmac runway I gripped the astrodome hatch clips, in case I needed to get out quickly, as I always did. We were away first. Torrens thundered down the runway (our bomb load was small because of the need for extra fuel). With flaps full on we climbed slowly into the sky above Waterbeach. I climbed into the front turret immediately (enemy fighters might already be about). Grinding away slowly we headed for Southwold, our point of departure.

'Nearing the coast of Holland I exclaimed, 'Enemy coast ahead!' As usual on any night raid, the first sign of enemy activity as our Wellington crossed the Dutch coast was a burst of *Flak* from the ground, fired it seemed with the intention of letting the RAF know that the defenders were alert. There were a few shots all was quiet again. The captain talked quietly to us, telling us to keep our eyes peeled. There followed a nerve-racking three hours during which very little anti-aircraft fire was encountered.

Instead, as the lone bomber edged its way towards Berlin at about 120 mph, it was passed in silence from one searchlight to the next until we could see the multitude of colored *Flak* bursts over Berlin. We had been told that there were 1000 guns at Berlin. Field Marshal Göring had only recently announced that the RAF would never get through to Berlin. Because a few had, he was determined to claw down every one in future. No land warfare was going on at that time. (The French had been defeated and the Russians were still nominally their allies). So Göring was able to concentrate as much heavy *Flak* as he wished and from less than 15,000 ft, which was as high as most laden Wellingtons could fly, that looked plenty. And to make his task easier, we were going over one at a time. They couldn't all fire at us but it felt like it. We could actually smell *Flak*. The Germans were very good gunners. Down below Lake Wannsee shone in the moonlight. Buildings or imagined buildings appeared in the Berlin suburbs below and at any moment an attack by night fighters was expected. One of my tasks when over the target was to report heavy *Flak* bursts on the ground to enable the pilot to take evasive action in the time it took the shells to lift themselves up to our level. For a while this ploy worked and our bombs went down, hitting the opera house we were later told.

'Then it happened.

'There was a loud explosion in one of the engines. Fortunately, it did not catch fire. Torrens feathered the prop but *M for Mother* could not maintain height and, though it succeeded in flying out of the heavy barrage, was down to 1000ft within half an hour. Nearing Brunswick Torrens came on the intercom.

'Sorry to tell you chaps but we will not make it back. You will each have to decide if you want to bale out or stay in the aircraft for a crash-landing.'

'I had previously decided that should such an occasion occur, then I would jump. I looked at the altimeter. It read 1100 ft (300 ft less than recommended). The ruddy bulkhead at the front prevented me from turning the turret door handle. (To bale straight out of the turret would have taken me into the turning props.) To my relief, Eric Berry opened it from the other side. F/O Goodwin, observer and I baled out. The remaining four crew, including P/O Palmer, rear gunner and Sgt Albert Smith, WOP/AG stayed with the aircraft and crash-landed at Wolfenbuttel near Hanover. They set fire to the aircraft before being captured and made PoWs. Goodwyn and I joined them.'[31]

On 10/11 April 53 bombers comprising 36 Wellingtons, 12 Blenheims and five Manchesters headed for Brest to try and finish off the *Gneisenau* which had been recently danmaged by a Coastal Command torpedo bomber. Meanwhile 29 Hampdens and 24 Whitleys went to bomb Düsseldorf and minor operations were flown to Bordeaux/Mérignac airfield and to Rotterdam. Four hits were claimed on the *Gneisenau.* One Wellington FTR while five Hampdens were lost on the raid on Düsseldorf.[32] On 12/13 April 66 aircraft including 35 Wellingtons returned to Brest. WOP/AG F/Sgt Edwin Wheeler in 214 Sqn was aboard one of them as he recalls:

'We found 10/10ths cloud over the target and the bombs were released through the cloud with unobserved results. We were getting sick of the sound of Brest and wondered how much longer those two battleships would survive. I suppose the Royal Navy were content to have them confined to port and not on the open seas to wreak their havoc. Three nights later, 15/16 April, five crews were detailed to attack Kiel on the north German coast – an important naval base and four to the Channel ports. We were airborne at 2040 hrs in very good weather conditions; heading out over Skegness to Sylt and Flensburg but on arrival at Kiel 8/10ths cloud covered the target. The town's batteries set up intense heavy anti-aircraft fire. Without radar we were obliged to bomb on dead reckoning and no results were observed so we scorched it back to base landing at 0410 hrs. Three aircraft set out on 17/18 April[33] for Mannheim but weather conditions were foul and we were unable to locate the target. As we were loathe to bring our bombs back – apart from the hazard of landing with same – we decided to off-load them on an aerodrome near Brussels, encouraged by the sight of a resultant large fire. The last days of the month [30 April/1 May] arrived and after a night flying test in a strange aircraft (R1495) we found ourselves being briefed to attack Kiel again. One of eight aircraft assigned, we took off at 2055 hrs, following the coastline down from Kappeln to the target where we found 10/10ths cloud at 10,000 ft. Bombing of any specific target was impossible but the searchlight activity was intense. We decided to let the searchlight crews have the benefit of our considerable bomb load following which there was an immediate extinguishing of all lights.[34]

'On 3/4 May once again cloud came to the rescue of the *Reich* and Cologne was totally obscured. Nevertheless this raid counted towards our first tour and we had clocked up our twentieth operation – about halfway to the desired total before being 'screened' to take up instructional duty at an OTU.[35] An uneventful raid on 5/6 May was to Mannheim and yes 10/10ths cloud again obscured the target area. *Flak* was of barrage type and only slight damage was experienced. We landed back at base at 0440 and were content to watch the dawn rise as we hungrily consumed our eggs and bacon. 7/8 May saw us on our way to St. Nazaire, the U-boat base. We were airborne at 0015 hrs, one of ten squadron aircraft detailed. A daylight landing at 0610 hrs, debriefing and the usual breakfast. We thought we might become egg-bound if we operated too frequently. The bad news was that the Wellington captained by Freddy Savage, who had previously flown with us as second pilot, had failed to return.[36] Replacement crews were to arrive in the next 48 hours. No respite for us as that same night we were despatched to Bremen but this time the weather was excellent and the target objectives stood out with complete clarity. All crews were satisfied with their results and we landed unscathed at base at 0455 hrs. It was so unusual to bomb in clear conditions and the crews eagerly scanned the displayed photographs of our bomb plots later in the morning.

'Forty-eight hours later (10/11 May) we were off again, this time to Hamburg. The weather was perfect. Nine of our aircraft were involved and we crossed the coast at Cromer, then on to Texel on the Dutch coast and then Hamburg clearly seen, ideal bombing conditions. We bombed from 15,000 ft and saw detonations in the target area. The depth of the searchlight defenses was incredible and it seemed that we were constantly illuminated in spite of continued evasive action. With the heavy *Flak* around we at least thought we would be safe from fighter attacks. Denny Denman was in the front gun turret and Bill Bassom in the rear turret. I kept a lookout in the astrodome. We had just emerged from the searchlight activity when Denny said he had to go to the Elsan toilet located in the rear beyond the main spar I was to relieve him in the front turret. Denny had passed me on his way and I was preparing to go forward to replace him when there was an almighty crack of exploding AA shells and I was convinced we had sustained a direct hit. I clambered over the main spar and nearly fell over Den's body lying prostrate on the floor. In the darkness it was necessary to feel my way around and I was about to pull his helmet aside to shout in his ear to ask if he was alright and was horrified to find his face a mass of 'gooey' fluid. I thought that he had been hit in the face, which seemed a gory mess. I stayed with him until we were clear of *Flak* and on our way home across that awful long stretch of the North Sea of which I had a dreadful fear of having to ditch in. He whispered that he had been hit but that he could feel no pain. My hands had become wet with this 'goo' from his face but it smelt like strong disinfectant. My eyes were beginning to focus in the darkness and suddenly I realized what had happened. The proximity of the bursting AA shell had been sufficient to dislodge the Elsan toilet from its mounting. It had hit the roof of the aircraft; struck Denny on the head rendering him unconscious and the Elsan contents had emptied over his face! Our 25th operation was achieved on the night of 12/13 May when eight squadron aircraft were detailed to bomb Mannheim. Weather conditions were so adverse, which made Ginger's dead reckoning navigation vital, that we released our load through 10/10ths cloud on DR and no results were observed. The heavy *Flak* barrage was the only thing of note on an uneventful trip but I'm sure Denny welcomed that after his previous experience.'

In May *Nachtjagd* claimed 41 bombers destroyed.[37] Operating from Schleswig airfield in northern Germany 5. and 6./NJG 1 destroyed 12 bombers in the *Helle Nachtjagd* over the Grossraum Hamburg on the nights of 9, 11 and 12 May. *Oblt* Helmut Lent, *Staffelkapitän*, 6./NJG 1, claimed his first two night victories on 11/12 May, shooting down two Wellingtons of 40 and 214 Squadrons when Bomber Command raided Bremen. In June *Nachtjagd* destroyed 66 aircraft, 22 of them by I./NJG 2.[38] On 26/27 June when Bomber Command raided Cologne, Kiel and Düsseldorf weather conditions were appalling and prevented good bombing. Two Wellingtons and two Manchesters were lost. F/L John Price, Wellington tail gunner in 150 Squadron recalls:

> 'On this raid the weather closed in completely, cloud cover was 10/10ths. The cumulo nimbus clouds towered to over 35,000 ft. In cumulo nimbus (thunderclouds) winds inside the turbulence can easily exceed 200 mph. To me it was unbelievable, the terrible turbulence, encountered in those storm centers can only be seen by an airman and I have actually been through them. You see the lightning (in close contact) it envelopes your aircraft with a sheet of blinding white light, millions of volts of electricity. If you are lucky the riggers have welded all your weak spots together, the metal are bonded together and are (hopefully) earthed. The next step for the unfortunate pilot is how to control an aircraft that is thrown about like a butterfly in a high wind. We weighed about ten tons but no pilot on earth could fly in these conditions. We were turned upside down and thrown about like a leaf in a winter storm, leaving it all to fate and destiny. Our pilot managed to obtain a lower altitude. Then by rotating my turret 180 degrees I saw ice forming quickly on the wings. I spoke to the captain, warning him of the danger. Even at a lower altitude our de-icers were not good enough to avoid an eventual ditching into the North Sea. At about 7000 ft

and out of those terrible cumulus towers of hail, ice and winds I sighed with relief as great chunks of ice broke off from the wings and blown away by our airspeed sailed past my rear turret. 'It was far worse than facing the *Flak* and German night fighters. Nature can throw better weapons at you than the enemy! We still had bombs on board, had used up most of our fuel and having escaped by a sheer miracle the terror of electrical storms and the icing etc, we decided to go home, cruising at about 7000 ft above the cold gray North Sea. Our first priority now was to get rid of the bombs, so we dropped them on or near Texel. We knew that German night fighters were nearby. Going home was a very strange and frightening experience to me.'

On 27/28 June *Oblt* Reinhold Eckardt of 6./NJG 1 destroyed four bombers in 46 minutes, including Whitley V Z6647 of 77 Squadron, during a *Helle Nachtjagd* sortie in the Hamburg area. The next night, 29/30 June, *Oblt* Helmut Lent, *Staffelkapitän* 6./NJG 1 destroyed Stirling Is N3664 and N6001 of 7 Squadron with the loss of all 14 crew. Apart from these two Stirling claims by Lent, *Nachtjäger* destroyed eight other bombers on the continent on 29/30 June. On 1 July Lent took command of the 4th *Staffel* at Leeuwarden and during the month he claimed seven kills to take his score to 20 victories.[39]

'Our losses, recalls Sgt Eric Masters, a 99 Squadron Wellington pilot:

'Were running at approximately five per cent so one believed one was living on luck after the 20th trip. One was just as likely to 'buy it' on the first as on the last and 7/8 July was my thirtieth and final operation of my tour, a sortie to Cologne.[40] P/O Don Elliott, my Canadian navigator, came to stand beside me. There were two areas of AA activity ahead and I decided to head between them so that Elliott could pick out the river reflecting the moonlight from the south and from his map would be able to place us exactly. We discovered we were just south of Cologne. I wanted to get a really good run at the target and needed to get north of the city. There was no need for navigation now and having passed over the Rhine I turned north and flew past Cologne on its eastern side watching the *Flak* exploding, flares dropping, flash bombs illuminating huge areas and bombs bursting. I felt remote from it all. North of Cologne I turned over the river and headed south. Elliott was now in the prone bomb aiming position, just below and in front of me, getting a very clear view of the river and giving me course corrections to keep us in line with the target. 'The activity over the target had practically ceased and it became very peaceful. One of the gunners remarked, 'Everyone else seems to have gone home, skipper'.

'In these last minutes I had kept straight and level and at the same speed for much too long. The Germans must have wondered about this crazy lone raider. We were caught in the bluish-white beam of a master searchlight. Six more standard searchlights coned us. Now the whole fury of the Cologne defenses concentrated on us. I increased speed, still heading for the target. The *Flak* followed us expertly, throwing the aircraft about. Johnny Agrell, the second pilot, who was watching all at the astrodome ready to deal with the flash-bomb, called out that we had been hit. 'I had felt a judder in the control column and then found it rigid in the fore and aft direction (elevator control). As I had been holding it in the dive I was now unable to bring the nose up. The *Flak* was still after us. I told Don to jettison the bombs (live) in a last hope to get the nose up but when this failed I realized that we were virtually out of control at 10,000 ft and losing height rapidly. I had no alternative but to give the order, 'Bale out!' I was thankful my chest parachute pack was in its storage position. At times I had been known to forget to take it on a trip and I had delegated Don Elliott to make sure it was always on the 'tumbril'. I was glad at on this occasion he had not let me down.'

S/L R P Widdowson captained one of the 75 Squadron RNZAF crews that attacked Münster and was fortunate to return. Their Wellington was badly damaged by a Bf 110 nightfighter, which hit the starboard engine and put the hydraulic system out of action, with the result that the undercarriage fell half down. The bomb doors fell open too, the wireless sets were put out of action and the front gunner was wounded in the foot. Worst of all a fire was burning up through the upper surface of the starboard wing where a petrol feed pipe had been split open. The crew thought that they would have to bale out so they put on their parachutes. Some got going with the fire extinguisher, bursting a hole in the side of the fuselage so that they could get at the wing but the fire was too far out along the wing for them to do any good. They tried throwing coffee from their flasks at it but that did not work either. By this time the Wellington had reached the Dutch coast and was flying along parallel with it, the crew waiting to see how the fire was going to develop. Finally Sgt James A. Ward, the 2nd pilot thought there was a sporting chance of reaching the fire by getting out through the astrodome, then down the side of the fuselage and out on to the wing. His courage was to earn the VC.

Ward recalls:

'Joe, the navigator, said he thought it was crazy. There was a rope there; just the normal length of rope attached to the rubber dinghy to stop it drifting away from the aircraft when it's released on the water. We tied that round my chest and I climbed up through the astrodome. I still had my parachute on. I wanted to take it off because I thought it would get in the way but they wouldn't let me. I sat on the edge of the astrodome for a bit with my legs still inside, working out how I was going to do it. Then I reached out with one foot and kicked a hole in the fabric so that I could get my foot into the framework of the plane. I punched another hole through the fabric in front of me to get a handhold, after which I made further holes and went down the side of the fuselage on to the wing. Joe was holding on to the rope so that I wouldn't sort of drop straight off.

'I went out three or four feet along the wing. The fire was burning up through the wing rather like a big gas jet and it was blowing back just past my shoulder. I had only one hand to work with getting out, because I was holding on with the other to the cockpit cover. I never realized before how bulky a cockpit cover was. The wind kept catching it and several times nearly blew it away and me with it. I kept bunching it under my arm- Then out it would blow again. All the time, of course, I was lying as flat as I could on the wing but I couldn't get right down close because of the parachute in front of me on my chest. The wind kept lifting me off the wing. Once it slapped me hack on to the fuselage again but I managed to hang on. The slipstream from the engine made things worse. It was like being in a terrific gale, only much worse than any gale I've ever known in my life. I can't explain it but there was no sort of real sensation of danger out there at all. It was just a matter of doing one thing after another and that's about all there was to it. I tried stuffing the cockpit cover down through the hole in the wing on to the pipe where the fire was starting from but as soon as I took my hand away, the terrific draught blew it out again and finally it blew away altogether. The rear gunner told me afterwards that he saw it go sailing past his turret. I just couldn't hold on to it any longer.

'After that there was nothing to do but to get back again. I worked my way back along the wing and managed to haul myself up on to the top of the fuselage and got to sitting on the edge of the astrodome again. Joe kept the dinghy rope taut all the time and that helped. By the time I got back I was absolutely done in. I got partly back into the astro hatch but I just couldn't get my right foot inside. I just sort of sat there looking at it until Joe reached out and pulled it in for me. After that, when I got inside, I just fell straight on to the bunk and stayed there for a time.

'Just when they were within reach of the English coast the fire on the wing suddenly blazed up again. Some petrol, which had formed a pool inside the lower surface of the wing, had caught fire. However, after this final flare-up the fire died right out much to the relief of all the crew. The crew pumped the wheels down with the emergency gear and Widdowson decided that instead of going to Feltwell, he'd try to land at another aerodrome nearby which had a far greater landing space. As he circled before landing he called up the control and said, 'We've been badly shot up. I hope we shan't mess up your flare-path too badly when we land.' He put the aircraft down beautifully but the Wellington ended up by running into a barbed-wire entanglement. Fortunately nobody was hurt.'[41]

S/L Ray Glass DFC a pilot in 214 Squadron was one of 57 Wellington crews despatched to Osnabrück two nights later, on 9/10 July, in a Merlin engined Wellington II:

> 'We carried a 4000-lb 'Dustbin' bomb. In a Wimpy the bomb doors and floor were removed and the bomb attached by a 1-inch wire hawser and toggle to a metal beam introduced under the main spar. An axe was supplied to cut the hawser in case it hung up. So much for technology! We reached the Zuider Zee but with a full moon silhouetting us from above and below we were a sitting target. We were attacked by a Me 109 and 110, which were beaten off by the rear gunner who claimed the 110 as a 'probable'. Our port engine was hit so we bombed Bergen airfield and observed a huge smoke ring of debris and the runway lights went out.'[42]

In the summer of 1941 ground trials of the new radar navigational aid *Gee*[43] were in progress at Marham, Norfolk. Twelve pilots and 12 observers from 115 and 218 Squadrons were involved in the trials and had been informed they would not be undertaking operational flying until these were completed. Understandably they were surprised to be notified of briefing for an attack on Sunday 13 July 1941. It was to be a 'maximum' effort consisting of 69 Wellingtons, 47 of which were targeted on Bremen, 20 on Vegesack and two on Emden. All crews would encounter heavy cloud and icing. Sixteen aircraft would claim to have bombed Bremen. Two Wellingtons would fail to return from the Bremen attack.[44] In 115 Squadron the all-sergeant crew of Wellington IC R1502, W.J. Reid, pilot and captain, Geoff T. Buckingham, observer, M.B. Wallis, wireless operator, M.G. Dunne, front gunner and T.W. Oliver, rear gunner, were short of their regular second pilot. He had been sent to London to attend a Commission Board. 27-year-old Sgt pilot Frederick Birkett Tipper, who was regarded as a jinx on the Squadron, took his place. The crew that he had flown with on his first sortie had suffered a very shaky 'do'. On his second operation the aircraft had crashed on take off, fortunately with no fatal result. Bremen would be his third operational flight.

The observer's chair in a Wellington moved backwards and forwards in tracks firmly fastened to the floor of the aircraft. When he boarded the aircraft Buckingham found to his intense annoyance that the tracks to his chair were broken leaving it free to slide all over the place in the event of violent evasive action. Furthermore, the chair cushion was missing. Instead of throwing his parachute pack on the bed as he usually did-he would have to sit on it in lieu of the cushion. Little did he realize that before the night was out the object of his annoyance would save his life.

The sky was clear in England but over the North Sea thick cloud was encountered. As they approached the enemy coastline there was a partial thinning of the cloud and Sgt Tipper was able to pass a pinpoint on the Dutch Coast to his observer. Tipper then left the cockpit and made his way aft to the astrodome where he would keep a constant vigil for night fighters. The Wellington was now at 9000 ft. Buckingham had just spotted Texel Beacon and was returning to this station from the cockpit when Sgt Oliver in the rear turret yelled over the intercom, 'Fighter'. Simultaneously he opened up with his guns racking the fuselage with vibration and filling it with the fumes of cordite. *Oblt* Egmont Prinz *zur* Lippe-Weissenfeld, the Austrian Prince and *Staffelkapitän*, IV./NJG 1 had just made his initial strike setting the starboard engine of the bomber on fire. He was now somewhere out in the darkness maneuvering for a second attack. Buckingham rushed forward to the cockpit and pressed the starboard engine fire extinguisher button. This put out the fire. Next he jettisoned the bombs and gave the pilot a reciprocal course to fly. He then returned to the cabin to check his log. At this moment – the second attack occurred and it was far more devastating than the first. Cannon fire from beneath the bomber raked the whole length of the fuselage wounding all members of the crew, some more seriously than the others. Buckingham blacked out. When he came round he was lying across the step, adjacent to the forward escape hatch. As the aircraft had gone into a dive the loose seat, which he had cursed so roundly at the beginning of the flight, had slid to the nose and deposited him on the floor by the escape hatch. His parachute pack, which he had used as a cushion, was lying on top of him.

He took stock of the situation. The bomber was on fire and he was wounded in face and arm with cannon shrapnel. There was a hole in the back of his leg, which was bleeding profusely. The door to the front turret was wide open. There was no sign of the pilot. Fastening his parachute pack to the harness he found that one J-clip had been- smashed by the cannon fire. He used the remaining clip then heaved on the edge of the escape hatch. In an instant he was out and away into the night. Hanging awkwardly beneath his parachute, suspended at an angle by one clip only, he made a bad landing injuring his anklebone. Tipper's body was recovered from the wreckage.[45] It was assumed that Tipper had been killed by the second burst of fire from the night fighter. Later *zur* Lippe visited the crew in hospital and expressed his regret that a member of the crew had died. He said he was after the bomber not the crew.

On 14/15 July 78 Wellingtons and 19 Whitleys were dispatched to Bremen where they were given three aiming points, the shipyards, the goods station and the Altstadt. One of the Wellington ICs that took part was *T-Tommy*[46] of 9 Squadron at Honington with an all-sergeant crew captained by Sgt J.C. Saitch, who came from Dunmow, Essex. R.D. Telling, who was from Epsom, Surrey was the second pilot. Navigator was Smitten, a Canadian from Edmonton, Alberta, while the three remaining members were an Englishman, Sgt E. Trott, from Sheffield and two more Canadians – Hooper from Vancouver, the front gunner and Sgt English, the rear gunner was from Picton, Nova Scotia. *T-Tommy* took off at 2330 on 14 July with seven 500-lb bombs on board. It seemed at first that Bremen would prove hard to find for the weather was very thick. Just before *T-Tommy* reached the city, however, it came out of the clouds into a clear sky carved by the sharp blades of searchlights. There was a slight haze over the rooftops 11,000ft below but Smitten found the target and Saich began his bombing run. It was just 20 minutes to two in the morning. One bomb was released, when the wheeling searchlights caught and held *T-Tommy* in a cone of light which grew in size and intensity as more and more beams concentrated upon the aircraft. Two heavy anti-aircraft shells burst just behind and below the rear turret and inside the fuselage itself level with the leading edge of the tail plane. The first shell wounded English in the shoulder and the hand and cut the hydraulic controls to the turret so that it could no longer be turned except by the slow process of cranking it. Fragments of the other shell riddled the rear part of the fuselage and set on fire the fabric covering it and the tail fin. Saitch said, 'The flames seemed to be the signal for every anti-aircraft gun in the target area to give full and uninterrupted attention to us.'

And all this time, be it remembered, the rear gunner was in the blazing end of the torch. Saich took violent evasive action and succeeded in throwing the German gunners momentarily off their aim. While he was doing so Smitten went to the help of English in the rear turret. He made his way down the rocking, shell-torn fuselage till he was brought up short by the fierce fire separating him from the turret. Here for the moment he could go no further. He crawled back a little way, snatched a fire extinguisher and returned to the fire in the fuselage, which he presently subdued. Above him the fin still flamed. He sprayed it with all that remained of the methyl bromide in the extinguisher, thrusting it through the hot framework of the fuselage from which the fabric had burnt away. He was able at last to reach the turret.

English was still there but he had made preparations to abandon the aircraft by swinging the turret round into the beam position and opened the doors to throw himself out backwards. The doors now refused to close. Back went Smitten and returned with a light axe. He leant out through a hole beneath the fin, which he had just saved from burning, the wind of the slipstream tearing at him and hacked away at the doors till they fell off. English was then able to rotate his turret by means of the hand gear and as soon as the gaping hole, where once the doors had been, coincided with the end of the fuselage, he extricated himself and entered the aircraft.

While this was going on astern more trouble broke out forward. The Wellington was hit again and a shell splinter set light to the flares carried in the port wing. These are for use in an emergency, when a forced landing has to be made in darkness. They burned brightly – so brightly that Saich thought the port engine was on fire. He promptly turned off its petrol, opened the throttle fully and switched off. Soon, however, the flames died down, for the flares had burnt their way through the fabric of the mainplane and fallen from the aircraft. Realising what had happened, Sgt Saich turned on the petrol again and restarted the engine. At his orders Telling was crouched beside the main spar behind the wireless cabin pumping all the oil which could be extracted from a riddled auxiliary tank. *T-Tommy* was still under intense anti-aircraft fire and the shell splinters, one of which wounded him, were described by Telling as 'angry hail tearing through the aircraft.'

One further misfortune had befallen the Wellington. At the moment when the Germans scored their first bit, the bomb doors were open, for the aircraft was completing its first bombing run-up and one of the bombs had just been released. The damage caused by the anti-aircraft shell was such as to make it impossible either to close the bomb doors or to release the remaining six bombs, since the hydraulic pipes had been punctured and the electrical wiring to the slips had been severed. As well as this and the damage to the fuselage, the rear turret, the rudder and the fin, there was a large hole knocked by a shell in the starboard wing. It had just missed the petrol tanks.

In this condition *T-Tommy* was headed for base. The chances of making it did not appear bright. The aircraft with bomb doors open and a heavy load still on board was very hard to control and Saich's task was not made easier by the hole in the wing through which the draught rushed, blanketing the starboard aileron which was for all intents and purposes useless. Nevertheless be held sternly to the homeward course given him by Smitten and at 0535 hrs on 15 July *T-Tommy* crossed the English coast dead on track. Its speed had been much reduced and the petrol gauges had been registering zero gallons for two hours out of the four on the return journey from Bremen, over nearly 300 miles of sea. With dry land beneath him once more Saich determined to make a forced landing, for he thought that at any moment the engines would stop for lack of fuel.

The sky was now 'pale as water before dawn' and he picked out a barley field where it seemed to him that a successful landing might be made. In the half-light he did not see the obstruction poles set up in the field to hinder an airborne invasion. He set about making his perilous descent. The flaps would not work and when be came to pump the undercarriage down with the emergency hydraulic band pump he found that, owing to loss of oil, it would only push the tail wheel and one of the main wheels into their positions. *T-Tommy* came in to land, lop-sided a little to take full advantage of the one sound wheel. On touching down, the aircraft swung round but its motion was violently arrested by an obstruction pole. It shuddered and then came abruptly to rest on its belly with its back broken. Save for many bruises none of the crew sustained further hurt. *T-Tommy* was little more than a wreck. It had flown to that East Anglian barley field with a huge hole in its starboard wing, with uncounted smaller holes in its fuselage, with nine ft of fabric burnt entirely away forward from the rear turret, with half the fin and half the rudder in the same condition. Yet it flew home. The operative word is 'flew.' Saich and Smitten were awarded the DFM.[47] Crews reported the 'whole town was ablaze'. Four Wellingtons were lost from the Bremen raid.[48]

F/Sgt Eddie Wheeler, WOP-AG in 150 Squadron, meanwhile, flew his next operation on 21/22 July:

> 'It was to be our most hair-raising experience. Entering the briefing room, we looked expectantly at the operations map and saw the red route ribbon targeting to Frankfurt, our first raid on that city. We were airborne at 2210 hrs and wondered if we were destined to return to Snaith in the early hours of next morning. The usual

searchlight and *Flak* activity was experienced near and over the target but once having released our considerable bomb load we felt relief and thought it was just a matter of getting home now – hopefully without incident.

'Not long after leaving the target, it was apparent that our starboard engine was not functioning satisfactorily. Paul was concerned that the engine was sounding like a bag of old bones and said that the oil was obviously not getting through to it. We gradually lost height and Paul directed Denny and myself to operate the manual oil pump located behind the main spar, in an effort to get oil through to the engine. We found, in turns, that the manual pump was almost inoperable, it took immense effort to force it one way and then the other It was intensely cold and our fingers became numb and we experienced cramp in our legs whilst in the crouching position. It was obvious that our efforts were not working, we could hear tremendous grinding noises coming from the engine and the strain was causing the plane to fly crab-like. Sparks and fire were spitting out from the engine cowling and we were losing more height. I had visions of having to ditch in the North Sea and cursed the possibility of our coming to the end of our luck on our 34th operation.

'The noises were becoming more pronounced and Paul was having great difficulty in maintaining course and height. Something drastic was obviously going to happen and it did – with flames and sparks and tremendous grinding within the engine, the propeller with an accompanying section of engine suddenly tore itself free and spun forward and upwards, fortunately, to disappear over the tail and downwards to the North Sea. If, in its final torment it had spun into the fuselage then without doubt I wouldn't have been around to pen this report! As it happened, the aircraft flew much better without it although we were still losing height and we were concerned at the risk of not reaching the mainland. I was instructed to send out 'Mayday' SOS signals – breaking the usual radio silence because of our dire circumstances. We aimed for the nearest coastal point and it seemed an eternity before we made landfall and made a successful one-engine landing on the grass field at Marham in Norfolk.

'We ran to a halt, clambered out to gaze at the gaping great hole in the engine nacelle and the surrounding ground crew stood there mouthing their amazement. It was not until very much later that Ginger informed us that we had a 1000 lb. bomb hang-up still in the bomb-bay and that we had unknowingly made a fairly heavy one-engine landing on the bumpy grass 'drome which might easily have dislodged the bomb. Ginger's character was such that he would have carried a guilt-complex over this incident but the crew immediately dismissed this notion out of hand by reason of his wonderful dedication to the job in hand. Hadn't he always navigated us to and from the target so expertly and got us back to friendly territory time and time again in spite of the many hazards and diversions? So, we thought, 'Well, we have got charmed lives, haven't we?' Furthermore, we had taken off from Snaith on two operations and not yet been able to land back there! Was this to be a feature of future operations from there?

'On 24 July 1941 we just couldn't believe our ears when the CO said that six crews were to participate in a daylight operation against the German battleships *Scharnhorst* and *Gneisenau* lying at anchor in the French port of Brest. A total of 150 aircraft were planned to make the attack in formation but at the last moment this had to be changed because of the departure of the *Scharnhorst* to La Pallice. The force to Brest was then to be composed of 100 aircraft of which three were to be Flying Fortresses flying at 30,000 ft in the hope of attracting German fighters prematurely. Then 18 Hampdens escorted by three squadrons of Spitfires with long-range fuel tanks were to attack in anticipation of drawing off more enemy fighters. Finally, the main force of 79 unescorted Wellingtons of 1 and 3 Groups were to attack in the final wave.

'This was to be our first daylight operation and without fighter escort and in the knowledge that our formation flying technique was far from efficient and enemy fighter prowess was widely known, we did not give much for our chances. As a diversion for this raid 36 Blenheims all escorted by Spitfires were to attack Cherbourg Docks in the hope of drawing German fighters from the main raid. Very apprehensive, we took off at 1050 hrs and it took quite some time before our six aircraft could take up some semblance of a formation and set course. The weather was good and visibility excellent, there being no cloud in which to hide in the event of attack.

'The German fighter opposition was stronger and more prolonged than anticipated by Group HQ but the crews involved had not shared their view. We were struggling to maintain formation and then found that our oxygen supply failed. With the target area sighted ahead with the bursting *Flak* – our engine-driven generator failed and discussion followed on the situation pertaining. With the generator out of action, so many of our electrics would not function and more importantly our bombs would not release. Having come so far, naturally we were disappointed but had to abandon our mission and turn for base.

'The remainder of the force pushed home their attack but they were badly mauled by the German fighter attacks. Ten Wellingtons were shot down – 12 1/2% of the total force but six hits were claimed on the *Gneisenau*. Of the 15 Halifaxes attacking La Pallice, five were shot down and all the remainder damaged but five direct hits were registered on the *Scharnhorst* putting her out of action for four months. Two of the 18 Hampdens were lost to fighter attacks. It was considered a highly successful operation but with heavy losses. We landed back at base at 1600 hrs somewhat disappointed but comforted in the knowledge that we had survived our 35th op. Each operation now was tempting fate – how much longer could we survive when so many crews were coming to grief before reaching double figures of ops completed? The strain was telling on each crewmember now and each flight seemed so much harder than ever before.

That night, 24/25 July, 34 Wellingtons and 30 Hampdens visited Kiel and 31 Whitleys and 16 Wellingtons went to Emden. One Hampden and one Wellington were lost on the Kiel raid. Two Wellingtons which FTR from Emden were shot down by nightfighters of 4./NJG 1. The following night, 25/26 July, 30 Hampdens and 25 Whitleys were despatched to Hanover[49] while 43 Wellingtons visited Hamburg. Flying his first operation this night was F/Sgt J. Ralph Wood a Canadian air observer on Whitleys of 102 Squadron at RAF Topcliffe, Yorkshire in 4 Group, Bomber Command. Ralph Wood recalls:

'I was a 'one-winged wonder' or as we affectionately called ourselves, 'a flying asshole.' Sure, we were occasionally asked when we would finish our training and get the other half of our wings.' At this time we were all on loan to the RAF as the RCAF Bomber Command had not yet been established. Later, when it became active as No.6 Group, some of the Canadians transferred to the Canadian squadrons. Several others and myself preferred to stay with the RAF. We got along fine with the Limeys and besides, we thought that where we were on loan we might get away with a little more murder and less discipline. (I'll never ever forget my introduction to this first operational squadron. Arriving around midday the OC informed me that I would be on tonight's raid. Who? Me? Why, I hadn't even unpacked my kit bag. The flight's chief navigator suggested that he went in my place and I would watch him go through his routine preparing for the flight. I watched him prepare his flight plan, get the meteorology report, go to the intelligence office for his secret coded information on rice paper (so you could eat it if necessary) and other pertinent things to do before going off into that treacherous looking sky. That navigator and crew never returned. This was a hell of an introduction, especially when stories were circulating about washing out the remains of a tail-gunner with a hose, there was so little left of him).

'On the night of 25/26 July 1941, 13 months after joining the RCAF, I found myself in the briefing room nervously preparing my charts for the raid. I was trying to appear calm and nonchalant, this being my first op and not wanting to appear to be too much of a greenhorn. After the briefing, the navigators gathered around the huge plotting table in the operations room and worked out our DR (dead reckoning) courses to get us to the target and far more important, home again. Our dead reckoning was based on the predicted winds as supplied by the Met section, the airspeed, the ground speed and the drift, as well as other information so important in our navigation. Many corrections and adjustments were made during our trip from new information obtained in flight. Our only navigational aids were from fixes obtained from our wireless operator and good only up to a limited number of miles from the English coast. I soon learned to jokingly call my navigation 'guestimation'! So here we were a crew of five; two pilots, a navigator/bomb-aimer (observer), a wireless operator and a tail-gunner. Bomb-aimers appeared later in the war and there weren't always enough to go around. I felt that if I could get us to the target I should have the pleasure of bombing.

'My navigator's table was behind the pilot's seat in the cockpit As we neared the target I unplugged my oxygen lead and my intercom and dragging my parachute with me, made my way to the bomb-sight in the nose of our flying coffin. It was a long crawl in the darkness and without oxygen the going was tough. Reaching the bombsight and front-gunner compartment I searched frantically for the oxygen connection to restore my strength. With the aid of a torch – partly covered so as not to attract any wandering enemy fighters – I found my connection and began breathing easier. I was now lining up the target with the bombsight, as I directed the pilot on our bombing run – Left, Left – Steady – R-I-G-H-T – Steady – Left 14 – Steady – Bombs Gone. Our aircraft leapt about 200 ft with the release of tons of high explosives. Now we flew straight and level for 30 seconds, the longest 30 seconds anyone will ever know, so that we could get the required photo of the drop for the Intelligence Officer back at base – Picture taken – Let's get the hell out of here'. With the flak bursting around and searchlights trying in vain to catch us I crawled back to my plotting table in a cold sweat. The pilot was still taking evasive action as I gave him the course for home. Black blobs of 'smoke' surrounding the aircraft were flak bursts. When you can smell the cordite it meant they were too damn close.

'Arriving back at our base without incident gave me a great feeling of relief and satisfaction. It was hard to believe that I'd been over Germany but harder to believe that I was back in England. Next came our debriefing by the intelligence officers, accompanied by a cup of coffee laced with overproof rum. I was tired but happy after our seven and a-half hour trip. I guess I had that blissful 'No.1 Op behind-me-look' written all over my face. I kept thinking, I've made it. That first op I'd been dreaming about and working toward for 13 months.

'As I settled into squadron life at Topcliffe I found that the best way to keep your sanity was to separate your pleasures from your work. I didn't want to become one of those casualties found walking around the airfield talking to himself. There was the odd one who cracked up mentally and you really couldn't blame him. Our commanding officer was a queer one. We called him 'Curly' but not to his face. He was RAF permanent force and had been stationed in India too long. We thought he'd gotten too much sun out there He was balding and had a remarkably long, red handlebar moustache, which he took great pride in. I noticed that anytime he put himself down to fly the operation would be comparatively easy. How unlike P/O Leonard Cheshire, who was later to become G/C Cheshire, winning the VC and other decorations. He was described as a mad man who always picked the dangerous targets like Berlin for himself. Some say this was partly because his brother was shot down over Berlin.[50] My second op on 6 August was Frankfurt – seven hours of misery accompanied by engine failure. We were very glad to arrive safely back at base.'[51]

F/Sgt Eddie Wheeler, WOP-AG in 150 Squadron meanwhile, was approaching his final op of his first tour:

'We were saddened to learn that P/O Landreth and crew were lost on the Frankfurt raid, which meant that we had lost all the earlier second pilots on our crew when they had received their captaincies. On 8 August 1941 we were assembled in the CO's office to be told at long last that our operation that night was to be our last and that we were then to be 'rested' at an OTU. The target was Hamburg, not the easiest of targets for our last excursion and we all wished each other good luck and promised ourselves a party if we were fortunate enough to return. We had come to rely on each other so much over a period of one year and had become the staunchest of friends. We almost regretted the necessary split-up to various stations after this last flight together. We reached the enemy coast and experienced *Flak* for the last time and as one engine was not functioning we were forced to abandon our task at Groningen. However disappointing this last sortie was we had survived where so many crews had not. When we taxied to our dispersal we climbed out of *'C-Charlie'* and kissed the ground in thankfulness. We embraced our faithful ground crew and invited them to a final party to show our appreciation of their marvellous service and dedication. The rivalry between the respected ground crews was great and they would all uphold the merits and achievements of their aircrews. While we were fully engaged on flying operations, the ground crews invariably had to hang around, sometimes in the coldest of weathers awaiting our return. Their smiles on our return were indicative of their delight that we had brought their aircraft home safely although sometimes with varying degrees of damage. Following this op I left Snaith for 27 OTU Lichfield and the rest of his crew also received various postings. We all expressed the hope that the war would be over before we had to undertake a second tour of ops but that seemed highly unlikely as the war had gone badly for Britain -virtually on her own but for the gallant help of the Commonwealth. However, against all odds we had survived Dunkirk, the Battle of Britain and in a smallish way were hitting back at the *Reich* with limited Bomber forces which compelled the enemy to retain Forces in defense which could have been so usefully employed in other theatres of war. I was now 21 years old, had completed 38 operations and was still fit and unscathed.'

Altogether during July 63 Bomber Command aircraft were claimed shot down.[52] In August a record 67 RAF bombers were shot down by flak and fighters.[53] One of the victims of the German defenses was Sgt Basil Sidney Craske, a Whitley pilot in 10 Squadron, 4 Group at Leeming Bar in North Yorkshire:

'Squadron life did not consist only of operational flying although this was its raison d'etre. Other flying duties could be considerable fun and air tests could amount to something more than ensuring that all facets of the aircraft were free from any defect. There were not too many rules and regulations to abide by and if there were as an operational squadron and pilot, they were not taken too seriously. Air tests invariably entailed a bit of relaxed flying and the Yorkshire Moors were a convenient venue for low flying which was exciting. There was one particular spot where there is a sheer drop of several hundred feet and it was something of a challenge to fly close to ground level and then see how quickly the stick could be pushed forward over the precipice. That takes some doing in a Whitley and one's in-built mental survival kit did not allow the aircraft to go over the edge too soon.

'I was only 20 years of age and there was no telling what tomorrow held. Indeed there were very serious moments particularly when some particular mate and crew did not return from a mission. As part of the attack force we were in the unfortunate position of having an aircraft that was being phased out and thus the performance was not being improved. On the contrary, the Whitley I think, was originally given as the stated bomb load about 2500 lbs but this gradually increased as the crew decreased to about 4500 lbs. It had a crew specification of two pilots, a navigator, a wireless operator, a rear gunner and a front gunner but in the second half of 1941 we were without a second pilot and the front gunner. Bombs were getting bigger. Even the modest 1000-lb job when slung in the bomb bay protruded below the fuselage line. Fortunately the bomb doors were kept closed by strong elastic bands (no joking) and thus the bigger bomb could be accommodated. It was a bit off-putting when at certain angles of climb or descent the flapping bomb-doors could be heard.

'The wireless operators, who were quite a unique breed, seemed to make them work most of the time. Navigation was pretty basic. Admittedly we had a bubble sextant, which would take accurate astro shots. But to calculate a 'fix' reference had to be made to copious charts and always assuming that the timing was correct to the second (no quartz movements in 1941), with a bit of luck we could get some idea of where we were! I usually relied upon a series of shots of Polaris, which could quickly be translated into lines of latitude giving a good indication of direction. It is quite amazing how we found our way to a particular target and hopefully back home again. It says a great deal for the training all members of the aircrew had received.

'In the briefing room the first indication of the target was the red tape affixed to the outsized map showing the shortest path to the target. It really was a matter of the Briefing Officer saying, 'We're bombing Essen tonight. Take off 2015 hrs. Bomb load 4000 lbs plus incendiaries. Best of luck, see you later'. Our usual route to the Ruhr, with Cologne, Düsseldorf, Essen and Dortmund the most frequently visited and peripheral targets like the marshalling yards at Hamm and Mannheim, would be Leeming to Coningsby beacon (in Lincolnshire) and leaving the shores of England at Orfordness. (The nature of the shoreline usually enabled us to obtain an accurate visual fix). After crossing the North Sea to the Hook of Holland it was then straight to the target. At least this was the theory but the line from the Hook to the Ruhr necessitated running the gauntlet of the searchlight barrier. With the experience of a few trips under my belt and from swapping 'gen' with other crews, it soon became obvious that the best approach was a more southerly line entering enemy territory around Dunkirk, thence across northern France and southern Belgium to bomb the target from an easterly direction. This route took about an hour longer but it was relatively free from enemy interference except over the target area. As the distance between Orfordness and the Hook of Holland was insufficient, with the extra bomb load, to reach the 'safe' height of 12,000 ft which meant a stooge back and forth to reach it, a Dunkirk entry just about enabled us to stagger up to the magic 12,000 ft.'

On 14 August F/Sgt Ralph Wood of 102 Squadron was one who went to Hanover:

'This was my third op and it proved as exciting as the first two. While over Europe we would drop thousands of propaganda leaflets down the flare chute. We also dropped flares out this chute as we approached the target area enabling us to pinpoint the target itself. Before taking off we usually had a nervous pee beside the aircraft. This was much easier than trying to manipulate in the air. On our homeward journey we would get into our thermos of coffee and spam sandwiches. Of course, our real treat was the flying breakfast of bacon and eggs back at the base and our discussions of the attack with the other crews on the raid. Bacon and eggs were otherwise scarce as hen's teeth. At the ritual breakfast after every mission there were empty tables, chairs, dishes and silverware aligned for the men who weren't coming back. Weldon MacMurray, a school friend of mine from Moncton, was a sergeant pilot stationed at RAF Dishforth about two miles from the village of Topcliffe as the crow flies. For relaxation we would frequent the Black Swan pub, or as we called it, the Mucky Duck and Weldon and I would exchange news from home. On one such meeting he informed me that Johnny Humphrey bought it. Another time that Graham Rogers' number came up. This was followed by news that Brian Filliter was missing in action. One day at lunchtime I answered the phone in the sergeant's mess and it was Weldon inquiring about me. He'd heard that I'd bought it the previous night. A few weeks later friends of Weldon phoned me from Dishforth to say that he had failed to return from a trip. I found out that he was a prisoner of war. Boy! Was I getting demoralized? Would I be next?'[54]

The chance of finishing a tour of 30 operations was remote but by mid-August Craske and his crew had completed 26 and the 27th, to Cologne on the night of 16/17 August was viewed as 'relatively easy'. Craske's crew of Whitley V Z6805 *G-George* consisted of 34-year old Sgt Harold P. Calvert, navigator, Sgt King, WOp/AG and Sgt Bruce Robertson, rear gunner. In view of promised cloud cover from the Dutch coast to the target Craske and Calvert agreed upon a track to the target as opposed to 'going in by the back door'. Craske was to recall:

'It was a relatively calm night and after a bit of a stooge across the North Sea we obtained a good fix and some flak around the Hook of Holland. It was fairly obvious by this time that the promised cloud cover was a figment of the Met man's imagination, as it was as clear as a bell. But our die was cast, our course plotted, so we continued as planned. The searchlights were obviously working overtime and it was not going to be easy to sneak through by playing the waiting game. However, this was our best bet and sure enough the dancing beams of light merged into strong cones both to port and starboard, balancing an aircraft in full glare on the tip of the cone like a jet of water holding a Ping-Pong ball on a fairground rifle range. Our chance had arrived and with all the power that *G-George* could muster I went for the gap. Alas, not much progress had been made through the searchlight belt when the cockpit was filled with dazzling light. Normally, with a few hectic maneuvers there was a fair chance of losing the lights but on this occasion the center light had a bluish colour and had fastened on to *G-George* and no amount of twisting and turning could shift it and its accompanying beams. I was so occupied with trying to get out of the illumination that it was something of a surprise to hear and to see cannon tracer shells flying around the aircraft and in particular flashing up through the unoccupied front gun turret. The attack was from below and mercifully the rear turret was missed but gaping holes were blasted in the underside of the fuselage even to the extent of losing the Elsan (I wonder who was the lucky recipient beneath). I concluded that the bombs, positioned beneath the cockpit, acted as armor plating and had saved the three of us in the cabin – a sobering thought

'I had no doubt in my mind what to do next. I put the nose straight down and kept it that way. The ASI registered 320 mph. In the meantime Robbie in the rear turret was more than a little disturbed and was yelling all sorts of things into the intercom. He thought we had all 'had it' and certainly I was not able at that time to put his mind at rest. We had been at our usual 12,000ft and at about 7,000ft I tried to get back on an even keel, which was easier said than done. The port wing had dropped and the only way I could get sufficient purchase on the 'stick' (a large wheel) was to put my feet against the dashboard and heave like blazes with the wheel turned as far to the right as I could get it. With some relief I got *George* out of the dive and regained straight and level flight once again. I calmed Robbie with the news that I was still alive and flying and took stock of our situation. The engines were sounding good and while we were somewhat battered, there seemed no reason not to go to the target. However, a further attack from the starboard saw cannon shells whistling through the starboard engine, through the cockpit and within inches of my feet and out the other side. The starboard engine caught fire. I managed to extinguish it but the port engine sounded a bit sick to say the least. It was amazing to me that the pilot of the night fighter did not finish us off but presumably he lost us in the darkness.'

Oblt Wolfgang Thimmig of 2./NJG 1 was credited with shooting Craske's Whitley down at 0230 hours near Winterswijk 20 km NE of Bocholt. Thimmig's kill was one of the earliest *Dunkelnachtjagd* ('dark night fighting') victories, being achieved in complete darkness and under the guidance of ground radar. The crew jettisoned the bombs and everything removable but Craske was unable to maintain height and he ordered his crew to bale out. Everyone survived and they were made PoW. (Harold P. Calvert was later shot in cold blood by a member of the *Polizei* after escaping from *Stalag IIIE*). In all seven Whitleys and a Wellington failed to return from the raid on Cologne, the majority of these losses being due to night fighters of I./NJG 1. Three Hampdens and two Manchesters meanwhile failed to return from a raid on Düsseldorf by 52 Hampdens and six Manchesters and one Wellington was lost on the raid against rail targets at Duisburg by 54 Wellingtons.

Rail targets at Duisburg were attacked again on 17/18 August when the weather was bad and bombing was poor and again on 18/19 August when the weather was clear and the bombing results were good. Raids were mounted against Kiel, Mannheim, Düsseldorf, Karlsruhe and Cologne until on 28/29 August rail targets at Duisburg were once again the objective of Bomber Command. The force this time was made up of 60 Wellingtons, 30 Hampdens, 13 Stirlings, nine Halifaxes and six Manchesters. Furthermore, six Hampdens of 49 and 106 Squadrons made searchlight suppression sorties near the target, as Sgt George Luke, WOP-AG in Sgt Eric Robert Holmes

Lyon's crew[55], one of the three Hampdens of 106 Squadron used in the operation, explains:

'The apprehension felt at the possible danger involved was counteracted to a degree by the feeling of pride, rather like being chosen for the first eleven at school. We 'intruders' were to take off early and reach the target 15 minutes ahead of the main force. We carried a small load of incendiary bombs to release at 14,000-ft and additional ammunition for the machine guns, which, after diving to low level, we would use against the searchlights on the target route. We were to continue to harass the searchlights, hopefully keeping them out of action for one hour allowing the main force to bomb, leave the target area and be well on route for home, then they would regain height and return to their bases. This would enable the main bomber force to avoid the searchlight cones and the resulting attention of the German fighter and *Flak* concentrations.

'We released the incendiary bombs, surprisingly meeting little opposition en route, then dived to low altitude and commenced our attack on the searchlights. I felt great exhilaration during the low level attacks, the sense of speed being much greater and in my position as under gunner in the Hampden I was kept extremely busy firing away left and right at searchlights as they were switched on. They were extinguished immediately, whether by our marksmanship or intentionally by the Germans, we were not sure. We continued our attack with the wireless operator firing from the upper gun position. I felt that we were successfully achieving our purpose, although in the hectic activity taking place I caught sight of one of the main force bombers, which was caught in a cone of searchlights, receiving a pasting from the *Flak* batteries. We were meeting only light *Flak* and machine gun fire from the searchlight defenses. At low level and in the dark you are upon your target and gone almost before they can react. The pace of events was so fast that the hour-long attack seemed to last but a few minutes. Then we regained height and set course for base. We had crossed the Dutch coast at about 10,000 ft and were approximately forty miles NW of Texel when because of a technical inability to switch fuel tanks we lost both engines and we were forced to ditch. We all survived but after drifting in a dinghy for three days we were in such poor physical condition that when we were found by a Dutch fishing boat they had no choice but to hand us over to the German Naval authorities in the small harbour of Zoutkamp.'[56]

For F/Sgt Ralph Wood of 102 Squadron the operation to Frankfurt on 29/30 August by 143 aircraft represented about nine hours flying time:

'I was getting to have a healthy respect for those searchlights When they had you coned they would shoot tons of crap up those beams at you. After a bit they'd quit, leaving us to the fighters for target practice. The Whitley was a tough old bastard in spite of its ugly appearance. The damn thing always flew with its nose down, slowly at that, but it could take a hell of a beating nonetheless. [Two Hampdens and a Whitley were lost]. Op No.5 on 31 August was Essen. This was a comparatively short trip over enemy territory but still consumed six hours and provided us with plenty of activity. Our tail-gunner decided to put his steel helmet used for air raids to some practical use. He'd take it on ops with him and when things got hot over the target area, he'd sit on his steel helmet. He said no way was he going to get flak up his ass! Frankfurt on 2 September presented us with an engine failure and we were unable to complete the operation. If you carried the attack far enough you were given credit for an op. An op behind you was one closer to a tour no matter how you looked at it. A rubber factory just north of Essen was next on our list on 6 September. This raid saw us with a rear-gun-turret malfunction and an early and uneventful return to base. One of my compatriots from Moncton, a navigator, missed Great Britain altogether when returning from a raid. He landed in southern Ireland, which was neutral and remained there in internment for the rest of the war enjoying good food and drink while his pay and promotion continued. (I still haven't decided whether he was a stupid navigator or a smart operator). While partaking of some cheer at a favorite watering hole in Harrogate I became involved in a heated discussion with my flight commander. I was complaining that I was not flying often enough and he came back with some derogatory remarks on my navigational ability. I told him that if that weren't a yellow streak down his back he'd put me down to fly with him. Sure enough, the next morning, 7 September, saw me listed as his navigator for that night, to Berlin. Berlin in a Whitley – I didn't believe it! A little under the weather, I made sure during our air test that afternoon to take a few good whiffs of oxygen to clear the head. This was a tried and proven method of aiding your recovery. Hours later, as we were being debriefed at interrogation, I felt quite elated. We had actually bombed the capital of Germany but the trip wasn't that pleasant.'

On 7/8 September 197 bombers went to three aiming points in Berlin while another 51 bombers headed for Kiel. The Berlin force comprised 103 Wellingtons, 43 Hampdens, 31 Whitleys, six Halifaxes and four Manchesters. WOP-AG in the Manchester I of 207 Squadron flown by F/L W.J. Mike Lewis DFC was Sgt Charles Hall, who recalls:

> 'The outward flight was uneventful until about midnight when at about 13,000 ft over the sea near Tönning in Schleswig-Holstein, Sgt 'Dusty' Miller the rear gunner shouted, 'Night fighter astern!' This was accompanied by a stutter of machine gun fire, which hit our aircraft in the area of the port engine. As Miller opened fire the night fighter continued over the top of the Manchester enabling me, from my mid upper gunner's position, to fire into the belly of the enemy aircraft at very short range. F/L Lewis had immediately dived our aircraft and sought cover of thick cloud and contact was lost with the enemy fighter. There were no casualties but we had a serious fuel leak so after dropping our 4000lb bomb and incendiaries on a searchlight concentration at Wilhelmshaven (which had given us much trouble in previous operations) we set course for Waddington. The port engine cowling began to glow red-hot, then white hot in turn. Lewis shut down the engine, feathered the airscrew and activated the fine extinguisher within the engine cowling. This seemed to extinguish the fire but thereafter 12 very anxious eyes were focused on the port engine for signs of further trouble! It soon became apparent that we were not capable of maintaining height on the one remaining Vulture engine so we gradually lost height. With the gunners keeping a sharp lookout we descended through cloud emerging at 1500 ft over Holland with the inhospitable gray-black waters of the North Sea clearly visible. At this point Lewis decided that we were not going to make the English coast and turned south aiming to reach the Friesian Islands. The Friesians eventually came into view and turning westward again Lewis kept the aircraft parallel to the shore. We took up our crash positions. Amidst noise, water and mayhem we hit, bouncing several times before settling in what turned out to be the surf of the North coast of Ameland.'

Lewis put Manchester EM-W L7380 down safely on the beach in about 5ft of water at 0010 hrs. The crew took to their dinghy and got ashore. As they had previously agreed not to compromise any Dutch civilians, they were taken prisoner. Their attacker was *Fw* Siegfried Ney of 4./NJG 1 who successfully claimed this as his fifth *Abschuss*. In all, 137 crews claimed to have bombed their allotted targets in Berlin. Fifteen bombers were MIA and at least ten, including two Wellingtons of 115 Squadron, are thought to have been shot down by nightfighters.[57]

One by one the returning bombers landed back at their stations in eastern England. P/O Mike Evans and crew of a 149 Squadron[58] Wellington returned to Mildenhall after what was an eventful trip, as Sgt Jim Coman, the WOp, recalls:

> 'All went fairly well until we were making our bombing run, straight and level, when we were coned in searchlights and received numerous hits by *Flak*. After releasing the bombs at 9500 ft we took evasive action but were unable to get out of the searchlights so we dived to roof top level and moved out of the target area as quickly as possible. The AA gunners were actually shooting bits off their own buildings trying to hit us. We gained height as soon as possible to regain our bearings and arrived back at the Dutch coast short of fuel. All the main tanks were empty so we had approximately 20 minutes flying time on the engine nacelle tanks. We were attacked by a Ju 88 over the Dutch coast south of the Friesian Islands and north of Rotterdam, which our rear gunner engaged and the fighter broke off trailing smoke from one of its engines. We made an emergency landing at the nearest airfield on the English coast, at Martlesham Heath, a fighter 'drome. As we landed the engines cut out. They had been running for nine hours after take off. We counted 150 holes in the aircraft before we left for Mildenhall but we failed to spot the most serious damage, which must have happened over the target when a shell must have penetrated the main spar when the bomb doors were open.'

On 29/30 September when Bomber Command sent 139 aircraft to Stettin northeast of Berlin F/Sgt Ralph Wood of 102 Squadron flew his 9th op:

> 'It turned out to be the best trip I'd made to date. We threw out our flares, which lit up the target directly beneath us. We made two separate bombing runs, dropping one stick of bombs on each run. We never reached our base that night as we were running short of fuel. My flight commander was particularly pleased with this 11-hour trip and my navigational abilities were never questioned again. My tenth op on 12 October was to Nuremberg but we ended up dropping our load on Frankfurt as the alternate target. This turned out to be a 9 1/2-hour trip. Our exactors, whatever they might be were u/s (unserviceable) and we had to land at Pocklington, returning to base later that day. At this stage of the game we didn't fly as a set crew. The members were interchangeable for various reasons.

For my part I always made a quick appraisal of the pilot I was to fly with. How much confidence could I place in him? For that matter how much would he have in me? We all had to depend on each and every crewmember. We were a team, each relying on the other to do his job to the best of his ability. Op No.11 to Duisburg on 16 October was one of the easier trips in that six hours saw the operation completed and to our satisfaction. Making a good landfall on the English coast on our homeward journey always boosted the navigator's morale. By a good landfall I mean approaching the coast and hitting it just about where you were supposed to, right on track. My pilot occasionally asked, 'Where are we?' I'd shove a map or chart in front of him pointing wildly to any spot over the North Sea or Germany depending on the occasion. This having satisfied him I returned to my plotting table to work out our actual position undisturbed.

'Operation number 12 was to Wilhelmshaven on 20 October and again we were forced to bomb Emden, the alternate target. This was an eight-hour trip but we managed to return to our own home base. The meteorology reports were very important to the success of our operations but the met section at times was not accurate and left a lot to be desired. We called the meteorology information 'met gen', which usually turned out to be 'pukka gen' ('good information') or 'duff gen' ('bad information'). There was a story going around about a Whitley crew becoming lost and running out of fuel. The pilot set the automatic pilot and told his crew to bale out. This they did, with the exception of the tail-gunner whose intercom had become disconnected and he failed to hear the order. A short time later the aircraft made a remarkably good landing on a sloping hill in Scotland. The tail-gunner upon vacating his turret commented loudly on the pilot's smooth landing. You could almost see him passing out when he discovered he was the only occupant of the aircraft.'

Thirty-four aircraft were shot down by *Nachtjagd* in September[59] and 20 more in October.[60] On the night of 26/27 October the RAF raided Bremerhaven. F/Sgt Derek 'Dick' Lord a Whitley pilot in 77 Squadron, wrote a letter describing the raid:

'My navigator said: 'Dick, if we are going to prang this place properly, it is about time we started looking for a gap in these bloody fog banks.'

I said, 'Right!' and stooged the plane to where the clouds appeared to be less thick.

'We found a hole in the black mass of tiny water particles. The Hun found it too with about 30 of his searchlights.

'The light from them seemed to penetrate the very floor of the Whitley. I made no attempt to evade them ... the navigator wanted a landfall. How he took it, glaring into those millions of candlepower, I cannot attempt to explain but he did so. He gave me fresh directions and we began our first run.

'An orange-colored searchlight followed our course, shining through the clouds as if such things never existed.

'Then the *Flak* came and the tracers and the bomb flashes. Some of the other boys were already on the job. We were flying at 16,000 ft; the remainder of the boys were lower. The shells were exploding at varying heights, mostly, I thought, at about 10,000 ft. I was wrong. We had just finished a tight turn when it happened.

'There was a terrific explosion somewhere at the back of my head ... everything went black and then red, punctured with little green and yellow dots. I heard my radioman say 'My God!' Then everything was silent.

'In the silence I could feel myself thinking 'This is it! This is the end of your run … you have not done so badly … what's this? The seventh raid? You've been lucky – some chaps don't last seven trips ...'

'Something spoke in my ear ... I say something because it sounded like a very weak loudspeaker ... 'For Christ's sake, Dick, pull your-self together ... we're not done yet!'

'A light flashed by my eyes ... it must have been a searchlight. It brought me to my senses with a jerk. I was sprawled over the steering column and the second pilot was puffing at me. I struggled into a sitting position. We were diving madly at the ground, spinning as we did so. The altimeter read 2,550 ft and was fast slipping back to 2000. Too late to bale out. If only I could have died with the explosion! My head was thumping and my right arm felt as heavy as lead. It was still resting on the joystick.

'Two thousand feet. The cloud had gone but the searchlights played on us. Shells burst around us still. In a flash I saw all these things and in the same flash realized that unless we did something very drastic quickly we were going to pile in. The second pilot and myself pulled on the stick. After what seemed an age there was a response from the controls. We stopped spinning and flattened out. The navigator down in the front turret shouted something but I couldn't make out what it was. The aircraft bucketed and I thought we had been hit again. Somehow we kept control of the old Whitley and climbed slowly into the shelter of the clouds.

'Someone said 'Are you OK Dick?' I replied that I was and was anyone hurt? The second pilot said 'No'. 'We'd better stooge back and get rid of our eggs,' I suggested.

'The navigator laughed, 'We dropped them from approximately 1200 ft, you ass!'

'Oh!' I said and asked for directions home. Over the North Sea we discussed the dive. 'We were only over Bremerhaven seven minutes', said the wireless-operator, 'but what a seven minutes!'

'What did we hit with the bombs?' I asked.

'God knows,' said the navigator. 'We were diving straight on to a portion of the docks just before you pulled out!'

'The Canadian rear gunner called over the intercom from his turret, 'The docks ain't where they used to be, Dick! We've gotta small portion in the fuselage right behind me. What the hell d'ya want to dive-bomb the place for? Jeez, we could ha' made just as good a show from 15,000!'[61]

When 181 aircraft were despatched to Hanover on the night of 30 November/1 December it was F/Sgt Ralph Wood's 13th op and it was destined to be his last in a Whitley:

'No. 13 – lucky or unlucky? I guess one had to call it lucky as we had a malfunction with our rear turret and we were forced to return to base. The next five months were occupied converting to the Halifax bomber at Dalton, a satellite station near Topcliffe and some temporary duty at Lossiemouth in northern Scotland, which gave us a nice change of pace, including a rest from those bombing raids over Germany. Our Handley Page bomber was a beautiful four-engined bird with three gun turrets, front, mid-upper and rear. She carried a 5 1/2-ton bombload, cruised at 300 mph and had a 3000-mile range. Our 'Hallybag', as it was fondly called, had a crew of seven – six in our case as I still acted as bomb-aimer, navigator and front-gunner – a pilot, a wireless operator, a flight engineer, a mid-upper gunner and a tail-gunner. The dinky little navigator's compartment was below and in front of the pilot's cockpit. You went down a few steps and entered a small section with a navigator's metal table down one side, ahead and below the pilot's feet. A curtain in the nose end hid the even smaller compartment where I would huddle with my Mk.14 bombsight and other instruments when we got reasonably close to the target. The gun I was supposed to operate when called upon was a Vickers gas-operated .303 machine-gun mounted on a swivel and stuck out through the perspex nose, high above the bombsight. I recalled the short introduction lecture on the VGO; the RAF sergeant telling us the gun was famous for jamming. All you had to do was look at it the wrong way and it would plug up on you. I hadn't fired a machine-gun since Bombing & Gunnery School at Mossbank late in 1940. That had been a Browning, not a relic like this. If a Junkers should suddenly make a pass I really couldn't tell how I'd make out at all. But I'd sure give it my very best try. We transferred to 76 Squadron and operated out of Middleton St. George, County Durham.'

Another of the new generation RAF bombers, the Manchester, which had been suffering from a plague of engine failures, was proving a big disapapointment. Ernie Rodley, who had joined the RAFVR in 1937 and had spent an 'exhausting and unrewarding' year and a half in Training Command, recalls:

'The Manchester could maintain height on one engine as long as the oil-cooler flap remained closed but the straining good engine would gradually overheat and the flap had to be inched open. This was followed by a slow loss of height, which continued until the crew had to bale out or ditch. The Manchester was grounded to give Rolls-Royce time to develop the Vulture engine to a more reliable state. By mid 1941 this had been achieved but to play safe it was decided that 97 Squadron should be re-formed and equipped with Manchesters but all pilots had to have at least 1000 hrs under their belts and so it rescued me from the thraldom of instructing. Somewhat awed by the size of this monster, I found it a delight to fly. Everything worked – after all, they were nearly new – and I was relieved to find that I had not completely lost the art of landing. Actually, the Manchester was even nicer to fly than the Lancaster was. With 12 feet less in the wing span and with a closer engine-mass, it had a rate of roll like a fighter. The landing, with a trickle of engine to offset the high wing loading, was like that of the Anson. Then once on the ground the huge 16 feet props bit into the air, decelerating the machine like wheel-brakes. The Vulture was now very dependable. The big-end trouble had been overcome and one only has to remember how the Manchester took the brunt of the work at the Lancaster Conversion Units to realize what a good job Rolls had done.[62] The re-equipped 97 Squadron was stationed at Coningsby, a grass field near Boston and happily boasting peacetime quarters. We shared the Station with 106 Squadron, flying Hampdens. One of their pilots was a press-on type by the name of Guy Gibson.[63] After posting to 97, we had to spend some time working up to operational fitness and we spent a lot of time wistfully watching 106 being bombed up and need I say, bearing their wisecracks in the Mess.'

A fellow contemporary in 97 'Straits Settlements' Squadron was F/O Brian 'Darkie' Hallows[64] who flew his first op on 15/16 November to Emden when 49 heavies were despatched. Hallows was at the controls of L7474 *'Z-Zebra,* which carried a bomb load of five 1000 lb bombs[65]:

> 'We took off at 1830 hours, 40 minutes late due to aircraft being unserviceable. Met forecast said there would be no cloud. We climbed to 5000 ft, met cloud, climbed to 10,000-ft, again in cloud up to 12,000 ft. Continued at 12,000 to DR[66] position off Borkum, thence to Emden. Cloud 8-10/10ths and observation was difficult. We spent 15 minutes in the target area but could not see anything. *Flak* was all round us all time. Fire was seen through cloud, which we bombed, causing more fires. Heavy ice was encountered in cloud and we landed at Coltishall. Time 6-30 hrs.'

Four Wellingtons were lost.[67]

After much preparation in formation flying Hallows second trip was to bomb the *Scharnhorst* and *Gneisenau* at Brest on 18 December in a daylight formation operation with ten other of the squadron's Manchesters. Altogether, 47 aircraft including 18 Halifaxes and 18 Stirlings were despatched and told to keep "Salmon and Gluckstein"[68] penned in. The weather was good and a fighter umbrella was provided. Hallows took off at 0930 hours at the controls of Manchester I L7525 *'D-Dog'* carrying a bomb load of one 4000 lb HE bomb and two 500 pounders, with ten other aircraft, two of them spares. There was some cloud at about 5000 ft with large holes so navigation was easy. All went well up to the target area when very intense flak was encountered. *'D-Dog'* was hit three times and Hallows and his navigator were hit on the head by flying perspex but with no lasting damage. 97 Squadron bombed in formation at 15,000 feet and dived away to the right. The leading aircraft of No 1 section had his starboard elevator shot off and the rear gunner was killed. On the way back a tight formation was maintained but P/O Stokes in the third Vic straggled and he was shot down by a Bf 109. Two crew were seen to bale out seven miles north of the French coast. Flak off Brittany had damaged the tailplane of the leading Manchester flown by W/C D.F. Balsdon and the lowering of flap on final approach proved too much for the remaining tail surfaces and the aircraft dived into the ground at Coningsby. All eight occupants were killed.[69]

In December 1941 *Nachtjagd* claimed 13 including three by 4./NJG 1 and another three by I./NJG 1 on the 27/28th. On 28/29 December 61 Hampdens of the 81 detailed reached their target, the Chemische Werke, a synthetic rubber plant at Huls west of Duisburg. The target was clearly identified in the moonlight and the factory was thoroughly bombed, fired and photographed. Four Hampdens were lost. P1165 of 408 'Goose' Squadron RCAF at Balderton, flown by P/O Stuart Bruce Keigh Brackenbury RCAF, who was on his eighth trip, fell to the guns of *Oblt* Helmut Woltersdorf of 7./NJG 1 and the Hampden crashed two kilometers west of Winterswijk (Gelderland). Brackenbury had reached the target and bombed it. The flare they could have used to illuminate the target had not been needed so they were still carrying it when a Bf 110 nightfighter attacked them while at 15,000 ft. The flare was hit and ignited. Brackenbury baled out. He was free for four hours before being found by some Dutchmen who led him down back streets to the police station, which was manned by Germans. He was taken to meet *Major* Wolfgang Falck, *Kommandeur* NJG 1 at Twente. Falck apologized, treated him well before he was taken to a prisoner of war camp.[70]

Hallows flew his third op with an attack on the *Scharnhorst* and *Gneisenau* at Brest again on 9/10 January 1942 in a night sortie. All told 82 aircraft were despatched. Take off originally was at 0320 hours on the 10th but it was put forward to 0004 hours because of weather. Crews had previously been briefed twice for this trip but each time it was cancelled. At take-off it was dark and no horizon with cloud at 1500 feet. They kept to 1000-1500 ft to Upper Heyford when the cloud thinned and they went up through it to 7000 ft. Pinpoint Start Point and on to Brest. Cloud 1-3 tenths Channel but 10/10 target. Twenty minutes were spent over the target. "Nickels" (propaganda leaflets) were dropped but as the target could not be identified they brought their bombs back. Flak was heavy but inaccurate. Hallows fourth trip was to Hamburg on the night of 15/16 January. He took off at 1700 hours in daylight and set course for Denmark, arriving there at 1915 hours. From there to Hamburg. Over the target Hallows saw little until another aircraft dropped a load of incendiaries. In the subsequent glare he saw the river and docks and the Binnen Alsten (inner harbour) clearly. He then ran in easterly and dropped his 14x400lb incendiaries across this first stick. It produced a 'lovely sight' of over 3000 small fires across the centre of the town. Fifty-two of the 96 aircraft despatched claimed to have hit Hamburg. Hallows left the target swiftly in a northerly direction and came home the same way. Three Wellingtons and a Hampden were lost and another eight aircraft crashed in England.[71]

Mainly because of a lull in Bomber Command operations just 16 bombers were claimed destroyed by *Nachtjagd* in January 1942. Twelve of these went to II./NJG 2 at Leeuwarden, which 23-year old *Hptm* Helmut 'Bubi' ('Boy')

Lent, innovator of the night fighter arm had established on 1 November 1941. On 20 January during a *Himmelbett*[72] sortie over the North Sea to the north of Terschelling, *Oblt* Ludwig Becker of the 6th *Staffel* NJG 2 destroyed three Wellingtons in 37 minutes.[73] A mere seven victories were claimed by *Nachtjagd* in February, all by II./NJG 2.[74]

21-year-old *Lt* Dieter Schmidt who had been posted from the Zerstörerschule at Neubiberg to III./NJG 1 on 1 September 1941 comments on the early wartime *Nachtjagd* procedures:

> 'The Third *Gruppe* of NJG 1 was at Twenthe, an airfield to the north of Enschede in Holland. The *Gruppe* was carrying out *Helle Nachtjagd* in a sector of the night-fighting defenses reaching from the Heligoland Bight to Belgium, together with the searchlight and fighter control units stationed there: when approaches by enemy aircraft were reported, a number of night fighters were sent up to readiness positions, then shoot down any enemy aircraft caught in the searchlights. At the time, the British used almost exclusively twin-engined aircraft, Wellingtons, Whitleys or Hampdens, flying loosely on a broad front, i.e. practically singly. In our opinion, we young crews had been over-trained for our task as nightfighters: to begin with, we were only permitted to take off for practice flights, especially for searchlight target indications and sometimes we were ordered to cockpit readiness for the more senior crews. So two months passed before I had my first operational flight and another two-and-a half months passed before I had my second one. But at that time the night air war was a slow business. Crews were trained for the *Himmelbett* method of the *Dunkle Nachtjagd*. In that, the abilities of the *Jägerleitoffizier* [JLO, or GCI-controller] were critical, as he directed the fighter to a position behind and a little below the enemy aircraft with a succession of courses, heights and speeds to fly, until he was able to make him out as a dark shadow against the lighter night sky. During the first half of 1942 we received the first Bf 110s specially built for nightfighting, recognisable by the large propeller spinners. Each DB601F motor delivered 1300 hp but suffered frequent engine trouble and caused some losses. New British aircraft such as the twin-engined Avro Manchester and the Short Stirling began to appear. One Manchester, its engines damaged by Flak, had force-landed in Holland on its return and we had taken a good look at it.'

It had soon become obvious that the *Helle Nachtjagd* with searchlights could only function in more or less clear weather. At the beginning of 1942 therefore, fighter controllers were equipped with radar sets, one *Freya* early warning one and two *Würzburg Riese* for individual guidance and the crews trained for the *Himmelbett* method of the *Dunkle* [Dark] *Nachtjagd*. In that, the abilities of the controller were critical, as he directed the fighter to a position behind and a little below the enemy aircraft with a succession of courses, heights and speeds to fly, until he was able to make him out as a dark shadow against the lighter night sky. Kammhuber's system resembled the British GCI-system and it took full advantage of Bomber Command's tactic in sending bombers singly and on a broad front and not in concentrated streams. All approaches to Germany and its main industrial centers were divided into *Himmelbett Räume* ('four poster bed boxes'), circular and partly overlapping areas in which one to three fighters orbited a radio beacon.[75] Positions near the coast were additionally equipped with a *Wassermann* or *Mammuth* long-range search installation. When approaching bombers were located by Freya radar its *Jägerleitoffizier* would vector an individual *Nachtjagd* crew towards a single bomber with one of the *Würzburg* radars at his disposal. The bomber was simultaneously plotted on a Seeburg Tisch (an accurate plotting table with a radius of 36 kilometers) by the second *Würzburg*. Night fighters were at first restricted to activity within the area of their boxes. Procedure was for one night fighter to be taken under GCI control in each *Himmelbett* Box affected by the raid, while any other night fighters available orbited the radio beacon at different heights in the waiting area. The first night fighter was vectored towards the bomber formation until such time as it picked up the enemy in its *Lichtenstein* B/C, whereupon it was released from control and the remaining aircraft were called up and sent into action one by one. *Lichtenstein* B/C airborne interception radar had been given industrial priority No.1 in July 1941 and the first four *Lichtenstein* B/C sets were installed in aircraft of NJG 1 at Leeuwarden in February 1942. Such was their effectiveness that by the spring successes obtained through the searchlight and GCI techniques were about equal.

These therefore, were the defenses which confronted crews in Bomber Command at the beginning of 1942 but a new and dynamic leader and the arrival of a new aircraft which was to prove the most successful bomber of the war, were about to usher in a new era in RAF Bomber Command.

Notes

1. So called from the American Disney cartoon character 'J. Wellington Wimpy in 'Popeye'.

2. 2 were credited to *Oblt* Günther Specht, 1 to *Hptm* Dickore, 1 to *Uffz* Pollack and 1 to *Uffz* Pirsch. On 3 December 1939 Specht was shot down by return fire from a Wellington and he ditched in the sea and he was later rescued. The German had been wounded in the face and later had to have his left eye removed. In May 1943, after a long convalescence and postings in fighter training schools Specht became *Gruppenkommandeur*, II./JG II. He scored 32 confirmed *Abschüsse* (victories), including 15 *4-mots (*4-motor bombers) and awarded the *Ritterkreuz* (Knight's Cross) before being reported MIA on 1.1.45 during the disastrous *Bodenplatte* operation.

3. P1319 of 49 Sqn. P/O A.H, Benson and crew were KIA. Förster went on to claim Hampden P4286 of 44 Sqn at Oosterhout on 14/15 May. P/O L.J. Ashfield and his crew were KIA. He also claimed Hampden I P1178 of 83 Sqn at Often (nr Aachen) on 3/4 June. F/O F.J. Hayden and crew were KIA. Förster joined 2./JG 27, scoring another 10 daylight victories. KIA 14 December 1941 in North Africa.

4. Meyer joined the RAF in 1937 on a Short Service Commission for a period of 4 years' active service and for 6 yrs in the Reserve. He was posted to 76 Sqn in April 1939, then in the process of re-equipping with the Hampden to replace the obsolete Armstrong Whitworth Wellesley.

5. Dead (corrupted from Deduced) Reckoning navigation is navigation based on known facts such at planned course and airspeed and variables such as wind velocity and temperatures forecast by the Met Office and used to calculate track and ground speeds. These items were used by the navigator at the pilot/navigator briefing to complete the Flight Plan at the top of the Log Sheet, RAF Form 441c, to give the navigator basic facts and to give the crew something to work on should disaster befall him.

6. After completing 37 operations Rothwell was posted to an OTU to instruct pupils converting from the Anson and Oxford trainers to Wellingtons. He had flown over 180 hrs on operations.

7. I., II., III./NJG 1, I./NJG 2 and I./NJG 3.

8. N1496 at 0250 hrs. Förster was a former soldier who trained as a pilot in 1936 and as a *Zerstörer* pilot he scored three day victories in 1940. After he was shot down and wounded he was assigned to the role of flying instructor and later served as a staff officer. In 1943 he retrained as a nigthfighter pilot and on 1 June 1943 he joined 1./NJG 1.

9. Förster achieved four more night victories in NJG 1.

10. Whitley V P5007 of 51 Sqn with F/L S. E.F. Curry (KIA) went down in the early hrs of 20 July 25 km NW of Kiel (3 others KIA, 1 PoW), followed on 21/22 July by Whitley V N1487 of 78 Sqn flown by Sgt V.C. Monkhouse (all KIA) 10 km N of Münster. Sreib soon added to his score, claiming 2 Wellingtons on 30/31 August 1940 and 3 bombers on 30 September/1 October 1940.

11. *Ofw* Paul Gildner of 3./NJG 1 claimed 3 aircraft over the Netherlands during September 1940. Hampden P4370 of 144 Sqn (which he identified as a Whitley) crashed near Sittard at 0045 hrs on the 3rd and on the night of 18/19th P5008 of 58 Sqn at 2230 hrs near Groenlo and N1425 of 77 Sqn two hrs later at Zieuwent.

12. P4964 of 78 Sqn near Hummelo, 21 km E of Arnhem.

13. These included Hampden Is X2910 of 44 Sqn and X2993 of 50 Sqn on a bombing operation to Berlin.

14. *Spanner* or *Spanneranlage (Spanner* installation*)* literally translated, a 'peeping Tom', was an infrared searchlight mounted in the nose of the aircraft to illuminate the target and a receiver to pick up the reflected energy. *Spanner I* and *Spanner II* (a passive device that in theory used the heat from engine exhausts to detect its target) were not very successful.

15. L7844 KX-T of 311 Czechoslovak Sqn flown by P/O Bohumil Landa crashed at 2145 hrs near Oosterwolde/Doornspijk. Landa and 3 crew KIA. Sgts Emanuel Novotny and Augustin Sestak baled out safely. It was Becker's first Abschuss.

16. *JLO* or fighter-control officer.

17. Becker, born in Dortmund in August 1911, volunteered for the *Luftwaffe* in 1934 and became a *Stuka* pilot before joining the Bf 110 *Zerstörer* and becoming a nightfighter pilot in July 1940. In 1941-42 Becker became one of the leading '*Experten'* in the Luftwaffe night fighter arm. He shot down 40 bombers in 1942 and taught the new and young crews from his experiences. To them Becker 'The Night Fighting Professor' was an inspiring fatherly figure. Instrumental in introducing the *Lichtenstein* AI radar into the night fighter arm in 1941 though most night fighter aircrew were sceptical about it (they liked to rely on the 'Mk I Eyeball'). Becker had one of the still experimental sets installed in his Do 217Z night fighter at Leeuwarden. Guided by the revolutionary radar, his and *Natchjagd's* first AI victory was in the early hrs of 9 August 1941 in a Do 215B-5 night fighter version of the Do 215 reconnaissance-bomber when 44 Wellingtons of Bomber Command attacked Hamburg. Becker shot down 6 RAF night bombers 8/9 August-29/30 September 1941.

18. As he recalls Robinson and the crew of W/O Snowdon in Wellington X9873 joined the toll on 31 October/1 November 1941 when they FTR from a raid on Bremen (X9873 was the only a/c lost while 4 Whitleys FTR from the raid on Hamburg). 'A Bf 110 [piloted by *Oblt* Paul Gildner of 4./NJG 1] operating from Leeuwarden made a copybook attack from astern and below on our Wellington at 1930 hrs. We never saw him until it was too late. We were never in with the chance of a shot. He just loomed up out of the murk with a startling suddenness and opened up with a prolonged and devastating burst of cannon fire. It was all over in a matter of seconds. No time to consider. One minute we were happily on course and the next we were plunging down and about to crash, ironically, on Schiermonnikoog itself. [It was Gildner's 20th victory and he added a 21st, a Whitley, later that same night]. Fate decreed that I should survive this, plus some enlightening even if somewhat dreary years in German prison camps before liberation by Russian troops in May 1945.'

19. L7859.

20. One Blenheim and one Whitley were lost this night.

21. *Oblt* Egmont Prinz *zur* Lippe Weissenfeld destroyed Wellington P9286 of 115 Sqn 10 km W of Medemblik on 16/17 November, the aircraft going down in flames at 0205 hrs to crash near Winkel, Holland and with the loss of the whole crew. *Fw* Hans Rasper of the same Staffel destroyed Whitley P5012 of 102 Sqn on 15/16 December 10 km NW of Petten off the Dutch coast at Egmond.

22. Six by the intruders of I./NJG 2 plus Whitley T4203 of 78 Sqn by *Oblt* Reinhold Eckardt of II./NJG 1 on the night of 9/10th, which went down between Millingen and Kekerdom, Holland and Whitley N1521 of 58 Sqn by *Oblt* Egmont Prinz *zur* Lippe-Weissenfeld of 4./NJG 1, which cr. near Callantsoog, Holland on the 15/16th.

23. Four-engined bombers went into action for the first time when 43 aircraft, including 3 Stirling Is of 7 Squadron, led by Acting S/L J.M. Griffith-Jones DFC bombed oil storage tanks beside the Waal at Rotterdam in a separate operation. Each Stirling carried 16 500 lb bombs and they dropped a total of 46 500lb bombs (2 hung up). 7 Squadron had been the first squadron in the RAF to receive the four-engined bomber, in August 1940.

24. 'Taffy' Rearden died trapped in his front turret, which sank beneath the ice. Jock Hall was badly injured with his foot almost severed and he had bullet holes in his burned clothing but surgery at the Queen Wilhelmina hospital in Amsterdam was successful and he survived. *H-Harry* was one of 4 losses on the Hanover raid and was credited to Hptm Walter Ehle of *Stab* II/NJG 1 from Middenmeer N of Schiphol for his 5th victory. Ehle poured 560 rounds of 7mm mg and 100 rounds of 20mm cannon into Wellington T2702, which cr. on the frozen Ijsselmeer about 17 km W of Kempen. Three other bombers were lost including Hampden X3001 of 49 Sqn, which was shot down by *Lt* Leopold Fellerer of 5./NJG 1 N of Alkmaar. Enemy intruders claimed 6 a/c over the UK: *Oblt* Albert Schulz and *Hptm* Rolf Jung of 2./NJG 2 claimed a Blenheim and a Wellington near West Raynham respectively and *Oblt* Paul Semrau of 3./NJG 2 claimed two Blenheims near Feltwell for his 1st and 2nd victories. *Oblt* Kurt Hermann of I./NJG 2 claimed 2 Hampdens near Waddington for his 5th and 6th victories. The intruders of I./NJG 2 claimed 12 bombers destroyed on intruding operations over the UK during February. On the night of the 15/16th Wellington T2847 of 15 Sqn went down near Barchem to *Fw* Kalinowski of 6./NJG 1 and Whitley T4164 of 77 Sqn shot down by *Oblt* Jüsgen of I./NJG 3 at Malden. *Ofw* Paul Gildner of 4./NJG 1 destroyed Blenheim T1895 at Oosterhoogebrug on 28 February/1 March. His 6th confirmed kill.

25. Halifax Is of 35 Sqn flew the first operational sorties on 10/11 March when 6 a/c and 8 Blenheims bombed Le Havre. The Halifax was the second four-engined bomber to be introduced into operational service and began equipping first line squadrons in November 1940. By spring 1942 12 squadrons of 4 Group were fully equipped. The prototype Manchester twin-engined bomber flew on 25 July 1939 and initially was fitted with twin fins, later increased to three. The Manchester I entered service with 207 Sqn at Waddington in November 1940 and the first operational flight took place on the night of 24/25 February 1941 when 6 Manchesters were part of a force of 57 aircraft that attacked Brest. 1 Manchester crashed in England.

26. 22 Hampdens, 13 Whitleys and 4 Manchesters.

27. L7303 EM-P.

28. In 1931 F/L J.N. Boothman, flying Supermarine S.6B S1595 won the Schneider Trophy outright for Britain setting an average speed of 340.08 mph (547 km/h)

29. L7303, which was shot down at 2350 hrs 1 km W of Hertogenbosch, was credited to *Oblt* Walter Fenske of I/NJG 1. Herzog, who shot down a Whitley of 78 Sqn at 2305 hrs at Helenaveen 2330 hrs (for his 2nd official kill) and scored his 2nd victory of the night at 2330 hrs at Bakel, 15 km SE of Helmond. In March *Nachtjagd* claimed 20 victories, including 14 over the continent.

30. On 9/10 April 80 a/c – 36 Wellingtons, 24 Hampdens, 17 Whitleys and 3 Stirlings – went to Berlin. 6 FTR.

31. T2879 was 1 of 3 Wellingtons, which FTR from Berlin. A Stirling which FTR was claimed by *Fw* Karl-Heinz Scherfling S-W of Lingen at 2335 hrs and a Whitley was claimed by *Ofw* Wilhelm Beier nr Chelmsford at 0235 hrs. 2 Wellingtons FTR from a raid on Vegesack by 9 a/c. WellingtonW5375 of 12 Sqn, which cr in the Ijsselmeer N of Harderwijk on a raid on Emden by 7 a/c was claimed shot down by *Oblt* Egmont Prinz *zur* Lippe Weissenfeld of 4./NJG 1 for NJG 1's 100th victory at 0059 hrs on 10 April. W/C Vivian Q. Blackden the CO and his crew KIA. Blackden was buried at Lemsterland in Holland. *Nachtjagd* crews actually claimed 7 Wellingtons, 3 of them over England.

32. Two were shot down by *Hptm* Werner Streib of *Stab* I/NJG 1 and 1 by *Ofw* Gerhard Herzog of 2./NJG 1. *Lt* Hermann Reese of 2./NJG 1 and *Lt* Hans-Dieter Frank of *Stab* I/NJG 1 claimed the other 2. Frank had joined the *Luftwaffe* in 1937 and was introduced to nightfighting in the spring of 1941. By mid-1942 he was a *Hptm* and *Staffelkapitän 2 Staffel* NJG 1 flying He 219s. Awarded *Ritterkreuz* on 20 June 1943, two nights later (21/22.6) he claimed 6 bombers destroyed. On 1 July 1943 he became *Kommandeur* I./NJG 1.

33. Eleven a/c were lost, the largest total lost on night operations so far in the war.

34. 40 RAF night bombers were claimed destroyed during April 1941 (including 25 by I./NJG 2, 6 by I./NJG 1 and 2 by III./NJG 1.

35. Operational Training Unit.

36. All 6 of F/L Freddy Savage's crew of R1374 KIA when the a/c was shot down by *Flak* near Nantes.

37. 14 victories were credited to I./NJG 2, 6 to 4./NJG 1 including Stirling I N3654 of 15 Sqn flown by W/C H.R. Dale (all KIA) by *Oblt* Egmont Prinz *zur* Lippe Weissenfeld on 10/11th nr Spanbroek and 4 to I./NJG 1.

38. This included the intruder *Gruppe*'s 100th victory, an unidentified Wellington 70-km E of Great Yarmouth by *Ofw* Hermann Sommer of 2./NJG 2 at 2355 hrs on 27 June. (During 1940-41 Sommer claimed 8 a/c over the UK including, on 29/30 April 4 Blenheims. He claimed 19 *Abschüsse* in NJG 2, NJG 1 and NJG 102 1940-early 1944. KIA during a daylight sortie on 11 February 1944). II./NJG 1 claimed 13 and I./NJG 1 8. I./NJG 3 at Werneuchen nr Berlin for protection of the Reich capital, scored 5 kills during June. One of these victories was achieved by *Fw* Kalinowski and his *Bordfunker Uffz* Zwickl of 2nd *Staffel* who destroyed Stirling W7430 of 7 Sqn over the 'Big City' in a *Helle Nachtjagd* sortie on 2/3 June. Only Sgt W.S. Bellow the rear gunner survived.

39. Lent was destined to rise to command of NJG 3 and to score an incredible final total of 113 victories, including 105 Bomber Command aircraft. He succumbed to severe injuries on 7 October 1944 after crashing on landing at Paderborn airfield 2 days earlier.

40. 114 Wellingtons bombed Cologne (3 lost) and 54 Whitleys and 18 Wellingtons attacked Osnabrück (3 Whitleys FTR) while another 49 Wellingtons raided Münster (3 FTR).

41. Ward was KIA on 15/16 September 1941, shot down in a 75 Sqn Wellington over Hamburg.

42. 2 FTR. 82 a/c bombed Aachen 1 Hampden and 1 Whitley FTR. Three crews of NJG 1 claimed 3 of these losses.

43. A navigational and blind-bombing device, which was introduced into RAF service during August 1941. It consisted of the reception by equipment in the aircraft of transmission from a 'master' ('A') and 2 'slave' stations ('B & C') situated on a base line about 200 mls long. The difference in the time taken by the 'A' & 'B' and 'A' & 'C' signals to reach the aircraft were measured and displayed on a CRT on the navigator's table in the aircraft. From then on the aircraft could be located on 2 position lines known as *Gee* co-ordinates. Accuracy of a *Gee* fix varied from less than 1/2 a mile to about 5 miles, depending on the skill of the navigator and the strength of the signal. *Gee* range varied with the conditions from 300-400 mls.

44. The starboard engine of a Wellington IC of 75 Sqn flown by Sgt F.T. Minikin cut as the bomber crossed the coast at 6000 ft and cr. in the sea nr. Corton, 2 mls N of Lowestoft. Both pilots, who were inj, were picked up. Rest KIA.

45. R1502 had crashed at 0028 on 14 July at Onderdijk, 5 km S of Medemblik.

46. T2619.

47. Telling was killed 6 months later on 19 January 1942 when his Wellington broke up during a training flight near Thetford, Norfolk. Saich and 5 others of *T-Tommy's* crew, including Sgt E. Trott, KIA on the Berlin raid of 7/8 September 1941 when their Wellington was shot down in flames by a German night fighter, believed to be flown by *Oblt* Helmut Lent of 4./NJG 1 nr Terwispel in Holland. 15 bombers FTR.

48. *Oblt* Lent (4./NJG 1), *Lt* von Bonin (6./NJG 1) and *Uffz* Benning of 1./NJG 3 each destroyed a Wellington. Lent's victim has been identified as W5513 of 104 Sqn and von Bonin's as R1613 of 214 Sqn. *Uffz* Benning's *Abschuss* was either T2737 of 149 Sqn or W5726 of 305 Sqn.

49. 2 Whitleys of 10 Sqn were lost to crews of 1./NJG 1 and 4./NJG 1. *Lt* Linke of 4./NJG 1 destroyed Hampden AD835 of 83 Sqn over Schiermonnikoog.

50. F/L Christopher C. Cheshire and Halifax I L9530 MP-L of 76 Sqn was shot down on 12/13 August over Berlin. Cheshire & 4 crew PoW. 2 KIA.

51. On 6/7 August 2 Wellingtons and 2 Whitleys FTR. *Hptm* Werner Streib, *Kommandeur* of 1./NJG 1 shot down Whitley V Z6488 of 51 Sqn SE of Eindhoven and *Fw* Reinhard Kollak, Wellington IC X9633 of 149 Sqn at Thorembais E of Wavre.

52. Including 21 by I./NJG 2, 16 by 4./NJG 1,14 by I./NJG 1 and 5 by III./NJG 1.

53. They included 15 by I./NJG 2, 12 by 4./NJG 1, another 12 by I./NJG 1 and one by III./NJG 1). *Oblt* Ludwig Becker and his *Bordfunker Uffz* Staub of 4./NJG 1 flew Do 215 G9+OM, the first Fu202 *Lichtenstein* AI-equipped night-fighter on operations from Leeuwarden during late summer 1941. With the use of this revolutionary radar set and skillfully guided by the fighter controller of *Himmelbett* box *Löwe* (Lion) W of Groningen they claimed 6 bombers. destroyed W of Groningen. On 8/9 August they shot down Wellington T2625 of 301 Sqn. On 12/13 August Manchester L7381 of 207 Sqn, 14/15 August, Whitley V Z6842 of 102 Sqn, 17/18 August Hampden AE185 of 50 Sqn, 6/7 September, Whitley V Z6478 of 10 Sqn and 29/30 September, Wellington IC X9910 of 115 Sqn.

54. Sgt A.W. MacMurray RCAF of 51 Sqn and his Whitley V crew were shot down over Holland on 7/8 November 1941. All PoW. Sgt Observer J. Graham Rogers, 21 (KIA). Sgt Brian F. Filliter MIA, 12 April 1941. Sgt Observer John W. Humphrey (19) KIA.

55. AE193 ZN-A.

56. 3 Wellingtons, 1 Halifax, a Hampden and 1 Stirling, were lost. The 2nd and 3rd searchlight suppression Hampdens (AD971 EA-O and AE126 of 49 Sqn), which FTR on 28/29 August were shot down and crashed into the Waddenzee S of Ameland. *Oblt* Helmut Lent, 4./NJG 1, shot down AD971 at 0340 hrs for his 21st victory. P/O Bernard Fournier and his 3 crew KIA. They were buried in Nes General Cemetery. 10 minutes earlier AE126 piloted by P/O Thomas Pratt had gone down in the same area, probably shot down by flak at 0043 hrs in the Waddenzee. 3 of the crew were buried on Vlieland and Texel Islands and Sgt A. Willis, under gunner, at Harlingen. In addition to the searchlight suppression losses, 3 Wellingtons, 1 Halifax, a Hampden and a Stirling of the Main Force on Duisburg were lost probably all to *Flak*.

57. R1772 piloted by Sgt R.B.D. Hill was shot down over Kiel Bay by a Bf 110. 5 crew baled out safely and were PoW. R1798 shot down on its return from Berlin by *Oblt* Helmut Lent of 4./NJG 1 as his 23rd *Abschuss* at 0458 hrs near Drachtstercompagnie in Friesland province with the loss of all Sgt Gordon's crew.

58. This was the squadron that featured in the well-known wartime propaganda movie, *Target For Tonight*. F/L Percy Pickard and Wellington '*F for Freddie*' took the 'leading roles' and for a short time Mildenhall was like a film set. Group Captain Pickard lost his life on the legendary attack by Mosquitoes on Amiens prison on 18 February 1944 when his Mosquito was shot down by *Fw* Wilhelm Mayer of II/JG 26 (KIA 4.1.45) in a Fw 190.

59. Including 4 by the intruders of I./NJG 2 and 9 by III./NJG 1). II./NJG 1's tally rose to over 100 kills on 15/16 September when *Uffz* Walter Geislinger of the 6th Staffel destroyed Stirling N6021 of 15 Sqn at Hemslingen, Germany, with the loss of P/O E.J.D. Guild and his crew.

60. Including 2 by I./NJG 2, 10 by 4./NJG 1 and 4 by I./NJG 1 including Manchester L7373 of 207 Sqn at 0530 on 14 October by *Gefr* Erhard Brühnke, which cr 2 km S of Gorssel nr. Beverlo, Belgium.

61. Lord, like so many others, carried out a dozen or more operations before his 20th birthday and he was not 22 when, with 30 or so ops and a 'rest' in an instructional job as his reward, he was killed in a flying accident.

62. The Lancaster resulted from the failure of the Manchester and was powered by four Rolls-Royce Merlin engines instead of the two Rolls-Royce Vultures.

63. Guy Penrose Gibson, born in Simla, India in 1918, joined the RAF in 1936 after leaving St. Edward's School, Oxford. At the outbreak of war he held the rank of F/O and in August 1940 he completed his first tour as a Hampden bomber pilot on 83 Sqn. He was promoted to F/L and won his first DFC (he was awarded a bar the following year). He was posted to instruct at an OTU before transferring to Fighter Command and a posting to 29 Sqn equipped with Beaufighters. In 99 operational sorties he claimed 4 e/a destroyed and was promoted to S/L with a bar to his DFC on completion of his second tour in December 1941. In March 1942 he returned to Bomber Command, was promoted W/C and posted to take command of 106 Sqn. He was awarded the DSO with a bar in 1943.

64. 11 years at Gresham's School, Holt, Norfolk, Hallows later passed through Sandhurst and took a commission in the King's Liverpool Regiment, which he later relinquished to take up civilian flying. He joined the RAF Reserve and was called up on the outbreak of war. On the sqn he was known as 'Darkie', not for his jet black hair and full moustache but for an episode when he got lost and invoked the R/T get-you-home service of those early days: '*Darkie, Darkie*'. Receiving no response, he had tried again but still no reply. Once more he had transmitted to the void: *'Darkie, Darkie...where are you, you little black bastard?* Hallows logged 24 hrs 50 mins during 4 trips on Manchesters. On 17 January 1942 97 Sqn began re-equipping with Lancaster Is though these gave some trouble and operations did not recommence in earnest until 8 April 1942.

65. L7474 FTR 12 March 1942 when it bounced on landing overshot and undercarriage leg jammed up. Abandoned 1/2 mile N of Winceby, Lincolnshire.

66. Dead Reckoning.

67. *Nachtjagd* destroyed 32 Bomber Command aircraft in November. On the night of 8 November III./NJG 1 were credited with 4 victories and I./NJG 1. 13 victories were credited to 4./NJG 1. *Lt* Ludwig Meister of 5./NJG 1 scored a triple victory on the night of 30 November/1 December when Bomber Command raided Hamburg, Kiel and Emden.

68. Battle cruisers *Scharnhorst* and *Gneisenau.*

69. Manchester I L7490. 4 Stirlings and 1 Halifax also FTR.

70. Hampden I AD804 of 144 Sqn crash-landed only 30 km from the site of the crash of P1165, at Gaanderen, 6 km E of Doetincham (Gelderland). Emergency landing was made to save the life of Sgt Cheesman, seriously WIA over Germany and who died in hospital shortly after his arrival. Woltersdorf KIA Twente on 2 June 1942 when he crashed into parked aircraft after being attacked by an e/a while landing with his *Bordfunker* Heino Pape WIA.

71. During 17 January-8 April 97 Sqn was re-equipped with Lancaster I aircraft after flying 36 raids with Manchesters losing 8 a/c from 151 sorties.

72. Literally translated, 'bed of heavenly bliss' or 'four-poster bed' because of the four night-fighter control zones.

73. Wellington II Z8370 of 12 Sqn flown by F/L W.H. Thallon, Wellington Ic Z1110 of 101 Sqn flown by S/L P.L. Chapman (all KIA) and Wellington IV Z1207 of 142 Sqn flown by P/O J.G. Scott RCAF (all KIA). Paul Gildner claimed Hampden I AT148 of 49 Sqn flown by F/O A.M. Harvey (all KIA).

74. *Hptm* Lent destroyed Hampden I AD750 of 106 Sqn W of Terschelling on the 5/6th and added Hampden AE308 of 455 Sqn in daylight on the 6th. Hampden Is X2969 and AT194 of 144 Sqn were claimed by *Oblt* Egmont Prinz *zur* Lippe Weissenfeld, *Staffelkapitän*, 5th *Staffel* on 24/25 February. Both a/c vanished into the North Sea at 2149 and 2202 hrs respectively. Whitley Z9280 of 77 Sqn went down to *Uffz* Heinz Vinke at Driesum at 2258 hrs on the 27th (1st of his 54 night victories). Destruction of 2 other 77 Sqn Whitleys (Z6943 and Z9148) credited to *Lt* Fellerer and *Ofw* Ney respectively.

75. Individual *Himmelbett* positions were equipped with a long-range *Freya AN early warning radar*, 2 *Würzburg Riese* ('Giant Würzburg') radar with a range in the direction-finding mode of 31 1/2-37 1/2 miles (50-60 km), a ground to air transmitter, 1-2 radio beacons and a visual beacon.

CHAPTER TWO

THE DEFENSE OF THE REICH 1942

On 22 February 1942, having been recalled from the USA where he was head of the RAF Delegation, Air Marshal Sir Arthur T. Harris arrived at High Wycombe, Buckinghamshire, to take over as Commander-in-Chief of RAF Bomber Command from AVM J.E.A. 'Jackie' Baldwin. (Baldwin had, since 8 January been standing in for Sir Richard Peirse, who had been posted to India). Harris was directed by Marshal of the RAF, Sir Charles Portal, Chief of the Air Staff to break the German spirit by the use of night area rather than precision bombing and the targets would be civilian, not just military. The famous 'area bombing' directive, which had gained support from the Air Ministry and Prime Minister Winston Churchill, had been sent to Bomber Command on 14 February, eight days before Harris assumed command. Harris warmed to his task and announced:

> 'The Germans entered this war under the rather childish delusion that they were going to bomb everybody else and nobody was going to bomb them. At Rotterdam, London, Warsaw and half a hundred other places, they put that rather naive theory into operation. They sowed the wind and now they are going to reap the whirlwind.'

Ron Read, a heavy bomber pilot who had completed Elementary Flying Training in Canada in 1941 and who was under training in England at the time, recalls:

> "Butch' Harris, as his crews were to call him, was a rough, tough, vulgar egomaniac. He was just what Bomber Command needed. He feared no foe, senior officers or politicians. He brooked no arguments from juniors and pooh-poohed any from those of equal or senior status who held a contra opinion. Harris knew what he was going to do and proceeded to move Heaven and earth to do it. Woe betide anyone who stood in his way. He was a firm believer in the Trenchard doctrine and with it he was going to win the war.'

Bombing German cities to destruction was not an entirely new concept. Ever since October 1940 crews were instructed to drop their bombs on German cities, though only if their primary targets were ruled out because of bad weather. During 1941 more and more bombs began falling on built-up areas, mainly because pinpoint bombing of industrial targets was rendered impractical by the lack of navigational and bombing aids. Harris saw the need to deprive the German factories of its workers and therefore its ability to manufacture weapons for war. From 1942 onward mass raids would be the order of the day, or rather the night, with little attention paid to precision raids on military targets.

F/Lt John Price, a wireless operator on Wellingtons of 150 Squadron, explains why:

> 'There have been many arguments for and against the indiscriminate bombing of civilian targets. For what it is worth, I have reason to believe that the High Command on either side knew that this course of events was inevitable even before the war started. Germany commenced this 'terror' tactic as long ago as the Spanish Civil War with the wholesale bombing of civilians in Guernica.[1] Both the Luftwaffe and the RAF avoided this during the early war years. In my year of bombing (1941) we were briefed in the Ops room to hit military targets only. In 1942 no Army was ready to invade the continent, the Royal Navy dare not put to sea in view of the *Scharnhorst, Gneisenau, Graf Spee* and *Tirpitz* etc., being

more concerned with the protection of convoys with food and ammunition from America. Therefore, in logical terms, the only weapon we had to retaliate was our own Bomber Command. In other words, the Germans were hitting us badly with their raids so we had no recourse except to fight with the only weapon we had – the bomber.'

However, 'Bomber' Harris did not possess the numbers of aircraft necessary for immediate mass raids. On taking up his position he found that only 380 aircraft were serviceable and only 68 of these were heavy bombers while 257 were medium bombers. Salvation though was at hand. In September 1941 the first of the new four-engined Avro Lancasters, a heavy bomber in every sense of the word, had been supplied to 44 (Rhodesia) Squadron at Waddington for Service trials. In early 1942 deliveries began to trickle through to 44 Squadron and on the night of 3/4 March four aircraft flew the first Lancaster operation when they dropped mines in the Heligoland Bight. That same night Harris selected the Renault factory at Billancourt near Paris, which had been earmarked for attack for some time, as his first target. A full moon was predicted so Harris decided to send a mixed force of 235 aircraft, led by the most experienced crews in Bomber Command, to bomb the French factory in three waves. It was calculated that approximately 121 aircraft an hour had been concentrated over the factory, which was devastated and all except 12 aircraft claimed to have bombed.[2]

During March also the first *Gee* navigational and target identification sets were installed in operational bombers and these greatly assisted bombers in finding their targets on the nights of 8/9 and 9/10 March in attacks on Essen. On the latter, 187 bombers including 136 Wellingtons bombed the city, which without *Gee* had been a difficult target to hit accurately. 44 Squadron flew the first Lancaster night-bombing operation of the war when two of the Squadron's aircraft took part in the raid by 126 aircraft on Essen on 10/11 March. Despite the new technological wonder the bombing was scattered on all three raids on the city which was covered alternately by industrial haze, and unexpected cloud. The same month 97 Squadron moved from Coningsby to Woodhall Spa nearby and became the second squadron to convert from the Manchester to the Lancaster but the early Lancasters gave some trouble, as David Penman[3] recalls:

'F/L Reginald R. 'Nicky' Sandford DFC of 44 Squadron flew a Lancaster in to convert a few pilots. Conversion consisted of one circuit by Nicky followed by one circuit each for the pilot to be converted. We then climbed into a Manchester and went to Woodford where we collected six Lancasters. I still remember with pleasure the surge of the four Merlins and the tremendous acceleration of the lightly loaded Lancaster after the painfully underpowered Manchester. Unfortunately, the Lancaster had teething problems and the first was a main wheel falling off F/O Deverill's machine when he took off from Boscombe Down. Then an outboard engine fell off after a night landing on the grass at Coningsby. More serious trouble came when six aircraft took off on the first operational sortie loaded with six 1500-lb mines. Over Boston F/O Rodley looked out to see first one and then the other wing tip fold upwards. Even at full power he was descending but luck was on his side, as he dropped the aircraft in the Wash without injuring the crew. A second aircraft diverted to a strange airfield and overshooting the runway ended in a quarry. Engine trouble, maladjusted petrol cocks and upper wing skin buckling restricted flying but all were overcome in the end. The Lancaster was easy to fly and after the Hampden and Manchester it was like stepping from an ancient banger into a Rolls Royce. After the wing tip failures, bomb load with full fuel was reduced from 9000 lbs to 6000 lbs and we stopped doing circuits and bumps with a full bomb load! It had always been customary to do night flying tests before operations with bombs on, though it was stopped on the Hampdens at Waddington when one enthusiastic low flyer skidded to a halt in a field with 4x500 lb bombs on board.'

On 28/29 March 234 bombers, mostly carrying incendiaries, went to Lübeck, an historic German town on the Baltic, with thousands of half timbered houses and an ideal target for a mass raid by RAF bombers carrying incendiary bombs. Eight bombers were lost but 191 aircraft claimed to have hit the target. A photo-reconnaissance a few days later revealed that about half the city, 200 acres had been obliterated. The increase in RAF night bombing raids in the more favourable spring weather met with a rapid rise in *Nachtjagd* victories. In March 1942 41 bombers[4] and in April 46 bombers[5] were brought down by German night fighters. II./NJG 1, which had recently moved to at St. Trond, scored its first six victories from this Belgian base during the month. On the night of 6/7 April 157 bombers went to Essen but the crews encountered severe storms and icing and there was complete cloud cover at the target. Only 49 aircraft claimed to have reached the target area and there was virtually no damage to Essen. Five aircraft were lost[6] and a 149 Squadron Wellington crew[7] had a narrow escape as Sgt Jim Coman, WOP/AG, recalls:

'We were returning from Essen when we were attacked by a Messerschmitt 110 over the Dutch coast just south of the Friesian Islands at about 18,000ft. The

110 hit us in our port wing, holing one petrol tank and causing us to lose about 400 gallons of fuel. The gunners returned fire and it broke off the attack and dived back through the clouds trailing smoke. Before landing at base we lowered the undercarriage to examine the port wheel for damage but nothing appeared amiss. However, the pilot decided to keep the weight off the wheel for as long as possible and landed port wing up but on reaching stalling speed and the wheel touching the ground, it collapsed. The wing hit the ground and swung us round 180 degrees and the wing broke across one of the fuel tanks. We all evacuated the aircraft quickly, as we could hear the engine sizzling in the petrol spillage. Fortunately, it did not catch fire.'

97 Squadron operations finally recommenced in earnest on the night of 8/9 April when 24 Lancasters carried out a minelaying operation in the Heligoland Bight. The main Bomber Command thrust by 272 aircraft was aimed at Hamburg. On 11 April 44 Squadron was ordered to fly long distance flights in formation to obtain endurance data on the Lancaster. At the same time 97 Squadron began flying low in groups of three in 'vee' formation to Selsey Bill, then up to Lanark, across to Falkirk and up to Inverness to a point just outside the town, where they feigned an attack, and then back to Woodhall Spa. Crews in both the squadrons knew that the real reason was that they were training for a special operation and speculation as to the target was rife.

'Despite frequent groundings', recalls David Penman:

'Training continued and early in April rumours of some special task for the Lancasters were confirmed when eight crews were selected to practice low level formation flying and bombing. The final practice was a cross country at 250 feet for two sections of three led by S/L Sherwood DFC* with myself leading the second section. We took off from Woodhall Spa and were to rendezvous with 44 Squadron near Grantham but because of unserviceability they did not take off. We flew down to Selsey Bill and then turned round and headed for Inverness. Due to compass errors the lead section got off track and were heading into an area of masts and balloons. With no communication allowed I eventually parted company with the lead section and we did not see them again until we were bombing the target in the Wash at Wainfleet.

'Our low level flight up valleys to Edinburgh was exciting, but over the higher ground in the North we climbed to a reasonable altitude over cloud, descending in the clear at Inverness for a low level run. Once beyond Edinburgh, on the way back, we descended again to low level and, full of confidence, really got down to hedgehopping. F/O Deverill on the left and W/O Mycock on the right maintained very tight formation and my only regret was the stampeding cattle when we could not avoid flying over them. Greater satisfaction came as we roared across familiar airfields a few feet from the hangar roofs and Waddington got the full blast of our slip stream as we rubbed in our success whilst they were stuck on the ground. A perfect formation bombing run with Sherwood's section running in behind completed a very successful day.

'A few days later I went to HQ 5 Group in Grantham with the Station Commander from Coningsby and S/L Sherwood. At 5 Group when the target was revealed, we were shattered and *suicide* was common thought. However, the briefing was thorough with an excellent scale model of the target area and emphasis on low level to avoid detection, massive diversionary raids and little ack-ack or opposition at Augsburg. This briefing was only a day or two before the 17th and no one else was to be informed until the briefing on the day of the raid when take-off was to be 1515 hours. On the 17th briefing was immediately after lunch with crew kitted ready to go. The scale model of the target was on display and the gasps as crews entered the room and saw the target were noticeable.'

At Woodhall Spa when the curtain was drawn back at the briefing there was a roar of laughter instead of the gasp of horror. The target was the diesel engine manufacturing workshop at the MAN[8] factory at Augsburg. No one believed that the RAF would be so stupid as to send 12 of its newest four-engined bombers all that distance inside Germany in daylight. Crews sat back and waited calmly for someone to say, 'Now the real target is this' but Augsburg was the real target. Air Marshal Harris wanted the plant raided by a small force of Lancasters flying at low level (500 ft) and in daylight despite some opposition from the Ministry of Economic Warfare, who wanted the ball-bearing plant at Schweinfurt attacked instead. Sixteen Lancaster crews, eight each from 44 and 97 Squadrons (including four first and second reserve) were specially selected and South African S/L John Dering Nettleton,[9] who had already completed two tours, was chosen to lead the operation. Crews were ordered to take their steel helmets on this raid. 'Darkie' Hallows, who after flying three days of long formation cross-countries was set to fly *B-Baker,* wrote:

'Plenty was said about how important it was and all that stuff. So we were obviously not intended to come back in any strength. Fighter Command had been on the job for several days, hounding the German fighters and when we were on the job we saw no fighters at all, all the way …' Just before the Lancasters took off thirty Bostons bombed targets in France in a planned attempt to force hundreds of German fighters up over the Pas de Calais, Cherbourg and Rouen areas. This was designed to draw the enemy fighters into combat so that the passage of the Lancasters would coincide with their refuelling and re-arming. Unfortunately it had the opposite effect and the incursion put the *Luftwaffe* on the alert.'

David Penman continues:

> 'Take-off was to be at 1515 hours with the two reserve aircraft taking off and dropping out when the two Vics of three set course.[10] We were to meet 44 Squadron near Grantham and then on to Selsey Bill, across the Channel, then down south of Paris before turning left and heading for Lake Constance. Take-off was on time, singly, with full fuel [2134 gallons] and 4x1000-lb RDX bombs with 11-second delay fuses to be dropped from 250 feet. Weather forecast was perfect with clear skies and good visibility all the way. I took off and soon had Deverill on my left and Mycock on my right. We joined the lead section of S/L Sherwood, F/O Hallows and F/O Rodley. Once again there was no sign of 44 Squadron near Grantham and we were never to meet. We maintained 250 ft to Selsey Bill and then got down as close to the sea as possible for the Channel crossing. As we approached the French coast my rear gunner informed me his turret was U/S and I told him it was too late to do anything about it and he would just have to do what he could with it. Crossing the French coast was an anti-climax as not a shot was fired and we flew on at tree top height to Lake Constance. We saw the odd aircraft in the distance but otherwise it was a very pleasant trip.'

44 Squadron meanwhile had not been as fortunate as 97 Squadron. Nettleton in R5508 took his formation flying in Vics of three down to just 50 ft over the waves of the Channel as the French coast came into view. Five minutes later, Nettleton's first two sections were intercepted by fighters in a running fight that lasted an hour. The Lancasters tightened formation, flying wingtip to wingtip, to give mutual protection with their guns as they skimmed low over villages and rising and falling countryside. The Bf 109s of II./JG 2 were forced to attack from above. L7536/H, flown by Sgt G.T. Rhodes was first to go down, a victim of Spanish Civil War veteran *Major* Walter "Gulle" Oesau, *Kommodore,* JG 2.[11] None of the crew stood a chance at such a low altitude in an aircraft travelling at 200 mph. The whole of 44 Squadron's second 'Vee' were shot out of the sky. R5506 flown by F/L Nicky Sandford DFC fell victim to the guns of Fw Bosseckert. L7548 piloted by W/O H.V. Crum DFM was shot down by *Uffz* Pohl of II./JG 2 and L7565 flown by W/O J.F. Beckett DFM was destroyed by *Hptm* Heine Greisert of II./JG 2 and all the crew were killed. Crum's crew survived and they were made PoW. Nettleton and F/O A.J. Garwell DFM piloting R5510 continued to the target alone, flying low in the afternoon sun across southern Germany until the South African sighted the River Lech, which he followed to the target. Coming over the brow of a hill on to the target the two Lancasters were met with heavy fire from quick-firing guns. The bomb aimers could not miss at chimney-top height on a factory covering an area of 626x293 ft. Nettleton and Garwell went in and dropped their bomb loads but Garwell's Lancaster was hit and set on fire. He landed in a field two miles west of the town and the fuselage broke at the mid-turret. Garwell and three of his crew survived and were taken prisoner.

The six Lancasters in 97 Squadron had flown a slightly different route and had avoided the fighters in France. On the way Brian Hallows' crew shot up a passenger train in a large station and saw an aerodrome crowded with Ju 90s. South of Paris Rod Rodley saw only the second aircraft he saw during the whole war. It was probably a courier, a Heinkel 111. It approached and recognizing them, did a 90-degree bank and turn back towards Paris. Rodley continued on flying at 100-ft. Occasionally he would see some Frenchmen take a second look and wave their berets or their shovels. A bunch of German soldiers doing PT in their singlets broke hurriedly for their shelters as the Lancs roared over. The next opposition was a German officer on one of the steamers on Lake Constance, firing a revolver at them. Rodley could see him quite clearly, 'defending the ladies with his Luger against 48 Browning machine guns.'

David Penman continues:

> 'Rising ground then forced us to fly a little higher and eventually we spotted our final turning point, a small lake. I had dropped back a little from Sherwood's section at this stage and mindful of the delay fuses on the bombs, made one orbit before turning to run in on the target. The river was a very good guide and the run in was exactly as shown in the scale model at briefing. A column of smoke beyond the target, presumably came from Garwell's aircraft and it was soon joined by another.'

Brian Hallows: 'The target was easily picked out and we bombed the hell out of it. The gunners were ready for us and it was as hot as hell for a few minutes.' Rod Rodley recalled:

'We were belting at full throttle at about 100 ft towards the targets. I dropped the bombs along the sidewall. We flashed across the target and won the other side to about 50 ft because flak was quite heavy. As we went away I could see light flak shells overtaking us, green balls flowing away on our right and hitting the ground ahead of us. Leaving the target I looked down at our leader's aircraft[12] and saw that there was a little wisp of steam trailing back from it. The white steam turned to black smoke with fire in the wing. I was slightly above him. In the top of the Lancaster there was a little wooden hatch for getting out if you had to land at sea. I realised that this wooden hatch had burned away and I could look down into the fuselage. It looked like a blowlamp with the petrol swilling around the wings and the centre section, igniting the fuselage and the slipstream blowing it down. Just like a blowlamp. I asked our gunner to keep an eye on him. Suddenly he said, 'Oh God, skip, he's gone. He looks like a chrysanthemum of fire.'

David Penman watched as Sherwood's aircraft received a shell through the port tank just behind the inboard engine and it crashed and blew up about ten miles north of the town:

'Escaping vapour caught fire and as he turned left on leaving the target with rising ground, the port wing struck the ground and the aircraft exploded in a ball of flame. (I was sure that no one had survived and said so on return to Woodhall Spa but Mrs. Sherwood would not believe it and she proved to be right. I met Sherwood after the war and he had been thrown out of the aircraft, still strapped in his seat, up the hill and had been the sole survivor). As we ran in at 250 feet, tracer shells from light anti-aircraft guns on the roof of the factory produced a hail of fire and all aircraft were hit. Mycock's aircraft on the right received a shell in the front turret, which set fire to the hydraulic oil and in seconds the aircraft was a sheet of flame. It went into a climb and swinging left passed over my head with bomb doors open and finally burning from end to end was seen by my rear gunner to plunge into the ground.[13] A shell ripped the cowling of my port inner engine and at the same time, F/L Deverill received a hit near the mid-upper turret and a fire started. Despite the distractions we held course and the front gunner did his best to reduce the opposition. My navigator, P/O Lister Ifould was then passing instructions on the bombing run and finally called, "Bombs gone." We pass over the factory, I increased power and dived to ground level just as Deverill passed me with one engine feathered and the other three on full power. His navigator, F/O Butler had managed to put out the fire near the mid-upper. I called Deverill and he asked if I would cover his rear as his turrets were U/S. However, as my turrets were also U/S and Ifould had no wish to relinquish the lead, I told him to resume his position. Our attack had been close to the planned time of 2020 hours and as darkness took over we climbed to 20,000 ft for a straight run over Germany. It says a lot for Deverill's skill that he remained in formation until we reached the English coast and eventually landed at Woodhall Spa just before midnight.'

It was close fighting; one rear-gunner spotted a German behind a machine gun on the roof and saw him collapse under his return fire. As the survivors turned westward, the light failed and the aircraft, led by Darkie Hallows flew back without any opposition under cover of darkness. Hallows noted, 'The quintessence of loneliness is to be 500 miles inside Occupied Europe with one serviceable turret! Time 8.15 hrs.'

Hallows returned safely and was one of eight officers to be awarded the DFC for his part in the raid. Winston Churchill sent the following message to Arthur T. Harris:

'We must plainly regard the attack of the Lancasters on the U-boat engine factory at Augsburg as an outstanding achievement of the Royal Air Force. Undeterred by heavy losses at the outset, the bombers pierced in broad daylight into the heart of Germany and struck a vital point with deadly precision. Pray convey my thanks of His Majesty's Government to the officers and men who accomplished this memorable feat of arms in which no life was lost in vain.'[14]

Later, Hallows wrote in his diary:

'One event sticks in my mind. Over half the bombs dropped failed to explode!' Five of the 17 bombs dropped did not explode and although the others devastated four machine shops, only 3 per cent of the machine tools in the entire plant were wrecked. 'A bad way to spend an afternoon!'

S/L John Dering Nettleton, who landed his badly damaged Lancaster at Squires Gate, Blackpool ten hours after leaving Waddington, was awarded the VC for his efforts. David Penman adds:

'Nettleton, it would appear, having increased speed to avoid fighters, bombed early and unable to cross Germany alone in daylight, turned back the way he had come. Due to navigational errors he eventually reached the Irish Channel and landed at Squires Gate. All surviving crews were grounded until a press conference, which I attended, was held at the Ministry of Information in London, when awards were announced.'[15]

Bomber Command continued its usual routines and for four consecutive nights, beginning on the night of 23/24 April, it was the turn of Rostock a port on the Baltic coast, to feel the weight of incendiary bombs. By the end only 40 percent of the city was left standing.[16] Australian Sgt Cal Younger, navigator/bomb aimer in F/O R.A.P. Jones RAAF's crew in 460 Squadron RAAF[17] flying Wellington IVs from RAF Breighton recalls:

'Rostock on 26/27 April was one occasion in my fairly brief aircrew career when pity almost overwhelmed me. Because so many of its buildings were old and built of timber, we carried incendiary bombs. We could see the blazing city from 140 miles away as we flew home in relative safety. True, night fighters claimed some victims but we did not see one and the *Flak* over the target had worried us little. There had been no challenge, no battle to carry out on our mission and so there was awe and pity and guilt. In the years since the war many aircrew who survived must have looked at their consciences many times and looked away again. Certainly, I wondered how much blood I had on my hands, or whether I had any at all. After all, in early 1942 RAF chiefs were worried about the lack of accuracy of the bomb aimers of whom I was one. The bomb aimer was also the navigator at that time. Later the two tasks were separated. On several occasions I brought back photographs which proved that we had been on the target, so it is likely that I caused some deaths at least. Mostly one felt dispassionate about bombing. Our job was to bomb a target and to do so we had to contend with fighters and *Flak* and searchlights (which could be very unnerving). One did not really give much thought to people below. I suppose their chances of survival were better than ours.

'In the air, on operations, we were in danger from the moment we took off until the moment we landed. Statistically we had small hope of surviving even one tour of operations. We became impersonal. We had been given a target and we faced in most instances, an awsome challenge from night fighters and from *Flak*. Frequently we were pinned in the sky by a cone of searchlights, often consisting of one hundred or more beams. We felt naked and as vulnerable as a butterfly. The target, even if it was a city like Essen, became for us almost an abstract, engendering no more emotion than a clay pigeon. That ordinary people were below us seeking what shelter they could from our dreadful cargoes did not impinge on our minds. Over the target the battle was usually intense. We saw our friends shot down in flames and our relief when finally we left the target was immense. There was no room for regret. There was little if any discussion of feelings on the squadron at the time. Just an occasional 'I felt sorry for the sods' or some such remark. There were some sensitive types who must have suffered conscience but they kept their feelings to themselves. It is difficult to convey the atmosphere in the Mess. We all knew we were very likely to die. We had only to watch our friends disappearing. We lived on a permanent 'high' and did not talk about death except in joke. When we were not on 'ops' we headed for York. Most went to pubs and bars. I always went to the cinema, more often than not by myself. Some became regulars at the local village pub.'

F/Sgt Ralph Wood of 76 Squadron was now flying as part of a regular crew and getting to know each other fairly well so off duty they too would frequent the pubs and dance halls in Darlington and York. On 8 May he completed his 14th op, the first in a 'Hallybag', with P/O McIntosh as his pilot:

'Our target was Warnemünde and it was successfully attacked. There were many times a navigator had to remove his gloves to work at his charts and at this height it was *C-O-L-D*. Of course a Hallybag was always a deep freeze proposition, even at the best of times. There were supposed to be pipes giving off heat throughout the aircraft but this was a laugh. I found my hands and feet were always cold by the time an op was half over. You simply had to learn to live with it. It was around this period that I was listed to fly with a Canadian pilot by the name of F/Sgt Bellows. We were all at least Flight Sergeants by now! Well, due to a rash on the inside of my thigh, the medical officer took me off the flying list that night. He figured wearing the parachute harness would only irritate the rash, making it worse. So it was an application of medication instead. F/Sgt Bellows and crew that included my replacement bought it over the City of York when their aircraft exploded on the way to Germany. Someone must have been looking after me that night or I would have crapped out as well. 'Op No.15 was to Mannheim on 19 May. Sgt Tackley was my RAF pilot. Our aircraft became unserviceable so we had to cut our trip short. Op No.16 on 22 May we raided St. Nazaire the only French target of my so-called 'career' in the air force. It was a quiet op but one more toward that ultimate goal – a tour.'[18]

Seven days later another overseas visitor, Sgt Cal Younger navigator/bomb aimer in F/O R.A.P. Jones RAAF's crew in 460 Squadron RAAF, prepared for his 13th operation:

'Ironically, the target which caused me to jump for my life was believed to be more or less undefended. Nor, it was hoped, were French civilians in danger. It was the Gnome-Rhône factory at Gennevilliers, near Paris. At briefing on 29 May we were told that our squadron was to provide four of 12 Wellingtons, which were to attack from 2000 ft and illuminate the target for the heavies who would bomb from 8000-10,000 ft.[19] (That the air chiefs believed there would be no casualties was proved the following night when the first raid of 1000 bombers took place. Aircraft and crews from operational training units had to be scraped up to reach the magical 1000, so casualties among experienced crews was neither wanted nor imagined). The four navigators worked out their flight plans together. Some time before midnight the four Wellingtons followed each other into a moonlit sky. I had a strange feeling, a presentiment of disaster. As we flew over Northampton, its roofs shining in the moonlight, I suggested to my wireless operator (Sgt Mellowes) that he should go to the astrodome to look at his home city. We flew over Reading, crossed the coast at Beachy Head then set course for Paris. As we neared our target we were stunned to see a network of tracer, a fireworks display on a scale I had never imagined. Perhaps we were unwise to stick to the height we had been given. It looked suicidal in the scintillating moonlight. We did not hesitate. As I prepared to go to the bombsight I heard a crunching sound behind me. We had been hit and the intercom had failed. I told the skipper we would bomb on light signals. A blue, master beam of a searchlight had fastened on us and our rear gunner (Sgt Loder) fired down the beam. Eventually he put it out but not before a red line of tracer traversed the length of our starboard wing, almost as if the gunners were operating a garden hose.

'Standing beside the pilot I could see that we were doomed. I took his parachute from its container and put it on his knee and then released the front gunner (Sgt Houghton) from his turret, gave him his parachute, opened the hatch and told him to jump. I clipped on my own parachute as I returned to the skipper. He had managed to clip on one side of his parachute. I did the other for him. He asked, 'Was there any chance? I told him 'No'. He smiled a gentle, almost serene smile and told me to jump. At that moment the aircraft went into a steep dive, screaming as if in agony or from some terrible frustration. I could see that the skipper did not intend to bale out. He really had no time but also he did not know what had happened to the wireless operator and the rear gunner and would never have abandoned them. The latter had baled out when he saw flames streaming past his turret. To this day I do not know what happened to the wireless operator. He had been standing, watching from the astrodome and I think the burst of fire amidships had killed or badly wounded him.

'I felt a strange calm and I am sure I would have gone down with the skipper had I not seen the front gunner standing by the open hatch. As he stepped down I yelled to him to jump. He didn't and thinking I had nothing to lose, I jumped. The parachute just broke my fall. I was unconscious for a time but suffered no injury. Eventually I got up and walked away. Eight days later, after many hard hours of walking at night, I was arrested by French police and handed over to the Germans. Several years later I repeated my trek and discovered from a hotelier who had been chief of resistance in the area that the police should have handed me over to him, I should have been hidden until flown to England in a surreptitious Lysander, perhaps to join in the battle once more and to add to my guilt.'

On the 29th it was apparent that something out of the ordinary was about to happen as F/Sgt Eddie Wheeler at 27 OTU Lichfield recalls:

'The ground crews were being pressed like mad to ensure the full serviceability of all the aircraft and air testing was more prevalent. Parachutes had to be taken for closer examination and leave passes were cancelled, so something 'big' was happening. At ten am the next morning we were formed into crews, mostly comprised of instructors with a sprinkling of the more advanced pupils and then allocated aircraft. I was assigned to Wellington IC 1645 under the captaincy of F/O Temperley with whom I had flown on some training exercises. Shortly after, we were in the air for an hour's formation flying and air testing. Our formation had to be seen to be believed and with rumours of a daylight raid to be carried out in these clapped out Wellingtons, which had seen better days, we weren't too happy.'

Top-level consultations between Harris and his subordinate commanders had revealed that the raids on Rostock had achieved total disruption. Whole areas of the city had been wiped out and 100,000 people had been forced to evacuate the city. The capacity of its workers to produce war materials had therefore been severely diminished. Harris had for some time nurtured the desire to send 1000 bombers to a German city and reproduce the same results with incendiaries. Although RAF losses would be on a large scale Churchill approved the plan. Harris, (now Sir Arthur), gave the order 'Operation Plan Cologne' to his Group Commanders just after mid-day on 30 May so that 1000 bombers would be unleashed on the 770,000 inhabitants. Some 599 Wellingtons, including four of Flying Training Command, made up the bulk of the attacking force, which also included 88 Stirlings, 131 Halifaxes and 73 Lancasters. The rest of the force was made up of Whitleys, Hampdens and Manchesters. All bomber bases throughout England were at a high state of readiness to get all available aircraft airborne for the raid. 12 Squadron at Binbrook, for instance, put a record 28 Wellington IIs into the air. To accomplish this task, however, all aircraft had to fly without second pilots and this placed added strain on the crews.

S/L Hughie Stiles, an instructor at 22 OTU at Wellesbourne Mountford since 14 July 1941 recalls:

> 'After completing my first tour in 4 Group Bomber Command on 58 and 104 Squadrons, on 27 September 1942 I was giving night instruction on a Wellington 1C. I had allowed the pupil to wander quite a few miles from the proper circuit so that he would find out for himself how difficult it would be to line up for the final approach. Suddenly, the cockpit became filled with acrid smoke accompanied by sudden loss of power from the port engine. Even with full power, I was unable to maintain height with the other engine and crashed into the approach zone a mere one hundred yards from the beginning of the runway. We were fortunate to escape before it blew up and was completely destroyed. This event may seem completely irrelevant and I mention it only because it impressed upon me the fact that aircraft which had been put out to pasture at an OTU after perhaps 60 sorties on a squadron were certainly not as nimble as they once were. This realisation was brought home to me when all ranks were confined to base on all stations serving Bomber Command, immediate bomb load flight tests were carried out and crews put together for a maximum effort against an unknown target. I was therefore, not too surprised to find the aircraft assigned to me would not safely become airborne with more than 1000 lb of bombs compared with 4500 lb currently carried by front line squadrons. In addition to an instructor wireless operator, the navigator, bomb-aimer and rear-gunner were assigned from pupils on the senior course. Some crews consisted entirely of senior pupils.'

Crews went to their briefings on the 30th wondering what to expect. F/Sgt Eddie Wheeler recalls:

> 'At 1830 hrs we were summoned to the briefing room in the Operations Block. A cloth covered the wall chart and the crews sat there fidgeting awaiting the CO's arrival to announce what was in store for us. Finally, from the back of the room came the order 'Attention' and all personnel leapt to their feet as W/C Jarman entered with S/Ls Bamford and Burberry. We were greeted with the news that the C-in-C Bomber Command – 'Butch' Harris was mounting the first raid in which over 1000 bombers were to be unleashed on the *Reich*. This could only be achieved by supplementing the operational squadrons with aircraft from OTUs Coastal and Training Commands.
>
> 'The concealing cloth was removed and revealed that our target was Cologne. It was announced that only 90 minutes would be allowed for 1000 plus aircraft to pass through the target area. The dramatic figure of 1000 planes was something like two and a half times the usual complement of aircraft available for night operations. The main danger was the prospect of collision but this was an acceptable risk to get the bomber stream through the night-fighter boxes as quickly as possible. We had to swamp the anti-aircraft defenses and put down such a concentration of HE (High Explosive) and incendiaries in a short period that the fire services would be overwhelmed and large areas would be consumed by the fires. The OTU Groups were providing 365 aircraft, including Wellingtons, Hampdens and Whitleys. It was suggested that the loss factor of 10% or about one hundred aircraft would be acceptable for this size operation. With the late withdrawal of the Coastal Command contribution it was necessary to make up numbers with totally trainee crews. The total dispatched was 1047 aircraft. The days of specific targets had gone and with such a concentration of bombers in so short a space of time there would be no question of evasive action from *Flak* or fighters due to the greatly higher risk of collision with devastating effect on probably many friendly aircraft. Sitting in the Mess prior to take-off, the topic of conversation was dominantly on the question of the adequacy of our aircraft, used day in and day out on training by various crews.'

F/L John Price, an instructor at 10 OTU, adds:

> 'The target area was the center of Cologne and the map clearly showed the red crosses of every hospital in the city. I would have nightmares after the war thinking

about all the women and babies we had killed that night. It is now obvious to me that we in England were determined to save our land at whatever the cost and killing the enemy, of whatever gender, the only answer.'

'Take-off', recalls S/L Hughie Stiles:

> 'Was a little before dusk to ensure complete darkness before arriving at the enemy coast although it was a clear, moonlit night. The two-and-a-half hours to the target were relatively uneventful; except that coaxing the aircraft all that time put me barely at 15,000 ft as I approached the target. It just refused to go a foot higher and I surmised that the other 999 were mostly above me and I wondered if the bombs coming down would exceed the *Flak* coming up!'

F/Sgt Eddie Wheeler took off at 2230 hrs:

> 'It seemed as if the sky was full of black shapes, gun testing had been disallowed because of the density of the formations. We staggered up to 11,000ft in our weary IC but with the bomb and fuel load it just wouldn't go any higher. This would make us a target for the accurate light *Flak*. We were not alone. Some old Whitleys were below us and a lot slower and this was a slight encouragement for us. Crossing the enemy coast, we were soon illuminated by searchlight batteries and we felt totally exposed. Aircraft were above and below and on all sides, impossible to take weaving action. Approaching the target area, all hell broke loose and there was no question of overshooting and going round for a second run. In running up, I was located in the astrodome and I could never recall having been so scared. Many aircraft above us with their bomb doors open revealed stocks of bombs which when released were more than likely to land on the aircraft below. At the point of release, there were showers and showers of incendiaries and HEs passing us on all sides. These obviously accounted for the many explosions around us with many planes ploughing and plunging in big balls of flame into the target area. It seemed like one sea of flame on the ground and I felt sick for the poor devils below and the terrors they must have been experiencing.'

S/L Hughie Stiles again:

> 'Shortly before approaching any target one always wondered what the intensity of the *Flak* and searchlights will be and who would be the 'Joe' while I was making my run. It seemed that at any moment there was always one aircraft, which the batteries of radar-controlled searchlights, maybe 30 or so to a group, would lock onto and form such a large area of intersection that it was almost impossible to fly out of it. And into which the heavy *Flak* would be poured. I didn't have long to wait. My track was between two distinct groups of searchlights aimed more or less vertically into the sky. I kept my fingers crossed and hoped that I would sneak through while they were perhaps monitoring someone else. I was watching the increasing *Flak* bursts ahead and above when in a single instant all the searchlights in both groups swung towards each other and coned me in a blinding zone of light. I was the 'Joe'. Seeking the comfort of the instruments for a second or two to rest my eyes from the shock, I put the aircraft into a steep diving turn to port in a frantic effort to escape.
>
> 'Superimposed upon the myriad lights which followed wherever I went, I was uncomfortably conscious of the more mellowed color of the shell bursts which were so close I could hear the hissing thuds as they exploded. Instinctively I wrenched it over to a starboard turn, to no avail and I felt sure a direct hit was inevitable. Continuing down in the maelstrom of blinding noise, weaving from left to right, I noticed we were now down to 10,000 ft and moving at nearly 350 mph; over twice normal speed. Flattening out required some effort at that speed. As I banked again to the left in a fairly steep turn I felt and heard a terrific impact, which jarred the whole aircraft. The wireless operator reported that about three feet of the top of the fuselage behind the astrodome had just disappeared. As we were now well within the target area I instructed the bomb aimer to jettison, as it looked as though I was going to need all the performance I could get, any second. Then, as if to confirm my action I saw a jagged tulip-like shape appear on the top of the port-engine cover. I scanned the engine oil pressure and temperature gauges for a reduction in one and an increase in the other. It seemed impossible for a piece of *Flak* to come out of the top of the engine cover without having first caused critical damage in its passage through the engine components.
>
> 'Now at 9500 ft the defenses regretfully turned their attention to the next one on the 'Joe' list, while I set a course for home alternately praying and watching those port engine instruments. The thought of having to keep this thing in the air, on one engine, for over two hours filled me with a great deal of apprehension after my last

experience on the Wellesbourne circuit but minutes ticked by with no unpleasant manifestations and I finally relaxed. The crew had suffered no injuries and everything was still working so what more could one ask?'

At Mildenhall 419 'Moose' Squadron RCAF had 18 first line Wellingtons ready. A quarter of the 1046 aircraft despatched came from 3 Group, which operated in a fire-raising capacity, carrying loads of 4-lb incendiary canisters. F/L, The Honourable Terence Mansfield, 419 Squadron Bombing Leader recalls:

> '419 were wholly equipped with Wellington IIIs and there were crews for every aircraft. 'Moose'[20] was not one to take over someone else's aircraft so he borrowed an elderly IC from the Blind Approach Training Flight. This normally spent its time flying along our Lorenz-beam training pilots to use it. 'We took off at 2325 hrs. Although 419 were in the first wave, we were not. At approximately 50 mph slower than the IIIs our IC was also handicapped by trying to get to the briefed height of 18,000 ft, 4000 ft higher than I had ever been before in a Wellington. We made visual identification on arrival at Cologne and made one circuit of the city before our attack. We then flew round the target again as Moose had a pair of night binoculars, which were remarkably effective but I made no notes of what I could see. I think I must have been more interested in looking down from what seemed such a great height; this being the occasion on which I had dropped bombs from over 10,000ft. Our attack was made as ordered. Height 17,500 ft. Night photograph taken and later plotted within 800 yards of the aiming point. The weather over the target was remarkably clear and not as we had come to expect from the Ruhr area.'

For 98 minutes a procession of bombers passed over Cologne. Stick after stick of incendiaries rained down from the bomb bays of the Wellingtons, adding to the conflagration. Almost all aircraft bombed their aiming point as briefed. The defenses, because of the attacking forces size, were relatively ineffective and *Flak* was described variously as 'sporadic' and spasmodic'. F/L Pattison, who piloted a 419 'Moose' Squadron RCAF Wellington, wrote:

> 'When I bombed there was a huge fire on the east bank of the Rhine and another just starting on the west bank. When I left the target area both sides were getting it thick and fast and eventually, large concentrations of fires were spread practically across the length and breadth of the entire built-up area.'

'When we got there,' said the Wing Commander of a squadron of Wellingtons:

> 'We saw many fires which had not yet taken real hold but I thought it had all the makings of a successful raid. It was easy enough to see the city, for we could pick out the Rhine and the bridges quite clearly. There was little or no opposition over the target, I think because there were so many aircraft that the ground defenses could not cope with them. We did meet with opposition on the outskirts but it was very indiscriminate. Before I left I saw the fires growing larger and larger.'

The Wellingtons were followed closely by the Stirlings. Flying with them in the second seat of a Stirling of 218 Squadron flown by W/C Holder was the 3 Group commander AVM J.E.A. 'Jackie' Baldwin:

> 'The weather forecast made it uncertain almost up to the last moment whether we should start. We had not been flying very long before we met much low cloud and this depressed me. The front gunner got a pinpoint on an island off the Dutch coast but the weather was still somewhat thick and there was an alpine range of cloud to starboard. Suddenly, 30 or forty miles from Cologne, I saw the ground and then the *Flak*. It grew clearer and clearer until, near the city, visibility was perfect. First I saw a lake, gleaming in the moonlight, then I could see fires beginning to glow and then searchlights which wavered and *Flak* coming up in a haphazard manner. The sky was full of aircraft all heading for Cologne. I made out Wellingtons, Hampdens, a Whitley and other Stirlings. We sheered off the city for a moment, while the captain decided what would be the best way into the target. It was then that I caught sight of the twin towers of Cologne cathedral, silhouetted against the light of three huge fires that looked as though they were streaming from open blast furnaces. We went in to bomb, having for company a Wellington to starboard and another Stirling to port. Coming out we circled the *Flak* barrage and it was eight minutes after bombing that we set course for home. Looking back, the fires seemed like rising suns and this effect became more pronounced as we drew further away. Then, with the searchlights rising from the fires, it seemed that we were leaving behind us a huge representation of the Japanese banner. Within nine minutes of the coast, we circled to take a last look. The fires then resembled distant volcanoes.'

When the Halifaxes arrived the raid had lasted for an hour. By this time Cologne was visible to late comers 60 miles away, first as a dull red glow over a large area of ground. The captain of one Halifax and his navigator thought that the fire towards which they were flying was too large to be anything but an especially elaborate dummy. The pilot of another Halifax thought that a heath or a whole forest must have been blazing. Ten miles off however, they knew that the glow came from a town on fire. As they drew near they could see more and more loads of incendiaries burning in long, narrow rectangles made up of pinpoints of bright, white patch, which swiftly blossomed each into a rose of fire. Like the others, the Halifaxes identified the target easily by means of the bridges over the Rhine. One captain reported:

'So vast was the burning that ordinary fires on the outskirts of the city or outside it, which I should usually have described as very big, looked quite unimportant. It was strange to see the flames reflected on our aircraft. It looked at times as though we were on fire ourselves, with the red glow dancing up and down the wings.'

F/O Brian 'Darkie' Hallows DFC could see the fires over 60 miles away on his way out and they were visible at Dutch coast on return. S/L Stiles landed back at base five hours and ten minutes after take-off:

'Holes in the fuselage and flaps were fairly superficial but a major repair was necessary to replace the geodetic structure missing from the top of the Wellington's fuselage. There was much discussion as to how this damage occurred but as we were in a steep turn it must have been caused either by a falling bomb or an up-coming shell fused for a greater altitude. We concluded that the *Flak* hole in the port engine cover could only have been caused by a piece of shrapnel passing through the propeller blades, missing the cylinders and coming out the top. There was obviously a lot of luck involved.'[21]

F/Sgt Eddie Wheeler continues:

'We sighed with relief after our bomb load had gone down and wondered whether Cologne's wonderful cathedral had been obliterated. The return flight was mainly uneventful and we eventually landed at base at 0430 am. De-briefing and breakfast occupied the next two hours and thankfully we climbed into our beds at seven am. It was announced that the raid had been a success. Amazingly, Cologne Cathedral had survived and losses totalled 41 aircraft – 3.9% of the total force operating. We thought how glad we were to get this 'one-off' operation over and could get back to our usual mundane but safer task of training. It was not to be for two nights later the effort was to be repeated, this time against Essen in the Ruhr and we were to suffer all the same agonies again. This flight duration was five-and-a-quarter hours but due to the considerable haze over the target it was not as successful as the Cologne raid and bombs were well scattered. Thirty-one of our aircraft were lost out of a total of 956 dispatched – 3.2% – which was lower than expected.

S/L Hughie Stiles concludes:

'Two of my friends who officiated at my wedding the previous month were captains of two Wellesbourne aircraft which failed to return and I believe also one pupil crew. A high price to pay for dropping about 3000 lb of HE on Cologne. It seemed to us the whole thing was a propaganda ploy aptly summed up by a cryptic announcement in the Daily Telegraph the following day: 'At a Bomber Command Station. Sunday. On the 1001st day of the war more than 1000 RAF bombers flew over Cologne and in 95 minutes delivered the heaviest attack ever launched in the history of aerial warfare.'[22]

The majority of the Luftwaffe night-fighter effort on 30/31 May was concentrated in the *Himmelbett* boxes on the coast and in the target area. The German defenses were locally swamped by the mass of bombers and *Nachtjagd* crews destroyed relatively few. Of the 43 RAF losses it is estimated that 30 were shot down by *Himmelbett* opearting night-fighters. these were mainly achieved on the the return journey when the bomber stream had been more dispersed than on the way in and was easier for the *Jägerleitoffizier* (JLO, or GCI-controller) to pinpoint individual target aircraft. Eight claims were submitted by four crews of II./NJG 1 at St. Trond, including three by *Oblt* Walter Barte and his *Funker Uffz* Pieper of the 4th *Staffel*, seven of which were later confirmed by the *Reichsluftfahrtministerium (RLM* or *Reich* Air Ministry).[23] Of the remaining RAF losses, 16 or 17 were downed by *Flak* over Cologne and 12 were shot down by anti aircraft fire on the legs to and from the target. At Venlo three victories[24] were awarded to *Oblt* Reinhold Knacke, *Staffelkapitän,* 1st *Staffel,* NJG 1 for his 18th-20th victories.[25] In all, 898 crews claimed to have hit their targets. Post-bombing reconnaissance certainly showed that more than 600 acres of Cologne had been razed to the ground. The fires burned for days and almost 60,000 people had been made homeless.[26]

Notes

1. A town in northern Spain almost completely destroyed in 1937 by German bombers aiding General Franco's forces in the war of 1936-39.

2. It was reported that 300 bombs fell on the factory destroying 40% of the buildings. Production was halted for 4 weeks and final repairs were not completed for several months. A post-war American estimate said that the production loss was almost 2,300 vehicles. Just 1 aircraft (a Wellington) was lost but 367 French people were killed, 341 were badly injured and 9,250 people lost their homes.

3. Later W/C Penman DSO OBE DFC.

4. Including 27 by II./NJG 2 with 6 of these being credited to *Oblt* Ludwig Becker and 4 each by I. and III./NJG 1.

5. Including 12 by II./NJG 2, 9 by I./NJG 1 and 4 by III./NJG 1

6. 2 of them Hampdens, a Manchester of 61 Sqn, 1 Stirling and a Wellington.

7. Of N3726 OJ-G flown by P/O Mike Evans.

8. *Maschinenfabrik Augsburg-Nurnberg Aktiengesellschaft.*

9. Born 1917 at Nongoma, Natal.

10. All 16 had taxied out so the second reserve cut their engines and watched the others leave and over Selsey Bill the first reserves swung round and returned to Lincolnshire, leaving 12 Lancasters flying low over the water.

11. Oesau had shot down 10 a/c in Spain and was the 3rd German pilot to reach 100 victories, on 26 October 1941. He was shot down and killed in air combat with P-38 Lightnings SW of St. Vith, Belgium on 11 May 1944 in his Bf 109G-6. At the time of his death, his score stood at 127 aerial victories, including 14 four engined bombers.

12. L7573 flown by S/L J.S. Sherwood DFC*.

13. R5513 was on fire over a mile from the target but W/O T.J. Mycock DFC continued on to drop his bombs on the factory and became enveloped in flames and crashed. There were no survivors.

14. 37 aircrew were lost, of which 12 were made PoW and 36 returned.

15. Although also recommended for a VC by Air Marshal Harris, Sherwood was awarded the DSO After a brief spell instructing with 1661 HCU and being promoted to W/C, Nettleton returned to 44 Sqn as OC in January 1943. He FTR from a raid on Turin on 12/13 July 1943.

16. The raids on Lübeck and Rostock prompted the Luftwaffe into reprisal, or *Baedeker* raids, after the German guide book to English cities, on Canterbury, Exeter, Norwich and York.

17. First RAAF Sqn in Bomber Command and which carried out its first operation on 12/13 March.

18. Between 11 May 1940 and 31 May 1942 of the principal targets in the Ruhr, Essen had been attacked 89 times, Duisburg 93 and Dortmund 33. Of the main German cities outside that great industrial area, Bomber Command had been to Cologne 144 times, to Mannheim 68, to Hanover 64 and to Magdeburg 26. The four German ports most directly concerned with the Battle of the Atlantic were heavily attacked. Targets in Bremen were bombed 110 times, Wilhelmshaven 88 and Kiel and Emden 82 each. Hamburg was attacked 115 times.

19. 65 Wellingtons, Lancasters, Halifaxes, Hampdens and Stirlings.

20. W/C J. 'Moose' Fulton, the CO.

21. Darkie Hallows flew his 27th and final trip on 9/10 January 1943 to Essen, 'a lovely night, clear and dark'. The city was bombed by 50 Lancasters of 5 Group and 2 PFF Mosquitoes for the loss of 3 Lancasters. 127 buildings were destroyed or seriously damaged and 28 people were killed. Hallows noted, 'We pranged the flares. Flak very hot and too close too. Bombs seen burning in built up area. Time 4.00. Load 1 x 4,000 12 SBC.' This trip brought Hallows' total flying time to 145.25 hrs. He was now posted to ground duties and non-operational flying – Group HQ, two different Bomber Conversion Units (Stirlings and Lancasters) – instructing again, until, in January 1945, he was posted to command 627 Pathfinder Mosquito Marking Sqn at Woodhall Spa, where he completed 4 operations. At the end of the war he was told that he was not needed for the Far East because he was on his second tour of operations and was sent on leave. He was then given a permanent commission in the RAF.

22. Stiles' navigator, S/L T. Hillier-Rose recalled that Stiles was 'ticked off' for having flown on the raid. At the time he was recovering from a severe wound to an arm, sustained in a crash whilst flying a Mosquito.

23. Barte's first claim of the night for a Wellington shot down N of Maastricht was later officially turned down.

24. Two Wellingtons and Halifax L9605 of 1652 CU, crashed near Weert.

25. Finally, 2 III./NJG 1 aces operating from Twenthe were successful on 30/31 May: *Oblt* Manfred Meurer destroyed Hampden P2116 of 14 OTU near Diepenveen and *Oblt* Helmut Woltersdorf claimed Wellington IA N2894 of CGS (a veteran of 403 flying hrs) near Apeldoorn and Wellington IC DV715 of 156 Sqn at Vorden.

26. 31 bombers were lost. I./NJG 1 at Venlo, southern Holland on 1/2 June shot down 12 Essen raiders. Although seemingly lacking the concentration of the earlier raid on Cologne the bombing nevertheless was effective enough to saturate the defenses. One skipper went as far as to say that the fires were more impressive than those of Cologne were. A belt of fires extended across the city's entire length from the western edge to the eastern suburbs. Many fires were also spread over other parts of the Ruhr.

CHAPTER THREE

UNDER COVER OF DARKNESS

Squadrons repaired and patched their damaged bombers and within 48 hours they were preparing for a second 'Thousand Bomber Raid', this time against Essen on the night of 1/2 June. A force of 956 bombers was ready. Again the numbers had to be made up by using OTU crews and aircraft as F/L John Price at 10 OTU confirms:

> 'We had only 700 first line bombers. To make up the difference the other 300 were drawn from the OTUs. I was doing my usual so called 'rest' period of six months between ops. The idea being to give seasoned aircrew a brief respite from real operations and also to teach others. I found it ironic that so many of us got killed on these OTUs. Pilot error (the pupil was flying), navigational errors, bad weather over England in wintertime – the losses were horrendous. To return to the thousand-bomber raid on Essen, at briefing we were told our part in the operation was to kill as many of the workers as possible. Other bombers would go for the Krupps factory itself. Real bombs were not used on an OTU station so I was a bit shaken to see them rolling onto our airfield at Harwell. We had Whitley aircraft, which were unbelievably slow and climbed at about 125 mph with a full bomb load. They had the same turrets as the Wellington. There was no protection for the poor old air-gunners front and rear, just perspex. I felt very sad. As an instructor I had been ordered to go but as there were not enough instructors to fill the aircraft pupil pilots were called upon – ditto navigators and air gunners. My pupils – 18-year old boys – pleading with me to let them go besieged me. I knew that half of them would not come back but I chose my dozen or so then prayed for their safety. None came back.'

Of the 37 bombers lost on the second 1000-bomber raid on Essen 20 were claimed by nightfighters. One of the RAF aircraft fell victim to *Lt* Karl-Heinz Völlkopf and *Uffz* Heinz Huhn of II./NJG 2 who took off from Leeuwarden at 2330 hrs. Huhn recalled in his diary what happened:

> 'We got a course to steer from ground control. Clouds were beneath us. Moon very big, very clear sky.
>
> '*Kurier*[1] still far away to the west. We approached him on incoming heading. Picked it up in Li-set at a distance of 4.5 kilometers [2.8 miles]. We turned round and chased him.
>
> 'Marie 2[2], slow down, slow down, can't see anything.
>
> 'We've overtaken the *Kurier*. Start the whole procedure again.
>
> 'Marie 4, Marie 3. Pick him up in Li-set at 2.6 kilometers [1.6 miles]. Height 3000m [9,700ft].
>
> 'I lead my pilot towards him. Marie 300 meters [970ft].
>
> 'Karl-Heinz: 'I have him!'
>
> 'We lose height. Underneath *Kurier*. It's a Hampden. Dangerous. Can see and fire downwards. We climb ever more. Distance 100 to 150 meters [110 to 160 yards].
>
> 'Attack.
>
> 'Keep firing. Burst of fire aimed very well. *Kurier* is burning.
>
> 'Sieg Heil! [Bomber destroyed!]'
>
> 'Karl-Heinz congratulates me: a *Lichtenstein* victory! I am feeling very pleased.'[3]

After Cologne and Essen Harris could not immediately mount another 1000-bomber raid and he had to be content with smaller formations. F/Sgt Ralph Wood of 76 Squadron flew on the Thousand bomber raids:

'30 May was my 17th op and we really pranged the target, leaving it looking like the red-hot embers of a huge bonfire. With all the aircraft over the target during a short period of time, one wonders how many may have collided! Op No.18, 1/2 June, F/Sgt Tackley and crew took part in the second 1000-bomber raid, on Essen. This was another spectacular raid reminding one of paintings of the Great Fire of London. It was a vision of hell, a vision I would never forget. There was plenty of opposition over this target which was part of the industrial center of Germany. Those long cold hours sweating it out in the navigators and bomb-aimer's compartment always chilled you through, even with heavy flying boots, extra socks thick gloves and your flying suit. The usual 'cold sweat' didn't help much either. Op No.19 was to Bremen on 3 June was a long haul over the North Sea. Every time we beetled down the runway I wondered if we were going to make it back. I guess I'd seen too many guys go for a Burton in the past year. *'Gone for a Burton,'* meaning, in barrack-room language, *'Gone for a shit'*. A Burton being a strong English ale, which caused one's bowels to move rather freely, necessitating a quick trip to the can.'

On the night of 3/4 June 170 bombers were despatched on the first large raid to Bremen since October 1941. Eleven aircraft failed to return – eight of them shot down by *Nachtjäger*.[4] One of these was a Manchester of 50 Squadron at Skellingthorpe flown by F/O John Heaton, which took off at 2110 hrs on 3 June. The Manchester lost power crossing the Dutch coast and refused to climb higher than 9000 ft but Heaton still managed to bomb the target and even completed two circuits to obtain the mandatory photographs. On the way home over the Veluwe in central Holland the Manchester was attacked and set on fire by a Bf 110 night fighter and crashed near Apeldoorn. Sgt Ken Gaulton, wireless operator, recalls:

'I switched to the aircraft inter communication system to advise the pilot that we were cleared to return to our base, this information having been received on the 0230 broadcast from Group HQ. A Messerschmitt 110 attacked us. The starboard wing of our aircraft was burning and the pilot advised that he was going to dive in an attempt to 'blow out' the fire. This did not succeed. The German aircraft did a victory roll near the tail of our aircraft and Sgt Peter Buttigieg our tail gunner shot him down. I was amazed to hear the yelling from the tail gunner who was engaging the Me 110 with his guns. After diving for thousands of feet I requested the pilot's permission to have the tail gunner and mid-upper gunner join me to prepare the rear escape hatch for evacuation. This was done and we jumped in turn; firstly the tail gunner (the only married man in the crew) then the mid-upper gunner and then came my turn. The aircraft kept on diving and crashed, killing Heaton, P/O John Steen, 2nd pilot, P/O Harold Sheen, navigator and Sgt Stan Thomas, front gunner, all of whom were in the front of the aircraft. I left the aircraft when it was slightly under 1000ft, quickly pulled the ripcord and was promptly knocked out by the chest parachute striking me under the jaw. I landed in the Zuider Zee on an ebbing tide and speared up to my chest in mud. An Alsation dog woke me by licking my face and its owner took me to a medical doctor at about 0530 am. I was unable to walk. The doctor quickly established that the man was a collaborator and was therefore unable to hide me. I was transported by car to Arnhem where I was interrogated by the *Gestapo* and then by train to Amsterdam, where I was gaoled in the Amsterdam watchtower for four days. While I was there a German captain from the fighter squadron visited me about 6 June and advised me that our aircraft had crashed on a hunting lodge owned by the Dutch Royal family near Apeldoorn. He told me that we had shot down one of his aircraft, killing two airmen. He claimed the Germans were two up as four of our crew had been killed.'[5]

On 5/6 June F/Sgt Ralph Wood of 76 Squadron completed his 20th op and took part in the raid on Essen by 180 aircraft[6]:

'It was a hot one and they were ready for us. The damn flak was like lightning flashing in daylight. All about us as the searchlights grabbed us over the target. The shell bursts made a squeaky, gritty noise. The smell of cordite was strong and you had the feeling that someone was underneath kicking your undercarriage, keeping time with the bunts. We were glad to get back without too much damage.'

On the night of 6/7 June three more Manchesters, three Wellingtons, two Stirlings and one Halifax were lost from the 233 aircraft despatched to Emden.[7] Two of the missing Manchester Is were from 50 Squadron. Sgt Leonard Thomas Baker's aircraft was shot down by *Oblt* Ludwig Becker of 6./ NJG 2 at 0044 hrs and crashed into the North Sea off Ameland. P/O A.D. 'Don' Beatty and his all RAAF crew ditched their Manchester I[8] off the coast of the Dutch Friesians after their Manchester developed engine problems. Beatty recalls:

'We could only climb to 9000ft with a bomb load, when bombs dropped on target we always put the nose down and headed for the deck to avoid night fighters and

Flak and to also fire at searchlights when necessary. We flew north of the Friesian Islands at low altitude when one engine packed up. The propeller would not feather, causing excessive drag and as I was in the front turret and the ocean getting too close I climbed back up behind the pilot while the two pilots struggled to control the aircraft. We were perhaps only 200 ft above the water and could not gain height, when the port engine stopped and the aircraft crashed nose first into the drink.

'I saw the second pilot [Sgt Ronald Burton] hit the dashboard, then we were under water. Both he and I were not strapped in. I picked myself up off the floor and got kicked in the face by the navigator [P/O Fred W.R. Allen] as he pushed open the escape hatch. I followed him and was about to jump into the water when I saw the navigator's curtain bobbing up and down in the escape hatch. I tore it off and helped the pilot who was badly injured out and helped him swim around to the dinghy on the starboard side of the aircraft, which was half submerged. The tail section had broken behind the mid-upper gunner's turret. The dinghy had inflated upside down and the mid-upper gunner cut it free, which was probably just as well as the aircraft sank in a couple of minutes. I heard the wireless operator [Sgt Arthur G. Tebbutt] calling in the dark that he could not see so I swam to where he was calling from and brought him back to the dinghy. We all got in the dinghy, which was upside down, as we did not want to lose anybody in the dark. We spent a wet and most uncomfortable night, as there were six of us who had survived. The 2nd pilot had a horrific head wound [Burton died from his injuries on 10 September]. The navigator, we found later, had a broken thigh. The wireless operator had a split lip and eyebrow and I had a head wound and badly bruised left side, arm and leg.

'When daylight finally arrived we had to all get back into the water and the two uninjured gunners turned the dinghy over and helped us all back in stiff and sore. About an hour after daylight two Me 109s on patrol spotted our florescent trail in the water, flew low over us, waggled their wings and disappeared. A very old biplane seaplane arrived, landed and picked us up. The injured were put on stretchers. The dinghy was slashed to sink it and we were flown to Nordeney where we were put into the *Luftwaffe* hospital for a week and were very well treated. We were covered in oil and florescence. The two uninjured were put in the cooler until we were fit to travel. One of the blond 109 pilots came to see me, gave me cigarettes and shook hands. As neither of us understood each other, I tried to thank him for his courtesy and in saving us. We joined the two gunners[9] and were then taken under escort by train to Frankfurt to *Dulag Luft* for interrogation. There we joined up with a number of Commonwealth and RAF aircrews and placed on a guarded train to *Stalag Luft III* at Sagan in Silesia, where we arrived 16 June 1942.'

Op No.21 for F/Sgt Ralph Wood of 76 Squadron on 8 June was Essen again:

'You began to wonder how much more it could take. Our crew consisted of two Englishmen, a Scotsman, an Irishman, a Welshman and myself as the Canadian. A very mixed crew and all nervous as hell. It must be remembered that each bomber was really a flying 25-ton bomb just looking for an excuse to blow up. The five tons or so of high-explosives and magnesium flares, plus another three or four tons of high-octane fuel, provided the ideal mixture for a violent explosion when hit in the right place by an explosive bullet or shell. We were losing too many of our friends. It was not very pleasant, when you awoke in the morning, to see them gathering up the personal effects of those who failed to return from last night's raid. The normal crew of a Hallybag being seven, three aircraft missing meant 21 wouldn't be around anymore. New replacements would soon arrive and fill these empty beds. And so the war goes on!'

Malcolm Freegard, a Wellington IC pilot in 115 Squadron at Marham, flew his first first op on 17 June to St. Nazaire followed by a minelaying operation on the 18th. Two days later he went to the port of Emden in north Germany and again on the night of 22/23 June when his aircraft[10] was damaged over the target:

'We came back on one engine and I struggled to reach home. Then the second engine went and I was obliged to ditch in the sea some 70 miles due east of Cromer. After 12 hours in a dinghy an ASR Walrus amphibian picked up my four crew and me. The ASR crew who had been guided to their dinghy by a Wellington and a Hudson and which took three attempts to take-off was pleased, as we were the first crew they had rescued. After patching us up we were taken back to Marham, where all except one of us recovered to go back on ops.'

Ralph Wood flew his 22nd op, to Emden, on 19/20 June:

'As we crossed the enemy coast we threw out many bundles of *Window* by way of he flare chute. *Window* packages consisted of hundreds of metal strips, which fluttered down over enemy territory. A few aircraft could completely confuse the German radar detectors with the use of *Window.* Occasionally we would take along a bag of beer bottles to drop out the chute, bottom first, over enemy built-up areas on our way to the target. We understood that these empty bottles with open top would create a whistling sound similar to that of a bomb dropping. We felt better thinking that our little effort may have caused someone on the ground to change his underwear. This trip was no better than the rest. You'd think that by now we'd be used to it. We were all getting the 'twitch' as we experienced one 'Shaky Do' after another. A rough translation of 'shaky do' is 'a very frightening affair'. I must admit, I was absolutely petrified on many occasions. You had to live with it, control it. But I was lucky. Once the danger was over, I got over it fairly fast, until the next op. One of our Hallybags crashed on landing back at the base. The crew and aircraft were a mixture of broken bodies and metal. My morale was sure taking a beating.

'Op No.23 the following night was Emden again. Another 'shaky do' but a little closer to the end of our tour. The target was burning like hell but the bombers were going down like flies.[11] One poor bastard got it right over the top of the target. Two guys got out and they held him in the searchlights all the way down. I heard in the Cracker's club in London one day, what the Jerries do with our guys that get down. They threw them into the fire. One of our warning aids against enemy fighters was a light on the pilot's instrument panel, which flashed when they were approaching. This was called IFF (Information Friend or Foe) and not to be confused with the familiar medical inspection term, FFI (Free From Infection). We usually called it 'Short Arm Inspection'. Sometimes one had to urinate on these long trips in spite of having a nervous one on the ground before take-off. This was accomplished by using a funnel and tube arrangement conveniently placed at various locations in the aircraft. The pilot had his own funnel and tube, as he wasn't supposed to go wandering around the aircraft, even though he had the automatic pilot at his disposal. Well, this night he had to use it and the damn thing was plugged. Guess what navigator, sitting at his table, below and slightly in front of him, received this addition to his plotting charts! Having it freeze before I could figure out what was happening just made further plotting very difficult As we had to land at Linton on our return, we did not witness yet another complete write-off of crew and aircraft as they attempted a landing at our base. Lately there were many rumors of sabotage as crews discussed the raids and allied events. On a cross-country practice trip we lost an engine (the engine had seized). The machine-gun-like noise and vibrations in the aircraft startled the hell out of us. It was so scary to our sensitive nerves that we nearly baled out. As a matter of fact, the flight engineer had already kicked out the door of the escape hatch in my compartment and away it went toward the English countryside. Who said we weren't nervous?'

On 22/23 June 227 aircraft comprising 144 Wellingtons, 38 Stirlings, 26 Halifaxes, 11 Lancasters and eight Hampdens, attacked Emden again for the third night in a row. Some 196 crews claimed good bombing results but decoy fires are believed to have diverted many bombs from the intended target. Six aircraft, four Wellingtons, one Lancaster and a Stirling, were lost[12] while Emden reported that 50 houses were destroyed, 100 damaged and some damage caused to the harbour. Six civilians were killed and forty were injured.

Then, on the night of 25/26 June the third and final 'Thousand Bomber Raid' in the series of five major saturation attacks on German cities took place when 1006 aircraft, including 102 Wellingtons of Coastal Command, attacked Bremen.[13] One of the many instructors involved in the 1000 Plan was F/O Harry Andrews. After completing an anti-shipping tour of ops flying Hudsons of 224 Squadron, Coastal Command he was posted to 1 (C) OTU at Silloth as an instructor on Hudson's in early 1942:

'The monotony of training was temporarily broken for us when 30 or so Hudsons took part in the 1000 bomber raid on Bremen. The instructors flew the aircraft but most of the crews were trainees, many of them from establishments in Canada. The Bremen raid was their first taste of operations. I think that many of us welcomed the news of the operation as a break from months of instructing. The ceaseless 'circuits and bumps', the constant reminders to student pilots to lead with the port throttle to prevent swing (and, to the over-confident type, a graphic description of the burn-up that often followed an uncontrolled swing). The warnings to 'watch your airspeed' on the approach, the fighting down of ones reaction to take over the controls when the student was holding off too high at nearly stalling speed and, not least, an encouraging word to the student whose white knuckles gripping the controls too tightly and whose knee tremors indicated both stress and determination. And later on when the student pilots had soloed on Hudsons teaching them low flying over the sea and holding one's breath at their first attempt to fly at 50 feet or so. Certainly we had no conception of the seriousness and moment of the 1000-bomber raids operation. Looking back I find it almost unbelievable how ignorant we all were on what was happening: in short, what it was all about and what part we were playing in the overall plan.

'After the abortive stand-by for the Cologne raid in May no one really took the orders for special operations on 23 June seriously until we flew to Squires Gate late on that day for bombing-up: ten 100 lb GP bombs – the maximum load a Hudson could take with the fuel required. We then flew on to Thornaby arriving late at night. The next day (24 June) was spent in the seemingly inevitable hanging about and it was not until the late afternoon that we were released from standby: another anti-climax. On the morning of 25 June we were briefed that Bremen was the target: 1000 aircraft would be taking part, the risk of collisions over the target was virtually nil if everyone kept to their timings and flight paths. Briefing included weather, night fighter tactics, anti-aircraft Flak concentrations and other standard Bomber Command data. All of us had a Coastal Command background involving anti U-boat, reconnaissance and anti-shipping operations. The Bomber Command type of briefing was entirely new to us. Many of the student navigators had been trained overseas and had little or no experience of night flying or European weather. The specific briefing for the Hudson crews was to climb to 10,000 ft after take-off, cruise at 140 knots to the target, bomb and then immediately descend to 1500 ft and return to base at that level. if I remember correctly, the designated targets were the Focke-Wulf aircraft works and the U-boat construction yards at Deschimag in the waterfront area of Bremen.'[14]

At 12 OTU Chipping Warden excitement pervaded the station and trainee bomber pilots like Ron Read watched the take off with mixed feelings:

'It would have been nice to be taking part but in a clapped out old training Wimpy, well perhaps it was as well we weren't. Chippy's aircraft were manned by mixed complements of instructor pilots and navigators, flying with trainee crews.'

F/L, The Honourable Terence Mansfield 419 'Moose' Squadron RCAF Bombing Leader, 'Moose' Fulton the CO's navigator/bomb aimer, who was on the 30th and final operation of his tour, recalls:

'We took off at 2325 hrs. Although briefed for a greater height, we found the target area completely covered by cloud and came down to 12,000 ft in the hope of getting some visual identification from which we could start a timed run. We ended up doing what others did, namely bombing what we thought was the most likely place. Not very satisfactory and nor were the results.'[15]

The heavy bomber crews were given the opportunity of bombing the red glow of the fires, using *Gee* as a check, or proceeding to a secondary target in the vicinity of Bremen. The cloud conditions prevailed at many of the targets of opportunity and many crews, unable to bomb, brought their lethal cargoes home. F/O Harry Andrews continues:

'The old Hudson I had, like many others, suffered from the faults brought by the hard usage from OTU training. Rate of climb at full throttle was something less than 1000 ft a minute and 3 or 4 degrees of lateral trim was required to fly level. Weather was good for the first 200 miles or so. The sky was clear and the surface of the North Sea was dark against the lightness of the sky. With some envy I could see the silhouettes of Halifaxes and the odd Stirling flying high above us and overtaking on a roughly parallel course. The weather then turned treacherous (as was not uncommon over the North Sea). Low stratus covered the entire sea long before we reached the enemy coast and medium and heavy cloud developed in layers. We were navigating solely on dead reckoning and had only a general idea of our position, flying in and out of cloud (no radar, Gee, Loran or H2S[16] in those days at least for our Hudsons). We saw groups of light and medium Flak to port and starboard with a heavier concentration ahead, which we assumed to be Bremen (a pious but hopeful assumption since we had not been able to fix our position on crossing the coast). In a somewhat detached frame of mind I noticed the colored AA tracer start slowly then corkscrew past one's line of sight almost unbelievably quickly. Cloud cover was such that no positive identification of the target could be made.

'A few minutes after our dead reckoning time over target the turret gunner shouted that a night fighter with an orange light was astern of us (we had been warned at briefing that some German night fighters carried a red/orange light – purpose unknown). It disappeared as quickly as it came and it may well have been the exhaust flame of one of our own aircraft. However, at that time violent evasive action seemed to be the prudent order of the day. Some minutes later we saw through a gap in the clouds a port complex which, from its geographical features, we took to be Wilhelmshaven. Since we were now well behind our scheduled time over target and Wilhelmshaven was a designated alternative target and, not least, mindful of the other 999 (theoretical) aircraft milling around in the general area we released the bombs. With some relief we dived to just above the lowest layer of stratus and set course for home. Fifteen or so minutes later a gap in the cloud layer showed us for a fleeting moment to be over a coastal airfield with one runway lit by flares. A few minutes on we had a glancing sight of one of the islands off the coast but we were too low to identify it and an uneventful flight home was made at low level. Not a herioc flight or one that made even a minuscule contribution to the defeat of Germany. The contribution made by Coastal Command OTU Hudsons in the main must have been to public morale – the 'magic' figure of 1000 bombers had simultaneously attacked a German city.'

The risk of collision and enemy fighter activity proved a constant threat and crews had to be ever watchful. S/L Wolfe's Wellington of 419 'Moose' Squadron RCAF was involved in an engagement with a Bf 110 night fighter north of Borkum at 4200 ft over the North Sea. Sgt D.R. Morrison opened fire and the enemy fighter's port engine was seen to burst into flames, which almost at once engulfed the entire wing. It dived into the sea, leaving a large circle of fire around the point of impact.

The total of 48 aircraft lost (including five Coastal Command aircraft) was the highest casualty rate (five per cent) so far. Of the 31 No.1 (C) OTU Hudsons on the Bremen raid, two returned early owing to cowling and engine trouble and three were lost.[17] The bomber OTUs of 91 Group suffered particularly heavily, losing 23 of its 198 Whitleys and Wellingtons. Altogether, 29 Wellingtons, four Manchester Is, three Halifaxes, two Stirlings, one Hampden and one Whitley were lost. F/O Leslie Thomas Manser of 50 Squadron at Skellingthorpe piloted L7301, one of the Manchesters lost. Manser's Manchester was caught in a searchlight cone and seriously damaged by flak on the approaches to Cologne. Manser held the bomber steady until his bomb load was released and despite further damage, set course for England although he and his crew could have safely baled out after leaving the target area. The Manchester steadily lost height and when it became clear that there was no hope of reaching England Manser ordered the crew to bale out. *Oblt* Walter Barte of 4./NJG 1 intercepted the Manchester at low level in *Nachtjagd* Box 6A and delivered the coup-de-grace with a burst in the right Vulture engine for his fifth victory. Manser, who went down with the aircraft and was killed, was awarded a posthumous Victoria Cross on 20 October 1942 after testimonies from five of his crew who evaded.[18]

Wellington T2723 of 20 OTU from Lossiemouth flown by Sgt N.W. Levasseur was shot down into the sea off Terschelling in an encounter with *Oblt* Egmont Prinz *zur* Lippe Weissenfeld of 5./NJG 2. All six crew were killed. 24 OTU sent 16 aircraft this night and three failed to return.[19] Ron Read at 12 OTU recalls:

'We lost two aircraft from Chippy. One resident from our hut, a Canadian wireless operator, didn't return. We watched his effects being collected the following morning. A first indication that operations weren't going to be all fun.'

Sgt Harris B. Goldberg, born in Boston, USA, who trained as an air gunner in the RCAF and in October 1941 had arrived in Scotland before joining a Wellington crew, flew the 1/2 June Millenium raid on Essen and the 25/26 June raid on Bremen:

'Went in at 12,000-ft got hit and damn near fell to pieces. Went down to 2000 ft and sort of stumbled home at about 90 mph. Don't really know how we got home. All my crew were English. We used to have some pretty wild arguments about the States staying out of the war. After that night over Bremen we argued but we never really got mad any more. Going through something like that brings you pretty close.'[20]

F/Sgt Ralph Wood of 76 Squadron flew on all three 1000-bomber raids and Bremen was his 24th op, which he described as 'pretty spectacular' but which was overshadowed by an incident he witnessed on their return to base:

'Another total loss of an aircraft and its crew. They crashed and burned on landing. I'll never forget the spectacle of bodies trapped in the aircraft, the reek of smoke and the fumes of death. Not a pretty sight! It was all I could do to keep from I throwing up. It's no wonder my nerves were wearing pretty thin. Again the word 'sabotage' was on everyone's lips. The rum and coffee was sure needed at interrogation this night.'[21]

Although the raid was not as successful as the first 1000-bomber raid on Cologne, large parts of Bremen, especially in the south and east districts were destroyed.[22] The German high command was shaken but at Leeuwarden airfield in northern Holland at least, morale soared. II./NJG 2 claimed 17 of the 48 bombers shot down. *Hptm* Helmut 'Bubi' ('Boy') Lent[23] destroyed a Wellington and a OTU Whitley.[24] III./NJG 1, operating from Twenthe aerodrome, claimed seven RAF aircraft. *Lt* August Geiger of the 9th *Staffel* shot down three of these bombers.[25] *Oblt* Werner 'Red' Hoffmann, *Staffelkapitän*, 5./NJG 3, operating from Schleswig, scored his first two night kills by shooting down a Coastal Command Lockheed Hudson and a Whitley.[26] Fifty-two bombers were claimed destroyed by the *Flak* and night fighter defenses on the Bremen raid for the loss of just two Bf 110s[27] and four NCO crewmembers killed or missing. A total of 1123 sorties (including 102 Hudsons and Wellingtons from Coastal Command) had been despatched and 50 Bomber Command aircraft and four from Coastal Command were lost. A 206 Squadron Hudson fell victim to 21-year-old *Lt* Hans-Heinrich 'King' Koenig of 8./ NJG 3.[28] An unidentified war reporter flew with *Lt* Koenig on 25/26 June:

> 'Far, far away the thin white fingers of the searchlights rise up. The first flashes of exploding shells flicker in the sky. Now the multi-colored streams from the light *Flak* join in. 'Take off!' The cabin windows slam closed. With one leap the mechanic jumps off the wing. The fuselage shudders in the slipstream of the propeller. The chocks are snatched away. We sweep over the concrete runway into the thick wall of cloud and climb and climb...We have reached our ordered altitude. Far below us the milky-gray mass of cloud shimmers, in many places already clearly marked by the muzzle flashes of the *Flak* guns, the bomb explosions, the searchlights and the core of raging red fires over my home town. And now, suddenly, we receive the call from afar! We commence our hunt. The moon is our guiding light.
>
> 'King' is sitting forward at the controls. The left hand on the throttle, the right on the button for machineguns and cannon. The head flashes to the left, to the right, the eyes bore into the night. 'There he is, ahead! Can you see him?' Throttle closed. It is a Lockheed Hudson; it is much slower than we and has not spotted us. The black camouflage shimmers in the silvery light of the moon. This is the attack: the fighter is snatched upward and fires from all barrels. The dull sound of the engines is overlaid by the clear crackling of the guns. For a moment we gaze into a fountain of deadly fireworks, were then pressed unremittingly backwards. The Lockheed had swung desparately away, we dive down after it. The Tommy must still have his machine under control. He twists cleverly, then we have him and are set for another merciless attack. Bright yellow, bright red, thin tracer at eye level, directed at the belly of the British bomber. He doesn't defend himself. Has the gunner been eliminated already? Now small flames appear on the port wing! 'He's burning, King, he's burning!' He is still diving down towards the layer of cloud which could be his salvation if he reaches it unscathed. We make another attack, a burst goes into his starboard wing. As the machine disappears reeling into the white veil there is a flash. We have to abandon our opponent to his inevitable fate. A fresh call has reached us. We turn in.
>
> 'How ghost-like is the confrontation with the enemy in the sky at night! Like a black shadow which discloses its bodily shape only in the aftermath, the duck-like profile of a Vickers Wellington suddenly appears before us. 'I am attacking!' says King and snatches the machine steeply upwards. But before the deadly fire leaves the fighter's barrels, a pulse beat ahead, there are flashes above us from the rear guns of the British bomber. Just tiny sparks, like someone striking matches far away. At the same time our guns sound with earsplitting crashing; it must be boring like red hot steel into the enemy's belly, who spreads his wings seemingly within one's reach. Missed.
>
> 'Like a plaintive call from far away I hear the words on the intercom: 'I am wounded! I'm finished! Get ready to jump!' My hand goes at once to the emergency lever. I take one last querying look at the radio operator. King also turns his head. Both have blood running over their faces. King must have a severe injury. To his right there is a gaping hole in the glass cockpit roof. Leaden silence. The hands are on the parachute straps. The body is tense. Then the releasing words. 'My right eye is gone,' says King, 'but I can still hold the machine. I will try to get you home.' The radio operator appears to have been only slightly wounded. Now that the immediate threat has been removed, the steady sound of the engines sounds like soothing music. What is the Wellington doing? Is this attack to have been in vain? It has been heavily hit. Then I see it tottering not far away to aft. 'King, it's burning! It's going down over the port wing! It's exploding!' I must have shouted this into the throat mike. I have to repeat it before they understand it up front. When King replies – in monosyllables, without pleasure at his success, I realize for the first time and with stifling certainty that the fight is not over yet. Now our lives are at stake and they are in his hands. If the left half of the face has also been hit, if the blood runs into the other eye, then we are lost.
>
> 'All around the lone aircraft, which had already sent out its emergency call, the battle continued with undiminished intensity. We are in deep shadows beneath the clouds; the muzzle flashes of the *Flak* only intermittently interrupting the darkness. Somewhere a blazing fire. Our comrades at the base would certainly be following our progress with all their good wishes. Only now, as the airfield appears before us with all its lights, we feel a certainty that we would master our fate. King approaches for landing. The pneumatics lower the undercarriage. A small bounce on the grass, then the

machine completes its run and stops. We only heard later on that, after landing, the last drops of coolant were dripping out of the damaged tank. Twice, three times King nearly collapsed on the way to operations. Time and again he rallies under our helping hands. Warm light receives us as we enter the hut. There is absolute quiet in the bright room; 20, 30 pairs of eyes gaze at the young pilot. Upright, with tousled fair hair and face covered in blood he stands before his commander: 'Obediently report: *Leutnant* Koenig returned from enemy encounter. One certain *Abschuss* in area Anton Two!'[29]

On 30 June Ron Read adjusted to life at Chipping Warden and prepared to start flying 'stumpy, black Wellington bombers':

> 'We shared a ten bed Nissen hut, ate in a Nissen hutted mess, took ground school in a Nissen hut and went into a Nissen hut at flights. At first sight a Nissen looked anything but cosy. However, as wartime servicemen we could settle down anywhere and a Nissen wasn't too bad. It was summertime so we escaped the condensation on the walls and the water on the floor that affected winter dwellers. Outside, the aircraft were old Vickers Wellingtons, the Wimpy. I know they said, 'If you can't take a joke, shouldn't have joined' but this was beyond a joke. It was my nightmare scenario and it was here. Most of our instructors were New Zealanders and tended to be rather serious. All the instructors had recently completed operations and we were avid for their advice. However, when we asked the inevitable, 'What's it like, going on ops?' they found it difficult to explain. At the commencement of flying we found our crews. I was assessed as 'Above Average' as a heavy bomber pilot. Now I hoped to fly Lancasters but I expected to be posted to Stirlings. (12 OTU primarily turned out pilots for 3 Group and it was converting from Wellingtons to Stirlings). When my posting arrived I was posted to 78 Squadron at Middleton St. George, County Durham, a Halifax squadron in 4 Group. I had missed Stirlings, which was a relief but I hadn't much hope of Lancasters now as 4 Group was all Halifax.'

A record 147 Bomber Command aircraft were destroyed by *Nachtjagd* in June 1942. No less than 62 RAF bombers (including 12 Halifaxes) were claimed shot down by II./NJG 2, the top-scoring night fighters based at Leeuwarden. On 31 June Hitler decreed that all searchlight regiments except one (which was kept in action in the Venlo area for experimental purposes against the possible resumption of the searchlight techniques at some later date) should be given up to the *Flak* for the protection of special industrial and urban targets, which eliminated any further use of the *Helle Nachtjagd* technique. Kammhuber, who strongly contested the decision (though he later decided that the step proved beneficial to the development of the *Himmelbett* system) compensated by further extending the existing radar positions. This had the double aim of leaving no gap through which attacking aircraft might penetrate and to put fighters into a position to attack bombers continuously along the penetration and return flights. By early 1942 *Himmelbett* was so advanced that all that was necessary to make good the loss of searchlights was the further extension of the existing radar positions. To achieve greatest density of interception, Kammhuber retained these positions intact, though for more coverage he might have spread them more widely apart. Further positions were equipped, first covering the entire foresector up to the coast, then gradually taking in the main target areas in the rear. The old *Grossraum* was combined with new positions to form the new *Nachtjagdgrossraum* under the command of a *Nachtjagdführer*. Night fighter divisions eventually consisted of four to six of these nightfighting areas. The Bomber Command tactics of staggered approach, involving a period of long duration (between one and one and a half hours) over a target were ideal for the successful operation of the *Himmelbett* system. From June 1942 until the British introduction of Window in July 1943 German night fighters inflicted heavy losses on the bomber forces. *Lt* Dieter Schmidt of III./NJG 1 comments:

> 'The British began now not only using heavier machines, they also changed their tactics by no longer approaching loosely on a broad front but, in order to overwhelm the defenses, coming tightly packed in what became known as a 'bomber stream'. The first of these attacks was the famous 1000 bomber raid on Cologne in the night of 30/31 May 1942. We responded with a defense network of nightfighting areas, the *Dunkle Nachtjagd*, which was independent of searchlights, reaching from the coast far back into the hinterland. The growing intensity of the air war but especially the difficulty of air operations at night, resulted in the first and for us young ones hard to bear losses of experienced crews: *Oblt* Woltersdorf, *Kommandeur* of the 7th *Staffel* was killed in a belly landing after 23 victories on 2 June. On 30 June *Oblt* Werner Rowlin lost his life while baling out and *Fw* Philipp of the 9th *Staffel*, who landed his aircraft on 9 June in spite of being shot through the lung was out of action for a long time.
>
> 'In mid-1942 our *Gruppe* not only got a new commander in *Hptm* Thimmig, our equipment was also

significantly improved by aircraft fitted with radar, the *Lichtenstein*-BC, which had been developed since August 1941 by IV./NJG 1. Until now, the success of the *Dunkle Nachtjagd* had been entirely dependent on the skill of the ground controller to direct the fighter accurately, especially during the final phase of the approach to the enemy aircraft. Now it would suffice to guide the crew close enough to be able to pick up the target with their on-board radar. Also, the aircraft were no longer painted black but in a light color and by the end of the year our Bf 110Fs with their unreliable engines were replaced by the G4 nightfighter version, which was to serve us well until the end of the war.'

On the night of 29/30 June Bomber Command dispatched 253 aircraft to Bremen and 11 aircraft failed to return.[30] W/O Len Collins RAAF a Stirling gunner in 149 Squadron at Lakenheath who had completed his tour and was awaiting a posting to an EFTS to train as a pilot volunteered for an extra op. He stood in for the mid-upper-gunner, who was ill, on the crew of S/L G.W. Alexander, who would be flying N6082. It would be Collins' 33rd trip. He recalls:

'Other than the second pilot, F/O W.G. Barnes, on his first trip to gain experience, the remainder of the crew were on their thirtieth. All were RAF. I was the only Aussie. The trip to Bremen was uneventful. Conversing with the squadron leader I found that he was most interested with the pyrotechnic display from the *Flak* and the colors of the searchlights as we crossed the enemy coast. I predicted we were in for trouble when a blue one slid off our wing tip. However, either our doctored *IFF* did not work or the Germans were given a tip-off. Over Bremen we received a direct hit from *Flak* on our inner starboard engine, killing Alexander and P/O C.W. Dellow, observer and injuring the WOp D.S. Hickley. The bombs were dropped live, a photo taken and we headed for home on three engines. Over the Zuider Zee a night fighter appeared.[31] I can still recall the flash of his windscreen in the darkness as he opened fire. As I was speaking to the rear gunner, Sgt R. Gallagher he was blown out of his turret. I was ringed with cannon shells and injured in the leg by shrapnel. Owing to the electrical cut out which protected the tail of the aircraft from the mid-upper guns, I was unable to fire on the fighter attacking us. Fortunately, the turret became jammed in the rear position, allowing me to vacate it. Forward, the aircraft was burning like a torch. I could not contact any crewmember. The position was hopeless. I felt I had no option but to leave the aircraft. My parachute was not in its storage holder. I found it under the legs of the mid-upper turret with a cannon shell burn in it. I removed the rear escape hatch, clipped on the parachute and sat on the edge of the hatch. I pulled the ripcord and tumbled out. The parachute, having several holes from the shell burn, 'candlesticked' (twirled) as I descended and I landed in a canal. I was apprehended the following day and was taken to Leeuwarden airfield for interrogation. Here I met the pilot of the Messerschmitt 110 who claimed to have shot us down. I abused him in good Australian. He understood, having spent three years at Oxford University.'[32]

Despite a brush with a Ju 88 on 29/30 June Sgt Neville Hockaday RNZAF in a Wellington of 75 Squadron RNZAF returned safely to Feltwell on what was his first trip with his own crew, having flown as a 'second dickey' on the Essen raid 2 June.[33] 'Three nights later, on 2/3 July,' continues Hockaday, 'the target was again Bremen to follow up the considerable damage reported as having been done to the Focke-Wulf factory last time. We got in sight of the Dutch coast when Bruce (Sgt Bruce Philip RNZAF, rear gunner) reported a sick stomach getting worse. Not wishing to risk combat with night fighters with a sick rear gunner we returned to base after jettisoning our 'Cookie' into the sea set 'safe'. On 7/8 July we were 'Gardening'[34] off Nordeney where we placed two mines without incident, the whole trip of four hrs flown at 2000 ft or below. Our next trip on 8/9 July was to the naval dockyard at Wilhelmshaven, a heavily defended target, which I decided to attack from 11,000 ft – low enough to avoid the night fighters which would be after the four-engined bombers at greater heights. We got a fairly hot reception and dropped our 'Cookie' against the outer wall of the dockyard and made our escape. However, all was not yet over and we were harrassed by *Flak* ships off Emden and Borkum. We landed after five hours and 15 minutes:

'The next two nights' operations were cancelled because of weather but on 13/14 July the target was Duisburg and this proved to be the first of four visits to that city during the next 12 nights, by which time we had named ourselves The Happy Valley Express, a great understatement for the Ruhr was anything but a happy place for Bomber Command. To reach it we crossed the North Sea and then Holland which held a network of radar units operating in co-operation with night fighters. Next there were radar controlled searchlights in which, a blue master light sought out the bomber and because of its blue color it was almost impossible to spot it before it made contact when the first warning was a blue glare full in the face. Then half a dozen white beams would cone the aircraft. All these combined threats added up to a chastening experience! Over the Ruhr itself the night fighters were the most audacious anywhere and would think nothing of flying amongst their own anti-aircraft fire. After bombing, the gauntlet had to be run again in reverse. A visit to the Ruhr involved two and a half hours of strain that it is almost impossible to describe. We made nine operational visits and came out unscathed, a fact at which I still marvel. On return from the first of these the greatest risk was faced on return to base where the cloud base had fallen to 300 ft. The next night, 14/15 July, we went 'gardening' again, this time to Terschelling without incident. The weather was unfit for operations for the next week or so but the next moon period was coming up and on 21 July the Happy Valley Express set off for its second excursion. We followed a direct route from Southwold to Duisburg, passing south of Rotterdam and to the north of the night fighter base on the island of Walcheren. Using our usual technique of seeking a gap in the *Flak* ahead we found it near the island of Goeree, crossing the coast and keeping north of Tilburg we arrived unimpeded at the outer defenses of the Ruhr. The searchlights and night fighters were showing their usual ferocity but somehow we got through without being intercepted. Duisburg lay on the east bank of the Rhine a few miles north of a sharp bend in the river. There were many dummy fires on the west bank but the bright full moon and silvery ribbon of water led us directly to our target. We dropped our 'Cookie' on some marshalling yards and turned for Geldern before returning, again crossing the Dutch coast near Goeree and again left alone by the defenses. Two nights later (23/24 July) we went there again and followed almost the same route but this time the aiming point was obscured by cloud and we had to make a *Gee* bombing run from the last visible 'fix'. The cloud also hampered the defenses and we were not intercepted.'

Malcolm Freegard of 115 Squadron had returned to ops on 11 July, with a minelaying trip and then it was off to Duisburg on the 13th:

'Minelaying trips were fairly cushy unless you saw a flak ship and people could and did get shot down. Duisburg was particularly well defended. It put the wind up you to see the old night fighters creeping around. I hated bombing cities, I really did. I was happier when I was given military targets. Saturation bombing of German cities was awful. Waging war on children and old people and historic cities is not what I wanted to do. I was 20 years old. I had wanted to be a fighter pilot where the war was one on one. When I joined 115 Squadron I was as patriotic as the next man. Then I began to think about all the energy and human ingenuity used to wage war that could have been employed in better ways. This war was an expensive spirit and a waste of shame.

'My seventh op, on the night of 21/22 July, we set out at 2349 hrs to bomb Duisburg again. Shortly after bombing we were attacked from underneath by a Me 110 night fighter close to Düsseldorf and my faithful Wellington caught fire and was damaged beyond any hope of recovery. Fortunately, I was again carrying no second pilot that night. As it was three of my five crew were killed in the aircraft (one of the lads had been married only three months).[35] After checking them to make sure they were dead, Sgt Bill Rogers the front gunner and I escaped with some difficulty. I had been wounded slightly in the thigh by an exploding cannon shell and I had a hell of a job getting out through the front hatch. When I finally opened my parachute I was well under a 1000 ft from the ground. I thought, this is it – I've had it. It's what I joined up for. But to my great relief, the chute opened and I landed in open countryside in a sodden wet field, breaking an ankle in the process. Guns were going off in the distance. Aircraft continued to fly overhead. I went to sleep wrapped up in my chute. When it started getting light I began walking along a road but I did not get far. A car with three Luftwaffe officers in it drew up and I was captured, Eventually, I ended up at the *Dulag Luft* interrogation center in Frankfurt. There the *kommandant* came to see me. He showed me a book and pointed out a photo of a group of people. One of them was my father! The book was about the Chiswick Convention, which my father and apparently the *kommandant*, had attended every year. The *kommandant* was genuinely pleased that my father was his friend.

'I was to be put on a train under guard for PoW camp. While we waited at Frankfurt railway station, a tiny, wizened, old lady, who was almost certainly Jewish, approached me. She was so small her head reached only as a far as my waist. She said to me, *'Got bless you.'* I patted her gently on the cheek. There was uproar all around me. I was put on a train and finally taken away to captivity. *'For you the war is over'*, the Germans would say. Some of them said it crowingly. Others said it with envy in their voices. They must have thought, 'Ruddy war. Sodding Hitler. We're all in the same boat.' To them, 'For you the war is over' meant 'you lucky bugger'. They thought that for me the war was over. It wasn't. The next three years were spent in Stalag Luft III, notorious as the setting of the *Great Escape*, following which, 50 allied officers were

> executed on the orders of the *Führer* himself.[36] I was one of those responsible for getting rid of soil from the tunnels. I was in the same hut as Tom Lees and two of the officers who were among the 50 who were executed. It was terrible. There were even one or two Germans who were as upset by the murders as we were. Now I look back on the whole experience like it was a book you read about someone else. Sometimes, suddenly, I am there again. An expensive spirit, a waste of shame.'

On 25/26 July Sgt Neville Hockaday of 75 Squadron RNZAF and the crew of the Happy Valley Express made it four in a row by setting course for Duisburg yet again, this time crossing the Dutch coast and setting off as if for Düsseldorf where some diversionary marker flares had been dropped. Just past Krefeld to their port Hockaday turned sharply northeast and headed once more for the tell-tale bend in the Rhine. Incredibly after three raids on Duisburg surprise was achieved and they saw their 'Cookie' blow up in the middle of a large factory fire. They brought back a very good photograph to prove it.

The next night, on 26/27 July, again in full moonlight, the target was Hamburg. In all, 403 bombers were despatched. Twin engined types like the Wellington and to a lesser extent the Hampden still formed the backbone of Bomber Command. AM Harris was gradually building up his numbers of four-engined types and the 181 Wellingtons and 33 Hampdens were joined on the raid by 77 Lancasters, 73 Halifaxes and 39 Stirlings. Sgt Neville Hockaday recalls:

> 'The plan was to make a long sea crossing wide of Heligoland, as though bound for the Baltic via Jutland before turning south east below Rendsburg to fly down the Elbe estuary to our target. All went well until crossing the Kiel Canal when without warning we developed a fault in the intercom. We flew in wide circles while Sgt Mike Hughes, WOp/AG frantically tried to locate the fault. After ten minutes we began to run out of time on the target and not wishing to take on the defenses all alone decided to go for the secondary target of Rendsburg, selecting the submarine pens as our aiming point. Communication was extremely difficult, everything having to be said several times to be heard over the static. The bombing run was done using hand signals for 'left', 'right' or 'steady'. Just as we were on the bombing run Mike found the fault and corrected it so the run was completed normally and the 'Cookie' fell in the shipyard on the canal. We cleared the area out to sea and descended to 200 ft to frustrate the radar screens at Heligoland, another fighter base that was considered a regular hornet's nest.'

At Marham at around 2200 hrs 115 Squadron had put up 14 Wellingtons and crews. W/C Frank W. Dixon-Wright DFC the 31-year-old CO popular with his crews and who had already completed a tour of operations led the briefing. Some members of his crew of Wellington BJ615 were second tour men. They too were well respected. Normally this crew would fly with S/L Cousens, OC A Flight but Cousens was on stand down. Twenty-year old Sgt Baden B. Feredey, an experienced pilot with 15 operational flights captained another 'A' Flight crew.[37] Not every crew flying-to Hamburg was as well experienced as these. Sgt Jim Howells RNZAF had completed five operations as a second pilot with other crews and he was given captaincy of a new crew in 'A' Flight.[38] There had been recent criticism of the Squadron for failing to obtain suitable photographs of the target so the New Zealander decided that his crew would bring back a superb photograph. Sgt Jim Burtt-Smith and crew had been with the Squadron for just over a month. They had been allocated to A Flight. Having overcome their operational teething problems, including writing off a Wellington when returning from a raid, they were now settled in to completing a tour of 30 operations flying Wellington B3723 *B-Bear*. Hamburg would be their ninth operational flight.

Howells, the novice captain, had managed to coax his Wellington up to 14,000 ft by the time he reached Hamburg. He was carrying a mixed load of high explosive and incendiary bombs. Despite the opposition from the defenses he was still determined to obtain a good photograph of his bomb bursts. Reaching the aiming point his bomb aimer released the bombs. This action automatically opened the shutter on the fixed camera and released the flash bomb. All the pilot had to do was fly a straight and level course until the flash functioned. The photograph would then be taken. More experienced, perhaps more prudent pilots would have had greater concern for the immediate safety of their aircraft than bringing back a photograph for the planners at base to study. The *Flak* at Hamburg was accurate and intense. In such situations following the release of the bombs it was usual to stick the nose down in a shallow dive, build up speed and corkscrew like Hell away from the target. Howells was resolute. Following a straight and level course he flew blissfully on. It was a golden opportunity for the *Flak* batteries and one they could not ignore.

Almost immediately the Wellington was ranged. *Flak* hit the port engine. It may have damaged the propeller as well as the engine. Intense vibration began to rack the airframe. Howells quickly feathered the propeller and switched off the engine. To his dismay the aircraft began to lose height. He managed to weave away from the target with no further damage to the bomber. Rapidly losing height he crossed the German coastline in an attempt to fly back over the comparative safety of the North Sea. It was all to no avail. The Wellington would not stay in the air. Below he could see clearly the tops of the breaking waves. He issued orders for ditching. The observer collected all the survival apparatus including the Verey pistol and cartridges and placed them in a bag. As the bomber hit the sea a wall of water cascaded through the fuselage. It tore the bag from the observer's hand. When they clambered into the dinghy they found the marine signals stowed aboard had perished. They were adrift in the North Sea with no Verey pistol or any means of attracting the attention of a passing ship or aircraft. They were to drift like this for three days. On the first day a Beaufighter came close to them but did not see them. That night they drifted within earshot of a fierce naval battle presumably between German *E boats* and a convoy. On the second day two Spitfires flew over without seeing them. On the third day a German seaplane from Nordeney rescued them and took them off to captivity.

B-Bear and Sgt Burtt-Smith's crew arrived in the target area about the same time as Howells. Fortunately for them the defenses were preoccupied with another aircraft and they quickly made their way to the aiming point, released their bombs and set course for the German coastline. Jim Burtt-Smith continues:

> 'We were on course, homeward bound and flying between Bremerhaven and Wilhelmshaven, when New Zealander 'Frizzo' Frizzell piped up from the rear turret, 'What about a bloody drink? I'm gasping.' Sgt Jack French, the WOP-AG was just about to hand me a cup of coffee when, BANG! We were hit in the port engine. The smoke and havoc was appalling. I feathered the port engine and managed to bring her head round. Fortunately, no one was hurt. The bomb aimer, Sgt Lionel 'Len' Harcus, came out of the front turret to hang on to the rudder bar to try to help counter the violent swing to port. I took stock of the situation and tried to increase boost and revs on the starboard engine, but to no avail. By this time we were losing height. I got Barney D'Ath-Weston, my New Zealander navigator to give me a new course for home. Heavy ack-ack was still pounding away. We were heading for the open sea and try as I might; I could not gain any height. As we headed over the coast the searchlights pointed our way to the fighters. We were now down to 1000 ft. I told Jack to let out the 60-foot trailing aerial. We were having a terrible time trying to keep the aircraft straight and level. The drag of the dead engine was puling us to port. I applied full rudder bias and Len hung onto the rudder for dear life. It was impossible to set a straight course. I gave instructions, 90 miles out over the North Sea, to take positions and prepare for ditching. It was as black as a November fog; no moon, no nothing.
>
> 'As Jack and Len left the cockpit I jettisoned the fuel, shut off the remaining engine and turned towards England. I had no idea of height because when the port engine failed, so did the lights and instruments. Jack clamped the Morse key down so our people could get a fix on us.[39] I told him to give me a shout when the aerial touched the water so I knew I had 60 feet of height left. I had to keep playing with the stick to keep her airborne, letting the nose go down then pulling her up a bit, just like a bloody glider. I prayed for a moon, knowing full well that if I couldn't see to judge which way to land we would plunge straight in and down. (One had to land towards the oncoming waves; any other way would be disastrous.) [The bomb aimer and the wireless operator retreated to their ditching stations. Jim Burtt-Smith shut off the starboard engine and began to glide, repeatedly dropping the nose and then pulling up gently].
>
> 'Jack shouted out, 'Sixty feet!' and there we were, wallowing about like a sick cow. I shouted to the lads to hold tight, we were going in. 'Frizzo' turned his turret to starboard so that he could get out when we crashed. This was it! Prepare to meet thy doom. Suddenly, the moon shone and, thank God, I could see the sea. The moonbeams were like a gigantic flarepath. We actually flew down them. We were practically down in the drink when I saw we were flying the wrong way. I lugged *B-Bear* around, head-on to the waves. I hauled back on the stick and there was one almighty crash. We were down! It was 0300 hrs.
>
> 'The water closed over my head and my Mae West brought me to the top. I got my head out of the escape hatch and there we were, wallowing in the sea. Then the moon went in! It was again as black as it could be. Len helped me out of the cockpit. Jack popped out of the astro hatch carrying the emergency kit, followed by D'Ath, who had stayed to destroy the *Gee* box and papers. 'Frizzo' scuttled along the fuselage and we all scrambled into the dinghy, which had popped out of the engine nacelle and was inflating in the water, still attached to the Wimpy, which was sinking fast. D'Ath slashed the rope and we pulled away as best we could before we got sucked under.'

At 0930 hours a German seaplane from Nordeney picked up the crew of *B-Bear* and they all finished the war as PoWs.

Sgt Baden B. Feredey and the crew of KO-K meanwhile, reached Hamburg without incident. The outward journey was relatively calm and there were no interceptions from night fighters. The inward flight was near Borkum and Feredey flew

Above: The Bomber Always Gets Through? This theory of the self-defending, daylight, bomber formations on which the RAF had based its ideas of strategic bombing during the 1920s and 1930s was rudely shattered during daylight Hampden, Blenheim and Wellington attacks on *Kriegsmarine* shipping in the German Bight and off Norway during the 'Phoney War', September 1939/April 1940. Here three 61 Squadron Hampdens I are flying a typical self-defending box formation for daylight operations. (Alex H. Gould)

Below: Handley Page Hampden I of 144 Squadron at RAF Helmswell, Lincolnshire in 1939. The Hampden was the last of the twin-engined monoplane bombers to go into service with the RAF during the pre-war expansion period. At the outbreak of war Hampdens equipped eight squadrons in 5 Group, Bomber Command and they were used on daylight operations until heavy losses caused the aircraft to be used only at night. Together with the Armstrong Whitworth Whitley and Vickers Wellington, Hampdens carried the night offensive to Germany until 14/15 September 1942 when the Hampden operated with Bomber Command for the last time. (via Jock Galloway)

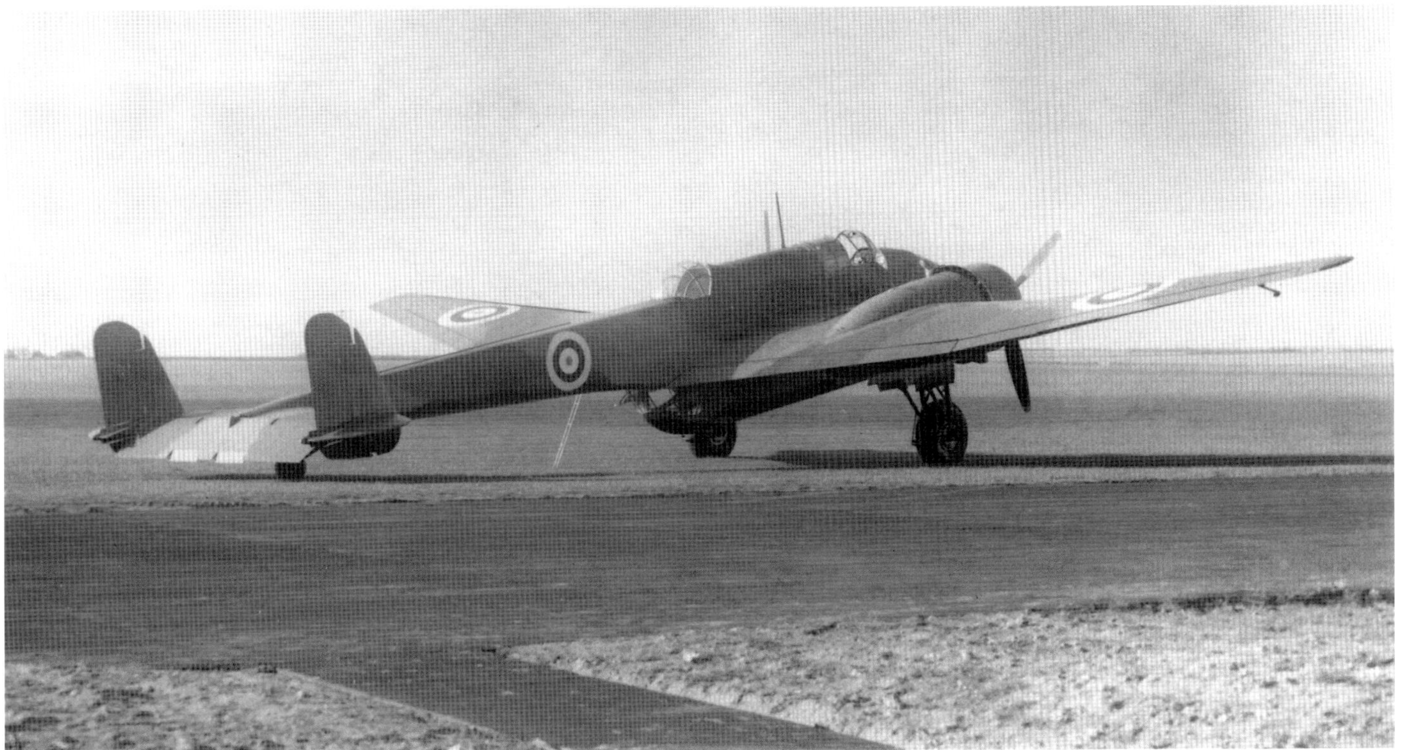

Right: *Hptm* Wolfgang Falck, born on 18 August 1910, was destined to become one of the legendary figures in the Luftwaffe. He had been one of the *Reichswehr* officer-cadets selected in 1932 to be sent to Lipetsk in the Soviet Union for training as a fighter pilot. By the outbreak of war in September 1939, *Oblt* Falck was *St.Kpt* of 2./ZG 76, which was newly equipped the Bf 110C-1 *Zerstörer*. During the Polish Campaign Falck scored three victories and on 18 December 1939 when ZG 76 were credited with 12 Wellingtons destroyed during the 30-minute Battle of the German Bight, Falck claimed two Wimpys shot down. In all, Falck scored eight kills as a *Zerstörer* pilot. Operating from Aalborg in Jutland during the Norwegian campaign in April 1940 Falck, who had meanwhile been given command of I./ZG 1 and promoted to *Hptm*, and his unit experimented with night interceptions of RAF aircraft over Denmark using details of approaching RAF bombers supplied by a local *Freya* early warning coastal radar installation. (via Steve Hall)

Far right: *Hptm* Wolfgang Falck, *Staffelkapitän*. 2./ ZG 76. On the night of 30 April/1 May 1940 when 50 Whitleys, Wellingtons and Hampdens attacked German airfields in Norway Falck, *Oblt* Werner Streib, Falck's communications officer and *Oblt* Günter Radusch, made a successful interception but they could not claim any bombers destroyed for certain. Falck wrote a detailed paper on his night fighting theories and after the successful Battle of France where he led his *Zerstörer Gruppe*, on 26 June 1940 his night fighting initiatives were duly recognized and he was appointed *Kommodore* of NJG 1, the first *Geschwader* dedicated to nightfighting. Falck was awarded the *Ritterkreuz* on 7 October 1940. (Falck)

Right: Bf 110C-2 G9+GA Werk Nr.3920 of *Hptm* Wolfgang Falck, *St.Kpt* 2./ZG 76 at Jever in early 1940. The *Haifischmaul* (shark's mouth) marking is missing from the nose of his aircraft but the 'England Blitz' badge designed by *Oblt* Victor Mölders, brother of then leading fighter *Experte* Werner (14 victories in the Spanish Civil War and top scorer in the French campaign with 25, who was grounded in July 1941 after scoring 101 victories), can be seen. The badge with a red lightning flash pointing at London, was adapted for use on *Nachtjagd* fighters simply by changing some of the colors. The diving silver falcon was inspired by the Falck family crest. (Falck)

Right: The *Nachtjagd* crest.

Far right: RAF Bomber Command crest with the motto, STRIKE HARD STRIKE SURE.

Below: Whitley I K7188 of 10 Squadron, which introduced this bomber type into RAF service in 4 Group at Dishforth, Yorkshire in March 1937 where it replaced the Heyford biplane bomber. (K7188 had been delivered to the squadron in 1937 and it was SOC on 10 October 1940). Thirty-four Whitley Is were built for the RAF and they were followed into service by 46 Whitley II and 80 Whitley III aircraft. In 1938 40 Merlin-engined Whitley IVs with a Nash and Thompson powered turret with four Browning machine guns in place of the manually operated rear turret were delivered. Delivery of the final variant, the Whitley V, began in 1939 and ceased in June 1943, by which time 1466 total examples had been built. At the outbreak of war in September 1939 six squadrons of Whitleys equipped 4 Group, Bomber Command. On the night of 19/20 March 1940, 30 Whitleys of 10, 51, 77 and 102 Squadrons joined 20 Hampdens of 5 Group in a raid on the German mine-laying seaplane base at Hornum, this being the first time when bombs fell on German territory in World War II. On 11/12 May 1940 Whitleys and Hampdens dropped the first bombs on the German mainland when they attacked the rail network near Münchengladbach. Whitleys were finally retired from Bomber Command in spring 1942. (AW)

Right: Vickers Wellington bomber undergoing maintenance in a RAF hangar. The Wellington, known affectionally as the 'Wimpy' after the character J. Wellington Wimpy in Popeye cartoons, formed the backbone of RAF Bomber Command in the early part of the night war uintil the advent of the four-engined heavies that came later. During 1941-42 there were no less than 21 squadrons of Wellingtons in front line service. The last operational flight of a Wellington in Bomber Command took place on 8/9 October 1943. (Authors' Coll)

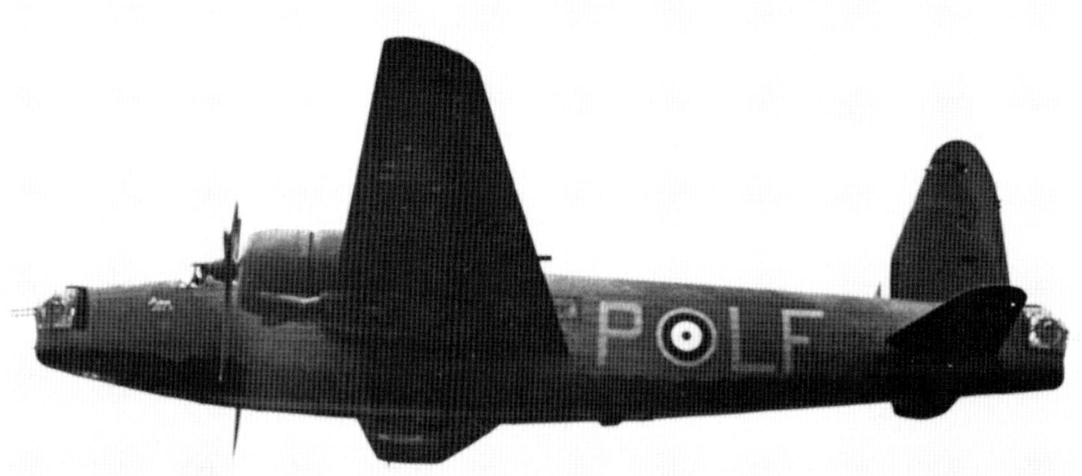

Wellington Ia L7779 LF-P of 37 Squadron at Feltwell in April 1940. In 3 Group at the outbreak of war, 37 Squadron was posted to the Middle East in November 1940. (F/L K. Haywood)

Wellington I L4387 LG-L of 115 Squadron in 3 Group on detachment with RAF Coastal Command in April 1940. L4387 was on loan to a crew of 75 RNZAF Squadron who used it for a daylight reconnaissance of Narvik, Norway. The aircraft passed to 11 OTU and crashed on take off at Bassingbourn on 13 August 1940, killing three of the crew. (Authors' Coll)

Right: Wellington IC T2468 'Y-Yorker' of 9 Squadron in 3 Group at RAF Honington, Suffolk in June 1940. This aircraft later served with 40 and 311 Czechoslovak Squadrons and various OTUs before being scrapped on 20 June 1944. (Rupert Cooling)

Below: Wellington IC L7788 KX-E of 311 Czechoslovakian Squadron developed engine trouble on 23/24 September 1940 on an operation to Berlin and the pilot, F/L Karel Trojáèek, was forced to put the aircraft down at Leidschendam in the den Haag in Holland. Five of the crew were taken prisoner but Sgt Karel Kuòka shot himself with his Verey pistol when German troops attempted to capture him. The aircraft was later tested by the Luftwaffe. 311 Squadron was formed in July 1940 from Czechoslovak airmen who had been serving in France. In April 1942 311 Squadron was posted to Coastal Command and flew Liberators on long-range maritime operations until the end of the war. (Bart Rynhout)

Right: On the evening of 26 August 1940 F/O Peter D. Tunstall and his crew of Hampden I P4324 QR-P in 61 Squadron headed for the Merseburg oil refinery. On their way back, the crew completely lost their way and with the fuel gauges showing 'zero' they decided on an emergency landing on a flat stretch of beach on the coast, which the navigator thought was Ireland. It was only when Tunstall looked though the window of a shack in the dunes and spotted a Dutch magazine that he realized where they were. Soon after, the four men were taken PoW by the German garrison of the Dutch Friesian Island of Vlieland, where they had come down. A few days later, a German crew flew their Hampden off the Vliehors sandbank and to Rechlin, Germany (the Luftwaffe equivalent of Boscombe Down). Unconfirmed reports suggest that the aircraft, although escorted by German fighters, was shot down by *Flak*. (Hille van Dieren)

Right: An apprehensive crew in 99 Squadron preparing to board their Wellington I at a desolate and snow-covered corner of Newmarket Heath airfield during the winter of 1940-41. (via Eric Masters)

Below: Wellington IC T2888 LN-R 'R-Robert' of 99 Squadron at Newmarket Heath airfield during the winter of 1940-41. This aircraft crashed in heavy fog at Stags Halt, Wisbech on the night of 11/12 February 1941 when 22 aircraft crashed in England returning from a raid on Bremen when unexpected fog descend on the majority of stations. Most of the crews baled out safely but five men were killed. of the 79 Hampdens, Wellingtons and Whitleys, only 27 claimed to have hit the target. (RAF Museum)

Right: In 1940 after high losses on daylight operations most Blenheim light bombers in 2 Group were employed in night attacks, initially on the Channel ports in support of Hampdens, Whitleys and Wellingtons of Bomber Command. During 1940-1941 *Flak* and searchlight defenses were a greater hazard for RAF bomber crews than the infant night-fighting arm, or *Nachtjagd*. Here the Oldenburg *Flak* defenses are putting up a barrage during the raid on Hamburg of 4/5 January 1941. Although a force of 24 Blenheims was dispatched to bomb Hamburg, poor weather prevented the crews from finding and attacking the primary target and Hamburg records for this night contain no mention of any attack. All participating aircraft returned to England safely on this occasion. Blenheim squadrons continued flying night operations until March 1941 when they were switched to daylight low level attacks on German shipping when losses again were high and the North Sea became known in RAF parlance as the 'Sea of Carnage'. (Erich Kayser)

Top: P/O R.F. Beauclair of 102 Squadron force-landed Whitley V N1377 DY-B at Hekelingen (15 km SW of Rotterdam) at 0130 hours on 27 July 1940 after being hit by *Flak* from Vlaardigen-Ambacht. The crew of five was taken prisoner. (Kees Wind)

Above: A Wellington IC of 149 East India Squadron at RAF Mildenhall, Suffolk in 1941. This squadron was in 3 Group at the outbreak of war and until the end of the war and flew Wellingtons, Stirlings and Lancasters from Mildenhall, Lakenheath and Methwold. (via Dr. Colin Dring)

Right: Short Stirling I MG-L of 7 Squadron at RAF Oakington. On the night of 10/11 February 1941 British four-engined bombers went into action for the first time when three Stirling Is of 7 Squadron, led by Acting S/L J.M. Griffith-Jones DFC bombed oil storage tanks beside the Waal at Rotterdam. Each aircraft carried 16 500 lb bombs and they dropped a total of 46 500lb bombs (two hung up). 7 Squadron had been the first squadron in the RAF to receive the Stirling, in August 1940. (via Theo Boiten)

Right: Wellington IC R1593 'N-Nuts' of 149 Squadron being bombed up at Mons Wood, RAF Mildenhall in 1941. The odd drawing beneath the pilot's window is of a drunken firefly and represented, variously, the wireless operator (antennae), the pilot (wings), the tail-gunner (Scorpion sting) and the eyes for the half-blind navigator. The whole portrayed a crew that flew by night and was supposedly drunk by day. On 14 July 1941, following a raid on Bremen R1593 was taken away in pieces, damaged beyond the possibility of local repair. (Lord Sandhurst)

Below: F/O B.G. Cook of 101 Squadron flew this IC home on one engine after an attack by a night fighter near Hamm on 7 August 1941. P/O Milton Pelmore, 2nd Pilot and Cook were wounded and Sgt Lackie, the rear gunner, who was hit badly by a cannon shell, could not bale out because two parachutes were badly burned. With hydraulics out, Cook skillfully bellied in at Oakington and the crew was evacuated before the Wimpy caught fire. It was only then that a 500-lb bomb was discovered still in the bomb bay! (B.G. Cook)

Right: An early infrared camera captures aircrew of 149 Squadron being driven to dispersal for a raid on Kiel docks on the night of 11/12 March 1941. L-R. W/C (later G/C) Powell OBE DSO Squadron CO; Sgt Petter, WOP of Wellington 'M-Mother'; P/O Coryat; Squadron Navigation Officer. Standing. F/O Trevor A. 'Happy' Hampton. Sitting. Sgt George Gray. Twenty-seven Wellingtons claimed many hits on the shipyards at Kiel and no aircraft were lost. (T.A. Hampton)

Right: Manchester I L7380 EM-W of 207 Squadron at low tide on the beach at Ameland on 8 September 1941. En route for Berlin L7380 was damaged by a night fighter flown by *Fw* Siegfried Ney of 4./NJG 1. F/L Mike Lewis DFC ditched the aircraft in five feet of water. The Manchester first entered RAF service with 207 Squadron at RAF Waddington in November 1940 and the first operational flight was on a raid on Brest on the night of 24/25 February 1941. (Frits Vos via Hendrik Cazemier)

Right: Bf 110D-0 *Dackelbauch* ('dachshund belly') of NJG 1, probably taken at Deelen airfield in the winter of 1940-41. In the background is Bf 110 G9+KP of NJG 1. A handful of Bf 110s fitted with this type of long-range belly tank were used in NJG 1 during summer 1940 mid-1941 at Deelen and at Bergen aan Zee. However, due to highly explosive gases developing in the emptying tanks, which led to aircraft exploding in mid-air, the *Dackelbauchs* were removed. (Marcel van Heijkop via Ab Jansen)

Below: Bf 110D-0 *Dackelbauch* G9+HR of 7./NJG 1 on a practice flight over Holland in early 1941. (via Rob de Visser)

Right: 'Bashful' Bill Williams' Wellington I of 75 Squadron RNZAF at RAF Feltwell, Norfolk. A number of the squadron's aircraft were similarly painted with Disney cartoon characters. (via Bob Collis)

Right: Remnants of a Whitley turret (registration number '324/A' only partly visible) with the tail gunner still inside after it was shot down by a Marine *Flak* unit at Juist, probably during a Bomber Command raid on Emden. (Emil Lechner)

Below: Whitley shot down at Kiel or Sylt. (Emil Lechner)

Right: F/L Johnnie A. Siebert RAAF pilot of Manchester I L7303 EM-P of 207 Squadron, which was shot down on the night of 27/28 March 1941 returning from Düsseldorf. (Kees Rijken)

Far right: *Ofw* Gerhard Herzog at his wedding. (Kees Rijken)

Right: The wreckage of Manchester I L7303 EM-P of 207 Squadron, which was shot down at 2330 hrs at Bakel, 15 km SE of Helmond on the night of 27/28 March 1941 returning from Düsseldorf. The Manchester was credited to *Ofw* Gerhard Herzog of 3./NJG 1 for his third confirmed kill. (Kees Rijken)

Below: Bf 110 nightfighters of I/NJG 1. M8+GH was flown by *Ofw* Gerhard Herzog, who on the night of 27/28 March 1941 also shot down a Whitley of 78 Squadron at 2305 hrs at Helenaveen (for his 2nd official kill). (Kees Rijken)

Above: Wellington IC's R1410 KX-M and R1378/K of 311 Czechoslovakian Squadron in March 1941. Returning from Bremen on 18 March 1941 R1378 suffered an engine failure and the pilot, Sgt Anderle, belly landed at East Wretham. R1410 passed to 12 OTU where, on on the night of 25/26 June 1942 when the third and final 'Thousand Bomber Raid' took place with a raid on Bremen, it crashed off the Friesians probably after being attacked by *Major* Kurt Holler of StII./NJG 2. 18-year old pilot Sgt J.T. Shapcott and his crew were killed. Twenty-four OTUs (Operational Trining Units) sent crews on Bomber Command operations in World War II. Most were by pupil crews. (via Zdenek Hurt)

Right: The right outer wing of Whitley V T4145 GE-P-Peter of 58 Squadron, which took off from Linton-on-Ouse at 2055 on the evening of 7 April 1941 for a raid on Kiel, in a farmer's field near Waterhuizen, Groningen Province, Holland. Shortly after midnight the aircraft was intercepted to the north of Groningen by *Ofw* Paul Gildner in a Bf 110 of 4./NJG 1 and the German *Experte*, who had six night victories, set it on fire. It flew over Groningen trailing a sheet of flames and exploded just to the SE of the city at 0027 hrs. Sgt Arthur R. Mason, the WOp was the only survivor from 21-year old P/O Ronald McC. Carrapiett's crew. (Coen Cornelissen)

Right: On 26 April 1941 a large celebration was held in the Amstelhotel in Amsterdam on the occasion of NJG 1's 100th Abschuss. The honor of this historic occasion fell to *Oblt* Egmont Prinz *zur* Lippe Weissenfeld of 4./NJG 1 who claimed Wellington W5375 of 12 Squadron at 0059 hrs on 9/10 April 1941, which crashed in the Ijsselmeer North of Harderwijk. Vivian Q. Blackden the CO and his crew were KIA. W/C Blackden was buried at Lemsterland in Holland. *Geschwaderkommodore Major* Wolfgang Falck, seated in the middle, is obviously very pleased, as is *Fw* Hans Rasper to his right. Falck commanded NJG 1 until 30 June 1943 when he was called to duty in various organizational tasks in the nightfighter arm. (Hans Rasper)

Above: *Ofw* Hans Rasper and his *Bordfunker Fw* Erich Schreiber (KIA in 1943) of 4./NJG 1 in front of their Bf 110 G9+BM at Bergen aam Zee. One of *Nachtjagd*'s first aces, Rasper had trained as a fighter pilot during 1939-40 and he and Schreiber claimed a 'Wellington' (more probably a Whitley) off Egmond on 15 December 1940 as their first victory. After his 7th *Abschuss* on 12/13 June 1941 (Wellington T2996 of 103 Squadron flown by F/O Chisholm, who was KIA along with his crew) Rasper was awarded the 'Bowl of Honor' – for 'exceptional achievements in the Air War' by *Reichsmarschall* Göring. After his 8th victory on 21 January 1942 Rasper was posted to a nightfighter training unit where he was an instructor for three years until he became operational again in early 1945 in II./NJG 101. On 16/17 March 1945 he claimed his 9th and last *Abschuss*, a *Viermot* over Nürnburg. *Lt* Rasper flew his last sortie, a ground attack mission on 26 April 1945, when his aircraft was caught in radar-directed American flak at low level. He baled out and was taken prisoner but his *funker* was found dead near the wreckage of their aircraft. (Hans Rasper)

Above: *Flak* over Emden in 1941. (Emil Lechner)

Right: *Flak* over Kiel and Sylt in 1941. (Emil Lechner)

Right: A smiling 22-year old *Lt* Eckart-Wilhelm 'Hugo' von Bonin of 6./NJG 1 in front of his first night victim, Wellington IC R1379 of 115 Squadron, which he shot down near Tönning, Schleswig-Holstein in the *Helle Nachtjagd* (illuminated night-fighting) on 10/11 May 1941 flying a Bf 110. 26-year old pilot Sgt John Anderson twice took the Wellington over their target at Hamburg before Sgt Bill Legg, the observer/bomb aimer, could get their bombs away because of the severity of the port defenses. Almost immediately they were picked up by three radar-controlled searchlights and coned in their beams by other searchlight batteries. Heavy flak peppered the Wellington and cut the hydraulic pipes to Sgt David Fraser's rear turret, which caused it to jam at an awkward angle and set the turret on fire. Fraser's vision was obscured by hydraulic fluid and oil, which had spread over the perspex windows of the turret and his electric gunsight was put out of action. As Bill Legg made his way towards the rear turret with the cabin fire extinguisher the flak batteries suddenly ceased firing and the crew knew that a nightfighter was closing in on them. Von Bonin opened fire with his machine guns (luckily for the Wellington crew he had overlooked the firing button for his 20mm cannon). Sgt Alex Kerr, the 20 year old Australian 2nd pilot, who was in the astrodome to direct the pilot in the event of attack, was hit and wounded in ten places including a bullet in his liver and knocked backwards onto the canvas bed in the aircraft and he lost consciousness. A fire started in the reconnaissance flares, which were amidships on the starboard side. Bill Legg, who was standing next to Kerr when the Bf 110 attacked, was hit in the lower part of his back and he fell unconscious to the floor with back and stomach wounds oozing blood. Anderson gave the order to bale out. Fraser managed to squeeze out of his turret and he got Alex Kerr's hand on the ripcord and pushed him out of the escape hatch before baling out himself. Sgt Bernard Morgan, front gunner, and Sgt Geoff Hogg, WOp, also baled out safely. Anderson set the automatic pilot and he baled out but he landed in the River Elbe and was drowned. Sgt Bill Legg regained consciousness but did not have the strength to bale out and his parachute slipped from his grasp and out through the escape hatch. With great difficulty he climbed into the pilot's seat and from about 600 ft Legg was able to crashland the aircraft on its belly near Tönning, Schleswig-Holstein. Two soldiers from a Flak battery nearby climbed into the burning Wellington and lifted Legg to safety. In captivity Alex Kerr recovered from his wounds and on 11 May 1942 he was recaptured after an escape attempt. Bill Legg's horrific injuries never fully healed and in October 1943 he was among PoWs who were repatriated. In August 1944 he recommenced flying duties as an instructor. Exactly 50 years later, on 10 May 1991, von Bonin and three of the Wellington crew met at Hohn air base. The German *Experte* said that he was angry at the time for not using his 20 mm guns but meeting them now he was glad he had forgotten to arm his cannons. Von Bonin died in January 1992. (Ab A. Jansen)

Above: Wellington II W5360PH-C of 12 Squadron at RAF Binbrook, which was the only Wellington that FTR from a raid on German warships at Brest on 6/7 July 1941 by 88 Hampdens and 21 Wellingtons. W5360 crashed at Guilers (Finistère) 7 km NW of Brest killing S/L A.G.G. Baird and his crew. One Hampden was also lost. One Hampden I was lost when AD856 EA-P of 49 Squadron flown by Sgt J. Flint ditched in the sea off Cromer, Norfolk after being attacked by an intruder, probably flown by *Ofw* Wilhelm Beier. All the crew were injured and Flint died later. He was posthumously awarded the GM and DFM. Beier, who was awarded the *Ritterkreuz* on 10 October 1941 after his 12th-14th long-range nightfighting victories with 3./NJG 2 on the night of 8 August 1941, survived the war with 38 night victories in NJG 2 and NJG 1. (RAF Museum)

Right: Whitley V Z6743 of 77 Squadron flown by Sgt P.J. McClean down at Berging on 10 July 1941. All of McClean's crew were KIA. This was the only Whitley lost from the 27 that set out with 39 Hampdens and 16 Wellingtons, for a raid on Aachen on 9/10 July. A Hampden of 144 Squadron was also lost. (Henk Wilson)

Right: Bf 110G-7 Werk Nr.2075 of 4./NJG 1 flown by *Uffz* Vinke in a wheatfield on Texel on 24/25 July 1941. (Rob de Visser)

Above: Sgt Basil Sidney Craske, a Whitley pilot in 10 Squadron, 4 Group at Leeming Bar in North Yorkshire. Craske, who was flying Whitley V Z6805, was shot down at 0230 hrs on the night of 16/17 August 1941 by *Oblt* Wolfgang Thimmig of 2./NJG 1 near Winterswijk 20 km NE of Bocholt (all crew PoW) on his 27 op, to Cologne on the night of 16/17 August 1941. Thimmig's kill was one of the earliest *Dunkelnachtjagd* ('dark night fighting') victories, being achieved in complete darkness and under the guidance of ground radar. (Basil Craske)

Right: Bf 110G-7 Werk Nr.2075 of 4./NJG 1 flown by *Uffz* Vinke in a wheatfield on Texel on 24/25 July 1941. (Rob de Visser)

Below: Merlin-engined Wellington II W5461 EP-R of 104 Squadron, which FTR fom Berlin with S/L H. Budden DFC and crew (all PoW) on 12/13 August 1941. Seventy aircraft set out to bomb the 'Big City' where the *Reichsluftfahrtministerium* (RLM or Reich Air Ministry) building in the Alexander Platz was the aiming point but only 32 aircraft reached the target and dropped their bombs. Nine aircraft, including three Wellingtons and three Manchesters, failed to return. (via Mike Bailey)

Above: Stirlings taxiing out. The first Stirling to be shot down by a *Nachtjagd* aircraft was N6011 of 7 Squadron by *Fw* Karl-Heinz Scherfling of 7./NJG 1 near Lingen, Germany on 9/10 April 1941. The Halifax was the second four-engined bomber to be introduced into operational service and the first lost on operations was Halifax I L9492 of 76 Squadron, which crashed at 0232 hrs on 24 June 1941 at Eilendorf, 20 km SW of Hamburg after being hit by *Oblt* Reinhold Eckhardt of 6./NJG 1. (IWM)

Right: The first Short Stirling to fall virtually intact into German hands was Stirling I N6045 LS-U of XV Squadron. F/L R.P. Wallace-Terry and his seven-man crew had left Wyton on the evening of 7 September 1941 for a raid on Berlin but when over eastern Holland they were shot up by the Twente airfield *Flak* defenses and were forced to crash-land near Hengelo. Note the feathered starboard outer propeller, the inflated dinghy on top of the starboard wing, parachute flares for target marking in the grass beside N6045 and personnel of the Twente-based III./NJG 1 inspecting the aircraft. The aircraft was on only its 5th sortie when it failed to return. Wallace-Terry, Sgt R. Harper, Sgt Jock Moir, Sgt C.S. Aynsley, Sgt R.D. Hooley, Sgt H.J. Dunnett and Sgt J.E. Dodd were all captured. Although badly burned and suffering from head injuries, Sgt Richard Bernard Pape, navigator evaded. He made his way on foot to Amsterdam where an organization made arrangements for him to be shipped back to the UK but Pape was arrested and subjected to severe torture in an unsuccessful effort to obtain from him details of his helpers. Inspired by Douglas Bader, who he met in his first camp, Pape made up his mind to escape from Germany at all costs. He made another bid for freedom when he escaped from a coalmine in Poland and made his way on foot to Krakow. At this time, his health was in much a poor state and he collapsed at the station while waiting for a train. He was re-arrested and after a period in a concentration camp was again put to work. A year later, Pape again escaped and walked through Slovakia, attempting to reach Yugoslavia. He was re-arrested and afterwards developed meningitis, temporary blindness and pleurisy, which kept him in hospital for about a year. Whilst in hospital, he continued his underground activities. He also gave secret propaganda talks to the other inmates. Pape, who was captive for 3 1/2 years, was awarded the Military Medal. After the war he wrote a book about his experiences called, *Boldness Be My Friend*. (Coen Cornelissen)

Above: Wellington IC R1781 SR-C of 101 Squadron a veteran aircraft of 30 ops, at Oakington late in 1941. This aircraft enjoyed a long wartime career with the squadron and then OTU service before being SOC on 9 July 1944. (Paul Todd)

Right: Hampden I AD911 OL-M of 83 Squadron prior to take off for Hamburg on 15 September 1941. L-R: Sgt George Mitchell, 2nd pilot; Sgt W.A. Bob Brooks, rear gunner; Sgt Doug Hedley, captain; Sgt E.W.E. Teddy Gough, WOP/AG. AD911 was shot down by *Ofw* Siegfried Ney of 4./NJG 1 on 10/11 October 1941 and the Hampden crashed in the Waddenzee off Harlingen. Brooks was killed and Hedley, Mitchell and Gough survived to become PoWs. (Frank Haynes via A. Wachtel)

Right: Ken Wright, navigator, at his station in a Wellington bomber. (Ken Wright)

Far right: S/L J.A. Ingram DFC who flew with F/O T. Wardhaugh's crew of 103 Squadron in Wellington IC X9609 meets his victor, *Oblt* Helmut Woltersdorf, *St.Kpt.* of 7./NJG 1 after being shot down on 20/21 September 1941. The Wellington crashed in the Ambt-Delden (Overijssel) 6 km WSW of Hengelo, Holland killing Wardhaugh and Sgt C.A.F. Thomas. The other three crew survived and were taken PoW. On this night 74 aircraft set out for Berlin and all were recalled because of worsening weather. Ten aircraft did not receive the signal and bombed alternative targets while none at all reached Berlin. Three Wellingtons and one Whitley failed to return and 12 more bombers crashed in England. Woltersdorf was KIA on 1/2 June 1942 in crash at Twente airfield, shot down by a 3 Squadron Hurricane. He had 15 night and 8 day victories in ZG 76 and NJG 1. (Dr. Schmidt-Barbo)

Above: Merlin-engined Vickers Wellington II W5379 PH-O of 12 Squadron, which FTR with P/O D.W.D. Faint and crew on 10/11 October 1941 when five Wellingtons were lost on a raid by 69 aircraft on Cologne. W5379, which had completed only 15 operations, crashed at 0325 hours at Haamstede (Zeeland) in Holland. Faint and three of his crew died and two men survived to be made PoW. (RAF Museum)

Right: Sgt J. Lenc (2nd from left) and his crew of 311 Czech Squadron in front of Wellington IC R1161 KX-X after their return to East Wretham on one engine after their starboard airscrew was torn off over the target at Hamburg on the night of 26/27 October 1941. Some 115 aircraft were despatched to bomb the shipyards and two city aiming points and three Wellingtons and one Hampden were lost. R1161 was operated from June 1941 until March 1942 and carried out 32 operations in total. (via Zdenek Hurt)

Below: Stirling I W7444 MG-G of 7 Squadron being bombed up with 250 lb bombs at Oakington, Cambridgeshire. On 31 October 1941 P/O N.E. Winch and his crew took off in W7444 at 1752 hours for the raid on Bremen but they had to return early due to oxygen failure and the aircraft crashed while trying to land. There were no serious injuries to the crew. Of the 40 Wellingtons and eight Stirlings that set off for Bremen only 13 crews claimed to have found their target and one Wellington was shot down. (Flight)

Above: Rolls-Royce Vulture engined Avro Manchester BIA L7515 of 207 Squadron, RAF Waddington, November 1941. This aircraft was SOC on 6 November 1943. Initial batches of the Manchester were built with triple fins but with the IA the center fin was deleted. Total production of the Manchester was 209, additional contracts for 300 Manchesters being cancelled. The Manchester's last Bomber Command operation was on the 1000 bomber raid on Bremen on the night of 25/26 June 1942, when 20 were despatched, after which the type was withdrawn. (BAe)

Right: Wellington IC Z8900 of 214 Squadron took off from Stradishall, Suffolk at 1719 hours on 15 November 1941 for the raid on Emden and en route to the target was damaged over the Friesians by a Bf 110, which tore a six-foot hole in the fuselage structure. The bomb load was jettisoned and Sgt Campbell nursed the ailing aircraft across the North Sea to Norfolk where at 2205 hours he put down at the fighter station at RAF Coltishall near Norwich where the Wellington was later certified as 'beyond economical repair'. Four of the 49 Wellingtons despatched failed to return. (via Mike Bailey)

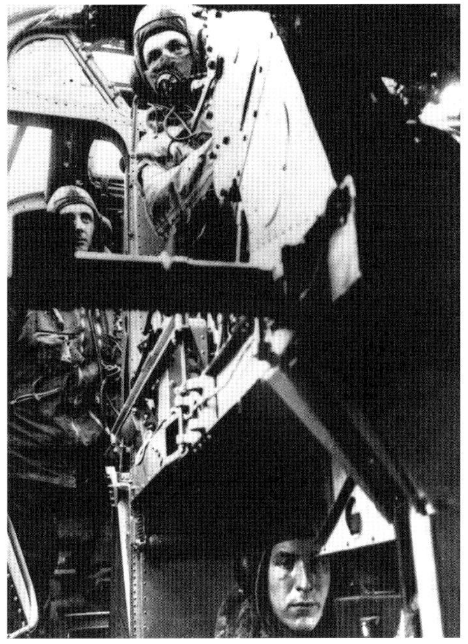

Right: Inside the cockpit of a Halifax B.Mk.I in October 1941 with the pilot, P/O Renaut at the controls, flight engineer (behind) and W/Op at his station. (AWM via John Williams)

Right: Wellington II Z8370 of 12 Squadron flown by F/L W.H. Thallon on the beach at Terschelling Island after it was shot down in a *Himmelbett* interception by 'Night Fighting Professor', *Oblt* Ludwig Becker, *Staffelkapitän*, 6./NJG 2 for his ninth Abschuss at 2100 hrs on 20 January 1942. Twenty Wellingtons and five Hampdens were despatched to Emden this night and three Wellingtons and one Hampden were lost. Sgt E.R.J. Fowler and Sgt W. Rutherford of Z8370 were killed in the encounter. Thallon, P/O P.R. Ross RCAF, F/Sgt F.W. Walker and F/Sgt G.H. Groves were taken prisoner. Becker went on to claim two more Wellingtons in the same area during a *Himmelbett* sortie in Box Tiger (Z1207 of 142 Squadron at 2107 hrs and Z1110 of 101 Squadron at 2137 hrs. There were no survivors. (Hille van Dieren)

Right: Some of the 6,947 Lancasters built in Britain under construction at Middleton near Manchester (another 430 Lancasters were built by Victory Aircraft in Canada). The most successful and one of the most famous bombers in history began in 1940 when a decision was taken to build a longer span version of the Manchester and re-engine it with four Rolls-Royce Merlins following the failure of the Vulture engine. 44 Squadron at Waddington was the first RAF squadron to operate the 'Lanc' followed by 97 Squadron at Woodhall Spa. 44 Squadron flew the first Lancaster operation on 3/4 March 1942 when four Lancaster Is dropped mines in the Heligoland Bight. On 10/11 March the Squadron made the first Lancaster night operation when two took part in the raid on Essen. Altogether, Lancasters dropped 608,612 tons of bombs in 156,000 sorties in World War II. (via Harry Holmes)

Right: Air Marshal Sir Arthur T. Harris, having been recalled from the USA where he was head of the RAF Delegation, became commander-in-Chief of RAF Bomber Command on 22 February 1942. Harris was directed by Marshal of the RAF, Sir Charles Portal, Chief of the Air Staff to break the German spirit by the use of night area rather than precision bombing and the targets would be civilian, not just military. The famous 'area bombing' directive, which had gained support from the Air Ministry and Prime Minister Winston Churchill, had been sent to Bomber Command on 14 February, eight days before Harris assumed command. (IWM)

Far right: F/Sgt Edwin Wheeler, WOP-AG in the crew of F/L Harry 'Rocky' de Belleroche in 214 Squadron. (Wheeler)

Above: Bf 110F-4a of III./NJG 1 with four nose-mounted FuG 202 *Lichtenstein* BC radar antennae, each with four dipoles and four reflectors used jointly for transmission and reception, flown by *Fw* 'Teddy' Kleinhenz and his *Bordfunker*, *Uffz* Hermann Gampe, from Leeuwarden, Holland, February-April 1942. (via Theo Boiten)

In March 1942 41 RAF heavy bombers were shot down including 27 by II./NJG 2 with six of these being credited to *Oblt* Ludwig Becker, *Staffelkapitän*, 6./NJG 2 (pictured) and four each by I. and III./NJG 1. Becker's victims were a Manchester and a Wellington on 8/9 March, a Whitley on 12/13 March, another Manchester on 25/26 March and a Stirling on 28/29 March, which took his score to 18 confirmed *Abschüsse*. (Rob de Visser)

Above: Bf 110F of 7./NJG 1 at Trondheim, Norway, in February 1942. (Dr. Dieter Schmidt-Barbo)

Below: Bf 110Fs of II./NJG 1 at Trondheim, Norway, in March 1942. (Anneliese Autenrieth)

Right: Wellington Z1147 KX-G of 311 Czechoslovak Squadron flown by Sgt Vladimír Pára was badly shot up by a Bf 110 in the target area at Emden on the night of 3/4 March 1942 when four Wellingtons were depatched to the German city on the night of the main raid on the Billancourt Renault factory. The 27-year-old tail gunner, Sgt Frantiçek Binder was badly wounded in the attack and died soon after the landing at East Wretham, Norfolk. He was buried in St. Ethelbert's Churchyard in East Wretham. (Vitek Formanek)

Below: Wellington II W5442 SRI GUROH BU-V of 214 'Federated Malay States' Squadron (note the Tiger's head in the white square below the cockpit), one of several aircraft paid for by funds raised by the Federated Malay States. W5442 later joined 12 Squadron (PH-B) and failed to return from Essen with P/O R. Buchanan's crew on 9/10 March 1942 when it was hit by flak and crashed at Beverwijk in Noor Holland. Buchanan and two of his crew were PoW. Three crew were KIA. (via Mike Bailey)

Right: *Oblt* Walter Barte (2nd from right wearing a British Irvin jacket) of II./NJG 1 at Sint-Truiden in March 1942 in front of Bf 110F-4a G9+FM. The aircraft has not yet had FuG 202 *Lichtenstein* BC radar fitted. (Kees Mol via Marc Debroeck).

Right: In June 1941 the Air Ministry had ordered the first prototype Mosquitoes, some PR models and 176 AI radar equipped NFII fighter versions (pictured) for RAF Fighter Command. Deliveries of the new fighter were slow to arrive but radar equipped night-fighters were desperately needed now that the Luftwaffe began its series of Baedeker raids against British cities of historic or aesthetic importance. Hitler had ordered the terror raids as retribution for an attack by RAF Bomber Command on the historic city of Lübeck on 28/29 March 1942. In the summer of 1942 Mosquito NFII fighters flew Intruder sorties over occupied France and the Low Countries Europe and it became the turn of the Luftwaffe to be the hunted. (GMS)

Right: Scattered remains of a 75 Squadron RNZAF Wellington III (either X3489 flown by W/C R. Sawtry-Cookson DSO DFC or X3661 flown by F/Sgt G.J.E. Thomas RNZAF) after impacting near Schladern Windeck, SE of Cologne after a raid on the Humboldt works in the Deutz area of Cologne on 5/6 April 1942. All aboard X3489 were KIA while Thomas and his crew survived to be taken prisoner. In all, 263 aircraft including 179 Wellingtons were despatched and 211 aircraft claimed 'good' bombing results but the nearest bombing photographs developed were 5 miles from the target. In all, four Wimpys and one Hampden were lost. (via Steve Smith)

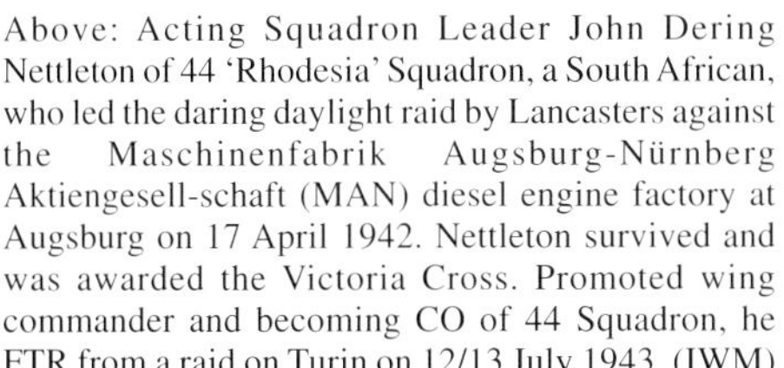

Above: Acting Squadron Leader John Dering Nettleton of 44 'Rhodesia' Squadron, a South African, who led the daring daylight raid by Lancasters against the Maschinenfabrik Augsburg-Nürnberg Aktiengesell-schaft (MAN) diesel engine factory at Augsburg on 17 April 1942. Nettleton survived and was awarded the Victoria Cross. Promoted wing commander and becoming CO of 44 Squadron, he FTR from a raid on Turin on 12/13 July 1943. (IWM)

Above: Wellington IC R1230 NZ-E of 304 Squadron was one of seven Wellingtons, which FTR from a raid on Essen on 10/11 April 1942 when it was attacked by *Hptm* Werner Streib, *Kommandeur* of I./NJG 1 and crashed near Kessel, Germany with the loss of Sgt J. Janik and his crew. In all 254 aircraft headed for the target but the bombing force became scattered in cloud and only 172 crews claimed to have bombed. Bombing accuracy was described as 'poor'. Fourteen bombers failed to return. (RAF Museum)

Right: Lancasters of 44 and 97 Squadrons bombing Augsburg in one of the most daring low-level daylight operations of the war on Friday 17 April 1942. (C. Stothard)

Left: Wellington III, possibly Z1290 of 460 Squadron RAAF, which was shot down by *Lt* Gustav Tham of 8./NJG 3 for his first victory and crashed at Bockhorst, near Neumünster at 0300 hrs on 28/29 April 1942 with the loss of F/Sgt L.M. Shephard RAAF and his Australian crew. On this night 88 bombers were despatched to bomb the shipyards at Kiel. *Flak* and fighters shot down five Wellingtons and one Hampden and 54 bombers claimed to have hit the target with 'good results'. (Peter Petrick)

Left: A Wellington IV of 460 Squadron RAAF flown by Sgt David G. Kitchen was hit repeatedly in four successive attacks by a Bf 110 night-fighter north of Sylt near the Danish coast on its way back from bombing Rostock on 26/27 April 1942. The Canadian rear gunner, Sgt D.A. Black was very severely injured and the second pilot, Sgt A.L. Moyle, was wounded in the head and thigh. The ASI and intercom were rendered U/S, the elevator trimming gear shot away, the rear turret put out of action, the port petrol tank holed, the fabric on the upper surface of the port wing between the nacelle and the fuselage and on the upper surface of the port tail plane were torn off and the bomb doors were damaged and open, which made the aircraft very difficult to control. Despite the enormous damage to his aircraft, Sgt Kitchen made the 400 miles sea crossing back to Breighton where he made a good landing without flaps and with both main wheels and tail wheel flat as a result of bullet holes, after having been at the controls for seven-and-a-half hours. Kitchen and his four crew were shot down, possibly by *Lt* Robert Denzel of 6./NJG 2, north of Schiermonnikoog on the Emden raid of 19/20 June 1942. The crew were later buried in Sage War Cemetery. (Cal Younger)

Far left: Sgt Cal Younger, nav/bomb aimer in 460 Squadron RAAF in front of Wellington IV Z1391 UV-R, in which he was shot down on 29/30 May 1942. 77 aircraft – 31 Wellingtons, 20 Halifaxes, 14 Lancasters, 9 Stirlings and 3 Hampdens – set out for the Gnome & Rhône factory at Paris/Gennevilliers. Four Wellngtons and one Halifax were lost, most probably all of them to *Flak*. (Cal Younger)

Left: F/O R.A.P. Jones RAAF stayed at the controls of Wellington III Z1391 to give his crew a chance to bale out after their aircraft was mortally hit by *Flak* over Gennevilliers on 29/30 May 1942. Only Sgt Cal Younger, navigator/bomb aimer, and Sgt G. H. Loder, tail gunner baled out safely before UV-R crashed near Dreux, Eure et Loire, France. (Cal Younger)

Right: Sgt G. Houghton, front gunner in Wellington III Z1391 failed to leave his stricken Wellington before it plunged down to earth and was killed in the crash. Houghton, his skipper F/O R.A.P. Jones RAAF, and Sgt K.R. Mellowes, WOp were buried in Dreux Communal Cemetery. (Cal Younger)

Far right: Sgt G.H. Loder, rear gunner of Wellington III Z1391 UV-R of 460 Squadron RAAF. (Cal Younger)

Right: Stirlings taxiing out. The newly introduced Stirling bomber invariably suffered from the German *Flak* and fighter defenses in daylight during 1941-42. (IWM)

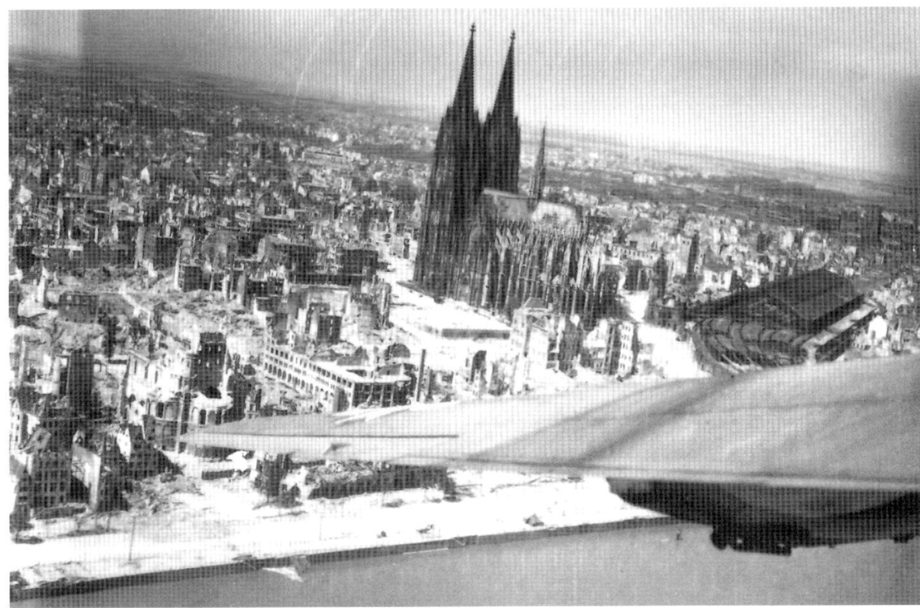

Right: On 30/31 May 1942 Cologne was the target of the first 1000 bomber raid by RAF Command when 1047 aircraft were despatched. Some 868 crews hit the main target destroying 3330 buildings, seriously damaging 2090 more and lightly damaging another 7420 dwellings. It was estimated that between 135,000 and 150,000 of Cologne's population of nearly 700,000 fled the city after the raid. Between 11 May 1940 and 31 May 1942 Cologne was attacked by RAF heavy bomber raids on no less than 144 occasions. By the end of the war when this photo was taken on a USAAF Trolly mission, only the blackened 13th century Gothic cathedral (its towers were not built until the 19th century) is recognizable. (USAAF)

Right: A common sight in many coastal communities in the Low Countries and NW Germany during the war. Crews of the B-Group 34th Minesweeper Flotilla form the funeral party for four British airmen in May 1942, who are buried with full military honors in Huisduinen War Cemetery. After the war, this large wartime cemetery in the dunes near the sea was cleared and the mortal remains of dozens of Allied airmen reburied in various War Cemeteries in the Netherland. (Alfons Borgmeier)

Below: *Obergefreiter* (later *Leutnant*) Otto Heinrich Fries with a 5./NJG 1 Bf 110 at St. Trond in May 1942. On completion of their nightfighter training Fries and his *Bordfunker*, *Uffz* Fred Staffa were posted to II./NJG 1 at St. Trond in January 1942. Under the prevailing conditions of the *Himmelbett* GCI system this green crew was hardly given a chance to prove their ability in combat as only the most experienced crews patrolled in the most 'profitable' boxes. By August 1943 therefore, Fries and Staffa had only fleeting encounters with a RAF bomber on two occasions without being able to score a confirmed kill. Their luck changed and during 1943-44 Fries and Staffa scored 18 night victories in II./NJG 1. (Otto H. Fries)

Right: A Wellington IC shot down over Dutch coastal waters is recovered from the sea. By the end of 1942, except for the Lancaster, the veteran Wellington still outnumbered all the types of bomber aircraft in Bomber Command. (Theo Boiten Coll)

Taken from the cockpit of a third Bf 110, a formation of III./NJG 1 Bf 110s are seen here whilst engaged on a practice flight sometime in the summer of 1942. Note the absence of AI radar aerials on these aircraft. (Coen Cornelissen)

Right: *Lt* Dietrich 'Dieter' Schmidt of III./NJG 1 inspecting his Bf 110 in Norway during '*Unternehmen Donnerkeil*' early in 1942. Schmidt achieved his first night victory on 24/25 March 1943 when he shot down Halifax HR665 of 138 Sqn off Enkhuizen. He was promoted to *Staffelkapitän* 8./NJG 1 after his 4th victory in May 1943. By the end of 1943 he had nine kills. On 13/14 January 1944 he shot down a Mosquito. During 1944 he claimed 3 kills in one night on 22/23 April (his 19-21st kills); 3/4 May (23-25); 22/23 May, 27-29 July and 28/29 (33-35 kills). Schmidt was awarded the Knight's Cross on 27 July 1944 after 32 night victories. On 12.25.44 Schmidt left 8./NJG 1 for the 9th *Staffel* of the same elite night fighter wing, again as *Staffelkapitän*. By the end of the war he had risen to *Hauptmann*, flown 171 operational sorties and claimed 40 RAF aircraft at night, 39 of which were *Viermots*. (Dieter Schmidt)

Far right: For the second 'Thousand Bomber Raid' against Essen on the night of 1/2 June 1942, a force of 956 bombers was put together by making up the numbers using young and inexperienced OTU crews and their aircraft. Of the 37 bombers that FTR from Essen 20 were claimed by nightfighters. Wellington IC R1266 of 23 OTU RAF Pershore flown by P/O W.J. Mawdesley RAAF fell victim to a Bf 110 flown by *Oblt* Hermann Reese of 2./NJG 1 from Venlo at 0208 hours. R1266 crashed near the Terwindt brickyard at Kerkdriel (Gelderland) on the west bank of the Maas in Holland with the loss of all five crew including 20-year old air gunner, Sgt Kenneth N. Kilby (pictured). All the crew are buried at Uden cemetery. Wreckage of their aircraft was discovered 17 years after the crash. (Marge Haynes)

Right: Wreckage at L'ecluse, Belgium, 20 km SW of Tienen of Stirling I W7508 OJ-D of 149 Squadron from RAF Lakenheath, which was shot down at 0227 hrs on 6 June 1942 by *Oblt* Walter Barte of 4./NJG 1 when Essen was the target for 180 bombers. Six of P/O P. Clayton's crew were killed. Sgt B. Goldsmith, one of the air gunners, evaded capture and was taken in by the Comète Line in Belgium while Sgt D. Pointer, air gunner, was taken prisoner. In all, 12 bombers, including eight Wellingtons and two Stirlings were lost on the Essen raid, 5/6 June 1942. (Hans Grohmann)

Right: *Hptm* Helmut 'Bubi' ('Boy') Lent, a *Ritterkreuzträger* and *Kommandeur* of II./NJG 2 in early June 1942, when his score stood at 34 night and eight day victories. Lent had become a national hero after the air battle of 18 December 1939 when flying a Bf 110C-1 *Zerstörer* in 3./ZG 76 he had claimed three Wellingtons IA destroyed. In fact N2888 and N2889 (both of 37 Squadron) only, fell to his guns, at 1440 and 1445 hrs near Borkum Island. (Lent previously had destroyed a PZL 24/11C on 2 September during the Polish campaign). (Anneliese Autenrieth)

Top: Bf 110F-4a flown by *Oblt* Walter Barte of 4./NJG 1. Note the nose mounted FuG 202 *Lichtenstein* BC radar array which worked on 490 MHz and could operate as far as 2 1/2 miles but slowed the nightfighter by about 25 mph. (via Peter Loncke)

Above: Bf 110F-4a flown by *Oblt* Walter Barte of 4./NJG 1 having its guns harmonised. This three-seat nightfighter had a ventral tray containing two 30mm Mk.108 cannon. Note the 'N' designator letter for the DB 601 engine on the cowling. (via Peter Loncke)

Right: Main undercarriage of Stirling I W7474 HA-K of 218 Squadron flown by 29-year old P/O James Garscadden and P/O John Richard Webber (19), one of eight shot down by *Nachtjäger* on the night of 3/4 June 1942 when 170 bombers were despatched on the first large raid to Bremen since October 1941. W7474 was claimed by *Oblt* Ludwig Becker of 6./NJG 2 South of Den Helder at 0027 hours. All seven crew were KIA. (Karl Fischer)

Stirling crews. Only 11 Stirlings survived to become veterans of 60 or more sorties. Stirling III LJ514 completed 75 ops with 199 Squadron (which was withdrawn from bombing operations on 1 May 1944 to join 100 Group for radar jamming duties). (IWM)

Right: Malcolm Freegard who enjoyed only a brief career as an operational Wellington pilot in 115 Squadron at Marham in June-July 1942. (Freegard)

Far right: *Uffz* Heinz Vinke of 5./NJG 2 in the cockpit of his Bf 110 night fighter at Leeuwarden in 1942. (Lowa via Rob de Visser)

Below: Bf 110 of II./NJG 2 not yet fitted with AI radar, at Leeuwarden airfield in 1942. (Rob de Visser/Heinz Hahn)

Above and left: Stirling I N3757 LS-G of XV Squadron, which was hit by Flak and force-landed at Hartward, Esens, Germany on 29/30 June 1942 on its 10th operational sortie to Bremen. Although at first sight the aircraft looks in reasonably good condition, its starboard wing burnt out completely after the landing on the northern German plains. S/L I.G. Richmond DFC and his crew escaped death and were taken prisoner. (Erich Kayser)

Below: Syncronising weapons of a Bf 110 of III./NJG 1 at Twente in 1942. (Dr Schmidt Barbo)

Right: Armorer working on a Bf 110 of 7./NJG 1 at Twente (Dr Schmidt Barbo)

Crews of II./NJG 1 in the Operations room at Leeuwarden airfield in 1942. L-R *Oblt* Helmut Lent, *Ofw* Paul Gildner, *Fw* Kleinhenz; *Uffz* Hätscher and *Fw* Kubisch (Lent's *Bordfunker*). (Schmitt via Rob de Visser)

Lt Werner Rowlin who was KIA baling out after air combat at Ehren/Westphalia on 29/30 June 1942. He scored four night victories in III./NJG 1. (Dr Schmidt Barbo)

Right: Sgt Neville Hockaday RNZAF (middle) and his 75 Squadron crew in front of Wellington III BJ837 F-Freddie during their tour of ops (June-October 1942). Note the swastika painted above the bomb log, which represents Sgt Bruce Philip's (rear gunner) claim for a Ju 88 destroyed over northern Holland on the Bremen raid of 29/30 June 1942. No *Nachtjagd* Ju 88s were lost this night although three Bf 110s of 8./NJG 1 at Ehren, Westphalia, 5./NJG 2 NW of Vlieland and 3./NJG 3 (which belly-landed at Vechta airfield near Oldenburg) were lost as a result of return fire. (Air Cde Peter Hughes DFC)

Right: Sgt Jim Burtt-Smith and his crew at 11 OTU Bassingbourn before they were posted to 115 Squadron at RAF Marham, Norfolk in June 1942. L-R: P/O Barney D'Ath-Weston RNZAF, navigator; Sgt W. 'Frizzo' Frizzell RNZAF, rear gunner; Sgt Lionel 'Len' Harcus, bomb aimer; Sgt Jim Burtt-Smith, pilot; Sgt Jack French, WOP-AG. Just over a month later, on the night of 26/27 July 1942 Burtt-Smith and his crew of Wellington III BJ723 KO-B were one of 14 Wellington crews despatched from Marham as part of a force of 403 bombers heading for Hamburg. B-Bear was hit on the way home and the crew ditched. Picked up by a German seaplane from Nordeney they finished the war as PoWs. (Burtt-Smith)

Above: *Hptm* Karl Helmer (left) of 7./NJG 3 was killed when his Bf 110E-2 (D5+FR Werk Nr.2429) crashed at Maquenoise near Hirson, France on 30 July 1942 at 0030 hrs after both engines sustained severe damage during an encounter with a bomber. His *Bordfunker* and *Bordschütze* baled out safely. It is possible that Helmer was unconscious when the aircraft crashed. (Steve Hall)

Top right: As a *Zerstörer* pilot in ZG 76, *Hptm* Karl Helmer had achieved *Experte* status with an estimated eight *Abschüsse*; he had yet to open his night scoring. (Steve Hall)

Right:W/C J. 'Moose' Fulton DSO DFC AFC, first CO of 419 Squadron RCAF (right) and F/Sgt Alexander inspecting their damaged Wellington after a raid early in 1942. Fulton failed to return from a raid on Hamburg in Wellington III X3488 VR-H on 28/29 July 1942 when all six crew including F/Sgt H.J. Dell RCAF who had completed his tour and who volunteered for one more op were KIA. Possibly, their Wellington was shot down by *Oblt* Rudolf Schoenert of 4./NJG 2, who destroyed a Wellington over the German Bight at 0328 hours for his 24th *Abschuss*. 419 'Moose' Squadron RCAF adopted Fulton's nickname in his memory. (via Dr. Colin Dring)

Below: Short Stirling I OJ-G of 149 'East India' Squadron in 3 Group at RAF Mildenhall in 1942. F/Sgt Rawdon Hume Middleton RAAF of 149 Squadron received a posthumous VC for his actions on 28/29 November 1942 when mortally wounded, he flew Stirling BF372 back to England after a raid on the Fiat Works at Turin, Italy. Five of his crew baled out to safety but when BF372 ran out of fuel it crashed into the English Channel and Middleton and his flight engineer and front gunner who had remained aboard to help their captain, drowned. 149 Squadron flew 2,628 Stirling sorties on 244 bombing and 160 minelaying raids, losing 87 aircraft, before converting to the Lancaster in August 1944. (Theo Boiten Coll)

down the side of the river to Hamburg. Sgt Frank Skelley, the youngest member of the crew at 19, jokingly remarked that his skipper wouldn't be able to find the aiming-point, as the only part of Hamburg he knew from his Merchant Navy days was the red light district. He had joined the Merchant Navy as a boy. After war broke out he had transferred to the RAF to train as aircrew. Skelley acted as bomb aimer and he manned the front turret. KO-K carried a 4000-lb bomb. This huge bomb was not designed for delivery by a Wellington aircraft. Modifications to the bomb bays were necessary. Host of the flotation bags had to be removed. These were the bags, which gave the aircraft buoyancy in the event of a ditching. As the perimeter of the bomb canister protruded below the bomb doors these had to be removed also. When the bomb was dropped the open space of the bomb bays would cause considerable drag.

Feredey continues:

'I approached Hamburg at about 13,000 ft. The place was well alight and the bombing was causing plenty of havoc on the ground and many searchlights illuminated the darkness. I bombed and flew around to take photographs. (There was some rivalry amongst the crews on the squadron to get good photos of our attacks. On a previous raid on Duisburg I had a photo of my bomb hitting the target and the photo was put on display on the Squadron for all to see). I flew over Hamburg taking pictures with the aid of other flash bombs exploding and then asked my navigator [Sgt G. 'Harry' Lindley] for a course to fly home on. He told me that in two minutes we should be crossing the German coast. Suddenly all hell broke out. North of Bremen a blue master searchlight pinpointed me and 20-30 other white searchlights coned me. At the same time Ack-Ack poured through to the aircraft and the first shell burst a few inches away from my face. I could smell the cordite from the explosion, which blew the fuel lines to the instruments, causing them all to go to zero. The oil from the burst pipes came down on the compass, blanking it out and making it impossible to use. The only thing working was the altimeter; I was at 12,000 ft. Both turrets were u/s and the guns were of no use. I was in this situation for three-quarters of an hour, diving and turning to try to get out of the glare of the searchlights. At the same time the guns were giving me hell from the ground. I went down to 8000 ft. Later the crew told me the aircraft was peppered with holes, through which you could map-read below. I gave instructions to Sgt Glafkos Derides [the wireless operator, who was in the astrodome] to come forward to destroy the paperwork and secret codings. At this point a piece of shrapnel caught him in the leg and caused him to collapse on the floor. His intercom plug came out of its socket. When he came to he was talking into a dead mike. He thought we had baled out so he decided to jump out through the rear escape hatch. Two searchlights followed him down to the ground. The Germans must have thought we were going to follow him or we were all dead as all the lights went out and the Ack-Ack guns were silent.[40]

'When I got out of the searchlights I found I was heading back to Hamburg so I decided to go home the same way I had entered Germany. The wheels and flaps had come down causing drag. I climbed to 14,000 ft and re-crossed the coast over Borkum where again the Germans shot at me. Then all was quiet. I checked the fuel gauge and found I had lost 200 gallons in 20 minutes. The rear gunner [Sgt Kelvin Hewer Shoesmith, a 21 year old Australian] had to tell me if and when I was turning, as I had no instruments to fly on. (While we had been in the dilemma of Ack-Ack and searchlights the rear gunner had been shot in his side. However badly I never knew but subsequently it hastened his death). I instructed Skelley to radio our troubles to base. (As my wireless operator had baled out, it meant that the front gunner was now sending out radio messages to warn the Squadron what was happening to us). All the time I was losing height and I went down to 1500 ft. Lindley put the nacelle tanks on so I estimated I had about one hours' fuel left. I was down to 500 ft by this time. Then the starboard engine started to cough and splutter. I sent out a Mayday on the radio. This was becoming the final phase in the drama. I told the crew to prepare for ditching. First the starboard engine and then the port engine stopped. I suddenly realized that the escape hatch over my head was still closed but I managed to get it open. As all this was going on I had turned away from the moonlight and was heading into total blackness for a ditching. My speed was about 140 mph. I had to land tail first to help slow the speed down.

'Finally we went into the sea. I wasn't strapped in so my head went through the windscreen. I may have been temporarily knocked out but the cold water soon brought my senses back. I was up to my waist in water with water pouring in through the escape hatch over my head. I wrenched my helmet off to release me to get out; I also lost one flying boot as I got out of the aircraft, which was already going under with the tail in the air. After getting onto the port wing I was chest deep in water. By this time the front gunner and navigator had made their escape via the astrodome. Sgt Kelvin Shoesmith RAAF jumped out of the rear turret but he got entangled with the trailing aerial and he shouted that the rapidly sinking bomber was dragging him under. [Frank Skelley and Harry Lindley swam over and released him. They all worked hard on the dinghy to inflate it but it was riddled with shrapnel holes. Their task was impossible]. The four of us managed to get hold of a loose wooden box, which one stood on to look out of the astrodome, that had floated out of the open hatch just before the aircraft sank. We each grabbed a corner with one hand and the other hand held on to the adjacent crewmember. We drifted with the waves breaking over us continually. All we had to keep us afloat were our Mae Wests. We were able to talk to each other and we tried to estimate how far from land we were. Shoesmith told us he had been wounded in his side but we were unable to ascertain his injuries. His Mae West was deflating so Harry Lindley had to blow it up with his mouth to keep him afloat. [The shrapnel, which had pierced his side, had also penetrated his Mae West]. At times we were up to our lips in water, this was causing us to swallow some of the salt water. The harrowing part of this tale was when Lindley began to pray and asked God to save us. When I tried to reassure him that we would be saved, he rubbed his hand down the back of my head and said that he was grateful for cheering him up. It seemed pretty hopeless at the time, as the water was up to our mouths as we floated around.

'After a few hours Shoesmith, who was directly opposite me, suddenly went quiet. He opened his eyes and they seemed to turn around. Some white foam came from his nose and mouth. At this point Skelley was unconscious. I tried to lift him on to the box to keep his head out of the water but minutes later he too died very quietly, again with white foam coming from his nose and mouth. He hadn't been injured but later I realized that he was pretty near to death. When the front and rear gunners died we let them go but they continued to drift near us. After six hours in the sea only two of us were alive. Then in the distance I saw a German seaplane flying towards us. I tried to attract the attention of the crew and Lindley started blowing his whistle. I kept telling him they couldn't hear him but his mind had gone blank. They circled around and the chap in the gun turret turned his gun towards us. I honestly thought he was going to shoot us. However he lifted his hand and saluted. Thank God, what a relief that we weren't going to die in this way. The seaplane landed and taxied towards us with its two engines ticking over but they were too fast to grab us as they passed. They returned on just one engine with crew on the floats holding boat hooks. I managed to grab hold but they had to hook Lindley by his jacket to stop him going past. They lifted me on to the float and tied a rope around my waist to lift me into the aircraft where I was laid on the floor and a blanket placed over me. Lindley was then brought in. Although they must have seen that the two gunners were dead the Germans did not stop to pick them up and they allowed them to continue floating in the sea. Shivering with cold I motioned to one of the crew for a drink but instead of a hot drink or a brandy they gave me soda water! I fell asleep as we took off for Nordeney where we landed and were lifted out of the water onto the beach. I was helped to my feet and out of the plane into the daylight where an ambulance waited to take us to hospital. The German crew came with us. At the hospital I thanked the crew for picking us up and I asked the pilot what time he had started searching for us. He told me it was 0340 am; the exact time I crashed in the sea. Lindley remembered nothing of the rescue or his journey to hospital and it was six pm that evening when he recovered sufficiently to be taken into custody.'[41]

In all, 115 Squadron lost four Wellingtons on the night of 26/27 July. At 0235 hours *Hptm* Helmut Lent of II./NJG 1 was patrolling over the North Sea NW of Vlieland in a Bf 110 night fighter when he brought down a Halifax.[42] His victim crashed in the North Sea north west of Vlieland. Four minutes later a dark shape loomed into his line of sight. Quickly closing the gap between himself and the other aircraft he perceived the unmistakable bulky outline to be a Wellington bomber. Not wishing to overshoot and lose the enemy aircraft in the darkness Lent eased back on his throttles. W/C Dixon-Wright and his crew of Wellington BJ615 were doomed. Their aircraft crashed into the sea NW of Vlieland near the crash position of Lent's Halifax victim at 0239. The only body recovered from the water was that of 25-year old WOp/AG P/O J. Whittaker DFM. Night fighters were active on 26/27 July because of the clear moonlight conditions along most of the route and over the target *Flak* was accurate. 115 Squadron's four missing Wellingtons were among 29 bombers shot down,[43] eight of them by night fighters of II./NJG 1 at Leeuwarden. Many of the missing aircraft came down off the NW German coast, in the northern part of The Netherlands and in the Friesian Islands area. *Oblt* Lothar Linke of 5./NJG 1 shot down a Lancaster[44] and it crashed at Rottevalle in Friesland. Hamburg suffered its most severe air raid to date and widespread damage was caused, mostly in the housing and semi-commercial districts. The Fire Department was overwhelmed and forced to seek outside assistance for the first time. 337 people lost their lives, 1027 were injured and 14,000 people were made homeless. Damage amounted to the equivalent of £25,000,000.

Bomber Command was stood down on 27/28 July but this was the full moon period and on 28/29 July a return to Hamburg was announced at briefings. Crews were told that the raid would be on a far bigger scale than two nights ago. At Feltwell Sgt Neville Hockaday, who was not to be denied his trip to Hamburg, which his crew had failed to reach on 26/27 July, heard that nearly 800 bombers were planned to bomb Hamburg. At Oakington, P/O Leslie R. Sidwell, rear-turret gunner in 23-year-old F/L Douglas W. Whiteman's crew of Stirling I W7565, *B-Beer* of 7 Squadron made a note that said it was another 'Thousand Raid'. He surmised, correctly, that the number was again being made up with OTU crews[45]:

'Out at dispersal we got everything finally checked and ready in the sweltering heat inside the aircraft before climbing out into the oh-so-welcome cool night air. It was lovely to relax outside on the grass and smoke casually before reluctantly putting on the flying kit which I knew would be badly needed for the cold later on, after the muck-sweat had gone. I donned flying kit, regretfully and knowing full well it would be freezing at height was soon in another sweat in the aircraft. We took off at 22.29 hrs. The weather was good. We passed over Cromer and out over the North Sea. I spent the time taking the usual sightings from my rear turret on flame-floats we'd dropped to check drift for the navigator. We'd been briefed to cross the German coast north of the Elbe estuary, then to turn south 20 miles north of Hamburg to run up to the target.'

Sgt Neville Hockaday continues:

'We made the sea crossing at 200 ft and planned to bomb from 8000 ft, which would be just below the forecast cloudbase. This was a dangerous place to be, as one would be silhouetted against the cloud background but flying above it would expose us similarly to fighters. There was plenty of activity around Heligoland as we passed safely five miles to seaward and taking advantage of the confusion crossed the coast without interference and began the long climb to bombing height, levelling out as we crossed the Kiel Canal near Rendsburg. Twice I had to break away to avoid interception by searchlights and began a time and distance run as a precaution against the target being obscured by cloud. Ten minutes from the target there was much activity ahead; more ferocious than I had expected. There were about six groups of searchlights; each of which held a bomber in a cone, the flak concentrating on each. At one time I saw five aircraft going down in flames. The cloud was barely 8000 ft and solid, having the effect of trapping the searchlight beams below it and turning the sky over Hamburg into a vast mirror. I could see that it would be no trouble identifying the aiming point if we could get to it! Just as I was preparing for the bombing run an Fw 190 came out of the target area, having flown through his own flak and we narrowly missed a head-on collision. He was almost on top of us before he spotted us and he sheered off as Bruce opened fire on him. A few seconds before [Sgt Alfie] Drew [RNZAF, front gunner/bomb aimer] released our bomb a blue master searchlight fastened on us and just as 'bomb gone' was called we were coned in about half a dozen searchlight beams. Standing on the rudder pedals I threw F for Freddie into a stall turn to port, the most violent turn I had ever made. With the engines screaming the Wimpy went down in a spiral dive, speed rising to 250 mph until, eventually, we broke free from the lights. Heading north westerly away from the target the vibration of the airframe and the over-revving of the engines died down and we regained level flight at 400 ft.'

Leslie Sidwell in the rear turret of *B-Beer* continues:

'There was heavy *flak* and we were hit just before the run up. Just after we'd bombed, someone on the intercom reported tracer coming up from below and we were hit by night-fighter attack from underneath. I reported a decoy headlight out on the starboard quarter and searched around for other fighters. I reported one coming in from above on the port side and told the skipper to turn to port. I think I hit him with a burst before my power went off. A fighter came in again from the rear and continued firing. My turret was shattered and we seemed to be in a steady dive. The skipper gave the emergency bale out order, quickly followed by what sounded like his cries of pain. Then the intercom abruptly cut off and we were on fire.

'When my turret power had failed I'd been left partly on the beam. I started to operate the dead man's handle (emergency winding gear) to centralize my turret so that I could get back into the fuselage to grab my parachute and bale out. (Chutes could not be stored in the rear turret as one did in earlier two-engined jobs, which were dead easy for rear gunners to quit in a hurry). I wound away like mad at the hand-winding gear behind me, very conscious that we were losing precious height. As if in a dream, I saw a Me 110 closing in from astern with his guns blazing away. I wound away as I watched him through the shattered perspex. My painfully slow progress was like a nightmare. I was conscious of the EBO order given in what seemed some time ago ... Would I be in time? He was extremely close to me when he eventually broke away and I finally managed to move the turret sufficiently to fall back hurriedly into the fuselage. I grabbed my 'chute from the stowage outside the turret doors, forced open the nearby emergency exit door and as quickly as I could, jumped out into space. In those seconds I was conscious of flame and smoke up front in the fuselage. I gave no thought at all to any dangers of baling out, or that I'd had no practice in jumping. I just concentrated in getting out of a doomed aircraft. In my haste to get out I banged my head on something as I quit poor old *B-Beer*, partly knocking myself out. I pulled the ripcord without counting as you were normally told to do. I must have done the right thing because I came to swinging in the air. I could see the waters of the Elbe shining below, with the full moon bright towards the south.

'After all the turmoil I was now swinging gently in a strangely contrasting silence, floating down and rather higher than I'd expected. This peace was suddenly interrupted by a dazzling searchlight, which probed around as if looking for me. It held me in its blinding beam. I felt naked, vulnerable and powerless hanging there, not knowing what to expect. I raised my arms and wondered, *'Is this It?'* But it soon switched off, as if satisfied that I'd been located and I was left to watch the Elbe more clearly as I lost height and to worry about landing in the wide waters. I'd never fancied coming down in the water and I pulled the rigging lines as instructed, hoping to spill air from the 'chute to alter my course. Probably more by luck than anything else, the Elbe disappeared and I braced myself for a landing, south of the river. The ground seemed to loom up very quickly in the moonlight and it wasn't possible to judge my first parachute landing expertly. I landed rather clumsily and hurt my right ankle on the hard ground but tall growing crops helped to cushion me. I remembered that my first duty was to hide my chute. As I struggled to gather it all up I thought I'd have a good view of a big 'Thousand Raid' but I was surprised. Little was seen or heard and I wondered, 'Where are they?' My watch showed 0110 hours just after landing.'[46]

Sgt Neville Hockaday meanwhile, crossed the Kiel Canal at 2000 ft when he saw tracer fire coming up over the port wing from behind:

'I called Mike who replied that it was from a chap on top of a building. Bruce had just fired back and all had gone quiet; he thought he had got him. Later I checked to find that we had wandered over Meldorf and the building was probably the local barracks. We went well out to sea to avoid Heligoland and just as I ordered, 'Watch out for 'flak ships'. One opened up at us but we were too fast for him and were soon out of range. Mike said that not all our aircraft had reported to base after bombing and as we approached Cromer we were all diverted to Methwold. We assumed that someone was in trouble and that Feltwell was being kept clear for him. It was six am by the time we walked into debriefing to learn that of the 14 aircraft of our squadron only eight had returned.[47] We then learned that far from there being 800 aircraft on the raid there had been only 165 as a late forecast had predicted bad weather on return and all except 3 Group had cancelled. If only we had been told we could have revised our tactics to meet the new situation.[48] We had all lost many good friends and our morale was temporarily very low but at about three pm we were advised that we were 'on' tonight, briefing at six pm. We snapped out of it, every survivor of the night's debacle wishing nothing more than the chance to 'get back at the bastards'. Morale rocketed. We had had very little sleep but this did not dampen our determination. The target was Saarbrücken, a town that had not been raided since November 1940. Before briefing began the Station Commander said that the C in C appreciated that we had taken a beating last night and that anyone who did not feel up to it could withdraw from tonight's operation without any blame. All ten captains stood and said as one man, 'Tell Butch Harris we'll bloody well go'.

'Thank you, gentlemen', said the CO. 'I told the AO I was sure that would be your answer.'

'Clearly this operation was intended as a morale booster for our Group after the trauma of yesterday as Saarbrücken would be taken by surprise after two years unmolested. Only four heavy *Flak* guns were believed to be there and if early arrivals could put them and the searchlights out of action the remainder would go in low for accuracy – although with a cookie we were limited to 5000 ft because of the enormous blast which would be felt to that height.

'The planned route was Beachy Head, Le Treport and then direct to the target returning via Le Cretoy and Brighton. There was much searchlight activity and a heavy barrage from Dieppe to Calais so searching for a gap I found it in the Somme Estuary. We avoided Abbeville and also Amiens where we had seen an aircraft attracting much attention. We weaved round other hot spots (as shown when others passed over them) of Peronne, St. Quentin, Sedan and Montmedy. In contrast to the lack of any such signs when flying over Holland the number of 'V for Victory' signals that were aimed at us were noticeable. One wondered at the contrast. We approached the target from Saarlouis to the north west and as we ran over the marshalling yards at 7000 ft we saw two Lancasters and a

Stirling below us, so we made a left turn and began our run once more. This time all was clear and we saw a great flash on the ground by the marshalling yards; seconds later the whole aircraft was lifted by the shock waves from the blast. I was very glad we were at 7000 ft. Two sets of searchlights and one heavy gun battery were still operative until silenced by two Lancasters firing from the front turret and a Wellington dropped a stick of 500 lb bombs on flares laid by another on the gunsite. As we turned away incendiaries ignited what appeared to be an oil tank and flame lit up the whole of Saarbrücken. Coming home over Brighton I could see the street where my wife and baby son were sleeping unaware that I was so close to them.'[49]

For the next Main Force raid, on Düsseldorf on 31 July/1 August 630 aircraft[50] were despatched. Again Bomber Command's training units made up the numbers. F/Sgt Eddie Wheeler at 27 OTU recalls:

'It seemed to us that if we were to operate we may just as well be back on a fully operational squadron with the best available aircraft and not lumbered with clapped-out training types with a lesser survival potential. As it transpired, we were soon back to our normal instructional routine and the thought of further 'ops' had disappeared. That is, until 31 July when we were detailed once again, this time to Düsseldorf and I was assigned to F/Sgt Chidgey, an exceptionally good pilot who originated from the West Country. We took off just before midnight and landed back just after five am. Our OTU contribution to the raid totalled 105 aircraft and our losses were heavy – over 10.5%. We now resigned ourselves to being called for 'ops' at any time in the future, there was no guarantee that being on a Training Station would relieve us of this likelihood.'

Sgt Neville Hockaday continues:

'We circumvented Eindhoven and weaved between Mönchengladbach and Krefeld until the Rhine once again made it easy to identify our target, which was already well alight by the time we got there, a column of smoke rising to about 4000 ft. Many searchlights made it difficult to see the ground and we were aware that the night fighters were now using airborne radar. We bombed from 9500 ft, Drew having a clear view of the target despite being held by the beams of a group of searchlights which I eluded by diving away once the photograph of the bomb strike had been taken.

'As we approached Domburg Bruce saw a Fw 190 turn to follow us but I gave him the slip by diving into cloud just below us and altering course 90° to starboard, towards the Hook of Holland – I hoped he would guess that I would turn to port, towards Knokke and Zeebrugge. We saw no more of him. Bomber Command lost 29 aircraft that night but some extensive damage was inflicted[51] and so ended the month of July and the 'moon period'.

Nachtjagd victory claims for July 1942 were 102 bombers shot down, 29 of which went to *Hptm* Helmut Lent's crack II./NJG 2 at Leeuwarden, ten to I./NJG 1 and seven to III./NJG 1. One hundred *Himmelbett* kills were claimed by *Nachtjagd* in August 1942 with II./NJG 1 at St. Trond, Belgium, recording the most with 25 confirmed victories. Much of the success in the *Himmelbett* night-fighting was achieved by excellent ground-to-air and air-to-ground communication using a combination of R/T codes and plain language.[52]

Arthur 'Johnnie' Johnson, rear-gunner of Wellington III Z1469 of 142 Squadron flew his first op on 16/17 August when Bomber Command went to Flensburg near the Danish border:

'There was a fair amount of haze over the target area and on the return journey the skipper, P/O Ron Brooks, reported a problem with the port engine. We landed safely at base with no further incident. My second op, on 18/19 August, was a mine-laying trip to Heligoland off the north German coast. The Wimpy carried two of these cylindrical shaped mines with parachutes on each end to lower them gently in to the sea. The navigator had to be spot on and able to identify the selected target area visually (this was before any radar navigation aids) so the navigator, or observer as he was then known, had to know his gen on these trips. On this occasion we had to return to base with the mines as ordered as the target area was covered in very low cloud. We were always instructed that the mines must only be dropped at a height of only 800 ft. the hazards became obvious to me in later mining trips to the Friesian islands and the French ports of St. Nazaire, Lorient and La Rochelle. All these were important areas for enemy shipping activities and the dropping zones were usually in between islands and mainland, or narrow channels in large bays. During the run in therefore, we were normally subjected to crossfire from islands and mainland and *Flak* ships that were always based in these waters. And of course, there was always the night fighter threat. After one of these trips, to Lorient, we got back to base and were informed that only half an hour after we left the target, it had been reported that the mines had sunk a large vessel. We all went to bed elated at this news.

'My 3rd op was a trip to Frankfurt on 24/25 August [when 226 aircraft were despatched]. The weather was perfect with a full moon. About 15 minutes from the target I spotted a Junkers Ju 88 fighter flying on a steady course about 1000 ft below just above a bank of cloud. I reported this to the skipper, who told us to keep an eye on him but after a few minutes he swung away and left us. We had just completed our bombing run over Frankfurt and began to weave our way out of the target area, when dead astern of us, approximately 400 yards, I watched another Wellington on its run in with bomb doors open. With the clear weather and moon I had a good view from my rear turret but I was not prepared for what was about to follow. I witnessed a huge explosion. Balls of fire, fragments and colored lights were falling all over the sky behind me. After a short while I looked again for the Wimpy but it was gone. On this night I had seen my first enemy fighter and witnessed my first aircraft shot down. I was 19 years of age.'[53]

Wellingtons came in for high losses on 27/28 August when 306 aircraft were despatched to bomb the German army headquarters and garrison at Kassel. Norman Child, radio operator in P/O Alan Gill's Wellington crew in 'B' Flight, 142 Squadron, at Waltham, Lincs, recalls:

'At briefing we were told to expect the target to be heavily defended. We carried a mixed load of 500-lb bombs and incendiaries. The Met report was 'good visibility' over the target. Wind, 'light westerly'. We were routed in ten miles south of Münster. Same route out. Flak ships were very active off the Dutch coast. There was no trouble so far. Visibility good. There was lots of Flak up ahead. Somebody must have wandered off course over Münster. Good pin point. Approaching target and all hell let loose approximately ten miles ahead. Very heavy barrage – town ringed with guns and searchlights. Several kites had been hit and gone down.

'Running into target now – terrific smell of cordite – searchlights were blinding but dropped bombs on schedule at 8500 ft. Weaved out of target area and for a few minutes everything was chaos. Set course for home. Same route as course in. Difficult to get a good pinpoint and aircraft ahead were running into heavy *Flak* ... there shouldn't have been any *Flak* on this course.

'Checked the wind again. There had been a sudden terrific wind change round to the north and the whole force had been blown over the Ruhr Valley. Searchlights and *Flak* were forcing us lower and lower and many aircraft were seen to go down. The *Flak* was so bad and the searchlights so blinding, we decided to go right down full power to below a thousand feet. Front and rear turrets were firing at the searchlights and between them they accounted for five. We burst our way out of the Ruhr, knowing that we had been hit many times and climbed up to 8000 ft again. We made for 'Over *Flak*kee' (an island off the Dutch coast just south of the Hook of Holland and an aiming point for a comparatively quiet exit from the Continent).

'Our aircraft looked a mess. Full of holes and big chunks off but miraculously, except for cuts and abrasions; none of the crew was hurt. The next day we were flown back to Waltham to discover, to our horror, that of the six aircraft from 'B' Flight, our crew were the only survivors. The Met report, or lack of one, could be held responsible for the debacle over the Ruhr Valley and the consequent loss of aircraft and crews force-landing all over south of England, out of fuel.'[54]

Stirlings too came in for heavy losses on occasion. AC1 Jack Bennett, who served as flight mechanic and fitter with 214 Squadron at Stradishall, had the onerous duty of helping remove a dead gunner from a Stirling which landed at Newmarket Heath after getting shot up on a daylight raid on Sylt in late August-early September 1942:

'The kite was silhouetted against a sky that was breaking dawn when we arrived. It looked like a giant lizard on tall front legs. As we pulled closer to it we could see damage to the fuselage. The front turret was at 45° and there was a figure still inside. As there was no movement I assumed that the gunner was dead. The only way the gunner's body could be moved was by breaking the perspex of the gun turret. As this was 15-ft or so from the ground a trestle was required. I was told to stay with the kite whilst the rest moved off in search of some help. I felt very lonely with a bloody great kite and a dead man in the nose. I wondered if he was the guy I had seen lean over a landing wheel vomiting just before take off. In the distance I could now hear the noise of vehicles and our Hillman Minx towing a mobile trestle with a 'Coles' crane following. They got closer and I was told, 'Get the fire axe out of the kite.' I entered the fuselage and peered at the partly turned turret with horror. After grabbing the axe I was told to smash the perspex. I got a closer look at the victim who was unrecognisable because of his flying helmet and intercom over his face. Blood spattered the perspex. Carefully I started to crack it but suddenly the axe was wrenched out of my hand by an orderly who shouted, 'You can't hurt the bugger now.' The mobile crane moved in and the crane driver was given the order, 'Take it up.' Within seconds shouts of 'he's coming in half,' echoed across the racecourse. In horror I could see half a body hanging on the crane and slowly being lowered to the ground. 'God almighty' I thought. 'Poor bugger.' The top half of the corpse was gently lowered. I felt quite sick and did not watch the rest of the operation but was jolted to my senses by Chiefy calling me to get aboard the Hillman truck and away we went back to Stradishall.'

Ron Read and his crew reported to Middleton St. George to join 78 Squadron on 3 September:

'It was a busy station. Apart from being at full blast on operations over Germany, it was preparing for a hand over to the Canadians as the first bomber station of their new 6 Group Bomber Command. Our squadron commander was 'Willie' Tait, later to become one f the legendary, elite bomber pilots, who commanded 617 the famous Dam Busters squadron. There he led the raid that finally sank the battleship *Tirpitz*. Already the possessor of a DSO and bar and a DFC and bar at Middleton, he was to become one of very few men to win four DSOS when he was awarded a further two bars later. Willie was a reserved man, dark and introvert and a tough CO. He had a strong motivation for being a bomber pilot. It was said that his young WAAF officer wife had been killed in the Blitz on London. He was, in RAF parlance, a 'Press On' type and he expected his crews to be the same.

'We spent the day checking in and making ourselves familiar with the station. In the mess at lunchtime the squadron crews were just getting up after their previous night's operations. We eavesdropped on their talk, not daring to say a word. This was the stuff of experienced veterans. Soon we hoped, we would be able to share these conversations, talking from our own experience. We learned that two crews were missing, one who had completed 25 operations. We were a little shocked to realize that even at 25 you weren't immune from the 'Chop'. These matters had been thoughts harboured secretly but never considered openly. Here was stark reality.

'We were invited to attend one briefing as observers. Willie Tait, cold and stony faced, gave a tough series of instructions to his crews. Now we felt the cold blast of the reality of life on operations, blowing right down our necks. The smart uniforms, the carefree flying, the girls, the dancing and the good times all faded into the background. Now was the time we had to pay the piper. It was obvious from the chat around us that Willie Tait demanded payment in full.

'We spent ten days waiting at Middleton without flying. Our Conversion flight was merged with that of 76 Squadron at Croft and moved to a new airfield at Riccall to become 1598 Heavy Conversion Unit. The squadron itself was moving to Linton on Ouse, which it would share with 76 Squadron. We flew down to Riccall with our instructors one wet Sunday morning 13 September 1942. We had time expired aircraft for training. They were pretty clapped out. Some were still original Halifax Is with low powered Merlin 5 engines. They all suffered from problems, not least glycol leaks. At Riccall Jimmy Goodwin, a 20-year-old fresh faced 6ft 2in quietly spoken Rhodesian, joined my crew as flight engineer. This was a new trade, to replace the old second pilot in the four-engined bombers. It was their duty to look after the management of engines and systems, constantly watching temperatures, pressures, outputs of hydraulics, electrics, pneumatics, fuel consumption and so on. They were intended to sit in the second pilot's seat and aid the pilot on take-off and landing but were unable to do this on the Halifax. The aircraft was designed in 1936 to provide for the earlier, two-pilot concept with a separate engineer. As a result, the instruments the flight engineer had to monitor were located in a large panel facing the wrong way behind the two pilots' seats.

'My rear gunner, sleepy old Sunshine Smith, was loaned to Linton and went missing with a 76 Squadron crew. We would have to find a new gunner.[55] Worse, my friend Geoff Hobbs had also gone missing on 2 October with an experienced pilot and crew on their 28th trip. Geoff was doing his obligatory 'second dickey' trip.[56] Three Halifaxes were lost from the 39 sent to Krefeld by 4 Group that night. I was shocked at the news of Geoff, the best pilot all the way through all our various courses, from elementary at Calgary, to heavy conversion at Riccall. We'd been best friends for over a year. Now he'd gone without even flying one operation as captain. What a waste! Now I knew ops were for real. A little chill ran down my spine. E.G. 'Morty' Mortenson, my long-standing friend from our training days who gave me the news when I called from Riccall, had completed his 'second dickey' trip and was about to start operations. 'You'd better hurry up Readey,' said Morty, 'or we'll all be chopped before you get here.'

During September 86 heavies were shot down by the *Nachtjagd* with 22 victories credited to II./NJG 2, 14 to I./NJG 1, nine to

II./NJG 1 and eight to III./NJG 1. Twelve bombers failed to return from the 4/5 September raid on Bremen by 251 Wellingtons, Lancasters, Halifaxes and Stirlings. *Oblt* Ludwig Becker, *Uffz* Karl Heinz Vinke, *Hptm* Helmut Lent and *Oblt* zur Lippe-Weissenfeld of II./NJG 2 at Leeuwarden claimed seven bombers including four Wellingtons destroyed.[57] On 6/7 September, when 207 bombers raided Duisburg for the loss of eight aircraft *Lt* Wilhelm Beier of III./NJG 2 scored a triple victory over southern Holland. On 8/9 September 249 aircraft were dispatched to Frankfurt-on-Main. Norman Child, radio operator in P/O Alan Gill's crew in 'B' Flight, 142 Squadron, at Waltham, Lincs, recalls:

> 'We carried one 4000-lb 'cookie'. Our route out took us via Overflakkee, south of Cologne, Koblenz and then due east to Frankfurt. The Met report said it would be probably hazy over the target but otherwise, good. Airborne at 2020-hrs. Set course for Overflakkee and climbed to 10,000 ft. Cloud thicker than expected over Holland and we fly in cloud up to the German border. Break in the cloud and we get a good pinpoint on the Maas. Steered well clear of Cologne but plenty of *Flak* to port suggests that a number of aircraft have wandered off course in cloud and are over the city. Cloud now clearing and only 3/10ths cover. North of Mainz a night fighter attacked us and he scored a hit on our tail fin. 'Jock' Sloan, the rear gunner, gave him a burst and we weaved and dived our way to safety.
>
> 'Approaching the target we detected a Halifax just overhead with its bomb doors open. We took quick avoiding action and prepared for our own run in. Very heavy defenses and well-predicted *Flak*. Enormous flash in the sky and flaming debris falling. It looked as though two aircraft had collided.
>
> 'We dropped our 'Cookie' into the middle of a huge circle of explosions and fires and dived away into the night. Checked on the damage to tail but although it looked a ragged sight, it was still functioning satisfactorily. Steered course for home north of Koblenz and south of Cologne. We had a brief encounter with *Flak* ship off the Dutch coast and a few more holes punched into us. None of the crew was hurt. Message from base: 'Weather closed in – visibility very poor. Divert to Waterbeach'. Landed at Waterbeach. Duration of flight: 6 hrs 55 mins. Riggers inspected the tail unit and the damage was so severe they were amazed that the whole structure hadn't collapsed. The Wellington was a tough baby.'[58]

On 10/11 September training aircraft of 91, 92 and 93 Groups swelled the numbers in a 479-bomber raid on Düsseldorf. Thirty-three aircraft failed to return and the OTUs were hard hit.[59] Sgt Derek Smith[60], a Wellington observer/navigator at Bircotes, the satellite of 25 OTU Finningley flew his first op, which he described in a letter to his father at his London office because the contents would have worried his mother if it had been posted to his home:

> 'Last night we were taking our bow over Germany at Düsseldorf. As you will have heard front the radio it was a large-scale show. We flew as a crew, which was a good thing as none of us had ever been under fire before and I must say the boys put up a grand show. We had an oil leak, which was not discovered, until our return. The Wimpy is supposed to cruise at 130 IAS but owing to the leak we could only get 110. We were supposed to attack at 14,000 ft but could only get 10,000. It was very quiet all the way to the target although I must say Jerry has very elaborate dummy fires and decoy towns. Anyway, we reached the target at 10,000 ft down below everybody else and then' the fun and games began. We had to get through four cones of searchlights to get to the target so we aimed for the widest gap. We were just in the middle, weaving like hell when the purple master searchlight swung smack on to us followed by about 30 others. I think we must have been coned for about five minutes but it seemed a lifetime with, what seemed every gun in Germany firing at us. We could hear the *Flak* bursting and were flying through the smoke of it but we were only holed twice. Gordon [F/Sgt Gordon Oldham, the Rhodesian born pilot] did some wonderful piloting and we were down to 7000 ft before we finally lost them. One good thing was that there was not the least sign of panic and the boys regarded it as a free Brocks Benefit Anyway, we got out of it and made our run over the target to drop our five 500 pounders. We then made off at the terrific speed of 100 knots!
>
> 'Over Holland Doc [Sgt Maurice Root-Reid, air gunner, a doctor in civvy street[61]] saw a fighter but we managed to evade it and reached base having had trouble with petrol gauges, boost control, cylinder head temperatures and the compass. She certainly was a ropey kite but we made it although we arrived back an hour after the others because of these faults. According to the radio it was one of the heaviest barrages ever, well if we never get worse we will be OK. We have a great crew and will come through every time. We lost two kites last night, both crews off our course, including a good friend of mine, Stan Southgate.'

Many training aircraft from various OTUs and Conversion Units were included in the force of 446 bombers which attacked Bremen on 13/14 September. Twenty-one aircraft failed to return.[62] Six were claimed by six crews of II./NJG 2. On the night of 14/15 September 202 aircraft attacked Wilhelmshaven for the loss of two Wellingtons. This was the last raid by Hampdens and all four aircraft of 408 Squadron RCAF returned safely. On 16/17 September during a 369 aircraft strong Bomber Command raid on the Krupp works in Essen *Oblt* Reinhold Knacke, *Staffelkapitän*, 1./NJG 1 claimed five victories to take his tally to 38. Thirty-nine bombers, or 10.6 per cent of the force dispatched were lost, 21 of these to *Nachtjäger*.[63] On 23/24 September 83 Lancasters of 5 Group bombed Wismar for the loss of four aircraft and 28 Halifaxes of 4 Group attacked Flensburg, losing five aircraft. Meanwhile, 24 Stirlings of 3 Group went to Vegesack and another eight Stirlings and 25 Wellingtons laid mines between Biscay and Denmark. Two Wellingtons failed to return. A Stirling I of 218 Squadron[64] lost on the Vegesack raid fell victim to a Bf 110 flown by *Uffz* Karl-Georg Pfeiffer of 6./NJG 2 at Wittmundhafen. It was his first victory since joining the *Gruppe* at Leeuwarden in late April. Pfeiffer had been banished to Wittmundhafen as a punishment for failing to lower the undercarriage of a new Fw 190 when landing on his 1st or 2nd training flight. Four Fw 190s had been allocated to NJG 2 for day operations against Coastal Command aircraft that were becoming a nuisance to shipping and coastal targets in the Dutch coast area. *Major* Helmut Lent, the *Gruppenkommandeur* was so angry that he told Pfeiffer he did not want to see him again. Pfeiffer recalls:

> 'The Leeuwarden *Gruppe* was commanded by *Major* Lent and was considered to be the best night fighter unit, especially as their aircraft, mostly Me 110, were already equipped with *Lichtenstein* radar. *Staffelkapitän Oblt* Ludwig Becker's *Bordfunker, Fw* Josef Staub, was a master in the operation of this highly sensitive device and unceasingly instructed the other radio operators in the finer points of its use. My *Bordfunker* was *Gefr* Willi Knappe from Berlin. After I shot down the Stirling I was recalled to Leeuwarden and a great victory party of the *Abschuss* tyro with my comrades! It had been a textbook *Abschuss*, ideal for a beginner: bright moonlight, white cumulus clouds and the island of Heligoland clearly visible below. The crew must have been asleep not to have seen me, especially as my guns had been badly sighted and my first burst missed. But then the Short Stirling burst into flames and several white parachutes emerged. The first *Abschuss* was always a psychological hurdle for a crew. Now we had taken it.'

A Bomber Command directive was now issued whereby crews stood down from night flying would be employed on daylight intruder missions to keep the German sirens wailing and disrupt industry by driving the workers into air raid shelters. The RAF crews' only protection was cloud cover and it was essential that there was sufficient cloud to hide in. A Wellington was no match for a German fighter and all aircraft captains had strict orders to return to base if the cloud cover broke up. On Monday 28 September three Wellingtons of 115 Squadron were detailed for a 'cloud cover' daylight bombing attack on Lingen on the Dortmund-Ems Canal. As the aircraft made their way east the-cover thinned out rapidly to a scattering of isolated clouds. Sgt Crimmin in BJ695 decided to turn back. S/L Sandes in BK272 made a similar decision. S/L Robert James Sealer Parsons in Z1663 decided to press home the attack buteight kilometers south west of Urk over the Zuider Zee, he was attacked by *Uffz* Kurt Knespel of 10./JG 1 in a Fw 190. As his cannon shells tore through the fuselage F/Sgt John Austin Parker, the Canadian WOP-AG was hit and died instantly. Flames from the ruptured wing gasoline tanks, fanned by the slipstream, spread rapidly. Parsons shouted over the intercom that he would try to ditch the bomber. The front gunner, Sgt Gilmour, entered the cockpit from his turret and saw F/Sgt William Leonard Clough, the 31-year-old observer with the cabin fire extinguisher in his hand vainly trying to subdue the raging furnace. The aircraft hit the sea and only the Canadian gunners, Sgts Gilmour and Stansell emerged.

With the coming of Fall weather and a decrease in Bomber Command activity during October 1942 38 bombers were destroyed by *Nachtjagd*. Twenty of these were credited to I./NJG 1 at Venlo and nine to II./NJG 2. Whilst flying from Melsbroek near Brussels and patrolling in *Himmelbett* box Hamster on 23/24 October, *Ofw* Lüddecke of 3./NJG 2 claimed a Stirling destroyed.[65] During the same month four aircraft were claimed by II./NJG 1 including two by *Lt* Hans Autenrieth.[66] Victories by IV./NJG 1, *Hptm* Helmut Lent's *Gruppe* at Leeuwarden (previously II./NJG 2, which had been renumbered on 1 October) included four victories by *Lt* Wilhelm Beier of *Stab* IV./NJG 1 on 15/16 October, which took his total to 36 kills. On 22 October Wellingtons were once more sent out on cloud cover sorties. Sgt Bill Rae a Wellington rear gunner in 142 Squadron at Waltham, Lincs, tells of this operation:

> 'When the operation was announced in the morning there was of course unusual excitement on the squadron and when we got out to the dispersal point all the other crews were there along with the non-flying members waiting for us to taxi to the end of the runway. Probably the other crews were glad that we were to be the guinea

pigs. Normally on a night trip the only people who would see us off would be the technical staff i.e. the ground crew who serviced our aircraft. One aircraft from each of three I Group Squadrons was detailed and take off was at two hours intervals. Having experienced the efficiency of the German defenses from the North Sea coast to the target and back we felt that we were being led like lambs to the slaughter. I know we all felt proud as one of the senior crews on the squadron to have been selected for this unique occasion, while at the same time wondering what was in store for us. Met had promised cloud cover but it was very slight over the North Sea so I got a nice view of the Friesians for the first time. Cover did then thicken and we reached Essen to drop the cookie. Using our new *Gee* navigation the navigator was certain we were over Essen when we dropped our cookie bomb and I just cannot understand why we were not attacked. German radar could have tracked us for most of the trip, so why was there no reaction from *Flak* or fighters? On part of the way back we were out of cloud cover but still no attack. I did see two aircraft but they were too far away to identify and did not seem to be interested in us. There was a marvellous reception awaiting us on our return and we were the heroes of the hour but having been keyed up to expect a life or death struggle, the whole thing was a bit of an anti-climax. It was a unique experience but not one we had any desire to repeat. Sending three Wellingtons to Essen may have had some effect but I doubt it.'[67]

On 23 October more cloud cover sorties were flown when 15 Wellingtons were sent to bomb Krefeld and 11 to Essen. Again there were no losses but Norman Child in 142 Squadron agrees with the same sentiments expressed by Bill Rae:

'Our black-painted Wellingtons were quite unsuitable for this type of work and, to the crews, plain suicidal but orders were orders. On 23 October the order was to penetrate well into Germany, circle for a while and return. The Met report was two layers of cloud and 10/10ths at 6000 ft with clear sky between the layers, 'these conditions extending from the English coast to central Europe'. We were airborne at 1240 hrs. Climbed to 8500 ft and flew in upper layer for approximately one hour. When over the Dutch coast, the cloud started to thin and we ran into clear sky. Immediately, we dived for the thick lower layer and continued on course at 6500 ft. It was noticeable that the cloud was beginning to thin and after three-quarters of an hour we suddenly ran out into clear sunshine, many miles short of the German border. We steep-turned back into cloud and headed home at full throttle, volubly cursing all the 'duff gen merchants' and what they could do with their forecasts. We came through unscathed amid light *Flak* at the Dutch coast and flew low in thick cloud to avoid fighters. Duration of flight: 3 hrs 30 minutes.'

On 23/24 October 122 heavies set out to bomb Genoa but the target was almost completely cloud covered and it was later determined that Savona, 30 miles along the coast from Genoa had been bombed. On 24 October 88 Lancasters of 5 Group attacked Milan in daylight with the loss of four Lancs. Then that night it was the turn of 71 aircraft of 1 and 3 Groups and the Pathfinders.[68] Norman Child recalls:

'We climbed to 9000 ft over France. Clear starlit night. Fighter reported on starboard bow cruising at same speed so we throttle back and descend to 15,000 ft to clear Swiss Alps – extremely cold. Good pinpoint on Lake Geneva to port and mountain range looming ahead. Mont Blanc identified quite easily in clear night air and set new course for target. 'Box barrage over target, which quietens down when bombing commences (unlike German targets) and we bomb through comparatively little opposition. Many fires started and large explosions seen. Bombed at 12,000 ft. Turned on course for base and climbed back to 15,500 ft. At course change at Haute Savoie we noticed the port engine was leaking oil badly and beginning to overheat. The port engine was throttled right back and we started a very slow descent across France to keep up a reasonable airspeed. Everyone was keyed up and anxious. We reached the French coast at 3000 ft and pinpointed St. Valery. Everything was quiet and we stole out to sea untouched. The port engine temperature was now so high we decided on a forced landing at West Malling. They cleared us for emergency landing and when we taxied to a halt the port engine died. The fitters found a shell splinter had damaged an oil-feed line and the engine was starved of oil. Across France we had the choice of feathering the prop and probably a forced landing there, or pressing on and risking the engine catching fire. We made the right choice – just. Duration of flight: 7 hrs 50 minutes.'[69]

In November 19-year-old Sgt John 'Jimmy' Anderson Hurst, a tail gunner in 21-year old George Barker's crew was one of several from the Halifax Heavy Bomber Conversion Unit at RAF Topcliffe who joined 102 Squadron. He recalls:

'We were all keen to go on ops. I was. Little did we know that of the ten crews who arrived at Pocklington in Yorkshire ours would be the only one to complete a tour. All the others were killed or seriously injured or became

PoWs. The majority of my ops 6 November 1942-13 May 1943 were over the Ruhr. We hit most of the main cities – Essen, Munich, Cologne, Frankfurt, Mannheim and Stuttgart, etc. Then of course there was Berlin and three to Italy – Turin and Genoa – a 9hr trip, as well as minelaying around the Friesian islands, so I had an exciting an eventful war and lived to tell the tale. We were a happy confident crew – no bickering or arguing. We just gelled. (We almost won the *Croix de Guerre* in 1943. The French Government sent our squadron seven of them. They must have been impressed with our efforts. The names of the crews involved were put into a hat and those drawn were given the medals. What a way to win or not to win the *Croix de Guerre*!)

'Our first operation was mine laying off Ameland in the Friesian Islands on 6 November. Mines were dropped from 200 ft and at such a low height we received a lot of attention from ground fire. Tracer was hosed around us but we were not hit. That was our 'baptism of fire' but we had yet to encounter night fighters. They were always a problem. The worst encounter that we had was with a Fw 190 that attacked us from astern. He was very determined but I had seen him before he was within range and warned the skipper. At the critical moment as he came in I told the skipper to corkscrew, this entailed the aircraft diving a few hundred feet to port or starboard and then climbing again on the opposite tack in a corkscrewing motion. This could be quite a violent maneuver but effective in shaking off a fighter. A few minutes later the fighter found us again and came in from port and I told the skipper to turn hard to port and as the Fw 190 broke away the mid upper and I gave it a short burst. He came at us again, this time from starboard and we repeated our evasive action and as he broke away he gave us a burst but did no damage and we did not see him again.

'Most of our ops entailed flying through areas heavily protected by anti aircraft guns, it sound like hail as it hit the aircraft after the shell had burst above us, this was not too lethal as it was in free-fall on its way to the ground. The most dangerous was from shells that burst close to the aircraft and the hundreds of hot jagged fragments had the momentum to penetrate the plane and kill or injure crew members and cause mechanical damage, often resulting in it crashing. On one occasion we were on our way to Essen in very heavy *Flak*, when there was a loud explosion in the aircraft and a rush of cold air and the plane bounced around. The skipper checked on the intercom that we were all OK and the flight engineer went to see what the damage was.

'What had happened was that a piece of shrapnel had detonated the photo flash which exploded and destroyed its launching tube and blew a jagged hole in the starboard side of the fuselage just behind my turret. We measured it back at base and it was about 5ft long by 3ft high. This resulted in a gale blowing through the aircraft and made it very difficult for George to handle. Never the less we flew to the target – Krupps – and bombed it – no photo of course – and set course for base. About half way home – still over enemy territory we lost an engine due to mechanical trouble, this reduced our airspeed even more and we lumbered home an hour later than the rest of the squadron. Being behind the main stream and flying low as we approached the English coast we attracted the attention of the Navy, who fired at us with pom poms. Despite us firing off the colors of the day, I recall sitting in my turret and hearing the pom, pom, pom of the guns above the sound of our three engines. When counting the hits on our plane-as we always did – we wondered how many were from enemy fire and how many from the navy. It was surprising how much damage the Halibags could sustain and remain flyable. I certainly owe my life to this factor. As well as *Flak* holes there were sometimes unexploded incendiary bombs embedded in our wings – and this is where our fuel tanks were! This was the result of flying through an incendiary shower dropped by Lancs flying above us at about 20,000-ft. Our gallant ground crew of whom I cannot speak too highly would remove these. They did a great job keeping our aircraft in first class condition whatever the previous night's battle damage had been. They waved us off and they were there waiting for us to bring 'their' aircraft home. Our CO, Gus Walker would also wave us off from beside the runway. He would stand there with cookhouse staff (who always waved us off) with the crew list in his hand. As each plane started its run down the runway, he would run beside it, waving to the crew and would be waiting in the briefing room when we returned to chat to each crew. He was popular with the crews, whom he called 'my boys'. He had flown quite a few ops but had to stop flying when he severely damaged a hand in a ground incident involving exploding bombs.

'The cold could also caused problems for crews, it was not unusual for the air temperature to be -20C and ice would build up on the wings of the aircraft, often adding weight and making the plane difficult to fly and sometimes causing it to crash. The crews had little protection against the cold and on one occasion when we were returning through the Alps from Turin, my oxygen tube frozen solid, cutting off my supply of oxygen. The crew became aware of this, because I had switched on my intercom and was singing into my mike. (This was due to me being starved of oxygen, which has a similar affect to drinking too much alcohol). The skipper sent the flight engineer to my turret to see what the problem was. On finding my oxygen tube solid with ice, he went back into the fuselage and returned with a flask of hot coffee. He removed my mask and poured coffee into it and this quickly thawed the ice in the tube, enabling me to breathe the oxygen vital to survival at 18,000 ft. I was so starved of oxygen that I was hardly aware of what was happening, the quick thinking of the engineer surely saved my life – another of my nine lives gone!'

Another recent arrival on operations in November was F/Sgt Jack Woodrow, observer in Sgt John Michaud's crew in 425 *'Les Alouettes'* French-Canadian Squadron flying Wellington IIIs at Dishforth, Yorkshire. Michaud was from Montreal. Sgt Frank Rowan from Orilla, Ontario was WOP/AG and Sgt M.T. 'Mac' McMillan from Vancouver was rear gunner. Their navigator was a Sgt from Alberta. Woodrow recalls:

'The Wellington was the only two-engined bomber still flying on operations. I had been hoping for a 4-engine squadron. The Wellington III had two Bristol Hercules engines. It had a maximum speed of 235 mph at 15,000 ft with a service ceiling of 18,000 ft and a range of 1275 miles with 1000-lb load and a 600-mile range with a maximum load of 4500 lbs. That load was more than the B-17 'Flying Fortresses' could carry but of course, at a much lower altitude. The Wimpy was not of stressed-skin metal construction. It was built instead on the 'geodetic' principle of countless strips of metal in a basket weave pattern, then fabric covered. It could take lots of punishment. In fact, it was said that it was built like the proverbial 'brick shithouse.' Because of the Wellington's limited range compared to the 4-engine Lancasters and Halifaxes, our targets were limited to the Ruhr, Frankfurt, Kiel and other targets in that area. The .303 calibre machine guns were as useless as peashooters against the four 20mm cannons on the attacking Me-110s or Focke-Wulf 190s. The only navigation aid on the Wellington was *Gee*. We sometimes used Astro navigation but only in special circumstances. *Gee* was an instrument that allowed a navigator to calculate the bomber's location by receiving pulse signals from a trio of widely spread out stations in Britain. *Gee* calculated the difference between the signals, giving the navigator an immediate fix of his own position. The range was about 400 miles, which meant it couldn't be used much beyond the Ruhr and a few North ports. However, *Gee* was pretty well jammed by the time we reached the enemy coast. The Lancasters and Halifaxes had H2S. It was self-contained and thus independent of any transmitting stations on the ground. H2S sent a directional beam of high energy directly toward the earth, the beam rotating with its antenna approximately once per a second. The aircraft's antenna picked up reflections from these beams. These reflections appeared on a cathode ray tube. Each signal received registered as a spot on the screen. The various reflections created the necessary contrast to 'paint a picture' of the terrain below. It sounds simple but it wasn't. Operators had to practice to interpret the screen accurately. Also at its early stage it had a terrible record of serviceability.

'There was lots of squadron training to be done before we were ready for operations. New crews were often put on mine-laying trips to help them get experience. This was especially true for Wellington crews because of its shorter range. A favourite target was the Friesian Islands off the coast of Holland and Germany. There was a lot of enemy coastal shipping and the mines caused a lot of damage. The normal load was two 1500-lb mines, which were also called 'Vegetables.' Our first trip was cancelled twice because of weather and we finally went on the third night, on 16/17 November. However our station did not have the capability of loading the mines, so we were sent to Middleton-St.George to be loaded up.[70] Right after planting our two 1500-lb mines, the captain asked me to take over the navigator's job. I ended up navigating the aircraft home. A satisfactory and a very memorable trip but which ended in a blaze of ignominy. Each day as part of our flying rations we were given two chocolate bars. So when we finally went on our trip, I had six chocolate bars. Anyway, through normal excitement and nervousness from it being our first trip and a problem with our navigator, I ate all six bars on the way home. Then I started to feel pretty sick. Right after landing, I jumped out of the aircraft and immediately upchucked on the dispersal pad. Very embarrassing.

'I don't really know what happened but it seems our navigator got into a 'blue-funk' and was not capable of doing the job. We returned to Dishforth and I never saw him again. Later on we heard he was accused of LMF[71] and whisked off the station. I heard from him several months later. He told he had been returned to Canada, discharged and then drafted into the Army. I never heard from him again and I feel very sorry that I did not make a greater effort to keep in touch. I have always felt disgusted with what the Air Force did with him. I think they should have been more understanding and compassionate instead of sending him home in disgrace as LMF. No rehabilitation was attempted. Maybe that first trip was an anomaly and he would have been OK with some help from the rest of us. But he never got the chance. I've always had the niggling thought that but for the grace of God, there go I. This was the saddest episode of my Air Force career. I heard very little talk about LMF while I was on operations and never had any connection with it other than our navigator. I think there is a fine line between battle fatigue and being a coward. There are of course two sides to the argument. The Air Force had to fight it because if you could get out of flying just by saying you didn't want to fly anymore, where would it all end. I think they had to have a strict policy but it should have been conducted with more compassion. (Our replacement navigator, F/O Don LaRiviera from Brockville who had about 11 trips was top-notch).'

On 18 November Ron Read rejoined 78 Squadron and his companions at Linton on Ouse:

'Willie Tait had been posted and we had a new wing commander, Gerry Warner, at 23, cheerful and brisk. I was allocated to 'A' Flight, whose Flight commander was Bertie Neal, a rough diamond of a New Zealander. A lumpy six footer, round faced with dark hair cut short in the approved RAF fashion, Bertie looked and talked like a sheep farmer, although he could have been a bank manager for all we knew, or cared. In Bomber Command we lived for the day ahead. We seldom had time for deep conversations on the pre-war past. In fact, such was our life style; the conversation seldom reverted to anything more recent than our activities of the preceding operation or last night out in York. Bertie had a raucous laugh and a slight speech impediment that gave him a sort of 'slussching' lisp.

'The morning of our arrival Bertie told me I was 'on' that night as second pilot to S/L MacDonald, B flight commander. I didn't mind that. A Sqn Ldr and a flight commander, I was sure he must be an experienced operational pilot. Reporting to him in the afternoon, I met a tall, fair-haired man, with a typical RAF pilot's moustache, who gave me a welcoming smile. Accompanying him to briefing, I noted his calm demeanor and the way he noted down points of importance. He's done this before I thought. I'll be safe enough with him and his experienced crew. His presence relieved some of the natural tension felt in going on my first op. The butterflies were there all right but they fluttered less with Mac as my skipper. Going on ops was the first real test of going into action under fire.

'The blitz had soon become easy to handle, the bombs had been impersonal and random. It was soon obvious that survival was a matter of pure chance. Our life style accepted that and we enjoyed ourselves, even during the worst times. Flying in hostile skies for the first time, was a different proposition. Highly trained people on the ground and in the air were spending their lives trying to stop RAF bombers reaching their target. Tonight we would be subjected to their attention. I felt added relief, when we learned the target was Turin. There were 77 aircraft going. Italian targets were supposed to be easy, the briefing certainly made it sound so. There had been two raids on Genoa previously.[72] After a day's rest, the squadron was going back to continue the pressure on the Italian defenses. The Italian targets came as a welcome relief to those crews who had been engaged in the nasty little battle of Flensburg, the week earlier. In the first attack five Halifaxes were lost out of 28. Two nights later 28 went again but they were recalled after two hours. One didn't get the recall and bombed the target all on his own, to return safely. A second who presumably didn't get it either failed to return.

'I was glad I was starting on such an easy target as Turin with such an experienced crew. Although nervous, it was more the sense of adventure of embarking on a new experience, rather than the fear of going into battle that I felt. I was fairly relaxed during the tense waiting period, between briefing and take off, confident that the experience of my captain and the easy target, would provide a smooth introduction to ops. We took off about 5.30, into the dark November night. I was surprised to note that Mac had a problem correcting the swing on take off. We almost had our starboard wheel on the edge lights before we got off. I assumed that she behaved more awkwardly than ever, with a full load. We had a quiet ride all the way to the Alps. The one scare came when we heard the rattle of a machine gun, very close indeed. It must be close, damn it! We could even smell the cordite. We frantically scanned the dark sky, until the bomb aimer in the front turret, called; 'Sorry skipper, don't worry, it was me. I leant on the button.' We all laughed and relaxed. No wonder it had sounded so close. Privately, I thought it was an odd happening for an experienced crew.

'We were over cloud as we passed Paris. There were a lot of searchlights underneath which looked as though they were following us. Feeling a pygmy among operational giants, I tentatively mentioned this to the skipper. He nodded his acknowledgement but took no action. I kept quiet after that, confident that he knew what he was doing. We had a marvellous view as we crossed the Alps under the rising moon. We could also see the unaccustomed sight of the lighted towns and villages of Switzerland, just down our port side. At 18,000 ft, progress seemed slow but eventually the Alps slid under us and there, ahead of us, I had my first sight of a target. It wasn't all that impressive. There were a lot of searchlights waving about rather aimlessly, some light flak was popping up but it didn't seem threatening at all. There were a few fires burning on the ground. Nonetheless it was a target and there were guns shooting at aircraft. Soon no doubt, they would be shooting at us. I felt the twinges of apprehension grow as we approached, although I was sure Mac would cope. It took a quarter of an hour to reach, then we let down to 8000 ft to make our bombing run. As we closed in, the searchlight activity seemed even less than before and the guns had almost stopped. Just the occasional flash at random. It was the reverse to all we had been led to expect.

'The run up came just as it had in training. A 'left, left', a 'steady' and finally, 'bombs away', from the bomb aimer and we were done. There were lots more fires below as we closed the bomb doors and climbed for the trip home across the Alps. The flak and searchlights were now inactive. Hope it's always like this, I wished silently to myself. It was a long, uneventful flight home and we made it to Linton, after being airborne for nine hours and ten minutes. We landed and were on our way back to flights in the crew bus.

'OK chaps,' said the Squadron Leader,' that's our third.'

'Pardon sir' I asked. 'You mean that was your third trip?'

'Yes, what did you think it was?'

'Well, I – er, I thought – er, we did our second dickey trips with an experienced crew.' I said, somewhat untactfully.

'Mac laughed. 'Well, we're getting to be an experienced crew now. Any complaints about tonight?'

'No sir, not me, I'm quite happy thanks.'

'That was it. My first op, my one and only second dickey trip completed. Now I knew how it felt to go on ops. Or did I? Thoughtfully, back in my own flight office, I crossed off the 'ops completed' square against my name, newly chalked on the crew board. There were 29 adjacent squares awaiting the same treatment. If they were all like tonight it wouldn't be too bad. But I had no illusions; there would be tougher nights than this. I didn't think too much about those. Next time I'd be on my own, except of course, for the anxious fellows who awaited me at flights the next day.

'How did it go skip? What's it like? Have any problems?'

'No. Piece of cake really. If they're all like that, we'll have nothing to worry about.' But I knew in my heart there wouldn't be many like that. Bomber Command didn't provide too many 'pieces of cake' for its crews. They knew that too. I also discovered that the 'What's it like?' question, was impossible to answer. Partly because we'd had such an easy trip, partly because I couldn't put into words, the unique experience of knowing that other people are trying to kill you.'[73]

In November 1942 just ten victories (three by IV./NJG 1 at Leeuwarden) were claimed by *Nachtjagd* and 37 during December. On the night of 17/18th *Hptm* Helmut Lent of *Stab* IV./NJG 1 shot down two Lancasters of 44 and 97 Squadrons.[74] *Oblt* Hans-Joachim Jabs downed an unidentified Stirling and a Lancaster[75] off the Dutch coast.[76] II./NJG 1 claimed three bombers during December. On the 21st *Lt* Heinz-Wolfgang Schnaufer claimed a Lancaster[77] and the bomber crashed at Poelkapelle. III./NJG 1 at Twenthe also claimed three victories and I./NJG 1 one.[78] Total *Nachtjagd* claims for 1942 were 687 aircraft destroyed.

Meanwhile, Bomber Command had to turn its attention to the U-boat menace which by the end of 1942 was threatening Britain's Atlantic sea lanes and the Gardening or aerial magnetic mine-laying campaign off the coastlines of the Third Reich was intensified and would last until the start of the Battle of the Ruhr in March 1943. 21-year old Australian Sgt (later F/O) Colin 'Col' Moir , who flew 25 trips with 420 'Snowy Owl' Squadron RCAF and five with 432 'Leaside' Squadron RCAF 30 May 1942-21 June 1943 as rear gunner in the crew of Canadian Sgt (later P/O) Jim Thomson, recalls:

'An important target group were the U-boat bases located at St. Nazaire, Lorient, Hamburg, Wilhelmshaven and Kiel. These places were consistently harrassed and heavily bombed. Special Intelligence officers at briefings impressed on us crews that the Battle of the Atlantic could be lost, or the war prolonged if supplies, personnel and trained reinforcements could not reach England. In comparison to the Ruhr Valley, these coastal targets were not heavily defended and in some ways jokingly referred to as a 'Cake Run' or a 'Piece of Cake'. We did our best but we were only of a nuisance value. The pens were protected by very thick reinforced concrete, which was hard to penetrate.

'When the day dawned, the weather had to be shocking and the then powers that be decided that 'Ropey' Thomson's crew needed a work out with a mining operation with one or two unlucky crews to keep them company but only in the briefing room, a Nissen hut – rarely did you see another aircraft in the air, when flying on this type of operation. The Nissen hut would have been more crowded for a maximum effort. During briefing, the W/C would state the target: 'Sea lane here off Borkum Island, or Heligoland Bight, etc. Drop Zone of the mine exactly here', marking it on the map. The navigator was briefed carefully as to the exact details, as timing was essential. I had to study the Islands carefully. They were quite flat. I had to memorise details, coves, inlets and bays, especially when the target was Borkum.

'On our way in, the English navigator Bill Shakespeare located the correct Island by his reckoning. The aircraft then descended through the 10/10ths weather to make visual identification. We were usually met with a hail of light flak. Enemy *flak* ships or gun emplacements only fired when your aircraft was in sight as you came out of the fog, cloud, rain or snow squalls. They knew you were alone and obviously they did not want to reveal their position. The Wellington bomber was very low and slow and the tracer shells and bullets were a brief but spectacular sight. Each time you went round or approached the shooting became more intense. They knew you meant business. I never fired back. Luckily they mostly missed. My important job was to read the ground accurately and ignore the fireworks. The correct cove identified, I notified our Canadian pilot Jim Thomson, 'Yes. That's it.'

'The mine was then primed by the bomb aimer or navigator. From the identified spot, a correct height of 500 ft was given, a course set, time in minutes and seconds given to follow the correct path – don't descend below 300 ft etc, keep straight and level with bomb doors open. The pilot decided which height to keep on according to the prevailing conditions. The minutes and seconds were counted off -and we didn't deviate. The 2000-lb mine was dropped on an attached parachute which opened. It then descended quickly into the sea right where we had been briefed it had to go. Naturally we did not stay around and set course for Middleton St. George in Yorkshire.

'Our fourth and most eventful mining operation, in Wellington 3926 'A', took place on the night of 14 December. Our Gardening target lay in the Heligoland Bight, briefing went as usual. When the target was due, I identified a flashing light off a headland jutting out into the sea. You could not miss it as the weather was clear and you could see for miles. Our run was made once and the course set, the mine primed, then all hell broke loose. The Flak was murderous and when you can smell it, it's bloody close.

'BANG'.

'On the intercom our pilot said,'Starboard engine gone. Hell I can't hold it; you can bale out.'

'I said: 'No bloody way Ropey. You can fly it on one engine. The water's too bloody cold and I like Yorkshire better.'

'Mine jettisoned. Get out of the bloody turret and hurry up here and help me.'

'That's just what I did. There was no alternative. I passed Jock McCaffer (WOp/AG) and Bill Shakespeare whose job it was to shut down the petrol lines to starboard and then later alter the petrol cocks to transfer fuel to the port engine. The forward part of the aircraft was full of activity. Tragically, we lost a young Canadian bomb aimer on his first – and last – operation. He must have panicked and jumped through an open hatch and perished. Luckily Jim Thomson and I were very fit and strong and flew the lopsided old Wimpy back over the English coast and belly-landed on a fighter aerodrome. We arrived back at Middleton St. George by train a very sorry lot. No one had noticed our new crew member leave and that was our story at debriefing.'

In December 1942 Sgt Derek Smith, a Lancaster navigator and the rest of his crew arrived at 61 Squadron in 5 Group at Syerston. It was a pre-war permanent station on the Fosse Way with two Lancaster squadrons (the other was 106, commanded by W/C Guy Gibson DSO* DFC*):

'The Station Commander was Gus Walker, who, at the age of 26, the youngest Group Captain in the RAF and an extremely popular CO.[79] We had joined a crack squadron, which considered itself to be among the cream of 5 Group. In its turn 5 Group considered itself to be superior to all other groups although 8 (Pathfinder) Group had just come into being. It still rankled that two squadrons had been removed to form the nucleus of 8 Group.[80] These were reclaimed in 1944 when 5 Group launched itself as the 'Independent Air Force' attacking small, specialized targets -this being Butch Harris's most important concession to the 'panacea target theory'. They proved that, within certain range limitations, small targets could be taken out at night more effectively than in the day by the USAAF, mainly because of the vastly superior bomb load carried). As for the 'crack squadron' theory it may have been just luck or careful selection and training of crews but 61's losses in the Battle of the Ruhr were much the lowest in 5 Group. The Group always did the same ops together but our sister squadron at Syerston, 106, suffered significantly higher losses than we did. Probably, this was just the luck of the draw, which was to play such an important part in our survival but the morale of the squadron was very high during our time there.

'Initially, we were accommodated in a barrack block next to the Sergeants Mess because the Mess was full but we moved over within a matter of days, as rooms became available quite quickly, I regret to say. Sammy Sampson and I moved in to a corner room on the ground floor in the front of the Mess and that was to be our comfortable home for almost six months. Being a peace time permanent station, these quarters were of the highest order and vastly superior to anything enjoyed by commissioned officers on the stations built in wartime.

'Just after we got to Syerston there was a nasty accident on 8 December when an ops kite [Lancaster I R5864 of 61 Squadron] with its bombs on caught fire on the ground. G/C Gus Walker went out to it and the kite blew up killing two men on the fire-tender and blowing his the Group Captain's arm off.[81]

'We considered ourselves to be a fully trained crew when we arrived but I was soon to realize just how wrong we were. I had heard mention of radar navigational aids coming on stream but had never heard mention of the name *Gee*. However, soon after our arrival, the Navigation Leader, a very amiable Australian by the name of F/L Cliff Giles took me to the 'Gee Room'. He introduced me to a *Gee* Chart, which was a normal Mercator's chart with diagonal crossing lines and the magic box called *Gee*. This had a cathode ray tube on its face with two lines of signals, which were transmitted from stations in this country, one far South and the other far North. From this the operator obtained readings which corresponded to the lines on the chart and at their intersection, the position of the aircraft over the ground with very little error. Consequently, by taking three such fixes at three minute intervals, one immediately found the track made good over the ground and the speed over the ground (ground speed) by measuring the distance from first to third fix and multiplying by ten. The technique of operation was logical to someone with my sort of mind, something, which could be assimilated quickly and I required only a short spell of practice. However, this was not so for everyone as quite a lot made very heavy weather of it. Why this was taught on the squadron I never quite understood as navigators had so much spare time on Conversion Units. Perhaps it was just that there were not enough sets to spare at that time.

'By 21 December 1942 we were fit to make our debut over Germany in a Lancaster *D- Dog* and were briefed for one of the longest German trips, Munich, with Cliff Giles along as flight engineer. I was rather nervous, not because, we were going to Germany but because Cliff was alongside (in the event, he left me to my own devices and he told me afterwards I had done an excellent job). We climbed to 20,000 ft and crossed the coast at Dungeness. A fighter was sighted off French coast but we evaded safely. The mountains were beautiful in the moonlight but the target was obscured by cloud and was badly marked. *Flak* was weak but there was some near Mannheim on the return. There was 10/10ths cloud Brussels to base. We were back first at Syerston in 7 hrs ten minutes having flown 1400 miles over England, France, Germany, Luxembourg, Belgium and Holland. 137 aircraft on – 8.8% lost.'

Meanwhile, Ron Read's call to arms in of 78 Squadron had come on 6/7 December:

'The target was Mannheim and we were 'on'. I had not yet been given any gunners so we carried two spares whose crews were otherwise occupied. At briefing we learned we were part of a force of 272 aircraft, Halifaxes, Lancasters, Stirlings and Wellingtons. Our route took us down England to Dungeness, south beyond Paris, into the heart of southern Germany itself and Mannheim. I was busy before take off keeping the crew in good spirits, seeing that they were doing their 'things' and having a chat with our two strange gunners. They all seemed unruffled and we cracked a few feeble jokes as we waited for 'start up'. On board the checks on the aircraft and the crew kept my mind busy and from thinking too much about what lay ahead. Taking off with a full load of bombs and fuel, she was slow. Mindful of Mac's swing, I took it easy and made sure that I had her under control all the way to the lift off. We took up a lot of runway that way but at least we stayed on it. She climbed slowly and was sluggish under the load but I expected that. What I didn't expect was the effect of the turning of the turrets at altitude. It quite shocked me. Over 10,000 ft they acted like a rudder and pushed the aircraft in the opposite direction to their turn. Worse, they pushed the nose down and lost a hundred feet of precious height. I asked the gunners not to turn too quickly or too frequently unless it was for real.

'The fun started while we were circling Dungeness waiting for our correct departure time for France. We became involved in a German air raid on Dover. While I wasn't too impressed with English flak I did think it would be too stupid for words to be shot down by our own guns before we'd left England ... The rest of the outward journey passed without incident. Our only sight of Paris was of gun flashes beneath the cloud and *flak* bursts in the sky. Not too near us, just close enough to aid navigation. The cloud persisted to the target. The forecast of a clearance over the target remained that, just a met forecast. It was covered too. We saw a few pathfinder flares go down before we reached the target area. I flew towards them but they had vanished by the time we arrived and had not been replaced. I stooged around for 20 minutes waiting for more flares. They never arrived but there were a few areas of fires showing through the cloud. I picked one, which I estimated had been closest to the Pathfinder flares we had seen and bombed through cloud on it. It was a flat and disappointing experience. We flogged back across Germany without incident. As we crossed the Channel Jimmy Goodwin, the engineer called:

'We're getting short of fuel skip.'

'I couldn't imagine how that could happen; we'd followed the recommended engine handling procedures and hadn't been hit. 'How short Jim? Can we make Linton?'

'Don't think so skip. I reckon we've got about half an hour's.'

'Down below, the beacon of a coastal airfield blinked invitingly. It proved to be Bradwell Bay. A check confirmed the runway was long enough for a Halifax, so in we went. A day bomber station, they were used to helping night bombers crews in trouble and we were well looked after. I called Linton to advise them of our safe landing. Our first operation was over but we slept in strange beds that night. In the morning, I had breakfast with Johnny McPherson a quiet American from Philadelphia I'd last seen 16 months earlier at Elementary Flying Training in Red Deer, Canada.[82] He was now at Bradwell flying Bostons on daylight raids to France and sounded reasonably happy with his lot. We flew back under very low cloud but we were a light-hearted crew who'd completed their first op safely. The crew's general reaction was that it couldn't be bad if it always went like this. It paid to be optimistic in Bomber Command.

'The next morning our rear gunner arrived. He appeared almost as a manifestation, standing in front of me as he was introduced: a slouching, gap toothed, sloppily dressed, thin faced cockney wearing a big grin and calling himself Jesse James. I wasn't too sure I really wanted him. I had a word with Shorty, our new Gunnery Leader. Shorty said he was good.

'But he looks so scruffy,' I protested.

'Depends on what you want a gunner for,' said Shorty. 'To look smart or shoot 'em down.'

'Finally, I conceded to Shorty's arguments and took him on.

'We were on ops again on 9/10 December. Once more the target was Turin. I was happy about that. It would be a good one to break in the full crew: a long run in operational conditions without, I hoped, too much opposition. There were 227 aircraft of which, 47 were Halifaxes, scheduled for the trip. I didn't have to do much cheering up of the crew in the wait before take off. Jesse James was irrepressible with his cockney humour. His outrageous, much exaggerated accent greatly amused the crews, especially the Canadians. Young Mac McQueen was also keen to get into action and not at all worried about his first trip. The rest were one-trip veterans and Turin was easier than our last target, Mannheim. All went well on the outward journey, except that soon into France, Gee, our wonder navigation-aid was jammed and we had to rely on Vic's dead reckoning for the rest of the trip. The flak around Paris and later the Alps sticking up ahead helped point the way well enough. At the target the scene was much the same as my first trip. Searchlights were ragged, the gunfire, not hostile to start with, was hardly present as we flew over the target. We didn't see much; it was still smokey from a Lancaster raid the previous night. The crew was quite professional in their actions and I was pleased with our performance. I noted that after I operated the lever to close the bomb doors they didn't close, so I pushed it down again and this time they did.

'We were high above the overcast in France when we got a scare.

'Mid-upper to pilot', came Mac's urgent call. 'Fighter overhead going port to starboard. Turn to port, go.'

'I flung her into a descending left turn. The recommended response at that time was to turn into the attacking fighter. I could see nothing in the black sky as I headed down for cloud cover, the Spit's superiority that morning strong in my mind.

'Anyone see anything?' I asked.

'It seems OK Skip', came Mac's voice again. 'Perhaps he couldn't have seen us, he went straight on over us to starboard.'

'I was now just on top of the cloud. We all looked for the fighter as we dropped into it. I sat tight about a hundred feet below the top for 15 minutes, changing course several times. When we popped up again nothing was in sight, the sky was pitch black anyway. En route again, Mac told us he was sure it was one of the new Me 210s, a formidable foe indeed. Upon reflection, Mac thought that he'd seen us and made a beam attack, heading straight for us. For some reason, he couldn't fire his guns.

'We were highly alert for the rest of the trip. But I noted Vic was irritatingly slow to give me an estimated time for crossing the enemy coast. We were well across before he pinpointed us in mid-channel with a *Gee* fix. I put it down to the long trip without any real help from any other aids. At the English coast Jimmy reported that we were again short of fuel. I really couldn't believe it but he insisted. I decided to go back to Bradwell Bay, where they had been so helpful. It was very bumpy as we came lower and there was a strong wind below cloud. We passed over Bradwell's runway at 6000 ft and obtained permission to land, number two. As I descended, unknown to me Jimmy opened the hydraulic valve that isolated the flaps (this was always closed over enemy territory to prevent damage to hydraulic pipes), causing the flaps to fall down inadvertently. At 2000 ft I opened up the engines to slow our rate of descent but the aircraft kept going down at a high rate. I couldn't understand why. 'Have we lost an engine?' I asked Jimmy, who replied in the negative. We continued down in a hurry. I opened more throttle while scanning the instruments for our problem. Finally I had full power and we were just about flying level at 600 ft. I couldn't think why the aircraft was so heavy and sluggish. We now had a big problem. I couldn't climb and when I put the undercarriage down I didn't see how we could stay in the air. What's more, I would have to be very late putting flaps down, if I could put them down at all. 'Flaps! Something stirred in my memory, hastily scanning the instruments, for the umpteenth time, I spotted the flap needle. It was showing 'Full Flap'. Thank God! That's it, we'd got full flaps down. I eased them up, gently at first, then a bit more, as we slowly regained circuit height.

'It was a very rough night and I flew gingerly around the circuit, working hard to keep her in line with the runway. As we made our final approach a strong gust pushed us hard to the right just before landing. I applied full left rudder and it went hard over to the stop. We were just above the ground and it only came back very sluggishly. We touched down on one wheel and bounced to an untidy landing along the edge of the runway. It was a nasty end to what had been a reasonable trip. I had found out the hard way two of the worst design aspects of the Halifax. First was the proximity and similarity of the flap and bomb door levers. They were together on the right hand side of the pilot's seat. The flap lever was a little longer with a small round knob on its end. It operated in the normal sense to put flap down, push down, flaps up, pull up. The bomb door lever was the same shape but with a little spindle protruding through the center of the knob. It operated in the opposite sense. Bomb doors open, pull up. To close, push down. Leaving the target, intending to close the bomb doors, I must have pushed the flap lever down in error the first time. Because the flaps were isolated from the hydraulic system, nothing happened. My second try using the correct lever closed the bomb doors. The flap lever remained fully down. When the engineer opened the valve to feed fluid to flaps they were already selected down and they came fully down without my knowledge causing us to lose height so rapidly. I was looking for the reason for the height loss in the engines and it took time to eliminate those instruments. Fortunately, I thought about the flaps just in time to retrieve our situation. The juxtaposition of two similar levers functioning in opposite senses, was a design fault that could easily have killed us.

'The other fault was in the rudders. They were designed so that at low speeds using heavy foot force it was possible to push the rudder fully to one side. Because of the design, it was not easy to force it back to a central position. Many Halifaxes were lost as a result of this fault, known as 'rudder stall'. I was fortunate that when it occurred we were so low that the wheels touched the runway before we could come to any harm. From more than 50 feet up it could have been an almighty prang. Later rudders were modified to correct it but not entirely successfully.

'But the whole situation arose because of the dreadful design of the fuel system. Back at base, I had a long session with Jimmy as to why we were always running short of fuel. He told me that he was changing the tanks when the gauges, notoriously unreliable, showed empty. He did this to save me from the problem of engines cutting if he waited for the tanks to run dry. Standard practice for a tank change was for the engineer to watch the fuel contents and pressure gauges closely. When fuel pressure started fluctuating, he warned the pilot, left his position and climbed over the main spar into the center of the aircraft. There, he had to look under the rest beds and make his choice of moving two of the five levers, which he could only see at night with a torch. He had to turn the tank in use off before turning the next on to avoid air locks. Then probably, just as he returned to his position, he'd have rush back to do the same for the tanks on the other side. All this time he was off intercom and couldn't hear the pilot. Jimmy wanted time to ensure he didn't, as so many engineers had, select the wrong lever and put engines onto empty tanks, thus cutting more than one engine. The whole system was a mess that was never satisfactorily resolved.

The Halifax fuel system instructions read like a Chinese puzzle. For crews with only a few hours on the aircraft it was frighteningly dangerous under operational conditions.

'There has always been conflict about the relative merits of the Halifax and the Lancaster. There is much to be said for both. The Lancaster had its gauges and a mere two fuel cocks next to the second pilot position. The engineer rode there in the Lanc. Whether seated there or standing up behind in the astrodome on look out, he had no need to move to change tanks. Indeed it was not difficult for the pilot to change the tanks himself: an impossible task in the Halifax. As a result of losses and strong criticism, the Halifax rudders were modified in later marks but the awful fuel cock system and the adjacent flap and bomb door levers stayed with them for the rest of the war. As a result of our experience Jimmy and I perfected a procedure to allow the tanks to drain till the pressure gauge fluctuated. He'd warn me of the engine concerned, hop back in double short time, quickly changing tanks to avoid a full engine cut. We had a couple of occasions when the engines lost power from loss of fuel flow but we never suffered from shortage again. From that night too he warned me whenever he was turning the flap isolating cock on. I checked the flap lever and we never encountered that problem again.

'We reported our encounter with the fighter (a Me 210) to the Intelligence officer at Bradwell, who was most interested. They were only just coming into service and had not been seen by any of their crews. At breakfast I saw Johnny MacPherson again and told him about the 210. He was in a thoughtful mood. On their sweep over France the previous day they had lost two aircraft to Me 109s. He said things were getting tough and looked rather pensive. It was the last time I saw him and I never heard how he fared.

'We were briefed for a trip to Duisburg on the 20th but our Halifax had developed a coolant leak and I said I was not taking her in that state. Our next scheduled trip was Christmas Eve. 'Butch' Harris was not at all popular for this one. We were briefed for Essen, the toughest target of them all. Not much of a Christmas present for anyone. The jokes, as we waited for our buses were more forced than ever; even Jesse was subdued. As we were glumly driving out in the bus there were a lot of Irish laborers working on the taxi track.

'Good luck boyos', they called out. 'Give him one for us. Wisht we was goin' wid yer'.

'I wish you were going instead', I called back.

'We reluctantly climbed into our aircraft and set about our checks. All completed, we were looking at the tower for the green Verey flare, the 'start up' signal. It was long delayed. Eventually a red flare soared into the dull December sky; it was the 'Scrub' signal, cancelling the operation. Cheers went up all round in and outside the aircraft. We piled into the buses, laughing and joking with genuine humour this time. It was a great relief not to have to spend Christmas Eve over the Ruhr. There was a party in the mess that night that went on until early Christmas Day. The next day we were stood down so the previous evening's celebrations continued. After the traditional serving of the airman's Christmas dinner by the officers we returned for our own. By then the mess waitresses, especially Peggy the pretty blonde for whom we all made a play, had to do a lot of dodging of mistletoe clasping, girl grabbing hands. It was a dreary bunch of bomber crews who fell into their beds that Christmas night in 1942.'

Notes

1. Bomber.

2. Luftwaffe code for distance to target.

3. Völlkopf and Huhn's victim was Hampden AT191/A of 408 Sqn, which they hit at 0006 hrs N of Harderwijk. P/O W. Charlton had taken off from Balderton at 2258 hrs. After the nightfighter attack the Hampden cr. in flames into the Ijsselmeer with the loss of the crew. F/Sgt Womar DFM, one of the gunners, was flying his 56th op. On 2 June 1942 *Hptm* Lent presented Huhn with the *EKI* (*Eisernes Kreuz I* or Iron Cross, First Class). *Lt* Heinz-Wolfgang Schnaufer and his Bordfunker *Uffz* Rumpelhardt of *Stab* II./NJG 1 scored their first victory in the early hrs of 2 June. At a height of 3500 m, they fired a burst of cannon fire into Halifax II W1064 of 76 Sqn, which was flying home on 3 engines. At 0155 hrs the a/c cr. nr Grez-Doiceau, 15 km S of Leuven, Belgium, with the loss of Sgt T.R.A. West, pilot and Sgt J.R. Thompson, air gunner. 4 crew baled out safely, 2 of which evaded. It was the first of Schnaufer's final all-time record of 121 night victories.

4. They included Stirling I W7474 HA-K of 218 Sqn flown by 29-year old P/O James Garscadden and P/O John Richard Webber (19) which was shot down by *Uffz* Heinz Vinke of II./NJG 1 S of Den Helder at 0032 hrs. All 7 crew KIA.

5. Peter Buttigieg, a Maltese national, Gaulton and F/Sgt John Farquhar, WoP/AG baled out and Manchester VN-Z L7432 cr. in flames at Beekbergen nr. Apeldoorn at 0233 hrs. German radio traffic on the morning of 4 June referred to a Bf 110 crashing at Deelen. Buttigieg tried to get back to England but was betrayed and fell into the clutches of the *Gestapo*. He survived the war.

6. 12 aircraft – 8 Wellingtons, 2 Stirlings, 1 Halifax, 1 Lancaster FTR. *Nachtjagd* was credited with 8 victories.

7. Stirling I W7471 of 7 Sqn, which was shot down between Blija and Holwerd was claimed by *Oblt* Ludwig Becker of 6./NJG 2 and N3761 BU-E of 214 Sqn flown by F/L R. W.A. Turtle DFC whose crew were on only their 2nd operation, was shot down by *Oblt* Egmont Prinz *zur* Lippe-Weissenfeld of 5./NJG 2 and cr. in the North Sea off Terschelling. Crew KIA. As well as the Stirling and a Manchester of 49 Sqn Becker was also credited with a Wellington of 150 Sqn E of Ameland.

8. L7471.

9. Sgt Alan F. Scanlan and Sgt Ronald Buchanan – and the 6th member of the crew, navigator, Sgt R.F. Davies.

10. X3555.

11. 8 bombers FTR, 7 to night fighters of II./NJG 2 and III./NJG 2 operating in *Himmelbett* fashion over N. Holland and only part of the bomber force identified the target.

12. 2 of which were destroyed by *Oblt* Rudolf Schoenert, *St Kpt* 4./NJG 2.

13. This raid was the last flown operationally by Manchesters, after which the type was withdrawn.

14. The entire 5 Group effort – 142 aircraft – were to bomb the Focke Wulf factory; 20 Blenheims the A.G. Weser shipyard; the Coastal Command aircraft the Dechimag shipyard and all other aircraft were to make an area attack on the town and docks.

15. 'Moose' Fulton and Terence Mansfield landed back at Mildenhall at 0445 hrs. Mansfield had completed his tour and later became Bombing Leader on a Sqn of Lancasters. Fulton FTR from a raid on Hamburg 28/29 July.1942. His nickname was incorporated in the official title of the unit.

16. *H2S* was a navigational radar developed by Dr. Lovell at the TRE (Telecommunications Research Establishment) at Malvern, Worcestershire, which produced a 'map' on a CRT display of a 360° arc of the ground below the equipped aircraft.

17. 29 crews reached the target area. All except 3 (1 of which, AM794, was shot down by *Oblt* Egmont Prinz *zur* Lippe-Weissenfeld, *St Kpt* 5./NJG 2 E of De Kooy airfield) returned safely, 2 with minor shrapnel damage. Hudson V AM762 VX-M of 206 Sqn cr. at Frel nr. Heide; it was shot down by *Oblt* Werner Hoffmann, *St Kpt* 5./NJG 3 for his first night victory of the war. F/Sgt Kenneth Douglas Wright (22) pilot, WOP/AG and an air gunner KIA. Other 2 men aboard PoW. Another 206 Sqn Hudson V AM606 VX-S flown by S/L Cyril Norman Crook DFC (29) cr. into the sea S of Fehmarn Island, shot down by *Lt* Konig of 8./NJG 3. No survivors. Hudson flown by F/L Derek Hodgkinson (later ACM Sir Derek Hodgkinson, KCB CBE DFC AFC) of 220 Sqn, CO of the temporary Operational Hudson Sqn, shot down by 2 u/i Bf 110s attacking simultaneously on the return leg over the Dutch coast. Hodgkinson skilfully ditched his burning aircraft off Ameland, where he and his badly wounded navigator were taken prisoner next day.

18. Barte also claimed a Wellington 30 km N of Hasselt and a Wellington NNE of Maastricht. *Oblt* Heinrich Prinz *zu* Sayn-Wittgenstein of E./NJG 2 claimed a Manchester and a Wellington. Oblt Reinhold Knacke StI/NJG 1, claimed a Halifax 3 km ESE of Weert, a Wellington 10 km E of Weert and a Wellington 3km SW of Middelbeerer. *StFw* Gerhard Herzog of I./NJG 1 claimed 2 Wellingtons as did *Oblt* Helmut Woltersdorf of 7./NJG 1 *Nachtjagd* claimed 30 heavies.

19. Whitley V BD266 of 'B' Flt flown by P/O J.A. Preston, shot down at 0254 hrs by *Major* Kurt Holler of II./NJG 2 N of Vlieland in the North Sea. All 5 crew KIA. (Holler KIA 22 June 1943. 19 victories). Whitley V BD379 piloted by F/O James Brian Monro RNZAF (21) was hit by *Flak* from 5./Marine Flak Battery 246 and cr. into the sea off Terschelling at 0418 hrs. All 6 crew (who were a 'screened' crew and all OTU instructors) KIA. 3 members of the crew removed from the wrecked a/c on 26 June and buried next day. P/O Ian Patterson Clark, WOP/AG washed ashore on 27 June and buried on 29 June. BD379 shot down by *Lt* Günther Löwa of 5./NJG 2 and cr. in the North Sea off Den Helder at 0426 hrs. *Lt* Lothar Linke, *Lt* Robert Denzel and *Lt* Hans-Georg Bötel, also of II./NJG 2, were responsible for 4 Wellingtons, Bötel claiming 2 for his first 2 combat victories. Linke KIA 13/14 May 1943, 27 victories; Denzel KIA 25/26 June 1943. 10 a/c destroyed. Bötel KIA 2/3 July 1942, 3 victories.

20. After flying 273 operational hrs in the RAF and surviving a crash in a 'Wimpy' in the Sinai desert in November 1942, Goldberg transferred to the 8th Air Force.

21. This is possibly the Halifax flown by Sgt A. Aston, which lost 1 or 2 engines on the port side on t/o for an air test on 25 June. On 28 June 1942 Ralph Wood was himself lucky to survive the crash of a Halifax (W7665) at the end of a cross-country exercise. F/Sgt S. Tackley, pilot, was taken to Darlington Hospital, where he died the next day. Wood recalls. 'The flight engineer and WOp were both pretty badly gouged but eventually recovered. A ground-crew member who filled in for the tail-gunner was found in the next field. The aircraft hitting first on one wing had slung him out of the turret like a clay pigeon from a catapult. He had a broken neck, a broken leg, a broken arm and many bruises. Apart from a few bruises and one hell of a scare, I was uninjured. Our Hallybag was literally in pieces. The fuselage was broken into at least 2 sections. The wings were torn off and the engines distributed around us. The meat wagon (ambulance) and fire engines were soon tearing across the fields and took us to the station hospital. We were given a large belt of overproof rum and quick medical, then dismissed. That is, those of us who were still mobile. As we made our way to the mess for tea I thought this had got to be a dream. I shook for 2 hours, as this dream became a startling reality. I came damn close to cashing it in. 24 ops and we had to crap out on a lousy training trip.' Wood was given 2 weeks sick leave in Scotland, flew 3 more ops 28 August-4 September 1942 and was posted to 19 OTU. Commissioned as a P/O, he returned to Canada and in June 1944 returned to fly another 50 ops on Mosquitoes of 692 Sqn. He completed a total of 77 ops in World War II and finished as a F/L with the DFC.

22. 5 Group destroyed an assembly shop at the Focke-Wulf factory when a 4000lb 'Cookie' scored a direct hit. 6 other buildings were seriously damaged.

23. who claimed 9 a/c during June to take his score to 48 *Abschüsse*.

24. Wellington T2612 of 18 OTU shot down at 0237 hrs and cr nr Andijk with the loss of P/O M. Niemczyk and his all-Polish crew. Whitley V BD201 of 10 OTU was shot down by Lent at 0256 hrs to cr. at Wervershoof.

25. Wellington Ic R1078 of 11 OTU near Rheine; Whitley V AD689 of 10 OTU in the vicinity of Lingen-Ems and Stirling I N3754 of 7 Sqn, which came down at Bimolton between 0120 and 0158 hrs.

26. The Hudson was shot down 6 km SE of Heide and the Whitley in *Himmelbett* box Heide/Büsum 6 km E of Busum. Hoffmann began his career as a fighter pilot in ZG 52 (later ZG 2) in August 1938 and he claimed his first victim, a Spitfire, over Dunkirk on 24 May 1940. After a spell of instructing he joined *Nachtjagd* early in 1942 as *Staffelkapitän* 5./NJG 3 and flew with *Bordfunker*, *Ofw* Rudi Köhler. Between June 1942 and the eve of the Battle of Hamburg they scored 8 night bomber kills in the illuminated and *Himmelbett* night fighting. Hoffman was appointed *Gruppenkommandeur* of I./NJG 5 on 5 July 1943, one of the *Gruppen* of NJG 5 stationed in the vicinity of Berlin. He and Köhler claimed a Lancaster N of Berlin as their 9th Abschuss at 0032 hrs on 4 September 1943 (Lancasters of 8 different Sqns crashed in this area during the raid). Their first Tame Boar kill was followed by 19 more Lancasters and Halifaxes, half of them in the Berlin area, in 6 months September 1943-February 1944. Hoffmann ended the war as *Ritterkreuzträger* and *Kommandeur* of I./NJG 5 with 52 *Abschüsse*.

27. of 4./NJG 2 and 4./NJG 3.

28. Koenig had 2 Blenheim day *Abschüsse* in 1941 with 5./ZG 76 before his unit was incorporated into *Nachtjagd* in November as 8./NJG 3.

29. Koenig lost sight in his right eye, which made him unfit for further night-fighting duties but he persuaded his superiors to allow him to join a day-fighting unit (*Jagdstaffel Helgoland*) in March 1943 and he soon made a name for himself in the air battles against the American combat boxes. He destroyed 8 *Viermots* during the ensuing summer months and rose to command 3./JG 11 in October. In April 1944 he was appointed *Kommandeur*, I./JG 11, claiming 4 American bombers shot down on 29 April. After shooting down his 20th *Viermot* over Kaltenkirchen on 24 May the ensuing explosion ripped off the left wing of his Fw 190A-7 and 'King' Koenig crashed to his death. Posthumously promoted to *Hptm* and decorated with the *Ritterkreuz* 19 August 1944.

30. 9 were shot down by nightfighters including 6 by II./NJG 2. 3 of these were Halifax IIs of 405 'Vancouver' Sqn RCAF. W1113 LQ-G piloted by P/O Echin shot down at 0148 hrs by *Oblt* Rudolf Sigmund of II./NJG 2 cr. between Wolvega and Noordwolde. W7714 flown by W/O Sidney shot down at 0214 hrs by *Major* Helm of II/NJG 2 cr. at Sybrandaburen. W7715 LQ-H flown by F/L Liversidge was claimed by two pilots within one minute of each other: *Lt* Rolf Bussmann of III./NJG 3 in into the Borger swamps S of Papenburg at 0145 hrs and *Uffz* Alfred Brackmann of 2./NJG 3 at Bimolton, 7 km. NNW of Nordhorn at 0146 hrs. 4 Wellingtons and 4 Stirling Is lost. Wellington III X3539 of 75 Sqn RNZAF shot down at 0308 hrs by *Oblt* Egmont Prinz *zur* Lippe Weissenfeld of II./NJG 2 and cr. in Waddenzee S of Ameland. P/O W.J. Monk RNZAF and crew KIA. A Wellington III of 57 Sqn, which returned to Methwold carried P/O Buston, RG KIA in a night fighter attack. Stirling I N3706 MG-S of 7 Sqn probably shot down at 0233 hrs by *Lt* Günther Löwa and *Fw* Möller of 5./NJG 2 in Bf 110 Werk Nr. 2669 R4+JN. Bomber cr. in North Sea 35 km NW of Vlieland. F/Sgt M.G. Bailey RCZAF, pilot and MUG and RG PoW. 5 KIA. (Both men in the Bf 110 KIA. Löwa probably collided with the bomber and cr. in the sea nr. his final victim). Stirling I BF310 OJ-H of 149 Sqn shot down at 0302 hrs by *Oblt* Leopold Fellerer of 5./NJG 2. It also cr. in the Ijsselmeer off Schellingwoude. P/O G.W. Simmons, an American from Winston-Salem, North Carolina, and his crew KIA and are buried at Amsterdam.

31. A Bf 110 of 6./NJG 2 flown by *Lt* Hans-Georg Bötel. Bötel KIA 2/3 July 1942, 3 victories.

32. N6082 was shot down at 0204 hrs and cr. in the Ijsselmeer near Wons S of Harlingen. Collins was the only survivor.

33. June-October 1942 75 Sqn RNZAF lost 35 Wellingtons and crews on ops, 10 of which FTR during the moon periods of July. Just 23 crewmembers survived being shot down to be taken prisoner, 2 escaped capture. The other 153 aircrew posted KIA or MIA.

34. Minelaying.

35. W/O II George Vincent Booth RCAF (USA), observer, F/Sgt Warnford Francis Victor Pink, WOP RAFVR and Sgt John Munro, rear gunner, were buried in Nijmegen (Jonkerbos) War Cemetery. Wellington III X3561 KO-X crashed 7km SE of Roermond. Two Wellingtons – both of 115 Sqn – were claimed by *Oblt* Reinhold Knacke, *St.Kpt* 1./NJG 1: X3561 5 km SE of Roermond and X3750 8 km E of Eindhoven for his 22nd and 23rd victories. Of 291 bombers despatched 12 aircraft – 10 Wellingtons, 1 Halifax and 1 Hampden FTR.

36. 76 prisoners escaped from the North Compound of *Stalag Luft III* on the night of 24/25 March 1944 before '*Harry*' (the name of the tunnel) was discovered. ('*Tom*' had been discovered in the summer of 1943 and was blown up by the Germans. '*Dick*' was used subsequently to store tools and equipment for *Harry*.) 50 of the escapers who were captured, including S/L Roger Bushell SAAF, who as 'Big X' organised the successful escape and Brettell, who was caught together with F/Ls R. Marcinus, H.A. Pickard and G.W. Walenn near Danzig, were taken to remote spots and shot in the back of the head by the *Gestapo*. Only Bram van der Stok, Royal Netherlands Navy; F/L Jens Einar Mueller, Royal Norwegian Air Force and F/L Peter Rockland RAF made 'home runs'.

37. 8 of the crews were from 'A' Flight, 6 from 'B' Flight.

38. He was to fly his first operation as an aircraft captain in Wellington X3412.

39. Listening stations in Britain would pick up the resulting continuous note. When the aerial touched the water the signal would stop. The listeners would have the DF loop fix of the position of the bomber when the signal vanished.

40. Clerides, a Greek Cypriot who had been educated at an English Public School, recovering his senses and finding the a/c plunging to earth immediately called up on the intercom. Not realizing he was no longer connected to the system and receiving no reply he assumed the others had baled out. Scrambling back to the emergency hatch in the rear of the fuselage he baled out. In the meantime Fereday had regained control and flattened out at 8000ft. Without navigational instruments he was flying by the seat of his pants. The undercarriage and the open bomb bay were causing excessive drag. Clerides landed safely in the outskirts of a town. A crowd of civilians soon surrounded him. Mistaking his Greek features for those of a Jew the cry of '*Jude*' went up from someone in the mob. In a trice they were rifling his pockets, punching and kicking him. Luckily a detachment of the Luftwaffe arrived and rescued him. He was whisked off to hospital in Bremen where an immediate operation was carried out on his leg. After the war Clerides qualified as a barrister. He became President of the Creek Cypriots.

41. On Friday 21 August 1942 the body of Sgt Kelvin Shoesmith RAAF was recovered from Ho Bay in Denmark. Frank Skelley's body was washed ashore on the Dutch coast.

42. W1153 of 102 Sqn.

43. 7.2% of the total force despatched – 15 Wellingtons, 8 Halifaxes, 2 Hampdens of 420 Sqn, 2 Lancasters and 4 Stirlings. 2 other a/c cr. on return.

44. R5748 of 106 Sqn at 0205 hrs. Most of Bomber Command's inward and outward routes on raids against German targets were over the Netherlands and during 1941-1943 the crack night-fighting *Geschwader* NJG 1 and NJG 2 were based at various airfields in the Low Countries. Operating from Leeuwarden II./NJG 2 destroyed an estimated 320 bomber aircraft. All *Major* Helmut Lent's first 65 night victories (May 1941-July 1943) were claimed whilst flying from Leeuwarden. *Oblt* Heinz-Wolfgang Schnaufer claimed 32 of his all-time record total of 121 night victories whilst serving with the Leeuwarden *Gruppe*.

45. Bad weather over the stations of 1, 4 and 5 Groups prevented their participation. Ultimately 256 aircraft – 165 of 3 Group and 91 OTU comprising 161 Wellingtons, 71 Stirlings and 24 Whitleys took part.

46. Sidwell, Sgt W.F. Carter, flight engineer and Sgt A.L. Crockford a new pilot on the Sqn who joined the crew late on to fly as 'second dickey' for experience, survived and were soon captured. F/L Whiteman, Sgt Albert Bates, a replacement for Sgt Paddy Leathem, the mid-upper gunner who had reported sick late on, Sgt Frank McIntyre, WOp/AG and Sgt John Boyle, navigator were KIA.

47. 5 went down in NW Germany, X3452 in the mouth of the Eider River to an u/i nightfighter; Z1570 was shot down by *Lt* Geiger of 8./NJG 1 at Hastenkamp nr. Neuenhaus. BJ661 was destroyed at 0305 hrs on its way back over the Ijsselmeer in a surprise attack from below and behind by *Lt* Wolfgang Kuthe of 5./NJG 2 with the loss of 3 crew. During the course of the night Nachtjagd claimed an estimated 24 a/c destroyed, mainly in *Himmelbett* fashion.

48. 16 Wellingtons and 9 Stirlings of 3 Group or 15.2% of those despatched FTR. A 10 OTU Whitley crashed into the sea and 4 Wellingtons of 16 and 22 OTUs also FTR. Only 68 crews reported bombing in the target area, their bombs scattering over a wide area and relatively little damage was done to Hamburg.

49. Saarbrücken suffered severe damage and casualties in the center and NW districts. 396 buildings destroyed and 324 seriously damaged. 155 people killed. Of the 291 aircraft despatched on 29/30 July, 9 aircraft – 3 Wellingtons, 2 Halifaxes, 2 Lancasters and 2 Stirlings – lost. Nightfighters claimed 7 of these losses.

50. 308 Wellingtons, 113 Lancasters, 70 Halifaxes, 61 Stirlings, 54 Hampdens and 24 Whitleys. 29 a/c FTR; 18 of which were shot down by *Himmelbett* nightfighters.

51. 2 a/c of 18 Sqn and 21 OTU shot down by *Hptm* Werner Streib *Kommandeur* I./NJG 1 and 7 by II./NJG 1. *Lt* Heinz-Wolfgang Schnaufer of *Stab* II./NJG 1 destroyed 2 Wellingtons (of 25 and 27 OTUs) and a Whitley of 24 OTU. 453 buildings in Düsseldorf and Nuess destroyed and more than 15,000 damaged with 279 people killed and over 12,000 'bombed out'.

52. On 12 August 1942 *Lt* Hans Autenrieth, adjutant of II./NJG 1 and his regular *Bordfunker Uffz* Adam worked in concert with the Ground Controller of Raum [area] 6B during a successful interception of Wellington BJ767 of 75 Sqn RNZAF, which cr in flames 700m SW of Vaals, the Netherlands at 0133; Autenrieth and Adam's 4th confirmed kill. *Lt* Autenrieth's first night *Abschuss* was Halifax I L9531 of 76 Sqn on 12/13 August 1941. By 26 November 1943 he had claimed 14 *Himmelbett Abschüsse*.

53. Of 16 bombers, which FTR, 5 were Wellingtons, all of whom were shot down by nightfighters. Crews of NJG 1 and NJG 4, patrolling in the *Himmelbett* boxes in Belgium and Northern France were credited with 14 victories.

54. 142 Sqn lost 5 of the 15 Wellingtons despatched from Waltham. At least 1 of these (Z1396) was shot down by a nightfighter on its way back from Kassel by *Oblt* Rudolf Altendorf of 2./NJG 3 at Erika, NW of Meppen on the Dutch-German border. 31 bombers, 21 of them Wellingtons FTR. *Nachtjagd* was responsible for the majority of these losses, being credited with 23 confirmed kills during the course of the night.

55. Sgt A.F. 'Sunshine' Smith was killed when on the night of 6/7 December 1942 P/O W.C. Hillier MiD's crew in Halifax II BB242 of 76 Sqn FTR from the raid on Mannheim.

56. On the raid on Krefeld on 2/3 October 1942 F/O Geoff M. Hobbs was flying in Halifax II W1275 with F/L G.C. Foers' crew who were on their 28th trip. Foers, who had been very seriously injured following a mid-air collision with a Hampden of 14 OTU near March, Cambridgeshire returning from ops to Cologne on 30/31 May 1942, and 5 of his crew, were killed.

57. IV./NJG 1 claimed 3 Halifaxes and 5 Wellingtons. Among them were Lancaster R5682 of 61 Sqn, which cr nr Wartena and Halifax W1220 of 103 Sqn, which cr. N of Leeuwarden.

58. Even so, 5 Wellingtons and 2 Halifaxes were lost, 4 of them to nightfighters.

59. At least 16 a/c, or almost half the losses this night were shot down by nightfighters of NJG 1 and NJG 2. These include 8 OTU Wellingtons. 16 OTU at Upper Heyford lost 5 of 13 Wellingtons despatched. I./NJG 2, the former intruder Gruppe flying the Ju 88C-6, had returned from North Africa earlier that month to resume *Himmelbett* night-fighting duties in the west from Gilze-Rijen and *Oblt* Schultz destroyed Wellington R1616 of 22 OTU at 2345 hrs near Biervliet.

60. 'All aircrew were Sergeants and above because of the dangers of being shot down over enemy territory to ensure slightly better treatment in captivity. Pay was very good by the standards of the day but I was one of the lucky ones who lived to enjoy it while so many of my friends and colleagues only received it for an extremely short period.'

61. Lost on the operation to Kassel on 3/4 October 1943 when all of W/C W.M. Penman DFC AFC MiD's crew were killed.

62. 15 Wellingtons, 2 Lancasters, a Halifax, a Whitley and a Stirling. *Nachtjagd* scored 13 confirmed kills, all but one of these achieved over the Netherlands and the Dutch coast.

63. On 17 September *Oblt* Schultz of II./NJG 2 probably shot down Wellington DV941 of 26 OTU at 0010 hrs 2 km W of Egmont. *Ofw* Lüddeke of the 3rd *Staffel* NJG 2 claimed an unidentified Stirling shot down at 2315 hrs on 19 September in box 'Gorilla' off the Dutch coast. On 19 September 1942 6 Mosquito IV bomber crews of 105 Sqn carried out the first daylight Mosquito raid on Berlin. Two crews were forced to return early. Another crew bombed Hamburg after finding Berlin covered by cloud. Another jettisoned their bombs near Hamburg. One crew succeeded in bombing the 'Big City'. One Mosquito was shot down.

64. R9187 of 218 Sqn flown by S/L C. Raymond DFC, a New Zealander serving in the RAF (all KIA) cr. 40 km N. of Nordeney.

65. A few days later I./NJG 2 moved further south and in February 1943 began flying *Himmelbett* sorties in Italy.

66. Lancaster I R5701 of 97 Sqn at Brunssem on the 5/6th and a Halifax, probably W7850 of 103 Sqn nr. Roermond on the 15/16th.

67. 22 Wellingtons made cloud-cover daylight raids on Essen, the Ruhr and the Dortmund-Ems Canal at Lingen again. 13 a/c bombed estimated positions through cloud. 1 Wellington came down low and machine-gunned a train near Lingen, setting some of the carriages alight. No a/c losses.

68. 25 Halifaxes, 23 Stirlings and 23 Wellingtons.

69. 4 Wellingtons and 2 Halifaxes FTR. All were shot down by nightfighters of NJG 2 and NJG 4 operating over France and on the SE Dutch coast.

70. 65 aircraft carried out minelaying to various places from Lorient to the Friesian Islands. 2 Wellingtons and 1 Stirling FTR.

71. 'Lacking in Moral Fiber', as it was euphemistically called, which next to the unknown was the greatest fear to be found. The layman has the harsher but more accurate word for it – cowardice.

72. 13/14 and 15/16 November.

73. 77 heavies were despatched to Turin. No aircraft lost. Another raid was made on Turin on 20/21 November by 232 bombers. 3 FTR.

74. Lancaster ED355 of 44 Sqn was claimed at 2022 hrs at Woudsend and Lent shot down Lancaster ED333 of 97 Sqn 16 mins later into the Ijsselmeer off Urk for his 55th and 56th kills.

75. Probably W4382 of 50 Sqn.

76. Jabs was a seasoned combat veteran who had his first taste of action during the Battles of France and Britain when he served as a Bf 110 *Zerstörer* ('Destroyer') pilot in ZG 76. He quickly became one of the leading fighter pilots in the Bf 110 day-fighter force with 7 a/c shot down during the Battle of France and another 12 Spitfires and Hurricanes over England during the summer of 1940. Decorated with the *Ritterkreuz* October 1940 and thereupon successfully led his 6./ZG 76 during the campaign in Crete. His *Staffel* became 9./NJG 3 in November 1941 and on completion of night fighter training Jabs became an operational night fighter pilot. He went on to claim his 1st night kill (an u/i Stirling) on 25/26 June 1942 and was appointed *Staffelkapitän* of the elite 11./NJG 1 at Leeuwarden in November 1942. By the end of 1942 he had shot down 4 RAF night bombers.

77. R5914 of 106 Sqn in Raum 6C at 2353 hrs.

78. *Hptm* Streib destroyed Wellington III BJ589 of 156 Sqn near Heijen on 20/21 December.

79. Later Air Marshal Sir Gus.

80. Formed originally from 3 Group, using volunteer crews, 8 Group started as a specialist PFF force on 15 August 1942 and on 13 January 1943 it became 8 Group (PFF). By March 1945 8 Group numbered 19 squadrons, ten of them equipped with Mosquitoes

81. Guy Gibson in his autobiography *Enemy Coast Ahead* writes of the incident, which occurred at dusk on the night of 8/9 December 1942 when 133 aircraft of 5 Group and the Pathfinder force set out for Turin: 'It all happened on one of the worst nights I can ever remember. We were sending a lot of aircraft off and it was dusk ... About 30 aircraft were taxiing around the perimeter track waiting for each other to take off. Gus and I were watching from the control tower. Suddenly, right on the far side of the aerodrome, we saw that a few incendiaries had dropped out of the gaping bomb doors of one of the Lancasters. Gus, thinking that this aircraft had a 'Cookie' on board, immediately rushed over to warn the crew to get out. I saw his car go speeding straight across the aerodrome, over the runways in front of aircraft taking off, to carry out his plan. But we knew it was a reserve aircraft and I had to stay in the watch tower, anyway, now that he had gone. Watching him through field glasses, I saw him get out of his car. I saw him run towards the aircraft, his arms waving against the lurid light cast up by the incendiaries. He was within twenty yards of the Cookie when it went off. There was one of those great slow explosions which shot straight into the air for about 2,000 feet and the great Lancaster just disappeared. We turned away, trying not to think of the horrible sight; we thought that Gus had surely been blown sky high. But he was too tough for that. He had been bowled over backwards for about 200 yards; he had seen a great chunk of metal swipe off his right arm just below the elbow but he picked himself up and walked into the ambulance. Ten other men, belonging to the fire tender crew, were also injured ... Before he was taken to a base hospital he said two things. He asked me if I would look for his arm, which had a brand new glove on it, and he told me to ring up the AOC and ask him if he would take a one-armed Station commander in two months' time. And Gus came back in that time to the day.' None of the crew was injured but Walker, who was within 20 yards away, lost his right arm.

82. There were153 training schools in the UK (which trained over 88,000 aircrew) and 180 overseas under the British Commonwealth Air Training Plan. Canada became the main center with 107 training stations (14 for the RAF's use) that turned out 137,000 aircrew. Australia trained 27,000 at 20 schools, New Zealand trained 5000 at 6 schools, South Africa trained 25,000 at 25 schools and Southern Rhodesia trained 10,000 at 10 schools. India had 9 schools. 6 more training schools were in the Middle East. In 1941 7 British Flying Training Schools were established. During May 1941-1945 21,302 airmen from 31 foreign nations graduated from flying and technical schools in the USA, 12,561 of which were British.

CHAPTER FOUR

RAF BOMBER OFFENSIVE 1943 AND THE BATTLE OF THE RUHR

By early 1943 Kammhuber's *Himmelbett* defenses had been completed and the Lichtenstein AI-equipped[1] *Nachtjagd* aircraft were now capable of exacting a toll of up to six per cent bomber casualties on any deep penetration raid into the Reich. Thus, Bomber Command losses rose rapidly during the first few months of 1943 although in early January operations were of neccessity, on a limited scale, normally to the U-boat bases on the Atlantic coast.

On 13/14 January 66 Lancasters were despatched to Essen. Sgt Robert S. Raymond, one of a small number of 'Yanks' in Bomber Command piloted a Lancaster of 44 Squadron. He recalled[2]:

> 'Briefing is always a by pretty grim business when that target is announced. Price, W/Op, said, 'You faint and I'll carry you out.' We took a second pilot, a new boy on the squadron, to give him some experience. It was his first operational flight and he was still shaking after we landed. My boys are absolutely steady and normal under fire now, although we had never seen so many searchlights nor so great a barrage as over the Ruhr. It still represents to me a marvelously beautiful picture, especially on such a night with a few scattered clouds and the moon in its second quarter.
>
> 'The sky was steel blue and everywhere below. There was the restless criss-cross pattern of long white beams. The bright pinpoints of the bursting heavy *Flak* shells at our level, left big, dark smoke puffs that were often mistaken for balloons by the uninitiated observer. The long strings of red tracers from the light *Flak* guns were being hosed up like liquid corkscrews. The brilliant flares that hang interminably between heaven and earth and never seem to move, the photoflashes exploding near the ground with a piercing blue-white light. Then the long strings of incendiaries being laid out in geometrical patterns among the buildings and the great red mushroom explosions of the 4000-pounders. It is destruction on a colossal scale and terrifying in its concentration and intensity.
>
> 'We carried a 4000-pounder and more than a thousand incendiaries. It was the shortest trip we've ever made. We're usually among the last to return to base, because both Griffiths and I believe in saving our engines. He's a miser with petrol, quite rightly and his most famous remark was in crossing the Alps when I asked for more power to gain height. He opened the throttles about half an inch and said, 'There, that's all you can have.' His knowledge of our engines, due to long experience, is amazing for a young man of 19 years. One of our engines overheated badly at more than half-throttle, so that it wasn't much help. He and I talked over the possibilities and procedures in such cases by cutting other crew members off the intercom; otherwise they'll have too much to think about. The air temperature was -30° C and the North Sea is pretty cold at this season.
>
> 'Interrogation after the trip is always a pleasant time. It is carried out in the warm, brightly-lighted mess while we are eating. WAAFs move about serving food; all our own officers are around and usually a number from the Air Ministry look on; much laughter, many inquiries among the crews about incidents en route. There is much kidding if you didn't land promptly in your turn. The whole scene was a complete contrast to that of half an hour ago when most of us were stacked on the circuit listening to the others and the WAAF in the control tower, cursing like troopers if any stooge didn't land on first try.'

On 16/17 January Berlin was bombed for the first time in 14 months by 190 Lancasters and 11 Halifaxes.[3] Air Marshal Sir Arthur Harris, C-in-C, Bomber Command sent them on their way with the words, 'Tonight you are going to the big City. You will have the opportunity to light a fire in the belly of the enemy that will burn his black heart out.' Only one Lancaster was lost but the raid was a disappointment. Thick cloud en route and haze over the target caused problems and the bombing was scattered. The Berlin flak had proved light and ineffective and it was assumed that the greater altitude of the attacking force had surprised the German gunners.

Harris repeated the raid on Berlin, sending 170 Lancasters and 17 Halifaxes back to the Big City the following night, 17/18 January, when the weather was better. Broadcaster Richard Dimbleby reported on the raid for the BBC, flying with W/C Guy Gibson, the CO of 106 Squadron at Syerston in Lancaster I R5611/W in a 9 hr 15 minute round trip.[4] Next morning British listeners tuning in to the BBC Home Service heard Dimbleby's broadcast on their wireless sets:

> 'The Berlin raid was a big show as heavy bomber operations go: it was also quite a long raid, and the Wing Commander who took me stayed over Berlin for half an hour The flak was hot but it has been hotter. For me it was a pretty hair-raising experience and I was glad when it was over, though I wouldn't have missed it for the world. But we must all remember that these men do it as a regular routine job. The various crews who were flying last night from the bomber station where I'd been staying had flown on several of the Essen raids, and that means that night after night they've been out over one of the hottest ports of Germany, returning to eat, drink and sleep before going out again. That's their life, and I can promise you it's hard, tiring and dangerous.
>
> Four-engined Lancasters, Halifaxes and Stirlings roared out over the North Sea. We flew among them, and turning back from the cockpit to look into the gorgeous sunset, I counted 30 or 40 Lancasters seemingly suspended in the evening sky. They were there wherever you looked – in front, behind, above and below – each a separate monster, each separately navigated, but all bound by a co-ordinated plan of approach and attack. Up above the clouds, the dusk was short The orange and crimson of sunset died back there where the coast of England lay, and ahead of us the brilliant moon hung with the stars around her; below us, the thick clouds hid the sea. We were climbing steadily, and as it grew dark we put on our oxygen masks when the air grew too rarified for normal breathing.
>
> As we approached the enemy coast I saw the German Ack-Ack. It was bursting away from us and much lower I didn't see any long streams of it soaring into the air, as the pictures suggest: it burst in little yellow, winking flashes, and you couldn't hear it above the roar of the engines. Sometimes it closes in on you, and the mid- or tail-gunner will call up calmly and report its position to the Captain so that he can dodge it. We dodged it last night, particularly over Berlin: literally jumped over it and nipped round with the Wing Commander sitting up in his seat as cool as a cucumber, pushing and pulling his great bomber about as though it were a toy.
>
> We knew well enough when we were approaching Berlin. There was a complete ring of powerful searchlights waving and crossing, though it seemed to me that most of our bombers were over the city. Many of the lights were doused: there was also intense flak. First of all they didn't seem to be aiming at us. It was bursting away to starboard and away to port in thick, yellow clusters and dark, smokey puffs. As we turned in for our first run across the city it closed right round us. Far a moment it seemed impossible that we could miss it, and one burst lifted us in the air as though a giant hand had pushed up the belly of the machine but we flew an.
>
> Just then another Lancaster dropped a load of incendiaries, and where, a moment before, there had been a dark patch of the city, a dazzling silver pattern spread itself a rectangle of brilliant lights – hundreds, thousands of them – winking and gleaming and lighting the outlines of the city around them. As though this unloading had been the signal, score after score of fire bombs went down, and all over the dark face of the German capital these great incandescent flower-beds spread themselves. It was a fascinating sight. As I watched and tried to photograph the flares with a cine-camera, I saw the pin-points merging, and the white glare turning to a dull, ugly red as the fires of bricks and mortar and wood spread from the chemical flares.
>
> We flew over the city three times, for more than half an hour, while the guns sought us out and failed to hit us. At last our bomb-aimer sighted his objective below, and for one unpleasant minute we flew steady and straight Then he pressed the button and the biggest bomb of the evening, our 3 1/2-tonner, fell away and down. I didn't see it burst but I know what a giant bomb does and I couldn't help wondering whether, anywhere in the area of the devastation, such a man as Hitler, Göring, Himmler or Goebbels might be cowering in a shelter. It was engrossing to realise that the Nazi leaders and their

Ministries were only a few thousand feet from us, and that this shimmering mass of flares and bombs and gun-flashes was their stronghold.

We turned away from Berlin at last – it seemed we were there far an age – and we came home. We saw no night fighters, to our amazement, nor did any of the flak on the homeward journey come very near us. We came back across the North Sea, exchanged greetings of the day with a little coastwise convoy and came in to England again, nine hours after we had flown out. There were so many machines circling impatiently round our aerodrome that we had to wait up above for an hour and twenty minutes before we could land and it was two o'clock in the morning when the Wing Commander brought us dawn to the flarepath and taxied us in.

We climbed stiffly out, Johnny from the tail turret, Brian who used to be a policeman from the mid-upper, Hutch, the radio operator, Junior the navigator – by far the youngest of us all. Then the Scots co-pilot, a quiet calm sergeant, and last the short sturdy Wingco who has flown in every major air raid of this war and been a night fighter pilot in between times. They were the crew – six brave, cool and exceedingly skilful men.[5]

Perhaps I am shooting a line far them but I think somebody ought to. They and their magnificent Lancasters and all the others like them are taking the war right into Germany. They have been attacking and giving their lives in attack since the first day of the war and their squadron went on that show too. 'Per ardua ad astra' is the RAF motto. Perhaps I can translate it 'Through hardship to the stars'. I understand the hardship now and I'm proud to have seen the stars with them.'

Nineteen Lancasters and three Halifaxes were lost[6] Nineteen of these were claimed shot down by *Himmelbett*-operating *Nachtjäger*. *Uffz* Karl-Georg Pfeiffer of 10./NJG 1 claimed one of the Lancasters[7] over the North Sea ten km west of Vlieland at 2329 hrs in bitterly cold weather as his second *Abschuss*:

'The 10th *Staffel* (*Oblt* Sigmund) to which I had been assigned had recently returned to Leeuwarden from Gilze-Rijen. (The *Staffel* had been sent to Gilze-Rijen for a few weeks because attacks had been expected on the towns of Tilburg, Breda and Eindhoven. The attack on the Philips works at Eindhoven had actually taken place on a bright Sunday [6 December 1942]. By the time we night fighters had arrived it was all over.) We took off at 2201 hrs and flew to the operational area *Tiger* (around Terschelling Island) and orbited for hours over the radio beacon. The *Jägerleitoffizier* announced monotonously at regular intervals: 'No *Kuriere* in sight' and we had to continue orbiting. We were at about 6000 meters. Suddenly the *Jägerleitoffizier* shouted, 'Have *Kurier* for you, Kirchturm 10 (1000 meters), course 300°, *Kurier* flying from two to 11.'[8] So power off quickly and I dived from 6000 to 1000 meters. Meanwhile ground control reported, 'Kirchturm 5' so the Britisher was down to 500 meters over the water on course for home. Unfortunately the visibility at this height was extremely hazy; no more than 500 meters in good but diffuse moonlight. Then it was '*Kirchturm* 2', so I went down even lower. Attack was impossible at this height and also, the *Lichtenstein* radar gave no indications close to the ground.

'We were now flying at no more than one hundred meters over the North Sea and strained our eyes. According to the information from the *Jägerleitoffizier* we were a little offset behind him: '1000 meters, 800 meters, 500, 400, 300 meters!' Power off and minimum speed in order not to overtake him, we had to attack from behind and that at the dangerous rear turret of the *4-mots*! Suddenly I saw about 200 meters on my starboard bow something gray in the thick soup. So he had not spotted us yet. Calm now! Guns armed? Night sight switched on? Everything OK! Now I could see that it was an Avro Lancaster. I applied a little more power and approached him cautiously. No sudden movement, that attracted their attention! Now I was exactly behind him at about 100 meters range. The rear turret was clearly recognisable. My radio operator kept silent. Suddenly the rear turret was lit up in a flickering light. The head of the gunner with his helmet appeared and I realized that the poor fellow was lighting a cigarette. He felt he was already safely home. Any further delay would be crazy. I pressed the gun button on the stick and was startled at the rattle of the cannon. I stayed behind him firing and observed the projectiles striking the rear turret and the fuselage. Suddenly both inner engines caught fire. The great night bird dipped down and crashed into the sea. The escaping petrol spread fire over the water and was still alight as we reported our success and set course for Leeuwarden, where I landed at 2346 hrs. For a beginner with only one *Abschuss* this was a precarious situation but at the time we were still optimistic and trusted that only the other one would suffer.'[9]

First trip in the New Year for Sgt John Michaud's crew in 425 *'Les Alouettes'* Squadron RCAF was to drop mines in Brest harbour on 2/3 January as F/Sgt Jack Woodrow, Wellington observer recalls:

'The mines were not dropped due to bad visibility preventing pinpointing and the *Gee* pulses also faded. We landed at Middle Wallop in southern England and returned to Dishforth on 3 January. On our next trip on 9/10 January we planted two 1500-lb mines from 800 ft off the Friesians and saw both parachutes open. On 14/15 January we dropped mines on *Gee* from 800 ft at Brest harbour again. Visibility was good and 'Mac' McMillan the rear gunner, saw the parachutes open. We landed at Harwell in southern England because of range difficulties. We took off from Harwell for our sixth trip and bombed Lorient from 15,000 ft with seven 500lb bombs. Fires were observed. We landed back at Dishforth.[10]

'For the first time on 26/27 January when we went to Lorient, we carried the 'Cookie', which the squadron had just started to receive. This was the first of the so-called 'light case' bombs: a mild steel tube into which molten RDX explosive was poured. This resulted in a bomb weighing 4000 lbs. It became a major weapon in Bomber Command's arsenal – a bomb noted for its tremendous blast. Bigger and more powerful 'Cookies' would appear later in the war carried by the Lancasters and the Halifaxes. They were ideal weapons for area bombing and were perfect partners for the incendiaries. These were 4-lb bombs packed into containers, which broke open when dropped. There was also a 30-pound phosphorus-filled incendiary bomb. Our bomb loads could vary considerably depending on what was being bombed. It could vary from one 'Cookie' to different combinations of 250, 500; 1000-pound bombs mixed with incendiaries. We bombed from 15,000 ft with the 'Cookie'. There was no cloud but hazy. Good visibility. Saw our bombs burst in southern part of town. There were plenty of fires on both sides of the river. Defenses were negligible over the target but there was much more flak when crossing the coast. I noted in my log, 'A successful trip.'[11]

Sgt Michaud's was one of 19 Wellington crews despatched to various targets in Germany on 30 January as F/Sgt Jack Woodrow recalls:

'The purpose, according to the Intelligence Officer was 'to create despondency and despair among the refugees from Cologne'. There was supposed to be low cloud cover that we could hop into if required. We had bad weather but we didn't have our low cloud cover. I noted in my log, 'Another Met cock-up. Who thought up this operation must have had rocks in his head. Pretty stupid'. Under these conditions we were allowed to turn back without bombing Oldenburg. I had some fun on this trip. I was in the front turret and shot at anything that moved – livestock, dogs, etc. Didn't see any people.'

Equally scathing was P/O Don Bateman was pilot of one of the eight Wellington crews of 466 Squadron RAAF dispatched to Emden:

'This operation was set up at very short notice and did not appear to be co-ordinated. A hurried briefing gave no mention of the primary target. My bomb aimer could not be located in time and a spare man had to be drafted in. I did not relish flying over Germany in daylight at this stage of the war. British bombers were heavily outgunned by cannon firing German fighters and were easily out maneuvered but I believe the majority of pilots when briefed to fly in daylight to Emden were more concerned about the weather conditions at take off, which were the worst I had experienced up to that time. Aircraft took off as soon as they were ready into heavy rain, low cloud and a strong gusty wind. The met forecast was accurate except for being two hours out in the timing of the dispersal of low cloud over Holland and Germany. I did not see any Boston aircraft. I spotted a Wellington approaching the Dutch coast but did not attempt to formate on it, as we were about to enter a layer of cloud. The height flown varied between 1500 and 2500 ft, my main concern being to fly within the densest cloud layer, given the forecast weather conditions. I did not anticipate any fighter attacks whilst flying in cloud. We were told at briefing that the German fighters were likely to be grounded by the weather.

'We had been told to expect barrage balloons protecting the target, the bomb bursts were both felt and heard, though no results were observed, the bombs being fused with several seconds delay. 'Reaching longitude 6'30' east on the return flight we emerged into clear skies and unlimited visibility. I was tempted to turn on a northerly course and get out to sea as quickly as possible but there being no ground fire or fighters to be seen. I decided to continue on my westerly course and to get down low. I may well have passed within a mile or so of Leeuwarden airfield but my main occupation was scanning the skies for fighters. Crossing the North Sea we ran into the cold front that had been over base at take-off. Visibility under the low cloud was poor so I climbed to 4000 meters to avoid the possibility of icing and was glad to break cloud just clearing the Yorkshire coast.'[12]

Attempts were now made to try to improve the Halifax as Ron Read in 78 Squadron recalls:

'Our aircraft changed in recognition of new German tactics. Some time in January 1943 the front turrets were removed and a new nose section fitted. There wasn't much point in carrying a front gun. Nothing was slower than we were and unless an enemy aircraft was foolish enough to fly in front of us and throttle back we weren't going to be able to shoot them down. In early February our mid-upper turrets were also taken out and faired over. This was a Cheshire modification. Again there was little use for them. Almost all fighter attacks were now being made from below. It was decided that the reduction of weight would give more speed and height. To help the illusion along, aircraft so modified were recoded from a Halifax II to a Halifax II Series 1 Special. Whatever they called it, it remained a lumbering, under-powered, sitting target for enemy night fighters. Now we had only the rear turret to fight back with. With four puny .303 inch Browning machine guns of limited range we were at a great disadvantage to the Ju 88 night fighters who now carried three 20mm cannon and three 7.9mm machine guns in the nose as well as a 13mm machine gun facing the rear. We asked for .5-inch machine guns to give us a chance of reaching them since sitting behind us out of range they could pump canon shells and heavy caliber bullets at us with impunity. We never got them, although later a few 5 Group Lancasters were fitted with them. We were slowly becoming aware that most of the attacks were now being made from the blind area beneath us. With the withdrawal of the mid-upper turret we had a spare gunner. To help to improve the total blind spot that existed below, a small blister window was fitted in the floor of the fuselage. Here, the poor mid-upper had to lie on his belly with his head poked into the blister to try to spot a climbing fighter. Someone could do this for a short period but lying on his stomach, head lowered through the floor into the blister; it was absurd to expect anyone to stay alert for the long hours over enemy territory.

'Another change was the removal of the shrouds covering the glowing exhaust pipes either side of each engine. Their effect on the airflow over the wings reduced performance. With their removal we gained a hundred feet or two in height but were left with eight red-hot glowing exhausts displayed to the world above and behind. A Beaufighter pilot flying in bad visibility thought the exhausts he saw from a Halifax was a flare path and tried to land along it. We were always vulnerable and the improving fighter radar was making life even more difficult.'

Read's crew returned from two weeks leave and did a trip to Cologne on 2/3 February:

'We now had our own aircraft, *C-Charlie* in squadron terms, HR657 in official documents. It was not new but had only done three trips. We didn't worry about that. She was ours, to me as pilot, my very own 'kite.' We mightn't have been so sanguine had we known that the average life of a Halifax was ten trips but we didn't know and were never told those unpleasantries. We would have ignored them if we had known. There was nothing you could do about it. Technically Cologne was not in the Ruhr but for us it was our first trip to the Ruhr: Happy Valley to all who'd been there and most that hadn't. It was a trip that brought out all the butterflies. The real thing at last and it was here that we started our own little superstitious rituals. Mac had been given a stuffed penguin mascot called Percy by a girlfriend. Fixed to the bulkhead behind the engineer's panel he became our travelling companion on all our trips. We had his image painted on the side of the cockpit riding a bomb and beneath him the ground crew painted small bombs for each trip we completed. Taxying out I started my own little ritual by singing, 'We're Off On The Road To Morocco' from the movie I had seen on my last leave. It was meant to keep us all cheerful and show my confidence in our venture of the next few hours. I never asked what the crew thought but no one complained. They were probably too numbed by my singing to do so. Completing the ritual, I patted the Percy painted on the outside of the cockpit on the rump. I don't know how useful these superstitious rituals were but they helped. Many crews had one and I'm here to prove ours worked.

'The Cologne trip was a good one. We were spot-on on heights and at turning points all the way. Our first sight of the Ruhr was impressive. In Bomber Command folklore was the story of the pilot who when asked what the flak was like over the Ruhr replied, 'Well, it was so thick over the target old boy that I put the undercart down and taxied across'. It wasn't quite as bad as that but there was a lot of it about and plenty was coming our way, accompanied by hundreds of searchlights probing the sky to seek us out. We bombed at midnight and that day Jimmy was 21 so we all sang 'Happy Birthday' to him as soon as I turned off target. I was feeling a little happy so I said a few rude words over the radio to the Germans. It was certainly a coincidence but they replied with a big thump under our tail. I shut up and we ran for the coast. We were quite a happy crew when we landed that night. We had gone to the Ruhr for the first time and what's more, we'd come back. We were destined to see a lot more of it during the next three months. While January had been a quiet time for operations, February was to be the reverse. The bad weather of the previous two months improved and we were to fly the hardest month of operations of our tour. On the 3rd we were 'on' to Hamburg. I had a bad trip and reluctantly turned back. I felt a little better on landing where I found several aircraft had turned back ahead of me because of heavy icing conditions over the North Sea. There were four missing out of 84 Halifaxes among the 323 aircraft operating that night. Sixteen aircraft were lost all told, 6 1/2% of the force.'[13]

Sgt Derek Smith, Lancaster *K-King*[14] navigator, 61 Squadron who flew on the raid, the first 200-plus raid for more than two weeks and wrote. 'Good trip. Lot of inaccurate *Flak*. Did target recce to observe results. Very scattered. 263 on, 6.1% lost. Wanganui.[15]

F/Sgt Jack Woodrow of 425 *'Les Alouettes'* Squadron RCAF's made his 9th trip in a Wellington, to Lorient again, on 4/5 February:

'We carried a full load of incendiaries. Visibility was good and the bombs fell in the target area. There was intense and accurate light and heavy flak and the searchlights were numerous. We saw large fires all over the area. On 8 February I was commissioned as a pilot officer and I moved into the Officers Quarters. My roommate was P/O Bill Maxwell from Detroit who was a rear gunner on 426 Squadron. We led strange lives, residing in reasonably comfortable civilized surroundings. This was especially true at Dishforth, which was a permanent RAF station. We had lots of free time when we weren't required to fly. The nearest town to Dishforth was Boroughbridge. We would visit the neighbouring pubs and maybe a little further afield to go to dance halls. There were lots of nice looking girls. We also spent a lot of time in the Mess. The food on the squadron was good. The only complaint would be the Brussels sprouts. They must have grown in profusion in England because there never seemed to be a shortage. We got so many that it was quite a few years after the war before I could eat one again. Many stations had four meals a day. Tea was roughly from 1530 to 1630 and supper from 1900 to 2000. As a sergeant I had been billeted in a two-bedroom Permanent Married Quarters row house with three other Senior NCOs. We slept one in each bedroom and two in the living room. All eating and entertaining was done in the Sergeants Mess.

'Our days had a familiar routine. We got out of bed when we woke up. At the Mess, a quick look at the Battle Order would show who was on operations that night. If you were on, it usually meant a flight test had to be done to make sure the aircraft was ready. The briefings were usually in the late afternoon. The navigators and the wireless operators were briefed ahead of the rest of us because they had more information to absorb. At the briefing the Intelligence Officer would tell about the defenses. The weatherman would tell us what to expect in the way of weather. In both cases there was a lot of guesswork. The Navigation Leader would discuss the route and the Bombing Leader would describe the target and the bomb load. These would be followed by short 'pep' talks from the squadron and station commanders. From this moment until the end of the operation everyone in that briefing room was incommunicado to the outside world.

'Then we went to supper. After that we picked up our parachutes. Pilot chutes were fixed to the harness so that they formed a seat, which he sat on. The other crewmembers carried their chutes as a separate brown-canvas parcel, which before use had to be fixed to their chest by metal clips. Each crewman would carry the chute with him wherever he moved. The pilots didn't have to remember their parachute but on the other hand, moving around in the aircraft's cramped interior with a pilot-style chute was difficult. We picked up our flying gear in the crew locker rooms and put it on. We then went out and got into trucks and drove across the airfield to be deposited beside our aircraft usually just as dusk was falling. After any necessary consultations with the ground crew, we climbed aboard and took up our various crew stations. The pilot proceeded with the engine start-up. This pumped life into the hydraulic systems and the gunners tested turret rotation and gun controls. Each crewman did their pre-flight drill and tested oxygen supplies and intercom connections. When time to go our fully laden aircraft moved slowly from its parking pad and took its place in the line-up on the perimeter track as the line moved slowly toward the end of the runway in use. Then we waited for the green light from the Aldis Lamp from the control van located beside the end of the runway before turning onto the run-up place. The run-up procedure did not take very long and we were soon turning onto the end of the runway. With Dishforth being a short length field the brakes had to hold the aircraft until the tail was up. Then the brakes were released. There was a gradual surge as the skipper applied full power. The Wellington rapidly gained speed as it went down the runway. The skipper compensated for torque swing with the throttle. Soon we were airborne. Then the pilot retracted the landing gear and then the flaps as we started our long climb to operational height. Ops were often scrubbed at the last minute. I think this happened close to half the time.'

Ron Read's crew had a break until the 11th. Then they were off to Wilhelmshaven:

'We had a long wait between briefing and take-off waiting for better weather. We found that the weather was still bad over the target so we were to bomb on 'Sky-markers'. This was the first use of a new Pathfinder technique. The colored markers floated high in the sky on parachutes. We had to pass over them on a given heading and bomb when they were in the bombsight. We had a few problems, as the clouds were so high that almost as soon as the markers were dropped, they disappeared. We had to chase three markers until we just managed to catch one before it disappeared. It was a frustrating experience but it was later reported that the bombing caused much damage to the port. There were only three aircraft lost from the 177 who operated. This was more like it.

'Two nights later, the 13th, fortunately a Saturday, we were on again, to Lorient. Lorient was an easy target and only seven aircraft were lost from the 466 despatched. We were on again the next night, the 14th, to Cologne once more. Over the target we again used sky markers and this time we had more time to line up before they dropped below cloud. It was a good trip for us, although the results were unsatisfactory, as there were no photographs because of the cloud cover. We liked sky marking nights though, as most of the fighters were grounded and the searchlights couldn't get you. Only nine of 240 aircraft were lost; about 60 crew.'

Nine aircraft were lost to nightfighters, three of which were Wellingtons and two were claimed by *Ritterkreuztrager* Paul Gildner[16] who after the death in combat of Reinhold Knacke on 3/4 February had been given command of 1./NJG 1 at Gilze-Rijen airfield. *Uffz* Heinz Huhn, his experienced radar operator recorded:

'On 14/2 we destroyed a Wellington and a Boeing [sic] in sector *'Hamster'* [Domburg/Holland]. There was no radio beacon in operation and we flew without being able to orientate ourselves. Our bearing set was unserviceable. Thank God we could still communicate over R/T with the ground station. Finally, a thought crossed my mind: could it be the *Lichtenstein* that was jamming our bearing set? I switched off the *Li*-set. Sure enough, I could then obtain a bearing. We proceeded towards the box flying at a height of 3000m [9,700ft]. We received a course to steer straight away but the *Lichtenstein* was not in operation. We flew between two layers of cloud; above us the clouds were very thin. We therefore climbed above these clouds and got a visual on a Wellington.

'I am engaging', Gildner announced and he attacked directly from behind. Its left engine and wing on fire, the enemy pulled up steeply and plunged down. We observed it crashing into the water: *'Sieg Heil!'* [Bomber destroyed!]

'Immediately, we received a new course to steer from the ground station. The moon brightly illuminated the sky as if it were daylight. I experienced interference in the R/T communications with ground control. At last we obtained visual contact.

'I am engaging' Gildner said, as got into an attacking position and he opened fire. The *Kurier* was identified as a Boeing [sic]. It was burning in the left engines and dived down out of control. It crashed into the sea. *'Sieg Heil!'*

'We were vectored onto another aircraft. We got a visual but we were too fast. We turned around to get into a good attacking position but contact was lost with the *Kurier* in the process. We were low on fuel so we set course for home right away. It was a smooth landing. Oblt Gildner's 39th and 40th night victories.'[17]

After the Cologne raid of 14 February Ron Read's crew were one who had a night off 'to catch their breath' but the break did not last long, as he recalls:

'We were 'on' once more to Lorient again. We had a good trip and could see the target clearly. Unfortunately we could only inflict accidental damage on the town, as the submarine pens were more than proof against our bombs. After three nights on operations out of four, I was very tired and could hardly keep my eyes open. As we flew up the length of England, I found myself falling asleep a couple of times. Reaching Suffolk and Norfolk, we started to pass through the landing traffic of the many bomber aerodromes there. I put my second pilot to good use and told him to keep a good look out for other aircraft and make sure I didn't go to sleep. I sucked a caffeine tablet to keep me awake and finally with the aid of my drug, Linton beacon hove into sight.[18]

'We had a whole night off on the 17th but we were off again on 18/19 February to Wilhelmshaven. I had F/Sgt Ginsberg Morton back again as navigator. I was happy about that. A good New Yorker from the Bronx serving in the RCAF, Ginsberg was an old hand and a very cool head.

I liked his style. He was positive about his work and seemed to have plenty of time to spare. He would come and stand between the second pilot and me for a lot of the time. (This was quite a novelty. I'd once asked Vic to come up and have a look at the *flak* and the target. Vic had popped his head over the cockpit coaming for about ten seconds, whispered '*Christ*' to himself and quickly disappeared back into his compartment below, never to be seen again). This time the target was clear but the bombing didn't seem very effective. (Although the Pathfinders claimed to have marked accurately in clear visibility, most of the bombs fell in open country west of the target). We had no problems but four Lancasters were lost out of the total of 195 aircraft sent.

'As the results were doubtful we were detailed to return to Wilhelmshaven the following night, 19/20 February. We never liked going to the same target two nights in a row. We always felt that the defenses would be more alert and more practiced the second time around. It seemed a good effort, though the resultant fires were subdued. We noted that the defenses now waited until they were sure that the target was marked before opening fire. This meant that the early Pathfinders ahead of us had a relatively quiet reception. Our task, as the second wave carrying mostly incendiaries, was to start fires to illuminate things for the Lancasters following up with their big 4000-lb 'Block-buster' bombs. Once they were sure that the target was identified, the German defenses gave us all they had. Their gunners at the start of a raid were always more accurate and quicker than later on.'

P/O Jack Woodrow, observer in a Wellington of 425 '*Les Alouettes*' Squadron RCAF, also noted the effects of the PFF force:

> 'We bombed on Pathfinder Force (PFF) markers with a mixed bomb load. The PFF Force was the elite group in Bomber Command. It had the best crews and the latest and best equipment. Their mission was to mark the target with flares, either ground or air. Then the rest of the force bombed on those flares. This was to improve the bombing accuracy and it did. However there were still many problems-most of them caused by our constant enemy, the weather. There was 8/10ths cloud and smoke over the target. Intense heavy and light *flak* was encountered but it was a very successful trip.'[19]

Despite the dreadful weather conditions on 19/20 February, three experienced crews were given permission to take off from Leeuwarden to try and intercept the returning Wilhelmshaven force. Twelve bombers failed to return. In adverse weather conditions *Oblt* Hans-Joachim Jabs, *Staffelkapitän*, 11./NJG 1 destroyed three Stirlings[20] of 15 Squadron in 44 minutes over the North Sea operating in *Himmelbett* box '*Schlei*' at Schiermonnikoog Island to take his score to 29 victories. *Lt* Wolfgang Kuthe of IV./NJG 1 destroyed a Stirling of 90 Squadron.[21] *Oblt* Paul Gildner, *Staffelkapitän*, 1./NJG 1 was also victorious, as *Uffz* Heinz Huhn recalled in his diary:

> 'We're in the Operations Room that night. A thick layer of mist and bad ground visibility prevail. Enemy bombers are reported approaching Wilhelmshaven. We can't take off. Still, Gildner wants to get after the bombers, if necessary he will fly the Dornier. The bombers fly back through the boxes in our area. We decide to take off all the same. There's a full moon. The Dornier is not fitted with flame dampers, so from the engine exhausts long flames trail back. The radio and radar equipment of the aircraft is completely worn out. I switch off the *Lichtenstein* and we have to search without it. We immediately get a course to steer for a mission in box 'Tiger'.[22] The first *Kurier* is a Halifax. Suspecting no attack, its crew must feel quite safe. Gildner attacks, the *Kurier* starts to burn and at 2105 hrs it crashes into the North Sea. *Sieg Heil.*
>
> 'The reflector sight has broken down and only one cannon still fires. We are guided onto another aircraft. At 21.10 hrs we obtain visual contact. A Halifax. A giant pillar of smoke from our first kill rises from the water. An attack, the *Kurier* trails a long banner of smoke, it explodes and crashes into the sea. Time is 2116 hrs.
>
> 'We are vectored onto another aircraft, this time we engage a Boeing [sic]. R/T connection is very bad, as a transmitter on the ground has broken down. I am dripping with sweat, have to switch all the time and tune the radio set. And my helmet fits miserably. Nevertheless, were still in business and remain in visual contact with the enemy bomber. We get into attacking position. Gildner opens fire, only three machine guns are still working. The aircraft is not burning yet. We charge in again and fire another burst, then have to turn away as a second *Kurier* is flying only 200 meters away from us. So, this one is getting away. We can only claim a damaged. Our own aircraft has been hit by return fire in the propellers.
>
> 'We immediately turn back for home and safely touch down. In the Operations Room we have a big party that same night with champagne and red wine. Jabs has shot down three bombers, all Short Stirlings. Our third probably

didn't make it back home either as it sent off a SOS. In the afternoon of the 20th our lightning visit to Leeuwarden comes to an end and we fly back to Gilze.'[23]

Sgt Derek Smith of 61 Squadron and his crew in 'K-King' returned safely on 19/20 February, the crew having dropped their load of one 4000 lb and 12 Small Bomb Containers (30 lb incendiaries). He noted:

'Good trip. Full moon and target was clearly visible. Bombed at 16,000'. Flak heavy but below us. Greatest danger was of collision with our own aircraft. Flew away from target alongside a Halifax. Lot of bombing well off target. 195 on, 2% lost. Five hours. The lads much enjoyed the eggs I brought back with me. Aircrew did well for eggs as bacon and egg was the usual meal on return but some extra was always appreciated. The weather was not too good at this time as we only flew on 21 February for 1.50 hrs doing some low level formation and bombing and then a Night Flying Test (NFT) prior to 25 February, when it was Ops to Nürnburg. Quiet a boring trip. Defenses were swamped. On the 400-mile leg from Mannheim we saw no Flak or searchlights. Paramatta.[24] 337 on, 2.7% lost. Nine hrs! Our longest trip.'[25]

On 24/25 February *Oblt* Paul Gildner, *Staffelkapitän,* 1./NJG 1, whose score stood at 44 victories, was killed when his his Bf 110G-4 crashed on final approach to Gilze-Rijen following an engine fire. *Uffz* Heinz Huhn managed to bale out at low level. At Leeuwarden on 26 February 30-year-old *Hptm* Ludwig Becker, *Staffelkapitan* 12/NJG 1 a great night fighting tactician with 44 night victories, waited to fly his very first daylight sortie. Shortly before taking off from Leeuwarden 1135 hours in a formation of 12 Bf 110s of IV./JG I led by *Hptm* Hans-Joachim Jabs, in pursuit of the American daylight raiders Becker was informed of the award of the *Eichenlaub* (Oak Leaves) to his *Ritterkreuz* (Knight's Cross), which had been bestowed on him on 1 July 1942 after his 25th night victory for his leading role in the development of the night fighter arm. They intercepted the B-17s and B-24s, returning with claims for two shot down but Becker's Bf 110 was lost without a trace. Completely at ease and master in the night battle against the British bombing offensive the 'Night Fighting Professor' and his *Funker Fw* Josef Staub fell victim to the gunners of B-17s or B-24s of the 1st and 2nd Bomb Wings. Losses to *Experten* like this was not good for German morale, which was under pressure due to the intensifying airwar over Europe, as *Oblt* Dieter Schmidt of NJG 1 recalls:

'The fall of Stalingrad [in February 1943] resulted in a change of fortunes in the east. For us operations became more difficult and stressful too. Not only did the night attacks of the British become increasingly heavy during 1943. On 27 January the Americans, who so far had only appeared over occupied territory, attacked a German town without fighter escort. They maintained these attacks and, as there were only very few day fighter units stationed in the west, our past as *Zerstörer* units was remembered and we were called upon to confront these attacks. The 3rd *Gruppe* took part in a number of these operations but had only had one major engagement with the enemy on 4 March near Texel. The successive re-equipment of the aircraft and the operational readiness by day and night proved a considerable strain. Also, the night fighter version of the Bf 110 had become cumbersome through additional equipment for day-fighting and the crews no longer had the necessary experience of formation flying and attacking tactics. So, losses of highly specialised and experienced night fighters could not be avoided. In the hitherto quiet Holland, where a large part of NJG 1 was stationed, the efforts of the resistance increased in 1943. It was necessary to guard the widely dispersed aircraft and hangars against possible sabotage. Shooting down single four-engined British aircraft dropping sabotage material from low level was also part of our task.

'The British intensified their bomber stream tactics and used four-engined aircraft – the Short Stirling, Halifax and the Lancaster – almost exclusively: The different performance of these three types and the different height of the individual waves were well known to us. On operations over the north German plain especially one could choose the type to confront; but there was no difference in the defensive power of the three types. The tight British bomber stream and the radar equipment of our own machines resulted in a change in our tactics. We became more independent of our controllers and we succeeded in shooting down several enemy aircraft in succession more frequently. The bomber stream required a concentration of the nightfighters on the supposed approach route, which could frequently be determined by our early warning radar on the coast and the monitoring of radio traffic. Now began the time of operational deployments at short notice, most frequently to St. Trond in Belgium. Also, during the short summer nights we would be reinforced by crews from *Geschwader* stationed in the hinterland.'

During the 1943 strategic night bombing offensive the life expectancy of a bomber crew was between eight and 11 operations, whereas each crew member had to complete 30 'trips' before being sent on 'rest' at an Operational Training Unit. F/O Harry Barker, a Stirling bomb aimer in 218 'Gold Coast' Squadron, May 1943-July 1944, adds:

'We all knew that in 1943 the average 'life' of a crew was ten operations so you can imagine that everyone was a bit jumpy at their 13th! If you really begin to analyse it the options open to us were limited. We had to consider the following: 1. We had all volunteered to do the job. 2. We all wanted to hit back at the enemy, who were attacking London, Coventry, Liverpool etc. 3. The camaraderie was so strong on the Squadron that no one would seriously consider letting his friends down. 4. There was a keen determination to achieve 30 ops and complete the tour. 5. The alternative was refusal – followed by a court-martial and the awful consequences. 6. The reward on returning from an op was a breakfast of bacon and egos, a luxury only available to successful aircrews. When you take this lot into account, together with the youthful confidence that 'only other crews get shot down', you may understand how we felt about the incredible risks we were taking. It is similar to the attitude of cigarette smokers who are all convinced that it is only other people who get lung cancer!

'In general the morale of aircrews was good. It was easier for the young unmarried and unattached men to cope than it was for those with wives, children or steady girlfriends. One could cope with the prospect of death if this did not result in the misery and hardships for others. This inevitably caused some differences in attitude to the war and the way we behaved under fighting conditions. I am not saying that the men with family commitments were any less dedicated to the job but I believe they were under much greater strain than many of the rest of us. 'We did tend to 'let ourselves go' when off duty. We drank a great deal of beer and used any excuse for a party commonly described as a 'piss up' either in the mess or at a local pub. We got to know the locals who were always friendly and understanding. Some shared their Sunday dinners with us and of course there were the girls. Life on the Squadron was a mixture of fun, laughter, friendships, excitement and hell, just around the corner. In the Officers Mess we had a very good standard of living. The food was very good. Sleeping quarters were comfortable and we had either a batwoman or batman to look after us, cleaning shoes, brass buttons etc and pressing uniforms and making beds. I usually had a cup of tea brought to me in bed every morning! I was one of the few who survived and it seems dreadful to admit that I enjoyed the life on the Squadron. The only way I can admit this is in the belief that my friends who were lost also shared the good side of this time of battle for survival. That is how we saw it. The tragedy was that so many did not survive.'

F/L Stanley Freestone, a Wellington pilot in 142 Squadron in 1942 and Stirlings of 199 Squadron in 1943, recalls:

'As an operational heavy bomber I felt the Wellington was a better aircraft than the Stirling. The Wellington could cruise fully laden around 15,000 ft and with its fabric covered geodetic airframe construction could take a great amount of damage. Of course the Stirling could carry a greater bomb load but its weakness was the inability to cruise laden much above 12-13,000 ft. A further weakness was a lack of performance on only three engines. However the Stirling had a strong airframe and violent maneuvers to escape from searchlight cones and fighters bore it in good stead. It was the best of the four heavy bombers for a tight radius turn.

'The most undying vivid memories I had were seeing a huge area – the target- covered in flame and explosions. Above the immediate target area the Germans maintained a 'box barrage' of heavy anti-aircraft fire. This was constant and fire only diverted when searchlights had captured an aircraft in a cone of intense light. Aircraft would be caught in these beams such as an octopus holds its prey with tentacles. The aircraft would twist and dive to extricate itself but would immediately receive a concentrated volume of fire. Sometimes a still fully laden bomber received a direct hit -then a huge ball of fire would explode as bomb load, hundreds of gallons of petrol, oxygen bottles and the huge photo flash bomb we all carried by which we photographed our target sighting, exploded. A terrifying cascade of brilliant colors would follow this explosion, as the whole inferno fell to earth. A very quick death for some but many airmen fell to earth without a chance to operate their parachutes. Often a bursting shell was so close one could hear the explosion above the din of the engines and through the helmet and earphones all crewmembers wore. One also heard the metal shrapnel as it tore through the aircraft. This made a rather strange tinkling bell-like sound. In the brilliant light over the targets both from enemy searchlights and ground fires and explosions one could see the hundreds of balls of smoke left after exploding anti aircraft fire.'

P/O Jack Woodrow of 425 *'Les Alouettes'* Squadron 425 RCAF adds:

'Like most aircrew I don't remember feeling any particular emotion toward the Germans. I had ended up as a bomb-aimer and it was my duty to drop the bombs as accurately as possible. It was all sort of remote and impersonal. Our operations encouraged the British who had suffered so much and seen so much damage to their country. I had relatives living in the east-end of London which suffered greatly. (I was staying with them once in 1944 when a V-1 Buzz Bomb came over and hit not very far away). On leave in London, I was always being thanked by the Londoners for giving it back to the Germans. I've never lost a moment's sleep from feeling guilty about bombing German civilians. They started it. Criticism of the Bomber Command bombing campaign surfaced after the war. The two main criticisms were the lack of effectiveness and the lack of morality of the campaign. Certainly, Bomber Command's effectiveness was reduced by the terrible weather conditions and lack of certain equipment but in the early part of the war, Bomber Command was quite literally the only force, which could carry the war to the Germans and do damage to the German homeland. The defensive effort forced on the Germans justified it. According to Speer, the *Reich*'s Munitions Minister, it tied up many thousands of Germans defending Germany and repairing bomb damage. As for morality, we were told what the targets were. With area bombing, we knew civilians were being killed. But killing people did not enter your mind. From the air, the human factor does not mean what it would to an Army soldier. When you are in a bomber you don't see people, you see things – buildings, bridges, docks.

'To undertake a tour of 30 operations, which was the requirement for a tour with Bomber Command in the central period of the war of 1941-43 and the first half of 1944, was to have only about a 50% chance of surviving. The stats seemed to show that the chances of a crew surviving a first tour got much better if it could survive the first 5 or 6 operations. After all our training, the deciding factor for survival seemed to be experience. When we started, we had no idea of what we were getting into. Well into the tour, you started to count up the crews that had not returned since you had started. Then you began to realize the lousy odds you were fighting. Having said all this, perhaps the most remarkable fact is that despite the cold, the dark, the lousy weather conditions, the flak, fighters and searchlights, the loss of comrades, the constant strain and fear, the general morale remained solid. I think most of us handled the strain well. We knew that ops were dangerous and stressful and that some crews would be lost but we also knew the trip was necessary. In my experience, the number of aircrew who from loss of nerve were unable to continue operating was near zero on our squadron. Statistics show that it was less than one in 200 for the whole command. For my crew, I think we went through stages. During the first few trips we realized that we had got ourselves into something very dangerous. I think our morale sagged a bit. Then we entered a stage of confidence. The enemy had done his best and we were still around. I think we all felt we had the measure of the job. Then came a stage of discouragement. We realized how lucky we had been so far and it was going to be tough to complete our tour. Then came the point that we might just complete the tour. By this time we had become highly experienced. We worked together as a highly efficient team. We each knew what to do and when.'

F/Sgt Maurice 'Frank' Hemming DFM, a flight engineer in 97 (PFF) Squadron flying Lancasters, recalls:

'The most frightening ops were those to the Ruhr (Happy Valley to the crews), these targets being heavily defended. The real danger was on the bombing run in, when the pilot had to fly straight and level under the bomb aimer's guidance, for what seemed like forever. Our five trips to Berlin 'The Big City' to us, were no picnic due to night fighters. We certainly saw more of our bombers either shot down, or hit by *Flak* and blown up than at other targets.'

'Any target in the Ruhr Valley struck a chill into any aircrew,' continues P/O Jack Woodrow observer in P/O Johnny Michaud's Wellington crew thart went to Cologne on the night of 26/27 February when the city was subjected to a heavy raid by 427 heavies. It was their 13th trip. Woodrow recalls:

'Cologne had *flak* guns by the thousands and radar-controlled searchlights and endless miles of factories spewing out a permanent layer of haze. Along with the often-lousy weather, it presented very difficult targets. The sight of a city under heavy attack was a totally new experience and like nothing you had seen before. It was like a huge fireworks display with the sound turned off. The sound you heard was the monotonous roar of the engines interspersed by the thuds of near misses and the clatter of bits of shrapnel hitting the skin of the aircraft. When you saw a target under attack for the first time, you were convinced that no aircraft could fly through the *flak* unscathed. Then you would see a bomber blow up and go falling out of the sky. You felt a twinge of guilt because a disaster suffered by another crew helped tipped the scales of chance a bit in your favour. The other problem was the congestion over the target. The RAF system was to concentrate their attack into a few minutes in an attempt to overwhelm the defenses. You had to keep your eyes open to avoid collisions. You just strained all the time looking for the silhouettes of other aircraft with no lights on. We bombed on a good concentration of PFF markers. There were lots of both light and heavy *flak* and some searchlights. Searchlights could be as unsettling as being shot at. If one nailed an aircraft, others would quickly get you and form a cone. Then the aircraft became the center of fire for the *flak*. This could be very bad. Immediate and harsh evasive action was required to escape.[26]

'On the trip to St. Nazaire on 28 February the PFF markers were good. *Flak* was heavy over the target and fires were seen for 70 miles after we left. We didn't fly another op for a while. While on operations I took advantage of the Nuffield Leave Scheme several times. The Foundation paid for your accommodation at many nice hotels in England. This usually included breakfast. On one occasion I stayed at the Queen's Hotel in Torquay. On my first evening there I struck up an acquaintance with an Aussie and a New Zealander. They were just finishing their week's leave. They offered to show me all the best drinking spots in Torquay. To celebrate their final night, they persuaded me to join them in a down-under drink. It was a pint of Stout with some lemon juice to alleviate the heavy taste of Stout. I found it enjoyable and drank it all night. The next morning I woke up with a dandy hangover. When the little lady came around with the morning cup of tea, my hand was shaking so bad I couldn't hold the cup. The little lady commiserated with me, thinking I believe that I was suffering from some kind of operational 'shakes.' To my knowledge the main effect of the stress from operations was over-drinking – whether in the Mess, in the local pub or when on leave. It could have a long-term effect. I know a couple of squadron mates who turned into alcoholics stretching into the post-war years. I don't know what finally happened to them. I certainly drank too much but luckily I suffered no long-term consequences. I think we all developed an attitude of fatalism. You always thought it would happen to someone else. Deaths were cases of bad luck or bad timing. I think our age helped. I was 19 when I started on operations and finished by age 21. A doctor told me that when you are on ops, your system is all keyed up and the op is your release. When you are off flying your system is still keyed up but there is no release. So most of us used drinking as the release. It made sense to me. I did notice some changes in a few of the guys. The odd one who was normally noisy became very quiet while a shy one would become boisterous.'

Ron Read adds.

'Cologne and St. Nazaire were good trips for us but we had a problem arriving home from Cologne. A lot of our incendiaries remained in the bomb bay, because they'd been iced up and failed to release. The groundcrew were beneath the aircraft, pointing this out as we climbed out. Vic, getting his nav' gear together, was last out, last to look at the hang-ups. As he did so, the ice must have melted and one case of incendiaries fell out onto him. Fortunately it just struck him a glancing blow on the shoulder. I was worried that they would light up and got ready to leap back into the aircraft to move it. However they remained dormant and safe. As we turned away, another aircraft landing spread a host of incendiaries along the side of the runway. They caught and burned spectacularly for a short while. I resolved to open the bomb doors somewhere on the way home and give the aircraft a good shake to get rid of them.

'Coming back from that St. Nazaire trip, to avoid a repeat of hung up incendiaries, I opened the bomb doors and shook the aircraft quite violently. I'd completely forgotten we were flying over France, until Mac called. 'Hey Skip, you've done something rotten there. I can see a good fire going down below. You must have set some farm or something alight.' I felt quite guilty about that and resolved to think more carefully about where I dropped any hang ups in future. Always assuming we had one. The operation to St. Nazaire by 437 aircraft cost five aircraft.

'February 1943 had been a month of hard operational flying for Bomber Command. I flew 72 hours, all but 3.30 on operations. We had been to 11 targets and my total of trips reached 15, including the abortive trip when we had failed to reach Hamburg but I discovered since we had crossed the enemy coast, it counted. That was half my tour. As we'd enjoyed a low casualty rate and I'd had some good trips, I began to feel that I knew a bit about operational flying. I wasn't over-confident and realized more than ever, that luck was going to play a major part in survival. I just hoped that with a sensible approach to any situations I might encounter, I could help luck along in my favour. We were getting along well as a crew, although our frequent change of navigator was unsettling and threw a lot of work onto me every time we had a new one. One result of our continuing good luck was, the squadron now had a hard core of good experienced crews.

This gave the new boys confidence and made them feel that there could be a future for them too.

'March 1943 came in with a roar, when on the 1st we were briefed for Berlin – 'The Big City' as we knew it. It was a feared target and there was no doubt it would be defended fiercely. Cheshire was going and Jock Hill, his wireless operator was going to Berlin for the 14th time. Jock, a good friend of mine, was determined to make a full tour of 30 trips to Berlin if he could. He was the Signals Leader of 76 and could choose his trips. They were always the difficult ones. He had made several to Berlin with Cheshire on their first tour.

'I had, for my last few trips given up trying to get our aircraft *'C-Charlie'* up to our briefed bombing height. She was dreadfully slow on the climb and wallowed like a waterlogged boat at maximum altitude. I always became impatient and levelled off a couple of thousand feet below the stipulated height. This gave me more time on the run-in and a steadier platform over the target. It also made me look rather daring, always bombing at a lower height than most, although I didn't realize that at the time. These tactics were not at all popular with my crew, who believed, probably correctly, that every inch of height should be taken. They insisted that going to 'The Big City' I should climb all the way up to our bombing height of 20,000 ft. I felt perhaps this time they had something and promised to do so.

'Setting off before dusk, it was dark when we got to the North German coast. The plan was to fly North along the coast across Schleswig Holstein and turn South somewhere east of Hamburg. It was intended to indicate that we might be going for one of several targets, Kiel, Hamburg, or Rostock. We would pass them closely, before making a last minute turn south to Berlin. Over Germany, the winds were all over the place and we were soon well off track. We flew over Kiel by mistake and got a very hot reception. It even woke Taff up from his job of monitoring and jamming German R/T transmissions by using tinsel.[27] All aircraft carried a microphone in an engine nacelle. When he heard any German broadcast, the wireless operator pressed his key and the noise of the engine was transmitted on the German fighter frequency, to distort any instructions.

'As we bounced about the sky, Taff, while listening out, had been reading his musical magazine 'The Melody Maker'. Seeing the title of a popular melody of the day, he came up on intercom: 'Hey Skip, it says here that, 'Anywhere On Earth Is Heaven'.'

'You're bloody right Taff.' I replied through my teeth, hanging on to the shaking control column. 'And I wish like Hell we were anywhere on earth now.' We ploughed on to the Big City, me hauling and coaxing old C-Charlie, higher than she'd ever been before. Finally I told them, we were at last, at 20,000 ft. There were muted cheers all round. When we reached Berlin the Pathfinders, affected by the fickle winds, were late, so we had to stooge around. After a while, some fires and flares appeared ahead and Harry led us to them. We were quite close to them, when Mac said that there were other flares going down behind us. I looked around over my shoulder. No doubt about these, they were the real ones and the ones we were chasing were dummies, well east of the target. Now I had to go back against the stream of incoming aircraft. There were over 300 that night. As I turned, I saw a few more aircraft doing the same. Making my turn fairly sharp, *Charlie* lost a bit of height. By now there were aircraft all around us, going in all directions. It was bloody dicey. Wanting to get over the target, drop the bombs and get out as soon as possible, I pushed the nose down to speed things up.

'We soon had a good view of the correct marker flares but I now had to go the full distance back across the target, among the heavy *flak* and against the oncoming stream before turning once more onto the correct heading. By the time we'd done that I was down to 17,500 ft for the bombing run. Once more I hadn't managed to bomb from the full height. However the crew wasn't complaining now; they wanted to get it all over with and get out just as quickly as I did. It was hot over Berlin all right. We saw several Halifaxes coned in searchlights. Having dropped our bombs in the approved fashion and spent ten long seconds waiting for our photo flash to go off, I turned for home at just about the correct position. At least we thought it was. Harry claimed another pinpoint, a junction of river and railway, just where they should have been. If we really knew where we were then, it was to be the last time for three more hours. As we headed back over Germany, we saw flak coming up at aircraft in almost every direction. Normally, the location of *flak* and searchlights was a good aid to navigation but this time they seemed to be everywhere. I was pretty sure that the *flak* ahead was the Ruhr. I noted two aircraft at least go down in flames. It was coming up in such quantity; there must have been a lot of aircraft ahead of us in the same predicament. I took some small consolation from that and pressed on. Fortunately, I had held height after we left Berlin and we were still at 15,000 ft. I wasn't crossing the Ruhr lower. We ploughed our way through the *flak*, getting bounced about in the process and eventually, 30 minutes later, came out the other side. Ahead lay the coastline, but we were headed for yet another concentration of *flak*. I flew north of most of it but we were hit just as we passed out to sea. It wasn't bad but noisy, as a lot of shrapnel rattled our tail.

'Back at Linton, waiting our turn to land a Halifax came flying along over the runway shooting off red Verey flares. We made way for him immediately. It was Roger Coverly, literally coming back from his spin to avoid the searchlights. He managed to pull out below 2000-ft. All his radios and electric's were out and he had to make a landing without any communications. He made it OK, the final happening of an eventful night. Counting the cost next day, we found that of the force of 302 aircraft setting out, 17 were lost: a nasty 5 1/2%. Six of them were Halifaxes. 76 Squadron lost two crews. P/O [N.S.] Black [RNZAF] and Sgt [J.L.] Fletcher [DFM MiD], both of whom had been with us since December. In 78 our luck still held but it was a frail thread, as we were to find out.'

IV./NJG 1 destroyed five of the 19 aircraft that failed to return from the 1/2 March raid on Berlin.[28] Sgt Derek Smith, navigator in 61 Squadron was on ops this night, in Lancaster *K-King* (W4236) again.[29] He recorded in his diary:

'Ops. Berlin K The Big One. On target on time after taking off 15 minutes late. About 100 searchlights but *Flak* poor. Lost port outer over City so set course for home on three. This was where we had our only failure of communication, which could have proved fatal and taught us a valuable lesson. I gave Gordon the course to steer, which he repeated back to me but either he repeated the right course back and put the wrong one on the compass or I misheard him. When we got back to extreme *Gee* range I was shocked to find I was getting fixes about 30 miles south of track and on checking, found we were steering a course 10° out and that on three engines! Our Guardian Angel was working overtime, as we had an extremely quiet return and saw nothing. And because of the Lancs great performance on three were back with the others. A case of least said soonest mended but we had learned our lesson and Woody always checked from then on. 302 on, 5.6% lost. 7.40 hrs.'[30]

Geoff Rothwell[31], now a S/L Flight Commander in 75 Squadron RNZAF at Newmarket, also took part in the 1/2 March Berlin raid:

'Because my crew had no operational experience we started my second tour with two mining sorties off the Friesian Islands on 26 and 27 February. We carried six mines and dropped them north of Terschelling on the first operation. The fifth mine exploded on contact. The second operation was to the north of Ameland. We were shadowed by a fighter, which did not open fire. After a one-night rest from operations we were briefed on 1 March for an attack on the German capital. It was the heaviest weight of bombs to be dropped on Berlin and fires were still seen 200 miles from the target. On the return journey we strayed off course and were engaged by intense heavy *Flak* over Osnabrück and fought off five attacks by German night fighters, one of which was claimed as destroyed by the front gunner. The aircraft had numerous holes from the *Flak*, which also shattered the windscreen. My impression after the first raid over Germany in just over two years was that there had been enormous changes in tactics, technology and the ferocity of the bombing. It was obvious that there had been tremendous developments in attack and defense by both sides.

'After nine operations with 75 Squadron I was posted to take command of a Flight in 218 (Gold Coast) Squadron at Downham Market. The Pathfinder Force had been formed in my absence from operations and the success of their target-marking techniques was most obvious from photographic reconnaissance after bombing attacks. From the point of view of the bomber crews, operations were made considerably simpler as Pathfinder markers were dropped at turning points so making adjustments to course possible without the necessity to obtain fixes and position-pinpoints continually. The responsibility for identifying target aiming-points had lifted from the shoulders of the bomber crews as TI[32] markers were dropped by the Pathfinders making the work of the crews easier.

'Although the actual bombing operations were more effective through the employment of new techniques, there was an added danger from the technological advancement of the German defenses. It was a terrifying sight to approach a target such as Essen or Düsseldorf and know that one had to run the gauntlet of searchlights, *Flak* and night fighters to reach the target. The display of these defenses could be seen from a great distance and there is little doubt that they had an effect on morale when the Ruhr Valley targets were attacked repeatedly in 1943. Strangely, although searchlights were not lethal in themselves, like *Flak*, they were feared far more, probably because of the psychological effect of being exposed since a night-bomber hoped the darkness would be a protection. However, there were very few cases of nervous breakdowns when crewmembers had to be taken off operations. In fact, those who completed tours and were given jobs on instructional units very often applied to return for a further tour of operational duty. Most applications were returned to the applicants marked 'not recommended' because there was a need for operational-experienced instructors on Operational Training Units. After completing my 55th operation on 24 June 1943 I was posted, once again, to an OTU. I had flown just over 115 operational hours on my second tour. Berlin was the target on three occasions; Hamburg, Nuremberg, Munich, Frankfurt, Kiel and Stuttgart once and the Ruhr Valley six times, with a special trip to bomb the Heinkel works at Rostock when we acted as the marker with an all-incendiary bomb load. It was an all-Stirling raid and we obtained a photograph of the aiming point. I must admit to being relieved when my tour ended. It had been stressful and I had come close to disaster on a number of occasions through enemy action and fuel shortage. On one occasion we hit a high tension electric pylon in Luxembourg whilst en route to Stuttgart when new tactics were being tried which required the Stirlings to fly at low level until nearing the target.'

At the OTUs airmen like Jack Short, a Wellington air gunner at 12 OTU at RAF Chipping Warden waited to fly their first op. Jack Short recalls:

'My crew, along with others was posted individuals to 12 OTU and after ground school to the satellite aerodrome at RAF Edgehill to form-up as crews and begin operational training in Wellington ICs. 'Crewing-up' was itself an interesting process. All aircrew specialization's on strength were put together in a large area, such as a gymnasium and all milled around chatting and choosing at random a pilot, navigator, signaller, bomb-aimer and gunners until a crew was formed. Although a haphazard arrangement, it apparently worked! My skipper, a F/Sgt, selected by chance, proved OK and our work-up as a crew was straightforward – least I have no recollection of being too badly frightened by our early flying experience as a crew. There was however, one incident towards the end of our training, which helped prepare us crew for what was to come! One leg of our night cross-country flight took us over East Anglia. As we approached the Wash our Wellington was suddenly coned in searchlights. The skipper was blinded by the intensity of the light and called for our signaller to fire the 'colors of the day'. He then put the appropriate cartridge into the Verey pistol above his head and fired. As the flare arched its way skywards the searchlights were rapidly extinguished, leaving us in what seemed an even darker night sky.

'Immediately however, there was a concerned cry over the intercom from the signaller exclaiming that the fuselage fabric above his was on fire! Evidently a rigger had covered the pistol vent hole with doped fabric. The signaller took the CTC fire extinguisher from its bracket and commenced pumping away, squirting the liquid on to the seat of the fire. This seemed to have little effect and the navigator was called to assist. The aircraft axe was brought onto use and they started chopping away at the geodetics. The situation was not improving and the skipper decided that a speedy descent to a diversion aerodrome was necessary. Frequency 6440 Kc/s was selected and 'Darkie' call was transmitted stating the nature of our emergency. No response was forthcoming, so the message was repeated. This time four sets of aerodrome lights appeared below us. The skipper selected one of the aerodromes on offer and initiated a steep diving descent to snuff-out the tyre. Calling regularly on 6440 the skipper made his way round the circuit on to finals. He touched down and immediately and immediately there was a roar over our heads as a Lancaster executed overshoot action having had its approach to land baulked by our arrival. It was obvious that the aerodrome lights had not been illuminated for our benefit! We were to learn later that we were in the middle of a squadron returning from a raid on Germany. The aerodrome we had selected was RAF Little Staughton with H2S equipped Lancs. We never quite forgave our pilot for his choice of aerodrome: it transpired that the other three, which had responded to our 'Darkie' call, were American bases. We had thus lost an opportunity to sample their noteworthy hospitality and food!

'Our adrenaline pumping evening was not yet over! Following our debriefing we were walking up the path to the Sergeants mess when we were forced to take cover as the aerodrome came under attack from a Ju 88 intruder. He had obviously followed the returning Lancasters and waited patiently until the aerodrome had started to relax and was at its most vulnerable before mounting its cannon and machine-gun attack. It was a terrifying racket and a chastening experience for a budding bomber crew!'

The night of 5/6 March has gone into history as the starting point of the Battle of the Ruhr. Essen, the city of Krupp steelworks, was on the receiving end of a heavy raid when 14 out of 442 aircraft failed to return, six of which were shot down by five IV./NJG 1 crews.[33] On 8/9 March 335 bombers went to Nuremberg and eight aircraft failed to return. S/L Ray Glass DFC pilot of a 214 Squadron Stirling recalls:

'On the way we were coned by one of the concentrations and again over the target, returning with 27 holes in the aircraft.'

'Searchlights caused problems on many ops', recalls Sgt John 'Jimmy' Anderson Hurst, a Halifax tail gunner in 102 Squadron:

'One would light our plane as it swept the sky but on 9/10 March when on our way to Munich [264 aircraft of Bomber Command attacked the city] we were locked onto by a blue beam. These were radar-controlled from the ground and referred to as master searchlights. Immediately it illuminated us several other searchlights locked onto us and George Barker our skipper took violent evasive action. He seldom flew straight and level. I was never airsick but invariably when a new member joined the crew they were sick on their first trips with George. To be aboard when he corkscrewed – descending 2000 ft weaving as we went, then up again – with a bomb load on, was something to experience but it worked and on several occasions enabled us to escape when coned by a group of searchlights. How he could see his instruments, I do not know, as so intense was the light from the beams that I was completely blinded. We seemed to be held for ages but it was maybe a couple of minutes before we were out of the beam. So violent had our evasive action been that the gyro in the compass toppled and we had to abort our op and return to base. The engineer thought that at one stage the skipper had rolled the Halifax onto its back. We still had our full bomb load aboard during these maneuvers and back at base we landed with them aboard. I can't recall just why we did not jettison them We were lucky that night, as usually when a plane is caught by a master beam, fighters come in and shoot it down, whilst the crew is disorientated.'

Eight aircraft were lost on the Munich raid. Sgt (later W/O) Arthur R. 'Spud' Taylor, a new arrival at Mildenhall noted in his diary that 'raids were on practically every night since their crew's recent arrival from OCU Bicester and that 'only three had been lost since we arrived; two riddled and a few prangs. One brought down a Ju 88 over Munich last night and returned with gunner wounded – he died later.' Spud was an observer in the Stirling crew captained by Sgt Victor Page who on 10/11 March gained experience flying as 'second dickey' with a regular 149 Squadron crew on a mining operation to Bordeaux. His own crew meanwhile, had to kick their heels because they were minus a navigator since OCU. Victor Page made it back, which was good news for Spud because he was wearing his Irvine. It was a 'pretty rough do' apparently. Some *Flak* through the kite.'

On 11/12 March Page went to Stuttgart when 314 Lancasters, Halifaxes and Stirlings were despatched. Eleven aircraft failed to return but Victor Page seemed to be leading a charmed life. On this night 21-year old *Bordfunker Uffz* Karl-Ludwig Johanssen of 11./NJG 4, flying with the experienced *Lt* Johannes Engels because his pilot, *Lt* Martin 'Tino' Becker (who he had teamed up with in January 1943) had gone sick, scored his first victory but at a cost as Johanssen recalls:

'At Gilze Rijen we collected a new machine, a Bf 110F with the markings 2Z+IU and equipped with *Lichtenstein*, a radar set I had never seen before. A local flight of forty minutes, then, on 11 March cockpit readiness and take-off at 2143 hrs for the box Bergziege (near Bergzabern). We had good radio contact with the *Jägerleitoffizier* (JLO, or GCI-controller) while climbing at maximum rate to our operational height of 5300 meters. The equipment was checked and the four machine guns and two MG-FF 2cm cannon, loaded and cocked. At my feet were the ammunition drums of the two 2cm cannon with 75 rounds each. The screen of the *Lichtenstein* was aglow with the green time base and the ground blips, which also showed our altitude. Our aircraft was over the radio beacon Bergziege. We were directed to the north-west corner of the box and waited there flying in large circles. At last we got directions from the controller. Course and height were changed as in the exercises, using brief coded expressions.

'2 times Lisa – Marie 7 – Hanni 5,2 – 1 times Rolf – Marie 6 – Rolf – Lisa – Marie 5'.

No indication yet on the *Lichtenstein*. We hoped to reach the 'Fat Car' before it left the range of the *Würzburg* ground radar.

'Rolf – Marie 4'. A slipstream shook our machine. There, a new blip on the screen. That must be the enemy aircraft. The controller continued with his orders but now the pilot only responded to my instructions:

'Rolf – more Rolf – Stop – Marie 2 – a little Lisa – same height – Lisa – Marie 1,5 – Rolf – Marie 1 a little Siegfried (climb) – Rolf – Marie 1 –Lisa – Lisa – Stop – Marie 0,8 – a little Rolf". With a jerk of the controls the pilot called,

'There he is!' To ground control: 'Making Pauke-Pauke'.[34]

'Our eyes looked out and clung to the black shape. Small, blueish exhaust flames made it easier to keep the target in sight. Four engines, twin tail, were recorded almost subconsciously. From about 200 meters aft and to starboard we fired our first burst but apparently without effect. But we had been spotted and the *Viermot* fired and took evasive action. Second attack: The tracer disappeared into its wing and fuselage. He must have been hit!

Continued twisting and turning; another burst but on breaking off the rear gunner had us in his sights. There was a crackling in our aircraft. The starboard engine trailed white smoke. Coolant! But it was still running. I tried to change the ammunition drums. Impossible! Our twisting made them either a ton weight or they flew up around my head. Another attack from the port rear. The shots from the four machine guns were on target. Breaking off to starboard below the *Viermot* we got so close too that, as he went down, at the same time our port wing tip touched his starboard wing. A brief strike but we were still flying. The starboard engine now packed up and stopped.

'The *Viermot* had turned off to port and while I tried to contact control and give the pilot a course for the radio beacon *Bergziege*, the cockpit was suddenly lit up by flames. The enemy aircraft had crashed and its fire lit up the wooded and hilly countryside. Our altitude was still 800 meters. Rounded peaks were below us and above a star-lit sky with a half moon. These impressions were interrupted by the order over the intercom.

'Jump, Johanssen! I cannot hold the machine.'[35]

'Released by the emergency lever, the cabin roof disappeared to the rear. Now out! My brain worked precisely. Best chance to starboard where the engine has stopped! Careful, you must get past below the tailfin! I climbed, no, rolled out of the cabin, still holding on as the pilot called over the intercom: 'Are you out?'

'Then I noticed that the cable from the helmet and the oxygen mask with its tube were still connected to the aircraft. I let myself fall back and disconnected the joints, although these should have released on their own. But one had heard of exceptions. Back on the wing alongside the fuselage. The front cabin cover opened, is flung backwards by the slipstream, the aerial mast disintegrated and at the same moment I let go. Slip along the wing, under the tailplane and count 21-22-23, before I pulled the ripcord of the parachute. Once clear of the machine it was suddenly quiet while doing a couple of somersaults in free fall. Tense expectation happened next. It was the first time, for baling out is not done as an exercise. First there was a rustling on my back (the parachute was worn like a rucksack), then a zishing noise and a heavy jerk. It had opened! Whatever now followed would not matter. Hanging on the 'chute I observed the crash of our aircraft and at almost the same moment a parachute glided past. The thought came as a relief: Engels, the pilot, had got out.

'But something else occupied my mind during these seconds. Down below, a river silvery in the moonlight but directly beneath me two similarly bright rectangles. Carp ponds? The thought had barely occurred to me when there is a swishing and the surroundings grew huge. A heavy impact. I was sitting on the ground, on garden soil, the rear parts somewhat bruised and I was amazed and almost frightened. Two meters away, silvery in the moonlight, there was the wall of a glasshouse and 30 meters further another such 'carp pond'. Swimming would have been no problem but this?!

'It was deathly quiet now, around midnight, with no one in sight. I sent up a green signal light as a sign for my pilot that I was safely down. I left my parachute where it was and, following the next wider path, reached a busy street. The air raid warning was still on. A soldier showed me the way to a telephone in a market garden. Picking up the receiver I heard two men talking. The conversation was about the events of the last minutes and about the parachutists, who they did not know whether they were friend or foe. As I made myself known as a friend there was silence in the line.

'Finally: 'Who's there?' After a brief reply and the request to look for my pilot, it was confirmed that Engels got out all right and was now in Weiblingen at the Gasthof zum Ochsen hostelry. The garrison doctor at Heidelberg, one of the speakers, invited me to go to his home close by. The soldier took me there and explained where I was and what he had seen of the fight. At the doctor's home I got a friendly reception from his family and was able to phone our base at Mainz-Finthen. Comrades congratulated me and said that they had already spoken with Engels. We were to be picked up the following day by a Fieseler *Storch*.

'After a quickly improvised meal a policeman suddenly appeared and asked for my identification. I had to decline, for at the alert I had put on my flying overall only and had left my uniform jacket containing my identity card hanging in the crew room. With his hand on my shoulder he declared that I was under arrest and required me to surrender my arms. The signal pistol was taken from its lanyard and placed, together with the remaining cartridges, upon the table. It must be said that during the preceeding nights some British crews had baled out and had not been found. The tension gradually subsided and I watched further developments almost with amusement. But for the authorities it was bitter earnest. My notebook did not count as evidence, neither the mention that I had just telephoned my unit. Finally Doctor B had a word with the policeman in an adjoining room. After several phone calls I was informed that a civil defense duty car would take me to the *Großdeutschland* Barracks. They were already expecting me in the mess. I was offered a glass of wine but the fact that I did not know that Heidelberg had an airfield, was suspicious. I recounted my experiences but these were discounted. In the end I spent a sleepless night in an *Unteroffizer*'s room whose usual occupants happened to be on leave. In the morning, having reported to the clerks' office, I was taken in a motorcycle side car to Wieblingen. We met *Lt* Engels by the wreckage of our aircraft. The remains were hardly recognisable as an erstwhile Bf 110. The *Storch*, with our *Staffelkapitän* at the controls, landed close by and took us first to the crash site of the Halifax in the Odenwald. The place was recognisable from afar. A new clearing had been made by the fire and the exploding bombs. Part of the crew had escaped by parachute. Beside the wreckage we found tins containing jam and other victuals. For a long time I kept The Story of the Naked Man, a well known English novel I believe, as a souvenir. Our take-off in the Storch from the small meadow and under a telephone line was criminal. The overloaded kite got airborne at the very last moment. Flowers and cigarettes from the enthusiastic spectators of Wieblingen and Odenwald covered the floor of the cabin.'

Engels and *Uffz* Karl-Ludwig Johanssen's first victory was most probably Halifax II BB212 of 405 'Vancouver' Squadron RCAF, which was shot down by a Bf 110 at 17,000-ft and came down near Schönau in the Odenwald. F/Sgt G.T. Chretien DFM and five of his crew had baled out safely and were taken prisoner. The rear gunner, Sgt R. Moore, was killed and later buried in Durnbach War Cemetery. The Stuttgart raid was 405 'Vancouver' Squadron RCAF first in Bomber Command and four of its 15 aircraft despatched failed to return to Leeming. At least three were shot down by night fighters of NJG 4.

Halifax pilot, Ron Read of 78 Squadron at Linton-on-Ouse, recalls:

'It would have been impossible to please aircrew in the choice of targets. The one place that was unlikely to be top on anybody's list was the Ruhr. But it was top of Harris' list in March 1943. On 5 March we were briefed for Essen again. The most heavily defended of the Ruhr towns; the big bogey one that had escaped serious damage to date. I sang '*Off on the Road to Morocco*' quite cheerfully as we taxied out. We were one of 94 Halifaxes from the total of 442 aircraft going. If we didn't know before, we found out what was meant by the Ruhr defenses being tough. On the way in it looked quite frightening from afar. There was solid *flak* ahead and already there was plenty of fighter activity. However, our own passage wasn't too bad and I managed to pick our way safely through the worst areas. We were in the first wave with a mixed batch of 4 and 30-lb incendiaries and a couple of 1000 pounders. Our task was to start the fires that the Lancasters and Stirlings following could use as a target guide. We got there on time and Pathfinder flares were going down as we made the target area. We had a good run up although it was through the heaviest *flak* we'd yet encountered. We dropped our bombs accurately on the flares below. We couldn't see anything of the target itself, as the usual haze covered Essen but it looked, as we turned for home, as though there were heavy fires breaking out. Leaving the target, we saw two aircraft shot down by fighters close by. [Fourteen bombers were lost]. I made a sneaky detour towards the scene on the basis that the attacking aircraft would be on their way elsewhere to seek some other unfortunate victim. It seemed to work out; we had no problems finding our way to quieter skies. Upon return two Linton aircraft were missing. A few days later we learnt that for the very first time the Krupps works was severely damaged by our efforts. We felt quite proud of ourselves.

'Although his main objective during spring 1943 was the Ruhr, to stretch the German defenses Harris varied the attacks with some long-range trips to southern Germany. On 9 March we went to Munich and on the 11th to Stuttgart. On the whole they were a softer option than the Ruhr, not quite such a frantic and frightening scene. Mind you could be killed going there just as easily as anywhere else. On the Stuttgart trip we saw a couple of night fighters flying over the target. One of them attacked us unexpectedly on the way out. I was surprised and thought he had us cold. I flung the aircraft around, expecting a long battle but we evaded him easily. We decided he must have been a 'Sprog'. On the Munich trip, out of 264 aircraft, eight were missing – none of them ours. On Stuttgart 11 out of 314 aircraft were missing. Once again at Linton, we had a charmed night, although six of the missing were Halifaxes.

'One reassuring story we were given by our intelligence staff, was that of 'scarecrow' shells. These were said to be anti-morale shells, fired in the path of a bomber stream to dishearten the crews. They represented aircraft being blown up. As they burst nearby, they showered flaming oil and petrol, together with the pathfinder flares and color signals carried by RAF aircraft. In fact all the symptoms of an exploding aircraft. Briefings referred to the probability of 'scarecrows'. Having been briefed, we would report that 'scarecrows' were active tonight'. We saw them often and used to say how realistic they were. We wondered how the Germans could portray an exploding aircraft so accurately. At the end of the war, when German anti-aircraft personnel were interrogated, it was discovered that they had no such thing in their armory. The 'scarecrows' that we dismissed so casually were real RAF aircraft blowing up. In a way, it was just as well that we didn't know. It was a comforting illusion that saved us some concern. Not that it would have made much difference if we'd known the truth. We were of the generation that would do what we were told, in the name of duty and honor. This was to be well proven in the winter's Battle of Berlin. Most of us were more afraid of being thought afraid than we were of flying over Germany. The period ahead of us in March 1943 was to test that loyalty to orders to the limits. We were entering the Battle of the Ruhr.

'Flogging night after night over enemy territory in our Halifaxes, with ever increasing numbers of Lancasters flying above us, slow Stirlings below and the dwindling Wellingtons around us, we were known in whole, as 'Main Force' squadrons, the work-horses of Bomber Command, making up the main body of any attack. We ploughed our way almost nightly, across Germany, to targets personally selected by our Commander in Chief. Our private hopes lay in doing as good a job as our aircraft and equipment would allow and to survive the night, get back home, ready to fight again.

'By March 1943, excluding the light daylight bombers of No.2 Group there were 51 main force squadrons operating, increasingly equipped with four engined aircraft. At an average of 24 aircraft per squadron there were theoretically 1224 aircraft available although it was probable that only about 50% were ever available at any one time. The rest were in use for training, under repair from damage, under routine maintenance or meeting other calls upon them such as mine laying or working for Coastal Command. Allowing for the ten squadrons still flying Wellingtons with five man crews, we numbered about 8000 trained-aircrew – the tip of an iceberg – reaching down all stages of training from HCUs to recruitment depots. With the five new squadrons of Pathfinders to lead us we were a formidable force. Down the bottom of the ladder at squadron level we were totally unaware of the momentous decisions taken in Bomber Command. At the time there was little of the mutual affection that was to blossom between our chief, 'Butch' Harris and his crews post-war. Then he was a remote, steely-eyed figure, who made announcements to the press about our activities. We basked in the glowing tributes the press paid to our efforts and believed the glossy interpretation of our results portrayed by Harris. We were unaware that much of his optimism was self-deception, brought on by his obsession, shared by many senior air chiefs, British and American, that the bomber on its own would be the war winning instrument. To us he was a man that sent us back to targets several times in succession, increasing the risk each time. He was responsible for sending us in bad weather to undertake almost impossible tasks which our aircraft and equipment was incapable of fulfilling.

'12th March 1943 dawned like any other day on an operational airfield of RAF Bomber Command. Kay, our mysterious WAAF batwoman, tapped gently on the door and slide quickly into the room, placing cups of tea beside our beds. She was out again before we were awake. She was an enigma, to my wireless operator roommate, F/O Bill Ramsey and myself. A lovely redhead with a pale, delicate complexion whose WAAF uniform failed to hide the fullness of her figure, nor could her Air Force issue lisle stockings disguise the shapeliness of her legs. As full-blooded young aircrew Bill and I thought it only a matter of time before we were on good talking terms with her, if nothing else. Kay had other ideas and every day slipped in and out of our room with averted eyes, rather like an escaped nun. Not that I knew many nuns, escaped or otherwise. They were too rare a breed to be entertained by wartime aircrew but just about the only breed that wasn't. Kay's major mystery was the intriguing *USA* flash she wore on her shoulders. What was an American girl doing in the RAF? And from the few occasions she did speak her accent was of Northern England. Her daily appearance was always a titillating start to the harsher facts of the day to come but alas the answer to our enigma was never revealed. Our relationship with her remained confined to day-to-day greetings, nothing else.

'Breakfast over, we wandered down to the flights to report to our flight commander, S/L Bertie Neal. Having counted the heads of his available pilots and learned that their crews were accounted for and available, he took himself off to the office of W/C Jerry Warner to learn of our fate for the next 24 hours. 'You never know,' said Bertie hopefully in his 'slussching' lisp. 'We might even get a shctand down, Ha, Ha, Ha!'

'We spent the next hour checking with our crews and ground crews, obtaining the serviceability state of our own aircraft after the night before.

'Shorry blokes,' said Bertie, when we returned to the flights an hour later. 'We're on again tonight. Maxshimum effort.'

'That meant all available crews and aircraft. Most of the crews departed to their various tasks. 'Morty' Mortenson, and I, as deputy flight commanders stayed behind to receive any further instructions. There wasn't much Bertie could say. No one was supposed to learn the target before briefing. 'By the fuel loads, its going to be 'Happy Valley' was all he could add. 'Happy Valley' was the RAF's euphemism for the Ruhr. The most feared and heavily defended targets in all Germany lay within its sprawling maw. The little knot, peanut size that always lay in the pit of my stomach on ops days, swelled a little more. I just hoped it wasn't going to be the hardest of them all, Essen again. We had been there the week before, on the 5th. It wasn't an experience I was anxious to repeat.

'The rest of the morning passed with the testing of equipment in the aircraft, culminating in an air test, where everything we could test, we did. We couldn't test the guns without going out to sea, which needed special clearance. We would test those after we crossed the coast of England, on our way to the enemy coast. Everything else we could test, we did. Navigation systems, radio, autopilot, bomb doors, turrets and hopefully, landing gear, upon our return. Everything worked and after a short discussion with the ground crew we repaired to our respective messes for lunch. Briefing was scheduled for 1600 hours.

'The briefing room was on top of Station HQ at Linton, reached by an outside wooden staircase. Extinguishing our cigarettes below, we clattered noisily aloft to take our seats inside. The big wall map at the end of the room was covered with a canvas curtain. The two wing commanders entered, followed by the Station Commander, G/C John Whitley. The chattering ceased and we stood until told to be seated. Briefing tonight was to be by W/C Leonard Cheshire, CO of 76 Squadron, our sister squadron at Linton. The two squadron commanders took it in turns to take the briefing. Gerry Warner was the CO of our squadron, 78 but we all preferred Chesh's briefings. They came from much more experience. W/C Leonard Cheshire DSO DFC and Bar had recently been promoted from squadron leader to take over 76 Squadron. At 24-years of age he was becoming a legend in Bomber Command because of his book; 'Bomber Pilot' published earlier in the year. For the first time, it put down on paper the experiences and feelings of a bomber crew at war. Reading it while in training, we had our doubts about the author. It flew in the face of the RAF tradition of never 'shooting a line'. Who was this chap, who was openly talking of his operational experiences not just in the mess but to the world at large? He must be a real lineshooter, putting it all down in a book. Many were the reservations we held about him.

'We looked at him as he first came into the mess. He looked harmless enough. Could he really be the chap who wrote that book? In fact he was and as soon as we had spoken and listened to him our doubts dissolved. He was a quiet, modest enough individual in any company. But he was also dedicated to the business of winning the war and wanted to share his experiences with other crews, to help them and the world at large to promote the war effort, especially that of the RAF. Before his 76 appointment, he had been a member of a British mission to the USA, on a tour to bring home to the American public the facts of being at war with Germany and to raise help for the RAF and Britain's cause. We soon found him an entirely open and helpful commander who would give assistance and advice to any member of aircrew who needed it, irrespective of which squadron he was in. He was now developing new tactics to assist in countering the German defenses. We had received the minimum instruction on this during our training. No formal lessons, just casual tips from those of our instructors who completed a tour and the 'no line shoot' tradition muted those too mere references. Chesh was providing a lot of light in our dankness.

'So we were all agog for his message that night. He stepped up onto the platform. We sat down and he pulled back the curtain across the map with a flourish, saying, 'Gentlemen, our target for tonight is Essen.'

'Glug! Our hearts dropped. There it lay, at the end of the red ribbon delineating our route, passing through the massed red hatched areas indicating the heavy anti-aircraft defenses and fighters of the Kammhuber Line, which protected the interior of Germany, from Denmark to south east of Paris. The section passing around the Ruhr, the most heavily defended of all.

'Not that the Kammhuber Line itself made a lot of difference. We had to fly through it to get to almost any North German target. It was just that going to Essen, the intensity of the defenses increased when you passed the line, rather than decreased as they did when you got through anywhere else. The little knot in my stomach grew to a pigeon's egg.

'Chesh told us that there were 457 aircraft going, one of the highest numbers for some time. 158 twin engined Wellingtons, 156 Lancasters; only 91 of our Halifaxes. Hallies had taken a beating on the previous two raids. There were 42 Stirlings and ten Mosquitoes, the latter acting as Pathfinder markers. Our role was that of fire raisers, following in immediately after the first pathfinders had dropped their marker flares. We were dropping incendiaries and two one thousand-pound bombs, to stir things up and light the fires for the following Lancasters to plaster them with their 4000 lb Block Busters. We were beginning to find our raising role a little onerous. The German defenses had the habit of waiting until they were certain that the target was properly identified. They held their fire until the initial markers went down and then gave the following aircraft – us – all they had.

'Having given us our route and general advice Chesh stepped down and we listened half-heartedly to the intelligence briefing on the defenses, which, as always, was optimistic. We knew what they were really like and didn't need to be told by an ancient, non-flying officer, what he imagined was in stone for us. The weather was good and the pathfinders were using the new *Oboe*[36] technique of marking the target with special flares dropped by the Mosquitoes, directly controlled by radio beams from England. At least we ought not to be hanging around waiting for the markers, as had been the case sometimes in the past.

'Take off was to be at 1900 hours. Briefing over, we left for our messes once more for our operational meal of real eggs and real bacon, which were unavailable to almost anyone else in wartime UK except through the black market. They were fattening us up for the kill. 'Morty' Mortenson had a macabre sense of humour. As this culinary treat was served he made the statement, 'The condemned man ate a hearty breakfast,' a statement that accompanied the notice of the hanging of a murderer. We ignored him and chewed doggedly on. By now the knot in my stomach was reaching the size of a hen's egg and the bacon tasted like leather.

'Leaving the mess we returned to flights to prepare for take off time. This waiting time was always the worst period. My hen's egg in the stomach grew steadily into an orange.

'The crews met in the locker room to dress up for the cold night skies. Depending on the anticipated weather, we could don Long Johns and string vests, on retain our normal underwear. We could wear our battle dress tops and cover them with the fur-lined Irvine suit, usually just the jacket. In between these was the long, heavy, white, submariner's jersey, which some quirk of supply branch humour labeled '*Aircrew, Frocks white*.' In summer, the battledress alone was sufficient. There was some heating in our Halifaxes, although it was not wholly reliable on effective. March though, was a time still for Irvine jackets over battle dress and jersey.

'Dressed, we stood around talking and joking with the other crews. By now, the jokes were pretty forced and we'd heard them all before. Nevertheless, they were part of the ritual and we laughed as best we could. Finally, the time came for us to step into the waiting crew buses, three crews to a bus, or the back of a three-tonner, if you weren't quick. I had my favourite little WAAF driver 'Blondie' to the squadron. Short, curly blond hair, sparkling blue eyes and a broad Glaswegian accent. The rest of her was enveloped in battle dress. Her sharp Glaswegian humour made her stand out from the other drivers. I managed as usual, to grab a seat in the cab beside her and her Glaswegian chatter kept me occupied until we reached the aircraft.

'My orange sized lump had reached jaffa proportions by this time. But now as I went to work it subsided. Outside checks in the company of Jimmy my Rhodesian flight engineer, were completed. I joined the nest of my crew aboard, already stowing their gear and busy checking what equipment they could before the engines started. I checked the fuselage interior on the way up to my seat. Once ensconced in the cockpit, I got to work in earnest, preparing for start-up. The lump that had been in my stomach all day, had disappeared. I was too preoccupied now to think about it. And so it would remain, at least unless some serious danger threatened later.

'Five minutes later the green Verey signal for 'Start Up' rose from the control tower and 30 Halifax captains gave the thumbs up to the crew chief standing below his cockpit. The fitter underneath the fuselage pressed the button on his battery cart and the skipper pressed his starter buttons. The noise reverberated around the airfield as 120 Rolls-Royce Merlin engines roared into life. Now that all power sources were operating, each crewmember tested the rest of his systems. I checked with Jimmy that all engines were running OK and he told me when they were ready for run up. Starting with the port inner we tested all four through each operating cycle.

'Run ups completed, each crewmember called in to say their equipments were OK. Now we were ready to taxi. Two on three aircraft were already moving, as we moved out of dispersal onto the taxiway. Our dispersal was quite a way from the runway, so I usually finished up about seventh on eighth in the line of aircraft waiting to take off. This gave me time to study their take offs and the possible side effect of a cross wind, as well as to gauge the length of take off likely to be needed. These useful little snippets of information could help in an emergency. Finally, on the end of the runway the green lamp from the runway control van cleared us for take off. Giving a quick wave to those lucky people assembled at the control van to see us off, I opened the throttles and we were away.

'Sluggishly and slowly the Halifax came to life. Watching the increasing air speed and feeling the beginnings of life flowing into the controls, I held hen down until the speed was 10 knots above the recommended take off speed. Every cautious pilot liked to have an extra ten knots for Mother. Then, wheels up and off on the long, slow, bomb laden climb that would not stop until we were somewhere over Holland. We circled Linton for 20 minutes before setting course at the specified time. Joined by another 50 on more Halifaxes from adjacent airfields, we climbed individually into the fading light towards our destiny. In an hour we would be the playthings of fate. We were all aware that some of us wouldn't return. The self-protective aspects of human nature made us believe that it couldn't be us. Although sometimes a little secret, traitorous voice kept asking, '*Why not*?' If I cared to think about it I knew quite well why not. The current chop rate was 4% per sortie. Since you had to complete 30 sorties before being taken off operations for a rest, there was a strong mathematical probability that you wouldn't. So I didn't think about it. Take each day and especially each flying night, as it came, was the common Bomber Command' crew's attitude.

'So 30 minutes later we lumbered across Flamborough Head to head for Egmond on the Dutch coast. This was our usual route and the Germans were aware of it. They had a fighter station adjacent to Egmond that could catch us on the way in and out. That seemed to make little difference to the plans of Bomber Command. We went that route with monotonous regularity when going to the Ruhr or north Germany. Going to south Germany, we departed via Southwold, the regular crossing point for the 5 Group Lancasters stationed around Lincoln and the 3 Group Wellingtons operating from Norfolk and Suffolk. Going further south we always left via Dungeness. And they said the Germans were inflexible! My aircraft, *C for Charlie* was slow on the climb and I often had to climb at 135 knots rather than the recommended speed of 140. I didn't mind this too much on the shorter trips. It gave me the opportunity to study the lay of the skies ahead and note what was happening to the 'press on types' rushing into the lead. It wasn't long before we could see the flashes on the horizon that indicated the arrival over Holland of the first wave of pathfinder aircraft. But it wasn't at the coast that the action began. The German flak ships stationed a few miles offshore were always ready to pop off a hostile reception for the unwary. One of the benefits of being behind the front runners was that I could pinpoint them and fly a course to avoid them.

'We tested our guns as we saw the flashes and I warned the crew to tighten up their look out for fighters. We saw nothing of anything in the black sky but every now and then we bumped across the slipstream of an aircraft in front. Although that meant he was probably dangerously close I took comfort from it. It showed we weren't entirely on our own. Crossing the coast, weaving through the growing bursts of flak we set a westerly course for our final turning point, before the nun to the target. Now above 16,000ft the aircraft was sluggish and slow to respond to controls. I tried to avoid sharp movements, as that led to a loss of precious height. But out of self preservation I always gave a bank to the left and night every five minutes or so just to give the lookouts a chance to note any crafty fighter climbing up from below. There was one on two bursts of air-to-air firing close to us, indicating fighters in action. We redoubled our lookout. Now, well into the heavily defended areas of the Kammhuber Line, the intensity of the flak was increasing. Just ahead of us was the Ruhr and there it was already an inferno of brilliant explosions, which appeared to fill the sky.

'Christ, it's worse than last time,' I called on the intercom. 'Come up and have a quick look at this Vic.' I invited the navigator.

'No thanks Skip.' I'm too busy. Anyway, I saw it the last time. Your course to the target is 156 in two minutes.'

'I knew he wouldn't come up. He'd only even looked out once. After a glance of less than a minute at the angry sky he returned to his little enclosed world of the nav cabin, never to appear again until we were ready for landing. He was lucky. Some of us had to look out. Apart from me and my two gunners Jimmy the engineer in the observation dome and Harry Laidlaw the bomb aimer, who was now going down on his pad, had to peer at it all through his bombsight. I banked steeply onto the last course, having a good look below as I did so. From now on we had to keep straight and level if possible.

'The flak was heavier than even before on the run up. We were bounced around by the bursting shells below and a stink of cordite from those bursting in front filled the cockpit. I clung onto the controls to try to keep things level for old Harry peering down through his sight. Taff, our wireless op back in his cabin, groped his way past me going back to the flare chute at the rear to make sure the large magnesium photoflash slid down the chute when we released the bombs. Shrapnel rattled against the fuselage. Our only consolation was that the flak wasn't predicted and aimed just at us. It was the usual blanket stuff, pooped up at random now they knew our approach path. Not that it was much of a consolation -flak was all a matter of luck – but looking out into the face of that inferno I needed all the consolation I could find, as well as all the luck. I could see the marker flares ahead quite clearly. So could Harry. I opened the bomb doors and told him we were all his.

'OK Skip', I've got the markers in sight. Steady, hold it at that.'

'Just as he said it, we got a roaring bang under the tail that pushed the nose down and way off to the left.

'Right, come right, you're a long way off. Come around about ten degrees right, quick', called Harry. I stomped on the rudders and swung us around. We were still a bit off to the left.

'More right,' Harry called urgently. I pushed her round against the *flak* bounces.

'A bit more – more – that's it. Steady, steady; hold her there!'

'The marker flares had disappeared under the nose but there was plenty to see. Some aircraft had already dropped their loads and fires were lighting up the ground. Among them I could see the flashes of HE bombs exploding.

'How far now Harry? We don't want to overshoot.'

'OK, Skip', it's coming up now. Steady – steady – steady.'

'I thought he'd never stop saying steady. Essen was at its worst. We were still bouncing around from the flak and I was sure Harry was over-shooting.

'Come on Harry, for Christ's sake. How much further?' Harry was not to be hurried and I shouldn't have been impatient.

'Just a little more, left, left, a little, steady,'

'Just as I reached bursting point, 'Bombs Gone' he called.

'Now came the most testing time of all. As the bombs were released, a little red light came up on the panel before me. It was the photoflash light. As the bombs fell they were followed by the photoflash, which, exploding above the site where our bombs would strike, would enable our camera in the fuselage to take a picture of that point. According to the height from which it had been dropped, that photoflash took between six and ten seconds to go off. I had to keep the aircraft flying straight and level across the target until the light went out, when every instinct screamed for me to fling the aircraft away from it and head for home. I closed the bomb doors and settled down for the longest ten seconds in the history of the world. The flak was getting worse, as more and more aircraft entered the target area. I hung on until, thank God, the light went out. I started a full right turn away. Just as I did I saw sparks going forward over my turning starboard wing. Now there were always sparks flying back from the engine exhausts when they were at full power but these sparks were going forwards. Christ! They weren't sparks; they were tracer bullets. We had a fighter, which none of us had seen.

'Halfway round my turn away from the target I could only go one way: down and back into it. I pushed the aircraft down into the *flak*-filled sky below and hoped for the best. Fortunately, the fighter either lost me or decided on discretion and not to risk being shot down by his own *flak*. Now down at 11,000 and still descending, my full turn had carried us right back over the target again. Now I had to get us out in the clear. I didn't want to go lower into the light *flak* at around 10,000ft. It looked unhealthily close already. A loud bang under the port wing pushed us into an even steeper turn. I wrenched the controls back into a steep turning, lumbering climb up and away from the target area. That's when the engineer, Jimmy, took a hand.

'Port outer engine is heating up, Skip'; it's going off the clock. You'll have to feather it.'

'Jesus, that bloody port outer. We'd had lost of trouble with it on previous trips. This was the fourth time it had let us down. That was if it hadn't been hit. The *flak* burst was certainly close enough. Anyway I couldn't leave it to run and not feather it; that would lead to a fire. There had been several engine fires in Halifaxes in the air recently. Not only would a fire probably force us to abandon the aircraft but also if really flamed, we'd be a clear target for every gun and fighter around. I feathered and our not very rapid climb dwindled to a slight upward stagger. That was when Taff re-entered the fray.

'Hey Skip'. I think there's a fire down here. There's a lot of smoke coming up from somewhere. What shall I do?'

'I couldn't think of another answer than, 'Put the bloody thing out then.'

While I pondered on our state (if you can call a quick mental debate of baling out now or trying to drag us away from an undoubtedly hostile Essen 'pondering') we somehow staggered to 12,000ft, gradually clearing the target area to quieter skies to the west. Taff called back quite soon.

'It's OK Skip, it's out. Don't know what it was but its clear now.'

'Thank goodness for small mercies. If you could call not having an engine on fire a small one. Now we could start the long haul home. It would be a long haul too on three engines. Once in the clear I checked to find all the crew still in one piece, excited and glad to be clear of the target area. But we were low and slow, lower even than the poor old Stirlings who usually caught the *flak*. It was not a good pace to be but I didn't want to descend in case we lost another engine and we couldn't climb at all.

'All right chaps but we're not home yet. Don't relax. Keep the look out going and Vic, what about our course? Any change after all that weaving?'

'Don't think so Skip. I think it's all night. Just keep her on 283. We should go out north of Antwerp.'

'Vic was never quite sure where we were until after we'd left it behind. We ploughed on at a snail's pace of 130 knots so that I could climb a little more to give us room for maneuver as we crossed the coast. I noted sporadic fighter action around us and kept giving a tilt to right and left for the gunners to view the sky below but there was little venom in that night for us. We made our departure from continental Europe quietly. Although a *flak* ship or two were still having a last word, it was not with us. After a long flog across the North Sea we saw the welcoming flashes of the red airfield beacons in England from 20 miles out and flew in over Filey Bay to land at Linton 5 hours 30 minutes after take off, glad to be once more on terra firma. The more firma the less terror, we always said.

'Once on the ground while waiting for the bus to take us back to our next chore, de-briefing, we discussed our night with the ground crew. We were in a mixed mood of relief, exhilaration and fatigue; pretty standard feelings after a hard flight. The one thing we wanted was to get to the mess and have a drink, eat our second bacon and egg meals, which I would enjoy much more than the first, simmer down and get to bed, but we had to be de-briefed first. That meant a joust in the briefing room with the intelligence staff, never a welcome task. Quite apart from the RAF tradition of understatement and never shooting a line, most aircrew were not ready to give long, detailed, descriptions of the night's events so soon after. On the other hand, the intelligence staff was anxious to obtain the immediate impressions, so that they would report to the group headquarters. Group itself was required to report to Bomber Command.

'Thus there was a little conflict between the crews and de-briefing staff. We tended to minimize events, whereas the intelligence staff tried to press us into revealing every detail. Our reports were normally laconic and tense while they tried to coax us into expanding them into detailed sagas. I was fortunate in that one of the WAAF intelligence officers, Pam Finch, had a sympathetic understanding of the way aircrew felt and was a good friend. She was smart and most popular. Short but well proportioned, her elfin face was surrounded by jet-black hair. Her voice and posture indicated a good girls-school background but all that breeding couldn't hide a slightly predatory air when she looked squarely into the eyes of the officer she was debriefing. She was a favorite with my crew and fortunately, I was one of her favorite pilots. I was always under pressure from the crew to take her out but I felt Pam was a little too high class and gentile for our rollicking evenings. We were good friends and that's how I liked it. As we walked into the briefing room to find several other crews waiting, Pam rounded off the de-briefing she was engaged in, just in time to call us to her desk. She almost always managed to do this. Aware of our feelings, she usually accepted our brief statements without probing too much for detailed expansion. Consequently, we said that it was a good 'prang' on the target. We had seen a fighter, though we couldn't see the type. The defenses were heavier than last time; otherwise it was pretty well a normal Ruhr trip.

'We learned the next day that 23 aircraft, five per cent of the force, some 140 aircrew, were missing. We had to do 30 trips for a tour of operations, then a six months rest before starting another tour of 20 trips. You didn't have to be a mathematician to wonder how it could be done. Still, this was just another mystery in the day of the life of a Bomber Command crew, vintage 1943. Sometimes I pondered on that other, greater, mystery. Just what was I doing here and how did I get roped into this bloody dangerous pastime? Not that I really had anyone else but myself to blame and anyway, in the words of every RAF flight sergeant listening to complaints from recruits, 'If you don't like it, yer shouldn't have joined.[37]

One of the losses on the Essen raid was Stirling I EF330/P flown by F/Sgt A. Pearson with Victor Page as his 2nd dickey. Page's erstwhile observer Spud Taylor noted:

'The rest of us are quite stunned at the idea of never seeing the laddie again. Went for a long walk tonight out along the Brandon road'.[38] On 27 March we left Lakenheath for 1657 Heavy Conversion Unit at Stradishall to acquire a replacement pilot. We got there long after others had already 'crewed up' and when we were shown into a large room there was only one pilot left. He looked rather thin and weedy but there was no one else. We introduced ourselves. He said his name was Bill. We asked him if he would be our pilot? He laughed and said,

'You'll regret it.'

'We laughed back, putting it down to typical British understatement.

'Stradishall was the usual monotony of circuits and bumps, which were brightened only by a remarkable series of lousy landings. Bill's weak point apparently was landing, whilc landings had been Vic's strong point. Bill hadn't much grip and we came pretty near to a prang on one landing. After bashing down in an unusually hearty manner on the deck, he suddenly decided to take off again (we were then about half way up the runway) and in a series of sickly swerves we closely missed the roof of the hangars. However, on 18 April we were posted to Downham Market and 218 'Gold Coast' Squadron, also flying Stirlings.'

Late in March meanwhile, Ron Read was promoted Flight Lieutenant and appointed deputy flight commander in 78 Squadron at Linton-on-Ouse:

'One day I had a long and controversial conversation with a couple of Intelligence Officers about 'Chop Rates'. They were averaging 4% per sortie, I mused, that with 30 sorties to complete, the average crew had a minus 20% chance of surviving. Their reply was instant and consoling but spoken from theory, not experience.

'Oh no,' they said. 'It doesn't work like that. The statisticians say it starts from zero, for every trip so it's only ever 4%.'

'Nonsense' I said. 'If you only had to go once, it would be 4%, as long as you don't go again. If you go again your percentage chance of the chop must go up. I've got to find a way to get on to some one else's percentage.' They laughed and tried to convince me by insisting the statisticians had proved it was only 4%. 1 said, if they'd find me a statistician who'd completed 30 operations, I might believe it. Otherwise I believed myself. By this time into a tour one became quite cynical. The illusions of youth had fallen away. Gone were the images fostered by the Battle of Britain of single-engined knights of the air jousting in the blue skies. We saw the raw, ugly face of death and destruction all around us when nightly flying those hostile skies across the North Sea.

'Giving the matter some thought I developed what I called my 'percentage' approach. I decided that we should go in a little behind our own wave to be able to assess what had gone before. This would take us round the course, over and through the target when, hopefully, the guns and fighters were still busy with the keen young pilots pressing on in front. There were always some. Whilst they were being attacked we would follow in the relative calm and slip through. A ground radar controller handling a box 30 miles deep dealt with each battery of guns and each enemy fighter. He picked an aircraft as it entered his box at its western edge and if it wasn't lost or shot down handed it over to the controller of the next box 30 miles east. I felt I could take advantage of this system. I decided that we should be up to two minutes late at each turning point. My theory was that when we entered a box the controller would be busy with the people in front.

'When I saw anyone being fired on by *flak* or fighters or coned in searchlights I would edge up to him, not too close but enough to feel shielded by the interest of the enemy forces in him. Once he escaped or was shot down I hoped to be too close to the controller's far boundary for him to bother with me. I reasoned that he would turn his attention back to his western boundary to pick up some one just entering it, thus missing me. In this way I thought I might get a little of the percentage of survival chance of those aircraft shot down near me. Hence my 'Percentage' system. Crude and cynical perhaps but flying a bomber over Germany in the spring of 1943 was a crude and cynical business. Morty Mortenson went on leave after the second Essen trip. We had a good break for 12 nights, as the weather was too bad to operate.'

On the night of 24/25 March 1943 *Oblt* Dietrich 'Dieter' Schmidt's name appeared on the 8./NJG 1 battle order for a different type of mission:

'During 1942-43 the British often penetrated with single, low flying aircraft over Holland to drop sabotage equipment, weapons and at times secret agents, to aid the Resistance. Dutch liaison people called in the material by radio and three or four simple lamps marked the dropping zones. For some time the *Abwehr* had succeeded in turning the whole thing around and the radio traffic was now almost completely controlled by German posts. Thus, the material, including the agents, could be collected immediately at the dropping zone. In order to make sure that the whole game looked real we received orders from time to time to shoot down one of the Special Operations machines. The whole exercise was difficult for us insofar as it was hard to track down machines by radar because of their low flying height. These missions were relatively unattractive for the 'old hands'. For us 'young hands' however, they were a welcome practice. We were briefed on the place and time of the established drop and we take off as soon as the intruder was confirmed.

'Shortly after midnight, as expected, the radio connection with the *Jägerleitoffizier* (JLO, or GCI-controller) faded out relatively soon. The last message we received was that the aircraft was homeward bound at a height of 200 meters. We proceeded at a height of one hundred meters in the direction of the Zuider Zee and beneath us – the night is not too dark – we saw the newly reclaimed land to the east of the Zuider Zee. Then suddenly my *Bordfunker* discovered him above – definitely four-engined. I sneaked up on him from behind. A short burst in the left wing. I could see hits registering but despite the low-level, at which we flew, he immediately peeled off to the right and levelled off just over the water. I could only still chase him because of a fire in his left engine, the glow of which reflected on the water. Immediately after everything was dark. Over and out? A red Verey light, which a few minutes later was fired into the sky from the spot, confirmed that it had crashed.

'Therefore we were deeply disappointed when on our return at the Operations Room we were greeted with the news that the intruder's outward flight had been reported over Northern Holland. Empty handed again! I gathered that I had, out of inexperience and for fear of detection, opened fire at much too long a range and with far too short a burst! With the obvious mixed feelings we drove to our quarters and tried to sleep. At dawn the phone rudely awakened me:

'My congratulations on your first kill.'

'Are you trying to pull my leg?' On the other end of the line was my friend Werner Rapp, who was duty officer and still in the Operations Room. He informed me that the crew of seven had been picked up in their dinghy between Enkhuizen and Stavoren. So the aircraft did crash! The report on the outward-bound machine was a second enemy aircraft.'[39]

On 26 March F/L Ron Read in 78 Squadron went back to the Ruhr, this time to Duisburg. Once again he was on special reconnaissance, which meant that he had to 'hang around' to report the efects of the raid:

'Special recce on Hamburg was one thing but the Ruhr was another. Wherever you hung around in the Ruhr you were over another town and the defences embraced both. They were fierce everywhere and growing more so. Once again we were in the first wave after Pathfinders so we could expect the same warm reception we got at Essen. Giving the matter some thought I extended my 'percentage' approach. I decided that we should go in even a little more behind our own wave to be able to assess what had gone before. This would take us round the course, over and through the target when hopefully the guns and fighters were still busy with the keen pilots pressing on in front. We would follow in the relative calm behind, slip through quietly if possible and observe. It worked on Duisburg like a charm. Four minutes late we sailed in and out having a good look at the action below as we went round. I worked my way in following two aircraft, one engaged by flak and the other by a fighter. Over the target we could see little on the ground and I couldn't say much in my recce report. I wasn't very enthusiastic about what I saw. I was right. Pathfinders had gone awry and the raid was scattered.

'We were briefed for Berlin on 27 March. There were 396 aircraft going. As it was beyond the range of our fuel capacity we were to carry 240 extra gallons in a bomb bay tank. It reduced our bomb load but as we were now fixed in our role as fire raisers, the loss of the two 1000 pounders made little difference. It was a fine Saturday evening as we taxied out. Well loaded with our extra fuel I knew we were going to use the entire runway for take off. When our turn came I was careful to give her full power as soon as I could and to hold her down for as much of the runway as I could get. She came off well but almost as soon as I got the wheels up Mac's voice came on the intercom: 'Hey. Is it raining outside Skip? There's all water coming into my turret' It was fine and clear outside and I wondered what was happening in Mac's turret. I was still thinking of a funny answer when Jimmy called urgently; 'Christ, it's fuel; the bloody over-load tanks leaking.' I felt him leap back into the fuselage. Looking back around my seat I could see a fountain of fuel spurting out of the bomb bay inspection cover in the floor. A light spray was flying back to the rear into Mac's turret. I was really glad that I had insisted on a strict no smoking regime at all times. Looking out of my cockpit window I saw all the sparks of red-hot soot flying back from the exhaust pipes. They always accompanied a take-off at full power and didn't bother us but tonight they were flying back into a stream of raw petrol. I hastily throttled back until the flow of sparks became a trickle. They weren't a pretty sight. We were still literally sitting on a time bomb. If a spark reached the fuel a flash back could see us finish up as a spectacular firework display.

'The smell of petrol was overpowering. Telling everyone to put on their oxygen masks I turned it on to full flow and opened the cockpit windows creating a flow of air through the aircraft. I glanced back at Jimmy and saw him face down on the floor, his arm down the bomb bay hatch immersed in a diminishing flow of petrol. Somehow he got the flow stopped. By this time I was at 1000 ft heading for Filey Bay on the Yorkshire coast. I knew we couldn't make it to Berlin and back without at least 150 gallons of the overload fuel. We flew on out to sea and dropped our bombs 'safe' in the approved area. Flying back we could see the other aircraft climbing outbound. With everything normal once more I felt guilty again. Perhaps we should have gone on but to finish up baling out over Germany or floating in a dinghy in the North Sea wasn't a future I sought. Normal Bomber Command activities exposed us to danger often enough without us making our own contribution. We made a quiet return and told our tale to an unbelieving Timber Woods, our engineering officer. Inside, the aircraft looked normal now. Next day our overload tank drained out at about 120 gallons. If I'd flown very slowly we might have landed in the North Sea just within reach of our rescue services.

'Post war analysis showed that the raid on Berlin that night was a failure. The pathfinders marked two areas but they were short of their aiming pints by five miles. Consequently, none of the bombs came within five miles of the target area in the center of the city so they didn't miss me much. Out of 396 aircraft despatched nine were missing.

'Two days after our last 'shaky do' on our Berlin take-off Jock Hill told me he was 'on' that night. I knew it was the 'Big City' again. Trying to make 30 Berlin trips, Jock only went there. I hoped we'd have better luck than the last time. Briefing was a nail biter. The weather forecast was awful. Thick cloud most of the way with a high icing index, just the formula I hatched. Miraculously, the cloud was supposed to clear over the target. At briefing we were told that Churchill particularly wanted a RAF presence over Berlin that night. There was a *Nazi* Party rally and Göring was to be present. We carefully checked the overload tank cap. At take-off time there were low clouds on the deck and pouring rain. We were all pleased when the red Very light for a 'scrub' went up from the control tower. We weren't so pleased when we learned that it was only a postponement. We were to take off two hours later at 2000 hrs. At 2000 we went out only to be told to position our aircraft on the taxiway for a 2200 hrs take-off. Our nerves by now were pretty taught. At 2130 we went out again to our pre-positioned aircraft. It was a terribly rough night. The wind was howling, rocking the aircraft as we sat in it. The rain was hammering on the wings and fuselage. We wished Churchill would go and get Göring himself.

'Engines started. '*The Road To Morocco*' was definitely not on the program. We still expected a scrub in such awful conditions when incredulously at ten sharp the first aircraft got a green light and lumbered off down the runway. I was number four for take-off and still hoping for the 'scrub'. I pointed *C Charlie* into the black night and got the dreaded green light. I crossed my fingers and gingerly poured on the throttles. The strong wind lifted us off in no time. It was a struggle to keep the aircraft on an even keel. She was being bounced all over the sky. We entered cloud at 600 ft and the bouncing got worse until at 6000 she settled down to a slightly smoother ride. We left the English coast at 6000 ft and she wasn't climbing very well. I knew what was happening; we were picking up ice. I felt sick. After the last debacle I really had to go on tonight. We struggled up to about 9000 and had been flying for just over an hour. Suddenly there was a big bang from the port inner engine and a great black mass sailed over the cockpit, striking the roof with a resounding clunk as it went. I thought we might have hit another aircraft. The port inner made a lot more noise and I was ready to feather it but scanning all the instruments I could see no malfunction and it still seemed to be turning. A check with the crew revealed no other problems.

'Peering out in the pitch black night I couldn't exactly see what had happened but it looked as though there was a big hole in the inner engine cowling. I still thought we might have clipped someone's tail wheel somehow. The port inner still sounded funny, noisy and rattling and still below 10,000 we weren't climbing much either. My thoughts ran riot. *'Christ! What would they think?* Two Berlin trips and we turned back on both. OK, we could do little else on the previous one but problems with the aircraft again, who will believe it? I gave it another ten minutes. We weren't climbing at all now and the engine still sounded very different. Somehow it was all wrong. Sick at heart I was forced to concede defeat and turn back for Linton. (The whole engine cowling had flown off. Passing over the aircraft it hit the top of the fuselage and carried away all our aerials. It appeared that it had not been properly fastened). When we called on the only communications we had left – the trailing aerial – we were No.7 to land. Out of 22 Linton aircraft setting out only five claimed to have reached Berlin. This made me feel a lot better.'

Nachtjagd scored 96 victories during March 1943. These included 18 by III./NJG 1 and nine by I./NJG 1. On the night of 29/30 March when 329 aircraft of Bomber Command raided Berlin[40] and 149 *Oboe*-guided Wellingtons bombed Bochum 21 Berlin raiders and 12 Wellingtons of the Bochum force failed to return.[41] Sgt Tom Wingham, a bomb-aimer in Sgt Dave Hewlett's Halifax II crew in 102 Squadron at Pocklington, Yorkshire was flying his 10th op (in *Q-Queenie* 'the oldest, clapped out Halifax on the squadron – quite notorious for its lack of climbing ability and poor ceiling'):

> 'We had been to Berlin two nights before and Harris was determined to get in another raid on the Big City before the light evenings. The weather forecast at briefing was ghastly and our station Met officers unofficially predicted a certain 'scrub'. Came take-off time and the weather was on the deck with heavy rain from the occlusion running N to S over Yorkshire to Lincolnshire. Cloud as solid up to 15,000 ft with severe icing predicted. Take-off was put back and we knew there had to be a 'scrub'. The weather persisted and take off was again put back. But Harris would not cancel and eventually we took off. The occlusion tailed back over Yorkshire and almost as soon as we took off we were in cloud as set course over the North Sea. We flogged our way upwards through the occlusion and at 15,000 ft we were still in cloud and were unable to climb another foot. Our climb had been so slow we had taken the whole of the North Sea to reach this height. Now straight and level and still in cloud, we found ourselves with iced-up windscreen and turrets and a maximum IAS of 135 knots. At this point we must have been somewhere near Flensburg for we suddenly became the object of some heavy AA fire. Even the Germans didn't seem to believe an aircraft could be flying so slowly since most of the bursts seemed to be ahead of us. With everyone operating 'blind' because of the icing, discretion now had to be the better part of valour. We dropped our bombs hoping against hope that they might give the German gunners earache but more in the hope of getting a bit more speed from the lightened aircraft.
>
> 'Thankfully, we turned for home and managed to recross the occlusion without incurring any further icing. As we reached the end of the runway we had to feather the starboard outer as the oil pressure dropped off the clock. Arriving at dispersal we got out and walked around the aircraft where one of the ground staff was getting rather excited. Both inner engines were shedding a steady flow of glycol. From one of the wing bomb bays two 4-lb incendiaries were protruding with the other 88 lying loose in the bomb-bay doors. The IFF aerial had disappeared. Had we gone on to Berlin it seems certain that we would have either have run out of engines, had a wing on fire, or in the last resort, have been shot down by Fighter Command. Sometimes it was easier to fight the Germans.'

Whenever an approaching bomber force was reported, the experienced *Nachtjagd Experten* crews were always the first to take off and take up their positions in the *Himmelbett* boxes. The young, green replacement crews were only rarely sent against returning aircraft. *Lt* Hans Krause and his crew in I./ NJG 3 operated for almost a year before they claimed their first two *Himmelbett* kills[42] on 6/7 October 1942. Then came recognition, as he recalls:

> 'At the end of January 1943 *Major* Knoetsch, my commander of I./NJG 3, honored me with the task of taking over a detachment of four aircraft at Wunstorf near Hanover. I felt this to be a preliminary to becoming a *Staffelkapitän* and was very proud and endeavoured do my job, which was similar to those of a *Staffel* commander, to the full. I was always on the ball, keeping my eye on everything. My experience as technical officer proved to be a great help. I was always able to report my aircraft as ready for action. Although the airfield at Wunstorf was relatively small, it had been built during peacetime and therefore had all possible modern facilities. We felt well off from the start. Because of its small size and short runway it was, however, necessary to retrain on the Bf 110, which caused us no difficulty as we had been equipped with this type for some considerable time. But, as a coin has two sides, the reverse of this one was anything but pleasurable for, during the two months we were stationed there, we flew but four operational sorties. In order not to get rusty we passed the time with training flights or day excursions such as to the Steinhuder Meer. It was really a lazy existence and had nothing to do with the war. I was beginning to get the impression that our presence had a more psychological reason, to show the inhabitants of Hanover that they were being protected by night fighters.
>
> 'Our transfer orders to Wittmundhafen had already been confirmed for the beginning of April when, after all, I was to be crowned with success on the last of our four operational sorties. As on every night, a weather briefing took place in the crew room on 30 March at 1800. According to the meteorologists, no operations could have taken place at all due to the miserable weather conditions; not because we could not have flown, as all-weather flyers we were able always to do that but because the enemy would not have been able to make out any target. The ceiling, as we were able to see for ourselves, was at about 500 meters, the tops at 7000 meters and in between compact cloud. There was no enemy activity at first, only later on were isolated targets reported over the North Sea and the Baltic, heading east.
>
> 'We knew that they would turn south at Stralsund or Greifswald and attack Berlin. Generally, bombs dropped through cloud always struck something but the air raid

warning alone would disrupt traffic and production more than one would generally assume. Towards 0200 the returning flights began, scattered over the entire area of northern Germany. One of these returning enemy bombers set course for Hanover to set off an air raid warning and thus came into our area. Cockpit readiness had already been ordered; then take-off was ordered. At around 0235 our Bf 110 thundered along the runway and into the pitch-dark night. Because of the risk of getting in each other's way in the clouds, the remaining aircraft stayed on the ground for possible operations later. I climbed in serpentines at two-three meters/second upward and it took an age before I came out of the clouds at 7000 meters. But then we found the sky starspangled and clear with a full moon making the cloud below appear like snow and visible afar. It felt like a bit of space opening up before our eyes.

'With the airfield below us, we flew a little to the east. The visibility was so good as to seem like daylight. After climbing another 400 meters we were able to observe an area of several kilometers around us. And then we saw him, the enemy bomber. He crept along looking like a fat beetle crawling over a ground-glass screen illuminated from below. We watched him for a while from a safe distance above and to his left. It was an Avro Lancaster. He flew on a westerly course and only a few meters above the bright layer of cloud, into which he would certainly disappear at any sign of danger. Otto Zinn, my radio operator, transmitted all the data to ground control and then ordered radio silence. We intended to attack shortly. The rear gunner had his quadruple machine guns pointing aft and so we could assume that we had not yet been made out by him. With the moon behind us, I then dived at him like a falcon on his prey and commenced firing at about 200 meters, aiming at the port wing which caught fire at once. He did not have a chance. He dived into the cloud and into the void below, leaving a ghostly reddish glow behind him. We followed but in an orderly descent of about five meters/second.

'We were unable to observe the actual crash but certainly its bright glow, clearly visible even through the cloud contrasting the dark of the night. We came out of the cloud at about 500 meters and were able to see the burning wreckage. The force of the impact had scattered burning pieces over several hundred meterst. To our surprise the crash site was only about ten kilometers to the north-west of our airfield. We landed at 0435 and drove to the crash site. The glow, visible from afar, gave us the direction. We were surprised to find so many people there already at such an early hour. Because of the still exploding ammunition and signal cartridges we parked the car at a safe distance in a country lane beside a *Flak* colonel and his adjutant. Their conversation indicated that their *Flak* battery stationed nearby would claim this *Abschuss* in order to paint another white ring on their gun barrels. But we had not seen a single burst of *Flak* during our entire sortie. During our conversation the colonel thought he had the better argument. We left, certain that the decision would be made at a higher level.

'While looking at the burning wreckage, we heard calls for help, faint at first but then louder, from the bushes 150 meters away. Otto and I looked at each other in amazement. Perhaps a local farmer had paid for his curiosity with a splinter from an exploding cartridge? Whatever, help was needed and so Otto and I went along a furrow towards the coppice. To our surprise we soon made out the rear fuselage of the Lancaster which had remained hidden in the dark. The fuselage had become entangled in the dense branches of the trees. Then we saw a member of the British crew lying on a soft bed of leaves and moss. He had gone clean through the fuselage and was in a pitiful state. His legs and arms must have been broken in several places as they were at strange angles to his body. His face and hands were covered in blood. A faint 'help' again came from his lips and also a call for 'water' but even the lightest touch caused him to cry out with pain. We were convinced that our British aviator comrade would soon breathe his last but we decided, in spite of his screams of pain, to release him. We pulled and pushed, seeking cover in the furrows, as far as the track through the field. He lost consciousness. Without the terrible screams of pain, the rescue operation became easier. Further helping hands were able to lay him on an available farm cart, then, out of the blue, our ambulance appeared and we knew that our patient was in good hands with the local military medical officer Dr Wesendorf.

'I sent the usual operations report to the *Gruppe* at Vechta for further transmission to the commanding officer. Dawn was breaking before I was able to retire for a well-earned rest. It was amost midday when the telephone rang. Our medical officer asked me to go to see him at the sick-quarters. Expecting the worst, he led me to the sickroom. But I was pleasurably surprised to find a man very much alive in the bed. Having been briefed by the medical officer, he knew who I was and we shook hands with a smile as is proper amongst flying comrades. The doctor had cleaned the patient's body of blood and abrasions, then set the broken limbs and put them in splints. A bullet had been removed from his buttocks which, in a macabre sort of way confirmed the *Abschuss* through night fighter and not *Flak*. He was taken to hospital the following day where the doctor expected him to have a good chance of recovery. Having exchanged home addresses, we parted with best wishes for the future. Unfortunately the address got lost in the turmoil of the war. He was the wireless operator, came from the Midlands and was 21-years old.'[43]

During April 1943 *Nachtjagd* claimed 161 bombers destroyed in the *Himmelbett* system.[44] Essen was bombed by 348 aircraft on 3/4 April for the loss of 14 Halifaxes and nine Lancasters. Four victories were credited to IV./NJG 1.[45] One of the pilots who flew a Halifax on the raid was F/L Ron Read in 78 Squadron at Linton-on-Ouse:

'This time I had a second pilot of some standing. We had four visiting Canadian Squadron Leaders – all, new appointees to the Central Flying School, Hullavington – visiting Linton as an introduction to an operational station. Learning that we were operating that night one made the usual visitor's remark that he wished he were going with us. Whether they meant it or not the others echoed this sentiment. Almost every visitor did and we were a bit sick of hearing it but someone took them at their word and obtained permission from Group for them to go. I'm not sure that they were really happy at such a premature and unexpected exposure to the realities of war but having expressed the wish they couldn't really refuse when permission was obtained. I noted that between briefing and take off all of our visitors were writing furiously, presumably to their loved ones; a sure sign that they had not expected to be going. All went well but the *flak* was heavier than ever over Essen. Back at Linton three of our aircraft were missing. Two were from 78 and one was from 76. Out of 348 Lancasters and Halifaxes, 21 were lost, 12 of them Halifaxes. The 'Chop Rate' was still 6%. I hoped my percentage' theory was working. If it was, there were enough RAF aircraft shot down near me that night to keep me going for a while. The next night, 4/5 April we went to Kiel. It was the largest number of aircraft we had operated with so far, 577, 116 Halifaxes. It was a cloudy night with sky marking to bomb on; not much *flak* and no sign of fighters. After Essen it was a 'Piece Of Cake'; everybody said so. Only 12 aircraft were lost, just 2%. If only they were all like that!

On 3/4 April Sgt John 'Jimmy' Anderson Hurst in 102 Squadron was detailed to fly as tail gunner in a crew piloted by the 'Wingco' who had no crew of his own as he seldom flew on ops:

'When he did he selected experienced men from other crews for the trip. I had been to Essen before [on 5 March] and I knew it was a heavily defended target. (I was always 'happiest' when flying with my regular skipper George Barker. To fly with another crew, as an 'odd bod' was something that I was not keen on doing. So many of my colleagues had failed to return from such ops). The flight to the target was normal, with the usual attention from *Flak*, searchlights and fighters but when we reached Essen, he seemed reluctant to leave! We started a normal bombing run through heavy *Flak* with bomb doors open. This was always a vulnerable situation – the bomb aimer doing his usual drill directing the pilot to our aiming point, the rest of us waiting to hear him say 'bombs gone' and feel the pilot put the nose down and head away from the target. But in the midst of our bombing run, the pilot told the bomb aimer that he was not happy with our run and we would go round again and make another run. So the bomb doors were closed and we flew a circuit around Essen, (which was well alight) and we came in for a second time. Again the bomb doors were opened and the bomb run began. To our 'dismay' the skipper aborted again and we were taken over the blazing city. The AA gunners were very active. So for a third time we made a bombing run. By now we all felt very vulnerable and that we were pushing our luck. This time the skipper was satisfied and our bombs were released into the inferno below. I had, on occasions, made two runs across a target but never three and it had then been the bomb aimer's decision to go round again, as he and not the pilot was in the best position to see if our aiming point could be hit.

'I finished my tour with a trip on 13 May 1943 to the steel works at Bochum, a routine one as ops went but we were all very much aware that it was not unusual for a crew to be lost on their last op. We were an experienced crew but many an experienced crew 'went for a Burton'. But we made it and the following day, we left 102 Squadron and went on leave after which I trained as an Air Gunner Instructor and was posted to No.4 Air Gunnery School at Morpeth in Northumberland. I enjoyed this posting but I loved squadron life and tried to get back on ops but I think they were so pleased to have a tail gunner on the staff that had survived a tour, that they would not release me. It was good for the morale of the trainee gunners. The rest of my 102 crew did return to ops, doing a second tour in a Pathfinder squadron, again in Halifaxes, this time in the BIII, a much superior aircraft to our Mark 2! I enjoyed life in the RAF, especially on the squadron, the adrenalin flow was terrific and nothing has matched it since.'

On the night of 4/5 April meanwhile, 577 bombers were dispatched to Kiel and 12 aircraft failed to return. NJG 3 'manning' the *Himmelbett* in NW Germany and Denmark claimed six kills. Nineteen bombers were lost on the Duisburg raid of 8/9 April from a force of 392 aircraft. Only one was shot down by a nightfighter. Johhny Michaud's crew in 425 *'Les Alouettes'* Squadron RCAF flew their 16th Wellington op as the observer, P/O Jack Woodrow recalls:

> 'We had 10/10ths cloud to 19,000 ft. No PFF flares were seen and we bombed on ETA. *Flak* was heavy. Of course bombing results could not be observed. It was certainly very poor weather for operations. Weather predicting over Europe was far from a science. They were sometimes 180° off. This unpredictable weather cut down on our effectiveness greatly. Sometimes, if there were no PFF flare or markers, we had to bomb blind. Sometimes we brought the bombs back. It was all very discouraging. The other effect of the weather was trying to return to base. Sometimes it would be socked in with fog and the only clear airfields would be too far away as you could be running low on fuel. You stacked up over your own or some other field and you hoped for the best. Preference of course was given to those with wounded on board or those about to run out of fuel. All in all it was very nerve wracking.'

Another eight Lancasters failed to return from a force of 104 Lancasters and five Mosquitoes that went to Duisburg on 9/10 April. IV./NJG 1 destroyed five Lancasters.[46] *Major* Werner Streib of I./NJG 1 claimed a Lancaster.[47] *Lt* Oskar Köstler[48] and *Uffz* Heinz Huhn were ordered off from Bergen in a Bf 110G-4[49] for a patrol in *Himmelbett* box 'Herring'. Huhn recorded his experiences on 9/10 April in his diary:

> 'Almost cloudless, moon, take-off at 2150. To begin with flying on radio beacon. After an hour at last contact with *Lichtenstein* at 2.2 kms. Köstler: 'I have him at 200 meters distance'. Sitting below him. Halifax or Lancaster at forty meters. I have to call out the speed. At last! Attack! The cannons start firing. Suddenly a blow from ahead, bright as day, boiling hot. What was that? Have we been hit? No, Tommy's exploding. Splinters rain onto our machine. We are burning. In front of me flames, a bright flood. We are going down. Heat is beating into my face. *Lt* Köstler is silent. I reach for the cockpit roof jettison lever. Helmet is singed, have to close eyes. At last the handle! Roof flies away. I rise up and shove myself off. Get away. Machine going down, burning. I somersault, cannot find the rip-cord. At last, a jerk, I float. Around me burning parts. I find that I am over water. Unlock parachute safety catch. I believe to be carried further out to sea, so I pull the parachute lines. Parachute collapses, falls. Icy cold, hands freezing. I notice that I'm drifting towards land. How high might I be? Attack was at 5500 meters, jumped at 5000? I reach for the signal pistol but it is not secured and my hands are almost rigidly stiff.
>
> 'Am over land ... pain, hang uncomfortably in the 'chute. Hands are stiff and without feeling. I had lost my boots during the jump. Bright patch below me. A lake? Would I drown in a puddle after all this? But I'm still very high. Swinging violently. At last the earth is coming up towards me. Woods, trees. Splintering, I am hanging between two trees. Helpless. No strength left and my hands frozen stiff. Parachute straps cutting into my flesh. Must wait until my hands have warmed. Pain. At last feeling returns to my fingers. I swing myself towards a tree trunk, am about four-five meters above ground. I grip the trunk. Release straps! Won't work. Lock frozen? With a final effort I clamber a little higher. Fortunately there is a branch which gives support, otherwise no strength left and fall down. Not to break my neck now, after all this! A little higher. Straps loosening at last. Chest straps are free but leg straps still pulling me upwards. A little higher still. At last the leg straps are released too. Climb, slide, fall down the trunk. Moss at the bottom. Dinghy off. I feel faint. Struggle up. Limbs unharmed. Signal pistol and torch still there. Have three red cartridges left. Must not use them senselessly.
>
> 'Start walking through the forest. Fall down again, get up, stumble, lose signal pistol, search for it and find it again. Move on. Feet cold, socks wet through the damp ground. Face burning, skin singed. Find a track, then past a meadow, finally a good road. Tread on sharp metal fragments of the Tommy lying around on the road everywhere. March on, pass a lone building. Fire one red. See no telephone wire in the bright light, so carry on. After an hour a railway crossing. Change direction and follow the rails. Painful for the feet due to sharp stones. Half an hour's laborious tramping along the rails. No signal cabin. Suddenly a noise behind me: a train. Load the last red cartridge. A shot in front of the engine. Brakes squeal. Train stops. Flash SOS. Freight train. Have to identify myself, get aboard. Face burning, eyebrows crusted over. Try to phone from next station. No connection. Continue on train to Harderwijk. Get out there. At the unit there I hear: *Lt* Köstler dead. Call Bergen: they think I'm a ghost as I had been reported dead. Karl Vinke had shot down three this night. Then into sick quarters. Eat, ointment on the forehead, sleep. In the morning I was taken to the crash

site. Had spoken during the night with Hptm Ruppel and made my report. At crash site. Bits from the Tommy strewn around for miles. Pieces of bodies everywhere. At the crash site of our machine also bits everywhere. Must have exploded in the air. *Lt* Köstler with open parachute dead beside the wreckage. The body whole, only the bloody head is put into the coffin. Then a car arrives from Leeuwarden to fetch the coffin. I go with it.'[50]

On 10/11 April a force of 502 Lancasters, Halifaxes, Stirlings and Wellingtons were detailed for a raid on Frankfurt. Sgt Jack Adams and the crew of Halifax II DT775 F-Freddie who had recently joined 78 Squadron at Linton on Ouse, on 28 March, were one of the crews. Sgt Stan Reed, one of the air gunners recalls:

'Including F-Freddie (which we had christened F for Firkin) 21 Halifaxes were detailed for this operation from our airfield. F Firkin was a fairly new kite and hadn't done too many operations. It was a Mark II Series 1 (Special) of which the nose and mid upper gun turrets had been removed to help improve the rather poor operational performance leaving only the rear turret for defense. The mid-upper gunner now manned a ventral position when on operations, looking downwards through a small perspex blister fitted to the floor of the aircraft just aft of the rear door. Not a well sought after position as it entailed lying flat out on the floor for hours with one's head in the perspex blister. This position had been brought in to reduce the heavy losses caused by the deadly attacks from below, which were so favoured by Jerry night fighters. Alas, the position was not armed until later with a .5 calibre Browning machine gun. An intercom point, oxygen outlet together with a signal light and switch were installed alongside the blister but no form of heating was provided and a cold, draughty and noisy position it was indeed.

'On the night in question our take off time was 2334 hrs. It was a very dark night with no moon and 10/10ths cloud cover. After leaving base we did not see another aircraft although on several occasions we became aware of their unseen presence as we flew through their slipstreams. I flew from Yorkshire to the south coast sitting up front alongside our Skipper on the second pilot's seat whilst Sgt Joe Enwright, our mid-upper gunner manned the rear turret until it was time for me to take over; somewhere over the English Channel. I very much enjoyed riding up front in the utter dark of the night, watching avidly all that went on about me with great interest. It was all so different to my normal lonely vigil in the rear turret. I studied Jack at the controls, clad in his leather Irvin flying jacket and helmet with his face half hidden behind his oxygen mask, in the dim red glow from the instruments on the panels before him. Being at the very heart of this huge powerful bomber made me feel privileged to be aboard. An enormous and deafening constant roar from the four big Rolls-Royce Merlins dominated everything up front. I was conscious of Sgt Nobby Clarke our flight engineer behind me, busy as always at his engineer's panel. P/O Phil Hyden, navigator, Sgt Cliff Price, wireless operator and Sgt Stan Hurrell, bomb aimer were at their respective stations on the lower deck of the Halifax, beneath and in front of me.

'My job during this part of the outward flight was to maintain a constant lookout for other aircraft in case one should come just a little too close for comfort. Flying blind on the aircraft's instruments alone in a night bomber stream with no radar could, to put it mildly; be disconcerting at times. Hopefully all the bombers were not at the same height even though we were all flying in the same direction or at least, should be doing so. Imagine if you can a corridor of air space one hundred miles long, ten or more miles wide and about a mile and a half high with the lowest strata being at least at 12,000 ft. In this corridor in the sky were at least 500-600 bombers all heavily laden with petrol and a large bomb load and all were heading in the same direction in the pitch darkness. Each wave kept to a specified height. The poor old Stirlings with their rather poor maximum operational ceiling were always at the lowest level. Behind and above them at 15,000-16,000 ft would come the Wellingtons and then the Halifaxes at about 18,000 ft, with the Lancasters bringing up the rear in the last wave at 20,000 ft or more. With all these unseen heavy aircraft around us collisions in mid air were known to occur but officially the percentage was less than half of one per cent of the total force. It had to be for morale purposes did it not? Many more aircraft were lost through enemy action!

'Having left the English coast we were soon well out over the Channel. I prepared to go aft and take up my normal station in the rear turret for the remainder of the operation. I gathered up my parachute pack and the rest of my gear including a big thermos flask of hot coffee. Then I discovered that my microphone in my face mask had gone unserviceable and no one could hear what I was saying. No amount of banging would clear the fault, although I could hear perfectly well through my flying helmet earphones. We didn't have a spare headset on board and I made a mental note to remind Cliff Price to draw a spare set from stores come the morrow. Jack decided that

Joe Enwright would now remain in the rear turret for the rest of the trip whilst I would take the ventral position in his place. It was essential that the rear gunner was able to communicate with the pilot. Joe was our sole means of defense. Even if the intercom system became unserviceable, communication was still possible between crew members and their pilot by means of small lights fitted at all crew positions. Any trouble would be flashed immediately to the pilot using the appropriate letter in Morse code like 'F for Fighter'! The pilot would then take immediate avoiding action by frantically weaving and corkscrewing the aircraft until hopefully clear of danger.

'I settled down in the blister position aft, laying on some none too clean canvas engine covers, which were stowed in the aircraft adjacent to the ventral blister position. I had done one operation with my head in the perspex blister which did not suit me at all but I could only try to make the best of the situation. After all it was my mike that had gone U/S wasn't it? I always felt very much at home behind four Browning machine guns in the rear turret with a little armor plate beneath my seat. Now I felt rather naked and very vulnereable laying flat out on the thin metal floor. I flashed Jack up on my signal light to let him know that I was in place and received a reassuring acknowledgement in return before settling down to gaze upon the awful nothingness below. We were flying around the 18,000 ft mark. Normally, with a full petrol and bomb load on board we couldn't get the old Mark II Halifaxes, even with all their recent modifications, much higher than this. I could see nothing below, just total blackness. It was damn cold too with no heating available. I could hear the rest of the crew going about their duties with Jack quietly in command and not saying much. Phil our navigator was trying to work wonders from his Gee set, which was being 'bent' by Jerry. Phil was telling Jack that the set was practically U/S and he would have to rely on his D/R plot from now on.[51] Stan Hurrell in his bomb aimer's position was busying himself looking out for PFF flares and markers, which should be showing up soon as we aproached our next turning point, a little to the north of Dieppe. Cliff Price was conscientiously searching his allotted wave bands hoping to pick up Jerry night fighter controllers nattering to their airborne charges so that he could give them a blasting from a microphone positioned alongside one of our Merlin engines and thus interrupt their broadcasts with some beautiful aero engine noise. Nobby Clarke was checking his petrol tank gauges and effecting change overs from one tank to another to maintain our center of gravity in flight as petrol was used. We used an awful amount of petrol per hour when airborne. Joe Enwright in the tail obtained permission from Jack to test his guns. I then heard the familiar rattle as Joe fired off a short test burst from the four .303 Brownings. That very morning he and I had harmonised those guns down to one hundred yards.

'Jack warned us that we were approaching the French coast just north of Dieppe per Phil Hyden's calculations. It was always a gut-tightening occasion and put everybody on their mettle. Jack then commenced a gentle weave (a winding course on a general heading of intended flight with variations of height) to distract enemy night fighters and predicted radar controlled Flak. I could see no Flak near us. No one mentioned seeing any close to us up front either. Stan Hurrell counted the yellow PFF flares aloud. We were heading towards Metz in eastern France where there was to be another change of course on PFF markers. Jack warned us that we were now in the Jerry night fighter belt. Nothing keeps you on your toes than the prospect of being caught by a Jerry night fighter. It concentrated the mind wonderfully. However, all was going well. F Firkin's four aero engines were all roaring on. All was quiet up front with just the occasional word from Phil warning Jack of a slight alteration of course. The golden rule was that no one spoke on the intercom over enemy territory unless one had to. Jack however did speak individually to us from time to time with quiet words of encouragement which always went down well. All was completely black below. It must have been 10/10ths cloud cover all over northern Europe. We duly turned onto our new heading over Metz amid a sprinkling of yellow PFF markers but other than that I saw nothing at all of the French city beneath me. We flew on, weaving more vigorously now with everybody on the 'qui vive' maintaining a close vigil of the black sky all about us.

'Suddenly from out of the utter nothingness below and a little astern came several blinding lines of very bright green lights. Tracer and lots of it! 'CHRIST!' I cried out loud. A bloody night fighter had caught us from below. The lines of tracer tore into us at a terrible speed. Our Hali was raked from tail to nose in just one long savage burst, which could not have lasted for more than three seconds. The noise was considerable and above the roar of the engines too. It was as if a giant was tearing up sheets of corrugated iron by hand and doing it very fast indeed. It was 20mm cannon fire that was hitting us and some of the cannon shells were exploding on impact in bright little splashes of light. How I was not hit I just do not know for the tracer appeared to go all around me lying there on the engine covers on the floor of the Hali as if frozen stiff. I was just 2° from being absolutely petrified. Faintly, over the intercom I heard that someone up front had been hit. Fire must have broken out immediately from amidships where the main petrol tanks and our bomb load, mainly incendiary bombs in metal containers, were and flames streamed back underneath the aircraft.

'I saw nothing of the Jerry night fighter that had caught us. He obviously knew his profession very well, creeping up quite unseen, entirely on his airborne radar no doubt and then hitting us plumb amidships just where he could do the most damage. And all in the one short burst too. He must have then stood off and watched our demise. I was told after my capture that a Bf 110 night fighter had shot us down and that we were one of 20 bombers brought down that night.[52] Cliff had been hit in the leg. I could now hear over the intercom and Nobby was saying that he had badly burnt hands. Fortunately, no one else appeared to have been hit in the attack, which was miraculous considering what had gone by me and struck up front. There was some shouting and a bit of a flap but no real panic. I heard nothing from Joe in the rear turret but that wasn't unusual as Joe never did say much nor had I heard his guns firing. He couldn't have seen the fighter either. I gathered quickly that we were now well alight and that it was impossible to control the fire, let alone put it out. All this had happened within seconds although it appeared to last for an age. In fact less than 20 seconds only were to pass from the moment of attack to the time Jack and the last to leave our doomed Halifax baled out. Time certainly seemed to stand still. I still couldn't believe that it was all happening to us. It was all so unreal. Was this a nightmare? I kept telling myself that this is what befell other crews; it just couldn't happen to us. I came back to reality rather abruptly when I heard Jack on intercom say very calmly, 'This is it chaps. Better get out quickly. We've had it'.

'Phil then shouted something about Switzerland but by then I had pulled my intercom plug out and was making my way to the rear door on the port side of the Halifax, having grabbed my parachute pack. I opened the door inwards up to the roof of the aircraft and saw fully for the first time the whole mass of flames tearing past underneath me. 'CHRIST' I said. It was damn noisy too. We had really had it all right. I had to get out fast before the kite exploded. I paused looking down into all that blackness I was about to jump into. Beyond the tearing flames I saw two bodies flash by so I knew that at least two members of the crew had managed to get out OK and wondered which two it might be. I sat down on the floor with my legs out of the doorway and prepared myself to abandon the Hali. I must have been sucked out or drawn out by the roaring rushing slipstream tearing past and in the mere seconds of receiving Jack's 'bale out' call I found myself out in the cold night air with the huge tail of the Halifax shooting past over my head. She was certainly well on fire amidships and diving away obviously out of control.

'Was I the last one out I wondered?'[53]

Altogether 144 Wellington crews made up the Frankfurt force on the night of 10/11 April. One of them was piloted by P/O Johnny Michaud of 425 *'Les Alouettes'* Squadron RCAF whose crew were on their 17th trip, as the observer, P/O Jack Woodrow recalls:

> 'The trip was fraught with 10/10ths cloud at 8000 ft. We bombed from 17,000 ft. The *flak* was heavy and increased during the attack. There were no sky markers. A twin-engined fighter attacked us 40 miles west of the target. Corkscrew action was taken and the fighter was lost. The major defense for a bomber's survival lay in evasive action or 'corkscrewing', which had been developed by the RAF. It was practiced over England with cameras instead of guns in both the bombers and the attacking Spitfires and Hurricanes. The gunner had to be alert to spot the faster moving enemy fighters flying around the bomber stream. Then when sighted he gave the warning 'Fighter attack, prepare to corkscrew'. Then at around 600 yards which was the point when the fighter would open fire, the gunner would give the command, 'Corkscrew port, go' or 'Corkscrew starboard go', depending on the side from which the attack was being made. If a port attack, the pilot would commence the corkscrew by applying violent port rudder, port aileron and diving elevators, which had the effect of instantly removing the bomber from the fighter's gunsight. After diving about 1000 ft, the pilot would recover from the descent by climbing in the opposite direction to recover his height and course to the target or home. Hopefully we had lost the fighter. We had an advantage in this struggle. Our pilot, Johnny Michaud, was extremely strong and could carry out this evasive maneuver without tiring.'[54]

19-year old Scot Sgt Charlie 'Jock' Baird from Edinburgh, mid-upper-gunner in 20-year old W/O Den Rudge's Lancaster crew in 103 Squadron at Elsham Wolds, Lincolnshire, began his tour on the night of 10/11 April, to Frankfurt:

> 'We were an all NCO crew and this bonded us all the more as we slept, ate, imbibed and flew together. Our pilot, an English lad, turned out to be a top grade pilot. Our

second trip, to La Spezia in northern Italy[55] lasted 9 hrs 45 minutes.[56] Our 3rd trip on 16/17 April had us wondering about our choice of going into action. This trip was to the Skoda arms works at Pilsen in Czechoslovakia and we were warned to be extra careful passing Saarbrücken. We were well and truly coned by about 25 searchlights and we took a bit of a hammering before eluding them. On arrival at Pilsen a blue master searchlight caught us and was soon joined by many more. We copped an awful beating and the port outer petrol tank was holed in the process. I reported it as smoke but it was petrol. I alerted the skipper and our engineer did a quick transfer of fuel. This all happened rather quickly but it made my hair stand on end. We finally broke clear and headed for home where we found 74 small holes and one shell had gone clean through the wing, fracturing the port outer petrol tank. We were more than fortunate several times during this trip but it went a long way to cementing us together as a crew. W4845 never flew on ops again having been badly damaged this night. It was a 9 hour 50 minute trip and 54 aircraft were lost.[57]

'Our tour of ops carried on through the battle of the Ruhr and we did 20 ops to that hotbed. Most evenings we were routed out over or between the Friesian Islands, Texel, Terschelling etc and then into the German fighter belt. We had about eight encounters with fighters but I had keen eyesight and always picked them up quickly and we evaded them. My skipper was very much alert and he never lost even a split second when I gave him instructions on evasive action, a great guy. We were a very alert crew and spoke only when absolutely necessary. No idle chatting and our turrets kept moving from take off to landing.This was a great comfort to our skipper. We finished our tour on 23/24 August to Berlin, when 58 aircraft went missing. Sadly we all had to part and go as instructors. Our skipper was awarded the DFC and navigator the DFM. Well earned; they were two fine men.'

By this time F/L Ron Read, in 78 Squadron was a deputy Flight Commander and as such no longer went on every trip:

'The first time I didn't was a novel experience when on 8 April they went to Duisburg without me. I had felt great relief at not going but considerable guilt, as I watched them take off. I was staying safely on the ground and it didn't seem quite right. Before start-up I had driven around with the W/C and 'Timber' Woods, wishing them luck. I forbore to tell anyone that I wished I were going; it would have been an outright lie. The next operation was on 10/11 April to Frankfurt. I was OC Flying for 78 that night and again I was not going. I was just beginning to get used to it. Having managed to get Group's permission, Group Captain Whitley the station commander was going. Normally station commanders were not allowed to go on ops. It was considered that they were privy to too many secrets. 'Groupy' Whitley was different. He'd been an operational pilot with the squadron in 1940-41 and he wanted to get an updated view of the problems of his crews. He was that sort of man. He was going with F/L Hull of 76 Squadron, an experienced pilot who'd started at the same time as me. Accompanying Gerry Warner we drove out to Hull's aircraft, saying 'good luck' to Groupy and the crew.

'I remember the long weary wait, as it became apparent that Hull wasn't coming back. The Group Captain was missing. A little shiver ran through us in the control tower. If they could get old Groupy we felt they could get anybody.[58]

'I went on leave a week after the Groupy went missing. I returned to London from leave in Torquay in not a very happy frame of mind. On the way I read about the latest RAF raid the night before [16/17 April 1943] on Pilsen. They had lost 36 aircraft; the highest loss to date. *'Phew! That's a bit hot',* I thought. When I arrived home on Saturday evening 17 April, there was a telegram that had arrived that afternoon from Pam. It said:

'MORTY MISSING LAST NIGHT 16TH, ON PILSEN.'

"Oh Hell! Morty gone!' It was a shock and yet not more than I had feared. I was somehow expecting it. I felt that he was going to go the minute he came back and told me he was married. It was just the way things were on the squadron at the time. He may have gone anyway but I had felt he was tempting fate, marrying in mid-tour. I know in his heart he thought so too. I had a couple of day's leave left but I went back to Linton the next day. I wanted to find out what I could and to screen Morty's effects. It was customary for a close friend to do this, just in case there were any articles that might have been embarrassing to the family. The return journey on Sunday seemed slow and dragging. I had a lot of time to think. As ever one felt there was always the chance that he and the crew would have baled out and would turn up eventually as prisoners of war. That was a standard palliative for friends and family. It saved the immediacy of the alternative. It had worked out that way for Geoff Hobbs.

'When I arrived I received a few tentative looks and words of sympathy. We had been very close, the sometime 'Terrible Twins'. Close friends were worried about how I would take it. I got what details were available. Pilsen should have been a 'Piece Of Cake': a long flight into Southern Europe well away from the heavy defenses. The Wingco had chosen to go himself. Unfortunately it was a night of bright moonlight and the fighters got into the bomber stream early. From then on it was a fight for survival with mainly luck deciding who was caught. There were 197 Lancs and 130 Halifaxes on the trip; 18 of each were lost – 11% of the force. The highest since the early days of the daylight raids and certainly since I'd been operating. It was soon learned that the raid did not affect the target, the Skoda armament factory. The major damage was to a lunatic asylum seven miles away. A terrible waste of crews, at least 252 and of poor old Morty – my closest RAF friend.

'I cleared up Morty's things the next day with a sympathetic padre. I didn't tell him that Morty went because he'd forsaken our pact with the Devil. He wouldn't have appreciated it, though Morty would. There were no skeletons in Morty's effects and they were sent off to his new wife. I sat down and wrote her a sympathetic letter with as much cheer as I could find in it. Then set out to get on with life. I had seen quite a few of my friends go and it was an accepted aircrew tenet that we put our lost friends behind us and forgot them as quickly as possible. Although he had been my closest friend for a year and a half I was determined to adhere to this philosophy. I reasoned that Morty was a good pilot and if any one could have made it he could. If he hadn't, well he was as aware as we all were of what could happen. He'd often philosophized on the, 'If you can't take a joke' joke. Unfortunately it was now on him. No doubt we should learn in due course what had happened.

'Meanwhile life had to go on and it was just as well to embrace that old secret aircrew belief, 'Whomever it happens to, it won't be me.' Though in deep thinking moments a little voice still murmured, 'Why not?' The answer, 'Don't think too often or too deeply about these things. Play the role of a light-hearted bomber aircrew. Remember that the Devil Looks After His Own. Eat, drink and be merry and to hell with tomorrow.'

'The Pilsen trip cut a swathe through the Linton aircrews, probably because they were in the second wave once more. Apart from Morty there were four others missing: F/L Paddy Dowse, a pleasant Irishman of 78 Squadron on his second tour and three sergeants and crews from 76.[59] It was our worst night to date – a total of five crews or 35 bods. I knew few of them personally, as many were replacements for recent casualties. There were lots of new faces in the mess now. Final news of Morty came a few weeks later with a letter from a PoW camp from his wireless operator [Sgt C.A.] 'Steve' Stevens. Hit by a fighter the crew had baled out. Meanwhile, the aircraft was getting lower and by the time they were all out it was too low for Morty to jump. He was killed in the ensuing crash. Typically Morty and typically a pilot's end. It had happened many times and would happen many more. Now to forget it. There was plenty to get on with.'[60]

For Sgt S.T. 'Tom' Wingham, a Halifax II bomb aimer in 102 Squadron at Pocklington, Yorkshire, Pilsen had been his 15th op and it had been in a full moon. With the moon still full it was with some trepidation that he realized from the petrol and bomb loads that he was in for another long trip on 20/21 April. All told 339 aircraft (194 Lancasters, 134 Halifaxes and 11 Stirlings) were to visit Stettin, an 8 1/2-hour round trip, while 85 Stirlings were despatched to bomb the Heinkel factory near Rostock. Wingham recalled that 'With briefing came enlightenment. Bomber Command had come up with a new plan to beat the German GCI – a low-level trip.' At Snaith F/Sgt Louis Patrick Wooldridge, a Halifax mid-upper-gunner in Claude Wilson's crew in 51 Squadron was also 'on' this night. Wooldridge explains the reason for the raid on Stettin:

> 'Information obtained from Russian intelligence sources revealed that a large quantity of German fighter and number aircraft had been concentrated at Stettin for use on the Eastern Front and the Soviets had requested that the RAF eliminate this menace to their forces on the Leningrad-Moscow fronts. Our Halifax II, HR750 MH-W, was fitted with an auxiliary petrol tank in the bomb bay for the 600 mile trip to Stettin and another pilot, on his first operation, accompanied us as a crewmember to gain operational experience. Judging by the number of bomb symbols painted in yellow beneath the pilot's window HR750 was a bit of a veteran. In addition the aircraft bore the words, 'WANCHORS CASTLE 'and carried an emblem of a small castle and a knight with a coat of arms on a shield.[61]
>
> 'We took off at about 2100 hours and on leaving Snaith the weather was clear and almost cloudless with brilliant moonlight. As a result of the forecasted weather conditions the operational flight to the target was carried out 50 feet, climbing to 12,000-ft at Stettin to release the bombload, thereafter dropping down to 50-ft for the flight to base. Approaching the Danish coastline I observed a *U-boat* on the surface of the sea. Wilson passed the details to Peter Finnett, navigator, who recorded it in his log and informed Don Hall, WOp who in turn sent a coded wireless signal to base. Receipt of this information after decoding, would then have been forwarded to the Admiralty in

London for appropriate action by naval units in the North Sea. Meanwhile, the *U-boat* crew had obviously seen us. There was feverish activity in the conning tower and the sea foamed about both sides of the *U-boat* as it blew its ballast tanks and crash-dived beneath the silvery surface of the sea. Neither Les Sharp in the rear turret or me could aim and fire our machine guns. The rear turret was unable to traverse to a suitable bearing and the mid upper's safety gear interrupter solenoid, which prevented a gunner causing accidental damage in the heat of combat, would have prevented my guns from firing. All the same, I do not think that any of the *U-boat* crew required any medical laxatives for quite a while.'

Tom Wingham's Halifax meanwhile, had climbed on take-off and crossed the North Sea at 10,000 ft, reaching the Danish coast near Esbjerg where they descended to 700 ft.:

'Now began one of the most exhilarating trips I took part in as 350 heavy bombers streamed across Denmark between 400 and 700 ft. Lying in the nose map reading did feel a bit hairy as we were constantly being hit by the slipstream from other unseen aircraft. In the brilliant moonlight all the ground detail was clear and Danes came out of their houses flashing torches and waving. Occasionally, a little light flak came up to port or starboard as aircraft strayed off course or the sky was lit up as an aircraft hit the deck.'

F/Sgt Louis Wooldridge continues:

'Flying at low level had its compensations in the exhilarating feeling of power and speed as the Danish countryside and gleaming rail tracks illuminated by the light of the brilliant full moon flashed beneath the wings of the speeding aircraft. We flew over an L-shaped farm with an orchard and the door to the farmhouse was suddenly flung open and a shaft of light appeared in the doorway. Four figures emerged and they ran out each frantically waving a large white cloth like a bath towel. I turned the mid upper turret slightly towards their direction and rapidly raised and lowered the four .303 inch Browning machine guns in acknowledgement of their greeting and the grave risk this family was taking. Shortly afterwards I saw two motor vehicles speeding along a road towards the German border. According to intelligence reports only German military forces, *Gestapo* personnel and their collaborators operated on roads after night curfew. I turned the mid upper turret to port and lowered the guns and waited until we overtook the speeding vehicles but they entered a large wooded area to stop until we had left the area.

'As the flight would be of 8 1/2 hours duration I decided I would use only two of my four guns so as to conserve ammunition. Normal ammunition supply for the four guns in the mid-upper turret was 2400 rounds (600 rounds in four metal boxes, one for each gun). In between my legs was a mechanism called the feed assister (in Lancaster, Stirling and late models of Wellington aircraft a mechanism of similar type was known as a Servo feed), which operated the rate of fire, approximately 1200 rounds a minute. In view of later events my decision was correct.'

Tom Wingham continues:

'We continued low level across the Baltic doing a cruise among the islands until on our last leg with the North German coast on our starboard we climbed to a bombing height of 14,000 ft. As we approached the target, Stettin was well alight and in the glare from the fires below and the brilliant moonlight. It was like carrying out an aircraft recognition test. It was the first time I had seen Fw 190s and Me 109s as well as 110s and Ju 88s, all clearly visible flitting about among the silhouettes of Lancs and Halifaxes. Somehow we were not singled out for attention as we went in and bombed. Immediately after completing the bomb run we dived for the deck and went out the same way we had come.'

F/Sgt Louis Wooldridge, approaching the Baltic, continues:

'Off the starboard bow at about 11,000 ft I could see 'white' flashing harbor lights in the vicinity of Lübeck and Rostock, as we awaited the 'yellowish' marker flares of the PFF Force about a mile ahead of the bomber stream indicating a course turning point. A mile west of Lübeck three Lancasters of the PFF Force released clusters of flares spaced across the night sky and burning brightly to indicate the way to Stettin. The flares, which floated slowly down on parachutes, could be compared in purpose with the 'Stave Leys' of times when knights of old found their way across Britain by staves or staffs interspersed across the country. Observing the marker flares Claude Wilson informed Peter Finnett who remarked; 'They're dead on time.' Suddenly two of the three Lancasters in the starboard beam about 3000 ft below were enveloped in black smoke and red flames and the bombers fell rapidly towards the moonlit sea 6000 ft below. No parachutes emerged from any of the stricken aircraft and Peter's casual remark on the Pathfinders' punctuality took on an entirely new meaning. A lack of flak puffs which always hung about the sky for some considerable time after the explosive burst seemed to indicate that enemy fighter activity was the cause but we failed to see any enemy aircraft in the area.[62]

'We left Lübeck and Rostock behind and had reached the bombing height of 12,000 ft as our Halifax altered course onto the final approach leg to Stettin. We were part of the first wave of Main Force bombers to arrive in the area, which was bathed in brilliant moonlight. The view from my turret gave the impression that the area below was peaceful but this was just an illusion. The air raid warning sirens would already have sounded to enable the inhabitants to take shelter and to alert the flak gunners. Suddenly, red and green TIs were released into the night sky by the Pathfinder aircraft directly ahead of us. (This type of target marking was known as *'Musical Parramatta'*, which was devised for visual ground marking. In the event of the target area being obscured by 10/10ths cloud conditions a sky marking technique consisting of similar colored flares attached to parachutes for a slow descent and known as 'Wanganui' was used. Both were reputed to have originated from the choice of the Commanding Officer of 8 Group, G/C Don Bennett. As Parramatta is a place-name in Australia and Wanganui a place-name in New Zealand it would appear that there is an element of truth in the matter). As the TIs cascaded through the air, burning brilliantly, all Hell was let loose. Numerous heavy flak bursts dotted the night sky and probing mauve (master) and white (coning) searchlight beams sought various individual aircraft of the bomber stream. Instructions broadcast from the Master Bomber of the Pathfinder Force informing the oncoming Main Force bomber crews to bomb the marker flares concerned were received over the bomber intercom system, as they commenced their run into the target area. As the flak bursts decreased tracer streams criss crossed the moonlit sky indicating the presence of night fighters over Stettin and aerial combats between the British bombers and German fighter aircraft. Miraculously, although troubled slightly by predicted flak, we managed to evade any engagement with any German night fighters and after the release of our bomb load our aircraft swiftly descended to 50 ft for the return flight to base.

'Suddenly the ditching hatch immediately forward of my turret swung downwards leaving a gaping hole about 2ft by 1 1/2 ft and 'Ginger' Anger the flight engineer waved towards me. I then remembered that he had a load of propaganda leaflets to dispose of. As 'Ginger' threw the leaflets out the air current of about 200 mph whipped them up into the air high over the turret to stream rearwards above the rear turret where Les Sharp observed them fluttering gradually to earth to give the impression of a gigantic paper chase over Germany. The military authorities always collected the British leaflets as soon as possible after they had been dropped but on this occasion their task would have been difficult as many settled on the roofs of numerous tall buildings that the Halifax bomber flew over. We flew over a large town with a tall white building in the main street, which I presumed was the town hall. A clock illuminated by the brilliant moonlight indicated that the time was 0130 am. To test the guns for sighting accuracy and to disrupt the German war workers dependent on the clock to rouse them from sleep, I fired at the building and observed two of the clock faces disintegrate. At the same time I felt a tug on my left leg and looking down I saw 'Ginger' Anger looking anxiously up at me through the open hatch. Apparently he had thought that I was engaged in combat with a German night fighter aircraft but after assuring him otherwise he carried on the disposal of the leaflets.

'Shortly afterwards we emerged over a German aerodrome. Turning our turrets to starboard Les and I fired tracer bullets into the glass panels in the hangar roofs and then we directed our fire against aircraft parked outside. The door of a long wooden hut suddenly opened emitting a shaft of light and numerous figures ran to a wood nearby or towards the parked aircraft. I presumed that the figures running towards the wood were to man anti aircraft guns so my gunfire was directed at them first and then again at the parked aircraft and the figures running towards them. Finally the wooden hut was strafed with gunfire. By now the Halifax was flying over the wood leaving the German aerodrome with its casualties and damage in the distance.

'Briefly relaxing for a few minutes the crew was suddenly brought into instant reaction by what seemed to be colored lights floating through the night sky towards us. The German aerodrome had obviously telephoned information of our approach to flak defenses ahead of us. Our arrival over what appeared to be peaceful meadow bounded by a small wood was suddenly marred by the criss crossing above and below of numerous red and green and white light anti aircraft shells. They rose ever so slowly from ground level giving the false impression that we could reach out and take hold of them as they sped towards the aircraft but a true indication of their speed was obtained when the shells whistled past the aircraft. Explosions carried away the external wireless aerial about two feet above my turret. Another shell exploded behind the Direction Finding (DF) loop immediately aft of the pilot's escape hatch in the upper fuselage. Allowing deflection to the right and behind I fired two of my guns at the fringe of the wooded area, my tracer fire speeding its way in a straight line before gradually curving slightly to the right of the source of the *flak* shells about half a mile distant. The gunfire suddenly ceased and was not renewed for a few minutes by which time our aircraft was leaving the area.

'About a quarter of an hour later I observed some light flak off the port bow about three miles ahead. As we neared the coastline I discovered that the gunfire originated from a source in the sea. We were approaching Kiel and observations revealed the silhouette of a surfaced *U-boat*. Allowing deflection I fired the two Brownings and observed the tracer fire snaking its way toward the vessel and then veer in all directions as it struck the *U-boat*. Apparently, Claude Wilson had hoped to pass the *U-boat* without attracting fire but I had cancelled that idea. By keeping an intense vigil on the source of the light flak I failed to notice about half a mile away a large *U-boat* depot ship with about half a dozen other surfaced *U-boats* positioned about the center of her starboard side. Suddenly I glimpsed the large dark shape of the depot ship emerging into view against the background of the moon. Figures could be seen running all over the ship and I turned the turret slightly more to port and concentrated my gunfire on to the vessel and its cluster of *U-boats*. Gunfire was returned as the Halifax continued its flight homewards over the Baltic towards the NW German coastline and Denmark. When I suddenly observed the dark shape of a Lancaster ahead of us off the port bow I realized that this was the reason for the solitary *U-boat's* gunfire.

'Our aircraft went off course and we suddenly emerged over the Danish port of Esbjerg, which was heavily fortified by the German forces. Our lone arrival resulted in the entire defenses being directed against us. Turning the turret to starboard I found that the guns could not be depressed far enough to return fire so I called Claude on intercom to bank to starboard. Obligingly, Claude banked the aircraft steeply to starboard so that the Halifax appeared to be standing on its wingtip, allowing me to return fire and eliminate the source. I had to return the favor for Claude as the searchlights were forming a cone on the aircraft and were blinding him as he endeavored to fly the Halifax towards the North Sea. Firing at the searchlights Les Sharpe and I managed to extinguish some of them as Claude weaved the aircraft over the rooftops and through the red, green and white tracer shells of the light flak defenses to eventually emerge unscathed over the North Sea. Settling down to a straight and level course Peter Finnett made some quick calculations and gave a corrective course alteration for the Yorkshire coast. The North Sea was covered with clouds at this time. Claude requested the second pilot to take over for a brief spell so that he could visit the Elsan toilet. While he was gone he was unaware that Peter Finnett gave the second pilot a course alteration for the flight to base. After a period of time on this course Peter said on intercom that base should be appearing at any second but minutes went by with no sign of base. Sqeaker noises on the IFF set were heard and everyone was mystified, as there were no barrage balloons for miles in the vicinity of base. Anti aircraft shell bursts were then heard and I briefly glimpsed a Heinkel 111 among the clouds, crossing ahead and slightly above the Halifax. As suddenly as it appeared it just disappeared from view. A quick check revealed that we were over the London area! Claude resumed control, obtained a reciprocal course and set off for base. We landed at Snaith at about 6 am amid the code words, 'Bandits in the area'. We were about the last aircraft of the squadron to return. Next day inspection revealed that there were only about forty rounds of ammunition left from the 2400 rounds in my mid upper turret boxes!'

Tom Wingham concludes:

> 'For such a long-range target, over 600 miles from England and well outside the range of *Oboe* it was probably the most successful raid during the Battle of the Ruhr. There were a lot of very tired pilots when we got home. We still lost between 6-7%[63], which was the going rate for the job, so presumably Harris felt there was nothing to be gained by repeating the exercise. As far as I know this was a one-off and the tactic was never used again on such a large scale.'

As was usual on nights when the heavies were operating the German defenses could expect 'night nuisance' raids on Berlin and other targets as a diversion for the Main Force operations but on 20/21 April Mosquito operations were also designed to 'celebrate' Hitler's birthday. Mosquito light bomber and night-fighter versions were a thorn in the side of the German air defense and the Bf 110 and Ju 88, the standard night-fighter types then in *Nachtjagd* service, lacked the speed to successfully intercept the Wooden Wonder. However there now occurred two Mosquito claims by a Bf 110 pilot. On 19/20 April (when there were no Main Force operations and six Mosquitoes of 2 Group failed to locate rail workshops at Namur in bad visibility returned without loss) *Major* Helmut Lent,

Kommandeur IV./NJG 1 claimed to be the second *Nachtjagd* pilot to destroy a Mosquito whilst flying a standard Bf 110.[64] Guided by *Lt* Lübke, *Jägerleitoffizier* of *Himmelbett* box *Eisbär* ('Polar Bear') at Sondel, Northern Holland, Lent power-dived onto a Mosquito west of Stavoren from superior altitude and at 500 kph fired a burst of cannon shells at the Wooden Wonder.[65] The experiment was repeated the following night, this time with *Oblt* Lothar Linke, *Staffelkapitän* 12./NJG 1 in the leading role when nine Mosquitoes of 105 Squadron and two of 139 Squadron led by the CO, W/C Peter Shand DSO DFC in DZ386 with P/O Christopher D. Handley DFM as navigator, carried out a bombing attack on Berlin. Over the target it was cloudless with bright moonlight and bombs were dropped from 15,000-23,000 ft. *Flak* was moderate and quite accurate but the biggest danger proved to be nightfighters. Linke, again led by *Eisbär*, overtook Shand's Mosquito in his Bf 110G-4 from high altitude and at high speed in a power dive and sent his quarry down over the northern part of the Ijsselmeer at 0210 hrs. Shand remains missing while the body of his navigator was washed ashore at Makkum.[66]

No Main Force operations were flown until the night of 26/27 April when F/L Ron Read of 78 Squadron had one of his nights 'on' and the target was Duisburg again. Altogether 561 aircraft including 215 Lancasters, 135 Wellingtons and 119 Halifaxes were despatched, 17 of which were lost – ten of them to *Himmelbett Nachtjager* of NJG 1 operating over the Netherlands. Read went 'with mixed feelings'; as he recalls:

> 'I felt better that I was not watching the others go while I stayed in safety but I felt once more that gnawing lump in my stomach. To keep me more occupied I had another young sergeant as a second pilot. We had a good run in, around and back. The Ruhr defenses were as nasty as ever but there was only one aircraft from 76 Squadron missing. Overall there were 17 lost including seven Halifaxes and that represented a drop from the previously high percentages to just 3%. Two nights later on the 28th, we were off again to the Kattegat, for another minelaying sortie. It was to be a big night for minelaying; a special effort to bottle up the German battleships still thought to be a menace, which was why senior crews were going. Normally minelaying was given to new crews and a total of 8, 10 or 12 aircraft were detailed. This time 207 aircraft were going – the highest number to date – so it wasn't just an exercise for beginners. But we were happy for the break from the fiery skies of the Ruhr. It looked a nice 'piece of cake' for a change.
>
> 'We were going back into the Baltic, east of Northern Denmark. Heights and timing were all set up for us by Group. There was some low cloud about but we had no trouble finding our dropping zone on this occasion. We flew low over Denmark on the way back. The gunners had loaded up with lots of ammo to shoot at ground targets, searchlights, gun positions etc. But it was black and we couldn't see much, so I wouldn't let them fire for fear of hitting civilians. They were extremely disappointed. We noted a few air-to-air exchanges but compared to the Ruhr it was nothing. The trip had just one thing in common with our previous visit. Half an hour on the way back we lost an engine. It was the same one: the port outer. By now I wasn't worried about flying on three. I climbed a bit higher just in case we lost another and we cruised in about half an hour behind the others. Although we lost nobody from Linton that night 22 aircraft – another 155 crew – were missing. It was the highest loss of the war on minelaying,[67] an unprecedented loss rate of 10% for these supposedly easy operations. Things were getting worse. Were there going to be any easy targets left?
>
> 'Two nights later, 30 April, we were off to Essen again.[68] My *C-Charlie* was still in the hangar having its engine replaced so I took the spare, *F Freddie*. We set off and I thought this kite ought to stay in one piece for a trouble free trip at least. To my dismay we were just on the outskirts of the Ruhr when Jimmy came up with the all too familiar, 'No pressure on the port inner. Feather her right away Skip.'
>
> 'I couldn't believe it. A nearly new aircraft! I pressed on for a while and decided to drop our bombs on the nearest Ruhr town of any size. I didn't feel like going to Essen on three at this stage. I was fed up with the jinx on every aircraft I flew. Somebody, somewhere didn't like me. Down below, tucked among the usual furious Ruhr *flak* in a town we thought was Oberhousen was a battery of nasty guns that were banging away at us. I thought that they might as well have our bombs. We unloaded them as accurately as we could and headed for home. We evaded a fighter going in the opposite direction. He must have been surprised to see us going against the stream. He didn't turn round as I feared so we made home two hours later with my usual three-engined landing. I got out cursing Halifaxes, ground crews and anybody who had anything to do with maintaining my aircraft. I was not at all happy. The only difference between *F-Freddie* and *C-Charlie* was that the former had a duff port inner instead of a duff port outer engine. I felt my fortunes were at low ebb that Friday night. Back at Linton Gerry Warner the CO told me that I would be screened after one more trip. That was good news. I was losing my appetite for ops because it seemed

that every aircraft I flew turned to ashes in my hands. It was this rather than any fear that I would be shot down that made me glad to see the end in sight.'

On 2 May F/Sgt Eddie Wheeler was delighted and excited when he and his crew, which had completed 16 hours day flying and 12 hours at night, were posted to 97 'Straits Settlement' Squadron in 8 Pathfinder Group at Bourn near Cambridge. The squadron was equipped with Lancaster IIIs and was commanded by W/C R.C. Alabaster DFC, a superb navigator. Wheeler recalls:

'Apart from being an efficient CO, he was an absolute gentleman and was most caring for the crews under his command. Our living quarters at Bourn were pretty spartan but we enjoyed the atmosphere of life on the squadron. Two days after arriving, we were called for our first operational briefing and the adrenaline started flowing again. We had during that morning undergone fighter affiliation with Thunderbolts based at Debden and we were amazed at the maneuverability of the Lancaster and with the fire power of the rear, mid-upper and front turrets we considered that we could face an adversary with greater confidence than ever before. We filed into briefing at 1700 hrs and saw that our target was Dortmund. We drew a gasp when we saw our bomb load totalled 12,000-lbs, comprising a 4000-lb. 'Cookie', four 1000 lb and eight 500 lb GP bombs. The all-up weight with our considerable fuel load was staggering and we wondered how we were going to get airborne on the comparatively short runway.

'At 2130 hrs we were aboard Lanc ED862 doing our pre-flight checks and then the four engines burst into life. The sense of power as 20 aircraft taxied in line from dispersal points to the take-off runway was frightening. When one thought of 240,000 lbs of explosive power, line astern and in close proximity it needed only one aircraft to spark off a major disaster. At 2210 hrs the brakes were released and with all available power we surged down the runway. It seemed we would never lift off before we ran out of runway. At long last we were up – just! It appeared as if we were brushing the treetops and ascent was painfully slow but sure. 'Hitch' [F/O H. Hitchcock, navigator] called out a course to steer to reach our coastal rendezvous with the main force. I tuned the radio to the Group frequency ready to receive the Command half hourly broadcasts which, in code, would transmit any relevant information as to target alterations, recalls etc. It was vitally important to listen to and log these transmissions as we were committed to radio silence except in the direst emergency. Transmissions from the aircraft would be picked up immediately by the German listening posts and we would give them ample opportunity to have a 'reception' party waiting for us.

'Over the sea, the gunners tested their guns after making a careful search for other friendly aircraft. This procedure had to be terminated after a time in view of the danger when forces became so concentrated. The gunners were always apprehensive at the thought that their guns would freeze up after flying at 20,000 plus ft. One normally had only a split second to act if attacked by an enemy fighter. The warmth of the cabin and the constant droning of the four engines had the effect of introducing drowsiness. To keep myself alert in between broadcasts I took a walk, positioned myself in the astrodome and peered into the blackness of the night – sometimes to see the red-hot exhausts of nearby aircraft or the tell tale vapor trails.

'Crossing the enemy coast brought the inevitable deep lines of searchlights and accompanying *Flak* – that had not changed after two and a half years – I remembered it well! We got to the target and the Ruhr was solidly defended. It was a new experience for Peter [P/O H.P. Burbridge, bomb aimer] as he took his position in front of his bombsight. After an initial 'Bloody hell' he directed Johnny [F/L Johnnie Sauvage, pilot] on to the aiming point with his directions of 'Left, left, steady' and it seemed an interminable period before he said 'Bombs gone:' The uplift after release of our full load was very dramatic. After the photo of our bomb plot was taken, Johnny said, 'Let's get the hell out of here,' and promptly threw the Lanc around the sky to escape the accurate anti-aircraft fire. As stood in the astrodome, the sight below was incredible – it seemed a sea of fire and I could imagine the hell being experienced by those poor unfortunates down there.

'The return flight was uneventful until we switched on our IFF equipment, which identified us as a 'friendly' to UK defenses. Listening in to the broadcast it was evident that the weather was deteriorating. A landing at base was considered out of the question and we were directed to divert to High Ercall. A landing at a strange aerodrome after six hours of tension was not good for morale – we just wanted to get back to our beds and relax. Not so, we had to wait our turn for de-briefing, then to follow the Duty Officer to find available sleeping accommodation here, there and everywhere. But at least we had survived the first trip of our second tour safely. As it was Bill's [F/Sgt William Waller, flight engineer] and Peter's first operation ever I don't think they could sleep at all. They had both done their jobs competently and we were confident that they would prove to be valuable crewmembers. We flew back to Bourn the next day and found that there was a stand-down from ops, so we all went into Cambridge to celebrate – which we did, in fine style.'[69]

On 4/5 May F/L Ron Read of 78 Squadron made his 30th trip and normally the last of a tour when 596 aircraft of Bomber Command carried out a heavy raid on Dortmund:

'I still had *F Freddie*, as *Charlie* was undergoing investigation as to why it had wrecked engine after engine. Just to round things off I was given special recce again. For us it was a good trip. There were 596 aircraft going, 141 Halifaxes. Outbound I noted that my artificial horizon was sluggish in recovering from a turn. It didn't worry me too much; it was a clear night. It worried me more on the way into the target, as searchlights coned us for a short while. I flung her around the sky and managed to escape, emerging with my head well down below the cockpit coaming, to avoid the dazzle from the lights. By the instrument's indications I was flying level but when I looked outside through the top left-hand corner of the cockpit I saw lots of fires and markers above. We were still in a steep descending turn although the artificial horizon recorded level flight. I pulled her straight just in time to start our run up. We ran in straight, Harry dropped the bombs in his usual slow way and we got a good picture as I carried on across the target to do our recce. On return I was able to say with all sincerity, that it was a good prang. Just right for our last trip. Once down I breathed a sigh of relief, both for the fact that for once we hadn't lost an engine and my last trip was over. I complained about the sluggish artificial horizon and an examination revealed the presence of small piece of lint or cleaning material in it, which affected the flow of air to it. Another mysterious maintenance failure that couldn't be explained. Well, it ought to be the last for a while. It had been a hard night for Linton. We had lost three on 78 Squadron and 76 had lost one; another 30 crew gone.[70] I felt relieved that I was to be screened and finished with ops.'

Ninety Stirlings had been part of the Dortmund force[71] and one[72] fell victim to *Uffz* Karl-Georg Pfeiffer of 10./NJG 1 for his third victory:

'We took off at 2350 hrs for fighting area *Schlei* (over the island of Schiermonnikoog). We orbited there until just before 0100 hrs and were sent hither and thither but it was only the disruptive activity of the British. Suddenly the *Jägerleitoffizier* (JLO, or GCI-controller) called, 'Have *Kurier*. But your time is up, make quickly Reise-Reise (course for home). Your relief is already on his way.' My radio operator asked, 'What is *Kurier* doing? We are not thirsty yet!' We wanted to tell our controller that we still had fuel for a good half-hour. As the relief had not yet arrived we were directed to the *Kurier*, flying southeasterly in direction of Dollart, probably in order to drop bombs on Emden. It was a pitch-black night and we had to do the entire sortie on instruments. At last ground control *Schlei* placed us behind the *Kurier* and my radio operator picked him up on his radar. He brought me ever closer to the target until the target and ground blips converged. But I could see nothing. The enemy must have been very close. He must be visible from below against the stars. So I went down 200 meters but still nothing. At long last I saw exactly and about 50 meters above me and little stars moving along with us. They were the exhaust flames, damped like ours. I carefully placed myself in an attacking position, exactly below him as *Oblt* Becker had taught us. I pulled slowly up behind him. Now was the moment when, using appropriate deflection, I would be able to fire without getting into the arc of fire of the rear turret (but don't forget to dip down again, otherwise we would get too high and give the rear gunner a perfect target). I pressed the firing button for 1 or 2 seconds but nothing happened. At last one cannon began to stutter. I caught my breath. A small fire started in the starboard inner engine but it did not get bigger.

'The Tommy now pushed his machine down onto me. He must have noticed where the enemy must be. I reduced power and remained, as if in formation, below and to the rear of him. The one cannon continued to stutter. Now we both increased speed and then the pilot of the Short Stirling suddenly pulled his machine upward. I followed all his moves. The one cannon (the others continued to remain silent) fired intermittently but struck home now and then. I wondered how much longer he would pull up his heavy machine. By now we were on our backs and had practically done a looping in formation. Now he was in a vertical dive and the speed increased from 450 to 500, 550, 650 and more. At this moment many searchlights lit up (probably from Emden) and had us both brightly illuminated. I was blinded and did not even notice that we were still in a dive towards the ground behind the bomber. The good people on the searchlights had probably meant to do us a favour, perhaps even to assist us but the opposite was the case. As thanks I wished they would go to the devil. Then my radio operator shouted,

'Watch the altimeter!'

'He was right: it only showed 2000 meters, 1500, 1200, 1000. I pulled the stick back as hard as I could. At last the good 'Cäsar X', as my 110 was known, pulled slowly out and we levelled out at about 400meters at probably 650 km/h. Now there was a heavy explosion beside us. The Short Stirling had struck the ground.[73] We had probably been chasing a dead crew all this time or they had not been able to recover from the looping. My knees were still trembling as we gave our *Abschuss* report to *Schlei*. The JLO congratulated us and gave us the shortest course to Leeuwarden, for now all four red lights of the fuel tanks were lighting up. But we made it and landed at 0120 hrs. The *Abschuss* had been at 0100 hrs precisely. Later the *Flak* tried to lay claim to the *Abschuss* but the required witnesses on the ground were able to confirm our claim, if with only one cannon and a stuttering one at that.'

The day after the Dortmund raid F/L Ron Read was summoned by the wing commander of 78 Squadron:

'I thought it was a little quick for a posting but assumed that was what he wanted to tell me.

'Ronnie, I know I said we would screen you after last night but you know Jimmy Church [B Flight CO] went and that makes things difficult.'

'I knew what was coming.

'So I'll have to ask you to stay on and take over B flight, until I can get a replacement. It should only be for a week and will probably only involve one more trip. Hope you don't mind?'

'What could I say? 'No sir, I don't mind.' I did but it wouldn't make any difference and it was good experience to take over a flight. So I went to B flight on 5 May. We lost three crews on Bochum on 13 May. A total of 24 aircraft, 13 Halifaxes were lost. For us, 21 more aircrew were gone. That night I learned that not going on ops was almost as wearing as going. The hours between take off and landing were spent in a partial vacuum. I went to control to see them land. There was a long lonely, sad wait until the time for all to be landed passed with the three unaccounted for.'

F/Sgt Eddie Wheeler also had to play a waiting game. He had waited a week after his first operation with 97 Squadron before being briefed for the attack on Duisburg on 12/13 May:

'The flight was in bright moon with no cloud and excellent visibility. The target was clearly identified visually which was a rarity. Our total bomb load of 11,000 lbs went down at 2am and the glow of the fires was seen from forty miles away. As usual, the *Flak* was intense and accurate but we came away unscathed and landed at base without incident at 0406 hrs.'[74]

Then, on 13/14 May 442 aircraft were sent to bomb Bochum while 156 Lancasters and 12 Halifaxes set off on a long haul to bomb the Skoda armaments factory at Pilzen in Czechoslovakia. Wheeler was one who was awakened at 11 am with news that 'ops' were on again that night and an earlier briefing than normal gave the hint of a longer target:

'Our flight engineer Bill Waller had to withdraw with a real stinker of a cold, flying at 20,000 ft on oxygen would do him no good at all. His deputy had to be Sgt Ken Fairlie. When we saw that the target was Pilsen in Czechoslovakia, we wished that we all had bad colds! We took off at 2140 hrs and we were not due back at base until approximately 5-am next morning. In the bomb bays we carried a 4000-lb 'cookie' and six 500-lb GP bombs, not inconsiderable for the distance involved. It was bright moonlight again, visibility very good but considerable ground haze. With such conditions, the gunners and lookouts had to be right on their mettle, we must have been so clearly visible to marauding fighters. A cluster of five red TIs went down as we did our bombing run at 13,000-ft and Peter saw our bombs going through the center of the cluster A vague glow was seen through the haze as we turned for home. Seven and a-half-hours after take off we saw the welcome sight of Cambridge and landed safely at Bourn at 0510 hrs. By the time we had been de-briefed and devoured our eggs and bacon breakfast it was nine am and tired as we were, it was difficult to get a satisfactory sleep. Up again to lunch, we were delighted to learn that we were not required for 'ops' and many 'cat-naps' were taken in the mess before embarking on another affray in Cambridge.'

In a Letter dated 15 May P/O Derek Tom Newell Smith, 61 Squadron Lancaster navigator, wrote:

'Ops. Skoda Works, Pilsen. K. *Newhaven.*[75] From our point of view it was a very successful trip as we got an aiming point photograph of Skoda. It was a very long and boring trip. It was getting dark as we were going out and dawn was breaking as we crossed the enemy coast coming back. We were one of the few to get an aiming point photograph due to Sammy spotting that the Pathfinders had marked a decoy' and we went round again. What I remember most is of seeing, five or six aircraft going down in flames in a few minutes as we passed through the Münster-Osnabrück 'gap', a supposed gap in the defenses, which had obviously been closed. 168 of 5 Group on. Nine lost. 7.45 hrs. 1x4000. 4x1000. 2x500.'

The 13/14 May 1943 raids on Pilsen and Bochum cost 33 bombers.[76] *Uffz* Karl-Georg Pfeiffer of 10./NJG 1 was one of the successful fighter pilots:

'We headed for night-fighting area *Löwe* (between Leeuwarden and Groningen). Very soon the *Jägerleitoffizier* (JLO, or GCI-controller) announced a *Kurier* flying over the Zuider Zee in a northeasterly direction. At last an incoming aircraft, which had not yet dropped his bombs. Ground control directed us to the target and *Uffz* Willi Knappe my *Bordfunker* soon had it on his *Lichtenstein* radar. As we got closer, we noticed that the Britisher[77] was constantly altering his course. Obviously an old hand who knew that he was passing through the German night fighter belt. I placed myself exactly beneath him and tried to follow his regular weaving movements. That was no simple matter. At long last we were weaving in unison like dancers to music and the time had come when I had to pull up. My neck was almost stiff through constantly staring upward. I pulled up quickly and was no more than 25 meters below and behind his tail. Then I remembered that I had not armed the cannon. Down quickly and away. He had not noticed us and I was able with shaking hands to repair my lapse. Now the maneuver had to be done all over again. I followed his movements, climbed a little, pulled up and fired! I intended to make certain by cutting through the fuselage from front to rear, when I realized that he would still have all his bombs on board. On firing I gave a little left rudder and the projectiles did not strike the fuselage but the port wing with the two engines, which caught fire at once. That was enough. Now away to the side and down I went. As I turned I noticed that the bomb doors were open and the whole load went down, narrowly missing my Me 110. We saw the Lancaster burning brightly. One could already see through the skeleton of the fuselage and still it continued to fly. Did the crew manage to bale out? They certainly had sufficient time. Suddenly the aircraft exploded and the burning parts fell into the North Sea.[78]

'We landed at about 0437 hrs after a half-hour flight and were glad that the night with its terrors was over. Once again all had gone well. The cockpit-clock showed 0329 hrs. Willi also gave a sigh of relief and remarked dryly, 'Congratulations on your EK I'.[79] It was my 4th *Abschuss*, for which a pilot received this decoration (the radio operator after the 6th). During May the well-known dance band Barnabas von Gécy was playing in the 'Harmonie' in Leeuwarden. Some of us got tickets and we hoped that we were not on the battle order that night. I was in luck and it turned out to be a wonderful evening. As I lay in bed later, still dreaming of the lovely melodies, the telephone suddenly rang. '*Uffz* Pfeiffer report at once to the officers mess!' I dived into my uniform, thinking that nothing good would come of this. When I arrived I found a party in progress, with ladies and many civilian guests. *Major* Lent came up to me and said, 'I hereby invest you with the EK I for your victories. Carry on like that!'[80] I was amazed and happy and only noticed now that the officers had invited the entire orchestra Barnabas von Gécy to join in the celebrations. I was allowed to remain and enjoy the party for the rest of the night. The next morning each and every hair on my head ached. A terrible hangover. But it had been worth it.'

For Sgt (later W/O) Arthur R. 'Spud' Taylor, observer in Stirling III BF480 '*I-Ink*' of 218 'Gold Coast' Squadron, one of 95 Stirlings on the Bochum raid, it was a nightmare trip, as he recalls:

'We were carrying incendiaries and were determined to the target at all costs. We crossed the Dutch coast off track and wandered pretty close to Antwerp. The searchlights and flak were pretty strong. It was a beautiful moonlight night and we managed to pinpoint quite easily. The *Gee* went u/s sometime before reaching target area and we turned up, all unaware, over Düsseldorf. (On the way out I pinpointed our position exactly on the Dutch coast and gave a fix to Shorty, our navigator. Through a fault in his calculations, he then gave an incorrect course to our pilot. This meant that by the time we reached the Rhine we were some 20 miles north of the main force and this in turn meant that we approached the target from completely the wrong direction. It was fortunate for us that we didn't collide with one of our own aircraft, who, by the time we reached it, were leaving the target in a northerly direction). Being the only kite over the place, they gave us all they'd got. Did my best to pinpoint but dazzled by all the lights.

'Bill panicked and circled about in a frantic endeavour to get out, losing height all the while. Before we left Düsseldorf we were at 6000'. Immense cones of 30/40 searchlights picked us up at a time and we were a sitting target for light, medium and heavy flak. There was plenty of it. I should think that something like 200-300 guns were firing at us at any one time. It was at this point that Bill gave the order to bale out. I replied that if we did no one would reach the ground in one piece. Bill then said,

'You bloody well fly it then!'

'I went up the steps and grabbed the 2nd pilot's controls and steered a straight course. In a few minutes we had left Düsseldorf behind. Some ten minutes after that Bill had recovered sufficiently to take over again. We then passed over the southern outskirts of Essen and for several minutes we were coned by searchlights and fired at continuously. When flak hit the aircraft there is a clap like thunder and a strong smell of cordite. Finally, we arrived at the target. The place was ablaze. Immense fires covered the ground and reflected red on a great pall of smoke, which hung above the town.

'Meanwhile, Jock, our rear gunner, had obeyed the order to bale out but he had pulled the ripcord too early and his parachute had partially opened, jamming him in the escape hatch. In this position, with his head, shoulders and arms out of the aircraft, he had received the full blast of the explosions. Having bombed I tried to get Jock on the intercom and had no reply, so I went back to see how he was, to find him half in and half out of the hatch. He was in a dazed condition when I pulled him back in. I then sat next to Bill. *I-Ink* was shaking so badly that I had to hold the throttles in position from then on. At last we lost the searchlights and headed north into the seemingly quiet fighter belt that ran right the way from Northern Denmark down to below Paris. *Gee* still u/s but I managed to pinpoint the Zuider Zee. There was only just enough petrol to get home.

'We arrived back at base in the half-light of early morning. The TR.9 was u/s so we landed without permission. Just as I thought everything was OK, I looked at Bill to find that he had let go of the controls and he had both hands over his eyes. The kite swerved suddenly to port and the next thing I knew we had cut a lorry in two, killing a couple of poor blokes just back from the raid. We also knocked two cars for yards and partially demolished the briefing room, where de-briefing was taking place, before finally pranging into the operations room with our right wing. A few people in there were injured. *I-Ink* finally came to rest on the control tower. I headed for the hatch but Paddy, who was wielding an axe in a desperate attempt to hack his way out, blocked the way. I tapped him on the back and asked him if he had tried the door and with that we all ran out of the kite, fully expecting it to burst into flames. We all went to the MO who gave us two little yellow pills each, which all but knocked us out before we reached the billet! Next day we looked over our kite. It had had it. We walked round counting flak holes and there were about 100 – several extraordinarily close to where we were sitting. Len's turret had five or six holes in it, one piece of shrapnel grazing his nose on its way through. The astrodome was whipped away while Paddy was looking through it and Jock had a deep cut in his head. I was lucky to escape injury myself as shrapnel broke off a six-inch piece of metal from my compartment, which hit me on the head but fortunately, my leather helmet saved my bacon.

'After breakfast we were told to report to the CO. When got to his office we gave him our account to do with the raid on Bochum. I told him that we had no confidence in Bill and did not wish to fly with him again. The CO looked at some papers on his desk and told us that we were Bill's sixth crew and that he had crashed the lot! This was news to us but the main thing was that he granted our request. (We thought that Bill would have been grounded but later, at Stradishall, we found him with another crew. I will never know for sure what happened to Bill eventually. Some months later I was in a pub chatting with a bomb aimer from another squadron who told me that he thought he had seen Bill's Stirling heading into the Channel for no apparent reason with all guns firing). As for Jock, in the month that followed, he went missing a few times and was found wandering around the fields near the aerodrome, barefoot and in his pyjamas. We never saw him again).'[81]

LMF was bad for morale and was kept out of the press. Morale was everything and Bomber Command and the British public received a huge boost when on 17 May 1943 listeners to the BBC tuned in to hear the news that the RAF had just mounted one of the most incredible and daring raids of the war. 'In the early hours of this morning a force of Lancasters of Bomber Command led by Wing Commander G.P Gibson DSO DFC attacked with mines the dams of the Ruhr Basin. Eight of the Lancasters are missing...' The rest of the bulletin was triumphal and morale boosting. Operation *Chastise* as it was called, had involved 19 Lancasters of 617 Squadron who took off from Scampton to breach the dams with 'bouncing bombs' invented by Dr. Barnes Wallis. It was, as Wallis said, 'the most amazing feat the RAF ever had or ever could perform'. The massive Möhne, Eder or Sorpe dams served the industrial Ruhr Basin and more than a dozen hydroelectric power plants relied on their waters. So did foundries, steel works, chemical plants and other factories fuelling Germany's war effort. Winston Churchill had authorized the operation and he used it as a coup to seek greater support from the USA. At the time, most of President Roosevelt's advisers were committed to targeting

Japan first. The 'Dam Busters' proved that the war in Europe was being prosecuted dramatically well. Two days after the operation, Churchill was given a standing ovation at the Trident Conference with Roosevelt in Washington. Gibson, who already had two DSOs and two DFCs was awarded the VC for leading the 'Dam Busters' and many of the officers got DFCs and DSOs.[82]

F/L Ron Read of 78 Squadron was on a ten day break when the Dam Busters raid went ahead. The news gave him and everyone else in Bomber Command and the country as a whole a great lift to see the results although as he said, 'Unfortunately it was never to be repeated.' Read meanwhile was due to do one more trip towards the end of May and he elected to finish up on the Ruhr with Dortmund, the fourth heavy Bomber Command raid of May on the night of the 23rd/24th:

> 'We were back flying *C-Charlie* again. They'd changed the port outer for the fourth time. They still couldn't find any sound reason why that engine always failed. I still viewed her with deep suspicion but hoped that she would last out one more trip. Shortly after reaching Egmond Jim took an all too familiar hand.
>
> 'Sorry Skip. You'll have to feather the port outer. The pressure's down again and she's warming up.'
>
> 'I moved to the feathering controls and hesitated. 'Oh Christ Jim, not again. You sure?'
>
> 'Yes Skip, 'fraid so. The bastard's gone again. Getting hot too.' He moved smartly into the cockpit to the feathering button and pressed it for me. He wasn't prepared to argue about it.
>
> 'I was angry but resigned. What could I do now? On my way round on the orbit I had noticed a night fighter station below. I'd actually watched a night fighter taking off on the subdued runway lightning. I thought we might drop our bombs on that. I'd have to go out to sea, come round and make a run over it in-bound. I didn't really want to head out against the bomber stream, which by now must be fairly thick over Egmond. However I did and as I passed by and made ready to turn back in the airfield lights went out. I was not able to guess accurately enough where they had been, to drop blind. I still had a long way to go around and the villages and towns below were Dutch. I couldn't unload at a rough guess over them. Sadly, we turned out to sea again. There were a couple of flak ships hosing the sky off the coast. More in hope than in anger I dropped them on one of them and turned for home.'

Of 829 aircraft despatched, 38 bombers failed to return.[83] A Wellington of 431 'Iroquois' Squadron RCAF which had just dropped its bomb load on Dortmund when it was hit by *Flak* was very fortunate. There was a terrific gust of air and the tail gunner and pilot vanished into the dark and then the bomber went into a spin. Of the three men left on board only F/Sgt Sloan, bomb aimer had done any flying and he had never handled a Wellington. Sloan, Sgt G.C.W. Parslawe, navigator and F/O John B.G. Bailey, WOP-AG stared at the wheeling mass of flame below and did not relish the idea of baling out into the inferno and so they decided they would try to fly the crippled bomber home, 300 miles. Bailey recalled:

> 'It was all very Heath Robinson. Sloan grabbed the controls and somehow managed to right us. We were down to 2000 ft and every gun seemed to be on us, not to mention searchlights. Parslawe and I bunched round him and we tried to think up everything we knew about piloting. We flew by conference. Sloan was grand. He got the plane well up again and even managed to dodge the *Flak* and searchlights. Thank goodness night fighters did not spot us! We were pretty shaky about the question of landing but Sloan was the calmest of the three. In fact, he was working up to a splendid landing when the starboard engine cut out. Even that did not rattle him. Somehow he got us down [at Cranwell]. He did nothing worse than overshoot the runway by a few yards. And nobody got hurt.'[84]

Now that it was all over, Ron Read was disappointed with his tour on 78 Squadron:

> 'Although it looked reasonable on paper I felt that I had not accomplished much more than the survival of the crew and myself. I had served my operational tour through the whole of the Battle of the Ruhr, unaware then that it would come to be known by that name. To us it was a series of operations, mostly unpleasant, to the most heavily defended area of Germany. It was the build-up to ACM Harris's plan for the systematic destruction of the German's capability to wage war by destroying its industrial capacity. It was also expected to break the morale of the civilian population to a point where they would abandon their towns and factories and perhaps rise up in arms against the Hitler regime. In spite of the failure of the London blitz to break British civilian morale the Air Marshals, as well as some of the politicians, not least Churchill, were convinced that German civilian morale was lower than British. They felt that it would collapse

under the much heavier bombardment that the new, 1943, Bomber Command could deliver.

'What we left behind didn't occupy our thoughts very much. We certainly didn't dwell in the past and in view of our circumstances didn't devote much time to the future either. The next day's activities or at longest the next leave was about the limit of our aspirations. Those Ruhr battles of 1943 provided the blueprint for the bomber offensive for the rest of the war. I was both sad and glad to leave 78 Squadron. In effect it was where I grew up. In my time with them I had seen 19 squadron crews go missing, approximately 150 aircrew members. In addition, 27 crews of our sister squadron 76, were lost – 195 aircrew. More friends were to go after I left. Just average Bomber Command figures for any station. I was relieved to be free of the constant knowledge that the next night I might have to stick my neck out once again. I should now be able to sleep easy in my bed. It was like a reprieve from the condemned cell of poor old Morty's corny, pre-ops statement: 'The condemned men ate a hearty breakfast.'[85]

On the night of 25/26 May 759 bombers were despatched to bomb Düsseldorf. 27 bombers (3.6 per cent of the force despatched) were lost – 21 of which, were due to nightfighters. The raid was a failure due to the difficulty of marking in bad weather. II./NJG 1 crews returned with eight victories, including *Major* Walter Ehle with four.[86] I./NJG 1 at Venlo destroyed ten bombers including Wellington X *Z-Zebra* of 431 'Iroquois' Squadron RCAF flown by Sgt Bob Barclay. Sgt Ken Dix, navigator, had misgivings from the off, as he recalls:

'I was concerned when I saw that our flight path took us one and a half miles north of the German night fighter base at Venlo. I said they could orbit their beacon and pick off bombers behind the main stream but no route change was made. On the runway the port engine would not start and the other bombers went off. As a specially selected crew usually we were the lead-machine. We carried 4000lbs of incendiaries to drop within less than ten seconds of the flares from the Pathfinder Force aircraft going down on the target; usually from as near to 18,500ft as we could reach with a full bomb load. But it was 22 minutes before we got the port engine going. So it left us well behind the main stream of bombers. The machine did not climb well enough and had not enough speed so we flew to Hornsea on the coast and flew across the North Sea to Ijmuiden. Then we headed between the *Flak* zones of Soesterberg and Hertogenbosch on our way to the Track Indicator Markers laid by the pathfinders. We had just seen it and were on the correct track when Sgt Harry Sweet in the rear turret shouted, 'FIGHTER!' He immediately fired his four Browning machine guns.'

At the same time as Harry Sweet opened fire, the fighter, a Bf 110 flown by *Oblt* Manfred Meurer *Staffelkapitän*, 3./NGJ 1, fired his cannons and he hit the Wellington along the starboard beam from the tail as Bob Barclay took evasive action. Ken Dix continues:

'The cannon shells had hit hard. They stopped just by my Gee radar set. The voice intercom failed and then our flashing intercom buttons also went off. Sgt Jeffries, the WOP/AG, was behind the main spar ready to launch the flare for our picture after the bombing run. He was killed. The aircraft was blazing with the port engine hit and on fire. We were spinning round and down. I managed to get my chest chute into my new harness. I couldn't go back to Sgt Jeffries because of the fierce flames driving me back. I went to the cockpit. The front hatch was open but F/O Bert Bonner, bomb aimer and Bob Barclay had baled out. They could have tried to contact us but the system had been hit. I had flown the aircraft when we were on exercises and I had also been on a pilot's course in Florida before becoming a navigator, so I decided to try and fly the Wellington back to base. I got into the pilot's seat and the Wellington at first answered the controls. I turned to fly northwest back to England then dived to try and put the flames out. It was going well when suddenly the control wires, hit by cannon fire, broke. I had no control so reluctantly I had to bale out. I pulled the ripcord and the turning Wellington just missed me. I saw it hit the ground.'[87]

When Essen was subjected to a Main Force raid by 518 aircraft on 27/28 May 23 bombers failed to return.[88] Minor operations were flown on the night of 28/29 May with 34 crews, some of them undoubtedly flying their first op sowed mines off the Friesians. This was the case a few nights earlier, on 25 May when F/O John Overton's Stirling III crew of 218 'Gold Coast' Squadron took off from Downham Market. Sgt Harry Barker, bomb aimer recalls:

'The mining trip was uneventful and lasted four hours but it gave us a gentle introduction into action over enemy territory. On the 29th of May we were briefed for an attack on Wuppertal in the Ruhr. This has stayed in my memory because during the briefing the target was designated a dormitory town serving the factories of the Ruhr and it was clearly intended to destroy housing to disrupt the workers production. We had a job to do and at that time bombing attacks on our own cities, London, Coventry, Birmingham and many others created a demand for retaliation. The view of many people has tended to forget that we were all fighting for our lives and the very real fear that defeat was possible and probably very likely has not been understood by the majority of people today. We were ordinary young men who had volunteered to undertake a special role in defending our country and our families. For my part I did not dwell on the damage and death resulting from our attacks. Instead I pictured the scenes shown in the press of Coventry and London burning. We were expected to hit back and that was what we did. The raid on Wuppertal was at times a bit scary. We saw flak and searchlights for the first time and our trip lasted 4hrs 25mins sleep. I remember the rewarding breakfast we had on return of bacon and egg and then getting back to our billet for six or seven hours sleep. I awoke and had my lunch in the sergeants' mess. Then I wandered off on my own and lay down on the warm turf outside our hut. It was beautiful day, a bright blue sky and birds were singing. I reflected on my incredible situation. I was a very immature kid at 20 years old stretched out on warm Norfolk turf having very recently flown as a crewmember of a huge bomber to drop bombs on a German town. Then I had helped to fly back to my well-earned bacon and egg before getting ready to do the same thing again. It all seemed so unreal. The other thoughts that I tried not to dwell on were the inescapable facts of losses by enemy action. They were just as determined to stop our attacks, as we were to carry them out.'

The area bombing of the Barman half of the long and narrow town of Wuppertal on 29/30 May involved 719 aircraft and the attack started a large fire area in the narrow streets of the old town centre. Wuppertal had never experienced a major raid before and being a Saturday night, many of the town's fire and air raid precaution officials were absent. About 4,000 houses were burned to the ground and about 3,400 people[89] died as a minor firestorm raged. Thirty-three bombers were lost, 22 of which, were shot down by *Nachtjäger*. I./NJG 1 claimed eight aircraft shot down, four of these being credited to *Oblt* Manfred Meurer *Staffelkapitän* 3./NJG 1[90] *Lt* Wilhelm Beier of 3./NJG 1 destroyed a Halifax at Limbricht.[91] In all 150 individual aircraft were plotted on the *Würzburg* radars flying through the *Himmelbett* boxes in eastern Belgium, in which 13 Bf 110Gs and three Do 217s of II./NJG 1 patrolled during the course of the night. For the loss of thee aircraft and two aircrew killed six II/NJG 1 crews scored 11 victories, three of which were credited to *Lt* Heinz-Wolfgang Schnaufer and his *Bordfunker Lt* Baro.[92] Schnaufer reported his encounter with one of the Stirlings:

> 'At about 0035 hrs I was directed on to an incoming enemy aircraft at an altitude of 3500 meters. It was located on the [airborne radar] and after further instructions [from Dr. Baro, his operator] I made out a four-engined bomber at 0045 hrs, about 200 meters away above and to the right. I attacked the violently evading bomber from behind and below at a range of 80 meters and my rounds started a bright fire in the left wing. The blazing enemy aircraft turned and dived away steeply, hitting the ground and exploding violently at 0048 hrs.'

In all 167 *Nachtjagd* victories were recorded in May.[93] By the early summer of 1943 there was only one effective tactical measure available to Air Marshal Harris and his staff officers to counter the German night fighter defense. This was the saturation of the German GCI system by concentrating the RAF bomber routes through relatively few GCI *Räume* (boxes) or through *Gebiete* (zones) in which few or no GCI stations existed. In 1942, when the RAF began attacking targets within a period of 30 minutes the narrow night fighter zone in the west was quickly penetrated and at the same time, only a few fighters came into contact with the bomber stream. *Flak*, emplaced in single batteries, was unable to cope with the concentrated attacks by the RAF. The carefully practiced system of concentrating several batteries' fire on a single target broke down because so many aircraft appeared over the target at the same time. As a result of all this the night fighter zone in the West had to be rapidly increased in depth and extended to Denmark in the north and to eastern France in the south. Operational control had to be developed whereby two or more night fighters could be brought into action in any one night fighter area at the same time. In addition, bombers over the target had to be attacked by fighters as well as *Flak,* which had to be consolidated into large batteries near the targets and concentrated at the most important targets. Above all, accuracy had to be increased by developing a large number of radar range finders.

In June the *Reichsverteidigung Himmelbett Nachtjagd* defenses claimed a record 223 victories.[94] On 11/12 June when 860 heavies were despatched to bomb Düsseldorf *Nachtjagd* claimed 30 bombers shot down. Just six weeks earlier F/Sgt B.J. 'Jim' Sprackling, flight engineer in P/O G.W. 'Bill' Lucas' crew of 10 Squadron (The Shining 10th) had had his first flight in a Halifax. Now the crew were detailed for their first operation from Melbourne, 15 miles southeast of York, as Sprackling recalls:

'My pilot had blond hair and very blue eyes. He was older than the rest, possibly nearly 30 and had been a sergeant in the Royal Artillery and had volunteered for aircrew after Dunkirk, so he was battle hardened. Jock, a young Glaswegian, was navigator. P/O Len 'Butch' Butcher was the bomb aimer. Paddy O'Neil, another older chap from Belfast, was wireless operator. The only other country lad was Digger, who was half Aboriginal and he had been brought up on a cattle station in Queensland. Digger was mid-upper gunner. Ronnie Pentlin, a cockney, was rear gunner. So began 14 months of very close association with six chaps from very different walks of life. Crews were alerted during the morning that there was a 'Call' and the flight commander detailed which crews were to fly and which aircraft. Group HQ nominated how many aircraft were required. Most bombing missions to German targets were maximum efforts, i.e. every available aircraft. During the afternoon the ground crew would prepare the aircraft, loading bombs and ammunition into gun turrets. The fuel load would be put on and everything checked over. The aircrew would go out to the aircraft and check that everything was to their satisfaction, each member checking his specialist equipment. The flight engineer would thoroughly inspect the whole aircraft, looking for any signs of trouble like small oil leaks and physically check the fuel tanks to see none had been missed – not too difficult with ten tanks on a Halifax. Then it was off to the mess for a meal before briefing.

'About three hours before the scheduled time for take off all the crews detailed to fly assembled in the briefing room. The airfield gates were shut and no one was allowed off camp. The briefing room at Melbourne was a standard Nissen hut. At one end there was a large map of France, Germany and the Low Countries, which at the time was covered by a curtain and a blackboard and easel holding a smaller map. There was a low platform with two or three armchairs in front of the maps and the rest of the room was filled with forms on which the crews sat. At that time the navigators had been doing preparatory work on their charts but no one, other than the briefing officer knew the details. On commencement of briefing the station commander, a group captain, took one of the chairs, the squadron commander, a wing commander, stood by the covered map and the station intelligence and meteorology officer stood by. Also, the most senior member of each non-pilot aircrew trade, known as 'leaders' hovered. With everyone inside the doors were shut and the roll was called, each captain answering for his crew. Then the curtain was raised and the target exposed. A large pin in the map indicated the city to be attacked and colored string showed the route in and out of the target. The squadron commander gave a brief description of the target, the time the squadron was to attack and the height from which the attack was to be made. There was a murmur from the experienced crews. *V-Victor's* crew remained very quiet. Then the intelligence officer took the stage. He gave a more detailed assessment of the target and what was expected to result from the attack. He pointed out all known German anti-aircraft batteries along the route, the known defenses of the target and also known night-fighter bases likely to be activated. The target was Düsseldorf, an industrial city south of the Ruhr Valley in northern Germany. The Ruhr cities were known as Happy Valley.

'The last briefing, from the met man was very important for many reasons. The navigators needed to know the wind strength and direction accurately because the aircraft flew at about 150-170 mph and wind speeds of 40-50 mph at altitude had a great effect on navigation. Also important was cloud cover. There were few navigational aids so crews needed to be able to see vital land marks like the coast and the Rhine but not too clear as some cloud cover made it difficult for the German night fighters. Cloud also broke up the searchlight patterns. What was ideal was low level broken cloud over the night fighter bases with clear weather conditions above and a hole in the cloud over the target. It seldom happened. Tonight it was to be clear above broken cloud and the moon set early. These were reasonable conditions. The engineer leader confirmed fuel, ammunition and bomb load and stick pattern. The station commander wished everyone luck and we all trooped out to the parachute and locker room where everyone put on flying gear and collected their parachute from the specially aired and heated store. And so, out to the crew busses. These were the standard pre-war Bedford 30-seaters, except that the seats were down the side to give room for the flying gear and equipment such as navigators' bags and sextants and engineers' tool kits etc: Each bus carried two or three crews for aircraft in adjacent dispersals. Usually, there was time to spare so those who smoked would move away from the aircraft and have a last puff. Superstitious members had a pee on the tail wheel. Don't ask why, it was tradition. Then we all waited and chatted to the ground crew until it was time to go aboard.

'A bomber airfield at night was an eerie place. There was absolute silence once the crew busses had gone. Just normal country sounds, owls, a cow mooing in the distance and, if it was really quiet, a night train chugging along a nearby railway line and the added rustle of small animals in the grass around the concrete pad. Then suddenly, the unmistakable crackle of a Merlin engine coming to life as the first aircraft due off started up. Then it was all aboard and time to get to work. Aircraft took off in alphabetical order so *V-Victor* (JD207) was one of the last. Bill and I worked to get the engines running from the external starter trolley, checking that all the gauges came to life as each motor started. Always the two inner-engines first, as they carried the essential auxiliaries. When all four were running, the ground flight switch was changed to 'flight.' This put all the electrics on the aircraft's own batteries and the ground crew removed the external connection and towed the trolley/AC away. We then went through all our pre-flight checks and the engines were given a quick run up. The captain set the first course on the compass and the correct barometric pressure on the altimeter and we were nearly ready for off. Chocks were waved away and the aircraft gently taxied out onto the perimeter track and in its turn, onto the runway. Twenty or so black monsters were trundling through the dark with only the faintest lights on the edge of the track to guide them. Except for the noise of the engines, all was silence. No radio or anything like that to warn Jerry that they we were coming.

'A green light flashed from the caravan at *A-Able*, or whichever aircraft was lined up first on the runway. Momentarily stopped another green light and then the roar of the four Merlin engines opened to full power and the aircraft started thundering down the runway. After what seemed an age, it slowly lifted off and started to climb away. The next aircraft was already lined up and off it went. At last it was *V-Victor's* turn. The green light flashed. Bill eased her onto the runway and held her straight on the brakes. He opened up the throttles to full power. I had a quick look at all the dials. They were OK. The brakes were released and *V-Victor* started down the runway. There were two points of apprehension at this time. This was the first take off with a fully loaded aircraft and *V-Victor* was a bit of an old lady – a Halifax I, with the nose turret removed and replaced by a hand-beaten fairing. So, she didn't really leap down the runway but eventually the magic speed was on the Air Speed Indicator. Bill eased the control column back and she slowly lifted off, out into the darkness over the Yorkshire countryside. No lights anywhere – just blackness. Gradually, we were gaining height and Bill turned on to course almost due south. I kept my eye on my engine gauges as the first five or ten minutes were the only time they would be on maximum power. Bill straightened up when on heading and at 2000 ft reduced the power and the long flog down the east of England began. Eventually over the Essex coast to the Scheldt Estuary of Holland. At 10,000-ft oxygen masks had to be worn and the superchargers' gears changed to S Gear i.e.- fully super supercharged, to pump more of the rarefied air into the engines. And so up to cruising height, which should have been 22,000 ft but we had been warned that poor *V-Victor* wouldn't go much above 19,000 ft until some of the fuel was used up. So at 19,000ft the throttles were eased back a bit as fuel consumption was critical if we were to get back safely. The object of the exercise was to carry the maximum bomb load so the minimum fuel safety margins were carried.

'As we approached the Dutch coast we could see that the early aircraft had alerted the defenses. Searchlights were throwing their beams in the air and occasionally, they would form a tripod and an aircraft would be illuminated for a few minutes. Tiny stars – anti-aircraft shells bursting – would appear round it but they didn't seem to be doing any damage. Except for this display nothing exciting was happening. Although there were another 400 aircraft with us we seldom saw another one. A black shape showing up against the skyline would stay for a while and then drift out of sight.

'We crossed the Dutch coast and entered enemy territory. Fortunately, searchlights did not bother us so we pressed on. The great rivers of the Rhine estuary were quite clear underneath and the Dutch islands were easy to identify. The navigator confirmed that we were on course and on time. Time was essential as every squadron had its precise time over the target to avoid hitting each other. The whole raid was scheduled to last under 30 minutes, the object being to swamp the defenses. Besides watching my engine dials and recording all their readings, I had to help with the lookout for enemy fighters. The astrodome was over my station and by standing up I probably had the best all-round view of any of the crew. And so we crossed Holland. The numerous glints of water below concentrated into one wide river, the Rhine, as wide as the Thames after it had passed London or the Severn opposite Avonmouth. They carried on south just west of the river. Then some way ahead what looked like a bright star appeared, which rapidly grew to look like a bonfire in the sky. Then it started twisting and dropping towards the ground. Bill remarked, 'Some poor sod has bought it, hope they baled out.' He warned every one of us to keep our eyes peeled for fighters. Then down below in front of the port wing tip fireworks' display began on the ground. The attack had started. It was easy to see the explosion of the HE bombs and then, what looked like streetlights, coming on as the incendiaries lit up. Then the whole area was a blaze of light as more and more bomb loads were dropped. The navigator called up a new course and Bill turned the aircraft toward the target. They were starting their bombing run. There was a screen of searchlights ahead to pass and numerous little pinpricks of light showed that anti-aircraft shells were bursting ahead. Other aircraft were appearing as the force was concentrating into the run in to the target.

'As the conflagration started to slide under the nose of the aircraft, Len's voice came over the intercom: 'Bomb doors open', bombs fused,' then calling 'left' or 'right', then 'steady'. Bill kept the aircraft dead steady, ignoring the white puffs of smoke flying past, which were caused by exploding shells and fighting the slipstreams of other aircraft. Suddenly the aircraft seemed to give a little jump and over the intercom 'Bombs gone, bomb-doors closed.' Poor old V-Victor seemed very relieved. Another minute straight and level for the camera to record what we had bombed when the photoflash went off and then turn north for home. But we had obviously stirred up a hornet's nest. We were just clear of the target area when a searchlight caught us and then two more joined in. Bill immediately started a corkscrew maneuver but the white puffs of smoke started to appear again and we could hear the shells exploding (We had been told not to worry about flak unless we could hear it). Then a loud explosion and I suddenly felt my left foot knocked from under me. This caused me to lose my balance and I fell into the gangway, sitting painfully on the edge of an armor-plated step just behind the instrument panel. I switched on my mike and announced that I had been hit. 'Bill said, 'There isn't much wrong with you or you wouldn't be making so much noise' and believe it or not there wasn't. A piece of 88mm *flak*, about half the size of the filler cap, had come through the starboard side of the cockpit and hit the heel of my flying boot and then rattled down among the oxygen bottles. Once I was back on my feet we had lost the searchlights and it was time to check for any other damage. Everything appeared OK. There was no vibration from the engines. All the gauges were normal and none of the ten fuel tanks appeared to be holed. A good look outside to see if there were any holes and a walk down the fuselage. No damage and nothing to report from the gunner. Next, a look into the bomb bay inspection hatch to check that all the bombs had gone and the doors were fully closed.

'Soon the Dutch islands were beginning to appear and then they disappeared under cloud. After about another half-hour Jock announced that he didn't know where we were. He wasn't sure where we had started from after taking evasive action from the searchlights and we had not been able to pick up a landmark over the Dutch coast because of cloud. Bill said he would hold his northerly course while we sorted ourselves out. Paddy was told to get his radio going and try and pick up a one of the J Beams, which were beamed out from the east coast of England across the North Sea, to help aircraft in trouble. After about half an hour Paddy called that he had found one and an interpretation by the navigator showed that we were due east of Yarmouth, so at least we were clear of enemy territory but how far were we from the English coast? It was decided to turn due west and make sure of making the coast, then if the fuel ran out we should be able to find an East Anglian airfield. After another half an hour we identified the coast and set a new course for base. It was now a question of would the fuel last? I set to work to make sure that it did.

'I set the engines at their most economic power setting and the aircraft was allowed to slowly descend. Then I drained all the six smaller tanks completely dry to concentrate all the remaining fuel in the four larger tanks; one connected to each engine, and kept a continuous watch on the fuel gauges. Eventually we spotted a chance light beacon flashing the letters *'MB' – MELBOURNE*. A quick half circuit and landing. We had only 15 minutes of fuel left. We had taken six hours to do a five-hour mission. The crew bus was waiting for us. While the navigators were packing up their gear Bill and I had a good look round the aircraft to see if there were any more holes. Surprisingly, none were obvious. Then debriefing, which for a new crew was fairly informal. I showed off my souvenir piece of Flak, which I had recovered from down among the oxygen bottles. The navigator's log would be thoroughly checked next day. A pat on the back from the CO and the station commander, then off to breakfast – bacon, eggs and baked beans. There was no rationing where aircrews were concerned. Then off to bed. Our first op was over.'[95]

Forty-three aircraft failed to return from the 11/12 June Düsseldorf raid, 29 of which were shot down by *Himmelbett*-operating *Nachtjäger*.[96] One of the victories went to *Uffz* Karl-Georg Pfeiffer of 10./NJG 1 who took off for the area *Hering* at 0115 hours. Earlier that day he had scored his sixth *Abschuss* when he shot down a B-17 during a daylight sortie.[97] Pfeiffer recalls his night sortie with *Bordfunker*, *Uffz* Willi Knappe:

'The weather was dreadful with rain, gusting wind and low cloud, all great favorites of pilots. We were sent all over the place by the *Jägerleitoffizier* without any result as the targets were mostly in cloud, then an order on 270° to the west. Willi, looking into his *Lichtenstein*, soon said, 'That's an old hand, he's weaving about all the time even though he'll soon be home'. By now we were so far away from area Hering that the voice of the JLO had grown quite faint. There was nothing to be seen. I was in cloud nearly all the time and had to keep my eyes on the artificial horizon. We were just able to make out, 'I cannot guide you any more' then all contact broke off. Willi Knapp was still watching the *Lichtenstein* and giving me new directions. Then he said, 'He must be somewhere here'. But I could see nothing. As I was worried that I might ram the enemy aircraft in the clouds I went a little lower and searched through the upper part of the windscreen. Willi was no longer able to help me and also stared. Without thinking I happened to take a look directly above me and spotted two tiny flames, the exhaust ports. Two engines? It could only be a Wellington.[98] This type did not burn easily and was well armored. However, I had to have a go at it. The red fuel warning lights were already on and blinded me. I had difficulty in matching his weaving about, then, as I had been taught, attacked. A long burst but without effect. A quick breakaway, then the same all over again. This time I fired a little to the left in order to hit an engine. At last there was a small flame, which grew slowly larger. Then it spread to the fuselage and the port wing. I kept my distance as the rear gunner might open fire. A number of crews had been lost this way. At last the burning machine dipped a little, tipped on its nose and went hurtling down into the sea 30 kilometers west of Ijmuiden at 0240. Now quickly homeward, hoping that the fuel would last out. After a while we heard the voice of the *Jägerleitoffizier* (JLO, or GCI-controller) to whom we reported, '*Sieg Heil'* [Bomber destroyed!] We landed happy and proud at Leeuwarden at 0315 hrs after exactly two hours flight. *Major* Ruppel congratulated us on our seventh *Abschuss* and he was relieved that the last crew had returned safely. Later I heard him saying to an officer in the operations room: 'The crew Pfeiffer is coming along, they're shooting themselves ahead'. 'But with fortune's powers…' as Schiller says!'

On 12/13 June 24 of the 503 aircraft raiding Bochum were destroyed by the German defenses. *Nachtjagd* was credited with 27 confirmed kills, an unusual overclaiming by three aircraft. Twenty-one *Abschüsse* went to NJG 1. *Hptm* Egmont Prinz *zur* Lippe Weissenfeld III./NJG 1 *Kommandeur* destroyed two Halifaxes.[99] III./NJG 1 patrolling the eastern Dutch-German border shot down eight Lancasters and Halifaxes.[100] *Oblt* Dieter Schmidt of NJG 1[101] recalls that *Hptm* Prinz *zur* Lippe Weissenfeld was a particularly experienced and successful night fighter:

'The *Gruppe* received its first distinction with the award of the *Ritterkreuz* to Lütje and Geiger and the Oak Leaves to *Hptm zur* Lippe, who soon after was posted to NJG 6. Besides *Major* Prinz *zur* Lippe, *Lt* Hans-Heinz Augenstein, later successful *Staffelkapitän* of 12./NJG 1 and *Oblt* Werner Husemann, at the time *Kommandeur*, 7th *Staffel*, headed the list.[102] Success for a night fighter did not depend solely on his flying ability. Technical competence and good night vision played a significant part as well and in the summer of 1943 the *Gruppe* was tested for its ability to see at night.'

IV./NJG 1, operating from Leeuwarden and Bergen, claimed three Halifaxes and eight Lancasters destroyed on 12/13 June.[103] Seven Lancasters were shot down by I./NJG 1 during the Oberhausen raid of 14/15 June when the *Himmelbett Nachtjagd* claimed 13 Main Force aircraft destroyed. Of 197 Lancasters despatched, 17 failed to return. Fourteen Lancasters were lost from a force of 212 heavies that raided Cologne on 16/17 June, the number of losses matching exactly the 14 kills officially credited to *Nachtjagd*. Three Lancasters[104] were shot down by *Uffz* Rudolf Frank of 2./NJG 3 to take his score to 12 kills.

On 19 June P/O G.W. 'Bill' Lucas' crew of 10 Squadron at Melbourne received another call for ops. F/Sgt B.J. 'Jim' Sprackling, flight engineer recalls:

'Something was different this time – more fuel and all 500lb HE bombs – no incendiaries. We had been given a brand new Halifax II with a plastic nosecone, a little Vickers machine gun for the bomb aimer to use and huge 'barn door' fins and rudders instead of the half diamond fins of the old one. And we had a new navigator. Young Jock had to go back to school for more training and we got old Jock, a Scottish schoolmaster, at least as old as Bill, probably 25, so we now had two old men in the crew. Old Jock was a flying officer so we now had two officers but Bill was still the captain and his word was law in the air. Briefing was a bit earlier and the target, the steelworks at Le Creusot on the eastern side of the Massif Central, 200 miles south east of Paris, was a surprise. It was impressed on the crews that this was to be a pinpoint target. If we could not clearly identify the target we were to bring our bombs home. It was hinted that the French Resistance would warn the French workers to take the night off. We were also told that we had very little fuel reserves so we would land at a south coast airfield and re-fuel.

'The operation went as planned. Butch could clearly see the target and the photos showed that very few bombs missed the target. There was little enemy opposition. (We learnt the next day that the Lancaster groups had attacked a German target so the night fighters went after them).[105] But we were getting very pretty low on fuel by the time we reached the south coast and were very pleased to land at Tangmere. We refuelled, had a meal and a few hours rest in the sergeants' mess, a magnificent pre-war building and then back to base. Two ops finished and 28 to go. (We were kept busy that week, only one day of rest then two nights in succession to the Ruhr area, Krefeld to the west of the Rhine on 21/22 June and Mülheim near Düsseldorf on 22/23 June. Next, one of the perks of Bomber Command aircrew was to have six days off with a rail warrant home every six weeks).'

By the 21st June F/O John Overton's crew of 218 Squadron had taken part in four attacks on Ruhr towns. Harry Barker the bomb aimer recalls:

'Krefeld on 21st, Mülheim on 22nd; Elberfeld on 24th and Gelsenkirchen on 25th. Now all the targets we attacked were either factories or rail centres in the towns concerned. Target maps were given to all crews and generally colored flares marked the aiming points and there was no question of simply dropping bombs just anywhere on the town concerned. In reality, after the first few minutes of the start of bombing, smoke obscured the target area and aiming depended on the markers so semi-blind bombing did result but I clearly remember the objectives being industrial targets.'

On 21/22 June 705 aircraft[106] attacked Krefeld and 44 were lost.[107] *Lt* Heinz-Wolfgang Schnaufer of *Stab* II./NJG 1 describes his encounter with a Stirling,[108] which resulted in his 13th victory:

'I recognized, 500 meters above and to the right, a Short Stirling and succeeded in getting in an attack on the violently evading enemy aircraft. It caught fire in the fuselage and the wings and continued on, burning. Then it went into a vertical dive and crashed three kilometers to the northeast of Aerschot.'[109]

I./NJG 1 at Venlo in the direct path of the approaching and returning bomber stream, claimed 14 victories. *Hptm* Hans-Dieter Frank, *Staffelkapitän*, 2./NJG 1 was his unit's top-scoring pilot for the night, returning with six victories.[110] *Hptm* Manfred Meurer of the 3rd *Staffel* destroyed two bombers[111] before he was hit by return fire from his second victim and he was forced to bale out wounded.[112] *Hptm* Wilhelm Herget, *Kommandeur*, I./NJG 4 celebrated the *Ritterkreuz* awarded to him on 20 June by scoring a triple victory.[113] Seven bombers were shot down by IV./NJG 1. *Fw* Rudolf Frank of 2./NJG 3 claimed his 13th victory[114] but he and his crew were forced to bale out due to return fire. On 22/23 June when 565 bombers raided Mülheim 578 people were killed and 1174 were injured in the twin towns of Mülheim and Oberhausen. Post war the British Bombing Survey Unit estimated that this single raid destroyed 64 per cent of Mülheim. Thirty-six bombers failed to return, 25 kills being credited to the *Nachtjagd*. Six of these were claimed destroyed by IV./NJG 1 and five by I./NJG 1. Two Wellingtons[115] by *Oblt* August Geiger and two Stirlings[116] were shot down by III./NJG 1. *Uffz* Karl-Georg Pfeiffer of 12./NJG 1 took off from Bergen at 0008 hrs and returned at 0152 hrs having downed a Halifax.[117] It was his eighth victory. Pfeiffer adds:

'During spring-summer of 1943 towards evening four aircraft were positioned to Bergen am See, which lies further to the west and allowed earlier intercepts. Though mainly responsible for the fighting area *Salzhering* (over the Zuider Sea) Bergen was the base for the more southerly areas (Zander-Zandvoort). I was one of the pilots who were frequently positioned at Bergen and I always looked forward to it. I was alone for the flight, which took place at low level in order to avoid detection by the British radar but the best part was flying at about three meters above the dam at the Zuider Sea. Then came the point at Den Helder with the water tower and then into Bergen. A tragic affair took place on one of these positioning flights: The crew of *Uffz* Ott flying with the others at about 200 meters was shot down by a two centimetre *Flak*, although information about the flight had previously been given. There was an inquiry but that did not help. A couple of good comrades were dead.

'It was always very cosy at Bergen am See because the senior officers remained in Leeuwarden and four or six crews were able to do their stand-by duty without great military ceremony. We either listened to music on the radio or played cards, chess, *Skat* and *Doppelkopf*. Standby duty had another positive side: At this time there were for the first time German airwomen on communications duty, quite a new sight for us. Previously no females had been permitted on the airfield, for security reasons. As long as there were no operations we flirted with the girls and some of us fell in love and even married. Unless there were test flights to be carried out or battle training took place, crews could nip into town and have an ice cream on the roof terrace of 'Vroom und Dreesmann' or go dancing in the 'Valhalla' and have some fun. But Leeuwarden was a main base of the German defence and when the American bomber attacks on Germany began and the British still came by night this was really the end of our best times, especially for our pilots.'

Wuppertal was the target for 630 aircraft on 24/25 June when Elberfeld, the other half of the town, unharmed on 29/30 May, was bombed. Thirty-four (or 5.4 per cent) aircraft failed to return.[118] On 25/26 June 473 bombers attacked Gelsenkirchen and Bochum and 31 aircraft were lost, including 13 Lancasters and seven Halifaxes. Sgt J.S. 'Johnny' Johnston was the flight engineer in Lancaster I ED528 PM-Z in 103 Squadron at RAF Elsham Wolds flown by F/Sgt Alan E. Egan RAAF, which was shot down at Bechtrup north of Lüdinghausen:

'Somebody shouted, 'There's a yellow marker.' Course we all looked away. Next minute I saw this great big wing above my head (as flight engineer I was standing up). We were hit just like as if it was a three-ton truck. *BANG*! We held together for a minute. Then she screamed right across the port wing, hit the propellers and we went out of control. Both engines burst into flames. I got thrown to the floor and banged my head. I got up, or tried to. I could see Alan trying to get her straight. Then she dipped her nose and I went straight down into the nose with all the junk that was on the floor and landed on top of the bomb aimer. All of a sudden, the nose broke off. I just saw it start to crack. The bomb aimer and I fell out. I was surrounded by bits of cowlings and pieces of metal all floating around me. I thought I was going up instead of the bits of metal going down. All the planes were coming in like little mosquitoes – line upon line of them. A yellow light from the fires that were just starting lighted up Gelsenkirchen. It was like a watery sunset. Bombs were going down like big golden darts in the yellow light. It was horrifying.

'I was captured and told to climb into the back of a truck. Up I got and in the darkness I could just see some boxes. I put my hand out and felt a flying boot. I thought, 'Gee, that's all right, I want a pair of flying boots'. I put it on and felt around for the other one. All of a sudden I realized that they were soaking wet. I felt horrible because I thought it was blood. Then it hit me. I was sitting on top of coffins. I counted them. There were five on the top layer and six on the bottom. Afterwards I found out that four of them were members of my crew and seven of others.[119]

'At the first stop on the train to my PoW camp with two Luftwaffe guards there was a Red Cross train just opposite and I saw little children with bandages round their eyes and their hands on one another's shoulders. A nurse in front and one behind were leading them to the train. This was the first time that I realized what war was really like. It was easy when you were dropping bombs up there. I turned to one of my guards, a good German and asked, 'Where's this?' He said, 'Mülheim' (which still smouldering from a raid the previous Tuesday). I kept silent. I had been on that one too.'[120]

Sixteen of the bombers lost on the Wuppertal raid were shot down by the Leeuwarden *Gruppe*,[121] five by III./NJG 1 and one, a 196 Squadron Halifax near Gouda, by *Hptm* Hans-Dieter Frank of I./NJG 1. *Oblt* August Geiger of III./NJG 1 scored a triple victory in 43 minutes.[122] *Uffz* Karl-Georg Pfeiffer of 12./NJG 1 had mixed fortunes, as he recalls:

'On 25 June we took off alone because according to information from *Fw* Huhn[123] at the small operations room a single aircraft was about to pass slowly, apparently damaged, through our area on its way home. I was directed southwards and caught sight of it from quite a distance, crossing my path from left to right. Without waiting for further instructions – I was by now a successful night fighter – I throttled back, put the nose down and placed myself 300-400 meters below the aircraft, a Halifax. There were no signs that we had been spotted. I pulled up to about 50 meters below the long fuselage and was about to pull up in a routine attack from below and behind when Willi suddenly shouted over the intercom:

'Look out, he's coming down on us!'

'I replied quietly: 'If the Tommy is coming down, then we need not go up!'

'I throttled back and indeed, the machine went down in front of me.[124] But I had pressed the firing button at just the right time and the kite went its full length through my burst. They struck true but a second later a burst rattled through our own machine and I felt a terrible pain in my right thigh close to the hip. I said painfully: 'Willi, I've been hit. Home quickly; give me a course to Bergen, give me a course for home!' I can still hear him saying continuously '300°' but my brain was unable to do anything with this figure because of the pain. I went into a slow turn to starboard and down. Then suddenly out engine nacelles were lit up from below and I said to Willy, 'Well, at least he's down. What is the course for home?' And he repeated it. I had assumed that the bomber had caught fire below us to light us up from below. I was wrong. Now there was a banging in our machine, the ammunition was exploding because we were on fire ourselves. Willi shouted,

'I can't stand it any longer, the flames ... we must bale out!'

'Then I heard a bang. He had jettisoned the cabin roof. I got no reply to my calls, 'Willi, Willi'. He had already baled out and I was alone. I became suddenly aware that we must by now be well out to sea. But just the same, I had no choice but to get out! I opened the roof and it went away with a bang, leaving the side panels flapping. What was it they had said? The pilot had to fly a half roll; push forward and the let himself fall out. Easily said. Stop – first release the straps. So – now the half roll! The flames were getting ever brighter and I could no longer see the horizon. I put the machine on its back, was caught by the slipstream and dragged out – but only half. One of my fur boots was caught between the seat and the starboard panel with the starters and I found myself with my head down half inside and half outside. The machine was hurtling down out of control. For a few seconds I thought, 'So that's what it's like when one dies'. But then the will to live returned.

'Breathing heavily – the slipstream sucked the air from my lungs – I tried to struggle back into my seat, managed it and got hold of the stick. I pulled and it responded. Having levelled out I said to myself quietly: 'Now you must fly the roll of your life, otherwise you will not get out'. I put her slowly on her back, waited until I was certain that I was upside down, then a push forward on the stick and I was flung out like a shot. Now the ripcord handle. Where was it? At last I had it and I pulled it right out until I had it free in my hand. For a few seconds nothing, then a painful jerk and the bright canopy opened up above me. Now all was strangely quiet, while I was swinging to and fro. My wound burned like fire because the parachute straps were tight around it. I felt ill and was sick as I went slowly downward. Thinking that I was still over the sea, I tried to pull the cords on one side to steer closer towards the shore, which I thought to be where the skies were darkest. Then suddenly it collapsed and I dropped like a stone. Startled, I let go and fortunately it opened up again. When I sensed that the ground could not be far away I held my arms in front of my face and there was a heavy bump, which brought a new heavy pain. I lay on the ground, breathing heavily and was unable to move my right leg. It was broken. I must have become unconscious. I awoke some time later and dragged the white silk of the parachute over and laid my head on it. It was freezing cold and my limbs were shaking.

'Suddenly I heard hoof beats and was startled to see cattle charging towards me. I fired some signal lights and the beasts retreated. My watch showed about half past three. In the course of time I fired off all my signal ammunition but no one came to help. At half past six, as the day dawned, a man wearing silk pyjamas came running along. He had been sleeping in a boat, which had been lying at anchor in a *Gracht*. It was a friendly Dutchman. He tore up his singlet and stuffed it into my wound, which was bleeding strongly. Then he ran off again and brought some farmers who offered me some cigarettes. They had apparently heard me but had not dared to come to help. Shortly after seven a German ambulance, which the man in the pyjama had called, came and I was carefully laid in it. Now I discovered I was in the vicinity of Leiden. I was taken to the university hospital and operated on straight away. Two days later my radio operator, head and arms bandaged with burns, called. He had no broken bones. He was able to return to Leeuwarden. Some days later *Fw* Scherfling brought me a new jacked with the epaulettes of a *Feldwebel. Major* Lent had promoted me. After 11 days *Oblt* Greiner turned up. He put me with my plastered leg into a car and took me to Bergen. We continued from there in a Fieseler *Storch* to Leeuwarden where I was taken into the Ziekenhuis in the Troelstrastraat. I had a high temperature but was happy to be 'home'. I was now taken good care of but it was many weeks before I could be discharged. Then I went on home leave. Meanwhile the *Gruppe* had been transferred from Leeuwarden to Quakenbrück and I was instructed to go there after my leave. After a couple of weeks I was back on operations. During this time I had to be helped into the cockpit and I was only able to walk with the aid of a stick.'

All told, Bomber command lost 275 bombers shot down in June 1943. Cologne was subjected to three consecutive heavy raids in late June and early July. W/O Eddie Wheeler, WOP-AG in 97 Squadron, recalls the raid on 28/29 June when 608 heavies were dispatched:

> 'After six days we resumed marking operations, this time against poor old Cologne again. We were allocated another *'N for Nan.'*[125] With no cloud and excellent visibility we bombed at 0140 hrs from 20,000 ft releasing our markers and 10,000 lb bomb load which resulted in a huge explosion at 0143 hrs. Landing at 0340 hours we decided on another thrash to Cambridge that evening. I had now completed my fiftieth operational sortie, which was as good a reason as any to celebrate.'[126]

Twenty-five bombers failed to return, all of which were probably destroyed by the *Himmelbett Nachtjagd*. A follow-up raid on Cologne on 3/4 July by 653 bombers cost another

30 aircraft. Twelve were claimed shot down over the target by single-engined Wild Boar fighter pilots of the *Nachtjagd Versuchs Kommando* (Night Fighting Experimental Command), which were employed for the first time this night. The Wild Boars had to share these victories with the local *Flak* defenses, who also claimed 12 successes. Twenty-one crews of II./NJG 1 at St. Trond returned with claims for 14 *Himmelbett Abschüsse*. Schnaufer and *Lt* Johannes Hager of *Stab* II./NJG 1 and *Oblt* Wilhelm Telge, *Staffelkapitän*, 5./NJG 1 each claimed two kills. F/O H.E. 'Harry' White and his navigator/radio operator F/O Mike Seamer Allen of 141 Squadron, who had still to claim their first kill, encountered a Bf 110 near Aachen while on patrol in their Beaufighter VIf to the German airfield at Eindhoven. White blasted the night-fighter at 200 yards dead astern in a two second burst. Then he gave the enemy a second burst of cannon and machine-gun fire before diving violently away to port to avoid collision but the enemy aircraft was not seen again and they could only claim a 'damaged'.[127] On 8/9 July when Cologne was raided again, seven out of 282 Lancasters were lost. Twenty-four II./NJG 1 crews manned the *Himmelbett* boxes in eastern Belgium and despite being hampered by thick layers of cloud destroyed three Lancasters and claimed another seven *Feindberührungen* ('encounters with the enemy'). The next Main Force raid was directed to Gelsenkirchen on 9/10 July when seven Halifaxes and five Lancasters went missing from a force of 418 aircraft. *Hptm* August Geiger of III./NJG 1, who was temporarily detached to I./NJG 4, destroyed a Halifax[128] at Eprave near Dinant, Belgium.

101 Squadron was the only one of its kind to combine Airborne Cigar (ABC) electronic countermeasure duties[129] with regular bombing operations, which meant that the squadron flew on almost every major bombing raid until the end of the war. Consequently, 101 Squadron lost 113 Lancasters on 308 raids, plus another 33 destroyed in crashes in the UK. F/L William Alexander 'Scrym' Scrymgeour-Wedderburn's crew was the only one to survive a tour on 101 during 1943. Sgt Les King, WOp in the crew, recalls one particularly memorable sortie in *N-Nuts*[130], the crew's 15th, to Turin on the night of 12/13 July 1943 when 295 Lancasters of 1, 5 and 8 Groups were dispatched:

> 'It was our first experience to Italy and we experienced very severe weather over the Alpine range. The electrical storms in the Mont Blanc area caused problems like flying blind hoping our altitude was sufficient to clear the highest peaks and St. Elmo's Fire was noticeable on the propeller tips and astrodome and when I wound in our trailing aerial it was like a Catherine Wheel firework. We developed engine trouble in an inboard engine when the magneto supercharger failed so we had to feather the propeller but we proceeded to the target and bombed accordingly at the required height of 16,000 ft. The problem now was knowing we would be unable to climb over the Alps but in an emergency we could follow our briefing instructions and proceed to Blida in North Africa. Sgt Robert Craddock our rear gunner became concerned, as he was due to become father and his wife certainly would be distraught if we went missing even if later we returned safely. Bill Wedderburn made a decision to get back to base by asking F/Sgt Roy Sidwell the navigator for a course to fly westwards over southern France, skirting the Pyrenees and reaching the Bay of Biscay to go down to sea level. (Being July daylight would be early so we would be sitting ducks on a more direct route home across France). Eventually we skirted Brittanny and reached the coastline of Cornwall. I had made more than one attempt to contact base to notify them of our situation but our signal was too weak at sea level. (I found out later that Gibraltar received my signal and being a powerful station had passed on my attempted message). We thought we would land at St. Eval in Cornwall and refuel but our skipper consulted the flight engineer regarding fuel remaining and decided to make base at Ludford Magna. After being airborne 11 1/2 hrs we landed with only enough fuel remaining for five more minutes when all three engines would have cut out'.[131]

W/O Eddie Wheeler, WOP-AG, Lancaster III *N-Nan* of 97 Squadron adds:

> 'Everybody said how much easier the 'Eyetie' trips would be after the Ruhr but of course we had to negotiate the Swiss Alps in each direction. Whilst passing through the Alps the Swiss, no doubt wishing to make a point of their neutrality, opened up with their AA fire, which although far from accurate was strange since it came down toward us instead of upwards! Visibility was good and the Alps was an awesome sight. Over Turin we came down to 13,000 ft as the *Flak* was haphazard and didn't present the problems we had come to be used to over Germany. With no cloud and clear visibility the target was defined and we took our time to ensure accuracy of bombing. Bomb aimer Peter Burbridge's words were, 'Piece of cake!'[132]

An area bombing raid on Aachen on 13/14 July officially ended the Battle of the Ruhr. Bombs released by 374 aircraft, mainly Halifaxes, devastated large parts of Aachen, reducing almost 3000 individual buildings conatining almost 17,000 flats/

apartments to rubble and killing or injuring over a thousand people for the loss of 15 Halifaxes, two Lancasters, two Wellingtons and a Stirling.[133] Aachen reported that that raid was 'a "Terrorangriff' of the most severe scale.'

The Battle of the Ruhr was fought over 99 nights and 55 days 5/6 March-23/24 July 1943 and 24,355 heavy bomber sorties were flown. The main Battle of the Ruhr lasted for four months, during which, 43 major raids were carried out. Two thirds of these were against the Ruhr and the rest were to other areas including Stettin on the Baltic, Munich in Bavaria, Pilsen in Czechoslovakia and Turin in Italy. Approximately 57,034 tons of bombs were dropped at a cost of 1038 aircraft (4.3 per cent). Though the *Flak* and searchlight defenses around the cities in the Ruhr were by now the most powerful in the *Reich* the large majority of these aircraft were destroyed by *Himmelbett Nachtjagd.*

Notes

1. Airborne Interception (AI).

2. Robert S. Raymond, *A Yank in Bomber Command,* Pacifica Press, 1998.

3. The Stirlings were withdrawn from an original plan so that only the higher-flying heavies would participate and most of the force came from 5 Group.

4. Gibson's 67th op.

5. Gibson's crew consisted of F/O 'Junior' Ruskell, Sub/Lt Muthrie, F/L Olivens; P/O E.G. 'Bob' Hutchinson, WOp/AG; F/O Wickens and McGregor. R5611 went MIA on 14 May 1943. Gibson, who led the famous Ruhr dams raid in May 1943, was KIA in a Mosquito of 627 Sqn on 19/20 September 1944. Hutchison, who flew as Gibson's WOp/Ag on the Dams raid, was KIA on 15/16 September 1943 on the Dortmund-Ems canal raid.

6. The routes taken by the bombers to and from Berlin were the same as those followed on the previous night and German nightfighters were able to find the bomber stream. On both raids the Pathfinders were unable to mark the center of Berlin and bombing was inaccurate. The experiments with the Lancaster-Halifax force using TIs against the Big City now ceased until *H2S* became available.

7. ProbablyW4772 of 1654 HCU.

8. Figures on a clock face, i.e. East to West in the northern part of the night fighting area.

9. 35 major attacks were made on Berlin and other German towns during the Battle of Berlin between mid-1943 and March 1944; 20,224 sorties, 9,111 of which were to the big City. From these sorties (14,652 by Lancasters), 1,047 aircraft FTR and 1,682 received varying degrees of damage. AM Sir Arthur Harris said later, 'We can wreck Berlin from end to end if the USAAF will come in on it. It will cost between 400-500 aircraft. It will cost Germany the war.'

10. On 17/18 January Berlin was the target for 170 Lancasters and 17 Halifaxes. 22 FTR, the large majority of which were claimed by *Nachtjagd.* IV./NJG 1 destroyed 5 *Viermots* over the sea N of Vlieland, Terschelling and Ameland. 2 of these claimed by *Ritterkreuzträger Hptm* Becker at 2220 and 2348 hrs for his 42nd-43rd kills. *Fw* Heinz Vinke destroyed a Lancaster, possibly W4321 of 101 Sqn, at 2030 hrs. On 23/24 January 1943 Lancaster W4308 *C-Charlie* of 460 Sqn RAAF shot down by the Bf 110F night fighter of *Oblt* Wolfgang Kuthe and his *Bordfunker, Uffz* Helmut Bonk of 11./NJG 1 at Warns village in Friesland.

11. 157 a/c were despatched. 2 Wellingtons and 1 Lancaster were lost.

12. P/O Mackeldon aborted the operation and 5 crews returned. F/L C.J. Simmons in HE397 and Sgt L.F. Axby in HE471 MIA. *Lt* Wolfgang Kuthe of 11./NJG 1 shot HE397 down over the North Sea off Terschelling at 1314 hrs. Of the 19 Wellingtons of 4 Group and 17 Bostons which went to many places in Germany and Holland, only 2 Wellingtons and 1 Boston found targets to bomb. 4 Wellingtons FTR. Mosquito BIV crews of 2 Group Bomber Command raided Berlin to disrupt speeches in the main broadcasting station by Hermann Göring and Dr. Joseph Goebbels for this was the 10th anniversary of Hitler's seizure of power. 3 Mosquitoes of 105 Sqn arrived over Berlin at exactly 1100 hrs and the explosion of their bombs severely disrupted the *Reichsmarschall's* speech. In the afternoon, 3 Mosquitoes of 139 Sqn arrived over Berlin at the time Goebbels was due to speak. However, the earlier raid alerted the defenses and flak brought down 1 Mosquito. In January *Himmelbett* Nachtjagd destroyed 44 bombers (including 9 by I./NJG 1, two by III./NJG 1 and 16 by IV./NJG 1) and in February 61 aircraft were shot down.

13. NJG 1 were credited with 13 kills. 3 crews of IV./NJG 1 destroyed 4 bombers over the northern province of the Netherlands. *Hptm* Reinhold Knacke, *Staffelkapitän,* 1./NJG 1 and a 44 victory *Experte* was killed in his Bf 110F-4 by return fire from his second victim that night, an u/i Halifax, near Achterveld, Holland.

14. W4236.

15. Method of marking a target where sky markers were put down in such a place where, if bombed on the correct heading, the bombs would fall on the target.

16. Gildner, a Silesian by birth, had volunteered for the Wehrmacht in 1934 as an infantry officer but had transferred to the Luftwaffe and he became a *Zerstörer* pilot, joining *Nachtjagd* in July 1940. As the third *Nachtjagd* pilot Gildner had been awarded the *Ritterkreuz* on 9 July 1941 after his 14th *Abschuss.* His score stood at 38 *Abschüsse,* 2 in the Battle of France and 36 at night.

17. His 39th victim was Wellington HE169 of 196 Sqn, which cr. into the North Sea at 2148 hrs 12 miles (20 km) W of Schouwen. F/L R.F. Milne, a New Zealander in the RAF and crew KIA. The 'Boeing' was Stirling I BF438 WP-D of 90 Sqn flown by Sgt L.W. Tabor RNZAF, which cr. 30 miles (45 km) W of Flushing (Vlissingen) at 2207 hrs with the loss of the whole crew. All 9 a/c lost were claimed by night-fighters. *Lt* Johannes Hager of 6./NJG 1 flying a Do 217 claimed Halifax II DT694 of 158 Sqn flown by S/L W. Fletcher DFC DFM nr Mechelen. (Fletcher and 4 crew KIA. 1 PoW. 1 Evd). *Ofw* Fritz Schellwat of II./NJG 1 claimed a 15 Sqn Stirling. *Oblt* Manfred Meurer, *Staffelkapitän* 3./NJG 1 destroyed 3 bombers on their homeward flight, including Wellington X3420 of 426 Sqn between Beegden and Heel to take his score to 14. I./NJG 1 claimed another Stirling and a Wellington destroyed.

18. 377 aircraft went to Lorient on 16/17 February 1943. 1 Lancaster FTR.

19. Though Woodrow believed it was a very successful trip the Pathfinder marking caused the Main Force – 338 aircraft were despatched – to bomb N of Wilhelmshaven. Later, it was discovered that the Pathfinders had been issued with out-of-date maps, which did not show up-to-date town developments.

20. Stirling III BF457 of 15 Sqn flown by F/O D.J. Hopson (all KIA), Stirling I BF378 of 15 Sqn flown by F/O B.V. Crawford RNZAF (all KIA) and Stirling I BF411 of 15 Sqn flown by P/O J.C. Monteith RCAF (all KIA).

21. Wellington I R9276 flown by F/L R.L. Knowles (all KIA). Kuthe KIA 14 April 1943 in a flying accident.

22. *Himmelbett* box on Terschelling.

23. *Lt* Wolfgang Kuthe destroyed Stirling R9276 WP-G of 90 Sqn over the sea N of Texel Island at 2225 hrs. Jabs' 3 victims were all Stirlings of 15 Sqn: BF457 (at 2100 hrs), BF378 (at 2114 hrs) and BF411 (destroyed at 2145 hrs). There were no survivors from these 4 Stirling crews. Both 'Halifaxes' which Gildner claimed were Lancasters, of 156 and 467 RAAF Sqns, both crashing into the North Sea, 20 and 15 km N of Vlieland respectively. The 'Boeing' was a Stirling, probably BK627 of 90 Sqn. On 29 April 1944 by now *Geschwader Kommodore* of NJG 1 with the *Eichenlaub* and 42 confirmed victories, on final approach to Deelen Hans-Joachim Jabs' was intercepted by Spitfire IXs of 132 Sqn. He shot down 2 Spitfires before being shot down by S/L Alan Geoffrey Page DFC and he crash-landed. Jabs survived the war with 50 victories. W/C Page DSO DFC* who had suffered severe burns in the BoB, scored 10 victories and 5 shared destroyed, 3 damaged.

24. Ground marking with colored target indicators.

25. 'In Bomber Command, in good weather we flew on two nights out of every three and often, when operations were scrubbed we had sat around for hours in case the weather cleared. From 25 February to 12 March 1943 we operated ten times in 16 days on Lancasters – over 68 hours airborne, mostly over enemy territory and breathing oxygen. On 25 February we took off at 1925 hrs for Nurnberg after the usual briefing for pilots and navigators, a flying meal followed by the briefing for the whole crews. We were airborne for 9 hours for the long haul there and back over southern Germany to land back at Syerston at 0425. We probably got to our pits at about 0630 after debriefing and the usual operational bacon and egg meal possibly followed by a wind-down game of snooker. Up again for a late lunch to repeat the process for Cologne, a short one of 5.55 hours, then our day off; probably in Nottingham or Newark. On 28 February, an easy one to the U-boat pens at St Nazaire in 6.30. To balance the books, Berlin on 1 March in 7.40 hours. 2 March would have been a day off until we did a Night Flying Test of 30 minutes around lunchtime on 3 March for Hamburg that night. It was normal to do NFTs in the aircraft to be flown that night but Hamburg in 5.05 was the first of six operations in ten nights when non-operational crews must have done all of the other tests. 4, 6 and 7 March were blank so most likely these were briefed and then scrubbed but we went to Essen on 5 March in 5.40. After 7 March weather must have been good as we did four in five nights starting with Nurnberg on 8 March in 8.40 hours. 9 March down south again to Munich in 8 hrs before a day of rest on 10 March. Another southern trip to Stuttgart on 11 March in 7.10 and then a quickie to Essen (the most heavily defended target in Germany) on 12 March in 4.35 before bad weather must have given us a well earned respite as we did not operate again until 22 March. However, we were probably briefed half a dozen times in those ten days before ops were called off at any time from mid-afternoon until midnight.'

26. 10 bombers (4 Wellingtons, 3 Lancasters, 2 Halifaxes 1 Stirling) FTR, 7 of which were shot down by NJG 1 and NJG 3. *Oblt* Meurer, *Staffelkapitän* 3./NJG 1 shot down a Lancaster at Wessem (possibly of 83 or 103 Sqn) and Wellington Z1599 of 426 Sqn at Erp NE of Eindhoven. *Ofw* Kruse of 3./NJG 1 destroyed Wellington BJ886 of 427 'Lion' Sqn RCAF at St. Oedenrode. *Uffz* Georg Kraft of IV./NJG 1 claimed a Lancaster, possibly W4792 of 12 Sqn over the sea in box 'Schlei'. Most of the bombs dropped fell to the SW of Cologne.

Right: Debriefing in 'Ops' Room of II/NJG 2 at Leeuwarden airfield. *Oblt* Ludwig Becker, *St.Kpt* of 6/NJG 2 has just returned from a sortie, probably on 17/18 August 1942. On this night, he claimed Stirling I BF330 of 214 Squadron at 0146 hours 19 miles (30 km) N of Terschelling Island (Sgt A. Fleming RCAF and crew all killed), and Wellington X3654 of 101 Squadron at 0202 hours near Harlingen (P/O R.H. Brown RCAF and crew all killed). (Horst Diener via Ab Jansen)

Below: 6./NJG 2 personnel relax on the grass in front of Bf 110F-4 R4+EN at Leeuwarden airfield in the summer of 1942. Note the early wartime camouflage pattern on the Bf 110 and the absence of AI radar yet which was slowly being introduced into *Nachtjagd* during this period. II./NJG 2 was re-named IV./NJG 1 on 1 October 1942. (Coen Cornelissen)

Right: *Lt* Rudi Röhr (left) and his *Funker*, *Uffz* Erwin-Gerhard Cobi of 5./NJG 1 were killed on 24/25 August 1942 when their Bf 110E-4 (G9+LN Werk Nr.4657) was shot down during night combat with the British bomber force. The aircraft crashed 800 meters NE of Kottenforst railway station north of Essen. (via Steve Hall)

Right: *Uffz* Otto Fries, pilot, 5./NJG 1, in hospital at Aachen in September 1942 convalescing after being shot down by a Stirling on 28/29 August 1942. He was shot down a second and third time later in the war while flying He 219s when he and his *Bordfunker* were able to eject to safety on both occasions. (Otto Fries)

Above: Halifax II W7676 TL-P of 35 Squadron, which was lost with Sgt D.A.V. John and his crew (all KIA) on the night of 28/29 August 1942 when it was hit by flak and crashed into the Westerschelde off Koewacht in Zeeland, Holland on the operation to Nuremberg. Of the 159 aircraft despatched, 23 including two Halifaxes and 14 Wellingtons were lost. Bombing was very accurate, crews having been ordered to bomb from as low as possible as Pathfinder aircraft marked the target with target indicators (adapted from 250lb bomb casings), for the first time. (Flight)

Right: Halifax II HR657C-Charlie of 78 Squadron with air and ground crew at Middleton St. George. Deputy flight commander F/L Ron Read, (3rd from right, front row) flew HR657 on his final op of his tour to Dortmund on the night of 23/24 May 1943. The other flight crew are L-R: 'Taff' Lewis; 'Mac' McQueen; Vic Freeman; Jimmy Goodwin and Harry Laidlaw. (Ron Read DFC)

Above: One wet day in late 1942 the air and ground crews of *Hptm* Lent's II./NJG 2 pose on the tarmac at Leeuwarden airfield in front of Lent's Do 215B5 R4+DC. Due to the aircraft's endurance of five hours (1 1/2 hours longer than the Bf 110, his regular mount) *Hptm* Lent flew this aircraft regularly on *Himmelbett* operations at that time, especially when bad weather prevailed. He claimed four *Abschüsse* in R4+DC. (Rob de Visser)

Right: New Zealand High Commissioner Mr. (later Sir William) Jordan shakes hands with W/O Bernet DFM during a visit to 75 Squadron RNZAF at Mildenhall on 8 October 1942. (via Dr. Colin Dring)

Below: Wellington IC Z1111 KX-N of 311 Czechoslovakian Squadron in October 1942 freshly repainted in Temperate Sea scheme in place of its original Bomber Command camouflage scheme after its transfer to RAF Coastal Command. Z1111's operational career stretched from November 1941 to June 1943, flying 23 ops in Bomber Command and 19 ops in Coastal Command. (Zdenek Hurt)

Above: Wellington IC of 311 Squadron being serviced at RAF Talbenny still in its Bomber Command scheme before being repainted overall white for Coastal Command operations. (Zdenek Hurt)

Left: The famous daylight raid on the Schneider armaments factory at Le Creusot on the eastern side of the Massif Central, 200 miles southeast of Paris was carried out on the afternoon of 17 October 1942 by a force of 94 Lancasters of 5 Group led by Wing Commander L.C. Slee of 49 Squadron, 88 of which made a direct attack on the factory and the other eight bombing a nearby transformer station which supplied the plant with electricity. The route was flown at tree top level with four aircraft being damaged by birds. Bombing was carried out from 7,500 to 2,500 feet and 140 tons of bombs were dropped. The only aircraft lost was a 61 Squadron Lancaster, which crashed into a building bombing the transformer station. Damage to the factory was not extensive and much of the bombing fell short and had struck the workers housing estate near the factory. The factory was bombed again by 290 Halifaxes, Stirlings and Lancasters of 3, 4, 6 and 8 Groups on 19/20 June 1943 for the loss of two Halifaxes. (Avro)

Below: Bf 110 R4+CC of *Oblt* Rudolf Sigmund, *Gruppen* Adjutant of II./NJG 2 in camouflaged dispersal at Leeuwarden airfield late in 1942. By this time Sigmund had seven night kills. He became one of the leading *Himmelbett* night fighter pilots, rising to the command of III./NJG 3 on 15 August 1943 shortly after receiving the award of the *Ritterkreuz* for 24 night *Abschüsse*, plus a B-17 and a B-24 in daylight. On 3/4 October 1943 *Hptm* Sigmund was killed when his Bf 110 (D5+AD Werk Nr.5560) was shot down by German *flak* or possibly, return fire from RAF night bomber at 2225 hrs SW of Göttingen. His *Bordfunker*, *Fw* Hugo-Albert Bauer and gunner, *Uffz* Johannes-Max Dittrich of *Stabskompanie* III./NJG 3 were also killed. (Schmitt, via Rob de Visser)

Fw Horst Schirmer, pilot and *Oblt* Albert Westhelle, gunner of 9./NJG 3 at Stade, Germany, were killed on 3 December 1942 when their Bf 110 (D5+AT Werk Nr.2425) crashed 300 meters N of Giessen/Sand, Germany during a flight check. By that time, Schirmer had scored two night victories. (via Steve Hall)

A *mechaniker* working on the elevator assembly of Bf 110 D5+GH of 9./NJG 3, which has six *Abschüsse* victory symbols on the tail. (via Steve Hall)

Mechanikers look over a crashed Bf 110 of 9./NJG 3. (via Steve Hall)

Above: Lancaster I R5689 VN-N of 50 Squadron at Swinderby, Lincolnshire was a well photographed aircraft when on 28 August 1942 S/L Hughie Everitt took her up to show her off to the press. Three weeks later, on 19 September 1942, Sgt E.J. Morley RAAF took R5689 off from Swinderby on a *Gardening* sortie at 1915 hours only to crash at Thurlby, Lincolnshire when both port engines failed as the crew prepared to land. Sgt J.R. Gibbons RCAF, the tail gunner, died in the crash. (Flight)

Right: Sgt Derek Smith, an observer/navigator at 25 OTU, flew his first bombing operation in a Wellington on 10/11 September 1942 and completed his first tour with P/O Gordon Oldham's Lancaster crew on 61 Squadron. Promoted to Pilot Officer, Derek Smith flew a second tour, 1 September 1944-12 March 1945, as a navigator on Mosquitoes in 692 Squadron, 8 (PFF) Group. He was awarded a bar to his DFC. (Derek Smith Coll)

Far right: Aircrew members of 61 Squadron at Syerston in early 1943 pose for the press (note the censored white area behind) in front of a Lancaster with the name 'Doris' and 35 bombs painted below the cockpit. P/O Gordon Oldham, Derek Smith's pilot with whom he flew his first tour, is in front of the Indian observer at the back. Oldham's mid upper gunner, F/Sgt A.F. 'Frank' Emerson is to his right in front of him. Emerson flew a second tour on 61 Squadron and was awarded the DFM for his actions on the night of 3/4 November 1943 when his pilot, F/L Bill Reid, brought their badly damaged Lancaster home and was awarded the Victoria Cross. Derek Oldham was promoted and awarded the DFC at the end of his tour on 61 Squadron. He was killed early into his second tour on 44 Squadron on the night of 26/27 April 1944 when his Lancaster was involved in a mid-air collision with another Lancaster on the operation to Schweinfurt. (via Derek Smith)

Short Stirling I N6101 of 1651 Conversion Unit being bombed up at RAF Waterbeach, Cambridgeshire in 1942. 26 Conversion Flight was formed at Waterbeach in November 1941 and merged with 1651 CU on 2 January 1942. Stirling I N6101, which had formerly served with 149 Squadron in 1941-42, belly-landed at Waterbeach with its port engines on fire on 9 December 1942. (IWM)

A buckled tail unit and burnt-out and scattered pieces of wreckage is all that remained of Lancaster I W4126 KM-B of 44 Squadron in a field called 'De Westen' near Den Hoorn, Texel. The aircraft was on its way to bomb Nienburg on the evening of 17 December 1942 when at 1845 hrs it was shot down by *Kriegsmarine Flak* at Texel Island, with the loss of 27-year old F/O Lawrence G.L. McNamara and five of his crew. (Andreas Wachtel)

German recovery crew with some of the wreckage of Lancaster I W4126 KM-B of 44 Squadron. (*Herr* Fahrenbach via Andreas Wachtel)

Canadian Wellington crew study their map before an operation. The decision to form a new Canadian Command had been taken in 1942 and a HQ was established at Allerton Park, Yorkshire, on 1 December 1942. Nos 420 'Snowy Owl', 424 'Tiger' and 425 'Alouette' Squadrons of the RCAF were selected in January 1943, along with other Canadian bomber squadrons, to form 6 Group RCAF, which officially became operational on 1 January 1943. 408 'Goose' Squadron, equipped with the Halifax, and 424 'Tiger' Squadron with Wellingtons were at Leeming and 419 'Moose' also equipped with the Halifax, and 420 'Snowy Owl' Squadron were stationed at Middleton St. George. 425 'Alouette' and 426 'Thunderbird' Squadrons were stationed at Dishforth while 427 'Lion' Squadron was at Croft. 428 'Ghost' Squadron was at Dalton and a sixth airfield, at Skipton-on-Swale was under construction. The first 6 Group RCAF bombing operation was flown by 427 'Lion' Squadron on the night of 3/4 January 1943. 429 'Bison' Squadron, unlike most Canadian squadrons, did not transfer from 4 Group to 6 Group until April 1943. Conversion of all RCAF Wellington squadrons in England to the Halifax and Lancaster was carried out from mid-1943. (RAF Museum)

Short Stirling at 1657 Heavy Conversion Unit in 1943. 1657 HCU was formed on 11 October 1942 at Stradishall by absorbing 7, 101, 149 and 218 Conversion Flights and 1427 Flight. (Graham B. Jones)

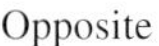

Formation of Short Stirlings of 1657 HCU (Heavy Conversion Unit) at Stradishall, Suffolk in 1943. Eight HCUs sent mixed crews flown by pupils and instructors on operations in WWII. Most of the operational flights by OTUs and HCUs ceased after the invasion of Normandy in June 1944 but the training units sometimes provided aircraft for diversionary sweeps over the North Sea and over France in 1944 and 1945. (Graham B. Jones)

Opposite
Top: F/L E.G. 'Bob' Hutchison and W/C Guy Gibson DSO* DFC* shortly before boarding Lancaster *G-George* for the Dams raid, 16/17 May 1943. On 106 Squadron Hutchison was Gibson's wireless operator on the night of 17/18 January 1943 when broadcaster Richard Dimbleby of the BBC flew aboard their Lancaster on the raid on Berlin. (IWM)

Bottom: L7540 the seventh Lancaster built began life on the production line as a Manchester. It is seen here in 83 Squadron markings (the letters OL-U freshly painted over the old 44 Squadron codes on which squadron it served from January 1942) awaiting 4000lb HC bombs. L7540 finished its career with 5 Lancaster Finishing School in 5 Group at Syerston and was SOC in April 1944.

W/C Guy Gibson DSO* DFC* (center), CO of 106 Squadron from 14 March 1942, with his two flight commanders, S/L John Searby (left) and S/L Peter Ward-Hunt DFC (right) pose for the camera at Syerston before leaving to form 617 Squadron. Behind is Gibson's Lancaster III ED593 ZN-Y 'Admiral Prune II' which survived at least 72 ops and finished the war as a ground instruction airframe. (Lancaster I W4118 ZN-Y 'Admiral Prune' which joined the squadron on 6 August 1942 was lost with Sgt D.L. Thompson RCAF and crew on 4/5 February 1943 on the operation to Turin. Outbound both port engines failed and 'Admiral Prune' crashed on a hill at Valsonne (Rhône), 30 km NW of Lyon. Thompson and three of his crew survived and were taken prisoner. Four other crew were killed). In mid-March 1943 Gibson, having completed two bomber and one night fighter tours, left to take command of 617 Squadron. (IWM)

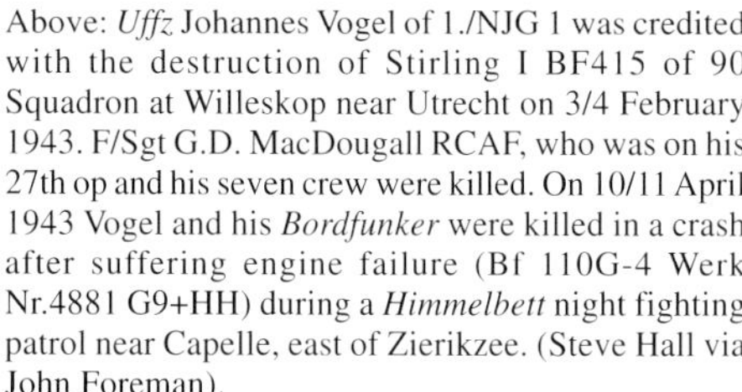

Above: *Uffz* Johannes Vogel of 1./NJG 1 was credited with the destruction of Stirling I BF415 of 90 Squadron at Willeskop near Utrecht on 3/4 February 1943. F/Sgt G.D. MacDougall RCAF, who was on his 27th op and his seven crew were killed. On 10/11 April 1943 Vogel and his *Bordfunker* were killed in a crash after suffering engine failure (Bf 110G-4 Werk Nr.4881 G9+HH) during a *Himmelbett* night fighting patrol near Capelle, east of Zierikzee. (Steve Hall via John Foreman).

Top right: German recovery crew attending to Bf 110 of IV/NJG 1 possibly flown by *Uffz* Naumann, which crash-landed on the beach at Ameland during *Nachtagd*'s first daylight operation against the 8th Air Force on 4 February 1943. When on 27 January 1943 55 B-17s carried out the first 8th AF raid on Germany it became obvious that more day fighters were needed and so some night fighters were pressed into daylight action, with disastrous results. Nightfighters were too large and cumbersome and their crews were scarcely trained in daylight interception and large numbers of valuable radar-equipped aircraft were lost along with their crews, including *Experten* such as *Hptm* Ludwig Becker, at the time of his death the top-scoring *Nachtjagd* Experte with 44 *Abschüsse*. (Ab A. Jansen)

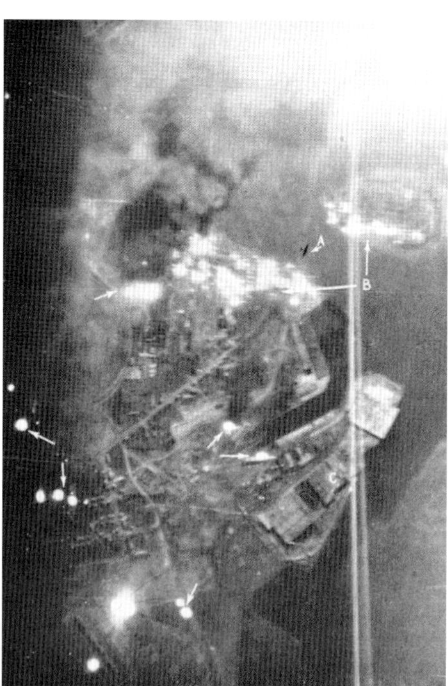

Left: *Oblt* (later *Hptm*) Reinhold Knacke, *Staffelkapitän*, 1./NJG 1. Knacke flew as a Bf 110 pilot in 3./ZG 1 in the French campaign of May-June 1940 and was one of the original pilots to be chosen for night fighting, joining 2./NJG 1. His first night *Abschuss* came in May 1941 and he soon became one of the top *Experten*, rising to take command of 1./NJG 1 on 4 April 1942. In July he was awarded the *Ritterkreuz*. On 16/17 September 1942 claimed five victories to take his tally to 38 and on the night of 3/4 February 1943 he shot down a Halifax and a Stirling for his 43rd and 44th victories. However, return fire from his last victim, a Stirling of 75 Squadron, damaged his Bf 110 and he ordered his crew to bale out. Knacke died when his parachute failed to open and his body was found near Achterveld, Holland. He was posthumously awarded the *Eichenlaub*. (Ab Jansen)

Right: Two Wellingtons (A) photographed over Lorient during the night attack by 128 aircraft on 4/5 February 1943. Sticks of incendiary bombs (B) are burning among port installations at La Perrière and on Ile St. Michel. This was an all-out incendiary raid on the French Atlantic port by 103 Wellingtons, 16 Halifaxes and nine Lancasters. (IWM)

Above: Wellington III BJ668 ZL-X, originally assigned to 419 'Moose' Squadron RCAF and then 427 'Lion' Squadron RCAF at Croft, failed to return with P/O C.M. Parsons' crew from the raid on Lorient on 4/5 February 1943 when the aircraft was hit by *flak*. (RAF Museum)

Right: *Oblt* Paul Gildner, 43 night and 2 day victories in ZG 1, NJG 1 and NJG 2, *Ritterkreuz* with *Eichenlaub* who was KIA on 24/25 February 1943 in a failed forced landing near Gilze-Rijen airfield after engine failure. (Horst Diener) Far right: *Lt* Hans Krause, Technical Officer (TO) of I./NJG 3 who on 29/30 March 1943 shot down Lancaster III ED469 EA-A of 49 Squadron flown by F/O George F. Mabee RCAF (26) for his third confirmed victory. ED469 crashed in flamers at Eilvese near Wunstorf killing six of the crew. Tail gunner Sgt G.A. Jones survived, although very seriously wounded and he was repatriated in 1944. (Hans Krause)

Below: Lancaster I of 61 Squadron at Syerston early in 1943. The squadron operated Lancasters from April 1942 first form Woolfox Lodge, then Syerston (May 1942-November 1943), Skellingthorpe and Coningsby and from April 1944, Skellingthorpe again and flew more operations (376) with the aircraft than any other Lancaster squadron in Bomber Command. (Peter W. Cunliffe)

A large crater and a smouldering heap of molten metal in a field somewhere on the Continent was usually all that remained of a once proud bomber. *Oblt* Hans Autenrieth, *Staffelkapitän*, 6./NJG 4 poses with the miserable remains of Stirling III BF469 BU-M of 214 Squadron, which he shot down 3 km SW of Chalons-sur-Marne at 0018 hrs on 12 March 1943 for his 10th victory. P/O A. Carruthers RCAF from Tonawanda, New York and five of his crew died. Only the tail gunner, F/Sgt A.J. Tyrell survived to be taken prisoner. (Norman Mackie)

Oblt Hans Autenrieth, *Staffelkapitän*, 6./NJG 4 and *Gefr* Rudolf 'Rudi' Adam, his *Bordfunker*, unstrap after getting out of their Bf 110. (Anneliese Autenrieth)

Oblt Hans-Joachim Jabs, *Staffelkapitän*, 11./NJG 1, who on the night of 19/20 February 1943 destroyed three Stirlings, all of 15 Squadron, in the North Sea off the Dutch Friesian Islands. (Helmut Conradi)

Right: *Ofw* Karl Haisch of 4./NJG 3 had nine kills, all achieved during 1942-43 with 4./NJG 3. These included a Short-Stirling of 218 Squadron on 25/26 April 1942, two Wellingtons (of 101 and/or 115 Squadrons) on 21/22 September 1942, an (unidentified) Lancaster near Kolding on 17/18 January 1943, a Halifax of 51 or 76 Squadron and a Short-Stirling, probably of 15 Squadron, on 3/4 March 1943 and a Wellington of 429 Squadron on 9/10 March 1943. Haisch was killed on 20 March 1943 while flying Messerschmitt Bf 108B1 Werke Nr.1638, which crashed near Neumünster, Germany. Wireless/Op *Uffz* Herbert Platzek and F/Engineer, *Fw* Ludwig Walter were also killed. (Steve Hall via John Foreman)

Sgt Dave Hewlett's Halifax II crew in 102 Squadron at Pocklington, Yorkshire. L-R, Back Row: Sgt Eric 'Joe' Holliday, flight engineer; Dave Hewlett, pilot; Sgt 'Blackie' Blackallar, navigator; F/Sgt Norman 'Chiefie' Beale, who had flown a first tour on Hampdens. Front Row: Sgt Andy Reilly, rear gunner; Sgt Tom Wingham, bomb-aimer; Sgt Jim Nightingale, WOp (It is his Alsatian dog in the foreground), Sgt Willie Hall, mid-upper gunner. (Tom Wingham DFC)

On the wet and wind-swept tarmac of Leeuwarden aerodrome in early 1943 *Lt* Karl Heinz Völlkopf (left) and his *Funker Uffz* Heinz Huhn get into their flying gear prior to an operational sortie whilst their Do 215B-5 is being topped up by one of the groundcrew of IV./NJG 1. Note the flame dampers on the 1075hp Daimler-Benz DB 601A liquid-cooled engine and the Roman IV (of the IVth *Gruppe*) painted on the side of the Dornier's cockpit. *Lt* Völlkopf, a 22-year-old *Experte* with six confirmed *Abshusse* in 5./NJG 2 and 9./NJG 1 was killed when his Bf 110G-4 G9+GT crashed whilst flying at low level near Rheine/ Wesfalen airfield on 21 June 1943. Huhn survived his three pilots – *Oblt* Gildner (KIA 24/25 February 1943), *Lt* Oskar Köstler (killed 9/10 April 1943) and Völlkopf – but after Völlkopf was KIA Huhn decided he had had enough and he never flew again. For the remaining years of the war he served as Operations Officer at Bergen/Alkmaar and St. Trond airfields. (Heinz Huhn via Rob de Visser)

By 1943 several Mosquito NFII, XII, XIII, XIX, XVII and FBVI squadrons were providing fighter support for Bomber Command main force operations and the intercept radar was continually improved. Pictured is DZ659/ G, a modified Mosquito NFII fitted with AI.Mk.X (US SCR 720/729 Eleanora) radar in the universal nose. AI.Mk.X radar, developed by the Radiation Laboratory, Massachusetts Institute of Technology and built by the Western Electric Co., had a range of 8-10 miles. (DH)

Right: Junkers Ju 88C-6b (powered by Jumo 211J engines) and Ju 88R-1 (basically a C-6 powered by two 1600 hp BMW 801MA or 801C engines) three-seat nightfighters were equipped initially with FuG 202 *Lichtenstein* BC from 1942-43. This was replaced on the Ju 88C-6 and R-2 from the summer of 1943 by the simplified FuG 212 *Lichtenstein* C-1 fitted in combination with SN-2b to the C-6 and R-2. The aerials for the SN-2b were carried on the wings. (Hans-Peter Dabrowski)

Right: On 9 May 1943 Ju 88C-6 D5+EV of 10./NJG 3 was flown from Kristiansund/Kjevik in Norway to Dyce, near Aberdeen after its crew defected during an aborted interception of a Courier Service Mosquito off Denmark. The fiancée of the pilot, *Flugzeugführer Oblt* Herbert Schmid, was Jewish and had been arrested and transported to a concentration camp, while his *Bordfunker*, *Obfw* Paul Rosenberger, was of Jewish descent. *Bordschütze/Bordmechaniker Obfw* Erich Kantwill went along with the defection. This aircraft was equipped with the FuG 202 *Lichtenstein* BC AI. Examination by TRE (Telecommunications Research Establishment) at Malvern, Worcestershire scientists enabled them to confirm that the Serrate homing device operated on the correct frequencies to home in on the FuG 202 *Lichtenstein* BC and FuG 212 *Lichtenstein* radars. Serrate could only home in on *Lichtenstein* AI radar and then only if it was turned on. The Ju 88C-6 is now on display at the RAF Museum, Hendon. (Martin Bowman)

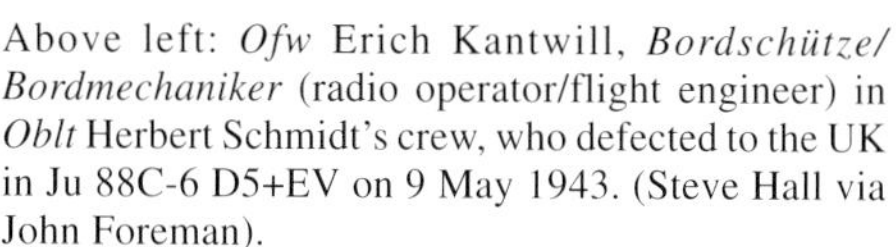

Above left: *Ofw* Erich Kantwill, *Bordschütze/ Bordmechaniker* (radio operator/flight engineer) in *Oblt* Herbert Schmidt's crew, who defected to the UK in Ju 88C-6 D5+EV on 9 May 1943. (Steve Hall via John Foreman).

Center: Nineteen-year-old Sgt John Hurst completed a tour of ops as tail gunner with 102 Squadron November 1942-May 1943. His photo was taken when training to be an air gunner and depicts him proudly wearing the white flash that all aircrew trainees wore on their caps. (John Hurst)

Right: Five of Sgt George Barker's NCO crew in front of Halifax II JB835 DY-X of 102 Squadron at Pocklington L-R: Sgt Dick Brown RCAF, wireless operator; Sgt John Dothie RAF, navigator and the eldest crewmember at 33; Sgt George Barker RAF, pilot; Sgt Ron Long RAF, mid upper gunner and Sgt J.W. Kilyon, flight engineer. Barker and Dothie were commissioned in February 1943. The crew flew six ops in Halifax JB835 (which was shot down on 27/28 August 1943 over Belgium by the legendary *Oblt* Heinz-Wolfgang Schnaufer of 12./NJG 1) when it was flown by Sgt G. Sproat. JB835 crashed at Auvelais (Namur) on the Sambre, Belgium, returning from Nürnberg. All the crew except the tail gunner Sgt R.W. Horten, who became a PoW, were killed. (John Hurst)

The crew of Lancaster I W4317 of 61 Squadron, which was one of 18 Lancasters lost on the Pilsen raid on 16/17 April 1943 when it was shot down by *Oblt* Rudolf 'Rudi' Altendorf, *Staffelkapitän*, 2./NJG 4 near Givry, France. All eight of P/O W. MacParlane's crew were killed. L-R: Sgt Donald A. Holdsworth, mid-upper-gunner (KIA); u/k; F/Sgt William W. Dawson, bomb aimer (KIA); Sgt Peter J. Keay RAAF, flight engineer (KIA), u/k, u/k. F/O C.F. Williams, Sgt E.R. Davidson and Sgt J.V. Rees also died. (P.W. Cunliffe)

Above left: When on 3/4 April 1943 348 aircraft attacked Essen it was the first time that more than 200 Lancasters had taken part. Twelve Halifaxes and nine Lancasters FTR and two other Halifax bombers crashed in England. Halifax II DT638 of 51 Squadron, which was heavily attacked by a nightfighter limped back to England and crashlanded at RAF Coltishall near Norwich where it was written off on 30 April. (via Mick Jennings) Right: Damage to the Boulton Paul E Mk.1 rear turret of Halifax II DT638 of 51 Squadron on 4 April 1943 which was caused by a German nightfighter probably equipped with FuG 227/1 Flensburg to home in on the Monica radar warning transmitter (note the tail mounted Monica aerial below the four .303 inch Browning machine guns). Flensburg had a range of 62 1/2 miles. (via Mick Jennings)

P/O Eric Wright's crew of Halifax V Series I DK178 who against all odds completed a tour of operations with 76 Squadron during the second half of 1943. L-R: John Barton, flight engineer; Harry Jones, WOp; Gilbert Darkie, bomb aimer; P/O Ted Strange, navigator; Eric Wright, pilot; George Halbert, AG; Arthur Everest, AG. (via Ted Strange DFC)

Arthur R. "Spud" Taylor ("Spud" Taylor Coll)

Stirling III BF480 "I-Ink" of 218 "Gold Coast" Squadron lies wrecked at Downham Market following the crew's disastrous operation to Bochum on 13/14 May 1943. "I-Ink" ploughed into a truck killing two airmen who had disembarked from Stirling BF413/T and were about to enter the Operations Block for interrogation. BF480 was damaged beyond repair. (via Arthur R. "Spud" Taylor)

The Möhne Dam the day after the raid on the Ruhr dams by Lancasters of 617 Squadron 16/17 May 1943. Nineteen Lancasters set out for the Ruhr dams but three were missing by the time that they arrived over the target. W/C Guy Gibson went in and sent his mine successfully bouncing up to the concrete wall of the Möhne Dam, where it sank and exploded. The next two Lancasters missed – one of them being shot out of the sky but both the fourth and fifth hit and finally breached the dam. The Möhne reservoir contained almost 140 million tons of water and was the major source of supply for the industrial Ruhr 20 miles away. Three Lancasters went on to bomb the Eder, 60 miles from the Ruhr, which was also breached. The Eder was even larger than the Möhne, containing 210 million tons of water. Eight out of the 19 Lancasters and 56 of the 133 men who flew on the raid failed to return. (René Millert via John Williams)

Left: On 25 May 1943 F/O (later Squadron Leader DFC) John Overton's Stirling III crew of 218 'Gold Coast' Squadron at Downham Market flew their first op when they sowed mines off the Friesians. In this photo, taken with their ground crew at Woolfox Lodge on 28 July 1944 on completion of their tour, Overton is in the center smoking a pipe. His bomb aimer, Sgt Harry Barker (now F/O with the DFC), is 2nd from left back row. F/Sgt Alf Aubrey, the flight engineer, also with a pipe, is far left, back row. F/Sgt Frank Dallman DFM, rear gunner, is far left front row. (Harry Barker)

Oblt Walter Barte, *Staffelkapitän* 4./NJG 1 (center) his *Bordfunker, Uffz* Pieper (right) and another crewmember at St. Trond. Barte survived the war with 19 night victories and four day kills in NJG 1 and NJG 3. (via Peter Loncke)

Oblt Walter Barte, *Staffelkapitän* 4./NJG 1, his *Bordfunker*, *Uffz* Pieper and *Oberwerkmeister* Adam, mechanic of II./NJG 1 at St. Trond. The victory tally displayed on the tail of Bf 110G-4a G9+FM shows nine *Abschuss* symbols, dating this photograph shortly after 11/12 June 1943 when *Oblt* Barte shot down an unidentified Lancaster and Halifax V Series I DK170 MP-C of 76 Squadron for his 8th and 9th confirmed victories. (via Peter Loncke)

F/Sgt B.J. 'Jim' Sprackling, flight engineer in P/O G.W. 'Bill' Lucas' crew of 10 Squadron who flew their first op on 11/12 June 1943. (Sprackling)

Halifax II Series I (Special) ZA-V of 10 Squadron at Melbourne, Yorkshire in 1943. The Halifax II Series 1A was the first Halifax with the longer molded Perspex nose and a Defiant-type dorsal turret re-designed engine cowlings and more powerful 1390 hp Rolls-Royce Merlin XXII engines. Late Series 1A models introduced large rectangular fins to dampen yaw effects and improve bombing accuracy. In March 1944 10 Squadron began re-equipping with the Halifax III. (Sprackling)

Seven *Abschuss* banners are hoisted in front of the Readiness Room of II./NJG 1 at St. Trond in the summer of 1943, indicating seven kills achieved by the *Gruppe*'s crews during the previous night's *Himmelbett* operations. (Otto H. Fries)

Sgt (later F/O) Colin 'Col' Moir RAAF at Middleton St. George, Yorkshire, late in 1942, completed a tour of ops as rear gunner in P/O Thomson's crew with 420 'Snowy Owl' Squadron RCAF and 432 'Leaside' Squadron RCAF May 1942-June 1943. 'Returning from one successful raid to the U-boat pens at St. Nazaire on the night of 28 March 1943 in Wellington *G-George* the visibility was quite clear. From nowhere, unseen by me, came this lightning fast fighter plane. It swung away, dived and approached quickly again. No shots were fired. I was so shocked and petrified as it happened so quickly. The plane had no propellers. We dived and weaved of course, after the event but it was too late. He came and was gone in a flash. Some frightening game to us! My words to the debriefing officer. 'The bloody thing had no fans (propellers)'. It was like a black evil bat but faster. Just as well no shots were fired. Our Canadian squadron always had a one-gallon barrel of rum at debriefing. I was one of the few aircrew who drank their portion of rum. Reason, it warmed me up a bit. No one believed me. 'Have another rum, Moir. You need a rest.' Next day we were on our way. A leave pass for Thomson's ropey crew. The outcome was to encourage me to see 'No Fans' on each successive trip and a warning from the upper echelon ('The Brass'). 'Don't talk about it. Forget what you saw. It upsets morale you know.' This dressing down and advice to keep what I saw to myself came from W/C O.A.R. Bradshaw, CO 420 Squadron. He said the orders came from Group HQ and it would be bad for morale to spread rumours. No one believes my story today.' (Colin Moir)

Returning from an attack on railroad maintenance facilities at Paderborn in the early evening of 16 March 1943 Mosquito BIV DZ497 XD-Q of 139 Squadron came under fire from *Kriegsmarine Flak* battery 11./ M.Fla.Abt.808 at Den Hoorn, Texel and at 1929 hrs crashed 1200 meters south of this village. 21-year old P/O Peter J.D. McGeehan DFM RNZAF and his 33-year old navigator F/O Reginald C. Morris DFC both died and were later buried in Den Burg cemetery. A member of the German island garrison is seen here with the wreckage. (Andreas Wachtel)

Halifax II DT775 EY-F The Firkin of 78 Squadron coming in to land at Linton-on-Ouse on a fine winter's day early in 1943. On the night of 10/11 April 1943 The Firkin and Sgt H.J. Adams' crew FTR when they were shot down by *Fw* Karl Gross of 8./NJG 4. DT775 crashed at Anoux, eastern France. Jack Adams and five of his crew survived to be taken prisoner. One crewmember was KIA. (Stan Reed)

Right: 24-year old Sgt Stan Reed who manned the unarmed mid-under blister position in Halifax II DT775 of 78 Squadron on 10/11 April 1943. Reed was taken prisoner. (Stan Reed)

Far right: Sgt Jack Adams, pilot of Halifax II DT775 of 78 Squadron. (Stan Reed)

Right: Canadian crew of 427 'Lion' Squadron RCAF at Croft, County Durham on 12 April 1943. L-R: Charles Lott, WOp/AG; Sgt Jack Hamer RCAF; rear gunner; Sgt Stuart Brown RCAF, navigator; Sgt Cletus Lunny RCAF, bomb aimer and Sgt Alex Mitchell, pilot. On the night of 3/4 January 1943 6 Group flew its first operation when six Wellingtons of 427 'Lion' Squadron RCAF were despatched to lay mines off the Friesian Islands. By March seven Canadian Wellington squadrons were operating within 4 and 6 Groups of Bomber Command. On 10 March Sgt Alex Mitchell (a Scot) and his crew, most of whom were Canadian, were posted to 427 'Lion' Squadron RCAF. At first the crew were given daily assignments to test the flight capabilities of their AI.Mk.X and to install new equipment. Stuart Brown, navigator, from Brandon, Canada, recalls. 'On 16 April we flew our first op; an uneventful trip to Mannheim with 3,500 lb of bombs. On 28 April we flew a very dicey do, minelaying near sea level on the Elbe estuary, from which only four out of ten aircraft from our squadron returned. Immediately following this trip 427 'Lion' Squadron RCAF was reorganized to become 1664 Conversion Unit for the training of crews to fly the larger Halifax bombers. Senior crews were posted in from other Wellington squadrons and in May our crew was posted to 428 'Ghost' Squadron RCAF to continue operations from Dalton, Yorkshire. May 1943 saw the beginning of the Battle of the Ruhr and our crew flew five trips. Following the trip to Düsseldorf on 11 June we were posted back to 427 Squadron for conversion to the Halifax.' (G. Stuart Brown)

Below: Wellington III X3763 KW-E of 425 'Alouette' Squadron RCAF which FTR with P/O A.T. Doucette DFC RCAF and his crew (all PoW) from a raid on Stuttgart on 14/15 April 1943. *Lt* Franz Draude of 4./NJG 4 shot X3763 down at 0146 hrs and it crashed at Mussey-Sur-Marne (Haute-Marne) on the west bank of the Marne 8-km S of Joinville. (IWM)

Hptm Herbert Lütje, *St.Kpt* 8./NJG 1 inspecting one of his six victims he shot down on the night of 13/14 May 1943. Lütje's claims this night included Lancaster I W4305 KM-G of 44 Squadron, which crashed between Bevergen and Hörstel on either side of the Dortmund-Ems Canal. Sgt J.G. Olding RCAF, pilot, survived but his six crew died. Lütje also claimed Lancaster III ED667 DX-W of 57 Squadron, which crashed at Albergen (Overijssel). P/O J.B.M. Haye, pilot, evaded. Four crew were PoW and two KIA. And, he also claimed Halifax II JB892 KN-E of 77 Squadron flown by F/O D.P. Puddephatt crashed into woods near Noordsleen (Drenthe). All the crew were KIA. (Dr. Schmidt-Barbo)

Dornier Do 217J of *Nachtjagdschule* (Night-Fighting School) 1 (later NJG 101) at Lechfeld in mid-1943. No radar or armament has been fitted to this aircraft. Although *Nachtjagdschule* 1/NJG 101 was primarily a training wing, its instructor crews had scored 200 day and night victories by the end of the war (Erich Kayser)

Oblt Hermann Greiner (left) and his *Bordfunker*, *Uffz* Kissing of IV./NJG 1 in '*Abschuss* pose' in front of their Bf 110G in 1943. Note the flame dampers on the 1475hp engines. Greiner joined *Nachtjagd* in October 1941 and although he claimed only two bombers shot down in the *Himmelbett Nachtjagd* during 1942, he was one of the nightfighter pilots who came to full maturity in the Tame Boar fighting from mid-1943. By the end of the war he had risen to *Kommandeur* of IV./NJG 1 with 51 victories (47 at night). he was awarded the *Ritterkreuz* after 36 *Abschüsse* in May 1944. (Ab Jansen via Hermann Greiner)

Right: Dornier Do 217 of *Nachtjagdschule* (Night-Fighting School) 1 (later NJG 101) at Lechfeld after a crash-landing in mid-1943. (Erich Kayser)

Right: During 10/11 April-23/24 August 1943 20-year old W/O Den Rudge and his crew completed a tour of 31 ops with 103 Squadron, 25 of which were flown in Lancaster III ED888 PM-M *M for Mother* (12/13 May-23/24 August). This aircraft completed the highest number of trips of any Lancaster – 140 in 103 and 576 Squadrons (the latter as PM-M2 Mike Squared) and 103 Squadron again, May 1943-December 1944 – in Bomber Command. ED888 went to Berlin six times with 103 Squadron and it was 'awarded' a DFC when it completed its 50th trip in November 1943. Four members of W/O Rudge's crew standing beside M-Mother in mid 1943 at Elsham Wolds are: L-R: Sgt George Lancaster, navigator; Sgt Jock Baird, mid upper gunner; Sgt Trev Greenwood, WOp; Sgt Jack Kilpatrick from Sidney, Australia, rear gunner. Clearly visible are many battle scars on the bomb doors and a large painted over patch on the aircraft roundel. The groundcrew of Bert Booth, fitter, Bob Draper, rigger and Tom Gean, aircraft hand were very protective of ED888 and did not care to see a few holes in her. (Charlie Baird)

IV./NJG 1, operating from Leeuwarden and Bergen, claimed three Halifaxes and eight Lancasters destroyed on 12/13 June 1943 including Halifax V DK183 of 427 'Lion' Sqn RCAF by *Major* Rolf Leuchs, which crashed near Den Hoorn on Texel Island at 0213 hrs. P/O A.M. Fellner RCAF, the pilot, survived to be taken PoW but he had head injuries and a broken leg. Two other crewmen were taken prisoner while three were killed. Sgt Imms, who was injured, died later. (G. Gerrits)

Halifax II Series I (Special) BB324 ZA-X of 10 Squadron photographed in April 1943 after completing four ops. Note the emblem below the cockpit of a cartoon of a terrier dog's head wearing a sailor's cap with Wings For Victory in white below it. On 22/23 June 1943 BB324 was shot down over the North Sea 15 miles (25 km) W of The Hague by a nightfighter probably flown by *Ofw* Bruno Eikmeier of 2./NJG 1. Sgt R.M. Pinkerton and his six crew were killed. Thirty-five aircraft, or 6.3 per cent of the force that attacked Mülheim were lost. At least 15 of these bombers fell victim to German nightfighters. (Tom Thackray)

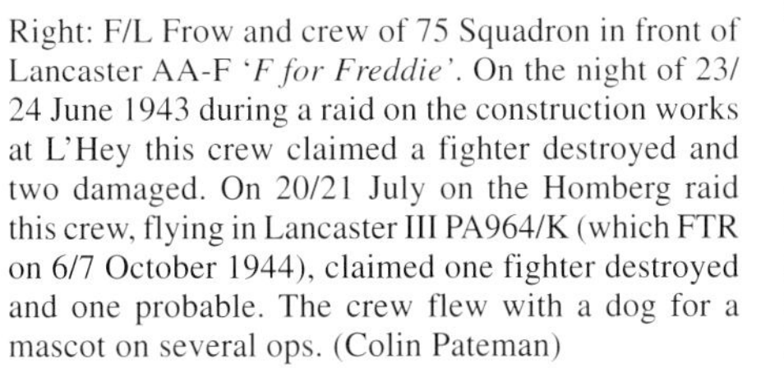

Below: In June 1943 the first of the Halifax B.Mk.II and V Series 1A aircraft were issued to squadrons, principally to 6 Group RCAF. Note the exhaust shrouds (later deleted) on the Merlin 22 engines and the Morris single-block radiators with series oil cooler, which replaced the earlier Gallay radiators, which proved troublesome. The Mk.V only differed from the Mk.II in having a different undercarriage. (via Mike Bailey)

Right: F/L Frow and crew of 75 Squadron in front of Lancaster AA-F '*F for Freddie*'. On the night of 23/24 June 1943 during a raid on the construction works at L'Hey this crew claimed a fighter destroyed and two damaged. On 20/21 July on the Homberg raid this crew, flying in Lancaster III PA964/K (which FTR on 6/7 October 1944), claimed one fighter destroyed and one probable. The crew flew with a dog for a mascot on several ops. (Colin Pateman)

Over Cologne on 28/29 June 1943 Halifax HR837 ND-*F for Freddie* of 158 Squadron had a bomb pass right through the fuselage without exploding. HR837 was repaired and served with 1656 HCU before it was SOC on 11 January 1945. (IWM)

Hamburg burning on 24/25 July 1943 when 'Bomber' Harris launched the first of four raids code-named *Gomorrah*. (IWM)

Right: Silhouetted against a background of fire and flak this Lancaster is over the target area of Hamburg. (IWM)

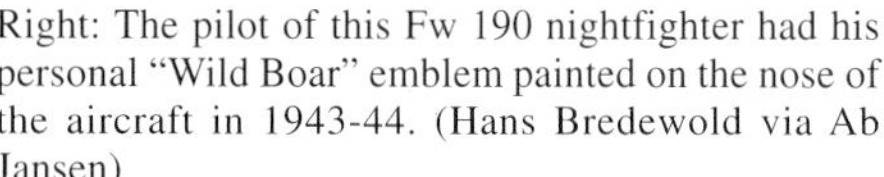

Right: The pilot of this Fw 190 nightfighter had his personal "Wild Boar" emblem painted on the nose of the aircraft in 1943-44. (Hans Bredewold via Ab Jansen)

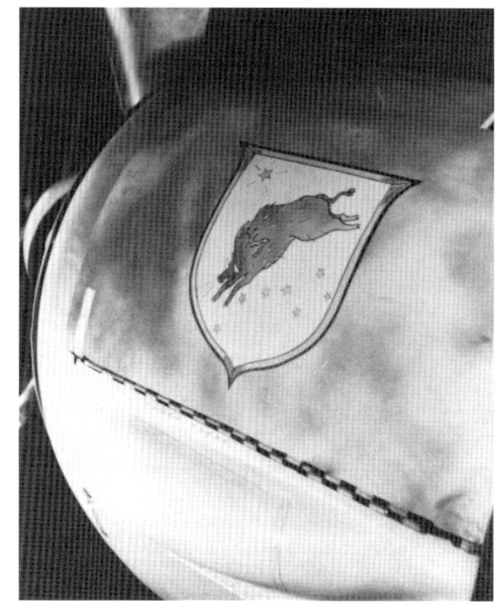

Far right: *Hptm* Peter Spoden was one of the leading "Tame Boar" pilots who made his first operational flight in a Bf 110 of 5./NJG 5 in the Battle of Hamburg 27/28 July 1943. Spoden's first victory came on the night of the Peenemünde raid 17/18 August 1943 when he shot down Lancaster III JA897 of 44 Squadron flown by Sgt W.J. Drew (KIA with five of his crew – only Sgt W. Sparks, bomb aimer, survived). On the night of 23/24 August 1943 during the RAF raid on Berlin Spoden was hit in the leg when his Bf 110 was hit by return fire from a Stirling and he and his crew had to bale out. Spoden baled out but he hit the tailplane and the speed of the aircraft pinned him for some time before he eventually broke free and pulled the ripcord. He lost consciousness and came too in a garden of a house in Berlin. His *Bordfunker* survived but his flight mechanic was killed. Spoden was hospitalized and only returned to action again in early November 1943. Late that same month he claimed his fourth *Abschuss* when he shot down a Lancaster. Spoden finished the war as *Gruppenkommandeur* of I./NJG 6 with 24 night and 1 day (the latter probably unconfirmed) victories (a USAAF B-17 on 6 March 1944) in NJG 5 and NJG 6. He was awarded the *Deutsches Kreuz*. Post war Spoden was a senior Lufthansa pilot. (Peter Spoden)

W/C 'Bob' Braham DSO DFC** CO 141 Squadron who, on the night of 17/18 August 1943 flying a Beaufighter VIf and with F/O W. J. 'Sticks' Gregory DFC (seen here, left) as his radar operator, shot down two Bf 110Gs of IV./NJG 1 flown by *Ofw* Georg Kraft and *Fw* Heinz Vinke to take his score to 18 victories. Braham finished the war with 29 victories. Gregory partnered Braham in four of his 8 victories in 141 Squadron 14 June-29 September 1943 and F/L Jacko Jacobs partnered him in the other four. (IWM)

Bristol Beaufighter undergoing maintenance in a RAF hangar. (Authors Coll)

With the change from close-controlled Himmelbett to broadcast-controlled Wild and Tame Boar night-fighting in the summer of 1943, the night air battles over the Third Reich were directed from five huge *Divisiongefechtsstände* or Divisional Battle Command posts positioned in Holland, France and Germany. The central HQ during the Battle of Berlin was the Battle Room of *Luftflotte Reich* in Berlin-Wannsee (pictured). *Generalmajor* Andreas Nielsen Chief of Staff of Luftflotte Reich and the officer in overall control (right) and *Oberst* Wolf Falck, since late 1943 'Ia Flieg', Senior Operations Officer responsible for the deployment of operational *Nachtjagd* units (left) keep a close eye on the development of a Bomber Command raid during the Battle of Berlin. Note the brightly painted telephone in front of Falck, which was his 'Hot line' with Göring. (Falck)

Halifax II HR738 '*Zombie Zephyr*' of 158 Squadron flown by P/O David Leicester RAAF being refueled at Lissett in July 1943. 'Zombie' Zephyr' and Sgt W. Kidd's crew FTR from the raid on Berlin on 31 August/1 September 1943 when the aircraft crashed near Lieberge, Germany after being attacked by a nightfighter. Kidd and four of his crew were killed. Sgt R.J.H. Prince was badly wounded and lay in a semi-conscious state for the best part of 48 hours before personnel from a Flak Battalion found him. (David Leicester)

F/Sgt William 'Bill' A. Burgum RAAF and his Halifax crew were posted to 158 Squadron at Lissett on 10 August 1943 and they flew their first op, to Peenemünde on 17/18 August. A second, to Leverkusen in the Ruhr, followed on 22/23 August. Their third and last raid was on 23/24 August when they took off at 2014 in HR980 NP-K, as part of a force of 727 aircraft detailed to bomb Berlin. The route took them in a direct line from England to a point south of Berlin where the bombers turned to run in from the south to the north of Berlin. The crew bombed the target and were 50 km N of Berlin when they were attacked by a German nightfighter flown by *Oblt* Rudolf Altendorf of 2./NJG 4. Burgum turned and flew south to what looked like an open field but it was a swamp and the Halifax crashed into in to it after part of the wing broke off on the approach. All seven members of the crew were killed in the crash. When the Germans arrived a few days later they were only able to recover the bodies of F/Sgt Harley C. Harber, rear gunner and Sgt Arthur Cox, WOP-AG. The bodies of Burgum, F/Sgt Gordon Harrison RCAF, mid-upper gunner, Sgt Peter L. Buck, navigator, Sgt Roland Hill, flight engineer and Sgt Don R. Hempstoch, bomb aimer, sank with the aircraft into the swamp. L-R: Sgt Arthur Cox, WOP-AG; F/Sgt William 'Bill' A. Burgum RAAF, pilot; F/Sgt Harley C. Harber, rear gunner; Sgt Don R. Hempstoch, bomb aimer. (John Williams)

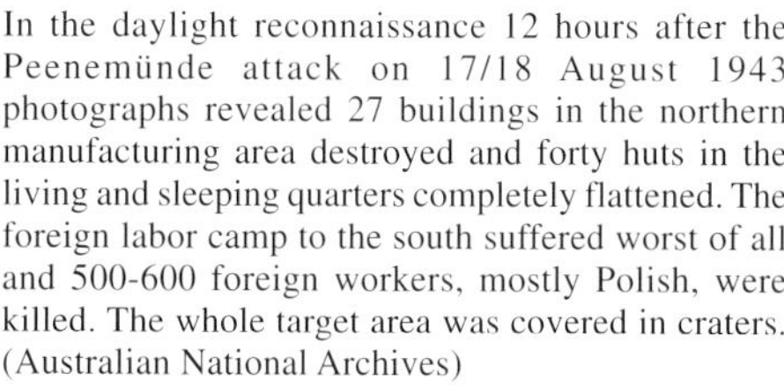

In the daylight reconnaissance 12 hours after the Peenemünde attack on 17/18 August 1943 photographs revealed 27 buildings in the northern manufacturing area destroyed and forty huts in the living and sleeping quarters completely flattened. The foreign labor camp to the south suffered worst of all and 500-600 foreign workers, mostly Polish, were killed. The whole target area was covered in craters. (Australian National Archives)

Opposite

Bottom: Lancaster III ED805 EA-S of 49 Squadron was involved in a non-operational taxying incident at Fiskerton on 11 August 1943. The aircraft and S/L R.N. Todd-White's crew (all KIA) was lost on the Peenemünde raid of 17/18 August 1943. (Leslie Hay)

Damage to the airfield and hangar installations at Peenemünde on 17/18 August 1943. The raid is adjudged to have set back the V-2 experimental program by at least two months and to have reduced the scale of the eventual rocket attack on Britain. (Australian National Archives)

Above: F/L Bill Scrymgeour-Wedderburn DFC and his crew chatting with their groundrew in 'B' Flight, 101 Special Duties Squadron at dispersal at Ludford Magna in August 1943, having just done a routine daily inspection of their Lancaster III W4995 N-Nuts. During 4 May-6 September 1943 F/L Scrymgeour-Wedderburn and crew completed a tour of 29 ops with 101 Squadron, all but three in W4995. During this period, 101 Squadron lost 20 aircraft and crews. Scrymgeour-Wedderburn and three of his crew did a second tour with 101 Squadron in 1944. Lancaster N-Nuts was finally SOC on 25 March 1948. (Les King DFM)

Right: Groundcrew sitting on the Lancaster's cockpit having just completed a routine daily inspection of Lancaster III W4995 *N-Nuts* in 'B' Flight, 101 Special Duties Squadron at dispersal at Ludford Magna in August 1943. The motif painted on the nose is a giant pair of nutcrackers with Hitler's head inside as the nut. Lancaster *N-Nuts*, which crashed at Lindholme on 16 May 1945, was finally SOC on 25 March 1948. (Les King DFM)

Right: *Ofw* Waack, *Jägerleitoffizier* (JLO, or GCI-controller) of *Himmelbett* box Rochen at the crash site of Lancaster III JA716 of 97 Squadron at Hanzinelle, SE of Charleroi, 11 August 1943. This aircraft was claimed by *Fw* Otto Fries and his *Bordfunker Uffz* Alfred Staffa of 5./NJG 1 at 0257 hrs for their first kill. F/L W.I. Covington DFC and his crew baled out and five men were taken prisoner. The skipper and his rear gunner, Sgt J. McKnight, evaded capture. (Otto H. Fries)

Far right: *Lt* Norbert Pietrek, a Bf 110 pilot who was ordered to take off for a *Zahme Sau* pursuit sortie on the night of 27/28 August when 674 heavy bombers attacked Nürnburg. Pietrek had become operational in 2./NJG 4 in January 1943 flying Bf 110s from Florennes airfield in southern Belgium. He had scored his first 'double' on 16/17 April 1943 when he shot down an unidentified Lancaster, which flew into a hill surrounding the River Meuse while being chased by Pietrek at low level and Stirling I BK653 BU-A of 214 Squadron flown by F/O D.E. James, which came down at Bonneuil-les-Eaux in the Oise district at 2345 hrs (Sgt E.M. Lee, tail gunner was KIA in the prolonged battle with Pietrek's Bf 110. James and three of his crew evaded. 3 PoW). Pietrek did not receive confirmation for the Lancaster, which had come down in the area of a neighboring *Himmelbett* box. (It was assigned to a comrade who claimed a Lancaster destroyed in that area at around the same time; his 3rd claim this night). However, Pietrek received confirmation for the Stirling and he was awarded the EKII (Iron Cross 2nd Class). On 9/10 August 1943 during a Bomber Command raid on Mannheim Pietrek scored another 'double' when he shot down Halifax II HR872 LQ-K of 405 'Vancouver' Squadron RCAF which crashed at Awenne, Luxembourg and Lancaster I W4236 QR-K of 61 Squadron 20 minutes later at Marbehan, Luxembourg. All seven crew of HR872 flown by F/L K. MacG Gray RCAF died and three crew of W4236 flown by Sgt J.C. Whitley were KIA. Barely recovered from head injuries he received when he belly-landed Bf 110 Werk Nr.4762 3C+BK at Kitzingen on 27/28 August, Pietrek suffered further head injuries when Bf 110G-4 3C+DJ crashed at Bieul near Dinant, Belgium on 1 October 1943 and he never flew operationally again. In October 1945 the Russians arrested Pietrek in Erfurt and he spent most of the next ten years in captivity in the Soviet Union. (Norbert Pietrek)

Bf 110s of I./NJG 4 in mid-1943. 3C+KK is closest to the camera. (Paul Gärtig)

Major Walter Ehle, *Gruppenkommandeur*, II./NJG 1, a veteran of the Spanish Civil War and one of the leading *Nachtjagd* aces during the *Himmelbett* period with 34 night and 3 day victories. (And) in his car in front of the ops room at St. Trond in 1942/43. (Hans Grohmann)

Award of the *Ritterkreuz* to *Ofw* Reinhard Kollak of 8./NJG 4 (left) and *Major* Walter Ehle, *Kommandeur*, II./NJG 1 (right) at St. Trond on 29 August 1943. *General* Josef Kammhuber is in the middle. *Stfw* Reinhard Kollak survived the war with 49 night victories in NJG 1 and NJG 4. (Otto H. Fries)

Fw Otto Fries and his *Bordfunker Fw* Fred Staffa of 5./NJG 1 at St. Trond in front of their Bf 110G in September 1943. This crew was credited with ten victories at night serving with II./NJG 1 and flying the Bf 110 August 1943-April-1944. (Otto H. Fries)

General Josef Kammhuber makes the award of the *Ritterkreuz* to *Major* Walter Ehle at St. Trond on 29 August 1943. (Otto H. Fries)

Left: *Reichsmarschall* Hermann Göring inspecting NJG 101 aircrew at Neuburg/Donau airfield in southern Germany in September 1943. As a protest against the meagre *Nachtjagd* results after the Battle of Hamburg, Göring is wearing only his white uniform (with his EKI (*Eisernes Kreuz* or Iron Cross First Class) of World War I vintage on his left breast) with red boots. (Dr. Karl Dörscheln)

Above: Messerschmitt Bf 110G-4d/R3 night fighters of 7./NJG 3 with FuG 220 Lichtenstein SN-2d AI radar, its antenna dipoles mounted at a 45° angle. SN-2d incorporated a tail warning capacity. This type of radar equipment, which required a larger (*grosse Hirschgeweih*/'Big Antlers') antenna array than the 212C-1 *Lichtenstein Weitwinkel* (Wide-angle) was fitted to the Bf 110G-4 from September 1943 onward. (Theo Boiten Coll)

Above and below: Stirling I EF393 BV-R of 214 Squadron, which took off from Chedburgh at 1910 hrs on 22/23 September 1943 was one of two of the squadron's Stirlings that FTR when it was shot down and crashed in the NW suburbs of Hannover. F/Sgt H. E. Hall BEM, pilot (KIA); Sgt D.L. Dean (KIA); P/O R.H. Nelson RNZAF (KIA); Sgt J.C. Todd (PoW); Sgt W. Thomas (KIA); Sgt J.L. Morgan (KIA); Sgt Geoff Parnell (PoW). (via CONAM)

Lancaster III ED702/D of 49 Squadron. L-R: Sgt Mick Mills, rear gunner; F/Sgt Keith Arthbury RAAF, bomb aimer; W/C Leonard Caine Slee, pilot; F/L Jim Bain, mid upper gunner; Sgt Joe Pass, WOp; Sgt ?, flight engineer. ED702 and P/O C.T. Anderson's crew (all KIA) went missing on the Mannheim raid on 23/24 September 1943. (Mick Mills)

Right: Stirling III EF464 ZO-P of 196 Squadron took off from Witchford, Cambridgeshire on 4 October 1943 but evasive action en route to Kassel caused the engines to over-rev and the port outer failed. F/Sgt G.H. Kogel, the pilot, turned back and made it across the North Sea but one mile from RAF Coltishall, a fighter station near Norwich, the port inner also failed and at 2143 hrs the Stirling hit trees and crashed at Scottow, a small village near the airfield. Sgt T.L. Dickie was killed and Sgt C.D. Williams, who was severely injured, recovered and later flew with 514 Squadron. (via Mick Jennings)

Right: Lancaster III LM326 EM-Z '*Z-Zebra*' of 207 Squadron, which on 18/19 October 1943 FTR from the raid on Hanover with F/Sgt Geoff Taylor RAAF and his crew after taking off from Spilsby at 1716 hrs. *Hptm* Friedrich Karl 'Nose' Müller, a *Wilde Sau* pilot of *Stab* JG 300, shot down '*Z-Zebra*'. LM326 crashed at 2030 hrs onto a road near Reinerbeck, 4 km WSW of Aerzen. Taylor, Sgt's Don J. Duff, A.G. McLeod, C.R. Smith RCAF, A.R. Burton, W. Worthington and F/Sgt W.J. McCarthy RAAF were taken prisoner. Post war Geoff Taylor wrote a book called *Piece of Cake* (George Mann, 1956) and in it he described the loss of his aircraft. 'As the dark horizon of Germany rapidly climbs higher round you, and *Z-Zebra* drops bumping into low cloud, rage grips you again this time at the thought of six men, six friends they are, riding with you and waiting for you to do something, hoping for the act of wizardry that will pull the rabbit out of the fire. Or is it the hat? You can't think which. There's Billy, married, by a few months. You never did meet his wife. Don; due to be married in a fortnight. Joe, long since married and content. The rest of the boys, like yourself, with light-hearted dates for tomorrow night. A bloody fine skipper you turned out to be. Thoughts like these loom rapidly into your consciousness to vanish as quickly, pursued by wishful-thinking calculations of fuel and range. Like a stab in the back, the starboard inner engine suddenly screams and spews flame. Don reaches for the feathering and fire buttons. He might just as well have sat back and sung the Lord's Prayer. Faithfully he plays out the little game he was taught but, in the language of the times, you have had it. Aching with the sheer muscular effort of holding up the plunging port wing, you feel the elevators tighten as the nose goes down with a lurch. Too tired to think, you hear your voice giving the queer little order they taught you one drowsy summer day at the operational training unit in pastoral Oxfordshire; the absurd jingle you had never really thought you would ever use: 'Abracadabra, jump, jump. Abracadabra, jump, jump.' (Frau Katherine Holterhoff Grote)

Left: *Lt* Heinz Grimm of IV./NJG 1 who died on 13 October 1943 from wounds sustained over Bremen from his own *flak* defenses. He was awarded the Ritterkreuz posthumously on 5 February 1944 for his 26 night kills and one B-17 (on 4 February 1943). (Ab A. Jansen) Right: *Hptm* Friedrich Karl 'Nose' Müller, a pre-war Lufthansa airline captain and a *Wilde Sau* pilot of *Stab* JG 300 who shot down Lancaster III LM326 EM-Z '*Z-Zebra*' of 207 Squadron on 18/19 October 1943 for his 19th *Abschuss*. (Fritz Krause)

Reichsmarschall Göring inspecting IV./NJG 1 at Leeuwarden airfield on 24 October 1943. Far right is by *Lt* Georg Fengler (who survived the war with 15 night and 1 daylight kills). To his left are Karl-Heinz Scherfling (estimated to have scored 35 night victories, KIA 20/21 July 1944) and Heinz Vinke (MIA 26 February 1944 off Dunkirk, 52 night victories). (Dr. Schmidt-Barbo)

Reichsmarschall Göring inspecting pilots of NJG 1 at Leeuwarden airfield on 24 October 1943. L-R: Göring, *Hptm* Hans-Joachim Jabs; (28 night and 22 day victories, ended the war as *Kommodore* NJG 1); *Oberleutnants* Heinz-Wolfgang Schnaufer (121 night victories, ended war as *Kommodore* NJG 4) and Martin Drewes (43 night and 6 daylight *Abschüsse*, survived war as *Kommandeur* III./NJG 1). (Dr. Schmidt-Barbo)

Right: Two engineers or *Schwarzemänner* (black men, so-called because of the colour of their tunics) of III./NJG 5 sitting on the right engine of a Bf 110G, 1943-44. Note the big flame dampers on the engine and the matt black camouflage paint applied to the aircraft's underside. (Herbert Fiedler)

Far right: *Hptm* Johannes Hager, *Staffelkapitän* 6./NJG 1 discussing the performance of his Bf 110G-4 on return from a NFT at St. Trond with T. Wart, his leading mechanic (left) and *Uffz* Hans Grohmann, a Daimler Benz engine specialist (center). Hager, who joined *Nachtjagd* in late 1942 soon became a leading *Experte* with 22 victory claims in 1943, including a B-17 *Abschuss* on the Schweinfurt raid of 17 August (which incidentally, was subsequently unconfirmed). He was awarded the *Ritterkreuz* on 12 March 1945 and finished the war with 42 night victories in NJG 1. (Hans Grohmann)

On 8 November 1943 100 Group (Special Duties, later Bomber Support) was created to consolidate the various squadrons and units using the secret ELINT (Electronic Intelligence) and RCM (Radio Counter Measures) in the war against the German night fighter air and defense system. '*Gertie*' and '*A Virgin's Prayer*' with Des Rice and his crew in front were two Wellington Xs that operated in 192 Squadron at Foulsham, Norfolk on ELINT duties November 1943-late 1944. The Wellington X, an improved version of the Mk.III with Hercules XVI engines served widely from 1943 with Bomber Command, the Middle East Air Forces and Operational Training Units and 3804 were delivered. It was the last of the Wellington bomber variants and the last version to see service with the RAF. Total production of Wellingtons was 11,461, the last being delivered on 13 October 1945. (via CONAM)

Above: In tandem with the electronic wizardry, 100 Group also accepted 'spoofing' as a large part of its offensive armory and it also controlled squadrons of Mosquitoes engaged purely on Intruder missions over Germany. The first Mosquito NFII nightfighters that 100 Group received usually had seen long service and mechanical troubles plagued the Serrate squadrons until finally, in February 1944, all reconditioned Merlin 21 engines were called in and, while stocks lasted, only Merlin 22s were installed. Note the AI.Mk.IV 'arrowhead' and wing mounted azimuth aerials. All four machine guns were deleted to make room for Serrate 'homing' apparatus. The all-black scheme could slow the aircraft by up to 23 mph. (DH)

Right: Five of the crew of Lancaster III LM360 *O-Oboe* of 61 Squadron, 5 Group at Syerston, near Nottingham, who flew the operation to Düsseldorf on 3/4 November 1943. Back row; L-R: F/Sgt Les Rolton, bomb-aimer; F/Sgt Frank Emerson, rear gunner Front row: F/Sgt Jim 'Taffy' Norris, flight engineer; F/L Bill Reid, pilot; F/Sgt C. Baldwin, gunner. P/O John Jeffreys RAAF, navigator was killed and WOp F/Sgt I.J. Mann died the next day from his wounds. Bill Reid VC and Rolton joined 617 Squadron after recovering from their ordeal. On 31 July 1943 Reid became a PoW and Rolton was killed when their Lancaster was brought down over France by a 1000-lb bomb dropped by an aircraft overhead during the bombing of both ends of a railway tunnel at Rilly-La-Montage, which was being used as a flying-bomb store. (Bill Reid Collection)

Right: Damage caused by German night fighters to Lancaster III LM360 *O-Oboe*. In the first of two attacks by night fighters, Emerson's turret was badly damaged, the communications system and the compasses were put out of action and the elevator trimming tabs of the Lancaster were damaged. In a second attack by a Wild Boar Fw 190 the Luftwaffe pilot raked the Lancaster from nose to tail with cannon fire. Despite the damage to the aircraft and being badly wounded, Reid and his crew managed to nurse *O-Oboe* back to England where they bellied in at the 44th Bomb Group Liberator base at Shipdham, Norfolk. (Bill Reid Collection)

Right: *Lt* Otto Fries' *Bordfunker Fw* Fred Staffa of 5./NJG 1 sitting on top of their Bf 110G-4 in a hangar at St. Trond in Belgium in November-December 1943. On the night of 22/23 October 1943 *Lt* Otto Fries and Staffa scored their second victory when flying Tame Boar they shot down a *Viermot* during the raid on Kassel. On 3/4 November 1943 Fries and Staffa shot down Halifax LK932 of 76 Squadron north of Maastricht. By May 1944 Fries and Staffa had 10 confirmed victories, plus two unconfirmed *Abschüsse* in daylight. After being posted to 2./NJG 1 in early July 1944 Fries and Staffa flew the He 219 from Venlo airfield and added another six victory claims (four of which were subsequently confirmed) to their score before the end of the war. This made their final tally 14 confirmed, and four unconfirmed *Abschüsse*. (Otto Fries)

Far right: *Lt* Otto Fries, pilot, 5./NJG 1 carrying decorations of *Major* Walter Ehle, *Kommandeur*, II./NJG 1 during the funeral ceremony on 19 November 1943. Ehle who with *Ofw* Ludwig Leidenbach, *Bordfunker* and *Uffz* Heinz Derlitzky, air gunner, was killed when their Bf 110G-4 G9+AC Werk Nr.5575 crashed in a dive at Horpmaal, Belgium at 2020 hrs on return from an operational sortie on 17 November 1943. The crew were buried at the Brustem military cemetery near St. Trond five days later. 31-year-old *Major* Ehle was one of the leading *Nachtjagd* aces with 35 night and 4 day victories. The cause of the crash, on final approach to St. Trond has never been explained. (Otto H. Fries)

Right: During a 'Bullseye' on 6 November 1943. Stirling R9192 of 1657 HCU at Stradishall (an ex-75 and 15 Squadron aircraft) collided with Wellington III X3637 of 27 OTU in shadow of cu nim cloud at about 2000 hours. The Wellington, which took off from Lichfield at 1940 hours for an evening navigation detail, crashed at Raden Stick Farm, Little Walden, 2 miles north of Saffron Walden, Suffolk. The all-Australian crew including the pilot, P/O M. E. McKiggan RAAF were killed. R9192 was captained by F/O D. W. Thomson RNZAF. Also on board were F/O Vern L. Scantleton DFC RAAF, QMSI I. Colley and F/Sgt W. Mitson, army gunners for experience of AA. The Stirling, which returned to Stradishall and landed safely was SOC on 12 June 1944. (CONAM)

Right: *Oblt* Heinz-Wolfgang Schnaufer *St.Kpt* of 12./NJG 1 at the funeral ceremony of *Major* Walter Ehle, *Kommandeur*, II./NJG 1 on 19 November 1943. (via Peter Loncke)

Far right: Pilot *Uffz* Karl Hartel IV/NJG 101 at Kitzingen, Germany was killed on 30 November 1943 when his Bf 110D (Werk Nr.3348) crashed NE of Kitzingen, SE of Würzburg and burnt out due to engine failure whilst on a training flight from Grosslangheim to Sassendort near Bamberg. His *Bordfunker, Uffz* Hans Tonn, was also killed. (Steve Hall)

27. To the Germans Tinsel, which had been first introduced in December 1942 and blotted out German R/T transmissions with engine noise, was *Seelenbohrer*, or 'soul-borer' because it sounded like a very unpleasant drilling noise.

28. Including Halifax II DT641 of 419 'Moose' Sqn RCAF flown by P/O A.J. Herriott DFM (all KIA) over the North Sea 8 km N of Ameland by *Major* Lent and Stirling I EF347 of 15 Sqn flown by F/Sgt H.S. Howland (all KIA) by *Lt* Kuthe at Schillaard. 3 Halifaxes were credited to III./NJG 1, 2 of which – Halifax II BB223 of 51 Sqn flown by F/Sgt J.D.W. Stenhouse (all KIA) at Voorst and Halifax II W7877 of 35 Sqn flown by S/L P.C. Elliott DFC (KIA) at Oost-Stokkum – went to *Lt* Geiger. *Oblt* Herbert Lütje claimed Halifax II DT797 of 408 Sqn flown by Sgt A.W. Cochrane RCAF (6 KIA. 1 PoW) at Zuidloo.

29. In all, the crew would fly 23 operations in *K-King* (W4236), which was shot down en route to Mannheim by *Leutnant* Norbert Pietrek of II./NJG 4 on the night of 9/10 August 1943. Sgt J.C. Whitley and 3 of his crew evaded. 3 were killed.

30. P/O Derek Smith flew a second tour 1 September 1944-12 March 1945, as a navigator on Mosquitoes in 692 Sqn, 8 (PFF) Group and was awarded a bar to his DFC.

31. After completing his first tour in 99 Sqn he had served as an Operational Liaison Officer with the USAAC in Alabama and Georgia in 1942 and on returning to England was posted to a 4-engine CU, which was equipped with Short Stirlings.

32. Target Indicators.

33. *Major* Helmut Lent shot down Halifax BB282 of 76 Sqn and Lancaster W4847 of 83 Sqn into the Waddenzee and the Ijsselmeer respectively. *Hptm* Herbert Lütje of 8./NJG 1 destroyed Halifax HR687 of 78 Sqn nr Staphorst.

34. Kettledrums, Kettledrums – going into attack.

35. The Bf 110F was unable to fly on one engine when carrying night fighting equipment.

36. *Oboe* was the most accurate form of high-level blind bombing used in World War II and it took its name from a radar pulse, which sounded like a musical instrument. The radar pulses operated on the range from 2 ground stations ('Cat' & 'Mouse') in England to the target. The signal was heard by both pilot and navigator and used to track the aircraft over the target, If inside the correct line, dots were heard, if outside the line, dashes, a steady note indicated the target was on track. Only the navigator heard this signal. When the release signal, which consisted of 5 dots and a 2-second dash was heard, the navigator released the markers or bombs. In April 1942 109 Sqn was established at Stradishall, Suffolk to bring *Oboe* into full operational service as a navigation aid for Bomber Command before moving to Wyton in August, where at the end of the year, it received the first *Oboe* equipped Mosquito BIVs. *Oboe* was first used on 20/21 December 1942 when the CO, S/L H.E. 'Hal' Bufton and his navigator, F/L E.L. Ifould and 2 other crews, bombed a power station at Lutterade in Holland. On 31 Decemeber.1942/1 January 1943, on a raid on Düsseldorf, sky-marking using *Oboe* was tried for the first time when 2 Mosquitoes of 109 Sqn provided the sky-markers for 8 Lancasters of the Path Finder Force. 'Sky markers' were parachute flares to mark a spot in the sky if it was cloudy. The *PFF* markers' job was to 'illuminate' and 'mark' targets with colored TI's (target indicators) for the Main Force and other 8 Group Mosquitoes. Air Cdre (later AVM) Donald C.T. Bennett's specialist PathFinder Force formed in August 1942 achieved Group status on 13 January 1943. 109 became the premier marking squadron in the RAF, carrying out the most raids and flying the most sorties in 8 Group, which it joined on 1 June 1943. On 10 December 109 Sqn at Marham received the first BXVI for the RAF, although 692 Sqn were the first to use it operationally, on 5 March 1944. In addition to its flare marking duties for the heavies, 109 Sqn's Mosquitoes carried bombs. On 23 December 1944 S/L R.A.M. Palmer DFC lost his life in an *Oboe*-equipped Lancaster borrowed from 582 Sqn when he led a formation-attack on the Cologne railway marshalling yards. His Lancaster was hit by *flak* and set on fire but Palmer got his bombs away before his aircraft went down out of control. He was awarded a posthumous Victoria Cross. On 21 April 1945 109 Sqn dropped the last bombs to fall on Berlin in World War II.

37. Essen was bombed by 457 bombers on 12/13 March. 23 a/c FTR, of which 13 were destroyed by the *Nachtjagd*. *Oblt* Manfred Meurer, *Staffelkapitän*, 3./NJG 1 destroyed 4 bombers for his 20-23rd kills, which earned him the *Ritterkreuz*. His victims were Halifax HR69 of 10 Sqn, Lancaster ED449 of 50 Sqn, Halifax DT774 of 78 Sqn and Wellington BK348 of 424 'Tiger' Sqn RCAF. All these a/c came down over S. Holland. 5 victories were credited to IV./NJG 1 including a triple (2 Wellingtons of 115 Sqn and 425 'Alouette' Sqn RCAF Sqn and a 'Lancaster', which in fact was Halifax BJ836 of 102 Sqn, which cr. in the North Sea SW of Den Helder) by *Lt* Oskar Köstler who operated from Bergen/Holland airfield. *Oblt* Eckart-Wilhelm von Bonin *Staffelkapitän* 6./NJG 1 shot down Halifax DT751 of 76 Sqn, which fell at 2148 hrs 4 km NNW of Amerika (Limburg) and he also claimed Wellington HE690 of 420 Sqn, which force-landed at Brielle at 2226 hrs but Sgt G.H. Cooke RCAF and his crew told their captors that they had been downed by *Flak* and von Bonin was not credited with a victory, which instead went to the *Flak* arm. (Ron Read meanwhile, beat the odds and survived his tour.)

38. All 8 of Pearson's crew KIA when at 2119 hrs *Hptm* Wilhelm Dormann, 9./NJG 1, shot them down at Beek, 8 km SSE of Zevenaar, Holland. 'Spud' Taylor and Page's erstwhile crew was posted to Downham Market and 218 'Gold Coast' Sqn, also flying Stirlings, on 18 April.

39. Schmidt's 1st victory was Halifax HR665 NF-L of 138 Sqn that had taken off from Tempsford for dropping at 3 different DZs. F/O E. Clow RNZAF was at the controls and on board were 2 secret agents, Gerbrands (code-name '*St. John*') and Bergman ('*St. Andrew*') and containers with supplies for the Dutch Resistance (*Leeks 5/Catarrh II*). 2 containers were successfully dropped nr. Limmen 25 km NW of Amsterdam and then Clow set course for Friesland to drop the 2 agents. While flying low over the Zuider Zee they were hit in the left wing by Schmidt's gunfire at 0036 hrs. Bergman was killed by the burst of fire and the aircraft was so heavily damaged that Clow had to ditch in the sea E of Enkhuizen. The crew managed to escape from the a/c before it sank and set sail in their dinghy but were soon picked up by the Germans. A second SD Halifax, of 138 Sqn, flown by F/O Rutledge successfully made 2 drops in Holland, at '*Lettuce 10*' and '*Parsnip 5*' before returning to Tempsford.

40. 162 Lancasters, 103 Halifaxes 64 Stirlings. 21 aircraft – 11 Lancasters, 7 Halifaxes, 3 Stirlings FTR – 18 of which were shot down by *Himmelbett*-operating nightfighters over the Netherlands and Germany.

41. *Major* Lent and *Fw* Vinke of IV./NJG 1 each shot down a Wellington; BJ762 of 426 Sqn at Nijemirdum and X3965 of 166 Sqn respectively, over the North Sea, as did *Major* Werner Streib and *Oblt* Martin Bauer of I./NJG 1. Streib's victim (HE545 of 166 Sqn) went down nr. Deelen a/f, whereas Bauer's victim (MS484 of 420 Sqn) went down near Wanrooy. III./NJG 1 claimed 9 Wellingtons, 5 Lancasters and a Halifax destroyed. *Lt* August Geiger, *Staffelkapitän*, 7./NJG 1 flying Bf 110G-4 G9+ER and guided by *Himmelbett* box 'Kröte' over the Dutch-German border was the night's top-scoring pilot with 5 victories in 2 sorties. At 2252 hrs he shot down Wellington HE182 of 431 'Iroquois' Sqn RCAF nr. Ahaus and at 2315 hrs Wellington HE385 of 196 Sqn went down nr. Barchem. On his 2nd sortie of the night Gieger destroyed Halifax BB244 of 51 Sqn, which was returning from Berlin, at 0347 hrs and it spun in at Vorden. At 0427 hrs this was followed by Lancaster ED596 of 106 Sqn at Delden and 17 mins later Geiger shot down Lancaster W4327 of 460 Sqn RAAF, which crashed at Lieveldeand. These victories took Geiger's score to 19.

42. Wellingtons BK313 of 115 Sqn and DF639 of 75 RNZAF Sqn on 6/7 October 1942.

43. Krause's 3rd victory was Lancaster III ED469 of 49 Sqn, which had taken off from Fiskerton at 2145 hrs on 29 March piloted by F/O George F. Mabee RCAF (26) on his crew's 1st operation since they joined 'A' Flight on 10 March. At 0326 hrs bomber cr in flames at Eilvese nr Wunstorf. Six of the crew perished. Tail gunner Sgt G.A. Jones survived, although very seriously wounded and he was repatriated in 1944.

44. At least 18 by IV./NJG 1 at Leeuwarden, 13 by I./NJG 1 at Venlo, 5 by III./NJG 1 at Twenthe and 3 by II./NJG 1 at St. Trond.

45. *Oblt* von Bonin, *Staffelkapitän* 6./NJG 1 downed Lancaster ED694 of 9 Sqn at Stevensbeek. I./NJG 1 destroyed a Lancaster and 4 Halifaxes, 3 of them by *Gruppen Kommandeur Major* Werner Streib, including DT808 of 405 'Vancouver' Sqn RCAF, which came down at Vierlingsbeek. *Hptm* Herbert Lütje, *Staffelkapitän* 8./NJG 1 claimed Lancaster ED334 of 83 Sqn at 2245 hrs at Winterswijk and Halifax DT617 of 419 'Moose' Sqn RCAF at 2337 hrs, the a/c coming down at Olst. *Lt* August Geiger and *Uffz* Emil Henzelmann both of III./NJG 1 destroyed an u/i Lancaster at Gemen, Germany and Halifax DT795 of 158 Sqn at 2350, respectively (the a/c crashing at Wapenveld).

46. 3 of these credited to *Ofw* Heinz Vinke of 11./NJG 1. ED554 of 207 Sqn went down at Jisp at 2242; ED566 of 9 Sqn went down in the North Sea at 2345 hrs 50 km W of Castricum. ED724 of 103 Sqn, which *Ofw* Vinke claimed destroyed over the North Sea W of Alkmaar at 0014. ED502 of 9 Sqn came down at 2345 hrs at Snelrewaard near Utrecht. ED724 of 103 Sqn, which *Ofw* Vinke claimed destroyed in the vicinity of Alkmaar at 2356 limped back to England. F/L K.G. Bickers flew the stricken aircraft back with Sgt R.H. Howell (rear gunner) dead. Attempting to land near Bodney airfield, the bomber was wrecked.

47. ED806 of 9 Sqn at Nistelrode. *Oberst* Werner Streib scored 67 *Nachtjagd Abschüsse* (including 30 *Viermots*) in 150 sorties with NJG 1 plus 1 as *Zerstörer* in I./ZG 1. *Ritterkreuz* with *Eichenlaub* and *Schwerter*. Died 15 June 1986 in Munich.

48. Köstler and original *Bordfunker Uffz* Völler were one of the newly-trained *Nachtjagd* crews posted to 10./NJG 1 in the Netherlands in the summer of 1942. They operated from Leeuwarden and its satellite Bergen/Alkmaar airfields, claiming their first victory on 1/2 March 1943. Within five weeks they were aces with 2 Wellingtons and two Lancasters destroyed, plus a B-17 in daylight on 4 March. Völler had fallen ill early in April and was replaced by Huhn, whose two previous pilots were KIA.

49. G9+CX (Werke Nummer (Serial) 4811).

50. There were no survivors from F/Sgt J.D. Steele RCAF and his 101 Sqn crew when Lancaster III ED618 exploded at 2243 hrs. *Lt* Oskar Köstler and *Uffz* Heinz Huhn's Bf 110 crashed a few km further N, at Elburg.

51. D/R being dead reckoning navigation on a time and distance flown basis with an allowance made for possible drift.

52. *Fw* Karl Gross and his *Bordfunker Uffz* Geck of 8./NJG 4 flying a Bf 110G-4 from Juvincourt were guided onto the tail of the bomber by the ground radar of 15./Ln. Regiment 203 and in a single long burst of cannon fire Gross shot DT775 down; his sole victory of the war. Whilst serviing in 11./NJG 6, Gross was KIA in a crash at Urzenici, Rumania, on 11 July 1944, cause u/k.

53. Halifax DT775 cr in a field at Anoux near Briey (Meurthe-et-Moselle) in E France, where it burned out. Sgt Jack Adams and 5 of his crew baled out safely and all were PoW. Sgt Joe Enwright, a married man with a small daughter, KIA by cannon fire and his body was found near the remains of his rear turret the next day. (Of the 10 78 Sqn crews who returned to Linton on Ouse from Frankurt, 6 were shot down on ops 16 April-15 July 1943). 22 aircraft FTR from Frankfurt – 10 of these losses were due to crews of NJG 4 and 1 to *Maj* Walter Ehle of *Stab* II./NJG 1, who destroyed Stirling III BK760 of 7 Sqn flown by S/L H.W.A. Chesterman DFC (2 Evd, rest KIA) at Tongelo. *Hptm* Wilhelm Herget, *Kommandeur*, I./NJG 4 claimed his 16th night kill when he downed Wellington X HE652 of 426 Sqn flown by P/O J.H. Sammet RCAF (all KIA) at Virelles (Hainaut). Halifax II DT806 of 35 Sqn flown by F/O G.F. Lambert (Evd) (4 KIA. 2 PoW) was shot down by *Lt* Helmut Bergmann of *Stab* III./NJG 4 for his 6th confirmed kill and it cr. at Fleigneux, Luxembourg. Halifax II JB871 of 76 Sqn flown by F/L A.H. Hull (found dead in the cockpit) (4 Evd. 3 inj) went down nr. Hirson (Aisne), victim of *Fw* Piwarz of 3./NJG 4 – his first victory. *Nachtjagd* lost 2 Bf 110s of NJG 1 and 2 Do 217s of NJG 4 and 3 crews, at least 2 due to accidents.

54. In the latter part of April crews were informed that 425 *'Les Alouettes'* Sqn RCAF was being sent to North Africa with tropicalised Wellington Xs to be part of 331 Wing along with 424 'Tiger' and 427 'Lion' Sqns RCAF. There were several crew changes and Woodrow was the only member of the crew who would fly his whole tour with Johnny Michaud.

55. On 13/14 April.

56. On the night of 14/15 April Bomber Command attacked Stuttgart with 462 bombers. 23 a/c FTR including 8 Stirlings. Again NJG 4 was successful, 12 of its crews scoring 17 confirmed victories.

57. 36 Lancasters and Halifaxes on the Pilsen raid and 18 aircraft on Mannheim. 34 of these losses were claimed by NJG 4 manning the *Himmelbett* areas in Northern France and Luxembourg.

58. F/L A.H. Hull was found dead in the wrecked cockpit of Halifax II JB871 MP-V. G/C J.R. Whitley and 3 others Evd. 3 inj.

59. F/L A.P. Dowse DFC and crew in Halifax II DT773, who were shot down by a Bf 110, survived and were PoW.

60. F/L E.G. 'Morty' Mortenson's Halifax II (HR659 EY-A) was brought down by the combined fire of a Bf 109 and a Bf 110 (possibly *Fw* Paul Faden of 11./NJG 4) & cr. nr. Trier. (Faden claimed a Halifax *Abschuss* S of Bitburg at 0307 hrs). 5 of the 7 crew were PoW. Sgt D.A. Pitman was KIA along with Morty.

61. This aircraft and W/O A.H. Beeston's crew FTR from Essen on 28 May 1943 when they were shot down by a nightfighter and cr. nr. Oud-Reemst 10km NW of Arnhem. (All KIA)

62. 5 Lancasters (and 3 Halifaxes) were claimed shot down by *Nachtjäger* crews who also claimed 5 of the 8 Stirlings lost from the 86 sent to bomb n the Heinkel factory at Rostock.

63. 21 aircraft (13 Lancasters and 7 Halifaxes) FTR from Stettin and 8 Stirlings FTR from Rostock. NJG 3 was credited with 12 and NJG 5 with another 6 confirmed victories.

64. On 28/29 June 1942 *Oblt* Reinhold Knacke, *St Kapt*, 1./NJG 1 had been the first *Nachtjagd* pilot to claim a Mosquito kill, when he shot down DD677 of 23 Sqn at Haps, S Holland).

65. NFII DZ694 of 410 Sqn. F/Sgt W.J. Reddie and his navigator, Sgt K. Evans, who were on a Night Fighting Patrol over Holland KIA. Lent was noted for experimenting with new methods of attack. He would practice and perfect a diving attack, which would give him sufficient speed to overtake a Mosquito and shoot it down. For being one of the first German pilot to overcome this versatile aircraft he received special praise from Göring. Lent eventually rose to the rank of *Oberst* with a position of high command in the night fighter arm. He would achieve 102 night-victories and 8 day-victories before being killed in a flying accident on 5 October 1944.

66. Linke, with 24 night and 3 day victories was killed on the night of 13/14 May 1943. After shooting down two Lancasters (W4981 of 83 Sqn and ED589 of 9 Sqn) and Halifax DT732 of 10 Sqn over Friesland, he suffered an engine fire (Bf 110G-4 G9+CZ, Werke Nr. 4857). He baled out near the village of Lemmer in Friesland but he struck the tail unit of his Bf 110 and was killed. Linke's *Bordfunker Ofw* Walter Czybulka baled out safely. In mid-July 1943 3 Fw 190s for Mosquito hunting were stationed at Bonn-Hangelar and which came under operational control of *Himmelbett* Box 6 in E Belgium. The subsequent Mosquito-hunting sorties by these single-engined fighters were without result.

67. 9 to *Himmelbett*-controlled crews of NJG 3 over Denmark and 13 to light *flak*.

68. 12 a/c FTR from a force of 305 bombers. Half the losses were inflicted by nightfighters.

69. Lancaster III ED862 and P/O D.J. Marks DFM were lost without trace on 30 July 1943.

70. 30 a/c FTR, 22 of which were destroyed by *Himmelbett Nachtjager* of NJG 1, all but 3 of which were achieved over the Netherlands and the Dutch coastal waters.

71. 31 aircraft or 5.2% of the bombing force were lost. (Another 7 bombers crashed in England in bad weather). 6 crews in IV./NJG 1 destroyed 12 of the bombers. *Gruppenkommandeur Major* Lent claimed 2 Stirlings (Stirling III BK773 of 7 Sqn flown by P/O W. Holden RCAF (all KIA) at 0008 hrs over the Ijsselmeer S of Enkhuizen and Stirlng I EF343 of 149 Sqn flown by F/O W.E. Davey (all KIA) 10 mins later at Heeg) to take his score to 66 victories. There were no survivors. III./NJG 1 claimed 6 bombers.

72. Stirling III BK658 of 15 Sqn flown by Sgt W.M. McLeod RNZAF. McLeod and 5 others PoW. 1 KIA.

73. At Midwolda, 31 km E of Groningen.

74. 572 aircraft attacked Duisburg. 24 of these losses are attributed to *Himmelbett*-operating nightfighters of NJG 1; all these victories being achieved over the Netherlands. I./NJG 1 at Venlo destroyed 10 bombers; III./NJG 1 5, including 2 Halifaxes of 35 and 77 Sqns and Wellington HE321 of 428 'Ghost' Sqn RCAF by *Oblt* August Geiger. These were Geiger's 24th-27th official victories. 34 aircraft or 5.9% of the force FTR.

75. Target illuminated by flares.

76. Bochum cost 24 a/c (13 Halifaxes, 6 Wellingtons, 4 Stirlings 1 Lancaster). Pilsen cost 9 aircraft. 27 a/c were shot down by *Nachtjäger* patrolling in the *Himmelbette* over the Netherlands, Blegium and Germany. I./NJG 1 claimed 9 bombers, including Stirling BF479 of 149 Sqn by *Lt* Walter Schön of the third *Staffel* at Kasterlee. III./NJG 1 at Twenthe destroyed 10 Lancasters, Halifaxes and a Stirling over the Dutch-German border. *Hptm* Herbert Lütje, *Staffelkapitän* 8./NJG 1 claimed 6 victories. His first 3 claims were against Pilzen-bound bombers. At 2332 hrs Lancaster ED667 of 57 Sqn went down at Albergen, followed 10 mins later by R5611 of 106 Sqn at Rossum/Weerselo. 6 mins before midnight Lancaster W4305 of 44 Sqn went down between Bevergern and Hörstel. When the Bochum raiders were on their return leg, Lütje destroyed Halifax JB966 of 405 'Vancouver' Sqn RCAF nr. Oud Avereest at 0225 hrs and at 0245 Halifax JD113 of 419 'Moose' Sqn RCAF at Dalen. 7 mins later he downed Halifax JB892 of 77 Sqn, which cr into woods near Noordsleen. These took Lütje's tally to 28 victories. Was awarded the *Ritterkreuz* two weeks later and appointed *Kommandeur* of IV./NJG 6 in Rumania. Lütje ended the war as *Kommodore* of NJG 6 with 50 kills.

77. Lancaster W4110 of 44 Sqn.

78. 20 km W of Den Helder.

79. *Eisernes Kreuz I* or Iron Cross 1st Class.

80. Pfeiffer scored his 5th victory when he shot down Stirling BF405 of 218 Sqn 70 km N of Terschelling on 27/28 May.

81. The 2 airmen killed in the incident – WOp/AG Sgt A.R. Denzey and the flight engineer, Sgt H. Lancaster, both of whom suffered a fractured skull, were from Stirling III BF413/T, flown by Sgt J.B. Smith. They had disembarked from their aircraft and were about to enter the Operations Block for interrogation. BF480 was damaged beyond repair.

82. Gibson was later sent to America as an air attaché but he begged the Air Ministry to allow him to return to operations. On 19/20 September 1944 he flew from Woodhall Spa in a Mosquito of 627 Sqn and crashed at 2300 hrs near Steenbergen, Holland, killing him and his navigator S/L J.B. Warwick. (21 other veterans of the Dams raid were also killed on ops).

83. NJG 1, the elite *Nachtjagd* wing, was credited with 21 confirmed kills; 18 of which were achieved over the Netherlands and Dutch coastal waters. *Oblt* Manfred Meurer, *Lt* Strüning and *Hptm* Friedrich of I./NJG 1 claimed 6 of the aircraft shot down on the Dortmund raid. 6 crews of III./NJG 1 destroyed 9 bombers. During a patrol in the *Himmelbett Raum* 4C and being guided by GCI fighter controller *Oblt* Freudenberg, *Hptm* Thimmig shot down Wellingtons HE290 of 166 and HE281 of 426 Sqns (both coming down at Rutbeek and Buurse nr. Enschede) and Halifax JD122 of 78 Sqn at Zuna W of Almelo between 0108 and 0134 hrs. 6 crews in IV./NJG 1 returned with claims for 8 kills.

84. Sloan received an immediate award of the Conspicuous Gallantry Medal, was commissioned and posted to pilot training. Bailey and Parslow received immediate awards of the DFC and DFM respectively. They later became part of the crew of W/C J. Coverdale MiD, Sqn CO but were lost without trace with Coverdale in a Wellington X on the night of 21/22 June 1943 raid on Krefeld, one of 44 aircraft that FTR. Sgt (later F/L) Sloan became a Halifax pilot on 158 Sqn and flew on ops from January 1945 to the end of the war.

85. F/L Ron Read was posted as an instructor to 1664 Heavy Conversion Unit, 6 RCAF Group. In a 4 1/2-month period he converted 11 pilots and crews to Halifaxes. Read adds. 'After this they really took old *C-Charlie* apart. Someone noticed the end of the oil tank supplying the port outer was deformed. They took it out and drained it, something they might have thought of before. Inside they found a loose piece of rag. It had been the cause of all the trouble. When on the ground and with the tank full it floated and allowed the oil to flow normally on ground tests. But airborne, as the oil level got lower, the rag floated closer to the engine pipe until the force of the pump sucking pulled the rag down to the pipe eventually stopping the oil flow. The rag was too large to go right into the pipe so after landing and refilling the tank, it floated away and was undetectable. No one thought about how it got there in the first place. It was just one of those wartime mysteries. Meanwhile, my reluctant aircraft *C-Charlie* continued true to form. On 21 June bound for Krefeld, Sgt Kitchen had to abandon the operation when the aircraft 'was unable to maintain height.' On the 22nd F/Sgt Wilson, going to Mülheim, had to abandon when he was 20 minutes late at the concentration point 'because the aircraft couldn't climb.' *C-Charlie* finally went out in a blaze of glory on the 24th when F/Sgt Wilson flew her on his second operation. Over the target a Lancaster dropped its bombs on *C-Charlie*, flying directly below. The 4000lb bomb went diagonally through the upper fuselage leaving two gaping holes. A number of incendiaries fell directly into the cockpit, one knocking off the earpiece from the engineer's helmet. The engineer threw these out of the cockpit windows. A few lodged in the wings, returning to Breighton that way. The port pouter propeller was shattered and the engine revolutions ran off the clock before Wilson could stop it. The port inner propeller had two blades severely damaged. One reduced to 3-4 ins in width in the middle. It ran very roughly all the way home but just kept turning. The young pilot dropped his bombs and nursed the damaged aircraft home. Looking at the aircraft the next morning I warmly commended him for a considerable feat of airmanship. No one was hurt but *Charlie's* wounds were mortal. Having done her one good deed she obviously felt life wasn't worth going on without me to plague her with her temperamental unserviceabilities.

86. His attack on Halifax II JB837 of 77 Sqn flown by Sgt R. Lewis near Jülich resulted in a massive explosion, which not only downed the Halifax but also two Stirling IIIs, EF361 of 7 Sqn flown by F/L J.F.E.G. Berthiaume RCAF (all KIA) and EH887 of 218 Sqn, flown by Sgt N.S. Collins (KIA).

87. Wellington X HE990, which cr. at Venray NW of Venlo, was the first of 3 RAF bombers Meurer shot down on 25/26 May. Dix and Barclay PoW. Meurer went on to claim Lancaster III LM320 of 100 Sqn at Vlodrop and Lancaster III W5001 of 207 Sqn at Neerbosch.

88. Again, I./NJG 1 was successful with 7 *Abschüsse*. III./NJG 1 claimed 8 victories, which included 3 Halifaxes and Wellington HE752 of 166 Sqn at Hengelo by *Lt* Augenstein. IV./NJG 1 claimed 4 victories.

89. Norbert Krüger, *The Bomber Command War Diaries*.

90. In May 1943 Meurer claimed 13 heavies shot down.

91. Halifax HR840 of 158 Sqn cr at Swalmen, Stirling IV EF398 of 75 Sqn at Roermond/Vlodrop, Wellington MS494 of 466 Sqn nr Reuver, Limburg and Lancaster EE123 of 44 Sqn at Castenray between 0033 and 0144 hrs. *Lt* Wilhelm Beier of 3./NJG 1, a successful intruder pilot who had earned the *Ritterkreuz* in October 1941 with 14 victories in 3./NJG 2, destroyed Halifax HR793 of 35 Sqn at Limbricht. (Beier was awarded the *Ritterkreuz*. In 1943 he claimed the last of his 38 night victories. At the end of the war he was undergoing night fighter training on the Me 262. He died in July 1977). 2 bombers were credited to *Major* Walter Ehle and *Ofw* Fritz Schellwat also destroyed 2 a/c, including Lancaster DS627 of 115 Sqn near Hechtel, Belgium. *Hptm* Ludwig Meister of I./NJG 4 claimed Stirling IV EF349 of 90 Sqn nr Cambrai, France. *Oblt* Rudolf Altendorf of the same *Gruppe* destroyed Halifax JB805 of 419 'Moose' Sqn RCAF at Péronnes-les-Binche and Wellington HE212 of 466 Sqn at Vollezele. *Hptm* Hoffmann, *Staffelkapitän* 4./NJG 5 from Greifswald destroyed a Halifax (possibly W7876 of 35 Sqn) over the Gilbach valley dams. On 17/18 November 1943 30-year old Ehle and his crew KIA when on finals to St. Trond, the flarepath was suddenly extinguished. Ehle's Bf 110G-4 G9+AC crashed near Horpmoel in Belgium. He had 39 victories.

92. 218 Sqn Stirling IIIs BK688 flown by F/Sgt W.A.M. Davis RAAF (all KIA) at 0222 and BF565 flown by P/O S.G. Allan RAAF (all KIA) at 0048 and Halifax II DT804 of 35 Sqn flown by F/O R. Hoos at 0143. (Hoos and 5 of his crew KIA. 1 PoW).

93. 58 by I./NJG 1, 43 by III./NJG 1, 24 by II./NJG 1 at St. Trond and at least 26 by IV./NJG 1.

94. At least 60 were credited to IV./NJG 1, 52 to I./NJG 1, 22 to II./NJG 1 plus 13 to 10 crews of NJG 3, 4 and 5 temporarily attached to the St. Trond *Gruppe*) and 20 to III./NJG 1.

95. Halifax II Series I (Special) ZA-V JD207 *V-Victor* was shot down by *Major* Werner Streib of I./NJG 1 over Holland on the night of 25/26 July 1943 when the target was Essen. S/L F.J. Hartnell-Beavis survived to become a PoW, 5 of his crew were killed and one evaded.

96. 4 of the losses can probably be attributed to IV./NJG 1 and 5 (4 Halifaxes 1 Lancaster) to *Major* Werner Streib *Gruppenkommandeur* of I./NJG 1 who with *Uffz* Helmut Fischer as his *Funker* was flying the first fully operational test sortie in a He 219A-0R2 Uhu (219009 G9+FB). Streib's victims included Halifax HR719 of 158 Sqn near Mook, Limburg at 0155 hrs, Lancaster DS647 of 115 Sqn nr. Mill at 0216 hrs and Halifax W7932 of 78 Sqn, which came down at 0222 hrs nr. Sambeek. The night's victories took his score to 54. Streib exhausted all his amunition and approached Venlo with fuel running low and several instruments u/s. On approach his canopy misted over and he was forced to fly on instruments. Streib lowered the electrically-operated flaps to the landing position and then lowered the undercarriage. The flaps did not lock down and they returned to the normal position. The He 219 hit the runway and disentegrated but remarkably, Streib and Fischer escaped almost uninjured.

97. Pfeiffer recalls: '*Oblt* Rudolf Sigmund congratulated me on my *Abschuss*. 'A Boeing is not easy to get,' he said. I appreciated his noble gesture. (Once, at 1600 hrs 22 March, I had contact with about 60 Boeings in the vicinity of Terschelling but the defensive fire was too strong and I did not dare to get too close. I fired a couple of bursts at one on the fringe but he did not go down). We always got on well and he was a fine fellow.' *Hptm* Rudolf Sigmund awarded the *Ritterkreuz* for 24 night victories and a B-17 and B-24 by day. Given command of III./NJG 3 on 15 August. KIA 3/4 October 1943 when his Bf 110 (G4+U7) was hit by German *flak*. 28 kills. *Fw* Hugo-Albert Bauer, *Funker* and *Uffz* Johannes-Max Dittrich, *Bordschütze* also KIA.

98. HE277 of 199 Sqn.

99. Of 408 and 76 Sqns.

100. Between 0122, when III./NJG 1 *Kommandeur Hptm* Egmont Prinz *zur* Lippe Weissenfeld destroyed Halifax JB790 of 408 Sqn nr Burgsteinfurt and 0237, when *Oblt* Geiger claimed Lancaster III ED584 of 49 Sqn at Luttenberg nr. Raalte with the loss of Sgt J. Hutchison and his crew.

101. Promoted to *Staffelkapitän* 8./NJG 1 after his 4th victory in May 1943.

102. Hans-Heinz Augenstein had joined 7./NJG 1 at the end of 1942 with his *Bordfunker Fw* Günter Steins. It was almost 6 months before Augenstein claimed his first kill, on 27/28 May 1943, when he destroyed 4 bombers in quick succession. *Uffz* Kurt Schmidt joined Augenstein's crew as Bordschütze in September 1943 as a precaution when the RAF night intruders began exacting an increasing toll on German nightfighters. Augenstein took command of 7./NJG 1 on 31 January 1944 and 12./NJG 1 came under his command a month later.

103. These included Halifax DK183 of 427 'Lion' Sqn RCAF by *Major* Leuchs, which cr near Den Hoorn on Texel Island at 0213 hrs.

104. ED840 of 156 Sqn, ED553 of 100 Sqn and ED785 of 49 Sqn.

105. 290 aircraft of 3, 4, 6 and 8 Groups bombed the Schneider armaments factory and the Breuil steelworks. 2 Halifaxes were lost. 26 Lancasters

of 8 Group were given a second target, the electrical-transformer station at Montchanin.

106. 262 Lancasters, 209 Halifaxes, 117 Stirlings, 105 Wellingtons and 12 Mosquitoes.

107. 17 Halifaxes, 9 Lancasters, 9 Wellingtons and 9 Stirlings. 38 of these losses were due to *Himmelbett* nightfighters operating mainly over the southern provinces of the Netherlands.

108. Stirling III BK712 of 218 Sqn flown by P/O W.G. Shillinglaw RAAF (all KIA).

109. All 7 crew were found dead in the wreckage.

110. A 100 Sqn Lancaster nr. Dinter, a 305 Sqn Wellington at Gramersweil, a 158 Sqn Halifax nr. Kaathoven, a 35 Sqn Halifax at Wamel, an u/i Halifax nr. Vechel and 2 408 Sqn Halifaxes nr. Lopik and Zeist.

111. Of 83 and 77 Sqns.

112. On 27/28 July *Ritterkreuzträger* Meurer, *Staffelkapitän* 3./NJG 1 claimed his 50th victory when he shot down a Mosquito flying a Ju 88R specially prepared for hunting Mosquitoes with much equipment removed to save weight and using GM1 (nitrous oxide, a power boosting device) to increase speed. Meurer was directed to Mosquito IV DZ458 of 139 Sqn flying at 8300m in a classic *Himmelbett* interception. Overtaking the Mosquito from below and behind with a surplus speed of 30-40k/ph, only one of his cannon fired a six-shell burst but his quarry exploded immediately. F/O E.S.A. Sniders-S/L K.G. Price, who had taken off from Wyton at 2305 hrs for a raid on Duisburg, survived to be taken prisoner.

113. A 619 Sqn Lancaster at Asten, a Wellington of either 166 or 429 'Bison' Sqn RCAF at Neerkant and a 460 Sqn RAAF Lancaster at Leuthlerheide for his 32nd-34th kills

114. A 305 Sqn Wellington E of Antwerp.

115. Wellington X HE326 of 466 Sqn, flown by P/O A.L. Ford (Ford & 2 others KIA. 1 PoW) nr. Haminkeln at 0133 hrs and Wellington X HZ312 of 429 'Bison' Sqn RCAF flown by 22-year old W/C J.L. Savard DFC RCAF (all KIA) nr. Rees/Niederrhein at 0135 hrs.

116. Stirling III BK656 of 15 Sqn flown by F/O J.V. Hawkins RNZAF (all KIA) by *Hptm* Dormann and Stirling I EF399 of 75 Sqn flown by F/Sgt K.A. Burbidge RNZAF (all KIA) by *Gruppenkommandeur Hptm zur* Lippe.

117. Halifax V DK225 of 427 'Lion' Sqn RCAF flown by F/L K. Webster at Oost-Mijzen, NE of Scharmerhorn at 0122 hrs. Webster & 5 crew KIA. 1 PoW.

118. *Himmelbett Nachtjagd* shot down 28 Main Force a/c. *Oblt* Gerhard Raht of 4./NJG 3 claimed Lancaster III ED595 of 7 Sqn E of Rilland, Zeeland. W/C R.G. Barrell DSO DFC* KIA when his parachute failed to deploy after he baled out. *Hptm* Werner Hoffmann, *Staffelkapitän* 4./NJG 5 destroyed a Lancaster (probably Lancaster III ED858 of 156 Sqn at Erkelenz) and Wellington HF594 at Dessel/Antwerp.

119. Egan and F/Sgt W. Miller RAAF were also captured. F/Sgt S. B. Elliott RAAF, navigator; Sgt J. Brown, WOp; Sgt H.A. Horrell, mid-upper-gunner and Sgt C.A. Britton were KIA.

120. ED528 was shot down at Bechtrup N of Lüdinghausen. Egan and the air bomber F/Sgt W. Miller RAAF survived and they too became PoWs. F/Sgt S.B. Elliott RAAF, navigator and Sergeants J. Brown, WOp, H.A. Horrell, mid upper gunner and C.A. Britton, rear gunner were KIA.

121. Including 3 Lancasters of 100, 101 and 103 Sqns by *Ofw* Karl-Heinz Scherfling.

122. Downing Stirling IV EF430 of 218 Sqn at 0126 at Empe, Halifax HR731 of 51 Sqn at 0200 hrs and a Lancaster, possibly ED831 of 9 Sqn at 0209, both of which disappeared into the Ijsselmeer off Edam.

123. *Fw* Heinz Huhn, who after his third pilot, *Oblt* Karl Heinz Völlkopf was KIA on 21 June decided he had had enough and he never flew again. For the remaining years of the war he served as Operations Officer at Bergen/Alkmaar and St. Trond airfields.

124. Halifax JB834 of 102 Sqn cr. in the North Sea at Breezand, 13 km S of Den Helder at 0240 hrs but this *Abschuss* was later credited to *Hptm* Jabs, *St Kpt* 11./NJG 1. It is highly probable that *Uffz* Pfeiffer's Halifax claim was subsequently turned down.

125. Lancaster III EE176.

126. 8 claimed destroyed by I./NJG 1 and 12 by II./NJG 1 over E Belgium. *Lt* Heinz-Wolfgang Schnaufer of the *Gruppen Stab* destroyed Lancaster LM323 of 97 Sqn at 0125 and 2 Halifaxes, HR812 of 35 Sqn at 0145 and DK137 of 76 Sqn at 0155. *Hptm* Hoffmann, *Staffelkapitän* 4./NJG 5 destroyed Stirling BK694 of 15 Sqn nr. Leopolsburg, Belgium at 0218.

127. On 15/16 July 8 miles SE of Rheims White and Allen, one of 6 Beaufighter crews providing Bomber Support for the Main Force of 165 Halifaxes whose target was the Peugeot Motor Works at Montbelliard, scored their first victory during an *Intruder* patrol to Juvincourt. Their victim was a Bf 110G-2 flown by *Major* Hubert Rauh who baled out safely. (Rauh later rose to command of II./NJG 4, was decorated with the *Ritterkreuz* (Knight's Cross) and survived the war with 31 night victories.

128. BB249 of 102 Sqn.

129. *Airborne Cigar (ABC)* was a device consisting of six scanning receivers and three transmitters designed to cover the VHF band of the standard German R/T sets and to jam 30-33 MHz (*Ottokar)* and later 38-42 MHz *(Benito.* R/T and Beam).

130. W4995.

131. Scrymgeour-Wedderburn and his crew flew two tours before the end of the war.

132. 13 Lancasters (4.4% of the force) including 1 flown by W/C John Deering Nettleton VC, CO of 44 (Rhodesia) Sqn (who had won the Victoria Cross for his leadership on the low level raid on Augsburg on 17 April 1942) were lost. An u/i night fighter shot his aircraft down over the Channel on the return.

133. NJG 1 and NJG 4 were credited with 18 *Himmelbett* kills. 5 bombers – all of them Halifaxes – were destroyed by I./NJG 1. Lancaster II DS690 of 115 Sqn flown by S/L The Hon. R.A.G. Baird shot down by *Hptm* Geiger, temporarily of I./NJG 4 and cr at La Cornette at 0210. (Baird, son of Viscount and Viscountess Stonehaven and 5 of his crew KIA. 1 PoW). *Oblt* Wilhelm Telge, *Staffelkapitän* 5./NJG 1 and Telsnig his Bordfunker shot down 2 Halifaxes – JD116 of 158 Sqn flown by S/L R.S. Williams DFC (Williams & 4 crew KIA. 2 PoW) NE of Gelsenkirchen and an u/i a/c that came down at Weissweiler at 0151 hrs.

CHAPTER FIVE

GOMORRAH

At the start of the Battle of the Ruhr 'Bomber' Harris had been able to call upon almost 600 heavies for Main Force operations and at the pinnacle of the Battle, near the end of May, more than 800 aircraft took part. Innovations such as Pathfinders to find and mark targets with their TIs and wizardry such as *Oboe,* which enabled crews to find them were instrumental in the mounting levels of death and destruction. Little it seemed could be done to assuage the bomber losses, which by the end of the campaign had reached high proportions. There was however, a simple but brilliant device, which at a stroke could render German radar defenses almost ineffective. On 24/25 July when Harris launched the first of four raids, code-named *Gomorrah,* on the port of Hamburg, Bomber Command was at last allowed to use *Window*. Although *Window* had been devised in 1942 its use had been forbidden until now for fear that the *Luftwaffe* would use it in a new *'Blitz'* on Great Britain. These strips of black paper with aluminium foil stuck to one side and cut to a length (30-cm by 1.5-cm) were equivalent to half the wavelength of the *Würzburg* ground and *Lichtenstein* airborne interception, radar. When dropped by aircraft in bundles of a thousand at a time at one-minute intervals, *Window* reflected the radar waves and 'snowed' the tubes. *Window* was carried in the 791 aircraft,[1] which set out for Hamburg.

W/O Eddie Wheeler, Lancaster WOP-AG, 97 Squadron, recalls:

> 'The target did not present too many difficulties in that most of the flight was over the sea and therefore we escaped the attentions of the *Flak* that was experienced during overland trips to places like the Ruhr. We took off at 2200 hrs with 8000 lb of bombs plus our target indicators. There was very little cloud but hazy visibility and at 17,000 ft we ran into the inevitable heavy *Flak* and released our load at 0105 hrs. Two minutes later there was the most violent explosion near the aiming point followed by a glow lasting for forty seconds. This was confirmed later by all the squadron crews at de-briefing. Many large fires and a pall of smoke were visible as we turned away for that journey back across the dreaded North Sea. Six hours after take off we touched down at Bourn at 4 am, another satisfactory night's work over. On this raid, first use was made of *Window* the metallic strips that were to cause such havoc with the German radar devices. The effect was noticeable because searchlights wandered all over the sky and the *Flak* was haphazard.'

Led by H2S PFF aircraft, 728 bombers rained down 2284 tons of HE and incendiaries in 50 minutes on the dockyards and city districts of Hamburg, creating a firestorm, which rose to a height of two and a half miles. Only 12 bombers[2] (just 1.5% of the force) were lost. The advantages enjoyed by Kammhuber's *Himmelbett* system, dependent as it was on radar, had been removed at a stroke. The German fighter pilots and their *Bordfunker* were blind. *Oblt* Wilhelm 'Wim' Johnen, *Staffelkapitän* 3/NJG 1 who was flying his Bf 110 in the direction of Amsterdam was one who was totally confused. Though the ground stations were giving the night fighters the positions of the bombers Johnen felt that the reports were hasty and nervous. No one knew exactly where the enemy was or what his objective would be. Radio reports contradicted themselves saying that the enemy was over Amsterdam and then suddenly west of Brussels and a moment later they were reported far out to sea. In desperation Johnen flew straight to Amsterdam but he found nothing. At 1000 ft his *Bordfunker* Facius reported the first enemy bomber on his *Li* set. Johnen swung the Bf 110 round on to the bearing in the direction of the Ruhr thinking he was bound to approach the stream. Facius continued to read out bearings of 'bombers' but they were travelling at very high speed and Johnen thought that they must be German fighters. Johnen lost his patience but the tense atmosphere was suddenly interrupted by a ground station calling, 'Hamburg, Hamburg. A thousand enemy bombers over Hamburg. Calling all night fighters, calling all night fighters. Full speed for Hamburg.' Johnen was speechless with rage. For half an hour he had been chasing an imaginary bomber stream while bombs were falling on Hamburg. It was a long way to the port and by the time Johnen got there Hamburg was blazing like a furnace – a horrifying sight'. Incredulously Johnen turned for home.[3]

Sgt Harry Barker, Stirling III bomb aimer in 218 'Gold Coast' Squadron the raid (during which the CO, W/C D.T. Saville DSO DFC and six of his crew fell victim to *Fw* Hans Meissner of 6./NJG 3 8 km NNW of Neumünster), recalls:

> 'The Hamburg raid was a horrendous event with vast areas set on fire. No doubt this was a clear signal that as a terror factor the Germans did not have it all their own way in bombing. If we had known the result of our effort I think we would have said that they started it. But we did not know. Our bosses sent us again in the 25th to Essen and on the 27th back to Hamburg.'

1st Lt John W. McClane Jr., B-24 Liberator navigator, 44th Bomb Group who flew a U.S. 8th Air Force daylight mission after the raids it appeared to him, 'that every section of this huge city was on fire. An ugly pall of smoke was blowing to the southwest. It looked the way that one might imagine Hell to be.'

Eric Phillips, a Stirling rear-gunner in 15 Squadron at Mildenhall, Suffolk recalls:

> 'The governor, Bomber Harris, addressed us. He said, 'I feel sure that a further two or three raids on Hamburg, then probably a further six raids on Berlin and the war will finish. Well done lads. You have flattened the Ruhr so you will be pleased to know you will not have to return there again.' But we did return to the Ruhr – the next night in fact. Because of bad weather over north Germany we went to Essen. There was full cloud over the target so pathfinders dropped a flare outside the target and the navigator gave the pilot a course on a timed run from the flare and dropped the bombs through cloud. The navigator asked me to watch out for the flare. Within seconds the flare was dropped and just as I reported this, a Ju 88 came in from the port quarter firing two cannons. My rear turret and the starboard outer engine were hit and set on fire. The pilot, thinking the starboard wing was also on fire, ordered bale out. Then the engine fell away from the aircraft and the order to bale out was cancelled. The Stirling lost height from 18,000 down to 8000. The bombs were dropped at this height in the Essen area and the aircraft then made a safe journey home with me keeping watch from the astrodome, as the rear turret was unserviceable.'[4]

During the Battle of Hamburg 24/25 July-3 August 1943 *Window* prevented about 100-130 potential Bomber Command losses.[5] Over four nights 3000 bombers dropped 10,000 tons of HE and incendiary bombs to totally devastate half of the city and kill an estimated 42,000 of its inhabitants. After the fourth raid on 2/3 August, a million inhabitants fled the city. Albert Speer, Minister of War Production, warned Hitler that Germany would have to surrender after another six of these bombing raids. Paralyzed by *Window*, *Nachtjagd* and the *Flakwaffe* were unable to offer any significant resistance. On average, British losses during the Hamburg raids were no more than 2.8%, whereas in the previous 12 months, losses had risen from 3.7 to 4.3%. *Window* neutralized the *Würzburg* GCI and GL radars and short range AI and completely destroyed the basis of GCI interception. Controlled anti-aircraft fire was almost completely disrupted at night and fixed box barrages only remained possible. The new British tactics also combined the use of PFF, the massed bomber stream and new target finding equipment (H2S). This combination resulted in total chaos to the German night fighter defense system, which was unable to obtain a true picture of the air situation or control the night fighters in the air. *Oblt* Dieter Schmidt, *Staffelkapitän*, 8./NJG 1, comments:

> 'On the screen of the *Lichtenstein* radar each such cloud of strips appeared as a target on opposite course and real targets could not be made out at all. Until we received better equipment, the only method we could use was the *Wilde Sau* (Wild Boar) tactic.'

To try to overcome the crisis caused by *Window*, in early July free-lance single-engined night-fighting was hastily introduced into *Nachtjagd* under the command of *Ritterkreuzträger Oberst* Hans-Joachim 'Hajo' Herrmann.[6] *Geschwader Herrmann* (renamed JG 300 in August 1943) was equipped with Fw 190s and Bf 109s thrown into the fray in *Wilde Sau* operations, a primitive form of night fighting in which the pilots tried to intercept and destroy the bombers over the target with the aid of searchlights and in the glare of fires burning below.

The first Wild Boar operation over Cologne on 3/4 July met with instant success and 12 bombers were claimed shot down. The force was expanded to three *Geschwader* with JG 300 based around Berlin, JG 301 defending the Frankfurt/Main area and JG 302 based in the Munich/Vienna area. A new divisional staff, JD30, was set up by *Oberst* Herrmann to control the Wild Boars and which operated independently from any other *Nachtjagd* or *Flak* authorities.[7] Of the record 290 *Nachtjagd* victories achieved in August 1943 only 48 were by the traditional *Himmelbett* method while the remaining 80% were credited to the Wild Boar units and to twin-engined crews operating in Wild Boar fashion.[8] Early Wild Boar successes were undoubtedly achieved by Herrmann's original band of ex-bomber pilots like *Oblt* Friedrich Karl 'Felix' or 'Nasen' ('Nose' on account of his aristocratic proboscis). Müller, a pre-war Lufthansa captain and now Operations Officer in JG 300 destroyed 29 *Viermots* and a Mosquito in just 52 sorties.[9] Herrmann claimed nine *Viermots* shot down in 50 sorties. Another *Wilde Sau* legend was *Oblt* Kurt Welter of 5./JG 301 who claimed 17 *Viermots* destroyed in only 15 sorties between September 1943 and early April 1944. The vast majority of the single-engined night fighter pilots though had no such tale of success to tell but lived on the reputation and glory of the skilful few. *Lt* Kurt Lamm, an experienced fighter pilot instructor who volunteered for Wild Boar duty in August 1943 recalls:

> 'I knew *Oblt* Kurt Welter from our instructing days at the Pilot Training School at Quedlinburg. We were both very experienced in flying on instruments. During August 1943 we were trained in the Wild Boar illuminated night fighting on the Me 109 and Fw 190. Kurt Welter was a brilliant pilot and soon after our posting to 5./JG 301 he scored his first kills in the Schleswig-Hamburg area. Only experienced pilots were able to achieve successes in the single-engined *Nachtjagd*, as became clear over the following months. They had to do the flying, navigating, calculating, reading the phosphorescent dials and digital clocks and interpreting the often strongly distorted and jammed information which came in over the R/T single-handedly. Moreover, they had to interpret the flares and waving searchlights correctly, combat the bombers, avoid being deluded by the glaring searchlights and finally, find an illuminated airfield and land with the last remaining drops of fuel. This all bordered on the limits of what our brain and body were able to cope with.'

Just six victories were credited to night-fighter crews on 9/10 August when 457 aircraft raided Mannheim. Four of these, three Halifaxes and a Lancaster were credited to four crews of the newly formed I./NJG 6 based at Schleissheim. In fact, Bomber Command lost nine aircraft (six Halifaxes and three Lancasters) or 2% of the force. Len Bradfield, bomb aimer of *J-Johnny* a 49 Squadron Lancaster flown by Johnny Moss reflects:

> 'When we first began flying ops in March 1943 losses were averaging 5% a night but we believed we were special and would survive. We were sorry other crews didn't make it back but we accepted that this was the way things were. We didn't think it could happen to us. We were an above average crew and expected to go to Pathfinders after our tour. On return from leave in August our spirits were high. Casualty figures had got significantly lower. It came as a sharp jolt when the crew we had trained with failed to return from the raid on Mannheim on 9/10 August. Next day, however, was beautiful. The NFT[10] went well. When we saw the fuel and bomb loading for we decided it would be a longish operation. After the flying supper we went to briefing. The target was Nürnburg with the MAN diesel factory at Furth being the aiming point. As it was in southern Germany the route was over lightly defended territory as much as possible.
>
> 'Climbing to a height of 21,000ft on track, we crossed the enemy coast at Le Treport, then flew on over France, directly to Nürnburg. '*Window*' was dropped at intervals on entering German airspace north of Trier. There was about 8/10ths cloud with tops at 14,000ft, which meant we would be silhouetted from above by the bright moonlight. We knew we were in trouble and we generally weaved to give a maximum sky search. All of a sudden, at about 0030hrs, near Wolfstein (south of Bad Kreuznach and NNW of Mannheim, where we could see the glow from our bombing the night before), we were attacked by a night fighter. Terry Woods, the mid upper gunner, spotted the incoming attack and shouted, ' Bandit 5 o'clock high!'
>
> 'I abandoned scrabbling about on the floor dropping '*Window*' and stood at my guns (being 6ft 1in I could work the turret better standing than sitting). Cannon and tracer fire hit our port wing and port outer engine, setting both on fire. Terry returned fire, followed by Ronnie Musson in the rear turret before he was put out of action because of the loss of the port outer, which produced hydraulic power for his turret.
>
> 'As our attacker broke away over the nose I got in a burst of 30 rounds from the front guns. Johnny started taking violent evasive action to blow out the fire. Sammy Small, the WOP/AG, was standing in the astrodome co-ordinating the defenses as we had practiced. Almost at once Ron Musson, the rear gunner, called out a second

attack. It began at 6 o'clock level, dead aft. All hell was let loose. Shells were exploding 'crunk' 'crunk' 'crunk' against the armored doors and the 4000lb cookie in the bomb bay. There was a smell of cordite and fire broke out in the bomb bay and mainplane. I dropped down to the bomb aimer's compartment and could see the fire raging. I told Johnny and he gave the order to jettison. I did. The attack was still in progress. The nightfighter was holding off at 600 yards, blazing away. He didn't close.

'The fire persisted and Johnny gave the order to bale out – 'Abracadabra, Jump, Jump!'

'From beginning to end it had lasted perhaps 1-2 seconds but it seemed like slow motion. The order was acknowledged, except for the rear gunner. I got my parachute on and pulled up, twisted and dropped the front escape hatch in order to bale out. Ernie Roden, flight engineer and David Jones, navigator were coming down the bomb aimer's bay. I dived out and fell clear and delayed opening my chute until I was below the cloud. I could still see red and yellow tracer flying by. It is possible that Ernie and David were hit when they baled out. As I broke cloud I could see several small fires, which reinforces the idea that the *B-Baker* exploded. On the ground I chucked my lucky woolly gollywog away. It was nothing personal (I had carried him on all my 18 ops) but I thought it had failed me. He hadn't because later, when I was captured, when I asked about my crew I was told, *Fünf Tot* (five dead). Johnny Moss was the only other survivor, probably blown clear when the Lancaster exploded. A *Luftwaffe* NCO told me three four-engined bombers had been brought down in a 10-km circle by his unit. At *Dulag Luft* interrogation center I thought about the attack and concluded that a professional, a real 'tradesman' had shot us down.'[11]

By now Halifax flight engineer Jim Sprackling had turned 21 and had been commissioned as a pilot officer. He and P/O Bill Lucas' crew had completed ten operations in 10 Squadron without turning back once and they were considered an experienced crew. This experience affected their next operation on 12/13 August, which was a long one for 321 Lancasters and 183 Halifaxes to Milan, Italy while 152 aircraft of 3 and 8 Groups went to Turin:

'All the fuel tanks were full and most of the bomb racks loaded with incendiaries, which, being made of magnesium, didn't weigh very much. But again, tight on fuel with the expectation of landing on the south coast to refuel. In fact some crews were to fly straight on to Malta and then to North Africa. Half of 10 Squadron had done this a few months before, expecting to bomb up and take another target on the way home. They didn't. Montgomery held on to them and they stayed out there for a year or more. At this time some bored army officers from the artillery regiments volunteered to see what a bombing raid was like. *V-Victor's* crew acquired one of these chaps. It was doubtful if he had flown before but he was put in the rumble seat next to the pilot and told not to touch anything.

'The route out involved crossing the French coast before dark. We were conned that the coast would be cloud covered and with *Window* to upset the Jerry radar there would be no bother. There was cloud, about five miles inland. Also, we were going through at a relatively low level of 10,000 ft to save some fuel by climbing very slowly. The ack-ack fire made a good firework display, seeming to come up in front of the aircraft and curve away astern. No one appeared to be hit and we were soon clear and in cloud cover. We climbed clear of the cloud and carried on south. The Alps was a beautiful sight in the moonlight above all the cloud. Mt Blanc was a pinpoint en-route and Len, the bomb aimer, called when we were clear overhead, Jock then called up that we were two minutes late and could he have another couple of mph? The Army chap commented that we were lucky to be there the same day let alone to be within two minutes.

'All went well. Milan was clear so a lot of Italians lost their sleep and then off home. On the way back Paddy, the wireless operator, announced that he was going to the Elsan, (a W/C bucket in the rear of the plane). When he got there he called up that the so-and-so ground crew had been using it and not emptied it. Bill said, 'Well open the rear door and empty it but be careful not to fall out!' We felt the rush of air as the door was opened. Then another call from Paddy, 'Navigator, where are we?'

'Just about over Geneva'.

'Well I've dropped the bucket!'

'On reaching the UK we landed at Ford in West Sussex. They made us welcome, fed and watered us, refuelled the aircraft and, after a few hours' rest, we flew back to base. The next week was spent in local flying and flying crews down to Ford to pick up aircraft that had been damaged and needed repair after the Milan operation.'

Milan was considered a successful raid and two Halifaxes and one Lancaster were lost. Turin was hit by 112 Stirlings, 34 Halifaxes and six Lancasters and two Stirlings failed to return.[12] Sgt Harry Barker, Stirling III bomb aimer and F/Sgt Arthur Louis Aaron, pilot, both in 218 Gold Coast Squadron, were two of the airmen who flew on the operation:

'Eight and a half hours with spectacular views of the Alps at 15,000 ft with Mont Blanc looking much the same height and glistening in the moonlight. There was very little opposition but F/Sgt Arthur Aaron's aircraft was shot up and he received severe injuries. His bomb aimer flew the crew on to North Africa and they landed at Bone. Aaron insisted on carrying out the landing and he later died of his wounds. His bravery earned him the VC. On 16 August we returned to Turin but on the return trip we had to land at Ford on the Sussex coast due to fog at Downham.'

On 17 August the USAAF attacked the German aircraft industry for the first time by day and that night, 17/18 August 596 heavies of Bomber Command raided the V-2 rocket site at Peenemünde.[13] W/O Eddie Wheeler, WOP-AG, 97 Squadron, Bourn, Cambridgeshire, recalls:

'On 17 August we were warned that a special target was to be attacked that night, that we would not be allowed off camp during the day and no outside telephone calls would be allowed. Briefing for only three crews was at 1800 hrs under a great veil of secrecy. Entering the Operations Room, we anxiously scoured the room for a hint of this 'special' target. A sheet obscured the route map until the CO arrived. When the unveiling revealed the target, we were none the wiser as it identified Peenemünde, which meant absolutely nothing to any of us. We had never hard of it!

'The Intelligence Officer rose to give his briefing and said that the target on the Baltic Coast was probably the most important target ever to be attacked. Whilst not revealing it was a site for the development and production of V-1 flying bombs and V-2 rockets he said that advanced radar equipment was its main function. Three aiming points, including scientist and production worker billets had to be destroyed totally – if not tonight, then tomorrow night and the night after if necessary. We were told that Peenemünde could alter the whole course of the war and had to be destroyed regardless of losses. This did nothing to encourage us especially when we learnt that there would be no cloud and a full moon and the attack would be from as low as 12,000 ft or lower. These conditions would be ideal for the German night fighters so the RAF would adopt 'spoof' tactics by sending a small number of Mosquitoes to Berlin, giving the impression that that was the night's target for the main force. Berlin was high on the RAF priority list and the Germans were very sensitive to attacks on their capital. It was hoped that their fighters would be concentrated nearer to Berlin and that by the time it was established that Peenemünde was to be the main target, the first two waves of bombers would have completed their task and been on the way home. The third wave provided by 5 Group could, however, expect to have a hot time.

'We took off at 2108 hrs and climbed to 18,000ft. Our primary target was the scientists' quarters. The whole force would be directed by a Master-Bomber. Group Captain John H. Searby of 83 Squadron at Wyton was selected for this task and he was to fly over the target for the whole attack giving a commentary and shifting the attack as was necessary. Forty minutes could elapse from first to last aircraft on target. Some aircraft were fitted with *Oboe* ground controlled radar, other PFF aircraft with H2S but the conditions would allow for full visual attacks, providing smoke did not obscure the aiming points. From 08°E we started to throw out *Window*.

'We began to lose height as we approached Rugen Island and saw many aircraft around us in the almost daylight conditions. Fortunately none were hostile so hopefully the Mosquitoes who had preceded us by one hour had lured the night fighters to the Berlin area. We sighted the target clearly at 11,700 ft. The enemy in the hope of thwarting the attacking forces had already started a smoke screen. Light *Flak* started piping up from the target zone as we went in with our green TIs and 7500 lb bomb load. Peter reported direct hits on the living quarters and just then we suffered a direct hit from *Flak*. Johnny shouted that we were going round in circles and could not fly straight and level. If the state of affairs could not be rectified we would have to consider baling out – a prospect which did not appeal one bit. To jump with the possibility of either landing in the sea or amid a hail of bombs just wasn't on. Bill beckoned me to follow him down the fuselage and with great trepidation I did so, regretting the fact that I was putting distance between me and my parachute. Bill indicated the trimming and aileron cables that had been severed by the impact. He busied himself with lengths of nylon cord and then Johnny said that he had recovered control of the aircraft. By now the target was a sea of flame and high explosions and we were intent on returning from whence we came with all speed.

'The German defenses were well alerted by now and fighters would be re-deployed from the Berlin area without delay. We felt sorry for the last wave of bombers entering the scene and who would have to take the full brunt of attacks in ideal night-flying conditions. Several aircraft were seen going down in flames. Seven hours after take-off we had the welcoming sight of Bourn and we hoped that the target had been well and truly plastered and that it would not be necessary to return again the next night, when the Luftwaffe would be ready and waiting to wreak their revenge.

'Initial reports that morning indicated that the raid had been a complete success achieved through the element of surprise, the decoy raid on Berlin and the sheer audacity of operating under a full moon and clear skies. Out of the total of 606 aircraft assigned, 44-engined bombers and one Mosquito were lost (6.7%) and 32 suffered damage. In the daylight reconnaissance 12 hours after the attack, photographs revealed 27 buildings in the northern manufacturing area destroyed and 40 huts in the living and sleeping quarters completely flattened. The foreign labor camp to the south suffered worst of all. The whole target area was covered in craters. It was inconceivable that the site could ever operate again and at least we had gained valuable time against V-1 and V-2 attacks on London and our impending second front assault forces. This raid probably gave us our most satisfaction against all other targets attacked.'

Although the ground controllers were fooled into thinking the bombers were headed for Stettin and a further 'spoof' by Mosquitoes aiming for Berlin drew more fighters away from the Peenemünde force, forty Lancasters, Halifaxes and Stirlings (6.7% of the force) were shot down. In the wild melée over the target, *Nachtjagd* actually claimed 33 aircraft, total claims from the Peenemünde force amounting to 38 victories.

A deadly new weapons system was introduced on this night. Two crews flying Bf 110s fitted with *Schräge Musik*[14] found the bomber stream and destroyed six bombers. This device, invented by an armorer, Paul Mahle of II./NJG 5, comprised two 20mm MG FF cannon mounted behind the rear cockpit bulkhead of the Bf 110 and Ju 88 night fighters and was arranged to fire forwards and upwards at an angle of between 70 and 80°. *Uffz* Hölker of 5./NJG 5 shot down two bombers and *Lt* Peter Erhardt destroyed four. Towards midnight, 13 II./NJG 1 crews left St. Trond for the *Gruppe*'s first Wild Boar mission of the war. They returned with claims for 13 victories, mainly over Peenemünde, nine of which were consequently confirmed by the *Reichsluftfahrtministerium (RLM or Reich* Air Ministry). These included five *Schräge Musik* kills by *Lt* Dieter Musset and his *Bordfunker Ogefr* Helmut Hafner of the 5th *Staffel*, which were their first (and last) victories of the war. Whilst attacking their sixth bomber of the night Musset's cannon jammed and their Bf 110G-4[15] was subjected to ferocious return fire. Wounded, Musset and his *Bordfunker* baled out to the north of Güstrow.[16]

Nachtjagd also successfully employed *Zahme Sau* (Tame Boar) free-lance or Pursuit Night Fighting tactics for the first time since switching its twin-engined night-fighting crews from the fixed *Himmelbett* system. *Zahme Sau* had been developed by *Oberst* Victor von Lossberg of the Luftwaffe's Staff College in Berlin and was a method used whereby the (*Himmelbett*) ground network by giving a running commentary, directed its night fighters to where the *Window* concentration was at its most dense. The tactics of *Zahme Sau* took full advantage of the new RAF methods. Night fighters directed by ground control and the 'Y' navigational control system[17] were fed into the bomber stream (which was identified by tracking H2S *transmissions)* as early as possible, preferably on a reciprocal course. The slipstream of the bombers provided a useful indication that they were there. Night fighters operated for the most part individually but a few enterprising CO's led their *Gruppen* personally in close formation into the bomber stream, with telling effect (*Geschlosser Gruppeneinsatz*). Night-fighter crews hunted on their own using SN-2 AI radar[18], Naxos *7* (FuG 350)[19] and Flensburg (FuG 227/1).[20]

'SN-2' recalls *Oblt* Dieter Schmidt, *Staffelkapitän*, 8./NJG 1:

'Was a great improvement on *Lichtenstein*, which worked on a wavelength of 53 cm, had a search angle of 24° and a maximum range of 4000 meters. SN-2 worked on a wavelength of 330 centimeters had a search angle of 120° and a maximum range of 6500 meters! With this equipment, wide-ranging nightfighting, independently of the target being attacked and dependent solely on general reports of the situation and one's own navigation, again became possible. For the individual crews, *Zahme Sau* frequently involved more than one sortie per night. Almost invariably landings were away from base; such as take-off at Laon, an approach via Osnabrück to Frankfurt and landing at Mainz-Finthen, or take-off at Laon, attack over Berlin, *Abschuss* of a departing bomber after three hours flight and landing after three and a half hours at Erfurt. (The usual airborne time was only three hours). The early finding and infiltrating of the bomber stream, whose progress was soon marked by *Abschüsse* of other crews but occasionally also by turning-point markers or the dropping of incendiaries was decisive. Now, during all major attacks, all available nightfighters were whenever possible assembled over radio or light beacons to be directed early on into the bomber stream. Although there was no traffic control at these assemblies – an unthinkable procedure in peacetime – resulting losses were rare.'

In what was to be his first and last *Geschlossener Gruppeneinsatz* using the Y-system, *Oblt* Heinz-Wolfgang Schnaufer, *Staffelkapitän* of 12./NJG 1 and three other Bf 110s of the unit took off from Leeuwarden airfield. Soon after take off

Schnaufer and *Ofw* Karl-Heinz Scherfling had to break off the operation, as they suffered engine failures. Schnaufer made an emergency landing at Wittmundhafen in NW Germany and the *Flak* defenses shot at him. It was a bad omen for what was to come for the crews of IV./NJG 1. Two other Bf 110s flown by *Fw* Heinz Vinke and 22-year old *Uffz* George 'Schorsch' Kraft pressed on to intercept what they thought were RAF heavies. They arrived north of Schiermonnikoog around 2300 hrs. Ten of 141 Squadron's Beaufighter VIfs patrolled German night fighter bases in Germany and Holland this night. One of them was flown by the CO, W/C J.R.D. 'Bob' Braham DSO DFC** and his radar operator, F/L 'Jacko' Jacobs DFC[21] whose Beaufighter VIf was fitted with the *Serrate* homer.[22] Braham bounced Kraft's Bf 110[23] and shot it down in flames. *Uffz* Rudolf Dunger, radar operator, baled out into the sea and was rescued two hours later by a German *Flak* trawler but Kraft's body was washed ashore four weeks later on the Danish coast near Heidesande (Esbjerg), where he was interred. Kraft had shot down 15 Allied bombers in a period of only seven months.

Immediately after shooting down Kraft's Bf 110 Braham got onto the tail of the second machine of IV./NJG 1[24] flown by *Fw* Heinz Vinke, a night fighter *Experte* with over 20 victories. *Uffz* Johann Gaa, the gunner, spotted the attacker and Vinke immediately turned away sharply. The German crew had already assumed that they had shaken off the Beaufighter, yet only moment's later Braham's attack from below and behind caught the German crew completely by surprise. Vinke's control column was shot out of his hands and the burning aircraft plunged down out of control with a severely injured gunner. Vinke and *Fw* Karl Schödl, his radar and radio operator, who was injured, baled out. Landing in the North Sea Vinke inflated his one-man dinghy. While he floated under the star-lit expanse of the night sky he was appalled to hear the desperate calls for help from his friend Schödl. This continued for quite some time but Vinke was unable to do anything to rescue his friend, who drowned. Next day, a ship sailed past quite close to Vinke's dinghy but the crew did not notice him. Only 18 hours after he was shot down by Braham and Gregory he was picked up by a Dornier Do 18 floatplane of the German ASR service. The bodies of both Gaa and Schödl were never recovered. Rudi Dunger crewed up with *Fw* Vinke and with their gunner, *Uffz* Walter they became a most successful team. After scoring 27 night kills Vinke was awarded the *Ritterkreuz* on 19 September 1943 and the Oak Leaves followed in April 1944.[25]

The third Bf 110 lost to a Beaufighter crew of 141 Squadron on 17/18 August was a Bf 110[26] of 9./NJG 1 flown by *Hptm* Wilhelm Dormann, a pre-war Lufthansa pilot with 14 victories, which was later credited to Flying Officers H.E. 'Harry' White and Mike Seamer Allen, their second victory of the war. Dormann's radar operator, *Obfw* Friedrich Schmalscheidt was killed when his parachute did not fully open.[27] Shortly after midnight White and Allen intercepted a Bf 110 of 12./NJG 1 flown by *Lt* Gerhard Dittmann, a 20-year-old pilot and his radar operator, *Uffz* Theophil Bundschuh, also 20 years of age. After raking the 110 with gunfire it plunged down steeply.[28] For once the tables had been turned. It had been a very black night for the night fighters from Leeuwarden.

Flying back to the General Staff HQ in East Prussia on 20 August *Generalleutnant* Josef 'Beppo' Schmid learned that the Chief of Staff, *Generaloberst* Hans Jeschonnek had died overnight (he had committed suicide by shooting himself because Hitler and Göring held him responsible for the deterioration of the Luftwaffe). Schmid therefore approached Göring directly with his proposals that the conduct of the entire defense of the *Reich* both by day and night should be placed in one pair of hands and that France, the territory of *Luftflotte 3,* should be incorporated into the defense of the *Reich.* He seems also to have convinced Göring that he was the man for the task. In any event Kammhuber was in disfavour because his night fighting system showed few signs of success. Göring gave Schmid command of *Fliegerkorps XII* on 15 September. Kammhuber remained *General der Nachtjagd* for two months longer before departing to command *Luftflotte 5* in Norway.[29]

With Kammhuber's departure the title of *General der Nachtjagd* was dropped, the relevant functions being taken over by a newly instituted *Inspekteur der Nachtjagd*, subordinated to the *General der Jagdflieger*. This was a great blow to the prestige of night fighting and resulted, according to *General* Schmid, in considerable neglect of night fighting interests. The change in the night fighter command had immediate repercussions. Schmid described the Divisional Operations Rooms, as they were when he took over command as 'Richard Wagner theatres.' They were, he said:

> 'Oversized, overstaffed, over-equipped and utilizing every device of electrical engineering, optics and cartography for the sole purpose of fixing the position of the enemy and one friendly night fighter on large scale maps, they were built almost as an end to themselves. They ceased completely to function when the British tactics of flying in a narrow stream deprived the *Himmelbett* system of its effectiveness.'

Schmid reduced the personnel of each Division by 75 officers, 14 officials, 3290 NCOs and men and 2630 female employees. On 1 October, in an extensive re-organisation *Fliegerkorps XII* was split into three separate commands: *Jagdkorps I, II* and *7.* This signalled the end of unified night fighter control and the adverse effect on night fighter efficiency was so great that Schmid, in command of *Jagdkorps I*, had no difficulty in obtaining the re-subordination of *7 Jagddivision* on 1 February 1944.

Since the introduction of *Window* few of the traditional *Himmelbett* GCI patrols were flown. The twin-engined German night-fighters thus released from GCI activity were employed at first on *Objektnachtjagd* (target interception). The *Jagd-division* carried out control, all the aircraft of a *Geschwader* operating as a unit, with no limitation of the area of activity. High power light beacons and radio beacons were set up and used as assembly and waiting points. At the same time single engined night-fighters were also employed in fairly small numbers on *Objektnachtjagd*.

The simultaneous operation of several bomber streams, the jamming of the *Lichtenstein* AI and the Mosquito screening of the bomber formations resulted in the splitting up of German night fighter forces and reduced (it) to a minimum the chances of success of individual *Zahme Sau* tactics. Indeed, owing to the inability to overcome RAF jamming, the *Zahme Sau* technique never reached its full development but it was used to great effect during the Battle of Berlin and remained the main night attack tactic until the end of the war. *General* Schmid thought that had the *Jagdschloss Panorama* ground radar set been perfected early enough, events might have taken a different course. Schmid concluded that in view of the high standard of RAF Bomber Command tactics, the Germans acted correctly in not depending on one method of night fighting alone but in employing the different methods singly and in combination in accordance with the situation. I.e. *Zahme Sau* against the massed bomber stream, *Himmelbett* against loose formations or single aircraft, *Objektnachtjagd* in the case of surprise attacks and against Mosquito formations.

On 23/24 August Berlin was the target for 710 Lancasters, Halifaxes and Stirlings and 17 Mosquitoes when Bomber Command suffered its greatest loss of aircraft in one night in the war so far. For W/O Eddie Wheeler, WOP-AG in 97 Squadron at Bourn, Cambridgeshire, it was his first trip to the 'big one':

> 'It meant a long trip over heavily defended enemy territory and the Berlin defenses were savage in the protection of the great city which, the *Nazis* had sworn would never be subjected to air bombardment. What a long way I had come since those dark days in 1940 when there appeared to be no salvation from the gloom and here we were attacking the German capital in strength and talking more and more of an invasion of Europe. This was to be my 57th operation, could I survive to see that sixtieth operation? It did seem to be inviting the inevitable with each further raid, so many crews had not even reached double figures and with so many more aircraft involved, losses mounted so that the likelihood of aircrews surviving 12 raids was still minimal. For this trip, we had an additional crewmember – a F/Sgt Penny who came as second pilot for the experience. Apart from the heavy *Flak* and searchlight activity, the flight was uneventful, far less frightening than any trip to the Ruhr and after bombing from 18,000 ft we were back at base in six hours 35 minutes.'

F/Sgt Arthur 'Spud' Taylor, Stirling observer in *M for Mother* of 90 Squadron at Wratting Common noted in his diary:

> '23.8.43. Berlin tonight. Over 800 kites went, all four-engined. Not much trouble on the way there. The visibility was good so we could watch the attack as it developed. In six short minutes of the raid the place was glowing with fires and enormous flashes were lighting up the ground. Searchlights and *Flak* not very intense but bags of fighters. Making our final run-up on to a marker we were suddenly attacked from very close range by a Dornier. She scored several hits on our kite but Len and John kept their heads and brought her down. Once in flames, the Dornier was picked up and finished off by searchlights and *Flak*. Bombed dead central on a marker and got out like bats out of hell. Counted six of our kites going down in flames in the short time we were over the target. Over the target there was a plane circling around the whole time with one of the Pathfinder laddies making a continual running commentary telling us where to bomb and cheering like mad whenever we scored a hit. This fellow[30] is called the Master of Ceremonies. They use him on all the big raids. On the way back we got quite considerably off track crossing the Baltic. There were doubts about us even reaching England. Also, one engine packed up for a while. We threw out quite a lot of things though. My guns, ammo, etc and just made Coltishall with 80 gallons. We were flying about 8 hrs 40. Damn tired.'[31]

P/O Jim Sprackling in P/O Bill Lucas' Halifax crew in 10 Squadron recalls that:

> 'Berlin, the 'Big City' in RAF jargon was another long flog. Mostly we carried an incendiary bomb load and only three HE bombs – only 4500lbs – although all the bomb stations were full with either cases of 4lb magnesium fire bombs or 25lb phosphorus bombs. The route to the target was mostly uneventful, across the North Sea to cross the coast between Bremen and what was left

of Hamburg. Then to the target, which was brilliantly illuminated by the Pathfinders and a great area of the city seemed to be burning. Some 700 aircraft were on the raid and 4 Group were the last wave. All aircraft had to cross the target before turning for home. The powers-that-be had discovered that if the turn was made over the target then the bombing pattern gradually crept back, as crews tended to release their bombs as soon as the edge of the fire area was reached, resulting in the later waves bombing before they reached the target. Also, now the Master Bomber would direct the attack at a specific area of the target required.

'Soon after leaving the target I spotted a small aircraft astern and slightly above. At first sight it looked like a Mosquito but as it started overtaking us both Digger and I were sure it was a Me 110. It obviously hadn't seen us. We were probably in a blind spot under his nose cone; or else he was creeping up on another aircraft. We debated whether to lie doggo in case shooting at him attracted attention and if our gunners missed, then the Me 110 would make short work of a Halifax. However he presented such a tempting target, well within the range of the gunners' .303 Brownings, both gunners opened up together and immediately their tracer bullets flew in all directions off the target, which promptly dived away and was lost to sight. No further sign was seen of it or any other enemy action, other than the odd searchlight and we soon cleared the coast between Kiel and Hamburg and set course home across the North Sea. We of course reported the fighter engagement at debriefing and were told that other crews had reported seeing a Me 110 going down. Next day we were credited 'a kill' by Bomber Command. This finished our ops for August and it was also the last time that Halifaxes went to Berlin. After, they were detailed to secondary targets to decoy the German defenses while the Lancasters, with their bigger bomb loads, went to Berlin.[32] We had now completed 13 operations and were among the most experienced crews on the Squadron. At this time Bomber Command were suffering losses of 5%on each operation, i.e. the whole force in 20 operations. However the worst losses were in crews during their first five ops and as a crew became more experienced so the chance of survival increased.'

Sgt Harry Barker of 218 'Gold Coast' Squadron in P/O John Overton's crew also went to Berlin:

'It was of course heavily defended and we had our hands full. We dropped our bombs and then the rear gunner shouted that a fighter was attacking us. He fired back and we were aware that we had been hit. The empty paper packets, which had contained the *Window* anti radar strips, had been set on fire and Benny our wireless operator seized a fire extinguisher and he and Alf [Aubrey], the flight engineer set about the flames. They managed to put out the fire and then Benny admitted that he had been hit. Frank [Dallman], the rear gunner also called on the intercom that he had been hit in the leg. In the meantime I had moved from the bombing position into the front turret to prepare for further attacks. John flew brilliantly and got us away from the target area, which was a huge mass of smoke and flames with searchlights by the dozen and anti aircraft gunfire to light up the sky. As soon as things quietened down I went back into the centre of the aircraft to help with the injured crew. There were stretcher-like beds and Benny lay on one with Frank on the other. Benny had received a bullet or shell splinter in his back and was beginning to feel poorly. Frank had two bullets in his leg and his flying boot was full of blood. We made them as comfortable as possible and proceeded to get home without any more aggro. I must admit to feeling decidedly dubious about the certainty of getting back to base on this occasion. Whilst I had been in the bomb aimer's position, I had been aware of unusual crack and bangs around me and later I found a couple of bullets on the deck which had ricocheted off the interior of the cabin and ended up harmlessly beside me. Our return route was north to the Baltic and then west to the Norfolk coast. We landed safely and the medics took care of Benny and Frank. Two days later three of us went to Littleport hospital to see them and we were pleased to find them in reasonable shape. Benny's injuries were more serious because of the damage to his lung. Frank's leg healed fairly well but he spent two or three months off on sick leave and did not return to rejoin the crew until November.'[33]

On the night of 27/28 August when 674 heavy bombers attacked Nürnburg *Lt* Norbert Pietrek, pilot of a of 2./NJG 4 Bf 110F-4[34] was ordered to take off for a *Zahme Sau* pursuit sortie. Free-lancing single-engined Wild Boars often obtained successes in good visibility which favoured searchlight operations. Sometimes, when twin-engined night fighters were illuminated by searchlights in the hectic and whirling chaos over the German cities under attack a twin-ruddered Bf 110 was mistaken for a Halifax or Lancaster and paid the price, as Pietrek recalls:

'The Tommies were attacking Nürnberg. *Uffz* Paul 'Paulchen' ['Little Paul'] Gärtig was still flying with me[35] together with my rear gunner Moritz. We were off at full throttle in the direction of Nürnberg and after about an hour we were in the vicinity of the city. The weather had created excellent defensive conditions, a so-called 'shroud'. This was a thin, high-level cloud layer on which, when illuminated by searchlights and fires from below, one could see the attacking Tommies crawling like bugs across a bed sheet. As we arrived we could see that the attack had already begun. A horrid-beautiful and colorful spectacle was presented to us. Seeking searchlights, exploding shells of the heavy *Flak*, multi-colored tracer of the medium *Flak*, the brilliant white, red, yellow and green 'Christmas trees' of the attacking Tommies, the explosions of the bombs below, the expanding rings around an exploding heavy mine, the bright white lanes of igniting incendiaries and the terrible multi-colored fires raging in the city. And added to all this, Tommies which had been shot down by night fighters going down in flames and the fires as they crashed. All very fascinating but bitter for those in this hell below. A spectacle which no painting could ever portray.

'The searchlights had caught a Tommy and they waited for a night fighter to shoot him down. The *Flak* was only permitted to fire to 4000 meters. We arrived and I made for the Tommy twisting about in the searchlight cone. Range 800 meters, 600 meters, 400 meters. But one went much closer in order to conserve ammunition and be more certain of a hit and that was a range of less than 50 meters! Then I was suddenly fired at from behind. A burst hit my starboard engine and I had to feather it. What rotten luck. Damn it! I had my fifth night *Abschuss* certain in my sights and then this had to happen! Moritz said it was a *Wilde Sau*! The 'Wild Boar' was the single-engined nightfighter unit of *Major* Herrmann, stationed at Bonn-Hangelar. The pilots were from bomber and reconnaissance units, which had been disbanded and converted to Bf 109 and Fw 190 fighters. Whether this fellow had, after firing at me, realized that it was not a four-engined Tommy but a twin-engined night fighter he had attacked, or whether he had fired at a range of 600-800 meters at the Tommy in the searchlights before me, remained a mystery. I think it had been the latter. No more hunting now and off I went to find a place for a single-engined landing.

'Now the weather conditions were not favourable for me for the 'shroud' hid my view of the ground. On feathering the engine I turned off to the west, for the port engine proved too powerful until I trimmed the kite and now I did not know my position. I asked Paulchen for a QDM to Stuttgart. The machine maintained height well on one engine and the new trimmers on the rudders made it easy to maintain course. I could therefore look forward to a single-engined landing with confidence. After all, it would be my fourth (the third by night) and it would not be the last by a long chalk. Then suddenly I saw an airfield through a gap in the cloud almost directly below me, so power off and down. From only 2500 meters I could clearly see flying activity only there was no sight of a Morse identification beacon. Had that become unserviceable? Paulchen was continuously firing the colors of the night plus a red, indicating an aircraft in emergency, until the trigger of his signal pistol failed and I circled, losing height.

'The landing as such presented no problem for me. The only snag was that the starboard engine operating the hydraulic system had failed and with it the extension and retraction of undercarriage and flaps. I could extend both pneumatically but then no longer retract. At a strange airfield by night one is not familiar with local conditions and one could make considerable errors in one's judgement. Get too high or too low with unpredictable consequences for survival. As I was responsible not only for my own life but also for that of my crew I decided on a belly landing, which would cause no problems but I did not want to interfere with the flying activities, especially landings, so I aimed 50 meters to the right and had Moritz continuously firing reds. We were still 30 meters high and 500 meters from the threshhold when the runway controller fired two reds at us, meaning that we should go round again. But that was quite impossible on one engine. We were just past the threshhold. I eased my straps a little and about to switch off the ignition of the port engine when there was a terrible crash and my head struck against the reflector sight, which broke off. I jettisoned the cabin roof at once and I found myself up to my belly in gravel and the tail unit of my machine hurtling forward above my head. The port engine and wing were torn off at the first impact. At the second the starboard wing with the stationary engine folded vertically upwards, then the third impact followed and then there was silence. Only the cockpit was left and that lay on the tip of a heap of gravel. I released my straps, jumped down the heap of gravel and drew my signal pistol, which was always loaded with a red, when I saw Moritz standing beside the pilot's seat shouting, 'The boy has gone!'

'No, here I am,' I replied and fired off my signal pistol. Then we got Paulchen out of the cockpit. He had struck his head against the radio equipment and had received a gaping wound like a parting. An ammunition drum from the rearward facing machine gun had been torn free and had also struck his right upper arm and fractured it. Moritz had only sprained the little finger of his left hand. My collision with the reflector sight had punctured my right eyelid and if I pulled it down a little, I could see through it. It could have been much, much worse. Everyone who looked at the wreckage later could hardly believe that the three of us were alive. It had been particularly fortunate that the still hot port engine, together with the wing and the fuel tanks, had broken away at the first impact; otherwise the kite could have caught fire and then what would have happened to us? I prefered not to think about.

'Having got Paulchen out of the machine we plodded towards the sick quarters. Reaching the first building, I went down to the air raid shelter in order to report to the operations room. Women and children – dependants of the station personnel – sat in the cellar and cried out in alarm as I entered. At first I did not understand why. Then I looked down at myself and realized that my face and overalls were covered in blood from my injured eyebrow. We went to the sick quarters where we got first aid for our injuries. There we discovered that we were in Kitzingen, an airfield which was closed for night landings because of repair work on the runway. We knew that, for it was mentioned at each briefing but how was I to recognize it from above with no Morse recognition beacon operating? Then we boarded the ambulance which would take us to hospital in Würzburg but before we left I had us driven to the operations room in order to phone my unit in Florennes and inform them what had happened. The commander of the night fighter school at Kitzingen must have heard and he raged at me.

'What do you mean by landing here when you know that it is closed for night landings!'

'I replied, 'Because some idiot had turned on the airfield lighting and switched off the recognition beacon.'

'That idiot was me!'

'You said it!' I replied. 'How could I in my situation, urgently needing an emergency landing ground and happening to see one, know that it is Kitzingen when the beacon is not operating? It could be any open field whose beacon had gone unserviceable for some unknown reason.'

'The *major* remained unconvinced and I left the fellow standing there. We went to the ambulance which got us to Würzburg towards five o'clock in the morning. I insisted on Paulchen being treated first. His head was terribly swollen and the doctor pressed hard a couple of times against the sides of the gaping wound, causing almost a litre of blood to spurt out. The swelling was gone and the wound sown up. His upper arm was also seen to, the bone being drilled in several places, then bandaged. Then it was my turn and my right eyebrow was stitched up. On my way to my sick room I passed a clock. It was 7.45. After the strain of the past weeks, during which we had to fly almost daily with up to five sorties by day or by night with hardly any sleep, I was so exhausted that I slept for ten days. Apart from my eye injury I had also suffered severe concussion.'[36]

'On 27/28 August 1943', recalls W/O Eddie Wheeler:

> 'We were back to Nuremberg with another 7000 lbs of 'goodies'. These were placed on workshops and marshalling yards, bombing with the aid of H2S. On return we were coned by searchlights and suddenly the heavy *Flak* stopped which indicated fighter activity could be expected. Jacky in the mid-upper turret spotted a fighter attacking from the starboard quarter and gave Johnny instructions to 'corkscrew' and he and Geoff in the rear turret gave a burst of fire which made *N for Nan* shudder and the smell of cordite in the cabin was pungent. I was sitting at my radio listening to the Group broadcast and as I looked up I saw that there was a clean hole through the crystal monitor about 18 inches above and to the right of my head. A cannon shell had pierced it and gone straight out through the front of the aircraft. I was rigid, not daring to move an inch. The contact was brief and the fighter sheered off – much to our relief. One of the crews, captained by F/L C.B. Robertson, did not return from this operation.'

On 30/31 August 660 heavies targeted the cities of Mönchengladbach and Rheyd. Approximately half of the built-up area in each town was destroyed for the loss of 25 aircraft, 22 of which were shot down by the by Tame Boars. II./NJG 1 claimed five victories whereas I./NJG 1 destroyed eight bombers, including a triple victory by *Gruppenkommandeur Hptm* Hans-Dieter Frank.[37] The very next night 622 bombers assembled in a giant stream and headed for the Big City once more. W/O Eddie Wheeler, WOP-AG in 97 Squadron, recalls:

> 'Our hearts dropped again when we saw that the target was Berlin again. It seemed that the targets were becoming so much harder these days and I gained the impression that time was running out for me and the odds were increasing. I was becoming more nervous then ever before and was looking forward to finishing my tour of ops. Although we had a satisfactory trip we were upset to hear that W/C Burns had been shot down. It was established subsequently that all except two of the crew had been taken prisoner of war.[38]

'The raids on Berlin were becoming monotonous when we found ourselves in flight again on 3 September against the 'Big City'. The seven and a half-hour return trip was carried out without too much trouble. There was no moon, no cloud and good visibility and our bombs released from 19,000 ft were seen to burst in a built up area. The *Flak* as usual was intense and accurate but we escaped damage. From the frequency of raids on the Capital City, it was only too evident that the 'Battle of Berlin' had started in earnest and we were repaying ten-fold the attacks on London in 1940/41. All our crews returned from this operation, one having to return early after two hours when Sgt Miller's mid-upper gunner Sgt Williams was rendered unconscious at 20,000 ft after his electrically heated suit and oxygen supply failed.'[39]

On 5/6 September 1943 a force of 605 aircraft was despatched to bomb Mannheim and Ludwigshafen. Reg Lawton navigator in Stirling 'U' of 196 Squadron piloted by S/L Edmondson recalls:

'This was our first trip to Germany. It was S/L Edmondson's second trip, as he had done one as observer and he came back and thoroughly alarmed us. Anyway this trip went well until we reached the target. As we approached, the pilot told me to leave the navigating in my curtained cabin and come and sit in the right-hand seat and open the bomb-doors. This was a big mistake. It was not my job. I didn't even know how to do it. I was horrified at the sight of what was going on outside. With enemy flares lighting up the sky many of our planes looked like they were in daylight and I lost my night vision. We were risking our lives for nothing because the target seemed to be one vast fire, without our load. We were hit repeatedly by *Flak* and I hurriedly got back to my navigation as the bombs were going. The bomb-aimer and rear gunner both called out 'enemy fighters attacking' and we went into violent evasive action for some minutes. I should never have left my work as I was now called on for a course for home, with all my timing lost as well as courses flown during the evasive action. The pilot was exhausted. He had operated the fire extinguishers in both inboard engines, which was successful and he then restarted both these engines. And they worked! Bristol radials – marvellous. The starboard outer engine, which gave all the power to our instruments, was just a mass of tangled struts in a huge hole in the wing. I gave a course for our next turning point (which was halfway between Paris and the coast).

'Having bombed at 17,500 ft, which was the maximum a Stirling could get to, we started back at 12,000 ft. We were very slow and steadily losing height. After a bit I took an astro-fix but the plane was vibrating so much I took no notice of it. It put us well south of track and actually I was dead right. I was just going to give the pilot the change of course north for the coast when we were plastered by *Flak* again. We had flown straight and alone into the defenses of Paris. We survived this and after some minutes the pilot called me up and told me to go forward and see if I could pinpoint our position as we crossed the coast. I gingerly went down the steps into the nose, because some of the extreme front had been shot away and the bomb-aimer was injured in the eyes, so there was quite a wind blowing and cold too. I saw the coast pass under us but could not locate the area and I didn't know in the dark where to plug in my intercom. When I climbed back the pilot was very relieved as he thought I had fallen out of the wreckage. We were now down to 1000 ft and the engines were on fire again. The flight engineer had been telling us long ago we were out of petrol and at this height we flew right through the London balloon barrage.

'I don't know why we didn't make for one of the 'crash' aerodromes but I got us back to our own station. As we were burning we came in to crash-land, without any preliminaries, such as doing a circuit. We had no flaps and came in much too fast. As we touched down the fuselage broke in two at the trailing edge of the wings. The front part we were in skidded a long way off the runway and headed straight for the control tower, which gave them a fright. We all scrambled out and were OK except for the bomb aimer who soon recovered. No one commiserated with us. No one praised us. No medals were offered. We were shaken and worried that all trips were like this but I was not frightened at any stage (6 hours 50 minutes flying time) nor did the rest of the crew seem to be. (Our next trip, the bombing of the entrance to the Mont Cenis tunnel in France was uneventful and that made us a lot happier. Then Stirlings were taken off bombing as they were outclassed by Lancasters and were deathtraps, 5000 ft below the Lancs where they were just right for all the *Flak* and bombs from above).'

Sgt Leslie Cromarty of 61 Squadron manned the rear turret of Lancaster[40] on 5/6 September:

'This was our first operation with the Main Force and it was a complete disaster from beginning to end. We were so excited when we heard we were flying that night and playing around in our dormitory Johnny Kershaw the WOP/AG swung a broom round his head and hit Harold Pronger, our mid-upper gunner in the eye. He had to go to the MO, who dressed it and advised him not to fly. There was no way that Harold was going to miss the trip. Then the WOP/AG left some of his notes in the Ops room and we had to wait on the tarmac for the WAAF driver to go and fetch them. Next, F/O Ginger Lyons accidentally opened his 'chute and we had another wait while someone brought another. By this time we were half an hour late taking off. We learned later that we should not have taken off so late but Flying Control thought we were a training flight and not part of the Main Force.

'We flew without incident until we were still some distance from the enemy coast. To my surprise I saw an aircraft approaching from the starboard quarter high. I identified it as a Fw 190. It came in very fast and we began corkscrewing. The Fw opened fire and I thought he had put his lights on. Then I realized it was his cannon. I opened fire at 200 yards with a long burst. Suddenly the Fw reared up and began climbing. He was almost out of sight when he seemed to hang on his nose for a few seconds and then the nose slowly began to drop and he began diving. His speed built up and I thought he was attacking again. I could not fire because he was still out of range. I had to wait until he pulled out of his dive and attacked again. Instead, the FW continued to dive, gathering speed all the time. I lost sight of him for a while. Then I saw a flash and a great white ring on the sea. There was no smoke or fire, just a white ring growing bigger. I did not feel elated or pleased. I realized that I had just killed someone. I switched off my intercom and had a bit of a weep.

'Our aircraft was damaged in the attack and we had trouble with the starboard outer engine so we headed back. Big sparks flew past my turret and when I leaned forward I could see the engine beginning to burn. We crossed the English coast and tried to feather the engine. The Skipper called 'Mayday'' and we got an immediate response when there was a bright flash from the engine and the Skipper ordered us to bale out. I had the choice of either leaving via my turret doors, or climbing out to the rear exit. I chose the latter in case anyone needed help. When I reached the rear door the mid-upper gunner was already there and the navigator, F/O Jennings, as coming down the fuselage. I sat on the step and he signalled me to go. I tucked my head into my knees and rolled out, just missing the tail. I landed in a field full of cows and went to a house for assistance but the only occupant was a woman. From an upstairs window she told me that her 'phone was disconnected. I walked to the road and flagged down a van. It was a RAF vehicle and the officer took me to the Police Station at Newark, which was only a couple of miles away. I contacted base and learned that my Skipper, F/O Fitch, had successfully landed the aircraft by himself. I was the first to report in and return. The others arrived unhurt some hours later. We were given a 48-hour pass. So-called 'Survivors' Leave.'

The raid was succesful but 34 aircraft were lost[41] while German losses amounted four single-engined Wild Boars and three twin-engined aircraft; three crew were killed.[42] Hanover was the target for 711 bombers on 22/23 September. At least 20 bombers were shot down over the target by both single-engined and twin-engined night fighters that engaged the bomber stream en masse and in Wild Boar fashion over the burning city under attack. On the night of 23/24 September 627 bombers attacked Mannheim when 42 bombers were lost, 21 of them to twin-engined night fighters and 11 to *Wilde Sau* single-engined fighters of all three Wild Boar *Geschwader* that operated in force over Mannheim. F/Sgt Arthur 'Spud' Taylor, observer on Stirling *'L-Love'* in 90 Squadron recalled:

'The target was pretty hot, lit up for miles around by fighters, flares and fires. Good prang. I noticed for the first time lanes of yellow flares dropped by fighters to show our route in and out and of course, the usual walls of searchlights with the fighters and us in between. We came off pretty lightly with one hole in Len's turret (the man led a charmed life!) and a few dents in the old bus. Damn strain on the eyes, these long trips. We lost one kite over the target and another (with Perce in it) was badly hit. Perce and the WOP baled out over the target, rear gunner dead in turret. One other came back on two engines and pranged just inside the east coast.'

W/O Eddie Wheeler DFC WOP-AG, 97 Squadron, whose 64th op this was, adds:

'We lost F/L [R.A.] Fletcher and crew, including P/O [W.H.] Layne, the wireless operator, was on his second tour and never learned that he had been awarded the DFC. The loss of this most experienced crew made me wonder how much longer our luck could hold out. I had exceeded 60 ops and wondered how soon I could be relieved. Searchlights coned us for six minutes. It seemed as if every *Flak* battery was concentrating on us and I thought it would be only a matter of seconds before they scored a direct hit. I virtually gave up any hope of escaping but after a battering during this interminable period Johnny finally gave them the slip by violent evasive action and we were away and on the return flight. If ever I prayed, it was never more earnestly than on this night. (It was to be just one more week before my operational career was to come to an end but in that week I was to fly to Mannheim, again, to Brunswick and finally to Munich).'

Bomber Command continued the offensive against German cities with four raids on Hanover in September-October. On 27/28 September Hanover was the target for 678 aircraft although of these only 612 dropped their bombs, but scattered them in open country. RAF crews were not yet expert with the new H2S navigational radar, which showed up an expanse of water very well but the Steinhuder See, a large lake, which was used as a way point, had been almost completely covered with boards and nets. Millions of strips of Window were dropped but losses were high. Some bombers experienced problems. P/O Bill Lucas' crew in 10 Squadron set out in Halifax V-Victor, which had just been overhauled but this time the crew did not make it, as Jim Sprackling recalls:

'Just as we were approaching the enemy coast, one of the engines started exhausting white smoke. I had seen this before. (It was an internal glycol (coolant) leak). The engine temperatures started to climb to the upper limit and the oil pressure began to drop. There was nothing for it but to feather the engine. It was rapidly decided that we could not reach the target with three engines, so we just crossed the coastline and jettisoned the bomb load, hoping that it might hit something and turned for home.'

F/Sgt Arthur 'Spud' Taylor's Stirling also had problems. He wrote in his diary:

'Just as we were about to taxi on to the runway for take-off, 'M' went u/s (engines again!) so we dashed into 'Q' and set course as we took off. Saw a good many fighters' flares on the way and also a fair number shot down but no trouble ourselves till on the bombing run (as at Berlin). Just as I was about to press the tit, I heard John's voice say 'Fighter!' I heard the rattle of guns and saw a dirty stream of tracer shooting under the bomb window. Dropped the bombs (19 cans) on to an inferno of fire below and weaved away out of the target. We damaged the fighter and it shot away into the darkness. Hanover is one of the toughest targets I have yet been to – enormous cones of searchlights and plenty of fighters. Weaving away from the town I looked back and saw it, one enormous sheet of flame and smoke, the sky filled with *Flak* puffs and searchlights and markers. Best prang I have ever seen. Near Emden I saw one of our kites shot down in a combat. The rotten swine of a Jerry followed the blazing bomber practically down to earth, pumping lead into her. [P/O] Ted [Mills, pilot] and I who saw it, swore. Apart from the usual dangers over enemy territory, there is the added one of hitting one of our own kites in the dark. On average, at least once in a trip we have all but pranged another bomber. For this reason I spend a lot of my time sitting next to Ted. Tonight, coming back to base, the weather closed in till nothing could be seen but an occasional glimmer of light in the blackness. I happened to glance out of Ted's window and saw an enormous black shape sweeping towards us. Ted hadn't seen it and there was no time to warn him, so I heaved the stick back as hard as I could and we just made it. Near thing. One kite pranged near Haverhill – mid-upper and engineer OK. Another came back with rear-gunner badly wounded and landed at 'Strad'. Otherwise OK. Took a look at 'Q' this morning and found that one of the tail planes was riddled and the starboard wing and one petrol tank were also holed.'

Meanwhile, it was just as well that Bill Lucas had aborted as Jim Sprackling concludes:

'As we neared base, another engine started playing up. This time something was broken and it had to be stopped. We re-started the first failure in the hope that if we were gentle with it we would get some power to go in and land but Bill knew it had to be first time, as it would not take full power for an overshoot. We made it – 4 1/2 hours mainly over hostile waters for nothing. An operation didn't count if you didn't reach the target. (*V-Victor* was unserviceable for most of October 1943, which was spent training the navigator and bomb aimer using *Gee*).'[43]

On 27/28 September also *Major* Hans-Dieter Frank, *Kommandeur,* I./NJG 1 with 55 night victories was killed. Approximately 25 km NW of Celle his He 219A-03 (190055 G9+CB) collided with Bf 110G-4 G9+DA of the *Geschwaderstab* of NJG 1 as they went down the two aircraft separated and crashed 5 km S of Bergen near Meisendorf. Frank, who three months earlier had received the *Ritterkreuz* while *Staffelkapitän* of 2./NJG 1, ejected from the *Uhu*. Frank landed safely but he was choked to death by the cable of his radio helmet, which he had omitted to disconnect and which compressed and crushed his larynx. His *Bordfunker*, *Obfw* Erich Gotter was either thrown from the aircraft or he baled out without the aid of his ejection seat, which was found in the wreckage with the seat harness undone. Frank, who most likely was being pursued by W/C J.R.D. Braham of 141 Sqn before the collision had 55 victories. He was posthumously awarded the *Eichenlaub*.[44]

Hptm August Geiger, *Staffelkapitän,* 7./NJG 1 who had scored three victories on 27/28 September and his *Bordfunker Fw* Koch, were lost on 29/30 September when 352 aircraft raided Bochum when they were shot down by W/C John Randall Daniel 'Bob' Braham DSO DFC** CO of 141 Squadron in a Beaufighter VIf over the Zuider Zee. It took Braham ten minutes of fierce maneuvering before he could finally out-turn the Bf 110 and five miles west of Elburg the 'Night Destroyer' gave Geiger[45] a three-second-burst from astern. It was Braham's twentieth victory and the eighth while on the squadron. The Bochum raid cost the RAF nine bombers, seven of which were claimed destroyed by the *Nachtjagd*.[46]

Fw Karl-Georg Pfeiffer of 12./NJG 1 was airborne once again this night after having baled out and broken his leg in June:

> 'It was a lovely moonlight night with nothing much going on. We had just passed over the two lakes to the east of Leeuwarden. Suddenly the pointer of the boost gauge of the port engine began going to and fro, although the engine continued to run normally. Carefully I throttled back, waited, then pushed the lever forward again, when suddenly the cowlings flew off and flames came from the rear, close to the wing. I tried to extinguish the fire and shut the engine down but all to no avail. The fire got stronger. I said to my crew (apart from Willy, *Gefr* Bauernfeind, a gunner, was with us because of the presence of many long range night fighters) 'We must bale out!' They had seen for themselves why. Based on our own experience, we had explained to the gunner the important points. I heard them jettisoning the roof, then felt a strong impact on the machine, as if someone had kicked the port rudder pedal. Unfortunately *Gefr* Bauernfeind had opened his parachute too soon and his head had struck the rudder. But we only discovered this afterwards after Willi and I had landed safely and the third man had been found dead. I had again done a half roll, like the first time and had almost been trapped by my fur boot. But this time I had not been wounded and had managed the roll so that I was flung out. I opened my parachute and landed at 2200 hrs precisely in a meadow beside a road. I took my parachute under my arm and started walking, meeting two Dutchmen, one with a bicycle, who accompanied me to the nearest village. I waited there with a Dutch family until I was picked up from Leeuwarden. There, in the operations room, I met Willi again and we heard the sad story that our companion had not reached the ground alive. As far as I know he came from Berchtesgaden and I later sent a letter of condolence to his mother but what use were words. Her boy had been killed. The following day *Oblt* Greiner took me back to Leeuwarden but Willi had had enough and although his wife visited, he preferred to go by train and did not arrive until two days later. I took his wife to the cinema in the evening to keep her company.'

A total of 178 victories were credited to *Nachtjagd* in the *Reichsverteidigung* for September. The arm was now in a downwards spiral that was not halted until the end of the year when the Tame Boar force had been fully built up and trained to counter the strategic night bombing offensive effectively.

When a bombing force of 294 Lancasters set out for Munich on the night of 2/3 October (8 Lancasters were shot down by night fighters) W/O Eddie Wheeler DFC WOP-AG, 97 Squadron had no prior knowledge that this would be his crew's final operation together:

> 'Perhaps it was just as well as we might have been even more nervous in our anxiety to survive. As it was the trip was largely uneventful except that we coaxed Hitch our navigator to leave his seat and take up position in the astrodome to see what was going on over the target area. His remarks over the intercom brought smiles to our faces when he said, 'Christ! Does this sort of thing go on every night?' Seeing the mass of fires in the target area he considered it was 'sheer bloody murder:' Ginger too was on this raid and he was to be involved in five further operations against Berlin. Our crew was stood down for a few days after this until Johnny called us together and said, 'Well lads, do we want to go on, or for some of us at least, shall we call it a day?' For Johnny, Hitch, Jackie Blair and myself, we had done our quota and would ask to be relieved of further operational duty. Bill (flight engineer), Peter (air bomber) and Geoff (rear gunner) had no option but to continue. Peter anxiously cleaned his pipe, Bill kept shuffling his feet and Geoff nervously fingered his lanyard whilst the rest of us tried to reach a decision. If we old-stagers decided to finish, then Bill, Peter and Geoff would be assigned to a new crew to finish their first tour. Whilst they were hopeful that the crew would not split up, they recognized that we had done our fair share of ops over a long period and in similar circumstances they would say, 'enough is enough:' Johnny posed the question to us again and there seemed a reluctance to reply. Finally, I said that the last half dozen trips had been a nightmare for me and I had been getting progressively more nervous, so I was going to call it a day. Hitch, said he agreed with me and so it was decided

to tell the CO, W/C Alabaster, we had made up our minds. Naturally, the other three lads were disappointed but they thanked us for the happy times we had enjoyed at Bourn and we wished them all the luck that was going.'

During October 149 RAF bombers were destroyed by *Nachtjagd*. On the Kassel raid of 3/4 October *Nachtjagd* claimed 17 heavies shot down from a force of 547 aircraft and for nine Tame Boar losses.[47] On 4/5 October when 406 aircraft attacked Frankfurt for the loss of 11 bombers it is highly likely that these were due to *Nachtjäger* as the Tame and Wild Boars claimed 12 victories. The raid by 343 Lancasters against Stuttgart on 7/8 October resulted in cliams by *Nachtjagd* for only two kills but on the Bremen and Hanover raids of 8/9 October *Nachtjagd* claimed 37 of the 623 bombers. *Lt* Erwin Ernst of 6./NJG 1 and *Lt* Hans-Heinz Augenstein and *Uffz* Heinz Amsberg both of 9./NJG 1 were among the successful Tame Boar crews.[48] Flying instructors of II./NJG 101 operating from Deelen in Holland scored three Wild Boar victories. Two German aircraft were lost and *Lt* Heinz Grimm of *Stab* IV./NJG 1, who had 27 victories, was hit by German *Flak* and he died of his injuries on 13 October. Three more large-scale Tame Boar operations were mounted by First *Jagdkorps* during October. On the 18/19th when Bomber Command attacked Hanover with 360 Lancasters, 190 twin-engined aircraft claimed 14 victories for two own losses, JG 300 and JG 301 claiming seven Viermot kills. On the 20/21st I JD scrambled 220 aircraft, which claimed 11 Lancasters destroyed from 358 sent to raid Leipzig for nine own losses. Three victories went to III./NJG 1. On 22/23 October, while 36 heavies bombed Frankfurt as a diversion, Kassel was subjected to an exceptionally accurate and concentrated raid by 569 Lancasters and Halifaxes, which created a firestorm destroying 63% of all Kassel's living accomodation. I JD action was hampered by strong Window jamming of the Fighter R/T Frequency and the diversionary raid on Frankfurt but the 194 Tame Boars dispatched made 40 kills, mainly in Wild Boar fashion in the target area and to the north of the target, for the loss of only six fighters Altogether, the RAF lost 43 aircraft.[49]

Aircraft of I JD flew 728 sorties during November 1943 but scored only 22 victories for 24 fighters lost. Total *Reichsverteidigung Nachtjagd* claims for November amounted to 128. Night-fighters destroyed all of the 18 heavies that failed to return from Düsseldorf on the night of 3/4 November when the city was raided by 577 bombers and 12 Mosquito I/IIs after a lapse of almost five months. AM Sir Arthur Harris was in the midst of a campaign of area bombing German cities at night using Lancasters and Halifaxes, while B-24 Liberators and B-17 Flying Fortresses of the U.S. 8th and 12th Air Forces stoked the fires by day. The Düsseldorf operation included a special force of Lancasters equipped with *G-H*, who were to test this precision device for the first time on a considerable scale in a raid on the Mannesmann steelworks. Fifty-two Lancasters, including 20 blind-markers and ten Mosquitoes were detailed to carry out a feint attack on Cologne 10 minutes before the start of the main raid on Düsseldorf. Thirteen *Oboe*-equipped Mosquitoes were detailed to hit Rheinhausen, two more, equipped with *G-H*, went to Dortmund and 23 Stirlings and Lancasters were detailed to lay mines off the Friesians.

Weather could affect the overall success or failure of an operation. A belt of layer cloud extended from the Dutch coast to 90 miles west of Düsseldorf. Contrails extended at all heights above 15,000 ft. The wind at 20,000 ft was 25mph and 28mph at 28,000 ft. Acting F/L William 'Bill' Reid RAFVR and his crew of Lancaster III LM360 *O-Oboe* of 61 Squadron crossed the North Sea without incident. Reid, the son of a Scottish blacksmith and not quite 22 years old who was on his 10th 'op' had enlisted for training as aircrew in 1941 and he trained as a pilot in the United States. Commissioned in 1942, Reid had reached his present rank in 1943 and had been posted to 61 Squadron at Syerston, a 5 Group unit near Nottingham, on 6 September. As they crossed the Dutch coast Reid's windscreen was suddenly shattered by fire from a twin-engined night fighter. F/Sgt Frank Emerson[50] in the rear turret was unable to open fire immediately because his hands were frozen owing to a failure in the heating circuit, and he could not operate his microphone for the same reason. The rear turret was badly damaged; the communications system and the compasses were put out of action, and the elevator trimming tabs of the Lancaster were damaged. The bomber became difficult to control. Emerson was unaware of the damage that the night fighter had caused to the rest of the aircraft, but it had registered hits in the cockpit area of *O-Oboe*, leaving Reid nursing wounds to the head, shoulders and hands. Reid said later:

'I just saw a blinding flash and felt as if my head had been blown off. My shoulder was a bit stiff and it felt as if someone had hit me with a hammer. Blood was pouring down my face and I could feel the taste of it in my mouth. It soon froze up because of the intense cold.'

Reid asked, 'Everybody OK?' Miraculously, the rest of the crew were unscathed and, on receiving answers, he said, 'Resuming course.' He didn't say he was hit, but 'the wind was lashing through the broken windscreen and pieces of the perspex had cut my face.' Despite his wounds and damage to the aircraft, Reid was determined to carry on to Düsseldorf. 'There were other bombers behind us and if we had turned we might have been a danger to them,' he said. F/Sgt L.G. 'Les'

Rolton, bomb-aimer added later, 'We gave all the oxygen to the pilot, who was navigating by the stars.' Soon afterwards, however, O-Oboe was pounced on again, this time by a Fw 190 *Wilde Sau*. The Lancaster was raked from nose to tail with cannon fire. Emerson put up a brave resistance, returning fire with his only serviceable machine-gun but the damaged state of his turret made accurate aiming impossible. F/Sgt Cyril Baldwin climbed out of his mid-upper turret, which had been hit to see for himself the extent of the damage to the aircraft. He found 22-year-old WOp/AG F/Sgt J.J. Mann, a Liverpudlian, lying full length over the body of P/O John Jeffreys RAAF, Reid's 30-year-old navigator from Perth, Western Australia who was dead with a bullet through his skull. The oxygen system aboard the aircraft had been put out of action. Baldwin helped the badly wounded wireless operator into his seat and put an oxygen tube from a portable supply into his mouth. Reid had also been hit once again. Though wounded in the forearm, F/Sgt Jim W. 'Taffy' Norris, flight engineer supplied him with oxygen from another portable supply and Reid was able to carry on.

En route the bombers encountered heavy flak with searchlights from Rotterdam, Antwerp, Krefeld (where one bomber was reported shot down by flak on the way home[51]), Duisburg, Eindhoven, Tholen and Herenthals.[52] Fighters shot down six bombers en route to Düsseldorf. Some 525 aircraft succeeded in reaching Düsseldorf, where the anti-aircraft guns opened up with a vengeance. Heavy *flak* reached 15-16,000 ft, occasionally aimed at aircraft held by searchlight cones above this level. Eighty fighters were reported over the city, as many as 55 of these being twin-engined. Fourteen returning bombers were damaged by the fighters while three enemy fighters were claimed destroyed, two Ju 88s to Halifaxes of 4 Group over Düsseldorf and a Me 210 to a 5 Group Lancaster near Gilze-Rijen. The 'heavies' opened their attack with three Red TIs dropped in salvo by an *Oboe* Mosquito. The serviceability of *Oboe* on this night was very poor with the result that only five bundles of sky-markers and three of TI were dropped. However, 72 Main Force aircraft carried H2S for navigational purposes and 55 reached the target with their sets in order. There was little cloud and an accurate ground-marking attack was delivered by the light of a half moon. Decoy fires at Macherscheid 5 miles south-south-west of Düsseldorf were started but the main force dropped their HE in the centre of the city. Their Aiming Point was situated in the extreme northeast of the city but with the usual undershooting the RAF attack spread rapidly south-southwestwards. Most of the 2000 tons of bombs dropped fell within the built-up area.

The *G-H* trial attack by 38 Lancaster IIs on the Mannesmann Rohrenwerke was successfully carried out at the same time as the main operation. Fifteen aircraft attacked the steel works according to plan but 126 found their sets unserviceable and bombed the city, five returned early and two were lost. Photographic evidence gathered later showed that the accuracy was such that 50 per cent of their bombs had fallen within half a mile of the works.

Bill Reid flew the course to and from the target by the Pole Star and the moon. He was growing weak from loss of blood, and the emergency oxygen supply had given out. With the windscreen shattered the cold was intense, and he occasionally lapsed into semi-consciousness. Rolton recalled, The Lancaster went into a dive and I saw the engineer pull the pilot off the stick and level the aircraft. That was the first I knew of anyone being wounded. I went back and helped the engineer to control the aircraft. The pilot several times regained consciousness. As one of the elevators had been shot away, the aircraft tended to go into a dive, and both of us had to hold the stick. Bill Reid confirms:

> 'Considering that I was in the pilot's seat with my left foot jammed on the rudder because of the effect of the elevator damage and having my hands clasped in front of the stick to hold it back – because of the fact that it acted nose heavy – I did have some effect on the plane's reaction. Les Rolton helped by pushing back on the stick from in front and sighting a beacon flashing, signifying land and asking for the wireless operator's 'flimsy' so that we could find out where we were.'

Norris and Rolton braved heavy anti-aircraft fire over the Dutch coast and, clinging to the stick all the way across the North Sea, kept the Lancaster in the air. Bill Reid continues: 'I do remember Jim shaking me and pointing to the fuel gauges and then downwards, meaning that it was time we landed as we were running out of fuel. I also saw the searchlights to the north of us, for which I headed and it was en route to them that the layout of Shipdham airfield[53] in Norfolk appeared below us.' Reid resumed control, and made ready to land. Ground mist partially obscured the runway lights and Reid was also much troubled by blood from his head wound getting into his eyes. With the hydraulics shot out, he had no brakes for landing, and the legs of the damaged undercarriage collapsed when the load came on, but he got *O-Oboe* down safely. The Lancaster skidded to a halt on its belly as ambulances and crash wagons raced over to the unexpected arrival to help get everybody out of the plane.

Reid was given a blood transfusion and spent four days at the Norfolk & Norwich Hospital, before being transferred to a military hospital. It was while convalescing that he was told he had been awarded the Victoria Cross. The citation reads:

'Wounded in two attacks, without oxygen, suffering severely from cold, his navigator dead, his wireless operator fatally wounded, his aircraft crippled and defenceless, Flight Lieutenant Reid showed superb courage and leadership in penetrating a further 200 miles into enemy territory to attack one of the most strongly defended targets in Germany. Every additional mile increased the hazards of the long and perilous journey home. His tenacity and devotion to duty were beyond praise.' Reid says, 'I nearly fainted. It was like getting 100 per cent in English at school – which I hadn't long left.' The citation went on, ... he showed superb courage and leadership and refused to be turned away from his objective ...' Reid was to say later, 'My VC is for those who did all the things I did but didn't make it back to tell their stories.'[54]

Altogether, 18 bombers[55] were lost on the night of 3/4 November while 37 were damaged. I./NJG 6 and II./NJG 101 were credited with a victory apiece and *Lt* Otto Fries of 5./ NJG 1 at St. Trond shot down a Halifax[56] at Lanaken (Limburg), 22 kilometers SE of Genk, Belgium. Fries' *Gruppe* in fact were credited with five Lancasters and Halifaxes in all. One of the Halifaxes that was lost was credited to *Oblt* Dietrich Schmidt, *Staffelkapitän*, 8./NJG 1, who was flying his seventieth operational sortie, for his seventh confirmed victory. Schmidt's graphic account reveals the chaotic conditions in which the *Nachtjagd* crews had to hunt for Bomber Command at this time:

'We took off from St. Trond for a Wild Boar sortie. Utter confusion reigned. We had only just arrived and had to collect our flight documentation first. Willi Schlosser, *Bordshütze*, accompanied me for the first time. We flew towards radio beacon *Kurfürst*. Nothing was going on. On a silly hunch I flew to the south again. There was bright moon in the southwest and a thin cloud layer at 5000 meters. Suddenly I saw four exhaust flames below to port. Then they were gone again. Then two of them drew away up ahead. We were right in the bomber stream! Then I saw a third – four-engined, twin fins – a Halifax – ahead and a little above. At the same time Schlosser saw one over to port. I closed in, fired into the fuselage and starboard wing, saw the shells hit and broke off! He burned very bright and white in the starboard wing. He returned fire and I heard a distinct 'click'. We'd caught one too! Schlosser was struck on the cheek but did not bleed. I fired at him again, scoring hits. Burning bits flew off and he entered the clouds to port. I fired again. More hits. No return fire. A brief bright glow, then we were in the clouds. I pulled up straight away. There was nothing to see above but below us there was a bright fire-glow. I went through the clouds again. There was one down below. Impact at 1936 hrs. We must have been in the area Mönchen-gladbach-Aachen-Maastricht. It was 060° to the target (Düsseldorf). One hit in our machine[57] went through a piece of equipment on the starboard wall. Willi Schlosser got a splinter in the earpiece of his helmet. A second hit in the tail unit, the skin near the landing light was damaged by wreckage. Confirmation of my eighth Abschuss was finally given by the *Reichsluftfahrtministerium (RLM or Reich* Air Ministry) in February 1945.'[58]

On the night of 4/5 November the RAF carried out mining of the western Baltic, with a Mosquito spoof towards the Ruhr. At 1819 hrs German radar picked up 50 to 60 RAF aircraft between Cap Griz Nez and the Westerschelde River at 23,000 to 30,000 ft. Their further course was southeast into the southern Ruhr area. As their speed at first was only about 250mph they were taken to be four-engined bombers but later, taking headwinds into consideration, the defenses identified them as Mosquitoes. Several aircraft of *1 JD* for *Himmelbett* night fighting in the area of the western Ruhr were ordered to take off but the operation was abandoned after the approaching aircraft were identified as Mosquitoes. Meanwhile, at 1802-1840 hrs 30 to 50 aircraft at heights between 3300 ft and 5000 ft flying at 200mph were picked up by German radar approaching the northern part of west Jutland. *2 JD* occupying two night fighter boxes in Jutland were scrambled to take on the heavies. They engaged 16 bombers and shot down four without loss.

On 8 November 100 Group (Special Duties, later Bomber Support) was created to consolidate the various squadrons and units using the secret *ELINT* and *RCM* in the war against the German night fighter air and defense system. In tandem with this electronic wizardry, 100 Group also accepted 'spoofing' as a large part of its offensive armory and it also controlled squadrons of Mosquitoes engaged purely on *Intruder* missions over Germany. It would need to hone and refine all of these techniques if it were to be of any value against the German night fighter defenses. Early in November about 50 German night fighters were equipped with the improved *SN-2* radar, which was relatively immune to *Window* but only 12 nightfighters and crews were operational, mainly because of the delay in training suitable operators to use the complicated and sensitive radar equipment.

To P/O Jim Sprackling, flight engineer in P/O Bill Lucas' Halifax crew in 10 Squadron at Melbourne 19 November was another ordinary autumn morning on the plain of York:

'I was having a 'lie in'. The previous night we had been to Mannheim. It had been a long flog but as we had taken off early we had finished 'debriefing' and got to bed soon after midnight. Normally, we would be left in peace until midday after an op and would wander up to the mess in time for lunch and then spend the afternoon up at the flights checking over the previous night's work. As flight engineer leader I would have to check through all the flight engineer's logs and discuss any irregularities with the squadron engineer officer whose job it was too oversee all aircraft servicing, repair damage and rectify faults. I would also check over my own aircraft – normally *V Victor* – and have a chat with the ground crew. Finally I had to check the sick, lame and lazy list to see who was able to fly. Just a quiet afternoon's work. But today was different. Soon after 9 o'clock my batwoman, a nice little girl of about 20, gave me a shake. She put a cup of tea on the bedside locker and said there was a 'CALL' (the code word that we were wanted for another raid that night). All crews were to report for duty by 10am. I never had any trouble sleeping no matter what the previous night's excitement, so I was soon up, washed and shaved and down to the squadron offices, where it was confirmed that there was to be another 'Maximum Effort'. Lunch was to be taken at 12 o'clock and briefing at 1pm. This meant another early takeoff and that all serviceable aircraft would take part if they could get crewed. Again we would be crossing the enemy coast in daylight and it was probably a German city. Other targets were usually restricted to experienced crews only.

'So a quick word with Bill, my skipper, to be told that we were on and that our own aircraft, *V-Victor* was still unserviceable and that we would be taking *X-X-Ray* again. We climbed into my old Morris and drove out to the dispersal where our own ground crew was getting it ready. There was no time for an air test but it had gone well the previous night so a quick look round would have to do. The fuel was already on – some 200 gallons short of a full load – so it wasn't going to be a long trip; probably the Ruhr, North Germany. A full bomb load was waiting to go on – 9x1000lb HE for the main bomb bay and six canisters of incendiaries for the wing bays. The incendiaries were a mix of 25lb phosphorous bombs, 12 to a canister and 4lb Magnesium bombs: about 60 to a canister – enough to start a private war. Some of the HE had delayed action fuses to keep the show going as long as possible. We ran the engines up to make sure that everything worked and that the ground crew had missed nothing. The gunners checked their turrets and ammo loads, which were still on from yesterday, as they had not been used. The navigator and bomb aimer checked their magic boxes, which, if the weather was to be the same as last night, they would need them.

'And then to lunch. The mess was quiet, the bar closed and there was none of the usual banter and horseplay. To the old hands (those crews with more than ten ops – and there were not many of these), it was just another job of work. The newer crews were either very quiet, or noisy, depending on their temperament. Then up to the briefing room. I joined the other leaders and flight commanders on the platform while the crews were lined up on benches in the main body of the room. On the platform was a weather map of Northern Europe and at the back a large map concealed by a roller blind. Dead on time, 'groupy,' the station commander and 'Wingco', the squadron commander, the only old men (over 25) in the room, came onto the platform.

'The flight commanders called a roll of the captains of their flight who confirmed that all their crews were present and the doors were closed. The met man was called to give the weather. The important news was that, like last night, fog and low cloud covered the whole of northern Europe. This meant that the German nightfighters would be grounded and the attack would be blind using target-markers dropped by the Pathfinder aircraft of 5 Group. The met man left and the screen was raised showing the target and the route to be flown in and out. The target was Leverkusen on the Rhine, about halfway between Cologne and Düsseldorf, a real military target as it was the home of the I.G. Farben works, a vast chemical plant. We had a go at it only a few weeks before, so already we knew it was heavily defended. It was confirmed that we would not see the target but that it would be marked by Oboe controlled Mosquitoes backed up by H2S equipped heavy bombers. The markers would be green, corrected if necessary, by reds. A Master Bomber, who would advise which marker to aim at, would control the raid.

'Then followed details of the bomb and fuel loads. Take off time 1500hrs. Height to be reached at each turning point en route, time and height and time on target. Attack the target from west to east and then circle south to miss Cologne, then across southern Belgium and NE France and home. Known anti-aircraft sites marked were to be avoided! Signal codes were given. These included the colors of the day. Verey pistols to warn off trigger-happy Navy ships or friendly? A/A gunners. Any questions and a final good hunting from the CO and away to the locker room to get into flying gear.

'The standard flying suit was kapok lined overall with loose fitting Morland's sheepskin boots. Bill and I had acquired a full Irvin suit of sheepskin jacket and trousers and properly fitting fur-lined boots, much more comfortable and a status symbol. Pilots carried a seat type parachute while the rest of the crew wore a harness with a detachable chute. Fully kitted and with a 38 Webley revolver pushed into my flying boot I joined the rest of the crew on the crew bus and we were taken out to the aircraft. In November they didn't waste much time hanging around. A quick smoke for the nicotine addicts and a pee on the tailwheel for the superstitious, then climb aboard and close the hatch. Other aircraft were already being started and soon the peace was shattered with the roar of some 80 Merlin engines. A green Aldis lamp from the control tower and the aircraft started rolling. We took off in alphabetical order so again 'X' was one of the last to go.

'A green light from the runway caravan and roll on to the runway. A few yards to get straight then brakes on as much power as the brakes would hold, then brakes off. As soon as the aircraft was running straight then full power was fed on. Acceleration was fairly rapid and at just over 120 mph the plane would lift off and a long slow climb began As soon as a safe height was reached we turned SSE. We were already being joined by 6 Halifaxes from North Yorkshire (all Canadians) and were soon joining Lancaster's from 1 and 3 Groups. There were even a few Stirlings but most of these had been relegated the glider towing for the Army. The total force would be about 600 aircraft and they would be so concentrated that the raid would be over in about 20 minutes. Although it was still daylight as we reached the enemy coast, below was a solid bank of cloud that the met man had promised. This didn't stop Jerry flak gunners from opening up but with no searchlights and their radar jammed by Window, they were not very effective but the light ack-ack tracer shells gave a good firework display.

'Once over Belgium and Holland things quietened down. We were now at our full operating height of 22,0000ft and although occasionally a searchlight illuminated the cloud, we could not break through so we were soon over the Rhineland and turning east for the target ahead. The first target marker appeared. It looked like a great green Christmas tree sitting just above the clouds. The master bomber's voice came over the radio. The first marker was good, clear for backup markers and commence bombing. So in we went. Now the natives really became hostile. Leverkusen itself was heavily defended and also we were in the range of the heavy guns defending Düsseldorf and Cologne. Bill, the skipper, was an ex-artillery Sergeant and knew a bit about guns. He would never weave about as that only increased the time we were in range. If we had spare height he would put the nose down a bit and increase speed. But now Butch was beginning his bombing run patter so it was 'press on regardless'. Fortunately, we were now using *Window*, so most of the flak was at random as the German radar would be overwhelmed. In fact, the flak never looked lethal, just pretty white puffs of cloud but if you could hear the shells exploding that was different matter.

'We ran in to the target. 'Bomb doors open, left, left, steady, steady, bombs gone, bomb doors closed' We could feel the aircraft lift as 5 tons of dead-weight dropped off. Bill and I adjusted the power settings of the engines a little but allowed the aircraft to climb to get away from the flak guns. There was no sharp about turn for home. Experience had shown the planners that if this was allowed then the bombing pattern crept away from the target as crews dropped their bombs early, also there was a danger of meeting late arrivals head on as they approached the target.

'Tonight we were to fly straight ahead for about 10 miles to clear the defended area then south for 20 miles to clear Cologne on the westerly run home across the Rhineland and the Ardennes South of Belgium. Once clear of the target are my job was to check that all my dials and what I could see of the aircraft for damage, or if any of the bombs had 'hung up'. It was my job to get it released preferably over enemy territory. Everything seemed OK so we settled down for the run home, when suddenly, things went wrong. We were bracketed by flak, in salvoes. We must have drifted out of the mainstream with its Window cover and presented the gunners with a clear single target. Bill opened up the engines to full power and Paddy, the wireless operator, started pushing bundles of Window down the chute as fast as he could go. This worked because the flak bursts drifted behind and then ceased.

'But this time our luck had run out. There was no visible damage and all four engines were running smoothly but the fuel tank supplying No.2 engine, the port inner, was losing fuel at an alarming rate. Switching tanks soon made it obvious that fuel pipes to the engine were damaged, so there was nothing for it but to shut down the engine and isolate it from the rest of the fuel. This in itself was no problem as the Halifax, with no bombs and only half its fuel load, flew quite well on three and could maintain height and speed. The problem was that the damage had almost drained No.1 tank on the port side which held 300 gallons and which had been held back for the return journey. Bill liked to use the outboard fuel first as this kept the weight of the fuel inboard and improved the aircraft's maneuverability. I got my pencil out and calculated how long we could fly on the remaining fuel. On checking with navigator it was obvious that we could not reach Yorkshire. So we decided to stay with the main bomber stream until over the Channel (we had enough personal attention for one night) and then head for the Sussex coast where there were several airfields just inland. We had recently called on the Navy at Ford on the way home from Milan so we chose that one.

'All went well across the Channel and we arrived over Ford with enough fuel to do a circuit and land. We called for priority and were given No.2 behind a Stirling, which was also in trouble. Everything was going smoothly. We could see the Stirling reach the runway, so wheels and flaps down. They all still worked. Paddy, the wireless op, could see the port wheel, which was in the port inner engine bay and it appeared to be OK. Bill called, 'Positions for landing' and started his landing run. Then just before reaching the airfield, a red Verey light was fired from the caravan and we were told to go around again. The Stirling had crashed on the runway.

'Bill opened up the engines and retracted the wheels and we seemed to be climbing away but suddenly Bill called, 'Can't hold her – we're going down. Everybody brace.' I was sitting on two bundles of unused *Window*, between my instrument panel and the pilot's seat and I stuck my head between my knees and waited for the inevitable crash. Then it happened. There was an enormous jolt and the noise of grinding metal as we crashed through hedge of small trees. Bill had got the wings level so the aircraft did not stick a wing tip in and cartwheel, which was always fatal but it slid along on it's belly through a herd of cows until the nose dropped in a rife (water meadow ditch) and it tore itself apart. I had the impression of being inside of a barrel being tossed in all directions, with a noise as though half a dozen blacksmiths were beating the outside with sledgehammers. Then everything came to a stop – no movement, no noise. There was absolute silence except for the gentle hiss of escaping oxygen from the bottles over which I had been sitting. This quickly brought me to my senses. I appeared to be in one piece and I realized that a mixture of oxygen and spilt petrol was something to get away from. There was some moonlight and fortunately no fire and I soon found a hole to scramble through. I unclipped my parachute harness and scrambled through. Once out I could see what was left of the plane. The whole nose section had been ripped away from the center section. Most of the starboard side of the cockpit was missing and there was a wheel in its place. Jock, Paddy and Digger appeared out of the center section, so that was four of the crew accounted for. Then help started to arrive from the nearby railway station but panic – they were carrying a hurricane lamp! I yelled at them to put it out. There was spilt petrol about.

'Now to find the rest of the crew. I crawled back in the hole I had left by and scrambling around, found Bill conscious but trapped in the remains of his seat. I got my harness and parachute undone but could not move him. He was moaning that his arse was cold – he was sitting in the bottom of the rife in six inches of pretty cold water! Paddy came and between us, by hauling his sheepskin jacket, we were able to haul him clear. Bill was also complaining that his shoulder hurt and that we were making it worse but we had got him out alive. Jock and Digger had found Ronny, the rear gunner, half out of his turret with a chunk of his knee missing. Six out of seven but where was Butch? There was nothing left of the aircraft where his seat had been so where to look? Then he appeared climbing out of the rife, wet and muddy but in one piece. He must have been thrown clear through the side window. Seven out of seven.

'The Navy soon arrived with stretcher. Bill and Ronny were loaded on two of them and they all trudged out of the field to an ambulance waiting on a nearby road. They were all given a standard Navy noggin to cheer them up and carted off to St. Richard's hospital in Chichester, where they were cleaned up and put to bed for the rest of the night. Next day they were more thoroughly checked by an orthopaedic surgeon who pronounced that except for Bill, dislocated shoulder and Ronny, badly damaged knee, they were all in one piece. Butch was very badly shaken up and was being checked for internal injuries but they were told that they were all being kept in for another day in case any other injuries became apparent.

'My answer to this was that if they didn't have to go back to base, he might just as well go home, which was only 12 miles away. The doctor thought this was a good idea and I was allowed to use the phone my parents. Half an hour later Paddy and I were on our way to the farm. No one made a fuss at home. Pop was a World War I survivor and Mum had been a VAD nurse, so they were not excitable parents. We were given a good lunch (rationing didn't apply on a farm) and I pinched Pop's chair by the fire and dozed off. When I awoke it was a different story. I ached in every limb and muscle and I didn't move from the chair all afternoon. To make matters worse, Paddy was OK, had been given a gun and was taken out rabbit shooting – my favourite pastime. He didn't hit anything – the report was that he couldn't hit a stationary barn door!

'After another night's sleep the bruises began to wear off and in the afternoon we were taken back to St. Richards, where after another check over we were pronounced fit to return to base the next day. That evening, we all gathered around Bill and Ronny's beds and it was agreed that we would all would wait until Bill was fit and we'd finish our tour of ops together. We had chuckle over a report in the local paper. A bomber had crashed into a herd of cows and killed 11 of them. I remarked that the owner was one of the wealthiest farmers in West Sussex and he could afford it! Next day five of us caught the morning train from Chichester and that evening we were back at base, the end of Op 19. But it wasn't quite the end. A few days later, a package of personal belongings arrived that had been salvaged from the wreck. In it was my tool bag and in it our mascot, the Scarlet Woman, a rag doll given to me by a girlfriend Ethel. The doll had lost a leg – the only permanent casualty.'[59]

From 18/19 November 1943 to 24/25 March 1944 Berlin was subjected to 16 major raids, which have gone into history as the Battle of Berlin. During the 18/19 November raid, only nine out of 440 Lancaster were lost. An effective Tame Boar operation was mounted against a second force of 395 aircraft simultaneously raiding Ludwigshafen-on-Rhine, a handful of crew shooting down the majority of the 23 aircraft that failed to return from this raid. Six crews of I./NJG 6 destroyed eight *Viermots*, *Hptm* Franz Evers of the *Gruppenstab* claiming one *Viermot* (Lancaster DS784 of 115 Sqn) shot down at 2210 hrs at Assesse. On 22/23 November, an estimated four out of 764 bombers raiding Berlin were lost to the *Nachtjagd*, which largely remained grounded due to adverse weather conditions. The very next night, 383 bombers again made the long haul to the Big City; this time, a handful of experienced *Nachtjäger* braved the elements, 12 Tame Boar crews shooting down 13 of the 20 heavy bombers that were lost. On the night of 25/26 November when 262 Halifaxes and Lancasters attacked Frankfurt, for the loss of 12 of their number at least six Halifaxes were destroyed by as many crews of NJG 3, NJG 4, NJG 5 and NJG 6. A raid by 450 bombers on Berlin and 178 on Stuttgart on the night of 26/27 November was met by a combined operation of target area and *Himmelbett* night fighting under difficult weather conditions, which resulted in only the best German crews being ordered to take off. Even so, 84 fighters engaged the RAF formations. *1 JD* downed most of the 28 main force bombers that failed to return while from the smaller force six aircraft were lost. Just two German night fighter aircraft were lost.

In the USA on 3 December 1943 radio listeners tuned in to hear their favourite foreign correspondent Edward R. Murrow, head of CBS European Bureau in London, begin his broadcast, *This Is London.* Murrow, who had become well known in America for his broadcasts during the *Blitz* when the USA was still neutral, proceeded to regale his listeners with a gripping account of his experience over Berlin in a Lancaster the night before. (Murrow had boarded Lancaster *D-Dog* of 619 Squadron RAAF at Woodhall Spa and flew with Acting W/C William 'Jock' Abercromby DFC* and his crew[60] to Berlin. *D-Dog* was one of 458 aircraft that took part in the raid on the Big City):

> 'Yesterday afternoon the waiting was over. The weather was right; the target was to be the big city. The crew captains walked into the briefing room, looked at the maps and charts and sat down with their big celluloid pads on their knees. The atmosphere was that of a school and a church. The weatherman gave us the weather. The pilots were reminded that Berlin is Germany's greatest center of war production. The intelligence officer told us how many heavy and light ack-ack guns, how many searchlights we might expect to encounter. Then Jock the wing commander, explained the system of markings, the kind of flare that would be used by the Pathfinders. He said that concentration was the secret of success in these raids, that as long as the aircraft stayed well bunched, they would protect each other. The captains of aircraft walked out.
>
> 'I noticed that the big Canadian with the slow, easy grin had printed 'Berlin' at the top of his pad and then embellished it with a scroll. The red headed English boy with the two weeks' old moustache was the last to leave the room. Late in the afternoon we went to the locker-room to draw parachutes, Mae Wests and all the rest. As we dressed a couple of the Australians were whistling. Walking out to the bus that was to take us to the aircraft I heard the station loud speakers announcing-that that evening all personnel would be able to see a film: *Star Spangled Rhythm,* free!
>
> 'We went out and stood around a big, black, four-motored Lancaster, *D-Dog*. A small station wagon delivered a vacuum flask of coffee, chewing gum, an orange and a bit of chocolate for each man. Up in that part of England the air hums and throbs with the sound of aircraft motors all day. But for half an hour before take-off the skies are dead silent and expectant. A lone hawk

hovered over the airfield, absolutely still as he faced into the wind. Jack, the tail gunner, said, 'It would be nice if we could fly like that.'

'*D-Dog* eased around the perimeter track to the end of the runway. We sat there for a moment, the green light flashed and we were rolling ten seconds ahead of schedule. The take-off was smooth as silk. The wheels came up and *D-Dog* started the long climb. As we carne up through the clouds I looked right and a 1eft and counted 14 b1ack Lancasters climbing for the place where men must burn oxygen to live. The sun was going down and its red glow made rivers and lakes of fire on top of the clouds. Down to the southward the clouds piled up to form castles, battlements and whole cities, all tinged with red.

'Soon we were out over the North Sea. Dave, the navigator, asked Jock if he couldn't make a little more speed – we were nearly two minutes late. By this time we were all using oxygen. The talk on the intercom was brief and crisp. Everyone sounded relaxed. For a while the eight of us in our little world in exile moved over the sea. There was a quarter moon on the starboard beam. Jock's quiet voice came through the intercom: 'That'll be *flak* ahead.' We were approaching the enemy coast. The *flak* looked like a cigarette lighter in a dark room – one that won't light. Sparks but no flame. The sparks crackling just about level with the cloud tops. We flew steady and straight, end soon the flak was directly below us.

'*D-Dog* rocked a little from right to left but that wasn't caused by the *flak*. We were in the slipstream of other Lancasters ahead: and we were over the enemy coast.

'And then a strange thing happened. The aircraft seemed to grow smaller. Jack in the rear turret, Wally, the mid-upper gunner and Titch, the wireless operator all seemed somehow to draw closer to Jock in the cockpit. It was as though each man's shoulder was against the others. The understanding was complete. The intercom came to life and Jock said; 'Two aircraft on the port beam.'

'Jack in the tail said, 'Okay sir; they're Lancs.' The whole crew was a unit and wasn't wasting words.

'The cloud below was ten-tenths. The blue green jet of the exhaust licked back along the leading edge and there were other aircraft all around us. The whole great aerial armada was hurtling towards Berlin. We flew so for 20 minutes, when Jock looked up at a vapor trail curling across above us, remarking in a conversational tone that from the look of it he thought there was a fighter up there. Occasionally the angry red of ack-ack burst through the clouds but it was far away and we took only an academic interest. We were flying in the third wave. Jock asked Wally in the mid-upper turret and Jack in the rear turret if they were cold. They said they were all right and thanked him for asking. Even asked how I was and I said, 'All right so far.' The cloud was beginning to thin out. Up to the north we could see light and the flak began to liven up ahead of it.

'Boz, the bomb-aimer crackled through on the intercom. 'There's a battle going on on the starboard beam.' We couldn't see the aircraft but we could see the jets of red tracer being exchanged. Suddenly there was a burst of yellow flame and Jock remarked, 'That's a fighter going down – note the position.' The whole thing was interesting but remote. Dave the navigator who was sitting back with his maps charts and compasses said, 'The attack ought to begin in exactly two minutes.' We were still over the clouds. But suddenly those dirty gray clouds turned white. We were over the outer searchlight defenses – the clouds below us were white and we were black. *D-Dog* seemed like a black bug on a white sheet. The flak began coming up but none of it close. We were still a long way from Berlin. I didn't realize just how far.

'Jock observed: 'There's a kite on fire dead ahead.' It was a great golden, slow-moving meteor slanting towards the earth. By this time we were about 30 miles from our target area in Berlin. That 30 miles was the longest flight I have ever made. Dead on time. Boz, the bomb-aimer reported, 'Target indicators going down.' The same moment the sky ahead was lit up by brilliant yellow flares. Off to starboard another kite went down in flames. The flares were sprouting all over the sky – reds and greens and yellows; and we were flying straight for the center of the fireworks. *D-Dog* seemed to be standing still, the four propellers thrashing the air. But we didn't seem to be closing in. The cloud had cleared and off to starboard a Lanc was caught by at least 14 searchlight beams. We could see him twist and turn and finally break out. But still the whole thing had a quality of unreality about it. No one seemed to be shooting at us but it was getting lighter all the time. Suddenly a tremendous big blob of yellow light appeared dead ahead, another to the right and another to the left. We were flying straight for them.

'Jack pointed out to me the dummy fires and flares to right and left but we kept going in. Dead ahead there was a whole chain of red flares looking like stoplights. Another Lanc coned on our starboard beam; the lights seemed to be supporting it. Again we could sea those little bubbles of colored lead driving at it from two sides. The German fighters were at him.

'And then, with no warning at all, *D for Dog* was filled with an unhealthy white light; I was standing just behind Jock and could see the seams of the wings. His quiet Scots voice beat into my ears. '*Steady, lads – we've been coned.*' His slender body lifted half out of the seat as he jammed the control column forward and to the left. We were going down.

'Jock was wearing woolen gloves with the fingers cut off. I could see his fingernails turn white as he gripped the wheel. And then I was on my knees, flat on the deck, for he had whipped the *Dog* back into a climbing turn. The knees should have been strong enough to support me but they weren't and the stomach seemed in some danger of letting me down, too. I picked myself up and looked out again. It seemed that one big searchlight, instead of being 20,000 ft below, was mounted right on the wingtip.

'*D for Dog* was corkscrewing. As we rolled down on the other side I began to see what was happening to Berlin.

'The clouds were gone and the sticks of incendiaries from yellow and started to flow to the preceding waves made the place look like a badly laid-out city with the street lights on. The small incendiaries were going down like a fistful of white rice thrown on a piece of black velvet. As Jock hauled the *Dog* up again I was thrown to the other side of the cockpit and there below were more incendiaries glowing white and then turning red. The cookies – the four 1000 lb high explosives – were bursting below, like great sunflowers gone mad. And then as we started down, still held in the lights. I remember that the *Dog* still had one of those cookies and a whole basket of incendiaries in his belly and the lights still held us. And I was very frightened.

'While Jock was flinging him about in the air he suddenly flung over the intercom, 'Two aircraft on the port. Beam.' I looked astern and saw Wally, the mid-upper gunner, whip his turret round to port and then looked up to see a single-engined fighter slide below us. The other aircraft was one of ours. Finally we were out of the cone, flying level. I looked down and the white fires had turned red; they were beginning to merge and spread. Just like butter does on a hot plate. Jock and Boz, the bomb-aimer, began to discuss the target. The smoke was getting thick down below. Boz said he liked the two green flares on the ground almost dead ahead. He began calling his directions and just then a new bunch of big flares went down on the far side of the sea of flame and flare that seemed to be directly below us. He thought that would be a better aiming point. Jock agreed and we flew on. The bomb doors were open. Boz called – his directions: 'Five left…five left.' Then there was a gentle, confident upward thrust under my feet and Boz said, 'Cookie gone.' A few seconds later the incendiaries went and *D-Dog* seemed lighter and easier to handle.

'I thought I could make out the outline of streets below, this time all those patches of white on black had turned caught us but didn't hold us. Then through the intercom, 'We're still carrying it.' And Jock replied, 'Is it a big one or a little one? I'm not sure – I'll check.' More of those yellow flares came down and hung about us. I hadn't seen so much light since the day war began. Finally, the intercom announced that it was only a small container of incendiaries left and Jock remarked, 'Well, its hardly worth going back and doing another run-up for that.' If there had been a good fat bundle left he would have gone back through that stuff and done it all again.

'I began to breathe and to reflect again – that all men would be brave if only they could leave their stomachs at home, when there was a tremendous whoomp, an unintelligible shout from the tail-gunner … *D-Dog* shivered and lost altitude. I looked out the port side and there was a Lancaster that seemed close enough to touch; he had whipped straight under us – missed us by 25-50 ft. No one knew how much.

'The navigator sang out the new course and we were heading for home. Jock was doing what I had heard him tell his pilots to do so often – flying dead on course. He flew straight into a huge green searchlight and as he rammed the throttles home remarked, 'We'll have a little trouble getting away from this one.' And again *D-Dog* dived, climbed and twisted and was finally free. We flew level then and I looked on the port beam at the target area. There was a red, sullen, obscene glare – the fires seemed to have found each other … and we were heading home.

'For a little while it was smooth sailing – we saw more battles and then another plane in flames but no one could tell whether it was ours or theirs. We were still near the target. Dave, the navigator, said 'Hold her steady skipper. I want to get an astral sight.' And Jock held her steady. And the flak began coming up at us. It seemed to be very close. It was winking off both wings. But the Dog was steady. Finally, Dave said, 'Okay, skipper, thank you very much' and a great orange blob of flak smacked up straight in front of us. Jock said, 'I think they're shooting at us.' (I had thought-so for some time) and he began to throw D for Dog up, around and about again. When we were clear, of the barrage I asked him how close the bursts were and he said, 'Not very close. When they are really near you can smell 'em.' That proved nothing; for I had been holding my breath.

'Jack sang out from the rear turret, said his oxygen was getting low, thought maybe the lead was frozen. Titch, the radio-operator, went scrambling back with a new mask and a bottle of oxygen. Dave, the navigator, said, 'We're crossing the coast.' My mind went back to the time I had crossed that coast in 1938 in a plane that had taken off from Prague. Just ahead of me sat two refugees from Vienna – an old man and his wife. The co-pilot came back and told them that – we were outside German territory. The old man reached out and grasped his wife's hand. The work that was done last night was a massive blow of retribution for all those who have fled from the -sound of shots and blows on that stricken continent.

'We began to lose height over the North Sea. We were over England's shore. The land was dark beneath us. Somewhere down there below American boys were probably bombing up Fortresses and Liberators getting ready-for the day's work.

'We were over the home field; we called the control tower; and the calm, clear voice of an English girl replied, 'Greetings D-Dog, you are a diverted to Mulebag.' We swung round, contacted Mulebag, came in. on the flare path, touched down very gently, ran along to the end of the runway and turned left and Jock, the finest pilot in Bomber Command, said to the control tower, 'D-Dog clear of runway.'

'When we went in for interrogation, I looked on the board and saw that the big slow smiling Canadian and the red headed English boy with the two week-old-moustache hadn't made it.[61] They were missing. There were four reporters on this operation. Two of them didn't come back – two friends of mine, Norman Stockton, of Australian Associated Newspapers and Lowell Bennett, an American representing International News Service. There is something of a tradition amongst reporters that those who are prevented by circumstances from filing their stories will be covered by their colleagues. This has been my effort to do so.

'In the aircraft in which I flew, the men who flew and fought it poured into my ears their comments on fighters, flak and flares – in the same tones they would have used in reporting a host of daffodils. I have no doubt that Bennett and Stockton would have given you a better report of last night's activities.[62]

'Berlin was a kind of orchestrated hell – a terrible symphony of light and flame. It isn't a pleasant kind of warfare. The men doing it speak of it as a job. Yesterday afternoon, when the tapes were stretched out on the big map all the way to Berlin and back again, a young pilot with old eyes said to me, 'I see were working again tonight.' That's the frame of mind in which the job is being done. The job isn't pleasant – it's terribly tiring – men die in the sky while others are roasted alive in their cellars. Berlin last night wasn't a pretty sight. In about 35 minutes it was hit with about three times the amount of stuff that ever came down on London in a nightlong blitz. This is a calculated, remorseless campaign of destruction. Right now the mechanics are probably working on *D-Dog*, getting him ready to fly again.'[63]

Predominantly crack night fighter crews again were sent to intercept the bombers on 16/17 December 1943 when the RAF made yet another night attack on Berlin. They were met with a combination of *Zahme Sau*, *Objektnachtjagd* (Target Area night fighting) and (in the Schleswig-Holstein and Jutland areas) *Himmelbett* night fighting tactics. German radar began picking up J beams from 1800 hrs and the assembly of the RAF formations, their leaving England and approach, were all plotted correctly by H2S bearings. Mosquito *spoof* attacks on Kassel and Hanover were clearly recognized as such. Large scale jamming of German radio and radar was carried out. *First Jagdkorps* VHF was jammed by bell sounds, R/T traffic was rendered almost impossible and *First Jagdkorps* HF was jammed by quotations from Hitler's speeches. *First Jagdkorps* alternate frequency and Division frequencies also were strongly jammed and there was a very sudden jamming of the *Soldatenrundfunksender* (Forces Broadcasting Station) '*Anne Marie*' by continuous sound from a strong British jamming station. Widespread mist and fog at 150-300ft in the North German plains reduced the overall effectiveness of the fighter defense and 23 aircraft, mostly Bf 110s had to abandon their missions prematurely. The 30 night fighters engaged in Target Area Night Fighting, 28 for *Zahme Sau* and 34 for *Himmelbett* (over Jutland) shot down 20 bombers. *Wilde Sau* night fighters and *Flak* brought down another five. Heinz-Wolfgang Schnaufer, *Staffelkapitän,* 12./NJG 1 shot down four Lancasters during a classic *Himmelbett* sortie over Friesland Province to bring his total to forty victories. Only three German aircraft were lost.

After a certain initial success *Objektnachtjagd* proved to have weaknesses easily exploitable by Bomber Command. It was not until the twin engined night-fighters were used for route interception that the *Luftwaffe* could begin to inflict heavy losses again. This technique was subsequently improved to such an extent that deep raids into Germany could only be carried out at a heavy price in bombers. However, Bomber Command's new tactics of multiple raids and shallow raids on invasion targets in France combined to offset the development of route interception.

Despite atrocious winter weather *Nachtjagd* claimed 169 victories during the final month of 1943 against 28 lost, 23 of which were written off I *Jagdkorps*' strength. I./NJG 1 claimed four aircraft destroyed, including a Mosquito by *Hptm* Manfred Meurer flying a He 219A-0 *Uhu* ('Owl')[64] on the 12/13th.[65]

On the night of 16 December a Lancaster II[66] was intercepted at 19,700 ft (6800m) by *Oblt* Heinz-Wolfgang Schnaufer, *Staffelkapitän,* 12./NJG 1 who shot it down for his fourth kill of the night and his fortieth *Abschuss* overall. The Lancaster careered over Leeuwarden trailing a sheet of flames and completely disintegrated on impact followed by the explosion of the bomb load. F/O W. Charles Fischer the American skipper and five of his crew were killed. During the 20/21 December raid I./NJG 6 destroyed ten Lancasters and Halifaxes. They included triple victories by *Fw* Günther Bahr[67] and *Oblt* Martin 'Tino' Becker.[68] II./NJG 1 was credited with three Halifax kills, including two[69] by *Gruppenkommandeur Oblt* Eckart-Wilhelm 'Hugo' von Bonin. In December II./NJG 1 was credited with four victories. III./NJG 11 claimed four victories on the night of 16/17 December and a Lancaster over Frankfurt by *Oblt* Hans-Heinz Augenstein on the 23/24th.

Fw Karl-Georg Pfeiffer of 12./NJG 1 who flying from Bergen on 4 December 1943 shot down a Stirling III[70] of 623 Squadron into the Waddensea at 0303 hrs for his ninth confirmed victory. On 16 December he had to make a belly landing at Bergen with engine trouble:

'One shook wildly and would take more petrol. I therefore did not dare to risk landing on my wheels and put the machine down on its belly beside the runway. They were not very happy about this at Leeuwarden and hinted that this had not been necessary, although there was a regulation about a situation such as this. I was annoyed about this but my life was more valuable to me. Our next sortie, on Christmas Eve, was criminal. We had hoped that the British would leave us alone. The worst of it was that on this night [23/24 December] only the northwest corner of Holland remained free of fog. All the airfields, even those in the *Reich* were already closed at mid-day. Against our wishes, the British had sent out several hundred bombers. They flew far to the south along the French west coast to bomb targets in southern Germany (Munich, as it transpired later) (sic). From Bergen or Leeuwarden the fuel was just sufficient to fly there and back, without time to fight over the target. We had just reached the area around Stuttgart, when we heard that Munich had already been hit (sic.)[71] There was no point in trying to get the returning aircraft because we were in cloud at whatever height we flew. We headed for the radio beacon Rhein-Main and from there to Bonn-Hangelar. That was as far as the fuel would last. I had already shut down one engine to save fuel. The cloud base was reported to be 120 meters but it was not enough because of the Siebengebirge where many crews had struck the ground in bad weather and exploded. I said so to Willi and had him enquire what the visibility was at St. Trond. 'Cloud base 80 meters and very hazy!' In spite of this I decided on St. Trond because it is flat and I knew the field very well. I flew on using the minimum of fuel and could see the place from afar. All the field's searchlights had been set vertically, brightly illuminating the cloud tops above. At least we knew where the field was but going down into this bright murk I could hardly make out my wing tips. But all went well. Bathed in sweat and with our last drops of fuel we touched down heavily on the runway after a confused blind-landing procedure and were safe. When the dawn broke the fog had become thicker and they would not let us go. But Willi wanted to get engaged to his girl friend and he kept urging me so hard until midday that I decided on a blind take-off on my own responsibility. All went well and as we got closer to Bergen the clouds broke up and we landed in bright sunshine. The following party with the happy couple was one of the highlights of our flying life.'

As 1943 neared its close German airmen like *Fw* Friedrich Ostheimer who had recently joined *Major* Heinrich Prinz *zu* Sayn-Wittgenstein, *Kommandeur* of II./NJG 2 as his new *Bordfunker* at Deelen, Holland reflected on the year's events which had not boded well for Germany:

'A few more weeks and the year of 1943 would be a thing of the past. The war, with all its distress and terror was at its height. Our troops were fighting from the North Cape to the Libyan Desert and from Russia to the Atlantic. Since America's entry into the war the Luftwaffe was utterly outnumbered and the crews under unceasing stress.

'At Arnhem-Deelen Prince Wittgenstein spent his time either in his bungalow or at the command post. We, the flight engineer, the first mechanic and I were on stand-by in a small hut beside the hangar, which housed our Ju 88. We only saw the Prince when he came to fly. After landing he returned immediately to his quarters. Once, a few nights before we were shot down, he invited us to his bungalow for an evening meal before stand-by commenced. Prince Wittgenstein was a tall, good-looking officer with a fine, reserved and very disciplined personality. As a nightfighter he did his utmost, shunned no danger and never considered his own life.

'Prince Wittgenstein, who had been commander of II./NJG 3 in Schleswig, was given a new task in December 1943. We were transferred with our machine to Rechlin[72] on the Mürlitzsee, where a new nightfighter experimental unit was to be established. This came as a surprise for *Uffz* Matzuleit, our flight engineer and myself. Within a few hours we were torn from the circle of our comrades. In Rechlin we knew no one and frequently sat unhappily around. Most of the time Prince Wittgenstein was away at meetings, frequently in Berlin at the Air Ministry.

'Our job was to keep the machine in constant readiness. There was no nightfighter unit stationed at Rechlin. It often took me hours to obtain the operational data for radio and navigation by telephone. For accommodation we had railway carriages with sleeping facilities. During our three weeks in Rechlin, we flew some sorties over Berlin. Two of these night flights in particular have remained in my memory.

'Kurt and I had a small room in flying control at our disposal. During reported attacks we waited there for possible orders. One evening it looked as if Berlin might be the target for the bomber stream. Prince Wittgenstein had already reported our imminent take-off. We climbed on a southeasterly course in the direction of Berlin. The distance Rechlin-Berlin is about one hundred kilometers. The speaker in the so-called *Reichsjägerwelle*[73] gave a running commentary of position, course and height of the enemy bombers. Their code word was *Dicke Autos* ('Fat Cars'). This kept all the airborne fighters constantly informed. Meanwhile Berlin had been recognized as being the target and the *Reichsjägerwelle* gave the order: 'Everything to Bär (Bear), everything to Bär!' Meanwhile we had reached the height of the bombers at about 7000 meters. We entered the bomber stream on a southeasterly course. The radar was switched on and we observed the air space around us as far as the visibility allowed.

'I soon had my first target on my screen. I passed the required changes of course to the pilot on the intercom. We were closing in on our target. 'Straight ahead, a little higher!' Very quickly we had reached the heavily laden four-engined one. It was, as nearly always, a Lancaster. Prince Wittgenstein set it on fire with a single burst from the *Schräge Musik* cannon and the enemy went down.

'Ahead of us the first beams of the searchlights were searching the night sky. The fire of the *Flak* defenses intensified and as a signal for the attack the British pathfinders dropped target indicators for the approaching bombers. And again I had a target on my screen. The distance to the enemy bomber decreased quickly. By this difference in speed alone we could see that it must be an enemy bomber. But suddenly the closing speed became very high indeed and I could only call out on the intercom: 'Down, down, the machine is coming straight at us!' A moment later a shadow passed above us in the opposite direction. We just felt the slipstream and the aircraft, probably another Lancaster, had disappeared into the night. The three of us sat rigid in our seats and we only relaxed when Kurt said, 'That was close!' Once more we had been lucky.

'Now for the next target. The approach was almost complete and both the pilot and engineer could recognize the aircraft. Then suddenly the starboard engine began to shake, the propeller revolutions quickly decreased and finally stopped completely. Prince Wittgenstein pushed the nose down to maintain speed, feathered the propeller and adjusted the rudder trim to counteract the thrust of the remaining engine. By the time Wittgenstein had done all this the Lancaster had disappeared into the darkness.

'We might have had further successes during this night. But with only one engine we now had only one aim: back to Rechlin. I obtained a course to steer from the D/F station. The port engine ran smoothly and we flew slowly losing height towards Rechlin. I told the D/F station that we had lost one engine and that we would have to try a single-engined landing. Every airman knows about the dangers and difficulties of such a landing at night. One should really have been terribly frightened. But that doesn't help in such situations at all. Although it wasn't really allowed, Prince Wittgenstein wanted to do a normal landing with extended undercarriage. That meant that if it shouldn't work out, an overshoot on only one engine would not be possible and both aircraft and crew would almost certainly be lost. But Prince Wittgenstein, as pilot and commander of our machine, was in command; he had the power to make the final decision. The airfield fired off signal rockets to aid our orientation, which we called *Radieschen* (radishes). When we had reached the airfield we first flew past it, then made a wide circuit towards the approach path. The Prince had to do this, as we could only turn towards the running engine. A turn into the stopped engine could easily have caused a crash. We commenced our approach on a VHF beam, a very accurate approach aid at that time. The power of the running engine had to be reduced and the rudder trim adjusted at the same time. The landing was perfect. As the machine rumbled over the runway we felt a great relief. We praised our pilot very highly of course and Kurt and I thought that we had earned some relaxation.

'After a few days the engine had been changed and our machine was again ready for action. Prince Wittgenstein was impatient again. At the next approach of enemy bombers – Berlin was the target again – we were once more in the air. The weather was good for a change. There was a slight layer of haze at medium altitude, above that the sky was clear. I tuned in to the *Reichsjägerwelle* and so we were kept well informed about the general situation. Everything was pointing to another attack on the *Reich*'s capital. At this time large parts of Berlin had been heavily damaged. Entire streets were in ruins. An unimaginable sight. I had once experienced a night attack on the city from the ground. I was in an underground station with many others, the earth shook with each explosion, women and children screamed, smoke billowed through the place. Anyone who did not feel fear and horror would have had a heart of stone.

'Back to our operation. We had meanwhile reached the altitude of the bomber stream and entered, like the Lancasters, the *Flak* barrage over the city. British pathfinders – we called them 'master of ceremonies' – had already dropped markers. The scene over the city was almost impossible to describe. The searchlights illuminated the haze layer over the city, making it look like an illuminated frosted glass screen, above which the sky was very light. One could make out the approaching bombers as if it were daylight. It was a unique sight.

'Prince Wittgenstein put the aircraft into a slight bank. At this moment we did not know where to make a start. But the decision was suddenly taken from us, as tracer flew past our machine. Wittgenstein put the machine into a steep turn and dived. As we went downwards I could see the Lancaster flying obliquely above us and its mid-upper-gunner who was firing at us with his twin guns. Fortunately his aim had not been very good. We had got a few hits but the engines kept running and the crew was unhurt. We went off to one side into the dark, keeping the Lancaster just in sight.

'We now continued parallel to the bomber for a while. The darker it got around us, the closer we moved towards the enemy machine. As the light from the searchlights decreased and the fires which the attack of the enemy had started lay behind us, we were well closed up to the bomber. The Lancaster was now flying above us, suspecting nothing. Perhaps the crew was relieved to have survived the attack and to be on their way home. But we, intent on the hunt, sat in our cockpit with our eyes staring upward, hoping that we had not been detected.

'Prince Wittgenstein placed our Ju still closer to the huge shadow above us, took careful aim and fired with the *Schräge Musik*. The tracer of the 2cm shells bored into the wing between the engines and set the fuel tanks on fire. We swung immediately to one side and watched the burning Lancaster, which continued on its course for quite a while. Whether the crew had been able to bale out we could not tell. They had certainly had enough time. The bomber exploded in a bright flash and fell disintegrating to earth. I got good contact with our D/F station right away. We flew without any problems to Rechlin and landed there.'

On the night of 29/30 December Berlin was again the target for RAF Bomber Command and 712 aircraft were despatched. Of these 457 were Lancasters. At the 1 Group aerodrome at Elsham Wolds, Sergeant Ben Frazier, *Yank Staff* Correspondent boarded Lancaster III ED888 V-Victor of 576 Squadron for the operation to the Big City with F/O Gomer S. 'Taff' Morgan and his crew. This famous Lancaster had originally served on 103 Squadron, as had Morgan (576 was formed from 'C' Flight of 103 Squadron on 25 November) and the Berlin op would be ED888's 58th sortie. Frazier wrote:

> 'England. A small village lay tucked away in the fold of a valley just below the high, windswept, bleak plateau where a Lancaster bomber station was situated. Housewives were busy in the kitchen preparing food, and the men had left their ploughing to come in for the noon-day meal. In the lichen covered Gothic Church, the minister's wife was arranging decorations, and placing on the altar freshly cut chrysanthemums that had managed to escape the north winds and were still blooming in December.
>
> 'The placidness of the village life was in sharp contrast to the bustling activity at the airfield. It seemed as remote from war as any hamlet could possibly be, although the provident farmers, living so close to an obvious military target had wisely provided themselves with shelter trenches at the edge of each ploughed field. Nevertheless, the name of this quiet, lovely village had spread far. By borrowing it, the bomber station had made it one to strike terror into the heart of the Nazi High Command.
>
> 'At the airfield, V for Victor's crew lounged around B Flight's Office waiting to see if operations were on. They kept looking up into the sky as if trying to guess what the weather was going to be like. Some of the men chuckled. 'Papa Harris is so set on writing off the Big City that he hardly even notices the weather,' one of them said. 'The last time, there were kites stooging around all over the place. The met boobed that one.'
>
> 'It was a strange new language. What the airmen were saying was that the last time out the meteorological men had given a wrong steer on the weather, and the planes had been flying all over looking for the field on the return trip. 'Papa' Harris was Air Chief Marshal Harris, chief of Bomber Command.
>
> 'V for Victor's captain came back from the operations room with the news that there would be ops. That settled

the discussion. You seemed to be aware, without noticing anything in particular, of a kind of tension that gripped the men; like they were pulling in their belts a notch or two to get set for the job ahead.

'And with the news, everybody got busy – the aircrews, the ground crews, the mechanics, the WAAFs, the cooks. The ships already had a basic bomb and fuel load on board, and the additional loads were sent out in ammunition trailers and fuel trucks. The perimeter track lost its usually deserted appearance and looked like a well travelled highway, with trucks and trailers, buses and bicycles hurrying out to the dispersal points. It was just like the preparation at any bomber base before taking off for enemy territory – but going over the Big City was something different. These men had been there before. They knew what to expect.

'In the equipment room, June, the pint-size WAAF in battledress, was an incongruous note. Over a counter as high as her chin, she flung parachutes, harnesses and Mae Wests. The crew grabbed them and lugged them out to the ships. You kept thinking they ought to be able to get somebody a little bigger for the job she was handling.

'In the briefing room, the met officer gave the weather report and the forecast over enemy territory. There would be considerable cloud over the target. The men grinned. An operations officer gave a talk on the trip. The route was outlined on a large map of Germany on the front wall. It looked ominously long on the large scale map. He pointed out where the ground defences were supposed to be strong and were fighter opposition might be expected. He gave the time when the various phases should be over the target. He explained where the 'spoof' attacks were to be made and the time.[74] He told the men what kinds of flares and other markers the Pathfinders would drop. There was the usual business of routine instructions, statistics and tactics to be used. The Group Captain gave a pep talk on the progress of the Battle of Berlin. And all the while, that tape marking the route stared you in the face and seemed to grow longer and longer.

'Outside it was hazy and growing more so. But this was nothing new. The men were convinced that the weather was always at its most variable and its dampest and its haziest over their field. What could you expect? Ops would probably be scrubbed after all. Hell of a note.

'In the fading light the planes were silhouetted against the sky. They looked, on the ground, slightly hunched and menacing like hawks. Seeing them there, in the half light you would never guess how easy and graceful they are in flight. Nor would you realise when you see them soaring off the runway, what an immense load they take up with them. It is only when you see the open bomb bay on the ground, that you get some idea of a Lancaster's destructive power. The open bomb bay seems like a small hangar. The 4,0001b-block buster in place looks like a kitten curled up in a large bed. It is a sobering sight.

'In the evening some of the men tried to catch a few winks; most of them just sat around talking. The operational meal followed. It was only a snack, but it was the last solid food any one would get until the fresh egg and bacon breakfast which has become a ritual for the proper ending of a successful mission.

'As there was still some time to wait before take-off, V for Victor's crew sat around the grounderew's hut near the dispersal point, warming themselves by the stove or chewing the rag with the groundcrew. The Wingco came around to make a last minute check-up. The medical officer looked everyone over. The engineer officer checked the engines.

'The minutes crept by until at last the time came to get into the planes. The deep stillness of the night was awakened by the motors revving up; one after another until each one was lost in the general roar. The crews scrambled into the planes and took their places. The great ships were guided out of their dispersal areas by the ground crews who gave a final wave as the Lancs moved off slowly down the perimeter track. They appeared more menacing than ever creeping along in the dark with their motors roaring. One by one they turned onto the runway and noisily vanished into the night.

'From now on, until they would return, the members of V for Victor's crew were a little world in themselves, alone and yet not alone. For all around them were other similar little worlds, hundreds of them with a population of seven, hurtling through space, lightlessly – huge animated ammunition dumps. For its safety, each little world depended utterly and completely on its members – and a large dash of luck.

'There was not much conversation over the intercom. When you're flying without running lights on a definite course, and surrounded by several hundred other bombers, you have not time for any pleasantries. The navigator was busy checking the air speed and any possible drift. Almost everyone else kept a look out for other aircraft, both friend and foe. A friendly aircraft is almost as dangerous as an enemy plane, for if two blockbusters meet in mid-air, the pieces that are left are very small indeed.

'Occasionally the ship jolted from the slipstream of some unseen aircraft ahead, and frequently others overhauled V for Victor, passing by to port and starboard, above and below. V for Victor gained altitude very easily for maximum ceiling. She was a veteran of over 50 ops and had the DFC painted on her port bow to celebrate the fiftieth, but she had the vitality of a youngster. Blondy [Sergeant J.R. O'Hanlon], the wireless-operator, broke the silence. 'Taff, the W/T has gone u/s.'

'The wireless is not used except in an emergency such as ditching, but it is nice to know it's there. We went on. Occasionally Taff, the pilot, would call into the intercom, 'Bob, [Sergeant C.E. 'Bob' Shilling] are you OK?' There would be a silence for a moment while the rear-gunner fumbled to turn on his intercom, until you wondered if he had frozen back there. Then he'd sing out, 'OK, Taff.' He and the mid-upper gunner [Sergeant A. Newman] were the only two outside the heated cabin. Inside the cabin it was warm and snug. You didn't even need gloves. Jock [Sergeant J.R. 'Jock' Mearns], the navigator, wore no flying gear, just the Air Force battledress.

'Up ahead the Pathfinder boys dropped the first route markers, flak shot up into the air and the men knew that V for Victor was approaching the Dutch coast. An enormous burst of flame lit up the night off to port. 'Scarecrow to starboard,' the mid-upper reported on the intercom. Jerry intended the 'scarecrow' to look like a burning plane but it did not take long to see that it was not.[75]

'Jock's Scots accent came over the intercom: 'Taff, we're eleven minutes late.' 'OK, we'll increase speed.' The engineer pushed up the throttles. Everything was black again below. Occasionally there was a small burst of flak here and there.

'Plane to starboard below!'

'OK, it's a Lanc.' As V for Victor passed it you could seen the bluish flame from the exhausts lighting the aircraft below in a weird ghostly manner. It was unpleasant to realise that our own exhausts made V for Victor just as obvious as the other plane.

'Away off the port bow, a glow became visible. It looked like the moon but it was the first big German searchlight belt, encompassing many cities. The beams were imprisoned under cloud.[76]

'That will be Happy Valley,' (the Ruhr) Jock said. Another route marker appeared ahead.

'Tell me when we're over it,' the navigator replied. Shortly the bomb-aimer [Flight Sergeant N.A. 'Digger' Lambrell RAAF] said, 'We're bang over it now.'

'OK, Digger.'

'Taff, we're nine minutes late.' The navigator took a couple of astro sights to get a fix. From this he could determine the wind and the drift of the plane.

'Another searchlight belt show up to starboard. It was enormous, running for miles and miles. It was all imprisoned under the cloud but it was an evil looking sight just the same.[77] The top of the clouds shone with millions of moving spots, like so many restless glow worms, but the impression was much more sinister – like some kind of luminous octopus. The tentacle-like beams groped about seeking some hole in the cloud, some way of clutching at you as you passed by protected by the darkness. The continuous motion of the searchlights caused a ripple effect on the clouds, giving them an agitated, angry, frustrated appearance. Once in a while one found a rift and shot its light high into the sky. Flak came up sparkling and twinkling through this luminous blanket. V for Victor jolted violently from close bursts, but was untouched. It passed another Lanc which was clearly silhouetted against the floodlit clouds.

'Another leg of the trip was completed. The navigator gave the new course over the intercom and added, 'Seven minutes late.'

'OK, Jock. Mac, [Pilot Officer E.M. Graham, flight engineer] make it 165.'

'V for Victor passed plane after plane and occasionally jolted in the slipstream of others. A third searchlight belt showed up, this one free of cloud. It was a huge wall of light and looked far more impenetrable than a mountain. It seemed inconceivable than any plane could pass through and reach the opposite side. You thanked your lucky stars that this was not the target. To fly out of the protecting darkness into the blaze of light would be a test of courage you would rather not have to face.

'Nevertheless, there were some facing it right now. The flak opened up and the searchlights waved madly about. It was a diversionary attack, the 'spoof. You watched in a detached, remote sort of way. It seemed very far away and did not seem to concern you at all. Until suddenly, one beam which had been vertical, slanted down and started to pursue V for Victor, and you realised that it did concern you very intimately. The seconds ticked by as the beam overtook the plane. But it passed harmlessly overhead and groped impotently in the darkness beyond.

'Four minutes late,' Jock called over the intercom.

'The target itself, the Big City, came into view like a luminous patch dead ahead. It was largely hidden by cloud and showed few searchlights. It seemed so much less formidable than the mountain of light just behind, that it came as a sort of anticlimax. Surely, you felt, this cannot be the Big City, the nerve-centre of Europe's evil genius.

'It was quiet. There was no flak as yet, no flares, and just the handful of searchlights. You tried to imagine what it was like on the ground there. The sirens would be about to sound; the ack-ack batteries would be standing ready, the searchlights already manned. You wondered if the people were in shelters.

'But it was too much of an effort. It was too remote. Your problems were flak, fighters, searchlights and whether you were on the course and on time. What happened below was an entirely different problem, which had nothing to do with you. What happened below might just as well be happening on Mars. V for Victor's own little world simply hovering off this planet and leading a life of its own.

'Ever so slowly V for Victor crept up on the target. The two worlds were coming inevitably together. But it still had the quality of unreality. It was like a dream where you were hurrying somewhere and yet cannot move at all. Nevertheless, Victor was passing plane after plane and jolted in somebody's slipstream now and again. The other Lancs looked ominous bearing down on the target, breathing out blue flame as they approached.

'The minute of the attack and still the target was quiet. One more minute ticked by – still quiet. The engineer opened up the throttles to maximum speed and increased the oxygen supply. Still quiet. The whole attack was a minute or two late. Winds, probably. Suddenly the whole city opened up. The flak poured up through the clouds. It came in a myriad of little lights. It poured up in a stream of red, as if shaken from a hose. It would be impossible to miss such a brilliantly marked objective. Bright flashes started going off under the clouds. That would be the cookies from the planes ahead. V for Victor started the bombing run. The bomb-aimer called the course now.

'Left, left ... Steady now ... Right a bit ... Steady ... steady ... Cookie gone!' V for Victor shot upward slightly. 'Steady ... Incendiaries gone ...' V for Victor surged again ever so slightly.

'Stand-by, Taff,' it was the voice of Bob, the tail-gunner. 'Fighter.'

'Instantly the pilot sent V for Victor over to starboard and rushed headlong downward. A stream of red tracer whipped out of the dark, past the rear turret, and on past the wing-tip, missing by what seemed inches. A second later the fighter itself shot past after the tracer, a vague dark blur against the night sky.

'Me 109,' Bob said calmly.

'V for Victor squirmed and corkscrewed over the sky of Berlin. You wondered how it could be possible to avoid all the other planes that were over the city. But the fighter was shaken off and V for Victor came back to a normal course again.

'Down below through rifts in the cloud, you could see that Berlin was burning. The bright, white flame of the incendiaries showed up as a carpet of light, always growing. And flash after flash went off as the blockbusters fell. The dark, black shapes of many Lancasters could be seen all over the sky, against the brilliant clouds below. They were like small insects crawling over a great glass window. It did not seem possible that these tiny black dots could be the cause of the destruction which was going on below. The insects crawled to the edge of the light and disappeared into the darkness beyond. They had passed safely through the target, V for Victor close behind.

'Shortly the course was set for the return and Berlin was visible for many miles on the port quarter. The attack was over now. It took only fifteen minutes. The ack-ack was silent. There was no flak flashing over the city, but the city was brighter than ever. The clouds were getting a reddish tinge which showed that the fires had caught hold below.

'And so the capital of Nazism dropped astern, obscuring the rising moon by its flames. The Government which came into power by deliberately setting fire to its chamber of representatives, the Government which first used wholesale bombing, and boasted of it, was now perishing in fires far more devastating than any it ever devised. It was perishing to a fire music never dreamed of by Wagner.

'But it was impossible to connect V for Victor with the death struggles of Berlin. There was no time for contemplation.

'Stand-by, Ju 88 starboard – corkscrew,' came Bob's voice. Again with lightning speed, the pilot put V for Victor over and dived out of the way. The Ju 88's tracers missed us and shot down another Lanc which had not been so fortunate.

'After that the route home was uneventful. Crossing the North Sea, V for Victor went into a gentle incline towards home base, as if by a sort of homing instinct. The searchlights of England sent out a greeting of welcome. For miles alone the coast they stood almost evenly spaced, vertical sentries guarding the island. Then they started waving downwards in the direction of the nearest airfield. No doubt they were helping home a damaged bomber. How different they were from the menacing tentacles over the German cities. V for Victor arrived over the home field. The wireless-operator called base over his repaired equipment. He said simply. 'V-Victor'.

'The clear voice of a girl came pleasantly over the intercom, 'V-Victor, prepare to pancake'. The short business-like message in service slang was a wonderful welcome home. V for Victor circled the field, losing altitude.

'V-Victor in funnels.'

'V-Victor, pancake,' the girl's voice said. V for Victor touched down, ran down the flarepath, and turned off on the perimeter track.

'V-Victor clear of flarepath.' The groundcrew met V for Victor and acted as a guide back into the dispersal area.

'How was it?'

'Piece of cake,' someone said. The crew got out, collected their gear, the parachutes, Mae Wests, the navigator's bag, the guns, etc, and then, as one man, lit up cigarettes. The pilot walked around the plane looking for any damage. There was one small hole through the aileron but it was too dark to see it then.

'The bus arrived and the crew clambered in with all the gear and were taken back to the locker room. June was there, and gathered all the stuff over the counter and staggered away, lost from sight under a mound of yellow suits and Mae Wests.

'Then back to the briefing room where a cup of hot tea with rum in it was waiting. Each captain signed his name on the board as he came in. Crew by crew, the men went into the Intelligence room, carrying their spiked tea with them. There were packages of cigarettes on the table and everyone chain-smoked, lighting up from the butt of the previous one.

'The Intelligence Officer asked brief questions and the replies were brief such as 'The heavy flak was light and the light flak heavy'. It was over in a very few minutes and you went back to the briefing room and bantered over the trip with the other crews. No trouble, any of them, but there were gaps in the list of captains chalked on the board.

'It's like that,' the Wingco remarked. 'In night flying, you usually get back intact, or you don't get back at all. If you get coned, or a fighter sees you before you see it, then very often you've had it, but if somebody else gets coned then its that much easier for you.'

'You thought of the other Lancaster the Ju 88 got with the same burst that missed V for Victor. And you lit another cigarette. The first signs of dawn were coming over the field now and off in the distance, on the bleak, windswept, little knoll, V for Victor stood guard over the empty dispersal points from which other men and ships had gone out a short while before. '...if somebody else gets coned then it's that much easier for you.'[78]

With his score standing at 68 victories, 27-year-old *Major* Wittgenstein became *Kommodore* of NJG 2 on 1 January 1944. That night he was airborne again in his Ju 88C-6 equipped with *SN-2* radar and *Schräge Musik when* Bomber Command went to Berlin with a force of 421 Lancasters. One of the crews on the Order of Battle[79] was captained by F/O James 'Gil' Bryson of 550 Squadron, who had joined the squadron on its formation at Waltham, Grimsby on 25 November 1943, having transferred from 12 Squadron at Wickenby where they had begun operations on 3 September. The crew's last two trips had been to the Big City before they had received two days of rest. Sgt Jim Donnan, the WOp recalls the events of New Year's Day 1944:

> 'We were engaged in routine pre-operational checks and testing of our equipment prior to the main briefing, which commenced in a tense atmosphere. When the curtain was drawn aside exposing the operational map, the target was Berlin for the third consecutive time, only this time our route to the 'Big City' was almost directly from the Dutch coast across an area, which was becoming increasingly dangerous because of nightfighter activity. Deteriorating weather conditions delayed our take-off for several hours. It was therefore difficult to relax during this period. As New Year's Day was drawing to a close we were preparing for take-off and at 14 minutes past midnight we were airborne and on our way at last. The sky was dark and overcast as we flew through layers of broken cloud, climbing to our operational height, heading east over the North Sea. As we approached the Dutch coast we could see that the anti-aircraft defenses were very active and we became alert to the dangers ahead. Flying over Germany, occasional bursts of *Flak* and flashes lit up the thick, unbroken cloud along the route. While searching the night-fighter waveband I was aware of considerable activity by the German control. We found it necessary to keep a sharp look out even though our trip had been uneventful so far. Our navigator Sgt Thomas 'Rocky' Roxby called for a slight change in course for the final leg to Berlin as we reached a position between Hanover and Bremen.
>
> 'It was almost immediately afterwards that a series of thuds vibrated through the floor and the aircraft seemed to bank away to starboard. I leapt up from my seat to the astrodome where I could see the starboard engines were on fire. As I switched over from radio to intercom, I saw that a fire had started under the navigator's table on the floor just behind the pilot. It was soon burning fiercely.
>
> 'The pilot gave the order to abandon the aircraft. I clipped on my parachute and as I moved forward it was

found that the front escape hatch would not open. The engineer joined the bomb aimer in trying to release it. As I stood behind the navigator waiting to exit, the rear gunner said that he was having trouble with the rear turret. I then signalled that I would go to the rear exit. The navigator was standing beside the pilot ready to exit as I scrambled over the main spar and along the fuselage to the rear door, losing my shoes on the way. When I got there, the mid-upper gunner was ready to leave and the rear gunner was out of his turret and preparing to come forward. I then jettisoned the rear door as the flames from the starboard wing streamed past, licking the tail plane. Grasping the release handle on my parachute I prepared to jump but I must have lost consciousness as I have no recollection of what happened next nor how I left the plane. When I regained consciousness, my parachute was already open and I was floating in pitch darkness, very cold and my feet were freezing. I seemed to be a long time coming down but as I descended through the clouds, dark shadows appeared and I landed on soft ground in an open space. Gathering up my parachute, I dashed over to a clump of trees, where I sat on the ground shivering and wondering how I could avoid capture.'[80]

The Lancaster's starboard wing and the incendiary bombs in the front of the bomb bay were set on fire by a surprise *Schräge Musik* attack. Most probably Bryson's Lancaster was one of the six shot down in quick succession by *Major* Heinrich Prinz *zu* Sayn-Wittgenstein[81], who had succeeded in penetrating the bomber stream bound for Berlin. Most of these *Viermots* were Pathfinders flying at the front of the bomber stream.[82] Twenty-eight bombers failed to return, 21 of which were destroyed by *Tame Boars*; two *Gruppen* of JG 302 that operated over the target claimed another four *Viermot* kills, two of which, were later officially confirmed to the single-engined claimants.

The next night, 2/3 January, 383 Lancasters went to Berlin again and 27 bombers were shot down, mainly over the target. On 5/6 January 358 bombers raided Stettin with the loss of 16 heavies (15 of which were destroyed by the *Nachtjagd*, including at least nine in the greater Stettin area). On 14/15 January when 498 bombers hit Brunswick, 38 bombers failed to return. This time 38 to 42 Lancasters were shot down by the *Nachtjagd*. On the night of 20/21 January 35 bombers were shot down by the German defenses (*Nachtjagd* claimed 35 victories), which operated the *Zahme Sau* tactics to excellent advantage and who seemed to have rendered *Window* counter-productive. *Oblt* Dietrich Schmidt, *Staffelkapitän*, 8./NJG 1 who had 11 confirmed night victories, recalls:

'Towards the end of 1943 the British started to attack pin-point targets using Mosquitoes equipped with a transponder-type navigation system, known by us as the Y-system, which guaranteed high precision from great heights. The Mosquito could operate at heights of 10-12,000 meters, which was unreachable for us. They even carried out attacks on moonlit nights, which would have been too risky for normal bombers. In my 8th *Staffel* we had modified a Bf 110G-4[83] especially for Mosquito hunting. The exhaust covers, drop tanks, armor and all the guns except two cannon with little ammunition was removed. In addition, the machine was polished and flown with only a two-man crew. All this allowed us to reach 12,000 meters in a relatively short time but as the engine performance dropped off above 6000 meters there was little maneuverability left. Also, the heating was no longer efficient at minus 50°. Obviously our only chance against the Mosquitoes was to get to 10,000 meters in time and then get precise directions to a target from the *Jägerleitoffizier* (JLO, or GCI-controller).

'On 14 January we were roused at 0445. The front was through. It was perfect weather, four days after the full moon. We took off and soon saw condensation trails above. We climbed to 9100 meters and then things began to happen. *Jägerleitoffizier Lt* Rauer directed us to an aircraft coming from the Ruhr. I approached well. Two kilometers, one kilometre, two kilometers, one and a half kilometers' range. I was going flat out and waited to see what the radio operator said. Then I saw him over to starboard at a height of 8500 meters. I turned in. Now I was close below him. It was a Mosquito. The wings and tail were clearly recognisable. On each engine I saw dark red exhaust flames. My speed matched his. I pulled up and I was behind him, my sights on his port engine. My first burst struck well. There were no misses. The engine burst into flames – large bluish ones – and he went down, first in a flat descent, then steeper. At about 5000 meters he exploded with a thick, dark flame. Small pieces broke off. One burning part plunged downward but was extinguished while still high above the ground. There was no crash fire. Probably there was not much of him left. I recorded our *Abschuss* at 0535. We were delighted. The 'Mosquito-hunt' had paid off after all. We phoned right away and were informed that our adversary crashed near Mehr, northwest of Kleve. One man escaped, the other was found dead. As far as I knew, this was the fourth fighter *Abschuss* of a Mosquito at night.'[84]

Despite all *Nachtjagd*'s continued efforts, the Mosquito continued to fly practically unchallenged over the *Reich*. By the end of World War II *Nachtjagd* had destroyed only about 50 Mosquitoes, mainly by He 219 and Me 262 jet crews.

One of the Mosquito intruder pilots at this time was American 1/Lt James Forrest 'Lou' Luma[85] of 418 Squadron RCAF stationed at Ford, Sussex. Luma recalls:

> 'Ford was located on the beautiful south coast of England. Like many RAF aerodromes, it consisted of two paved runways at right angles to each other. Circling the perimeter of the aerodrome was a paved taxiway. The aircraft were parked in blast bays located outside this perimeter. Blast bays were 'U'-shaped revetments that protected the aircraft from all but a direct hit by a bomb. The blast bays were in clusters with a taxiway leading from each cluster to the perimeter taxiway. The taxiways and runways were lighted at night but only when aircraft were using them. Life at Ford was good. We had a comfortable officer's mess and were billeted in private homes that had been taken over by the government. We had our own rooms and were awakened and brought tea in the morning by a batman, who was a RAF enlisted man.
>
> '418 Squadron consisted of 'A' Flight and 'B' Flight, which alternated duty. Fin and I were posted to 'A' Flight. The squadron's Mosquitoes had the paintings of Al Capp's 'Li'l Abner' characters on them; each aircraft had a different character from Dogpatch. The aircraft that was assigned to Fin and me,*'D for Dog'* had a painting of *Moonbeam McSwine* on it.
>
> 'Sometimes when we were on standby, we would conduct a night-flying test. Fin and I would fly the airplane for 30 minutes or so to determine its mechanical fitness. Sometimes we would also practice air-to-air gunnery, using a camera gun. At other times we would do an in-flight compass swing. After landing we would leave our parachutes and helmets in the seats in order to save time in case of a scramble. The 'erks' (ground crew) would correct any mechanical problems we might have experienced and would top off the fuel tanks. The erks were a hard-working, dedicated, loyal part of the team, and they did not receive the recognition they deserved. At least not from me. I was too young and egotistical to think that anyone other than myself was contributing to any success that I might achieve.
>
> 'After we had finished our night-flying test, we would have supper at the officers' mess before reporting in at the ops room for the night's duty. The ops room was a medium-size room with reasonably comfortable chairs to lounge in while we were on standby. It had planning tables for the navigators, and the walls were plastered with silhouettes of German aircraft for boning up on aircraft recognition. We killed time by reading, talking, and listening to the radio. Sometimes we would listen to the English-speaking 'Lord Haw Haw,' who broadcast Nazi propaganda from Germany. The music on his station was usually better than what the BBC offered.
>
> 'Usually we were given our targets as soon as we arrived at the ops room, and would plan our flight accordingly. At other times, we reported to the ready room and remained there on standby, waiting for a scramble. We were dressed and ready to go. Pilots had flying gloves made of thin chamois that fit tightly to the hands. The preferred style of flying boots had a dress shoe on the foot with fleece lined uppers. In the event you baled out over occupied territory, you would cut off the uppers after you were on the ground by using a small knife carried in a pocket in the boots. This left you with black, low-cut dress shoes that could pass as part of your civilian attire when being helped by the Underground to get out of the country. Each crewmember carried a packet containing the currency of the country they would be flying over (usually French francs) and a map printed on cloth.'

Luma carried out his most memorable flight on the night of 20/21 January when 648 bombers attacked Magdeburg. (Berlin was also bombed in a diversionary raid by Lancasters and Mosquitoes and flying bomb sites were also hit). Luma's 17th mission was the one that entitled him and his navigator to have their first swastika painted on the side of their Mosquito FBVI, as he recalls:

> 'My navigator, Fin [Colin Finlayson] was sick so another navigator, F/L Al Eckert, was assigned to my plane. We took off from Ford at 2215 hours on a *Flower* to Hildesheim, Germany, near Hanover. By now ops were pretty much routine for me. On each of my early flights I fully expected that I would see an enemy aircraft but it didn't happen. Now I was pretty much resigned to the fact that I might put in a whole tour without ever seeing an enemy aircraft. It was possible; some of our crews did come up scoreless. When Al and I took off, there was no reason to believe that this wouldn't be just another uneventful op. The weather was sour with a lot of low cloud and haze, which made navigation difficult. We reached an airfield that was lighted with perimeter lights. After orbiting the airfield we found a pinpoint that fixed the airfield as Wunstorf. Shortly after that we saw two bright lights on the other side of the airfield. We came in to meet them very nearly head-on. They proved to be on an aircraft that had just taken off from the base. We were at 1500 ft and the enemy aircraft passed over us at 2000

ft. As he passed over us we identified him as a twin-engine aircraft with one white light just under the nose and one under the tail.

'We did a quick orbit to port, coming in behind him and chased him for 15 to 20 miles. As we closed, he was climbing through about 4000 ft. In my excitement at seeing my first enemy aircraft, I very possibly came close to losing the opportunity to chalk up my first kill. I had overestimated our closing speed and overshot him. As I threw down the landing gear to slow us down, the thought that my buck fever was going to cost me the chance of destroying my first enemy aircraft left me with a sick feeling in the pit of my stomach. With the gear down, the Mossie rapidly slowed but we were still not in a position to shoot at him. We were directly below him. By now the nervous excitement had disappeared. I did a quick turn to port, followed by one to starboard. This brought us under his tail – about 500 ft below and 250 to 100 yards behind. I was calm, and I knew we had him in the bag. We were in position. I pulled back on the stick, placed the center of the gunsight slightly forward of and midway between the points where the exhaust flames emerged from the engines. Then I fired all my cannon and machine guns. Strikes on the fuselage were followed by a big ball of fire, which enabled us to identify the aircraft as a Me 210. A large piece broke off to the left and he went down. Al Eckert saw him go in, explode and burn on the ground. After our return to base the erks found two pieces of plywood from the enemy aircraft embedded in the leading edge of the Mosquito's starboard wing.

'Not long after destroying the Me 210 there was an article in the Air Ministry Weekly Intelligence Summary about a Luftwaffe ace by the name of *Major* Prinz Heinrich *zu* Sayn-Wittgenstein, a highly decorated Luftwaffe night-fighter pilot who was killed in air combat on the night of 21/22 January 1944. The Intelligence Summary went on to say that he had shot down 83 aircraft. It also said he had shot down five RAF aircraft within a few hours of meeting his death. I found it interesting that I was the only RAF/RCAF pilot who had shot down an enemy over the Continent that night.'[86]

On 21/22 January German night-fighter defenses destroyed 57 bombers. In less than 40 minutes *Major* Wittgenstein, *Kommodore* of NJG 2 flying a Ju 88C-6[87] on a Tame Boar sortie in the vicinity of Magdeburg shot down three Lancasters and two Halifaxes. His third kill of the night was probably the Lancaster[88] flown by F/L L.B. Patkin RAAF of 467 Squadron RAAF, which Wittgenstein set on fire with a single burst. The bomber flew on for a few moments before plunging down and crashing in flames at 0230 at Altmerdingsen, near Burgdorf, Germany. The aircraft exploded so violently on impact that roofs and windows of nearby houses were shattered and the crater caused was approximately 25 yards in diameter. Wittgenstein was about to press the trigger to fire a second burst into the fifth Lancaster when the fuselage and port wing of the Ju 88 was riddled with enemy fire, probably from below. This happened shortly before 2300 hrs to the east of Magdeburg. The Junkers went into a dive, whereupon Wittgenstein jettisoned the cabin roof and ordered his crew to bale out immediately, which they did successfully. Early next morning the body of Prinz Wittgenstein was discovered close to the crash site at Lübars. On baling out, his head had probably struck the tailplane, rendering him unconscious and unable to pull the ripcord.[89] Another leading *Experten*, *Hptm* Manfred Meurer, *Kommandeur* I/NJG 1 was also killed.[90]

Fw Karl-Georg Pfeiffer's career almost ended in January 1944 too:

'The days and weeks were filled with sorties without any success. Once we were over Heligoland where we had scored our first victory. 12./NJG 1 operated from Bergen, Quakenbrück and Leeuwarden. On 14 January 1944 we operated over Holland from Quakenbrück, take-off at 1812 hrs. There was not much going on. I wanted to refuel at Leeuwarden, in spite of or perhaps because of bad weather. Cloud base was only 120 metre. I also had the feeling that my port engine was not working quite as it should and Leeuwarden, with its long runway and well-illuminated approach lights, was just the very thing. With clearance from flying control, I set about letting down over the radio beacon ten kilometers east of the airfield, going round and round, ever lower, with the beacon indicator steady in the left-hand corner of the instrument. I had inherited 99+CZ only a few days before from *Lt* Holland who had been given a new machine. He probably knew why he had given the kite away. It took an age before I got down, orbiting over the radio beacon, from 2500 meters to 550, 400 and finally 300 meters and still no sight of the ground. The engines were running at half power. Willi had already switched on the VHF approach beam. Still in cloud, I suddenly noticed that the starboard engine was failing. It started to stutter. This looked like being a fine thing, to have engine failure during an instrument approach. It got worse and worse and I stopped the engine. I was in a left-hand turn so it was not so bad if the starboard engine had failed. We were down to one hundred meters and I went carefully onto about 250°. Now I could not go any lower. I still had no ground contact. The clouds broke up a little and I could see the approach lights way ahead. Would we make it? I pushed the port throttle lever fully forward. It was said that the Me 110 could maintain height on one engine (some wizards maintained one could even climb). In my case it was unfortunately not so. The port engine was also failing to give full power; I took the throttle back and pushed it fully forward. In my fear I even increased the propeller pitch to 11.30, even 12.00. But there was no increase in power.

'Suddenly Willi shouted from behind: 'Watch your height, we are down to 30 meters!'

'But I was unable to pull the machine up without risking a stall. I realized that I would have to put the kite down in an open field. Quickly I switched on the landing light and noticed just in time that we were heading for a barn at 200 km/h. I lifted the port wing a little and also gave a little right rudder. And we missed it by inches. But the aircraft had lost too much speed in this maneuver. It dropped; there was an impact and then sudden silence. Then I heard *Gefr* Krause calling: '*Herr* Oberfeld, out quickly, hurry!' He was trying to open my cockpit roof from outside but he did not succeed.

'I replied quite calmly: 'I'm coming', unlatched the cabin roof and stepped out onto the wing. It seemed odd that one could simply step down from this onto the ground. My two crew took me by the arm and we ran away from the machine. The fuselage was broken in several places and the two still steaming engines had been torn off. Ten meters beyond was a deep ditch. Fortunately the machine had not slithered that far, otherwise there would probably have been an explosion and we would not be standing here now. Suddenly I felt sick. I went to one side and vomited. Now we heard a disturbance and klaxons far away. Oho, flying control had noticed that we had gone down and now the fire engine, ambulance and some cars were on their way. We fired off a red to show them where we were and finally they reached us. They stared at us because we were uninjured. A forced landing in a pitch-black night with chances of survival far less than baling out! We were taken straight to the sick quarters and examined by *Stabsarzt* Dr. Schreiber. I had a gaping wound on my left eyebrow, which I had not noticed before. I had apparently hit my head on the reflector sight. Dr. Schreiber tested my reflexes by scratching around my stomach with a pointed stick. 'Well, everything is in order', he said. Or so he thought. If the *Herr Stabsarzt* had taken a little more trouble with me right away, an X-ray would have shown that I had a fractured skull, which would cause me a lot of trouble later on. Only after I was unable to lay my head on my pillow without feeling dizzy and complained about constant headaches, did he send me to the eye clinic in Osnabrück but there was nothing wrong with my eyes. Then I was taken to the Luftwaffe hospital in Brunswick for a thorough examination. After four weeks of tests they discovered my skull fracture, which was unable to heal because after an eight-day rest after the accident I had continued to fly. With the decrease of air pressure at height the fracture had widened each time I went up. I was forbidden to fly for four months, which did not please me at all.

'At Easter 1944 I had to go to the decompression chamber at Köln-Ostheim, where I was cured. At long last I could fly again but by then the 'classical' night fighting was over. The war continued and became more difficult for us night fighters too. For some months we continued to fly from St. Trond and Brussels-Melsbroek. I got one more *Abschuss* (my 11th)[91] then it was all over. When we were transferred, after the invasion, to Dortmund, virtually our last station as night fighters, it was just a case of staying alive. Many good comrades still lost their lives, such as *Lt* Holland and others.'

Meanwhile, on 30/31 January 1944 Berlin was attacked again, this time by a force of 534 aircraft. Thirty-three bombers were shot down, all of them by twin-engined *Tame Boar*s. Two Mosquitoes were put up by 169 Squadron, including *P-Pluto* flown by B Flight Commander S/L Joe Cooper and F/L Ralph Connolly.[92] Cooper recalls:

'I had to orbit 50 miles from Berlin on one of the German beacons. We tootled along and just got into position when I picked up a blip in front of me. He was orbiting slowly Turning down the gunsight I could see the shape. There was no moon and it was very very dark. I got into position, slightly below and astern, went up to him and gave him the treatment; cannon – a lot of cannon. We were at about 25,000 ft. He was a complete flamer. Actually I gave him a bit more. 'That's for Coventry', I said. But I got in too close. I was mesmerized by it all. Rafe said, 'Look out Joe, you're going to hit the bastard.' I pulled the 'pole' back hard and the result was I stalled and went into a spin. We were not allowed to spin or acrobat the Mosquito because of our long-range belly tanks, which moved the center of gravity of the aircraft. I put on the usual drill: full opposite rudder, stick forward. I'd done this before but never in a Mossie. Went straight into a spin the other way! I went into the spin about five times, heading for the ground all the while. During the spins I could see this 110 out of the corner of my eye; most extraordinary!

'One's thoughts were, what a bloody shame. This is going to be the first Hun the Squadron's got and I won't be there to tell the boys. I wonder who's going to hit the ground first, him or me? What a bloody shame the boys aren't going to know I told Rafe, 'Bale out. We've had it!' He had an observer-type parachute under his seat. In the spin he couldn't bend down to pick it up! He took his helmet off and put it on again. I said, 'Get out!'

'Rafe replied, 'If you can get us out of this spin, I could!'

'I thought, 'I'll try something else.' I centralized the pole and the rudder and eased it out of the dive. At 7000 ft I straightened up. I had not been frightened but boy was I frightened now. Our radar blew up in the spin. I said to Ralph 'You can kneel and look backwards and keep an eye out for the Huns!' We had light *Flak* all the way back to the coast. Approaching Snoring I called up the tower 'Is S/L Ted Thorne in the tower?' I asked. 'Yes,' they said. I said, 'Tell him he owes me ten bob.' (I had bet Ted ten shillings I would get a Hun before him!) Ted took the camp Tannoy – it was one in the morning – and announced, 'For your information everybody S/L Cooper is coming into land and he's got the first Hun!' When I landed there were 300 airmen and WAAFs around P-Pluto! Most extraordinary! I gave them a little talk and off we went.'[93]

The month ended with the *Nachtjagd* scoring an all-time monthly record of 308 Bomber Command aircraft shot down. I *Jagdkorps* claimed at least 223 victories (including 114 during the three Berlin raids 29 January - 1 February) but lost 55 aircraft and crews during January 1944. Losses had reduced the front-line strength to 179 operational aircraft and crews by 31 January. It was clear that new British tactics and new countermeasures would be necessary before a resumption of raids deep into Germany and the *Reich* defenses too, were in need of an overhaul.

Notes

1. 347 Lancasters, 246 Halifaxes, 125 Stirlings and 73 Wellingtons.

2. 4 Halifaxes, 4 Lancasters, 3 Stirlings and a Wellington, all but one falling to night fighters of NJG 3 and IV./NJG 1 operating over NW Germany, Schleswig-Holstein and the northern part of the Netherlands.

3. On the night of 27 April 1944 Johnen landed his 8./NJG 6 Bf 110G at Dübendorf airfield in Switzerland after claiming a Halifax nr Strasbourg as his 17th victory (in fact Lancaster III ND759 of 35 Sqn). The German authorities fearing that he had defected immediately ordered the arrest of his family but Johnen had simply made an emergency landing after being hit by return fire from a second bomber that he intercepted over the Swiss-German border. He was soon repatriated and a German agent was permitted to blow up his Bf 110 and destroy the radar equipment. The Swiss Government received a *Staffel* of Bf 109E fighters as reward! Johnen was awarded the *Ritterkreuz* in October 1944 and he took his score to 34 victories. He survived the war as *Gruppenkommandeur* of III./NJG 6.

4. The 25/26 July raid on Essen caused severe damage to the industrial areas in the eastern parts of the city. The Krupps Works suffered its most damaging raid of the war and 51 other industrial buildings were damaged with another 83 heavily damaged. 26 bombers or 3.7 % of the force FTR of which, 19 were destroyed by nightfighters – 15 of these to crews of NJG 1 and NJG 3 manning the *Himmelbett* boxes in Holland and over the Dutch-German border. Wild Boar single-engined night fighters that engaged the bomber stream over the blazing city of Essen claimed the 4 remaining a/c losses.

5. On 27/28 July *Nachtjäger* claimed 16 bombers shot down, including 4 by single-engined Wild Boars. During the third raid on Hamburg on 29/30 July the *Nachtjagd* was credited with 34 kills, equally divided between single-engined Wild Boars and twin-engined crews that were allowed to leave the confines of their *Himmelbett* boxes for the first time. On 2/3 August 19 of the 30 bombers that FTR from Hamburg were shot down by the *Nachtjagd.*

6. A bomber pilot and one of the foremost blind flying experts in the Luftwaffe, who had been agitating for a long time without success for permission to practice freelance single-engined night fighting. Hermann had reasoned that the light of the massed searchlights, pathfinder flares and the flames of the burning target below could easily identify enemy bombers over a German city. By putting a mass concentration of mainly single-engined fighters over the target, his pilots could, without need of ground control but assisted by a running commentary from a *lentraler Gefechtsstand* (Central Operational Headquarters) visually identify the bombers and shoot them down. A *Fühlungshalter* (shadowing) aircraft, usually a Ju 88 or Do 217 would fly in or near a penetrating bomber stream and keep the plotting room at the *Zentraler Gefechtsstand* informed on course, height and speed of the bombers. Around May.1943 Hermann had begun trials at Jüterborg in the use of the Bf 109G6 as a night fighter. On 27 June 1943 he transferred his activities to Blind Flying School No 10 at Altenburg, where he gathered together some experienced pilots and began forming a *Nachtjagd Versuchs Kommando* using 12 Fw 190-As fitted with 300 litre (66-gallon) drop tanks. As a result of his suggestion, *Helle Nachtjagd* was again tried, in July and, after the first trials in Berlin and the Ruhr proved successful (12 RAF 'heavies' were shot down on 3/4 July over Cologne), was put into operation over the whole of Germany. This procedure, termed *Wilde Sau* (Wild Boar) for short, called for close co-operation by the night fighters and the *Flak* over the target and a dependable control of single-engined night-fighters throughout wide areas. Co-operation was achieved by visual signals and by radio. Flare paths and a system of radio beacons was established. The single engine night fighter was particularly favoured by virtue of its high rate of climb to participate in this primitive form of night fighting the Germans were now forced to adopt. Herrmann's pilots were a motley collection, loosely organized and rather like guerilla bands in their attitude to authority, composed as they were by volunteers drawn from all sections of the Luftwaffe, including highly qualified ex-bomber pilots and even pilots in disgrace seeking reinstatement. They were equipped with the Focke Wulf 190F-5/U2 and the Bf 109G-6/U4N. Additional FuG 25a and FuG l6zy radio equipment and the FuG 350 *Naxos-7* radar-receiving set, which could pick up *H2S* radar emissions from up to 30 miles away, were installed.

7. July 1943-early March 1944 Wild Boar *Geschwader* claimed 330 bombers destroyed at night. Such was the immediate success of *Wilde Sau* that in September they were expanded into three *Geschwader* named JG 300, 301 and *302*, under *Major* Kurt Kettner, *Major* (later *Otl*) Helmut Weinreich and *Major* Manfred Mössinger, respectively. JG 300, for instance, claimed 173 victories between July 1943-March 1944, including 13 RAF bombers on 23/24 August, 8 on 27/28 August, 11 on 31 August/1 September and 16 on 5/6 September. Herrmann conducted his operations without the slightest regard for losses. Only when the last of the best pilots had been expended and bad weather set in, late in 1943, it became quite normal for up to 25 *Wilde Sau* aircraft to be lost from 60 engaged. Wastage on this scale continued into the winter of 1943-44. JG301 flew on 21 nights from September 1943, losing 58 pilots killed or severely injured for 87 victories. From November 1943, Fw 190s and Bf 109s of JG 302 operated on 22 nights, claiming 70 bombers for the loss of 43 pilots. In 1945, *General* Schmid estimated Wild Boar losses at 45% between 1 August 1943 and 1 February 1944. The diminishing Wild Boar results in late 1943 were compensated for by the twin-engined free-lancing Tame Boars, which were gradually getting over the shock of Window during the autumn of 1943. On 16 March 1944 *Jagddivision 30*, the divisional staff, which controlled the three *Geschwader*, was scrapped and shortly afterwards the remnants of Hermann's three *Geschwader* were subordinated to *Jagdkorps I* and re-trained for day and all-weather fighting.

8. *Nachtjagd* lost 61 aircraft in action that same month. Mainly they were flown by green and inexperienced crews.

9. Müller, who received the *Ritterkreuz* in July 1944, was the most successful *Wild Boar* pilot, claiming 30 victories in this fashion.

10. In ED625 *B-Baker* (the flight commander's aircraft which was fitted with *Monica* tail warning apparatus.

11. *B-Baker* was one of 6 Lancasters lost and was shot down by *Major* Heinrich Wohlers *Kommandeur* I./NJG 6 flying a Bf 110 who claimed a 'Halifax' at Spessbach, NW of Landstuhl at 0230 to take his score to 18. (Dave Jones died when he landed in a vineyard and was impaled in the throat. Len Bradfield was incarcerated in PoW camp and in March 1945 he attempted escape during the forced march through Germany. He hid in a sugarbeet field for 3 nights but both his feet were badly frostbitten and his toes had to be removed later by a Polish surgeon). On 10/11 August 653 heavies caused widespread destruction in Nürnburg. 7 Halifaxes, 3 Stirlings also FTR making a total of 16 aircraft lost overall, or 2.4%. Twelve of the losses are attributed to *Nachtjagd.* I./NJG 6 claimed 4 victories; *Hptm* Wohlers scoring a triple kill. *Fw* Otto Fries and his *Bordfunker Uffz* Fred Staffa of 5./NJG 1 shot down Halifax JA716 of 97 Sqn at Hanzinelle, Belgium, SE of Charleroi for their first kill. (F/L W.I. Covington DFC and crew all baled out safely). *Oblt* Heinz-Wolfgang Schnaufer, StII/NJG 1 claimed a Lancaster at Hahnlein and *Oblt* H.J. Birkenstock, StI/NJG 6 a Lancaster nr Alsenborn.

12. *Nachtjäger* operating over France were credited with four kills, including three by two single-engined pilots of 2./JG 2.

13. Germany's ineffective air defenses caused an upheaval in the highest echelons of the German command system. *Generalleutnant* Josef Schmid, whom it was intended to place in command of the day fighter units of *Fliegerkorps XII* under Kammhuber, was ordered to report on the state of the fighter defenses. Schmid was particularly struck by the eccentric organisation of Command, which seemed to belong to two separate worlds – *Luftflotte 3* covering France and *Fliegerkorps XII* covering Germany and the Low Countries. Schmid happened to be at Deelen in Holland, where, owing to the failure of a division in the *Luftflotte 3* area to report on the air situation, the target was not known until the following day.

14. 'Oblique Music'.

15. G9+JN.

16. Musset's ankles had been broken. When he had recovered from his injuries Musset joined *Stab* II./NJG 1. He died in a flying accident at Harderode on 9/10 February 1945.

17. Which escaped jamming throughout the war but owing to its limited number of channels was restricted to use by individual reconnaissance aircraft and formation leaders.

18. whose longer wavelength, unlike early *Lichtenstein* AI, could not be jammed by Window.

19. A device which homed onto the H2S navigation radar.

20. Which homed onto the Monica tail warning device widely used on Bomber Command heavies.

21. The son of a World War I RFC pilot, Braham shot down his first aircraft during the Battle of Britain and at 23 had become the youngest wing commander in the RAF. An outspoken individualist, unsurpassed in his sheer aggressive fighting spirit and relentless determination, Braham was already a living legend when he assumed command of the Sqn in December 1942, having shot down 12 e/a, 11 of them at night. 'The Night Destroyer', as he was dubbed in the press, had an overdeveloped sense of modesty and could see no reason for the press having an interest in him. On 9/10 August 1943 Braham notched his 4th victory since joining 141 Sqn and his 16th overall, when he destroyed a Bf 110 on a patrol to the German fighter a/f at St Trond in Belgium. F/O William J. 'Sticks' Gregory DFC DFM who as usual flew as his

navigator and operated the radar, was then rested and replaced by F/L H. 'Jacko' Jacobs DFC who had been instructing at 51 OTU Cranfield. Gregory earned his nickname as a result of having been a drummer in Debroy Somer's band.

22. Since the end of 1942 RAF nightfighters had been able to 'home' onto the radar impulses emitted by the FuG 202/212 *Lichtenstein* (AI) radars in the 490 Megacycles band by using the *Serrate* homer, which could only home in on the *Lichtenstein* AI radar and only if the sets were turned on. *Serrate* had first been used by 141 Sqn Beaufighter FVIs on 14 June 1943. The first victories to be credited to Mosquitoes fitted with *Serrate* occurred on the night of 28/29 January 1944 when a Bf 109 and a Bf 110 were shot down.

23. G9+E7 Wrk Nr 5469.

24. Bf 110G-4 G9+BY Wrk Nr 4874.

25. The *Eichenlaub* were awarded posthumously because on 26 February 1944 two Typhoons of 198 Sqn (F/L R.A. L'Allemand and F/O G.E.A. Hardy) shot down Vinke during an ASR operation 15 km NW of Dunkirk. The crew of *Ofw* Vinke, Dunger and Walter had scored 54 victories in about 150 sorties.

26. Wrk Nr 6228.

27. Dormann also baled out and suffered severe head injuries and burns. He never flew operationally again.

28. Dittmann may have tried to crash-land Bf 110 G9+FZ (Wrk Nr 5479) on the Friesian coast but the Bf 110 exploded near Marrum at 0015 hrs, Both crew KIA. Dittmann had claimed no night kills during his short time with 12./NJG 1 but he had shot down two B-17s on 25 and 26 July 1943. F/L Harry White DFC**-F/L Mike Allen DFC** finished with 13 victories and 3 damaged.

29. Kammhuber was appointed Inspector of the West German Air Force in 1956. He died in Munich in January 1986.

30. Master Bomber, W/C J.E. 'Johnny' Fauquier, CO, 405 'Vancouver' Sqn RCAF.

31. *M-Mother* was left at RAF Coltishall, its tailplane and rudder full of holes. 56 a/c (or 7.9%) – 23 Halifaxes, 17 Lancasters and 16 Stirlings – FTR. *Nachtjagd* was credited with 58 victories. I./NJG 1 at Venlo scored 6 kills.

32. The Berlin raid of 23/24 August cost Bomber Command 62 aircraft – 25 Halifaxes, 20 Lancasters and 17 Stirlings, or 8.7% of the force despatched. 31 bombers fell victim to fighters in the target area with another 7 crashing on the way home as a result of fighter attacks over Berlin. 5 German nightfighters were lost to return fire or to their own *Flak*. A 6th crash-landed at Hanover after a combat with a bomber on the inward flight and a 7th, a *Naxos*-equipped Bf 109 of II./JG 300 crashed in Sweden. Another 6 Bf 110s of NJGs 1, 2 and 3 made emergency landings at Berlin-Werneuchen a/f with *Flak* damage. Flak defenses did not always distinguish between friend and foe and German nightfighters fell victim to their own *Flak* over the bombers' targets. In an effort to minimize losses, the ceiling of fire for the *Flak* batteries over the German cities was reduced to 14,600ft (4500m) just as in 1941-42 during *KoNaJa* (Combined Night Fighting). However, the *Flak* arm was not placed under a unified battle control as it had been in the *KoNaJa* era so during night raids *Flak* units tended to ignore the agreement with *Nachtjagd* and fired as high, as much and as long as the local *Flak* commanders considered necessary. As a result, between 15 September 1943 and 20 April 1944, at least 15 German nightfighters were destroyed by *Feindbeschuss* (friendly fire) and many more limped back to base badly damaged with dead and wounded on board. In December 1943, *General* Schmid made another determined effort to ensure close co-operation with the *Flak* arm and reduce the losses among his crews in the target area. But he overplayed his hand by demanding direct control over the local *Flak* units during a British raid on any given city. This was unacceptable to the *Flak* commanders and co-operation between the two arms became virtually non-existent.

33. On 27 October Harry Barker and 2 others in Overton's crew were commissioned. At the end of January 1944 John Overton DFC was now a S/L. On.28 July 1944 the crew completed their tour of ops. Barker was awarded the DFC and F/Sgt Frank Dallman, rear gunner, the DFM.

34. Bf 110F-4 Werk Nr. 4762 3C+BK.

35. Otto Bauchens, his original radio operator had been hospitalised with hepatitis.

36. Barely recovered from his wounds, *Lt* Norbert Pietrek suffered further head injuries when Bf 110G-4 3C+DJ cr. at Bieul nr. Dinant, Belgium on 1 October 1943 and he never flew again. Twin-engined *Nachtjagd* crews operating in Tame Boar fashion claimed 12 of the 33 bombers shot down on 27/28 August 1943. Total *Nachtjagd* claims were 28 kills this night.

37. A Stirling over Mönchengladbach, a Wellington (JA118 of 432 'Leaside' Sqn RCAF, cr. at Siggerath near Mönchengladbach) and a Lancaster that came down at Brüggen, W of Mönchengladbach.

38. W/C K. H. Burns DFC lost a hand.

39. Three heavy bombing raids in ten days by RAF Bomber Command on Berlin had resulted in the loss of 137 aircraft and great loss of life to Berliners in the Siemensstadt and Mariendorf districts and also to Lichterfelde. It was but a prelude to the Battle of Berlin, which would open with all ferocity in November. On the 3/4 September raid, 20 out of 316 Lancasters were lost, 12 (possibly even 15) of which were destroyed by *Nachtjäger*.

40. LM360.

41. 13 Halifaxes, 13 Lancasters and 8 Stirlings, or 5.6% of the force. III./NJG 1 claimed 4 of these aircraft over Germany, including a Lancaster (W4370 of 12 Sqn) by *Hptm* August Geiger, which cr at 0024 hrs near Oppau/Stutenheim. Geiger went on to claim a Halifax at 0045 hrs at Rheinhausen. *Lt* Hans-Heinz Augenstein also scored a double victory shooting down Stirling IV EH878 of 623 Sqn at 0045 hrs at Rödern/Schönborn and a Lancaster 22 mins later at Boechingen nr Landau. II./NJG 1 operating from St. Trond claimed a Stirling and a Lancaster destroyed and *Hptm* Hans-Dieter Frank, *Kommandeur* of I./NJG 1 shot down an u/i Lancaster NE of Pirmasens. I./NJG 6 at Mainz-Finthen was credited with 7 Stirlings and Halifaxes.

42. One of these was *Oblt* Heinz Strüning's (*Staffelkapitän* 3./NJG 1) *Bordfunker Ofw* Willi Bleier. Their He 219A-0 (219010 G9+FB) was damaged by return fire during a sortie in the Ludwigshafen-Mannheim area and a bullet severed the control cable from the fule tank selector lever and during the flight back to Venlo Strüning was unable to switch to Tank 1. The He 219's engines quit one after the other and Strüning and Bleier decided to abandon the aircraft. However, the ejection seats refused to fire and so both men climbed out. Strüning hit the antenna mast and tail surfaces of his Uhu and suffeerd bruised ribs and contusions. Willi Bleier probably also hit the machine and he was found dead the next day with an unopened parachute. At the time of his death Bleier had participated in the destruction of 40 RAF bombers. On 24/25 December 1944 Strüning, *Staffelkapitän* 9./NJG 1 was shot down by a Mosquito; either NFXIII MM462/T of 604 Sqn or by NFXIX TA404/M of 157 Sqn flown by S/L R.D. 'Dolly' Doleman DFC and F/L D.C. Bunch DFC. Strüning was KIA after he hit the tail unit of his Bf 110G-4 baling out. His total of victories was 56 *Nachtjagd Abschüsse* in NJG 1 and 2 in 250 sorties. Holder of the *Ritterkreuz* with *Eichenlaub*.

43. 33 victories for 5 a/c lost were claimed by 207 twin-engined Tame Boars. 38 RAF heavies were lost. 7 victories were credited to III./NJG 1. *Hptm* August Geiger scored a triple victory destroying a Lancaster at 2210 over the Ijsselmeer, Halifax LWE230 of 78 Sqn at 2330 at Hattendorf, Germany and at 0001 a Halifax (possibly HR907 of 35 Sqn) went down at Wippingen. *Oblt* Heinz Knigge of 2./NJG 6 and *Hptm* Heinz 'Hannibal' Hadeball of 3./NJG 6 claimed a Stirling 20 km NE of Hanover at 2308 and Halifax HX159 of 10 Sqn 13 km NE of Minden at 2335 hrs respectively. Hadeball became an *Experte* with 33 night kills with NJG 1, 4, 6 and 10 and he was awarded the *Ritterkreuz* in July 1944.

44. The Bf 110 cr. 2 km from the He 219. *Hptm* Friedrich, *Oblt* Gerber and *Obgefr* Weisske died.

45. *Hptm* Geiger had become *Nachtjagd*'s highest-scoring *Experte* March-September 1943 with 41 *Himmelbett* victories, which took his total to 54 *Abschüsse* by the end of September 1943.

46. On 25 June 1944 Braham and his navigator F/L D.C. Walch DFC RAAF flew a *Day Ranger* to Denmark and Braham scored his 29th and final victory. Braham had just completed an attack on a German Staff car on a road on Fyn Island when 2 Fw 190s, one flown by *Lt* Robert Spreckels, attacked and set the Mosquito's port wing and engine on fire. Braham tried to crash-land on the shore of a fiord when he was attacked again but he managed to set it down and fortunately the aircraft did not explode. Walsh and Braham made a run for it and got behind sand dunes. Troops from a nearby radar station advanced towards them and opened fire with automatic weapons. Unhurt, Braham and Walsh were marched away into captivity.

47. *Hptm* Rudolf Sigmund, *Kommandeur*, III./NJG 3 KIA either by *Flak* or by return fire SW of Göttingen. He had 27 victories. *Oblt* Fritz Lau of 9./NJG 1 destroyed Stirling III BF470 of 15 Sqn at Haste, Germany and *Lt* Hans-Heinz Augenstein of the same *Gruppe* shot down Stirling EF158 of 623 Sqn to crash at Windhausen, Germany. *Ofw* Engel of 3./NJG 6 destroyed Halifax LK925 of 431 'Iroquois' Sqn RCAF at St. Vith at 2315 hrs.

48. Ernst destroyed Halifax LW236 of 78 Sqn, Augenstein a Stirling SSW of Hanover at 0142 and Amsberg a 'Lancaster' at Schwarmstedt – in fact Halifax LK647 of 434 'Bluenose' Sqn RCAF. Amsberg and his *Bordfunker* KIA 7/8.2.45 when their Bf 110G-4 was shot down by a 239 Sqn Mosquito XXX crewed by F/L D. A.D. Cather DFM-F/Sgt L.J.S. Spicer DFM.

49. *Hptm* Manfred Meurer of *Stab* I./NJG1 claimed one victory, 61 Sqn Lancaster W4357 that crashed at Bühne-Haarbrück, N of Kassel at 2120 hrs. *Oblt* Werner Husemann of 7./NJG 1 got a Lancaster, DS778 of 408 Sqn NW of Minden at 2130 hrs while *Lt* Otto Fries of 5./NJG 1 destroyed Lancaster EE175 EM-R of 207 Sqn. S/L McDowell RCAF and his crew KIA when the Lancaster cr at Nettersheim at 2030 hrs. All buried at Rheinberg War Cemetery.

50. Emerson had flown a first tour on 61 Sqn in Gordon Oldham's crew.

51. This was in fact a night fighter kill.

52. 2 a/c seen by the bomber crews shot down by flak on the outward route, one at Tholen and another at Herenthals, again were night fighter kills.

53. A U.S. 8th AF 2nd Bomb Division base occupied by B-24 Liberators of the 44th BG where earlier, at 2115 hrs Halifax B.II HX 179 ZA-L of 10 Sqn flown by P/O Robert Cameron (22) cr. and exploded in flames while attempting a landing after it was apparently forced to turn back, possibly after being hit by flak or fighters, or with engine trouble. Cameron circled the a/f 3 times before finally. As he descended, the Halifax struck telephone lines and crashed and burst into flames. Cameron, Sgt Samuel Eyre (37) flight engineer, Sgt John Hutton WOP/AG, F/L Roland Fielder, bomb-aimer, F/Sgt Roy Tann, navigator and Sgt Adam Williamson (21) mid-upper gunner all perished in the fire. Ernie Bowman, a member of the Home Guard, was sitting with his wife and their newborn child as the Halifax crashed 60 yds from his home. Emie could see the flames but noticed that the rear of the bomber was not alight, and tried to get 19-year-old rear gunner, Sgt Jack Winstanly, who was unconscious, out of the rear turret. The latter's parachute was snagged, and Ernie had to rush home and get a knife. On the way he met his brother-in-law, Sgt Williams Wilkins of Norfolk Police behind a tree that earlier Ernie had sheltered under for safety and they returned to the a/c. They removed Winstanly's parachute and got him out on to the ground but he died of his injuries in hospital 2 days later. Bowman was awarded the BEM and 2 American servicemen were awarded the Soldiers Medal for the rescue.

54. Mann wounded by shrapnel, died in hospital on Thursday morning. He was buried later in Bootle Cemetery on East Merseyside. John Jeffreys was buried in Cambridge City Cemetery. Taffy' Norris, who had shrapnel wounds in the shoulder and left arm, did not reveal that he was wounded until he was getting out of the aircraft. (He was awarded the Conspicuous Gallantry Medal for his heroic efforts, while Joe Emerson was awarded the DFM. Baldwin went on to complete his tour.) Reid's Lancaster was repaired and rejoined 61 Sqn on 7 August 1944. 3 days later it was transferred to 50 Sqn at Fiskerton and was lost in a crash near the station on 11 November 1944 when F/O Hickling and crew were returning from a raid on Harburg. Reid, meanwhile, went back on ops in January 1944, this time with 617 Dam Busters Sqn. With him went Les Rolton. On 31 July during a raid on Rilly La Montagne near Rheims, a RAF bomber put paid to the rest of his tour when an a/c overhead released its bombs and a 1000-pounder hurtled through Reid's Lancaster. 5 crew, including Les Rolton, were KIA. Reid and his WOp/AG, F/O David Luker, were thrown clear when the nose of the plane broke off as it spun down. Both spent 10 months behind the wire at *Stalag Luft III* Sagan and *Stalag Luft IV* Bellaria. Bill Reid left the RAF in 1949 and back in his native Scotland he became a student again. He studied at Glasgow University and the West of Scotland Agricultural College and in April 1949 gained his degree and was awarded a post-graduate travelling scholarship from one of the Lady MacRobert Trust schemes (Lady MacRobert lost 3 sons in the RAF during World War II) to study agricultural methods in India, Australia, New Zealand, Canada and the USA.

55. Or 3.1 per cent of the attacking force. 3 German fighters were claimed destroyed.

56. Halifax V LK932 MP-X of 76 Sqn. F/L D.G. Hornsey and crew evacuated the a/c safely. Hornsey evaded and 5 crew were PoW. (Sgt R.W. Glover evaded also but he was caught on the French-Swiss border on 23 December). Fries' 4th victory was Stirling III LJ442 JN-F of 75 Sqn on 19/20 November 1943 at Horrues, Belgium. 4 of the crew KIA. His 5th victory followed on 29/30 December 1943 when he shot down Lancaster II DS834 KO-F of 115 Sqn, which had left Witchford at 1728 hrs. It cr nr Tungelroy, Holland 18 km (11 miles) W of Roermond. F/Sgt J.Y. Lee and his crew were on their way back from Berlin. Lee and Sgt Pike, navigator, PoW. Sgt A.F. Gunnell evaded. Other 4 crew KIA.

57. G9+AS.

58. Halifax LW298 of 158 Sqn, which cr. 500m W of Vlijtingen, 13 km NE of Tongeren, Belgium was piloted by Sgt V.E. Horn and was one of 20 158 Sqn crews from Lissett bound for Düsseldorf. Sgt R.C. Graham perished and was later buried in Heverlee War Cemetery. 2 of the crew, including the skipper, evaded. 4 others PoW. The *Gruppe*'s 4 other victories were awarded to *Lt* Henseler of 4./NJG 1 (Halifax LK948 of 76 Sqn SE of Rheydt); *Hptm* Manfred Meurer of I./NJG 1 (Halifax JD321 of 77 Sqn at Helvoort) while *Ofw* Becker and *Fw* Günther Bahr of I./NJG 6 claimed a Lancaster at Düsseldorf and a Halifax 25 km S of Düsseldorf respectively.

59. Of 266 aircraft which were despatched to Leverkusen, only four Halifaxes and 1 Stirling were lost, as very few *Nachtjagd* fighters were operating probably because of bad weather as their airfields. Three crews of NJG 1 and NJG 5 were credited with three Halifax kills, and *Lt* Fries of 5./NJG 1 was credited with the shooting down of 75 Sqn Stirling III LJ442 near Horrues.

60. Abercromby, who had been promoted to S/L on 19 November, was born in Inverness-shire.

61. F/O J.F. Bowyer RCAF and 2 of his crew of Lancaster III JA847 PG-C were killed, the aircraft crashing into the Tegel, a heavily wooded area near Berlin. 4 crew survived and were taken prisoner. P/O J.F. Ward and 5 of his crew were killed after Lancaster III EE170 PG-N was hit by flak N of Magdeburg and burst into flames. As the crew prepared to bale out the Lancaster exploded. Sgt G.W. Cross regained consciousness at 5,000 ft and landed safely, albeit with several broken ribs.

62. Murrow's account of the 2/3 December raid, which cost 40 bombers, 37 of them Lancasters, appeared in the morning edition o the *Daily Express* under the banner headline, *'Berlin – Orchestrated Hell of Light and Flame'*. Tame Boar crews claimed 40 kills, 7 pilots of 2 Wild Boar *Gruppen* (I. and II./JG 302) claiming another 8 *Viermots* shot down over Berlin. At least 32 bombers went down in the main air battle that was concentrated in the target area. It was a one-sided battle; only 3 *Nachtjäger* were lost in return fire. 460 Sqn RAAF at Binbrook lost 5 of its 25 Lancasters on this raid, including 2 carrying press correspondents. Capt J.M.B. Greig of the Free Norwegian Army representing the *Daily Mail* who flew with F/O A.R. Mitchell RAAF and crew of Lancaster III LM316 AR-H2 died, as did all the crew. The Lancaster crashed at Döberitz. A night-fighter attacked Lancaster I W4881 AR-K, which exploded killing P/O J.H.J. English RAAF a native of New South Wales and 3 crew and 40-year old Australian, Norman Stockton of the *Sydney Sun*. 3 crew survived to be taken prisoner. Stockton is buried in the Berlin War Cemetery. F/L I.D. Bolton of 50 Sqn from Skellingthorpe flying Lancaster I DV325 VN-B was shot down by a night-fighter and crashed in the target area. 2 crew died. Lowell L. Bennett, a 24-year old war correspondent employed by the *Daily Express,* and Bolton and 4 of his crew survived and were made PoW. Bennett escaped from captivity and managed to file his story at one point but he was later recaptured and held prisoner until the end of the war. Walter King an Australian war correspondent returned safely.

63. Wing Commander Abercromby and his crew of Lancaster III ND354 OL-A of 83 Sqn, 8 (Pathfinder Force) Group was one of 28 aircraft lost from a force of 421 Lancasters sent to bomb Berlin on the night of 1/2 January 1944. Sgt L.H. Lewis, flight engineer, was the only survivor. Murrow continued to report on the war from Europe and North Africa throughout World War II. A heavy smoker, he died on 22 April 1965 aged 57.

64. The He 219 might have turned the tide for *Nachtjagd* had it been introduced in quantity. Fast, manoeuvreable and with devastating firepower of six cannon the 'Owl' was fitted with SN-2 radar and the world's first operational nosewheel undercarriage and ejection seats for the 2 crew. I./NJG 1 had been equipped with the anti-Mosquito version of the He 219 *Uhu,* a modified version of the He 219A-2 which was lightened by the reduction in armament from 6 to 4 20-mm MG 151/20 cannon and had its performance improved by the installation of a nitrous oxide fuel injection system to its engines. It had FuG 2205-N26 airborne radar system, a service ceiling of 37,000ft and was one of the few Luftwaffe night fighters fast enough to catch the Mosquito. During the first 10 days of operations in June 1943 with I./NJG 1 which operated from Venlo and Münster, it proved the only Luftwaffe piston-engined night-fighter capable of taking on the Mosquito on equal terms, the unit claiming 6 Mosquitoes destroyed (+ claims for 25 4-engined bombers). But like the Me 262 jet fighter in the day-fighter arm was never available in sufficient numbers to have a significant effect on the course of the air war. In late May 1944 the *Uhu* was abandoned in favour of the Ju 88G series, an aircraft that had sufficient performance to take on 4-engined bombers but incapable of combatting the 'Wooden Wonder'. Only 268 *Uhus* were built, 195 of which were delivered to operational units. The majority went to I./NJG 1 and to NJGr 10, a specialist anti-Moskito *Gruppe* at Werneuchen near Berlin.

65. DZ354/D of 105 Sqn (F/O Benjamin Frank Reynolds-F/O John Douglas Phillips) which cr. nr. Herwijnen in Holland on the N bank of the Waal River. Both later buried in the Herwijnen General cemetery.

66. D5831 QO-N of 432 'Leaside' Sqn RCAF, which cr. at Wytgaard S of Leeuwarden at 1841 hrs.

67. Three Halifaxes between 1924 and 2000 hrs, two of which were possibly Halifaxes of 10 Sqn.

68. Who downed Lancaster DV234 of 50 Sqn at Bodenrode/Bad Nauheim, Halifax LK644 of 427 'Lion' Sqn RCAF at Weilmünster/Hessen and an u/i Halifax at Ellar/Hintermeilingen in just 6 mins 1950-955 hrs.

69. LK928 of 428 'Ghost' Sqn RCAF and LK732 of 76 Sqn.

70. LK387 flown by P/O N.J. Veech RAAF (all KIA).

71. 379 bombers including 364 Lancasters were headed for Berlin but Pfeiffer might have received confused signals from the German controller who was temporarily deceived by a diversion by seven Mosquitoes at Leipzig and possibly by other Mosquitoes heading for Aachen and Duisburg.

72. *Erprobungsstelle* (*E-Stelle*) Rechlin.

73. Reich fighter frequency.

74. 8 Mosquitoes to Magdeburg, 6 to Düsseldorf, 5 to Leipzig. 4 to Bristillerie – a suspected V-weapon site near Cherbourg – and 3 to Leverkusen, 6 RCM sorties, 2 Beaufighters on *Serrate* patrols.

75. It was only after the war that it was discovered that the Germans did not use an explosive device to simulate an exploding bomber. What the men saw, in fact, was a fully loaded bomber exploding, having either been hit by flak or night fighter attack.

76. A *Spoof* raid was in progress.

77. Leipzig, where the bomber stream appeared to be heading before turning north-east for Berlin.

78. In all, 20 aircraft (11 Lancasters and 9 Halifaxes) failed to return. A long approach route from the south, passing south of the Ruhr and then within 20 miles of Leipzig together with Mosquito diversions at Düsseldorf, Leipzig and Magdeburg, caused the German controller great difficulties and there were few fighters over Berlin. Bad weather on the outward route also kept down the number of German fighters finding the bomber stream. 182 people were killed; more than 600 were injured and over 10,000 were bombed out.

79. DV189 T2.

80. Jim Donnan remained at large for the next 24-hrs but when he asked some German civilians for some food and drink he was taken into custody. Lancaster DV189 cr. between Holtrup and Schweringen and blew up with its full bomb load, including a 'cookie', in a deafening explosion. Bryson and Roxby had been trapped in the cockpit and were killed in the crash. They were interred at Hassel and at Hoya, later re-buried in Hanover War Cemetery. F/Sgt Paul Evans, the bomb aimer and Sgt Don Fadden, flight engineer had a very lucky escape. They were also in the nose section when the aircraft suddenly dived, pinning them down with the centrifugal forces. They were released when an explosion blew off the front of the nose section, enabling them to escape by parachute just before the bomber crashed.

81. His 69-74th victories.

82. DV189 was probably Wittgenstein's third kill of the night.

83. G9+FS.

84. Oblt Schmidt's 12th victim, Mosquito IV DZ440 HS-F of 109 Sqn, cr. at 0535 hrs at Landwehr, near Kleve, Germany. F/O P.Y. Stead DFC a 2nd tour pilot, PoW His 2nd tour navigator, W/O A.H. Flett DFM died in the crash.

85. Luma was born in Helena, Montana, on 27 August 1922. After joining the RCAF he was posted to England in January 1943, where after a sorting-out process, through some sort of error or mix-up, Luma received an exceptionally high grade in a night-vision test. As a result, he was assigned to night intruders, though at the time he had no idea what a night intruder was. At 60 OTU he learned to fly the Mosquito and practised air-to-air gunnery and air-to-ground gunnery. After several weeks at OTU intruder trainees were instructed to informally pair off into crews. Colin Finlayson, a Canadian from British Columbia and Luma agreed to crew up together. While at OTU Luma decided to transfer to the U.S. Army Air Forces. The official policy at the time, agreed to by the Americans and British, was that a crew would not be broken up, so after he was sworn in as a 1st lieutenant he was permitted to return to the RCAF to finish his tour of operations before returning to the USAAF. Luma was a USAAF pilot on detached duty with the RCAF. After finishing OTU Luma and Fin were assigned to 418 Sqn RCAF.

86. 9 other Mosquito victories went to 29 Sqn crews in NFXII HK197 and NFXII HK168 who got a Fw 190 and a Ju 88 respectively S of Beachy Head. NFXII 'N' of 85 Sqn destroyed a Ju 88 off Rye. W/O H.K. Kemp-F/Sgt J.R. Maidment of 151 Sqn in NFXII HK193 got He 177A-5 Wk Nr 15747 of I/KG40 which crashed at Whitmore Vale, nr Hindhead, Surrey, the first He 177 to be shot down over the British Isles. Sub-Lt J. A. Lawley-Wakelin-Sub-Lt H. Williams of 96 Sqn in NFXIII HK414 destroyed a Ju 88 at Paddock Wood Stn. F/L N.S. Head-F/O A.C. Andrews of 96 Sqn in NFXIII HK372 claimed 2 Ju 88 'probables' S of Bexhill and another 96 Sqn crew in NFXIII HK425 got a Ju 88 at Tonbridge. F/O C.K. Nowell-F/Sgt F. Randall of 85 Sqn in a NFXI destroyed He 177A-3 of 2./KG40 6m SE of Hastings. F/L J.A.S. Hall-F/O J.P.W. Cairns of 488 Sqn in NFXIII HK380/Y destroyed a Do 217M-1 13m off Dungeness and a Ju 88A-14 at Sellindge, Kent.

87. Werke Nr. 750467 R4+XM.

88. Lancaster III ED547 PO-M.

89. Wittgenstein's 83rd victory (one more than Lent) elevated him to the position of highest scoring night fighter pilot ever. After his death, only *Oberst* Lent and *Major* Heinz-Wolfgang Schnaufer were to overtake him with a higher score.

90. *Eichenlaubträger* Meurer and his *Funker*, *Ritterkreuzträger Ofw* Gerhard Scheibe in He 219A-0 'Owl' 190070 G9+BB were hit by debris from their 2nd victim and they crashed to their deaths 20 km E of Magdeburg. In less than 2 years Meurer had claimed 65 *Nachtabschüsse* (night victories) (including 40 *Viermots* and 2 Mosquitoes) in 130 sorties. Meurer was succeeded by 42 year old *Hptm* Paul Förster, who had 6 night victories prior to being named *Kommandeur* of I./NJG 1, with which he added 2 more victories while flying the He 219. On the evening of 1 October 1944 *Maj* Förster, St./NJG 1 and his *Bordfunker Oblt* Fritz Apel who were testing a new instrument landing system, were killed in He 219A-0 190194 G9+CL in a landing accident at Münster/Handorf airfield.

91. A Lancaster on 1/2 May 1944. This victory was probably unconfirmed; Pfeiffer ended the war with nine confirmed kills.

92. S/L Joseph Aloysius Hayes 'Joe' Cooper and F/L Ralph D. Connolly an Income Tax Inspector from Dulwich, London, had been posted from 141 Sqn where Cooper had been one of Bob Braham's flight commanders. In the early 1930s Lance Cpl Joe Cooper or 'Trooper Cooper' had been a cavalryman in the 4th Hussars. When it mechanized in 1936, Cooper decided he did not wish to drive tanks – he wanted to fly aeroplanes -so he borrowed £25 from a friend and bought his discharge from the Army He applied for and surprisingly got a short service commission in the RAF. 'I'd left school at 14 without the School Certificate but to their credit, the RAF took me in', he recalls. Apart from being a keen horseman, Cooper was an accomplished boxer and he became Lightweight Boxing Champion of the RAF in 1938/39. Cooper soloed on the Tiger Moth and went on to fly Audaxe and Hart biplane bombers, Blenheim night-fighters and then Beaufighters in 141 Sqn where he was B Flt Commander. 'The Beaufighter was for men not boys,' he fondly recalls. 'I could out-turn the Mosquito in a Beau.' Flying a Beaufighter he and Connolly damaged a Ju 88 on the night of 18 January 1943. In 169 Sqn Cooper had no problems converting to the new steed, Mosquito NFII HJ711 VI-P, which he christened, *P-Pluto*.

93. Cooper and Connolly's victim was Bf 110G-4 Wrk Nr 740081 D5+LB of *Stab* III/NJG 3, which cr. at Werneuchen, 20 km E of Berlin. *Oblt* Karl Loeffelmann, pilot (with one night kill to his credit), KIA. *Fw* Karl Bareiss, *Bordfunker* and *Ofw* Oscar Bickert, *Bordschütze* (both WIA) baled out.

CHAPTER SIX

NIGHT FIGHTER WAR 1944

On 30 January the first move to effect closer liaison between *Luftwaffenbefehlshaber Mitte* and the operational side of the Air Defense of the *Reich* saw the creation of *Luftflotte Reich. Generaloberst* Weise was relieved from his *Flak* command of Air Defense of the *Reich* and replaced by *Generaloberst* Hans-Jurgen Stumpff. Stumpff had previously commanded *Luftflotte 5* in Norway and Finland. His new command was now responsible for all day and night fighter aircraft and all anti-aircraft regiments. These changes were part of a belated attempt to reverse the decline of the defense of the *Reich*, which, after the situation created at the end of 1943 by the Bomber Commands of the RAF and USAAF, could no longer be ignored. Göring had opposed improvement but the Allied air forces had forced a number of changes to be adopted.[1] Changes too were made in the *Flak* units and the Aircraft Reporting Service, the former being considerably strengthened by increasing armament and bigger batteries. The entire direction of Air Defense rested, as far as command was concerned, with *Luftflotte Kommando Reich.*[2] *Jagdkorps I* directed the operations of day and night fighter formations, as well as the establishment and training of fighter units and their technical equipment. The night fighter control was improved by the extension of the 'Y' system. The day fighter formations were appreciably strengthened numerically and improved types of aircraft were introduced.

Defensive *Nachtjagd* operations over the *Reich* during February 1944 began relatively quietly, no First *Jagdkorps* claims being submitted before the night of the 15/16th when 143 crews were deployed against a 891 aircraft raid against Berlin. They claimed 39 victories, mainly over the *Reich* capital for the loss of 11 night fighters. *Oblt* Helmuth Schulte, Technical Officer of II./NJG 5, destroyed three *Viermots* in the greater Berlin area for his 5th-7th confirmed kills.[3] A few days later, on 20 February, the Americans launched 'Big Week'. Bomber Command and the USAAF dropped 19,000 tons of bombs on the Reich in a true round the clock offensive but losses were high with 224 American and 157 British bombers failing to return in just one week of sustained operations.

The Leipzig raid of 19/20 February cost Bomber Command 82 Lancasters and Halifaxes and one Mosquito of 692 Squadron; its worst casualties so far. The majority was destroyed by a very efficiently deployed Tame Boar operation involving 294 I *Jagdkorps* sorties (17 of which were lost). *Fw* Rudolf Frank of 3./NJG 3 destroyed five Lancasters to take his score to 34 kills. *Oblt* Martin 'Tino' Becker, *Staffelkapitän*, 2./NJG 6 aided by his *Bordfunker Uffz* Karl-Ludwig Johanssen claimed two Halifaxes and two Lancasters to take his score to ten victories. Becker's *Gruppe*, I./NJG 6 claimed eight victories.

Lancaster III D-Dog[4] of 57 Squadron flown by Johnny Ludford had a close encounter with a Ju 88, which 18-year old P/O Maurice Stoneman, flight engineer, describes:

> 'The skipper and I used to go out to our aircraft and, blindfolded, we would identify each control switch button, etc. Still blindfolded we would practice such things as closing down an engine and feathering the airscrew and other routines. This paid dividends on more than one occasion, in particular on this Leipzig raid. We were attacked by a Ju 88, our mid-upper Frank Fox saw him at the last minute and shouted 'Dive starboard GO.' We did just that. As I was standing up with my seat retracted I was thrown to the side but managed to recover by grabbing the small 'Window' handle. We were however, hit in the starboard engine and also lost three inches of a propellor blade. This of course caused great vibration but

unfortunately I was looking at the engine at the time of impact and the flash of the impact temporarily blinded me. The skipper ordered me to 'Feather starboard inner'. I did and the 'blindfold practice' paid off. I also pressed the fire extinguisher button. I was still unable to see properly but was beginning to recover my eyesight and vision. The fire was put out but the feathering mechanism was damaged and the propeller had to 'windmill'. This was a good thing as the engine drove the mid-upper turret hydraulics and one of the two generators. We also lost certain hydraulics and collected a large gash on the starboard side just above the main wing, which at 20,000 ft and in that temperature was more than uncomfortable. We went into a dive and lost 10,000 ft and only managed to pull out of it by the skipper and me with our feet on the instrument panel and hauling like hell on the stick. We got back to East Kirkby with difficulty. During 30 ops I only had to feather an engine once through malfunction and during many a ten hour trip the engines did not miss a beat. You just have to love the Merlin and also the rugged build of the Lancaster.'

One of the 34 Halifaxes that failed to return from Leipzig was shot down at 0241 hrs near Rotenburg between Hamburg and Bremen by *Lt* Otto Fries and his crew of *Fw* Fred Staffa, *Bordfunker* and *Uffz* Konrad Deubzer, air gunner of 5./NJG 1. Fries described what was his ninth *Abschuss* (possibly a Halifax of 35 or 102 Squadron):

'We were to have carried out an operational transfer to Wittmundhafen during the early afternoon of 16 February under extremely unfavourable weather conditions. The weather at our base of St. Trond did not appear to be very promising for night operations. There was heavy haze over the field, bordering on fog. Above that a thick layer of cloud with a base of about 200 meters reaching, according to the weather wizard, up to about 5000 meters, with risk of icing from about 400-500 meters upward. The light was so poor as if the sun had not been there at all. A further deterioration of the weather was expected but over the British Isles it was supposed to be good throughout. A cold front was expected to cross northern-Holland and northwest Germany during the early part of the night, followed by an improvement of the weather. Because of this weather forecast, Fighter Division had ordered the II. *Gruppe* to transfer to Wittmundhafen for operations.

'To be on the safe side we had put our 'QBI-kit', soap, towel, razor and toothbrush into the pockets of our flying leggings before the crew bus took us out to the dispersals towards three pm. I was the Technical Officer (TO) of the *Gruppe* and had been given orders by the CO to lead it to Wittmundhafen. During the journey to the airfield we had agreed to fly in a 'wild heap' in visual contact and to remain throughout the flight on the frequency of our home base. But transmissions were to be kept to the minimum necessary and even then to essentials.

'Ten crews took off towards 1545 and assembled at about 150 meters over the field in a circuit to port. When all were airborne I gave the signal to set course by wobbling my wings. Fred Staffa signed us off from base operations. I went onto the course, which I had calculated with my radio operator and remained below cloud at 150 meters. I switched on the automatic course keeping in order to save manual flying. The flying time had been calculated as a bare hour. Fred had already set the frequency of the beacon of our destination before take-off in order to take bearings for course correction in due course. During the flight I kept taking cross-bearings on other beacons abeam of our course just for the fun of it, as I remarked and in order to keep my hand in. Konrad, who had nothing to do, dozed on his jump seat. My nine companions were behind me in a loose echelon to starboard at the same height. The haze was so thick that I was barely able to make out the gray outline of the last machine. The countryside passed beneath us, gray and without contours. We crossed the River Meuse, which remained invisible under a bank of fog. It looked like a winding strip of spilt milk out of which odd chimneys and church towers stuck out and, like ranks of skeletons, the tops of bare poplars. The lower Rhine appeared out of the haze, a broad band of fog with frayed edges. We passed over villages, smaller and larger ones, compact or strung out, over meadows, fields and moors with fog-bound water pumps, strangely formed woods with patches of fog nesting in their fringes.

'The cloud base lowered as we progressed northwards. The River Ems was completely hidden by fog. It was a strange atmosphere: the clouds hung down like fat gray stomachs, frequently below our level forcing us to plunge down so as not to lose visual contact with each other. There were lighter patches of fog below us. In between, in a pale-cold light, the haze through which our machines passed on our way. Meanwhile, I had switched the Wittmundhafen radio beacon onto my autopilot and its reactions showed me that we were approaching our destination. As I saw the airfield appearing in the haze, I turned off the autopilot and turned into the concrete runway; a white cross on the grass beside the runway indicated the landing direction. When I was in the right position I throttled back the engines and extended the undercarriage and flaps. I touched down precisely beside the cross and continued to the end of the runway. To my right, somewhere in the haze, I recognized the control tower. I turned right onto the taxiway and as I was approaching the tower I could see the marshaller waving me in. I taxied into position and stopped the engines. One after the other the other machines came and parked beside me. Fuel bowsers arrived and the gunners attended to the filling-up. Later on, after the engines had cooled down, we carried out the 'mixture run' for a cold start, a necessary procedure for a quick take-off without first having to warm up the engines which would otherwise have been necessary. The saving of minutes could be decisive for the success of a sortie.

'We assembled in the tower where a readiness room, sleeping quarters and washing facilities were assigned to us. We were also told where we could get a meal. Fred attended to communications with operations at Division and I made my way to the meteorological office. The forecaster was amazed: 'What are YOU doing here in Wittmundhafen?'

'Nightfighting – what else! In St. Trond the weather is so bad that even the birds are walking and over at the Tommy's it is supposed to be good. Therefore we had to go where we would be able to get up aloft ourselves.'

'You won't have much luck with that tonight here!'

'Why – I don't understand, we had been sent here just for that!'

'Well, we shall have the best of snowstorms here within the hour!'

'I called Divisional Operations – they already knew about the unexpected development in the weather situation. As our own base was fog-bound and other places not much better off by now, we were to remain at Wittmundhafen for the present. It was now too late for anything else anyway. We were fortunate in having brought along our QBI-kit! The snowstorm began after a bare hour, quite a heavy one and when it was over it thawed accompanied by thick fog, which did not begin to lift until the evening of 19 February.

'We were stuck fast and after one day I had got through all the reading matter, except for files and regulations, that was available on the station. There was no chessboard to be found either in the canteen or the mess – the others played cards from morning until night without pause. I was bored to distraction and I set out for a walk around the airfield. I soon turned back; the fog was too thick for comfort. 'Come, watch us playing a round or two. The game of Skat is quite easy to learn!' I had always considered card games as plebeian and below my dignity – I must have played 'Sixty six' as a child but for years now all I had played was chess. But a day such as this was long, very long and boring. I joined them in the end, had the rules of the game explained to me, watched a few dozen rounds and then joined in. Had we been playing for money, I would have lost half a years pay in a day -but it was only noted down, for the 'honor' of it. After one day I thought myself to be a reasonable player and changed over to the 'double-headed' round; after a further day I had mastered this game too.

'During the late afternoon of the fourth day the fog thinned and good flying weather was forecast for the night. The gunners – for they were all former aircraft mechanics – saw to the machines and did engine runs. The radio operators checked their equipment. Deficiencies were attended to with the assistance of the local technical staff. At dusk the meteorologist explained the weather situation on his chart. There were no problems to be expected during the night. Division issued the code word 'Fasan' ('Pheasant') and we went into readiness. As the weather conditions had also improved at our home base in Belgium, we did not expect a return to Wittmundhafen and so we stuffed our small kit into the voluminous pockets of our flying leggings, which provided plenty of stowage space.

'Midnight came – no orders had been given and we considered whether it might not be better to get into the horizontal. I called Division and inquired about the situation regarding enemy activity. I was informed that considerable radio activity had been reported and that something could still be expected to happen. At 0115 cockpit readiness was ordered and soon after the green Verey light from the tower ordered the take-off. The engines sprang to life and somewhere on the other side of the field a light flashed at the take-off point. We taxied in single file along the perimeter track towards the light. The cockpit clock showed 0137 as I opened the throttles.

'When we had reached 4000 meters on a course of 270°, my radio operator called Y-procedure control:

'Kunibert from Adler 98 – on our way – course 270 – Kapelle 40 – over.'

'Adler 98 from Kunibert – received – switch over!'
'Viktor [Roger] – have switched over.'

'The Y-procedure consisted of a pulse being transmitted from the ground, which was modulated and retransmitted by the aircraft. This enabled control to establish the position of the aircraft. Control then attempted to guide the nightfighter into the bomber stream.

Then it was the radio operator's job to find enemy aircraft with his radar and guide the pilot into visual contact with the bomber. The Y-procedure enabled control to guide several nightfighters at the same time.

'Adler 98 from Kunibert – course 45 – Kapelle 45 – switch back.'

'I went on a northeasterly course and climbed to 5000 meters to be on the safe side. I could always turn the extra height into more speed. Control reported in from time to time. We were sent into the Heligoland Bight and were about abeam of the island when we were ordered eastward. Just short of the coast they were instructed onto a course of 130°; the 'Kuriere' (enemy bomber aircraft) were on the same course and at a height of 40 and 50. Also we were to go Express-Express if we were to catch up with them.

'I switched the propellers to automatic and increased the boost pressure. I went into a slow descent and did not level off again until the altimeter showed 4000. Fred switched on his radar.

'Nothing on the tube yet?' I asked after a while.

'Nothing yet – no *Düppel* (Window) either.'

'I'll weave back and forth, perhaps that will help you to find something.' I weaved slowly 30° to port and starboard of my course. This way a wider band could be covered by my radar without leaving the original course.

'Hamburg must be somewhere on the starboard bow. It was foggy down below, or at least very hazy for nothing could be made out. In spite of all the blackout measures something could always be seen from this height. The brief flash of a light, the flashing letters of a radio beacon or as marker for an aircraft in an emergency or the weak glow of a lamp, which someone had forgotten, to turn off. There was an even black-gray darkness beneath us, bordered by a narrow milky zone and the cloudless sky with its countless sparkling stars above.

'Adler 98 from Kunibert – switch over!

''Viktor – have switched over.'

'Adler 98 from Kunibert – switch back – course 175 – Kapelle 43 to 46 – single *Kuriere* – question Viktor – out.'

'Kunibert from Adler 98 – all Viktor – out.'

'Well, light up Aladdin's wonderful lamp and see that you find some blips,' I said, 'I'm maintaining course and going to 4000, a little lower than the Tommy, it can't do any harm.'

'Down below on the starboard bow quite a lot was going on. I saw faint flashes through the haze and seconds later, at our own height, there were explosions followed by small ball-like cloudlets. The cloudlets were lit up as by flashes of lightning and each new explosion resulted in yellow-brown cloudlets like a foul orange. From the distance it looked almost funny, like the release of yellow-brown balloons at a fair. 'The fellows from the other side are on the approach,' I said to Fred, who could not of course see the spectacle as he had his head down under the screens of his radar gear. 'It appears to be the Hamburg Flak banging so merrily away.'

'Again I weaved about to cover a wider area of search. I was about to weave to port when my radio operator's voice stopped me:

'I have a blip, hard to starboard, a little higher – 320.' He turned further to starboard. 'Ahead, a little higher, 290 – a little to port, a little higher, 270 – a little to port, a little higher, 250.'

'It looked as if the bomber would cross our course at a sharp angle from starboard to port. I kept altering course according to the instructions from my radio operator and when I was on a course of 100° the target remained dead ahead. I had got myself behind the bomber in a wide turn.

'Ahead, a little higher, 100.'

'I raised my seat until my eye was level with the reflector sight and switched it on, adjusting the intensity slightly. Then I cocked the guns; the breeches rattled aft. To be on the safe side, I jettisoned the auxiliary tanks; they must be empty by now, anyway. Each time I regretted this waste but it was a case of safety first: should one of these be hit by the defending fire of a tail-end-Charlie, then the petrol-air mixture remaining within it would explode with the effect of a Flak shell.

'Ahead, very high, 070, you must climb higher!'

'I eased the stick back; the altimeter showed 4200 as my machine began to shake. We had got into the slipstream of the bomber ahead, which had to be at the same height. I pushed my Bf 110 a little lower. 'Slightly to starboard, slightly higher, 090.''

'I reduced power a little and scanned the horizon on my starboard bow. Then I saw a shadow and the glow of the exhausts of the four engines. 'I have him, you can leave your screen'. Fred searched along the horizon.

'I can't find him, where is he?'

'On the starboard bow, right above the top of the dipole, a thumb's width above the horizon.'

'I can see him!' called both radio operator and gunner almost together; 'he has a twin tail.'

'It could be a Lancaster but also a Halifax; I went a little lower to get a better view against the sky. It was a Halifax; a Lancaster's engines protruded further forward from the wings.

'I turned the trigger lever on the control column downward and moved a little to port. When I estimated to have approached to about 50 meters I again moved over to starboard until I was under the port wing of the bomber. Slowly, very slowly I eased the stick back. When my sight had almost reached the lower edge of the wing between the engines I pulled the trigger for a short burst of fire. The clatter of the breeches joined the dull bangs of the cannon and the barking of the machine guns whose muzzle flashes blinded me. The entire machine shook and the cabin was filled with the powder smoke from the machine guns. For a moment I lost sight of the bomber but then I saw the flashes of the 2-cm shells in the wing and the port outer engine. Diving away, I registered a bright flame coming from between the two engines. The bomber dived away in a violent turn and a long flame of burning petrol trailed from the stricken wing.

'The tail end-Charlie had not reacted; it had all happened too suddenly. I dived after it in order to have the burning Halifax above me. It contrasted better against the lighter sky and I would not lose it, even if the fire should go out. The port wing burned fiercely and parts of it were torn away. The crew did not have a chance and they appeared to have realized this for the Halifax was now quite steady in the air. It did not take long and six bundles dropped from it in quick succession. The bomber slipped over to port and we watched it going down in a steep, burning spiral, which ended in a violent explosion on the ground.

'The cockpit clock showed 0241. 'Note the time and get our position!' 'Kunibert from Adler 98 – report *Sieg Heil* – request position – I am switching over.'

'Ground control gave us letters and figures, which Fred noted down. Later, after landing, we found that the map reference we had been given was between Hamburg and Bremen, that the Halifax must have crashed in the vicinity of Rotenburg and that was where the wreckage was found.

'Adler 98 from Kunibert – course 105 – single *Kuriere* between Kapelle 40 and 45 – out.'

'Viktor-Viktor-out.'

'I weaved about on a course of 105° but we got no further contact on our SN2. We landed at 0337 at Rheine and returned the following morning to St. Trond.'

Also on 19/20 February Allied countermeasures gained new impetus when a *Spoof* attack was carried out over the North Sea by a OTU force while 816 bombers attacked Leipzig. The main disadvantage of the *Spoof* was that the aircraft had to turn back before reaching the enemy coast, thus reducing the period during which they appeared a threat to the enemy. (On 23 July the addition of a small force of special *Window* aircraft, which flew with the OTU aircraft but carried on when the *Spoof* Force turned back, solved this weakness). The '*spoof*' raids met with limited success, while the Germans reported that about '100' (RAF figures are 19) *Intruder* attacks on airfields at Gilze Rijen, Deelen and Venlo caused only minor damage. A Mosquito *Spoof* attack on Berlin kept German fighters back but another Mosquito spoof, on Dresden, failed. Pursuit Night fighting procedure by *SN2* was an essential factor in the heavy losses meted out by *I Jagdkorps* this night. They were also helped significantly by plotting accurately the H2S bearings and gauging correctly the significance of a turn in the sea area NW of Terschelling by the main force while 49 minelayers continued the original course due east (they dropped their mines in Kiel Bay). Altogether, 294 twin-engined and single-engined fighters were sent against the bomber stream. The RAF lost 44 Lancasters and 34 Halifaxes, with approximately 20 of the 78 bombers shot down by *Flak* and four aircraft destroyed in collisions while the *Nachtjagd* lost just 17 fighters.

An attack on Stuttgart on 20/21 February 1944 by 598 bombers was outstandingly successful. This was due mainly to the North Sea sweep and a diversionary feint towards Munich, which successfully drew the German fighters up two hours before the main force flew inland. Nine bombers only were lost (All were shot down by night fighters. Four other Lancasters and a Halifax crashed in England on their return). Two further effective Tame Boar operations were directed against Bomber Command raids before February 1944 was out. On the 24/25th 209 First *Jagdkorps* Tame Boar crews destroyed 31 Lancasters and Halifaxes of a 734 strong force raiding Schweinfurt (Bomber Command lost 33 aircraft). I./NJG 6 claimed a Lancaster and a Halifax destroyed but NJG 6 lost five Bf 110s and four crewmen in air combat. *Ofw* Fritz Schellwat of 6./NJG 1 downed a Lancaster SE of Saverne at 2222 hrs for his 17th victory and *Hptm* Eckart-Wilhelm 'Hugo' von Bonin, *Ritterkreuzträger* and *Kommandeur* of II./NJG 1 destroyed two *Viermots* for his 28th-29th kills.[5]

The next night 165 twin-engined Tame Boars claimed 19 heavies during an outstandingly accurate and successful raid against Augsburg. Seven crews of I./NJG 6 operating from Mainz-Finthen claimed eight kills, or almost half of *Nachtjagd*'s tally for the night. Four other bombers were lost in collisions and three were probably lost to *Flak*. Total *Nachtjagd* claims for February were 183 bombers destroyed. I *Jagdkorps* casualties amounted to 14 aircraft and crews during the 24/25 and 25/26 February operations.

February 1944 had been an auspicious month for P/O Jim Sprackling who was appointed Engineer Leader of 10

Squadron, which meant promotion to flight lieutenant and another substantial pay rise. His pilot, P/O Bill Lucas, who was now fit again, was also promoted as senior pilot of C Flight. Sprackling recalls:

> 'It made no difference to the crew. We were a team and all mates, each a professional who's sole object was to carry out the duty given them and get home in one piece. At the end of February we were back on operations again and a new experience called *Gardening:* laying anti-shipping mines in enemy waters. We were detailed to do this first of all in the Kattegat, the narrow sea channel round the north of Denmark. The following night we went right into the home of the German Navy in Kiel Bay. Both were uneventful. Each time four mines, about 7ft long and 18 inches in diameter, with a parachute fitted to one end. They had to be dropped from low level for accuracy. Fortunately there are no mountains in Denmark!'

February 1944 had also been an auspicious month for 418 Squadron RCAF, which scored nine confirmed victories, two of them by 1/Lt 'Lou' Luma, pilot of Mosquito FBVI SWEET MOONBEAM MCSWINE. On 13 February Luma's scored his second victory when he and F/O Colin 'Fin' Finlayson destroyed a He 177 over Bordeaux, France. Luma recalls that a large degree of co-operation was needed to get kills like this:

> 'British intelligence was excellent. Each time the Germans sent bombers to raid England, the British knew where the bombers were taking off from, how many aircraft there were in each flight, and where they were returning to. In many cases, they knew the names of the officers leading the flights. The RAF control center would dispatch night intruders to each of the aerodromes that the bombers were expected to return to and to those from which German night fighters were operating. This type of operation was known as a '*Flower.*' The Mosquitoes would time their takeoffs to arrive at the German aerodromes when the Hun aircraft were preparing to land. Since the intruder had no radar, he had to hope that the Germans would turn on their navigation lights prior to landing. Normally they didn't, but if they did, consequences were usually fatal. I can recall being at a German airport on a black night, seeing nothing but every once in a while getting a jolt when the Mosquito flew through the slipstream of a Hun aircraft. If the Germans were returning to a field deep within Germany they would feel safer and be more likely to put their navigation lights on. One of our crews was at Munich one night, deep inside Germany. The Germans apparently felt they were too far from England to be in any danger and they put on their navigation lights prior to landing. The Mossie pilot immediately shot two of them down. The crew said the sky was full of aircraft with their nav lights on but they had to leave after shooting down the two because they lacked fuel to remain any longer.[6] The Germans did not like the night intruders, and it made them uneasy knowing they were being stalked. One night a squadron of German bombers was diverted to an alternate airport because a Mosquito was lurking at the destination airport. The alternate fogged in before they got there, and all of the aircraft ran out of fuel and crashed.
>
> 'There was a green phone on a raised dais at one end of the ops room. The phone was a direct link to some mysterious place (mysterious to me, at any rate) from which we received the word to scramble. The target would be given to us, and we were to take off as soon as possible. The navigator would quickly draw some courses on our charts, and we would be driven to our airplane by an enlisted WAAF (Womens Auxiliary Air Force). We were expected to have our engines started within five minutes from the time we were given our target. Included in that five minutes was a nervous pee behind the airplane before climbing in.
>
> 'After starting our engines and calling the tower, we were given the runway in use for takeoff. We did not use our navigation lights. There was the possibility that some Hun could be waiting to do unto us as we would do unto him. After takeoff we would set course across the English Channel, flying several hundred feet off the water. Even on a clear night, we were completely on instruments. Crossing the Channel could be nervewracking. You were inside of a pitch-black nothingness. You knew the water was a few hundred feet below you, because you had a radio altimeter that told you so. In training, we had been warned that we would eventually experience vertigo, where your senses tell you that you are in a turn, yet your instruments tell you that you are wings level. The compulsion to believe your senses is overpowering. You swear that the instruments are lying, that they are malfunctioning. You really believe that you are in a turn. Fortunately, in training we were emphatically told, 'Believe your instruments!' In the beginning, there were times that I had to force myself so hard to believe the instruments that it made me sweat. Later in my combat career, I learned little techniques to more rapidly dispel the vertigo, like forcing myself to make a gentle bank one way followed by another gentle bank the other way. Another means of diminishing the vertigo was to take my

eyes off the instruments and slowly look around the cockpit. This would reset the inner ear to neutral (wings level). Then, when you returned to the instruments, everything was normal (hopefully).

'One night on a Channel crossing we saw RAF bombers being shot down, most probably by some Luftwaffe night fighters. We would see a light glow appear at the bottom of the overcast, followed by the burning bomber spinning out from underneath. It was an unforgettable sight, to say the least.

'For navigating across the Channel and making an accurate crossing of the enemy coast, we were aided by *Gee*, the forerunner of *Loran*. It generated a single 'line of position' that could be followed to intersect the enemy coast. This gave us a very accurate means of crossing the coast exactly where we wanted to. After crossing the coast we would climb to a thousand feet above the ground if there were no mountains below us or 2,000 feet above the ground in mountainous areas. Usually we were flying on instruments because black sky blended into black ground. Yet it was possible to navigate by planning a course that went between pinpoints that were unique. On the blackest of nights a point on the ground where land meets water is visible when looking straight down at it. The navigator planned his course utilizing unique pinpoints – oddly shaped bends in a river, for instance.

'We were given permission to shoot at trains, an option later withdrawn. Shooting at a train on a black night was deceptively dangerous. A train could be spotted when the engine's firebox door was open to shovel in more coal. You could not see the rest of the train or the surrounding terrain, just the firebox. We would dive on the firebox and I would fire when I got it in my gunsight. My navigator would read out the altitude, and tell me when to break off the attack and pull up. It was always tempting to fire for just a second or two more but that could be fatal because of to your close proximity to the ground. German trains were known to deliberately stop in a cut and open their firebox. When the intruder dived on it, the crew would see the firebox but not the high ground. The high risk involved in shooting trains was probably why the option was later withdrawn. A locomotive wasn't worth the loss of a Mosquito and its crew.

'Sometimes the Germans flew decoy aircraft at night. The decoy would fly with its navigation lights on. The gunner in the tail would be just waiting for you to suck in. Fortunately for the intruders, the navigation lights of the decoys were inordinately bright, because they wanted us to be sure to see them. We were told to stay away from bogeys with extremely bright lights.

'The Germans used different combinations of colored flares as a means of identifying friend and foe. These color combinations were changed daily. British intelligence was so good that we usually knew what the German colors for the day on every mission that we flew. If we mistakenly flew over an area heavily defended by antiaircraft guns, we could fire the correct colors of the day, and the enemy, thinking we were a friendly aircraft, would cease shooting at us. The Mosquito flew close to the ground so the amount of time that the aircraft was within range of the guns was not very long. Because we didn't want the Hun to know that we knew his colors for the day, we used our speed to our advantage. The navigator would fire any flare other than the correct colors of the day. In the brief time it took the gunners on the ground to associate the correct colors of the day with the colors that we shot, we would be out of range.

'When returning to England from ops, we would turn on our IFF after crossing the enemy coast. IFF (Identification, Friend or Foe) was an electronic device that would identify us on British radar screens, both ground and airborne, as friendly aircraft. When we were well on our way back to England, we would use our VHF radio to contact our radar control center, which would give us vectors or steering to base. As we neared the base, we would pick up the outer circle, a ring of lights over a mile in diameter that surrounded the aerodrome. We would follow this outer circle as we prepared for landing. From the outer circle another set of lights funneled the aircraft into the runway in use. These lights guided the pilot as he descended to the runway. It was thus possible to make an approach and landing under extremely poor weather conditions.

'After landing, we would have a debriefing session with the intelligence officer. That would be followed by breakfast, where we were rewarded with fresh eggs. Fresh eggs were a precious commodity in wartime England, and only young children and aircrew got them.

'On one of our early ops, we inadvertently flew over a defended area, where we encountered our first enemy flak. When the flak was behind us, the compass needle was swinging wildly because of the violent maneuvering that we had done to evade the exploding shells. The British aircraft compass was like a marine compass, with the glass on top. Under normal circumstances, it was customary to gently tap the glass to get the compass needle to settle down. My first experience with enemy ground fire resulted in an adrenaline high, causing me to 'tap' the glass so hard that I broke it, rendering the compass unusable. Fortunately, we still had heading information available from the directional gyro. It was a clear night, so we had the North Star to crosscheck the accuracy of the precessing gyro. Unfortunately, we were unable to spot any good pinpoints on the ground to accurately determine our position as we pressed on in a westerly direction. As a result, we crossed the coast at Abbeville, which was one of the Germans' most heavily fortified coastal areas. Fortunately, Fin and I were the beneficiaries of techniques developed by preceding night intruder crews, who had learned through experience to develop ways to cope with a situation where the night turns to day because of the seemingly infinite number of searchlights and obscene amount of flak.

'Our best defense was our low altitude and high speed. The procedure in this situation was to turn into the searchlights and away from the flak, which was visible because of the tracers. By turning into a searchlight, you made it more difficult for the searchlight operator to lock on to you. The reason for turning away from flak is self-evident – the farther from it the better. I would duck my head down so as to be just a few inches from the instrument panel. Fin would hold his map over the top of my head to shield me from the glare of the searchlights. He would tell me when to turn, and which way. Our turns were steep and violent. In addition, I would abruptly change altitude several hundred feet up and down. At one point during that night over Abbeville, we were so low that, during one of the steep turns to the left, I saw nothing but water out of the corner of my eye. I hopefully asked Fin whether we were over the Channel. He replied that we were still over Abbeville, that it was a river I saw.

'I do not remember any night-intruder crew that liked a clear, moonlit night. Although it was easier to see and thus to navigate under such conditions, it was also easier for the Hun to see us. We didn't have the security of a moonless night's total blackness. Whenever we did have an op on a moonlit night, we always entertained the hope that we might spot and destroy enemy aircraft that didn't have any of their lights on. Spotting such aircraft was called a 'cat's eye.' One night, we finally realized our dream – at least the cats-eye part – when we spotted a bogey over France. We immediately took out after him, since all bogeys over the Continent were fair game. Because the bogey was flying in a direction that put him up-moon, I had to position the Mosquito behind so that we were down-moon from him. As I eased into position to shoot at him, Fin shouted, 'Don't shoot, Lou! It's a B-24!' I immediately broke off the attack.'[7]

On 6 March Luma and Finlayson got a Fw 190 over Pau, France and achieved ace status on 20 March. Luma and Finlayson and F/L Donald MacFadyen and 'Pinky' Wright flew a long-range *Ranger*[8] over France. Luma and Finlayson attacked Luxeuil airfield, where they shot down a Ju W34 liaison aircraft and a Ju 52/3m transport and damaged two Gotha Go 242 glider transports and two Bf 109s on the ground, while MacFadyen and Wright shot down a Bü 141, which was coming into land. Moving on to Hagenau airfield, MacFadyen proceeded to destroy nine Go 242s and a Do 217 on the ground.[9] Luma flew his final RCAF mission with 418 Squadron on the night of 30 April 1944. He then transferred to the 8th AF and flew a Mosquito weather plane until in November 1944 he rotated to the USA. Finlayson was killed on 18 October 1944 when he and his pilot, F/L S.H.R. Cotterill DFC, were returning to England from Italy after landing there at the end of a *Day Ranger* to the Vienna area on the 17th.

In Bomber Command circles meanwhile, the first half of March 1944 was relatively quiet. Bomber Command's first heavy raid of the month was directed against Stuttgart on 15/16 March. Ninety-three First *Jagdkorps* crews were fed into the 863-strong bomber stream just before the force reached the target and they returned with claims for 30 kills for the loss of nine aircraft and crews. Bomber Command lost 37 aircraft, or 4.3% of the total force. Five *Viermots* were credited to I. and II./NJG 6 for the loss of six Bf 110s, which crashed due to lack of fuel. II./NJG 1 operating from St. Dizier, claimed four four-engined bombers destroyed, two of which were downed by *Hptm* Eckart-Wilhelm 'Hugo' von Bonin.

Frankfurt was raided on the night of 18/19 March by 846 aircraft, including 620 Lancasters. For the loss of six twin-engined night-fighters (including two of I./NJG 6)[10] the German defenses claimed 22 heavies, 11 of which were attributed to the Tame Boars of I *Jagdkorps*. Five crews of I. and II./NJG 6 destroyed four Halifaxes and a Lancaster. The same city was subjected to another devastating raid by 816 aircraft on 22/23 March, from which 26 Lancasters and seven Halifaxes failed to return. Frankfurt all but ceased to exist. Almost 1400 people perished in these two raids and 175,000 inhabitants were bombed out. I *Jagdkorps* crews claimed 38 heavies destroyed. Six of these (four Halifaxes and two Lancasters) went to *Oblt* Martin 'Tino' Becker, *Staffelkapitän*, 2./NJG 6 and *Uffz* Karl-Ludwig Johanssen, his *Funker*, during a Tame Boar sortie from Finthen aerodrome. After being led into the bomber stream, all their victims went down within an hour between 2142 and 2239 hrs. Four victory claims were credited to I./NJG 2, three of which were destroyed by *Oblt* Heinz Rökker.

Target for the night of 22/23 March was Frankfurt and for P/O Dickie Atkins' Halifax crew in 578 Squadron at Burn (which was 'cold, wet and full of mud') it would be the final trip of their first tour. No other crew on the squadron had finished their tour because of heavy losses sustained in the Battle of Berlin. G/C Nigel Marwood-Elton DFC Burn's Station Commander flew as Atkins' second dickey in Halifax III R for Robert[11] and F/Sgt Eric Sanderson manned the four Brownings in the rear turret. Sanderson recalls:

> 'We had an early evening take-off. The last turning point was Hanover at about 2200 hrs and we were on the run down to Frankfurt. Nightfighters were active and combats were to be seen. A little after 2200 we were at about 20,000 ft when I saw a Ju 88 slide underneath my turret. My evasive action was always a steep diving turn to port. We lost about 3000 ft, got back on course and I expected to have lost the Ju 88 but he was still there underneath us! We tried a corkscrew. The Ju 88 followed us through the lot and we did another diving turn. I was worried for this one was special and now I made my error for which he had been waiting! I told my pilot to bank the aircraft so that the mid-upper might shoot downwards. The fighter was still below whilst our Halifax hung there with the pilot fighting to get control of the fully loaded bomber. That was when the Ju 88 hit us in the bomb bay and in the petrol tanks on the starboard wing. Dickie Atkins ordered, 'Parachute, Parachute, Jump, Jump!' I opened the turret doors and pulled my chute in. My helmet, mike and oxygen were off. Now which side? Port, or starboard? Most of the fire was on the starboard side and did my WOp/AG have his trailing aerial out? (Not the best thing to meet baling out of the port side of a rear gun turret). So starboard side, a fast-roll through the flames and away! But No! My feet were caught in the turret and I was hanging half in and half out. I tried to get back in the turret to free my legs and try again but after several attempts I gave up. I now thought of pulling the ripcord but the thought of being pulled out of my legs delayed my decision. However, life with or without legs was sweet and preferable so I pulled the string. I shot out of the turret like a cork out of a bottle. I must have been only about 500 ft from the ground. The next thing my chute was fully open and I was swinging on the end of it. Looking down I saw that I was about to enter trees below. I was knocked out and must have been out for some time because when I started getting out of my parachute, Mae West and flying gear and checking if I still had my legs, I saw the burning aircraft only a few hundred yards away. Men were shouting to each other around the fire. I was unable to walk and my hands and face were burnt so evasion was out of the question and I called to them.'

Eric Sanderson was taken to a village nearby and next day was transported to Herborn 15 miles from Frankfurt where he met G/C Marwood-Elton. Happily, he was re-united with the other members of his crew over the next few days. All eight men had baled out safely before their Halifax crashed. *Oblt* Heinz Rökker, *Staffelkapitän*, 1./NJG 2, flying a Ju 88R-2 had shot down Atkins and his crew, his third victim that night, as Rökker recalls:

> 'I took off from our operational airfield Langensalza at 2010 hours and I shot down my first adversary at 2130 hrs near Emmen, Holland. A second *Abschuss* followed at 2227 hrs near Koblenz and at 2235 hrs I claimed Atkins' Halifax in Steinringsberg near Herborn. I landed safely back at Langendiebach at 2330 hours.'[12]

On 24/25 March the 'Big City' was visited for the last time during the Battle of Berlin by 811 aircraft. Sgt Roland A. Hammersley DFM, Lancaster WOP-AG, 57 Squadron recalls:

> 'A memorable day. On arrival at the Flight Office we found our names on the battle order for the night's operations. The aircraft we were to fly was *T-Tommy.*[13] We set off on bicycles that had been issued to each one of us, to look the aircraft over and check the equipment. The ground crew responsible for the maintenance of *T-Tommy* were a fine bunch and gave us much information as was possible about it as we went through the checking procedure. The bomb load was one 4000 lb, 48x30 lb and 600x4 1b. Later we were fully briefed both as individual crewmembers and then all crews together. We soon learned that the target was Berlin – the Big City. At the briefing we were told at what time there would be signals broadcast from Bomber Command; when we would receive weather reports; where the searchlight belt and anti-aircraft guns were known to be and also the positions of known German night fighter units and airfields en route. A weather report was given by the Station Met Officer: the indications being that the weather conditions were not too good and we would be meeting quite strong winds at 18,000-20,000ft. We were issued with amphetamine (Wakey-Wakey) tablets, these were taken just prior to take-off and would keep the crews wide-awake and on a 'high' for the duration of the flight. If the operation was cancelled, it meant a sleepless night which, for the most of the crews, meant that a wild night of drinking would take place in both the Officers' and Sergeants' mess until the effects of the drug wore off and sleep could take over.
>
> 'It was customary for a meal to be prepared for the crews before we-flew. We were then issued with a flask

of tea or coffee, with chocolate, sandwiches and an apple; armed with a 0.38 revolver and parachute. Codes and Verey pistol with cartridges which when fired would give the coded colors of the day. We were even given what were understood to be those in use by the German forces that day. After emptying my pockets and locking my personal items into my cage type locker, I joined the crew in the crew bus with WAAF Connie Mills at the wheel. Connie often drove the bus that collected the crews from near the control tower. We were then taken out to *T-Tommy*. We had another look around the aircraft with the ground crew and about an hour before we were due to take off we settled into our places to await the take-off order. When the first part of the take off procedure commenced, we were lined up on the airfield perimeter with 17 other Lancasters from the squadron. All crews would by now have taken their amphetamines and would be wide awake.

'The first Lancaster was given the 'Green Light' from the mobile watchtower and we watched as it slowly climbed away. The remainder all slowly moved around the perimeter track towards the runway and then it was their turn for destination Berlin! The smoke from the engines and the smell of burning high-octane fuel eddied across the airfield. Sixty tons of explosives and incendiaries were to be dropped by 57 Squadron that night and the sight of 17 Lancasters, each under full throttles roaring away into the evening sky was an awesome spectacle. Sergeants' Frank Beasley and Leslie Wakerell with their ground crews and a number of other well wishers watched us away before returning to while away the long hours before our return. The smoke and smell slowly thinned and drifted away over the silent airfield and we were on our way to our first bombing operation with the squadron.

'We were airborne at 1845 hours. This was to be the order of things for some time to come. As the weather reports came in and I decoded them, it became apparent from Mack's findings that they were not as he expected them. We were faced with greater wind speeds than those indicated in the signals being sent out to us from Command, so we used our own. We were late arriving over the target and we could see there were great fires as the run in towards the target commenced. We bombed successfully and headed back towards home.'

For P/O Richard 'Dick' Starkey and his Lancaster crew in 106 Squadron at Metheringham it was their twentieth trip. They had joined the squadron in October 1943, flying their first op to Leipzig on the 20th. Starkey, who was commissioned two hours before taking off for Berlin, recounts:

'The outward route was over the North Sea to Denmark then south-east over the Baltic Sea crossing the German coast and continuing south-east before turning south through the target. The trip was one of the worst we encountered because of the strong winds. On the way out over the North Sea the navigator, Sgt Colin Roberts, was finding winds with speeds far in excess of those in his Flight Plan and coming from a more northerly direction than predicted at briefing. We were 'windfinders' this night and the navigator advised me that the wind speed was approaching 100mph and should he broadcast his findings back to Bomber Command? I said if he was satisfied with his calculations he must transmit them to England. (A number of aircraft were detailed as windfinders on every raid. When the navigator had calculated the actual wind speed and velocity they were transmitted back where an average wind speed was calculated from those sent back by aircraft and then relayed to the Bomber Force to use on their journey). I ordered my navigator to work from his own calculations and ignore the wind speeds being sent back to us because they were far too low. By the time the Danish coast was crossed we were many miles south of track as a result of the high wind speed from the north. (At that time nobody had heard of the Jet Stream. Bomber Command met this phenomenon on this night). The force was scattered over a very wide front as we approached Berlin well before zero hour. Some captains ordered their navigators to work to the winds broadcast from England and found them hopelessly off track. Others navigated on their own findings and were reaching points well in advance of ETA but they were not as far off as the others were. We arrived over the target early and I decided to risk going round the city on the eastern side, by which time the PFF markers would be going down and start our bombing run.

'The activity in the sky over the city was awesome and frightening, as were all raids on Berlin. The sky was full of sparkling flashes as anti-aircraft shells from 1200 guns, the equivalent of an ammunition dump, burst in a box barrage every two minutes. I estimated that anyone getting through that would be very lucky indeed especially as the aircraft had to be flown straight and level with bomb doors open during the bombing run and take photographs after dropping the bombs. There were also hundreds of searchlights, making two cones over the city, which the bombers had to try and evade. The fighters no longer waited outside the perimeter of the target where they were in little danger from their own *Flak* because we were now severely damaging their cities. They flew amongst us in this area of death ignoring their own safety, meeting the anti-aircraft fire in order to get amongst us and many a bomber was shot down when most vulnerable with bomb doors open. When we were on our bombing run with two other Lancasters whose bomb aimers had chosen the same markers as my bomb aimer, Sgt Wally Paris, a twin engined fighter flew past our nose with cannon and machine guns firing at one of the Lancasters. There were tracers flying all over the sky as my gunners, Sgts Jock Jameson, mid-upper and Sgt Joe Ellick, rear gunner and the others in the third aircraft joined the targeted Lancaster to return the fire. However, the stricken Lancaster turned over on its back and went down in flames. We did not see anyone escape because we were concentrating on the bombing run.

'The Luftwaffe were now using single-engined fighters in the battle, generally over the target and as I took a quick glance down at the fires I saw 12 of them circling up line astern towards the bombers whose bellies were red from the reflection of the flames below. The searchlight cones held two bombers like moths round a candle; the pilots were tossing their aircraft all over the sky but they were held like stage artists in a spotlight. The next move was from the fighters who came in and inflicted the coup de grace, the bombers plunging down in flames before exploding and cascading in balls of fire to splash among the inferno below. A pilot had to take whatever action he could to get across the target area. One practice was to fly near a coned aircraft and hope the action against it would help him get across. This wasn't always possible because although the brightness was less intense they could be seen.

'When a raid was at its peak with 800 aircraft bombing in a 20-minute period, the illuminations have to be seen to be believed. The target indicators – red and green chandeliers, 200 ft in length – cascaded down with a shimmering brightness, Flak was bursting, filling every part of the sky with twinkling bursts and as you flew towards them there was no escape. You thought you would never get through it. Many years afterwards I read that a bomb aimer who flew on the raid was so awed by the experience, he just repeated, 'Jesus Skipper, look at that Flak, just look at it, we'll never get through it, just look at it'. That summed it up perfectly.

'After bombing the target I gained height to 25,000 ft and with relief at surviving the anti aircraft, searchlights and night fighter defenses but we had another fight on our hands before we reached England. The strong head winds and night fighters had not finished with us. It soon became apparent that our ground speed was very slow and we did not appear to be making much progress. As we crawled our way west to the next change of course, which was to take us north-west between Hanover and Osnabrück, the navigator was continuously amending his air plot to try and keep us on course but we were being blown south of our intended track. It soon became apparent that the conditions were getting worse and because of the effect of the wind on navigation found ourselves further west than the point where we should have turned northwest to fly between Hanover and Osnabrück. Instead we amended our course to fly between Osnabrück and the Ruhr making sure we kept well clear of the latter area.

'We had seen many aircraft shot down since we left Berlin, proof that the force was well scattered and aircraft were being picked off. As we looked towards the Ruhr we saw many more that had wandered over that area shot down, so they had flown into the two heaviest defended areas in Germany – Berlin and Ruhr – in one night. I was concentrating our efforts to get to the coast without further trouble when a radar-controlled searchlight was suddenly switched on just below the aircraft. (These searchlights had a blue-white beam and more often than not hit the aircraft at the first attempt). The searchlight knew they were near us because the beam started creeping up in front of the aircraft. I put more power on and raised the nose to maintain our position above the beam but it still continued creeping towards us. I was just on the point of putting the nose down and diving through it when it was switched off. Talk about a dry mouth. If the searchlight had found us it would have been joined by others and as was the customary practice a night fighter in the vicinity would have attacked us as we were caught in the beam.

'Our last turning point was near the Dutch border. Although our ground speed was very slow the intensity of the defenses had slackened off and for the first time in the raid, fighter activity had ceased. Maybe they had landed to refuel because we were approaching their airfields in Holland. We did not have any further trouble and eventually reached the North Sea coast where I pushed down the nose of the aircraft and did a very fast descent to 2000 ft to the relief of the crew who were thankful to have the raid almost behind them.

'As we flew towards the English coast the wireless operator, Sgt George Walker, received a signal ordering us to divert to Wing, an OTU near Luton. It was a dark night and normally as you approached the coast you saw the odd searchlight. But we did not see one light and I was surprised when the navigator told me that according to his calculations we had already crossed the coast and gave me a course to Wing. We were by then well inland with navigation lights on flying at 2000 ft but could not see a thing. Suddenly a searchlight switched on to us followed by two more. They could not have been practising because they could see the lights of our aircraft. I cursed as they held us, thinking back to the hundreds we had evaded over Germany only to be caught in the beams of a searchlight battery in England. I was told afterwards that a crew of ATS girls operated the lights. We eventually landed at Wing, after a flight of seven and a-half-hours on the last big raid to Berlin.'

T-Tommy of 57 Squadron made it back to England but they had to land at the fighter airfield at RAF Coltishall in Norfolk. Sgt Roland A. Hammersley DFM concludes:

'The time we spent flying was seven hours, 30 minutes. We were debriefed and fed, then shown to our sleeping quarters. We made the 35 minutes flight back to East Kirkby the following afternoon, leaving at 15.00 hrs by which time the fog that had prevented our landing the previous night had cleared. Of the 17 Lancasters from the squadron that flew this operation, one made an early return and two others failed to return. We made our reports at the squadron office before heading for our huts to await the evening meal.'

F/Sgt Larry Melling, a Halifax pilot in 51 Squadron at Snaith, Yorkshire, also put down at Coltishall:

'I suspect that we probably never came near to Berlin and, on the way home, found ourselves far to the south of where we were supposed to be. Directly ahead of us was the Ruhr Valley with its heavy defenses and we elected to head to the north and pass between Hamburg and Hanover on our way to the North Sea. We were lucky enough to get to the coast without any trouble but by now we were running considerably late because of the extra distance we had flown. Fuel became a major concern as we crossed the North Sea and at one point my flight engineer, when asked, reported that all gauges were reading zero but, according to his calculations, we had about 30 minutes' fuel left! His calculations proved correct and we landed at Coltishall, whereupon all four engines quit and we had to be towed off the runway!'[14]

P/O Dick Starkey and his 106 Squadron Lancaster crew were nearing the end of their tour when on the night of 29 March they were scheduled to take part in a raid on Brunswick. 'But', as Starkey recalls:

'Four crews were on the last ten trips of their tours and it looked as though they would complete the 30 operations (a complete tour) at about the same time, so it was decided to stagger the remaining trips. Following this decision we were to stand down for the Brunswick raid. However this operation was cancelled because the Met forecast was not good. On 30 March Nuremberg was the target and again I was told by the Flight Commander that my crew would be stood down. I informed the lads of the order but as one man they said that as we had been a stand down crew for a cancelled operation one of the other crews should do so for the Nuremberg raid and they asked me to see the Flight Commander again. Although I had to decide whether or not to let the order stand I agreed that we should be put on the Battle Order and gave my views to the Flight Commander. At first he said the order would not be reversed but after some thought to our request changed his decision. It was our last trip.

'With only three weeks to go to the end of our tour after the afternoon briefing some of the crew had reservations about the operation. The attack was planned for what would normally have been the middle of the stand down period, when a near full moon would be visible. The forecast was for high cloud on the outward route with the target clear. However in the early afternoon a reconnaissance aircraft reported that the route would be clear of cloud but the target would probably be covered. This was after the crews had been briefed for the operation but it was not cancelled.

'We took off[15] and climbed on course over the Norfolk coast towards Belgium. The moon was bright and almost full making near daylight conditions. At our cruising height of 21,000 ft the air temperature was very low and the bomber stream began making condensation trails as we flew on route, over Belgium towards the log leg which ran from south of the Ruhr east to a turning point Northwest of Nuremberg. It was this long leg that crews were apprehensive about because it ran for over 200 miles. Flying conditions over Germany were ideal for fighter aircraft against slow bombers who had inferior armament and the sky was absolutely clear with a near full moon and four-engined bombers making condensation trails which could be seen for miles. The fighters began their attack and from the number of tracers being fired, it appeared there were combats everywhere; I saw around 30 aircraft go down in a short period and as we continued to the target the ground became covered with burning aircraft.'

S/L Arthur William Doubleday DFC RAAF (later W/C Doubleday DSO DFC and CO of 61 Squadron), 'B' Flight Commander in 467 Squadron RAAF in 5 Group at Waddington, said to his crew of Lancaster I LL843[16]:

> 'Look boys it's on for young and old tonight. Just keep your eyes on the sky because they started to fall within ten minutes of crossing the coast and from then to the target the air was not only of good visibility but seemed to be bright. The moon was really shining brightly although it wasn't a full moon.'

Night fighting in good visibility was ideal and on 30/31 March the weather over Belgium and eastern France was 0/10ths to 4/10ths thin cloud while Holland and the Ruhr were cloudless. At Nürnburg, destination of 795 RAF heavy bombers and 38 Mosquitoes, there was 10/10ths cloud at 1600 to 12,000 ft but the cloud veiled at 16,000 ft with generally good altitude visibility. Jamming was carried out on a large scale but Mosquito spoof attacks on Cologne, Frankfurt and Kassel were identified for what they were because to the German defenses they were apparently flying without H2S. The heavies on the other hand could quite clearly be followed on radar by their H_2S bearings. As the bomber stream was clearly recognized from the start, it was attempted to switch in night fighters as far west as possible. All units of *3 JD* were switched in over radio beacon Bonn. *2 JD* was brought near via radio beacons Bonn and Osnabrück and switched in by radio beacons Bonn and Frankfurt respectively. *1 JD* was brought near via radio beacons Bonn and Harz and switched in by radar station north of Frankfurt, as was *7 JD*. Single engined units from Oldenburg, Rheine and Bonn were directed via radio beacon Frankfurt to radio beacon Nürnburg. Night fighter units from Ludwigslust, Zerbst, Jüterborg and Wiesbaden were led directly to radio beacon Nürnburg. Altogether, 246 twin- and single- engined night fighters were engaged. Despite the British jamming the first interception of the bomber stream in the area south of Bonn was successful. From there on in the bomber stream was hit repeatedly and the majority of the losses occurred in the Giessen-Fulda-Bamberg area. A staggering 82 bombers were lost en route to and near the target.

Oblt Dieter Schmidt, *Staffelkapitän*, 8./NJG 1 who took off from Laon-Athies[17] at 2326[18] recalls:

> 'On the night of 30 March we were on our way to the radio beacon Ida. A bright moon in the west, first quarter and not to set for another two hours. Would the Tommy really come? – They were coming! Suddenly we were right in amongst them, course 120° to 150°. *Flak* fire, a bomber was going down! And another one! More and more! Soon we also had one in front of us. I was not accustomed to the prevailing bright light and fire at too great a range, Missed! At the second burst there was only a miserable 'bum-bum'. The guns had failed! I broke off briefly, reloaded, test fired – partial success (two cannon had failed completely). Now of course my adversary had gone! '*Abschüsse* all around us, wild dogfights. 'There's one behind us,' 'Break off', '*Flak* to starboard!' 'No, aircraft guns!' It's a madhouse; aircraft exchanging fire everywhere, bombs and aircraft falling all around, a night such as this I had never experienced before.
>
> '0045hrs. I was flying at an altitude of 5700 meters, 'Look out, one coming from port, 300, 200 meters'. He passed in front of us. I had almost rammed him! Turn in, full throttle, at him, one hundred meters. He turned. I took better aim, a little deflection and fired. He passed through the burst from the right and caught fire at once in the fuselage and starboard inner engine. That was enough for him. I passed to the right. He returned fire. I broke off, saw the roundels, believed to be the letters N and MP. Then he was behind us to port. It went down to crash at 0049, 50 to 100 kilometers Northwest of Würzburg in the mountains and on the approach to Nürnburg. We heard later that the Halifax crashed at Vogelsberg. We landed at Langendiebach at 0155. We had a hit in the port wing and the port spinner was dented. Our *Gruppe* had six *Abschüsse*.'[19]

P/O Starkey of 106 Squadron continues:

> 'We continuously operated the 'banking search' looking for enemy aircraft coming up from below. This was achieved by turning steeply to port for 15 degrees to see if fighters were preparing to attack and then banking to return to the original course. Our Fishpond aircraft detector failed to work on the Nuremberg raid. [The bombers were attacked just before they reached the Belgian border and the attacks lasted for the next hour]. 'We had been flying the long leg for many miles. When we were in a position 60 miles northwest of Nuremberg our luck changed. A fighter attacked with tracer and cannon fire, which hit the port mainplane and outer engine, flashed past outside the perspex covering of the cockpit and between my legs. I remember praying we would not go up in flames. However, within three or four seconds the port outer engine and mainplane were alight. It was always the one you didn't see that shot you down as in our case and if Monica[20] had been available we would have been aware of the fighters' approach.

'There was only one action to take; I gave the order to abandon aircraft. The engineer, Sgt Johnnie Harris feathered the port engine as he helped me with the controls because we were going down at a very fast rate and the next few seconds I remember vividly. The bomb aimer, Sgt Wally Paris, acknowledged my order to bale out and said he was leaving the aircraft. The navigator, Sgt Colin Roberts, came to the cockpit to escape through the front hatch. The rear gunner, Sgt Joe Ellick, also acknowledged the order but said he could not get out of his turret (this was because the port outer engine powered the turret; the alternative way was to turn the turret by hand controls in order to fall out backwards). There was no reply from the mid-upper gunner, Sgt Jock Jameson and the wireless operator, Sgt Jock Walker, I assumed they must have been killed by the burst of fire which ran along the side of the aircraft.

'Johnnie Harris handed me a parachute from one of two in the rack at his side. I managed to connect one of the hooks on the chute to the harness I was wearing (we did not wear seat type chutes), at the same time trying to control a blazing aircraft which was diving at well over 300 mph. I gave up all hope of survival and waited for the impact; a terrifying experience. That is the last thing I remember because the aircraft exploded with a full bomb load (we had no time to jettison) and 1500 gallons of high octane fuel which must have ignited and caused the explosion. As I lost consciousness I did have a feeling of being lifted out of the cockpit and must have been propelled through the perspex canopy. When the petrol tanks exploded in the port wing outside my window a fireball must have been created in the aircraft which would incinerate anything in its path and I must have been just ahead of it as I was blown from the aircraft. Many years later I was told an unopened parachute was found next to the body of the flight engineer who had landed in a wood six kilometers from the wreckage of the aircraft. We were only two feet apart in the cockpit when the aircraft went up and Johnnie Harris must have been blown out like me but I was lucky my parachute had opened, probably by the force of the explosion.

'When I regained consciousness and realized what had happened my first thought was, 'where am I?' Then I heard the sound of aircraft engines as the main force passed overhead and I was suspended somewhere over Germany. I expected to feel the parachute supports in front of my face but could not find them. I thought I was coming down without a parachute! I desperately groped around and located the one hook attachment and hung on. This attachment was well above my head, evidently the part of the parachute that once it opens rises to a position over your head. I wasn't aware of this. By this time I did not know how quickly I was descending. I was coming down without flying boots. As I looked up I saw the canopy of the parachute quite clearly in the bright moonlight. It was riddled in parts with a number of burnt small holes, some of them half an inch in diameter. It was terrifying because I was afraid that my descent might be too fast for a safe landing. Although the moon was bright I could not see the ground but there were several fires burning, which I took to be from our aircraft. The fires did not help me to judge my altitude because I did not know the size of them. I also had facial injuries and a nosebleed. These must have occurred when I was blown out of the aircraft.[21]

'As my thoughts dwelt on landing, I hit the ground with an almighty wallop and rolled backwards down a small hill. When I reached the bottom I regained my wind and could see hills silhouetted against the night sky. My neck and back were very painful and when I attempted to stand, my right leg collapsed. It was out of line just above the ankle and I knew it was broken. I must have then lost consciousness again and when I came to the moon was low in the sky behind the hills. I could not walk and waited for someone to arrive. I soon heard shouting in German and realized I had left Metheringham a few hours before where everyone spoke English and here I was for the first time listening to a German voice. I saw a torch about 200 yards away so I shouted back and the torch came towards me. A number of people arrived and the torch was shone in my face. I could make out both young and elderly men; one of the younger men started shouting and was about to hit me in the face with a rifle when he was stopped by one of the elderly men. One or two of them went off to search the wreckage and the others wrapped me in the parachute, placed me on a stretcher and carried me to a horse-drawn cart, which took me to a small village called Köningsberg about 1000 meters away.'

S/L Arthur William Doubleday DFC RAAF was first back at Waddington and Air Marshal The Hon. Sir Ralph A. Cochrane KBE CB AFC commanding 5 Group, called him up to the control tower:

'He asked, 'How did it go?'

'I said, 'Jerry got a century before lunch today.' He didn't quite – he got 95.'

Sixty-four Lancasters and 31 Halifaxes (11.9 per cent of the force dispatched) were lost (and ten bombers crash-landed in England); the worst Bomber Command loss of the war. P/O

Starkey and his crew were possibly shot down by a Bf 110 flown by *Oblt* Martin 'Tino' Becker, *Staffelkapitän*, 2./NJG 6 as the 37th aircraft to go down on the Nürnburg raid. Becker and his *Bordfunker Uffz* Karl-Ludwig Johanssen had taken off from Finthen airfield for a Tame Boar mission. (I. and II./NJG 6 operated 19 Tame Boar Bf 110s and four in *Himmelbett* sorties). They were guided by 3 JD into the bomber stream to the south of radio beacon 'Ida' whereupon they intercepted and shot down six bombers between 0020 and 0050 hrs with their '*Schräge Musik*' cannons. After returning to base to re-fuel and re-arm, Becker and Johanssen took off on a second sortie and they claimed their seventh kill of the night when they destroyed a Halifax[22] south of Luxembourg. Next day Becker received news that he was awarded the *Ritterkreuz*. Of the 17 Lancasters of 106 Squadron that had been dispatched from Metheringham, three failed to return, all probably falling victim to a night fighter. For just nine First *Jagdkorps* Bf 110s and Ju 88s lost (four of which went down to return fire), the Nuremberg raid had turned into a black affair for Bomber Command. It was *Nachtjagd*'s finest hour[23] and brought its total for March to 269 RAF bombers destroyed. Since the start of the Battle of Berlin Bomber Command had lost 1047 aircraft and another 1682 returned with severe battle damage.

The Nürnburg raid brought, for a brief period, the virtual cessation of heavy attacks. During April Bomber Command became engaged in the preparations of D-Day, mainly focussing on transportation targets in France and on raids against Luftwaffe airfields in the Low Countries and France. On 10/11 April *Hptm* Helmut Bergmann, *Staffelkapitän*, 8./ NJG 4 at Juvincourt destroyed seven Lancasters in 46 minutes (his 17th-23rd kills – all the Lancasters failing to return from a raid against Aulnoye). Also operating from Juvincourt *Hptm* Gerhard Friedrich, *Staffelkapitän*, 1./NJG 6, a former transport pilot who had joined the *Nachtjagd* in 1942, claimed two Halifaxes in the Montdidier area.[24] On 11/12 April 352 heavies raided Aachen, for the loss of nine aircraft.[25] Towards the end of the month a series of deep penetration raids into Germany were mounted again, to which First *Jagdkorps* replied with successful Tame Boar operations. On six nights April 21-28 1407 night-fighter sorties were dispatched, which resulted in claims for 135 bombers destroyed.[26]

On 18/19 April Harry White (promoted F/L on 14 April) and Mike Allen of 141 Squadron gave chase during a *Serrate* patrol to Swinemunde and the western Baltic but their intended victim escaped. Their ninth kill would have to wait just a little longer. Eighteen Mosquitoes operated from West Raynham this night, including ten from 141 Squadron, its best effort so far. White and Allen were one of eight 141 Squadron Mosquito crews dispatched to patrol over France on 20/21 April when Main Force targets included Cologne and three rail targets in France, as part of the preparations for what was to be the Normandy invasion, and one in Belgium. Some 247 Lancasters of 5 Group and 22 Mosquitoes of 5 and 8 Groups were despatched to the rail target at La Chapelle just north of Paris and 175 aircraft of 6 and 8 Groups attacked Lens, while 14 Sirlings attacked a rail depot at Chambly. 196 aircraft of 4 and 8 Group meanwhile, attacked rail yards at Ottignies in Belgium.[27] Harry White wrote:

'We took off and set course over base at 6000 ft at 2252 hrs and continued uneventfully on course until 2350 hrs when our first *Serrate* contact was obtained to starboard and below, crossing starboard to port. We gave chase going down hill and obtained an AI contact at 12,000-ft range, which was found to he jinking considerably. Height was decreased to 12,000 ft and range closed to 1500 ft when *Senate* and AI contacts faded. We turned starboard and back to port hoping to regain contact – no joy. Enemy aircraft switched off *Serrate* as we broke away. Throughout this attempted interception our elevation was behaving most erratically and it is believed that the enemy aircraft was directly below us at 1500 ft when contact faded, the usual reason for fading blips.

'The gyro having spun during the interception, I had little idea of where this interception had taken me, so set course towards the estimated position of Paris, which I hoped shortly to see illuminated and fix my position. At 0020 hrs various contacts were obtained on the bomber stream leaving the Paris area. *Window* was much in evidence. At 0025 hours an AI contact at 15,000 ft to port and below was obtained a few miles west of stream and chased. We decreased height and followed contact through gentle port and starboard orbits reducing height to 12,000 ft and eventually closing range to 600 ft where I obtained a visual on four blue-white exhausts, later positively identified at 300 ft as a Ju 88. For five minutes I followed enemy aircraft patiently through gentle port and starboard orbits at 200 indicated air speed, eventually opening fire, still turning, at 500 ft with a one-second burst allowing 5° deflection; no results. Enemy aircraft, completely clueless, continued to orbit. Apparently clueless also, I tried again with a one-second burst. Again no results. A third burst was fired as enemy aircraft peeled off to starboard and disappeared from view I have no idea why I continually missed enemy aircraft and can only attribute it to the dot dimmed out from the gunsight and gremlin interference.

'At 0100 hrs, being in the proximity of the bomber stream, second attack on Paris, we obtained another *Serrate* contact starboard and below which we followed for three minutes. This *Serrate* momentarily faded and enemy aircraft was presumed to be orbiting, at least turning. This was confirmed within a few seconds by a head-on AI contact at 15,000 ft range well below. We turned behind and closed rapidly to 600 ft and there obtained a visual on four quite bright blue exhausts, identified from 300 ft as a Do 217 now flying at 10,000ft. Enemy aircraft was now turning very gently port and was followed for five minutes not wishing to repeat above. At 450 ft only exhausts could be seen, though these, unlike the Ju 88, quite clearly. Not wishing to approach closer I opened fire at this range with a two-second burst and was gratified to see enemy aircraft exploded with a blinding flash and disintegrate. Several pieces were flung back at us and I instinctively ducked as they splattered over the windscreen and fuselage. Apart from two broken Perspex panels, which were causing more noise than worry, we appeared to be OK but visions of damaged radiators caused some concern for the first minutes. We had no trouble in that respect and returned uneventfully to base.'[28]

The other confirmed victory this night was a Bf 110 in the Ruhr that went to F/L Gordon D. Cremer and F/O R.W. 'Dick' O'Farrell of 169 Squadron, who flew a *Serrate* patrol in support of the bombers targeting Köln. As the 110 was diving away to starboard Cremer closed astern and gave a short burst at about 100 to 50 yards' range from slightly above. Strikes were seen instantaneously inboard of the port engine followed by a large flash of flame, which clearly illuminated the cockpit, fuselage and tailplane. It disappeared in flames through the clouds at 10,000 ft and a few seconds later there was an explosion, followed by a red glow on the clouds. (Cremer fired just 40 rounds of 20-mm ammunition to down the German aircraft.) On the debit side, two Mosquito NFIIs that were providing Bomber Support, for the Cologne raid and the attacks on rail targets, and eight of the bombers failed to return.[29] No aircraft were lost on the raid on Ottignies. One of the Halifax III bomber crew who flew on the raid was bomb-aimer F/O S.T. 'Tom' Wingham. He had completed his first tour, on 102 Squadron, in June 1943. On 28 March 1944 he and the crew captained by S/L S.A. 'Stan' Somerscales DFC had arrived at RAF Holme-on-Spalding Moor, a bleak wartime airfield with very few comforts, to start their second tour with 76 Squadron. A few days followed in getting acquainted with the station and squadron routine as well as the Halifax III, before pushing off for some leave prior to commencing operations. They made their 76 Squadron debut in a brand new Halifax III, MZ578 *I-Ink* on 22/23 April when the target for 596 heavies was Düsseldorf. It was well known to Tom Wingham and all of the crew who had been there twice before during the 'Battle of the Ruhr' April to July 1943, as Wingham recalls:

'Briefing followed the usual pattern that had become all too familiar to those who had operated before. The Ruhr always produced apprehension even in the most experienced veteran and tonight was no exception. I had been over the Ruhr ten times in 1943 and losses sustained during that period were always heavy and in terms of average aircraft numbers put up each night it would hardly be an exaggeration to say that the Command had been wiped out nearly twice in that time. The route was always a matter of great interest and tonight the colored string on the wall map took us down to the south coast and then east across northern France before swinging north east at the last moment over Belgium and south east Holland to reach Düsseldorf. Two other major operations to Brunswick and Laon were also being mounted that night to keep the German defenses guessing and at full stretch, in all around 1100 heavy aircraft would be attacking. The Station Intelligence Officer had his usual say on the target giving an update on any known alterations to the defenses on the way in before the Met Officer was able to promise good clear weather on route and over the target. He was followed by navigation, bombing and W/T briefings before the CO W/C Hank Iveson finally rounded-off the briefing with a few well-chosen words.

'We drifted out of the briefing room and went about our various tasks before using the last hour or so stretched out on a bed. At the appointed hour we made our way to the Mess for an operational supper of bacon and eggs, afterwards filling our flasks with hot coffee before making our way to the crew room. The time-honored routine followed. Turn out pockets removing all forms of identification, put on flying boots, for gunners heated flying suits as well, Mae West and harness. Collect rations and parachutes, codes, signal cartridges of colors of the day and any other paraphernalia required before moving out to the waiting bus or truck which was to transport us to our waiting aircraft a mile or more away around the perimeter track at dispersal. We were somewhat quieter than we had been 24 hours earlier in the 'Half Moon' at York. Jim Lewis, a tall, thickset Herefordshire farmer, had a Morris 8 open four-seater but somehow it always managed to carry six. The previous night, on our return from a raid on the marshalling yards of Ottignies, photographers and reporters from a press agency had been visiting 76 Squadron and as the most experienced crew on the squadron we had been interviewed and photographed leaving our aircraft. So we were celebrating in good style and we had a rumbustuous ride back to Holme. Pride, literally, doth go before a fall!

'At dispersal we climbed into the Halifax, which had that smell of all things new, stowed our parachutes and carried out last minute checks. A last smoke in the cold night air and then all in again to take up position as the time came for start-up. Each of the four engines roared into life and after warming up checked for magneto drop to minimize the risk of engine cut out during take-off. One of the groundcrew brought the Form 700 to Stan for signature. (This ritual accepted by the pilot indicated that a RAF aircraft was in a satisfactory condition before leaving the ground). Following the groundcrew departure the hatch was closed and we were on our own. Slowly we moved out of dispersal in the inky darkness on to the perimeter track to wend our way to the end of the runway to take our turn for take-off with the rest of 76 Squadron; 22 aircraft in all. We lifted off at 2236 hours in clear conditions with no moon and settled down to the slow climb with full bomb load to operational height of 19,000ft. Having assisted Stan with the take-off I folded down the second pilot's seat to allow Jim and F/O Jack Reavill to come forward, as I also moved down to the nose. Very little conversation took place on the intercom other than routine chat on course and height between Jim Lewis and the skipper and comments by the gunners of other aircraft. The usual thoughts passed through our minds as we crossed the English coastline. Open seas were always viewed as a potential grave. God knows how many bomber boys they swallowed up. However, tonight was a short sea crossing and it was not long before I was reporting 'enemy coast ahead'. We roared ahead with everything completely obscured by the blackness of the night and with only the stars glowing above us. Apart from the odd bit of AA fire, as some poor aircraft strayed, life was rather quiet, if one ignored the thumping drone of the four Hercules engines. Occasionally we were assured that we were not alone by a bump as we hit the slipstream of another bomber. There was little sign of enemy activity as the aircraft reached the end of our easterly run and the navigator gave Stan the new course for the last leg of our approach to Düsseldorf, tracking north across the east of Belgium and Holland.'

As usual Mosquito bombers were flying a diversion raid (on Mannheim) while 100 Group operated ten RCM sorties and dispatched 19 *Serrate* and seven intruder patrols over the continent to hunt for enemy nightfighters. Two Mosquito NFII crews of 169 Squadron, Welshman P/O Wilfred Handel 'Andy' Miller and his radar operator P/O F.C. 'Freddie' Bone, a 38-year-old policeman from Birkenhead[30] and F/L Tim Woodman and F/O Patrick Kemmis, were successful. Miller and Bone claimed a Bf 110 at Cologne and Woodman and Kemmis another Bf 110 in the Bonn area as Woodman recalls:

'The Y-Service[31] had informed us that when the bombers were approaching targets in northern Germany and the Ruhr, night-fighter squadrons in the Munich area were being directed to the suspected target area. On this night, therefore, I flew from the Ruhr towards Munich as the bombers approached the Ruhr We picked up a *Serrate* contact coming towards us and when it was within AI range turned port and came up underneath him. He had not spotted us on his radar. It was a 110 with a small white light on his tail and he was probably escorting Me 109 *Wilde Sau* fighters to the bombers' target area as there were four other aircraft flying in formation with him, two to port and two to starboard. I switched on the gunsight but it did not light up. I changed the bulb and it still did not work. I banged the sight with my gloved fist and the socket and bulb fell out on its lead, blinding me with its brilliant white light as it lit up. I switched off and fired a short burst at the 110 tail light but with no strikes. We were fast approaching the Ruhr searchlight zone so I fired a longer burst, stirring the stick as I did so to spread the shells. There were a number of strikes and the 110 seemed to have blown up. Black sooty oil covered my windscreen (and when we got back we found the nose and starboard wing damaged). Pat, on radar, said that he could see large pieces going. (Seeing their escort aircraft shot down they would all have dived down to ground level, not knowing what was behind them. Maybe this is what Pat Kemmis saw on radar). Now the Ruhr searchlights were after us and I did not want them to recognize me as a Mosquito. The Y-Service came to my aid. I reached back and pressed the trigger of a fixed Verey pistol. Red and green Verey lights spread across the night sky. The searchlight crews counted them and doused their searchlights. I had fired off the German 'colors of the day' using information supplied by the Y-Service. It was the only time I did so.'

All told, Ist *Jagdkorps*, which had reacted to the mass raid by despatching 294 sorties lost only seven fighters while claiming no less than 42 victories. In fact 37 RAF bombers were lost. One of these was Halifax *I-Ink* of 76 Squadron flown by Stan Somerscales, which had crossed Belgium and began to move up Holland between Maastricht and Aachen. Suddenly there was a soft muffled thud. P/O Sid Stephen was in his normal position as flight engineer directly behind the pilot when the Halifax was hit by a Bf 110G-4 night-fighter with *Schräge Musik* cannon, piloted by *Ofw* Rudolf Frank of 3./NJG 3 for his 43rd 'kill'.[32] *Schräge Musik* seems to have been a secret kept just as well by the Air Ministry in late 1943 and early 1944, as it was by the Germans. Certainly, very few operational aircrews were made aware of this type of attack at the time. Three voices including the skipper's and Stephen's cried out, *'What was that?'* For probably no more than two or three seconds there was silence. Then F/Sgt Harry Poole the mid-upper shouted, *'The wing's on fire!'* Again, silence, which was quickly shattered by Somerscales' order: *'Bale out!'* Tom Wingham continues:

> 'It was an order, which one did not have to agonize over. A fire in an engine or in the fuselage could be dealt with by fire extinguishers but with hundreds of gallons of high-octane petrol in each wing it did not need much imagination to visualize the inevitable end. I looked up into the cockpit. Jack Reavill, who had keyed a distress call to base and then half clipped his parachute on as he made his way up to the cockpit, was standing there with the pilot's parachute, which he was trying to clip on the Stan's harness. Behind him was a dull red glow and smoke was drifting in from the fuselage. To give Stan a lighter aircraft I jettisoned the bomb load, hoping to make the aircraft easier to handle while everyone got out. That done, it was time to go! I threw off my oxygen mask and helmet, clipped on my parachute and turned to help Jim Lewis remove the escape hatch just behind me under the seat where he had been sitting. Being new, the hatch was proving troublesome but the combined effort of the two of us quickly overcame the problem and we dropped the hatch into the night. Jim Lewis crashed into trees on the edge of some woods and with his parachute caught in the branches he was still a number of feet from terra firma. As I dropped through the hatch I felt a bit muzzy and so I pulled the ripcord almost immediately. The last thing I remember was the black bulk of the port wing above and then nothing until I awoke on the ground.'

There was an explosion, one of the wings broke away and the aircraft went into a spin, rendering those left in the aircraft helpless in the grip of 'G' forces. Sid Stephen, who was levering at the hatch with his feet, was thrown out into space but Harry Poole the mid-upper gunner was trapped in the fuselage and he never left the aircraft. F/Sgt John Rowe had great difficulty in getting out of the rear turret, which had to be rotated to the 'fore and aft' position for baling out. Finally he did it manually, then putting his hands behind his back, he slid open the turret and bulkhead doors to find his chute in the rack, unclipped it and pulled it over his head into the turret. Once he fell clear Rowe pulled the cord and the noise, smoke and flame suddenly stopped. He was only just in time, as he had but a few hundred feet left but he broke one knee and badly damaged the other. Another explosion threw Reavill clear. He woke up to find himself in space with no parachute on his chest and then he realized that it was there but it was attached by only one strap. Reaching over his shoulder and grabbing the strap he drew it back and pulled the ripcord. Barely had the canopy opened when he hit trees in Wachelder woods. Somerscales had probably been blown clear by the same explosion, as he was found dead not far from the aircraft with his parachute streamed out in the trees above him.[33]

Somerscales' Halifax was one of 16 lost on the raid. Thirteen Lancasters also FTR. Ernst-Wilhelm Modrow of Venlo-based 1./NJG 1 flying a He 219 destroyed three Lancasters.[34] Earlier that night several more German kills were claimed over Norfolk and Suffolk by Me 410A-1 *Hornisse* (Hornet) intruders of *II Gruppe, Kampfgeschwader* (KG) 51 *Edelweiss* led by the *Staffelkapitän* of 5./KG 51, *Major* Dietrich Puttfarken, a former bomber pilot. Puttfarken had been awarded the *Ritterkreuz* and he had three victories to his name. The intruders took off from Soesterberg, Holland to infiltrate a returning USAAF bomber stream over England. The Luftwaffe had discontinued intruder operations over England late in 1941 because Hitler believed that German morale would be greater if British bombers were seen to fall on German soil rather than on England. Over the North Sea after the official blackout time of 2138 hours the attackers spotted a formation of twin-tailed bombers with their lights on heading for East Anglia. KG 51 crews identified their targets and were credited with nine Halifaxes shot down. Two of the victories were credited to Puttfarken while a B-17 and a UEA were also awarded to the unit. However, the 'Halifaxes' were American Liberators returning late from a raid on the Hamm marshalling yards.[35] KG 51 lost two Me 410A-1s and their crews. *Oblt* Klaus Kruger and *Fw* Michael Reichardt, his *Bordfunker* in 9K+HP and *Hptm* Dietrich Puttfarken and his radio-operator-gunner, *Ofw* Willi Lux in 9K+MN, were lost. Just who shot them down is open to conjecture. Three Me 410A-1s were claimed shot down by B-24 gunners. The Me 410 flown by Kruger crashed and exploded in a field at Ashby St. Mary. Uncertainty surrounds the disappearance of Puttfarken and Lux's Me 410 because no trace of it has ever been found. Quite probably they crashed in the North Sea.

On 23/24 April F/L Graham J. Rice and P/O Ron Mallett of 141 Squadron, one of four Mosquito Serrate patrols despatched, shot down a Fw 190 employing *Zahme Sau* tactics against RAF bombers carrying out mine-laying in the Baltic. It was Rice's second victory on the squadron. Four Halifaxes and a Stirling failed to return. Among claims for seven kills was a Halifax at radio beacon Chameleon by *Lt* Otto Fries of 5./NJG 1 and a *Viermot* at Laaland Island by *Ofw* Rudolf Frank of 3./NJG 3. When on the night of 24/25 April 637 aircraft bombed Karlsruhe and 234 Lancasters and 16 Mosquitoes raided Munich. 100 Group flew 11 RCM, 21 Serrate and eight Intruder Bomber Support sorties for the raid on Munich which coast nine Lancasters. Eleven Lancasters and eight Halifaxes from the Karlsruhe raid were lost while two OTU Wellingtons went missing on a diversionary sweep over the North Sea by 165 aircraft.[36] P/O Bill Lucas and his Halifax crew on 10 Squadron had a close shave, as P/O Jim Sprackling, recalls:

> 'On the way home I saw a dim shape of what looked like a 'hostile' astern and below on the port side, which was rapidly overtaking us. It disappeared under the tailplane so I asked Bill to bank the plane so that we could look underneath. As he did so, fortunately quite violently, a stream of tracer shells came up between the wing and the tailplane, followed by a fighter aircraft. Digger, in the mid-upper turret, got a full burst at point-blank range. We could see his tracer hitting and bouncing off the target, which quickly fell away and disappeared from view. Our luck was still holding. I had now completed 28 operations but the crew had done 29 because they had all gone to Leipzig one night without me when I was doing Halifax Mk.III training.[37]
>
> 'Our final op, to Essen on 26/27 April [when Bomber Command raided Essen, Schweinfurt and Villeneuve-St.George] Bill managed to coax the aircraft up to 24,000 ft, the highest we had ever attacked a target. All the crew put on parachutes over the target, the first time we had done that. The markers were clear and we were attacking from the south. We had plenty of fuel so we left the power on and put the aircraft into a shallow dive to get maximum speed. We were back over the Rhine estuary north of Antwerp in 14 minutes and then we eased up and made for home.'

At Asten near Eindhoven *Ritterkreuzträger Ofw* Rudolf Frank of 3./NJG 3 flying a Bf 110G-4[38] night-fighter with *Schräge Musik* cannon from Vechta claimed his 45th and final *Abschuss*[39] before he and his crew were hit by debris from their quarry. Frank and *Oberfeldwebel*'s Schierholz and Schneider crashed to their deaths. (Frank was posthumously promoted to *Leutnant* at the end of April on Hitler's birthday). F/O William Ranson Breithaupt RCAF and F/O J.A. Kennedy of 239 Squadron shot down a Bf 110 in the Essen area for the first of their five victories together. S/L John C.N. Forshaw and his navigator P/O Frank Folley of 141 Squadron failed to return. II./NJG 5 and I. and II./NJG 6 despatched 33 Tame Boar Bf 110s against the stream of 206 Lancasters heading for Schweinfurt. Sgt John B. Johnson, a Lancaster mid-upper turret gunner in 57 Squadron at East Kirkby, who flew his first op on the operation to Schweinfurt on 26/27 April, recalls:

> 'On my first day I was flying with F/O Walker and crew and P/O G.J.L. Smith would be flying with S/L M.I. Boyle DFC, the 'B' Flight Commander's crew, as the 'second dickey' for operational experience before taking his own crew on an operation. I did not have time to unpack my kit before meeting my crew and start the preparations for that night. After briefing we went out to the aircraft and went through a routine pre-operation check of equipment. After shutting the engines down we got out of the aircraft and the crew went one way and I made my way towards the next aircraft. It was strange but the other crew did the same thing; they walked one way but the one member walked towards me. As we approached each other I realized that it was my pilot, he took his helmet off and he had a very large red band across his forehead from the helmet that was far too tight for him. I can still see him standing there because within a few hours he was dead. Two aircraft crashed into each other over the target. One man baled out. I am sure that it was my pilot in one of those two aircraft I saw go down.'[40]

P/O Bill Lucas and his Halifax crew returned safely to Melbourne and their tour was now complete, as Jim Sprackling recalls:

> 'At the debriefing we were targeted by the press representatives who had been allowed in. I made the mistake of talking. It was nearly a year since we had attacked Düsseldorf for our first operation. I said that the defenses were now so weak that they must be short of ammunition. This made the center page of the *'Daily Mirror'* next day and drinks were demanded in the bar – very expensive! And then began 48 hours of one enormous 'booze up'. None of us would have to go on operations again unless we volunteered, except for me. After a thrash in the mess bar, where amends were made for the remarks to the press the previous night, we agreed that we would all go to London, so we all drew warrants home via Kings Cross. The plan was to have a short afternoon sleep and then catch a night train to London, which we did. We parked our baggage in the Left Luggage and set out for town. Ronny, being a Londoner, knew where to start. Covent Garden Market pubs opened at 3am for the porters, so that is where we started. As soon as the locals found out what we were celebrating, that was the end for the need for money and we were feted until he market closed at about nine o'clock. Then back to the Strand for some

breakfast and by that time the Irish Pubs were opening, which kept us going until early afternoon when Bill said he knew an Afternoon Club which was open from 1pm-6pm. So, off we went. By the time that closed we were hungry again so a meal somewhere around Piccadilly Circus. Then we thought we would give the booze a rest and all go to the Windmill where we cheered the girls and booed the comedians but were not thrown out. After the show we decided to finish the job properly and set off for Shepherds Market. Somehow we got back to King's Cross station in the early morning and collected our kit and went our various ways. I never saw three of them again. Bill was killed instructing on Whitley bombers. Someone flew into him at night. Butch (Len), who was sure we would never complete a tour, volunteered for a second tour on Mosquitoes and was killed in a training accident. Digger presumably went back to Australia.'

On 27/28 April NJG 5 and NJG 6 again struck hard against a stream of 322 Lancasters heading for Friedrichshafen. Thirty-one Bf 110s and three *Luftbeobachter* (air situation observer) Ju 88s were successfully guided into the stream via radio beacon Christa and they wreacked havoc. Thirteen confirmed victories plus a probable were credited to I./NJG 6, a Ju 88 *Luftbeobachter* crew and to Austrian-born *Hptm* Leopold 'Poldi' Fellerer of II./NJG 5. 239 Squadron Mosquito crews landed back at West Raynham and submitted claims for three enemy aircraft destroyed. S/L Victor Lovell DFC and his navigator W/O Robert Lilley DFC failed to return from their patrol to Stuttgart/Friedrichshafen. In all the Friedrichshafen force lost 18 Lancasters. I JD's casualty figures for the period 21-28 April were 71 night-fighter aircraft lost, or almost 20 per cent of its total first-line battle strength. By 28 April, I JD had only 378 aircraft and crews ready for action. 100 Group RAF was partly responsible for bringing this about, turning *Nachtjagd* from hunters into the hunted with both its highly efficient radio and radar countermeasures campaign and the Mosquito screening of the bomber formations. In spring 1944 the Germans made huge advances in preventing the jamming of their radar sets and *SN2* was fully operational. RAF Bomber Command was almost completely limited to continual attacks by Mosquitoes. German night fighter crews developed a healthy respect for the twin engined British fighter, which late in 1944 developed into what became known as *Moskitopanik*. German pilots now flew very low, or at *Ritterkreuz Height.* If they flew higher they would never survive to receive their Knight's Cross. This caused many accidents and German night fighters often flew into the ground.

During May-June Bomber Command was, apart from three major raids against German cities towards the end of May, fully committed to destroying the Wehrmacht's infra-structure in France and bomber losses were relatively light. One exception, however, was on 3/4 May when Bomber Command attacked a *Panzer* depot and training center at Mailly-le-Camp near Epernay to the east of Paris, about 50 miles south of Rheims, which was reported to house up to 10,000 Wehrmacht troops.[41] Some 346 Lancasters and 14 Mosquitoes of 1 and 5 Groups and two Pathfinder Mosquitoes of 617 Squadron (one flown by W/C Leonard Cheshire, the 'Marker Leader') were despatched. F/L J.R. 'Benny' Goodman DFC[42] a Mosquito BIV pilot of 627 Squadron at Oakington in 5 Group, who with his navigator, F/L A.J.L. 'Bill' Hickox DFC flew on the Mailly Le Camp operation, recalls:

'Cheshire was to lead the low-level market aircraft and eight Mosquitoes of 627 Squadron were to be at a slightly higher level and were to dive bomb the light *Flak* positions which were known to be around this depot. The raid was timed to begin at 0001 hrs, when all good troops should be in bed.'

Mailly-le-Camp was P/O G.E. 'Ted' Ball's crew in 49 Squadron's 16th operation.[43] Sgt Ronnie H. 'Squiggle' Eeles, the rear gunner recalls:

'The morning of 3 May commenced as any normal routine day at RAF Fiskerton, Lincolnshire. the home of 49 Squadron (Lancaster) in 5 Group, Bomber Command. The day was uneventful until we were advised operations were on that evening. I cannot recall whether an NFT was carried out prior to briefing. Briefing details stressed the importance of Mailly Le Camp which was a training camp for tanks and the need to destroy it in company with 1 Group. As a crew, we were apprehensive of the raid arrangements in view of the planned concentration of aircraft over the target in a short space of time, particularly as crews were given bombing heights with only 100 ft variations in altitudes which obviously increased the risk of collision. Our individual bombing height was to be 7,100 ft and the target was to be marked by W/C Leonard Cheshire in a Mosquito. Our bomb load was high explosive bombs only. F/O Martin DFM (AG) was to accompany us. I understood his task was to observe anti-aircraft activity. As far as I recall he was not attached to squadron strength. Our take off time was 2157 with the usual 'wave off' by Station personnel at the end of the runway. I had a sense of foreboding that something was different, as I did not have the usual exhilaration when taking off on full power. I thought that something was going to happen and I would not be coming back. What had also stuck me as strange was that when I entered my turret at dispersal, for the first time ever the WOP/AG (Kernahan) had closed the turret doors behind me, as they were difficult to close oneself with full flying clothing due to the restriction space. I had thanked him – the last I was ever to speak to any member of the crew. The flight to the target area was uneventful. At the lower than usual operational height I found my electrically heated suit was unnecessary and I kept switching it on and off to maintain a reasonable temperature.'

F/L J.R. 'Benny' Goodman DFC continues:

'The Mosquito force arrived over Mailly, five minutes before zero hour as briefed. Although the target was marked accurately and Cheshire passed the order to bomb, confusion occurred. The first wave did not receive instructions and began to orbit the target. This was fatal and the German night-fighters moved in and began to shout down the Lancasters. Eventually the situation was sorted out and bombs began to crash down unto the depot. From our worm's eye view, Bill and I could see bomber after bomber coming down in flames towards us. We had a scary time as we dived on the light *Flak* batteries, dropped out bombs singly on them, avoided light *Flak* and burning Lancasters and contrived to keep ourselves out of harm's way. When out fourth bomb had gone I called Marker Leader and was told to go home. Bill gave me a course to steer for the French coast and I should have climbed to 25,000 ft but because of the mayhem in the target area I stayed at low level. All went well for a few minutes and then a searchlight shone directly on us, followed immediately by two or three more. Light *Flak* batteries opened up and the pretty blue, red, green and white tracery associated with light AA fire came shooting up the beams and exploded all around us.

'We were at 500-ft and I did not dare to lose height, not could I climb because this would have been a 'gift' to the German gunners. With Bill's exhortation '*watch your instruments*' ringing in my ears I ruined steeply to port through 30 degrees, levelled out for a few seconds, then tolled into a steep turn to starboard and repeated the performance. Although we were in searchlights and *Flak* for quite a long rime, we were not being held by any one light or being shot at by any one gun for very long; and we zig-zagged our way steadily towards the coast. It was a tense rime for us and we did not speak; we could hear the explosions around us from light AA shells but incredibly, were not hit. Deliverance came eventually as we breasted a low hill and ahead of us lay the sea. Now we were treated to a rare sight. The final group of searchlights was shining through the trees on top of the hill we had just passed and the beams were actually above us and lighting us on our way. We roared along a river estuary, below the level of the lighthouse at Le Treport and then were away over the 'drink' and climbing to safety, home and bed.'

The Mosquito crew had been lucky. For the heavies it was a different story as a tail gunner on the raid recalled:

'We circled and circled for what seemed an eternity without receiving any instructions. During this time the German fighter activity became more intense. There was tracer everywhere and aircraft were going down in flames all around us but still no instructions. One could sense the bombing force getting restless, like a herd ready to stampede. This was emphasised by the remarks made over the air, some of which should have turned the night sky blue. I heard one pilot's voice, 'For Christ's sake shut up and give my gunners a chance'. When I heard this remark I thought – 'God help them if they are being attacked with this lot going on'. But always the same stock phrase 'Don't bomb. Wait.'

The control of the raid in the target area failed to go according to plan. The initial Mosquito low level spot flares were accurate and were well backed up by Lancaster marker aircraft. Cheshire ordered the Main Force, who were orbiting at a holding pattern to the north, to come in and bomb. However, the 'Main Force Controller', W/C L.C. Deane, could not transmit the order because his VHF radio was being drowned by an American forces broadcast and his w/t was not tuned in correctly. *Nachtjagd* fighters arrived during the delay with deadly results. The main attack eventually began when the Deputy Controller, S/L E.N.M. Sparks of 83 Squadron took over.

A RAF pilot wrote:

'I switched on for the Main Controller's commentary and was surprised to hear him ordering the Main Force to wait, as the target had not yet been marked. The air was really blue with a succession of replies from the Main Force. I had never before heard R/T indiscipline and this was really the measure of the panic and fear that was abroad that night. This was quite enough for me – I had no intention of joining the crowd round those death-trap markers, so we turned east towards the darker sky…We heard brief snatches of R/T, on one occasion what sounded like an English voice saying.

'For Christ's sake! I am on fire!'

> 'This was replied to by a rough Australian voice saying: 'If you are going to die, die like a man – quietly.'
>
> 'A wing commander came up on the R/T, identified himself and said, 'This has got to stop. Cut your R/T and wait for instructions to bomb.' But the frightened voices continued. 'When the order to bomb was finally given the rush was like the starting gate at the Derby,' recalled a pilot.

Fw 190 fighters working without radar but by searchlight and moonlight and the bombers' 'marker flares' destroyed six bombers.[44] F/Sgt L.H. 'Lizzie' Lissette RNZAF, pilot of a Lancaster III of 207 Squadron, was attacked by a Fw 190. A third attack soon finished off the bomber. Tracer hit the port wing, blowing off the dinghy hatch. The dinghy then commenced to inflate and then shot back over the tailplane like a big hoopla ring. Lissette could see down through the wing to the ground. The port undercarriage was partially down. A little later the rear gunner reported a fighter coming in port quarter down. They were hit again in the bomb bay and a small fire started. Lissette, who remained at the controls to the end, was critically injured and he died later in a French hospital.[45]

Oblt Dietrich Schmidt, *Staffelkapitän*, 8./NJG 1, destroyed three Viermots for his 23rd-25th confirmed victories:

> 'We took off from Laon-Athies at 2323 hrs.[46] It was bright moonlight, four days after the first quarter. Our destination was the nightfighting area Chamäleon. It seemed that the enemy were going to attack targets in France again. We had hardly arrived in our area when Schönfeld, my Bordfunker got indications on his SN-2. Soon I saw one. Was it a Tommy? It was flying on an easterly course. To be on the safe side, I swung about from left to right below him, the moon high on the starboard quarter. I could not make out four engines for certain, so I swung again to the left. This time he had seen us and turned in. We passed at a hair's breadth and lost sight of each other. But there were more of them about. Schönfeld assisted with the SN-2 and I soon had another one ahead of me, which was confirmed as four-engined. We approached on course 120°-150° and at 2500 meters height passing close to the north of Paris from behind and below. I fired at 200 meters range, 2300 meters high, followed by a second burst to make sure. He burst into flames in the port wing and a little in the fuselage; a typical fuel fire. As we passed on his left I saw a pot-like thing below his fuselage (belly guns?) He went vertically down to crash at 0003. The flames were mixed with bluish-white phosphor fire. He lay in an open field beside a village.
>
> 'It was difficult to use our radar as we were flying at about 2000 meters where range was limited and it was also affected by ground echoes. But it was light enough to see them anyway. We flew to the target, ascertained the direction of the attack by the bomb bursts and went on to the departure course. Schönfeld assisted a little and soon we could see several, at 1800 meters and on course west. I chose the most suitable one but before we were close enough he fired and I went down a little to be on the safe side. But then my attack was just right. Just like with the first one, range about 200 meters, from behind. I opened fire at 0018 hrs. He was on fire at once in the fuselage and both inboard engines. The rear gunner fired again but without success. We passed to the left. Evidently it is a Lancaster. Burning bits flew off. He pulled up and then went down steeply. Our adversary crashed at 0019 hrs in an open field beside a small clump of trees, about 30 kilometers and 240° from the target.
>
> 'To the northwest of us the main attack was still going on. We flew there and observed close to it two bombers going down and then a third. While still on the approach from the southeast, we met no end of them head-on. One had to take care not to be rammed. We turned in and saw several around us in the bright moonlight. Following one, I lost him against the bright moon (in the south-west) but there were enough of them in sight. Although flying at full throttle, we had difficulty in getting closer, especially as they were climbing! We passed close to the south of a Flak area at Romilly sur Seine, which was firing heavily. At last we were close enough. I fired a first burst at 0045 hrs from behind, about 200 meters range, followed by a second one to make sure. He burned brightly in the port wing and fuselage at 3000 meters and on course west. I saw that it was four-engined with twin rudders, apparently a Lancaster. He pulled up to port and then went down burning in a shallow dive.
>
> 'Looking around I saw that we had a heavy trail of coolant from the starboard engine! We turned to port onto north in the direction of base and climbed with full throttle as long as the starboard engine held. Behind us we noted the crash of our third Abschuss at 0046 hrs. Meanwhile the starboard coolant temperature had reached maximum (over 120°). The trail of coolant had disappeared. Black smoke was coming from the exhaust. The engine began to vibrate; high time to stop it (ignition off, fuel off, propeller to feather). We were at about 3000 meters and passed back through the *Flak* area with Tommies still passing us on opposing course. I was unable to hold the aircraft on one engine and had to slowly lose altitude.

(Single-engined flight was only possible without the two 300 litre fuel tanks below the wings but we found out later that they had failed to release when the jettison lever was pulled). Although we fired emergency flares, the airfield at Romilly was not illuminated, so we continued to the north with steady loss of altitude. We were finally so low that, in spite of radio contact, we were unable to see Laon-Athies. We therefore had no choice but to bale out. We made that decision whilst flying at 800 meters but as Schlosser had difficulty in getting clear, we lost another 400 meters before I could think about getting out. Even then, I almost failed to get clear! The opening of the 'chute, the crash of the machine and the landing in the top of a tree were almost simultaneous. The aircraft and I both landed in a small wood, the two others in an open field, where both sprained ankles. Time was about 0110. We found each other with the assistance of flares. The relief was enormous. We went along a minor road northwards to the next village (Le Breuil Marne) which took us two hours, as the other two were limping. Le Breuil had no railway station and it was difficult to find anyone to help us. We finally managed to telephone from the post office, where our commander picked us upafter handing us a chicken which he had run over in his haste. Later we examined our crashed machine and, apart from the business with the drop tanks, found a bullet hole in the starboard radiator. Other hits were, as far as we could examine the wreckage, not found.'[47]

Uffz Erich Handke[48] *Bordfunker* describes how his pilot, *Hptm* Martin Drewes *Kommandeur* of III./NJG 1 flying a Bf 110G-4/U1 and one of the few fitted with the upward-firing *Schräge Musik*[49], also from Laon-Athies, 65 miles away, shot down five Lancasters on what was his 113th operational sortie:

'In the area of Chamäleon (south of Compiègne) we were directed into the bomber stream and at a height of 2500-3000 meters [8100-9700 ft] I immediately had contacts on my radar on a reciprocal course but by the time we had turned, they were out of our radar range. We flew on and finally saw the target burning in front of us and this enabled us to get into the bomber stream. I guided my pilot with the *SN-2* onto the nearest bomber and at 600 meters we could see it. The weather was wonderful, almost full moon. The *Flak* was putting a barrage over the target. We decided not to follow the Lancasters over the target for fear of being hit by their bombs. Twenty kilometers [12 miles] to the south we again headed after the bombers, descending all the while, as they had in the meantime lost height to 2300 meters [7500 ft]. We sat under a Lancaster, which was only at 2400 meters and shot from underneath into the wing, which burned at once. Almost immediately the bomber went down in flames. It was our 41st *Abschuss*.

'I had already found another target on my screen at 270°, which meant that it was a homebound aircraft. It was flying away to the west at 2000 meters [6500 ft] and at a distance of 500 meters [550 yards] we spotted it; it was another Lancaster. We got 500 meters underneath it and then climbed to within about 70 meters under the cockpit area and we fired this time into the fuselage because we could now be sure there were no bombs there. The Lancaster erupted into a bright fire and it soon crashed, ten minutes after our first victim.

'Then I again caught a machine on my radar while we were already overtaking it. It flew just in front and underneath us. We dived down fast and we spotted it 500 meters [550 yds] to our left and over us. Again we positioned ourselves quite far underneath, pulled up slowly and fired into the middle of it. There was a bright fire and immediately the Lancaster plunged down. It exploded into several parts and crashed eight minutes after our second and just like our 42nd, it came down on the banks of the river Seine near Romilly. This was our 43rd kill.

'Then 'Schorsch' our *funker* suddenly saw one passing diagonally over us. We immediately banked towards it. As visibility was so splendid we could keep our eyes on it easily. Again we dived down re-position ourselves low underneath, as of course we didn't want to be seen and slowly pulled up but the Lancaster also climbed, so that only at a height of 3000 meters [9700ft] did we get into effective firing range. We fired a long burst of fire vertically with our *Schräge Musik*, again aiming into the middle of the bomber. The whole tail unit broke off and engulfed in bright flames the Lancaster plunged down. It was six minutes after our third *Abschuss*.

'The next one was immediately spotted by Petz, which weaved quite violently whilst climbing all the time. We adapted to its weaving pattern and flew along 500 meters [550 yds] underneath it. After ten minutes when we had reached a height of 4300 meters [14,000-ft] Schorsch saw another one closing in from behind but this one flew on a steady course. Then I spotted two more to the right and over us, of which we picked out the aircraft that cruised on most steadily. The others were only 600 meters [660 yds] away when we shot up this one from below, at a distance of 80 meters. At the same instant, it plunged down in flames and my pilot had to pull away sharply. This caused us to lose contact with the others and unfortunately, we didn't succeed in finding them again. All our kills were Lancasters. Our final victim crashed 50-km [32 miles] southwest of Paris near Dreux.'[50]

S/L E.N.M. Sparks, deputy controller, continues:

'As we left the target my rear gunner, W/O 'Tiger' Teague, reported four fighters on our tail. I immediately started a corkscrew intending to lose height rapidly from 3000-ft to return as near ground level as possible and I took a straight line from Mailly towards England. During our second steep bank to the left I saw another fighter directly beneath us, perhaps 1000-ft below. I pressed on with the corkscrew but this chap somehow put perhaps a dozen cannon shells into my starboard wing fuel tanks. We had no nitrogen suppression and in a short time the top skin of the wing had burnt through with a mass of flame. I had seen so many Lancasters with burning wings that I knew my aircraft had at most two minutes before the main spar failed with a consequent uncontrollable spin. I gave the order to bale out in my No.2 method, which was unofficial but known and practised by my crew. This method was that the crew were to get up and get out without delay and any intercom. This they did and I was sitting there keeping an eye on the burning wing and calling up all crew positions to check that no one was left on board. None was and all lived. As I was calling the last position, the wing folded up and I immediately made a turning dive through the front hatch.'[51]

Sgt Ronnie H. 'Squiggle' Eeles recalls:

'On arrival at Mailly we were directed to proceed to a point 15 miles away and there orbit a yellow marker. After a few minutes we did not like this at all and the crew were worried as visibility was clear and good and we knew from experience the danger of hanging around enemy territory any longer than absolutely necessary. We were circling this flare for approximately half an hour and becoming increasingly worried, as it appeared impossible to receive any radio instructions due to an American Forces Network Broadcasting Station blasting away. I remember only too well the tune 'Deep in the heart of Texas' followed by hand clapping and noise like a party going on. Other garbled talk was in the background but drowned by the music. Whilst this noise was taking place I was suddenly aware from my position that several Lancasters were going down in flames; about five aircraft and the fire in each was along the leading edge of the mainplane. I saw some of these planes impact on the ground with the usual dull red glow after the initial crash. My job was to keep my eyes open for enemy aircraft so I did not dwell for more than fleeting seconds on these shot down planes. At this stage I did not see any night fighter activity nor anti-aircraft fire but with regard to the latter we were still orbiting 15 miles from Mailly.

'At about 0030 hrs my pilot commenced his run in to the target and I could then see several planes burning on the ground. I do not remember hearing any instructions to the pilot from outside sources but obviously he would have obtained clearance to proceed with the bombing. During the bombing run, with the Bomb Aimer directing the pilot, there was a sudden huge bang and a blinding pink red flash along the port side of the aircraft, followed immediately by the pilot saying (not shouting) 'Christ, put on chutes chaps.' Within a second of this the plane was hit again by anti aircraft fire along the fuselage. Then was a sizzling sound in the intercom system and then it went dead. The pink red glow on the port side persisted and I assumed we were on fire.

'I was disconnecting my electrical suit plug and leaving my flying helmet on the seat with intercom and oxygen connected when I now come to a point which has always mystified me and to this day I still think of it at times. I had a vision of my mother's face outside my turret and she said, 'Jump son, jump.' I was at this stage about to vacate the turret anyway. On leaving my turret and attaching my parachute, I saw the mid upper gunner (Sgt 'Speedy' Quick) already at the fuselage door. He was using an axe to open the door and this came as no surprise as this door had previously given trouble due to difficulty in opening. Our ground crew had checked it out more than once and said they could find nothing wrong with it. By the time I reached the door Sgt Quick had left the plane. I could see nothing in the fuselage as it was full of smoke and the plane itself seemed to be out of control.

'I rolled out of the plane in the recommended way to avoid hitting the tailplane but my legs did in fact brush along the underside. Fortunately my flying boots remained on. I have no recollection of pulling the parachute's 'D' ring although I had it in my grasp as I baled out. I have simply no idea of when it was pulled. Being at a low level the descent did not take long but it was quite a pleasant sensation whilst it lasted. I was unaware of any noise but would have been a distance from Mailly. I came down somewhere in the area of Rheims. On looking down during the descent I thought I was heading towards what I thought was a small lake surrounded entirely by woodland. Suddenly and unexpectedly I landed heavily in what turned out to be a clearing (not water). Although I did not realize it I was actually floating backwards but on hitting the ground my head was protected by the padded collar of my Taylor suit otherwise I would probably have been injured about the head.

'On the ground I could hear bangs, maybe bombs in the distance and shouts and dogs barking in the near vicinity. I freed my parachute harness and discarded my Taylor and inside electric suits. The chute drifted across the open space and came to rest against the nearby trees. I tore off my brevet and sergeants chevrons and placed them in my battle dress pocket. I made no attempt to hide or bury the chute and left the area. I recall at this time a Mosquito flying past very fast and low in the direction of Mailly presumably, probably to take a last look at the target.

'For the remainder of the night I kept walking and at dawn heard voices in a nearby field by a large fire. As I was uncertain if this was a crashed aircraft with military or merely farm workers I gave the area a wide berth. At this time an observation plane approached at low altitude and slow speed, very close to where I was. I hid behind a tree and do not think I was noticed. Walking on, I came to the outskirts of a village and saw German troops and motorcycles and sidecars manned by soldiers. Cautiously approaching the end small cottage in this village, I rushed through the front door. A very elderly Frenchman and his yapping dog were naturally surprised and he tried to push me out, shouting 'Allemandes, Allemandes'. In view of the noise and perhaps his fear that I was in his cottage, I immediately left and ran out of the village. All I really wanted to know was where I was as I had my silk escape map with me. I next remember coming up towards an isolated large house but remember nothing further. Although I was not injured in any way I must have passed out. I suppose by then it was probably about nine am.

'When I came to, I was lying on the ground and I was being kicked about the body. On opening my eyes a German officer was pointing a pistol at my head and I was surrounded by several soldiers. I was walked back I believe to the same village I had left, searched in some presumably Army HQ and then taken to a cell. Whilst there I was told a rear gunner had been taken out of the turret of a crashed plane and was very badly injured. I asked if I could see him but the request was refused. After two days I was taken to another town where I was placed in a cell with a navigator from 50 Squadron but after a few hours we were separated. Thereafter I was taken under guard to Oberursel Interrogation Center at *Dulag Luft* near Frankfurt. Arriving in Frankfurt in late evening a bombing raid was in progress and I was taken by my guard into a large air raid shelter. Local inhabitants did not seem concerned although there would be no doubt I was a shot down flyer. After 12 days in solitary confinement apart from two interrogations, I was passed out to the transit camp. I met Speedy Quick who was attached to the small HQ staff working in the kitchen and distributing clothing and Red Cross food, etc. He had no news of any other members of the crew and we concluded they must have all been killed. I was then moved to *Stalag Luft III*, Sagan, in Silesia (East Compound).[52]

No.5 Group, which supplied nearly all the marker aircraft and the entire first wave, lost 14 of its 173 Lancasters. No.1 Group, which dispatched 173 Lancasters also, in the second wave of the attack and which were subjected to the greatest delay at Mailly, lost 28 bombers, including five out of 17 crews from 460 Squadron RAAF from Binbrook. Nos.12, 50 and 101 Squadrons each lost four crews. One Mosquito *Intruder* and one RCM Halifax were also shot down. Approximately 1500 tons of bombs were dropped on Mailly and 114 barrack buildings, 47 transport sheds and workshops and some ammunition stores were hit. 218 Germans were killed or missing and 156 were wounded. 102 vehicles were destroyed, including 37 tanks. Damage to the buildings was German assessed as '80 per cent destroyed, 20 per cent worth repairing'. The only French civilian casualties in the village of Mailly nearby occurred when a Lancaster crashed into the house.

On 6/7 May 149 aircraft attacked railway installations at Mantes-La-Jolie, a suburb of Gassicourt, for the loss of two Lancasters and one Halifax. Lancasters and Mosquitoes also raided Sable-sur-Sarthe and 52 Lancasters of 1 Group attacked an ammunition dump at Aubigne for the loss of one bomber. Mosquitoes were out in force too, with 28 of them attacking Ludwigshafen and others, including five to Leverkusen, making 'nuisance' raids on German targets. S/L H.B. Stephens DFC and F/L N.H. Fredman DFC and Mosquito IX ML958 of 109 Squadron who failed to return from the raid on Leverkusen was shot down over Holland at five minutes to midnight by *Oblt* Werner Baake and his *Bordfunker Uffz* Rolf Bettaque of 2./NJG 1 in a Heinkel 219A-2 *Uhu*. Stephens and Fredman were killed. Baake was able to dive on his victim from above and gain enough airspeed to overtake the Mosquito because it was flying below its usual operating altitude.

On 7/8 May 471 sorties were flown against five targets in France for the loss of 12 aircraft. On 8/9 May another five French targets were bombed in 452 sorties and again 12 aircraft were lost, seven of them Halifaxes and four, Lancasters. The largest operation of the night was an attack by 123 aircraft on rail yards at Haine-St-Pierre, which cost six Halifaxes and three Lancasters. Tim Woodman and Pat Kemmis of 169 Squadron were aloft in a Mosquito NFII as Woodman recalls:

> 'We could clearly see the bombers, as many as ten at a time but no sign of German night fighters. We sniffed around for 109s and 190s over the target area but saw none. I saw three Halifaxes weaving like dingbats up at 6000 ft. Below the leading bomber was a twin-engined aircraft climbing up to it.'

The Bf 110 flown by *Leutnant* Wolfgang Martstaller and his radar-operator/air gunner of I./NJG 4 had taken off from Florennes at 0300 hrs. In a letter to his parents on 12 May, Martstaller wrote:

> 'The sky was fully lit, so we could easily see the Tommy. Our crew saw at least ten bombers. However, we could only concentrate on one aircraft.[53] When I was near him and fired (and my burst of fire bloody well blinded me!) the Schwinehund fired off a flare with a signal pistol, so that an enemy night fighter could post us).'

Woodman fired a two-second-burst and Martstaller dived into the darkness, Kemmis following him on *Serrate.* Martstaller soared up in a steep climb and Woodman fired from 800 yards Woodman continues:

> 'This time he opted out and took us on a chase across the French countryside at treetop height, not seeing him as he flew away from the moon but following him on *Serrate.'*

Martstaller wrote:

> 'I went into a steep dive to almost zero feet (at night!) but still we could not escape from the Mosquito's attention.'

Woodman continues:

> 'He made the mistake of flying towards the moon and I saw the moonlight glint off his wings. I fired and got some strikes on his fuselage and wings as he flew across a wide-open space, which looked like an aerodrome. He went into a steep turn and firing 50 yards ahead of him to allow for deflection I hit him again. White smoke poured from his port engine and closing to 150 yards I gave him another two seconds burst and hit him again.'

Martstaller concludes:

> 'I was fortunate to spot a field in which to belly-land. We were slightly injured from shrapnel. When we found that we were OK we then saw a large explosion two miles away from us. Next day this turned out to be my Viermot with seven crewmembers burned to death. We were so happy!'[54]

On 10/11 May F/O Vivian Bridges DFC and F/Sgt Donald G. 'Spider' Webb DFM of 239 Squadron in a Mosquito NFII attacked a Bf 110 of 1./NJG 4 near Courtrai, setting one engine on fire. It crashed at Ellezelles, Belgium. *Oblt* Heinrich Schulenburg, pilot and *Obfw* Hermann Meyer, *Bordfunker* baled out near Flobeq. Meyer recalled:

> 'We were shot down with one engine on fire. We could save ourselves by baling out and came down near Flobeg. I was wounded on the skull and was badly concussed. I spent three weeks in hospital at Brussels and then had four weeks leave at home.'[55]

On 11/12 May 429 bombers of the Main Force made attacks on Bourg-Leopold, Hasselt and Louvain in Belgium. The target for 190 Lancasters and eight Mosquitoes of 5 Group was a former Belgian *Gendarmerie* barracks at Leopoldsburg (Flemish)/Bourg-Leopold (French), which was being used to accommodate 10,000 *SS Panzer* troops who awaited the Allied invasion forces. The weather was bad with low cloud and poor visibility and a serious error was made with the broadcast winds. As a result, the aircraft were late over the target area and consequently flare-dropping was scattered and provided no adequate illumination. An *Oboe* Mosquito flown by Flight Lieutenants Burt and Curtis of 109 Squadron dropped a yellow marker. The Mosquito marking force of 627 Squadron arrived late over the target with the result that the *Oboe* proximity marker was seen by only one of the marking aircraft and the proximity marker, unfortunately, seemed to burn out very quickly. Flare dropping was scattered and did not provide adequate illumination of the target. Haze and up to 3/10ths cloud conditions hampered the marking of the target. The 'Marking Leader' then asked the 'Master Bomber'(S/L Mitchell of 83 Squadron), if he could drop 'Red Spot Fires' as a guide for the flare force. The Master Bomber agreed and 'RSFs' went down at 0024 hrs in the estimated vicinity of the target. Unfortunately, the 'Main Force' started to bomb this red spot fire immediately it went down and half of the main force bombed this. The result of this was the five Mosquitoes of 627 Squadron returned to Oakington with their bombs and were unable to mark the target. Immediately Mitchell ordered

'Stop Bombing', as he realized it was impossible to identify the target but VHF was very poor, particularly on Channel 'B' and the Germans had jammed Channel 'A'. Only half the main force received the 'Cease Bombing' instruction and 94 Lancasters bombed the target. At 0034 hrs a wireless message, 'Return to base' was sent out to all crews.

One of the aircraft that failed to return on 11/12 May was a Lancaster of 166 Squadron flown by P/O Geoffrey J.R. Clark, which was probably shot down by *Oblt* Gottfried Hanneck of 6./NJG 1 for his first victory[56]:

> 'In the early morning of 11 May my crew and I were detached from Deelen to Düsseldorf. In the evening we came to immediate readiness at around 1800 hrs and one hour later, I was ordered to fly to Melsbroek near Brussels and 'towards the enemy' as I was told. I touched down at Melsbroek at 2042 hrs and came to immediate readiness again. Our patience was really tested as only just before 2300 hrs our nightfighter *Jägerleitoffiziers* reported aircraft flying in. After having been ordered to scramble at 2320 hrs, we flew in the direction of the Ruhr area in the hope of intercepting the *Viermots* during their outward flight. And we succeeded; we caught one on our *SN-2!* My radar operator gave me courses to steer to get a visual on the target. However, before we caught a first sight of our target, a steam of tracer appeared before me, which smashed into a *Viermot,* putting it on fire and it plunged down out of control. All of a sudden, the night sky was turned into daylight by the burning bomber and I had to break off and 'hide' into the darkness some distance away, fearing that the massed firepower of other *Viermots* would 'fry' me!
>
> 'In the meantime, I had arrived over the edge of the *Flak* Zone, so I turned away and started searching for a new target in the withdrawal route of the British. We were successful in our search, as we flew several tracks to the west and northwest. Thus, we got a new contact on the *SN-2,* a four-engined aircraft that tried to get home and away at high speed, whilst slightly losing height. This time, no 'colleague' was chasing the same target. I slowly got closer, until I could make it out with my bare eyes. Approaching at the same altitude (4000m/13,000ft) I gradually lost some height and positioned myself 100 to 150m beneath my target. It now hung over us, as large as a barn door I put my sights on the fuselage and with the *Schräge Musik.* I fired through the whole length of it, by slowly pushing my aircraft down and away from the bomber. We watched how many hits registered in the whole fuselage; our target dived down steeply and crashed onto the ground in the area of the mouth of the River Scheldt. We saw how it exploded on impact, with a huge detonation and a sheet of flames. Time of our *Abschuss* was 0048 hrs. Fifty minutes later we touched down on our aerodrome at Deelen, it was a good landing and we were unhurt. Later on, our weapons mechanics established that I had used ample ammunition. This was quite understandable, as I was only a novice who wanted to make sure of the kill. During my later *Abschüsse* I was more economical![57]

George Vantilt, a 15-year-old Beverlo boy, recalls:

> 'The raid of 12 May had brought the terror of war again to the doorstep of the people of Beverlo. Eighty-four people were killed and many more were wounded. One lady died one year after the raid. She lost her whole family and could not get over her grief. Low flying aircraft woke us up that night. We lived in the Korspelstraat No.3. We had no air raid shelter. Together with my parents and sister we ran to the neighbours who a shelter in the garden. Once inside, the first bombs were falling very close. We were thinking they bombed the coalmine at Beringen.[58] We all prayed. The constant change of air pressure hurt our ears. I can assure you it was hell on earth! The family escaped unhurt and our house too was lucky. As we came out of the shelter, fires were all around. Most of the people had small farms and even today when I smell burnt hay I think of that terrible night in May. The day after the raid we all went to the village. The road called Zuidstraat was hit the most. It was totally destroyed. The dead cows in the fields spread a terrible smell. The people were shocked and in one house a complete family were killed. Everybody in the village lost a relative or friend that night. The next Sunday after the raid we went to church as usual. After the service, my friend and I went to the crash site of a Lancaster, which had exploded in mid-air during the raid. The place where one of the crewmembers had died could still be seen as a print in the cornfield. Parts of the aircraft were scattered over one kilometer.'[59] (Five Lancasters were lost on the raid).

F/L Harry White DFC* and F/L Mike Allen DFC* of 141 Squadron in a Mosquito NFII reached double figures by bringing down a Ju 88 a few miles north of Amiens. Flying another 141 Squadron Mosquito NFII[60] over the country of his birth this night was 44-year-old bespectacled Belgian pilot F/L Lucien J.G. LeBoutte and his radar operator F/O Ron S. Mallett. LeBoutte had flown over 50 *Instep, Ranger,*[61] nightfighter and *Serrate* patrols and had damaged three trains in strafing attacks but the cherished air to air victory he sought had eluded him. Now his luck was about to change.[62]

Mitchell and Marauder bombers had been reported approaching from the Calais-Brussels area and a Ju 88G-1 of 6./NJG 2 crewed by *Fw* Wilhelm Simonsohn, pilot and *Uffzs*' Günther Gottwick, his *funker* and Franz Holzer flight engineer, which had taken off from Köln-Wahn, a satellite field to the main base at Köln-Butzweilerhof, was one of those sent to intercept them. Like LeBoutte Simonsohn was still chasing his first aerial victory of the war. As with so many relatively inexperienced *Nachtjagd* crews, only occasionally did they get into a position to fire their guns in anger. One *Abschuss*, which was claimed in April in the Cologne area was not credited to the crew but was instead given to one of the *Flak* batteries defending the city. During another sortie that same month the crew tracked a Lancaster in the vicinity of Hanover. Having positioned his aircraft underneath the huge bomber Simonsohn pressed the gun button of his 2-cm *Schräge Musik* but a shell jammed in the barrel of his starboard cannon and he was unable to fire a single shot and the Lancaster had escaped unscathed. Simonsohn now recounts the events of 11/12 May:

'We took off at around 2200 towards Brussels and flew at about 6500 meters in the direction of the Channel coast. Here and there scattered *Flak* could be seen. Compared to the nightly major attacks on German cities with their widespread fires it was almost 'peaceful'. We had been in the air about 1 1/2 hrs and had reduced our height a little (to about 6000 m) leaving the thin veil of cloud above us for better visibility, when a burst of tracer from port and below struck the port Jumo engine and set the tank on fire. I pushed the machine down to force the enemy to break off the attack. My eyes, used to the dark, were blinded by the flames. I shouted into the throat mike, 'Bale Out!' Franz knelt on the floor hatch to operate the lever on the hinge side and disappeared with the hatch cover. Günther, sitting back to back to me, tipped stiffly sideways towards the hatch and also disappeared into the night.

'Meanwhile I had released my harness and taken off my helmet after having closed the fuel cut-off valve at full power and switched off the ignition (what the human brain is capable of!) Lowering the nose had caused the aircraft to increase speed considerably. I tried, half standing, to pull back the stick with all my strength to get the speed back. At this stage the port wing must have come off (was the main spar shot through?). The aircraft (or what was left of it) went into an irregular spin. Apparently I was flung across the cockpit and was able to catapult myself out with a kick. My next thought was not to pull the rip-cord right away but to allow myself to fall for about five seconds. Then I pulled with such force that I had the entire bowden cable in my hand and felt a violent jerk. I would never forget the feeling of utter bliss, hanging in the parachute and hearing the soft rasping of the cotton lines.

'Far away I saw burning bits of aircraft like torches falling down. To the side and above me a parachute appeared in the light of a white Verey light. I drew my signal pistol to reply but while cocking it, it slipped from my stiff hands and dropped into the void. I landed like a wet sack in the vegetable patch of a farm. The parachute collapsed in the calm air. Far away the all-clear sounded. I collected some youngsters, holding my pistol like a warning finger and told them to take me to the nearest German post. The following morning all three of us were together again, slightly ruffled but happy and taken to Brussels.'[63]

On 12/13 May Viv Bridges DFC and 'Spider' Webb DFM destroyed a Ju 88G-6 when 239 Squadron dispatched *Serrate* patrols to Belgium in support of the bombers raiding Hasselt and Louvain again.[64] F/Os Bill Breithaupt RCAF and J.A. Kennedy DFM also downed a Bf 110 in the Hasselt-Louvain area. Mosquito crews in ADGB and 2nd TAF were also successful. On the night of 14/15 May nine German aircraft were claimed shot down, four of them over England. The night of 15/16 May was a grand Mosquito affair also. Thirty Mosquitoes of 8 Group went to Ludwigshafen and smaller numbers visited as far afield as Carpiquet airfield near Caen and Leverkusen while 43 Lancasters mined the waters from the Kiel Canal to Biscay. Three Lancaster minelayers went missing but the Mosquitoes returned without loss. Two *Serrate* patrols were despatched and one of them, P/O Wilfred Handel 'Andy' Miller and P/O F.C. 'Freddie' Bone of 169 Squadron returned with claims for a hat trick of victories. They destroyed two Ju 88s on the German-Danish coast and the Kiel Canal area and a Bf 110 to take their score to five enemy aircraft destroyed in 100 Group and eight all told. Then there was a lull though Berlin received another visit by Mosquitoes of 8 Group on the 16/17th.

On the night of 19/20 May RAF Bomber Command resumed operations with raids by 900 aircraft on five separate rail targets in France, two French coastal gun positions at Le Clipon and Merville and a radar station at Mont Couple. Mosquitoes raided Cologne and Halifaxes and Stirlings dropped mines off the French coast. Seven Lancasters were lost on the raids. One of them was a victim of *flak* while the raid on Le Mans claimed three Lancasters, including the aircraft flown by the Master Bomber and his deputy, which collided over the target. *Nachtjagd*'s only claim this night was by *Oblt* Jakob Schaus of 4./NJG 4 for a *Viermot* near Vimoutiers. Mosquito nightfighters flew eight Serrate and 23 Intruder sorties over France and the Low Countries and they returned with one claim though the Luftwaffe lost two Bf 110s to long-range night fighters, one at Venlo (4./NJG 1), Holland and one near Chartres (1./NJG 6), France.[65] W/C Norman John 'Jack' Starr DFC and P/O J. Irvine of 605 Squadron in a FBVI flew the successful Intruder sortie. Starr had taken command of the squadron on 11 April after a successful career with 23 Squadron in the Mediterranean where he had destroyed two Ju 88s and damaged two other aircraft. On 6/7 May he scored his first victory for the 'County of Warwick' Squadron by destroying a Bf 110 at St. Dizier airfield for this third kill overall. Starr and Irvine took off from Manston at 0100 hours for their patrol over France on 19/20 May and they headed for the vicinity of Florennes where landing lights were obligingly switched on, as a twin-engined aircraft prepared to land. Starr and Irvine, whose Mosquito was at 2000 ft, were assisted further when a searchlight on the NW side of the airfield was switched on and began sweeping the area before it was switched off, the operators presumably satisfied that there no intruders following the landing aircraft. Starr dived to attack while his prey, oblivious to the Mosquito's presence, blinked its landing light on and off sufficiently for Starr to estimate his position on the runway. Just as he was about to open fire the German aircraft switched on its landing light again and appeared to be travelling at about 20 mph. Starr gave the aircraft a 1 1/2 second burst of cannon only and strikes were seen in front of the machine and then strikes all over the aircraft. (Starr and Irvine were unable to identify their victim). By this time the Mosquito was very close to the ground in the dive and Starr had to pull out very sharply. As he pulled out Starr and Irvine saw the German machine catch fire and all the airfield lights were switched off. They orbitted the airfield and saw a motor vehicle with powerful headlights on dash up to the now blazing aircraft, which the fire crew took about 12 minutes to extinguish the flames.[66]

Bomber Command directed its might against German targets once again on 21/22 May when 532 aircraft raided Duisburg. Twenty-nine Lancasters were lost, Tame Boar crews claiming 26 bombers shot down, most of them over the southern provinces of the Netherlands.[67] Dortmund was severely hit by 361 Lancasters and 14 Mosquitoes the next night, 22/23 May for the loss of 18 Lancasters while a second stream of 225 Lancasters and ten Mosquitoes headed for Brunswick. There, 13 Lancasters failed to return. This time the *Nachtjagd* claimed 38 kills (a slight overclaiming to actual Bomber Command losses). F/L D.L. Hughes and F/O R.H. 'Dickie' Perks of 239 Squadron destroyed a Bf 110, as did W/C Neil B.R. Bromley OBE and F/L Philip V. Truscott of 169 Squadron.[68] Hughes and Perks were one of three 239 Squadron Mosquito NFII crews who were succesful two nights later when 100 Group dispatched six RCM aircraft and 31 *Serrate* and eight *Intruder* Mosquitoes on Bomber Support. With invasion of France imminent, Bomber Command's main objectives for 264 Lancasters, 162 Halifaxes and 16 Mosquito bombers were theWestbahnh rail station in Aachen and the Rothe Erde marshalling yard east of the town. Aachen was an important focal point for traffic moving from the Ruhr to France.[69] Hughes and Perks and F/L Denis J. Raby DFC and F/Sgt S.J. 'Jimmy' Flint DFM each destroyed a Bf 110G-4 of 7./NJG 6.[70] while F/O W.R. Bill Breithaupt RCAF and F/O J.A. Kennedy DFM added a Ju 88 to their score.[71] One of the three RCM Fortresses[72] despatched by 214 Squadron was flown by P/O Allan J.N. Hockley RAAF, which provided support for 44 Lancasters and seven Mosquitoes of 5 and 8 Groups attacking the Ford Motor factory at Antwerp. Hockley was intercepted by *Oblt* Hermann Leube, *Staffelkapitän* 4./NJG 3 flying a Ju 88G-1.[73] *Fw* Eberhard Scheve served as *Bordfunker* in the crew and *Stabsfeldwebel* Druschke was the *Bordschütze*. Leube went off in pursuit of the bomber stream, as Scheve recalls:

'Until this day our night fighting radar *SN-2* was jammed only by *Düppel (Window)*. On this night however a flying transmitter, which caused a flickering of the waves over the full width of the picture tube and which completely prevented the blips from appearing normally jammed our equipment. I tried a few tricks, switched off the transmitter of my *SN-2* set, then dimmed the amplifier on the receiver and then had two different flickering bands to the left and to the right of the middle line. I told my pilot to alter his course and established that the flickering bands changed accordingly. I therefore decided that I could use this jamming transmitter as a flying beacon to home on to. As the jamming transmitter probably flew inside a bomber stream to give protection to the formation, we decided to investigate this. It took us a long time before we spotted the bomber and we attacked it no less than six times before we were able to shoot it down. At once when the bomber exploded the jamming of the *SN-2* ended. Our *Staffel* comrades, who had also flown around aimlessly for several hours, confirmed the vanishing of the jamming at this instant. At debriefing we told of our observations but we were then told that no such thing existed as a

> jamming transmitter for the *SN-2* and that we had experienced jamming by the overlapping of other *SN-2* sets.'[74]

No aircraft were lost on the raids on Eindhoven (where bad weather prevented bombing), the French coast or Antwerp but 25 Lancasters and Halifaxes failed to return from the attacks on Aachen-West (which was well hit) and the Rothe Erde yards (which escaped serious damage). *Nachtjäger* claimed 32 kills. Before the bomber stream reached Aachen, the 'Night Ghost of St. Trond', *Oblt* Heinz-Wolfgang Schnaufer of St.IV/NJG 1, claimed five Halifaxes destroyed in 14 minutes.[75] He 219 *Uhu* aircraft of I./NJG 1 at Venlo destroyed another seven of the Aachen raiders. II. and III./NJG 6 were guided to the Aachen force via radio beacon *Ida*. Despite strong intruder activity and jamming of the SN-2 radar these claimed five Lancasters and Halifaxes destroyed plus one 'probable' *Viermot* for the loss of three Bf 110G-4s.

After a night of minor operations on 26/27th May when two Mosquitoes were lost to German nightfighters on the raid on Ludwigshafen, the men of Bomber Command steeled themselves for a Main Force attack on Bourg-Leopold again. This time 331 aircraft (267 Halifaxes, 56 Lancasters and eight Mosquitoes) were returning to try to finish the job that had ended in disaster a few nights earlier. Not surprisingly there some like Sgt George Burton; flight engineer in P/O William Kalle's crew in Halifax '*G-George* of 420 'Snowy Owl' Squadron RCAF at Tholthorpe, Yorkshire, who were apprehensive:

> '27th May 1944 was a day in my life I would never forget. After waking at 0730 hrs and shaving (in cold water) etc we made our way half a mile, to the Sergeant's Mess for breakfast Then walked another half a mile to the group section on the main drome. At approximately 11 am we heard that ops were on that night. We then spent the rest of the day preparing our aircraft. In the late afternoon we attended briefing and heard that our target was the military camp of Bourg Leopold in Belgium. We were hoping to catch a *Panzer* division there. We then marshalled our aircraft around the perimeter track, one side for 420 'Snowy Owl' Squadron RCAF the other for 425 'Alouette' Squadron RCAF. Then back to the Sergeant's mess for our supper of bacon and eggs.'

At Skipton-on-Swale, Yorkshire where 424 'Tiger' Squadron RCAF was stationed, F/L B.L. Eric Mallett RCAF, pilot of Halifax III HX313 *Blonde Bomber* prepared for the difficult trip:

> 'After leaving the briefing room I mentioned to the crew that we were being sent on a mission for the sole purpose of killing people. We carried 14.000 lbs of anti-personnel bombs and the aiming point was to be the officers quarters. This mission did not sit well with the crew. We had already been through some tough missions against industrial targets but this mission made us uneasy.'

His bomb aimer, W/O2 Ken Sweatman thought that the raid would be 'a piece of cake':

> 'Located in the NE corner of Belgium it was little more than two-hour flight from Skipton-on-Swale. I remember the Wing Commander's caution, however,'The target is a rectangle image of lines dividing it diagonally. Our prisoners are on the close side and to your left. Don't undershoot.'

Meanwhile, Mosquito nightfighters provided the usual Bomber support for the Main Force raids on Aachen and Bourg-Leopold.[76] F/L Harry White DFC* and F/L Mike Allen DFC* were one of seven Mosquito crews in 141 Squadron. At 0235 hrs a little to the west of Aachen, Allen obtained two AI contacts at 14,000 ft and 12,000 ft, crossing right to left. At a range of 8000 ft the two blips merged into one and Allen remarked to White: A bomber's about to be shot down in front of us at any minute. 'Still crossing,' White wrote:

> 'We turned to port in behind this contact and at 1200 ft, obtained a visual on two white exhausts. We had not increased speed as range was closing quite rapidly but as we assumed the line astern position. The exhausts faded from sight and range was increased to 8000 ft before, at full throttle, we were once more able to decrease the range slowly to 1200 ft again, obtaining a visual on two white exhausts. We closed to 600 ft where I was able to identify this target as a Me 109. I closed further to 300 ft and opened fire with a two-second burst from 15° below. It exploded with a colossal flash, which completely blinded me for about a minute and a half. I asked Mike to read my instruments for me but his attention was at that moment elsewhere. The flash had attracted his attention from his box and he looked out in time to see a second Me 109 slip slowly by under the starboard wing. With his head now well in the box, Mike commenced reading off the range as this 109 emerged from minimum range behind. But even the best navigator cannot carry out an interception with the help of a blind pilot and the range had increased to 6000 ft astern before I could even see my instruments.

We turned hard port but contact went out of range at 14,000 ft.'[77]

Sgt George Burton meanwhile was en route to Bourg Leopold, having taken off at 0011 hours, climbing on course, 5000 ft over England then down to 1000 ft over the North Sea. They hoped that this would be below the German radar. Over the enemy coast they climbed up to 9000 ft, on track to the target and made their turning into their bomb aiming run. Burton recalls:

'At 9000 ft flying straight and level, bomb-doors open and bombs primed live, Bill Haliburton, the bomb aimer, was giving our skipper instructions: 'Left, left, steady. Our position was over the village of Oostham five miles due West of the target. It was exactly 0210:30 hrs when Sgt Metcalfe our rear gunner yelled, 'Corkscrew port go!' A Fw 190 was on our tail but Metcalfe had the satisfaction of hitting the enemy fighter, see it slowly turn over, burst into flames and crash. The next thing the fuselage was on fire and full of cordite. I got the fire extinguisher from my position and went back to fight the fire and was pleased that this soon went out. Then back beside the pilot, only the starboard inner engine and wing were on fire! I pressed the circuit breaker 'inner engine' and 'graviner fire system button' to extinguish the fire but after a few minutes it was still burning. Consulting the skipper we decided that the only alternative was to try to blow it out and we dived to 350ft. Kalle gave the order to prepare to abandon the aircraft. I got his parachute and made sure that it was clipped on properly. Then I got my own. The three crewmembers in the front of the aircraft stood by the escape hatch waiting for the words, 'Jump. Jump!' I looked out onto the wing; the fire had blown itself out! I shouted, 'Pull her out skipper – the fire's out!' After a few moments he ordered us back to our positions. The wireless was unserviceable so Sgt Cusack the WOp/AG was unable to send a Mayday call and he went aft to man the mid-upper turret. Then a roll call but there was no reply from the mid-upper, Sgt John Elslinger. Our skipper ordered me to go and see what happened to him. I found Elslinger's helmet plugged into the intercom and blood on his helmet and then noticed that the rear escape hatch was open so he must have baled out.[78]

'Then once again it was 'Corkscrew starboard go!' and we evaded another fighter. Our three engines were OK but now it was time for another tank change. Back to the rest position and I looked so see what damage had been done. As luck would have it, the only tank controls not damaged on the starboard side were the ones I wanted to change. Once more another corkscrew to evade trouble. When I went back to check for bomb hang-up I found damage in the bomb bay and the floor of the Halifax and we still had seven 500lb bombs on board! They were all mixed up and one bomb had its fins off. I tried to jettison the bombs but the bomb-doors would not operate.

'At last we had the pleasure of seeing the Norfolk coast line. It was a wonderful feeling. After flying inland for a few miles the skipper said he wanted us to bale out and he would fly the plane back towards the coast and bale out at the last minute so that the Halifax would crash into the sea. But we said we had come so far together we would stick it out. Sgt Magson, the navigator gave a course to Tholthorpe but I saw a light on port side and said, 'It looks like a drome' [North Pickenham, an American B-24 base]. I fired a red distress flare and then the colors of the day and after a few minutes the airfield put the landing lights on. I lowered the undercarriage and with great relief the green light came on saying it was locked down. On the final approach I lowered the flaps then the skipper ordered me to go at rest position with the others in the crew. Kalle made a wonderful landing if rather bumpy as the starboard tyre was soft. We got a great reception from the personnel of the 491st Bomb Group. The following morning we were taken out to see the extent of the damage to our Halifax. The undercarriage fairings from starboard engine had come off and hit the rudder and elevator. There was a hole behind the starboard engine that you could have put a jeep in. The aircraft was like a pepper pot with hundreds of shrapnel holes. The main floor under the mid-upper was like tissue paper and you had to be careful where you walked or you would have fallen through the bomb bay. A piece of shrapnel had made a hole in the astrodome where I had been standing during the attack. A senior American officer came to have a look and commented that, 'aerodynamically it was impossible for this kite to fly!' Later that day we were flown to Tholthorpe in a Lancaster.'[79]

Nine Halifaxes and one Lancaster were lost on the Bourg-Leopold raid. In all probability they were all shot down by prowling *Nachtjäger* over Belgium. One of the Halifaxes lost was '*N for Natch*' of 432 'Leaside' Squadron RCAF flown by *Natch's* regular skipper, P/O Howard Menzies of Vancouver. The flight across the Channel to the Belgian coast had been uneventful. Sky markers led them to Bourg Leopold. In the nose, F/O Don Rutherford, an Ontarian, huddled over the bombsight like a priest before his altar, lining the plane up with the sparkling target indicators dropped by the pathfinders. Busy with his charts, P/O Gouinlock navigator, who was on his tenth operation, heard Rutherford sing out, 'Bombs gone'. Now it was his job to plot their course home. He gave the pilot a heading and the aircraft swung around. They were just south of Eindhoven when they 'bought it'. Tail gunner F/Sgt Tom McClay, an Irishman, sounded the first and only warning, 'Fighter coming in – six o' clock, low.' The sound of his guns was all but lost in the roar of the engines as the pilot gave '*Natch*' additional boost for some violent evasive action. Then the Halifax shuddered under the impact of cannon shells and both port engines burst into flame.

'She's going down,' Menzies shouted over the intercom. 'Bale out.'[80]

F/L Eric Mallett RCAF of 424 'Tiger' Squadron RCAF in Blonde Bomber arrived at the target after weaving his way around *Flak* stations and avoiding getting coned by searchlights. A lone Mosquito bomber had already dropped a yellow flare on the target and it was backed up by a Pathfinder Force dropping flares. In all, five *Oboe* Mosquitoes dropped TIs and the third and most accurate salvo fell 320 yards of the aiming point. The early visual markers were wide to the south but a salvo of 'whites' went down 250 yards SW. W/C S.P. Daniels of 35 Squadron, the Master Bomber, saw early bombs fall among the camp buildings and the aiming point soon became obscured by smoke. Daniels reported:

> 'Our load for the trip to Leopoldsburg was 4x7 hooded flares, 6 TIs yellow. 5 TI yellow, 1 4000-lb 'cookie' The weather over the target was no cloud and the vertical visibility good. The target was identified visually, aided by a red TI and flares. On approach to the target at 0159 hrs 2 red TIs seen on aiming point. I broadcast from 0201 hrs to 0213 hrs. Our own yellow target indicator was dropped on the NW end of the red TI. I instructed the Main Force to bomb on the yellow target indicators. White TIs were well backing up yellows. I instructed the Main Force during the last 3 mins to bomb on whites to port and this with 1-second overshoot. The Main Force bombing was good. One large explosion from the center of target, rising well above ground with minor explosions in the air and this at 0207 hrs.'

The target began to look like a 'bullseye' to the crew of *Blonde Bomber* by the time the first wave of bombers began their bomb run. Ken Sweatman, the bomb aimer, was about to put the fusing switches down when he reported an enemy aircraft passing below from port ahead. The rear gunner Sgt Vic 'Pop' Poppa saw him too:

> 'The aircraft lurched upwards as if struck by a gigantic hammer. Flames ran down our left side. A few seconds later there was the clatter of machine gun bullets and cannon shells slamming through the plane. The Plexiglas nose was shot out and I could hear the patter as they came close. Our bombs did not explode. Inside the fuselage it was cherry red. There were fires from the front to the rear.'

Mallett reported:

> 'Port inner engine on fire'. Then, Mallett's voice, very faint, said, 'Abandon aircraft! Jump! Jump!' I gave the order 'abandon aircraft' immediately, as I knew from past experience that we only had seconds before the flames reached the tanks and the 100-octane gasoline would blow. (Strange as it may seem we were not able to drop our load. Just a few seconds prior to being hit I had an urge to take evasive action but I didn't want to spoil the bomb aimer's sighting, as there was no indication of the attack). The whole crew was supposed to go out of the top forward escape hatch in the navigator's position so that I would know when all were out. However, F/L Bob Irwin, our navigator couldn't open the hatch [which had melted together where an incendiary bullet had passed through the door jam]. The second pilot [F/O W.J. Elliott, who was along for his first trip to gain experience as a pilot] and flight engineer Sgt M. Muir [the only Englishman on the crew] took off and went out of the rear entrance hatch. I went forward to see how our navigator was doing and by good fortune he was beginning to have some luck so I went back to my seat and straightened out the aircraft.'

Sgt Vic Poppa called on the intercom but there was only static:

> 'I pulled my flying helmet off, opened my turret doors and snapped my parachute onto my chest but I stayed in my position until I saw another parachute open. Then I swung my turret 50 degrees to the fuselage but I could not get out because of the fire and wind. Twice I tried but to no avail. By this time the ground appeared quite close. Reaching the aft fuselage exit would have entailed too much time and by then it would be too late anyway so I sat there awaiting my end. The aircraft went into a flat spin, my turret rotated free and the brute force flung me out. My left leg came free. I was falling flat on my back. I looked on my chest for my parachute. It was not there! The parachute had been pulled away from my chest by the wind force and was now three feet from my face and above. I pulled on the harness and brought the parachute down close enough so I could grab the 'D' ring and pulled. It opened with a sharp snap. A pain knifed through my groin.'

Ken Sweatman and Bob Irwin between them managed to force the escape hatch open and W/O Wilf Wakely, WOp/AG went first followed by Irwin and Eric Mallett. Sweatman could remember little of the bale out. He assumed that he had gone out feet first facing forward but when his chute cracked open the casing must have hit him under the jaw and he landed unconscious, taking quite a beating. His ankle hurt as someone ripped the leggings off his escape boots and Mallett and someone with him said, 'Oh, good, it's Ken.' Sweatman had no idea who Ken was and what was more, he 'didn't give a damn.'

Vic Poppa hit and collapsed to the ground with his parachute falling on top of him. He was sure the chute had opened at less than 100 ft and the aircraft had been at 11,900 ft when they were first hit by *Flak* and then shot up by the Junkers 88. Poppa was soon apprehended and three days later he was placed in the back of a truck with four caskets. A German NCO pointed to one and said, *'Kamerad Irwin'*. Poppa again gave a negative response. The NCO then pointed to another casket and said, *'Kamerad Wakely'*. Again Poppa gave a negative response. Poppa was not questioned about the third casket, which must have contained the body of his close friend, Sgt George Freeman, the mid-upper gunner. The fourth was empty, as Poppa had moved it with his foot. The Belgian underground found Mallett and Sweatman and hid them in a forest for ten days. After this began a series of moves that eventually led to them being liberated by American troops not long after D-Day, 6 June 1944.[81]

F/Sgt Louis Patrick Wooldridge DFC, a Halifax mid-upper-gunner who had flown a first tour with 51 Squadron, was now a second tour man in Sgt Jim Allen's crew in 578 Squadron[82] and they also flew the 27/28 May Bourg-Leopold raid:

> 'We arrived at the target with no difficulties. We attacked with 18x500lb GP bombs at 0213 hrs from 10,000 ft. Smoke obliterated ground detail but bombs were seen to burst among the markers. There was moderate to heavy *Flak* over the target. After attacking the target area without incident, course was set for the return to base. Due to bad weather conditions in Yorkshire at that time, wireless signals sent to the squadron aircraft on the return leg instructed everyone to divert to the RAF Silverstone, Northamptonshire where we landed at 0434 hrs the next morning. The next day all the squadron aircraft left Silverstone to return to base.'

In Belgium after the raid Marcel Heselmans (a resistance fighter code-named *'Sixtus'* whose brother Leon was also in the resistance) cycled to see the damage to Bourg-Leopold so that he could transmit information to England. According to *'Sixtus'*, 7000 German soldiers were killed or missing and 218 German women, who arrived on 26 May to receive nursing training, were also killed. He added that the spirit of the German soldiers at Leopoldsburg was totally destroyed. Many were still absent and hiding in the surrounding woods and had deserted. Civilian casualties were 22 killed. All the buildings 'including the big messes' had been destroyed. The 'Cavalry Camp', which held many Belgian political prisoners survived the attack. The guards had closed the doors and ran away leaving the prisoners locked up unattended. Marcel, together with other members of his team, was taken prisoner a few weeks later and was shot on 15 July 1944 as he tried to escape when he was transported from the interrogation office to the prison of Hasselt.

In England meanwhile German fighter-bombers had been active during *Steinbock,* an operation commanded by *Oberst Generalmajor* Dietrich Peltz, *Angriffsführer* (Attack Leader) England. Peltz had assembled a small fleet of all types of bombers and fighter-bombers for dive-bombing over England as retaliation for RAF heavy bomber raids on German towns and cities.[83] On 18/19 April, when the last 'Baby Blitz' raid was made on London, eight intruders were shot down by Mosquito nightfighters.[84] From 20-30 April, Mosquitoes claimed 16 enemy raiders as *Steinbock* raids were made on Hull, Bristol, Portsmouth and Plymouth using He 177, Ju 188 and Do 217 aircraft. Mosquitoes shot down nine raiders on 14/15 May when over 100 Luftwaffe raiders attacked Bristol. A Ju 188 and three Ju 88s were destroyed on 22 May when Portsmouth was again the target. On 28/29 May W/C C.M. Wight-Boycott DSO, CO 25 Squadron at Coltishall and F/L. D.W. Reid were directed by Neatishead GCI towards a 'bogey' over the North Sea. It was a Me 410 *Hornisse* of KG 51, flown by *Fw* Dietrich and *Uffz* Schaknies, which was returning from an intruder mission in the Cambridge area.[85] Dietrich and Schaknies sped off towards the coast and headed home. Wight-Boycott approached the Me 410 almost at sea level and fired a half-second burst into it from 700-ft. Dietrich and Schaknies fell into the sea 50 miles off Cromer. The wreckage could be seen burning on the water from 20 miles away. It was the final day of the 'Baby Blitz'.[86] (Though this was the last all out series of raids by enemy aircraft that Britons would have to endure there would be one more mass intruder operation over their island in spring 1945).

On 31 May/1 June 219 aircraft[87] in another operation in suport of the forthcoming invasion, attacked the railway marshalling yards at Trappes, Paris in two waves. For F/Sgt Louis Patrick Wooldridge DFC, mid upper gunner in Halifax III MZ617 LK-D of 578 Squadron, it was to be his crew's last operation before a seven-day period of leave:

'The purpose of the operation, carried out in brilliant moonlight, was to disrupt German troop movements and war materials from eastern France, central Germany and the occupied countries. As we approached the target area, flying high above the almost 10/10ths low lying cumulus cloud I observed a Ju 88 nightfighter about 7000 ft below, streaking away at an angle of about 45 degrees in the direction of our starboard quarter. It was soon several miles away and posed no danger to us but the target area was apparently full of nightfighters. The Master Bomber called for assistance but the anguished reply from the Deputy Master Bomber was, 'I bloody can't. I've been hit', whether by one of the numerous bursts of heavy *Flak* in the target area at that time or enemy fighter activity. Several aircraft [four Lancasters all shot down by NJG 4 and NJG 5 FTR] including some squadron commanders, were lost. On the whole enemy fighter activity was considered intense in the target area. Presumed to be a relatively easy target, Trappes apparently lived up to its name and had become an operational aircraft trap.'

The presence of 14 Bomber Support RCM aircraft and 16 *Serrate* and nine *Intruder* Mosquitoes may have had something to do with the low loss rate.[88] 239 Squadron at West Raynham dispatched ten Mosquito NFII nightfighters on *Serrate* sorties and two of these crews returned with claims for two Bf 110s destroyed. F/O Viv Bridges DFC and F/Sgt D.C. Webb DFM[89] destroyed a Bf 110 near Trappes while F/L Denis Welfare DFC* and his Welsh navigator F/O David B. 'Taffy' Bellis DFC*[90] shot down a Bf 110 West of Paris. It was the latter's first victory since they had flown their first op together on 19 March, when they had patrolled Holland and France with no contacts. Similarly they had had no luck with further patrols during the following weeks:

'Success came at last', Bellis recalled, 'on the night of 31 May when we picked up a *Serrate* transmission north of Paris. Our first priority was to make certain that the transmission did not come from a fighter homing on us from behind! We then maneuvered our Mossie to get behind the transmitting aircraft. To our dismay, it switched off its radar before we were in AI range. However, we kept on the same course and picked up an AI contact a minute or so later and converted this to a visual and the shooting down of a Me 110.'

Success had also proved elusive for the Mosquito NFXVII pairing of F/O Desmond T. Tull and his radar operator, P/O P.J. Cowgill of 219 Squadron. On the night of 24/25 May they claimed a Ju 88 55 miles east of Orfordness but the Intelligence Officer would only award them a 'probable'. Then, on the night of 3/4 June Tull and Cowgill claimed an unidentified enemy aircraft over the Friesians while on patrol in HK248. The Intelligence Officer listened to Tull and Cowgill's description of the aircraft and after studying his identification manuals he concluded, correctly as it turned out, that the twin-engined aircraft must have been a He 219, although this was not confirmed until after the war. Their victim was He 219A-0 190188 G9+BL of 3./NJG 1, which crashed near Wilhelminsdorp where the body of the *Bordfunker*, *Ofw* Heinz Gall was found in the wreckage. *Hptm* Heinz Eicke, the pilot, was able to parachute to safety. Tull and Cowgill claimed seven more aircraft destroyed during 1944 in 219 Squadron and the FIU. In November Tull was awarded the DFC before he and Cowgill were KIA on 18/19 December when they accidentally rammed a Bf 110 landing at Düsseldorf.

On the night of 5/6 June the *D-Day* invasion, postponed by 24 hours because of bad weather, finally began with thousands of ships and aircraft setting out for five beach landing areas on the Normandy coast.[91] Most everyone had known for several weeks that the invasion was imminent but only the Chiefs of Staff knew when and where. W/C Rollo Kingsford-Smith[92] RAAF, CO of 463 Squadron, which operated Lancasters at Waddington, recalls:

"In June I heard more and more accounts about the masses of Allied troops, guns and tanks building up in the south of England. It was obvious a very substantial army operation would soon begin but I was too busy with my own war even to think about the Army's activities let alone find out any more details. On the evening 5 June the Operation Order coming through on our Teleprinter began: "Main force aircraft from 53 Base will attack" "Objective to destroy enemy gun positions at 450 am 6 June." The location given in the operation order was on the Normandy coast and to me it meant that Allied forces could be landing there immediately after we had finished with the enemy gun battery. I say, "could be landing" because the weather forecast for the English Channel for the 6th was terrible and it seemed quite unsuitable for the small craft that the invasion forces would be using.

'We took off at about 2am on 6 June. We had a leisurely flight down England to the south coast and across the Channel to the Normandy coast flying between 6-7000 ft. There was low cloud most of the way but it started to break up as we approached France. I still did not know whether the Allied Forces would land. But about five miles out from the coast, when I could just discern the dark grey surface of the sea beneath in the early twilight, the fleet of invasion barges right below opened their throttles for the dash to the beach. It was too dark for me to see the boats but their increased speed made white wakes and these showed up clearly. I knew it was 'on'. Some of the wakes were all over the place. There must have been a few collisions at that level. Undoubtedly it was the most thrilling and emotional experience for me in all the years of the war. Until that moment Bomber Command had alone been taking the war to the Germans. For all I knew it would continue on and on until my crew and I finally joined the killed-in-action list. A massive army on the continent meant it was not unreasonable to think that the war might finish and I might get to see Grace and Sue (wife and daughter) again.

'The enemy gun battery was at Pointe Du Hoc, a high point surrounded by cliffs overlooking *Omaha* beach. In my mind this attack would be about the most important my squadron had ever made and we were all determined it would succeed. The battery was well marked by the Pathfinders and from a relatively low height, about 6500-ft, we all took our time, each aircraft dropping 13,000 lbs of bombs. The whole Pointe was battered; the battery including its concrete bunkers was destroyed. Even a part of the cliff tumbled into the sea. US soldiers, who about two hours later (had they been on time they would have seen and heard us), scaled the cliff to attack and silence the guns not knowing of our attack, reported the shambles of shattered concrete and steel they saw when the reached the top.

'On the first day after the Allied armies had landed, their foothold on French soil was still precarious and they could have been in real trouble had the German armored divisions been able to get there rapidly. Our squadrons were taken off the long flights into Germany and were kept busy attacking both the German tanks and their rail transport routes in and around the Normandy area. We went back to Normandy to destroy a rail and road junction at Argentan about 50 kms from the beachhead. I was Controller for this raid and as it would have been a vital transport junction for the Germans on the following day I was determined it would be pulverized with nil or absolute minimum damage to the adjacent village. At the planning conference I agreed to a bombing height of 6000 ft but we all bombed lower. The target was accurately marked. I held up the attack for about five minutes to avoid confusion with another target under attack a few miles away. There were a few complaints but not many and it was another successful raid. Milling around the target in the dark and held back by their CO, the operational discipline was always excellent but the radio comments (always with no call sign) were typically Australian – pertinent, disrespectful, sometimes rude and usually funny. The raid report given by S/L Vowels, my most experienced Flight Commander in briefing session on return.

'Sortie completed. Cloud base 6,000 ft. Vis good. Cluster of green TIs 0127 hours. 2x1,000 lb and 14x500-lb bombs drop height 5,000 feet Bomb bursts all around and on TIs – straddling and on road junction. Attack went very well, even though it opened about 5 minutes late through the Controllers order. Control very good and there was no hitch to original plan. T/Is were practically bang on. Max error was about 30 yards. Was fired on by British Navy who ceased fire when colours of the period were fired.'

'Alec Vowel's comment of being fired on by the British Navy was not unusual around D-Day. The English Channel was full of allied Naval ships who continued to fire on us as we went across backwards and forwards – fortunately they were not as accurate as the Germans and I was not aware that they did any harm.

'I think I was the last to bomb at Argentan and my approach to the bomb release point was made on a shallow descending dive. Our bombs were always dropped rapidly one after the other and on this occasion they were dropped at about a micro fraction of a second intervals so they fell in a stick right across the target. I was possibly over keen and was too low, so when the first bomb exploded, its blast hit my aircraft with a really severe thump. In a flash I realised that as I was still losing height each successive blast would be harder and heavier. At this late stage being brought down by my own bombs may have showed my determination to press home the attack but it would have been a stupid way of finishing my career. My own report to the intelligence officer at debriefing states: Sortie completed. Thin layer cloud, base about 6,000 ft. Bombing appeared good and attack successful. Train on fire possibly ammunition train. 4000 ft. 0140 hours. 2x1000 lb mc, 14x500 lb GP. Attack delayed 5 mins to avoid any possibility of the force bombing green TI's of the eastern target which were put down late. Markers quite good. Majority of bombs appeared overshoot slightly and were to the west of the road junction – in the rail siding.' We landed back at base after a very short return flight – one of the best aspects of fighting so close to base. The self-inflicted damage the ground crew found was a fairly small dent under the tail plane.'[93]

On 5/6 June Luftwaffe activity was almost non-existent.[94] 21 *Serrate* Mosquitoes were despatched to northern France[95] but only two victories were claimed by 100 Group crews and both were in 239 Squadron. F/L Denis Welfare DFC* and F/O

Lancaster III ED547 PO-M of 467 Squadron RAAF at Bottesford in October 1943 with F/L L.B. Patkin RAAF and his crew who were shot down by *Major* Heinrich Prinz *zu* Sayn-Wittgenstein, *Kommodore* NJG 2 for his 71st *Abschuss* on 1/2 January 1944. Back row L-R: Sgt Cliff T. Cooper, mid-upper gunner (grounded with a head-cold on 1/2 January, later posted to 582 (PFF) Squadron and finished the war with 56 ops); Sgt Ralph Chambers, flight engineer (MIA 1/2 January 1944); F/L L.B. Patkin RAAF, pilot (KIA 1/2 January 1944); F/O W.N. 'Bill' Fisher RAAF, rear gunner (WIA 3/4 November 1943 in night-fighter attack over the Ruhr and taken off ops). Front, L-R: Sgt G.A. Litchfield, bomb aimer (KIA 1/2 January 1944); F/O R.J.A. Maidstone, navigator (KIA 1/2 January 1944); F/Sgt W.D. 'Blackie' Blackwell RAAF, WOp (KIA 1/2 January 1944). ED547 and P/O B.A. Tait RAAF and his crew failed to return from a raid on Berlin on 29/30 December 1943. It crashed at Grossziehten near Berlin killing all seven crew. (Jim George)

Below: The Heinkel He 219 *Uhu* ('Owl') might have turned the tide for *Nachtjagd* had it been introduced in quantity. Fast (670 km/h at 23,000 ft), maneuverable and heavily armed with four or six forward firing cannon and a twin 30mm Mk.108 *Schrage Müsik* installation, the *Uhu* was *Nachtjagd*'s only aircraft capable of meeting the Mosquito on equal terms. But by the time the first He 219A-6 Mosquito hunters (with all engine and ammunition tank armor and oblique armament removed) was delivered, use of the *Uhu* against the Wooden Wonder had officially been banned. On 23 April 1944 a daylight raid by the American 15th Air Force halted production of the He 219A-0 at Vienna-Schwechat and in May 1944 the 219 was officially abandoned in favour of the Ju 88G series. Heinkel He 219V33 Werk Nr.190063 +DL, which was used by *Telefunken* for equipment and antenna testing at Munich-Riem (and air firing at Tarnewitz in February 1944) is equipped with FuG 220 SN-2b and FuG 212C-1 *Lichtenstein Weitwinkel* (Wide-angle) attenna (in the center of the nose), which was deleted from late 1944. (Hans-Peter Dabrowski)

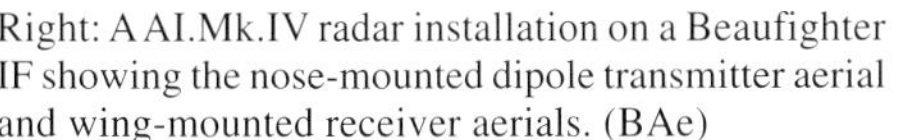

Right: A AI.Mk.IV radar installation on a Beaufighter IF showing the nose-mounted dipole transmitter aerial and wing-mounted receiver aerials. (BAe)

In the USA on 3 December 1943 radio listeners tuned in to hear their favourite foreign correspondent Edward R. Murrow, head of CBS European Bureau in London, begin his broadcast, "This Is London". Murrow, who had become well known in America for his broadcasts during the Blitz when the USA was still neutral, proceeded to regale his listeners with a gripping account of his experience over Berlin in a Lancaster the night before. (CBS)

Lancaster III DV238 of 49 Squadron being towed by a tractor driven by WAAF driver LACW Lillian Yule at Fiskerton in the summer of 1943. DV238, which formerly served with 619 Squadron, was later transferred to 44 Squadron at Dunholme Lodge where it became KM-M. DV238 and P/O D. A. Rollin DFC's crew were lost on the Berlin raid on 16/17 December 1943 when the Lancaster crashed at Diepholz. Rollin and six of his crew were killed. One man survived.

On 20/21 December 1943 *Oblt* Martin 'Tino' Becker of *Stab* I./NJG 6 was credited with the destruction of a Lancaster and two Halifax bombers. Born at Wiesbaden on 12 April 1916, Becker joined the Luftwaffe just before World War II and at first trained as a reconnaissance pilot, flying Bf 110Cs, until early in 1943 he transferred to night fighters, scoring his first victory on 23/24 September when he destroyed a Lancaster (possibly DV174 of 460 Squadron) near Speyer during a raid on Mannheim. He would fly in all weathers and in the weeks following he scored a further five *Abschüsse* against RAF *Viermots* before the year was out. (Bundesarchiv)

Left: On 23/24 December 1943 when 390 bombers raided Berlin, F/L Howard Kelsey DFC and P/O Edward M. Smith of 141 Squadron, pictured here in front of their Beaufighter VIF V8744 at RAF Wittering, scored the first 100 Group victory. They shot down a Bf 110 G-4 of 4./NJG 1 based at St. Trond and it crashed at Unteresbach, near Cologne. *Oblt* Lenz Finster, pilot and *Staffelkapitän* was KIA. *Fw* Siegfried E. Beugel, *Bordfunker* (WIA) baled out. (Tom Cushing Collection)

Right: III./NJG 1 officers at Christmas dinner at Twente airfield, Holland in December 1943. L-R: *Major* zur Lippe; *Oblt* Dietrich Schmidt; *Staffelkapitän*, 8./NJG 1, Dr. Thiele, (meteorology), *Lt* Rolf Ebhardt. (Dr Rolf Ebhardt)

Above: A brilliant pilot of aristocratic descent, *Major* Heinrich Prinz *zu* Sayn-Wittgenstein served with distinction in KG 51 1940-41 flying operational sorties as a bomber pilot in France, Britain and Russia. In August 1941 transferred to *Nachtjagd* and rapidly became a legend. Appointed *Staffelkapitän* 9./NJG 2 in November 1941, scored his 1st confirmed victory 6 months later on 6/7.5.42, launching him in a meteoric night fighting career. During the following 6 months he scored 22 victories, receiving the *Ritterkreuz* in October of that year. Over the next 12 months he added 40 more victories, 23 of these on the Eastern Front whilst serving as *Kommandeur* of IV./NJG 5 and I./NJG 100. Award of the Oak Leaves for 54 kills followed at the end of August 1943. On 15 August Wittgenstein took over II./NJG 3 at Schleswig. On 1 December appointed *Gruppenkommandeur* of II./NJG 2 based at Deelen, Holland. During 1943 was the second highest scoring *Nachtjagd* pilot (after Lent). At the time of his death in combat on 21/22 January 1944 Wittgenstein had 83 *Nachtjagd* victories (including 23 on the Eastern Front) in 170 sorties with NJG 2, 3 and 5. And he had been awarded the *Ritterkreuz* with *Eichenlaub* and *Schwerter*.

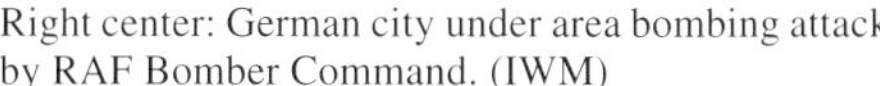

Right center: German city under area bombing attack by RAF Bomber Command. (IWM)

Right: Specially modified Bf 110G-4 G9+FS of 8./NJG 1 for Mosquito hunting, which was flown by *Oblt* Dietrich Schmidt, *Staffelkapitän*, 8./NJG 1 on 13/14 January 1944. Schmidt's 12th victim, Mosquito BIV DZ440 HS-F of 109 Squadron, crashed at 0535 hrs at Landwehr, near Kleve, Germany. F/O P.Y. Stead DFC a 2nd tour pilot, PoW His 2nd tour navigator, W/O A.H. Flett DFM died in the crash. (Dr Rolf Eberhardt)

418 'City of Edmonton' Squadron RCAF crews in front of a Mosquito FBVI. 1/Lt James Forrest 'Lou' Luma, pilot of *Sweet Moonbeam McSwine*, is smoking a pipe and his navigator, F/O Colin G. 'Fin' Finlayson is far right. (Colin Finlayson DFC* was killed on 18 October 1944 when he and his pilot, F/L S.H.R. Cotterill DFC, were returning to England after landing in Italy after a Day Ranger to the Vienna area on the 17th. Both men are buried in Belgrade British Military Cemetery). W/C 'Howie' Cleveland (far left) with his navigator, F/Sgt Frank Day DFM. January 1944 proved rewarding for the Canadian squadron. On 21/22 January Luma and F/O A. Eckert destroyed a Bf 110 20m SW Wunstorf. On 27 January F/L J.R.F. Johnson destroyed a Ju 88 at Clermont-Ferrand airfield and two Ju W34s 10m SE Bourges. P/O J.T. Caine and P/O E. W. Boal destroyed a Ju 88 at Clermont-Ferrand and two Ju W34s while F/L C.C. Scherf destroyed a Fw 200 SE of Avord airfield. (Stephen M. Fochuk)

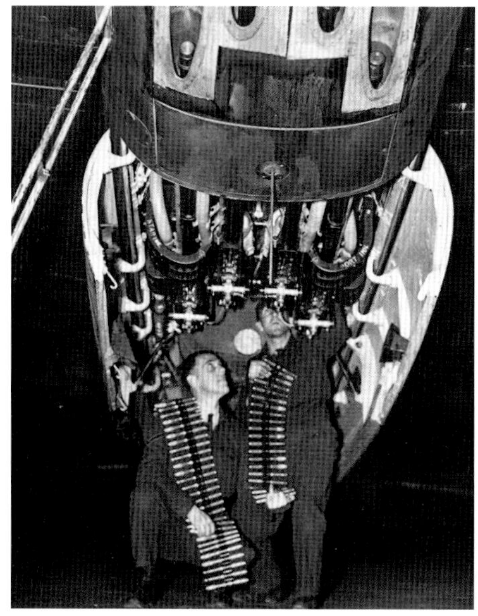

Above: Armorers, 20mm belts around their necks at the request of the cameraman, attend to a Mosquito FBVI fighter-bomber armed with four 20mm cannon and four .303 inch machine guns. The FBVI could also carry two 250-lb bombs in the bomb bay plus two more under the wings. (Tom Cushing Coll)

Right: F/Sgt Schumann and his Halifax BIII crew of 466 Squadron RAAF are debriefed at Leconfield, Yorkshire after the 20/21 January 1944 raid on Berlin. 769 aircraft set out for the 'Big City' and 22 Halifaxes and 13 Lancasters were lost. (Syd Waller)

Right: B Flight, 169 Squadron at Little Snoring, Norfolk. Back row L-R: P/O Harry 'Shorty' Reed; Logan; D.C. Dunne; Bob Tidy RCAF, F/L S.L. Dickie Drew. Middle row, L-R: P.A.J. 'Pete' Dils; W/O Hays; F/O Pat Kemmis; Len 'Tiny' Giles; F/O Stuart Watts; Robinson; F/L R.W. 'Dick' O'Farrell. Front row L-R: F/L Ralph Connolly; F/L R.G. 'Tim' Woodman; S/L J.A.H. 'Joe' Cooper, 'B' Flt CO; F/O Gordon F. Cremer; F/L A. Paul Mellows. 'B' Flt had a very successful period January-August 1944. On 30/31 January Cooper and Connelly shot down *Oblt* Karl Löffelmann of *Stab* III./NJG 3. During February-May Woodman and Kemmis destroyed four Bf 110s and in August, a Fw 190. On 20/21 April Cremer and F/O B. C. Farrell shot down a Bf 110 and in June-July Harry 'Shorty' Reed and F/O Stuart Watts destroyed a Bf 110 and a Ju 88. Mellows and Drew had to wait until 31 December 1944/1 January 1945 before they got their first victory, a He 219A-2 in the Köln area, their second kill – a Bf 110 – following on 1/2 February 1945. (Joe Cooper)

Above: *Oblt* Karl Löffelmann served in 9./NJG 3 and *Stab* III./NJG 3, being credited with one night *Abschuss* before he was killed flying Bf 110G-4 Werk Nr.740081 D5+LB on 30/31 January 1944 when he was attacked by Mosquito NFII HJ711 VI-P flown by S/L J.A.H. 'Joe' Cooper and F/L Ralph Connelly of 169 Squadron at Leuenberg near Werneuchen, 20 km E of Berlin. *Fw* Karl Bareiss, *Bordfunker* and *Ofw* Oscar Bickert, *Bordschütze*, both WIA, baled out. It was 169 Squadron's first victory in 100 Group. (Steve Hall via John Foreman).

Top right: Bf 110G-4 of *Gruppenstab* I./NJG 1 equipped with both FuG 220 SN-2 and FuG 212 *Lichtenstein* C1 and underwing 300 liter auxiliary tanks for long-range free-lance Tame Boar operations. Left is G9+DK and right, G9+BB. Although barely visible, of particular interest is the teardrop-shaped plexiglass cupola above the pilot's seat housing a Revi 16N gunsight, used to aim the obliquely-mounted *Schräge Musik* cannon (Otto H. Fries)

Two at right: The Gnome & Rhône aero engine factory at Gennevilliers, near Paris after the raid by a dozen Lancasters of 617 Dam Busters Squadron on 8/9 February 1944. The attack was led by W/C Leonard Cheshire DSO* DFC, the Dam Busters new CO (who had completed four operational tours of duty) who made three low level runs on the factory in bright moonlight to warn the French factory workers to escape. On his 4th run he dropped a load of 30 lb incendiaries from between 50 and 100 ft and each of the other 11 Lancasters dropped a 12,000 lb bomb with great accuracy. Ten bombs hit the factory and the remaining one fell in the river alongside the factory was severely damaged and production almost completely ceased. There were few if any French casualties and all the Lancasters returned safely. (IWM)

Above: Downed RAF aircrew member being interogated by his German captors. (IWM)

Top center: On 19/20 February 1944 *Lt* Otto Fries of 5./NJG 1 scored his 9th *Abschuss* when he and his crew of *Fw* Fred Staffa, *Bordfunker* and *Uffz* Konrad Deubzer, *Bordschütze* shot down a Halifax of possibly 35 or 102 Squadron during the disastrous Bomber Command raid on Leipzig. (Otto Fries)

Top right: *Lt* Paul Szameitat of 6./NJG 3 wearing the EKII (*Eisernes Kreuz* or Iron Cross Second Class) with ribbon on the day of receiving the award, 27 February 1942. The previous night, Szameitat had scored his first kill, shooting down Wellington W5423 of 305 'Ziemia Wielkopolska' Squadron near Jejsing, NE Tonder. Szameitat went on to score 27 more night *Abschüsse* and one kill in daylight (a Liberator on 8 October 1943) and was appointed *Kommandeur* of I./NJG 3 on 14 December 1943. Whilst engaging a bomber on 1/2 January 1944, he was seriously injured in return fire. Szameitat attempted a crash-landing in a clearing in woods near Bückeburg in the Weser Mountains SE of Minden but his Ju 88C-6 D5+EN Werk Nr.750444 somersaulted killing him, his *Bordfunker Fw* Richard Kübler and *Bordmechaniker* (BM/flight engineer) *Fw* Herbert Blokus. *Bordschütze Fw* Heinrich Henning baled out and was slightly injured. Szameitat was posthumously awarded the *Ritterkreuz* on 6 April 1944. (Steve Hall via John Foreman).

Bottom left: F/Sgt Louis Patrick Wooldridge DFC who flew a first tour as a Halifax mid-upper-gunner in Claude Wilson's crew in 51 Squadron. By January 1944 Wooldridge was a second tour member in Sergeant Jim Allen's newly picked crew who went on to fly 39 operations over Europe on 578 Squadron at Burn, Yorkshire. (Wooldridge)

Right: Pilot, *Lt* Gerhard Rheinheimer of II./NJG 1 (right, standing) at Venlo, Holland, was killed on 9 February 1944 when his Bf 110G-4 (Werk Nr.720055) crashed at Helden/Panningen, 12 km SW of Venlo during a practice interception flight. His *Bordfunker*, *Uffz* Herbert Layer also died. (Steve Hall)

Below: In mid-1944 *Oblt* Fritz Krause was a *Staffelkapitan* in the experimental I./NJGr. 10 commanded by *Hptm* Friedrich Karl Müller which operated Fw 190As and Bf 109Gs with AI radar and a long-range fuel-tank for *Wilde Sau* sorties against Mosquitoes of the LNSF (Light Night Striking Force). *Hptm* Fritz Krause survived the war having scored six *Abschüsse*. (via Hans-Peter Dabrowski)

Above: Fw 190A-5 '*Weisse Elf*' – 'White 11' (Werk Nr.550143) fitted with FuG 217 J2 (*Neptun*) AI radar, flown by *Oblt* Fritz Krause (later *Kommandeur* III./NJG II) of 1./NJGr. 10 at Werneuchen in 1944. Originally, *Neptun* was designed as a tail, warning radar for twin-engined aircraft and the J2 version was used as an AI radar in single-seater fighters. At 0040 hrs on 8 July 1944 Krause took off in 'White 11' from the research station at Werneuchen, NE of Berlin and near Brandenburg he intercepted Mosquito BXVI MM147 of 692 Squadron, which after his three attacks went down and crashed W of Granzow, 9 km NNW of Kyritz at 0155 hrs. The pilot, F/L P.K. Burley DFC was KIA. F/L E.V. Saunders DFC, navigator, survived and he was taken prisoner. It was Krause's only *Abschuss* in 1./NJGr. 10. Three days later at 0120 hrs on 11 July Krause was shot down over Berlin by his own flak and he had to bale out of his Fw 190. (Fritz Krause)

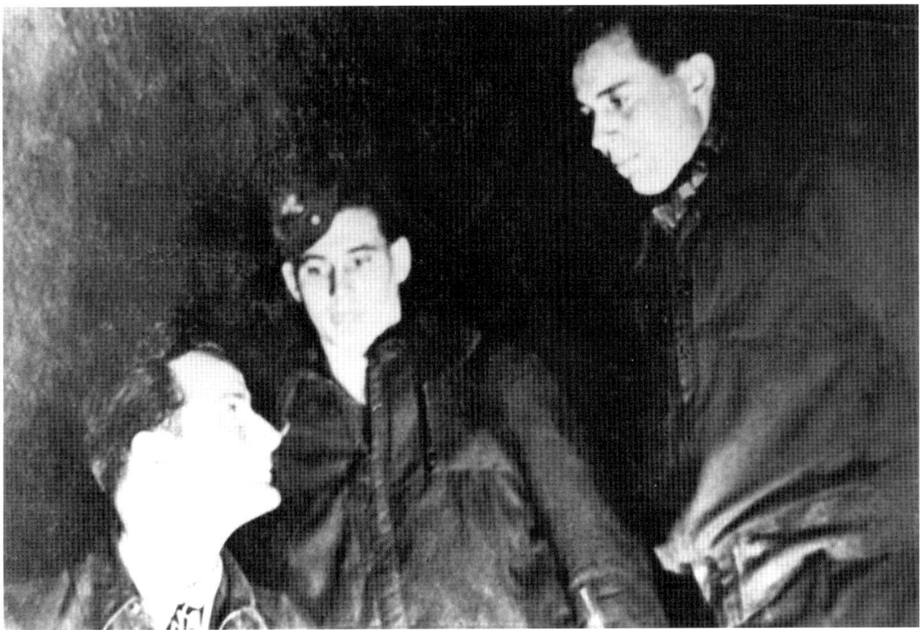

Above: *Oblt* Martin 'Tino' Becker *St.Kpt* 2./NJG 6, *Uffz* Karl-Ludwig Johanssen, his *Funker* and and air gunner *Ogefr* Eugen Welzenbach. On 19/20 February 1944 Becker reached double figures and on the night of 22/23 March he claimed six Lancasters and Halifaxes shot down. Becker ended the war as *Kommandeur*, IV./NJG 6 with the rank of *Hauptmann* and the *Ritterkreuz* and *Eichenlaub*, claiming 58 night kills (all four-engined bombers) in 2./NJG 6 and IV./NJG 6. (Karl-Ludwig Johanssen)

Below: 128 Squadron Mosquito BXVIs of the LNSF (Light Night Striking Force) taxi out at Wyton fitted with 50-gallon underwing drop tanks for another visit to Berlin. Mosquitoes flew so often to the 'Big City' that its raids were known as the Berlin Express and the different routes there and back, as platform one, two and three. LNSF Mosquitoes raided Berlin 170 times, 36 of these on consecutive nights. (via Jerry Scutts)

Above: The Short Stirling squadrons were withdrawn from the Battle of Berlin after very high losses late in November 1943 and they were used in other roles, including Special Duties (SD), dropping agents and equipment to resistance groups in occupied Europe while Stirling IVs of 190, 196, 295 and 620 Squadrons of Transport Command towed gliders to Nortmandy and Arnhem in 1944. (IWM)

Top center: *Major* Hans-Joachim Jabs, *Kommodore* NJG 1 in 1944. Jabs's final tally was 28 night and 22 day victories in ZG 76, NJG 3 and NJG 1. He was awarded the *Ritterkreuz* with *Eichenlaub* and he survived the war. (Ab Jansen)

Top right: As one of 100 Group's most successful pilots, Harry White had joined the RAF as a 17-year old in 1940, having lied about his age. On 4 August 1941 he crewed up with 18-year-old Mike Seamer Allen at 54 OTU at Church Fenton. The following month the two of them were posted to 29 Squadron at West Malling, where they started defensive night patrols in Beaufighters. White was eventually commissioned as a pilot officer on 26 March 1942 and after scoring three kills and two damaged in July/August 1943 both he and Allen were awarded DFCs – Bars followed in April and October 1944. White and Allen's first Mosquito victory came on 27/28 January 1944 when they destroyed a Bf 109 near Berlin. On 15/16 February they claimed a He 177 Beleuchter (Illuminator), which was being used in conjunction with single-engined fighters conducting *Wilde* and *Zahme Sau*, tactics against RAF bombers. The pair continued to score until their lengthy tour with 141 Squadron came to an end in July 1944, by which time their tally had risen to 12 destroyed and three damaged. Their final claim was for a Ju 88 damaged whilst flying an NFXXX with the BSDU in January 1945. (Mike Allen DFC**)

Stirling IV LJ923 ZO-D-Dog of 196 (SD) Squadron at Shepherds Grove, Suffolk in 1944 with its skipper F/O Henry 'Chock' Hoysted DFC RCAF and his crew. *Per Lager ad Aspro* (a reference to drinking beer and needing an aspirin for the hangover) completed 11 sorties with 196 Squadron and was scrapped in 1947. L-R: John Barker, navigator; Jack Hooker, air gunner; F/O Henry 'Chock' Hoysted DFC RCAF; Ray Owen, bomb aimer; Bill Garretts, flight engineer; Mike Stimson, WOp. (Mike Stimson)

Right: *Oblt* Heinz-Wolfgang Schnaufer, *Staffelkapitän* of 12./NJG 1 at Leeuwarden points out his 47th *Abschuss* – he scored his 45th-47th victories on 15/16 February 1944 during a Bomber Command raid on Berlin when 43 aircraft were lost. Victory number 47 was Lancaster I W4272 of 622 Squadron, which he shot down into the Ijsselmeer 1 km south of Medemblik at 2333 hours. F/L T.L. Griffiths RAAF and his crew were killed. (Hans Bredewold via Ab A. Jansen)

Right: Mike Seamer Allen DFC** of 141 Squadron who shared in 12 victories with Harry White DFC**. (Mike Allen DFC**)

Far right: On 24/25 February 1944 209 I *Jagdkorps* Tame Boar crews destroyed 31 Lancasters and Halifaxes of a 734 strong force raiding Schweinfurt (Bomber Command lost 33 aircraft). *Hptm* 'Hugo' Eckart-Wilhelm von Bonin, *Ritterkreuzträger* and *Kommandeur* of II./NJG 1, seen here with his regular *Bordfunker Ofw* Johrden when they were together in II./NJG 1 in 1944, destroyed two *Viermots* for his 28th-29th kills. (His 28th *Abschuss* was Lancaster III JB721 of 156 Squadron flown by F/L J.A. Day DFC, which crashed at Briey, NE of Metz at 2136 hrs. Day and one other of the crew were PoW while five men died. Day fractured a leg and he was later repatriated). *Major* Eckart-Wilhelm von Bonin was decorated with the coveted *Ritterkreuz* on 5 February 1944 while *Kommandeur* of II./NJG 1. He ended the war working for the Luftwaffe Inspector of Jet Aircraft and had 32 victories. Two of his brothers, also serving in the Luftwaffe, were killed on the Eastern Front and his father, *Oberst* Bogislav von Bonin, was captured by the Russians in March 1945 and never seen again. (Hans Grohmann)

Right: Sylt, March 1944. L-R: *Uffz* Walter Bräunlich, *Bordschütze/Bordmechaniker* (radio operator/flight engineer), two ground crew and *Uffz* Brandt, *Bordfunker*, with Bf 110G D5+BV 'Bertha' flown by *Lt* Walter Briegleb. In March-May 1944 this 10./NJG 3 crew scored three kills in this aircraft (Briegleb's 2nd-4th confirmed victories). These three aircrew had a lucky escape on the night of 6/7 October 1944 while flying in Ju 88G-1 710639 D5+EV, which crashed at Beetsterzwaag, SW of Groningen after being shot down by F/L A.C. Gallacher DFC and P/O G. McLean DFC of 141 Squadron. (*Fw* Paul Kowalewski, 2nd radar operator was KIA). At that time Briegleb was one of the most successful replacement pilots in the *Nachtjagd* with 17 victories. He survived the war as *Staffelkapitän* of 7./NJG 2 and had 25 night victories. (Soren Flensted)

Below: Lancaster II DS771 of 426 'Thunderbird' Squadron RCAF, which went missing with F/Sgt A. G.S. Simard RCAF and his crew (all KIA) on the Stuttgart raid of 15/16 March 1944 when 863 aircraft were despatched for the loss of 37 aircraft including 27 Lancasters. Simard and his crew are buried at Dürnbach War Cemetery. (BAe)

Right: *Oblt* Heinz Rökker, *Staffelkapitän*, 1./NJG 2. On the night of 22/23 March 1944 he was flying Ju 88R-2 R4+BB when he scored three victories to take his tally to 17. Decorated with the *Ritterkreuz* and Oak Leaves, his 65 aerial victories made him the 8th highest scoring Luftwaffe night fighter pilot of the war. (Heinz Rökker)

Far right: Sgt Roland A. Hammersley DFM, Lancaster WOP-AG, 57 Squadron who on 24/25 March was one of those who went to the 'Big City' when the German capital was visited for the last time during the Battle of Berlin. (Hammersley)

Center right: The final stages of a night interception once radar contact had been made, ideally at 2-3 miles range, the Mosquito radar operator would aim to turn his pilot onto a heading that would bring him on to the target's heading and usually slightly below its height. The radar operator would call out range and the pilot would adjust his speed so that he would close to a range of about 1000-ft behind his target at the same speed and about 100-200 ft below it. From that point he might, on a dark night, see a flicker of exhaust flames, for the minimum range that his radar operator could work to was about 600-800 ft. having seen the exhausts or an outline of some aircraft, the pilot closed in very slowly right beneath his target so that its identity could be established. Then having satisfied himself that it was a RAF aircraft, he then had to very gradually move back and up to a point immediately behind and about the same level and then, as the target gradually sank down into the gunsight, the Mosquito pilot fired. On 24/25 March 1944 F/L Edward R. Hedgecoe and F/L Norman Bamford of 85 Squadron had a narrow escape when their Mosquito NFXVII *O-Orange* was damaged severely by burning fuel while shooting down a Ju 188 at 300-ft range. Hedgecoe ordered Bamford out but the flames went oiut and he hauled his navigator back into the cockpit and nursed *O-Orange* back to West Malling where a piece of debris from the Ju 188 – his fifth victory of the war – was removed from the port wing. Note that the cockpit canopy is completely blackened with soot and all the fuselage madapolan and wing surfaces are burnt and the fabric on the rudder is completely burnt away. Hedgecoe and Bamford received the DFC after this encounter. This harrowing experience appears to have had an effect on Hedgecoe who employed a more judicious approach in future. Hedgecoe and Bamford scored one more victory together on 16/17 September 1944 at FIU (a UEA at Ardorf airfield) before his navigator was killed in a flying accident. Hedgecoe went on to claim two more victories and a Ju 88 'probable' and a Bf 110 'damaged' with F/Sgt J.R. Whitham before the end of the war. (DH)

Right: The Lyons Engine factory taken from 10,700 ft during the marking by 8 Group Mosquitoes on 25/26 March 1944. In 8 Group, marking for the LNSF and the Main Force was carried out by 109 and 105 Squadrons using Oboe, and 139 Squadron, using H2S. In 5 Group the target areas were identified on H2S and a carpet of hooded flares laid making it as bright as day. This enabled a small number of 627 Squadron low-level visual marker Mosquitoes – four or possibly six – to orbit, locate and mark the precise aiming point in a shallow dive with 5001b spot-fires. 5 Group Lancaster bombers would then destroy the target. (Jim Shortland)

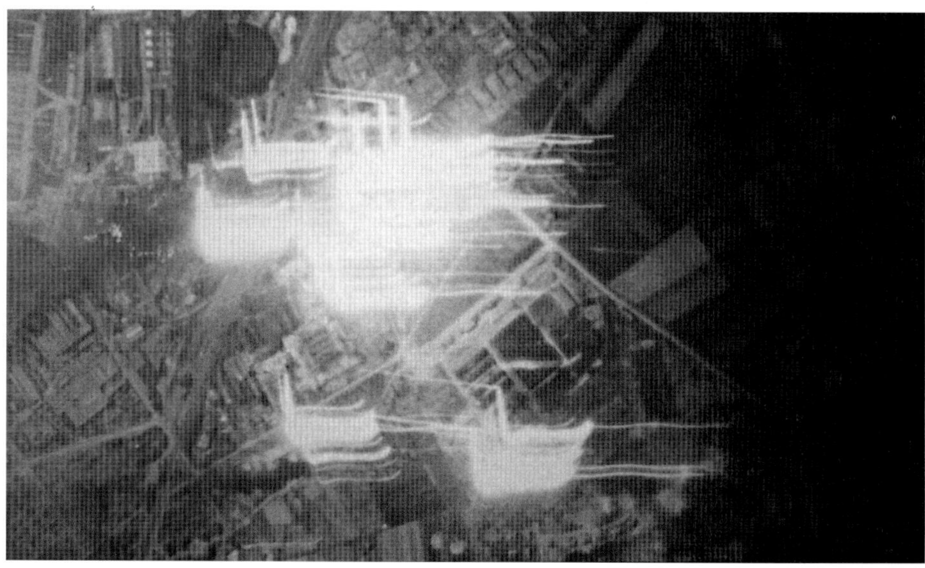

On the Nürnburg raid on the night of 30/31 March 1944 Bomber Command lost 64 Lancasters and 31 Halifaxes and ten bombers crash-landed in England; the worst Bomber Command loss of the war. Lancaster ND466 of 156 Squadron flown by F/O J.V. Scrivener RCAF was claimed by Oblt Martin 'Tino' Becker, Staffelkapitän, 2./NJG6 and it crashed at Eisfeld. L-R: F/O J.V. Scrivener RCAF (PoW); F/O H.C. Frost RAF (KIA); W/O J.C. Baxter RAF (KIA); F/O E.H.J. Summers RAF (PoW); S/L P.R. Goodwin RAF (PoW); P/O C.A. Rose RAAF (KIA) and W/O V. Gardner RAF (KIA). F/O W.C. Isted RAF (PoW) took this photo.

Right: Short Stirling which dropped into Horsham St. Faith airfield near Norwich, Norfolk and caused some curiosity among the men of the 458th Bomb Group, 8th Air Force who flew Liberators from the former RAF base. (the late Jake Krause)

Below: Bf 110G-4 night fighters of 5./NJG 5 airborne during a daylight sortie against the U.S. 8th AF in January 1944. (Peter Spoden)

Above: 57 Squadron aircrew in front of Lancaster III JB526 *D-Dog* of at East Kirkby in late 1943 or early 1944. JB526 was intercepted and shot down by a night fighter at Koslar near Jülich, Germany, on a raid against Wesseling on 21/22 June 1944. P/O S. Weightman the pilot, was the only survivor. The raid cost 57 Squadron six aircraft and at least three of these were victims of the night fighters. (Maurice Stoneman)

Below: *Ofw* Heinz Vinke, 54 victories in NJG 1, *Ritterkreuz* with *Eichenlaub*, was KIA on 26 February 1944 when he was shot down by Typhoons of 198 Squadron. (Ab Jansen)

Right: FuG 202 *Lichtenstein* BC radar-equipped Messerschmitt Bf 110G-4a night-fighter (2Z +OP) of 6./NJG 6, which landed in error at Dübendorf, Switzerland on 15 March 1944. (The twin Mk.108 cannon tray was omitted when FuG 202 *Lichtenstein* BC was carried). (Hans-Peter Dabrowski)

Bottom right: On the Messerschmitt Bf 110G-4d/R3 the FuG 220 *Lichtenstein* SN-2d AI radar's low drag antenna dipoles were mounted at a 45° angle to avoid the trajectory of the two nose mounted 30 mm Mk.108 and twin 20mm MG 151/20 cannon in the ventral tray. (via Hans-Peter Dabrowski)

L-R: *Fw* Herbert Scholz, *Bordfunker* (WIA 20/21 July 1944), *Ofw* Karl-Heinz Scherfling, FF (who had 33 to 35 night victories when he was KIA 20/21 July 1944) and *Fw* Herbert Winkler, *Bordshütze* who joined the crew late in 1943 (KIA 20/21 July 1944) at *General* Schmidt's HQ at Jüterborg on 8 April 1944 on the occasion of the award of the *Ritterkreuz* to Scherfling. (Herbert Scholz via Didier Hindrychx)

Lancaster I DV397 QR-W, which operated with 61 Squadron from 30 November 1943 to the night of 24/25 March 1944 when it was one of 44 Lancasters that FTR from Berlin. P/O D. Carbutt and 5 of his crew were killed. One man survived to be taken prisoner.

Right: The most successful nightfighter crew ever. L-R: *Ofw* Wilhelm Gänsler, gunner; *Oblt* Heinz-Wolfgang Schnaufer and *Lt* Fritz Rumpelhardt, radar operator. By August 1943 Schnaufer's score had reached 23 and he was promoted to *Staffelkapitän* of 12/NJG 1. By mid-December he had scored 40 victories and in 1944 he scored 64 victories, a feat unequalled by any other night-fighter pilot. In 1945 he scored 15 victories, including nine in one 24-hour period on 21 February, to reach a final score of 121. Schnaufer shared 100 victories with Fritz Rumpelhardt, 12 victories with *Lt* Baro and eight with Erich Handke. Wilhelm Gänsler shared in 98 of Schnaufer's victories. (Ab A. Jansen)

F/O Viv Bridges DFC and F/Sgt Don 'Spider' Webb DFM of 239 Squadron who on 10/11 May 1944 destroyed Bf 110 Werk Nr.740179 3C+F1 of 1./NJG 4 piloted by *Oblt* Heinrich Schulenburg near Ellezelles, Belgium. Two nights later they shot down Ju 88C-6 Werk Nr.750922 of 5./NJG 3 flown by *Uffz* Josef Polzer at Hoogcruts near Maastricht. On 31 May/1 June Bridges and Webb scored their third kill (a Bf 110) followed on 7/8 July by another Bf 110 near Charleroi for their fourth and last victory of the war. (Don Webb Collection)

Relaxing between ops. 617 Squadron 'Dam Buster' aircrew in the sergeants mess at Woodhall Spa, Lincolnshire probably in the spring of 1944. (Dennis Cooper)

Lancaster III ND787/F of 49 Squadron in a lovely spring setting at Fiskerton in the spring of 1944. This aircraft became operational with 49 Squadron on 5 April 1944 and flew 49 ops before it was replaced by a 'Village Inn'-equipped Lancaster. (Leslie Hay)

Dennis 'Lofty' Wiltshire, pictured early in 1940 aged 19 when he was a Fitter IIE serving with 82 'United Provinces' Squadron operating Blernheim IVs before he remustered for air crew duty as a flight engineer on Lancasters in 90 Squadron. His tour ended abruptly when he cracked mentally during an operation to Cologne, probably in the first half of 1944. (Wiltshire)

Left: P/O Freddie Watts at the controls of Lancaster III ND554 LE-C *Conquering Cleo* at East Kirkby on 25 March 1944. Having joined 630 Squadron in January 1944 P/O Watts and his crew completed 11 operations before the end of March. F/Sgt Dennis Cooper, the WOp/AG recounts: 'After the 30/31 March Nuremberg raid, we were asked to go to the Pathfinders but we did not want to drop flares so we went to 617 (Dam Busters) Squadron at Woodhall Spa for Special Duties. ND554 had our mascot *Conquering Cleo* painted on the nose. As we did not want to lose it we took the aircraft with us; surely the only crew in Bomber Command to steal an aircraft! We kept the aircraft at Woodhall Spa for almost three months before they missed it and fetched it back.' P/O Watts and crew flew four ops in *Conquering Cleo* with 617 Squadron before it was returned to 630 Squadron in mid-June 1944. The crew completed their tour on 29 October in LM695/N, bombing the battleship *Tirpitz* in Tromsö Fiord with a 14,000 lb Tallboy on their 37th trip. ND554 and F/O R.B. Knight RNZAF and crew were lost without trace on the 8/9 February 1945 raid on Pölitz. (Dennis Cooper)

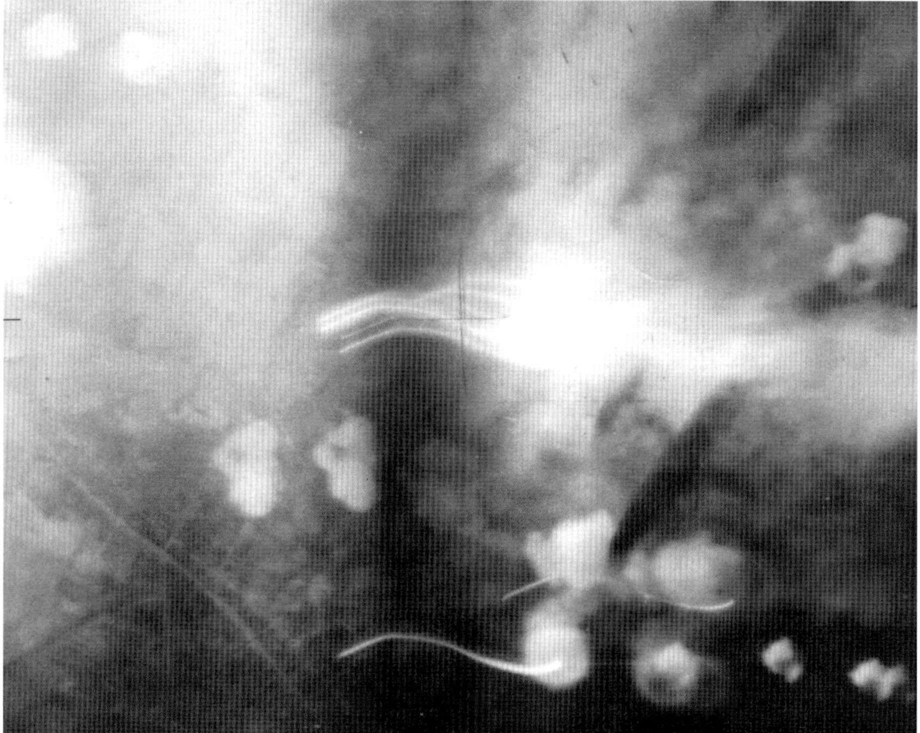

Left: Target photo taken on 10/11 April 1944 from 11,000 feet of a raid by 148 Lancasters and 15 Mosquitoes of 3, 6 and 8 Groups on the rail yards at Laon, France. One Lancaster was lost and the marking was not completely accurate with only a corner of the rail yards being hit. Note the silhouettes of two Lancasters crossing the target below. (Spud Taylor Coll)

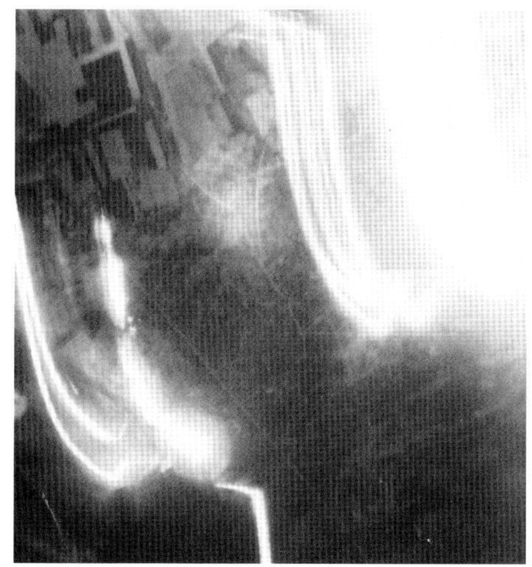

Above: F/Sgt Bob Heuston brought this target photo back from his crew's first operation, to the marshalling yards of Tergnier on 18/19 April 1944. 171 aircraft, including 139 Halifaxes blocked 50 railway lines in this bombing attack but most of the bombs fell on residential areas to the southwest of the railway yards. Six Halifaxes failed to return, two of which collided over Seraucourt-le-Grand with the loss of all 14 crew members. (John Cook)

Top right: Halifax III LV792 NP-E *E for Easy* of 158 Squadron at Lissett, Yorkshire in April 1944. This aircraft was written off after a Ju 88 attack on 2/3 June 1944. (Bruce Bancroft)

Below: Mailly-le-Camp before and after the raid on the night of 3/4 May 1944 by 346 Lancasters, 14 Mosquitoes and two PFF Mosquitoes. Despite good marking the main force delayed its attack and paid dearly, losing 42 Lancasters, or 11.6 per cent of the force, probably all to *Nachtjäger*. 1500 tons of bombs were dropped with great accuracy and hundreds of buildings and vehicles, including 37 tanks, were destroyed. (G/C J.R. Goodman)

Above: Halifax II HX189 of 419 'Moose' Squadron RCAF, which was shot down by *Oblt* Dietrich Schmidt, *St. Kpt*, 8./NJG 1 on 22/23 April 1944 and crashed at Couvron-et-Aumencourt (Aisne) 12 km NNW of Laon. F/O C.A. Thomas USAAF and three others evaded. One crewmember was KIA and two were taken prisoner. (Rolf Ebhardt) Below: Crashed remains of Halifax II HX189 of 419 'Moose' Squadron RCAF, which was shot down by *Oblt* Dietrich Schmidt, *St. Kpt*, 8./NJG 1 on 22/23 April 1944. (Rolf Ebhardt)

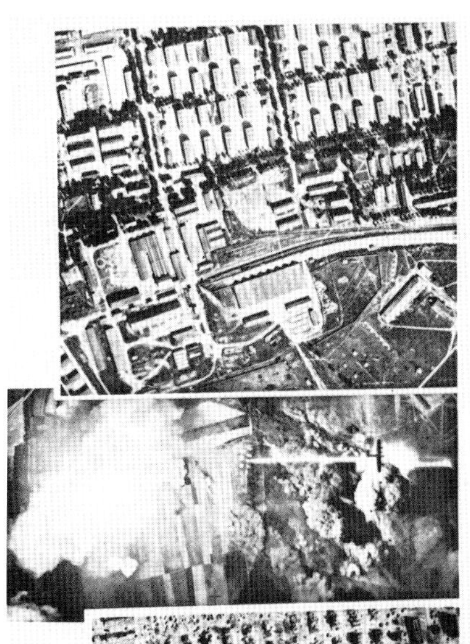

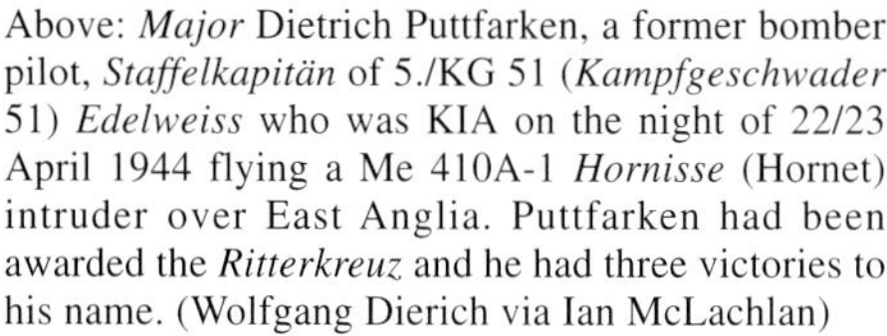

Above: *Major* Dietrich Puttfarken, a former bomber pilot, *Staffelkapitän* of 5./KG 51 (*Kampfgeschwader* 51) *Edelweiss* who was KIA on the night of 22/23 April 1944 flying a Me 410A-1 *Hornisse* (Hornet) intruder over East Anglia. Puttfarken had been awarded the *Ritterkreuz* and he had three victories to his name. (Wolfgang Dierich via Ian McLachlan)

Top center: F/O Gordon W. Oldham DFC, a Rhodesian Lancaster pilot who flew his first tour on 61 Squadron, was killed on his second tour, on 44 Rhodesian Squadron, on the night of 26/27 April 1944 when his Lancaster I was involved in a mid-air collison with Lancaster I ME679 DX-K of 57 Squadron flown by S/L M.I. Boyle DFC on the operation to Schweinfurt. There was only one survivor from the Boyle's crew. All seven of Oldham's crew died. (via Derek Smith)

Top right: S/L Harold 'Mick' Martin DSO DFC (right) of 'Dambusters' fame with W/C Freddie Lambert, CO, 515 Squadron at Little Snoring in spring 1944. Martin was supposed to be 'resting' after a Lancaster tour in Bomber Command, but instead he flew many Mosquito Intruders and destroyed an unidentified enemy aircraft on 26 April 1944 and a Me 410 over Knocke in Belgium on 25/26 July. F/O J.W. Smith was his navigator on both occasions. (Tom Cushing Collection)

Two Me 410A-1 *Hornisse* (Hornet) in formation. (Wolfgang Dierich via Ian McLachlan)

Dornier Do 217N-2 3C+IP of 6./NJG 4 in the hangar at an airfield near Basel on 2 May 1944. By early 1944, the heavily armed but relatively slow Do 217 was largely phased out of operations in *Nachtjagd* and relegated to the training role. (Anneliese Autenrieth)

Left: *Hptm* Martin Drewes, *Kommandeur* III./NJG 1 who on the night of 3/4 May 1944 flying a Bf 110G-4/U1 and fitted with the upward-firing *Schräge Musik*, shot down five Lancasters on what was his 113th operational sortie. Drewes, who was awarded the *Ritterkreuz* on 27 July 1944 and *Eichenlaub* on 17 April 1945 ended the war with the rank of *Major* and a score of 43 night and 6 day victories (including four claims for B-17s and B-24s) in ZG 76, NJG 3 and NJG 1. (Ab A. Jansen)

Right: Juvisy railway marshalling yards, Paris, before and after the attack on 18/19 April 1944. The yards were marked at each end with red spot-fires by four Mosquitoes of 627 Squadron, 5 Group, and with three Oboe Mosquitoes of 8 Group. The 202 Lancasters bombed between the Target Indicators (TIs) so effectively that the yards were not brought back into service until 1947. One Lancaster was lost. (G/C J.R. Goodman)

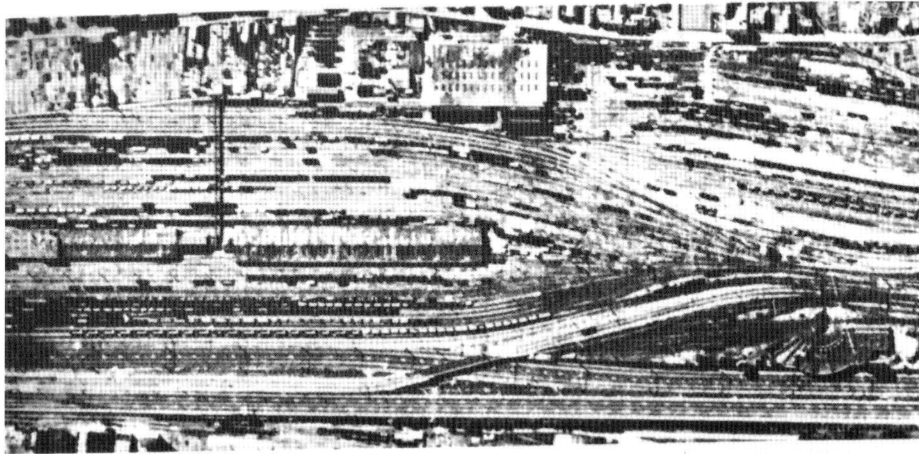

On 7 May 1944 *Ogefr* Arno-Heinrich-Lorenz Seibert, pilot and his *Bordfunker*, *Ogefr* Hermann Hasel (pictured) of II./NJG 5 at Parchim, Germany died when their Bf 110G-4 (C9+EM Werk Nr.5433) crashed at 0002 hrs at Schlieffkopf, Schwarzwald after combat. (Steve Hall)

The crew of Lancaster III ND347 of 405 'Vancouver' Squadron RCAF (when they were with 427 'Lion' Squadron RCAF). Back Row, L-R: Don Copeland, rear gunner; F. Constable, original navigator, Alex Nethery, bomb aimer; P/O Arthur Darlow, pilot. Front: Trevor Utton, mid upper gunner; Pip Richards, flight engineer; Allan Burnell, WOp. (via Steve Darlow)

Left: *Oblt* Hermann Leube, one of the free-lancing Tame Boar night fighting Experten, scored 22 night *Abschüsse* in NJG 3 August 1943-September 1944. After his 15th *Abschuss* he was appointed *St. Kpt*. of the 4th *Staffel* in April or May 1944. *Hptm* Leube claimed 22 bombers destroyed before he was killed on either 27/28 or 28/29 December 1944 in a failed crash-landing at at Reeuwijk near Gouda during a free-lancing night fighting sortie in Ju 88G-6 Werk Nr.620889 (Steve Hall via John Foreman).

This photo of the crash site and wreckage of Lancaster ND347 of 405 'Vancouver' Squadron RCAF at Bon-Secors, which was lost on the night of 8/9 May 1944 returning from the raid on Haine St. Pierre, was taken by the French Resistance. In the foreground is Raymonde Rock's head. She hid George Lorimer, navigator and Alex Nethery, bomb aimer until the area was liberated. P/O Arthur Darlow, pilot and the rest of his crew were KIA. (via Steve Darlow)

Fortress BII (B-17F) SR384 BU-A of 214 Squadron at Oulton on 24 May 1944 before F/O Allan J.N. Hockley RAAF and his crew took off on a bomber support sortie to Aachen near Antwerp They were intercepted by Ju 88G-1 D5+KM flown by *Oblt* Hermann Leube *Staffelkapitän* 4./NJG 3 who attacked the Fortress no less than six times before it finally exploded over the Oosterschelde at 0057 hrs. Hockley and Sgt Raymond G.V. Simpson, his mid-upper gunner were KIA. The other seven in the crew survived. Leube, his *Bordfunker Fw* Eberhard Scheve and air gunner, *Stabsfeldwebel* (W/O) Druschke landed back at Plantlünne, a satellite airfield between Rheine and Lingen/Emsland. (Gerhard Heilig via CONAM)

Right: S/L R.G. 'Tim' Woodman DFC. On 30 March 1944 he and his observer, F/O Pat Kemmis DFC had a very eventful night in their Mosquito night fighter while the fatal raid on Nürnburg by bomber Command was in progress. A devastating loss of 95 bombers was recorded; Woodman saw 44 of them go down. Flying with 169 and 85 Squadrons Woodman destroyed six aircraft in 1944 including, on 8/9 May at Braine-Ie-Comte, a Bf 110 of I./NJG 4 flown by *Lt* Wolfgang Martstaller. He and his radar operator/air gunner had taken off from Florennes and at 0300 hrs shot down Lancaster III ND587 of 405 'Vancouver' Squadron RCAF before their combat with Woodman. The Bf 110 belly-landed in a field. In 1945 Woodman took his final score to eight enemy aircraft destroyed and one damaged while flying Mosquito NFXXXs in 85 Squadron and BSDU. (Tim Woodman)

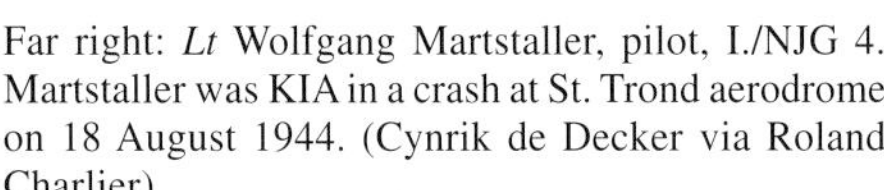

Far right: *Lt* Wolfgang Martstaller, pilot, I./NJG 4. Martstaller was KIA in a crash at St. Trond aerodrome on 18 August 1944. (Cynrik de Decker via Roland Charlier)

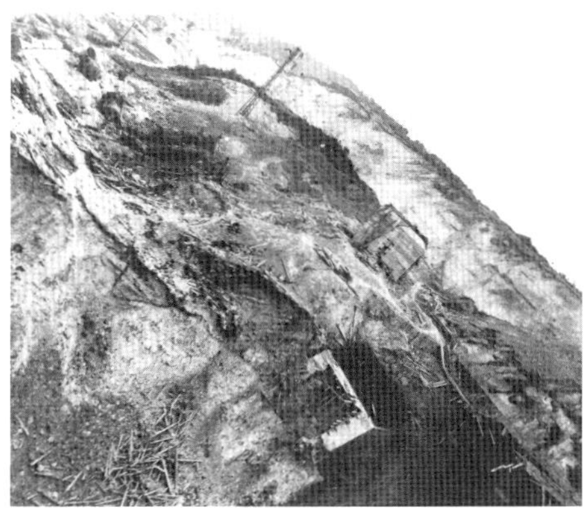

A low level photograph taken after the attack on Wizernes V-2 rocket site under construction in Northern France on 17 July 1944 by 16 Lancasters of 617 Squadron with a Mosquito and a Mustang as marker aircraft. The 'Dam Busters' aimed 12,000 lb Tallboy earthquake bombs with 11-second delay on the huge concrete dome, 20-ft thick, which lay on the edge of a chalk quarry protecting rocket stores and launching tunnels that led out of the face of the quarry pointing towards London. One Tallboy that apparently burst at the side of the dome exploded beneath it, knocking it askew. Another caused part of the chalk cliff to collapse, undermining the dome, with part of the resulting landslide also blocking four tunnel entrances, including the two that were intended for the erected V-2s. Ironically, though the construction was not hit the whole area around was so badly 'churned up' that it was unapproachable and the bunker jeopardized from underneath so the Germans abandoned the site and the V-2s were pulled back to The Hague in Holland where, in September they began firing them from mobile launchers. (IWM)

Australian and RAF crews of 192 Squadron, 100 Group in front of Halifax *BIII Matthews & Co. Express Delivery Service* at Foulsham, Norfolk. F/L Matthews RAAF, 4th from left. W/C David Donaldson CO is to his left. On D-Day, 6 June 1944, when 100 Group aircraft jammed enemy radars and made spoof attacks on the French coast, 192 Squadron maintained a constant patrol between Cape Griz-Nez and the Cherbourg area to see if the enemy was using the centimetric band for radar, all the known enemy radars being effectively jammed. Though jamming and spoofing were crucial to the war effort, the Australians in 100 Group (462 Squadron RAAF and its Halifax BIII aircraft moved to Foulsham from Driffield, Yorkshire in 4 Group in December 1944) felt they were not hurting the enemy and insisted that they carry bombs on ops! (John Crotch)

Right: The wreckage of Halifax VII NP716 of 408 'Goose' Squadron RCAF, which took off from Linton-on-Ouse at 2235 hrs and crashed at 0145 hrs in the vicinity of Heide after being attacked by *Lt* Rolf Ebhardt of 8./NJG 1 on the night of 28/29 July 1944. Among the dead in S/L G.B. Latimer RCAF's crew was 2/Lt A.A. Hauzenberger USAAF, who rests at the U.S. Military cemetery at Neuville-En-Condroz, Belgium. (Rolf Ebhardt)

Right: *Uffz* Wilhelm Simonsohn during flying training in 1940/41 before he joined 6./NJG 2 as a night fighter pilot flying the Ju 88C-6 and G-1 with his crew of *Uffz*'s Günther Gottwick, *funker* and Franz Holzer, flight engineer. (Simonsohn)

Left: *Lt* Rolf Ebhardt of 8./NJG 1, who on the night of 28/29 July 1944 claimed three Halifax IIIs shot down from the force of 187 Halifaxes, 106 Lancasters and 14 Mosquitoes, which raided Hamburg. Ebhardt shot down MZ816 of 433 'Porcupine' Squadron RCAF flown by F/O J.K. Armstrong RCAF (KIA) and crew (3 KIA, 3 PoW) at Prinzenmoor at 0123 hrs. Six minutes later in the vicinity of Heide he shot down NP716 of 408 'Goose' Squadron RCAF and S/L G.B. Latimer RCAF and crew (KIA). Ebhardt's 3rd Halifax (possibly MZ589 and F/O J.B. Collver RCAF and crew (KIA) of 431 'Iroquois' Squadron RCAF disappeared into the North Sea 25 km E of Heligoland at 0137 hrs. In all, 18 Halifaxes and four Lancasters were downed. (Rolf Ebhardt)

Right: *Uffz* Martin Siegel, one of the young replacement pilots in the *Nachtjagd* during the latter phase of the war, had only a short career before being killed in action. Serving with 2./NJG 2, Siegel scored two night *Abschüsse* (a Lancaster near Dunkirk on 12/13 May 1944 and a Viermot on 7/8 June 1944) before he was shot down in air combat near Le Havre on 9/10 June 1944. He baled out of his Ju 88G-1 but his body was found 4 km E of Harfleur. (Steve Hall via John Foreman).

Far right: F/O Bob Stainton, 34-year old Mosquito navigator of 29 Squadron at Hunsdon. (Frank Pringle)

Below: On 13 July 1944 *Ogefr* Hans Mäckle of 7./NJG 2 landed his Ju 88G-1 night-fighter 4R+UR at RAF Woodbridge, Suffolk after taking off from Twenthe at 2305 and became lost in thick cloud, which had a ceiling of about 14,000-ft. For 45 minutes the *Bordfunker* tried to establish radio contact but without success. After four hours in the air and very low on fuel Mäckle told his crew they might have to bale out but the *Bordmechaniker* (flight engineer informed him that he had not packed his parachute. Mäckle therefore put the Ju 88 down at the nearest available airfield, which unfortunately for him was Woodbridge! Scientists from TRE (Telecommunications Research Establishment) investigated the Ju 88's FuG 220 *Lichtenstein* SN-2, FuG 227/1 and FuG 350 Z Naxos radars, the last two types being previously unknown to the RAF. They confirmed Serrate's ineffectiveness and discovered that the *Nachtjägd* was using the FuG 227/1 equipment to home on to the Monica radar warning device and the FuG 350 Z Naxos to home on to H2S radar bombsight transmissions. RAF bombers were ordered immediately to restrict the use of H2S while Monica sets were removed from the Lancasters and Halifaxes. Window was modified to jam the new *Lichtenstein* radar. The Ju 88G-1 was added to 1426 Enemy Aircraft Flight at Duxford, which was used to evaluate enemy aircraft and display them at operational stations like Great Massingham, where this photo was taken. Note the Hirschgeweih (antler) aerials of the FuG 220 radar. (Mellows)

Right: Mosquito crews of 29 Squadron. (Frank Pringle)

Cockpit of Mosquito NFXIII HK524 of 29 Squadron of the ADGB (Air Defense of Great Britain) showing the AI.Mk.VIII radar equipment on the right. In the run up to D-Day, 29 Squadron had been the first Mosquito unit equipped with the superior AI.Mk.VIII radar to be released for intruding over the Continent. At most altitudes, the set had a maximum range of 6 1/2 miles straight ahead, falling to two miles when the target was at a 45° angle to the transmitter. (Frank Pringle)

On 14 July 1944 *Oblt* Joachim Fincke of 2./NJG 1 and his *Bordfunker*, *Uffz* Felix Petzold were KIA when they crashed at Venlo at 1545 hrs in He 219A-0 190212 G9+LK after they had possibly been attacked over Belgium by Lieutenant Armour RN of the Fighter Interception Unit, who claimed a Do 217. Fincke had claimed his first and only victory a few days earlier on 1/2 July when he scored hits on Mosquito XVI ML931 of 109 Squadron at Beacon Gorilla though F/L L. Gatrill and F/O A.J. Burnett limped home and crash-landed at RAF Woodbridge. (Steve Hall via John Foreman)

Center left: Light *Flak* was always a great hazard during low-level operations. F/O Kneath and his navigator/radar op. P/O George Kelsey of 151 Squadron flew Mosquito FBVI LR384 back to Predannack on one engine, a distance of 390 miles, after taking direct hits in the starboard engine and wing during a Ranger sortie to the Naval barracks at Château Rongnet, Vannes, France on 22 July 1944. Clearly visible are the 12 square feet of wing surface missing. Late in 1944 151 Squadron provided night defence for the invasion forces and in 1945 commenced fighter support for night bombing operations. (George Kelsey DFC)

Center right: F/L (later Squadron Leader DFC and 'A' Flt Commander) Geoffrey E. Poulton and F/O (later F/L DFC) Arthur J. Neville of 239 Squadron, who destroyed a Ju 88 (in all probability Ju 88G-1, Werk Nr.710866 of 8./NJG 2, which crashed near Volkel airfield at 0253 hrs. *Lt* Harald Machleidt, a replacement pilot with no victories and one of his crew KIA) and damaged another near Eindhoven on 17/18 June 1944. (IWM)

Right: A Polish crew gather for a group photograph in front of Wellington II Z8343 of 305 'Ziemia Wielkopolska' Squadron. This aircraft first saw service with 142 Squadron and was struck off charge on 27 July 1944 when it was serving with 104 Squadron. Note the bomb log painted above the fin flash. (RAF Hendon)

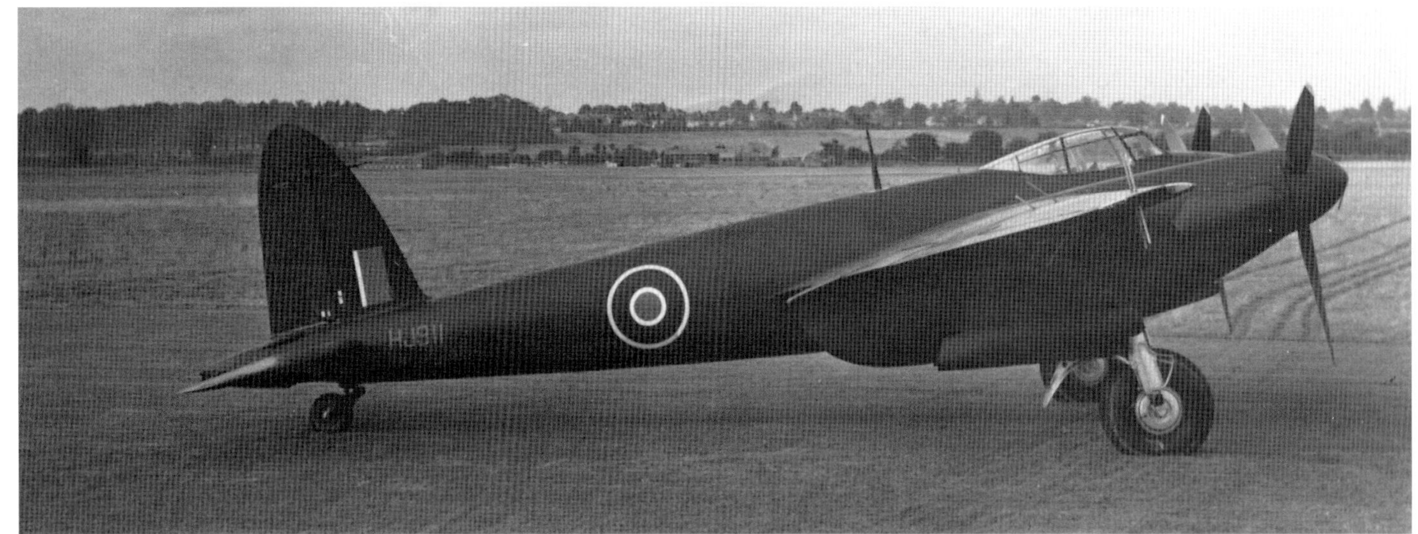

Above: Mosquito NFII HJ911/A, which S/L Graham J. Rice and F/O Jimmie G. Rogerson of 141 Squadron flew when they destroyed a Ju 88 at Cambrai on the night of 27/28 June 1944 and on 7/8 July, a Bf 110G-4 which crashed 5 km west of Chièvres, Belgium, the latter being Werk Nr.730006 D5+ of 2./NJG 3. The pilot (name unknown) and *Gefr* Richard Heiff, *Bordfunker*, who was wounded, both baled out safely. *Obgfr* Edmund Hejducki, *Bordschütze*, was killed. (DH)

Right: F/O Les Sutton and his crew of Lancaster K-King of 514 Squadron at Waterbeach. L-R: John Britain, Alf McBurrugh, engineer; WOp; Bob Tores, rear gunner; Les Sutton, pilot; Shorty Evers, Mid Upper Gunner; Joe Speare, bomb aimer; Ray Hilchey, navigator. (Les Sutton)

Above: 19-year old Sgt Ernie Reynolds in the rear turret of Wellington 341 of 26 OTU. This aircraft crashed into a wood at Fairwood Common airfield on 2 August 1944 during a cross-country flight with F/Sgt Dawson RAAF at the controls and was written off. (Ernie Reynolds)

Right: F/O Les Sutton and crew of 514 Squadron perched on top of Lancaster *K-King* at Waterbeach. L-R: Shorty Evers, Mid Upper Gunner; Alf McBurrugh, engineer; Ray Hilchey, navigator; Joe Speare, bomb aimer; Bob Tores, rear gunner; John Britain, WOp; Les Sutton, pilot. (Les Sutton)

Right: *Fahnenjunker-Feldwebel* Hermann-Walter Stähler of 2./NJG 3 had scored four victories when on 23 August 1944 he was taking off from Nordhorn and a searchlight blinded him. Stähler crashed into a building from an altitude of 60 ft and he was badly injured together with his crew. (Steve Hall via John Foreman)

Far right: Lancaster III W5005 L-Leather served with 460 RAAF and 550 Squadrons and completed 94 operations before it hit the water in the Humber Estuary on 27 August 1944 on approach near Killingholme Haven, Lincolnshire. (Keith Wardell)

Below: Liberator BVI of 223 Squadron at Oulton, Norfolk in 1944. This squadron formed on 23 August 1944 as part of 100 Group for jamming duties. Note the *Jostle* IV transmitter mast on top of the fuselage. The B-24 was capable of carrying up to as many as 30 of these sets for jamming of German HE and VHF signals. Unfortunately, 223 Squadron's B-24s, some of which had accumulated as many as 350 flying hours in 8th AF service, had seen far better days. Throughout 1944 besides *Jostle* the Fortresses of 214 Squadron and the Liberators of 223 Squadron were fully equipped with Carpet (anti-Würzburg) and Piperack (anti-SN-2). (CONAM)

A 100 Squadron Lancaster awaits bombing up with 1000 lb bombs in 1944. (Maurice S. Paff)

Above: The crew of Halifax III MZ559 LK-F of 578 Squadron. L-R: F/Sgt R.F. Bob' Burn RCAF, navigator; Sgt R.G. 'Sam' Browne, rear gunner; F/O R.D. 'Bob' Davies, pilot; Sgt F.E. 'Wally' Scarth, flight engineer; Sgt M.U. Hayward, top turret gunner; F/O B.A. 'Ron' Corbett RCAF, bomb-aimer; Sgt Tither, radio operator. Bob Davies flew 16 ops on Halifaxes before being posted to 100 Group RAF and serving with 171 Squadron before taking command of 'A' Flight, 214 Squadron, flying ten ops on Fortresses. (Bob Davies AFC)

Top right: USAAF personnel of the 453rd Bomb Group inspect the damage to Halifax III MZ559 of 578 Squadron after it landed at Old Buckenham, Norfolk on 3 September 1944 after sustaining a direct hit from a 1000-lb bomb dropped from a Lancaster overhead during a daylight bombing run on Venlo airfield. The pilot, S/L Bob Davies, managed to land safely. Afterwards Davies was having a drink in the bar at Old Buckenham when he felt a tap on his shoulder: 'What are you doing here Bob? It was Captain (now Major) Murray who had been Davies' BT-13 Vibrator instructor at Shaw Field, South Carolina in 1942, now an operational pilot of a B-24 Liberator! Repaired and returned to operational service, MZ559 incredibly was destined to be involved in another incident two months later, on 18 November 1944, when it was involved in a collision with Halifax III NR241 on approach to Snaith on the return from a raid on Münster and crashed at Camlesforth near Selby, Yorkshire. There were no survivors from F/O T.I.M. Evans' crew in MZ559 and everyone in W/O J.W. Bruce's crew of NR241 also died. (Bob Davies AFC)

Lancaster X KB745 VR-V of 419 'Moose' Squadron RCAF flown by F/O Rokeby photographed over Normandy in the summer of 1944 by 1/Lieutenant Joseph H. Hartshorn DFC, an American pilot on the squadron who flew 34 ops. The gray streaks on the wing were caused by the exhaust gases from the leaded petrol. KB745 and F/O G.R. Duncan RCAF and crew flew into a hillside at Goldscleugh near Rothbury, Scotland setting course for Norway and an attack on the U-Boat pens at Bergen on 4 October 1944. All the crew died.

Right: *Fw* Robert Koch's Bf 110 (Wrk.Nr.440130) G9+MN of 5./NJG 1 explodes near Peer, Belgium at about 2320 hrs on 7 October 1944 as a result of an attack by F/O Ross Finlayson and F/O Al Webster of 409 'Nighthawk' Squadron RCAF in Mosquito NFXIII MM560. In the minutes prior to this interception Koch had made a 180° turn to port and set course for his base at Düsseldorf, totally unaware that the Canadian nightfighter had been alerted to his presence by Allied GCI. The NFXIII crew approached unobserved from astern, the GCI controller bringing them in to visual range because the Mosquito's radar had gone 'wonky'. Once close enough to see the contact, it was discovered that the enemy aircraft boasted external wing tanks, leading Finlayson to believe that his target was a four-engined aircraft. He therefore misjudged the closing speed and distance between himself and the Bf 110, scoring hits in the port wing and fuselage with his first burst but ending up right below the Messerschmitt with his wheels and flaps extended. However, before Koch had time to take evasive action, a second burst was fired which rendered the Bf 110's controls useless and set the port wing alight, whereupon the pilot who was flying his 70th operation, gave the order to bale out. Koch was slightly injured whilst taking to his parachute but his *Bordfunker*, *Uffz* Heinrich Ferster and gunner *Uffz* Ernst Karg were both KIA. Koch, who had seven four-engined RAF bombers to his credit (February-August 1944) had previously been shot down near St. Trond during a daylight mission on 14 October 1943 by a USAAF P-47 shortly after joining 6./NJG 1. He baled out wounded and did not fly again until February 1944 and in August joined 5./NJG 1. A highly experienced Bf 110 pilot, Koch had also flown with 7./NJG 1. (Ross Finlayson)

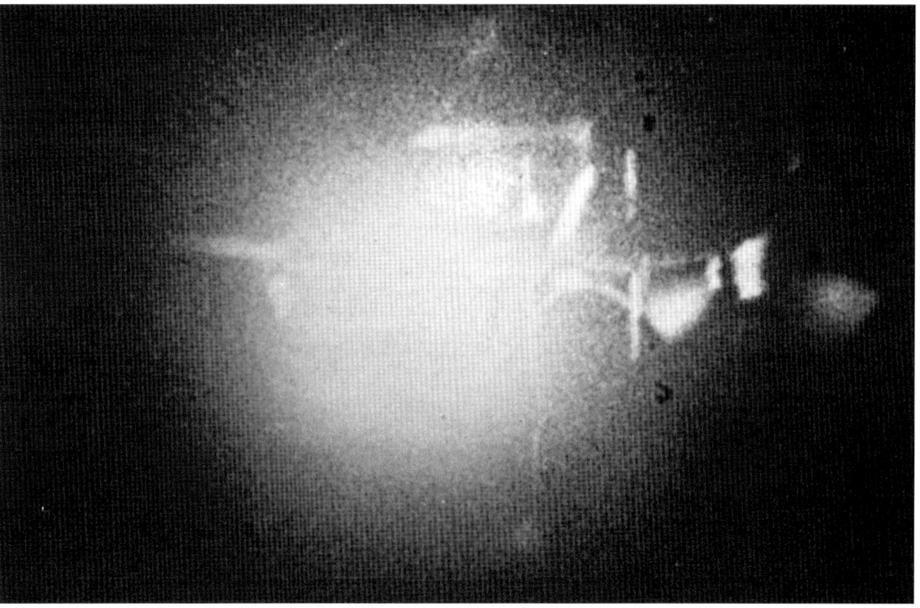

Right: F/O Al Webster (left) and F/O Ross H. Finlayson of 409 'Nighthawk' Squadron RCAF. Behind is NFXIII HK425/KP-D Lonesome Polecat. On 25/26 November 1944 F/O I.E. Britten RCAF and F/L L.E. Fownes shot down a Ju 88 and damaged a second Junkers' bomber at Rheindahlen in this aircraft. By the war's end Britten and Fownes had destroyed five aircraft. (Ross Finlayson)

Mosquito NFXIII MM560 of 409 'Nighthawk' Squadron RCAF at Le Culot in Belgium on the morning of 7 October 1944 following Finlayson and Webster's shooting down of Koch's Bf 110. MM560 was written off in a belly landing at Lille-Vendeville on 13 March 1945 after the undercarriage had jammed during an air test. Behind MM560 is the 410 Squadron NFXIII in which F/Ls Ben E. Plumer DFC and Hargrove had been vectored onto a second Bf 110 on the night of 6 October and lost an engine to return fire. Plumer weaved to dodge the German's bullets and the Bf 110 pilot lost control and crashed. (Ross Finlayson)

S/L Robert Daniel 'Dolly' Doleman of 157 Squadron who on 19/20 October 1944 with his radar operator F/L D.C. 'Bunny' Bunch DFC (right) in a Mosquito XIX shot down a Ju 88 and claimed a Ju 88 'damaged' on their High Level Support Patrol to Nürnburg. Doleman finished the war with ten and two shared victories. (Doleman)

F/Sgt John Cook DFM in front of his rear gun turret of 578 Squadron Halifax III MZ560 J-Jig at Burn, spring 1944. (John Cook)

Mosquito NFXXX MM767 of 410 'Cougar' Squadron RCAF rests on PSP (Pierced Steel Planking) in a muddy dispersal at either B48/Glisy or B51 Lille-Vendeville in the winter of 1944/45. On 29/30 October 1944 Lt A.A. Harrington USAAF and P/O D.G. Tongue shot down a Fw 190 whilst flying this aircraft in the Venlo area. On 25/26 November this crew, again in MM767, destroyed three Ju 88Gs at Muntz, Jackerath and North of Hunxe thus raising their final tally to seven. (Stephen M. Fochuk)

L-R: *Ofhr* Manfred Tangelst, pilot and *Uffz* Herbert Rockel, *Bordfunker*, a typical late-war replacement crew serving with 7./NJG 6 at Wiener Neustadt late in 1944. Flying the Bf 110G-4, the crew had eight *Feindberührungen* (contacts with the enemy) with RAF aircraft but they never scored a kill. (Manfred Tangelst)

F/O Bob Heuston and his crew and ground crew in front of Halifax III MZ560 J-Jig of 578 Squadron at Burn. This crew completed a tour of 37 operations between April and October 1944. Back row, L-R: Sgt (later F/O) Johnny Cook DFM, rear gunner, Sgt Jock Campbell, mid upper gunner; F/Sgt Eric Dishart (later F/O DFC) bomb aimer; F/Sgt Harry Harris, navigator; F/O Bob Heuston DFC pilot, W/O Andy Andrews DFC wireless operator, Sgt J.W. Kindred, flight engineer; F/Sgt Jimmy Grogan, spare engineer (took over from W/O Andrews on completion of his second tour, later KIA). Front row: ground staff, with Corporal in charge in center. Note Rip van Heuston painted below the cockpit (which was coined by the ground crew for their skipper and was based on Rip van Winkle) and the three symbols of combats with German night fighters which the crew of J-Jig survived and which were painted over the bombs by the ground crew. (John Cook)

Acting Squadron Leader Ian Willoughby Bazalgette DFC RAFVR (seated, far left, second row) of 635 Squadron stationed at Downham Market, Norfolk lost his life on 4 August 1944 while flying as 'master bomber' in Lancaster ND811 (F2-T) during the bombing of Trossy St. Maxim, which was thought to be a V-1 storage site. Bazalgette's aircraft was badly hit by flak and set on fire but he pressed on to the target and dropped his markers. With only one engine still running and the starboard wing a mass of flame the order to bale out was given. Bazalgette however saw that the bomb aimer and mid upper gunner were incapacitated and so elected to try to put the aircraft down in a field. This he did successfully but the Lancaster exploded and killed all three on board. It was only when the surviving crew returned to the UK and told the story that Bazalgette was awarded a posthumous Victoria Cross, on 17 August 1945. After the war captured German documents revealed that Trossy-St-Maxim, which cost 2 Lancasters, and Bois de Cassan, which was also bombed on 4 August, with the loss of 2 Halifaxes, were dummy sites. (via Tom Cushing)

Right: After running out of fuel this Bf 110G of III./NJG 6 made an emergency landing at Tapoleu airfield in the summer of 1944. Note the aerial array associated with the FuG 220 *Lichtenstein* SN-2d AI radar, its antenna dipoles mounted at a 45° angle. SN-2d incorporated a tail warning capacity. (Georg Punka)

For Canadian F/O Jack F. Hamilton, mid-upper gunner in the crew of Lancaster JO-J *Jumpin' Jive* of 463 Squadron RAAF, the trip to Königsberg on the night of 29/30 August 1944 when 189 Lancasters of 5 Group carried out one of their most successful attacks of the war, was his 21st trip (and longest at almost 11 hours) in a tour of 33 trips 6 June-17 October 1944. Hamilton had started out as a tail gunner at OTU but as he was 6ft tall and too big for the gun turret, he had problems with the gun sights, so he had to switch to the mid-upper position. (Jack Hamilton)

Right: Target photo of an oil depot at Bordeaux, France being bombed by 15 Lancasters of 5 Group in daylight on 13 August 1944 taken from Lancaster 'X' of 61 Squadron flown by F/O Watkins. Bombing was accurate. One Lancaster failed to return. (Edgar Ray)

Above: Lancaster JO-J *Jumpin' Jive* of 463 Squadron RAAF at Waddington in 1944 in which F/O Jack F. Hamilton RAAF and his crew flew 33 trips of their tour, which was cut from 35 to 33. (Jack F. Hamilton)

Below: Mosquito NFXIII HK382/T of 29 Squadron at Hunsdon, 1944. 29 Squadron had begun conversion from the Beaufighter to the Mosquito NFXII in the summer of 1943 for the continuance of night intruder operations over occupied Europe and by the end of 1943 had destroyed about 600 enemy aircraft. Intruder operations continued in 1944, apart from October/November, when the Mosquitoes were used briefly for night interception of V-1 flying bombs. Intruding then continued unabated until VE Day 1945. (Frank Pringle)

Above: Bombs ready for loading aboard a 463 Squadron RAAF Lancaster at Waddington in 1944. The Lancaster normally carried a 14,000 lb bomb load. The 4000 lb Cookie (right, with its three transit plugs in place) or the 8000 lb 'Block Buster' (which was two Cookies in tandem) were the largest bombs dropped until the advent of the 12,000 lb 'Tallboy', which could be enclosed within the aircraft, and the 22,000 lb 'Grand Slam' of which 41 were delivered before the end of the war in Europe. (Jack F. Hamilton)

Above: *Hptm* Heinz Rökker, *Staffelkapitän*, 2./NJG 2 gets strapped into his Ju 88G-1 at Twenthe airfield. On the night of 7/8 August 1944 Rökker claimed three Lancasters NE of Le Havre for his 38th-40th victories. Rökker survived the war having scored 63 *Nachtjagd* victories (including 55 *Viermots* and one Mosquito), plus one in daylight in 161 sorties with I./NJG 2. He was awarded the *Ritterkreuz* with *Eichenlaub*. (Heinz Rökker)

Top right: *Oblt* Dietrich Schmidt, *Staffelkapitän*, 8./NJG 1 at Leeuwarden airfield in August 1944. Schmidt was decorated with the *Ritterkreuz* on 30 July 1944 after his 32nd kill. He ended the war with forty night victories in 8. and 9./NJG 1. Apart from one Mosquito claim on 13/14 January 1944 all his other victories were against four-engined heavies. (Dr. Schmidt-Barbo)

Right: Bf 110G-4s of 8./NJG 1 or '*Zirkus* (Circus) *Schmidt*' during a daylight training flight over France in the summer of 1944 and taken from the Bf 110 flown by 8th *Staffelkapitän Oblt* Dietrich Schmidt. Clearly visible are the large SN-2 antennae and long-range drop tanks for Tame Boar missions on these night-fighter aircraft. G9+RS, nearest to the camera, was the mount of *Ofw* Ruge and the furthest away is flown by *Lt* Rolf Ebhardt. (Dr. Schmidt-Barbo)

Right: Lancaster III EE139 'B-Baker' of 550 Squadron, better known as *Phantom of the Ruhr* at North Killingholme with F/O Joe C. Hutcheson's crew just before its 100th op on 5 September 1944 on a daylight raid against Le Havre, France. (Note the mustard-colored circular gas detection panel, which appeared on aircraft of 1 Group Bomber Command and the four ice-cream cones in the first two rows of the bomb log denoting raids on Italian targets in 1943). EE136 began it career in 100 Squadron at Waltham near Grimsby in May 1943 and flew at least 29 sorties with this unit until in November 1943 it joined 550 Squadron. The name and the ghoulish figure were the creation of Sgt Harold 'Ben' Bennett, the aircraft's first flight engineer who had been a ground engineer in Fighter Command in the early part of the war. Len Browning)

Above: F/O Joe C. Hutcheson of 550 Squadron taxying Lancaster III EE139 *Phantom of the Ruhr* out at North Killingholme on 5 September 1944. Some 348 Lancasters, Mosquitoes and Stirlings raided German positions around Le Havre in good visibility without loss. During 11/12 June 1943-21 November 1944 PHANTOM OF THE RUHR completed 121 trips, surviving five night-fighter attacks and returning with severe *Flak* scars on five occasions. (Len Browning)

Left: Bf 110G-4 of II./NJG 6 at Grosssachsenheim airfield one moonlit night in September 1944. (Dr. Günther Lomberg)

During the daylight hours of 14 October and the night of 14/15 October 1944 in Operation Hurricane Duisburg received nearly 9000 tons of bombs dropped by RAF Bomber Command. During the da 957 RAF heavies dropped 3574 tons of high explosive and 820 tons of incendiaries and that night 1005 more bombers dropped 4040 tons of high explosive and 500 tons of incendiaries on the city. (via Ben Jones)

Lancaster EE176 QR-M *Mickey the Moocher* of 61 Squadron at Skellingthorpe in 1944. L-R: Jim Leith, flight engineer; Den Cluett, rear gunner; Pete Smith, bomb aimer; F/O Frank Mouritz RAAF, pilot; Arthur Bass, mid upper gunner; Laurie Cooper, navigator; Dave Blomfield, WOp. Aircraft lettered 'M' were usually known as M-Mike or M-Mother. (Frank Mouritz)

Left: Lancaster EE176 QR-M *Mickey the Moocher* showing 91 ops on the nose. EE176's nose had received a Walt Disney cartoon of Mickey Mouse, pulling a bomb-trolley on which sat a bomb and this Lanc became Mickey The Moocher; a name derived from singer Cab Calloway's popular slow blues song, 'Minnie the Moocher'. (Frank Mouritz)

Right: Lancaster EE176 QR-M *Mickey the Moocher* of 61 Squadron was flown by F/O Frank Mouritz RAAF and crew on her last operation on 6/7 November when 235 Lancasters and seven Mosquitoes of 5 Group attempted to bomb the Mittelland Canal at Gravenhorst. (Frank Mouritz)

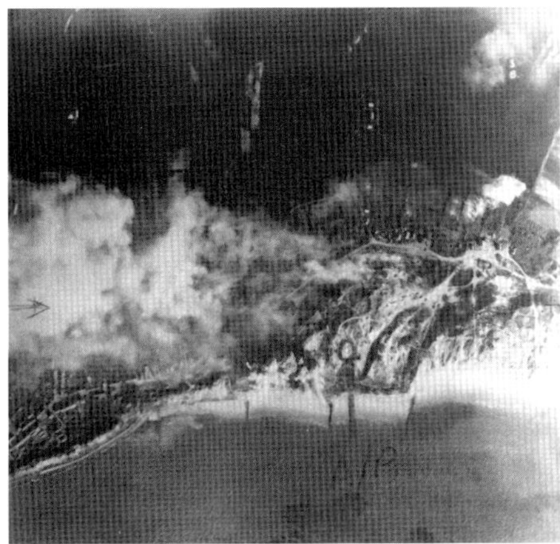

Target photo of the Zoutelande (Walcheren) gun positions raid on 29 October 1944, which was brought back by Halifax III MZ399 NP-Z of 158 Squadron, flown by F/L Humphrey F. Watson. A force of 358 aircraft – 194 Lancasters, 128 Halifaxes and 36 Mosquitoes – of four Groups attacked 11 different German ground positions in good visibility for the loss of one Lancaster. (Don L. Simpkin)

F/Sgt R.B. 'Doc' Dockeray DFM and P/O Terry A Groves DFC of 515 Squadron destroyed a Bf 110 in the air and damaged several Bf 109s on the ground during a legendary Day Ranger with F/L F.T.L' Amie and F/O J.W. Smith on 29 October 1944. All told these two crews were responsible for nine aircraft shot down and five damaged. (Tom Cushing Collection)

Above: On 4/5 November 1944 S/L Branse Burbridge DSO* DFC* and F/L Bill Skelton DSO* DFC* of 85 Squadron shot down three Ju 88s and this Bf 110 of 6./NJG 1 north of Hangelar airfield. The Messerschmitt crashed into the Rhine at 0150 hours, killing pilot *Oblt* Ernst Runzel, although radar operator *Ogefr* Karl-Heinz Bendfeld (WIA) and the gunner baled out safely. Burbridge and Skelton finished the war as the top scoring nightfighter team in the RAF, with 21 aircraft destroyed, two probables, one damaged and three Vls also destroyed. (IWM)

Left: Mosquito crews confer before a sortie over the Reich. (DH)

Major Heinz-Wolfgang Schnaufer, *Kommodore* NJG 4 (middle) and his crew (*Ofw* Wilhelm Gänsler, air gunner, left and *Lt* Fritz Rumpelhardt, *Bordfunker*, right) preparing for a night sortie late 1944/early 1945. (Theo Boiten Coll)

Right: A Mosquito NFXIX crew of 68 Squadron prepare for a night sortie in late 1944. The bulbous nose contains the AI.Mk.X radar equipment. This squadron was successful in shooting down four V-1 carrying He 111H22 aircraft over the North Sea during November-December 1944, the first on the night of 5/6 November 1944 by F/Sgt Neal and F/Sgt Eastwood in NFXIX TA389. 68 Squadron destroyed another V-1 carrying aircraft in January 1945. (DH)

Ju 88G flown in daylight by *Lt* Horst-Rüdiger Blüme who flew in 8./NJG 2 and 11./NJG 3 during 1943-44. Note the FuG 220 *Lichtenstein* SN-2 nose mounted aerial array and FuG 227 *Flensburg* wing mounted antenna, which enabled German crews to home onto *Monica, Mandrel* and *Piperack/Dina* jamming devices. During the early months of 1944 *Nachtjagd* units were frequently called upon to attack the mass American formations and nightfighter losses were usually quite high. On 30 January 1944 NJG 2 lost seven Ju 88s to P-47 Thunderbolts and other units lost five more and many badly damaged. (Steve Hall via John Foreman)

Lt Horst Rüdiger Blume claimed one victory in 1943 and two more in 1944, a *Viermot* on 12/13 August and a Lancaster on 4/5 November before he was killed in a crash south of Lübbecke during a non-operational flight ten days later on 14 November 1944. (Steve Hall via John Foreman)

Target photo taken from 20,000-ft showing bombs from 169 Lancasters of 3 Group raining down on the Kalk Nord rail yards at Cologne during the G-H attack on 27 November 1944. Results were described as 'good'. One Lancaster failed to return. (Les Sutton)

'Taffy' Bellis DFC* claimed a Bf 110 North of Aachen[96] while F/Os Bill Breithaupt RCAF DFC and J.A. Kennedy DFC put in a victory claim for a Ju 88G-1 off the Friesians.[97] The AI.Mk.X[98] radar equipped NFXVIIs of 85 Squadron and 157 Squadron's NFXIXs at Swannington officially began operations on 5/6 June, when 16 sorties were flown. Twelve Mosquitoes in 85 Squadron operated over the Normandy beachhead, while four in 157 Squadron patrolled night-fighter airfields at Deelen, Soesterberg, Eindhoven and Gilze Rijen in Holland. 85 Squadron despatched 12 Mosquitoes over the Normandy invasion beaches and four Mosquitoes of 157 (and ten of 515 Squadron) made *Intruder* raids on Belgian and Dutch airfields and strafed road, rail and canal traffic. Two 515 Squadron FBVIs failed to return. S/L J.L. Shaw and his navigator, Sgt P. Standley-Smith were shot down by *Hptm* Heinz Strüning, *St.Kpt* of 3./NJG 1 flying a He 219 *Uhu*, for his 49th confirmed kill. S/L W.R. Butterfield DFC MiD and his navigator Sgt C.S. Drew were lost without trace off Dieppe heading for the Lille area.[99] The Luftwaffe had put up just 59 fighters to intercept the invasion forces but only two *Nachtjäger* submitted one claim each.[100] Finally, *Oblt* Helmut Eberspächer, a fighter-bomber pilot of 3./SKG 10 flying a Fw 190G-3 claimed three Lancasters at Isigny and Carentan while *Fw* Eisele of the same unit claimed another Lancaster at Isigny-Lessay-Vire.

On 6/7 June 1065 RAF four engine bombers and Mosquitoes dropped 3488 tons of bombs on rail and road centers on the lines of communication behind the Normandy battle area for the loss of ten Lancasters and a Halifax. Raids on the communication targets continued on 7/8 June when 19 Lancasters and 11 Halifaxes were lost and on 8/9 when three Lancasters and a Mosquito bomber were missing. *Nachtjäger* and 100 Group Mosquito nightfighter claims were to the fore and there was always the unexpected. On 8/9 June W/C Neil Bromley OBE and F/L P.V. Truscott of 169 Squadron shot down a Dornier in the Paris area.[101] 141 Squadron Mosquito nightfighter crews had mixed fortune. F/O A.C. Gallacher DFC and W/O G. McLean DFC destroyed an unidentified German aircraft over Northern France after they had chased it into a flak barrage at Rennes where it was brought down by a single burst. Capt H.J.B. D'Hautecourt and Ltn C.E. Kocher, a popular Free French crew who had been with the Squadron since February returned from their seventh operation on one engine and landed at Ford, Sussex but the NFII swung off the runway and crashed into two fighter aircraft. Both Frenchmen later died of their injuries.

On the night of 10/11 June when 432 aircraft attacked rail targets in France 15 Lancasters and three Halifaxes were lost. *Nachtjagd* claimed 21 Lancasters and Halifaxes with *Hptm* Paul Zorner *Gruppenkommandeur* of III./NJG 5 being credited with three Halifaxes and a Lancaster in the Dreux area to take his score to 52. *Lt* Walter Briegleb of 10./NJG 3 was credited with four Lancasters[102] to take his score to eight confirmed victories. Two Mosquitoes also failed to return from a raid by 32 of the Wooden Wonders on Berlin. One of the German nightfighter crews on patrol this night was *Oblt* Josef Nabrich and his *Bordfunker*, *Uffz* Fritz Habicht of 3./NJG 1 who were flying a cleaned up He 219 *Uhu* with the armor plating and four of the cannons removed especially for hunting Mosquitoes. Nabrich was looking to add to his claims for four bombers destroyed during May, including two in one night (on 24 May). This crew began their patrol high above the Zuider Zee until ground controllers reported the approach of a formation of Mosquitoes at a slightly lower altitude. Habicht looked at his *SN-2* radar display and directed Nabrich to reverse course for about 10 1/2 kilometers towards a Mosquito flying east at high speed. Over Osnabrück the He 219 crew obtained visual contact and Nabrich closed to within firing range. He opened up with a short burst from the He 219's wing cannon. The starboard engine of the Mosquito (BIV DZ608 of 692 Squadron) immediately burst into flames and started down in a spiral, out of control. Before Nabrich could attack again the Mosquito's bomb load exploded and the blast caused the *Uhu* to stall. Nabrich finally managed to recover just above the cloud layer. Only pieces of the Mosquito were found but F/O I. S.H. MacDonald RAAF and F/O E.B. Chatfield DFC had baled out immediately after the first attack, convinced that a new anti aircraft weapon and not a nightfighter had shot them down. Both men survived and were made PoW.

This same night another Mosquito, BXVI MM125 of 571 Squadron flown by F/L Joe Downey DFM, was shot down returning from Berlin by *Hptm* Ernst-Wilhelm Modrow of 1./NJG 1 flying a He 219 *Uhu* for his 19th victory. Downey's navigator, P/O Ronald Arthur Wellington, recalls:

> 'The attack on our aircraft consisted of a short burst of cannon fire, no more than five rounds. The starboard engine was hit and burst into flames. The aircraft immediately went into an uncontrolled dive and on receiving the order 'Bale Out' I made my exit from the normal escape hatch. At the time Joe was preparing to follow me. Very shortly after pulling the ripcord I saw the aircraft explode beneath me. It is therefore, very unlikely that Joe was alive when the remains of the aircraft crashed onto the dunes near Bergen, a small seaside town three miles NW of Alkmaar.'[103]

Airborne again on the night of 11/12 June *Oblt* Josef Nabrich and his *Bordfunker*, *Uffz* Fritz Habicht of 3./NJG 1 in their He 219 *Uhu* sought more victories as the LNSF sent 33 Mosquitoes to Berlin again as the heavies bombed rail targets in northern France. West of Salzwedel Habicht was able to pick up a Mosquito, so near that he could see it clearly without radar. Nabrich had difficulty getting into a firing position because the Mosquito pilot, F/L O.A. Armstrong DFM MiD RNZAF of 139 Squadron, was carrying out wild evasive action. Finally, he gave the BIV two bursts of 20mm cannon and DZ609 went down vertically and exploded seconds later killing Armstrong and his navigator, F/O G.L. Woolven. Now it was time for Nabrich to have concern. He had made his pursuit at full power and seconds after the Mosquito went down the port DB603 engine of his He 219 seized. He feathered the propeller and was able to make a single-engine landing at Perleberg. *Generalleutnant* Josef 'Beppo' Schmid sent Nabrich and Habicht a congratulatory telegram and a gift of several bottles.[104] The *Nachtjagd* did not have it all its own way. W/C Charles M. Miller DFC** CO of 85 Squadron and F/O Robert Symon, in a Mosquito NFXIX fitted with AI.Mk.X shot down a Bf 110 over Melun airfield at 0035 hrs. Denis Welfare and Taffy Bellis of 239 Squadron on patrol between Paris and Luxembourg, on radar watch for night-fighters picked up a German airborne radar transmission about ten miles away on their *Serrate* apparatus and homed on to it. They made a contact 10,000 ft away with their own AI and in a few minutes converted it to a visual, showing clearly the twin fins and faint exhausts of a Me 110 which Welfare quickly despatched from about 50 yards and the 110 immediately blew up. Their Mosquito flew into debris and was enveloped in burning petrol but fortunately the fire did not get hold, though the fighter was damaged. The crew jettisoned the escape hatch ready to bale out but Welfare was able to control the aircraft and flew 300 miles home in a plane without an escape hatch.

Raids on flying bomb sites and communication targets in France and synthetic oil targets in Germany were high on the Bomber Command target list. On 12/13 June 671 aircraft attacked communication targets, mostly railways in France and a stream of 286 Lancasters and 17 Mosquitoes headed for Gelsenkirchen. F/L James Gilles 'Ben' Benson DFC and F/L Lewis 'Brandy' Brandon DFC of 157 Squadron[105] chased a contact during a low-level patrol of three airfields near Rheims (Laon-Athies, Laon-Couvron and Juvincourt). Finally, Brandon could see the blip on his AI.Mk.X coming in to 800 ft. It was a Junkers 188. At 150 yards' range Benson fired a three-second burst at the Junkers. There were strikes on the starboard wing roots and the starboard engine caught fire. A further two-second burst blew pieces off the port wing tip. A short third burst produced strikes on the burning starboard engine. Then the whole of the port wing outboard of the engine broke off and passed under us. A second later the Junkers hurtled straight down in flames and exploded on the ground in the Forest of Compiègne. It had taken the crew just under four minutes from obtaining contact on this aircraft to seeing it hit the ground. From the light of the burning starboard engine they had seen a swastika on the tail and dark green camouflage on the upper surface of the wing. It took Benson's personal tally to five.[106]

Seventeen Halifaxes and six Lancasters failed to return from the communication raids and 17 Lancasters were brought down on the Gelsenkirchen raid by the German defenses. At 0145 hrs *Hptm* Gerhard Friedrich, *Staffelkapitän*, 1./NJG 6 and *Hptm* Joachim Böhner of St.I./NJG 6 at Deelen both claimed a Lancaster from the Gelsenkirchen force.[107] *Oblt* Lau, *Uffz* Sarzio and *Lt* Gottfried Hanneck[108] of II./NJG 1 also operating from Deelen, each claimed a *Viermot* destroyed.[109] *Oblt* Dieter Schmidt, *Staffelkapitän*, 8./NJG 1 and his crew, Schönfeld and Schlosser, who were all on their 126th operation claimed one of the Gelsenkirchen raiders.[110] Schmidt recalls:

> 'We took-off from Leeuwarden at 0035 hrs in Bf 110 G9+AS (Anton Siegfried) and approached the Ruhr for the first time in this period of darkness. We were fairly late. I was flying at full throttle. The attack was already in full swing, mainly explosive bombs. The last bombs were falling as we got close to the target. Where was the departure route? I guessed over to port, across the Zuidersee and therefore continued towards north. I was right. Soon we had them before us. Kurt guided with the SN-2. Soon I saw one directly in front. At short range I could clearly make out the eight exhausts – a *Viermot* – distance 500 meters and relatively fast. It was fairly hazy but not bad. I attacked from a distance of one hundred meters and from behind as usual, between the engines, aiming a little low, pressing the buttons and pulling a little up and there it was. Time was 0123 hrs. The entire starboard wing was on fire. For a moment I saw clearly the port one with the low-mounted engines brightly lit. It looked like another Lancaster. Then we broke off quickly to port and up. Blazing fiercely he passed below our starboard wing. Pieces were breaking away. Kurt saw two parachutes. Then he went vertically down to crash at 0124. The radio beacon *Kurfürst* was 10-20 kilometers to the southeast. We landed back at Leeuwarden at 0206. (On 9 August we got confirmation: crash of a Lancaster near Warminghaven, 30 kilometers east of Arnhem. Further confirmation by the *Reichsluftfahrtministerium (RLM or Reich* Air Ministry) followed in February 1945).'

On 14/15 June, 100 Group and 2nd TAF wreaked havoc on the continent. Two victories went to 85 Squadron Mosquito NFXIXs. F/L H.B. Thomas and P/O C.B. Hamilton brought down a Ju 88 near Juvincourt. F/O Branse A. Burbridge DFC and F/L F.S. Skelton DFC destroyed a Ju 188 southwest of Nivelles.[111] A Ju 88 trying to land at Juvincourt was shot down by F/L J. Tweedale and F/O L.I. Cunningham of 157 Squadron in another Mosquito NFXIX. Eleven other enemy aircraft were shot down over the continent by Mosquito crews[112] including one by S/L Russ Bannock RCAF and F/O Bob Bruce, their first victory since joining 418 Squadron a few days earlier.[113] Bruce recalls:

> 'We wasted no time and after practice trips on the first three days set off on our first *Intruder*, a two-hour patrol off Bourges-Avord airfield. Luck was with us and after some time we spotted the exhaust of a night-fighter as it passed overhead. We picked it up as it turned on final approach but had to break off to the south due to heavy anti-aircraft fire. Fortunately for us the pilot switched on his landing lights. We attacked in a shallow dive and fired a burst of cannon and machine guns. As it exploded and caught fire we recognized it as a Me 110. We were subjected to a barrage of AA fire from the north side of the airfield and we turned sharply to the left to avoid this wall of fire but Russ was reefing so hard on the elevator we did a high-speed stall just as we almost turned 180 degrees. We exited to the west of the field still carrying two bombs under the wings and by the time we reached Holmsley South our fuel reserves were getting low. It was a memorable first trip.'

On 15/16 June another inspired Mosquito pairing, S/L F.S. 'Gon' Gonsalves and F/L Basil Duckett of 85 Squadron were on patrol over Belgium. They made a wide orbit of St. Trond airfield and picked up a contact. Closing to 200 ft and right below they recognized it as a Bf 110 with long-range tanks. Gonsalves dropped back to 600 ft and fired a one-second burst, which produced a strike on the back of the fuselage. He closed in to 400 ft and gave a further burst, which blew up the starboard engine then broke to starboard to avoid the debris flying back. From 3500 ft both men watched the enemy aircraft going down in a starboard turn until finally it hit the ground and blew up in the dispersal area east of the airfield. Resuming their patrol Duckett again reported a contact head-on at one-mile range and Gonsalves closed in to recognize another Bf 110 with long-range tanks at 4000 ft. He fired a short burst with no results and then closed in but he was too fast and he found himself flying in formation with the Messerschmitt 100 yards away on their port side. Gonsalves turned to port and gave a good long burst and scored strikes near the port engine but there was no fire. He pulled up to have another look but visual was lost and contact could not be regained so Gonsalves concluded that he must have gone down.[114]

The following night, 16/17 June, 405 aircraft of Bomber Command began a new campaign aginst V-1 flying-bomb launching sites in the Pas de Calais with raids on four targets accurately marked by Oboe Mosquitoes. A Ju 88, which crashed in the Pas de Cancale was possibly shot down by F/O Andy Miller DFC and F/O Freddie Bone of 169 Squadron.[115] Another bomber force comprising 321 Halifaxes, Lancasters and Mosquitoes of 1, 4, 6 and 8 Groups raided the synthetic oil plant at Sterkrade/Holten. No aircraft were lost on the raids in Northern France but 31 RAF aircraft were missing from the operation to Sterkrade/Holten though Tame Boar Nachtjagd claimed 37 kills. The route of the bomber stream passed near a German night-fighter beacon at Bocholt just 30 miles from Sterkrade and the *Jägerleitoffizier* (JLO, or GCI-controller) had chosen this beacon as the holding point for his night fighters. Fifteen crews of II./NJG 1 took off from Deelen and returned with seven victories without loss. These included two Viermot kills in the Venlo-Arnhem area by *Oblt* Johannes Hager, *St.Kpt* of the 6th *Staffel.* Twenty-two of the bombers that were missing were Halifaxes including seven out of 23 depatched by 77 Squadron from Full Sutton near York.

On 17/18 June 54 Mosquitoes were on *Serrate, Intruder* and *Diver* patrols and their patrols over Holland produced results for two 100 Group crews. Near Eindhoven F/L Geoffrey E. Poulton and F/O Arthur John Neville of 239 Squadron came across Ju 88s orbiting a beacon and fired at two of them. One was claimed destroyed after it plunged earthwards on fire[116] and the second, which went down with one engine on fire and fairly soon went out was claimed as 'damaged'. When F/O Philip Stanley Kendall DFC and F/L C.R. Hill DFC of 85 Squadron reached their patrol area at Soesterberg airfield it was not lit so they proceeded to Deelen, where similar conditions prevailed. They returned to Soesterberg and this time lights were seen and an aircraft with navigation lights on was landing. A red Verey light was fired from the ground and almost immediately another aircraft put on its navigation lights and began flying round again. Kendall gave chase, putting down wheels and flaps to reduce speed and at 140 IAS intercepted the aircraft at 700 ft, just as it was turning onto the flarepath to attempt to land again. He fired two bursts, one second and two seconds, with half-ring deflection, at 150 yards range closing to 100 yards. Strikes were seen on the wing and in the fuselage abnd the aircraft caught fire, climbed to 1500 ft, still burning navigation lights and then dived vertically and exploded on the ground 200 yards short of the end of the runway. Kendall broke away, retracted the undercarriage and flaps and climbed to 3000 ft and took cine shots from approximately three miles range of the aircraft burning on the ground. The Mosquito continued its patrol near Soesterberg but nothing else was found and the crew set course for base and laned at 0243 hours.[117]

During a *Day Ranger*[118] to northern Holland and the Friesians in a Mosquito FBVI on 21 June S/L Paul Wattling Rabone DFC and F/O Frederick C.H. Johns of 515 Squadron destroyed a Bf 110G-4 of 8./NJG 1, which had just taken off from Eelde airfield.[119] Rabone and Johns approached from astern and promptly attacked with a 3 1/2-second burst of cannon. No strikes were observed, so Rabone fired again. This time the two-second burst hit the starboard engine and pieces flew off before it crashed on the northern side of Eelde airfield. Later, Rabone wrote graphically:

> 'Before the Hun got his breath back a delightful third burst of cannon was presented at 50 yards range at a height or about 100 ft. This created havoc – the Me 110's starboard wing and starboard engine burst into flames, the port engine belched forth black smoke and the enemy aircraft dived into the ground enveloped in a mass of flames, smoke and destruction. Mosquito landed at Little Snoring at 1630 hrs after a most enjoyable afternoon's sport.'[120]

That night, 21/22 June, 133 Lancasters and six Mosquitoes headed for the synthetic oil plant at Wesseling, a town nine miles south of Cologne and 123 Lancasters and nine Mosquitoes of 1, 5 and 8 Groups set out for another synthetic oil plant, at Scholven/Buer. Clear weather conditions were forecast for both target areas, which were to be bombed simulatenously and it was planned to use the low-level marking method but both targets were covered by 10/10ths cloud so at Wesseling H2S was used and at Scholven/Buer Pathfinder aircraft provided Oboe-based sky-marking instead. Eight Lancasters of the Scholven/Buer were shot down and while this was bad enough for the squadrons concerned, the Wesseling force lost 37 aircraft (27.8 per cent of the force) all of which, falling victim to an effective Tame Boar operation. I./NJG 1 was credited with 16 kills that were claimed by eight Owl crews and II./NJG 1 received credit for six victories. Three squadrons (44, 49 and 619) each lost six Lancasters and there were individual losses too. F/L Ron Walker DFC and his very experienced crew of 83 (Pathfinder) Squadron had lifted off from Coningsby's long runway in Lincolnshire at 2318 hrs in Lancaster OL-V (ND551). Their 45th operational flight proved relatively uneventful until they reached Eindhoven when they were attacked by *Hptm* Heinz-Wolfgang Schnaufer, *Kommandeur* of IV./NJG 1. Schnaufer's cannon shells ripped into the Lancaster that was still loaded with bombs and the bomber exploded. ND551 had become the *Nachtjagd Experte's* 81st confirmed victim. Walker was blown from the bomber and though unconscious he miraculously survived with only a bruised leg and back. Walker's crew died in the aircraft and were buried in the Cemetery at Woensel near Eindhoven. Walker was quickly helped by Dutch Resistance workers and after a series of adventures and hair-raising escapes evading German troops he reached the home of a very brave woman, Jacoba Pulskens in Tilburg on 8 July. With two shot down navigators Roy Carter RCAF and Jack Knott RAAF they awaited their next move across the Belgian border to safety but six members of the *Gestapo* burst into the house and in a flurry of shots the three aircrew were killed. Jacoba Pulskens was arrested and after much suffering at the hands of the Germans was put to death in the gas chamber in February 1945. (In June 1946 the Germans responsible for the shooting were put on trial in Essen and four sentenced to death).

On 23/24 June 390 heavies and 22 Mosquitoes of 3, 4, 6 and 8 Groups carried out attacks on four V-1 sites in the Pas de Calais Area and 203 Lancasters and four Mosquitoes of 1 and 5 Groups set out for rail yards at Limoges and Saintes. F/L R.G. Wharton, rear gunner in *F for Freddie,* a 7 Squadron, 8 (PFF) Group Lancaster at Oakington flown by F/L Brian Prow, whose target was the V-1 site at L'Hey on the edge of a forest not many miles inland, recalls:

> 'Prow had recently been promoted Master Bomber in the PathFinder Force (a highly prized position) the members of which were chosen carefully and had to pass stringent tests before being accepted by D.C.T. Bennett (soon to be AVM Bennett, a legend in the RAF). Our crew had been granted the honor of leading the attack on the L'Hey site and we carried special multi-colored bombs, which on exploding marked the target with the chosen color of the day. The color was not disclosed to crews until just before take off in order to ensure that the enemy did not have the opportunity of duplicating the color before the main attack began or during it. 'Jerry' quite frequently did just that, much to our discomfort, for that meant we had to go in once again to re-mark. It also meant that the following bomber force was torn between the choice of two targets; ours and Jerry's and his were always well away from the real target. Brian did not disguise the fact that he intended this trip to be a success. With all preliminaries duly completed we took off at 0030 hrs and headed for the target. The outward flight was uneventful. Only sporadic anti-aircraft fire was directed at us as we crossed the French coast and soon we were approaching our target. We found the site very well camouflaged but as we had special equipment, coupled with radar co-

ordinates, which gave our navigator pinpoint accuracy, we quickly found our marking point and dropped our markers. On this occasion the Main Force bombers arrived precisely on time and began their bombing. A couple of aircraft passed over our marker when suddenly there was an almighty 'Bang' followed by a display of pyrotechnics that was a joy to behold. At least it was to us for that told us that the raid had been successful. The whole scene convinced us that a fuel dump or maybe an ammunition dump had been hit for shell-bursts were taking place hundreds of feet in the air and in all directions.

'The successive explosions were rocking us at 5000 ft, providing everyone with a grandstand view until Brian's voice came over the intercom, 'There is a Lancaster being attacked by a Junkers 88' and he ordered our bomb aimer in the front turret to open fire on the attacker. After a short burst from his two Brownings everything went quiet and the bomb aimer reported a stoppage, whereupon Brian maneuvered the plane to enable the mid-upper turret and me to fire at the attacker. The mid-upper gunner had chosen that moment to visit the Elsan so it was left to me to deal with the situation. The rear turret was fitted with four Brownings, which were capable of firing 1000 rounds per minute from each gun; a *very* formidable hail of bullets to encounter. Immediately I got the enemy aircraft in my sights I opened fire with a five-second-burst and that was sufficient. I hit the Junkers on the starboard engine. He went down steeply and exploded just before he entered the clouds.

'There was a certain amount of excitement, which I think contributed to a lapse in concentration so necessary to maintain at all times, particularly over enemy territory and we failed to spot another Me 210 positioning for an attack. As he straightened up I called the mid-upper gunner and told him to open fire. Our combined firepower proved too much for him and he broke off the engagement. We learnt later that we had scored hits and he had force-landed in a field near some Resistance fighters who at the first opportunity set his plane on fire. We had hardly regained our breath however, when suddenly we were hit. The starboard tailplane received a large hole and the line of fire continued up the fuselage tearing an even larger hole in the mainplane. In fact it shot a petrol tank in the wing clear out; just one gaping hole. As the aircraft broke away to position itself for another attack I recognized it as a Me 210 and it was equipped with the fixed angled firing cannon on the top of the fuselage. The pilot could position himself well under his target and adjust to the direction and speed of its prey, then drift slowly upward and slightly astern to make his attack. This was no time for aircraft recognition and I lost no time opening fire on the attacker. I was lucky for I definitely scored hits. The tracer bullets that I used were obviously hitting him for there were no ricochets and my bullets were not going past him. Soon I had verification for he suddenly dived through the clouds and we observed a brilliant and widespread flash of light from the ground.

'Brian was by now wrestling with the controls, attempting to keep the Lancaster flying and gradually he was able to steer a course for home. 'Bloodied but unbowed'. A more detailed assessment was made to the extent of the damage. To put it into the words of our flight engineer. 'A bloody great hole in the tailplane with attendant damage to the tail-fin, part shrapnel holes in the fuselage all the way from the rear turret to the main wing member and another bloody great hole in the starboard wing that you could drop a bloody piano through. Other than that, I cannot possibly see why we are still flying.' 'I dared not tell him that there was nowhere to rest my feet for there was nothing but a gaping hole when I looked down. Also, my guns were useless for the hydraulics had been shot away. I reckoned that Brian had enough on his mind concentrating on getting home. He asked for a course for Woodbridge, a recognized emergency-landing site and called for silence on the intercom to allow him to nurse our faithful *F for Freddie* home. Lurching, swaying, crabbing but always fighting to reach home we at last crossed the English coastline practically in line for landing at Woodbridge but on asking permission to land we were told to identify ourselves before they would switch the flarepath on. Brian was livid but we had to obey regulations and fire flares, which were the color of the day, We landed not knowing whether our wheels had locked, and the flight engineer fired all six of the remaining flare cartridges over the airfield. We gently rolled to a stop. A second or two later *F for Freddie* tilted slowly to starboard and the wing settled down on the grass, then slowly the port wing dropped too. I swear I heard a sound very similar to a sigh, as if to say, 'Well I managed it lads. I got you home'. I manually wound the rear turret to astern, opened the two small doors to evacuate the turret and then I placed my head in my clasped hands, resting on the sight, relaxed and said a little prayer.'[121]

On 24 June 321 aircraft including 200 Halifaxes and 106 Lancasters of 1, 4 6 and 8 Groups attacked three V-1 sites in the clear over the Pas de Calais without loss. Sixteen Lancasters and two Mosquitoes of 617 Squadron bombed the flying-bomb site at Wizernes with their *Tallboy* bombs the Dam Busters losing one one Lancaster. That night 739 aircraft including

535 Lancasters of all groups attacked seven V-1 sites. It was a clear, moonlit night and 22 Lancasters were lost, mostly to nightfighters. A 139 Squadron Mosquito XX, one of 27 that went to Berlin, was shot down 30 km NW of the 'Big City' by *Lt* Ernst-Ewald Hittler of 3./NJG 1 for his fifth and final victory.[122] Next day 323 aircraft of 1, 4, 6 and 8 Groups pounded three more V-1 sites for the loss of two Halifaxes that bombed a flying-bomb site at Montorgueil. V-1 sites were very difficult to hit and W/C Leonard Cheshire, the CO of 617 Squadron, who always tried to increase bombing accuracy, accompanied 17 Lancasters and two Mosquitoes to the Siracourt flying-bomb store in a P-51 with thepurpose of using it as a low level marker aircraft. What is remarkable is that the Mustang had only arrived that same afternoon courtesy of the U.S. Eighth Air Force and this was Cheshire's first flight in it! His Lancasters scored three direct hits on the concrete store with *Tallboy* bombs and Cheshire landed safely back at Woodhall Spa in the dark.

On 24/25 June F/L Denis Welfare DFC* and F/O Taffy Bellis DFC* of 239 Squadron destroyed a Ju 88 near Paris. they shot down a Me 410 east of the French capital two nights later when 100 Group *Serrate* Squadrons supported 1049 bombers in attacks on V-1 sites and other targets in northern France. In all Mosquito crews claimed six enemy aircraft shot down on 27/28 June. F/L Donald Ridgewell 'Podge' Howard and F/O Frank A.W. 'Sticky' Clay of 239 Squadron destroyed a Ju 88 near Brussels where a Fw 190 was also destroyed by their CO W/C Paul M.J. Evans and navigator F/O R.H. 'Dickie' Perks DFC. Near the French side of the Channel they picked up an IFF contact which turned out to be a Fw 190. Evans shot it down from behind but it exploded covering the Mosquito with burning petrol, which burnt off most of the doped control surfaces and made the aircraft difficult to control. Evans made a very fast landing at Manston after numerous trials at height to determine at what speed he would lose control. Two 141 Squadron crews FTR to West Raynham. F/L Herbert R. Hampshire and W/O Alan A.W. Melrose, who were on their last operation, were shot down in Belgium by *Oblt* Heinz Ferger of 3./NJG 3 7 km SE of Roeselare (Roulers) for his 18th *Abschuss*. Both men were killed, their NFII crashing at Izegem. F/L P.S. 'Paddy' Engelbach and F/O Ronald S. Mallett DFC meanwhile had patrolled north Holland for an hour and Mallett could tell that they were being picked up by a German night-fighter. Near Weert in Limburg their pursuer shot the tail off their Mosquito NFII killing Mallet. Engelbach was thrown through the canopy by the explosion and he survived.[123] S/L Graham J. Rice and F/O Jimmie G. Rogerson of 141 Squadron destroyed a Ju 88 in the Cambrai area for their third victory while W/Os Harry 'Butch' Welham and 'Gus' Hollis tracked and hunted an AI contact five miles north of Eindhoven. Their Mosquito[124] was the same aircraft they had used to shoot down their first enemy aircraft on 14/15 June when a Me 410 had fallen to the NFII's guns. Clearly painted in large white letters on the pilot's side of the Mosquito's nose was the double entendre '*SHYTOT*'. Welham reduced height to 14,000 ft and closed in on the contact. He recalls:

> 'A Ju 88 appeared dead ahead, slightly above but we looked as if we were going to overshoot. Gus came on the intercom and in his lilting Welsh accent said, 'Throttle back, pull the nose up butch.' His nose was in his set, keeping track of the fir-tree-shaped blip on the Serrate scope. 'Left, left, right, right,' he ordered. 'Thirty degrees above. Dead ahead, 2000 ft.' I steered to the ideal spot, 400 yards behind (the four 20-mm Hispanos were synchronized for 400 yards). I lined him up through the circular gunsight, my right thumb ready to press the firing button on top of the stick and aimed between the cockpit and engine. Gus said clearly, 'Go on, shoot!' I said, 'OK,' and I let fly a two-second burst. As the cannons fired beneath our feet the seats vibrated and dust flew up from the floor all around the cockpit. A fire started in the engine and the wing and the kite went down in a spiral burning all the while, exploding on the ground about six miles south of Tilburg.'[125]

P/O C.W. Chown and F/Sgt D.G.N. Veitch of 515 Squadron meanwhile, had set off from Little Snoring to patrol Gilze-Volkel-Venlo-Eindhoven. For three-quarters of an hour they bombed Venlo airfield and created a substantial fire emitting flashes for 15 minutes before returning to Eindhoven for a second look. There was no cloud, visibility was 'good' and the airfield had its north-south flarepath well lit. On their approach four red cartridges were fired from another aircraft and three of the airfield identification bars at the southern end almost immediately were switched off and a single red cartridge was fired from the ground. Chown gave chase at 1500 ft and spotted the outline of an aircraft with a green bow light and red downward identification light under the tail. He closed to 200 yards and recognized it as a Ju 88[126] Chown delivered a stern attack with a two-second-burst of cannon fire, which recorded one strike on the Junker's fuselage. The Mosquito pilot closed to 150 yards and he delivered a second stern attack with a three second burst. The Ju 88 immediately exploded and scattered debris through the sky as it disintegrated before crashing into a house, killing three children. Chown and Veitch orbited the scene and took photos of the burning enemy bomber before breaking away and returning home

On 28/29 June 230 bombers hit the railway yards at Blainville and Metz for the loss of 18 Halifaxes and two

Lancasters (or 8.7 per cent of the force)[127] while 33 Mosquitoes of the LNSF[128] went to Saarbrücken and another ten were despatched to drop 4000 lb 'Cookies' from 32,000 ft on the Scholven/Buer oil plant in the Ruhr. All the Mosquitoes returned without loss but F/L David 'Russ' Russell and his navigator F/O 'Barks' Barker of 109 Squadron, who had completed a tour on Stirlings and who were on their third Mosquito trip[129] had a close shave after dropping their 'Cookie', as Russell recalls:

'Heading for home at 30,000 ft it was clear and with bright moonlight. At almost one o'clock near Venlo on the German/Dutch border we were feeling relaxed and were trimmed for a gradual fast descent with an hour or so return to base. Suddenly and without warning lines of orange colored 'blobs' flashed past underneath, then gracefully and lazily fell away in the distance – quite fascinating. Shocked, we felt the dull thud of shells striking the Mossie. A fighter must have closed to within a hundred yards or so and attacked from below and dead astern. We must have been the perfect target, silhouetted against the light. Shells crashed between us, cold fluid from the compass got into my boots and poor Barker kicked his legs in the air. I opened up to full power and went into a tearing, climbing turn to starboard toward the attack but with the Mossie shuddering it became more of a sluggish stall turn. Looking around for some cover I could see a few wisps of cloud below us but they were so sparse that the moon shone through in a watery way. After a few more violent turns and looking around hopelessly for any sign of our attacker, who must have overshot, I levelled out hoping that we had shaken him off but the thud and clatter of shell strikes began again. This time our attacker seemed closer. He really 'caned' us. I responded like a scalded cat, turning toward him with full power and varying my height at the same time. After what seemed an age I levelled out cautiously, weaved and looked around, wondering if our tormentor was standing off to have another go. I was frustrated at not being able to make out any sign of him. We were still at about 23,000 ft and speed was now of the essence so I stuck the nose down and scarpered at about 400 or so. Either he had run out of ammunition or thought we had 'had it' and left us to our fate.

'I reduced speed and we assessed our damage. The radio and compass and the gyro were out of action and the port engine felt a little rough. There was the possibly that our fuel tanks were damaged but all the gauges seemed normal and all aircraft controls appeared OK. The intercom was still functioning. No physical damage to either of us but our real annoyance was, 'Why us?' I tried in vain to feather the port propeller so I decided to use the power for as long as possible. A windmilling or dead propeller may well have been the worst choice, particularly in view of the distance to cover. We set course for Woodbridge and hoped that the weather had improved. A feeling of calm after the storm now set in and with it reaction to the exertion of sheer survival against an unseen enemy. Poor Barks; he had just had to sit there hoping and I'd like to think, trusting in me! The adrenaline uplift and feeling of elation and achievement in beating the odds loosened our tongues on the return home.

'Crossing the Dutch coast at about 20,000 ft we received a farewell gesture of light Flak, the tracer rising slowly and then increasing in speed as it neared us before falling away. I reduced power slightly to ease the loading on the port engine and we had a good look around. Weather conditions and visibility were good with 3-4/10ths broken cloud to the South but complete cloud cover was forecast at base. I decided therefore to head for Manston airfield in Kent, which like Woodbridge had three very long runways and grass undershoot and overshoot areas for emergencies such as ours. With some relief we made a straight-in approach in a gentle descent but at 16,000 ft flames started in the port engine cowling. Again feathering proved useless so I cut the fuel and the ignition off, reduced the revs and activated the fire extinguisher, all to no avail. Ditching was a possibility and so the roof panel was jettisoned but without radio and my own firm reluctance, I assured Barks that ditching was the last thing I intended. I was confident we would make the airfield and we could always bale out over land but the fire appeared to be gaining and spreading back over the wing and the inner wing tanks and control was beginning to fall off with a tendency to increase the rate of descent. Not trusting the hydraulics and with no flaps I advised Barker that we would land wheels-up to give us a better chance of getting out through the roof and away more quickly. At about 2000 ft I told him to fire off the colors of the day. Despite a marked increase in roughness on the closed down port engine I felt confident of hitting the threshold. At around 1000 ft and having crossed the coast we could see rooftops below from the glare of our burning aircraft. Final approach was made at about 500 ft with elevator control virtually non-existent and maximum trim. It was with an almost casual feeling of anti-climax that we glided, or fell the remaining few feet at about 160/170.

'We must have touched down on the grass undershoot area. Skidding and bumping along, our speed carried us to the threshold of the tarmac runway where the Mossie stopped suddenly, broke up and jack-knifed with the tail end of the fuselage folding forward, the tail-plane ending up against the trailing edge of the mainplane. Although my straps were secure they were not locked and I pitched forward, pranging my forehead on the screen frame. We appeared to be engulfed in fire and Barks left through the roof hatch. Dazed and my left foot jammed by the rudder, I thought about my new escape boots and was determined not to leave without them. Eventually I freed my foot and I clambered through the roof onto the starboard wing. It was hot and surrounded by glaring fire. I turned and escaped through a gap between the nose and the starboard engine. Jumping off the wing into darkness as the fire and ambulance crews ran toward me, all I could see behind was the huge bonfire of the poor old Mossie.'[130]

On 30 June/1 July S/L Paul Rabone DFC and F/O F.C.H. Johns of 515 Squadron destroyed a He 111 and a Ju W34 at Jagel and Schleswig to take Rabone's score to nine confirmed victories.[131] F/L D.J. Raby DFC and F/Sgt S.J. Flint DFM of 239 Squadron in a Mosquito FBVI destroyed a Ju 88 over France. They stalked the Junkers and were fired at by the enemy air gunner but his tracer passed harmlessly over the top of the Mosquito, Raby fired a two-second burst from 450 ft and saw strikes all along the port fuselage and wing and the port engine burst into flames. He pumped another two-second burst into the doomed Junkers, which exploded, scattering debris into the path of the charging Mosquito. As it fell vertically to earth Raby continued to pepper the machine, finally breaking away just before another explosion tore the wings off the night fighter. It crashed south east of Dieppe in a massive explosion.[132]

On 4/5 July W/O R.E. Preston and Sgt F. Verity of 515 Squadron took off on a *Night Ranger*[133] *to* Coulommiers airfield via Southwold and North Beveland. They reached the enemy night-fighter base at 0205 hrs but the base was inactive so they stooged around for three-quarters of an hour before returning. This time their approach signalled the double flarepath to be lit. Obviously, the base anticipated that one of its fighters was returning. Preston reduced height to 1000 ft. Verity obtained a visual sighting of the enemy aircraft at 300-400 yards range. It was a Ju 88 and it was on a southerly course at about their height. Preston gave chase but the Junkers started weaving before turning starboard and diving. Undeterred, Preston followed. As the Ju 88 pulled out of its dive at treetop height, it appeared right in his sights and Preston gave it a three-second-burst of cannon at 200 yards. It set the Ju 88's starboard engine on fire and the aircraft instantly disintegrated, scattering burning debris into the air like an exploding firework. Preston circled the scene before bombing the airfield with two 500-lb GP bombs, which exploded in the south side of the airfield. There was no opposition and only four inefficient searchlights vainly probed the cloudy sky. Not satisfied with their night's work, Preston and Verity attacked two small freighters moored side by side in the Zuid Beveland Canal at the Westerschelde lock gates with a three-second-burst of cannon fire. Strikes were seen on the how of one of the ships.

On 5/6 July four Mosquito FBVIs of 23 Squadron flew the first Squadron *Intruder* operation from Little Snoring since returning from the Mediterranean with sorties against enemy airfields. F/O P.G. Bailey and F/O J.O. Murphy of 169 Squadron destroyed a Ju 88 while a Bf 110G-4 crashed near Compiègne.[134] On 7/8 July S/L Graham J. Rice and F/O Jimmie G. Rogerson of 141 Squadron in a Mosquito NFII took off from West Raynham at 2317 hrs on a *Serrate* patrol in support of Bomber Command attacks on St. Lou D'Esserent and Vaires. They crossed the enemy coast between Calais and Dunkirk and about 20 miles south of Abbeville at 15,000 ft Rogerson picked up an AI contact dead ahead and slightly below. Rice turned hard port and the contact passed overhead, when a visual was obtained on very bright exhausts. At 1000-ft range the contact was identified as a twin engined aircraft travelling at high speed and Rice followed at full throttle but after about three minutes the contact disappeared in interference and could not be recognized. It was thought that the contact was probably a Me 410. Rice turned back on track and five minutes later an AI contact was obtained dead ahead and below at about eight miles NW of Amiens at 10,000ft. The contact was allowed to come in to 4000-ft range and Rice went into a hard turn through 180° as Rogerson obtained contact dead ahead and still below at 8000-ft range. It was weaving gently and made two hard turns of 90° to starboard with Rice following hard and losing height to come in from below. After about ten minute's chase a visual was obtained at 2000-ft range at 10,000-ft and Rice closing in quickly to 600 ft could make out an aircraft with twin fins and exhausts peculiar to a Bf 110.[135] At this moment the German pilot apparently became aware of the presence of the Mosquito and made a hard turn to starboard. Rice gave 1 1/2 ring deflection and opened fire with a four second burst at 600ft range. Strikes were seen all along the top of the mainplane leading to a large explosion in the fuselage, which was quickly well on fire. The 110 turned over on its back and passed underneath the Mosquito and Rice and Rogerson followed down to 3000-ft range on AI before the blip disappeared. As Rice straightened up and orbited to look for the aircraft a terrific explosion was seen directly below them and scattered pieces floated down in flames. One large remnant hit the ground with a further explosion.[136]

The increased tempo of operations in 1944 produced great strains on RAF aircrew and those worse affected had their logbooks stamped 'LMF' (Lack of Moral Fibre) and as such were considered unfit for flying.[137] Dennis 'Lofty' Wiltshire's tour on Lancasters in 90 Squadron ended abruptly when the flight engineer cracked mentally during an operation to Cologne, probably in the first half of 1944.[138] (He does not wish to mention the full names of his crew, nor does he remember the exact date when he suffered the incident):

'We were part of a 300 bomber force attacking the city. As always the crew of G-George were anxious, alert and apprehensive. A Bedford 2 ton truck with drop tail-board and canvas hood took us out and with Mae Wests, 'chutes etc, we clambered aboard our aircraft and, with a little banter, took up our respective positions. I shared the flight deck with Leslie the skipper and I went through our respective pre-flight checks: Fuel cocks open (or closed) as appropriate, main engine switches 'OFF' – all the usual routine. We were given the all clear to 'START'. Each engine in turn burst into life, over-rich combustion gasses belching from the exhaust stubs. The earth seemed to tremble into life with us. It was pitch black outside. 'Maps' (Reg, the navigator) had his map table illumination 'ON'. There was very subdued light from the instrument panels. We could see the various ground crew struggling to pull away the 'trolley accs' (starting battery trolleys). Leslie opened the throttle of each engine in turn. He looked at me. I looked at him:'RPM, thumbs up, radiator shutters 'OPEN' oil pressure steady, thumbs up and so through the whole pre-take off procedure, the ASI, the artificial horizon levelled up from its drunken position. There was an ever-present odour in the kite from 100 octane fuel, new rubber, exhaust gasses and hot engine oil as well as the constant shaking, shuddering and engines roaring. A quick check of the boost gauges. Had the pitot head cover been removed? Damned if I could see. The NCO i/c ground crew thrust the Form 700 at the pilot to sign.

'The green Aldis light went on for G-George. Leslie eased the throttles forward and set the elevator trim tabs. Stick forward, stick backward, left foot forward, right foot forward and a rap on the compass glass. My eyes flitted from gauge to gauge: boost pressure gauges, fuel gauges, oil temperature gauges, oil pressure gauges, air pressure, hydraulic pressure. The gyros were spinning. All was now alive on G-George, which shuddered and rattled as if it would fall to pieces. A wave from the pilot signalled 'chocks away' to the ground crew outside. Les glanced at me and gave a wink amd a thumbs up. I returned a thumbs up and the skipper released the brakes. The throttles were gradually opened and the propeller pitch controls were at their selected positions. Leslie and I cast a steady glance over the instrument panels and the Lancaster rolled forward. Three of the squadron were already airborne and now we had left dispersal and were at the end of the runway ready for take-off. Again the green Aldis lamp for G-George, mutterings on the R/T and then the crescendo of our four Merlin engines deafening all other sounds as the skipper selected through the gate for 'Take-off' on all four throttle levers. Leslie concentrated on his take-off procedures. Flaps were set and the propeller blades slapped at the cold night air as I firmly held the throttle levers at 'Take-off' position. 'Flaps set – wheels up.' I repeated each command in turn to the pilot. Each instrument danced to its respective tune: RPM, boost pressure, altimeter, compass – red lights went out, green lights came on. We were airborne, all 65,000 lbs of us including a little over 2150 gallons of 100 Octane fuel and four 5000 lb bombs. The fact that we were airborne in itself brought sighs of relief!

'The squadron headed for the coast to position ourselves with our contemporaries ready for the onslaught ahead of us. We had 'grouped up' and after a long incident free journey we were nearing our target area. It is was a dark night. No moon and a little broken cloud at 1000 ft below. R/T silence was being maintained with only our own aircraft R/T intercom 'ON'. Almost simultaneously Tom ('Piper') the mid-upper gunner and Les the pilot said, 'Pathfinders ahead'.

'I looked forward and saw a pale orange glow in the sky. Nick, the rear gunner ('Tail-end Charlie') and Tom had fired off a few rounds previously to ensure satisfactory operation of the guns. We each in turn – Jim (bomb aimer, 'Bomber'), Fred (wireless operator, 'Nosy') and Dennis (flight engineer, 'Lofty') now confirmed our readiness for action and positioned ourselves accordingly. At this stage of the proceedings my stomach was in knots. I felt terribly sick, long to be going home to base and found extreme difficulty in repeating 'The Lord's Prayer' to myself. The orange glow ahead had now turned red. Our Pathfinders had done a wonderful job, as always and the target was well illuminated. The glow now pin-pointed other aircraft flying with us, aircraft which we knew were there but had been unable to see because of the darkness.

'There was a sudden burst of gunfire from the rear guns. 'Bloody Hell!' 'Sorry Skip', I thought I saw a fighter.'

'Dont' think, look! You'll have one of ours down in a minute.'

'We moved ever nearer the target zone; the red glow changed in color as the first Lancs in dropped their green flares to keep the target illuminated. I could see the flashes as the first 5000 pounders fell in the target zone. Now things were livening up; searchlights were beginning to pierce the darkness; flash bolts were being hurled into the sly to illuminate our presence. The navigator, in a calm steady voice called, 'Three minutes to ETA', followed almost immediately by the bomb aimer, 'Keep her as she is skip', I have greens and reds straight ahead.'

'We were now feeling the blast effect from the ack-ack shells. We were all at our respective tasks: the bomb aimer at his window, the navigator at his charts, complete with his shaded light and curtains drawn. The skipper and myself were in almost total darkness apart from the occasional flash of moving searchlights. Les had his eyes fixed out to port, mine to starboard. Necessary adjustments were executed after sign language to each other. The pilot made various left and right deviations to our set course, as both searchlights and ack-ack shells became more numerous.

'Bomb doors open', came the bomb aimer's call and the whole aircraft seemed to want to fall apart as the skipper operated the bomb doors lever with his left hand. I was feeling pretty awful now. I always felt sick over the target but this time I was in a cold sweat and felt very light-headed. The skipper almost screamed at the bomb aimer.

'For Christ's sake, Jim, hurry up. What in God's name are you doing?'

'There was a very pregnant pause, then a voice so calm and collected that I wanted to scream. Jim, the bomb aimer, said, 'Left, Left, Left, right a little, steady! Bombs gone!'

'The aircraft seemed to take-off for a second time as the weight of the bombs was released. All of us looked in every possible direction outside the aircraft for fear of collision with another of the 300 aircraft out there in the dark. The bomb doors closed and the skipper made a steep turn for home but we were now in the thick of a heavily defended area. The blast of shells rocked us continuously and tracer shells, bomb bursts and screaming shells were everywhere. 5000 pounders burst below us. It was Dante's Inferno! I was frozen in my seat. The skipper completed his turn for the home run. This in itself was a major operation. The pilot was flying almost blind and was negotiating a maneuver with several dozen other aircraft making the same move. Something crashed through the perspex window behind me. It streamed past my head, buried itself in the cockpit floor and there was a sickly smell of burning and phosphorous. I released my harness, leapt from my seat and stamped and stamped on the object, finally using the cockpit fire extinguisher on it. The bomb aimer had, at this stage, been unable to leave his station due to the turn we were negotiating and various other maneuvers. He suddenly screamed, 'Fire!! For God's sake my suit's on fire!' Like anyone else in such a predicament in a confined space, he kicked and scrambled to get away from his window and then quite suddenly he crumpled up and was perfectly still.

'There was suddenly an horrendous, blinding flash. The whole aircraft shook as if it was a fish in its final thrash of life. Something had passed clean through our forward perspex nose window, taking parts of the bomb aimer's equipment. I thought of all those famous last words, 'Keep calm, Don't panic.' I wondered if the person who couched those words had ever been in such a position. I tried to struggle into the bomb aimer's station. The pressure from the ice cold blast now entering the nose section was immense. I put on my oxygen mask, not for oxygen but to help me to some state of normal breathing. The wind tore at my Irvin jacket. Debris was everywhere. Odd bits and pieces tore at my face. This was an impossible task. 'Skipper. I am on the R/T. 'This is bloody hopeless! I can't even stand up.'

'There was another explosive crash somewhere aft in G-George. 'How is Jim?'

'I can't get near him but I think he's had it, Skip. He's bleeding from ears, nose and mouth.'

'With the added assistance from the unbelievable force of the wind coming through the damaged nose, I returned to the cockpit to find chaos reigning supreme. The skipper was as calm as always. He was a wonderful guy. There was glass, oil and various liquids everywhere. Several of the pilot's instruments were U/S but he just sat there as calm and collected as is humanely possible under the circumstances. For a moment our eyes met. Were we both thinking alike? Then one eye winked. I think there was a hint of a smile, perhaps of encouragement. 'Check the fuel levels, Den. I don't know what the situation is, you tell me.'

'I don't know if we have lost any. Poor old George is like a bloody sieve at the moment, holes everywhere.'

'I hoped to God we'd got enough to get home. If we had lost any of our precious fuel, it was not much. I checked the levels of the tanks, opened the relevant bleed/transfer cocks and pumps and transfered the 100 octane fuel, as was the normal procedure. From hereon I am not truly aware of what happened. I do recall the inferno below us at the target area. I remember a Lanc', minus tail end, with all four engines on fire, hurtling to earth. From then on my mind was a blank. I was told many months later that I released the harness I had been wearing at my station, pulled off my helmet and started to walk aft. Apparently I was quite oblivious to frantic calls and abusive screams to sit down and I apparently failed to utter even one word or sound. I also failed to negotiate the main spar, which protrudes upward from the deck of the aircraft and fell to the deck remaining motionless. The navigator had apparently left his station to assist me but finding no visible wounds or blood and being unable to obtain any word from me, returned to his table and charts to plot the homeward journey. On landing it was confirmed that Jim was dead and I was taken from the kite by ambulance, which had been forwarned of our arrival by Les, our skipper and I was taken to station sick quarters. With de-briefing, breakfast, etc., etc., the other lads in the crew lost touch with my treatment. After all, a mission such as we had endured, plus de-briefing, breakfast and a good sleep, they each had their own problems. All the lads came to pay their respects but regrettably I was never aware of their presence. I was in station sick quarters for approximately four days. I learned eventually that I was as much a problem to the crew on their visits as I was to station medical officers. I was diagnosed as having no wounds, no broken bones and no physical disabilities but I was apparently quite content to remain in bed oblivious of anything and everything. I could not stand or sit. I ate and drank nothing. I did not seem to understand any sproken word and, despite attempts by all medical staff, nothing would register in my mind. A civilian consultant psychiatrist from a nearby hospital was requested to attend the station sick bay. I only learned of this many months later, either by letters from my colleagues or from third or fourth hand word of mouth.

'I was taken to an RAF pyschiatric hospital at Matlock in Derbyshire (known to in-patients as 'Hatter's Castle', after the Mad Hatter in Alice's Adveventures in Wonderland)[139] where air-crew types there were referred to by our RAF colleagues as 'A right load of nutters'! For many weeks my life was just a blank. A nurse accidentally knocked a steel dish of medical instruments from a trolley on to the floor and it seems I sprang to my feet, fell flat on the floor, because of my weak state and screamed, 'There's another poor sod going down, let's get the hell out of here. Look at the flares, look at the flares, shoot the Bastard down, they're coming closer, for God's sake shoot the Bastard down!' I then collapsed. I recall coming round. I was in bed with wonderful snow white sheets and beautiful soft white pillows. A nurse was seated at my bedside in a beautiful crisp, blue and white uniform. 'Doctor! Doctor! He's awake, please, doctor.' It was presumably the doctor who spoke to me. He was in white but his shoulders bore epaulettes bearing 'Air' rank.

'Well, laddie and how are we today?'

'A little bit confused, sir. No, very confused, hungry and feeling very weak thank you, sir.'

'There followed a series of questions, from which I did not make an awful lot of sense. Instruments were inserted in my ears; instruments were put up my nose. He peered into my eyes from all angles, rubber mallets struck me here and there! For several weeks I was subjected to the most unbelievable set of tests. I do not recall all the details though I do recall 'ECT' (Electrical Convulsive Treatment) whose letters remain with me forever. The best part of this treatment was a super cup of strong tea 15 minutes after completion. The effects are not a suitable subject for print. In late 1944, still a patient at Matlock, my service life came to an abrupt end. I attended a RAF Discharge Medical Board and then a further medical board. I confirmed my name, rank and serial number but I had to admit that the previous years were a complete blank in my mind. I now find all this difficult to believe. There is no real end to this particular episode in my life. Even to this day the RAF remains prominent in my mind. I think of 'Skipper' and the 'boys' and of 'Hatter's Castle' with its abundance of broken lives.'

Meanwhile, the war continued with a vengeance. During the prelude to the invasion of Normandy, Bomber Command was controlled by the Supreme Allied Commander and *Nachtjagd* was given a brief respite as the RAF heavies and American bombers were switched to bombing targets in France. Although the *Nachtjagd* had little reaction time to counter these shallow penetration raids, these ops were no picnic for the bomber crews as Bob Hillard of 35 Squadron PFF, who had completed 11 ops with 466 Squadron RAAF at Leconfield, seven on Wellingtons and four on Halifaxes, recalls:

'When we were posted to PFF we were feeling reasonably confident with just over a third of a 30-op tour completed. We suddenly found ourselves back behind the starting line with another 34 trips needed for a 45-op PFF tour (the trips with 466 still counted). In April 1944 when French rail targets became common, prior to D-Day, with a noticeable decline in the loss rate, our masters decreed that ops to France, Belgium and Holland only rated as a third of an op, so many totals shrunk as the new rule was retrospective. French ops didn't stay 'easy' and casualty rates sometimes equalled German targets. In July the masters relented to the extent of allocating three points for French targets and five points for Germany. A Main Force tour became 150 points and a PFF 225 and this applied for the rest of the war. In my own case it took 55 ops to reach a final tally of 228 points. A tour at the beginning of the war was 200 hours operational flying and then a 'normal' tour became 30 operations. A PFF tour was 45. At some time a normal tour was increased to 35 or 40 operations. Towards the end of the war some trips were classed as only a third of an operation.'

'Towards mid-1944,' recalls *Oblt* Dieter Schmidt, *Staffelkapitän*, 8./NJG 1:

'The final turn of the fortunes of war became apparent in the west. It was the time prior to the invasion of France, when our bases suffered increasing attacks by low-flying aircraft and bomber formations. From then on the ground personnel too suffered losses and the foxhole became a regular part of our mechanics' equipment. In mid-May the *Gruppe* was transferred back to Holland, at first with all three *Staffeln* at Leeuwarden and from mid-June with the 8th *Staffel* at our old and familiar Twente. In order to protect our aircraft from attack, these had frequently to be taken to small satellite airfields during the day, such as Eelde south of Groningen.

'The Bf 110, which we had flown since the beginning of nightfighting, was constantly being improved. In 1944, the four upper machine guns were replaced by two 3-cm cannon, the electrically fired MK 109, yet another example of the excellent guns and ammunition we used throughout the war. But the aircraft itself had become so slow and cumbersome through the fitting of extra equipment that the empty bombers, especially the Lancaster and the Halifax III were often faster than we were. In the search for a new aircraft, especially one with a greater endurance, many other nightfighting units had opted in part for the Ju 88. We also used these on occasion during the second half of 1944 but in the end we stuck to the Bf 110 until the end of the war; this applied also to the other *Gruppen* of NJG 1, apart from those which could be equipped with the specially for nightfighting conceived Heinkel 219.'

To meet the threat posed by the Allied invasion 20 day fighter *Gruppen* and one night fighter *Geschwader* were withdrawn from the defense of the *Reich*, together with 50 light *Flak* batteries and 140 heavy batteries, which included the bulk of the railway *Flak*. 3500 medium and light guns had already been moved from the *Reich* to the Channel coast. *Oblt* Dieter Schmidt, who became a *Ritterkreuzträger* on 27 July after achieving 31 night kills, recalls:

'Many crews were posted to us from disbanded Luftwaffe units and other nightfighting ones, such as *Hptm* Geismann and *Hptm* Strüning.[140] At the same time, all non-flying officers were to be transferred to Army or Luftwaffe ground units. We managed to circumvent this order by allowing them to fly as third crew members, such as our former *Gruppen* adjutant, *Lt* Scheel, who came to us from a Luftwaffe ground unit six months before.'

The deterioration of *Nachtjagd* after the Allied invasion of France was caused by various factors. 'Long' *Window* made its appearance on the invasion front and *SN2*, previously unsusceptible to *Window,* was now effectively jammed. These innovations were developed as a result of a stroke of luck in July when an inexperienced german night fighter crew in a Ju 88G-1 equipped with the *Lichtenstein* SN-2, Naxos and Flensburg landed in Suffolk.[141] Within ten days British scientists had developed 'long' Window for jamming the SN-2 radar (which previously was unsusceptible to Window) and the use of H2S was restricted, which rendered Naxos virtually useless. Finally, in an effort to counter the Flensburg homing device, all Monica radar warning sets were rapidly removed from the RAF heavies. Thus, virtually all the tools which the Tame Boars had used to their advantage during late 1943-early 1944 were gone at a stroke. It was a decisive blow from which the arm would never recover.

2nd TAF and ADGB destroyed at least 230 aircraft at night over the Channel, France, the Low Countries and Germany, June 1944-April 1945. In the run up to D-Day, 29 Squadron of the ADGB had been the first Mosquito unit equipped with the superior AI.Mk.VIII radar to be released for intruding over the Continent. Whilst still equipped with Beaufighter VIFs, the unit had had its first taste of offensive night operations in spring 1943 when it began Night Rangers over airfields in German-occupied France. After converting to the Mosquito in the summer 29 Squadron reverted to defensive operations in the ADGB, finally mounting its first Intruders over France on the night of 14 May 1944. F/O R.G. 'Bob' Stainton, a 34-year old navigator in 29 Squadron at Hunsdon has vivid memories of a narrow escape he and his pilot F/L George E. Allison had during a Night Intruder on the night of 5/6 July 1944 in Mosquito NFXIII MM553:

'We night-prowlers liked the 'blanket of the dark' better than any romantic moonlight and this night we were to visit the Coulommiers district again – Bretigny, Melun, Orly. There was a full moon. It was like daylight, as it had been on the night of the Nuremburg raid. The moon shone on French villages, woods and roads a thousand feet below us; for we had decided that at this height a 'cat's eye' Fw 190 had less chance of spotting us, although light Flak had more and we were still not low enough to escape German radar detection. No aerodromes seemed to be lit – ominous inactivity amid the luminous tones of a countryside so peaceful and still. The Seine was a bent silver ribbon but we saw one aerial beacon flashing. This was awkward, as was the fact that Bill Provan[142] had already been a nuisance, shooting at trains and stirring up wasp nests. It was our choice of height, however, that directly led to trouble. We failed to pinpoint an important small lake and shortly after narrowly missed the Melun wireless masts. At least we now knew exactly where we were.

'Suddenly, near Bretigny, we were lit by a searchlight and tracer shells passed behind the tail. 'What's the time, Bob?' It was 0242 and we were both wishing the clock would go faster, when there was a series of explosions under us. We felt the shock and shudder of their impact. Other tracers wove light-tracks behind and above and as suddenly stopped. The Mosquito was shuddering (us with it). It even seemed to me that the fuel cocks were hot. I got my parachute on as George, without speaking, though I could hear him snort, dived almost to the ground. For a second I wasn't sure that he had control and began feathering the port propeller. There was no further attack. We managed to make a little height, 1800 ft and in spite of a spasmodic shaking at the tail-end of the fuselage the aeroplane seemed to be holding her own. To lighten the load we dropped the wing-tanks and fired our cannon with empty bravado over that tranquil landscape. Headway was slow at 170 IAS (with the wind from port and against us, our ground-speed was about 145 mph) but it gave me time to double check our course and track and ETA at the coast. We prayed for accuracy and that no part of the ship would fall off. I kept my parachute on, hoping that no predator would creep up behind us for we could not have taken evasive action. And how that black hole in the propeller-blade eyed us! We decided that if we met Flak at the coast we would bale out. 'We'll paddle round to the beach-head in the dinghy.' Mild laughter. To our relief, neither event occurred.

'The crossing seemed age-long and George asked every few minutes exactly how far we had to go. However we did not quarrel. At last we could see the flashing 'K' of the Friston beacon west of Birling Gap. 'May Day! May Day!' There was no reply. We reached Ford to my wry satisfaction exactly as calculated and from 1800 ft went straight in to land at 170 knots. High speed is vital when you have only one engine and too slow a turn becomes an immediate and fatal stall. The wheels were down but we used no flaps. Half way along the runway the wheels still had not touched nor had the speed dropped. We both lifted the undercarriage lever. She dug her nose in like the 'wheels' in a wheel-barrow race, hit something, threw her tail up and turned an exact somersault amid a splintering of wood and perspex. Something cold and sharp closed on my left hand, twisting it behind me. We were stuck fast, upside down. Metal creaked, petrol escaped with an overpowering stench. There followed the long drawn-out waiting for the gas to burst into flames as it touched hot metal. I remember only one thought: 'At least you had your cricket.'[143] No? No fire? An age of waiting followed while I struggled in vain to free my left arm and the sweat dripped from my face.

'Forty-five minutes later the blood-wagon and crash crew arrived and began trying to hack us free. It was some time before they realized that if the aeroplane was upside down they were trying to cut their way through the guns. Someone had an attack of good sense and broke open the escape-hatch. It was the doctor. He also stuck a needle into my elevated bottom. They freed my arm. We were both very wide awake when they pulled us clear and I remember lying on the stretcher in a delicious twilight of sensation, comfortable and still conscious enough to appreciate this unbelievable freedom. Only later did I discover that the crash crew had stolen my torch, commando knife and the box of escape equipment we always carried.'[144]

The operational use of the Mosquito bomber had forced the *Nachtjagd* to reconsider the *Wilde Sau* method to hunt these high-performance aircraft at high altitude with Fw 190A-5s and A-6s and Bf 109Gs with *Neptun* AI radar and a long-range fuel-tank. *Oblt* Fritz Krause, a *Staffelkapitan* in the experimental I./NJGr 10 at Berlin-Werneuchen commanded by *Hptm* Friedrich Karl Müller whose main task this was, recalls:

'The new Heinkel 219 two-motor night-hunter to combat the Mosquito was not quite ready while the jet-hunter, the Me 262, was not available in sufficient numbers. So the task of testing the new methods fell mainly to one *Staffel* of the *Wilde Sau*. We had to meet the two quite different uses of the Mosquito. Firstly, there was the nightly to bomb Berlin and secondly their use as pathfinders at high altitude in the Ruhr. Night after night, 30 to 40 Mosquitoes flew to Berlin and dropped bombs and the psychological stress on the Berliners was considerable. *Flak* and searchlights were moved to Berlin without having any considerable or lasting effect. The

Mosquitoes flew at altitudes above 30,000 ft and after crossing the Elbe lost height to fly over Berlin at the highest possible speed to avoid the concentrated *Flak*. The direction of the flights across Berlin was different with each operation.

'A number of different tactical methods using night-hunters was tested but the following method, which I used with success, was the most effective. When the first of the incoming Mosquitoes crossed the Rhine, five single-engined hunters took off from Werneuchen and climbed to orbiting positions at 35,000 ft in the NE, NW, SE, SW and the center of Berlin, each position being marked by a strong master searchlight. This made it possible for at least one night-hunter, irrespective of the direction from which the attack was coming, to spot the Mosquitoes before they flew across the city. (As the single engined fighter's speed advantage over the Mosquito was only 60 kph there was only a short time available for hunting so a greater speed was required to catch the Mosquitoes and this was obtained by making a steep dive from the waiting position). Of course this method depended on good weather and visibility so that the searchlights could pick up the plane at high altitude. Up to 25,000 ft the *Flak* had a fire-free zone but the area above this limit was reserved for the hunters. The Mosquitoes usually entered Berlin at around 20,000 feet and the problem now was that the hunters had to avoid their own *Flak*. I often experienced shells exploding near me, disturbing me while hunting. On one occasion [at 0120 hours on 11 July] I received a severe hit and I was only able to save myself by baling out.'

Success was limited although *Hptm* Müller took his score to 23 kills with four *Abschüsse* while in command of I./NJGr 10. At 0040 hrs on 8 July Fritz Krause took off from Berlin Werneuchen in '*Weisse Elf*' – 'White 11', a FuG 217 J2 (*Neptun*) equipped Fw 190A-5 and destroyed a Mosquito near Brandenburg, as his only victory in this unit, as he recalls:

'I was flying over Berlin at a height of 8500 meters when I saw a twin-engined plane flying west caught in the searchlights. I closed in until I was 700 meters above, gave full throttle and dived. I went in too low and opened fire from approximately 200 meters from below and behind and kept firing as I closed. My first shots hit the right motor and an explosion followed. There was a burst of sparks and then a thick white trail of vapor. As I had overshot I had to stop the attack momentarily and found myself on the right, alongside the enemy aircraft, whose cockade and external fuel tanks I saw clearly and so was able to identify it without a doubt as a Mosquito. I fired ESN to draw the attention of the *Flak* and the searchlight to my presence. The enemy 'corkscrewed' in an attempt to evade. Because of the thick 'white flag' of vapor I was able to follow him, although he had already left the searchlight zone in a northwesterly direction. Following the trail, I managed to attack twice more. At the third attack I noticed a further explosion on the right wing and an even stronger rain of sparks. At 2000 meters he disappeared, turning at a flat gliding-angle under me. I did not see the impact on the ground as this was hidden from my angle of view.[145] On my return flight, passing Lake 'Koppeln I could estimate the crash-point as 60-70 km NW of Berlin. When I returned to base a report had already reached them about the crash of a burning enemy aircraft at 0155 hours at EE-25 to the west of Kürytz. My own plane was covered in oil from the damaged Mosquito.'[146]

Nachtjager successes against Mosquitoes were few. On 10/11 July *Major* Hans Karlowski of 2./NJG 1 shot down a Mosquito XVI of 692 Squadron off Terschelling and the crew were lost without trace.[147] On the night of 18/19 July *Hptm* Heinz Strüning of 3./NJG 1 flying a He 219 *Uhu* claimed a Mosquito west of Berlin during a raid by 22 Mosquitoes of the LNSF on the 'Big City.'[148] When navigator, P/O George W. Cash of 571 Squadron went into briefing he saw that 'A' Flight were going to the Ruhr and 'B' Flight to Berlin and so he began to get out the charts for the Ruhr. However he noticed that his name and that of S/L Terry "Doddy" Dodwell his pilot, were not on the 'A' flight list and when he told "Doddy" he said he had swapped with another crew and that they were going to Berlin instead! A momentary cold shiver went down his spine! One did not volunteer for anything unless you were mad or going 'hunting'. If in the line of duty, you were detailed for a hazardous mission that was one thing, but you did not 'stick your neck out' and ask for trouble. For the first time in 50 odd trips Cash had a premonition of doom. At dispersal Dodwell was checking the instruments and running up the engines when there was a magneto drop on the port engine and so they had to clamber out and send for the flight van to take them to the reserve aircraft, V for Victor MM136. They settled in and after hurried checks took off after the others. As they crossed the enemy coast they began to siphon the fuel from the drop tanks and settled at their operational height of 28,000ft. Cash continues:

'Near Arnhem, a sudden stream of tracer shot past us announcing the presence of a night fighter. Doddy took vigorous evasive action never easy with a bomb load and for a few hectic minutes that seemed like an age, we ran the gauntlet of what we thought were two Ju 88s. We felt a few thuds in the fuselage but there did not appear to be any serious damage. At this point Doddy realised that he was losing precious fuel into the slipstream. He had not stopped the siphoning pumps and the tanks were overflowing. I switched them off and neither of us knew how much fuel had been lost. Somehow I wasn't particularly worried. I knew deep down that we wouldn't be needing it anyway.

'At the turning point in our route which was to take us on a dog-leg to Stendal, the starting point for the bombing run we decided to fly straight there to make up for all the lost time. I worked out a course to steer and then began to window 'like mad'. Unfortunately the route took us over the flak at Wittingen, which immediately opened up on us. Suddenly we found ourselves in a box of heavy predicted flak with shells bursting all around. Shrapnel rattled down on to the cockpit of the aircraft and we could smell the cordite. Doddy put the aircraft into a steep dive; a chunk of flak smashed through the fuselage and hit the Gee set putting it out of action. The evasive action finally took us clear of the flak and on an ETA for Stendal we climbed back to 32,000ft. On course for the 'Big City' about 15 mins flying time away we could see the TIs going down as the raid began. Over on one side, we could see aircraft coned in searchlights and receiving a warm welcome from the defences. We had hardly settled on our approach when we too, found ourselves coned. We were blinded by the brilliance of the beams. More evasive action was taken but the searchlights hung on. Doddy began to climb rapidly and just as I was beginning to wonder if we would ever get clear, the beams moved away. Strangely there had been no flak, but such was our relief, that we relaxed our vigilance – we ought to have known better!

'The TIs were now dead ahead, and nose down, gathering speed we were going in. I wrote in my log '0200hrs target sighted. Preparing to bomb. "I undid my seat belt, and knelt down to go into the nose of the aircraft. Suddenly there was a thump, thump and a tremendous crump. As I straightened up again I could see that the port engine and wing was a mass of flames. I sat back on my seat and pulled up the flap to the escape hatch and it was then that I realised that I was alone in the aircraft. Doddy had gone out of the top escape hatch. Flames were licking around the side of the cockpit and the aircraft began to go down in a spin. I was pressed into my seat by the 'g' forces and I did what many in similar circumstances must have done – I prayed, "God help me."

'The spiralling stopped for some unknown reason; my mind was cool and clear despite the heat in the cockpit. Reaching behind my seat I pulled my parachute towards me, knocking my elbow on the damaged Gee set in the process. The parachute dropped into the escape hatch but fortunately it stuck halfway and I was able to retrieve it and clip it on. At this point I suddenly recalled an escape by a navigator described in the "Tee-Em" magazine, and so, instead of going through the navigator's escape hatch I climbed out of the cockpit and rolled on to the starboard wing before being swept away by the slipstream. After 3 seconds I pulled the release handle on the chute but it did not open so I reached up and pulled the flaps open. There was a clop, a slight jerk and I was floating down with a beautiful white canopy above me. Looking down, I saw the aircraft crash into a field in a blaze. The 'Cookie' had not exploded and I thought for a moment what would happen if I drifted down near to the aircraft and it blew up but I drifted away from the scene. All of a sudden I found myself hanging from a tree in the darkness. I pressed the release button on the harness and fell about l0ft into some bushes, which broke my fall. All I had were a few minor scratches and I was firmly on 'terra firma.''[149]

Two nights later, on 20/21 July during a LNSF raid on Hamburg by 26 Mosquitoes, Strüning shot down another 571 Squadron BXVI (ML984). F/L Thompson baled out but Jack Calder RCAF was killed. Thirty Lancasters and seven Halifaxes also failed to return from Main Force raids[150] but it was a famous night for 169 Squadron, which destroyed '100 Group's 100th Hun' during a hat trick of victories by three crews. P/O Harry 'Shorty' Reed and F/O Stuart Watts got a Ju 88 in the Homberg area while F/L J.S. Fifield and F/O F. Staziker claimed a Bf 110 at Courtrai. The CO, W/C Neil B.R. Bromley OBE DFC and his navigator F/L Philip Truscott DFC destroyed a Bf 110G-4[151], which crashed near Mol in Belgium. The pilot was 25-year old *Ofw* Karl-Heinz Scherfling of 12./NJG 1, who was a *Ritterkreuzträger* since 8 April 1944 and he had 33 to 35 night victories. It was the third time in six weeks that Scherfling had been shot down but this time he failed to bale out. *Fw* Herbert Winkler, the 31-year old *Bordschütze* was killed also and *Fw* Herbert Scholz, the 25 year-old radar operator, baled out seriously injured. (Bromley and Truscott were killed on the night of 6/7 September when their Mosquito was hit by flak near Oldenburg while they were providing Bomber Support for Mosquitoes bombing Hamburg).

The crack team of *Hptm* Martin Drewes, *Fw* Erich Handke, *Bordfunker* and *Ofw* Georg 'Schorsch' Petz, air gunner of *Stab* III./NJG 1 were one of the nightfighter crews that were sent up to meet the bombers as Handke recalls:

'We were the last to take off, as the situation was not clear. In the box *Eisbär* we were merely told, 'Situation uncertain', so we continued to box *Hase* on the southern edge of the Zuiderzee where we were informed that a formation was entering the Schelde estuary. We at once flew towards this on a southwesterly course but I remained on the frequency of GCI station *Hase*, which suddenly reported a new formation of one hundred aircraft near Amsterdam. We turned back immediately to *Hase* where six machines of our *Gruppe* had arrived in the meanwhile. The *Jägerleitoffizier* (JLO, or GCI-controller) of *Hase* gave an excellent commentary, according to whom the enemy aircraft should fly tightly through the area. When we were back at the beacon I initiated a turn to port. We must have been very close to the bombers. Schorsch spotted three of them at 5500 meters high flashing past on an opposite course. As we turned I saw one more. Immediately afterwards I had the first two in the *SN-2*, two kilometers ahead, when I discovered a weak blip at 300 meters, probably behind us. But before I had said anything Schorsch saw him behind and above. We adjusted our speed to his and slowly placed ourselves beneath him. (Meanwhile we had discovered another half dozen machines all around us. we had excellent visibility, up to 800 meters). It was a Halifax and we were under it. Drewes fired from 50 meters into the port wing. It caught fire at once but also in the fuselage and in the starboard outer engine. Probably one of the cannon mountings had come loose, causing our fire to scatter. The Halifax went into a left turn downward. The fire went partly out, increased again and the Halifax dived ever steeper. Finally a long flame shot out of the fuselage and at about 2000 meters the plane exploded into three parts.

'We went straight back on to the approach course (100°) and were immediately right again in the bomber stream and tucked ourselves under a Halifax, which weaved back and forth. I had been giving a running commentary not only to ground control but also to our other machines. All of them had seen our first *Abschuss but* none had found the stream and they had failed to make an attack! Our Halifax now cut under a Lancaster coming from starboard, which was flying a steadier course. As I saw the Halifax disappearing to the right, Drewes had already placed himself under the Lancaster. Schorsch said we were too close but before I could say anything at 50 meters range Drewes aimed at the port inner engine and close to the fuselage (as I could see by the aerial mast on top of the cabin roof). Then it happened. We must have hit the bomb-load because the Lancaster disintegrated into a thousand pieces! Our machine was struck several times and we went down steeply out of control. All around us were white flames and a thousand green stars. The Lancaster must have been a Pathfinder. We had no intercom. We were thrown about. Most of the time I was stuck against the cabin roof. We went down perhaps 1000 meters (the attack had been at 5800m) when I said to myself, 'It is no use. Drewes can never regain control; I must get out.' I gave two tugs of the roof jettison lever. (Schorsch had done the same at the rear). The rear cabin roof flew off. I pushed off a little to the rear and was caught at once by the slipstream and pulled upwards. My heel just touched the tail. I was clear of the machine and went down, somersaulting. Suddenly there was no more engine noise and briefly I saw our machine and the burning wreckage of the Lancaster going down. I was angry that we had been torn out of a beautiful stream where we could have shot down so many more.'[152]

Handke, Drewes and Petz baled out safely 30 kilometers from Twente where their 8th *Staffel* was stationed and they were picked up in a car by *Oblt* Dietrich Schmidt, who had also scored two *Abschüsse*[153] and driven to the nearest hospital. Schorsch, who had a bomb splinter in the left forearm and a flesh wound in the right, had his arms put into plaster casts. Drewes had released his harness straps and he was catapulted out through the cockpit roof which was torn off and left hanging around his neck. He had only managed to lose it with some difficulty and had dislocated his arm in the process but at a farmhouse shortly after landing it had snapped into place again when he leaned on a table.

Handke continues:

'Drewes and his wife Putzer, 'Schorsch' and his wife, our first mechanic with his wife, our armourer and me were sent to a convalescent home of the *First Jagdkorps* in Hellbeck on Seeland, Denmark for four and a half weeks. (I was the only one of my crew who was unmarried but here I met my future wife). We were allowed eight days at home and on the journey back to Heidelberg via Berlin I caught a bad cold, which did not get better until I had returned to Leeuwarden. On 23/24 July, the night we left, Mosquitoes shot down three more crews of our *Gruppe*. *Hptm* Jandrey and crew were killed. *Uffz* Huxsohl, *Fw* Heinrich Lahmann's radio operator died and the crew of *Lt* Hettlich baled out![154] Drewes still could not fly because of his arm. We expected daily that Leeuwarden would again be bombed.'[155]

On 24/25 July 461 Lancasters and 153 Halifaxes were despatched to Stuttgart in the first of three heavy raids on the

German city in five nights. Seventeen Lancasters and four Halifaxes were lost.[156] On 25/26 July when 412 Lancasters and 138 Halifaxes returned to Stuttgart and other large forces bombed Wanne-Eickel and flying bomb sites in France[157] two 2nd TAF[158] and two 100 Group Mosquito *Intruder* crews were successful over the continent. F/L D.J. Griffiths and F/Sgt S.F. Smith of 23 Squadron recorded the *intruder* Squadron's first air-to-air victory since returning from the Mediterranean, with a UEA at Laon Pouvron. Ex Dambuster, S/L Harold B.M. 'Mick' Martin DSO DFC[159] and his navigator F/O J.W. Smith of 515 Squadron in a Mosquito FBVI shot down a Me 410 *Hornisse* on a *Night Ranger* to Stuttgart and Boblingen. They had arrived over the area shortly after midnight and stooged around 'for as long as possible' but the patrol was uneventful and Martin headed home. Just after crossing the Belgian coast at Knokke at 0350 hours in very hazy conditions, an aircraft was seen about one mile to port flying very fast. Martin swung the Mosquito around to dead astern and below the illuminated aircraft at a height of about 3000ft. He closed to 50 yards and identified it as a Me 410. Martin gave the starboard engine a short second burst of cannon fire from astern and slightly below at 70 yards (so close that the 410's tail light literally blotted out the spot on Martin's ring sight). The *Hornisse* pilot dived to port but an almost simultaneous short second burst of cannon, directed on the port wing, blew the wing off and the *Hornisse* went down in a screaming dive and in flames. It was seen to crash on the sea and continued burning.

On 26/27 July 178 Lancasters and nine Mosquitoes of 5 Group attacked rail yards at Givors for the loss of four Lancasters and two Mosquitoes. Two of the Lancasters were claimed by *Lt* Otto Huchler of 2./NJG 2 for his first two victories. A Mosquito of 627 Squadron, one of the 30 in the LNSF that went to Hamburg, was also lost. Twenty-three Mosquito patrols were flown and S/L R.S. Jephson and F/O J.M. Roberts of 409 Squadron RCAF of 2nd TAF destroyed a Ju 88 over Caen but their NFXIII was brought down by the flying debris and both men were killed in the crash. The only other Mosquito claim was a Ju 188 at Melun by F/O Frank E. Pringle and F/O Wain Eaton of 29 Squadron. On 28/29 July when 494 Lancasters attacked Stuttgart again, 141 Squadron destroyed three aircraft. F/L Harry E. White DFC* and F/L Michael S. Allen DFC* got two Ju 88s in the Metz-Neufchateau area. In the same area, P/O Doug Gregory and P/O D.H. Stephens destroyed their second Ju 88 of the month, as Gregory recalled:

'We took off from West Raynham at 2315 hrs, set course for enemy coast, crossing in at Overflakkee at 16,000 ft at 2357 hrs. Route uneventful until leaving *Ida* on way to *Christa*. At 0031 hrs at 16,000 ft we got an AI contact slightly port and below crossing port to starboard. We turned in behind him and went down. A/C then led us on a vector of 210°M. we closed and after an eight-minute chase obtained visual. Closing still further we got into various positions and finally when about 200 ft directly below, identified A/C as a Ju 88. He was flying quite straight at 14,000 ft without a clue. We pulled up to his level and at approximately 100 yards and let fly with a 1 1/2-second burst. Our shells apparently found their mark for his port engine immediately gave up the ghost and burst into flames and smoking pieces came back at us. We broke off to port and watched him burning satisfactorily and going down. He entered cloud at 8000 ft and after a few seconds he lit up the cloud as he exploded on the ground. Time was now 0045 hrs and his grave may be found 16 miles NW of Metz. We then set course for base via Overflakkee, crossing out at 0140 hrs. Here endeth the second lesson.'[160]

Nachtjagd units intercepted the stream on the outward flight and aided by the bright moonlight, 39 Lancasters were shot down. Six crews of II./NJG 1, operating from Echterdingen, were credited with eight of the Stuttgart raiders.[161] Another force of 187 Halifaxes, 106 Lancasters and 14 Mosquitoes raided Hamburg but again Tame Boars were directed to the bomber stream on the bombers' homeward flight. Eighteen Halifaxes and four Lancasters were downed, eight of which were credited to III./NJG 1. *Oblt* Dietrich Schmidt, *Staffelkapitän*, 8./NJG 1 claimed three Viermots and *Lt* Ebhardt three Halifaxes[162]:

'After the Stuttgart operations' recalls F/Sgt Louis Patrick Wooldridge DFC '578 Squadron reverted to tactical targets, assisting the Army against the German *Wehrmacht* and operations against the 'V' bomb weapon sites. In consequence, operations, both by day and by night, were carried out against such place names as Thiverny, Bois de Cassan, near Paris, Forêt de Nieppe, Forêt de Mormal and Hazebrouck.' In all, 1114 aircraft – 601 Lancasters, 492 Halifaxes and 21 Mosquitoes – made bombing attacks on these targets and Trossy-St. Maxim flying bomb stores in northern France. Six Lancasters were lost on the raid on Trossy-St. Maxim and one from the Bois de Cassan raid on 3 August. Louis Wooldridge witnessed its loss.

'Flying at about 16,000 ft; 1000 ft below our height and about 1000 yards astern of our aircraft, it received a direct hit from an anti aircraft shell and blew up. The aircraft and its bomb load erupted in a huge pall of dense black smoke centered by bright reddish orange flames.

Several minutes later, when the dense black smoke began to disperse and thin out, a vacant space could be observed where the Lancaster had been.

'About the first week of August the squadron was informed that a decision had been made to commence a 'Round the Clock' bombing campaign against Berlin. Instead of returning to our bases in Britain after bombing Berlin, we were to continue our operational flight eastwards, to land at pre-arranged bases in Russia, where the Lancaster and Halifax bombers would be refuelled, bombed up and re-armed for the return flight. Meanwhile during the day period, the U.S. 8th Air Force would commence their operational day flights to Berlin and Russia, to land at the Russian bases vacated by the RAF air crews on their return flight to Berlin and Britain. 'Arrangements were made by RAF Bomber Command, the U.S. 8th Force and the Russians but after a few false starts, the operation was scrubbed. Annoyed, we questioned the reason for this. Apparently, Stalin himself had cancelled the operation because of supposed difficulties of aircraft recognition between unfamiliar British and American bomber aircraft by Russian aircraft. It is possible that if Stalin had agreed to the original operation code-named *Thunderclap*, upon Berlin in August 1944, Dresden might possibly have escaped destruction later in the war, 13/14 February 1945.'

Notes

1. *Fliegerkorps XII* was deprived of *Jagddivision 4* (Metz) and became *Jagdkorps I* to which *Jagddivision I, II* and *III* were subordinated. Owing to increasing pressure on the industrial areas of the Vienna basin and Upper Silesia, the *Jagdfliegerfuhrer* Ostmark and Oberschlesien and a little later Ostpreusen, were established. In south Germany *Jagddivision VII* (envisaged as *Jagdkorps III*) at first remained independent but later, deprived of *Jafü Mittelrhein*, to whom the defense of the Frankfurt basin was given, was also subordinated to *Jagdkorps I*. On 16 March *Jagddivision 30* (single-engine fighters) was dissolved and the personnel distributed among the remaining *Jagddivisionen*.

2. At the beginning of April 1944 the staff of *Luftflotten-Kommando* moved to Berlin-Wannsee to the newly extended Battle HQ (formerly the *Reichsluftschutzschule*.

3. Schulte was awarded the *Ritterkreuz* for 25 victories on 17 April 1945.

4. JB526.

5. One of his victims was Lancaster JB721 of 156 Sqn over Briey, E France with the loss of 5 crew. Three 156 Sqn aircraft FTR from Schweinfurt.

6. On 24/25 February F/L C.C. 'Charlie' Scherf RAAF and his navigator in FBVI 'R' destroyed 2 Ju 88s at Ansbach a/f. In 3 months, January-May 16 1944 Scherf racked up 23 destroyed, 13 of them in the air.

7. After Luma returned to the USA he was based for a while at Victorville, CA. One night in the bar at the officers club he was talking to a B-24 pilot. Luma recalls, 'We had become barroom buddies, because he, too, had flown at night out of England. He had flown clandestine trips over France to make drops to the French Underground. He related a story of one night when his tail gunner spotted a bogey on their tail and was about to open fire when he recognized it as a Mosquito. The barroom buddy and I rushed to our quarters and compared dates in our logbooks. We had indeed crossed paths over France!' Luma who was awarded both a British and U.S. DFC left the service in September 1945.

8. Operation to engage air and ground targets within a wide but specified area.

9. MacFadyen later operated in 406 'Lynx' Sqn RCAF where he flew the NFXXX on night intruders, finishing the war with 7 a/c and 5 V1s destroyed and 5 a/c destroyed and 17 damaged on the ground. On 14 April S/L Robert Allan Kipp and F/L Pete Huletsky of 418 Sqn shot down two Ju 52/3m minesweepers fitted with de-gaussing rings and 2 Do 217s on the ground, plus they damaged one more. S/L Kipp DSO DFC final score included 10 a/c shot down and 7 and 8 destroyed and damaged on the ground. (Kipp died in a flying accident in a Vampire at St Hubert, Canada, 25 July 1949). F/L S.H.R. 'Stan' Cotterill DFC and 'Pop' McKenna destroyed 4 in a night sortie. (Cotterill KIA Oct 18 44 on a *Day Ranger*). During April-May 1944 418 (City of Edmonton) Sqn shot down 30 e/a in the air and destroyed a further 38 a/c on the ground. 418 scored its 100th victory in May and in June flew anti-*Diver* patrols at night, destroying 123 V-ls July-21 August. 418 finished the war with the distinction of destroying more enemy a/c both in the air and on the ground, than any other Canadian squadron, in both night and daylight operations.

10. F/O J.C.N. Forshaw-P/O F.S. Folley of 141 Sqn in Mosquito NFII DZ761 'C' destroyed a Ju 88 nr Frankfurt. F/O Harry White-F/O Mike S. Allen DFC destroyed 2 Ju 88s during a patrol in the Frankfurt area. Ju 88C-6 Wrk.Nr. 750014 R4+CS of 8./NJG 2 cr. at Arheilgen near Darmstadt, 25 km S of Frankfurt. *Ofw* Otto Müller, pilot, *Ogefr* Erhard Schimsal, *Bordfunker* and *Gefr* Gunter Hanke, *Bordschütze* KIA.

11. LW540 LK-R.

12. In November 1978 Sanderson and Rökker came face to face for the first time at a meeting of the German Air War Historical Society at Hetschbach, Germany. They shook hands and from that very moment became friends. Rökker concludes. 'I think that such a friendship between former adversaries can only develop, if both sides approach each other unreservedly. Our contact is the same as I have with my German friends. Not the past but the present rules our close friendship.'

13. ND405.

14. On 24/25 March ferocious German defenses, aided by unforecast winds that scattered the bomber stream, claimed 44 Lancasters and 28 Halifaxes, or 8.9% of the force, the majority of which were claimed by 279 I *Jagdkorps* a/c (14 nightfighters were lost including Ju 88C-6 Wrk Nr 360272 D5+? of 4./NJG 3, which cr 10 km SW of Bayreuth and was shot down by F/Sgts J. Campbell DFM-R. Phillips of 239 Sqn. *Oblt* Ruprecht Panzer, pilot, WIA, *Bordfunker* and *Bordschütze,* all baled out safely. *Fw* Rudolf Frank of 3./NJG 3 claimed 3 a/c, including Lancaster ME640 of 460 Sqn RAAF at Teglingen, and 630 Sqn Lancaster ND657 at Altharen. *Oblt* Rökker, *St.Kpt* 1./NJG 2 destroyed 2 Lancasters and a Halifax 2250-2348 hrs. At 2235 hrs *Oblt* Martin 'Tino' Becker of 2./NJG 6 claimed a Lancaster at Wörlitz/Passau. Rökker claimed another Lancaster nr Mönchengladbach at 2255 hrs on 26/27 March, when a 705-strong force went to Essen. 9 Lancasters and Halifaxes FTR, most probably all being shot down by twin-engined Tame Boars. At least 16 *Nachtjagd* a/c were lost.

15. In Lancaster III ND535 ZN-Q.

16. LL843 PO-D survived the war as one of the few Lancaster centenarians with 118 ops on 467 RAAF and 61 Sqns.

17. Schmidt recalled that: 'By January 1944 my 3rd *Gruppe* had spent more than two years relatively quietly, in spite of everything, at its home base of Twente but in mid-February we were moved to Wittmundhafen and from then on we never remained at one place for longer than two months. At the beginning of March we moved to St. Dizier and in mid-March to Laon-Athies. The crews were housed in the Palais Marchais, which belonged to the Princess of Monaco, a noble if somewhat dusty accommodation.'

18. In Bf 110 G9+CS.

19. *Oblt* Schmidt's 18th *Abschuss* was possibly a 76 Sqn Halifax (code MP). Three 76 Sqn Halifax IIIs were shot down by night-fighters during the Nurnberg raid. MP-P LK795 went down nr. Hamm. LN647 MP-W went down in the Nieder-Moos 6 km NNW of Greiensteinau and LW696 MP-X cr. at Daubhausen 12 km NW of Wetzlar. (LW628 MP-J cr. at Tangmere on the way home).

20. *Monica* was a radar-warning transmitter with a tail mounted aerial and had a range of between 1000 ft and up to 2-4 miles.

21. Apart from Starkey, only Sgt Wally Paris the bomb aimer survived when he was hurtled from the exploding aircraft.

22. Halifax III LW634 of 158 Sqn, which had been hit by *flak* nr Metz, cr. at Eischen at 0315 hrs. 4 of F/Sgt S. Hughes crew were PoW. 2 Evd.

23. *Oblt* Martin Drewes, *St.Kpt*, 11./NJG 1 claimed 3 Lancasters. *Oblt* Witzleb and *Oblt* Prues of III./NJG 1 each claimed a *Viermot* at 0012 and 0031 hrs respectively. *Oblt* Helmuth Schulte of 4./NJG 5 scored 4 kills and *Fw* Rudolf Frank of 3./NJG 3 three.

24. At 0003 and 0011 hrs. One of his kills was possibly Halifax LV880 of 51 Sqn, which went down nr. Montdidier after a most unusual head-on attack by a night fighter.

25. Lancaster III ND395 of 83 Sqn was destroyed by the Aachen *Flak* defenses. All the other eight losses were due to *Nachtjäger*. One *Viermot* each by *Oblt* Werner Baake and *Fw* Rauer (on his 1st combat sortie) of I./NJG 1 at Venlo and *Major* Heinz-Wolfgang Schnaufer of *Stab* IV./NJG 1 at St. Trond claimed 2 heavies (Lancaster III ND389 of 83 Sqn W of Turnhout and Lancaster I LL899 of 49 Sqn nr. St. Leonhard) destroyed.

26. During the whole of April 215 victories were claimed by *Nachtjagd* crews.

27. 5 Fortresses of 214 Sqn, including one captained by the CO, W/C Desmond J. McGlinn DFC flew their first jamming operation this night. The Sqn's role was to jam the night fighter controllers on the ground and the German night-fighters in the air. Among other countermeasures, they also jammed the FuG 216 *Neptun* tail warning system.

28. White and Allen's victim either Do 217N-1 Wrk Nr 51517 of 5/NJG 4, which cr. nr Meulan, N of Paris. *Obfw* Karl Kaiser, pilot and *Uffz* Johannes Nagel, *Bordfunker* WIA, baled out. *Geftr* Sigmund Zinser, *Bordschütze*, MIA. Or Do 217E-5 Wrk.Nr. 5558 6N+EP of 6./KG 100. *Fw* Heinz Fernau, pilot, *Hptm* Willi Scholl, observer, *Uffz* Josef Bach, *Bordfunker* and *Obfw* Fritz Wagner, Flight Engineer KIA.

29. F/L G.R. Morgan (evd) and F/Sgt D. Bentley (PoW) of 169 Sqn in DD616 were lost on the Köln raid. S/L E.W. Kinchin-F/O D. Sellors of 239 Sqn (both KIA) who had downed a Bf 110 nr Frankfurt a month earlier, were in the 2nd *Serrate* Mosquito (HJ644) lost. They were last heard on R/T at 0220 hrs, *'We are OK now'*. (HJ644 cr. 4 km SE of Nijkerk (Gelderland). *Hptm* Paul Zorner, *Gruppenkommandeur* of St.III/NJG 5 at Mainz-Finthin, was credited with a Mosquito, which he saw flying on one engine at 0300 hrs NW of St. Trond for his 42nd victory (his only Mosquito *Abschuss* in a total of 59 Nachtjagd victories). Zorner was originally a transport pilot who transferred to nightfighting in 1940 and served with NJG 3, NJG 5 and finally *Kommandeur,* II./NJG 100.

30. In 1943 when sgts in 125 Sqn they had destroyed a Do 217 and two Ju 88s flying Beaufighter VIs. Both were commissioned and in Oct 1943 they were posted to 169 Sqn. Their first kill in 100 Group was a Bf 110 on Feb 5/6 1944.

31. *Ypsilon*, *Y-Verfahren*, *Ypsilonverfahren*: Luftwaffe ground-controlled navigation by means of VHF.

32. Frank claimed Halifax III MZ578 *I-Ink* as a 'Lancaster'.

33. MZ578 cr. nr. Gulpen in Limburg Province 16 km ESE of Maastricht. Wingham and Lewis evaded capture and after 4 1/2 months returned home to RAF service. The official German communiqué stated Somerscales, Poole and 1 u/i airman KIA. Stephen, Reavill and Rowe were PoWs. This information was later passed to the International Red Cross at Geneva. No satisfactory explanation has ever been discovered for the 'unidentified body' given out by the Germans. One can only speculate that, perhaps, the local German commander was seeking to discourage the local Resistance from helping two evaders or was covering his own back against charges of allowing two aircrew to escape rather than one. After compulsory 2 months leave and being given an open invitation to decide his own posting, Wingham volunteered for Mosquitoes and after a navigation refresher course at OTU ended up in 8 Group (PFF) on 105 (Oboe) Sqn at RAF Bourn at the end of March 1945, with whom he completed 4 ops before the war finished. In April 1946 on recommendation of AOC-in-C Bomber Command he was awarded the DFC, American, for his successful evasion, the list for British awards having been closed in June 1945.

34. His 2nd and 3rd victims were probably Halifaxes (LW633 of 425 'Alouette' Sqn RCAF 30 km SE of Gilze-Rijen at 0155 and LV780 of 424 'Tiger' Sqn RCAF 25 km SE of Gilze-Rijen at 0204 hrs). Modrow was a former tranpsort who trained as a nightfighter pilot late in 1943. *Major* Hans Karlewski of 2./NJG 1 and *Uffz* Heinz Filipzig of 4./NJG 1 and *Oblt* Johannes Hager of 6./NJG 1 (both flying from St. Dizier) each claimed a Halifax. *Lt* Hans Zettel of 2./NJG 6 at Illesheim downed a Lancaster at 0138 hrs 10 km NW of Düsseldorf.

35. 12 Liberators crashed or crash-landed as a result of KG 51's actions. 38 American crewmen were killed and another 23 injured.

36. *Nachtjagd* claimed 28-31 kills with *Hptm* Heinz-Wolfgang Schnaufer destroying four *Viermots* for his 53rd-56th victories. Two nights later Schnaufer claimed two more kills (Lancasters of 156 and 408 Sqns).

37. In March Bill Lucas and Jim Sprackling had been awarded the DFC. This was uncommon before completing a tour and unusual for a flight engineer. The rest of March and early April 1944 were spent converting 10 Sqn to Halifax III aircraft. When they went to Düsseldorf on 22/23 April it took only 4 1/2 hours, which showed the improvement in the Mk.III. *Gardening* in Kiel Bay again on 23/24 April, a 'long flog' to Karlsruhe on the 24th and then to Essen on the 26/27th made six operations in eight nights: the previous 23 had taken the crew nearly a year!

38. 720074 D5+CL.

39. Lancaster III ND873 of 12 Sqn.

40. He was. Smith was killed when Lancaster I ME679 DX-K of 57 Sqn was involved in a collision with Lancaster I of 44 Rhodesian Sqn piloted by F/O G.W. Oldham DFC who it will be recalled was a Rhodesian who had flown his first tour on 61 Sqn. There was only one survivor from Boyle's crew. All 7 of Oldham's crew died. Two I./NJG 6 Bf 110s were lost to *Flak* and return fire but the *Nachtjagd* crews returned with 8 *Abschüsse* plus 3 probables. The Schweinfurt force lost 21 Lancasters, or 9.3%.

41. Mailly actually accommodated a *Panzer* regiment HQ, 3 Panzer battalions belonging to regiments on the Eastern Front and elements of 2 more as well as the permanent training school staff.

42. Later G/C DFC* AFC AE.

43. The crew flew their first operation, an 8.05 hr trip to Schweinfurt in Lancaster ND573 on 24/25 February, followed by 14 further ops 25/26 February (Augsburg)-1/2 May (Toulouse).

44. All from I./SKG 10, a single-engined fighter-bomber and fast recce unit. One pilot, *Fw* Otto Heinrich of the 3rd *Staffel*, claimed 3 destroyed for his first and only three combat victories. Heinrich was KIA on 22 May.

45. Lancaster III ND556 went down at Chaintreaux in Seine-et-Marne, 12 km SE of Nemours. 4 crew Evd. 1 PoW. 1 KIA.

46. In Bf 110 G9+HS.

47. *Oblt* Dietrich Schmidt's 23rd victim cr nr Chavanges at 0003 hrs, followed by a second Lancaster kill 16 mins later near Mailly-le-Camp. His 3rd victory of the night came down at 0046 hrs near Romilly.

48. Handke, born 2 November 1920 in Darmstadt trained as a *Bordfunker* during 1941-42, crewing up with *Fw* George Kraft and joining 12./NJG 1 in October 1942. The team rapidly made a name for themselves, scoring 14 kills during the following months. Their partnership came to a violent end on 17/18 August 1943 when Kraft, flying with another *Bordfunker* was shot down by W/C Bob Braham DSO DFC* of 141 Sqn. Kraft's body was washed ashore in Denmark 4 weeks' later. Handke then joined the crew of *Oblt* Heinz-Wolfgang Schnaufer with whom he claimed five *Abschüsse*, before briefly flying on sorties with *Ofw* Karl-Heinz Scherfling and contributing to the destruction of 2 more bombers. Shortly before the end of 1943 Handke had teamed up with *Hptm* Martin Drewes, who at the time was *Staffelkapitän* 11./NJG 1 and an *Experte* with 7 victories and *Ofw* Georg 'Schorsch' Petz, *Bordschütze*). On 1 March 1944 Drewes assumed command of III./NJG 1 and this team went on to score 37 kills in less than 5 months.

49. *Schräge Musik* ('Jazz' or 'slanting Music', first used in August 1943) a twin 30mm MK 108 cannon installation in the aft cockpit bulkhead. These fighters did not need to attack *von unten hinten* ('underneath, behind'). They could attack from the blind spot underneath the bomber with cannon raked at 15°, fired by the pilot using a *Revi C/12D* reflector sight.

50. Drewes 5th victim (Lancaster EE185 KM-A of 44 Sqn, which cr. at Dreux with the loss of P/O Allen W. Nolan RAAF and his crew) almost fell on top of the Bf 110 and Drewes had to dive steeply to avoid his flaming victim. The 5 Lancasters shot down in a 40-minute period took Drewes' score to 34 victories. On 3/4 May also *Hptm* Helmut Bergmann (23) *St.Kpt* 8./NJG 4 at Juvincourt destroyed 6 Lancasters in 30 mins for his 29th-34th victories (which earned him the award of the *Ritterkreuz*).

51. Sparks and 5 others in his crew (2 PoW) evaded after baling out of Lancaster III JB402 OL-R. The French Resistance found Sparks and told him that his rear gunner had shot down one of the German fighters. Sparks was back with 83 Sqn at Coningsby seven weeks later.

52. Eeles learned later that of the 346 bombers despatched to Mailly-le-Camp 42 Lancasters (or 11.6 per cent) were lost (2 more were so badly damaged that they had to be written off). Ball's crew, less the 2 gunners, returned to base in their severely shot up Lancaster even though the aircraft had been further holed in a night-fighter attack after the anti-aircraft damage. P/O Ted Ball was awarded an immediate DFC. On completion of repairs, ND647 was relegated to 1653 CU, where it was lost during fighter affiliation on 8 April 1945. P/O Ball's crew, with two other Sqn gunners, went on to fly on ops but towards the end of their tour they were shot down, probably by 'friendly fire' from another Lancaster, on 7/8 July 1944 during an attack on a flying bomb storage depot at St. Leu d' Esserent (Creil, France). There were no survivors. Their average age was 22.

53. F/L Chase and crew of Lancaster ND587/D of405 'Vancouver' Sqn RCAF, which cr. at 0345 hrs at Gallaix (Hainaut) 12 km E Tournai.

54. Martstaller was killed in a crash on St Trond aerodrome in August 1944. The 8 other losses at Haine St Pierre were: Lancaster I ME620/C of 35 Sqn flown by W/O Kemp, which cr. at Estinnes-au-Val (Hainaut) 12 km ESE Mons, Lancaster III ND347/W of 405 'Vancouver' Sqn RCAF, flown by P/O Darlow which cr. at 0340 at Bon-Secours (Hainaut) 18 km SE Tournai and Halifax MZ598/J of 426 Sqn flown by 1st Lt Smith, which was lost without trace were possibly shot down by *Fw* Konrad Beyer of 1./NJG 4. ND587 D F/L Chase Martstaller 1./NJG 4. Halifax LK798/A of 425 'Alouette' Sqn RCAF flown by F/O White, which cr. at Walle-'t Hage (W. Vlaanderen) 2km SE Courtrai and Halifax LW583/L of 432 'Leaside' Sqn RCAF flown by F/O Martin, which cr. at Posthoorn (W. Vlaanderen) 2km SW Courtrai were shot down by either *Hptm* Adolf Breves or *Oblt* Georg Herrmann Greiner, both IV./NJG 1. Halifax LK884/X of 431 'Iroquois' Sqn RCAF flown by F/L Mead cr. at 0330 at Rance (Hainaut) 26km SE Mons and was shot down by *Lt* Georg Fengler of IV./NJG 1. Halifax MZ521/T of 431 'Iroquois' Sqn RCAF flown by F/O Wilson cr. at Zwevezele (W. Vlaanderen) 10 km NNE Roeslare and was shot down by *Lt* Friedrich Potthast of IV./NJG 1. Halifax LW594/G of 432 'Leaside' Sqn RCAF flown by P/O Hawkins cr. at Grand Reng (Hainaut) 16km SE Mons and was shot down by *Oblt* Heinz-Wolfgang Schnaufer of IV./NJG 1.

55. Bf 110 3G+E1 Wrk Nr. 740179 was attacked at 0010 hrs.

56. Hanneck had entered the Luftwaffe in July 1939 and trained as a fighter pilot during the next year. Expecting a posting to an operational unit, he was selected to serve as an instructor instead. Throughout 1942 he served in a liaison unit on the Eastern Front but he became so bored that he volunteered for nightfighter pilot training. He had finally been posted to 6./NJG 1 in April 1944 and on 1 May he started flying at Deelen near Arnhem.

57. Geoffrey Clark and 3 crew KIA when the aircraft cr. at the hamlet of Elkerzee NE of Haamstede. 3 survivors PoW. After *Nachtjagd*'s successes during the Mailly-le-Camp raid, just a few Tame Boar operations were mounted by First *Jagdkorps* during the remainder of May. On the nights of 11/12 May and 12/13 52 and 65 night-fighter crews respectively scored 12 and 13 victories.

58. 28 houses flattened, 40 houses evacuated and 528 houses damaged.

59. The crashed a/c George Vantilt saw was most probably Lancaster I LL792 of 467 RAAF Sqn, flown by P/O J.F. Ward with W/C J.R. Balmer OBE DFC RAAF and crew, which was making its final bomb run when it was attacked by *Oblt* Fritz Lau of 4./NJG 1. LL792 exploded with a full bomb load, killing the 8 crew and it came down 2 km W of Beverlo.

60. White-Allen were flying DZ726/Z and LeBoutte-Mallett were in DZ240/H.

61. *Instep* was a patrol seeking air activity in Bay of Biscay, *Rangers* operations to engage air and ground targets within a wide but specified area.

62. LeBoutte had joined the *l'Aviation Militaire* (Belgian Armed Forces) in April 1919. In 1924 he joined the *Militaire Vliegwezen* (Air Component of the Belgian Amy). LeBoutte had a successful career, rising to *Capitaine Aviateur* (Captain-Flyer) and commander of the IIIrd Group of the 2nd Regiment by 1930. In January 1940 LeBoutte was sent to the Belgian Congo on an assignment to form three Sqns at Leopoldville, Stanleyville and Elizabethville. Having successfully completed his mission in Congo, he left this Belgian colony on 16 May 1940 but the war and the rapid advance of the German Armed Forces in the West interrupted his voyage home and he was ordered to return to Belgium. LeBoutte went into hiding in Belgium and in 1941 he escaped to England. LeBoutte, aged 43 and wearing glasses, was declared unfit for all flying duties. He stole a friend's identity card and set off for the recruiting center for night fighter aircrew at Uxbridge. The interviewing board was impressed by his flying career, hardly glancing at 'his' identity card and the medical board declared him 'perfectly fit'. LeBoutte immediately joined the RAF as P/O. He did not care for his rank of Major, as he only wanted fly! His training on Oxfords and Blenheims was soon successfully completed and at OTU he crewed up with young Sergeant Harry Parrot, who wanted to improve his French. Despite his age and the fact that he wore glasses, LeBoutte was finally commissioned into the RAF as a P/O in January 1942 and that summer he and Parrot were posted to 141 Sqn.

63. Ju 88G-1 Werke No. 710575 cr between Mechelen and Leuven to the NE of Brussels. This was LeBoutte's first and only kill during his time on 141 Sqn. On 24 May Lucien LeBoutte and Mallett were awarded DFCs. In June LeBoutte was officially 'tour expired'. (Mallet was on his third tour). LeBoutte was given a staff position in London, reaching the rank of W/C DFC *CdeG*. (After the war G/C LeBoutte served in Brussels at SHAEF and he was one of the founder members of the Belgian Air Force. He served with distinction until retirement in 1956). At the end of June 1944 Simonsohn had to belly-land his Ju 88G-1 at Kassel-Rothwesten after a starboard engine failure caused by machine gun fire from a bomber gunner. Simonsohn and his crew suffered several broken bones in the crash. Having recovered from his injuries in hospital Simonsohn was posted to 4./NJG 100 based in Hungary in November 1944, where he flew a handful of night interdiction ground attack sorties. He completed 28 operational sorties before the end of the war.

64. Ju 88G-6 Wrk Nr 750922 of 5./NJG 3, which cr. at Hoogcruts nr. Maastricht. *Uffz* Josef Polzer (a replacement pilot who had yet to open his score) and *Ogefr* Hans Klünder, radar operator KIA. *Gefr* Hans Becker, *Bordschütze* WIA.

65. He 219V-16-0 G9+DC (Wrk.Nr. 190116) on test at EHF, flown by *Lt* Otto Fries, II./NJG 1's technical officer at Arnhem/Deelen and his *Bordfunker Fw* Alfred Staffa, was heading back to Deelen when their starboard engine suddenly erupted in flames. Fries shut it down and as a precuation he jettisoned the canopy. As he pulled the lever he was hit and he lost consciousness. When he came to Fries discovered that Staffa had already ejected and blinded by blood from a gash on his forehead, Fries abandoned the aircraft. (He 219V-16 was powered by Jumo 222 engines and had a larger wing). Fries and Staffa had 11 victories in May 1944 and they went on to add another 6 kills. They used their ejection seats again on 16/17 January 1945 when they were shot down by a Mosquito.

66. Starr destroyed a Me 410 and a UEA in 1944 to take his final score to 6 destroyed, 1 probable, 2 damaged, 2 destroyed on the ground + 1 V-1 destroyed. Starr was killed early in January 1945 when he was flying as a passenger aboard an Avro Anson, which crashed nr Dunkirk killing everyone on board. He was en route to get married at the time.

67. Over England *Fw* Johann Trenke and *Uffz* Beier of 6./KG 51 claimed three Lancasters and two Liberators shot down respectively.

68. Bf 110G-4 720050 05+2 of 3./NJG 3. *Fw* Franz Müllebner, *Flugzeugführer* (pilot), *Uffz* Alfons Josten, *Bordfunker* and *Gefr* Karl Rademacher, *Bordschütze*, all WIA baled out successfully. The Bf 110 cr. at Hoogeveen, S of Groningen.

69. Another 59 Lancasters and 4 Mosquitoes were dispatched to Eindhoven to bomb the Philips factory, over 200 bombers were to attack coastal gun positions on the French coast and a smaller force of Lancasters and Mosquitoes were sent to bomb the Ford Motor Factory at Antwerp.

70. Wrk Nr 730106 2Z+AR cr. at 0230 hrs in forest between Zweifall and Mulartshuette, SE of Aachen. *Oblt* Helmut Schulte, pilot and *Uffz* Hans Fischer, *Bordschütze* both baled out. *Uffz* Georg Sandvoss, *Bordfunker* KIA. The other Bf 110G-4, Wrk.Nr. 720387 2Z+HR, flown by *Uffz* Oskar Völkel, cr. 5 mins later at the Wesertalsperre nr. Eupen, S of Aachen. Völkel and *Uffz*'s Karl Hautzenberger, *Bordfunker* and Günther Boehxne, *Bordschütze*, baled out safely. F/O D.T. Tull of 219 Sqn flying Mosquito NFXVII HK345 claimed a Ju 88 as a 'probable' 55 miles E of Orfordness.

71. The Ju 88 was claimed 15 miles ESE of Bonn. They also damaged a Bf 109 NW of Aachen.

72. Fortress II BU-A SR384/A (ex-385th BG B-17F-130-BO 42-30970, one of 14 B-17Fs received from the 8th Air Force in spring 1944 for training (4 a/c) and jamming duties).

73. D5+KM, which took off from Plantlünne, a satellite airfield between Rheine and Lingen/Emsland at 2303 hrs on 24 May.

74. Leube's victims were the first Fortress crew lost by 214 Sqn on operations. He first set the fuselage of SR384 on fire, then the wings and finally the Fortress exploded over the Oosterschelde near Antwerp at 0057 hrs. Hockley and his mid-upper gunner Sgt Raymond G.M. Simpson KIA; the 7 other men in the crew escaped alive. The victorious Ju 88G-1 crew returned safely to base at 0220 hrs. Leube was KIA 27/28 December 1944. He had scored 22 victories.

75. Between 0115-0129 hrs LK885 of 51 Sqn cr. at Acht, HX320 of 158 Sqn went down nr Tilburg, MZ622 of 76 Sqn cr W of Goirle (Schnaufer's 71st victory), LW653 of 158 Sqn cr between Dongen and Tilburg and LW124 of 429 'Bison' Sqn RCAF SSW of Tilburg.

76. 239 Sqn provided 8 Mosquitoes on Bomber Support. 'A Flt' CO S/L Neil Reeves DSO DFC and P/O A.A. O'Leary DFC** DFM destroyed Bf 110F Wrk Nr. 140032 G9+CR of 7./NJG 1, which cr. at Spannum in Friesland province in Holland at 0115 hrs. *Uffz* Joachim Tank, 26, pilot, slightly wounded. *Uffz*'s Günther Schröder, 19, *Bordfunker* and Heinz Elwers, 24, *Bordschütze* KIA.

77. Although the second Bf 109 had escaped, the 11th victory of Harry White and Mike Allen was duly recorded in 141 Sqn's record book.

78. Elslinger, thinking that the aircraft was out of control had jumped for his life. He came down with his parachute on fire and he had a wounded wrist. He hid his parachute and took care of his wound and made contact with the local resistance who took him to Overpelt where Mr. Bergh, a policeman and his family hid him for 18 days and he received medical treatment from Dr. Poelmans. On 16 June Elslinger moved to the home of Van der Feeten ho and he and another RAF member were moved to Antwerp. He had to follow a man with ginger hair and was told that after a few days he would leave for Spain but the man handed him over to the Germans and he was put into jail at Antwerp. Elslinger was wearing civilian clothes and had a false ID card. He travelled back and forward to Brussels for interrogation and twice he was put in front of a firing squad. At last he was recognized as a PoW and Elslinger was sent to *Stalag Luft VII* at Bankau. He survived a long march to Berlin at the end of the war and was liberated by the Russians.

79. Halifax LW432 *G-George* was scrapped. P/O Kalle was awarded the DFC, Sgt George Burton the DFM. On 30 July 1944, a new *G George* took off to attack Amye-sur-Seulles. The target was successfully attacked but one bomb hung up. Back over England the pilot was forced to make a crash landing at the Air Transport Auxiliary airfield at White Waltham. Kalle overshot the short landing run and ran into a railway cutting. The 500-lb bomb exploded. All the crew were injured except John Elslinger's replacement. Some of the crew were badly burned and the rear gunner later died. Burton injured an arm and became one of Sir Archibald McIndoe's patients at East Grinstead.

80. Menzies was killed in the crash. The rest of the crew, including F/Sgt John Clark, the English flight engineer, WOp/AG Jock Rowan from Edinburgh, mid-upper gunner W/O Herb Rogers of Vancouver, who was making his 24th trip. Sgt R.S. Hall, an American serving in the RCAF, from a small Illinois town with the improbable name of Normal riding in the co-pilot's seat, survived.

81. F/O W.J. Elliott RCAF and Sgt M. Muir also evaded.

82. Halifax LW675 LK-B.

83. First in a series of revenge raids on Britain (where they were known as the 'Baby Blitz') was made by 92 aircraft on London 21/22 January 1944.

84. They included a 4./KG 2 Ju 188E-1 flown by *Hptm* Helmuth Eichbaum was shot down off Southwold and a 5./KG 2 Ju l88E-1 piloted by *Fw* Helmuth Richter was also destroyed while a Me 410A-1 of 1./KG 51 was downed over Brighton.

85. At 0239 hrs Dietrich had attacked a Stirling I of 1657 OCU on approach to Shepherd's Grove. F/O W.A.C. Yates, pilot and all crew killed when it crashed on a dispersal, hitting and badly damaging another Stirling to such an extent that it too had to be w/o.

86. On 23/24 June Wight-Boycott added a Ju 188 destroyed to his score.

87. 125 Lancasters, 86 Halifaxes and 8 Mosquitoes.

88. 1 Mosquito *Intruder,* 1 Stirling minelayer and 2 Halifaxes and a Hudson, which were on Resistance operations, FTR. *Fw* Wilhelm Morlock of 3./NJG 1 claimed the Hudson SE of Tholen Island and a Halifax off Walcheren. A 2nd Halifax was claimed by *Oblt* Hans Krause 30 km S of Subotica. *Hptm* Fritz Söthe claimed 2 *Viermots.*

89. In Mosquito NFII DZ297.

90. In Mosquito NFII DZ256 'U'.

91. 1012 RAF aircraft bombed coastal batteries, 110 aircraft of 100 Group carried out extensive bomber-support operations. 2 Halifaxes and 1 Lancaster were lost. 24 *ABC*-equipped Lancasters of 101 Sqn patrolled all known nightfighter approaches. (2 Intruders and 1 *ABC* Lancaster were lost). 58 a/c of 3 & 5 Groups flew diversion operations (2 Stirlings of 149 Sqn FTR). 31 Mosquitoes bombed Osnabruck w/o loss. In all RAF Bomber Command flew 1211 sorties.

92. A nephew of Sir Charles Kingsford-Smith MC who with fellow pilot C.T.P. Ulm and crew made the first trans-Pacific flight 31 May-9 June 1928 in Fokker F.VIIB/3m *Southern Cross.*

93. 'The final raid of my tour of operations was a few days later on 14 and 15 June when we attacked a German Panzer (tank) force concentrated at night hiding, under cover of trees in a wood. With information from the French Resistance we knew exactly where they were. On 17 June my replacement, W/C Donaldson RAAF, arrived and the next day I started my end of tour leave.'

94. Fewer than 50 plots were made. 2nd TAF's 1st aerial victory of *D-Day* is credited to F/O Roy E. Lelong RNZAF (later F/L DFC*) of Auckland & navigator P/O J.A. McLaren of 605 Sqn in a FBVI who destroyed a Me 410 7 miles SE of Evreux a/f during a *Night Intruder* patrol. (On 10 February 1944 Lelong t/o from his forward a/f at St Dizier and over the Baltic claimed 6 e/a destroyed plus 1 'probable' & 5 'damaged'. Lelong returned to base on 1 engine. His final score was 7 destroyed and 3 V-1s shot down). F/O Pearce-F/O Moore of 409 Sqn in a NFXIII claimed a 'probable'. During June 85 Base Group Mosquitoes destroyed 76 e/a & claimed 5 probables. On 6/7 June F/L E.L. Williams DFC of 605 Sqn in a FBVI shot down a Ju 88 at Orleans-Bricy a/f. F/L Don MacFadyen DFC RCAF-F/L 'Pinky' Wright of 418 Sqn flying HR155 destroyed a Ju 52/3m N of Coulommiers a/f. (MacFadyen finished the war with 7 a/c and 5 V-ls destroyed and 5 a/c destroyed and 17 damaged on the ground). W/C Keith M. Hampshire DSO CO, 456 Sqn RAAF -F/L T. Condon in NFXVII HK286 destroyed a He 177 3 miles E of Barfleur. F/L Allison-F/O R. Stainton of 29 Sqn destroyed a Ju 52/3m and a UEA over Coulommiers. On 7/8 June when Mosquitoes shot down 8 a/c over France 456 Sqn destroyed 4 He 177s and 3 more on the 8th. On 9/10 June 456 Sqn shot down a He 177 & a Do 217. (On 5 July the Australians claimed 3 e/a to take its score to 30 victories since 1 March). 604 Sqn alone destroyed 10 e/a on 7 & 8 June. On 8/9 June F/L J.C.I. Hooper DFC-F/O Hubbard DFM of 604 Sqn in NFXIII MM500 destroyed a Bf 110 NE of Laval & F/O Wigglesworth-Sgt Blomfield of 29 Sqn downed a Ju 88. On the 9/10th 29 Sqn destroyed 2 more e/a & 409 and 410 Sqns destroyed 2 Ju 188s. On 19/20 June S/L F.J.A. Chase-F/O A.P. Watson 264 Sqn shot down a Ju 88 over the Channel.

95. One of the dozen Mosquitoes of 141 Sqn was crewed by W/C Winnie Winn, the new CO and R.A.W. Scott.

96. Remotely possible that it was Wrk Nr. 440272 G9+NS of 8./NJG 1, which cr. at 0054 hrs on the N beach of Schiermonnikoog. *Uffz* Adolf Stuermer, 22-year old replacement pilot (no victories credited); *Uffz* Ludwig Serwein (21) *Bordfunker* and *Gefr* Otto Morath (23) *Bordschütze* KIA.

97. Wrk.Nr. 710454 of 5./NJG 3 cr. 20 km N of Spiekeroog. *Uffz*'s Willi Hammerschmitt (yet another inexperienced replacement pilot) and Friedrich Becker, *Bordfunker* and *Fw* Johannes Kuhrt, *Bordschütze* KIA.

98. AI.Mk.X radar (US SCR 720/729 Eleanora) developed by the Radiation Laboratory, Massachusetts Institute of Technology and built by the Western Electric Co had a range of 8-10 miles. AI Mk X (unlike AI.Mk IV) had no backward coverage so before it could be used on high-level operations a quick interim answer was provided by a modification to *Monica I,* which until the tail warner was fitted, 85 and 157 Sqns flew only low-level airfield intrusions.

99. Shaw and Standley-Smith's NS950 cr. between Hank and Dussen in the Noord-Brabant. Butterfield and Drew were flying PZ189.

100. Apart from the 515 Sqn Mosquito kill by *Hptm.* Strüning, *Lt* Otto Teschner of 11./NJG 1 dispatched a 36th BS/801st BG Carpetbagger Liberator SE of Brussels.

101. Possibly Do 217K-3 Wrk Nr 4742 6N+OR of *Stab* III./KG 100. *Oblt* Oskar Schmidtke, pilot and *Uffzs* Karl Schneider, observer; Helmuth Klinski, *bordfunker,* and Werner Konzett, flight engineer, were killed.

102. 3 in the greater Paris area, his 4th victim crashing 25 km E-SE of Rouen at 0132 hrs.

103. MM125 was shot down at about 0055 hrs (continental time) as it approached the Dutch Coast at 27,000-ft. Wellington was taken prisoner. It was the crew's first operation on 571 Sqn. Downey, who was approaching his 26th birthday, had enlisted in the RAFVR in November 1938 and when war broke out he was called up in December 1939. Qualifying as a bomber pilot at 16 OTU he was posted to 83 Sqn, which was flying Hampdens at Finningley, Yorkshire. During December 1940-July 1941 he completed 32 ops before he was posted to instruct at 16 OTU (where he volunteered for 2 ops whilst with the unit). In 1941 he was awarded the DFM for saving his crew and his aircraft when his Hampden suffered an engine failure on take off. Joe married LACW Margaret Mary Monk in 1941 and in 1943 they had a son, Patrick. In 1942 Joe volunteered for another tour and was posted to 218 Sqn, which was flying Stirlings and during November 1942-April 1943 he completed a further 23 ops.

104. Nabrich, *Staffelkapitän* of 3./NJG 1, was killed in his vehicle during a strafing attack by RAF fighter-bombers on *Eichstrasse 54* from Handorf to Telgte on 27 November 1944. *Fw* Fritz Habicht was WIA on 3/4 February 1945 when he and his pilot, *Hptm* Alexander Graf Rességuier de Miremont baled out of He 219A-2 290070 G9+CH. Over the Ruhr they were pursuing a Lancaster (possibly Lancaster I PD221 BQ-R of 550 Sqn) coned by 4 searchlights but as they went to attack 2 of the searchlights suddenly moved and illuminated the *Uhu.* The Lancaster gunners set the He 219A-2 on fire while the nightfighter crew's fire caused the Lancaster to go down nr. Roermond. (PD221 cr. nr. Westerbeek, Noord Brabant, 9 km SW of Boxmeer. F/O R.G. Nye and crew were KIA). Habicht jettisoned his canopy and his pilot ejected. Habicht's ejection seat handle had been shot off in the attack but he nevertheless managed to get free of the a/c and immediately pull the ripcord of his parachute. He had been hit in the shoulder and chest in the attack and he suffered worse injuries when he hit some tall trees but Habicht survived although his operational flying was over. He had been involved in 17 victories.

105. In NFXIX MM630/E.

106. F/L Micky Phillips and F/L Derek Smith of 85 Sqn destroyed a Bf 110 near Paris.

107. Probably LM158 of 90 Sqn, which cr. 2 km W of Laag Soeren. Friedrich, who was awarded the *Ritterkreuz* on 15 March 1945, was KIA on 16/17 March when his Ju 88G was hit when it collided with or was destroyed by the explosion of a 576 Sqn Lancaster he was attacking.

108. *Oblt* Hanneck shot down 5 Lancasters and Halifaxes in June/July.

109. Their victims were all Lancasters, respectively LL812 of 622 Sqn (cr. nr. Eindhoven); LM465 of 15 Sqn (NW of Venlo) and DV286 of 300 Sqn (cr. into the Ijsselmeer off Wijdenes at 0143 hrs).

110. Lancaster LL678 of 514 Sqn.

111. NFXIX 'Y'. Ju 88 G-1 Wrk Nr. 710833 flown by *Major* Wilhelm Herget, *Kommandeur* I./NJG 4. Herget baled out uninjured, both his crew were wounded but also managed to bale out before the Junkers crashed near Charleroi. 58 of the 73 victories Herget gained were at night.

112. Two 604 Sqn Mosquito crews claimed a probable Fw 190 nr Carentan and a He 177 and a 456 Sqn XVII crew claimed another He 177 off Fecamp. 25 miles SE of Caen F/L Walter G. 'Dinny' Dinsdale RCAF -P/O Jack E. Dunn RCAF of 410 Sqn in NFXIII HK476/O were the first crew to shoot down a *Mistel* (Mistletoe) (piggy-back Bf 109 and a bomb-laden Ju 88) (*Vater und Sohn*) of KG101. Off Normandy F/L J.H. Corre-P/O C.A. Bines of 264 Sqn in NFXIII HK502 also shot down one of the guided bombs. S/L I.A. March-F/L Eyolfson of 410 Sqn in a Mosquito NFXIII, a Ju 88. S/L R.A. Kipp DFC RCAF-F/L P. Huletsky RCAF of 418 Sqn in a FBVI, a He 111 S end Sagnkop Isle. S/L R.B. Cowper DFC RAAF -F/L W. Watson of 456 Sqn in XVII HK356/D, a Ju 88 at sea. F/O P.F.L. Hall-F/O R.D. Marriott of 488 Sqn in NFXIII MM513/D destroyed a Ju 88 10m SW St Lô. W/O H.W. Welham-W/O E.J. Hollis of 141 Sqn in NFII DZ240/H got a Me 410 N of Lille.

113. Bannock was a pre-war civilian pilot and had been an instructor and ferry pilot until finally getting a posting to England in February 1944. After completing a Mosquito OTU course at High Ercall and Greenwood, Nova Scotia he joined 418 Sqn at Holmsley South in May. 418 Sqn had been engaged in *Night Intruding* against enemy airfields as well as conducting low level *Day Rangers* against airfields when operating in pairs. While at Greenwood he teamed up with navigator, Robert Bruce, who recalls. 'In 1939 I was a graduate of Edinburgh University with a first in Music, a brilliant outlook and no money. Deeply influenced by the poetry of Wilfred Owen, who was KIA in November 1918, I joined the Friends Ambulance Unit (as gallant a bunch as any military). But after 2 1/2 years I knew the war was ruinous and I

must be part of the ruin. I was accepted for aircrew training. I was almost 28. Russ on the other hand was young in years – 23 – and old in flying experience and leadership. I arrived at Holmsley South about the 10th of June, Russ a few days earlier.' Bannock and Bruce went on to destroy 8 more e/a and 18 and 1 shared V-1s.

114. Gonsalves and Duckett's victim in the first encounter was Bf 110 5664 G9+IZ of 12./NJG 1. It cr. 9 km W of Tongres, between St. Trond and Maastricht. *Uffz* Heinz Bärwolf (replacement pilot, no victories), who was injured and *Uffz* Fischer, *Bordfunker*, baled out. *Ogefr* Edmund Kirsch, 23-year-old *Bordschütze* KIA. F/L Jimmy Mathews-W/O Penrose of 157 destroyed a Ju 188 the same night. He 219A-0 G9+RK 190180 of 2./NJG 1 was also lost. *Uffz* Willi Beyer and *Obgefr* Horst Walter both KIA.

115. Ju 88 710590 of 1./NJG 2. *Hptm* Herbert Lorenz (1 night victory), *Fw* Rudolf Scheuermann, *Bordfunker* and *Flieger* Harry Huth, *Bordschütze* KIA.

116. Ju 88 G-1 710866 R4+NS of 8./NJG 2, which cr. nr. Volkel a/f. *Lt* Harald Machleidt (a replacement pilot with no combat victories) and *Gefr* Max Rinnerthaler, *Bordschütze* KIA. *Uffz* Kurt Marth, *Bordfunker* WIA.

117. Kendall and Hill's victim was a Bf 110 of NJG 1. Müller, pilot and 2 others KIA.

118. Operation to engage air and ground targets within a wide but specified area.

119. FBVI PZ203/X. Bf 110G-4 Wrk Nr 740076 G9+NS of 8./NJG 1, which had just taken off from Eelde a/f shot down at 1519 hrs. *Uffz* Herbert Beyer, 21 (with one night victory), pilot, *Uffz* Hans Petersmann (21), radar op and *Ogfr*. Franz Riedel (20) AG, all KIA.

120. It was Rabone's 7th victory. Born in England and raised in New Zealand, Rabone had been a pilot in 88 Sqn on Fairey Battles and in May 1940 his a/c was hit by *Flak* during an attack on a bridge at Maastricht. He baled out behind enemy lines before escaping in civilian clothes with a refugee column. Returning to England he was shot down again on 12 June by a Bf 109 during a raid on a Seine bridge and he baled out once more. In August 1940 Rabone transferred to RAF Fighter Command and flying Hurricane Is in 145 Sqn, shot down a Bf 109E off Dungeness. Rabone added 2 more victories in late 1940. In October he had joined 422 Flt, which became 96 Sqn in December as a night fighter unit, flying Hurricanes and Defiants. On 13 April 1941 Rabone and his gunner had to bale out over the Derbyshire Peak District after an engine failure. After a spell on Havocs in 85 Sqn by the summer of 1943 Rabone was flying Mosquito NFIIs in 23 Sqn in the Mediterranean and on 15 August, while flying a Spitfire Vc carrying spare parts to Palermo, Sicily, he shot down a Ju 88. Flying a Mosquito NFII on 8 September he destroyed another Ju 88 and a Heinkel 111 and damaged another Heinkel.

121. From raids on the V-1 sites, whch were all hit, 5 Lancasters FTR. 2 Lancasters MIA on the Saintes raid.

122. F/L W.W. Boylson DFC* RAAF and S/L G.H. Wilson DSO DFC were killed.

123. On 2 February 1955 S/L Engelbach was killed when taking off from RAF Coltishall his Venom NF2 clipped a tree and crashed.

124. DZ240.

125. Possibly Ju 88G-1 Wrk Nr. 710455 of 4./NJG 3, which cr. at Arendonck, Belgium. *Uffz* Eugen Wilfert, yet another inexperienced replacement pilot, *Ogefr* Karl Martin, *Bordfunker* and *Gefr* Rudolf Scherbaum, *Bordschütze* KIA.

126. 300651 B3+LT of 9./KG 54 flown by *Uffz* Gotthard Seehaber, which was returning after a mine laying operation in the invasion area. Seehaber, *Gefr* Kurt Völker, *Ogefrs* Walter Oldenbruch and Hermann Patzel KIA.

127. 13 Tame Boar crews were credited with 21 *Viermot* kills.

128. Light Night Striking Force.

129. In ML960.

130. After a week or so in the station hospital Russell was given leave and returned to Little Staughton. Having suffered quite severe burns to his wrists on leaving the aircraft, Barker was grounded until on 4/5 October, when on only their second trip together after the 28/29 June incident, Russell and Barker's Mosquito was hit by *Flak* N of Luxembourg returning from an attack on a precision tool shop at Heilbronn. MM153 was beyond control, pitching and going down in a spin. Both men baled out over liberated Belgium near Verviers and they returned to 109 Sqn. Russell was then attached to the Mosquito Service Unit at Upwood, which brought his operational flying to an end.

131. In mid-July Rabone rejoined 23 Sqn and his run of luck finally ran out when he and Johns FTR from a *Day Ranger* on 24 July. Rabone's body was washed ashore on Heligoland Island 3 months later

132. Ju 88 711114 of 5./NJG 2 *Uffz* Erich Pollmer WIA. Other crew details unknown.

133. Night operation to engage air and ground targets within a wide but specified area.

134. Ju 88 751065 R4+? of 5./NJG 2 cr. nr Chartres. *Obfw* Fritz Farrherr, pilot (no kills to his credit) and *Ogefr* Heinz Boehme, *Bordschütze* KIA. *Gefr* Josef Schmid, radar operator WIA, baled out. Bf 110G-4 110028 C9+HK of 2./NJG 5, which cr. nr. Compiègne is believed to be 1 of 2 a/c shot down by S/L J.S. Booth DFC*-F/O K. Dear DFC of 239 Sqn. Lt Joachim Hanss, pilot and *Fw* Kurt Stein, *Bordschütze* KIA. *Uffz* Wolfgang Wehrhan, *Bordfunker* WIA. *Lt* Hanss was an *Experte* with 9-12 night *Abschüsse.*

135. Most likely Bf 110G-4 730006 D5+? of 2./NJG 3.

136. The Bf 110G-4 cr. 5 km W of Chièvres, Belgium. Pilot and *Gefr* Richard Reiff (WIA) baled out safely. *Ogefr* Edmund Hejduck, KIA.

137. LMF cases remained a very low percentage of total numbers of Bomber Command. Throughout the war, 4,059 cases were considered – 746 officers and 3313 NCOs. The 'charges' against most were dismissed and only 2726 (389 officers, 2337 NCOs) were actually classified as LMF; a total less than 0.4% of all the aircrews of Bomber Command. The NCO's total was higher, because there were more of them than officers.

138. During 1940-1941 Lofty Wiltshire served as Engine Fitter II E with 82 Sqn on Blenheims at Watton before he was posted overseas. In 1943 he remustered to flying duties and during training in Canada he survived a bad crash and remained in the wreck of the aircraft in sub-zero temperatures for two days before being rescued. He then spent 2 months in hospital recovering from frostbite and snow blindness. He recovered and became a Flight Engineer on Lancasters, being posted to 90 Sqn at Tuddenham.

139. This institution with twin turrets, high on a hill overlooking the town had been the Rockside Hydro, a 160-bed spa hotel before the war.

140. Geismann scored no victories in the *Nachtjagd*, whereas Strüning, who, after 56 victories was KIA on 24 December 1944 while commanding the 9th *Staffel*.

141. *Ogefr* Hans Mäckle (a young replacement pilot with one night victory to his credit) and his crew of Ju 88G-1 night-fighter 4R+UR of 7./NJG 2 completely lost their bearings during a sortie over the North Sea and inadvertently landed at RAF Woodbridge on 13 July 1944. Scientists from TRE investigated the Ju 88's FuG 220 *Lichtenstein SN-2,* FuG 227/1 and FuG 350 Z *Naxos* radars, the last two types being previously unknown to the RAF. They confirmed *Serrate's* ineffectiveness and discovered that the *Nachtjagd* was using the Flensburg FuG 227/1 equipment to home on to *Monica* tail-mounted warning device and the FuG 350 Z *Naxos* to home on to H2S radar bombsight transmissions. RAF bombers were ordered immediately to restrict the use of *H2S* while *Monica* sets were removed from the Lancasters and Halifaxes.

142. F/O William Wright Provan, another 29 Sqn pilot.

143. In 1938 Bob Stainton had been a brilliant captain of the Sussex cricket team.

144. George Allison was killed on 22 July on the squadron's first *Day Ranger*. His navigator Sub Lt (A) C.W. Porter FAA also died.

145. BXVI MM147 of 692 Sqn, which cr. W of Granzow, 9 km NNW of Kyritz at 0155 hrs. F/L Burley DFC (KIA). F/L E.V. Saunders DFC baled out (PoW).

146. *The Mosquito Log* by Alexander McKee. Souvenir Press. 1988. Krause, later *Kommandeur* of III./NJG 11, claimed a Lancaster shot down on 4/5 November 1944 during a Bomber Command raid on Bochum and survived the war despite 3 parachute jumps.

147. PF380. W/C S.D. Watts DSO DFC MiD and P/O A.A. Matheson DFM RNZAF.

148. *Uffz* Wittmann of 1./NJG 10 claimed a Mosquito at Gardelegen-Berlin at about the same time as Strüning. It could be that both claims were for the same Mosquito, as only one FTR from the Berlin raid and no others were lost this night.

149. S/L Terry Dodwell's death remains a mystery. MM136 crashed near Laudin, 35 miles W of Berlin. S/L Terence Edgar Dodwell RAFVR DFC* was 29 years old. He had completed part of a Mosquito tour with 1409 Met Flight before joining 571 Sqn. Before this he had completed a tour with S/L Peter Ashley on 110 Sqn, flying Blenheim IVs. The Germans buried him in the small cemetery at Laudin and later removed and reburied him in the cemetery at Heerstrasse in Berlin.

150. 971 sorties were flown on 20/21 July for the loss of 38 aircraft, or 3.9%. 87 heavies bombed V-weapon sites at Ardouval and Wizernes and 302 Lancasters and 15 Mosquitoes of 1, 5 and 8 Groups bombed rail targets at Courtrai. 153 heavies and 13 Mosquitoes of 4 and 8 Groups attacked the syn-

thetic oil refinery at Bottrop while another 147 Lancasters and 11 Mosquitoes of 1, 3 and 8 Groups attacked an oil plant at Homberg. 106 a/c from training units made a diversionary sweep over the North Sea while Lancasters and Mosquitoes made a spoof raid to Alost. More Mosquitoes raided Hamburg and RCM aircraft and Stirlings made other sorties to further stretch the resources of the *Nachtjagd.* 9 Lancasters were lost on the Courtrai raid (2 of which were destroyed on their way back by *Obstlt* Lent, *Kommodore* of NJG 3, within sight of the British coast off Dover for his 106th and 107th victories). 21 Lancasters and 7 Halifaxes FTR from the Bottrop/Homberg raid. *Nachtjagd* shot down an estimated 15 aircraft from the Bottrop/Homberg force. 75 Sqn RNZAF at Mepal lost 7 of its 25 aircraft.

151. Bf 110G-4 730218 G9+EZ.

152. The two victims of the Drewes crew have been identified as Halifax MZ511 of 578 Sqn which cr. at Apeldoorn/Heerde and Lancaster PB174 of 405 'Vancouver' Sqn RCAF (at Tubbergen, NE of Almelo).

153. Lancasters: HK569 of 75 Sqn at Kessel nr. Venlo and LL859 of 622 Sqn that cr. at Dongen, 30 km NW of Volkel.

154. F/L R.J. Dix-F/O A.J. Salmon of 169 Sqn in FBVI NS997/G claimed a Bf 110 at Kiel. This was Bf 110G-4 Wrk Nr 730036 G9+ER of 7./NJG 1, which was shot down at very low level around midnight and cr. nr. Balk in Friesland Province, Holland. *Fw* Heinrich-Karl Lahmann (25) pilot, *Uffz* Günther Bouda (21) AG, baled out. (Lahmann was KIA in March 1945. He had 2 combat victories) *Uffz* Willi Huxsohl (21) *Bordfunker* KIA. F/O N. Veale and F/O R.D. Comyn of 239 Sqn in NFII DZ661 also claimed a Bf 110 at Kiel. At 0125 hrs Bf 110G-4 730117 G9+GR of 7./NJG 1 was shot down 5 km N of Deelen airfield. *Lt* Josef Hettlich, pilot and *Fw* Johann Treiber, *Bordfunker* who were both slightly injured and the *Bordschütze* all baled out safely. F/L A. C. Musgrove-F/O G. Egerton-Hine of 29 Sqn in NFXIII claimed a Bf 110 nr Leeuwarden a/f. This was 441083 G9+OR of 7./NJG 1, which was shot down at 0147 hrs during landing and which cr. at Rijperkerk, N of Leeuwarden a/f. *Hptm* Siegfried Jandrey (30) pilot and *Uffz* Johann Stahl, (25) *Bordfunker*, KIA. *Uffz* Anton Herger (24) *Bordschütze* injured.

155. Drewes' Bf 110 G-4 720410 G9+MD cr. to the NE of Tubbergen, nr. the Dutch-German border. His first victim was Halifax MZ511 LK-M of 578 Sqn, a veteran of 32 sorties, which had left Burn at 2305 for a raid on Bottrop. Although the crew was warned of a possible night fighter attack when a blip appeared on the *Monica* set, Drewes' attack came as a complete surprise. F/L Alastair T. Hope-Robertson gave the bale-out signal 'J' over the visual intercom. F/O Kenneth Parsons, bomb-aimer and P/O Jack Smith, navigator were probably thrown clear when the Halifax exploded and they landed unconscious beneath opened parachutes. At 0130 MZ511 cr. nr Heerde where Hope-Robertson and 4 of his crew were later laid to rest. 578 Sqn lost 4 a/c all told. 2 more collided in thick cloud on their return. Drewes' 2nd victim was Lancaster PB174 LQ-P of 405 'Vancouver' Sqn RCAF, a PFF unit. F/L J.D. Virtue RCAF (28) Toronto, Ontario and 6 crew KIA when their a/c exploded. They were laid to rest in the Roman Catholic Cemetery of Tubbergen on 24 July. The Dutch Resistance hid sole survivor F/Sgt M. S. Stoyko RCAF, rear gunner. Whilst still recovering from his wounds, on 27 July *Hptm* Martin Drewes received the *Ritterkreuz* for his 48 victories. He added 1 more kill to his total before the end of the war, on 3/4 March 1945. He was decorated with the Oak Leaves to his *Ritterkreuz* 3 weeks before the capitulation of *Nazi* Germany. *Fw* Erich Handke's 58th and 59th *Abschussbeteiligungen* earned him the rare award for a *Bordfunker* of the *Ritterkreuz,* which he and his pilot received from *Gen* Schmid, C-in-C of the *Nachtjagd*, on 27 July.

156. Twin-engined *Nachtjäger* claimed 17 kills.

157. 8 Lancasters and 4 Halifaxes were lost on the Stuttgart raid and 1 Mosquito *Intruder* FTR. 11 of these including the 141 Sqn Mosquito (F/L A.J. Smitz (PoW) and F/O J.J. Bambury (KIA) who were shot down W of the Rhine WSW of Ludwigshafen, were claimed destroyed by the *Nachtjagd.*

158. W/C Reid-F/L Peacock of 409 Sqn in NFXIII MM587 got a Ju 88 while F/O D.T. Tull of 219 Sqn in a NFXVII got a Ju 88 50 miles ENE La Havre for his 4th victory. Tull's first victory was a He 219 on 3/4. June 1944 (He 219) followed by a Me 410 (7/8. June 1944) Ju 88 (11/12 July 1944). Posted to the FIU he scored 4 more kills, 3 on Mosquitoes (Ju 88 11/12 September 1944, Bf 110 23/24 September 1944, Ju 88G 14/15 October 1944) He 111 flying a Beaufighter VI on 25/26 October 1944. He and navigator F/O P.J. Cowgill DFC KIA 18/19. December 1944.

159. Harold Brownlow Morgan Martin, an Australian flew Hampdens and Lancasters, including *P-Popsie* on the famous 617 Sqn dams' raid of 18 May 1943. He had been grounded by the AOC 5 Group in February 1944 and was sent on 'rest leave' to 100 Group HQ at Bylaugh Hall, Norfolk but in April he inveigled his way onto 515 Sqn and flew *Night Intruder* and bomber escort operations. On 26 April 1944, flying a Mosquito VI Martin-F/O Smith had destroyed a UEA at Gilze Rijen a/f. By war's end Martin had flown 83 sorties.

160. Ju 88G-1 713649 R4+KT of 9./NJG 2, flown by *Hptm* August Speckmann, pilot (no victories to his credit) KIA, which cr. 20 km SSW of Toul, France. *Ofw* Wilhelm Berg, flight engineer and *Uffz* Otto Brüggenkamp, *Bordschütze* KIA. *Ofw* Arthur Boos *Bordfunker* WIA. Probably one of the Ju 88s destroyed by Gregory-Stephens and Harry White DFC*-Mike Allen DFC* of 141 Sqn.

161. On 20/21 July II./NJG 1 destroyed 3 *Viermots* (two by *Uffz* Sarzio and Lancaster III NE164 of 550 Sqn, which cr. at Ottrott nr. Strassburg by *Oblt* Gottfried Hanneck, *St.Kpt*, 6./NJG 1.

162. Ebhardt's victims were: MZ816 of 433 'Porcupine' Sqn RCAF at Prinzenmoor at 0123 hrs and NP716 of 408 Sqn just 6 mins later in the vicinity of Heide. Ebhardt's 3rd Halifax (possibly MZ859 of 431 'Iroquois' Sqn RCAF) disappeared into the North Sea 25 km E of Heligoland at 0137 hrs.

CHAPTER SEVEN

'ROUND THE CLOCK'

In July 1944 the six squadrons of 85 (Base) Group, 2nd TAF formed for the purpose of providing fighter cover over the continent leading up to and after D-Day, downed 55 German aircraft and claimed two probables.[1] On the night of 29/30 July F/L George 'Jamie' Jameson DFC RNZAF and his navigator, F/O A. Norman Crookes, from Derbyshire, were on patrol in the Coutance-St. Lô area in their Mosquito NFXIII. This 488 Squadron RNZAF crew were hunting for any German fighters in the vicinity with zeal born of personal tragedy.[2] When they saw against the dawn an unidentified aircraft approaching head-on at 5000 ft Jameson recognized it as a Junkers 88. He turned hard to port and followed him through the cloud tops. As the Kiwi closed to 300 yards there was a series of explosions from the ground caused by the Junkers dropping his bombs on Allied troops below. He tried to get away but Jameson gave two short bursts as they entered the next clear patch and after a fire in the port engine and fuselage the Ju 88 went down through the clouds vertically and hit the ground near Caen. Jameson circled the crash scene when Crookes picked up another contact on his radarscope. A visual sighting was soon obtained of an aircraft flying just over the clouds at about 280 mph. Whilst closing on it, another Ju 88 suddenly appeared through the cloud about one mile ahead, flying in the same direction as the first aircraft. As Jameson drew closer the second Ju 88 seemed to see him and did a hard port turn, diving towards cloud cover. Jameson and Crookes followed on the turn and opened fire from dead astern at 350/400 yards range. A large fire started in the Ju 88's starboard engine and it disappeared vertically through clouds, well ablaze.[3]

Jameson and Crookes continued on patrol. Almost immediately Jamie obtained a brief visual on an aircraft crossing from port to starboard some 5000 ft away and identified it as a Ju 88. Crookes confirmed this and took over on his 'box-of-tricks' keeping Jameson behind the enemy aircraft, which was now taking most violent evasive action and at the same time, was jamming their equipment. When they were down almost to tree-top height Jameson regained the visual at only 250 yards, opening fire immediately and causing the Junkers to pull up almost vertically, turning to port with sparks and debris falling away. The Ju 88 eventually stalled and nose-dived into a four-acre field near Lisieux where it exploded. As the time was now 0515 hours Jameson climbed to 5000 ft and requested Control to vector him back to any activity, as he had already observed further anti-aircraft fire through the clouds ahead. Norman Crookes soon obtained two more contacts and Jamie decided to take the nearest, chasing this until a sighting was obtained at 4000 ft range where it was identified as a Do 217. The Dornier pilot evidently spotted the Mosquito at the same time because he immediately began intensive evasive weaving and climbing before entering cloud where it straightened out just as Jameson opened fire at 300 yards. Strikes were seen on the Dornier's fuselage, which began to burn furiously as the enemy aircraft turned its nose up and to starboard with the rear-gunner opening fire but the gunner's dying burst missed and the aircraft dived into the ground with a terrific explosion. Jameson had fired 320 20mm shells to destroy all four aircraft in the space of just 20 minutes, a feat which took the New Zealander's score to nine enemy aircraft destroyed.

In August 77 enemy aircraft were destroyed in the air by the seven night-fighter and fighter-bomber squadrons of 2nd TAF. On 1/2 August Canadians S/L James D. Somerville and F/O G.D. Robinson of 410 'Cougar' Squadron RCAF in a NFXIII equipped with AI radar[4] intercepted a Ju 188 near Tessy. Somerville fired a short burst and the port wing of the

Ju 188 disintegrated outward of engine nacelle. It flicked over into a steep half spiral to starboard and dived vertically into the ground. A violent explosion followed.[5]

The night following, 2/3 August Somerville and Robinson scored their 3rd victory when they shot down a Do 217 six miles NW of Pontorson at 2255 hrs.[6] The situation in the invasion area was becoming so desperate for the Germans that night-fighter units like NJG 4 were now ordered to make low-level attacks on Allied positions. After being taken prisoner of war in August 1944 *Hptm* Hans Autenrieth, a Ju 88G-1 pilot in 6./NJG 4 and *Staffelkapitän*, was one who described this type of operation as pointless. His aircraft were neither bombers nor fighter-bombers and his night fighter crews were only trained and equipped for air combat. On the night of 2/3 August whilst on low level sortie in the area of Avranches his Ju 88G-1 had recieved several hits from U.S. anti-aircraft and having lost an engine he had to make an emergency landing at Coulommiers. At around 2230 hrs on 3 August Autenrieth took off from the base on a night-fighting patrol in the area of Brest as the German night fighter control was expecting the landing of American or British paratroops or other airborne forces in the area. With him in the Ju 88 was his *Bordfunker Fw* Rudolf 'Rudi' Adam, who before the war was a trumpeter in a dance-band and gunner *Uffz* Georg 'Schorsch' Helbig. In over three years of flying together this *Nachtjagd* team had destroyed 23 British night bombers in air combat. Autenrieth headed towards the Brest area accompanied by six other Ju 88s of his *Staffel*:

> 'We experienced a dreamlike beautiful night during our climb to 3000-4000 meters; clear skies, bright moonlight and gleaming white cumulus clouds continually approaching and then slipping by below us. We had the impression of flying over huge snow-covered mountains and were fascinated by this display of nature under a star-spangled sky. We were soon brought back to the hard facts of life when we heard over the radio that the operations in the area of Brest had been cancelled and we received orders to fly low-level atatcks on enemy postions in the area of in the area of Avranches-Rennes as during the night before. As we abandoned our course to Brest and headed for Avranches, we were suddenly hit by *Flak* from the American occupied area. A loud bang indicated that we had received a hit in the fuselage of our Ju 88. I tried to avoid further hits by twisting about and checked the instruments in the cockpit. Suddenly Rudi shouted, 'Aircraft behind!' At the same instant we were fired upon by a Mosquito night-fighter. He hit the port engine and wing of our machine, which caught fire at once. I gave my crew orders to bale out and had my hands full keeping the aircraft level long enough for Rudi Adam and then Schorsch Helbig to get out.'

Autenrieth sprained his left ankle on landing and limped to a farmhouse where the French occupants told him that the area he had parachuted into had been taken by the Americans two days earlier and he was advised to surrender to them. Autenrieth refused and was at large for two days before he was found by French partisans on the third day. They interrogated him and took him to a forest nearby where they clearly intended to shoot him. He was only saved when an American truck appeared and he was handed over to the U.S. troops. After further interrogation in Cherbourg and a spell in captivity in England Autenrieth was sent to the United States where he spent the next one and a half years in a PoW camp.[7]

On 6 August 604 'County of Middlesex' Squadron became the first England-based Mosquito fighter squadron to move to France when it transferred to A.8 at Picauville on the Cherbourg Peninsula. On the night of 5/6 August F/L J.A.M. Haddon and F/O R.J. Mcllvenny of 604 Squadron took off on a night patrol in NFXIII MM514.[8] When Haddon saw a tiny speck ahead in the sky at a distance of 3500 ft his navigator, who was using night glasses, voiced the opinion that it could be a Ju 88. Pilots seldom believed that navigators could tell a Lancaster from a Lysander but Mac was much above average and Haddon decided discretion was the better part of valor. He slid well to one side and below so that they were not silhouetted against the moon as they had been. It also gave them a chance to see the aircraft from the best angle. As Haddon closed it was clear that the target was a 188 and he did not know the Mosquito crew was there. Haddon closed to 800 ft, checked for the tenth time that his guns were set to fire, that the props were in near fine pitch and that the gunsight was dim enough to see through. Then he pulled up behind and opened fire hitting the Ju 88's port engine, then the fuselage. Something left the aircraft which was on fire on the way down and the Mosquito crew ducked. The Ju 188's pyrotechnics exploded and it finally went in near Domfront in the area of Rennes.

Before they had time for the usual mutual admiration to begin Haddon and McIlvenny got a call to turn southeast again because there was more 'trade' at 25 miles and below. Haddon put the nose hard down and eventually McIlvenny got a number of contacts. Haddon ended up overshooting one of them and it was clear that this was no sitting duck. He knew the Mosquito crew was there and what he had to do about it. After several visuals on an 88 that was all over the sky, doing steep turns, climbing and diving, Haddon finally managed to hold him visually and fly as in a day combat. He and Mac had developed a drill for such circumstances and the navigator called height and airspeed to Haddon every few seconds so that they would not fly into the ground. As he tried to turn inside the 88 to get his gun-sight on him Haddon found him flying in a very tight turn, much too low for comfort. Suddenly the Ju 88 went on his back and dived, perhaps having stalled. Shortly afterwards there was a great flash from the ground and Operations and Mac lost contact. Later the French Underground confirmed time and place near Antrain where it had gone in.

On 6 August F/L 'Jamie' Jameson and F/O Norman Crookes of 488 Squadron took off on their last sortie together in *R-Robert*. The controller informed them that 'Bandits' were making for the front-line. Jameson gave a '*Tallyho* '(enemy sighted) over his R/T and he claimed a Ju 88 damaged five miles W of the Vire before notching his 11th victory, a Ju 88 15 miles east of Avranches. *R for Robert* landed back at Colerne to a rapturous welcome.[9] Also returning successfully to Colerne were W/C J.D. Somerville and F/O G.D. Robinson of 410 RCAF Squadron in NFXIII MM566/R equipped with AI.Mk.VIII after a patrol south of St. Malo. At St. Hilaire they picked up a contact at two miles range, 30-35° above at 12 o'clock. The Mosquito was at 4000 ft and Somerville's starboard engine was missing badly but he managed to climb to about 5500 ft where a visual was obtained about 1000 ft above, dead ahead. Flak was starting to explode ahead and this seemed to frighten the German pilot, as he made a turn to port and started to let down slowly. This suited Somerville because the starboard engine was giving considerable difficulty. When he saw him start to turn Somerville cut across the inside of his turn and pulled in to about 900 ft, slightly below, where he recognized him as a Ju 88. The Canadian closed in, pulled up and opened fire at 700 ft. A few strikes were seen on the starboard engine, which caught fire, before the Ju 88 did a wide sweeping spiral to port from 3000 ft and struck the ground with an extremely violent explosion, scattering debris over a large area. It was Somerville's fourth victory.

In all on the night of 6/7 August Mosquitoes of 2nd TAF claimed nine enemy aircraft over France. Among the missing was *Hptm* Helmut Bergmann, a *Ritterkreuzträger* and *St.Kpt* of 8./NJG 4 with 37 kills, during a sortie in the Invasion Front area of Avranches-Mortain. No trace was ever found of his Bf 110G-4 or his crew.[10]

On the night of 7/8 August when 1019 heavy bombers blasted the Normandy battle area Mosquitoes of 2nd TAF claimed ten more victories,[11] almost one for each bomber lost. Ten heavies fell victim to *Nachtjäger* and one to flak. *Oblt* Heinz Rökker of 2./NJG 2 claimed three Lancasters NE of Le Havre for his 39-41st victories. The night following 2nd TAF Mosquito crews scored another three victories,[12] as 170 Lancasters and ten Mosquitoes of 1, 3 and 8 Groups attacked oil depots and storage facilities at Aire-sur-Lys and the Fôret de Lucheux in France for one Lancaster lost.[13] Though they destroyed three enemy aircraft on 8/9 August,[14] 100 Group Mosquito victories meanwhile were on the wane. This was largely due to successful German counter-measures to the *Serrate* homing device used in the Bomber Support units. In August, 331 *Serrate*/AI.Mk.IV sorties yielded just eight successful combats. 141 Squadron claimed just one, while 239 Squadron destroyed only three but lost two crews. 169 Squadron destroyed four. Two of the 169 Squadron Mosquito victories went to F/O Andy Miller DFC and F/O Freddie Bone DFC. Their Bf 109 over Dijon on 10/11 August when 104 Halifaxes of 4 Group and 20 Lancasters of 1 and 8 Groups attacked the town's rail junction and rail yards was their tenth victory of the war.[15] Their 11th on 11/12 August when 179 Lancasters and ten Mosquitoes of 1 and 8 Groups carried out a raid on rail yards at Givors[16] was not confirmed until after the war for Miller and Bone failed to return from a patrol near Heligoland. Freddie Bone picked up a contact crossing slightly at quite a rate and eventually the Mosquito FBVI caught up with it. Vertically above Miller identified it as a He 219 *Uhu*. He dropped back to about 150 yards before giving it four two-second bursts. The Mosquito was so close that it was hit by debris and lost coolant in both engines. Miller glided in over the coast of Holland and Bone baled out at 1200 ft. Miller followed at 800-900 ft.[17]

On 12 August 117 bombers attacked fuel dumps in the Fôret de Montrichard while 68 Lancasters of 1 Group and two Mosquitoes of 5 Group blasted *U-boat* pens at Brest, La Pallice and Bordeaux. Eight Mosquitoes of 100 Group provided a fighter escort for the bombers attacking the French Atlantic coast and no bombers were lost during the day's operations. However, on 12/13 August when Bomber Command mounted 1167 sorties for attacks on Brunswick, the Opel motor factory at Rüsselsheim, German troop concentrations at Falaise and flying-bomb sites in France a staggering 49 aircraft, or 4.2% were lost. The worst casualties were at Brunswick where the German defenses destroyed 17 Lancasters and ten Halifaxes while 134 Lancasters and seven Halifaxes failed to return from Rüsselsheim. *Schwerterträger Hptm* Heinz-Wolfgang Schnaufer, *Kommandeur* IV./NJG 1 was credited with the destruction of four Lancasters, all from the Rüsselsheim force, which took his score to 93 victories at night. Altogether *Nachtjagd* claimed 47 *Viermots*, mainly Lancasters and Halifaxes.

Between the nights of 12/13 and 20/21 August 2nd TAF and 100 group Mosquito crews destroyed 14 enemy aircraft. On the night of the 14/15th S/L Somerville and F/O G.D. Robinson of 410 Squadron RCAF again in NFXIII MM477/U equipped with AI.Mk.VIII went in search of their fifth victory.

Fifteen miles due West of Le Havre they picked up a contact and Somerville pulled in behind it about 1 1/2 miles behind before he started to close. Robinson maintained contact on the AI as Somerville closed the range untill finally the enemy aircraft leveled off at about 10,500 ft after turning a complete 360°. Somerville got to within 1800 ft and almost directly above before he started to pull up. The enemy machine's exhausts disappeared but visual was regained at 800ft range and Somerville closed to 600 ft and saw that it was a Ju 88. Robinson looked through his Ross Night Glasses and from directly underneath he confirmed his pilot's recognition. Somerville dropped back to 450 ft, pulled up to dead astern and opened fire. The fuselage of the Ju 88 burst with a violent explosion and disintegrated without firing a shot. Somerville pulled up in a very steep climb and broke away to starboard. He asked control for a fix and was given 15 miles due west of Le Havre.[18]

On 26/27 August Bomber Command raided Kiel for the loss of 17 Lancasters, all of which were probably shot down by Tame Boars. W/O Les Turner and F/Sgt Frank Francis destroyed a Ju 88 near Bremen to add to the Bf 109 they had shot down on 14/15 July. They allowed their target to pull away to 1000-ft range and then Turner opened fire. The port engine immediately burst into flames and turned gently starboard into a diving turn leaving a long spiral of gray smoke. Turner followed, firing intermittently, observing strikes all over the fuselage. A tremendous flash was seen as aircraft hit the ground. At the time of the interception Turner had a feeling of extreme anger because just before take off he read Press reports of the discovery of the extermination ovens at Lübeck. He was so incensed that he was determined that any *Nazi* within range was not going to aid that war effort.[19]

On the night of 29/30 August 402 Lancasters and one Mosquito of 1, 3 and 6 and 8 Groups attacked Stettin for the loss of 23 Lancasters and 189 Lancasters of 5 Group carried out one of their most successful attacks of the war on Königsberg. For Canadian F/O Jack F. Hamilton, mid-upper gunner in the crew of Lancaster JO-J 'Jumpin' Jive' of 463 Squadron, Königsberg was his 21st trip (and longest at almost 11 hours) in a tour 6 June-17 October 1944. Hamilton had started out as a tail gunner at OTU but at six foot tall he was too big for the gun turret and he had problems with the gun sights:

'Our English tail gunner was much smaller than me. Tail gunners were in the coldest part of the Lancaster and had to wear a lot of heavy bulky flying clothing, some of which was electrically heated. I also wore heavy flying clothing and this created a problem regarding urinating. I often had to urinate in my flying clothes and the piss usually ended up in my flying boots where it sometimes froze!

'We flew across southern Sweden on the way in, which was against international law. After that our course on our starboard side was along the German Baltic coast, sometimes over water and sometimes over the land close to the shore. This is when the German night-fighters first attacked. One night-fighter flew right over us. I thought that he was attacking us but he overshot and shot down a Lancaster a little below on the port side over the water. Several more Lancasters were shot down from this point all the way to Königsberg. There was also a lot of *Flak* along our route. Just short of Koningsberg we were attacked by what I thought at first was a Mosquito but turned out to be a Me 210, which looks very much like a Mosquito. However he over-shot us and missed. There appeared to be a lot of Mosquito Pathfinder aircraft over the target and they closeby resemble twin-engined German aircraft in the dark of night. We bombed the target (we think) and headed back down the Baltic during which time we could see several Lancasters shot down but we were not attacked and I assume that we again crossed Sweden. About this time we were advised by radio to expect heavy concentrations of night-fighters over Denmark. They hit us over Denmark and a considerable battle ensued at a medium altitude, as we started to descend to the North Sea. Our aircraft was not hit but several Lancasters were shot down at this point and we had to take evasive action to evade the night-fighters who appeared to be in great strength. We decided to reduce altitude and increase our speed to the coast but the fighters were still on our tail. We did not fire back so as not to give away our position from our tracer fire. We had some minor damage, which had to be from the fighters as there was little or no *Flak*. Finally, in desperation, we increased speed and dropped down to ground level when about half way across Denmark to the coast. Just as we crossed the coast at zero level, a *Flak* battery opened up on us and we had to climb up to a few hundred feet to get out of the low *Flak*. After we left the Danish coast we could look back and see the air battle continuing but I did not see any more Lancasters shot down.[20] We made it back safely to our drome at Waddington in Lincolnshire, where I received a commission as a pilot officer the day after the raid.'

During August in 1520 sorties *Nachtjagd* aircraft scored 164 victories, or 1.6 per cent of all Bomber Command sorties dispatched, losing 38 aircraft. *Nachtjagd*'s effectiveness further declined during September when the arm was deprived of ground radar control, the 'Y' service and its forward airfields in France. Just 76 kills were made in 1301 sorties or just 1.1 per cent of 6,400 Bomber Command sorties.

S/L Geoff Rothwell's career by now was anything but eventful. He had soon tired of instructing and commenced a barrage of applications to return to operations but they were all turned down by his CO. After nearly ten months at OTU he obtained a posting through Air Ministry, which his CO was unable to block, to 138 Special Duties Squadron at Tempsford, which was engaged in dropping secret agents and supplies to the Resistance Movements in Norway, Denmark, Holland, Belgium and France. He recalls:

> 'The squadron was equipped with Halifax aircraft, which I found easier to fly than Stirlings, which had a very high undercarriage and were difficult to land. The work was entirely different from the normal bombing operation and infinitely more satisfying. I welcomed being amongst highly skilled aircrew, few of whom had not completed at least one tour with a Bomber Command squadron and it was noticeable that there was an air of dedication and determination amongst them. Although the work was dangerous the skill of the personnel prevented serious losses and it was satisfying that much more individuality was permitted with heights and routes to dropping zones than was possible on an ordinary bombing operation when it was necessary to fly within certain limits to ensure safety. My tour with 138 Squadron ended on the night of 8/9 September when I flew my 71st operation to drop the agents Pieter de Vos and Tobias Biallosterski, codenamed '*Backgammon*' and '*Draughts*' at the dropping zone *Mandrill*, which was operated by a farmer, J. Schipper, near Spanbroek. After successfully completing the operation I crashed at De Cocksdorp on Texel and I was taken prisoner by the Germans.'

With the Allied armies advancing into France the Chief of Air Staff once again gained control of Bomber Command, which resumed its area bombing campaign and also mounted a new precision bombing campaign against oil and transportation targets. On 6 September Emden was bombed in daylight by 181 heavies escorted first by Spitfires and then American Mustangs, for the loss of one Lancaster. It was the final Bomber Command raid of the war on the city. Another daylight raid, on eight different strong points at Le Havre on 10 September, involved 992 heavies and all the bombers returned safely. A follow up raid the next day also saw the return of all 218 aircraft involved. On 11 September escorted by 26 squadrons of Spitfires, Mustangs and Tempests, 379 bombers pounded synthetic oil plants at Castrop-Rauxel, Kamen and Gelsenkirchen (Nordstern) in Germany. German fighters were noticable by their absence though eight heavies were lost to flak or to 'friendly' bombs. *Nachtjagd* made several claims on the night of 11/12 September when 12 Lancasters failed to return from a raid on Darmstadt by 226 Lancasters and 14 Mosquitoes of 5 Group. Three Lancaster minelayers were lost in the Kattegat and *Lt* Kurt Welter of 10./JG 300 was credited with shooting down a Mosquito, one of 47 which went to Berlin.[21]

On the night of 12/13 September *Wilde Sau* pilots *Lt* Kurt Welter and *Ofw* Baltenschat of 10./JG 300 claimed two Mosquitoes each. No Mosquito bombers were lost, though a NFII crew in 239 Squadron failed to return to West Raynham. Graves containing F/O Bill Breithaupt DFC RCAF and F/O J.A. Kennedy DFC DFM were found on 15 January 1947 when it was determined from witnesses that they had been shot down by a Bf 110 but had in turn brought this down at Ranschhack before their Mosquito crashed. The German crew baled out and confirmed that this was so. Four other German aircraft were claimed shot down by 100 Group and 2nd TAF Mosquito Intruders.[22] There was little if anything that the *Nachtjagd* could do to staunch the night offensive and while RAF raids by over 1000 bombers became fairly commonplace operational losses began to fall quite dramatically. This was due in part to the resourcefulness of Mosquito night fighter crews of 2nd TAF and 100 Group. Navigator-radar operator F/Sgt Robert Denison MacKinnon had never been to Night-Flying Training School but 85 Squadron had been short of navigators at the time and he was posted straight from training to the unit. He teamed up with F/L Bill House and they had flown their first op over Europe on the night prior to *D-Day* when they flew an intruder patrol over the Cherbourg Peninsular in support of the hundreds of U.S. gliders crossing the Channel. MacKinnon's first encounter with the enemy, in a NFXIX on 13/14 September was eventful, as he recalls:

> 'I guided Bill onto a Me 110 near Koblenz and managed it without the crew being aware of us. Bill opened fire and I thought it was us who were being attacked. The noise to me was terrifying but to the enemy it must have been terrible. I think that we must have hit its oxygen bottles because the whole plane just blew up in front of our eyes.'

Their victim was Bf 110G-4 G9+EN of 5./NJG 1 piloted by *Oblt* Gottfried Hanneck, who recalls:

> 'I took off at 2234. My crew consisted of *Unteroffiziers* Erich Sacher, radar/radio op and Willi Wurschitz (who on this sortie served as air gunner but normally was a radar operator). We had been ordered to

fly to a radio beacon in the Frankfurt area and await further developments. At the beacon we flew around in wide circles and listened on the radio frequency to the messages from our controllers relating to the developments in the air. Then Sacher reported a blip on his *SN-2* radar set. He could not quite determine it but gave me courses to steer to the target. The target flew in a westerly direction at a distance of about 6000 meters. It could be a homebound enemy aircraft. I followed and tried to reduce the distance by increasing my airspeed. The blip on the radar screen however, did not become clearer. Since we had been chasing it for about 20 minutes and by now we had probably arrived over the frontline, we had to turn around and return to the radio beacon. At this instant we were fired upon and many hits struck the wings of my aircraft. The control column was shaking – a clear indication that the controls were heavily damaged – and I ordered, 'Prepare to bale out'. The intercom was still functioning and my crew was not injured. We received another burst of gunfire and the 110 immediately caught fire in both wings and the pressure on my control column was completely gone. The aircraft was plunging down out of control! There was only one option left: save our lives – the parachute. I counted for four or five seconds to give my crew the opportunity to 'hit the silk'. Then I opened the roof of my cockpit and jumped out through the ball of fire. I counted for several seconds before I pulled the ripcord for fear of colliding with my crashing plane. The canopy unfolded and I floated down towards the dark earth. To estimate my height I fired off a Verey light towards the ground. It fell into a meadow and I swung to and fro a few more times before I hit the ground. I glanced at my watch and saw it was 2335 hrs. I landed East of Pruem in the Eifel and stayed under cover at the edge of a small wood for the remaining hours of darkness, as I did not want to walk into the arms of enemy soldiers. When dawn broke I sneaked to the East and soon ran into German soldiers. I had suffered second and third degree burns to my head and hands. My crew had been killed in the crash. In this way, a RAF long-range night fighter 'revenged' my six night kills of four-engined bombers.'[23]

Two Mosquito bombers, which failed to return from the attack on Berlin on 13/14 September were claimed shot down SE of the capital by *Ofw* Egbert Jaacks of I./NJG 10 and at Braunschweig by *Lt* Karl Mitterdorfer of 10./JG 300.[24] Two nights later, on 15/16 September, 490 aircraft bombed Kiel for the loss of four Halifaxes and two Lancasters. Three Mosquitoes and a Stirling of 199 Squadron in 100 Group were lost on Bomber Support and a Mosquito XX of 608 Squadron failed to return from a raid on Berlin.[25] *Lt* Kurt Welter claimed two of the Mosquitoes, one south of Berlin and the other north of Aachmer and *Fw* Reichenbach of 10./JG 300 one other northwest of Wittenburg.[26]

On 16/17 September Bomber Command's operations were in support of the Allied airborne landings at Arnhem and Nijmegen in Holland. Six Mosquitoes of 239 Squadron supported attacks on German airfields in Holland and Germany during the night and 141 Squadron took part at dawn on the 17th. W/C Charles V. 'Winnie' Winn and five other Mosquito crews carried out a low-level attack on Steenwijk, one of three airfields bombed during the night. Four Mosquitoes were damaged by *Flak*. Winn damaged a twin-engined Junkers on the ground and buildings and personnel were strafed. Trains were attacked on the way home. Six more Mosquitoes of 239 Squadron kept up the momentum, with support raids on the airfields again on the night of 17/18 September.[27] At last light on 18 September, two Mosquitoes of 141 Squadron flew protective patrols for nine Fortresses of 214 and 223 Squadrons supplying a *Mandrel* screen[28] off the Dutch coast and the action was repeated again at first light on the 19th. The Fortresses were covered by two 141 Squadron Mosquitoes again at last light on the 22nd.

Chas Lockyer, a Mosquito BXX pilot in 608 Squadron, 8 Group, had begun his second tour of operations with a trip to Berlin on 15/16 September, having flown a tour of ops in Hampdens on 106 Squadron in 1941, flew his second trip to Bremen on 17/18 September. He recalls:

'Naturally enough, with 635 Lancaster Squadron and 608 Mosquito Squadron sharing the same airfield at Downham Market there was a lot of good-humoured rivalry and banter between the respective aircrews. Our cause wasn't helped by some idiot naming the Mosquito squadrons of 8 Group 'The Light Night Striking Force', which left us wide open to sarcastic suggestions that the qualification for service on a Mosquito squadron was presumably an inability to see in the dark! It was later changed to 'The Fast Night Striking Force'; equally clumsy but less ambiguous. The Mossies were given a wide variety of tasks including such niceties as dropping route markers and target indicators over a false target while the main force pressed on elsewhere. With the introduction of the 'pregnant' Mosquito version [BXVI, which the squadron began receiving in March 1945] adapted to carry a 'Cookie' (4000-lb bomb, or 'blockbuster'), we became a reasonably lethal bombing force in our own right, particularly as we could operate in weather conditions that grounded the heavies. The inhabitants of Berlin would be the first to acknowledge that 100 Mosquitoes each carrying a 'Cookie' weren't the most welcome visitors night after night. When bad weather grounded the main force, small groups of Mosquitoes could be sent to a wide variety of targets in the *Reich*. Their objective was to get a large part of Germany out of bed and into the shelter so there were very few nights when the sirens were silent. Our second trip, to Bremen, promised to be a bit of an anti-climax. The Intelligence Officer assured us that owing to the demand for manpower to stem the Allied and Russian advance women and old men were now manning the anti-aircraft guns.

'We'd just completed our bombing and camera run when all hell broke out around us as we were introduced to one of the problems of ops in Mossies. We were often used on diversionary raids involving extensive use of '*Window*' to fool the enemy and tempt the fighters away from the main force of heavies. '*Window*' could be used in a variety of permutations to confuse the enemy and give the controllers problems where to send up their fighters. One popular ploy was for the Mosquitoes to overfly the main force of heavies and heave out masses of these strips as the heavies either continued or diverted to its target while the Mossies carried on to an alternative target. Sometimes the Germans got it right and sometimes they didn't. But the net result as far as we were concerned was that only a limited number of us would finally bomb our particular target and Jerry was able to dispense with his usual box barrage and concentrate on one aircraft at a time. What was happening left us in on doubt that we'd drawn the short straw. Climb and dive, twist and turn as we might, the *Flak* was deadly accurate and it was only a matter of time before the flying shrapnel found a vulnerable spot. That spot turned out to be the cooling jacket around the starboard engine and a violent juddering accompanied by belching smoke signified the imminent loss of interest of the engine in any further proceedings. Jock feathered the propeller while I throttled back and trimmed the aircraft for single engine flight and his finger hovered anxiously over the fire extinguisher button as we watched the trailing smoke but there was no fire. The smoke ceased and we breathed again.

'We were now faced with a further problem. As returning Mossies would be tracked by German radar they would soon know our course for home. We would be spotted as a straggler at our reduced speed and fighters would be sent up to intercept. Some more accurate *Flak* near Groningen convinced us it would be unwise to continue on this course and a hasty cockpit consultation resulted in our turning due North to get out to sea as quickly as possible. This wasn't going to get us any nearer home but it would help to throw off the tracking radar and also deter the German night fighters, who were always reluctant to venture too far out to the sea. The bright red *Boozer* light receiver tuned to the transmissions of the different types of German radar in the cockpit soon turned to dull red and finally went out and we thankfully turned westward for home. On learning that we only had one engine, Downham control promptly diverted us to Coltishall on the well-worn principle, 'We're all right, Jack but if you're going to make a clobbers of your landing we'd rather you cluttered up someone else's flarepath rather than ours'. Welcome home!

'After two operations like this Jock and I were somewhat thoughtful about our chance of doing another 53 to complete the tour but the good old Law of Averages prevailed and the next half a dozen ops were comparatively uneventful'.

On 23/24 September *Ritterkreuzträger Hptm* Ernst-Wilhelm Modrow, *Staffelkapitän*, 1./NJG 1 in a He 219 *Uhu* destroyed two heavies[29] for his 30th and 31st victories. *Oblt* Dietrich Schmidt, *Staffelkapitän* 8./NJG 1 claimed a Lancaster[30] while *Lt* Theodor Adamski of Schmidt's *Staffel* downed another Lancaster at 2327 hrs.[31] By October 1944 the fuel crisis had reached such proportions that only the *Experten* were sent against incoming raids. They flew 866 sorties, resulting in just 56 victories (or 0.5 per cent of 10,000 Bomber Command sorties). *Nachtjagd* ranks were further depleted by 54 aircraft and crews (or 6.2 per cent) during October. (During the remainder of the war, with only one or two exceptions, *Nachtjagd* never succeeded in exacting a toll of an average of more than 1 per cent of the British night raiders). November saw 959 night-fighter sorties dispatched, crews returning with claims for 87 kills (or 0.9 per cent of Bomber Command's night raids).

Over the *Reich* airwaves triumphant German battlecries of a few months previously had now given way to '*Achtung Moskito*': the bed of heavenly bliss' had become a bed of nails. As well as having to contend with the heavies for the last few months of the German night fighter defenses also had to contend with increasing numbers of *Intruder* aircraft in the circuit over the night-fighter bases. 100 Group Mosquitoes made a very important contribution to Bomber Support. They also took part in the *Window* feints flying with them to add to the effect of deception and then fanning out to take advantage of enemy reaction. In October the *Serrate* Squadrons destroyed six enemy aircraft and the AI.Mk.X Mosquito Squadrons' five. 141 Squadron shot down three enemy aircraft, although these were accomplished using AI and not *Serrate* 239 also scored three. 169 Squadron, which damaged three enemy aircraft that month, was already having nine of its *Serrate* homers replaced by *Perfectos*.[32] The first of the victories by 141 Squadron occurred on 6/7 October when F/L A.C. Gallacher DFC and P/O G. McLean DFC destroyed a Ju 88 during a *Serrate* patrol to Dortmund and Bremen.[33] The night following, 7/8 October F/L John Owen 'Jimmy' Mathews and W/O Alan 'Penny' Penrose of 157 Squadron picked up a contact at six miles range west of Neumünster while on a high level support sortie. Mathews narrowed the range and as they got a visual at 1000 yards the target straightened out. It was recognized as a Me 410 with long range tanks. Mathews opened fire with a short burst from 100 yards dead behind. Strikes were seen and a small explosion occurred in the starboard engine. Another burst and the starboard engine caught fire. It dived burning to the ground and exploded.[34] Victories by Mosquito nightfighter pilots were as much down to their skilled radar operators as piloting and gunnery skills, as F/L Paul Mellows a pilot in 169 Squadron confirms:

> 'When the AI.Mk.IV came out the RAF thought that anybody could read the two tubes but when they sent up radar mechanics they found that there was somewhat more to being a navigator/radio. It was insufficient just to know where the target was when you were flying straight and level. As you banked so the horizontal base from the one tube became the vertical base and vice versa. They also had to be able to read at what angle you were approaching the target and whether you were head on or whatever. The result was that the RAF started recruiting people deemed to be highly intelligent and they also seemed to waive certain medical and age requirements. We had a university lecturer, a schoolmaster and F/L S.L. 'Dickie' Drew, my radar operator, who was a chartered accountant. When we teamed up I was just 20 and he was 36 and married with two children. I was teetotal and Dick was virtually the same. He was also colorblind. He could not see poppies in a green field or tell the difference between the green, brown and red snooker balls. This was all right while he was looking at his CRT but it when it came to reading *Gee* maps with their red and green lines he found he had to dot the red lines in order to differentiate in the cockpit.
>
> 'The usual tour for intruders was 35 trips. We were on the point of taking a rest but on 7/8 October we at last came across a Ju 88 on our 35th trip on a Support patrol to Egmond. We arrived in the Patrol area at 2005 hrs flying at 15,000 ft. Two beacons flashing 'QC' and 'CT' respectively were observed near two airfields 15 miles to the North so we proceeded to the area to investigate. At 2022 hrs Dickie got an AI contact hard port at maximum range, our height being 14,000 ft. I closed to 7000 ft when the target started making hard urns to port through a number of orbits. It then straightened out and climbed at low IAS and we closed to 100 ft to identify enemy aircraft as Ju 88 vertically above height 18,500 ft in climbing at 140 IAS to attack. We dropped back and I opened fire at 500 ft at 2037 hrs. Strikes were observed between the starboard engine and fuselage and the enemy aircraft immediately peeled off to port and visual was lost but contact was held at 10,000ft range and we closed again losing height to 14,000ft. Another visual was obtained on the enemy aircraft while in hard starboard turn at 500 ft. It was losing height and turning starboard. However visual could not be held and no further AI contact was obtained on the enemy aircraft, which was inside minimum range. We continued to patrol the area where three aerodromes were now lit, until 2120 hrs at heights ranging between 7000 and 15,000 ft but no further contacts were obtained and we set course for base. Unfortunately, I didn't keep my finger on the button long enough. However this encouraged us to go on for another 15 as we were allowed to do.'

Duisburg received a pounding by RAF bombers on 14 October in Operation Hurricane when nearly 9000 tons of bombs fell on the city in less than 48 hours. According to the directive issued to Sir Arthur Harris, Hurricane's purpose was, 'In order to demonstrate to the enemy in Germany generally the overwhelming superiority of the Allied Air Forces in this theater ... the intention is to apply within the shortest practical period the maximum effort of the RAF Bomber Command and the U.S. 8th Bomber Command against objectives in the densely populated Ruhr.' Escorted by RAF fighters just over 1000 Lancasters, Halifaxes and Mosquitoes raided the city while 1251 American bombers escorted by 749 fighters hit targets in the Cologne area. At Duisburg 957 RAF heavies dropped 3574 tons of high explosive and 820 tons of incendiaries for the loss of 13 Lancasters and a Halifax to *flak*. American casualties were just five bombers and one fighter. That night, 14/15 October, which was fine and cloudless, 1005 RAF heavies attacked Duisburg for the second time in 24 hours in two waves and dropped 4040 tons of high explosive and 500 tons of incendiaries and losing five Lancasters and two Halifaxes. Bomber Support and forces on minor operations had played their part with 141 training aircraft flying a diversionary feint towards Hamburg and turning back before reaching Heligoland and 46 Mosquitoes raiding Hamburg, Berlin, Mannheim and Düsseldorf while 132 aircraft of 100 Group flew RCM, *Serrate* and *Intruder* sorties. *Uffz* Hans Durscheidt of I./NJG 10 in a Fw 190 claimed a Mosquito, which failed to return from the raid on Berlin and crashed north of Duisburg.[35] One Halifax of the diversionary force was also lost. One of the five Lancasters that was lost[36] fell victim to *Lt* Arnold Döring, an experienced 27 year old fighter pilot of 7./NJG 2 at Volkel aerodrome in Holland flying the Ju 88G-6. It was his twentieth aerial victory.[37] Döring recalls:

> 'Because of the continuing strafing and bombing attacks by Thunderbolts, Mustangs and Lightnings by day and the Mosquitoes by night in mid-October the *Gruppe* had been split up and our *Staffeln* dispersed to several 'dromes. The *Stab* and 7th *Staffel* were now based at Gütersloh, the 8th in Bad Lippspringe and the 9th at Werl. Our operational region was the Ruhr area, where I destroyed a Lancaster over Duisburg. During this operation Mosquitoes shot down *Lt* Hoevermann and *Stfw* Piewartz on return over Gütersloh airfield. *Hptm* Ernst-Karl Schneider belly-landed his burning aircraft on the drome and the crew was rescued.'[38]

Despite the enormous effort involved in Operation Hurricane that same night RAF Bomber Command was even able to despatch 233 Lancasters and seven Mosquitoes of 5 Group to bomb Brunswick. F/O Frank Mouritz RAAF, one of the Lancaster pilots who flew on the raid, was flying only his fifth operation since joining 61 Squadron at Skellingthorpe from 5 FLS Syerston nearby. He had carried out his first operation that first night, 27/28 September, a six and a half-hour trip to Kaiserlautern flying with another crew with no duties except to gain experience. The trip was uneventful and the young Australian was amazed at the sheer brilliance of searchlights and explosions of bombs, flak and photoflashes at the target. Even the biggest firework display he had ever seen was nothing compared to this. During the next ten days or so Mouritz and his crew carried out their first two operations, a daylight to Wilhelmshaven on 5 October and another daylight to Bremen on 6 October. They were then allocated a permanent aircraft, Lancaster EE176 QR-M MICKEY THE MOOCHER, a veteran of 119 trips. (Aircraft lettered 'M' were usually known as *M-Mike* or *M-Mother.* EE176's nose had received a Walt Disney cartoon of Mickey Mouse, pulling a bomb-trolley on which sat a bomb and this Lanc became MICKEY THE MOOCHER; a name derived from Cab Calloway's popular slow blues song, *'Minnie the Moocher'):*

'It was quite something to have our own plane,' Mouritz recalls:

> 'Another milestone in our air force career. The ground crew was very proud of their plane and the number of trips completed. This showed good maintenance and a lot of luck. We hoped that the luck had not all been used up as it was usually considered that to survive a tour required about 70% luck and 30% skill. By this time *Mickey* was nearly worn out. The four engines were close to the hours for a complete change, the controls were sloppy and she had dozens of patches on wings and fuselage. She took a lot of runway to get off the ground with a full load of fuel and bombs. We were the new crew given the oldest Lanc on the squadron but we were proud of her. She took us on our first trip on 11 October, a daylight one to the Dutch coast, with a fighter escort to bomb sea walls (dykes) in an attempt to flood German artillery batteries that were holing up the advance of the British ground forces. The raid was not successful although we bombed from low level. At this stage I could sense through *Mickey* the feelings of all the crews that had survived over 100 trips in this special aircraft, passing on their experience and good luck for a successful tour; a sort of feeling of comradeship and well-being which is hard to describe. *Mickey* was something to look up to, a guiding star.
>
> 'The 7 1/2-hour night flight to Brunswick was an area attack with Cookies and incendiaries. This was also a milestone as 15 October was my 21st birthday and we had our first fighter combat. Nearing the target area the mid-upper gunner spotted a fighter approaching from the port quarter above. It then appeared to side-slip into position behind them, he ordered the pilot to corkscrew as he opened fire, while also giving the rear-gunner the fighter's position and who, upon seeing it too, also opened fire. The fighter dived quickly away; the mid-upper gunner giving it a final burst as it disappeared out of range.[39]
>
> 'Our next trip[40] was another night area bombing one, 7 hrs to Nürnburg with 263 Lancs and seven Mosquitoes, with a large amount of casualties and damage inflicted. We were beginning to get a little confident now with our navigator keeping us on time and track and hence in the middle of the stream and our bomb-aimer directing the bombing run with precision and we were obtaining good target photos. Our next trip was another daylight one to the Dutch coast to attack the same batteries as before, also unsuccessful.'

Success though, came the way of S/L Branse Burbridge DFC* and F/L Bill Skelton DFC* of 85 Squadron again on 19/20 October. Flying a NFXIX they added to the two Ju 88Gs they had destroyed at Gütersloh on 14/15 October by shooting down a Ju 188 at Metz for their 11th victory. W/O P.C. Falconer and F/Sgt W.C. Armour of 239 Squadron in a Mosquito FBVI also shot down a Bf 110 at Strasbourg and two Ju 88s fell to the guns of 141 Squadron. About 15 miles northwest of Nürnburg a Ju 88 was claimed by P/O J.C. Barton and F/Sgt R.A. Kinnear as 'damaged', which they attacked on three separate occasions. It was confirmed as a victory upon their return to West Raynham when an inspection revealed the leading edge of the Mosquito's starboard spinner and starboard mainplane were extensively covered in oil from their victim while several indentations in the aircraft were found to be caused by flying debris. The second Ju 88 destroyed was by F/L G.D. 'Charlie' Bates and F/O D.W. Field ten miles southeast of Karlsruhe after a ten-minute chase. Bates gave the Ju 88 a two-second-burst of cannon fire at 300-ft dead astern. After what seemed like 'hours' the enemy aircraft's starboard engine burst into flames and the Ju 88 pulled up in a hard starboard turn. Bates turned hard port and came in to deliver a second attack. However, the Junkers was by now well alight and after firing red and white Verey lights, went into a steep dive into cloud. Two seconds later two explosions of great force were seen below: the second one lighting up the whole cloud. The Ju 88 split into three pieces, which were picked up on AI scattering into the night.[41] S/L Robert Daniel 'Dolly' Doleman and F/L D.C. 'Bunny' Bunch DFC of 157 Squadron in a Mosquito NFXIX shot down a Ju 88 and claimed a Ju 88 'damaged' on their High Level Support Patrol to Nürnburg.[42]

On 22/23 October the Main Force was grounded but 20 Lancasters and 19 Halifaxes dropped mines in the Kattegat.[43] W/O Les Turner and F/Sgt Frank Francis of 169 Squadron who were on a *Serrate* patrol to Denmark obtained a contact, which was held. After three minutes of hectic dog-fighting range was closed to 2000-ft where aircraft was identified as a Ju 88 travelling at about 150 mph. They throttled back and put down full flap opening fire at about 400 yards observing large strike on port wing root. The enemy aircraft peeled off to starboard and Turner fired off an ineffective burst which left the Mosquito in an 'awkward position' at about 145-mph (full flap and being curiously knocked about by slipstream from the Ju 88). Turner and Francis followed down on AI to about 4000-ft height where contact was lost in ground returns. Though they could only claim a 'damaged' Turner was convinced this aircraft crashed subsequently as there was a fire on the ground ten minutes after the attack.[44]

October had signalled a great decrease in the effectiveness of *Nachtjagd* opposition to the night bomber.[45] This was a combined result of the Allied advance into the continent and the technical and tactical countermeasures employed. The German warning and inland plotting systems were thrown into confusion. Low-level and high-level *Intruder* played no small part by causing the enemy to plot hostile aircraft over very wide areas as well as forcing him to broadcast frequent warnings of the presence of hostile aircraft to his own fighters.[46]

Meanwhile, on 23 October 112 Lancasters of 5 Group bombed battery positions at Flushing (Vlissingen) for the loss of four aircraft. On the night of 23/24 October Bomber Command despatched 1055 aircraft to Essen to bomb the Krupps works. This was the heaviest raid on the already devastated German city so far in the war and the number of aircraft – 561 Lancasters, 463 Halifaxes and 31 Mosquitoes – was also the greatest to any target since the war began. Altogether the force dropped 4538 tons of bombs including 509 4000 pounders on Essen. More than 90% cent of the tonnage carried was high explosive because intelligence estimated that most of Essen's housing and buildings had been destroyed in fire raids in 1943. Five Lancasters and three Halifaxes FTR from the raid. None were claimed by *Nachtjagd*. On the night of 24/25 October there was no Main Force activity. Sixty-seven Mosquito bombers visited Hanover and other cities while 25 Lancasters and nine Halifaxes again sowed mines in the Kattegat and off Oslo. One aircraft, Stirling *D-Dog*[47] of 196 Squadron, 38 Group at Shepherds Grove, Suffolk, flown by F/O Chuck Hoysted DFC went on an SOE[48] operation to the Zwolle area. WOp Mike 'Taff' Stimson remembers:

> 'This was our twentieth operation and we were an experienced crew. We did not talk at all over the intercom unless we had something to say so we flew in silence as much as we could. We went to the Zuider Zee to drop 24 containers of supplies but the weather was atrocious. Cloud was from the ground to right above us. Our aircraft was jumping all over the place, as we were going over England and we were not above 500 ft. We left by Cromer ('The Gate'). Our job was to deliver at night over Holland, France and Norway, arms, food, and clothing and money and jeep tyres – anything at all required by the resistance fighters. Our altimeters were not very accurate at low level but in August on an op to Liege we had been told by one of the briefing officers who had been on the Dam Busters operation, 'When you get low enough, you will see that the sea is illuminated by plankton'. Sure enough when we got down low we could see thousands of lights in the sea. I was standing in the astrodome where I could look right around through 360° with an unhindered view. I could see past Chuck that there was a light shining on the sea and I asked what the light was. Chuck said, 'It looks very much like a lighthouse Taff. It's flashing'.
>
> 'We had been told at briefing that the northern end of every one of the Friesian Islands had a searchlight and an anti-aircraft gun on to cover anybody travelling down the straits between any of the two islands. Was that light on the northern end of Texel or was it on the southern end of

Vlieland? We wanted to be in the middle of the sea channel so that nobody could shoot at us. If we went on the wrong side of that light we might well finish up on either of the islands. As we neared this flashing lighthouse we saw that it was on the eastern or northern end of Texel. Whenever we came to any coast crossing, Chuck would gear up his engines to give the best power. We were going 'like a bomb' as we entered this channel and went by the lighthouse and the light was level with our wing tips. That's how low we were. We had been warned that the Germans would turn off the lights on the sea channels to prevent us using them for navigation at low level. Of course, this light being left on helped us greatly.

'The next obstacle was to get over the dyke across the top of the Zuider Zee. We did not know if they had any *Flak* positions or *Flak* trains on it so we kept down, put full speed on and leapt over it then back down on the sea again. '*D-Dog* now flew at low level over the Zuider Zee to Enkhuizen, then turned to Emmeloord, the Dropping Zone (DZ). At the end of the timed run from Enkhuizen to the DZ Johnny Barker [navigator] announced over the intercom: 'Right, we are here' and Chuck automatically climbed to 500 ft. All the time we had been flying at sea level we occasionally went through fog or sea mist or even little bits of cloud and once we climbed to 500 ft it was hopeless. There was broken cloud all over the place, no visible moon and no hope of seeing the ground. As soon as we started circling the DZ I went back, opened the lower door and stood behind my panniers. We circled for a few minutes and it was obvious that we would not see the ground so the bomb aimer asked if we could go back to the TRV and come in a bit lower. We went back but it was just the same; cloud all over the place. Then Ray Owen the bomb aimer asked,

'Could we go down as low as we dared, on our altimeter and come in?' Chuck agreed and Ray Owen, said, 'If I see any lights on the way back (to the DZ), I'll press the bomb tit and drop the lot'.

'Running back to Enkhuizen I felt the bomb bay doors opening and then I heard something strike the fuselage, as if somebody had thrown a handful of stones against it. I said to Chuck, 'I think that we have been shot at'.

'What makes you think that Taff?'

'I told him that something had struck the fuselage.

'No, we are in cloud and probably over the sea and there's no sign of any *Flak*.'

'Without thinking, because I was looking down the open hole and could see about a hundred yards or more into this cloud, I said, 'Well, we must have struck a tree'.

'Taff, they don't have 500 ft bloody trees in Holland. It's flat!'

'We turned over Enkhuizen and ran back to Emmeloord and searched for half an hour but there was no hope. In the end Chuck said, 'Let's pack up and go home'. He turned around and closed the bomb bays while I closed the hatch and withdrew the packages back to the base of the winch root. 'We must have awakened half of Holland up by now and if the Germans are waiting for us between Texel and Vlieland we will have no chance of survival so we'll route straight out from Enkhuizen to Cromer at low level.'

'Four times on the sea leg to Cromer the aircraft did a violent sideslip to the left and almost went into a nosedive. Ray, now sitting in the second pilot's seat and Chuck were pulling back on the sticks with their feet on the dashboards. At one time the navigator was standing on the steps leading to the bomb aimer's compartment in the nose pulling back on the base of both control columns. Each time we managed to level out not far off the sea and when we did so we had to climb back up again. Arriving over England we put the aircraft into a bank and it sideslipped again and nearly hit the ground. We levelled off and flew to our base but we were diverted to Earls Colne where we were met by the ground staff who invited us to see what was sticking out of our bomb bay. The parachute on the middle container of the three nearest the tail of the aircraft had opened in the bomb bay and had streamed to the tailplane! This is what I heard hit the fuselage as it cracked open and it had been fouling our tailplane – hence the dives. It was a most exciting experience but I would never like to have had it happen again.'

The same could be equally said by F/O Elwyn D. Fieldson DFC pilot of Halifax *Clueless I*[49] of 76 Squadron, one of 992 aircraft,[50] which went to Düsseldorf on 2/3 November:

'All was pretty routine on the outward trip. Frequent turbulence from the wash of aircraft ahead gave a comforting reassurance that we were nicely in the stream, although only rarely was another aircraft sighted. We arrived over the target on time to find the city well ablaze and made our run. The call of 'Bombs gone!' from the bomb-aimer F/Sgt Gerry Tierney was immediately followed by 'Dive starboard', which I did. Another aircraft, perhaps a Halifax, was turning towards us not waiting for those critical two miles beyond the target. Then there was a God-awful thump on our rear end, which knocked us into a near vertical dive with the whole aircraft vibrating madly. A propeller had sliced through our fuselage, leaving the tail unit attached by the top half only. The gun rams were bent into hairpins and the tail surface was considerably damaged. Remarkably F/Sgt Jimmy 'Junior' Ross the rear gunner was not even scratched. After losing about 2000 ft I seemed to be getting some control back, only the aircraft became increasingly tail heavy and even with full forward elevator trim I soon had to push hard on the stick. P/O Frank Newland the engineer surveyed the damage and tied the dinghy mooring rope and the escape rope across the gap to prevent further opening. After a quick conference with F/Sgt Malcolm 'Mac' McLeod the navigator, we decided to try to follow the planned route as far as the French coast in order not to become easy prey for a fighter, then dodge across to Manston, which had a nice long runway. I had my elbows locked trying to hold the stick forward far enough to keep descending to the planned 8000 ft but my arms were getting very tired and the crew took turns to stand alongside me and help push the controls forward. Thus we arrived at Manston, where I planned a flapless landing, as I did not think there was enough control left to cope with the flap extension. But it wasn't quite over yet. On final, up went the red Verey lights. (We had no radio as the aerials had been carried away). So I overshot and went round again ('staggered round' might be a better description) at about 500 ft coming in very fast at 160 mph, this time I was allowed to land, only to end ignominiously in the mud at the end of the runway. (The Halifax always had lousy brakes). But at least the tail didn't break off. I had feared it might. Three days later we were back on ops.'

The next major night raid was on 4/5 November when Bochum and the Dortmund-Ems Canal were the objectives for the Main Force. Some 749 aircraft of 1, 4, 6 and 8 Groups attacked the center of Bochum and more than 4000 buildings were left in ruins or seriously damaged. Three Lancasters from the 174 despatched by 5 Group failed to return from the raid on the Dortmund-Ems Canal and 23 Halifaxes and five Lancasters were missing from the raid on Bochum, where 346 *Groupe Guyenne* Free French Squadron alone lost five of its 16 Halifaxes. Most of the night's bomber losses were due to *Nachtjagd* fighters. *Hptm* Heinz Rökker of I./NJG 2 was credited with two Lancasters and two Halifaxes and *Hptm* Hans-Heinz Augenstein of IV./NJG 1, thee Lancasters. *Oblt* Erich Jung of 6./NJG 2 claimed two Lancasters shot down north of Essen and *Hptm* Hermann Greiner of IV./NJG 1, two Halifaxes. *Fw* Karl Neumann of 8./NJG 1 scored his first two kills when he downed two Halifaxes. Over 60 Mosquitoes flew Bomber Support operations and five 100 Group crews were credited with the destruction of eight German aircraft. Foremost among them with four victories were S/L Branse Burbridge DSO DFC* and F/O 'Red' Skelton DSO DFC* of 85 Squadron who were credited with three Ju 88s in the South of Bonn and North of Hangelar areas and a Bf 110 north of Hangelar.[51]

On 6/7 November when 235 Lancasters and seven Mosquitoes of 5 Group again attempted to cut the Mittelland Canal at Gravenhorst, crews were confronted with a cold front of exceptional violence and ice quickly froze on windscreens. F/O Frank Mouritz RAAF of 61 Squadron said goodbye to an old friend when he flew MICKEY THE MOOCHER on her last operation. The marking force had difficulty in finding the target due to low cloud and the bombers were told to bomb at low level. Mouritz had to select full flap and wheels down to enable him to lose height in time and he was one of only 31 Lancasters that bombed before the Master Bomber abandoned the raid due to low cloud.'[52] Ten Lancasters FTR from the Mittelland debacle. Three of these were shot down west of the Rhine in just 16 minutes by *Lt* Otto Fries and his *Bordfunker Fw* Alfred Staffa of 2./NJG 1 flying a He 219.[53] Of 128 Lancasters of 3 Group that raided Koblenz, two failed to return. A Mosquito BXX of 128 Squadron failed to return from Gelsenkirchen and a RCM Fortress and two Mosquito Intruders were lost, one flown by C. 'Mickey' Phillips and F/L Derek V. Smith of 85 Squadron (who had destroyed a Ju 188 on 28/29 September).[54] A British bomber fired on them, setting one engine ablaze and they were finished off by a He 219. Phillips and Smith baled out and were captured. 100 Group crews claimed two Ju 188s and a Bf 110 and a Ju 88 and Ju 188 as probables.[55] *Hptm* Ernst-Karl Schneider who on 14/15 October had been fortunate to survive an attack by a Mosquito at Gütersloh airfield was the pilot of one of two Ju 88G-6 aircraft lost,[56] as *Lt* Arnold Döring of 7./NJG 2 recalls:

'Schneider was killed though his crew [*Ofw* Mittwoch, *Bordfunker* and *Uffz* Kaase *Bordschütze*] saved their skins by baling out. A few days later on 11/12 November the crew of *Uffz* Wuttke crashed in bad weather and only the *Bordfunker* escaped death. From mid-November, following an order from the powers that be we flew with a crew of four in the narrow cockpit and could hardly move any more. Eight eyes could see more than six and the *Bordfunker* should cover our backs because of the increasing Mosquito threat. From being the hunter we had become the hunted!'

Meanwhile, the bombing offensive against German cities and oil targets continued unabated with raids in November on Homberg, Wanne-Eickel, Harburg, Homberg and Dortmund among others and the Mittleland Canal again on 21/22 November. This time the canal banks were successfully breached near Gravenhorst. Lancasters flying as low as 4000 ft also breached the Dortmund-Ems Canal near Ladbergen. Then on the night of 26/27 November 270 Lancasters and eight Mosquitoes of 5 Group went to Munich. Before the main briefing at Fulbeck, Sgt 'Ricky' Dyson, rear gunner in the crew of F/O Desmond 'Ned' Kelly RAAF in 189 Squadron, was officially introduced to F/Sgt Doug Presland's crew, as he would be flying in Lancaster I PB745 CA-Q as a replacement for the rear gunner who was sick. Dyson was a pre-war ground crew regular who trained as an air gunner during 1944 and had flown on ops in 9, 106 and 44 Squadrons before being posted to 189 Squadron that October. He recalls:

'I knew Presland's crew by sight having mixed socially in the Sergeants Mess, so this helped enormously and I found them to be a great bunch of lads. It was moonlight when we reached the dispersal area but by the time we took off at 2335 hrs the weather had closed in and within a few seconds we entered a thick layer of low cloud. As the aircraft climbed the flight engineer called out the air speed (90-95 mph) to the pilot and it seemed to remain at that speed while we made a climbing turn. After reaching about 1000 ft for some reason we lost height and 'sank'. I looked out of the turret and saw trees and hedges whipping past at about 100ft and was about to warn the pilot when we hit a hill 500 ft above sea level. We had been airborne just 11 minutes. There was a terrific dull thud, then a crunching and screeching sound as the aircraft hurtled and tore its way along the ground, shuddering from nose to tail as it went. There was a series of loud bangs and thuds as the aircraft broke its back, followed by a blinding flash and a huge explosion. Then silence. Whether I was 'knocked out' I cannot remember but I do remember still sitting in the rear turret with a piece of fuselage burning fiercely behind me. The turret with this piece of fuselage attached had been thrown about 50 yards clear of the main wreckage but the doors had jammed and it was getting hotter by the second. I managed to free myself of the yellow Taylor flying suit I'd been wearing. With the aid of the axe on the turret wall I chipped away at the heavy duty perspex of the Clear Vision Panel in front of me. With great difficulty I managed to squeeze sideways and I went head-first through the opening over what remained of the four Browning machine guns. I fell to the ground, landed on my back and scrambled to my feet. I ran petrified into the darkness ahead and only stopped when I came to a hedge to look back. The whole field seemed to be alight with burning debris. Seeing the flames I realized with horror that somewhere in that inferno was the rest of the crew! I shouted something and raced towards the main part of the wreckage. As I got nearer I could hear groans and cries for help! Eventually I found some of the lads and tried to help and comfort them until the rescue services arrived. Doug Presland was semi-conscious, in great pain and calling for help. Half in and half out of the burning cockpit trapped by both legs, he was in great danger of being roasted by the terrific heat. Somehow I managed to free him and pull him to safety. The mid-upper gunner, F/Sgt Fender was also trapped. He was unconscious when I found him in his turret, his back and legs jammed hard against the twisted metal and his head embedded in the electrical junction box in the roof. In my shocked condition I tried in vain to release him. Later he was cut free from the wreckage, alive but with terrible injuries. Like me he had been thrown clear still in his turret. only days later did I realize how lucky I had been to survive a similar experience without serious unjury.

'F/Sgts Probert, McClune and Venning and Sgt Bayliss all perished on this dreadful night. As I ran into the wreckage, shocked and panic stricken calling for help I saw some of the bodies engulfed in flames with their clothing alight. On one occasion, I tried to put the flames out with my hands. When I thought I had succeeded, it was to find the person was already dead from other injuries. By the time the rescue services arrived, the field in which we had crashed, between Saltby and Croxton Kerrial resembled an inferno. The aircraft was fully laden with fuel and a mixed load of HE and incendiary bombs and wreckage was spread over a large area. The heat was terrific as the fuel tanks, bombs, oxygen bottles and ammunition from the gun turrets exploded, causing flaming debris to be flung high into the air and many pieces landing on the dead and injured. There was great danger as fragmented bomb cases and exploding ammunition whistled through the air in all directions. This scene, with the pungent and awful smell of burning flesh, burnt cordite and petrol and the pall of acrid smoke is one that I have never been able to obliterate from my mind.

'The three of us who survived were taken in an ambulance to an American base hospital a few miles away. Doug showed great courage. Although in great pain from his very serious injuries and burns to his face, hands and parts of his body, he managed to crack jokes, especially about the welfare of his moustache! His first concern was the fate of other members of his crew. Doug later had to have a leg amputated. After a long time in hospital and discharge from the RAF he became a schoolmaster and later a headmaster in Essex. F/Sgt Fender had to undergo numerous operations and he had a metal plate fitted in his head. After about two years in hospital he married his nurse. Having had excellent treatment for the few injuries I had sustained (mainly shock and minor burns to hands and face) I was discharged from hospital within two weeks and sent home on leave. Three weeks later I returned to Fulbeck and to 189 Squadron and resumed flying duties with Ned Kelly and crew. During the days and weeks which followed, the squadron was actively engaged on operations, both by day in support of our forces in France and by night against targets deep into Germany.'[57]

As a result of large-scale use of the Mosquito late in 1944, the German night fighter defenses were made to change their tactics and this seriously reduced their efficiency. One *Geschwader*, with a strength of about 100 crews, lost, in three months, 24 crews killed, ten missing and 15 wounded. It was at around this time that the real '*Moskitopanik*' started and from then on all the normal run of crashes through natural causes were attributed to the Mosquito. The Mosquito's increased reputation heightened the German night fighter crews' despondency and their demoralization was complete late in 1944 when they had to resort to throwing out *Düppel* (*Window*) as a routine, to mislead and distract the Mosquito night fighters. Few if any of the top German night fighter pilots dared to climb until the last moment and all remained very low or at '*Ritterkreuz Height*', as if they flew higher they would never survive to receive the decoration. *Hptm* Hans Krause, *Kommandeur* of I./NJG 4 with 28 destroyed; quoted an instance in the Ruhr when he was intercepted in the target area and pursued for 45 minutes having frequent visuals on a Mosquito as it came into range. He took violent evasive action in azimuth and height and by going through cloud but this failed to shake off the fighter. He finally succeeded in evading only by flying to a district in the Ardennes that he knew really well, flying, as he said, 'Down a valley below the level of the hills.' This confirmed in his mind the exceptional standard of the British AI radar. German night-fighter crews now flew at tree top height to the beacons. This caused many accidents and German night fighters often flew into the ground. An alternative technique of returning to base provided the pilot could go straight in and land was to approach straight from 10,000ft. When possible, Krause preferred to do this for as he said, 'It had the added advantage that if you were shot down by a Mosquito you had plenty of time to bale out.'

Moskitopanik was at its height during December 1944 when 36 German night fighters were shot down. When on 2/3 December 504 bombers were dispatched to Hagen and 66 Mosquitoes to Giessen the operations were supported by 44 RCM sorties and 62 Mosquito patrols of 100 Group. F/L William Taylor and F/O Jeffrey N. Edwards of 157 Squadron destroyed a Ju 88.[58] Capt Tarald Weisteen, a Norwegian in 85 Squadron, claimed a second nightfighter kill after obtaining a contact at five miles going west across the target area. Range was closed to 4000-5000 ft and at 2000 ft it was identified as a Bf 110. Weisteen opened fire at 200 yards and portions of the aircraft broke off and the starboard engine caught fire before the Bf 110 spun down. The explosion could be seen through the cloud half a minute later.[59] A Halifax and a Lancaster were lost when they crashed in France and a Mosquito NFXIII *Intruder* of 29 Squadron was also missing.[60] *Nachtjäger* could only claim a Wellington, which *Oblt* Walter Briegleb of 7./NJG 2 shot down north of Baltrum and *Ofw* Giesecke of 3./NJG 3 a Stirling, one of ten on Resistance operations this night.[61]

On the night of 4/5 December there was a spoof on Dortmund while 892 heavies set out for Karlsruhe, Heilbronn, Hagen and Hamm in the north and south of the Ruhr. The spoof Force of 112 aircraft of 100 Group went straight into 'Happy Valley' supported by PFF marking and not less than 90-100 German night fighters were sent to the spoof. They waited in the area for about 15 minutes for the attack to start. However, they found nothing but high intruders and they were too late for their deployment against the heavies. Losses to the Main Force were 15 aircraft or 1.5 per cent of the force. A handful of *Nachtjäger* from NJG 6 and NJG 11 engaged the bomber stream on their run in to the target at Heilbronn and shot down 12 Lancasters. 100 Group Mosquito nightfighters equipped with AI shot down five and probably destroyed another. Two 85 Squadron crews, F/L R.T. 'Dickie' Goucher and F/L C.H. 'Tiny' Bulloch[62] and F/O A.J. 'Ginger' Owen and F/O J.S. Victor McAllister DFM destroyed two Bf 110s at Germesheim and a Ju 88 near Krefeld respectively. Owen's was 85 Squadron's 100th victory.[63] Meanwhile, in the Karlsruhe area Captain Svein Heglund DFC*[64] and F/O Robert O. Symon of 85 Squadron obtained contacts on bombers and later two targets, with violent evasion, which were chased eastwards. At 2005, Schwabish Hall airfield was seen lit and several fleeting contacts appeared well below. The Norwegian pilot, whom Symon described as 'a delightful and modest young man' went down to 2500 ft to investigate but all lighting was doused. The Mosquito regained height and at 2015 hours NE of Heilbronn, Symon obtained a contact. Recognising it as a Bf 110 Heglund fired a one-second burst, pumping just forty rounds into the German machine and obtaining strikes immediately on the starboard engine and wing root. The *Luftwaffe* aircraft burst into flames and sideslipped into the ground and exploded. Heglund and Symon set course for base via the Frankfurt area where several airfields were seen active but their fuel was low and Heglund had to put down at Brussels before they could return to their base at Swannington in Norfolk.

On 5/6 December when Bomber Command sent 497 aircraft to Soest, 53 Mosquitoes went to Ludwigshafen, 32 to Nürnburg and four to Duisburg, only two Halifaxes were lost. Reports were that: 'There was probably no fighter reaction. Only a few contacts were obtained. This was probably due to adverse weather conditions over enemy airfields.' If there was no 'trade' to be found then the *Nachtjagd* bases had to contend with Mosqutio Intruder attacks and that night forty Mosquitoes of 100 Group alone were despatched. At Münster-Handorf *Lt* Otto Fries of NJG 1, pilot of He 219A-0 190193 G9+EK, was one who was aware of the ever-present danger the Mosquitoes posed:

> 'The duty long-range night fighter had turned up pretty late that night. When we heard the distinctive sound of the Rolls-Royce engines it was already shortly before 1900. The Mosquito stayed mostly to the east of the airfield and we suspected that the 'friends from the other postal address' were using our own radio beacon, although its frequency was changed each day. At 1915 the order was given for cockpit readiness. We grabbed our kit and ran to the crew bus, which promptly did its rounds. I sat beside my radio operator in the bus. My *Bordfunker*, *Fw* Fred Staffa, said, 'I hope that they have found the bug in the long-wave transmitter. When I tested the sets today and set the frequencies, it didn't give a squeak.'
>
> 'I merely growled. The constant short-circuits in the eletrical system and radio gear really were a nuisance but the aircraft were exposed to wind, rain and snow, fog and frost inside light camouflaging hangars, which hid them from sight but offered no protection against the weather. In the fifth year of the war the cable material did not appear to be of the best either. We flew our machines every second or third day in order to warm them up and dry out the condensation in the equipment and the cabling but we still kept getting the most ridiculous short circuits. When in the last week we had taken off for a 'drying-out flight' and I had wanted to retract my undercarriage, all six guns commenced firing. They would have continued firing until all their ammunition had been exhausted, had not my radio operator pressed the circuit breakers of the guns. A week before this I was behind a Lancaster and when I pressed my firing button the landing light in my port wing suddenly came on but not a single gun fired! I had never dived away so quickly! Fortunately the over-voltage switch was still functioning and Fred was able to break the circuit. Otherwise on our way home we would have been illuminated and an easy victim for any Mosquito. The whole area was alive with them!
>
> 'We were still fastening our seat belts in G9+EK when the green signal light was fired for take-off. I started the engines and taxied out. The clock showed 1934. It was typical winter weather with no wind. It had been sunny, though at briefing the weather wizard recommended that we land before 2200 if possible for ground fog was expected to form rapidly. After take-off it seemed as though we were flying into a dimly lit opaque void. Powerful criss crossing searchlights in the Ruhr from Cologne to Münster lit up the ground haze, showing the way to the nearest emergency airfield cleared for night landings. (Groups of searchlights with differing dispositions marked nearby cities. Münster at the northern end of this path had an 'X' as identifier). British long-range night fighters would easily be able to make out aircraft against the light background so I made it a habit not to begin the climb immediately after take-off. I kept my aircraft at between 50 and a hundred meters until, having made a wide and flat turn to port onto opposite course, I was able to see the airfield lit-up on my beam. Only then did I feel safe enough to start my climb, endeavouring to reach more than 8000 meters as quickly as possible. The altitudes between 2000 and 5000 meters were 'contaminated with Mosquitoes' and I tried to avoid this band by flying over or under it. When approaching the operating area I generally chose the higher altitude so that I could use the height to dive with greater speed. On return I usually preferred the lower level, but this depended on circumstances.
>
> 'One night when we were flying with the bomber stream at about 4500 meters towards Berlin we tussled with a Mosquito for nearly an hour without ever catching sight of it. According to Y-control we were right in the bomber stream but Fred tried in vain for a long time to get an indication. The screen showed only a permanent blip. I weaved back and forth in order to scan a wider area. (Our radar not only covered targets ahead but also ones behind and these became apparent in a turn). Soon Fred reported, 'There's one approaching fast from behind – a little lower and 2000 meters behind us but closing fast.' 'If only we knew whether it was one of ours or a Mosquito. Well, we'd soon find out!' I switched off the autopilot and reversed course in a steep turn to port. Then I counted to five and went back onto my old course.

'I have him – a good four kilometers ahead and a little lower.'

'Well, let's have a look at the fellow.' I opened the throttles and turned the propellers to automatic. Then I pushed the aircraft a hundred meters lower and primed the breeches of my guns. The speed increased rapidly.

'Two-five – two – three – now he's gone, dived away to port!'

'Well, we've got rid of the fellow! We're on the old course – watch carefully whether he turns up again!' I reduced power and turned the propellers to manual. While I was synchronising the engines my radio operator reported, 'The swine is behind us again!'

'I repeated the maneuver and was again behind the other machine. When I had approached to about 400 meters, he dived away again. The entire procedure was repeated three more times before the other one had apparently had enough of it and finally disappeared. After this experience I always went to an altitude of over 8000 meters in order to make an undisturbed approach. Only when I was sure to be close to the bomber stream, or when the bombers were recognisable, did I go down to the level of the enemy aircraft.

'I had just retracted my undercarriage and flaps when I heard my radio operator swearing.

'Damn it! Both transmitters, long and short wave, have gone unservicable. They were both all right when we started our run, now they are both gone – to hell with them! What do we do now – turn back or continue?'

'We ought to have aborted for we were unable to make contact with any ground station by Morse or voice. There could also be difficulties on return as we could not report in and get landing instructions. On the other hand, the weather was fair, at least for the next couple of hours, if the forecaster had not made a mistake. We could always get our own bearings back to base. We could receive information about the enemy's movements on the Reich Fighter Broadcast but that would not be absolutely necessary as we could listen in to our Y-frequency and orient ourselves with the instructions being given to the other aircraft of our *Gruppe*. We'd just have to manage somehow. We would not be able to use the emergency strip because during the afternoon fighter-bombers had pitted it with two bomb craters. Well, we'd get down somehow – no one yet had remained in the air forever!

'Are both your receivers really working – or have they too given up the ghost meanwhile?'

'No, not so far, but I cannot of course guarantee that they will hold out.'

'Very well then, let's try it! The weather was reasonable and if the weather wizard was right it would remain so for a while yet. If all else failed we still had the 'Ruhr-Hiking-Path', which ended more or less on our own doorstep, although I did not particularly like the idea of sneaking along the line of searchlights. As long as there wass no fog we should find our way home. 'You'd better tune to the Y-frequency and listen in to the instructions Willy[65] gets. He is Adler 94. He took off immediately before us so we should not go very far wrong if we fly the same course as he gets from ground control. So, let's keep our fingers crossed!' (We had known each other for two years, an interminable length of time, when old familiar faces kept disappearing and new ones turned up, became familiar and in turn, disappeared. We had been together in the second *Gruppe* of our *Geschwader* until Willy was transferred to the first Gruppe to hunt down Mosquitoes after the re-equipment of the second *Gruppe* to He 219 had been cancelled. As I had had some experience with the He 219 as Technical Officer (TO) a few months later the *Geschwader* ordered my transfer to the first *Gruppe* which was equipped with the He 219, while the second *Gruppe* continued with the Bf 110 as its standard machine). When the airfield lights were abeam to port I commenced my climb. I opened the throttles to increase power in order to reach 8000 meters as quickly as possible. Fred had tuned in to the Y-frequency and had me listening in. We were being called by ground control:

'Adler 98 from Harlekin – come on frequency!'

'Would but for laughing!', grumbled my radio operator.

'Adler 98 from Harlekin – come in – come in – come on frequency!' The call was repeated several times but as there was no reply Adler 94 was called.

'That's Willy – note down what instructions he gets!' Adler 94 was instructed to fly a course of 260° for eight minutes and then turn onto 180°. I turned to starboard until the compass showed 260° and then I turned on the autopilot and pressed the stopwatch. When we reached 4000 meters we put on our oxygen masks. When the eight minutes were up I turned onto 180°. After a further four minutes the altimeter showed 8000 meters. I levelled off and throttled back to economic cruise power, synchronised the propellers and retrimmed the elevator. Adler 94 was instructed to alter course to 160° and we did likewise. Somewhere close by my friend Willy must be flying parallel to me. 'Listen in to the *Reich* Fighter Broadcast to hear what they have to say!' Fred switched over but there was so much interference on the frequency that only indistinct snatches of words could be made out; it was impossible to get even the slightest information about the air situation from it. He went back to the Y-frequency but on this too only the 'soul borer' was to be heard.[66] Fred did his utmost to obtain some useful information but whatever frequency he tried, only the 'Dudelsack' or 'Bag pipe' and the 'soul borer' could be heard.[67]

'My aircraft was still on a southerly course. I let my eyes wander from left to right and up and down but apart from isolated specks of light there was nothing to be seen. There was nothing to hear either, for Fred had switched off the intercom as he always did when there was difficulty tuning in a particular transmitter or taking a bearing. Off to starboard and at almost the same height there was a flash, followed by green and red cascades going down and in the darkness below bright white magnesium fires appeared, which spread rapidly outwards. Dull red flashes in between indicated the first exploding bombs. The inferno had begun.

'The *Reich* Fighter Broadcast says that Soest is being attacked', my radio operator said. 'I can already see the fireworks!'

'With my left hand I knocked the course switch on the control column downward. In the same movement I opened the throttles to the gate and pressed the switches of the automatic propeller down to obtain maximum power from the engines before I dived in a steep turn to starboard. The airspeed indicator needle passed the 600 km/h mark. The high speed caused the wings to vibrate and this spread to the entire aircraft. I found this unpleasant but high speed offered the only chance to reach the scene of action as quickly as possible. Fred switched on the radar but the screen was hopelessly covered with interference.

'Nothing doing with the SN2; it is completely jammed.'

'When we reached Soest we were still at 5000 meters altitude. The constantly spreading fires caused the strong ground mist to appear like a huge opaque screen and some Lancasters a few hunderd meters below passed from starboard to port like shadows. I dived down in a steep turn into the approach path of the bombers. I endeavoured not to lose sight of them however; the lower I went, the narrower my field of view became and when I had reached their altitude they had disappeared into the dark above. Then I spotted the next group of Lancasters below. They were on an opposite course. I dived in a steep turn to port but it seemed that we were bewitched for they too were swallowed up by the dark. I went back and forth but I was unable to find them. Back over the burning town the airspace below was clear. Only the flashes of exploding *Flak* shells and the remaining puffs of smoke were to be seen. Looking up I recognized in the reflection of the fires the next wave of attacking Lancasters about 200 meters above and on opposite course. Then ahead and on the other side I saw black shapes passing close by; we had got right into the dropping bombs and it was a weird feeling, I felt as if someone was rubbing a wire brush along my spine from my neck to my buttocks. I pulled my machine around to port in a steep turn and tried to gain some height. Back and forth I circled the town, constantly changing my height but I had no luck. The fires raged below but there were no more explosions to be seen. Tthe attack was over.

'Listen in to see whether they are giving a departing course!'

'Fred twiddled with the knobs. The equipment rustled, whistled and roared in the headphones. Finally we were able to make out from the jumbled snatches of words that the course of the departing bombers lay between 280 and 310 degrees at about 4000 meters. My altimeter showed 4300 meters. I turned onto a course of 300 degrees and switched on the autopilot. Slowly I went down to 4000 meters. The radar was still being jammed. Slowly I weaved to starboard and to port and kept a look-out but I was unable to make anything out and I felt no air disturbance, as it would be if one were to get into the slipstream of an aircraft flying ahead.

'Still nothing on the screen?'

'No, completely jammed.'

'I weaved around a basic course of 300 degrees and continually changed my altitude. Fred had turned his radar off and we strained our eyes in all directions in the hope that somewhere the shadow of a bomber might show up against thc starlit sky. But all to no avail. Up ahead and down below muzzle flashes of guns and the exploding of shells indicated the front line, which ran approximately along the Maas, and I abandoned my search. I turned onto an easterly course and dropped down to 2000 meters, the right altitude for the flight home. We would be below the Mosquitoes and beyond the range of our own light *Flak*, which at night was known to fire at everything that moved within our range in the sky. I corrected my course a number of times in accordance to the bearings taken by my radio operator on our base radio beacon and when we were closer and the transmission was strong enough I switched the autopilot onto it. After about half an hour we had reached our airfield.

'Oh bother', my radio operator said, 'the *Gruppe* from Dortmund[68] is landing because of fog at their base. As our transmitter is unservicable and I am unable to announce ourselves, you will have to see how you can wangle your way in. The tower keeps repeating 'Watch out for competition' – so the duty long-range night fighter or his relief must still be around. Well, good luck!'

'We would really need it, for with both transmitters out we were dumb and unable to get a number for landing in sequence. The usual procedure for landings at the operational night fighter bases was that each approaching crew would report shortly before arrival:

'Adler 98 makes Reise-Reise[69] – about ten minutes.'

'If other crews wanted to land and had already reported in, we would be given an approach altitude (also our level for holding), which we would carry out doing wide circuits of the field to port until we were called in. If one was the first to land, one would get the instruction: 'You are clear to make Luzie-Anton!' Aircraft circling the airfield awaiting their turn to land were usually separated by a height interval of one hundred meters. When the aircraft flying at the lowest level was called in for landing, all the other aircraft automatically went one hundred meters lower. The next call followed at the moment when the landing aircraft had left the runway. Until then the runway was closed. The closing and opening of the runway was done by the runway controller using the 'closing chain' at the runway approach. It consisted of a row of lights placed across the runway and could be switched to green or red. When an aircraft touched down, the runway was closed by turning on the red lights. When the machine had completed its landing run and had turned off onto the perimeter track, the lights were turned to green. By this means a relatively large number of aircraft were able to land within a very short time. This was particularly important during a sudden deterioration in weather conditions such as fog or when crews had reached the end of their fuel endurance and, as they had all taken off at the same time, had to land at the same time. A crew, which for some reason had not been able to announce its approach, was faced with a problem in sneaking into the landing sequence. Either they had to wait until the last one had landed or put down on the grass emergency strip to the right of the concrete runway. One could of course be lucky and get in before the aircraft that had just been called in but then that one would have to overshoot as the barrier would have been turned to red, indicating that the runway was occupied. The risk of colliding with an approaching aircraft could not be ignored as landings were carried out without navigation or landing lights because of the danger from the 'duty long-range night fighter'.

'We were now in the awkward situation of having to land without being able to announce our presence. Fred had tuned into the communications between the waiting machines and the tower and he let me listen in to it. There were more than 20 aircraft waiting to land. The communication was somewhat hectic. Each crew that took too long to get down or failed to leave the runway quickly enough was urged along by many voices. This was not really surprising for the weather had deteriorated considerably since we had taken off and the haze had increased in intensity and it looked as if it would turn to thick fog very quickly.

'I circled the field at 500 meters in a wide orbit to port to orientate myself. It could hardly have been more unfavourable. To the west, in the direction of the landing, the searchlights marking the northern end of the 'Ruhr-Hiking-Path' illuminated the haze over the town and the airfield to such a degree that from the east it looked like an opaque screen. To the east in the approach path the British competition with a Mosquito would usually be hanging around. Each of the approaching aircraft must be visible like a shadow against a white wall. We were aware of this problem so we used a special landing technique. We orbited the field in a relatively tight circle to port and landed as we came out of the final turn. The flaps were only lowered half way and only fully at the last moment together with the undercarriage. A waiting Mosquito would only be able to spot the aircraft just before it touched down and by then it was usually too late for an attack. Although flying turns with partially extended flaps was not entirely without danger, especially at low levels, if one were familiar with one's machine, had sufficient speed and power and used little bank in the turns, this landing procedure could be carried out without any trouble.

'Quite some business going on!' remarked my radio operator.

'We'll just have to try it – we have no choice. We can't use the emergency strip, the Thunderbolts have made a couple of craters in it during the day. They would hardly have filled them in yet, with all this flying going on. Into battle then, Torero!'

'On my first approach I quickly retracted my undercarriage and flaps again for immediately ahead of me a Bf 110 of the Dortmund *Gruppe* was touching down. I went straight into a turn to port, steeper than usual in order to make my next attempt before the next aircraft was called in if possible. But as I approached the threshhold lights were still red and I did an overshoot. It was the same on my third and fourth attempt. I checked my fuel state and had cause for concern. We must have used up quite a lot during that business over Soest. Perhaps I could use the emergency strip if all else failed but the bomb craters on were invisible in the dark. To simply have a go and try to avoid them using my brakes seemed too risky as the landing speed of my machine was too high for that. The haze increased rapidly. I made another attempt at landing but the lights were again on red.

'It's no good – we must get down now! The haze is increasing by the minute. We have to swallow the bitter pill and make a wider approach – in spite of the presence of the Mosquito!'

'Wouldn't you rather try the grass strip after all? If you keep as far as possible to the right it should be all right.'

'I don't think I'll try that – the risk is simply too great for my taste. If we hit one of the craters we'll break all our bones – and our machine is also done for. Now listen, put the colors of the day into your signal pistol and have a red ready in your hand. I'll take a wider turn and when I'm on the final turn in I'll let you know. Then fire off both cartridges. They must see that emergency signal and perhaps someone will take pity on us and let us land! But keep your eyes skinned that no one gets at us from behind!'

'I went further to the east and as I made my final turn. I said, 'Now! Fire!' I waited for the report but it did not come. 'What's up? Fire!'

'My radio operator swore: 'Shit – the second dud!'

'Go on! We're almost there!' The flaps were already half extended. I put them down fully and pressed the undercarriage lever. The altimeter showed 140 meters above ground. I dragged the aircraft in with half power and a speed of a little over 200 km/h. The rate of descent varied between four and five meters. Suddenly there was an infernal banging and shaking and the cockpit was lit up brightly by explosions. I was blinded and black spots danced before my eyes. At the same time I felt a strong jerk in the rudder. It was so strong that my feet slipped from the pedals. For a moment I thought that my radio operator had fired off the signal cartridges in the cockpit but he shouted excitedly, 'Long-range night fighter – I believe the fuel tank is on fire!'

'Instinctively I pulled the cockpit roof jettison lever and shouted, 'Away! Out! Away with the seat and open the 'chute!' The roof flew away and the slipstream almost tore the helmet off my head. I released my straps and felt for the safety catch of the ejection seat on the right-hand panel. I was still blinded. The black specks on the retina were performing a devil's dance. I raised the safety catch and felt for the release pin. The bang of the radio operator's ejection must come any second now. I would follow him right away. Why did the bang not come? Time was running out!

'Quickly, get out!' For a moment, silence. Then I heard the voice of my radio operator in my earphones; it sounded as if it came from a deep well:

'I can't – my ejector seat won't work!' It struck me like a heavy blow!'

'Get strapped in again – I'm going to put the kite down on her belly!'

'The engines turned steadily as if nothing had happened. Gradually the glare diminished and I was able to see again. With great relief I found that the aircraft was not burning after all. In his initial excitement my radio operator had taken the flashes at the rear, where the fuel tank was situated, as a fire. The vivid flashes of the striking projectiles had blinded him too. There were gaping holes in the wings, the rear of both the engine cowlings were like sieves. But the machine was still flying steadily. I decided despite the bomb craters to drag the aircraft in to the field and make a belly landing on the emergency strip to the right of the concrete runway. I opened the throttles a little to gain some speed and then retracted the undercarriage but as I tried to turn to starboard I found that the rudder no longer reacted. I increased the power of the port engine a little and put on some bank to starboard. When I saw the lights of the emergency strip in a straight line in front of me I levelled off and pulled the port throttle back again. The lights of the perimeter track came closer. When I considered I was in the right position I closed both throttles and the fuel cocks, pushed both ignition keys up and removed them. The aircraft floated. I pushed it closer to the ground and slowly eased the control column to my chest, endeavouring to keep the aircraft just off the ground to touch down very softly.

'Seconds can turn into an eternity! I saw the grass flashing past like a shadow and I waited for the familiar grinding sound of the machine ploughing into the ground. With all my strength I jammed both feet into the rudder pedals and stiffened my body because I had had no time nor the opportunity to refasten my straps. Even if there had been time, it would hardly have been possible to fish them up from the depth of the cockpit. At touch down when I no longer needed to hold the stick I intended to snatch up my arms to protect my face. My nerves were stretched to breaking point. In a moment the fuselage would touch the ground. I hoped to be able to counteract the braking effect. The thought of striking my head against the instrument panel, 'to have all the instruments in his face', as we used to jest, was not very attractive. Suddenly the aircraft was bumping over the uneven grass surface; the undercarriage had not been retracted because the Mosquito had shot up the hydraulic system. 'The bomb craters! At the last moment I saw the dimly lit edge of the first crater. A second one was beyond it a little to the left. With all my strength I jammed my foot into the right brake pedal. The aircraft slewed to the right with considerable speed and just missed the crater. I wanted to brake but they had completely been drained of oil from the damaged pipes. Our speed gradually diminished and the machine finally came to a stop just short of the perimeter track. I released the parachute harness, let down the 'chicken ladder' and swung myself over the side of the cockpit. As I climbed down my knees felt soft like rubber. My radio operator followed me down. 'Phew!' We walked around our *Emil-Kurfürst*[70] to inspect the damage. The rear fuselage, tail unit and wings were full of holes and fuel was dripping from the tanks. When, some days later, the aircraft was dismantled in the hangar, an unexploded cannon shell was discovered in the fuel tank. For two days we celebrated our 'birthday' and 'poured oil into all available lamps'. On the third day we sweated it out and on the fourth day we did the first test flight on our new *Emil-Kurfürst*.'[71]

During December *Nachtjagd* flew 1070 sorties, which resulted in 66 victories or 0.7 per cent of all Bomber Command night bomber sorties. Despite the declining effectiveness of *Nachtjagd* during late 1944, an all-time record of 2,216 aircraft destroyed was claimed that year. *Luftflotte Reich* had 905 operational night-fighter aircraft on 17 November but losses in air combat, in ground attacks and in accidents rose steeply and 114 aircraft were destroyed during November-December 1944. Among the losses in December were *Experten* such as *Hptm* Hans-Heinz Augenstein, one of *Nachtjagd*'s favourite sons. It was on 6 December when a very severe ground frost heralded a bright and clear morning and all anticipation was for a maximum effort. Low-level *Intruders* bombed and strafed *Luftwaffe* airfields but the weather conditions were not good for this type of operation. That night, 1291 aircraft attacked Bergesburg, Osnabrück, Giessen, Berlin, Schwerte and Hanau. Eighty-nine aircraft of 100 Group supported the operations and lost one aircraft. The heavies lost 21 of their number, or 1.7 per cent of the force. (*Nachtjäger* claimed 14-19 heavy bomber kills). *Uffz* Kurt Schmidt, since September 1943 Augenstein's *Bordschütze* and who took part in the destruction of 27 'Dicke Autos' ('Fat Cars') with Augenstein, recalls the events of that fateful night:

'The Fourth *Gruppe* of NJG 1 was based at Dortmund. Shortly after the weather briefing the first incoming aircraft were reported. We went to immediate readiness at 1830 hrs, which shrortly after was called off. Around 1900 hrs we went to immediate readiness again and the first long range night intruders arrived over the airfield. They had been a real plague of late. A few minutes later we were ordered to take off. Our left engine refused to start. I unstrapped and assisted *Hptm* Augenstein with the engine. In the meantime, the light *Flak* was firing to drive away the intruders. Suddenly, the engine burst into life and I was almost swept off the wing. *Hptm* Augenstein was in a bad mood, as he was now not the first one to take off. He didn't say a word as we taxied to the take off point. The 'drome was enveloped in darkness. Just one mechanic walked in front of our machine and showed us the way with his dimmed electric torch. We were the last one to take off. The only light was a lamp at the end of the runway, in which direction we took off.

'Over the R/T we heard, 'Watch out for small Indians in your immediate vicinity'. We peered into the darkness until our eyeballs were almost out of their sockets but we took off unscathed and immediately disappeared into a layer of cloud at 1000 meters (3,250 ft) and set course for a radio beacon near Münster. The weather conditions were ideal for us. We arrived over the beacon and waited there at 7000 meters (22,700 ft). *Hptm* Augenstein didn't fly in a corkscrew as he normally did. Steins and I made our objections to this, as a long-range intruder had already shot us down once before over the invasion front in June. *Hptm* Augenstein replied, 'There are no small Indians at this height'. The main force of '*Dicke Autos*' was now over Osnabrück and flew straight at us. Their target was probably Berlin. We discussed where we should land when we flew with the bomber stream. 'Suddenly, our machine was rocked. Tracer bullets flew all around me. We plunged down. I believe *Hptm* Augenstein was trying to shake off our attacker and I asked him what was going on. The cockpit was full of smoke and the engines were screaming at full power. We still dived down. Augenstein shouted, 'Get out, I can't hold her anymore!' The control cables were probably shot through. Steins, who was not yet fully recovered from the last time we were shot down, had slumped forward. I jolted him and shouted, 'Get out!' He did not move. He had probably been hit. The intercom was dead and smashed and the cockpit canopy would not budge. Only when *Hptm* Augenstein jettisoned his cockpit roof did mine also fly away. I was pushed against the cannons of the *Schräge Musik* and though I exerted all my strength I could only get my upper body out of the machine. My parachute straps were jammed somewhere and unable to move I was glued to the fuselage with my legs still inside the cabin. I almost lost my senses from the noise and the air pressure. I gave in! Whilst spinning down I was hurled away. Immediately I came to my senses again and I went into free fall until the somersaulting slowed down. I pulled the ripcord. Thank God my 'chute opened immediately. Now swinging and turning started. I didn't know where the top and where the bottom were any more. Some of the cords had snapped and all I could do was swing. I moved my arms and legs to check if everything was still OK. I saw our machine crash in flames. I got a fright, as during the fumbling I suddenly had the lock of my parachute harness in my hand. I had pulled the cover of the harness lock loose. Carefully I grabbed some cords in order to hold on to them in case of emergency. Yet, with the vicious swinging I couldn't hold on to them.

'I had come out of the machine at 3000 meters (9,700 ft). Nearby I heard the noise of an aircraft. Then, with a deafening noise *Flak* shells started exploding above me and with every salvo I counted on being hit. I fired off the colors of the day and everything was quiet. I floated through a thin layer of clouds then everything turned black and I fire off a couple of flares. I was still a few hundred meters off the ground. I spotted a farmhouse and a silvery line, which I was floating towards. It looked like a canal (it was an asphalt road which had become wet in the rain) so I looked to see if the pressurized air bottle in my Mae West was still functioning and it was. Just before I landed I intended to fire off another couple of flares but I had no time left to execute this. I was unable to take off the harness, as the lock was broken. Fortunately, I had a hunting knife. I couldn't get up on my feet. The inside my head resembled a combination of a steam-hammer and a sawmill. Still, I was alive! I crept laboriously towards a house 100 meters away and knocked on the door. A woman answered and looked at me appalled. A small girl asked, 'Mummy, is that St. Nicholas? Steins was found the same night. He was hurled from the aircraft in the crash. During the next few days, not a trace of *Hptm* Augenstein was found. Only after three days, a farmer found his body in a ditch on his land with his unopened parachute. Both my comrades were buried at the military cemetery in Münster. After the war *Hptm* Augenstein's mortal remains were re-buried in his hometown at Pforzheim.'[72]

Also on 6/7 December F/L J.O. 'Jimmy' Mathews DFC and W/O A. Penrose DFC of 157 Squadron destroyed a Bf 110 and a Ju 88.[73] In the Kitzingen area S/L Dolly Doleman and F/L 'Bunny' Bunch DFC of 157 Squadron closed in on an almost head-on contact at 15,000 ft at six miles, same level. Their target dived to 11,000 ft on the bomber withdrawal route and then did a figure of eight before flying away eastwards. Doleman closed in and identified it as a Me 110 before he shot it down at 2040 hrs. on the night of 9/10 December *Fw* Reichenbach of 4./NJG 11 claimed a Mosquito near Berlin but the 60 Mosquitoes that attacked the 'Big City' returned without loss. Two nights later when 89 Mosquitoes went to various city targets one of the aircraft that failed to return from the raid on Hamburg was claimed by *Oblt* Kurt Welter of II./NJG 11.[74] *Uffz* Scherl of 8./NJG 1 claimed a Mosquito east of Hagen on the night of 12/13 December when 540 aircraft attacked Essen but though six Lancasters were lost, all 28 Mosquitoes that attacked Essen and 49 others that raided Osnabrück returned safley. (The only Mosquiito lost was a 306 Squadron NFXXX that was hit by a V2 in mid air during an *Intruder* patrol! W/O S. Wieczorek and W/O H. Ostrowski belly-landed at Hunsdon). 100 Group Mosquitoes shot down five German night fighters. F/L Edward R. Hedgecoe DFC and F/Sgt J.R. Whitham destroyed two more Bf 110s[75] while S/L Branse Burbridge DSO* DFC* and F/L F.S. Bill Skelton DSO* DFC* of 85 Squadron added a Ju 88 and a Bf 110 to their rising score. They shot down a Ju 88G-1, which crashed at Gütersloh airfield.[76] Flying towards Essen another contact was obtained at four miles and 12,000 ft and they dashed towards the target area at high speed and climbing. Luckily, a burst of *Flak* illuminated a Bf 110 and Burbridge closed to 400 ft for final identification. He gave the Bf 110 a half-second burst from 500 ft and the *Nachtjagd* aircraft exploded before spinning down in flames, the tail unit breaking off. It crashed about two miles west of Essen.

When the 13th day of December broke it was under a very heavy frost and towards mid-morning thick fog enveloped stations in Norfolk and operations were scrubbed very early. That night 52 Lancasters and seven Mosquitoes of 5 Group flew to Norway to attack the German cruiser *Köln* but by the time they reached Oslo Fiord, the ship had sailed so instead other ships were bombed. On 15/16 December 327 Lancasters and Mosquitoes of 1, 6 and 8 Groups raided Ludwigshafen for one Lancaster lost. Two nights later, on 17/18 December 96 aircraft in 100 Group, including a *Spoof* raid by four Mosquitoes of 141 Squadron on Mannheim, supported a massive operation by 1174 aircraft, which bombed Ulm, München, Duisburg, Hanau, Münster and Hallendorf. Two Tame Boar *Nachtjäger* of NJG 5 and NJG 6 each destroyed a Lancaster over Ulm. Three Halifaxes of the Duisburg force were shot down by three crews of 4./NJG 1 and *Hptm* Fritz Lau and *Uffz* Reinecke of 4./NJG 1 each claimed a Mosquito *Abschuss*.[77] In reply three Bf 110s were claimed destroyed by Mosquito crews of 85 and 157 Squadrons.[78] One of the 'Bf 110s' was probably He 219A-2 290188 G9+WL of 3./NJG 1 flown by *Lt* Jürgen Prietze and *Uffz* Frithjof Haake, both of whom were killed in air combat two kilometers SE of Sonsbeck.

On 18/19 December 308 bombers attacked Danzig (Gdynia), Münster and Nürnburg. in the Gotenhafen and Danzig areas three crews of I./NJG 5 claimed all four Lancasters that failed to return from the Main Force raid on Danzig. Forty-eight aircraft of 100 Group supported the operation and Mosquitoes of 2nd TAF and FIU intruded over the continent. Four 2nd TAF crews were successful. 410 'Cougar' Squadron RCAF destroyed a Ju 88 while 409 'Nighthawk' Squadron RCAF achieved three victories.[79] Four heavies and a FIU Mosquito flown by F/O Desmond T. Tull DFC and F/O Peter J. Cowgill DFC of the FIU failed to return.[80] F/L William Taylor and F/O Jeffery N. Edwards of 157 Squadron at the end of an uneventful patrol achieved a second victory. Having set course for base, they ran into *Window* but they were able to pick up a contact at about six miles' range. Their target was climbing steeply and orbiting. At 2000 ft and 800 ft above they obtained a visual. Taylor was nearly overshooting so he dropped back and weaved gently. Another visual was obtained 30° above him. After chasing for another five minutes the contact was correctly identified as a He 219A-0. Taylor opened fire from 250 yards but the Mosquito was caught in the night-fighter's slipstream and his shooting was erratic. Strikes were observed and minor explosions appeared in the fuselage before the *Owl* turned slowly to port and peeled off. Visual was lost but the Heinkel was followed on AI until contact was lost at 12,000 ft. A few seconds later, it exploded on the ground at Südlohn.[81]

Bad weather interfered again before operations resumed on 21/22 December when 475 heavies attacked Köln, Bonn, Politz and Schneidemuhl. Three bombers failed to return from the raid on Politz.[82] W/C K.H.P. Beauchamp DSO DFC and F/L Leslie Scholefield DFC of 157 Squadron in a NFXIX flew in support of Bomber Command operations against Bonn and Cologne and returned with a claim for a Ju 88 north of Frankfurt. They had identified their quarry in the light of a half-moon from 200 ft on his starboard quarter below. Beauchamp dropped back to 200 ft dead astern and fired a short burst, causing strikes. The Ju 88 immediately peeled off port and went down on to the top of some stratus cloud and visual contact was lost but as there was no resultant explosion Beauchamp followed down and regained a visual on him as he was weaving away violently just above cloud. The Mosquito crew closed in on his port quarter and slightly above. Beauchamp opened fire at about 600 yards. He set the port engine on fire before pulling up and doing a port orbit over the Ju 88, watching the fire increase until the aircraft flew into the ground in a shallow dive and exploded.

On 22/23 December 166 Lancasters and two Mosquitoes attacked Koblenz without loss while 106 aircraft including 90 Halifaxes of 4 Group raided the Bingen marshalling yards on the Rhine 30 miles south-west of Frankfurt. S/L Branse Burbridge DSO* DFC* and F/O F.S. Skelton DSO* DFC*[83] of 85 Squadron destroyed a Bf 110 at Koblenz-Gütersloh. Not to be outdone, F/O A.J. Ginger Owen and F/O J.S.V. McAllister DFM claimed a squadron hat trick of victories. They destroyed a Bf 110 north of Saarbrücken and then they got a Ju 88, which Owen despatched with a 'medium' burst from 150 yards, which set the port engine on fire before crashing. Twenty minutes later, a third contact was obtained four miles ahead. Closing to 2000 ft a visual was obtained well above him. It was another Ju 88 and it was taking evasive action. A short deflection burst scored strikes on the port wing and pieces flew off. The Ju 88 dived vertically and contact was lost at 7000 ft. Four minutes later, an explosion occurred on the ground.[84] S/L R.D. Dolly Doleman DFC and F/L D.C. 'Bunny' Bunch DFC of 157 Squadron also returned triumphantly to Swannington having destroyed a Ju 88 and also claiming another as a 'probable'. Their first contact was obtained North at Bingen at 1835 hrs when the Mosquito NFXIX was at 15,000ft. Doleman chased it to 20,000ft just north of Bingen but as they staggered up the last few thousand feet a *Monica* contact was picked up and Doleman had to break away. As he turned to port the *Monica*, which had been jammed, cleared and they saw their pursuer behind showing IFF. Doleman neared the bomber stream and dived into a cloud of *Window* where they lost him. This used up about 20 minutes and as the bombing had finished the Mosquito crew flew north of Frankfurt to have a look at Limburg. There they obtained a contact at ten miles range and well below. Doleman and Bunch were at 15,000 ft and range was closed. They descended to 8000 ft and Bunch obtained visual at 3000ft and at 1500 ft from below the target was identified as a Ju 88. The German pilot foolishly slackened his turn and Doleman was able to close to 500 ft and with only o-ring deflection pump shells into his fuselage and port engine, which burst into flames. Doleman remained behind just to make sure but the Ju 88 dived straight in five miles west of Limburg at 1935 hrs. Doleman and Bunch wished their victim 'a Merry Christmas on the way down – literally cooking his goose for him.'

Two Halifaxes and one Lancaster were lost on the Bingen raid.[85] F/L Neville E.G. Donmall, a Halifax navigator on 578 Squadron at Burn, near Selby, in Yorkshire, recalls:

> 'Halifax LK-X was airborne at 1611 hrs, climbing to 18,000 ft on a cold sleeting December evening. We cleared cloud at 17,000 ft and set course for Southampton. Leaving

our coast behind we were soon over Eastern France where the cloud started to break. Fifty miles from the target there was only 5/10ths cloud. Our flight to Bingen was fairly uneventful, with moderate *Flak* in places. There was also some *Flak* over the target. All markers went down on time and the main force was assembled over the marshalling yards within seven minutes. On the run in we could see the Rhine and the target and our bombs went down directly on the aiming point.

'After bombing the target, we turned south for about ten miles, then set course for home. Over Bad Kreuznach, after a few minutes on the new heading of 280°, our gunners reported there was a Ju 88 on our tail. The enemy fighter-bomber and our rear and mid-upper turrets opened fire together. Both gunners reported hits on the Ju 88, which dived away beneath us. They also reported minor damage to our own tailplane and fuselage. About two minutes later the mid- upper gunner called out that another Ju 88 was attacking from beneath us. Returning fire, our aircraft shuddered as more hits were registered on our starboard wing. Flames appeared near the petrol tank and our pilot ordered the crew to bale out. All crew positions acknowledged the call. Lifting my seat, I clipped on my parachute and released the emergency escape hatch beneath my feet. Positioning myself on the edge of the escape exit, I baled out at 17,000 ft. I recollect counting up to three and pulling the ripcord but remembered nothing more until I found myself swinging beneath the parachute, with my jaw hurting and feeling a little sick. I must have been in the prone position when the chest-type chute deployed, for it had hit my chin and nearly knocked me out.

'I started to look for the ground but couldn't see it, due either to cloud or fog. The next second I clouted it with a hell of a wallop, once again hitting my chin, this time by my knee. Luckily I'd landed in a foot or so of snow, which somewhat reduced the full impact of my landing. Shaking my head and gathering up my chute, I got my compass out and set off at a run towards what I hoped was Luxembourg. I knew how imperative it was for me to clear the area before the Germans found me.'[86]

No aircraft were lost to German action on the night of 23/24 December when 52 Mosquitoes of the LNSF bombed rail yards at Limburg in Germany and another forty attacked Siegburg. 2nd TAF Mosquito NFXXX, NFXIII and NFXVII crews and 100 Group NFXIX and NFXXX crews destroyed 14 Luftwaffe aircraft.[87] Four of the victories went to crews of 488 Squadron RNZAF and F/L Kenneth William 'Chunky' Stewart, a solicitor from Dunedin and his navigator/radar operator F/O H.E. 'Bill' Brumby[88] got two of them for their first kills since joining the squadron. While on patrol near Roermond Stewart noticed clusters of white flares and obtained permission to investigate. His controller said that there was no activity in that direction but Brumby succeeded in putting Stewart onto an aircraft. After a short chase, with the target taking mild evasive action, they identified the aircraft as a Ju 88 but for positive identification Stewart closed to 100 ft whereupon the Ju 88 fired off a red flare which illuminated the black crosses on the fin, fuselage and mainplane. Stewart dropped back to 150 yards and fired a short burst observing strikes between the port engine and fuselage. With a second burst the port engine caught fire and the Ju 88 spun down in flames, exploding before hitting the ground near Maeseyck. The controller told Stewart to climb to 7000 ft and whilst doing so he saw further flares and again requested permission to chase. After changing Controls Brumby seized an opportunity and, after the Luftwaffe aircraft had throttled back, turned, climbed and straightened out, Stewart obtained a visual at 2000ft which Brumby confirmed with his glasses as another Ju 88. At 300 yards this aircraft also dropped reddish flares and the Mosquito plainly saw black crosses and also the bomb racks. Stewart closed to 200/150 yards and gave two short bursts, which started a fire in the fuselage. The Ju 88 did a diving turn to starboard and when the Mosquito was down to 1000ft the enemy aircraft hit the ground and exploded.[89]

On Christmas Eve, when 104 Lancasters of 3 Group bombed Hangelar airfield near Bonn, losing one aircraft and 97 Lancasters and five Mosquitoes of 1 and 8 Groups attacked the marshalling yards at Cologne/Nippes Mosquito squadrons in 100 Group and 2nd TAF celebrated the festive season in style. Thirteen German aircraft were shot down, five of them by four crews of 100 Group and eight by seven crews of 2nd TAF[90], which dispatched 139 Mosquitoes to targets in southwest Germany. Low-level *Intruders* covered Luftwaffe airfields and carried out *Ranger* operations in the Breslau area. Locomotives, rolling stock and motor transport were bombed and strafed by the AI.Mk.IV Mosquito squadrons operating as low-level *Intruders*. The AI.Mk.X Mosquitoes enjoyed almost total air superiority over the *Nachtjagdgeschwader* this night. S/L James Benson DFC* and F/L Lewis Brandon DFC* of 157 Squadron in Mosquito NFXIX on High Level Support Patrol for Bomber Command attacks on Cologne and Hangelar destroyed a Bf 110 to take their score to nine. F/L Jimmy Mathews and W/O Alan Penrose of 157 Squadron blasted a Ju 88 out of the night sky with a 1 1/2 second burst, which resulted in the starboard engine bursting into flames. As it turned to port, three parachutes came out in quick succession and three bodies sailed to earth. The aircraft then spun down and crashed three miles southwest of Köln. Another success went to Capt

Svein Heglund DFC and F/O Robert Symon of 85 Squadron, who claimed a Bf 110 destroyed.[91] S/L Dolly Doleman and F/L 'Bunny' Bunch of 157 Squadron returned from a high Level Support Patrol for Bomber Command attacks on Cologne and Hangelar with claims for a Bf 110 west of Cologne and a second at 8000 ft in the Duisburg area.[92]

The nights of 25/26-27/28 December were much quieter with no Main Force operations on the 25/26th because of bad weather. Six claims were made by Mosquito crews in this period, including two Ju 88Gs at Kaltenkirchen by F/O R.I.E. Britten RCAF and F/L L.E. Fownes of 409 Squadron on the 27/28th. During the day 200 Lancasters and 11 Mosquitoes attacked rail yards at Rheydt for the loss of one Lancaster and a Mosquito of 109 Squadron, which crashed behind the Allied lines in Holland. F/L W.McK Hodgson DFC was killed but his navigator, F/O A.J. Cork DFM, survived and returned to the squadron. German claims in the same period were equally low.[93] *Oblt* Dieter Schmidt, *Staffelkapitän*, 8./NJG 1 comments:

> 'Winter 1944-45 can be said to have been the toughest time of all for us. With the front line getting ever closer, early warning times became shorter and consequently operational control more difficult. In mid-September NJG 1 had got its final nightfighting task: the protection of the Ruhr. The Third *Gruppe* transferred first to Werl, then to Fritzlar-Wildungen and finally, as it was too far from the area to be protected, back again to Werl, Düsseldorf and Dortmund and the 8th *Staffel* on 20 November to Krefeld in the Rhine bend near Uerdingen. In mid-December we got the final task. Because of our *Zerstörer* background we were to support the Ardennes offensive with low-level night attacks on ground targets but bombs were not obtained in time. By the beginning of 1945 the 7th and 9th *Staffels* were in Störmede, south of Lippstadt and the 8th *Staffel* back again in Fritzlar. Large-scale nightfighting was no longer possible. Added to this, since mid-1944 there was jamming on the SN-2 frequency and only the most experienced of us were able to make out targets with it. The ever-increasing British long-range nightfighter activity was especially dangerous with growing losses. Not only was the Mosquito superior to our Bf 110 in performance, it carried radar working on 3 cm which was fully functional down to low levels. Our own SN-2 was virtually blind below 1000 meters due to ground echoes. However, our equipment had an unintentional but under the circumstances, life-saving side effect. Using the so-called 'side-bands' we were able to 'see' behind to some degree and thus occasionally were able to escape the otherwise surprise attack of an intruder.
>
> 'Whenever we got the order for cockpit readiness, the intruder on duty at Krefeld was already circling above the field. We countered this by taking off using the minimum of airfield lighting, then immediately crossing the Rhine into the Flak area of the Ruhr which was dreaded by all, having first made arrangements for a ban on firing below 1000 meters in the area around Uerdingen. The same applied for our return. At Störmede airfield to the east of the Ruhr, take-offs and landings during light nights took place in the valleys of the Sauerland. During the dark ones we flew by the radio altimeter at 50 meters in the Münsterländer Bay to gain sufficient distance from the field before climbing through the blind zone from zero to 1000 meters. In spite of this, our crew losses were exceptionally high, especially during December 1944. This was the only time during the war that crew losses from enemy action were greater than in operational accidents. Under these circumstances there was hardly any point, especially during spring 1945 to use young pilots or radio operators and so only the few remaining experienced crews were sent on operations during this time.'

On New Year's Eve crews of the *Gruppenstab* and the 8th and 9th *Staffeln* of III./NJG 2 at Marx/Varel were given the usual meteorological and signal' briefing. The *Kommandeur* told the crews that 'in view of the suitable weather conditions, a RAF raid was to be mounted that night.[94] At 1800 hrs his eight Ju 88s were ordered to take off. The first was 4R+CS and sat at the end of the runway awaiting the signal when a Mosquito *Intruder* dropped a bomb which exploded on the runway about 30 meters from the Junkers. 4R+0S apparently suffered no damage and it took off after a short delay. The crew made for Hanover and soon they saw the first cascade flares. On arrival, they saw the incendiary bombs and fires. A four-engined bomber was seen to be held in searchlights and heading southwest. The *Naxos* and *SN-2* of 4R+0S had been u/s for some time and the four-engined aircraft was lost. The Ju 88 first turned west-northwest in the hope of finding the bomber stream but after 15 minutes the starboard engine cut out. It was a coolant leak, caused by the *Intruder's* bomb.[95] *Intruder* incursions over *Luftwaffe* bases were being made with haunting regularity and there was much 'joy' as the predators enjoyed rich pickings from among the returning flocks of unsuspecting, weary and chiefly inexperienced replacement *Nachtjagd* crews. The last of 39 aircraft to fall to 100 Group in December were two Ju 88s and a He 219 on New Year's Eve. It is no coincidence that 85 Squadron, which claimed 18 victories and 157 Squadron, which claimed 13, were the only squadrons in

100 Group which were equipped with the excellent AI.Mk.X radar. This situation annoyed other Mosquito nightfighter crews like that of F/L A. Paul Mellows and F/L S.L. 'Dickie' Drew of 169 Squadron as Mellows recalls:

> 'It had always riled us that 85 Sqn, who had been on defensive work, were allowed to go intruding and had success such as we had never dreamed of. Many of the Mosquitoes we were provided with in 169 Squadron had come from OTUs. The AI transmitted in all directions and the range was limited to a thousand or more feet less than your height. In December 1944 we were sent to 85 Sqn with one or two other crews. Dick and I trained on the AI.Mk.X, which was superb with very long range and 180 degrees coverage from side to side with no problem from ground returns. When on 31 December we were told we were doing our first trip, on the night of a spoof raid, Dickie was very annoyed indeed. He felt that we needed a little more time for training and also we did not want to waste one of our valuable last six trips on a night when there were no bombers but only *Window* was being dropped. However, on our patrol point a few miles NW of Cologne we got a contact at six miles at 15,000 ft.'

The contact was closed at 2000 ft and they could clearly see four white exhausts and twin tail fins. Shortly after black crosses on the blue undersurface of the wings were seen in the light of a searchlight. Mellows fired a two-second burst from slightly below causing debris to fly off and a small fire in the fuselage. Another two-second burst caused an explosion by the light of which Drew clearly saw the dihedral and slanting fins of a He 219, which Mellows confirmed. A further short burst set him well alight and from 1000 ft to starboard they saw him climb for a few seconds before plunging to earth, where he exploded with a bright orange flash at 1824 hrs in the Köln area.[96]

Mellows concludes:

> 'After the He 219 went down the temp on the port engine went off the clock and I had to feather the prop and we returned on the starboard engine to Manston. When we got out of the aeroplane we noticed glycol spurting from the starboard engine. I wrote to my fiancée, Jean and told her that there was no coolant left in the starboard engine and would probably have not kept going for more than another 5-10 minutes.'

Two of the New Year's Eve victories[97] were the first claimed using ASH. The first went to S/L C.V. Bennett DFC and F/L R.A. Smith of 515 Squadron. In the Lovns Bredning area during an *Intruder* patrol to Grove, Bennett and Smith's Mosquito was fired at with tracer from an unidentified Ju 88. Bennett returned fire at 400 yards and with a two-second burst of cannon. Strikes were seen on the port wing. A second burst cut the Ju 88 in two, the wreckage dropping into Lim Fiord. During the New Year's party that followed at Little Snoring Bennett and Smith[98] were joined by S/L J. Tweedale and F/L V. Cunningham of 23 Squadron. They had claimed their Squadron's first victory (a Ju 88 at Alhorn) using ASH.[99]

Also on the night of 31 December 77 Mosquito bombers of the LNSF went to Berlin. One of them was Z-Zebra[100] of 128 Squadron, which was flown by F/L Leicester G. Smith RNZAF.[101] He recalls:

> 'The big Cookie carrier BXVI was a wonderful aircraft to fly and although it had a pressurised cabin it was not used on operations in case of internal damage from *Flak*. Take off time was 1615 hrs. The flight plan kept our aircraft to 10,000 ft to 6° East and an indicated airspeed of 215 knots at that height. It was a glorious evening for flying, as so many evenings were and mainly over 7/10ths cloud. The reason given was to miss the cumulo-nimbus cloud tops. We climbed to operational height and levelled out at 26,000 ft. *Flak* was heavy between Lübeck and Hamburg (commonly called the Gap). Shrapnel was whistling around everywhere but our sympathy went out to one Mosquito crew who was coned by at least 20 searchlights. *Flak* was bursting all around him, at least 2000 ft above and below. I was about two miles north of this aircraft and he flew straight through it all. It was an unforgettable sight. Otherwise we had a comfortable run to the Big City. Over Berlin all was quiet as the target indicators, reds and green, went down. A warning was issued that fighters were in the area but none were seen. Bill reported contrails 2-3000 ft above. We put our 'Cookie' down on schedule, took the photo and had a relatively quiet flight back to England. We were coned by many searchlights over the Woodbridge area (must have been an army exercise), landing at Wyton from an operation of five hours airborne.'

The Luftwaffe was powerless to stop the inexorable advance westwards but there was one last attempt to try to halt the allies. Since 20 December 1944 many *Jagdgruppen* had been transferred to airfields in the west for Operation *Bodenplatte,* when approximately 850 Luftwaffe fighters took off at 0745 hours on Sunday morning 1 January to attack 27 airfields in northern France, Belgium and southern Holland. The four-hour operation succeeded in destroying about 100 Allied aircraft but it cost the Luftwaffe 300 aircraft, most of which were shot down by Allied anti-aircraft guns deployed primarily against the V-1s and by 'friendly' *flak*.

On 1/2 January Mosquitoes of 2nd TAF and 100 Group Mosquitoes on bomber support covered heavy operations over Germany and eight German nightfighters were claimed shot down.[102] Eight crews in 85 Squadron participated in a maximum effort in the Kiel and Ruhr areas while the Main Force attacked the Mittelland Canal, rail yards at Vohwinkel and Dortmund. F/L R.T. Dickie Goucher and F/L C.H. Tiny Bulloch chased a contact for 11 minutes before obtaining a visual. It was a Ju 188. Goucher gave the Junkers a couple of bursts and it fell in flames, crashing ten miles north of Münster. Almost immediately, Tiny Bulloch got a second blip on his AI.Mk.X scope apparently dropping *Düppel.* Goucher got closer and they could see that their enemy was a Ju 88G. Dickie Goucher gave it a long burst from dead astern as the Junkers turned to port. Flying flaming debris struck the Mosquito causing it to vibrate badly and lose height. Goucher jettisoned his drop tanks and the port tank came over the top of the wing, damaging the tail plane and at the same time shearing off the pitot head. They landed safely at Brussels/Melsbroek and were flown home in a C-47 the next day.[103]

On 2/3 January when 514 Lancasters and seven Mosquitoes of 1, 3, 6 and 8 Groups bombed Nürnburg and 389 aircraft raided Ludwigshafen Mosquito fighters claimed three nightfighters shot down.[104] Four Lancasters were lost from the Nürnburg force and one Halifax from the Ludwigshafen raid. *Hptm* Kurt-Heinz Weigel of 11./NJG 6 claimed two four-engined bombers west and southeast of Stuttgart for his 2nd and 3rd victories. *Hptm* Martin 'Tino' Becker *Kommandeur*, IV./NJG 6 claimed a Lancaster south of Mannheim-north of Bruchsal and another Lancaster over Luxembourg for his 44th and 45th victories. No night bombing operations were carried out by the heavies on 3/4 January but on the night of the 4/5th 347 Lancasters and seven Mosquitoes of 1, 5 and 8 Groups controversially attacked Royan at the mouth of the River Gironde. Upwards of 800 French civilians were killed. Four Lancasters were lost and two more collided behind the Allied lines in France and crashed. The number of aircraft lost in mid-air collisions is not known but it is generally accepted that the numbers were few. Sgt David Fellowes, a Lancaster rear gunner on 460 Squadron RAAF during 1944-45 recalls:

'The morning of 7 January 1945 started much the same as many others. The last minute scramble to complete ones ablutions, into battle-dress and a quick dash to the Sergeants' Mess for the last remains of breakfast. Then to the anti-room for a look at the previous day's papers and with the crew complete, a gentle walk to the hangers and B Flight office. Our skipper Art Whitmarsh followed us in. Soon, amid the noise and smokey atmosphere the telephone rang. An Aussie voice yelled, 'Quiet!' The noise stopped and Bob Henderson, our Flight Commander, replaced the phone. 'OK its on'. We all knew what he meant. We had heard it all before. Last night the crew had been to Hanau, a successful operation with all our aircraft returning safely. Crews dispersed to their individual sections leaving the pilots with the Flight Commander. Ken de la Mare, the mid-upper gunner and I departed for the Gunnery Section in the same hanger and carried out the routine daily inspection of our .303 Browning machine guns. A quick pull through with 4 by 2, check the return springs, read the latest Orders and sign the book. A walk to our dispersal where we were met by Sgt Spud Murphy with his team of fitters and armorers who were responsible for our aircraft. Spud, with his black curly hair, always had a wide grin is more like an Irish gipsy than a real Aussie digger.

'The turret covers had already been removed and with the help of the armorers the guns were fitted, the systems checked, spare sight bulbs, fuses and finally what little perspex we had was given a quick polish. Most of the perspex had been removed, which was more draughty and a lot colder but it improved night vision and made less work. As a last job, I fitted the celluloid caps over the flash eliminators. I then replaced the turret cover, met up with the other crewmembers and hot footed it back to the Mess. As we entered the foyer there for all to see was the 'Battle Order'; a list of names, aircraft, main briefing time etc but there without mistake under 'B' Flight was ours; Aircraft O-Oboe ND968/G. Flying Meal 1530 hrs. Briefing 1615 hrs. Back to our married quarters No.13 where Sgt Art Sheppard, the flight engineer and I shared a small room upstairs. Soon a fire was burning in the grate. The kettle was on and a quick brew up, feet up and relaxation for soon the game would be on again and one more operation less to do. A call at 1500, flying sweaters on and we walked to the mess. We went into the servery with its large trays of fried eggs, streaky bacon, baked beans and fried bread, plenty of bread and margarine all to be washed down with hot tea or coffee. Somebody dropped his plate and a mighty roar went up, then quietness for a few seconds before the low murmurings returned but not for long as it was time to leave. We put our greatcoats on and joined the growing crowd on its way to the Briefing Room.

'In a few minutes we saw the Corporal SP outside the double doors which we passed through. Past the rows of tables and chairs, the low stage with black curtains closed to the front, we took our seats in line with the Skipper and navigator sitting in the aisle seats. The room was thick with with cigarette smoke and noise, for the room was almost full. Eighteen crews were operating tonight; 126 men. The Intelligence Officer, Flight Commander and specialist officers took their place on the platform either side of the curtains. Loud and clear came the call, 'Atten-shun'. Everybody stood. It was quiet and down the aisle walked the Station Commander, G/C Keith Parsons and Squadron Commander Mike Cowan. A curt 'Good evening Gentlemen' was followed by a mass murmured reply and followed by 'Be seated,' as the Intelligence Officer drewsthe curtains apart and the target was revealed – MUNICH.

'A large groan went up. For all to see the thin red tape stretched from Binbrook southwards to Reading then altered course to Beachy Head, over the Channel south-east towards a point north of Mulhouse where the track turned north-east and headed towards Stuttgart. Just before Stuttgart a right turn onto a southeasterly heading, passing Ulm on our port side on to Memmingen and then a left turn heading directly for Munich. This was to be the second attack on Munich this night. 5 Group squadrons were to attack with an H hour of 2030. Us in 1 Group at H hour 2230. The briefing went on. We could expect moderate to heavy *Flak* with fighter activity. The target marking would be Paramatta with emergency sky marking. Finally the Met-man. A small cheer went up as he told us '10/10ths cumulus from France to the target area with tops to 8500-ft with a frontal belt lying south-east of Paris with winds at 18,000 ft of 27-30 knots and tops to 8-10,000-ft near the target'. There would be no moon during the operation and there was the likelihood of snow on return with possible diversions. Thus, the briefing came to an end. The Squadron Commander wished us well. The Station Commander wished he were going. Everybody stood as the hierarchy left.

'The crews dispersed to the changing rooms where they emptied their pockets. Then into flying overalls, long socks, flying boots, gloves, helmet, check the oxygen mask, collect parachute and harness (oh yes sign for it). I then put on my Mae West and harness and collected the escape kit, which was placed in the inner battle-dress pocket. Then it was out into the cold night. The crew bus soon arrived and with other crews with aircraft in adjacent dispersals, we were soon there we were met by Spud Murphy. He told us all was well and the aircraft serviceable.

'We climbed aboard, stowed our chutes and carried out the necessary pre-flight checks. I stuck wakey-wakey tablets onto a strut with a piece of chewing gum. With time to spare the crew gathered at the small ground crew shelter for a last cigarette. Art Whitmarsh signed the Form 700 and most of us went for a quick 'leak'. Then with harness fastened, it was into the aeroplane. While Art Sheppard; F/Sgt D. Collett, navigator, F/Sgt P. Turnbull, bomb aimer and F/Sgt J. Wilson, W/OP went forward I clambered over the Elsan, turned onto my back and slid over the tail spar. Legs down and you were there. I checked to see if my chute was secure, removed the cotton reel from the oxygen economiser, closed the doors, plugged in the intercom and connected the oxygen tube to my mask tube. I fastened the seat belt, opened the breach covers and armed the four Brownings, making sure they were all cocked and Fire/Safe to Safe. This was followed by a call to the Skipper, 'Rear Gunner ready, turret serviceable'.'OK' came the reply and one heard the others reporting. At last it was time to start the engines.

'Now it was time to check the turret's operation, full rotation, guns elevated and depressed. I switched the gunsight to 'dim', checked the radar systems and reported all systems serviceable. One could hear the power increased to the engines. We moved forward, then almost stopped as the brakes were checked. A quick thumbs up to the ground crew as we taxied out of the dispersal and onto the perimeter and joined the queue of Lancasters. We slowly went past the hanger and Control Tower, down hill past the bomb dump and then to the end of Runway 22. In turn we moved onto the runway, where I did my final checks. We got a steady green from the runway controller, the engines roared, the brakes were released and the take-off run started. The mighty Merlins gave full power, the tail came up and I was airborne. The tail swung a little and was corrected. I heard the engineer call, 'Full power, temperatures and pressures normal' and we were airborne at 1847.

'The flaps and undercarriage came in and the Skipper called for 2,650 +9 and Oboe climbed away with a 4000-lb cookie and incendiaries. We turned onto course for the rendezvous at Reading. As we climbed to our first height the guns were set to 'Fire' and I started the gunners' methodical search pattern, reporting other aircraft that may put us at risk. Occasionally the whole aeroplane shuddered from the turbulence made by other Lancasters joining the bomber stream. Eventually we reached our flight level and the navigator gave the Skipper a time for Reading and a new course to steer. At the appointed time we turned onto the new course and started to climb to our next flight level, carrying on to the next turning point at Beachy Head. So far, so good and soon we altered course again, crossing the Channel to the French coast and the long leg towards Mulhouse. Paris was passed well to the south of us. A shower of red sparks flew past my turret but this was no cause for alarm as it was the engineer clearing the engines. So on we droned, soon to run into the front with its associated cloud as forecast by the Met-man. The thought of flying in cloud in daytime was bad enough but at night in a bomber stream was not at all pleasant. The turbulence, sometimes in the tops then in the clear seeing the stars in the dark sky above, there were times when you couldn't see the wing tips, the dampness but we keep going. Sticking to the briefing we flew on toward the high ground of the Vogeses that rises up to more than 4600 ft and close to the German border.

'The weather worsened with more frequent turbulence. A voice on the intercom suggested that we should climb above the weather. There was unanimous agreement and after a second or two the Skipper called for climbing power. I felt the mighty bomber climb through the murky skies and in a few minutes we were in and out of the tops, seeing the stars in the dark sky and the dim shapes of other Lancasters who had climbed earlier. Then 'CHRIST' came a shout over the head phones together with a crash and the tearing of metal. Oboe rocked. 'We've been hit' said another voice.'Did you see that other Lanc?' 'It's falling away'. Our port wing dropped and Oboe fell back into the clouds in a spin. Art Whitmarsh was fighting with all his strength to regain control and after what seemed an eternity we were straight and level. The Skipper called for bomb doors open and Jock jettisoned the bombs 'Safe'. The clouds lightened with a flash; our bombs or the other Lanc, who knew?

'Our four engines were still running, the Skipper still struggling to maintain control as he told us that the ailerons were jammed. He called for a head count and serviceability check. The Skipper decided that we must return if possible. The wireless operator was instructed to advise Binbrook on W/T. The IFF was switched to 'ON' and a gentle turn was started for a course to the emergency airfield at Manston. The engine power was increased and slowly we started to climb to clear the cloud and the front, also to reduce the risk of icing. Eventually we reached 20,000 ft and were able to see and estimate the extent of the damage. The trailing edge of the starboard wing was well chewed up, the aileron and wing tip missing, Ken in his mid-upper turret reported that the floor and starboard side of the fuselage were missing as was the H2S assembly for about ten feet. Ken was assisted out of his turret by using the escape rope and the help of the W/Op to the relative comfort and safety of the flight deck.

'The tail end of the aircraft was swinging with lots of vibration. It was impossible for me in the tail to come forward. I was given the option of baling out but I prefered to stay and stick with each other. Besides, we were still subject to enemy fighters. The Skipper reduced the power and this helped reduce the vibration, so we flew on but with a lower speed. Not a lot was said. The Skipper had his hands full maintaining our crippled machine.

'Eventually the Channel came up, with a descent to Manston which could be seen. The Skipper decided to make a flapless landing. The undercarriage was lowered. Thank Goodness they both extended as indicated by the two green lights and with a long flat approach a safe landing was made at 0049 hrs. We taxied slowly behind a 'Follow Me' ATC truck and parked the aeroplane. The engines were closed down. It was so quiet. Slowly we emerged from the exits, me from the door, the rest of the crew via the front escape hatch down the ladder. We looked at the damage. I suppose we said a silent 'Thank You'. Then it was into the transport for a de-briefing in Air Traffic Control. The night's events were recalled, then a phone call to Binbrook to confirm that we were safe. A meal was soon provided and then we had a long sleep.

'It snowed during the night but next morning we inspected the aeroplane. It was not a pretty sight. The way she held together was a tribute to Avros. The starboard side of the fuselage from the trailing edge almost to the entrance door was missing, as was the floor from the bomb bay, three ft of wing tip and the trailing edge were all mangled and chewed up by the other Lancaster's propellers with little left of the aileron. A phone call from Binbrook instructed me to remove parts of our radar system as we operated with 'Village Inn'[105] and 'Z' equipment and to bring these back with me. However, due to bad weather at Binbrook and snow at Manston an aircraft was unable to come for us and whilst having a snowball fight outside Air Traffic Control we were told to clear off and get the train. We were given money, railway warrants and transport to Ramsgate but what a scruffy dishevelled crew we looked There was not a razor between us, so into a barber's shop we went where we were given shaves by ladies running their husbands' business. Now feeling more human, after a well earned drink we had a crew photograph taken, then we boarded the train to London. But it was no wonder we were stopped by the RAF Service Police. We wore no hats and were in flying boots, Mae Wests etc but their attitude was soon put to right by good Australian phraseology. A few hours later we were back at Grimsby with transport to take us back to camp for another debriefing. Our next flight was a short cross country and then the 'Game' was on again.'[106]

In January 2nd TAF and 100 group Mosquito night fighters claimed over 30 Luftwaffe aircraft. On the night of 5/6 January when 664 aircraft bombed Hanover, Capt Svein Heglund DFC and F/O Robert O. Symon of 85 Squadron who were seeking their 15th victory in their Mosquito NFXXX flew an eventful High Level Support Patrol north of Osnabrück. After patrolling a beacon in the Münster/Osnabrück area without any contact they set course for Hanover and arrived just as the target indicators were being dropped. They got a contact and chased it in a westerly direction for 20 minutes but when they got a visual of exhaust flames it looked like a Mosquito and they took it for one of the pathfinder force and turned back towards the target. At 2223 hrs they got another head-on contact north of Osnabrück and turned in behind it. It was slightly above and they closed in to about 2000 ft when Symon lost contact owing to scanner trouble. Heglund made one orbit and Symon picked up contact again at four miles' range. The Mosquito team closed in again and visually identified it as a Bf 110. As he was slightly overshooting Heglund weaved underneath the German aircraft, keeping visual contact all the time. At 500 ft range he pulled up behind it and gave it is a short burst, which caused an explosion in the fuselage. There was a lot of smoke and debris flew off but the 110 continued flying straight and level. Heglund thought that the crew was killed right away. He fired another burst, which missed but a third burst set the enemy aircraft well on fire and it crashed with a large explosion at 2230 hrs. It was the Norwegian's final victory of the war, which made him the top scoring RNoWAF pilot with 15 and one-third victories. F/L 'Ben' Benson DSO DFC* and F/L Lewis 'Brandy' Brandon DSO DFC* also notched their final victory of the war, shooting down a He 219 *Uhu* for their 10th confirmed kill.[107] F/L A.S. Briggs and F/O Rodwell of 515 Sqn destroyed a Ju 88 at Jägel airfield and W/C Russ Bannock DFC* RCAF and F/L Robert Bruce DFC of 406 'Lynx' Squadron RCAF in a NFXXX destroyed a He 111 at Josum airfield. It was the Canadian's seventh victory of the war.[108]

Despite these successes 23 Halifaxes and eight Lancasters FTR from Hanover, the majority shot down by an effective Tame Boar operation. Two Lancasters were lost on a raid on a bottleneck in the German supply system in the Ardennes in a valley at Houffalize in Belguim. Two Mosquito bombers were lost raiding Berlin while two 100 Group Mosquitoes also FTR, making 37 aircraft lost in total. Thirty-one bombers were claimed destroyed by *Nachtjagd*. *Hptm* Werner Hopf of 8./NJG 5 claimed four Halifaxes (for his 15th-18th *Abschüsse*), *Hptm* Werner Baake *Kommandeur* of I./NJG 1 and *Maj* Hans Karlewski of *Stab* NJG 2 each claimed three and *Oblt* Walter Brieglеb *St.Kpt* of 7./NJG 2 two. *Hptm* Hermann Greiner of 11./NJG 1 claimed three Lancasters over Hanover for his 43rd-45th victories.

On 6/7 January over 600 aircraft set out to bomb two important German rail junctions at Hanau and Neuss. Many of the bombs dropped by 468 Halifaxes and Lancasters of 1, 4 and 6 Groups at Hanau and 147 Lancasters of 1 and 3 groups at Neuss missed the targets and fell in surrounding districts. Hanau was reported to be '40 per cent destroyed' while in Neuss over 1700 houses, 19 industrial premises and 20 public buildings were destroyed or seriously damaged.[109] The following night Bomber Command returned to area bombing with the final major raid on Munich, which was carried out by 645 Lancasters led by nine Mosquitoes. F/O Ken Lee's Lancaster crew in 49 Squadron at Fulbeck, Lincolnshire were one of the 'supporters' for the Pathfinder Flare Force (83 & 97 Squadrons).[110] His bomb aimer was F/Sgt John Aldridge, who despite the nature of his job for the most part did not think in terms of people being killed but of areas that had to be hit:

> 'Nine of the 33 operations I flew September 1944-April 1945 were on built-up areas. Tom Gatfield (nav) and I had been working *LORAN* and obtained some decent fixes and we managed to keep to time, however predicted winds were all to cock that night and we arrived over Munich on time ... but on our own! I went forward into the bomb aimer's compartment to prepare for the bomb run in our supporting role. The sky was one mass of flak bursts and we seemed to be the only aircraft around and we were leaving a contrail at that. We were well and truly hammered. One piece of *flak* came through the front perspex and ripped the sleeve on my battledress blouse. Searchlights also dazzled us and the skipper nearly stalled the aircraft taking evasive action. Tom called out that the airspeed was 110 knots and falling and there was a shout of 'Get the bloody nose down skip!' Thankfully he did. We were then hit in one engine, which had to be feathered. This was the only occasion on which I removed my parachute from it's stowage and laid it on the floor beside me. I looked down at the snow covered landscape and thought, 'it's damned cold down there' if I have to jump.
>
> 'We had to keep an altitude of about 14,000ft as our route home was above the Alps skirting Switzerland. We saw the lights of that neutral country. Everything went well till half way across France (by now mostly occupied by our own troops since *D-Day*) when another engine started vibrating badly and shaking the whole aircraft. The skipper and Lou Crabbe our flight engineer decided to feather that engine, so now we were on two! We decided that rather than land at an airfield in France we would go for a landing at the emergency runway at Manston in Kent, entailing a short sea passage on two engines. This was

managed successfully although the skipper risked unfeathering the last engine to give us trouble, to get a little more power if required.'

On the night of 13/14 January 274 aircraft were dispatched to Saarbrücken and a second force of 218 aircraft attacked the oil plant at Pölitz, near Stettin.[111] This was, for F/O Frank Mouritz RAAF, pilot of Lancaster III *M-Mike* of 61 Squadron 'the night that he and his crew nearly 'bought it':

'It was our 20th operation. We were an experienced crew (but not too experienced to be over-confident) and we were to attack, for the second time, a synthetic oil refinery at Politz, near Stettin on the Baltic coast in Northern Germany. This was our maximum range on this route and we carried full fuel tanks of 2154 gallons and 12, 000 lb of 500 and 1000lb High Explosive bombs – some with delay fuses. The route out was over the North Sea to Denmark, across the Kattegat to Southern Sweden, then turning south across the Baltic to the North German coast. The return route was to be similar. Denmark, being occupied, was heavily defended by German armed forces, Sweden however, although neutral, shot up quite a lot of light *flak* but never in our direction so it was relatively safe to fly across their territory.

'The attack, purely a 5 Group operation, was planned as a blind attack through cloud but was changed to a visual one as the target was clear. Although we carried out our usual fighter search there was no real danger till we neared the target after crossing the Baltic. We bombed on time through very heavy flak and numerous searchlights as the refinery was very heavily defended. After bombing we set course for home over the Baltic, on the briefed route over Sweden, and then over Denmark. This meant that the Luftwaffe had little trouble working out the probable times and position that the returning bombers would cross Denmark. No doubt the Nazis had agents in Sweden that radioed their passing to Germany.

'The skill of the navigator and bomb aimer in map reading kept us on track as there was little cloud cover and the coast lines were fairly visible. On nearing Denmark we went into maximum banking searches at every 1 or 2 minutes, and saw several flashes of gunfire from aerial combats. We were about 15-20 minutes on the route home after crossing the Western Danish coast and I was easing up on the banking searches thinking that a couple more would be sufficient, when the silence of the intercom was broken by the mid upper gunner. 'Twin engined aircraft underneath'. He did not say which side down but as he could not see straight down it must have been on the starboard side. My reaction, which luckily must have been the correct one, was to put the Lancaster into a violent diving turn to starboard and called out 'going down starboard'. The wing had just started to drop when we heard explosions and saw flashes under the starboard wing between the inboard engine and the fuselage. Possibly 5 or 6 shells probably 30mm hit us and as we dived I heard our guns firing. One of the gunners called out excitedly 'we've got him and he is heading for a cloud bank below on fire'.

'In retrospect, we assumed that the mid-upper gunner had sighted him before he was in his best position and our violent diving turn had spoilt his aim. He had to break away to avoid a collision and as we were nearly on our side the two gunners were able to rake him with our six Browning machine guns across his top. As I straightened out the Lanc I found that our emergency signal lights at each crew station had come on and we were lit up and in full view if the fighters were hunting in pairs. I called out to the w/op to get to the fuse panel and pull out the appropriate fuses. Dave's reply in his slow Queensland drawl was 'Hell, I'm just taking a broadcast'. The calmness in Dave's voice reduced the panic that was beginning to appear in the crew. This all took place in a few seconds. The problem of the lights was solved by the rear-gunner smashing his light with his cocking toggle, short circuiting the bulb and blowing the fuse. By this time, of course we had all lost our night vision.

'I levelled the plane and returned to our course and started to take stock of our damage – from the front we could not see any fires – by calling each member of the crew in turn from back to front, asking for a report on themselves and their equipment. No one had been wounded and all the equipment, except the flight engineers, was functioning. He reported that we had lost some power on the starboard inboard engine, and that he was possibly losing fuel from the starboard inboard tank. The Lancaster has three tanks in each wing, all interconnected, and it was the rule to draw them all down together so that no tank held maximum fuel, as this could be lost if punctured. The air space above the fuel in the tank was filled with inert nitrogen gas to help prevent fires. Jim Leith, the flight engineer, immediately started to run down the holed tank by feeding the fuel from it to all engines. We also adjusted the controls to bring the bad engine up to the others and carefully watched the gauges. The navigator had a problem with his protractor and calculator etc as they were tangled due to the violent maneuver we had carried out. He had them all tied to a center point with pieces of string but they took some sorting out.

'We had just settled down and began to analyze the combat when the rear gunner reported an object going past his turret followed by another one. The flight engineer managed to have a look at the damaged wing with his torch and reported that the dinghy cover was missing and so was the dinghy. We assumed that was what the rear gunner had reported. The navigator, F/E and myself had a discussion on the distance to base, fuel consumption and remaining fuel. Having lost our dinghy, a ditching in the North Sea was out of the question. The other alternative was to return to Denmark and bale out. However we worked out that if we flew at our most economical airspeed and height we could make the English coast with a small margin to spare. I did think about putting out a mayday call but left it for the time being as we still had 3 1/2 engines and probably enough fuel.

'We discussed the combat and concluded that the fighter plane, a Junkers 88, had probably been following us on his radar for some time, waiting until we stopped the banking searches and that the decision to bank to starboard was the correct one. If we had turned to port he could have followed us down and used his front guns as well. Many years later when reading the accounts of the Luftwaffe night fighters, I learnt that their preferred aiming point, when attacking from below, was between the inboard engine and the fuselage. This was possibly to give the crew a chance and also that a loaded Lanc has bombs stretching along underneath the center section of the fuselage and a strike on the fuse of a bomb would blow up both aircraft. So we headed for home at the most economical speed with the rear gunner keeping a lookout for any more pieces of wing flying past the turret. Nothing further happened and I was tempted to try to lower the undercarriage, to test it, soon after we crossed the coast but decided to leave it until we entered the circuit in our normal manner. On arriving at base I lowered the undercarriage, which made the right sort of noises and vibrations and the indicator light came on, so I completed the approach. As soon as we touched the runway I knew that something was wrong. The aircraft tried to drop the starboard wing and I managed to hold it up with full aileron till we lost speed. Then it dropped down; something dragged on that side. We left the bitumen and slewed around in an ever-decreasing circle till we ended up, luckily almost in our own dispersal point. The starboard tyre had been shot to pieces.

'An inspection of *M-Mike* next morning showed that most of the underneath starboard wing plates were missing or holed. There were some holes in the lower section of the fuselage but no major structural damage. The loss of power had been due to some ignition leads being cut. Repairs were carried out at our aerodrome but the Lanc was out of action for nearly six weeks. The Junkers 88 was later confirmed as damaged as another crew had seen the combat and the Junkers 88 going down into cloud, on fire. He may have ended up in the North Sea. When we analysed the action we realized that the sighting by the mid upper gunner had saved us, and that on future operations extra banking searches would have to be carried out on the return journey and at irregular intervals.

'I was very pleased with the overall crew reaction with little or no panic. We realized that constant surveillance and not allowing ourselves to relax on the way home would be necessary for survival on the remaining operations. This had been our longest trip, 10 hrs 30 mins airborne. Photo reconnaissance stated that the plant was reduced to a shambles. However, we attacked it again in three weeks time and the production of oil ceased, proving to be a great setback to the German war effort.'[112]

F/L Kenneth D. Vaughan and F/L Robert D. MacKinnon of 85 Squadron shot down two enemy aircraft during January. The first of these was on the night of the 14/15th during a High level Patrol supporting the attack on Merseburg. They were on the last leg of their patrol when MacKinnon reported a contact 4 1/2 miles at 11 o'clock. Vaughan chased and caught the target and closed in to 100ft directly beneath to identify it. He could see by its pointed wings and underslung engines that it was a Ju 188. Vaughan increased range to 600ft and fired a 1-second burst dead astern, which produced a large explosion in the starboard engine. He pulled away to starboard but seeing no further results followed again with MacKinnon on AI and closed in to 900ft where he fired a 2-second burst. Results were inconclusive so he closed in to 600 ft and fired another 1-second burst. This time strikes could be seen and there was an explosion in the starboard engine again. Pieces flew past the Mosquito and then the Ju 188 disappeared straight down to explode on ground at 2143 hrs. Explosions lit up the countryside and the Mosquito cockpit was illuminated by a large orange glow.[113]

On 16/17 January F/L Tommy Smith and F/O 'Cocky' Cockayne,[114] an intruder crew of 23 Squadron were on ops in their Mosquito FBVI. Smith, who was within two or three operations of completing his second tour, recalls:

'It was a dirty night – thick as a bag up to 16,000 ft – and we went on an ASH patrol to Stendal fighter airfield near Berlin. I used a square search system for nearly an hour but picked up nothing and when the time was up, we set course for home. At the point when we should have been over the area of the Steinhuder Lake, we came across an airfield where aircraft with nav lights on were taxiing. This was unheard of. I went in to have a bash. There was a chap sitting at the taxi point. He was my target: his nav lights and the hooded runway lights were *on.* I opened up and saw a good cluster of cannon strikes on the aircraft and was about to break away when I saw exhaust flames of another aircraft half way up the runway. 'God, someone's taking off! I'll have him,' I thought. (I was trained to recognize an aircraft by the number, type and disposition of its exhaust flames and I reckoned it was a Ju 88.) So instead of breaking off; I closed in and opened up. My muzzle flashes lit up the Hun right under my chin! (I was so close I was practically looking at the back of the pilot's head.) It wasn't a Ju 88; it was a Me 109! (What I had taken for exhausts of two engines were the flames from either side of one engine.) Because of the difference in line between my gunsight and the guns beneath my feet, I was shooting low, being so close and ripped the bottom out of the Me 109. He crashed at the end of the runway.

'However, as I was pursuing this chap, I had passed between two flak towers at the downwind end of the runway. Light *flak* [from eight guns, the Germans said later] had the cannon flashes to aim at and my Mosquito was hit coming in over the perimeter track at a height of about 200 ft in a dive. *Flak* set my right engine on fire and I automatically feathered the prop and pressed the extinguisher button. I zoomed up to 1000ft. My mind was running on how to get organized to fly home on one engine, when, all of a sudden the other engine stopped! The first engine was blazing merrily and the prop was feathering and unfeathering. I said to Cocky, 'That's it! Bale Out!' It's not easy to get out of a Mosquito. Cocky was having trouble jettisoning the hatch door. Time and height were running out. I switched on the landing lights. Treetops showed up below. We were too low. I shouted, 'Knock it off. Do your harness up. Cocky didn't answer. A burst of flame lit up the open hatch. He had baled out. I found out later that his parachute didn't open fully and he had broken his neck.

'The forest came up and I was skimming over the treetops and preparing to stuff the nose in while I still had flying speed. I could feel the 'whiffle' which indicated the approach of the stall. Suddenly, there was a field covered in snow. I stuffed it in at about 200 mph. Next thing; I was hurtling along the ground heading for more trees. I thought it was a wood but it was only a line of trees; a windbreak! The trees ripped off the outer wing sections and something, possibly a stump, knocked a hole in the cockpit alongside me. I still had my hand on the throttle control and it was ripped away by the tree stump! Then I was out of the trees and into the snow again before the aircraft came to a stop. A feeling of relief came over me. All I could think was 'a forced landing in the dark! What fantastic luck to be alive!'

'All I had to do now was lift the roof emergency hatch, climb out and run away. Except that in the crash, the whole of the seat had come adrift and shot me underneath the instrument panel and the cockpit cabin was full of earth. The left rudder bar had taken my foot back under the seat and locked it. I had some grim moments trapped in the middle of a bonfire trying to extricate my foot. By the time I got out of the hole the port radiator and its contents were burning fiercely right outside the hole. I crawled out badly burned and stuffed my face and hands into the snow. When I got up, I found I had a broken leg, caused by the rudder pedal. [He had also lost an eye]. By the light of the fire I could see a farmhouse and crawled over to it. Two soldiers hiding in the hedge, expecting the bombs to explode, carried me into the barn and about an hour later a Luftwaffe ambulance from Fassberg collected me. I was sadly aware that my wartime flying was over.'[115]

Despite being an *Experte* pilot and flying the state of the art He 219 Owl in 2./NJG 1, *Lt* Otto Fries and his *Bordfunker*, *Fw* Fred Staffa, experienced the rare fate of being shot down for the second time by a Mosquito on the night of 16/17 January, this time by F/L Kenneth D. Vaughan and F/Sgt Robert Denison MacKinnon of 85 Squadron. *Lt* Fries recalls:

'Our operations were hopeless, depressing and mostly unsuccessful. Even before we were ordered to cockpit readiness, the duty long range nightfighter was around our base. When we heard the noise of his Rolls-Royce engines, that typical high-piched sound, we knew that a half hour later at most we would be driving out to the dispersals. There was a deathly silence in the crew bus, which took us out to our machines. Each of us tried to cope with the thought of the forthcoming operation in his own way. We thought about the Mosquitoes, which made us the hunters, the hunted. The boarding of our machines, the donning of rubber life jacket, parachute, helmet, throat microphone and the tightening of the straps took place in complete silence. Then the unnerving wait, the gut-churning anticipation, the 'arse-twitch' as we called it. The red Verey light signalled 'cockpit readiness 'cancelled' and the inner tension eased. The bus came and collected the crews. The return journey to operations was noisy. The pressure had given way to merriment; we had to let off steam. Once more we had escaped unscathed! The green Verey light signified the order for take-off. The ensuing activity dispersed the anxiety and fear and once in the air and the engines throbbed in their alternating rythm all the unease was forgotten. The night flight fascinated time and again in spite of all the adverse factors.

'The *Gruppe* had a good dozen crews, just about flight strength. Only rarely did more than ten machines take off for operations at night. Mostly they were fewer and frequently half of these aborted early because of damage or malfunction. In most cases it was the electrics that failed. Aircraft stood in the camouflaged revetments at the edge of the field or in the neighbouring wood unprotected against rain and storm, snow and frost. Condensation frequently caused unservicability, especially with the radio and directionfinder, even though test flights were carried out every second or third day to 'fly them dry'. In this fifth winter of the war the wiring was evidently past its best. Retracting the undercarriage would suddenly make the guns fire, even after all the appropriate circuit breakers were turned off, or, during an attack on an enemy bomber, the guns failed to fire but the landing lights would come on. 'I have never in my life broken off so quickly' reported the pilot to whom this had happened, 'but the Tommy was evidently so surprised that he forgot to pull the trigger. What luck!'

'That January night it was very cold and the snow lay unusually deep – the *Gruppe* had been ordered to take off shortly before 1900. Eight machines had taken off from Münster-Handorf and were controlled by the Y-method.

'Adler 98 from Wagenrad. Course 190. Kapelle 45.'

'Viktor. Going on 190. Out,' acknowledged my radio operator.

'But not at this height,' I said. 'There are too many Mosquitos around!' The number of enemy long-range nightfighters was depressing. The Mosquito was an excellent aircraft and the Serrate homer was unsurpassed but during this phase the SN2 suffered constantly from interference. Almost every week one of us was shot down! But relatively few crews were lost as the ejection seat of the He 219 (provided it had not been damaged) made exit easy when the red button was pushed.

'I went onto the given course in a turn on instruments and flew my machine up to a height of 9000 meters as quickly as I could. This was a very high altitude for flying. The decrease in air pressure made control response unpleasantly poor; it was no longer flying, just 'wobbling' about. Each turn resulted in a loss of height and the indicator would show 1400-1600 ft per minute but one would be fairly safe from the Mosquito night fighters, which were usually active at between 2-3000 meters. (Their radar covered a funnel-like area above and the band between 3000 and 6000 meters was the most dangerous). The other advantage was that the altitude diving speed enabled us to reach the attacking height of the bombers of usually between 4000 and 5500 meters more quickly.

'The situation was unclear. We were sent back and forth east of the Ruhr. Communication with control was very poor. My *Bordfunker* had barely said a dozen words when the 'soul destroyer'[116] blocked the frequency. Communication was therefore limited to the briefest of messages. We must have been somwhere to the east or northeast of Cologne when my oxygen system failed. I noticed it at once, closed the throttles and went into a steep dive. I knew that at this height I would suffer badly from anoxia within two to two and a half minutes and be dead within four or five. My *Bordfunker* was startled by the sudden dive.

'What's up?'

'I told him about the problem and said that I would like to go down to 1000 to 1500 meters in order to get below the Moskitoes.

'Don't go too low! Almost all of the transmitters are suffering interference, the lower you are, the more difficult it is to get a bearing. Stay at 4000 until I know where we are and am able to give you a course for Münster. Then you can do as you like.'

'I levelled off at 3500 meters, trimmed the machine and went onto a northerly heading where I assumed our home base to be. I knew that we were at a height which must be virtually saturated with Mosquitoes. I had evolved a system based on my own experience for such emergencies. I knew that a nightfighter normally needed three to four minutes to get into an attacking position or to slow down to that of his intended victim for the attack so, using my stopwatch I remained on the given course for just three minutes. After three minutes of level flight I would turn 30 or forty degrees to starboard to simulate a normal alteration of course. As an attacker, I would then have veered to port and complete this change of course before commencing my attack. With the word 'Now', I would have ordered my *Bordfunker* to scan the area behind, while snatching the aircraft out of its normal turn to starboard to a steep turn to port. Any Moskito in an attacking position behind us at this moment was bound to be spotted by my *Bordfunker*, who, on the other hand, would hardly be in a position to fire due to this unexpected and violent maneuver. Even if the pilot, startled by this sudden move, had pressed the firing button in a reflex reaction, he would surely have missed.

'We continued on our northerly course, interrupted every three minutes by this maneuver. Meanwhile my *Bordfunker* attempted to find an unjammed transmitter and obtain a usable bearing. After some difficulty he managed to get a bearing from a strong radio beacon lying abeam in the Osteifel and then he tried to get the local beacon at Münster-Handorf. Just before the end of another three-minute period, I announced the next maneuver.

'Wait a moment! I have just got Handorf, just a few more seconds!'

'Hurry up!' I urged. No more than 30 seconds had passed when there was a crashing and banging in our machine. The stick was torn from my hands and my earphones went dead. The intercom had failed.

'Long-range nightfighter!' shouted my *Bordfunker*.

'I was unable to hear him through the roar of the engines but I had understood, anyway. Then I saw, off to my right and about 20 meters higher, a Mosquito rush past. 'What a fool,' went through my head. 'Never heard about speed adjustment? Now I'll show you how it's done!' I turned the gun switch with my left hand and the breeches rattled. My hand reached for the control column and my index finger seeked the trigger. As I tried to move the stick back and forth to raise the nose to let the Moskito pass through the sights there was no response. The elevator control cables had evidently been shot through. Fortunately, the ailerons were still working. The aircraft began pitching. It went up, lost speed and nosed down, gaining speed as it did so and then did it again. I tried to counteract this with the throttles and then I tried trim but it was all to no avail. It was clear that I would not be able to land the aircraft. At some point we would have to bale out but the longer I was able to keep the machine in the air, the closer we would be to our home base.

'The pitching caused a loss of height. My altimeter reached the 1000 meter mark and the time had come to get out. I closed both throttles and shouted, 'Get out! – Out!' The machine dropped immediately and I opened the throttles to recover. The safety lever on the ejection seat was on the right-hand ledge with all the switches. I turned it up and placed my feet in the 'stirrups'. Then I released the throat microphone and tore the helmet off. I pulled the cord securing the torch around my neck over my head and let it drop to the cabin floor because in the slipstream after ejection it could cause me an injury. Then I jettisoned the canopy and waited for the 'bang', which would indicate that my *Bordfunker* had ejected. As soon as I heard this, I struck the release button with my fist and I was blown out. I wanted to land as close as possible to my *Bordfunker*. It was dark and very cold and deep snow lay on the ground. One could never tell where and how one would land and we might have to call upon one another's assistance.

'I was caught in the slipstream, which hurled me about. I released the straps and got clear of the seat and then I waited another couple of seconds before pulling the ripcord. The parachute opened and I pulled the signal pistol from the right-hand pocket of my trousers and loaded a parachute flare from the ammunition belt, which was strapped to my left boot. The bright light of the magnesium flare showed me my *Bordfunker* below me to my right. We drifted slowly across a coppice towards a clearing, which opened up like a funnel and a village within it. I fired off two more flares, which lit up our landing ground like day. On the furthest side there were very tall firs, while on the nearest side there were oaks, which would be easier to climb down from, so I reached up with both arms and pulled on the left-hand strap of the parachute. I miscalculated a little so I let go the strap but twigs cracked under my weight and I hung in the top of a huge oak. The canopy silk covered the tree like a large, white blossom. This was my third bale out and I had never landed so softly with a parachute before. I swung onto the nearest branch and operated the release before removing the straps. The flares had gone out and so I fired off another one. As far as I was able to make it out in the flickering light I was in an oak on a steep incline, which ended in a valley with a brook and a narrow road over a bridge leading to the village.

'As my flare went up my *Bordfunker*, who had landed in the village street, called, 'Come down to the village but take care and don't fall into the brook!' I climbed down, branch for branch. My right knee was very painful and it appeared to be swelling. When I reached the lowest branch I still seemed to be high above the ground and the thick trunk was hardly suitable for climbing down. I removed the rubber dinghy from my back, inflated it and let it glide down into the snow. 'A buffer can't do any harm', I thought. The descent with my damaged knee worried me. Then I thought of my ancient predecessors who, according to Darwin, must have been practised climbers and commenced my descent. I clung to the trunk with arms and legs – the knee hurt damnably – and slid slowly down. Luckily I was still wearing my flying gloves. I should have taken off my lifejacket. Slipping, I felt the air bottle on my left hip and thought, 'I hope it doesn't go off" but friction opened the valve. It hissed and inflated the life jacket, which pushed me away from the trunk and I went down like a lift but the deep snow and my rubber dinghy cushioned my fall.

'I made my way painfully down the slope and through the snow, which went into the tops of my fur boots. My *Bordfunker* was waiting for me at the bridge near an inn. It turned out that we were in Landenbeck. The villagers had been very alarmed at the sound of aircraft , the firing of the signal pistol and the 'Christmas-tree' flares and most had rushed to their cellars in fear of an attack on their village. Now they were happy to have been spared that experience! So was I and so too was my radio operator! We telephoned operations and made our report and then we were taken to a farm where we were entertained royally. Next morning a car took us back to our *Gruppe*. My knee had swollen so much that I had to cut open the stitching of my uniform breeches but this did not prevent me from pouring oil on all available lamps that evening.'[117]

Notes

1. 85 Group was created by the transfer from RAF Fighter Command of 29, 264, 409 'Nighthawk' Sqn RCAF, 410'Cougar' Sqn RCAF, 488 Sqn RNZAF and 604 Sqns. NFXVIIs of 219 Sqn Fighter Command at Bradwell Bay also shot down six Ju 88/188s in and around the beachhead.

2. George Esmond 'Jamie' Jameson DFC RNZAF had flown Beaufighter IIs and VIs in 125 Sqn and had his first combat during night raids on Cardiff and Swansea in the summer of 1942. After a Heinkel 111 had bombed his own airfield, Jamie pursued the e/a and shot it down into the Bristol Channel. He landed to find that the bombs had killed the WAAF fiancée of his Sqn friend. In August Jamie destroyed another He 111 and while on detachment in the Shetlands he claimed a Ju 88 as 'damaged' although later information indicated that the bomber had crashed on landing at Stavanger. He was credited with the destruction of a Do 217 on 11/12 February 1943 and he then went on 'rest', becoming a gunnery instructor. In January 1944 he joined No. 488 Sqn, which lost 9 crews in flying accidents for just 2 e/a destroyed. Morale at that time was very low but that soon changed. At the end of July the New Zealand Sqn moved to Colerne near Bath, where Jameson was devastated to learn that his both his brothers had been killed. His elder brother was serving with the New Zealand Army in Tunisia and his younger brother died in a Beaufighter during training at East Fortune. Tragically a cable from New Zealand informed Jamie that his father had died on hearing the news of the death of two of his sons. Jameson's mother immediately appealed to the New Zealand Government to allow Jamie to return home and take over the family farm of nearly 2000 acres in Rotherham nr. Canterbury. The High Commissioner, Mr. (later Sir William) Jordan, visited 488 Sqn and told Jamie that he had done more than his duty and that he should return to his mother. Jamie was persuaded to apply for a passage on the next ship repatriating time-expired New Zealanders and Australians via the USA and Panama. However, before Jameson departed he was determined to avenge the untimely deaths of his brothers.

3. Later confirmed destroyed by a navigator of 410 'Cougar' Sqn RCAF who saw the Ju 88 hit the ground 5-6 miles S of Caen, explode and burst into flames.

4. NFXIII MM477/U equipped with AI.Mk.VIII intercepted a Ju 188 10 miles NE of Tessy at 0100 hrs. It was their 2nd victory of the war. They had begun their long string of victories on 13/14 February when they destroyed a Ju 88 over Essex and damaged a Ju 188 in Mosquito NFXIII HK466.

5. F/L P F.L. Hall-F/O R.D. Marriott of 488 Sqn in NFXIII MM498 got a Ju 88 10m E of St Lô. F/L F.C. Ellis-F/O P.C. Williams of 604 Sqn in a NFXIII destroyed a Ju 188 SE Caen.

6. S/L F.J.A. Chase-F/O A.F. Watson of 264 Sqn in a NFXIII destroyed a Ju 188 (or 88) 10 miles W of Argentan. W/O T.G.C. Mackay-F/Sgt A.A. Thompson of 488 Sqn in NFXIII MM439 claimed a Ju 188-8m S of Avranches. F/L A. S. Browne-W/O T.F. Taylor of 488 Sqn in NFXIII HK532 got a Do 217-4m S of Avranches and F/L B.E. Plumer-F/O V.W. Evans of 410 Sqn in a NFXIII destroyed a Ju 188.

7. *Uffz* Georg Helbig who had also baled out before the Ju 88G-1 712343 3C+KP cr at Fougeres NE of Rennes at 0130 was soon taken prisoner by Allied troops. No trace was ever found of the *Bordfunker*, *Fw* Rudi Adam, who may have been shot out of hand by French partisans. Claims for 4 Ju 88s were made by Mosquito crews on the night of 3/4 August (14 German a/c were claimed by Mosquitoes). Autenrieth may have been shot down by F/L 'Jamie' Jameson DFC RNZAF and F/O A. Norman Crookes of 488 RNZAF Sqn in Mosquito NFXIII MM466. Jameson's 10th victory was a Ju 88 (he also claimed a 2nd Ju 88 which was not confirmed), which was about to dive-bomb British Army troops near St. Lô and it was brought down by a burst of just 60 20mm cannon shells. Four other claims for Ju 88s were another 488 Sqn NFXIII crew flying HK504 ENE of Vire; W/O G.S. Patrick-F/Sgt J.J. Concannon also of 488 Sqn, in NFXIII HK420 W of Avranches; S/L I.H. Cosby DFC-F/L E.R. Murphy of 264 Sqn in NFXIII 'S' and F/L Beverley-F/O P.C. Sturling in another 264 Sqn NFXIII (this Mosquito FTR and the crew baled out). Next day came news of Jameson's sailing date for New Zealand.

8. According to Haddon. 'By the time 2nd TAF came into existence the Allies had had 4 years of night warfare experience to devise airfield systems that could function well at night as well as protect aircraft on the ground from attack, largely using wide dispersal, aircraft blast sheltering and minimal visibility from the air as defensive systems. As a/c became heavier, grass surfaced fields fell out of use. By D Day engineers had perfected systems of construction that could carry entire airfields overseas, not too different in facilities from any modern field of that time. A8 at Picauville, W of St Mere Eglise in the American sector was built in about 48 hrs, including runway, dispersals, taxi paths, control and refueling, using a base of sand covered with tarpaper. Designed to last 30 days, it lasted 55 or so and was home to 3 American day fighter-bomber sqns and 2 RAF night sqns. The RAF was doing night cover from A8 because someone, quite wrongly, had convinced the planners that the U.S. night fighters were inadequate.

9. Jameson returned to New Zealand and the award of a DSO followed. Crookes, who after the war became a teacher in Kent, received a bar to his DFC. Jamie's score made him the highest scoring New Zealand fighter pilot of the war.

10. Bergmann's Bf 110G-4 Wrk Nr 140320 3C+CS probably shot down by F/L John C. Surman-P/O C.E. Weston of 604 Sqn in Mosquito NFXIII MM449/B who also claimed 2 Do 217s. (Only in 1956, Bergmann's badly burnt remains, which had been recovered from a crash site nr. St. James in mid-August 1944, were formally identified. Since then, the Nachtjagd *Experte* rests in the large German military cemetery of Marigny, Manche). F/L A.E. Browne-W/O T.F. Taylor of 488 Sqn in NFXIII HK420 destroyed a Ju 188 SW of Avranches and also claimed two UEA, which flew into ground trying to evade. Other 604 Sqn victories went to: F/O R. M.T. MacDonald-F/Sgt C.G. Baird in NFXIII MM500, a Ju 188 and W/C F.D. Hughes DFC**-F/L L. Dixon DFC* in NFXIII MM465 a Ju 88 S Avranches and F/L P. G.K. Williamson DFC RAAF-F/O F.E. Forrest of 219 Sqn in a NFXXX a Ju 188 in the Argentan area and F/L R.M. Currie-F/O A.N. Rose of 410 Sqn in a NFXIII a Ju 88. On a night when the Main Force was grounded, Mosquito XX KB118 of 139 Sqn flown by F/O B.E. Hooke (PoW) and F/O J. Stevenson (KIA) FTR from a raid by 40 Mosquitoes on Castrop-Rauxel. Mosquito NFXIII MM621 of 604 Sqn, 2nd TAF was lost in an engagement with a Me 410 over France and was also hit by flak. F/L J.C. Cooper DFC and F/O S.C. Hubbard DFM KIA. *Ofw* Willi Glitz of *Stab.*/NJG 2 claimed a Mosquito at 'BJ-BI' at 2340 hrs.

11. Three NFXIII crews in 604 Sqn claimed 5 victories. Nr Rennes F/O J.S. Smith-F/O L. Roberts in MM429 destroyed 2 x Do 217s. F/O R.M.T. MacDonald-F/L S.H.J. Elliott in HK525 got a Ju 188 S of Nantes. F/L J.R. Cross-W/O H. Smith in MM517 destroyed a Ju 188 E of Falaise and a Ju 88 nr. Conde. W/O Henke-F/Sgt Emmerson of 409 Sqn in NFXIII MM555 claimed a Ju 188. F/O W.W. Provan-W/O Nicol of 29 Sqn in NFXIII HK524 got a Bf 110 at Melun, W Orly. F/L Davidson-F/O Willmott of 264 Sqn in a NFXIII got a Ju 88. F/L M.J. Gloster DFC-F/L J.F. Oswold DFC of 219 Sqn in a NFXXX got 2 x Ju 188 W Vire. (On 9/10 August Gloster-Oswold got a Fw 190E Évreux and on 16/17 August 1944 a Ju 188 nr Caen. Michael John Gloster scored 10 e/a destroyed inc. 3 He 111s flying a Beaufighter VIf in N. Africa 5/6 December 1942. Gloster and James F. Oswold awarded bars to their DFCs November 1944.

12. F/O T.R. Wood-F/O R. Leafe of 604 Sqn in NFXIII MM528/H got a Do 217 and a 219 Sqn NFXXX crew got 2 Ju 188s.

13. Tame Boar *Nachtjagd* claimed 2 Lancasters and a '4-engined bomber' destroyed. Two of these could be Halifaxes (probably) which were lost on Resistance operations.

14. F/L D.J. Raby DFC-F/Sgt S.J. Flint DFM of 239 Sqn in a Mosquito NFII got a Bf 109 in N France. F/L D. Welfare DFC*-F/O B. Bellis DFC* of 239 Sqn in NFII DZ256/U destroyed a Fw 190 at St Quentin and F/L R.G. 'Tim' Woodman-F/L P. Kemmis of 169 Sqn in FBVI NT156/Y got a Fw 190E Abbeville.

15. Seven other Mosquito victories were awarded: S/L F.J.A. Chase-F/O A.F. Watson of 264 Sqn in a NFXIII destroyed a Ju 188 at Caen. F/L G.R.I. 'Sailor' Parker DSM-W/O D.L. Godfrey of 219 Sqn in a NFXXX a Ju 88 10m SW Le Havre and a Fw190 5m S Le Havre. S/L Hatch-F/O Eames of 409 Sqn in NFXIII MM504 a Fw 190. F/O Collins-F/O Lee of 409 Sqn in NFXIII MM523 a Do 217. F/O Daker-F/Sgt J. A. Heathcote of 264 Sqn in a NFXIII a Ju 188 and W/C G.A. Hiltz-F/O J.R. Walsh of 410 Sqn in a NFXIII a Ju 88. On 15/16 August 'Sailor' Parker-Godfrey claimed a Ju 88 15 m W of Le Havre and damaged a Ju 188 to take their score to 3 e/a destroyed. Gartrell Richard Ian Parker had after the outbreak of war with Italy joined 830 Sqn FAA as a Sgt Observer on Swordfish torpedo bombers and later flew night interdiction sorties over Sicily in Fulmars of 800X Sqn. Awarded DSM by the Royal Navy. Parker's score 9 confirmed, 1 probable, 1 damaged and 6 V-1s destroyed. Awarded DFC October 1944 and a bar in February 1945. Godfrey awarded DSM and DFC.

16. Other operations included a raid on Berlin by 33 Mosquitoes of the LNSF, 9 RCM sorties, minelaying off Biscay ports by 8 Stirlings and 6 Lancasters and 14 a/c on Resistance operations. 1 Mosquito FTR from Berlin.

17. Bone was captured early next morning and later sent to *Stalag Luft III*. Miller evaded for 4 weeks and he was sent along the Dutch Underground. Then the network was betrayed. He was among evaders captured at Antwerp and handed over to the *Gestapo*. At *Dulag Luft* he was confronted by the pilot

of the He 219 he had shot down in August and whose arm was still in a sling! Miller was sent to *Stalag Luft I*. Freddie Bone DFC* returned to the police force after the war and returned to the beat. On 11/12 August 1944 a 219 Sqn NFXXX crew destroyed a Ju 88 and W/O Henke-F/Sgt Emmerson of 409 Sqn in NFXIII MM619 got a Fw 190.

18. On 20 October 1944 Somerville and Robinson were awarded the DFC. Somerville was promoted W/C and command of 409 'Nighthawk' Sqn RCAF.

19. Ju 88G-1 710542 D5+BR of 7./NJG 3 flown by *Lt* Achim Woeste KIA. *Uffz* Anton Albrecht KIA. *Uffz* Heinz Thippe and *Gefr* Karl Walkenberger, both WIA, baled out. A/c cr. nr. Mulsum, 42 km E of Bremen. Woeste was an *Experte* with 10 night victories and 1 day kill.

20. 5 Group lost 15 Lancasters on the Königsberg raid. 23 Lancasters FTR from Stettin. *Nachtjagd* claimed 47 *Viermots* destroyed, for the loss of 7 Tame Boars. 100 Group Mosquitoes submitted only one claim: F/L D.L. Hughes-F/L R.H. Perks of 239 Sqn in NFII W4097, a Ju 88 at 0205 hrs at 5340N 1250E during a patrol in the Neuruppin area. Ju 88G-1 Wrk.Nr. 710861 of 3./NJG 2 reportedly cr. at Tellow nr. Hörkow after a *Fernnachtjäger* (long-range intruder) attack, 20 km SE of the location where the Mosquito crew reported their victim went in. *Uffz* Volkhard Petzold, an inexperienced replacement pilot was KIA. Crew baled out uninjured.

21. XX KB227 of 139 Sqn. F/L J.A. Halcro RCAF and F/L T.J. Martin RCAF KIA. 6 victories were claimed by RAF Mosquitoes. F/O D.T. Tull-F/O P Gowgill of the FIU in a XVII, a Ju 88 10m S Bonn; S/L B.A. Burbridge DFC-F/L F.S. Skelton DFC of 85 Sqn in XIX 'Y' a Ju 188 over the Baltic; F/L P.A. Bates-P/O W.G. Cadman of 141 Sqn in FBVI HR180/B, a Bf 110 SW of Mannheim; S/L J.G. Benson DFC-F/L L. Brandon DFC of 157 Sqn in XIX MM630/E, 2 x Ju 188 at Zeeland and F/L P.S. Kendall DFC*-F/L C R. Hill DFC* of 85 Sqn in XIX 'A', a Bf 109G in the Limburg area.

22. F/L R.D. Doleman-F/L D.C. Bunch DFC of 157 Sqn in XIX MM643/F, a Bf 110 Frankfurt; F/L W.W. Provan of 29 Sqn in XIII HK469, a Bf 110 SE Frankfurt; S/L R. Bannock RCAF-F/O R.R. Bruce of 418 Sqn in a VI, a UEA at Kitzingen and F/L L Stephenson DFC-F/L G.A. Hall DFC of 219 Sqn in a XXX, a Ju 88 on the Dutch border.

23. Bf 110G-4 G9+EN 440384 cr. at Birresborn in the Eifel at 2335 hrs.

24. S/L C.R. Barrett DFC and F/O E.S. Fogden of 608 Sqn (KIA) and P/O G.R. Thomas and F/O J.H. Rosbottom of 692 Sqn (KIA) both cr. nr. Nauen.

25. F/L B.H. Smith RCAF and Sgt L.F. Pegg KIA.

26. One of Welter's victims was a 515 Sqn FBVI flown by S/L C. Best DFC and F/Sgt H. Dickinson (KIA). S/L J.H. McK Chisholm and F/L E.L. Wilde of 157 Sqn disappeared w/o trace. Reichenbach's victim was a FBVI of 239 Sqn flown by F/O E.W. Osborne and P/O G.V. Acheson (KIA). Welter claimed another Mosquito N of Wittenberg on 18/19 September (B.XV DZ635 of 627 Sqn, which cr. at Schiffdorf in the E outskirts of Bremerhaven. F/L N. B. Rutherford AFC and P/O F.H. Stanbury KIA) when 1 Mosquito FTR from a heavy raid on Bremerhaven.

27. 11./NJG 1 lost Bf 110 G-4 740358 G9+MY shot down E of Arnhem by F/O Ginger Owen-F/O McAllister DFM of 85 Sqn. Walter Sjuts and *Uffz*'s Herbert Schmidt and Ernst Fischer KIA. This RAF crew also shot down Bf 110G-4 740757 G9+GZ of 12./NJG 1 in the same area. *Uffzs*' Heinz Gesse and Josef Kaschub and *Ogefr* Josef Limberg KIA.

28. *Mandrel* was a jamming device designed to jam German EW (Early Warning) ground radar in the 10-MHz bands (*FuMG 80 Freya, Freya Fahrstuhl, [Freya Lift] FuMG 404 Jagdscloss* [*Hunting Castle*], *FuMo 51 Mammut* [*Mammoth*] and *FuMG 402 Wassermann [Aquarian]*).

29. His 2nd kill of the night was MZ763 of 78 Sqn, which Modrow claimed shot down 75 km. WNW of Düsseldorf. This matches the crash location of MZ763, whch occurred near Weert. On 21/22 June 1944 Modrow destroyed 4 Lancasters flying a He 219 *Uhu*. His final tally was 34 combat victories.

30. On the southern edge of the Zuider Zee, which has not been identified.

31. In grid square position HN 4, which is in the Brummen-Zutphen area. This, in all probability, applies to the loss of Lancaster PD318 of 207 Sqn, which came down at Uddel, WNW Apeldoorn at 2330 hrs.

32. A homer, which gave a bearing on the enemy night-fighter's *IFF* set and had a range of 40 miles. Stop-gap arrangements were made to fit some 141 Sqn Mosquitoes with ASH (Air-Surface H), a centimetric radar originally developed in the USA as an ASV (air-to-surface-vessel radar for U.S. Navy aircraft and the Fleet Air Arm. ASH was a wing mounted radar but could not be fitted to the Mosquito wing it was installed in a 'thimble' radome in the nose.

33. Ju 88G-1 710639 D5+EV of 10./NJG 3, which cr. into a wooded area at Beetsterzwaag, SW of Groningen. *Oblt* Walter Briegleb, pilot, *Uffz*'s Brandt, flight engineer and Walter Bräunlich, *Bordschütze* WIA. *Fw* Paul Kowalewski, radar operator KIA. At the time Briegleb was one of the most successful replacement pilots in the *Nachtjagd* with 17 victories. He survived the war as *Staffelkapitän* of 7./NJG 2 and had 25 night victories. On 6/7 October also *Lt* Kurt Welter and 2 other 10./JG 300 pilots claimed 3 Mosquitoes over Berlin. Mosquito losses this night were P/O W.S. Vale RAAF-F/L A.E. Ashcroft DFC (KIA) of 157 Sqn in a NFXIX, a BXVI of 571 Sqn, and 2 NFXIIIs of 29 Sqn, 2nd TAF on *Intruders* to Stade, NW Germany and Handorf.

34. On 9/10 October 435 aircraft (375 Halifaxes, 40 Lancasters, 20 Mosquitoes of 1, 4, 6 and 8 Groups) attacked Bochum for the loss of 4 Halifaxes and 1 Lancaster. All were probably shot down by 4 crews of NJG 1. *Hptm* Schnaufer, *Kommandeur* of IV./NJG 1 reached the historic 100 *Abschüsse*, dispatching 2 *Viermots* S of Bochum and at Bocholt.

35. XVI MM184 of 692 Sqn. F/O F.H. Dell (Evd) and F/O R.A. Naiff (KIA).

36. In Grid Square LN-KN, or the Venlo-Goch area, at 0343 hrs.

37. In summer 1943 Döring had completed 348 operational sorties as a bomber pilot in KG 53 and KG 55, seeing action during the Battles of France and Britain and in the Russian campaign, where he destroyed 10 aircraft in the air (inc. 3 4-engined TB-3 bombers over Stalingrad one night) flying a He 111 fitted with extra machine-guns. He claimed a further 8 a/c destroyed as a *Wild Boar* pilot in JG 300 and 3 more night victories in NJG 2 and NJG 3.

38. S/L Branse Burbridge DFC* and F/L Bill Skelton DFC* of 85 Sqn in NFXIX 'Y' for their 9th-10th victories. *Nachtjagd* lost 3 other fighters to Mosquitoes. F/L Donald R. 'Podge' Howard and F/O Frank 'Sticky' Clay of 239 Sqn in a FBVI shot down a Fw 190 at Meland after a considerable dogfight. F/O Desmond Tull and F/O Peter J. Cowgill DFC of the FIU destroyed a Ju 88G W of Kassel. F/O G.S Irving-F/O G.M. Millington of 125 Sq in NFXVII HK245 claimed a He 219 nr Duisburg. He 219A-0 190059 G9+EH of 1./NJG 1 cr. at 2000 hrs. *Uffz* Franz Frankenhauser baled out. *Uffz* Helmut Biank KIA. Frankenhauser (and his *Bordfunker*, *Uffz* Erwin Fabian) KIA 30 November/1 December after engine failure of their He 219A-2 on approach to Handorf.

39. 1 Lancaster FTR from Brunswick.

40. On 19/20 October 565 Lancasters and 18 Mosquitoes of 1, 3, 6 and 8 Groups in 2 forces 4 1/2 hrs apart also went to Stuttgart. 6 Lancasters FTR, 5 of which, were shot down by Tame Boar *Nachtjäger*.

41. Probably Ju 88G-1 Wrk Nr. 712312 2Z+EB of I./NJG 6, which cr. at Vaihirgen/Marksdorf ENE of Pforzheim, Germany. *Oblt* Wilhelm Engel, pilot WIA. Radar operator safe. On 23/24 February 1945 Engel was again shot down and injured by an intruder, this time whilst coming in to land at Grossachsenheim airfield. By that time, his tally stood at 18 night and 2 day victories.

42. Doleman-Bunch's victim possibly Ju 88G-1 714510 2Z+CM of 4./NJG 6, which cr. at Murrhard SE of Heilbronn, Germany. *Uffz*'s Georg Haberer, pilot, who had yet to open his score and Ernst Dressel, radar op KIA.

43. Also, 54 Mosquitoes of 8 Group made attacks on Hamburg and other German cities. 6 Stirlings flew on Resistance operations. No a/c lost.

44. There were no night fighter losses over Denmark this night. S/L W.P. Green DFC-F/L D. Oxby of 219 Sqn in NFXXX MM792 destroyed a Ju 88 in the Verviers area. Mosquito crews rounded off the month with 3 more victories over *Nachtjagd*. On 29 October F/L P.T. L'Amie-F/O J.W. Smith of 515 Sqn in VI PZ344/E destroyed a Fw 190 (and a Ju W34) and P/O T.A. Groves-F/Sgt R.B. 'Doc' Dockeray, also of 515 Sqn, in FBVI PZ217/K destroyed a Bf 110. (L'Amie and Smith KIA 21 November 1944). On 29/30 October 1/Lt A.A. Harrington USAAF-F/O D.G. Tongue of 410 'Cougar' Sqn RCAF in NFXXX MM767 destroyed a Fw 190 nr. St Antonis, their 4th victory. On 14/15 March 1944 in NFXIII HK521 they destroyed Ju 88A-14 B3+CK of 2./KG 54 at Hildenborough. On 18/19 June 1944 in NFXIII MM571/Y they got a Ju 88 in the Vire area. On 26/27 September 1944 in NFXXX MM743 they destroyed a Ju 87 12m N of Aachen. Their 5-8th victories came on 25/26 Novemebr 1944 when in NFXXX MM767 they destroyed 3 Ju 88Gs at Muntz, Jacberath and N of Hunxe.

45. Even in broad daylight, Bomber Command was able to operate in relative safety. During October-December 1944 15 out of 20 raids on the Ruhr were in daylight. 100 Group's RCM bombers caused further confusion and disruption by its faint raids and jamming of the Luftwaffe's radio traffic and radar and often prevented German night fighters from reaching the bomber streams at all. 100 Group Mosquitoes, which had claimed 257 German aircraft (mainly night-fighters) destroyed by 1945, hunted down the *Nachtjagd* crews and complimented the offensive by 2nd TAF, ADGB and 8 Group over the continent.

46. On 7/8 October, in riposte to the enemy R/T communications used in its *Zahme Sau* operations, Lancasters of 101 Sqn, fitted with *Airborne Cigar (ABC)* carried out jamming of the enemy R/T frequencies. These Lancasters also carried a specially trained German-speaking operator. This night the order *'All butterflies go home'* was broadcast on the German night-fighter frequency, resulting in many German night-fighter pilots returning to their airfields! The most outstanding *Window* success of the month was perhaps on 14/15th when 1013 heavies went to Duisburg and 200 to Brunswick. It was anticipated that the Duisburg raid, by low approach, radar silence and shallow penetration, would get through with little trouble but that the Brunswick force might be strongly opposed. A *Window* Force was therefore routed to break off from the Brunswick route and strike at Mannheim. This had success beyond all expectations, for the Brunswick attack was almost ignored because the Mannheim area was anticipated as the main target. Just one bomber from the Brunswick force was lost: Lancaster ME595 of 61 Sqn was shot down by flak at Rieseberg, 6 km NW of Köningsbutter, around 0245 hrs; there were no claims by *Nachtjäger*. October also saw the introduction of *Dina;* the jammer used against FuG 220 *Lichtenstein SN-2. Dina* was installed in the *Jostle*-fitted Fortresses of 214 Sqn. This was frequently used in the *Window* force, as were *Jostle, H2S* and *Carpet,* thereby more effectively giving the simulation of a bombing force. A further realistic effect, also born in October, was created through the co-operation of *PFF,* which, on several occasions *Oboe*-marked and bombed the *Spoof* target. (The *Window* Force itself had not yet arrived at the bomb-carrying stage.) The noise of *Oboe*, which had until that time always preceded real attacks only, was thought to give still more confusion to the German controller.

47. LJ923.

48. Special Operations Executive similar to the American OSS or Office of Strategic Services.

49. LW639.

50. 561 Lancasters, 400 Halifaxes and 31 Mosquitoes supported by 37 RCM sorties and 51 Mosquito fighter patrols. More than 5000 houses were destroyed or badly damaged in the N half of the city, plus 7 industrial premises destroyed and 18 seriously damaged. This was Bomber Command's last major raid on Düsseldorf. 11 Halifaxes and 8 Lancasters FTR, 4 of these a/c crashing behind Allied lines in France and Belgium. 92 crewmembers were lost, 28 becoming PoWs. 5 men evaded and 6 were hospitalised, 1 dying later from wounds received. About 40 *Viermot Abschüsse* were claimed by the *Nachtjagd*, an unusual over-claiming by more than 100%! This included a claim for 6 destroyed and 1 probable in just 12 minutes S of Düsseldorf by *Ofw* Wilhelm 'Willi' Morlock and his *Bordfunker, Fw* Alfred Soika of 3./NJG 1. (Morlock was KIA two nights later, on 4/5 November, when his He 219A-0, 190182 G9+HL was attacked by a Mosquito and cr. in the Teutoburg Forest nr. Ibbenbüren. Soika ejected and sustained only minor injuries). *Nachtjagd* lost 1 a/c; Bf 110G-4 G9+PZ of 12./NJG 1 cr. N of Düsseldorf due to *Feindbeschuss* (enemy fire). *Uffz* Johannes Kischke and crew KIA.

51. Bf 110 of II./NJG 1, which crashed into the River Rhine nr Hangelar airfield at 2150 hrs. *Oblt* Ernst Runze, pilot, KIA. *Ogefr* Karl-Heinz Bendfield, *Bordfunker*, and *Bordschütze* bailed out. F/O A.J. 'Ginger' Owen and F/O J.S. V. McAllister DFM of 85 Sqn destroyed a Ju 88 SE of Bielefeld. A Bf 110 was shot down at Osnabrück by W/C K.H.P. Beauchamp and P/O Money of 157 Sqn and 2 more were destroyed at Bochum by F/O J.N.W. Young and F/O R.H. Siddons of 239 Sqn and S/L R.G. Woodman DFC and F/O A.F. Witt of 85 Sqn. Bf 110 of 6./NJG 1, shot down by Mosquito NF at 1900 hrs at 20,000 ft. *Uffz.* Gustav Sarzio (pilot, inj, 5 night kills) baled out; *Uffz.* Heinrich Conrads, *Bordfunker* and *Ogefr* Roman Talarowski, *Bordschütze* both KIA. (F/O Arthur F Witt and F/L T.W. Redfern, pilot died 26/27 January 1945 when their Mosquito NFXXX cr. nr Oulton, Norfolk in bad weather during night training exercise). Bf 110G-4 Wrk.Nr. 440648 G9+PS of 8./NJG 1 possibly shot down by Mosquito NF, cr. at Bersenbrück, 30 km N of Osnabrück. *Fw.* Willi Ruge, pilot (WIA), baled out; *Uffz* Helmut Kreibohm, *Bordfunker* and *Ogefr* Anton Weiss, *Bordschütze*, both KIA. Bf 110 Wrk.Nr. 730272 G9+E2 of IV./NJG 1 shot down by Mosquito NF SW of Wezel. *Lt* Heinz Rolland (26, pilot, 15 night victories including 1 this night); *Fw.* Heinz Krüger (25, *Bordfunker*); *Uffz.* Karl Berger (22, *Bordschütze*) all KIA.

52. Mouritz and his crew were later allocated a new QR-M. He recalled, 'What a difference to fly. When doing our first air test with no bombs and limited fuel, I opened the throttle on take off and we were flung back in our seats. She behaved like a sports car. We had now completed 12 trips and flew the new *Mickey* (although no art was ever painted on the nose) to the end of our tour except for a few weeks in January and February when she was being repaired after getting shot up and having a dicey landing.'

53. Fries and his *Bordfunker Fw* Fred Staffa had become a very experienced night-fighting team. They were credited with 10 confirmed night kills August 1943-April 1944, plus 2 unconfirmed *Abschüsse* in daylight, a B-17 on 17 August and a P-47 on 14 October 1943. On 9 July 1944 they had been posted to 2./NJG 1 at Venlo airfield.

54. And a FBVI flown by F/L T.N. Cooper and F/O K.H. Bonner of 515 Sqn (KIA). B-17 from 214 Sqn. F/O J.M.S. Jackson and crew KIA.

55. F/O Turner-F/O Partridge of 151 Sqn claimed a Ju 188. Ju 88G-6 620583 R4+TS of 11./NJG 3 was shot down in air combat and cr. SW of Paderborn. *Oblt* Josef Förster, pilot, ended the war with 16 night victories. *Fw* Werner Moraing, *Bordfunker* and *Fw* Heinz Wickardt, *Bordschütze* WIA. Capt T. Weisteen RNWAF of 85 Sqn in Mosquito NFXIX 'A' claimed a Ju 88 as a 'probable'.

56. Ju 88G-6 620396 R4+KR of *Stab*/IV./NJG 3, which was shot down by a Mosquito and cr. at Marienburghausen, Germany. Schneider had no victories credited.

57. 'Ricky' Dyson was awarded the George Medal for his attempt to save the lives of the crew and he was presented with the award by King George VI at an investiture at Buckingham Palace when the war had ended.

58. Possibly Ju 88 714819 3C+WL of 3./NJG 4, which cr. a little E of Stagen at 2136 hrs. *Oberfähnrich* Erhard Pfisterhammer, pilot (no victories credited), *Uffz* Wolfgang Sode, radar operator and air gunner WIA.

59. Bf 110G-4 180382 of 12./NJG 1, which had taken off from Bonninhardt at 2047 hrs cr. at 2145 hrs near Lippborg near Hamm. *Lt* Heinz-Joachim Schlage, pilot, survived. Fiebig and *Uffz* Kundmüller KIA.

60. NFXIII HK530. F/L K.J. Pamment KIA. F/Sgt H.C. Wiles PoW/WIA.

61. Stirling IV LK143 of 138 Sqn, which was lost w/o trace heading for Denmark. F/O G.F. Nicholls and crew were killed.

62. Richard 'Dicky' Goucher (23) and C.H. 'Tiny' Bullock (33) crewed up in North Africa in 1943 and remained together until the end of the war, being posted to 151 Sqn at Hunsdon on 18 January 1945.

63. Probably Ju 88G-1 714152 of 6./NJG 4. *Uffz* Wilhelm Schlutter, pilot (no victories) WIA and *Uffz* Friedrich Heerwagen, radar operator and *Gefr* Friedrich Herbeck, *Bordschütze*, KIA.

64. Heglund had joined 85 Sqn in October 1944 having scored 13 and 1/3 kills flying Spitfires with 331 Sqn.

65. *Oblt* Wilhelm Henseler, *St.Kpt* 2./NJG 1 who survived the war and scored 10 night victories in 4./NJG 1 and 2./NJG 1.

66. *Seelenbohrer* or 'soul borer' was the night-fighter's nickname of the British use of 'Tinsel', whereby a British German-speaking crew member blotted out German R/T transmissions with engine noise. Tinsel sounded like a very unpleasant drilling noise.

67. *ABC* (*Airborne Cigar*) emitted a warbling note which German crewmen christened Dudelsack or 'Bagpipes'. The British successive transmission of 6-8 jamming tones on the *Nachtjagd* R/T frequencies sounded like a child's cheap music box and it was very nerve-wracking to German night-fighter ears.

68. IV./NJG 1.

69. Literally 'journey'. R/T code as in '*Machen Sie Reise-Reise!* – Break off engagement.

70. He 219A-0 190193 G9+EK was involved in another crash-landing at Münster-Handorf of 25/26 September 1944 when *Lt* Günther Schirmer and *Gefr* Wilhelm Rosenberger (both rescued with serious injuries) were unable to lower landing flaps or undercarriage as a result of battle damage. F/L R.J. Foster DFC-F/L M.F. Newton DFC of 604 Sqn in Mosquito XIII MM462/T claimed a He 219 55 miles S Nijmegen.

71. *Lt* Fries and *Fw* Staffa added another 6 *Abschüsse* (4 of which were officially confirmed) flying the He 219 before the end of the war.

72. Bf 110G-4 140078 G9+HZ, cr. 6 miles (10 km) NW of Münster-Handorf, probably shot down either by F/L Edward R. Hedgecoe DFC-F/Sgt J.R. Whitham of the FIU at Ford (attached to 85 Sqn at Swannington) in a Mosquito XXX or remotely possibly by an RAF Fortress gunner, F/O Corke of 214 Sqn, while on *a Jostle* patrol, who claimed a Ju 88 as 'damaged'. On Christmas Eve *Hptm* Heinz Strüning (32) *Staffelkapitän* 9./NJG 1, Oak Leaves holder, who had 56 night kills died in similar circumstances to Augenstein. At 2200 hrs following a skirmish, probably with a Mosquito, Strüning baled out and struck the tail unit of his Bf 110G-4 and he was killed. Other *Experten* KIA around this time were *Hptm* Hans-Karl Kamp of *Stab* JG 300 (estimated 28 night and 2 day *Abschüsse,* killed in a crash N of Hamburg 31 December 1944)) and *Hptm* Hermann Leube of 4./NJG 3 with 22 victories, killed in a crash-landing nr. Gouda 27/28 or 28/29 December 1944. *Hptm* Alfons Köster who had 25 night victories and 1 daylight kill was killed when he crashed into a farmhouse on landing at Varel in heavy fog on 7 January 1945.

73. 712268 of I./NJG 4, which cr. nr. Giessen killing the air gunner, *Gefr* Alfred Graefer.

74. XVI MM190 of 128 Sqn. F/L R.C. Onley and F/O G.B. Collins RAAF KIA.

75. On 1 January 1945 Hedgecoe and Bamford, his navigator, died in a crash-landing. Hedgecoe had shot down 8 e/a and Bamford had taken part in the destruction of 10.

76. Wrk Nr 714530 of 6./NJG 4, *Uffz* Heinrich Brune, pilot, *Uffz* Emil Hoffharth, *Bordfunker* and *Uffz* Wolfgang Rautert, *Bordschütze* KIA. 23-year old Bransome Arthur Burbridge and Frank Seymour 'Bill' Skelton were deeply religious. Burbridge had been a conscientious objector on religious grounds for the first 6 months of the war before joining up. Both were commissioned from the ranks and served individually on Havocs in 85 Sqn in October 1941 and January 1942 respectively. They only crewed up on their 2nd tour on the Sqn in July 1943. Their 1st victory was a Me 410 *Hornisse* (Hornet) on 22/23 February 1944.

77. Probably NFXIII HK529 of 29 Sqn, which was on an *Intruder* over Germany. F/L N.R. Schwartz and Sgt R.W. Donaldson KIA.

78. W/O D.A. Taylor-F/Sgt Radford of 157 Sqn in NFXIX MM627/H. F/Sgt J. Leigh and his navigator of 157 Sqn in NFXIX MM653/L. F/L R.T. Goucher-F/L C.H. Bullock of 85 Sqn in NFXXX 'J' Bf 110 40m from Ulm.

79. F/L C.E. Edinger RCAF-F/O C.C. Vaessen of 410 'Cougar' Sqn RCAF in NFXXX MV527 shot down a Ju 88S of Bonninghardt. W/C J.D. Somerville DFC CO 409 scored his 6th confirmed victory, flying NFXIII MM456 with F/O G.D. Robinson DFC when they despatched a Ju 88 in the Kaiserworth area. P/O F.S. Haley-W/O McNaughton of 409 Sqn in NFXIII MM569 claimed a Bf 110 and F/O Ross H. Finlayson-F/O Al Webster of the same Sqn in NFXIII HK415 claimed a Ju 88.

80. Tull accidentally rammed Bf 110 G9+CC of *Stab* IV/NJG 1 flown by *Hptm* Adolph Breves (with *Fw* Telsnig, *Bordfunker* and *Uffz* Ofers, *Bordschütze*) who was coming into land at Düsseldorf airfield at 2230 hrs. Tull and Cowgill are buried in Reichswald Forest Cemetery nr. Kleef. A large part of one of the wings of the 110 was torn off but Breves landed without further damage. He subsequently received official confirmation of his Mosquito '*Abschuss*'. Breves finished the war with 18 victories. (The Bf 110 was repaired and test-flown on 31 December).

81. He 219A-0 Wrk Nr 190229 G9+GH of 1/NJG 1. *Uffz* Herbert Scheuerlein, an inexperienced replacement pilot (WIA) and his *Bordfunker*, *Uffz* Max Günther Heinze, *Bordfunker* (WIA) baled out safely. They had been airborne for just 15 minutes. Taylor and Edwards died on 22/23 December when they crashed while attempting to make an approach to land at Swannington after informing Flying Control over the R/T that they had no aileron control.

82. There were no *Nachtjäger* claims.

83. Burbridge and Skelton finished their 2nd tours early in 1945 and were the top-scoring night-fighter crew in the RAF with 21 victories. Bob Braham and W/C John Cunningham both destroyed 19 e/a at night. Post-war Burbridge became a lay preacher, while Skelton was ordained as a clergyman in the Church of England and became chaplain at Clare College, Cambridge.

84. Ju 88 621441 27+HK of II./NJG 6 cr. at Landstuhl killing *Ofw* Max Hausser, pilot, who had yet to open his score, *Ofw* Fritz Steube, radar operator and *Fw* Ernst Beisswenger, *Bordschütze*. Ju 88G-6 621436 2Z+DC also of II./NJG 6, cr. at Lebach, N of Saarbrücken. *Hptm* Kopp, pilot with one night victory to his credit, baled out injured, one of his crew was KIA. W/C Peter Green DSO DFC-F/L Oxby DFM** of 219 Sqn in NFXXX MM792 shot down a Ju 88.

85. All were shot down by *Nachtjäger*, including NA501 of 578 Sqn, which, in all probability, fell victim to *Oblt* Peter Spoden of 6./NJG 6, for his 18th *Abschuss* (Spoden claimed a Halifax shot down at 1859 hrs and at a height of 4,000 m, in Grid Square QO 7, which was in the Kylburg area.

86. Donmall successfully evaded and reached the Allied lines. *Hptm* Kurt-Heinz Weigel claimed a Halifax SW Bingen (his 1st *Abschuss*, pr. NP975 of 466 Sqn), *Ofw* Richard Launer of 1./NJG 6 claimed a Lancaster W of Koblenz (his 8th kill claim, pr. PA977 of 405 'Vancouver' Sqn RCAF). *Lt* Wolfram Möckel of 4./NJG 2 claimed a Mosquito at Hasselt, for his 10th *Abschuss*, but none were lost from the raids on Koblenz, Bingen and patrols over the continent.

87. 219 Sqn got three kills. W/C Peter Green DSO DFC-F/L Oxby DFM** in NFXXX MM706 shot down a Ju 88 S of Huy. F/O W. B. Allison-W/O Mills and F/O R.L. Young-F/O N.C. Fazan got a Ju 88 apiece. F/L McPhail-F/O Donaghue of 409 Sqn RCAF in NFXIII MM461 destroyed a Ju 188, F/O Mackenzie-F/O C.F.A. Bodard of 410 Sqn RCAF in a NFXIII brought down two Ju 88s. Four others and one damaged fell victim to 488 Sqn RNZAF at B48/Amiens-Glisy. The CO W/C R.G. Watts and F/O I.C. Skudder in NFXXX NT263 got a Ju 188 and F/L Johnny Hall DFC-F/O J.P.W. Cairns DFC in NFXXX MT570/P shot down a Me 410 in the U.S. Sector. Nr Koblenz F/L R.J.V. Smythe-F/O Waters of 157 Sqn in a NFXXX destroyed a Ju 88. F/L G.C. Chapman-F/L J. Stockley of 85 Sqn in NFXIX 'N' got a Bf 110 at Mannheim-Mainz. F/L R.W. Leggett-F/O E.J. Midlane of 125 Sqn in XVII HK247 shot up a V-1 carrying Heinkel He 111H22 of 7./KG 53 over the N Sea and it crashed in Holland. Four crew KIA. 1 gunner survived. F/Sgt Bullus-F/O Edwards of 68 Sqn in a NFXVII got another He 111H-22 over the N Sea. (The *Vergeltungswaffe 1* (Revenge Weapon No.1) or Fieseler Fi 103 *Kirschkern* (Cherry Stone) was a small pilotless aircraft with a 1870-lb high explosive warhead, which detonated on impact. Altogether, about 1200 V-1s were air-launched against Britain, although of these only 638 approached the coast. KG 53 ceased operations having lost 77 Heinkels, 16 of them claimed by Mosquitoes. On the night of 6 January 1945 a Mosquito of 68 Sqn claimed the last shooting down of a He 111H-22.)

88. In NFXXX MM822.

89. Stewart and Brumby destroyed a Ju 88G at Groenlo on 21/22 February 1945, a Bf 110 8 m NW of Bocholt on 26/27.3.45 and a Bf 110 20 miles SE Osnabrück on 7/8 April 1945 to take Stewart's final score to five destroyed and one damaged (He 111 on 26/27 March 1945) to earn him the title in the sqn records of 'the Last of the Aces'.

90. Two crews of 410 'Cougar' Sqn RCAF at Lille/Vendeville (B.51) claimed two Ju 87s of *Nachtschlachtgruppe* 1 (used for harassment of troops and transport). In the Wassemberg area F/L C.E. Edinger DFC-F/O C.C. Vaessen DFC in NFXXX MV527 destroyed one Stuka and S/L I.E. MacTavish-F/O A.M. Grant flying NFXXX MT485 got the other. F/O J.A. Watt-F/L E.H. Collis of of 410 'Cougar' Sqn RCAF destroyed a Ju 88 of 2./NJG 2, which cr. nr Roermond. *Ofw* Heinrich Tetzlaff, pilot, with one confirmed night victory, MIA. 3 crew survived and made PoW. Two crews in 219 Sqn claimed 3 victories. F/L G.R.I. 'Sailor' Parker DFC DSM-W/O D.L. Godfrey DFC DSM in NFXXX MM698 with AI Mk.X claimed 2 Ju 188s destroyed. F/L L. Stephenson DFC-F/L G.A. Hall DFC claimed a Bf 110 destroyed. W/C Russ Bannock DFC* CO, 406 'Lynx' Sqn RCAF in NFXXX MM693, shot down Ju 88G-l 714132 3C+CT of 9./NJG 4 10 km W of Paderborn. *Obfw* Manfred Ludwig (pilot, no victories) and *Fw* Hans Fischl KIA. F/L R.J. Foster DFC and F/L M.F. Newton DFC of 604 Sqn in NFXIII MM462/T claimed a He 219 destroyed 5 miles E of Nijmegen.

91. Heglund's 15th victory of the war.

92. One of their victims was Bf 110G-4 740162 G9+OT, flown by *Hptm* Heinz Strüning, *Ritterkreuz mit Eichenlaub* (Knight's Cross with Oak leaves), *Staffelkapitän*, 9./NJG 1, which was shot down at 2200 hrs and cr. in Referather woods nr. Bergisch Gladbach/Rheinland. *Bordfunker* and *Bordschütze* baled out safely but the 32-year-old *Experte* who had 56 night victories was killed when he hit the tail of his 110. Strüning's body was found two months later. Luftwaffe losses included Bf 110 of 7./NJG 1, which cr. nr Roermond killing the crew and a Ju 88 of 5./NG 1 which cr. S of Afferden, 1 KIA, 2 MIA and 1 PoW.

93. On the night of 26/27 December *Hptm* Kamsties of II./NJG 2 flying a Ju 88C claimed a Mosquito for his 4th victory. NFXXX MM705, which was on a defensive patrol, was shot down at 0030 hrs and cr. Holsbeck, Belgium. S/L D.L. Ryalls and F/L J.B. Hampson were killed.

94. 149 Lancasters and 17 Mosquitoes of 1 and 8 Groups attacked the railway yards at Osterfeld. 3 Lancasters FTR, 2 claimed by *Hptm* Johannes Hager, *Staffelkapitän*, 6./NJG 1 in the Essen area at 1900 and 1905 hrs. 28 Lancasters of 5 Group attacked cruisers in Oslo Fjord. 1 Lancaster lost. In minor operations 77 Mosquitoes went to Berlin and 12 to Ludwigshafen. 33 RCM sorties, 33 Mosquito patrols, 16 Halifaxes and 10 Lancasters' minelaying in the Kattegat. 1 mine-laying Lancaster FTR. (PB894 of 630 Sqn, shot down by *Hptm* Eduard Schröder of 3./NJG 3 into the sea 50 km NW of Hanstholm at 1900 hrs).

95. The *Intruder* was crewed by Lewis Heath-Jack Thompson of 23 Sqn, who had taken off from Little Snoring at 1700 hrs on 1 January. The Ju 88 pilot turned due E to return to Marx/Varel but soon afterwards, the crew believing themselves to be over German territory and anxious to find their exact whereabouts, fired a recognition signal followed by two 'reds' which they repeated. They were then surprised by a night-fighter attack from aft. The pilot lost control and all the crew baled out. They all landed in Allied territory and were taken prisoner. It was considered that splinters hit 4R+S from bombs dropped on the airfield by the Mosquito crew before take off.

96. He 219A-2 290194 G9+KL of 3./NJG 1 cr. near Schleiden, 50 km SW of Cologne. *Oblt* Heinz Oloff, pilot, with 9 or 10 night victories in I./NJG 1 and *Fw* Helmut Fischer, radar operator both WIA baled out and survived.

97. The other Mosquito victories on 31 December 1944/1 January 1945 went to a 604 Sqn crew in NFXIII MM569/J who got 2 Ju 87s while F/L L.F. Endersby 169 Sqn (attached to 85 Sqn) in NFXIX 'R' destroyed a He 219 and two NFXXX crews of 410 Sqn – S/L Currie-F/L Rose and F/L Dexter-F/O Tongue, got a Ju 188 nr Antwerp and a Ju 880 respectively. S/L J.P. Meadows-F/L H.M. Friend of 219 Sqn in a NFXXX got 2 Ju 188s.

98. On 13 January Bennett and Smith were KIA when they went down in the North Sea on the way home.

99. AN/APS4/AI.Mk.XV (ASH) 3 cm radar with horizontal scanner; maximum range 8 miles. This small torpedo-shaped installation more often seen on Fleet Air Arm Fireflies was originally intended for searching for surface vessels and reading coastlines. It had the tiniest plan position indicator (PPI) of all airborne radars, measuring about 3-ins by 1 1/2-ins and was proportionally efficient for air interception.

100. HM409.

101. Who with his navigator W/O Bill Lane, completed 52 operations in 128 Sqn on the Mosquito BXVI October 1944-April 1945. 20 of these were to Berlin.

102. In 2nd TAF F/L R.J. Foster DFC-F/L M. F. Newton DFC of 604 Sqn in Mosquito NFXIII HK526/U destroyed 3 Ju 88s; F/L F.T. Reynolds-F/O F.A. van den Heuvel of 219 Sqn in NFXXX MM790 destroyed a Bf 110 and S/L D.C. Furse-F/L J.H. Downes of 604 Sqn in NFXIII HK529 got a He 219 at Mönchengladbach. 'Over Holland on 1/2 January 1945' recalls Arnold Döring of 7./NJG 2 'a Mosquito shot down *Fw* Werthner and he was the only one who could escape by baling out. His crew was KIA in the attack.' (Ju 88G-6 Wrk Nr. 620880 of 10./NJG 3 cr. N Twente. Werthner PoW).

103. The German loss card for Ju 88G-6 621364 27+CP of 5./NJG 6, which cr. at Dortmund indicates that the a/c had been hit by 'friendly' *flak* fire; on return to Dortmund a/f. One of the wings broke off due to flak damage causing the loss of the a/c and crew. *Oblt* Hans Steffen, pilot and *Uffzs* Josef Knon, Helmut Uttler and Friedrich Krebber KIA. F/O York of 85 Sqn scored the other victory this night, a Ju 88.

104. F/L R.G. Woodman-F/O Simpkins of 169 Sqn in Mosquito NFXXX 'N' claimed a Ju 188 near Frankfurt. F/L J.O. Mathews DFC-W/O A. Penrose DFC of 157 Sqn in NFXIX TA393 'C' claimed a Ju 88 3m W of Stuttgart. S/L B.A. Burbridge DSO DFC*-F/L F.S. Skelton DSO DFC* of 85 Sqn in NFXXX 'X' got a Ju 88 15m SW of Ludwigshafen. On 4 January 1945 F/O P.W. Nicholas-F/O W.M.G. Irvine of 604 Sqn in NFXIII MM563 claimed a Ju 88 W of Hostmar.

105. Tail Warning radar (AGLT).

106. Of 645 Lancasters and 9 Mosquitoes of 1, 3, 5, 6 and 8 Groups despatched, 11 Lancasters FTR. 4 more crashed in France. Despite the extensive damage sustained in the mid-air collision ND968/G was subsequently repaired and returned to B-Flight 460 Sqn RAAF. The aircraft survived the war, finally to be SOC on 4 October 1945. Lancaster I NN766 PM-R of 103 Sqn, which had left Elsham Wolds at 1823, was most probably the aircraft that collided with O-Oboe. The unfortunate aircraft flown by F/O W.J. McArthur RCAF crash-dived into a hill near Hohrodberg (Haut-Rhin) during a snow storm about 23 miles SE of where the collision had taken place. The remains of the 7-man crew were not recovered for more than a week until the snow receded and they were buried 25m from the crash site by a party of local people and a nun. A/c and crew were identified by the crew identity discs and parts of the aircraft wreck. After the war the crew of NN766 were reburied in the Münster Communal Cemetery, French Military Plot in a comrades grave, which the French community considered a great honor. At the crash site, a memorial has been placed in commemoration of the crew, 6 of whom were Canadians.

107. Their victim was He 219A-0 190188 G9+CK of 2./NJG 1 flown by *Obfw* Josef Ströhlein (KIA) and his *Bordfunker*, *Uffz* Hans Kenne who were shot down at 2008 hours 5 km S of Wesendorf.

108. Benson-Brandon's victim was He 219A-0 190188 G9+CK of 2./NJG 1, which cr. 5 km S of Wesendorf. *Ofw* Josef Ströhlein, pilot with 4 night kills (KIA). *Uffz* Hans Kenne, *Bordfunker* baled out safely. Ju 88 620513 R4+CD of III./NJG 2, possibly the aircraft shot down by F/L A.S. Briggs-F/O Rodwell of 515 Sqn, cr. at Jägel airfield. *Oblt* Bruno Heilig, pilot with 12 *Abschüsse*, *Uffz* Günther Kulas, *Bordfunker*, *Gfr* Johan Goliasch, flight engineer and *Obgftr* Horst Jauernig, AG KIA. Bannock-Bruce's 8th victim was a UEA on 4/5 April 1945 in NFXXX NT283/Y and his 9th and final victory was on 23/24 April 1945 when a Ju 88 was destroyed at Witstock in NFXXX NV548/Z. Bannock's final tally included 4 a/c damaged, 2 destroyed on the ground and 18 and 1 shared V-1s destroyed.

109. Four Halifaxes and two Lancasters FTR from the raid on Hanau and 1 Lancaster which FTR from the raid on Neuss crashed in Belgium.

110. Supporting the Pathfinder Flare Force meant arriving at the target at the same time but flying at 2,000ft below them to attract the flak and enable the PFF to carry out a straight and level run. After drawing the flak the 'Supporters' then re-crossed the target to drop their bombs.

111. Despite the distant nature of the Pölitz raid, only one *Nachtjäger* submitted a claim for an a/c destroyed. *Ofw* Hans Schadowski of 3./NJG 3 claimed a Lancaster *Abschuss* 50-km NW of Hanstholm at 0028 for his 21st kill. This may have been Lancaster PB842 of 619 Sqn, which was attacked by a 'Me 410' after bombing Stettin. The bomber was so severely damaged in the attack that it headed for Sweden, where it force-landed at a satellite of Rinkaby airfield.

112. Frank Mouritz returned to Australia in July with the probability of starting a second tour as part of Tiger Force, the new name of 5 Group, bombing Japan. The Atom Bomb prevented this.

113. Their victim was possibly Ju 88G-1 710818 05+EP of *Stab*/NJG 3, which cr. 3 km SE of Friedberg, N of Frankfurt. *Ofw* Johann Eels, pilot, with no victories, *Uffz* Richard Zimmer, radar operator and *Gefr* Werner Hecht, *Bordschütze* KIA. F/L B. Brearley-F/O J. Sheldon of 141 Sqn in Mosquito VI HR294/T also destroyed a UEA at Jüterborg.

114. Tommy, formerly a Glaswegian accountant, had earlier completed a tour of ops with 96 Sqn on Defiants and Merlin-engined Beaufighters, which ended with a trip to the RAF Head Injuries Hospital in Oxford and a non-operational medical categorization. He spent his 'rest' as a PPCI (Permanent President of Courts of Inquiry), in 81 and 9 Groups, which administered the OTUs of Fighter Command. Everyone had the same burning ambition to get back on ops and Tommy was no different. Smith crewed up with Arthur Cockayne, a schoolmaster from Walsall, whose wife was a schoolmistress. 'Cocky', who was in his mid-30s, quite old for aircrew, had been called up late in the war and had trained on Catalinas at Pensacola in Florida before becoming a 'radar detective' on bombers in 100 Sqn.

115. Tommy Smith was treated at Fassberg sick quarters. The Germans confirmed his destruction of the two 109s he had shot at and also credited him with another 109 which spun in due to the presence of the intruding Mosquito. It crashed and burnt out, killing the pilot. Tommy stayed at Fassberg for a month before being transferred to *Dulag Luft* at Frankfurt for another month. He was bombed out by the RAF then transferred to Homemark, a convent hospital being used for RAF PoWs. On 28 March 1945, he and the other inmates were released by the U.S. 3rd Army and flown home from Paris. At the PoW reception center at RAF Cosford his assorted burns were treated in hospital. After discharge he was given a posting to Fighter Command HQ at Bentley Priory where the 'Prang Basher' once again took up crash investigation duties. When it came to demob he was invalided out of the RAF and sent to East Grinstead for further plastic surgery. It was there that he met a nursing sister who was to become his wife. Her name was Joy. After the war, a Feldwebel, who had befriended Tommy when he was blind, sent him photos of Cockayne's grave. It showed Tommy's grave, on the left, waiting for him! Tommy adds, 'The Huns were a tidy-minded lot and would have put the two of us alongside each other. Luckily I was 'late for my own funeral'.'

116. *Seelenbohrer* or 'soul borer' was the night-fighter's nickname of the British use of 'Tinsel', whereby a British German-speaking crew member blotted out German R/T transmissions with engine noise. Tinsel sounded like a very unpleasant drilling noise.

117. Three other Mosquito victories were achieved this night. Two 141 Sqn FBVI crews, F/L D.H. Young-F/O J.J. Sanderson in HR200/E and F/O R.C. Brady-F/L M.K. Webster in HR213/G each destroyed a Bf 110 at Magdeburg and F/L A. Mackinnon-F/O G. Waddell of 157 Sqn in NFXIX TA446/Q were credited with a Ju 188 at Fritzlar. Ju 88G-1 Wrk Nr. 710818 D5+EP of *Stab*/NJG 3 cr. 3 km SE of Friedberg/N of Frankfurt. *Ofw* Johann Fels, a replacement pilot who had yet to open his score (KIA); *Uffz* Richard Zimmer, radar op (KIA); *Gefr* Werner Hecht, *Bordschütze* (KIA).

W/C K.H.P. Beauchamp DSO DFC, CO, 157 Squadron, with his navigator F/L Leslie Scholefield DFC at Swannington, Norfolk in late 1944. On 12/13 December 1944 they damaged a Bf 110 SE of the Ruhr during a chase that took them over Aschaffenburg airfield during a patrol in support of Bomber Command attacks on Essen. Scholefield initially got a contact at six miles range, which Beauchamp chased, before dropping back to 600 ft astern and firing two short bursts. Strikes were seen on the starboard wing, followed by a large shower of sparks but visual contact was then lost. As was so often the case, the firing of the guns had also upset the AI radar resulting in the target being lost. Beauchamp and Scholefield had better luck just over a week later, however, when they destroyed a Ju 88 W of Koblenz on 21/22 December. (Mrs Edna Scholefield)

Lancaster I LL847 JO-D *Digger* (Australian slang for an Australian) of 463 Squadron RAAF, which FTR from München with F/O K.E.H. Bennett RAAF and crew on 17/18 December 1944 on the Lanc's 93rd sortie. *Digger* crashed at le Gros-Theil with the loss of all eight crew. The two Aussie cartoon characters are 'Bluey' and 'Curley' who are playing a game with coins called '2-Up'. (A long-term restoration of Lancaster VII NX622 of the Aviation Heritage Museum of Western Australia was completed with the authentic nose art of LL847). (Jack Hamilton)

Lt Gustav Mohr was one of the few Wild Boar night fighters who scored a handful of victories flying the Bf 109 at night during the latter stages of the war. He was credited with five night Abschüsse whilst serving with 2./NJG 1 1 September-December 1944. Whilst shooting down his 5th victim (a Lancaster on 12/13 December 1944) he was injured by return fire and was forced to bale out of his Bf 109G-6, which effectively ended his career in the *Nachtjagd*. (Steve Hall via John Foreman).

Above: Christmas 1944 and a 4,000 pounder, inscribed "Happy Xmas Adolf", is wheeled into position to be hoisted aboard Mosquito BXVI MM199 M5-Q *Q-Queenie*, a 'Cookie carrier' of 128 Squadron at RAF Wyton, flown by F/O B.D. McEwan DFC and F/O Harbottle. On 28/29 August 1944 McEwan returned from a raid on Essen with his 4,000 lb bomb still aboard. MM199 FTR from the raid on Hanover on 4/5 February 1945 when at 1948 hrs, it was hit by flak from the 8th Flak Brigade and exploded, pieces falling down over a wide area NW of Ronnenberg, 9 km SW of Hanover. F/L J.K. Wood RAAF, pilot and F/O R. Poole, navigator were killed. (via Jerry Scutts)

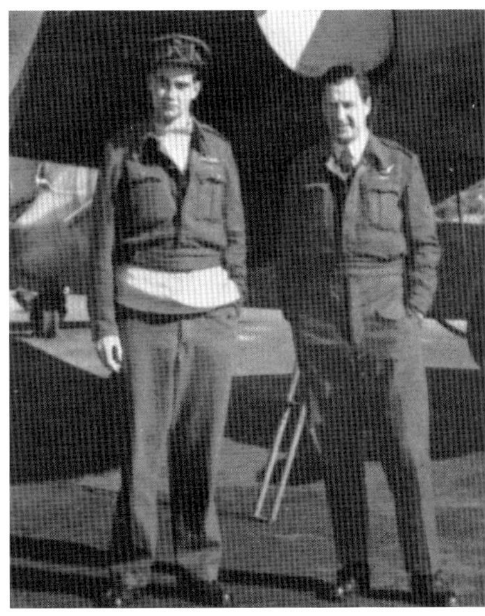

Right: Squadron Leaders Giles 'Ben' Benson DSO DFC* and Lewis Brandon DSO DFC* who shared in eight victories flying in 157 Squadron 1943-45. Benson, whose first victory with Brandon as his radar operator was in a 141 Squadron Beaufighter If on 15/16 February 1940 scored his 9th victory on Christmas Eve 1944 when he destroyed a Bf 110. Benson finished the war with ten victories, four damaged and six V-1s destroyed. (via Theo Boiten)

Right: Dozens of *Nachtjagd* crews were lost during ground interdiction sorties in the German Ardennes Offensive in the latter part of December 1944. *Uffz* Friedrich Eisenhauer of 1./NJG 2 was shot down and killed by flak while flying Ju 88G-6 4R+OH (Wrk.Nr.620575) during a ground interdiction sortie over Belgium on 27/28 December 1944 (Steve Hall via John Foreman).

Far right: *Lt* Arnold Döring (right) with *Lt* Lothar Sachs before starting Wild Boar flying from Bonn airfield with 2./JG 300 in the summer of 1943. Sachs was credited with three night kills in JG 300 and NJG 11. He survived the war. (Arnold Döring)

Below: Mosquito NFXIII HK415/KP-R of 409 Squadron RCAF at Lille airfield in November 1944. Note that the hangars in the background behind the Spitfire have been camouflaged as farm buildings. On 18/19 December 1944 F/Os Al Webster and Ross H. Finlayson destroyed a Ju 88 in this aircraft, which was lost in a take-off accident at the airfield on 18 January 1945. (Ross Finlayson)

Lancasters LS-M and LS-Q, (flown by Geoff Claydon's crew) of 15 Squadron in formation in 1944. (via M.J. Peto)

Messerschmitt Bf 110G-4 fitted with FuG 220B *Lichtenstein* SN-2b (the four antenna dipoles) and FuG 212 *Lichtenstein* C-1 *Weitwinkel* (Wide-angle) (central array in the nose). SN-2 was not affected by Window and the *Serrate* homer fitted to the Mosquitoes of 100 Group. C-1, which, with a range of only 2-km, was often used in conjunction with SN-2 because of the latter's poor resolution at close range. (via Hans-Peter Dabrowski)

Above: FuG 212 *Lichtenstein* equipped Ju 88C-6 of I./NJG 3 at Vechta airfield in early December 1944. Forward firing armament consisted of three MG 17 machine guns in the nose and three 20 mm MG FF/M cannon in a ventral gondola. Early Ju 88C-6 aircraft carried two 7.9 mm MG 17 machine guns for rear defense while late production models were armed with a single 13 mm MG 131 in a refined cockpit canopy layout. (Engelbert Hasenkamp)

Right: F/O Arthur 'Art' Whitmarsh DFC of 460 Squadron RAAF, skipper of Lancaster III ND968/O at Binbrook who on 7/8 January 1945 skilfully nursed the badly crippled *O-Oboe* back to force-land at Manston after a collision with Lancaster I NN766 of 103 Squadron whilst en route to Munich. NN766 crashed onto high ground near Hohrodberg (Haut-Rhin) with the loss of P/O W.J. McArthur RCAF and his crew. (David Fellowes)

Right: Ramsgate, 8 January 1945, the day after the crew of *O-Oboe* had a mid-air collision with Lancaster I NN766 of 103 Squadron. Back row, L-R: Sgt David Fellowes, R/G; F/Sgt Dennis Collett, navigator; F/O Arthur Whitmarsh, pilot; F/Sgt Jack Wilson, WOp. Front, L-R: Sgt Arthur Sheppard, flight engineer; Sgt Ken de la Mare, mid upper gunner; F/Sgt Jock Turnbull, bomb aimer. (David Fellowes)

Below: Lancaster III ND968/G AR-*O-Oboe*, the aircraft of the 'Whitmarsh Wonders' at the 'B' Flight dispersals at Binbrook shortly before the 7/8 January 1945 raid. (David Fellowes)

Destroying the Luftwaffe's life blood. The large oil plant at Politz, near Stettin, Poland under attack on 13/14 January 1945, taken 17,300-ft by Lancaster 'U' of 106 Squadron, flown by Lt Howes SAAF. After accurate marking from low level by seven Mosquitoes, 218 5 Group Lancasters reduced this oil plant to a shambles on an accurate bombing attack, for the loss of two Lancasters from 619 and 630 Squadron. Both these aircraft headed for Sweden in damaged condition, where the crews were interned until 10 March and 19 April respectively. (Ted Howes)

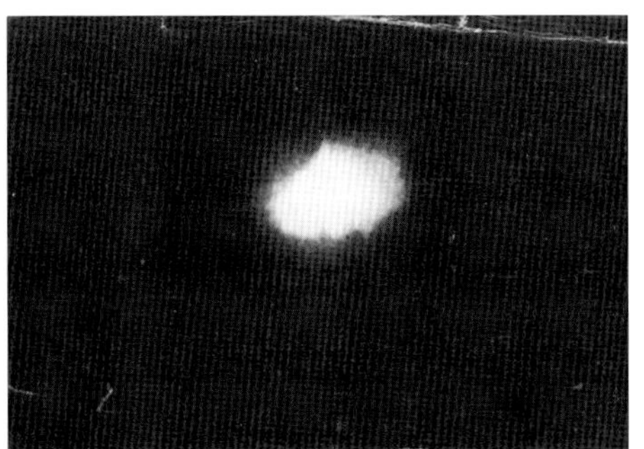

On 16/17 January 1945 F/L Kenneth D. Vaughan and F/Sgt Robert Denison MacKinnon of 85 Squadron in Mosquito NFXXX NT334/S destroyed a He 219 Owl of 2./NJG 1 flown by *Lt* Otto Fries. Fries and his *Bordfunker Fw* Alfred Staffa survived when they ejected from their doomed aircraft. On 19/20 May 1944 they were the second aircrew ever to eject under combat conditions after their He 219 suffered an in-flight engine fire. (The first to use ejection seats in combat were *Uffz* Herter and *Gefr* Perbix of 2./NJG 1, who ejected from their He 219 on 11 April 1944. They each received 1000 *Reichmarks* from Prof Dr. Heinkel.) (K.D. Vaughan via Theo Boiten)

Center right: The He 219 'Owl' like He 219V33 Werk Nr.190063 +DL used by Telefunken for equipment and antenna testing, was fast, had devastating firepower and could reach alttiudes in excess of 41,600 ft. It was also the world's first operational aircrfat to have a nosewheel undercarriage and ejection seats for the two crew. (Hans-Peter Dabrowski)

Right: Ju 88G-1 flown by *Hptm* Hans Krause of I./NJG 4 being serviced at the snow-covered Parndorf airfield in February 1945. (Hans Krause)

'J' John (right) F/O LJW Sutton & crew on route to
Langen Dreer Wanne Eickel works -Ruhr Jan 15 1945

Lancasters of 514 Squadron en route to Langen Dreer Wanne Eickel works in the Ruhr on 15 January 1945. Aircraft (right) is J-John flown by F/O L.J.W. Sutton. No aircraft were lost. (Les Sutton)

Right: Ju 88G-1 nightfighter 3C+FK, which was the regular mount of *Hptm* Hans Krause, *Kommandeur*, I./NJG 4 in early 1945. (Hans Krause/Charles F. Kern)

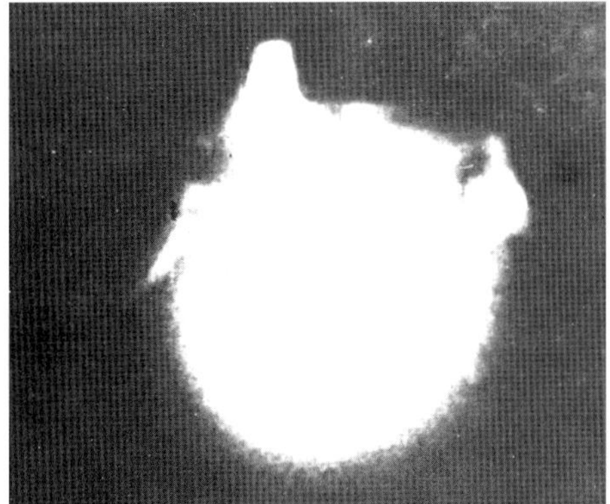

Above: The instant a Bf 110 probably 730370 2Z+EL of 3./NJG 6, flown by *Oblt* Willy Rathmann, fell victim near Stuttgart to the guns of F/L Paul Mellows who was flying Mosquito NFXXX NT252 with F/L S.L. 'Dickie' Drew as his radar operator on the night of 1/2 February 1945. The Bf 110 crashed 25 km S of Stuttgart. *Oblt* Willy Rathmann, with no victories, *Fw* Erich Berndt, *Bordfunker* and *Ogefr* Alfred Obry, *Bordschütze* were KIA. (Paul Mellows)

Right: Although this photo was specially staged and lit for the cameraman (Mosquito nightfighter crews never used tracer in their ammunition because if they did not hit their target immediately they would not want to advertise their presence and alarm their target), it nonetheless shows the formidable firepower of four Browning Mk.II .303 inch machine guns and four 20mm cannon available to Mosquito crews. (via Tom Cushing)

Above: This graphic photograph shows the damage suffered by NFXXX NT252 as a result of F/L Paul Mellows and F/L S.L. 'Dickie' Drew's combat with a Bf 110 near Stuttgart on the night of 1/2 February 1945. Mellows had opened fire at 300 ft range from slightly below with a two-second burst from which, a small explosion sent debris flying back. A second burst resulted in a very large explosion and for a few moments the Mosquito was enveloped in flame, the heat of which was felt in the cockpit. Mosquitoes were famed for their strength – NT252 operated after the war with 609 Squadron until 1948! (Paul Mellows) Right: Sgt Richard 'Ricky' Dyson, rear gunner with 189 Squadron survived a bad crash in Lancaster I PB745 whilst setting out for Munich on 26/27 November 1944 and was the only survivor of his crew when PB840 exploded in mid-air whilst on its bombing run over Karlsruhe on 2/3 February 1945. When he arrived home on 25 July 1945, he was informed that he had been awarded the George Medal for his brave actions on 26/27 November 1944 when he tried to save badly injured members of his crew from the blazing wreckage of PB745. (Ricky Dyson GM)

Above: The raid on Dresden in progress on the night of 13/14 February 1945. (IWM)

Top right: Flight Sergeant John Aldridge and his fiancée Jean in 1945. They married in 1948. (Aldridge Coll)

The destruction of Dresden photographed a short time after the city was devastated by 796 Lancasters on the night of 13/14 February 1945 and by 311 bombers of the 8th Air Force the following day. (via Geoff Liles)

Above: Lancaster I PD336 WP-P of 90 Squadron, blows up after taking a direct hit at 23,000 ft over Wesel on 19 February 1945 killing the CO, W/C P.F. Dunham DFC, F/O T. Metcalfe RCAF, F/O H.F.J. Carlton, Sgt L.A. Page, Sgt J.E. Bozeat, P/O F.A. Creswell and Sgt J.E. Bennett. PD336 came down in the Rhine near Xanten and the bodies of the crew were recovered at nearby Bislicker. Dunham had only recently taken command of 90 Squadron following the death on 2/3 February of W/C W.G. Bannister who died when his Lancaster I HK610 was involved in a mid-air collision with PD336 33 minutes after take off from Tuddenham at the start of the operation to Wiesbaden. Bannister was a pre-war athlete who had represented Great Britain in the 1936 Olympic Games in Berlin. (IWM)

Right: On 21/22 February 1944 *Ofw* Günther Bahr of 1./NJG 6 flying Bf 110 2Z+IH with *Fw* Rehmer as *Bordfunker* and *Uffz* Riediger as *Bordschütze* shot down seven Lancasters of the Worms force in quick succession 2034-2050 hrs, all on their bombing run to the target with their bomb loads still on board. Bahr survived the war having scored 35 night and two day victories in SKG 210, NJG 1, NJG 4 and NJG 6. He was also awarded the *Ritterkreuz*. (Günther Bahr)

Fw Helmut Bunje, *Flugzeugführer*, 4./NJG 6 who shot down three Lancasters on the night of 23/24 February 1945 on the Pforzheim raid. Bunje survived the war and he scored 12 *Abschüsse* in 4./NJG 6. (Helmut Bunje)

Halifax BIII NA221 came on 158 Squadron strength on 20 December 1944 and was first coded NP-A. After just one operational flight it became NP-Z for Zombie with characteristic 'grim reaper' nose art and completed another 34 operations before being heavily damaged by a *Flak* shell whilst on the bomb run at Cologne in daylight on 2 March 1945. F/L Humphrey F. Watson (center) and his crew in front of the aircraft at Lissett in early 1945 when 'Zombie' sported a bomb log of 22 operational sorties. (Don L. Simpkin)

Right: English Electric built Halifax BIII MZ717 DT-O *Rich(d)ale Express* was delivered to 'B' Flight, 192 Squadron and was used mainly by the crew of F/L G. Ward. Named after the Richdale Brewery in Sheffield where the crew stayed at the Albany (a temperance hotel) and ate and drank at the Atholl Bar. On 30 November 1944 this aircraft took off at 1819 hrs on a Feint Force mission between Mönchengladbach and Krefeld. On the outward-bound journey the starboard outer engine failed and flying speed was reduced to 110 mph. The op was aborted with the pilot knowing that if he was to lower the undercarriage, this speed would have been reduced even further, and the aircraft would have stalled, so he made a successful belly landing at RAF Manston. The aircraft was taken off squadron strength, repaired and transferred to 44 MU RAF Edzell, Scotland before being SOC and scrapped. P/O N. Irvine, pilot; F/Sgt A.C. Searle, rear gunner; P/O J.E. Nixon, navigator; Sgt L.A. Howard, flight engineer; F/Sgts J.A. Martin, WOp and S. Smith, air gunner; F/O D.E. Bankes, bomb aimer-front gunner), and F/Sgt W.J. McCullough, mid-upper gunner, escaped without injury. On 6 March 1945 this crew together with W/O Scotty Young as Special Operator flying in NR180 DT-S collided with another Halifax whilst en-route to Chemnitz. The aircraft crashed behind Russian lines near Krakow, Poland. All the crew survived but remained in Russian hands for some time. Young wrote *Descent into Danger* about his capture by the Russians. (Phil James via CONAM)

Far right: Lancaster G-H Leader, identified by the two yellow lines on its fins and rudders on daylight ops early in 1945. The G-H radar-ranging device came into use on a regular basis in 3 Group (Lancasters) from October 1944 and with Oboe and H2S proved accurate for effective blind bombing. (Ernie Reynolds)

Above: F/O Arthur 'Art' Whitmarsh DFC and crew of 460 Squadron RAAF pose on top of Lancaster I NN799 at Binbrook prior to taking off for a raid on Essen on 11 March 1945. NN799 was a temporary replacement for their original O-Oboe, ND968, which had sustained extensive damage in a mid-air collision on the night of 7/8 January 1945. ND968 was repaired and returned to F/O Whitmarsh and his crew on 4 March 1945 as AR-O and NN799 was re-designated AR-M. (David Fellowes)

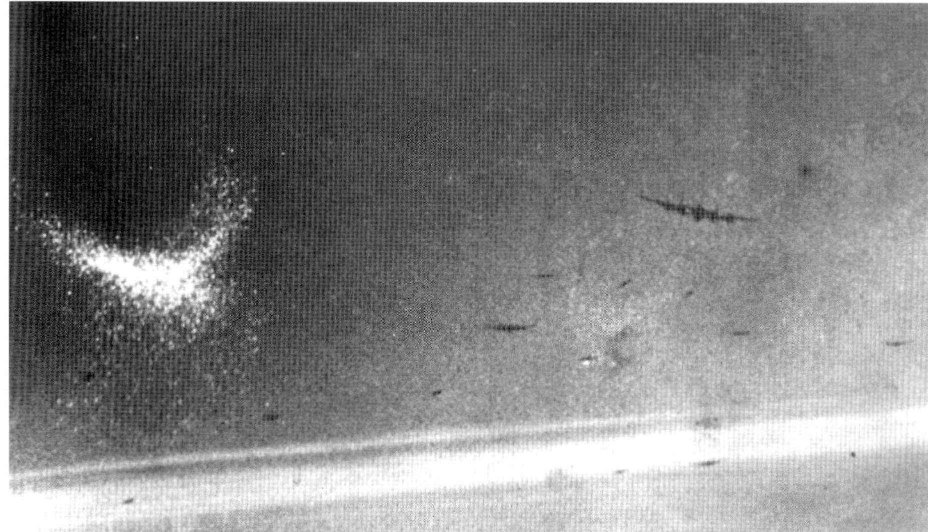

Right: Lancasters dropping 'Window' on 11 March 1945 during the greatest RAF Bomber Command daylight raid of the war when 1,079 aircraft went to Essen. Only three Lancasters were lost. (IWM)

Above: Lancaster I LM130 JO-N *Nick the Nazi Neutralizer* of 463 Squadron RAAF flown by F/O Ray Hattam at Waddington, Lincolnshire, with 48 completed operations on the bomb log represented by a satanic trident in red or yellow. On 11 March 1945 *Nick the Nazi Neutralizer* and its crew captained by P/O N.H. Orchard RAAF were lost while participating in a fighter affiliation exercise with Hurricane IIC PZ740 of 1690 Flight flown by F/O S.F. Parlato DFC RNZAF. The Lancaster crashed into The Ashholt Field at Blankney village 4 miles NE of Sleaford, Lincolnshire killing all the crew. Parlato too was killed. (Jack Hamilton)

Above: H2S equipped Lancaster I NG142 J-Jig of 514 Squadron in 3 Group flown by F/O Les Sutton taxies out at Waterbeach on 14 March 1945 for a raid on Wanna-Eickel. In all, 169 Lancasters of 3 Group made G-H attacks through cloud on benzol plants at Datteln and Hattingen, near Bochum. One Lancaster was lost from the raid on Hattingen. NG142, which had joined 514 Squadron in September 1944 went on to serve with 1668 CU and was SOC in December 1945. (Les Sutton) Below: Lancasters of 514 Squadron prepare to take off from Waterbeach on 12 March 1945 for a raid on Dortmund. At the head of the procession is K-King flown by F/O Les Sutton. This was the largest number of RAF bombers despatched to a single target in World War II and involved 1108 bombers – 748 Lancasters, 292 Halifaxes and 68 Mosquitoes – who dropped a record 4851 tons of bombs, mainly in the center and south of the city, which was left in ruins. Two Lancasters failed to return. (Les Sutton)

The first and only experimental German night-fighter unit was called 10./NJG 11 or *Kommando* Welter, which was created in December 1944 with ten Me 262B trainer versions, redesignated -1a/U1 fitted with FuG 218 *Neptun* and FuG 350 radars, four Mk 108 cannon and drop tanks under the nose. The unit was called *Kommando* Welter after its commanding officer *Oblt* Kurt Welter, supposedly one of the top scoring Wild Boar pilots during the Battle of Berlin. (Hans-Peter Dabrowski)

Above: Lancaster X KB832 WL-F of 434 'Bluenose' RCAF blows up shortly after take off from Croft on 22 March 1945 for the daylight operation to Hildesheim. F/O H. Payne RCAF took off at 1055 but the Lancaster was caught by a sudden blast of wind, which took the bomber onto the grass. Payne tried to bring the aircraft back onto the runway but he over corrected and he then closed the throttles but he was unable to avoid racing across the airfield. A tyre burst and a collision occurred involving Lancaster KB811 SE-T of 431 'Iroquois' Squadron RCAF before KB832 came to a halt near East Vince Moor farm. A fire started in the port engine and this spread rapidly. The crew managed to get clear and a general evacuation order was broadcast. At 1127 hours the bomb load exploded and the force of the blast removed the roof of the farmhouse and set fire to hay and nearby buildings. Incredibly, no one was injured but it was late afternoon before the airfield was declared fit for use. (George Kercher)

Center right: On 24/25 March 1945 two Mosquitoes were claimed destroyed by Me 262 jet fighters of 10./NJG 11 (Me 262A-1 single-seater jet of *Kommando* Welter with nose-mounted FuG 218 *Neptun* radar and four 30mm Mk.108 cannon pictured). One was claimed by *Oblt* Kurt Welter and another was credited to *Fw* Karl-Heinz Becker. (Hans-Peter Dabrowski)

On 24 March 1945 175 aircraft of 6 and 8 Groups attacked Gladbeck, a town situated on the northern edge of the Rhur and not far from the battle area for the loss of one aircraft, Halifax III MZ759 NP-Q *Wizard of Aus* of 158 Squadron, piloted by W/O E.Y. Yeoman, which took off from Lisset at 0905 hrs is seen here enveloped in flames shortly before it crashed. It is believed that all seven crew baled out but only three men survived. Yeoman, Sgt J.R. Williams, F/Sgt J. Brown and W/O W.H. Hulme RAAF were killed. F/Sgt J.E.D. Taylor, F/Sgt G.D. Lunn and F/O W.H. White were taken prisoner. The target was reported as 'devastated'. (IWM)

Flight Lieutenant R. Kemp's crew of Halifax III LV937 MH-E Expensive Babe of 51 Squadron back at Snaith from a raid on 25 March 1945 in support of the Battle of the Rhine. On this date the aircraft completed its 100th operational sortie.

Above: Pilot of a Ju 88G-1 nightfighter of 2./NJG 4 (right) with, facing aft, his *Bordfunker* (left). Note the refined canopy of the late production Ju 88C-6. A gunner manning a single 13mm MG 131 machine gun was also carried for rear defense. The aircraft also carried a forward firing armament of four long-barrelled 20mm MG 151/20 cannon in a ventral tray, the ventral gondola having been removed. The Ju 88G-1 was placed in production in the spring of 1944 and was also equipped with FuG 220 *Lichtenstein* SN-2c or 2d. (Charles F. Kern)

Mosquito BXVI ML963 *K-King*, which flew 571 Squadron's first sortie on 12/13 April 1944 to Osnabrück. Major repair work on the aircraft had recently been carried out following severe Flak damage sustained on the operation to Scholven, 6 July 1944, when it was flown by W/O Russell Longworth and P/O Ken Davidson. (ML963 had also been damaged on 12 May, on a raid on Brunsbuttelkoog, repaired on 25 May and returned to the Squadron on 26 June). ML963 returned to the squadron on 18 October 1944. On 1 January 1945 it was used by F/L N.J. Griffiths and F/O W.R. Ball in the precision raids on railway tunnels in the Eiffel region during the Battle of the Bulge. Their 4000lb delayed-action bomb totally destroyed a tunnel at Bitburg. ML963 FTR from Berlin on 10/11 April 1945 following an engine fire. The 'Cookie' was jettisoned and F/O Richard Oliver and F/Sgt L. Max Young, who baled out near the Elbe, returned safely. (Charles E. Brown)

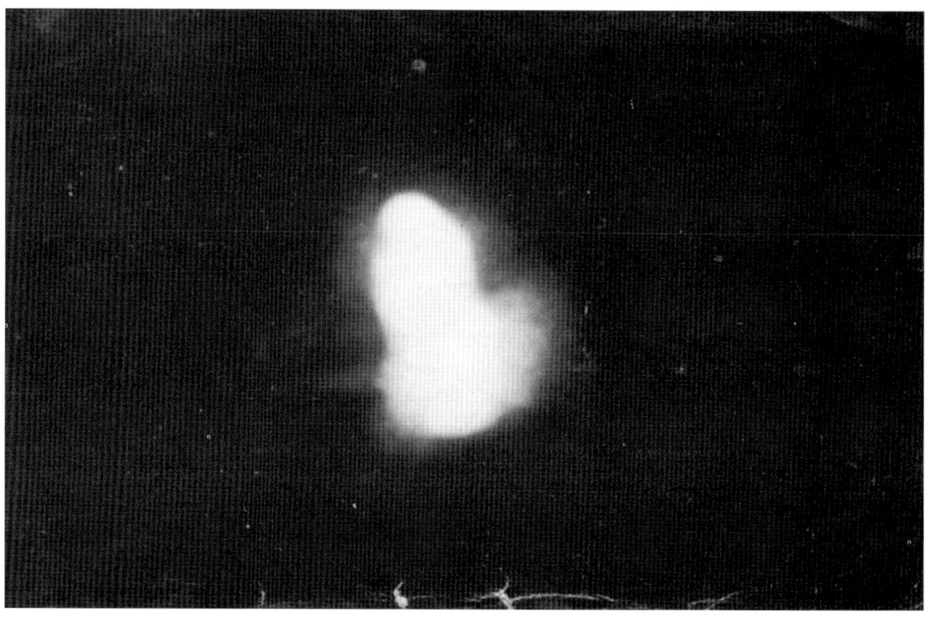

On 13/14 April 1945 F/L Kenneth D. Vaughan and F/Sgt Robert Denison MacKinnon of 85 Squadron in Mosquito NFXXX NT334/S destroyed a He 219 Uhu near Kiel. On the third occasion that Vaughan closed range to 1000 ft Vaughan thought that their twin-engined quarry had caught fire but MacKinnon got his head out of radar set and confirmed that it was the exhaust glow of his BMW 109-003 turbojet below the fuselage. Vaughan immediately pushed the Mosquito's throttles fully open before giving the Owl a half-second deflection shot on his jet at about 900-ft range. However, this burst produced no strikes, so he got dead astern in the turn and at 700 ft range fired another burst, which caused a large explosion and strikes on his starboard side. Vaughan gave him another burst 'for luck' and another explosion appeared on the port side. The Owl burned from wingtip to wing tip and went down in a spin to starboard. (K.D. Vaughan via Theo Boiten)

Mosquito NFXXX of 85 Squadron in 100 Group taxiing at RAF Swannington, Norfolk. 85 Squadron and 157 Squadrons had recommenced Intruder operations in 100 Group from Swannington in August 1944 after their brief sojourn south to West Malling in July for a month on anti-Diver patrols against V-1s. 85 Squadron began receiving NFXXXs in September 1944 and 157 Squadron, in February 1945. These squadron's last bomber support operation was flown on the night of 2/3 May 1945. 157 Squadron disbanded at Swannington on 16 August 1945 but 85 Squadron continued operating Mosquitoes in front line service until November 1951. (IWM)

For F/O Maurice Bishop (standing, center), pilot of Lancaster III PD270 *Winsome Winnie* of 218 'Gold Coast' Squadron at Chedburgh the raid on Potsdam just outside Berlin on 14/15 April by 500 Lancasters of 1 and 3 Groups and 12 Mosquitoes of 8 Group was his crew's 'most remembered'. Bishop's navigator and WOp are missing from this photo, which shows (L-R) F/Sgt Moon; Sgt Nichols, F/O Maurice Bishop, F/Sgt Smith and Sgt Brownlee with their three ground crew (kneeling). One Lancaster was lost to an unidentified nightfighter over the target. (Bishop)

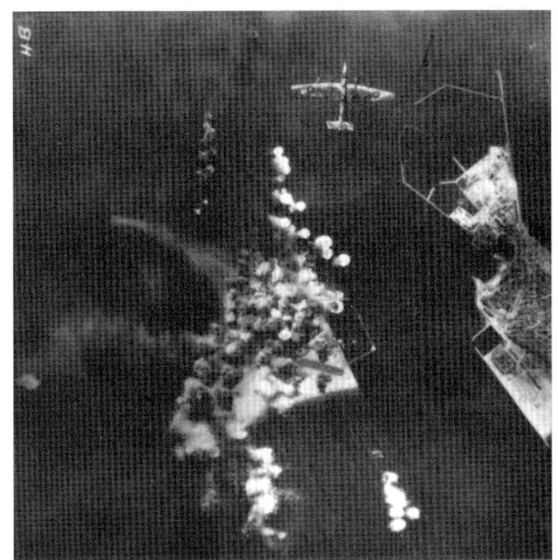

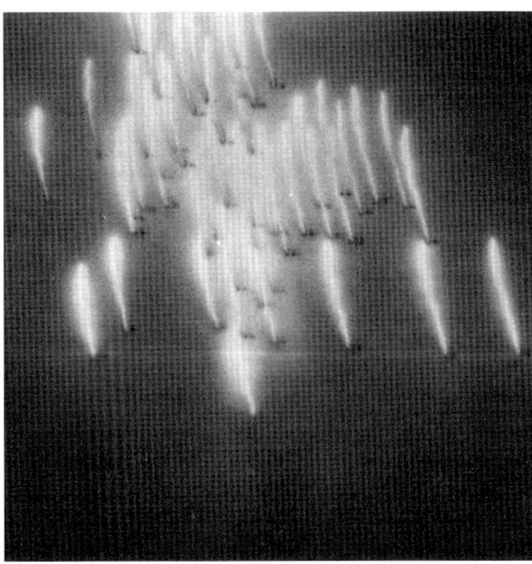

Above left: A Halifax at 17,500 ft over the airfield on the small island of Heligoland on 18 April 1945 during a daylight attack on the U-boat base, the airfield and the town by 969 aircraft – 617 Lancasters, 332 Halifaxes and 20 Mosquitoes. A total of 11,776 bombs were dropped on Heligoland between 1224 and 1325 hrs. Bombing was accurate and the target areas were turned almost into crater-pitted moonscapes. Ninety-five per cent of all the houses on Heligoland were destroyed leaving 2000 civilians homeless. Fifty German soldiers were killed and 150 injured. Three Halifaxes were lost. Between August 1944 and April 1945 one third of all Bomber Command sorties were flown in daylight, which underscored both the overwhelming allied air superiority and almost complete impotence of the Luftwaffe by this time. (Bill Harvey) Right: A TI (Target Indicator) dropped by a PFF Mosquito falling on Komotau in Czechoslovakia on 18/19 April 1945 the last major raid in a long communications offensive. In all, 114 Lancasters and nine Mosquitoes of 5 Group attacked this town (now called Chomutov). All aircraft despatched returned safely. (Bill Burke)

Above: Aerial photo of Bad Oldeslow taken at 18,600 ft during the raid on 24 April 1945 by 110 Lancasters on the town's rail yards. The town, located midway between Hamburg and Lübeck, was unprepared for air attack and precuations were described as 'slack'. Some 700 civilians were killed and 300 injured when bombs fell in areas near the rail yards. (Maurice Bishop)

Right: Destruction of Germany's rail network was almost total by April-May 1945. (Authors' Coll)

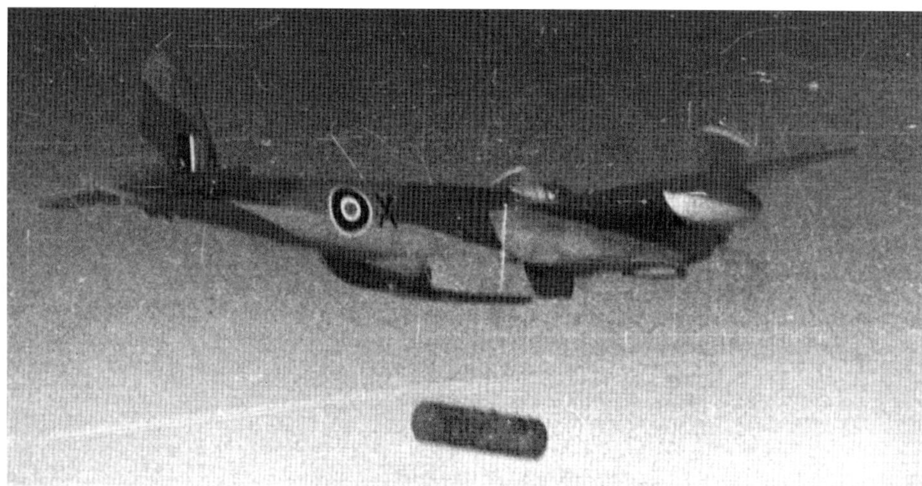

A 4000 lb bomb being released by Mosquito BXVI MM200/X of 128 Squadron. During the final months of the war, Mosquitoes of the Light Night Striking Force were the scourge of the battered German cities, especially the Reich capital. Berlin, suffered severely at the hands of 4000 lb Cookie-carrying LNSF Mosquitoes. These 'nuisance' raids culminated in a devastating series of 36 consecutive night visits against Berlin, beginning on 20/21 February 1945. Of 1896 sorties flown, only 11 Mossies failed to return from the 'Big City'. MM200 overshot landing on one engine at RAF Valley, Wales on 27 August 1945. (Graham M. Simons)

F/L Leicester G. Smith RNZAF, a Mosquito BXVI pilot in 128 Squadron at Wyton, who with his RAF navigator W/O Bill Lane completed 52 operations October 1944-April 1945. Twenty of these ops were to Berlin. (Leicester G. Smith)

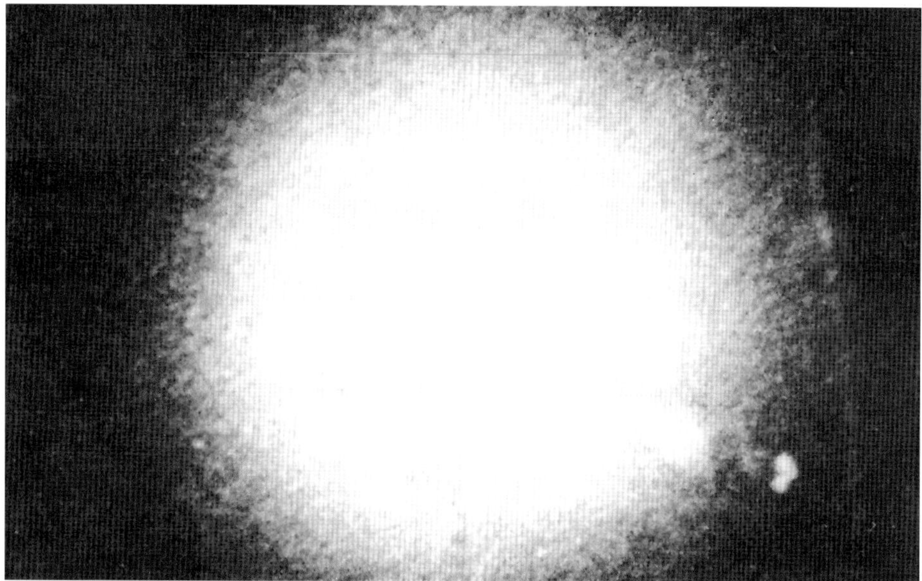

Above: Camera gun frame showing the last moments of a Dornier Do 217 shot down 6 miles N of Prague-Ruzyne, Czechoslovakia on 24/25 April by W/C Howard C. Kelsey DFC* CO 515 Squadron and F/L E.M. Smith DFC DFM in Mosquito VI RS575/C. Their victim was one of *Nachtjagd*'s most distinguished aces, *Major* Rudolf Schoenert, *Kommodore* of NJG 5, who had shot down four Russian bombers east of Berlin earlier that night, for his 62nd-65th victories. Schoenert and his crew all baled out safely. Kelsey and Smith therefore had the distinction of scoring 100 Group's first and last victories of the war. It took Kelsey's overall score to 8 destroyed, 1 probable, 2 damaged and 3 destroyed on the ground. (Tom Cushing Collection)

W/C Howard C. Kelsey DFC* drawn post war by Wren. The award of the DSO was gazetted after the war.

Opposite
Top: Ju 88G-1 C9+AS flown by *Lt* Herbert Altner of 8./NJG 5 1944-45. Altner's last successses with a Ju 88 were on 8/9 February 1945 when he shot down three aircraft over Stettin. Barely three weeks later he was posted to 10./NJG 11 or *Kommando* Welter. (Herbert Altner) Bottom: Me 262B-1a flown by *Lt* Herbert Altner of 10./NJG 11 or *Kommando* Welter 1944-45. When he first joined Kommando Welter the unit had only single-seat versions of the Me 262 and were awaiting delivery of Me 262B-1a/U1 two-seaters so much of Altner's jet fighter training, beginning 7 March 1945, was on the single-seater – after a theoretical introduction with *Oblt* Welter standing beside him on the wing! Altner performed several take-offs and landings and was so impressed that he could only confirm *General* Adolf Galland's words, 'It was as if an angel were pushing'. Altner flew his first jet nightfighter sortie, in a Me 262B-1a/U1 on 27 March 1945 but he and Reinhard Lommatzsch, his radio operator had to bale out after both engines failed when he throttled the powerplants too quickly. A restart of of the engines of a Me 262, especially at night, was impossible. Altner survived the bale out near Havelberg but Lommatzsch was killed when he struck the tail, lost consciousness and hit the ground without having opened his parachute. Flying from Lübeck on 6/7 April 1945 with Hans Fryba as his radio operator, Altner shot down a 305 'Ziemia Wielkopolska' Squadron Mosquito of 2nd TAF flown by S/L Hanbury. During the day his unit transferred their machines to the Lübeck-Hamburg autobahn near Reinfeld to avoid bombing attacks and only operated from Lübeck after dusk. Altner, whose last flight in a Me 262 was on 6 May finished the war with 24 night and 1 day victories in NJG 3, NJG 5 and NJG 11. He was awarded the *Deutsches Kreuz*. (Herbert Altner)

Herbert Altner

Leutnant Herbert Altner flog zunächst in der 5./NJG 3 und in der 8./NJG 5 die Bf 110G. Am 17. Juli 1944 erzielte er innerhalb von 33 Minuten 5 Luftsiege über britische Lancaster-Bomber. Ab August 1944 flog Herbert Altner die Ju 88G beim NJG 5. In der Nacht vom 15. März 1945 wurde er mit seiner vierköpfigen Besatzung, die sich retten konnte, von einer „Mosquito", geflogen von einem norwegischen Piloten, abgeschossen. Anschließend kam Herbert Altner zur 10./NJG 11 und flog die Me 262B-1a/U1.

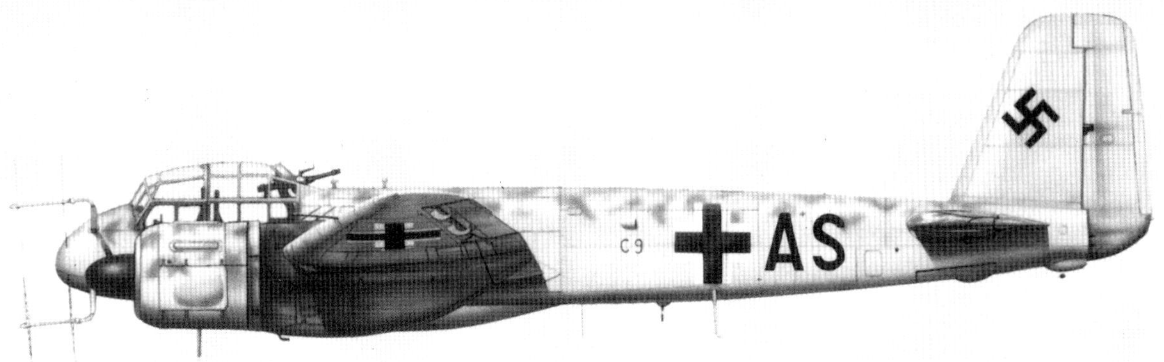

Ju 88G-1 „C9+AS", geflogen von Leutnant Herbert Altner, 8./NJG 5, März 1945

Herbert Altner

Leutnant Herbert Altner flog zunächst in der 5./NJG 3 und in der 8./NJG 5. Im März 1945 kam er zur 10./NJG 11, zum „Kommando Welter" und flog dort die Me 262B-1a/U1.

Me 262B-1a/U1 „Rote 12", geflogen von Lt. Herbert Altner im Frühjahr 1945

Above left: 239 Squadron personnel outside their crew room at West Raynham, Norfolk. L-R, at the rear, Squadron CO, W/C Walter Frame Gibb DSO DFC; u/k, Dicky Da Costa, W/O Tanner (obscured and wearing dark glasses). F/Sgt Briggs, F/L Wimbush and W/O 'Chalky' White. Front row, L-R: u/k; S/L Anthony J. Holderness; Peter Poirette and an unknown Australian. On the night of 7/8 February Holderness and F/L Walter Rowley DFC destroyed a Bf 110. On 5/6 March 1945 Gibb and F/O B.C. 'Killer' Kendall DFC destroyed two Ju 88s at Nürnburg to add to their Bf 110 and Fw 190 claims during February. (Graham 'Chalky' White) Right: Crew of the ill-fated Halifax III LV955 G-George of 192 Squadron, which crash-landed in flames at Ainlies Farm, Fulmodeston, Norfolk near the Mosquito base at Little Snoring on the night of 3/4 March 1945 after being caught with its navigation lights on by a Ju 88 night-fighter. F/O R.C. Todd, the Special operator, baled out before the second attack by the fighter. F/O E.D. 'Robbie' Roberts, pilot (front row: center) survived the crash with a fractured spine and severe burns, as did Sgt Ken Sutcliffe, who suffered burns to his body and face. W/O William Darlington, navigator, Sgt John Anderson, flight engineer and F/Sgt Reginald Holmes, air bomber, were found dead in the burnt out wreckage. After treatment at RAF Hospital, Ely and East Grinstead, Sussex where he underwent lengthy plastic surgery under the famous Sir Archibald McIndoe and thus became a member of the famous 'Guinea Pig Club', Roberts was finally discharged from the RAF in 1947. (via Bob Collis)

Lt Arnold Döring, 13 night victories and ten day victories in KG 53, KG 55, JG 300 and NJG 3. Two of his night victories were during Operation Gisela on 3/4 March 1945 when he was credited with a 'Lancaster' and a Fortress destroyed over England. His 'Lancaster' victim was actually Halifax III HX332 ZA-V of 10 Squadron flown by F/L J.G.L. Laffoley RCAF, which crashed on Spellow Hill, Staveley, 6 miles SE of Ripon, Yorkshire, returning from a raid on the Fischer-Tropsch synthetic oil plant at Kamen. Laffoley and three of his crew were killed and three others were critically injured. Döring was recommended for the Knights Cross only days before the final collapse of the Third Reich but he never received it. Twenty years later the documents were found and Döring was awarded his decoration, when this photo was taken. (Arnold Döring)

Above left: P/O H. Bennett DFC who piloted HB815/J BU-H, a 214 Squadron Fortress III, which was shot down in the circuit at Oulton by a Ju 88G possibly flown by *Lt* Arnold Döring of 10./NJG 3 based at Jever on the night of 3/4 March 1945. Bennett and seven members of his crew were KIA. (via CONAM) Right: 20-year old Sgt Leslie E. Billington, flight engineer of Fortress III HB815/J BU-H of 214 Squadron who was one of the eight crewmembers KIA in the intruder attack at Oulton on 3/4 March 1945. (via CONAM)

Right: P/O Leslie George 'Dutch' Holland of 515 Squadron at Little Snoring, Norfolk in 1944 in front of FBVI PZ459 3P-D *D-Dog*, which is equipped with AI.Mk.XV ASH (Air-Surface-H) radar. ASH was a wing mounted radar but could not be fitted to the Mosquito wing so it was installed in a 'thimble' radome in the nose instead. Holland and F/Sgt Robert 'Bob' Young, who on 15/16 April 1945 destroyed a Ju 52/3M near Schleissheim, flew 'D-Dog' almost exclusively. (Leslie Holland)

Oblt Hans Krause (2nd from right) discussing fighter tactics with his *Ofw* Otto Zinn, *Bordfunker*; *Fw* Mitschke; and *Ofw* Fritz Specht, flight engineer. Krause and his crew of Zinn, Specht and *Oblt* Hans Kretschmer took part in Operation Gisela on 3/4 March 1945 when they flew Ju 88G-6 Werk Nr.622056 3C+BC, a test aircraft. Specht was injured in a Mosquito attack over the North Sea returning from the operation. (Hans Krause)

Top right: F/L Geoff Liles' Fortress III (B-17G-60-VE 44-8336) KJ103 BU-*M-Mike* of 214 Squadron with four tail-mounted 'Yagi' transmission aerials, which from May 1944 were part of the Airborne Grocer device used to jam FuG 202 and 212 AI radar. When it became known that German nightfighters were homing in on Airborne Grocer it was replaced by AN/APT-I or Dina II, an American-development of the Mandrel IV, which when used against FuG 220 AI radar was known as Piperack. However, the 'Yagi' aerials were removed only from some aircraft and it is believed that they were used at a later date for the interim Dinah installation. (German night fighters were also able to home in on the Monica tail warning installation (the transmission aerial is hidden by the two crewmen) from up to 45 miles away and this was deleted). Behind KJ103 can be seen another BIII with plastic H2S nose radome (fitted to all 214 Squadron aircraft during June-August 1944 to aid navigation). KJ103 crash-landed at Oulton and burned out on 15 January 1945. (Geoff Liles via Murray Peden QC DFC)

Fortress III (B-17G-40-BO 42-97111) HB774 GU-G of 214 Squadron. Note the prominent Jostle transmission mast behind the radio room, H2S scanner nose radome and rear-mounted Airborne Grocer or Dina II/Piperack aerials. This Fortress was one of several flown to Great Falls, Montana in February 1944 and then Dorval, Canada for the transatlantic delivery flight to Britain for RAF service. (via Martin Staunton)

F/L Johnny Wynne, who brought Fortress III HB799/K (B-17G-40-VE 42-98029) back alone from Lützkendorf near Leipzig on the night of 14/15 March 1945, in the cockpit of another Fortress, *Take It Easy*. (CONAM)

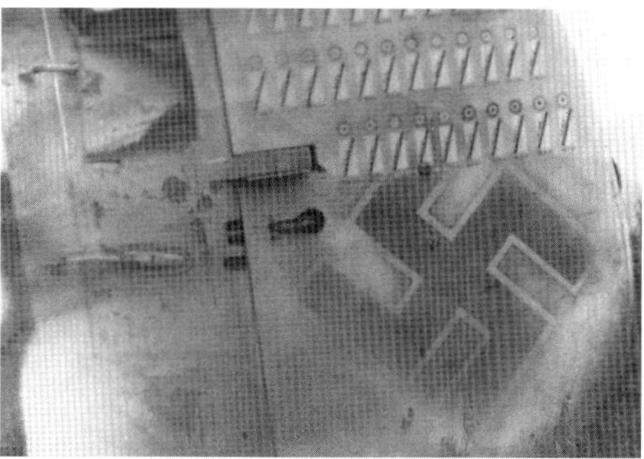

Above left: Victory tally painted on the tail of Bf 110G 2Z+MK of 2./NJG 6 flown by *Hptm* Martin 'Tino' Becker St.Kpt 2./NJG 6. In September 1944 Becker had been promoted *Hauptmann* and given command of IV./NJG 6, which flew the Bf 110G-4b/R3, which was armed with two 30mm and four 20mm forward-firing cannon and two further MK 108 cannon in a *Schräge Musik* oblique mounting. On the night of 14/15 March 1944, flying a Ju 88 this time, Becker was credited with nine bombers destroyed to take his score to 57. His final score at the end of the war was 58. (James V. Crow via Peter Petrick) Right: On the night of 14/15 March 1944 18 Lancasters were lost and 100 Group lost two Mosquitoes and a Fortress III of 214 Squadron during Jostle radio countermeasure duties in support of the Main Force. *Hptm* Martin 'Tino' Becker of Stab IV./NJG 6 and his *Funker Uffz* Karl-Ludwig Johanssen in a Ju 88G-6 claimed nine bombers, the highest score by a German night-fighter crew in any single night. Becker shot down six Lancasters before expending his last ammunition and Johanssen, manning the twin rear facing machine guns, then destroyed two Lancasters and Fortress III HB802 (B-17G-40-VE 42-98032) BU-O, piloted by F/L Norman Rix DFC. Johanssen's three victims counted towards the grand total of his pilot so the B-17 was Becker's 57th official victory. Johanssen is pictured receiving the *Ritterkreuz* two days later. (Karl-Ludwig Johanssen)

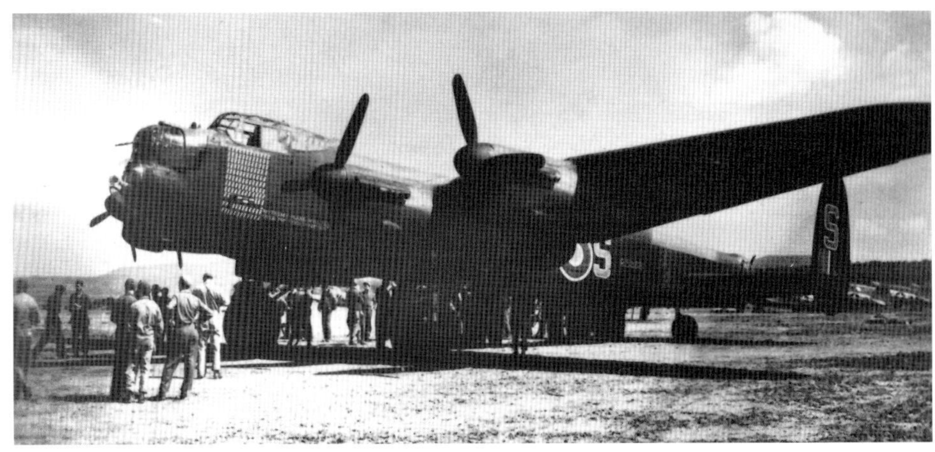

Lancaster I R5868 *S-Sugar* of 467 Squadron RAAF at Kitzingen airfield, Germany on 7 May 1945 for the repatriation of British ex-PoWs during Operation Exodus. S-Sugar flew her 100th operation a year earlier and went on to complete an official operational record of 137 ops, 68 operations with 83 Squadron as Q-Queenie at Scampton, Lincolnshire and 69 operations with 467 Squadron RAAF at Bottesford. The Göring quotation, "no enemy plane will fly over the Reich territory" was added in mid-March 1945 by LAC Willoughby. 'S-Sugar', which completed her 137th and final operational bombing sortie on 23 April 1945 to Flensburg, is now on permanent display at the RAF Museum, Hendon, London. (IWM)

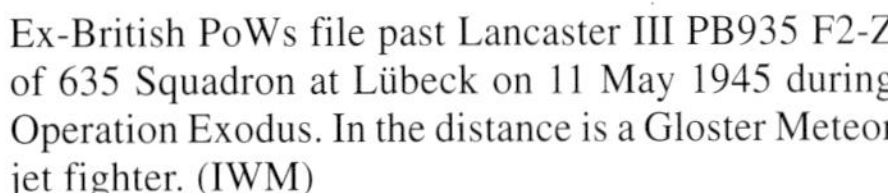

Ex-British PoWs file past Lancaster III PB935 F2-Z of 635 Squadron at Lübeck on 11 May 1945 during Operation Exodus. In the distance is a Gloster Meteor jet fighter. (IWM)

Halifax BIII PN375 FE-X of 199 Squadron (note the Mandrel airborne radar-jamming aerials under the fuselage) after take-off from North Creake for participation in Operation *Post Mortem* on 7 July 1945. This exercise proved the overwhelming success achieved by 100 Group in the final 18 months of the war. (via Jerry Scutts)

To the victor the spoils. A Me 262B/-1a/U1 night-fighter fitted with FuG 218 *Neptun* and FuG 350 radars, four Mk.108 cannon and drop tanks under the nose in RAF hands at the end of the war. (Tom Cushing Collection)

CHAPTER EIGHT

ARMAGEDDON

During January-February 1945 *Reichsverteidigung Nachtjagd* crews flew 1820 sorties, claiming 302 victories against the odds – 117 in January and 185 in February – but *Nachtjagd* lost 94 aircraft and the majority of the crews flying them. The German nightfighter arm was slowly but steadily bleeding to death. At this time Ju 88S-3s of 1./KG 66 and *Lehrgeschwader 1* were carrying out bombing and mining operations against Allied river traffic in the Scheldt estuary in an attempt to stem the flow of supplies to Antwerp. On 23/24 January LG 1 lost three Ju 88s, one of which, was claimed by a 409 'Nighthawk' Squadron crew over the mouth of the Scheldt.[1] While there is some doubt about which victim this was there is no doubt about a Ju 188E-l shot down three miles west of Dienst by the CO W/C James D. Somerville DFC and P/O A.C. Hardy.[2] *Ogfr* Heinz Hauck, who was on a clandestine mission for KG 200's *Kommando Olga* from Rhein-Main, flew this German machine. Hauck successfully dropped two agents near Gilze Rijen in the liberated part of Holland before heavy AA bursts and searchlights gave away their position to the Nighthawk crew, who were returning from patrol. '*Rejoice*', a GCI station directed the Mosquito crew towards the bogey, now six miles distant at 4000ft. Somerville reduced height and Hardy was assisted by '*Bricktile*' and '*Laundry*' GCI stations. Finally, they came upon the Ju 188E-1, which was now flying at 3000ft. Hardy had difficulty keeping their quarry out of the ground clutter on his AI.Mk.VIII scope at their height of 2500ft until finally, he got a contact at two miles. Somerville closed to 1500ft for a positive identification. Satisfied, he closed still further and opened fire with his cannons at 200ft. His first burst set fire to Hauck's port engine and the 20mm shells caused a brilliant explosion, which forced the Mosquito pilot, momentarily blinded, to break away. Somerville came in again for a second burst as Hauck desperately dived and stall turned in a vain attempt to extinguish the flames. Somerville's second burst missed but his third ripped the Ju 188's port wingtip off and the enemy aircraft dived steeply into the ground.[3]

The early months of 1945 saw a tremendous increase in Bomber Command's operations, both in tempo and number, forty raids being mounted in February alone. That same month *Nachtjagd* flew 772 sorties and claimed 181 *Abschüsse* for the loss of 47 fighters. 100 Group and 2nd TAF Mosquitoes shot down 18 German aircraft at night and probably destroyed one other. On the night of 1/2 February F/L Paul Mellows and F/L 'Dickie' Drew of 169 Squadron, attached to 'B' Flight. 85 Squadron of 100 Group, were also airborne this night on a High-Level Support patrol to Stuttgart. Mellows wrote:

> 'We arrived at our patrol point and after ten minutes proceeded in a northwesterly direction. A red star cartridge was fired some way off to the north so we proceeded to investigate. Losing height to 10,000 ft a head-on contact was obtained and after being once lost was converted to an intermittent visual on a blue light at 2000 ft range, height then being 11,000 ft. We closed on AI to 1000 ft where Dick Drew identified it as a Me 110 with the aid of night glasses. The target was climbing and weaving 30° each side of course. We closed to 200 ft to confirm and I opened fire at 300 ft from slightly below with a two-second burst from which, a small explosion sent debris flying back. A second burst resulted in a very large explosion and for a few moments the Mosquito was enveloped in flame, the heat of which was felt in the cockpit. We broke to starboard and watched enemy aircraft in the light of which a black cross and all details of the aircraft were plainly visible. I have always felt that we must have hit a partially empty drop tank because after the explosion the

Bf 110 continued to fly straight and level for some time. A further explosion occurred whilst it was going down and enemy aircraft eventually exploded on the ground at 1910 hrs. As combat had affected rudder control, the patrol was terminated.[4]

'When we got back another member of the squadron said he had seen the aircraft burning and had thought he might go and shoot at it. However, it plunged to earth before he got to it. The Sergeant in charge of the camera guns at Swannington had fixed an overrun switch to the gun button so that the camera continued to operate for several seconds after one had taken the finger off the gun button. He said that a number of frames on the film were completely exposed but he had to send them up to Fighter Command for verification and the person in charge there would not believe it and accused him of shining a torch into the camera to improve the effect. The result was that much of the film was cut out. However, we went on leave and when I came back there did not seem to be any point in remonstrating with the gentlemen of Fighter Command. We went to the BSDU where there were boffins inventing forms of radar for intercepting night fighters. We were allowed to fly when and where we wished but by March 1945 there weren't many German night fighters around and we had no more luck.'

Oblt Gottfried Hanneck of 5./NJG 1[5] returned to Bf 110 operations at Düsseldorf airfield with a new crew of *Fw* Pean, radio/radar operator and *Uffz* Glöckner, air gunner:

> 'By this time the night fighter control organization was experiencing severe problems when trying to assess the plans of the enemy, as we had lost the complete advanced defense line (Holland, Belgium and France were already occupied by the enemy). Therefore, a number of crews were ordered to fly to several night fighter beacons and wait there at the height at which the bombers were expected to fly in. I received orders to take-off at 1945 hrs,[6] proceed to a beacon in the Frankfurt area and wait for any reports of enemy aircraft movements. Thus, we were flying around in wide circles and figures of eight in the prescribed area and waited for the enemy reports. These however, did not reach us but something else did – the enemy in the shape of a Mosquito (which we were expecting because who else would have come?), which completely by surprise gave us a short burst of fire. We were hit. The intercom was put out of action and the landing light in the wing came on. I stood the aircraft on its nose to avoid a second attack and to find shelter in a layer of clouds beneath us. My crew, who couldn't contact me any more, must have assumed I was hit as I was slumped over the control column. They baled out and landed safely.
>
> 'I was now alone in the machine. I safely reached the layer of clouds and was now confronted with the question: should I bale out or attempt a crash-landing? There was no question that I should continue with my flight without any radio contact and with the light on. I decided to crash-land. I could only switch off the light by stopping both engines and glide towards the ground in an aircraft which weighed several tons. But where should I land? Fortunately, I could distinguish between the dark forest and the snow-white fields and I steered towards such a field where I let the tail unit touch the ground first (to avoid nosing over) and then with retracted undercarriage, slid over he ground on the motor gondolas. I had come down two kilometers west of Kettenhausen in the Westerwald. The time was 2110 hrs. My face slightly hit the gun sights but I was able to scramble out of my seat and withdraw from the machine through the snow and shouted for help. A farmer 'collected' me on his horse-drawn sleigh and took me to the nearest Army post. There I received first aid and large quantities of Cognac as a remedy for the shock and pain. Then I was transported to the nearest hospital, which was at Wissen on the Sieg.'[7]

On 2/3 February Bomber Command mounted raids on Mannheim, Wanne Eickel, Wiesbaden and Karlsruhe by 1200 aircraft, about 250 being ordered to raid Karlsruhe. Due to adverse weather conditions and extensive Luftwaffe night fighter activity near and over the targets operations were only partially successful. Twenty-one aircraft failed to return, including 11 from the Karlsruhe force and another 13 crashed in liberated French territory.[8] It was a bad night for 189 Squadron with four aircraft failing to return to Fulbeck, as air gunner Sgt Ricky Dyson, who on the night of 26/27 November 1944 had suffered such a tragic flying accident, recalls:

> 'My last memories of Ned Kelly and the boys were at briefing and at the dispersal area before take-off. As fate was to ordain, Frank Cowlishaw, our mid-upper gunner was on the sick list and Frank Fox was destined to fly in his place (the Fortunes of War?). We were timed to take off about 2000 hrs and arrive over the target at 2320 hrs so we had quite a long night ahead of us. We were all in high spirits, laughing and joking with other aircrew and among ourselves. We all must have had our own form of anxiety before a raid – the tenseness and butterflies in the tummy were common to us all I think. Once inside the aeroplane however, this nauseating excitement

disappeared, as one became occupied with one's tasks and checks etc. The outward leg was uneventful. I tested my guns over the Channel as usual and received confirmation from Frank Fox that he too had done the same ('chat' over the intercom was kept to a minimum and was mostly of a technical nature). The weather was cold and clear when we joined the main bomber stream but over France we did encounter icing-up conditions and an electrical storm, with cloud formations thickening from above. When we reached Germany we were flying at 17,000 to 18,000 ft. To our dismay on reaching Karlsruhe we encountered solid cloud beneath us at about 16,000 ft obscuring the target. To make matters worse we became 'sandwiched' since the cloud above had thinned considerably, allowing the moon to shine through. These conditions certainly assisted the enemy night fighters and greatly added to the difficulties of the bomber force.

'We were on time as we neared the target area but owing to the weather conditions we had to bomb on the colored sky markers, which together with chandelier flares glowed through the cloud. These had been dropped by the Pathfinder Force giving a diffused illumination to the whole target area. Whether we dropped our bombs or not I wasn't sure because there was a blinding flash and a terrific explosion and what happened just before was a bit of a blur! The whole of my body seemed to be propelled upwards and yet at the same time my head and neck felt as though they were being forced down below my shoulders and into my stomach. Then I must have passed out! The next thing I remembered was somersaulting earthwards in mid-air. I had been blown out by the force of the explosion with my rear turret being blown to pieces around me! (Yet another miracle it seemed!) My six friends and companions all died in that tragic moment in time as Lancaster PB840/K plunged earthwards in a ball of flame. I doubt whether the exact cause of the explosion will ever be known. We either fell victim to an enemy night fighter, or, as I believe, we may have collided with another Lancaster, which could have been taking avoiding action away from fighters or searchlights. This was not uncommon and was rated a calculated risk as the bomber stream narrowed at varying heights to converge on the Aiming Points. Tragically, whatever the cause the terrible result remains the same.

'To return to my sudden and dramatic departure from the rear turret. The realisation that I was still alive came as a great relief but, as I recovered my senses, I was also aware, with a feeling of deep anxiety, all was not yet over, since I was still somersaulting and falling towards the ground! In a fearful panic I reached for my parachute pack, which thankfully was still there and dangling behind me (it was a seat type pack that was a normal issue to pilots and also to rear gunners). I felt for the D-ring release on my harness and pulled until the ring and wire attachment came free in my hand. I prayed that the pack itself was not burnt or damaged in some way and for an awful moment I thought that it wasn't going to open! Then I felt a terrific jerk. I looked up and with great relief saw the huge canopy filling with air. My brain was by now quite clear and I was soon in an upright position with my hands grasping the parachute guide lines with which I was able to steer. The full horror of what had happened now came over me, as I saw what appeared to be a huge box-like inferno falling like a stone in the dark part of the sky. I could see bits and pieces falling from it, burning and aflame as they fell. With horror I realized that I was witnessing the death of some, if not all of my friends with whom I had been joking with a few hours before. Their average age was only 22-years and like so many were so young to die during those terrible years of war.

'As the exploding and flaming mass disappeared into the cloud below the despair for my friends turned to thoughts of my own self-preservation, as I realized I was being blown back to the target area. I quickly pulled on the chute guide lines, praying I would be able to avoid being caught in the many searchlights with their beams weaving menacingly about the sky. However, I was soon out of range and gazed, fascinated, at the sight below and to my left. Karlsruhe it seemed was alight from stem to stern. It was like looking down on a carpet of gold with the chandelier flares suspended above illuminating rivers of red from bursting incendiaries. The green sky markers winked intermittently with yellow and black smoke billowing skywards. Streams of multi-colored tracer shells were bursting from the anti-aircraft guns and there was a series of explosions as sticks of high explosive bombs burst, sending red and yellow flames high into the air. It was an awsome spectacle of great beauty, which I had seen many times before from the rear turret of a Lancaster bomber on its return leg to England!

'Whilst watching this terrible and beautiful scene, my attention was drawn to my feet. They were freezing cold! I looked down to discover I had neither boots nor socks (they had, I think, been sucked off by the blast as K-King exploded). Thoughts now crowded in on me and with apprehension I wondered whether I had any injuries? Was my face burnt? Were my legs and feet OK? I felt and tasted blood but as I felt around my eyes, nose, ears ec. all seemed OK. I entered broken cloud and was more conscious of my rate of descent and the exhilarating sensation, as I swayed and floated at the end of a parachute. Through the gap in the cloud I glimpsd woods and snow-covered fields and the target area was now a diffused red glow. I pulled on the parachute guide lines and steered myself away from the woods and prayed that when the time came I would make a safe landing. I could faintly see what I thought to be a cluster of buildings and steered to avoid them also. I was just beginning to enjoy myself when I realized that the fields were getting a lot closer. Then suddenly, without warning, the ground seemed to rush up to meet me and I landed with a bump in a snow covered field. Directly my feet touched the ground, I tried to relax, allowing my legs and body to glimp as I rolled over. I was dragged a short distance across the field as the parachute canopy collapsed. On recovering my breath, I remembered the release button on my harness. I banged it hard and the harness fell away. I had landed safely with no bones broken!

'As quickly as I could I gathered up the parachute canopy and stumbled to a wooded spiney nearby. After tearing up some of the silk to bind my feet, which were bruised and freezing from the cold, I buried the remainder beneath a pile of leaves and then tried to take stock of the situation. My wristwatch was missing but I estimated the time to be about 0100 hrs. I felt scared, cold and miserable, very much alone and I wondered again about the fate of the rest of the crew. I thanked God for my own survival. My only injuries were slight burns to my hands and face, a few cuts and bruises, very cold feet and scorched hair. As I realized how lucky I had been I became aware that the yellow flying suit I was wearing was conspicuous so reluctantly, I took it off and hid it beneath another pile of leaves. I thought about escaping and checking I still had my escape pack containing a compass, silk map, chocolate and foreign money etc, I wondered how far I was from the French border. Without my flying suit I was feeling the cold and became increasingly concerned regarding the state of my feet and the danger of frostbite. I thought that the best thing was to go in search of some boots or socks while it was still dark. Rightly or wrongly, I left the comparative shelter of the wooded spiney, with the hope of finding some in a barn or a shed. However, by this time I must have been suffering from delayed shock. I wandered across a field, ankle and sometimes knee deep in mud, hearing dogs barking and whistles blowing in the distance. I guessed they were search parties out looking for survivors. I must have wandered about for some time, as it was beginning to get light when I came across a shed in a farmyard. While I was searching for footwear I so urgently needed, the door burst open and I was confronted by a uniformed German soldier. And so it was; with his rifle and bayonet pointed at me, I reluctantly became his prisoner.'[9]

On 7/8 February 239 Squadron Mosquito crews were prominent. This night Main Force targets included strong German defense positions at Goch and Kleve, which had to be smashed before an attack by the British XXX Corps across the German frontier near the Reichswald. The Dortmund-Ems Canal was also targeted and Mosquito bombers carried out raids on Magdeburg, Mainz and five other targets. F/L D.A.D. Cather DFM and F/Sgt L.J.S. Spicer BEM of 239 Squadron shot down a Bf 110G-4 in the Ruhr.[10] F/L Anthony J. Holderness and F/L Walter Rowley DFC also returned triumphant to West Raynham as Holderness reported:

> 'We carried out the first part of our patrol at Zandvoort quite uneventfully before and while the targets, Kleve and Hussum were being bombed. Towards the end of the bombing we moved closer in to the targets and were doing a short 'square search' patrol when, at 2200 hrs 13,000 ft, we got a contact at 2240 hrs at about six miles range and heading towards the targets. It was only slightly above but difficult to close, as it was taking what appeared to be precautionary evasive action, diving and climbing through a series of steep turns. Throughout this part of the chase our altimeter was reading anything from 11,000 to 15,000 ft. Several times I caught sight of the exhausts glow but was unable against the starlit sky to hold them for-more than a few seconds at a time. After about ten minutes of this, when we had closed to 1000 ft we suddenly found ourselves overshooting very fast and some way above and had to turn 60° to port, then back onto our original course to recover the blip. This time the contact was headed away from the target, flying on an easterly course and at a height of about 12,000-ft. The pilot must have thought either that there was no longer any need to evade, or that he had shaken us off because he was flying straight and level. We closed in fairly fast and from only about 200 ft below and behind identified as Me 110. I dropped back to about 250 yards and opened fire. Quite a lot of debris flew back past us and the port engine immediately caught fire. Then the nose came up and he went into steep climb, which I tried to follow, still firing. Although I throttled right back we were – rapidly overtaking him and had to pull away quickly to starboard. Just then he seemed to stall and flick over to port. I turned as slightly as our low airspeed would allow and saw him diving very steeply with the port engine now a mass of flame. My navigator could still see burning pieces coming off when he went into the cloud. Almost

simultaneously there was a terrific white flash which lit up the clouds. We followed through about 3000 ft of cloud to come out at 4000 ft on the altimeter and there it was, burning immediately beneath us and only about a mile from a white beacon flashing the letters 'L F.'[11]

On 8/9 February Bomber Command returned to attacks on synthetic oil plants when Pölitz was bombed by 475 Lancasters and seven Mosquitoes.[12] Wanne-Eickel and Krefeld were also attacked. There followed a series of minor operations involving Mosquito bombers mainly while the Main Force was grounded, 9-12/13 February. Bomber Command though was merely building up for an operation that has since gone down in history as one of the most controversial bombing raids of the war. For most of the participating aircrew the Dresden raid of 13/14 February was another well executed and very efficient area bombing attack. Dresden was targeted as part of a series of particualy heavy raids on German cities in Operation Thunderclap with a view to causing as much destruction, confusion and mayhem as possible.[13] The campaign was to have started with an American raid on Dresden on 13 February but bad weather over Europe prevented any U.S. involvement until the 14th. Dresden was to be bombed in two RAF assaults three hours apart, the first by 244 Lancasters of 5 Group and the second by 529 Lancasters of 1, 3, 6 and 8 Groups. F/Sgt John Aldridge of 49 Squadron who flew 33 operations as a Lancaster bomb aimer September 1944-April 1945 and who took part in the 5 Group bombing of Dresden, recalls:

'The plan of attack was as follows: 5 Group was to attack at 2215 hrs on 13 February, using its own pathfinder technique to mark the target. This was a combination of two Lancaster Squadrons; 83 and 97, to illuminate the target and one Mosquito Squadron (627) to visually mark the aiming point with Target Indicators from low level. The aiming-point was to be a sports stadium in the center of the city situated near the lines of railway and river which would serve as a pointer to the Stadium for the Marker Force, especially since it was anticipated that visibility might not be too good. At 2213 hrs 244 Lancasters, controlled throughout by the Master Bomber, commenced the attack and it was completed by 2231 hrs. A second attack was timed for 0130 hrs on the 14th by another 529 aircraft of Bomber Command.[14] Calculations were that a delay of three hours would allow the fires to get a grip on the sector (provided the first attack was successful) and fire brigades from other cities would concentrate fighting the fires. In this second attack target marking was to be carried out by 8 Pathfinder Group.

'By the time of this attack cloud cover had cleared to 3 to 7/10ths but despite this the Master Bomber could not identify the aiming point due to the huge conflagrations and smoke and a decision was made to concentrate bombing on areas not affected. An area was marked by the Pathfinders both to the left and to the right to assist in concentrating the bombing and good concentration was achieved. So great were the conflagrations caused by the firestorms created in the great heat generated in the first attack that crews in the second attack reported the glow was visible 200 miles from the target. To assist the night operations of Bomber Command various 'spoof' attacks were made by Mosquitoes on Dortmund, Magdeburg and Hanover and 344 Halifaxes attacked an oil plant at Böhlen near Leipzig at the same time as the first attack. In addition to the above the routing and. feints carried out by the Main Forces involved caused night fighter reaction to be minimal. In the case of the 5 Group attack our outward route consisted of no less than eight legs with feints towards the Ruhr, Kassel, Magdeburg and Berlin using *Window* at the same time. An indication of the effectiveness of these operations was that out of over 1000 aircraft taking part only six were lost.'

F/Sgt Ray Base of 115 Squadron at Witchford, flight engineer on Lancaster I NG205 captained by Major Martin DFC SAAF was on his twentieth operation:

'We took off at 2145, taking G/C Reynolds as an observer. Bomb load consisted of one 4000 lb 'Cookie' and seven incendiary clusters, making a total of 7820 lb, plus 2114 gallons of fuel to make the deep penetration raid and back. It was a very clear night with good visibility apart from the odd small cloud. We flew right down France, along by Stuttgart, up to within 50 miles of Berlin and then on to Dresden. The attack was on the old part of the city which was covered in snow. We arrived over the city about three-quarters through the raid, so things were well alight by then. The marking TIs (target indicators) were mostly red and green and showed up clearly among the fires. It was a very good attack, with the whole city burning, the streets being outlined in fire. Of the fires themselves the burning buildings were very bright and around the outskirts were large dull red glows from the region of the railway station, gasworks and other industrial buildings. We experienced moderate *Flak* over the target. As we left the target and turned on course for home we saw a Lancaster about 1000 ft below silhouetted by the glow of the fires. I could see the Lanc's exhausts. Our mid-upper gunner then spotted a Ju 88 following the Lanc and then we saw a Ju 188 (clearly identified by its pointed wings) to the left and behind the Ju 88. There was a small cloud below and the three aircraft went into it and the cloud lit up with a large explosion typical of a bomber blowing up. There were lots of searchlights over the Ruhr on our way back and very strong headwinds restricted our ground speed to 80 mph. We went down to 5000 ft over France to get more favourable winds. We got back with five minutes fuel left – we drained all our tanks while in the circuit and all four fuel warning lights came on as we landed at 0650 hrs. Flight time was 9.05 hrs.'[15]

In a firestorm similar to that created in Hamburg on 27/28 July 1943, an estimated 50,000 Germans died in Dresden. *Oberleutnant* Wilhelm "Wim" Johnen, *Staffelkapitän*, 5/NJG 1, described the horrors of Dresden[16]:

'... the bomber formations appeared over the city and enveloped it in a single sea of flames by dropping phosphorus bombs. Hundreds remained stuck in the melting asphalt and were burnt alive like flaming torches. Hundreds jumped with their clothes on fire into the icy waters of the Elbe or into the 9ft deep water basins from which they could not clamber out. Those who could swim were dragged down into the depths by non-swimmers. The Exhibition grounds in the Dresden gardens were filled with refugees who had taken cover there when the sirens wailed. But even the lawns with their centuries old trees were sprayed with bombs and phosphorus canisters until a forest fire was raging. The burning city was again subjected at 2 o'clock in the morning with a second carpet of bombs, which transformed the center of the city into a ruined wilderness. The casualties that night are estimated at over 100,000. Most of the bodies could no longer be identified. The human remains were placed on huge steel platforms, sprinkled with petrol and burnt in the open air.'

As tons of explosives plummeted from the sky, an 800°C firestorm tore through the heart of the Saxon capital, burning thousands of Dresdeners alive. In a firestorm similar to that created in Hamburg on 27/28 July 1943, an estimated 25,000 to 40,000 Germans died in Dresden. Bill Gough was a British PoW in a camp near Dresden having been captured in the Western Desert in June 1942 by the *Afrikakorps* and he endured the bombing and its after effects:

'13th and 14th February gave all of us in the camp an experience almost impossible to describe. On the night of 13 February we were all in our bunks after lights out when the sound of' planes approaching and flying over became so loud it was as if the planes were just above the rooftops. The thump of the bombs was frightening and I am sure we all expected our camp to be struck at any moment. The relief was immense when all was quiet again. The following morning 14 February, instead of small gangs being sent under guard to various work locations, we, the whole camp were marched into Dresden. The situation was chaotic. Civilians who had survived were fleeing the city and every street we could see was just a smouldering ruin. The intention was that we would assist the SS and civilian railway men to repair damage sustained to the tracks outside the main station. We refused and stood around doing nothing, whilst the Germans were trying to do the impossible. The whole situation was unbelievable. Germans were frantically removing rails with sleepers still attached pointing vertically from gaping holes. The total area was cratered and littered with burnt out rolling stock including steam engines in the skeleton of workshops. We stood in the center of this carnage and confusion like bewildered schoolboys doing nothing. I suppose we were fortunate that no one reacted against us or attempted to force us to take part in the clear up operation. Then the U.S. air force arrived in formation. We did not wait to welcome them, just ran for shelter which we found in the boltholes built into the walls of a brick railway cutting. This saved us. A bomb dropped on our side of the cutting about 20 yards away. The blast ripped past and two of our lads were cut with shrapnel. Following this we were moved to an army barracks about ten miles from Dresden. Here we suffered more machine gun assaults from the U.S. Air Force and two of our party were killed. Enough is enough I thought, the Russians were getting ever closer from the east, so I took off with a friend who could converse in German. We eventually met the Americans who flew us from Leipzig to Reims and the greatest honor for me was flying home in the rear gunner's seat of a Lancaster bomber.'

In the sky above Germany F/L Donald R. 'Podge' Howard DFC and F/O F.A. 'Sticky' Clay DFC of BSDU[17] were airborne from Swanton Morley, Norfolk in their Mosquito NFXIX. Their patrol of beacons, *Kolibri, Ida, Elster, Nachtigall* and *Otto* with AI.Mk.X and *Serrate IV* proved very rewarding, as Howard reported:

'At *Ida* a visual was obtained on an aircraft at 1000 ft and at 600 ft was recognized as a Me 110. A short burst was fired but no strikes were seen. I increased deflection and fired another burst, which caused strikes all over starboard engine, wing root and starboard side of cockpit.

A fire started in starboard wing root and the Me 110 turned over to port burning well and dived straight down and entered cloud. Shortly after there was a vivid white explosion on the ground at 2033 hours. Two minutes after another Mark X contact appeared crossing starboard to port and above range 12,000. We turned after it and range closed fast. A visual was obtained on an aircraft at 1000 ft and at 600 ft this was identified as another Me 110 in a port turn. I opened fire at 600 ft and missed and the Hun promptly rolled into a starboard bank during which he presented no deflection and he received a one-second burst, which caused strikes on the cockpit fuselage and port wing root. He then dived away to starboard and we gave him another burst, which set his port engine on fire and caused bits to fly off. He dived vertically into cloud, burning very well. We had to pull up and out of our dive and we didn't see it hit the deck but he was well on fire. At 2040 hrs at 5000 ft we obtained yet another Mark X contact almost at once. Although we chased him in an easterly direction for about 20 minutes at full bore we could not overtake him so we decided he was very fortunate and returned to our patrol area and came back to base via *Kolibri* and West Kappelle.'[18]

Winston Churchill later tried to distance himself from Dresden and declared that:

'The destruction of Dresden remains a serious query against the conduct of Allied bombing.'

This was the same Winston S. Churchill who on 22 June 1941 had said:

'We shall bomb Germany by day as well as night in ever-increasing measure, casting upon them month by month a heavier discharge of bombs and making the German people taste and gulp each month a sharper dose of the miseries they have showered upon mankind.'

Sgt Frank W. Tasker a Lancaster mid upper gunner in 622 Squadron says:

'The most successful of our nightly operational flights and the ones that I remember so well were those on Dresden and Chemnitz. Since World War II some Germans have complained about those raids having taken place. Have they conveniently forgotten, how for the first TWO YEARS of the war, the Luftwaffe was bombing London (where I lived) and elsewhere in UK day and night! Have they also forgotten the V-1 flying bombs and V-2 rockets they were still indiscriminately sending to kill innocent women and children in England? Surely they haven't also forgotten about the gas chambers they used!'

F/Sgt John Aldridge concludes:

'Much has been written about the tragedy of Dresden. Probably the primary factor (and here I may be prejudiced!) was the highly successful first attack by 5 Group which resulted in an almost perfect 'sector' attack. Also the great strength of the wind helped create the firestorm conditions and spread the conflagrations. At my own bombing height of 13,000 ft the wind speed was 70-75 knots. An interesting point here is that on the very next night Chemnitz was to be the target of a similar attack, 330 aircraft to make the first and 390 the second attack three hours later. In this case Harris at Bomber Command (probably under pressure from Bennett of the Pathfinder Group) decided that 8 Group's Pathfinders would carry out the marking for both attacks and we in 5 Group would carry out a separate attack on an oil plant at Rositz near Leipzig. However, with cloud cover and with 5 Group low level marking, 8 Group had to rely on sky marking and no concentration of bombing was achieved. I saw personal evidence of this as our (5 Group) withdrawal route linked up with the force returning from Chemnitz and I well remember the fires were scattered over 20 miles. Would Chemnitz have been a second Dresden if the same procedure as in that attack had been carried out? Afterwards, when I read criticism of the bombing, I did wonder what I'd been a part of but at the time it was just a job we had to do. We knew the time on target was between 10 and 10.30 pm and joked that we'd catch the Germans just as they were coming out of the pubs. In hindsight I don't feel good about that but for the most part, we didn't think in terms of people being killed but of areas we had to hit. That was how things were in 1945.'

On 14/15 February Bomber Command attacked Chemnitz and an oil refinery at Rositz near Leipzig. P/O Leslie George 'Dutch' Holland and his navigator F/Sgt Robert 'Bob' Young[19] of 515 Squadron, returning from a *Night Intruder* patrol in Mosquito FBVI '*D-Dog*' to Hailfingen airfield in the area east of Stuttgart had a low-level encounter with a He 219. Returning from a *Night Intruder* patrol in Mosquito FBVI '*D-Dog*' to Hailfingen airfield in the area east of Stuttgart they had a low-level encounter with a He 219 as Holland recalls:

'After we had mooched around the vicinity of the airfield for the best part of an hour Bob announced that he thought there was something on the *Monica.* A port turn caused an increase in range whereupon I immediately opened the taps and made the turn as steep as possible. The blip disappeared so we started a starboard turn to make a sweep. A head-on contact came up on the ASH at about two miles closing fast. As he appeared to be on a parallel course slightly right we went straight into a hard right turn. The bogey must have done exactly the same because he failed to appear on our screen after the turn. I reversed course again and had another go. Sure enough, another head-on. Port turn this time and we lost him again. Suddenly, Bob yelled into the intercom, 'He's coming in from.'

'*WHOOSH* and a Heinkel 219 flashed by under our nose about 20 ft away – the radar operator clearly visible in the after part of the canopy. There was no time to depress the nose and have a squirt, not even to get the ginger on the button. And he was in a 600 bank to his right going to my left so he probably had *Lichtenstein* radar with all-round performance superior to our miserable little ASH. Our only course was to try and outguess him and at the same time bear in mind that we have now been making inroads at full throttle into our get-home fuel. We made a sweep and tried to make a bit of westing but a break in the clouds revealed that the North Star was to port. I had been steering by the directional gyrocompass and it had spun in the tight turns. A quick look at the compass which had just about settled down confirmed the 'astro' observation and we were actually working our way deeper into enemy territory. Obviously our adversary had been expecting us to do exactly as we had intended so we must have ended up going in opposite directions at a separating speed of something over 500 mph. We never saw each other again, which may be just as well considering the performance of his mount and the great superiority of his radar.'[20]

On the night of 20/21 February 514 Lancasters and 14 Mosquitoes of 1, 3, 6 and 8 Groups set out for Dortmund, another 173 bombers raided Düsseldorf, 128 aircraft attacked Monheim and 154 Lancasters and 11 Mosquitoes attacked the Mittelland Canal.[21] Twenty-two aircraft FTR.[22] Worst hit was the Dortmund force, which lost 14 Lancasters. These raids were followed on the night of 21/22 February by 1110 sorties against Duisburg, Worms and the Mittelland Canal and another 27 aircraft were lost plus seven Lancasters crashed in France and Holland. During the course of the operations on 21/22 February *Nachtjäger* claimed 55 heavy bomber kills (an overclaiming by at least 21 aircraft, 34 Bomber Command Lancaster and Halifaxes were actually lost). The two consecutive nights, 20/21 and 21/22 February proved a profitable 24 hours for several German pilots. *Hptm* Adolf Breves of IV./NJG 1 took off from Düsseldorf airfield at 0213 hrs on 21 February in his Bf 110 and claimed three aircraft in the Ruhr area to take his score to 16. Another Bf 110 pilot, *Hptm* Johannes Hager, *Staffelkapitän*, 6./NJG 1 claimed two *Viermots. Major* Heinz-Wolfgang Schnaufer, *Kommodore,* NJG 4 took off from Gütersloh at 0105 hrs in Bf 110C G9+MD. Employing *Schräge Musik* attacks delivered below the bombers in an *Einsatz* (sortie) lasting two hours nine minutes he shot down two Lancasters at 0153 and 0158 hrs about 11,000 ft[23] to take his score to 109.

Bordfunker Uffz Walter Schneider who contributed to the last 13 of Hager's victories recalls:

'On 21 February we took off at 0024 hrs. I soon spotted a *Viermot*, which our pilot shot down after a short chase at 0112 hrs. On the outbound flight from Düsseldorf I managed to get hold of another one on my radar and this one was made to crash at 0123 hrs.[24] Later the same day, at 2248 hrs we again received orders to take off. This time we had to fly in the direction of Duisburg. Soon we encountered the formation of bombers and we succeeded in shooting down six *Viermots* between 2309 and 2321 hrs. By skilful use of the oblique cannon, my pilot was able to set the bombers on fire with short bursts into the engines. The crews thus had more time to safely bale out. After this exploit I was commissioned.'[25]

After shooting down the two Lancasters over Dortmund and returning to Gütersloh Schnaufer and his crew had a rest period until a *Werkstattflug* (air-test) was called at 1815 hrs for Bf 110 G9+EF. The flight lasted 21 minutes and the Messerschmitt was declared 'serviceable.' *Lt* Fritz Rumpelhardt, Schnaufer's radar operator, recalls:

'The late night sortie on 21 February 1945 was to become Schnaufer's most outstanding achievement in two-and-a-half years' service as a nightfighter pilot. It was always a point of honor with him to be the first in the air after the order to scramble so that he could assess the situation and brief his squadron. Chance played quite an important part in the second operational sortie on 21 February. I was alone in the squadron mess having my supper, having missed the order 'Heightened Preparedness,' so when the order to scramble came the *Major* was ready but I was not. He did not mince his words about my apparent dilatoriness. In spite of the ensuing mad rush, the rest of the squadron was already airborne, on its way to Düsseldorf. By the time 'EF' lifted off from the aerodrome it was 2008 hrs. Events now turned in-our favour. Following the instructions received from Ground Control we believed that the others had reached the engagement area but we were somewhat puzzled when we could see neither bombers, nor night-fighters nor, in fact, any anti-aircraft fire ahead of us. Schnaufer was debating whether to follow our present track when we suddenly noticed over to the North, probably in the Münster area, a lot of light anti-aircraft fire. Again this puzzled us. Guns of that calibre were effective up to 2000 meters only, yet the British bombers usually flew between 3500 and 6000 meters over the Fatherland. Without further thought Schnaufer altered heading to the Northwest to cut off the bombers returning home.

'At 2500 meters we flew through a thin layer of cloud and our radar showed us several targets. Suddenly we were in a condition of 'Shroud,' above us a thin layer of stratus through which the moon shone giving us an opaque screen above which we could see clearly the black silhouettes of the bombers from quite a distance. Schnaufer closed upon a Lancaster flying along unsuspectingly slightly to our starboard at altitude 1700 meters. We had been airborne just over half-an-hour. The *Major* closed with the target, left to right, from below and delivered the first attack with the two vertically mounted 20mm cannons, just behind him, in the cabin. He aimed between the two engines on the right-hand side. The fuel tanks were located there and this method brings the quickest results. The time was 2044 hrs. The right wing of the bomber was badly damaged; a huge flame illuminated the sky. The Lancaster held steady for a while, long enough to allow the crew to escape by parachute before it fell to earth and crashed.

'There followed attack after attack, the sky seemed to be full of bombers! Now the British crews knew we were there and began their violent maneuvers, twisting and turning in an effort to escape us. Schnaufer had to follow all their corkscrew movements, to remain in a position under the bombers' wings where the return fire could not be brought to bear upon us yet ready, himself, to use the *Schräge Musik*. In one case we practically stood upon our wing tip whilst firing. Things became more difficult for us when we crossed the front line and the American anti-aircraft batteries opened up. Within a period of 19 hectic minutes we managed to shoot down seven bombers – without so much as a scratch – testimony to the *Major*'s great skill and ability to get in quickly, line up his target and dive away quickly. Normally during this wild fighting I would hardly have had time to note the details thoroughly but because of the 'shroud effect' the pilot did not need my assistance at the radar to guide him on to each target and I had more time than usual to observe the effects. *Ofw* Wilhelm Gänsler[26], our gunner, gave great support as usual but even he could not help when we attacked our eighth Lancaster bomber. At the crucial moment we exhausted the ammunition to the upward-trained guns and as a result had the greatest difficulty in getting away from the concentrated fire from the bomber crew.

'We still had our four horizontally mounted cannons in the nose of our fighter but these too refused to function during our ninth attack and we had to stop chasing the bombers. On the way back to base we had to fly again over the American batteries and by now the major was thoroughly weary, almost spent. I called, therefore, upon Dortmund to give us all possible assistance to clear us back to Gütersloh with all expediency and with this help Schnaufer greased our faithful G9+EF on to the ground. The night's work was done, we were back at base and it was just short of 2200 hrs. Once we had taxied in and shut down the engines, we sat in silence for a couple of minutes, thankful to have got through it and thought about the men who had gone down that night and hoped that they had managed to parachute to safety. Many years later I received a letter from an Englishman, Stanley Bridgeman. He had been a crewmember of Lancaster JO-Z of 463 Squadron shot down that night at 2102 hrs above Holland. All his crew had managed to escape by parachute. My prayers had been answered in part.'[27]

On the night of 21/22 two 2nd TAF Mosquito crews claimed two more victims. East of Stormede airfield F/L Don A. MacFadyen DFC of 406 'Lynx' Squadron RCAF in NFXXX NT325 destroyed a Bf 110.[28] F/L K.W. 'Chunky' Stewart and F/O Bill Brumby of 488 Squadron RNZAF were patrolling over Holland when they were warned by ground control that they were being followed by a strange aircraft. A dogfight ensued in complete darkness between the two night-fighters guided entirely by their own radar. With a great deal of weaving around Chunky Stewart managed to get behind the other aircraft. After brief visual contact it was identified as a Junkers 88G nightfighter. Following a quick burst of cannon fire it exploded in mid-air near Groenlo.[29]

On 22 February all 2nd TAF crews and serviceable aircraft were pressed into action for Operation *Clarion*. This was intended to be the 'coup de grace' for the German transport system with 9000 Allied aircraft taking part in attacks on enemy railway stations, trains and engines, cross roads, bridges, ships and barges on canals and rivers, stores and other targets. It was to be the last time that the Mosquitoes operated in daylight in such numbers. 2 Group put up every available aircraft, flying

215 sorties, 176 from the Continent and the remainder by 136 Wing in England. It was to be the last time that the Mosquitoes operated in daylight in such numbers. 138 and 140 Wings lost nine Mosquitoes and many more were damaged. 2 Group lost a total of 21 Mosquitoes on *Clarion,* with forty damaged. It appears that elements of NJG 11 were used in daylight to counter the Mosquito attacks, three crews claiming five Mosquito kills. *Fw* Reichenbach of the 4th *Staffel* and *Oblt* Kurt Welter (flying a Me 262) of the 10th *Staffel* (better known as *Einsatzkommando Welter*) each claimed two Mosquitoes shot down, *Fw* Richards of the IInd *Gruppe* claiming a 5th Mosquito kill. The large majority of the Mosquito losses however, were due to (mobile) *flak.*[30]

The second in a series of terrifying area-bombing raids on German cities, which had thus far escaped the bombing, went ahead on 23/24 February. Over 360 Lancasters and 13 Mosquitoes of 1, 6 and 8 Groups carried out the first and only area-bombing raid on Pforzheim, a city of 80,000 people, from only 8000ft and 1825 tons of bombs were dropped in just over 20 minutes. More than 17,000 people were killed and 83% of the town's built up area was destroyed in 'a hurricane of fire and explosions'. Ten Lancasters failed to return.[31] *Oblt* Wilhelm "Wim" Johnen, *Staffelkapitän*, 5/NJG 1 was one who vented his anger on the RAF[32]:

> 'With the attacks on Pforzheim and Dresden, the Allies mad-dog rage for destruction reached its peak. Just as in antiquity the city of Pompeii was destroyed by the sudden eruption of Vesuvius ... the Allies annihilated the cities which had so far been spared, with a burning rain of incendiaries. In particular the cities of Pforzheim, Dresden and Würzburg. Pforzheim was the first of these Pompeii's. The city was laid in ruins and ashes and about 17,600 people met their deaths in a hurricane of fire and explosions. During the attack the fire fighters were powerless but even after the raid the fires could not be put out since the water mains had been damaged and the walls of the houses had collapsed and filled the streets. The ashes lay ten feet high in the streets. This storm of fire reached its peak after ten minutes. It was so powerful that the rain of ashes was carried as far as Stuttgart and the sky turned blood red over a radius of 50 miles. On account of the raging flames and the explosion of delayed-action bombs after the attack, the inhabitants dared not leave their cellars and were suffocated. Any who dared to come out collapsed in the white heat of the huge fires. Thousands of blackened and mutilated corpses lay among the ruins.'

Meanwhile, the *Nachtjagd* was planning a large operation of its own. Not since Operation Steinbock in early 1944 had Britons suffered from German intruder operations. *Nachtjagd*'s final large-scale offensive effort was *Unternehmen* [Operation] *Gisela*, an intruder operation which had been mooted almost a year and a half earlier when H2S plots enabled German night fighters to accurately follow British bomber streams. In December 1943 *General* Schmid, C-in-C of *Nachtjagd*, intended to employ intruders not in routine operations against night raids but from time to time with all available forces (600-700 aircraft) when the bomber stream was on its way home and while landing. He expected to take Bomber Command by surprise as RAF crews were accustomed to landing without precautions on fully lit bases. By destroying at least 200 bombers in one operation, Schmid hoped to bring the Bomber Offensive to a temporary halt. Finally, in October 1944 *General* Schmid received approval and *Gisela* was to take place at the end of February but details of the plan were obtained and the British made it known by broadcasting the contemporary hit tune *'I Dance With Gisela Tonight'* on the Allied propaganda station *'Soldatensender Calais'*. *Gisela* was therefore postponed. *Hptm* Hans Krause, who was decorated with the coveted *Ritterkreuz* on 7 February after his 28th victory and at the same time appointed *Kommandeur*, I./NJG 4 at Vechta was among those who could not understand the delay:

> 'Inexplicably this operation was put off time and again, for weeks on end, although there were ample opportunities for entering the homeward bound British bomber stream coming from Berlin. In spite of intensive speculation, we were able to find an explanation for this strange conduct of our higher staff. Even an inquiry by our Kommodore brought nothing concrete to light. So we remained at readiness.'

When on 21 February 1945 the green light was given for the attack, the *Reich* was already staring certain defeat in the face. *Oberst Generalmajor* Dietrich Peltz committed only 142 Ju 88Gs of NJG 2, 3, 4 and 5 to *Gisela,* which went ahead on 3/4 March the 2000th night of the war. Some 234 aircraft raided the Fischer-Tropsch synthetic oil plant at Kamen (the fourth raid on this target in eight days) and 222 aircraft attacked an aqueduct on the Dortmund-Ems Canal at Ladbergen. 100 Group meanwhile, dispatched 61 aircraft on RCM sorties to jam the German radar and radio-networks and thus hamper the *Flak* and night-fighter defenses. One of the 100 Group aircraft was a Halifax of 192 Squadron piloted by the CO, W/C David Donaldson. His tail gunner was Gunnery Leader Jack Short:

'We went out in daylight, surrounded by Lancasters of 5 Group – the 'Death or Glory Boys', who were to punch a hole in the canal. Our lone Halifax caused a great deal of interest. They must have wondered if we had the right raid! It was a comfortable feeling though being with all these aircraft in daylight. At the target there was altostratus at 15,000 ft; bloody annoying because the searchlights silhouetted us against the cloud and we were picked up by the ack-ack. I saw three Lancs go down, one fairly close, in flames.[33] We were keyed up. Donaldson tipped the Halifax on one wing to look underneath for fighters. If suddenly your right wing crumples ... but we encountered no opposition and we headed back to Foulsham at 10,000 ft.'

Hptm Hans Krause takes up the story again:

'On 1 March my *Geschwader Kommodore* had asked me to go to Gütersloh where the *Geschwader* staff was based. So we climbed aboard our Ju 88 and flew to Gütersloh. There *Major* Schnaufer informed us that we were to try out a new search radar and also that a test flight with a Do 335[34] was to be carried out. The version of the machine placed at our disposal was a single-seater with a forward and a rear engine driving a traction and a pusher propeller respectively. After having received instructions by a works pilot from Dornier, first *Major* Schnaufer and then I each flew for about half an hour around the airfield. We were both enthusiastic about the handling qualities and speed of this aircraft. It was supposed to be the fastest propeller driven aircraft in the world at the time. Unusual for us was the nosewheel and the ejection seat,[35] which latter fortunately we did not have to use. Unfortunately we had to decline the usefulness of this single-seater version for Tame Boar night fighting. We needed a two-seater at least to accomodate the radio operator with his radio and radar gear. As far as I know a two-seater version had also been built by Dornier but neither of these saw action by the time the war was over.

'We were now able to attend to our other task, the testing of the new radar gear. It was called the *Kiel-Gerät*[36] and worked on the principle of heat emissions and was therefore free from interference. Every heated object emits infrared waves. The *Kiel-Gerät* made use of this by means of a parabolic aerial installed in the nose and displaying the received waves on the radio operator's screen. This was of course something entirely new for us and had to be tested. We made contact with a crew from the *Geschwader* staff who were to act as target. We arranged for a take-off in daylight and then continue through dusk into the night. We were in radio contact both with operations and the target crew. We agreed to begin at a height of 3000 meters and a speed of 400 km/h. We found that the range was about 4000 meters and this did not vary with height, remaining constant from 500 meters up to 7000. That was a significant difference to the SN2-gear used so far. The latter's range was reciprocal to the altitude and liable to interference by *Window*. The *Kiel-Gerät* was free from interference and was able to pick up targets even at low level due to the fact that aircraft engines develop a great deal of heat. Meanwhile it had become dark and we asked our target crew to turn on their position lights and change height and direction. Initial difficulties were overcome, particularly at sudden changes of course and height but we hoped to master these probems too. Practice makes perfect.

'Suddenly we received orders from operations: 'Land at once! Operation *Gisela'*. We would have preferred a little more warning. After about 30 minutes we made our approach to land, just as the last aircraft of the *Geschwader* staff had taken off. Our target crew remained on board their aircraft, refuelled and was able to take off for England after 20 minutes. But we had first to get into our own Ju 88G, which cost a lot of time and then we found that our starboard engine was running very rough at idling. The aircraft was unservicable for operations and there was no other machine available. Although the test aircraft was not to be used over enemy territory for reasons of secrecy, I simply decided to risk a court martial and use it against the foe.

'For me it was shameful and dishonorable towards my comrades as their commander not to take part in the long prepared Operation *Gisela*. The objective was for all night fighter *Geschwader* stationed in the north-west, Holland, Belgium and Germany to infiltrate the British bomber stream, follow it to their home bases and there attack them. Each unit was assigned a certain area for which they were to prepare themselves. My own *Gruppe* was assigned the area around Hull. We had the test Ju 88G-6[37] refuelled and armed and took off with considerable delay at 2239. When I say 'we' I mean my crew of four, consisting of the radio and navigation officer of the *Gruppe*, *Oblt* Hans Kretschmer, the radio operator *Ofw* Otto Zinn, the flight engineer *Ofw* Fritz Specht and myself, *Hptm* Hans Krause, *Kommandeur* of I./NJG 4. We first set course for our home base Vechta, firstly as it was practically on our way to England but also in order to tell our operations room under what difficulties and however delayed, we were taking part in the operation. After all, we had done all our preparations at Vechta.

'At first we flew at 300 meters knowing that there would be no obstructions for us at this altitude. Then we went ever lower until we were at 20 meters on crossing the coast. The pointer of our radio altimeter vibrated a lot, causing us to climb to about 30 meters, as this was indicative of a rough sea. This low-level flight was necessary in order to underfly the enemy radar system and not to be made out. We held course for London and were in the middle of the southern North Sea where the Channel towards the north has widened to 200 kilometers. In spite of the dark night, with a cloud ceiling of 3000 meters, we were soon able to make out the gray-white cliffs of England. Whenever I have seen these I got a queer feeling in my stomach. There was something threatening about them, like the walls of a castle which none would violate unscathed. Just before the coast I pulled the machine up towards the protective clouds. Soon we were over the suburbs of London. The sole reason for overflying London was to set off an air raid warning and with it the disruption of industry and traffic. Searchlight and *Flak* activity commenced at once. We found ourselves in a milky-white soup and some *Flak* shells exploded threateningly nearby.

'Now full watchfulness and concentration was required. I frequently altered height and course to make it difficult for the British radar, which was coupled to the *Flak* and the searchlights. I turned onto north for our real target, the area around Hull, where most of the 4 Group Halifax bases were situated. When *Flak* and searchlight activity were no longer noticable we left the protective cloud cover and we looked for lights on the ground. After 200 kilometers we were in our target area. During the following 30 minutes in the triangle Sheffield-Leeds-Hull we saw neither lights, *Flak* or searchlight activity. Total darkness. Our comrades who had taken off long before us were well on their return flights and some of them must have already reached their home bases. We were certainly the only ones still over England. Disappointed over the effectiveness of our sortie we turned for home, though not without triggering off an air raid warning in London again. We re-entered the protective cloud above 3000 meters, not least to avoid presenting a target for any British night fighters, which might have been sent up against us. Neither the British or us were able to score hits using radar alone. One had to have eye contact with the enemy before one could aim and fire. In my old aircraft we had a rearward-looking warning device installed, which would have shown up any British nightfighter behind us. This was not the case with the new test Ju 88, as it had not been intended for use in operations against the enemy. Again strong *Flak* and searchlight activity commenced over the suburbs of London and once more we were immersed in a ghostly milky-white soup but the bursting *Flak* shells were mainly too low. Suddenly the *Flak* ceased and warning bells started to ring in our minds. Our own experience told us that a British night fighter had us on his radar. Extreme vigilance was now essential. As long as we were in cloud we were safe. Flying on an easterly heading, our radio operator took bearings and obtained a fix. Then we were over the center of the southern North Sea, still in cloud.

'It was still about 100 kilometers to the coast and another 300 to our base at Vechta. I could not imagine that the British were still following us. This turned out to be a great mistake. I flew a complete circle to make sure and then went back to my old course. Now I left the cloud. The last scraps of cloud were still about me when there was a crackle and a burst struck the port engine which caught fire. The fuselage was slit open and the port landing flap hung loose. Fritz Specht was hit in the upper left arm but fortunately it was only a flesh wound. The entire radio gear was destroyed and with it our intercom. It was only my immediate slipping down to port which prevented the British from scoring further hits. Now I had my hands full keeping the machine under some sort of control. First I stopped the port engine and feathered its propeller and after closing the fuel and oil cocks the fire went out. By now Fritz Specht's arm had been bandaged so he would not bleed to death. Having now trimmed out the aircraft for single-engined flight we continued our journey homeward. Our intercom system being unservicable we were only able to communicate with each other by shouting. Although our evasive action had taken us more than 1000 meters lower, I was convinced that the Britisher would attack us again. Finding us would be easier for him as the fire in the port engine had not completely gone out. I therefore urged my crew to keep a particularly good look-out to the rear. Very soon a shout from Fritz Specht showed that he had been the first to make out the attacker with his radar eyes. The shout and my own reaction were almost simultaneous. I slipped the aircraft to port and the burst of fire from the Britisher went into empty space. Owing to our single-engined flight, he had overestimated our speed. He flew past us and was suddenly visible in full broadside above and to starboard. That put him within reach of our large-calibre movable defensive machine gun. I shouted Fire! and at the same time Fritz Specht fired in spite of his injury into the fuselage of the Mosquito 20 meters away, raking him several times from nose to tail. The Mosquito rose strangely up into the air, then flipped over to starboard and hurtled down. We could assume that the crew had been mortally wounded and that the Mosquito had crashed into the sea, for we were no longer troubled by it.[38]

'The succession of skirmishes with the British night fighter had cost us valuable altitude. Normally the Ju 88 was quite capable of single-engined flight, though at a reduced speed. But in our case, due to the disrupted aerodynamics, I was only able to maintain the required speed of around 230 km/h by a descent rate of 2-3 m/sec. We were hoping to be able to reach the coast where I would then do a belly landing in the shallows. But as time went on it became increasingly certain that we would have to ditch in the open sea 10-15 kilometers from shore. That would mean that at best we would have to abandon the aircraft and entrust ourselves to our lifejackets. But that would only put off the moment when we would suffer a hero's death through hypothermia. Or we would strike a wave which would have shattered and then swallowed us like a submarine. 'Failed to return from operations' would then have been the comment. Meanwhile we were down to one hundred meters with no land in sight. I noticed that my crew had become resigned to their fate; no panic, total aquiescence, silence, complete calm. Meanwhile I counted down the few meters we still had at our disposal. At about 70 meters I suddenly had the idea to try to restart the damaged engine. After all, when it was hit and before I had stopped it, it had not completely given up the ghost. I had first to unfeather the propeller, then switch on the ignition and open the oil and fuel cocks. If the engine did not start, the idling propeller would cause additional drag and the reduced speed would cause us to crash. But if it did start, we would be saved.

'This maneuver had cost us more height. But then it sounded like music in our ears, coughing at first but then with some regularity the engine ran and enabled us to climb to about 500 meters, which should enable us to reach the coast. Our hopes rose. But then the engine began to stutter and I had to stop it again. It was clear that we would not be able to reach base. We crossed the coast and agreed on a belly landing at Twente in Holland, an airfield which I knew from a number of night landings. We could see the light beacon from afar but had to restart the port engine for a short while and finally reached the airfield at an alttiude of 300 meters. As radio communication was not possible and the listening post made out only a single engine, the meagre airfield lighting was extinguished altogether. Firing off a recognition cartridge made no difference. I recalled that sometimes on an approach a lake caused a shimmer of light and I noticed this now. Still in the turn, the starboard engine now gave up the ghost. The long period at full power had been too much for it. The Ju 88 lost height rapidly. Just short of the ground the crew jettisoned the rear cockpit cover and I put her down on her belly on the rough surface. The lower fuselage was torn off with a resounding crash and indescribable dirt was flung into the cabin. Then I saw a large tree which would have crushed us completely but our speed was still sufficient to enable us, by using the rudder, to swerve past it. It tore off the entire port wing with an earsplitting noise. The aircraft turned a couple of times around its own axis and then there was silence. I watched the crew leave the aircraft in a panic and take cover to escape the explosion which usually followed a crash. I was incapable of doing anything at all. I was fully conscious but was unable to move. I seemed paralyzed. For whatever reason I felt absolutely certain that no explosion would follow. An indescribably happy and thankful feeling went through me, a sensation which I could not put into words.

'After some time, as no explosion had taken place, my crew returned and with some difficulty released me from my deformed pilot's seat. After a while strength returned to my body. We shouldered our parachutes and set out in the direction of the airfield. After about 100 meters we came to a water-filled hollow and realized that the tree which had caused us such trouble had in fact been our saviour. Without it we would have run into the opposite bank and certain death. Disturbed by the crash two Dutch farmers suddenly appeared. Once they had been informed about the events by our Dutch speaking radio operator Otto Zinn, they invited us into their house. Evidently impressed, they provided us with drinks and something to eat. Then Hans Kretschmer sat down at the piano and played Franz Liszt's Rhapsody No.2. He was a veritable virtuoso. Son of a teacher in Breslau, he had learned to play the piano in his youth. We listened to him in silence, deeply moved. We were still in shock. Each of us had our own thoughts. It had not been the first time that we had experienced a miraculous escape literally in seconds. More than once I had thought my life was finished but time and again some sudden brainwave would initiate a last-moment escape. This could not be put down to the simple notion of 'chance'. It must have had deeper reasons and causes. I was of the firm conviction that some 'Guardian Angel' had been responsible. Why one should be saved and another one not, is a question I cannot answer.

'After we had taken our grateful leave from our hosts a car, which had been summoned by telephone took us to the airfield Towards 0300 we introduced ourselves to the *Staffelkapitän* of the local unit which had also taken part in Operation *Gisela*. We courteously declined the offer to spend the rest of the night there and asked for the use of a car to take us to Vechta. This request was granted and a car with driver took us the remaining 200 kilometers to our unit, though several times we had to take cover in ditches because of low-flying British aircraft. Towards midday I was able to report to my *Kommodore*, *Major* Schnaufer. Gushing congratulations were not usual among operational airmen and with the dry comment, 'Well, you were lucky this time' the matter was closed. With the remark, 'we have removed the new *Kiel-Gerät* from the wreckage and it is in a secure place.' I knew that there would be no court martial or other consequences. Fritz Specht received medical attention and was then taken to a hospital in Rügen. We only flew a few more sorties and then the capitulation came on 8 May 1945 which, after the bombing of Vechta and subsequent transfer, we moved to Eggebeck in Schleswig-Holstein.'

Hptm Krause's Ju 88G-6 was officially classified as 30% damaged after the crash-landing near Twente airfield. I./NJG 4 lost another four Ju 88G-6s on *Gisela*, mainly due to aircraft running out of fuel on their return trip. Altogether, 33 Ju 88G night intruders were lost during *Gisela*. Five German aircraft crashed on British soil[39] and eight other crews were reported missing. Three more crews perished in crashes on German territory. Six crews baled out due to lack of fuel and 11 crashed on landing. In all the intruders shot down 24 aircraft.[40] *Lt* Arnold Döring of 10./NJG 3 at Jever shot down a Fortress over Norfolk and claimed a Lancaster. Döring recalls:

'I positioned myself beneath a *Viermot* with all his navigation lights on. It was a B-17, as I could see from its wide tailplane. I aimed a burst from my oblique cannons into the fuel tanks, the fuselage and wings. The bomber started to burn. The fires in its fuselage flickered up and then became fainter. The crew probably switched on the fire extinguishers. The *Viermot* crashed hard in a pile of dust and smoke but without a fire. We clearly saw it in the bright moonlight as we flew low and away over the wreckage. Despite the fact that we flew very low the navigation lights of a bomber even flashed past beneath me. As I was not familiar with the surroundings and the moon disappeared behind a bank of clouds, I let this *Viermot* escape and attacked another one on its final approach. I destroyed this Lancaster with my oblique cannons; it immediately burst into a bright fire and crashed in an enormous sheet of flames.'

Low on fuel Döring landed at Nordholz after a sortie lasting over five hours.[41]

In March 1945 Bomber Command flew a record 53 day and night operations. On 4 March 128 Lancasters of 3 Group carried out a daylight raid on Wanne-Eickel. W/O Arthur 'Spud' Taylor, who began a second tour[42] as a Lancaster observer on 149 Squadron at Methwold in F/O Bill Passlow's crew, recalls:

'We were woken up in the early hours at 0230(!), which was a thing I never did agree with and were briefed to bomb the railway yards at Wanne Eickel – a goodish target since our armies had reached the Rhine and Jerry troops were everywhere being rushed by rail. We were to take off at seven o'clock but the time was put on to 9.30. We were trying out a new sort of formation, more compact than the usual string of vics and boxes and very different to the old efforts. We flew in loose formations in boxes or Vs, each formation with a GH leader. The three behind bombed on the leader. Loose formations were a good idea. It made weaving possible and bombing remarkably accurate. We were No.3 in the last vic. A thick layer of cloud covered the target with brilliant sunshine above. There was a certain amount of highly inaccurate *Flak* and we were nearly bombed by some damn fool and then we started back for base passing over Bochum on the way. I dropped a large store on Bochum for old time's sake and took a few snaps of the kites and *Flak*. Crossing the English coast we ran into thick cloud and drove through it in blinding rain till we reached base and made one of the good old split-arse landings.

'On the afternoon of the 7th we were briefed for a night trip to Dessau, an evacuation center for Berlin, about forty miles SW. We set out over France in broad daylight. It became dark just as we cut through the Ruhr. Cologne was ablaze and the gun flashes were reflecting on the cloud. (Cologne and the Rhine were our front line now). We passed by a number of attacks going on in the Happy Valley. It was quite like old times to see the TIs and *Flak* and flares and all the 101 other mysterious lights that came out on a night trip. Our H2S and *Gee* were both u/s so we went round on DR and kept remarkably close to track all the way. The target was well ablaze when we left it – good prang. I saw about 15 kites' shot down all told and saw one fighter. I felt really worn out when we came back – 9 1/2-hour trip. (39 kites down last night).'

During early March Luftwaffe intruders made brief but damaging reappearance over eastern England and many

Mosquito crews talked confidently of getting more victories. At West Raynham, Norfolk the nights went by with excitement at fever pitch because 239 Squadron were chasing their fiftieth victory. This was achieved on the night of 5/6 March when W/C Walter Frame Gibb DSO DFC the CO and F/O R.C. 'Killer' Kendall DFC destroyed two Ju 88s at Chemnitz.[43]

On the night of 14/15 March 244 Lancasters and 11 Mosquitoes of 5 Group attacked the Wintershall synthetic oil refinery at Lützkendorf near Leipzig. S/L 'Dolly' Doleman DSO DFC and F/L Bunny Bunch DFC of 157 Squadron shot down a Ju 88G at close range at Lützkendorf. American pilot F/O (2/Lt) R.D.S. 'Hank' Gregor and his navigator/radar operator, F/Sgt Frank H. Baker in a Mosquito FBVI scored 141 Squadron's final air-to-air victory of the war during a lone ASH patrol in the Frankfurt-Mannheim area in support of the bombers attacking Zweibrücken. Near Saarbrücken they picked up a contact coming into land at Lachen airfield. Gregor planned to intersect just short of the runway when a floodlight lit up the runway and the enemy aircraft was seen. At about 2000 ft Gregor opened fire at the 'silver shape' giving it one ring deflection and then spraying the area. He rapidly closed range to 100 ft and just as the Mosquito started to pull out the enemy aircraft exploded under their nose illuminating the area. Almost immediately they came under fore from light and not too accurate flak and they were coned by a searchlight. Gregor dodged the searchlight by turning into it and diving before hooking back on the stick and heading for home.

Eighteen Lancasters were lost (7.4 per cent of the force) and 100 Group lost two Mosquitoes and two Fortress IIIs of 214 Squadron during *Jostle* radio countermeasure duties in support of the Main Force.[44] *Hptm* Martin 'Tino' Becker of *Stab* IV./NJG 6 and his *Funker Uffz* Karl-Ludwig Johanssen in a Ju 88G-6 claimed nine bombers, the highest score by a German night-fighter crew in any single night. Becker shot down six Lancasters of the Lützkendorf force. After expending his last ammunition on the sixth Lancaster he positioned his Ju 88G to the side of two more Lancasters and finally Fortress III HB802, piloted by F/L Norman Rix DFC and *Uffz* Karl-Ludwig Johanssen manning the twin rear facing machine guns shot each one down in turn. Johanssen's burst of gunfire hit the Fort's No.2 engine and the RCM aircraft went down five kilometers SE of Baiersbronn, west of Eutingen at 2337 hours. Johanssen's three victims counted towards the grand total of his pilot so the B-17 was Becker's 57th official victory. Johanssen was awarded the *Ritterkreuz* two days later.[45]

Another 100 Group Fortress III also failed to return to Oulton. HB799 BU-K flown by F/L Johnny Wynne DFC flew at around 24,000 ft while the Lancs flew towards the target at 20,000 ft. For the homeward trip the Lancs and the Forts were to fly at 3000 ft above sea level to make it difficult for the German night fighters to locate and attack them. However, this of course made the heavies more susceptible to *Flak* and small arms fire. Wynne comments:

> 'I had to obey orders … I had trusted that the planners had routed the force away from towns, airfields and other places which would be defended by guns. We now know that this was not the case. Of the 16 bombers shot down on this attack on the Lützkendorf oil installations almost all were brought down by light *Flak* between Nuremberg and the Rhine.' (Wynne's Fortress was within half an hour's flying time of the Rhine when his aircraft was hit). 'I thought that we were being attacked by a night fighter from below. The fact that I did not see the flash means the gun was more or less vertically below us or slightly behind us. It would not have made much difference if I had seen the flash. We would still have been hit, perhaps in a fuel tank instead of the front wheel bay, which would have been bad news for us.'

Wynne flew on as the Fortress gradually lost height. By now he had flown 80 miles with the No.2 engine on fire and the fuel tank, which by now was half full, could explode at any time. He was 60 miles from the Rhine where the land south west of the river was occupied by the Allied armies. Unfortunately, strong winds had caused the Main Force to fly further south and east of the planned track and the Fortress had been hit 25 miles east of the position recorded in the navigator's log. The No.2 engine gradually disintegrated but Wynne was sure that they had by now reached the safety of French territory though his navigator, when asked, was unable to confirm their position. Wynne decided to give the order for his crew to bale out. All nine men vacated the aircraft in less than five minutes. Wynne managed to keep the airborne but by the time he was ready to leave baling out was no longer an option, he was far too low and the aircraft refused to climb. Incredibly, the flames died down and finally the engine fire went out. Wynne somehow managed to level the aircraft off and cross the English Channel at 0240 hrs and amazingly reached England, where he crash-landed at the American 91st Bomb Group Flying Fortress base at Bassingbourn in Cambridgeshire. Wynne was sent on leave to await the return of his crew from France. However, five of the nine men who baled out of HB799 never returned.[46]

On 15/16 March when 267 bombers made an area attack on Hagen and another 257 Lancasters and eight Mosquitoes raided the Deurag oil refinery at Misburg two 100 Group Mosquito crews were successful. Norwegian pairing Captain Eric Fossum and F/O S.A. Hider of 85 Squadron destroyed a Ju 88 in the Hanover area and F/L Jimmy Mathews and W/O

Alan Penrose of 157 Squadron got another Ju 88 20 miles south of Würzburg. Six Lancasters and four Halifaxes FTR from Hagen and four Lancasters were lost on the Misburg raid while a RCM B-17 was also lost.[47]

The night following, 16/17 March 231 Lancasters of 1 Group and 46 Lancasters and 16 Mosquitoes of 8 Group attacked Nürnburg and 225 Lancasters and 11 Mosquitoes of 5 Group bombed Würzburg, the old cathedral city famous for its historic buildings and which, contained little industry. 5 Group dropped 1,127 tons of bombs with great accuracy in 17 minutes. Würzburg suffered 89 per cent of its built up area destroyed and it was estimated that between 4,000 and 5,000 people were killed. During the night's operations 30 aircraft were lost, 24 of them Lancasters of 1 Group on the Nürnburg raid, mainly to German night fighters, which found the found the two Bomber Streams on the way to the target. *Oblt* Erich Jung, *St.Kpt* of 5./NJG 2 in his Ju 88G-6[48] with his *funker Fw* Walter Heidenreich and flight mechanic *Obfw* Hans Reinnagel alone knocked down eight Lancasters,[49] which took Jung's personal score to 28 kills. S/L D.L. Hughes and F/L R.H. Perks of 239 Squadron destroyed a Ju 88 flown by *Major* Werner Hoffmann[50] near Nürnburg. *Hptm* Wilhelm 'Wim' Johnen, *Kommandeur* of III./NJG 6 claimed his 32nd and final victory of the war, a Lancaster SE of Würzburg. *Oblt* Kurt Welter of II./NJG 11, *Kommando Welter*'s controversial *Kapitän*, supposedly one of the top scoring Wild Boar pilots during the Battle of Berlin claimed two Mosquito victories the following night, 17/18 March when there was no Main Force activity.[51] A sweep by 66 Lancasters and 29 Halifaxes was made over Northern France to draw German fighters into the air and formations of Mosquito bombers carrying 'Cookies' visited targets in Germany. All of the 81 Mosquito bombers returned safely but 100 Group and 2nd TAF each lost a Mosquito.[52]

On 18/19 March when 324 aircraft of 4, 6 and 8 Groups carried out an area bombing raid on Witten F/L V.D. Win RNZAF and F/O T.P. Ryan RNZAF of 85 Squadron destroyed a Bf 110. W/C W.F. Gibb and 'Killer' Kendall of 239 Squadron shot down a He 219 *Uhu* at Witten to take their score while with the squadron to five victories. *Hptm* Werner Baake, *Kommandeur* of I./NJG 1 and his radar operator, *Uffz* Rolf Bettaque baled out safely.[53] The Witten force lost eight aircraft including six Halifaxes.[54] Meanwhile, 277 Lancasters and eight Mosquitoes of 12 and 8 Groups carried out an area raid on Hanau and just one Lancaster was lost.[55] W/O D.A. Taylor and F/Sgt Radford of 157 Squadron, one of the Mosquito NFXXX crews covering the Hanau raid, destroyed a Ju 88.[56]

On 19 March 79 Lancasters of 3 Group attacked the Consolidation benzol plant at Gelsenkirchen without loss.[57] W/O Arthur 'Spud' Taylor recalls:

> 'We skirted Düsseldorf and Essen and came in for a heavy pasting from all the guns there. I didn't see one kite go down. The target was the old benzol plant at Gelsenkirchen, which was still half-intact and still was, as not a bomb landed on it. Every kite on the station had at least one *Flak* hole in it and some had a pretty thin time of it. One bomb-aimer was smacked through the head on the run up and pegged out before we could get him back.'

It seemed that *Nachtjagdgeschwader* crews had little defense against the Mosquitoes. Even their *SN-2* AI band could now be jammed since several Fortresses of 214 Squadron had each been fitted with six installations of the latest development of *Piperack*.[58] Bomber Command's tactics of deception and radio counter-measures had reached a fine perfection. On 20/21 March no less than three feint attacks took place in support of the Main Force attack on the synthetic oil refinery at Böhlen, just south of Leipzig, by 235 Lancasters and Mosquitoes. The *Window* Force left the Main Stream soon after crossing the front line and made for Kassel, which was bombed. Further on, when closer to the true target, another *Window* Force broke off and bombed Halle. The third feint force was provided by the *Mandrel* screen which, after the passage of the heavies, re-formed into a *Window* Force and attacked Frankfurt with flares. The Main Force's zero hour was set at 0340 hrs on the 21st. Almost simultaneously, 166 Lancasters headed for the oilfield at Hemmingstedt in Schleswig-Holstein far to the north of the first target. This attack was to commence at 0430 and together with the other attack involved Bomber Command's main effort.

The evening's diversions had begun at 2114 hours with a large-scale nuisance raid on Berlin when 35 Mosquitoes of the Pathfinder force bombed the city. Just after 0100 hrs the main Böhlen force crossed the English Channel on a southeasterly heading, while a few miles to the south a feinting formation, comprising 64 Lancasters and Halifaxes from training units crossed the Channel on an almost parallel course. Here complications for the German radar operators began. By 0205 an 80-mile long *Mandrel* screen comprising seven pairs of Halifaxes from 171 and 199 Squadrons was in position over northern France throwing up a wall of radar jamming through which the German early-warning radar could not see. Shortly after crossing the coast of France, the Böhlen force split into two streams. Hidden behind the *Mandrel* screen 41 Lancasters broke away and headed off to the northeast. Meanwhile, 14 Mosquito fighter-bombers of 23 and 515 Squadrons fanned out in ones and twos and made for German nightfighter airfields. Once there they orbited overhead for hours on end dropping clusters of incendiaries and firing at anything that moved.

At 0300 the training aircraft, which had by now almost reached the German frontier near Strasbourg, turned about and went home, their work done. At the same time, the two formations making their separate ways to the Böhlen refinery burst through the *Mandrel* jamming screen. Seven Liberators of 233 Squadron and four Halifaxes of 171 Squadron went five minutes (about 18 miles)-ahead of the larger Böhlen force, laying a dense cloud of *Window,* which effectively hid the bombers following them. Once over the Rhine, the more southerly of the two streams of bombers turned northeast straight towards Kassel. So far, there was no way in which the fighter controller could tell the real target for the night. At the time the bomber forces crossed the German frontier *Major* Rüppel, *Jägerleitoffizier* (JLO, or GCI-controller) of the Central Rhine defense area, seriously under-estimated the strength of the two approaching formations. He thought each force involved about 30 aircraft and that both might be *Window* feints. As the reports from the ground observation posts began to come in however, it became clear that the southernmost of the two was much larger than he had estimated. No amount of jamming could conceal the roar of 800 aircraft engines. The spoofs, diversionary attacks and counter measures helped keep losses down to nine Lancasters. One was lost on the attack on Hemmingstedt. Three aircraft of the support and minor operations forces were also lost. *Nachtjäger* claimed 11 Lancasters shot down. Three of the missing aircraft this night were shot down SW and W of Kassel by *Hptm* Johannes Hager, *Staffelkapitän* of 6./NJG 1 flying a Bf 110G-4[59] and whose crew consisted of *Bordfunker*, *Uffz* Walter Schneider and *Ogfr* Bärwald, gunner.

RAF Mosquitoes found victories hard to come by. F/L Kennedy of 125 Squadron and his navigator in NFXXX NT450 destroyed a Ju 188 over the sea. On a high-level escort of the bombers to Böhlen F/L G.C. Chapman and F/Sgt Jimmy Stockley of 85 Squadron in NFXXX NT324/T claimed a Bf 110 and He 219 destroyed. While en route to patrol their first *Perfectos* contact appeared at 0255 hrs just after passing Hamm at 12 miles range and 12,000ft. Chapman closed range to one mile but no AI contact was obtained and the range began increasing again so he carried out a hard diving turn to port and down to 9000ft where the target was found at seven miles range. Chapman and Stockley closed to six miles range and an AI contact was obtained at 6 o'clock. The target was climbing and they closed rapidly, obtaining a visual at 900 ft, height 13,000 ft. it was a Bf 110 with a pale blue light between the starboard nacelle and fuselage. Chapman closed to 600 ft and pulled up to dead astern when the 110 started to turn to port. He gave it a o-ring deflection and a three-second burst whereupon the German aircraft exploded in the port engine with debris flying back and it exploded on the ground at 0305 hours 25-30 miles NW of Kassel. Chapman reported that, 'all this excitement was too much for the Perfectos, which went u/s unfortunately, so we set course for the rendezvous with the bomber stream.'

Chapman and Stockley reached the bomber stream at 0322 hrs. Their patrol was uneventful until the stream left the target at 0400 hrs when Chapman noticed to port and 15 miles south a ball of yellowish flame taking off [from Plauen airfield] and climbing very rapidly. He thought it was a flare or a V-2 until it began emitting a meteor tail several hundred feet long. The Mosquito crew turned port towards it, lost height to 7000 ft and continued watching. It travelled in a NW direction very fast and suddenly to their astonishment fired off some rocket projectiles, four singles and one pair, in the general direction of the departing bomber stream. Chapman and Stockley were amazed and decided that it must be a Me 163. Chapman continued turning port and got behind the UEA, which by now was travelling at about 260 mph. With Stockley using the AI to check range Chapman closed to 1000 ft and visually identified a twin-engined aircraft with rocket apparatus slung under the fuselage. They realized that it was a He 219.[60] Considerable quantities of flames and sparks flying back prevented the Mosquito crew from identifying the tail unit so Chapman decided to open fire at long range. He gave the *Owl* several longish bursts as two of his cannon had stoppages and he was gratified to see an explosion take place somewhere in the fuselage and debris fly back. The *Uhu* nosed straight down through the patchy cloud and exploded on the ground with a tremendous glare.[61]

On 21 March 178 aircraft of 4, 6 and 8 Groups carried out an accurate attack on the rail yards at Rheine and the surrounding town area for the loss of one Lancaster. Some 160 Lancasters of 3 Group raided the railway yards at Münster and a railway viaduct nearby for the loss of three bombers. Another 133 Lancasters of 1 Group and six Mosquitoes of 1 and 8 Groups headed for Bremen and accurately bombed the Deutsche Vacuum oil refinery without loss. Twenty Lancasters of 617 Squadron attacked the Arbergen railroad-bridge just outside Bremen and destroyed two piers of the bridge for the loss of one Lancaster.[62] That same evening 151 Lancasters and eight Mosquitoes of 5 Group set off to raid the Deutsche Erdölwerke refinery at Hamburg and 131 Lancasters and 12 Mosquitoes of 1 and 8 Groups sought a benzol plant at Bochum. Five Lancasters were lost, four of them from the Hamburg force and a RCM Fortress, which was supporting the Bochum force, also failed to return.[63] No less than 142 Mosquitoes of the LNSF carried out two attacks on Berlin, some of the aircraft and crews making two sorties, while three moreMosquitoes attacked Bremen and seven of 5 Group dropped mines in Jade Bay and the River Weser. Fifty-six

Mosquito patrols were flown and 2nd TAF squadrons too were airborne over the *Reich*. Two Mosquitoes, one from the attack on Berlin and a NFXXX of 2nd TAF, failed to return,[64] though claims for four Mosquito kills were submitted by II./NJG 11, one of them 10 km SW of Berlin by *Fw* Karl-Heinz Becker. *Fw* Reichenbach and *Oblt* Kurt Welter each claimed two Mosquitoes.

On 22 March raids on rail yards continued with 227 Lancasters and eight Mosquitoes of 1 and 8 Groups raiding Hildesheim for the loss of four Lancasters. Also, 130 Halifaxes, Lancasters and Mosquitoes of 4 and 8 Groups bombed Dülmen in an area attack without loss and 124 Halifaxes, Lancasters and Mosquitoes of 6 and 8 Groups raided targets at Dorsten, again without loss. Another 102 Lancasters of 5 Group in two forces attacked bridges at Bremen and Nienburg without loss and the bridge at Nienburg was destroyed. Completing the night's proceedings, Lancasters of 3 Group carried out an area attack on Bocholt, as 'Spud' Taylor recalls:

> 'Bocholt, a small town, came in for the next wallop from about one hundred of us. We were among the first to bomb and I saw them burst smack in the center of the town. Ten minutes later, looking back on the place, there was a pall of smoke, black and ominous, rising to about 15,000 ft where once was a town. I noticed a tremendous smoke screen stretching from Arnhem to Duisburg along the west bank of the Rhine. Apparently, this was to cover troop movements, as a large-scale attack was pending. On Saturday night, 23/24 March our army broke across the Rhine from behind this smoke screen and on the 26th they had about three good bridgeheads and were swarming east, north of the Ruhr.'[65]

On 24/25 March when 67 Mosquitoes visited Berlin and eight went to Nordheim (38 RCM sorties and 33 Mosquito patrols were also flown) Mosquito nightfighters destroyed four German aircraft.[66] There were no losses but two Mosquitoes were claimed destroyed by Me 262 jet fighters of 10./NJG 11. *Oblt* Kurt Welter claimed one and another was credited to *Fw* Karl-Heinz Becker. The small number of German jets were operating under the most drastic conditions, always on the move it seemed from one place to another (from Magdeburg to Lübeck and finally Schleswig) as their airfields were bombed and strafed constantly by the advancing Allies. Me 262s needed a big airfield with a runway up to 2000 meters, which the pilots called *Silberplätze* or 'silver fields' but the situation became so bad by April that they had to operate from the Hamburg/Lübeck autobahn. On 25 March Bomber Command flew 606 sorties against the main reinforcement routes into the Rhine battle area and Hanover, Münster and Osnabrück were heavily hit. Four bombers were lost (three to flak and one due to being struck by a bomb over the target). That night, as eight Mosquitoes raided Berlin, Mosquito fighters claimed four German aircraft shot down and a Ju 88 as a 'probable'. There were no RAF losses but *Oblt* Fehre of 5./NJG 3 claimed a Mosquito for his seventh *Abschuss* On 26/27 March 86 Mosquitoes attacked Berlin and Mosquito nightfighters claimed five aircraft shot down.[67]

On 27/28 March a Mosquito FBVI of 605 Squadron failed to return from an evening *Intruder* sortie to Germany.[68] Three Mosquitoes of the Light Night Striking Force were missing from a raid on Berlin[69] and a 627 Squadron Mosquito was lost during a 5 Group minelaying operation in the River Elbe. One of the Berlin losses was a Mosquito of 692 Squadron which was lost without trace and the other two were involved in a collision. F/L Leicester G. Smith RNZAF and his RAF navigator W/O Bill Lane of 128 Squadron in Mosquito BXVI MM202 V-Victor who were on their 44th op were on the outward leg to Berlin over Holland at 25,200 ft under a full moon when at about 2000 hrs they were involved in a collision with Mosquito RV326 of 571 Squadron. Smith recalls, 'We were waiting for the arrival of the Yellow Route Markers which was but a couple of minutes away when the collison occurred. There was a sudden jolt, the sensation of which was like being bounced off a trampolone. The aircraft started to go into a spin to the right with the nose well down and for a time out of control.' RV326 spun in, crashing in a cornfield near the village of Zevenhuizen, or Seven Houses, near Groningen. F/O Gordon 'Huddy' Hudson AFC RNZAF and his Canadian navigator F/O Maurice G. Gant, who were on their 11th consecutive sortie to Berlin, were killed. They were later buried in a single coffin the local cemetery of Leek.[70] Smith's starboard propeller had been torn away before it could be feathered and it cut a huge hole in the fuselage near the nose and splintered the cockpit windscreen. A small explosion followe and a fire broke out but Smith quickly extinguished it with the graviner and after falling to 16,000 ft Smith was able to jettisopn his 'Cookie' and regain control. He nursed V-Victor back across the North Sea and put down safely at Woodbridge. Throughout the attack on Berlin the searchlights were active across the city and a jet fighter was spotted in the area on the 128 Squadron bombing run. F/L Jim Dearlove and Sgt Norman Jackson's Mosquito was coned on the bomb run and it was attacked by a Me 262 of 10./NJG 11 just after they had dropped their 'Cookie'. He fired two short bursts of cannon fire, which missed the Mosquito and Dearlove was able to take evasive action and escape. Two other Mosquitoes, which failed to return were claimed shot down by Me 262 jet fighters. *Ofw*

Karl-Heinz Becker flew one of 10./NJG 11's three Me 262A-1a's this night and claimed his sixth *Abschuss* and the *Staffel's* 27th:

'I took off at 2058 hours for a night sortie over Berlin. The visibility was bad and I did not succeed in getting a target aircraft that was caught in the beam of a searchlight so I flew back on a reciprocal course. I spotted a long vapor trail from a Mosquito, which was dropping cascades. I turned towards it and slowly got closer to the target. At 2138 hours and flying at a height of 8500 meters [27,600ft] I clearly saw the target and opened fire at 150 meters whilst pulling up the nose of my aircraft. I hit him squarely. Pulling away to the left I observed large burning parts of the Mosquito falling and scattering the ground in sector FF5 near Nauen. After landing I found that a part of the Mosquito had left a dent in the right turbine cowling of my Me 262. I had used 20 nine-shells of 30mm ammunition.'[71]

Lt Kurt Lamm, one of *Kommando Welter*'s pilots,[72] adds:

'I flew my first operational mission in 10./NJG 11 on 27/28 March. With four aircraft we took off for a sortie over Berlin, as Mosquitoes were reported approaching the *Reich* capital. Kurt Welter instructed me: 'You will be the last one to take off, as this will enable you to see the illuminated flare path in time on your return. The vertical *Flak*-searchlights positioned to the left and right of our path of final approach are our 'gate' through which we must fly'. Soon after taking off, whilst still at low level, the undercarriage of my aircraft dropped all of a sudden. This was the first surprise. My vast flying experience and fast reactions came to my rescue. I immediately put the aircraft's nose down, went over into horizontal flight, pressed the button for 'undercarriage up' and I was lucky. The undercarriage stayed locked up. I made my way toward Berlin whilst climbing at 20 m/s. The thought crossed my mind that most other, less experienced, pilots would have crashed in similar circumstances.

'Over Berlin, concentrations of searchlights attempted to catch the enemy bombers in their cones. Then we got into range of our adversary. The first one I heard over the R/T was Welter. He exclaimed *Pauke* and *Horrido* to announce his first success of the night. Subsequently, each one of us shot a Mosquito down in flames to crash into the ruins of Berlin. Then once more, Welter shouted '*Horrido*'. Two successful interceptions in one sortie, he was the only one who could pull that off. He had an exceptional feeling for the game of night fighting. 'Bonzo', his cloth dog talisman, accompanied him on every sortie.

'During our flight back to base at Burg, we received the warning of Mosquito intruders lurking in the vicinity. It was their tactic to try and pick us off from behind on final approach. After having passed through the 'gate' the two searchlights immediately formed a cone and the light *Flak* defenses hosed up their ammunition into the cross of light. This saved my skin. When I had touched down and taxied into the dispersal area I was informed that one Mosquito, which had actually followed me in had been shot down.

'Whilst my machine was being towed into the hangar, the mechanic groundcrews observed. 'You have brought home the confirmation of your kill. Look at the dents in the leading edge of the wing'. I had rushed towards the fast bomber aircraft with a speed of 850 kph [530mph] and was so fascinated by the action that I had opened fire a bit on the late side. The burst of fire from my four 30 mm cannons had torn up the Mosquito and I had to pull away steeply to avoid getting hit by the debris flying around. Kurt Welter was not pleased when he saw the dents in my machine and warned me to keep a better eye on the difference in speed during the coming missions.'

In April *Nachtjagd* scored 33 victories to take the arm's total claims for 1945 to 528 kills but the writing was on the wall and nightfighter crews knew it. *Ritterkreuzträger Hptm* Dieter Schmidt, commander of the 7th *Staffel* of NJG 1 recalls:

'The Americans advanced ever closer to the Ruhr in the south and the British to the north. For the Third *Gruppe* the final phase of the war began with the transfer in March to Hildesheim. Technical personnel and material were taken out of the Ruhr area by night through the closing gap between Paderborn and Bielefeld. The 8th *Staffel* at Fritzlar was less lucky, it was overrun by American armored formations advancing from Marburg, not without losses of flying and ground personnel. From then on, successful night operations were hardly possible any longer. The remains of the *Gruppe* moved to Lüneburg at the beginning of April and to Neumünster in the middle of the month, where they finally got the order to park their aircraft to the north of Husum and to place themselves at the disposal of some army unit for fighting on the ground. But in the end it was agreed that the four *Nachtjagdgeschwader*, which had meanwhile collected in the 'wet triangle' should form a division of their own with orders to form a 'last line of defense' roughly on the line Husum-Schleswig. It was our good fortune that on the

> day of the capituation the British were near Rendsburg. So the III./NJG 1 together with the other four *Geschwader* was able to enter the demobilisation camp south of the Eder.'[73]

During April RAF Mosquitoes claimed 45 German aircraft destroyed, the first on 3 April when F/L D.L. Hughes and F/L R.H. Perks of 239 Squadron in a NFXXX destroyed a Ju 188. Later that night eight Mosquitoes of 157 Squadron made a *Spoof* raid on Berlin in support of 95 Mosquitoes of 8 Group. Over the 'Big City' F/L J.H. Leland was coned by the searchlights and a Me 262 seeing its chance, made four attacks on the Mosquito. Two strikes were recorded on Leland's engines but he escaped his pursuer after spinning his aircraft and heading flat out for friendly territory. A 139 Squadron BXX Mosquito, one of five that went to Magdeburg, went missing. (*Lt* Herbert Altner and *Oblt* Welter of 10./NJG 11 both claimed a Mosquito shot down).[74]

On 4/5 April 141 Squadron dispatched its first Mosquito NFXXX sortie when three joined 12 from 239 Squadron in a bomber support operation for the heavies attacking synthetic oil plants at Leuna, Harburg and Lützkendorf in southern Germany. S/L Tim Woodman and F/L John Neville, who were serving at BSDU, destroyed a Bf 109 west of Magdeburg (Woodman's seventh confirmed victory of the war). F/L C.W. 'Topsy' Turner and 20-year old F/Sgt George 'Jock' Honeyman from Edinburgh of 85 Squadron destroyed a Ju 188 near Magdeburg.[75] On 9/10 April W/C Howard C. Kelsey DFC*, CO, 515 Squadron and his navigator F/L Edward M. 'Smitty' Smith DFC DFM flew an *Intruder* to Lübeck, a night-fighter base that was still active. Smith recalls:

> 'After a while we spotted a Ju 88 taking off in dark conditions and had difficulty keeping it in radar contact and slowing down sufficiently to keep behind it. The Ju 88 was climbing very hard, probably with flaps, however, it was shot at and we saw several strikes. After that all was quiet and we headed off towards Hamburg. I spotted an aircraft coming in behind us. We feinted to the right then circled hard to port, coming in behind him in part moonlight. We had no trouble in shooting the Ju 188 down. We continued over Hamburg and dropped the *Intruder* load of two 500 lb HE and 160 incendiaries.'[76]

On Sunday 8 April F/Sgt John Aldridge, bomb aimer in a Lancaster crew in 49 Squadron at Fulbeck was among those briefed just after lunch for a raid on Lützkendorf. The oil refinery would be the target of 231 Lancasters and 11 Mosquitoes of 5 Group while 440 aircraft of 4, 6 and 8 Groups bombed the shipyards at Hamburg. It was a day for reciting 'there but for the grace of God' because fate took a decsive course, as Aldridge recalls:

> '1 Group Lancasters had attacked the Lützkendorf refinery [on 4/5 April] achieving 'moderate' success and 5 Group was to finish the job. At the conclusion of the briefing W/C Botting, with a piece of paper in his hand, told us that we were tour expired since the signal he had received during briefing had reduced the number of operations required from 36 to 33. We were scrubbed from the operation and the reserve crew (F/O Roger Cluer's) would take our place. Our rear gunner, Roy Wilkins had completed about three trips less than the rest of the crew (because of illness) and since Sgt Pollington the rear gunner in the reserve crew had contracted ear trouble Roy volunteered to take his place. We all went out to the runway to see the lads take off and Sgt Pollington came with us. Sitting on the grass on this pleasant early spring evening awaiting F/O Cluer to swing *N-Nuts* onto the main runway we idly picked clover. Pollington actually picked three four-leafed clovers in succession! Laughingly, we all remarked, 'You lucky bastard ... it looks like your crew will get the chop tonight'. Many a true word spoken in jest! Roy gave us thumbs up from his rear turret as *N-Nuts* roared down the runway at just after 1800 hrs. Later we all went to the 'Hare and Hounds' in Fulbeck village for a drink before rolling back into our hut. Although we never had the pleasure of knowingly flying our last op, the feeling of having finished was never the less fantastic. Next morning Roy's bed was still empty and we thought he might have landed elsewhere but nothing more was ever heard of him or the crew with which he was flying. Roy's loss was a very tragic experience coming right at the end of a long and distinguished tour. The raid itself was a total success with the refinery being rendered inactive. The cost had been six Lancasters and their crews.'[77]

On 9 April 40 Lancasters of 5 Group carried out the last raid on Hamburg by Bomber Command aircraft when they raided oil-storage tanks and 17 aircraft of 617 Squadron blasted the U-boat shelters in the already devastated city with Grand Slam and Tallboy bombs. Two Lancasters failed ot return from the raid on the oil-storage tanks. Next it was the turn of 1, 3 and 8 Groups, which raided Kiel on the night of 9/10 April when 591 Lancasters and eight Mosquitoes bombed the Deutsche Werke U-boat yards. The pocket battleship *Admiral Scheer* was hit and capsized and the *Admiral Hipper* and the *Emden* were badly damaged. Three Lancasters were lost and a Halifax III of 462 Squadron RAAF failed to return from a diversionary operation to Stade when it crashed in France. *Lt* Arnold Döring and *Hptm* von Tesmar of IV./NJG 3 and *Hptm* Heinz Ferger of III./NJG 2 were the *Nachtjagd* pilots who claimed the Lancasters. A Halifax and a Lancaster were lost on 10 April when 230 bombers attacked the Engelsdorf and Mockau rail yards at Leipzig. *Nachtjagd* pilots claimed six Lancasters, a Halifax and a Mosquito on 10/11 April when 307 Lancasters and eight Mosquitoes of 1 and 8 Groups attacked the rail yards in the northern part of Plauen and 76 Lancasters and 19 Mosquitoes bombed the Wahren railway yards at Leipzig. All the bombers returned safely from the raid on Plauen but seven Lancasters were lost on Leipzig where the eastern half of the yards were destroyed. A RCM Halifax III of 100 Group and a 571 Squadron Mosquito BXVI, one of 77 engaged on a LNSF operation to Berlin also failed to return.[78] Six of the losses were due to crews of NJG 5 and NJG 100, at least four of their victims crashing in the target area at Leipzig. *Fw* von Stade and *Oblt* Kurt Welter of II./JG 11 both claimed a Mosquito kill. The RCM Halifax was NA240 of 462 Squadron RAAF, which was flown by P/O A.D.J. Ball RAAF, and it was the one claimed by *Hptm* Herbert Koch of I./NJG 3 northeast of Anholt. Ball and everyone in his crew except one died.

More attacks on rail yards took place on the 11th when Nürnberg and Bayreuth were the targets for the Halifaxes of 4 Group who in part were supported by Pathfinder Lancasters and Mosquitoes of 8 Group. Another LNSF Mosquito went missing on a raid on Berlin that night when 8 Group launched its most complex attack on the 'Big City' to date. Some 107 Mosquitoes in three waves bombed the capital with Oboe aircraft marking the target for the first time. Eight other Mosquitoes attacked Munich without loss. *Oblt* Kurt Welter made the only Mosquito claim this night when a Mosquito of 163 Squadron failed to return.[79] Welter claimed another Mosquito on the night of 13/14 April (when a 100 Group Mosquito failed to return) and one more the night after when a Lancaster was the only aircraft shot down.[80]

On 12/13 April 28 Stirlings flew on SD ops. W/O James Harding in Halifax *F-Freddy* of 296 Squadron at Earls Colne, Essex piloted by F/L Watson flew a SOE op to northern Holland:

> 'My last tour we flew many operations over the Netherlands flying under Fighter Command for administration. Though they were shorter than our other covert operations (e.g. northern Norway) they were far more hazardous. Our Halifax was loaded with an armed Jeep in the bomb bay with the doors removed. We took two SAS drivers and made our take-off at 2240 bound for a dropping zone north of the Zuider Zee. Earlier another Stirling[81] took off for the same DZ to drop several SOE and SIS five to ten minutes before we were due to arrive. They were to immediately take charge of the Jeep and supplies and with the aid of the SAS drivers, complete their mission. We crossed the English coast low enough to avoid detection by German radar but high enough so that German fighters could not splash fire us (firing from above and drawing their bullet splashes in the sea in a line across our plane). We made landfall about the Hook of Holland. Jack, the navigator gave instructions to the pilot to turn south to cover our objective and he hedge-hopped as much as we could with such an awkward cargo, turning north later on a vector to the DZ.
>
> 'As we saw the Zuider Zee in the distance we could see the Stirling on a parallel course well in front and above. We then became aware of two enemy aircraft, which were assumed to be Fw 190s, approaching his starboard side. We turned on a course parallel with the lake using our camouflaged fuselage to give us cover against the dark ground. The enemy aircraft broke formation, one circling behind the slow Stirling, the other one flying in front and dropping flares whilst continuing in a semi-circle from the port side. This made the slow-flying Stirling a perfect silhouette. They both attacked alternately, their tracer looking like a string of beads. Indeed we did hear vaguely a May Day call, as it seemed to disappear somewhere over the Zuider Zee.
>
> 'We were still flying low on a diagonal vector keeping strict R/T silence. The enemy aircraft had broken off their contact with the Stirling and were flying in a line, which would bring them nearer to us. We were expecting a recall signal because our operation could not be completed without the other Stirling. As the enemy aircraft came within 800 meters I fired a short burst. It was a mistake, as it appeared to alert them to our presence. For a moment they maneuvered then flew off westward, probably running out of fuel or ammunition. Our recall came at that moment and we gave a direction for our return. Alas, as we reached the Netherlands coast two more enemy aircraft came into view, obviously alerted. They could easily out-gun and out-fly us. We had already decided to use our intercom as our best defense with the bomb aimer in the nose keeping them to our starboard. Jack in the dome and myself in the tail turret, passed the information one to the other. I directed the pilot in the maneuvers to keep both planes and flares at one side of us when possible and turning directly into any attack after the fighters had been committed and turning when the fighters were momentarily blind to us in the turn. This went on right across the sea to the English coast. We were concerned as we were still carrying the Jeep under our bomb bay and

though it helped us in making the fighters overshoot, we still had the problem of landing at our base. No one had ever landed with a jeep hanging underneath. If the fighters followed us we would be a sitting target. To our relief American Mustangs met us. We landed with a slight crosswind. It was an awful landing, possibly due to our nervous tension. It felt as if we had been in the air for hours but the whole operation was only 3 hrs 30 minutes. There was a de-briefing and the usual ham and egg breakfast, then to bed with the sure knowledge that we would not sleep due to the caffeine tablets we had taken to keep us awake and alert. Unfortunately they always lasted longer than needed.'[82]

Air to air victories were now few and far between but on the night of 13/14 April F/L Kenneth D. Vaughan and F/L Robert Denison MacKinnon of 85 Squadron achieved the last victory over a He 219 *Uhu* at Kiel. MacKinnon picked up a fast moving contact below them and Vaughan dived after the unidentified aircraft. Twice Vaughan closed range to 1000 ft. Then on the third time he closed in he thought that their twin-engined quarry had caught fire but MacKinnon got his head out of radar set and confirmed that it was the exhaust glow of his BMW 109-003 turbojet below the fuselage. (It was a He 219A-010/TL (V30 190101 of *Erprobungsstelle Rechlin*) which Heinkel had been testing for months). Vaughan immediately pushed the Mosquito's throttles fully open before giving the *Owl* a half-second deflection shot on his jet at about 900-ft range. However, this burst produced no strikes, so he got dead astern in the turn and at 700 ft range fired another burst, which caused a large explosion and strikes on his starboard side. Vaughan gave him another burst 'for luck' and another explosion appeared on the port side. The *Owl* burned from wingtip to wing tip and went down in a spin to starboard. (The aircraft reportedly suffered 40 per cent damage after crash-landing).[83]

On 14/15 April 500 Lancasters of 1 and 3 Groups and 12 Mosquitoes of 8 Group took part in an operation against Potsdam just outside Berlin. Although Mosquito bombers of the LNSF had attacked the Big City almost continually this was the first time the *Reich* capital had been attacked by heavies since March 1944. One Lancaster was lost to an unidentified nightfighter over the target. Maurice Bishop, pilot of Lancaster III PD270 *Winsome Winnie* of 218 'Gold Coast' Squadron at Chedburgh, recalls:

'This flight, which took 8 hrs 55 minutes, was our most remembered. About an hour from the target my mid upper gunner suddenly shouted, 'Down skip!' I pushed the stick forward hard and saw another Lanc sliding over the top of us on a slightly different heading, same height. My gunner saw the exhaust flame just in time as it was closing in on us. The searchlight activity over Berlin was intense and we were just sliding past one that was fixed when it suddenly locked straight on to us and I was completely blinded. I started to change height, speed and direction .as taught and went into a diving corkscrew pulling out the bottom dive quite hard and throwing the old Lanc around by feel as I was still blinded by the searchlight. Then suddenly we were clear before the night fighters spotted us and we dropped our load on the target and came home OK.

'The next day down at dispersal the ground engineer said, 'What were you up to last night?'

'I said, 'Why?'

'He said, 'Look at this' and he took me up the steps and showed me the upper wing between the fuselage and the starboard inner. The skin had a wrinkle in it. We must have pulled out of the dive with our full bomb load on board and the old Lanc had taken it under protest.'[84]

Nachtjagd scored its final heavy Bomber Command aircraft kill on 16/17 April when *Ofw* Ludwig Schmidt of 2./NJG 6 shot down a Halifax, which was engaged on a Bomber Support operation in the Augsburg area.[85]

'The morning of 18 April,' recalls W/O Arthur 'Spud' Taylor of 149 Squadron:

'Was a fine clear day. We set out for Heligoland flying straight there across the North Sea. Almost 1000 kites took part in this trip. The island guarded the entrance to Bremen and Hamburg, which key ports the Germans were fiercely defending against British troops. Next to Heligoland is a smaller island, which was almost entirely taken up by an aerodrome. The aerodrome was bombed first – then our island. From 70 miles away we could see the black smoke belching from these two places, although they themselves would be pretty well invisible from that range. Denmark, lying low in the water, stood out clearly in front of us, each island well defined. As we got closer we could see what was happening very clearly. A huge column of smoke belched up and from inside the smoke a continuous series of angry red flashes showed where the bombs were exploding. I don't think there was one square foot of that island which escaped the rain of bombs. I had never seen such absolute destruction before.'

On the night of 19/20 April F/L Podge Howard DFC and F/O 'Sticky' Clay DFC of BSDU at Swanton Morley were on a patrol to South Denmark and Island of Fyn airfields in a Mosquito NFXXX equipped with AI.Mk.X, *Serrate* IVA and

Wolf. They carried out a patrol of Fyn Island for an hour, during which time only one airfield was observed at Beldringe where they attacked a dispersed barrack site with two bursts of two seconds each. Strikes were seen. The airfield was not lit and no *Flak* was experienced. Many small convoys were seen on roads. At 2316 hours course was set from the island at 2000 ft. Eight minutes' later Clay picked up a AI.Mk.X contact crossing starboard to port, range four miles and above. Howard turned behind the contact at 5000-ft range when a visual was obtained on a Ju 88, which was identified with the aid of night glasses at 1500-ft range. It was flying at 3000 ft at a speed of 240 mph. Howard gave the Junkers a short burst from dead astern at 250 yards, which caused the outer half of the port wing to fall away. The Ju 88 rolled on its back and hit the ground spreading wreckage over a wide area and causing a large number of small fires. Their duty done the Mosquito crew set course for Norfolk, crossing out at Farre at 2340 hours and landing back at Swanton Morley at 0104 hrs.[86]

'On 21 April,' recalls W/O Arthur 'Spud' Taylor of 149 Squadron:

> '149 led the Group and the Wingco led the Squadron. We were on his right hand, being 2nd in the lead in case anything happened to the old man. Our route took us across Holland (by Ijmuiden), into Germany, north to Emden, east towards Wilhelmshaven, skirting that town and then south to the target. The Wing Commander led us over Wilhelmshaven into an accurate barrage of *Flak*, causing damage to every kite in the squadron. We bombed in a small hail of *Flak* and got away to the clear area around Hanover. Got back to base about nine pm. The story behind the raid is that our army was lining the west bank of the Weser, facing the main part of Bremen. The Germans on the east bank were picked *SS* troops, fanatical men determined to fight to the end. Shortly after our raid the 52nd Division crossed the Weser, stormed the east bank and spread out to surround the town. Absolute accuracy of bombing was required and achieved on this occasion. Not one of our bombs landed on our troops on the west bank of the Weser.
>
> 'On 22 April, with the war in Europe fast coming to a close, I thought that the number of raids before its end would be very limited – for us anyway – though I daresay the T97 would be kept pretty busy till the last moment. We had started practicing supply dropping by flying low-level across the drome and lobbing sandbags on to a white cross (I landed one on a runway!) Now that we were right across Germany, some pretty horrible things were coming to light. We were finding concentration camps complete with enormous cremation ovens and torture devices, filled with men, women and children looking like skeletons – hundreds of whom died every day in spite of all we could do. The numbers killed in these places was colossal. In one camp alone over a million died and were cremated. In another (Belsen) a laboratory was found where German doctors practised on live prisoners and lampshades were made out of tanned human skins. Russians, political prisoners and European civilians seem to have suffered most. Ours were mostly under nourished – thousands had already been freed. Germany was beaten all right but she had left Europe in a terrible state. There could hardly be one family on this side of the globe, which did not have a personal cause for hating the Germans.'

On 24/25 April when the Mosquitoes of 100 Group and 2nd TAF ranged far and wide over the rapidly diminishing *Reich* fortunes were varied. P/O K.A. Norman and his navigator F/O C.B.L. Warwick of 406 'Lynx' Squadron RCAF were fortunate to survive when their NFXXX was shot down by flak during an *Intruder* to Flensburg airfield. Norman crashlanded in flames from 50 ft and both men were captured. W/C Howard C. Kelsey DFC* CO and F/L E.M. Smith DFC DFM of 515 Squadron in a Mosquito FBVI[87] got 100 Group's last air to air victory of the war when they shot down a Dornier Do 217 six miles north of Prague-Ruzyne, Czechoslovakia. Their victim was one of *Nachtjagd*'s most distinguished aces, *Major* Rudolf Schoenert, *Kommodore* of NJG 5, who had shot down four Russian bombers east of Berlin earlier that night, for his 62nd-65th victories. Schoenert and his crew all baled out safely. Kelsey and Smith therefore had the distinction of scoring 100 Group's first and last victories of the war.[88] Also, *Nachtjagd*'s 7308th and final kill of the war went to *Hptm* Herbert Koch, *Staffelkapitän*, 1./NJG 3, his 21st of the war. In a classic *Himmelbett* operation, the *Experte* destroyed a Coastal Command Halifax over the North Sea off Denmark.[89]

For S/L R.G. 'Tim' Woodman a Mosquito pilot of the BSDU[90] 25 April was his 59th and final operation of the war:

> 'It was not the normal anti-German night fighter operation that F/L Paul Mellows, F/L Callard, F/O Terry Groves and I carried out, just a last crack at the Germans. We flew our NFXXXs, which were fitted with various radar and electronic devices, up to Peterhead from Swanton Morley and refuelled. We took off again at dusk and then, in loose formation in the moonlight, crossed the North Sea, through the Skaggerak and up the Oslo Fjord. I thought that with the war virtually over the Norwegian airfields would have lots of German aircraft on them. We attacked Lister where there was concentrated *Flak* but no aircraft, Rygge (same again) and Kjeller (where there was

no *Flak* or aircraft) and Gardermoen (now Oslo airport). There was a lot of activity at Gardermoen with searchlights and star shells and the *Flak* was intense, F/O Groves getting a cannon shell through a wing. Eventually the airfield was plunged into darkness with only the searchlights probing for us and the *Flak* snaking up. I called the chaps off and said, '*Let's go home*.' I would never have forgiven myself if either of us had been shot down'.

Bomber Command's last bombing operations were the obliteration of Wangerooge and a failed attempt at destroying Hitler's 'Eagle's Nest' at Berchtesgaden in daylight on 25 April and the oil storage depots at Tonsberg in Southern Norway on the following night. Yet, the war was not over for the weary bomber crews. Four days later they were called upon again but this time it was to drop food and not bombs. With the Germans at the brink of defeat, thousands of people in the western and northwestern provinces of the Netherlands, which were still in German hands, were without food. Parts of the country had been under German blockade and 20,000 men, women and children had died of starvation during a very short period and the survivors were in a desperate plight. From 29 April to 7 May Lancasters of 1, 3 and 8 Groups flew 2835 food sorties and PFF Mosquitoes made 124 sorties to 'mark' the dropping zones and Bomber Command delivered 6672 tons of food to the starving Dutch people during Operation *Manna*. Maurice Bishop, pilot of Lancaster III PD270 *Winsome Winnie* of 218 'Gold Coast' Squadron, recalls:

'On 30 April we did our first food drop on Operation *Manna* to Rotterdam and 2nd May to The Hague, both marvellous low flying 250 ft. The '*Thanks*' messages on the roofs with towels and sheets I will always remember.'

W/O Arthur 'Spud' Taylor of 149 Squadron flew a *Manna* operation on 1st May:

'Holland, from Rotterdam to the North was still occupied. To stop our advance the Jerries had flooded half the country, with a result that large towns were packed full of homeless, hungry Dutch. By arrangement we were dropping food on the towns, without any opposition. We set out about 11 in the morning with 6000 odd pounds of food for a place just outside The Hague. Crossed the Dutch coast at low level just north of Overflakee. The whole coastline and the edges of the rivers were all pitted with defense posts and gun positions, though I never saw a German the whole time. I daresay they had orders to keep under cover in case we shot at them. With the Germans all under cover the population turned out in strength and waved at us. It was a heartening sight! Some of them were madly waving flags (mostly Dutch but all red, white and blue). One little man I saw had one enormous flag in each hand and a terrific grin on his face; when he caught sight of the kite, he leaped off the ground in his excitement! A woman was perched perilously on the roof of a house waving like mad and shouting something. I should think every person in The Hague turned out to cheer us. Our dropping ground was in a sports field north of the town complete with a grandstand. With remarkable confidence in our aim, the grandstand was packed with the good people. I wouldn't swear to it but somebody looking remarkably like the mayor was there in his robes of office. The grandstand was only a stone's throw from our dropping point, which was marked by a white cross. We came back at nought feet above the sea very pleased with ourselves.'

Nineteen year old F/Sgt Bob Pierson who joined F/Sgt Leo Hughes' crew in 100 Squadron in February 1945 and completed 23 operations as tail gunner on Lancasters before the end of the war, has vivid memories of Operation Manna:

'I did several food drops at 200/300 ft to Rotterdam and Bergen. The first such trip we did was on 3 May and we flew in M-Mother from Elsham Wolds near Grimsby, Lincolnshire. We took off at 1130 hrs and we were very apprehensive, this being the first time we had flown at such a low height, without any training. The last trip we had done was to Bremen at 20,000 ft! Although there had been a temporary truce set up with the German Army, not many of us really trusted them very much. I remember thinking as we skimmed the waters on our way and crossing the Dutch coast, this really was something different. I could see the German soldiers standing by at their positions on their shore batteries so clearly and some of the Dutch people were waving, that it did not seem possible that we were still at war! It was not long however before we were flying so low over the fields and on to our 'target', which was a white cross in a field. I could see the previous drops made by other aircraft.

'Part of the truce was that we could make only one pass at 200 ft and immediately turn for home and we had to have all our guns in an elevated position or the Germans would open fire! This was quite nerveracking. However, we did see the Dutch people very clearly waiting at the dropping zone and wildly waving their greetings to us with sheets or anything else they could get hold of. We hoped that not too much of our load would miss the target.

The food was stored into what is best described as sandbags and we did a lot of the loading ourselves. The bags would be pushed into the open bomb doors and then gradually closed shut. The bomb aimer would then at the appropriate time release the switch that would open the doors and release the load. This would hit the ground and no doubt some of the bags would be split open but most of them were intact for collection.

'We made a second trip on 7 May in the same aircraft taking off at 1500 hrs. The trips usually took three hrs. The final drop our crew did was a very special occasion as it was made on 8 May, which was VE Day. I was actually crossing the Dutch coast at 200 ft in Lancaster C for Charlie at the very hour that Winston Churchill was announcing to the world that war in Europe was at an end. That day was such a contrasting episode in our lives, for only a few days before we had been on a killing mission in Germany and now were on a life saving operation in Holland. What could be more of a contrast than that? On one trip we were flying through Flak and on the other through a sea of flags it seemed. What a dramatic change. By the time we had reached the Dutch coast on 8 May the Dutch were also aware that it was all over and they waved British and American flags. Even the Germans standing on the top of their gun batteries were waving, truly an amazing sight. To experience the transformation that took place on that day will be something I will never forget.'

Large convoys of ships were now assembling at Kiel on the Baltic and it was feared that they were to transport German troops to Norway to continue the fight from there. 142 Mosquitoes of 8 therefore attacked Kiel on 2/3 May in the last operation of the war for Bomber Command. Mosquitoes of 23, 169, 141, 239 and 515 Squadrons in 100 Group made attacks on airfields at Flensburg, Hohn, Westerland/Sylt and Schleswig/Jägel. Hohn and Flensburg airfields were bombed with Napalm and incendiaries directed by a Master Bomber. Support for the night's operations was provided by *Mandrel/ Window* sorties and a *Spoof* operation with *Window.*[91] All told, a record 106 aircraft of 100 Group took part. A Mosquito of 169 Squadron was shot down by flak and the crew killed and two Halifaxes of 199 Squadron collided while on their bomb runs.[92] These were the last Bomber Command aircraft to be lost on operations. Six days later the European war was over.

On 8 May W/O Arthur 'Spud' Taylor wrote in his diary:

'VE Day! The war has lasted so long I can hardly believe it is over. I can't remember very clearly now what it was like to live without a war; it seems so long ago. Stayed in the flat this evening as the West End was pretty crowded and got through two bottles of wine. Went upstairs afterwards and watched people lighting fires and firing Verey lights (I wish I'd brought some). Singing and shouting went on to the early hours but we were in bed by then.'

Maurice Butt a pilot in 149 Squadron recalls:

'VE Day found many hundreds of RAF and other recently liberated prisoners of war on the tarmac at Brussels Airport, awaiting transport back to England. The boys of Bomber Command gave up their celebration leave to come and get us out and we piled into the Lancs, the most excited 'bombloads' ever carried. I was lucky, being the first on our plane and scrambled forward to the bomb aimer's station, spotting everything approaching after about half an hour, there were the white cliffs of Dover. At that moment, the front gunner handed me his helmet. Incredibly, Winston Churchill was speaking from the House of Commons, announcing the victory news and I could hear it quite clearly on the earphones.'

• • •

By the end of the war no less than 73,741 casualties were sustained by Bomber Command of which 55,500 aircrew had been KIA or flying accidents, or died on the ground or while prisoners of war. It is a casualty rate that compares with the worst slaughters in the World War I trenches. Operational bomber losses were 8655 aircraft and another 1600 were lost in accidents and write-offs. Approximately 125,000 aircrew served in the front-line, OTU and OCUs of the Command and nearly 60% of them became casualties. In addition, almost 9,900 more were shot down and made PoWs to spend one, two or more years in squalid, desolate *Oflags* and *Stalags* in *Axis* held territory. Over 8000 more were wounded aboard aircraft on operational sorties. Bomber Command flew almost 390,000 sorties, the greatest percentage of them by Avro Lancasters, Handley Page Halifaxes and Wellingtons. Theirs of course were the highest casualties.

On 12 May ACM Sir Arthur T. Harris KCB OBE AFC issued a 'SPECIAL ORDER OF THE DAY':

'...You for long alone, carried the war ever deeper and even more furiously into the heart of the Third Reich. There the whole might of the German enemy in undivided strength and – scarcely less a foe – the very elements, arrayed against you. You overcome them both. Through those desperate years, undismayed by any odds, undeterred by any casualties, night succeeding night, you fought... isolated in your crew stations by the darkness and the murk and from all other aircraft in company. Not for you the hot emulation of high endeavor in the glare and panoply of martial array. Each crew, each one in each crew, fought alone through black nights rent only, mile after continuing mile, by the fiercest barrages ever raised and the instant sally of the searchlights. In each dark minute of those long miles lurked menace. Fog, ice, snow and tempest found you undeterred. In that loneliness in action lay the final test, the ultimate stretch of human staunchness and determination.

'Your losses mounted through those years, years in which your chance of survival through one spell of operational duty was negligible; through two periods, mathematically nil. Nevertheless survivors pressed forward as volunteers to pit their desperately acquired skill in even a third period of operations, on special tasks.

'In those five years and eight months of continuous battle over enemy soil, your casualties over long periods were grievous. In the whole history of our National forces, never have so small a band of men been called upon to support so long such odds. You indeed bore the brunt...To all of you I would say how proud I am to have served in Bomber Command for four and a half years and to have been your Commander-in-Chief through more than three years of your saga.

'Your task in the German war is now completed. Famously you have fought. Well you have deserved of your country and her Allies.'

But for thousands of Bomber Command aircrew, the war was far from over. 'Spud' Taylor, who on 20 July 1945 received the award of the DFC, says:

'For some months after the war I used to wake up in a cold sweat on the floor next to my side of the bed. The dream was always much the same – my clothes were on fire and I was baling out of a burning aircraft. My wife Marguerite would say,

'You OK Spud?'

'I would reply, 'Yes thanks' and she would say, 'Well get back into bed then and stop mucking about.'

'And that is all the counselling I ever received. But it worked and I soon forgot about those dreams. I have never however, forgotten my time in the RAF, or the comrades I flew with.'

Many years later Peter Richard[93] had this to say:

'Losses in Bomber Command are usually shown as percentages of aircraft missing or shot down of the total number despatched. In aircrew members, the total of those killed over the 68 months of the war was 55,358. As the war progressed after D-Day the enemy lost the advantage of their forward bases in the occupied territories and their aviation fuel reserves dwindled whereas our numerical strength in crews and aircraft increased dramatically thus the percentage losses in relation to sorties despatched declined. However, from September 1942, when incidentally PFF was founded, the average of the losses each month did not fall below 1000 aircrew members killed and during 1943/44 that average figure topped 1500. The steady monthly erosion of 1000 aircrew translates to the equivalent of a squadron a week written off, a minimum of 50 squadrons each year until the war ended. When one considers the potential of the airmen killed one begins to realize the grave loss there casualties were to the future of this country as they were all Officers and Senior NCOs whose training and eventual duties necessitated that those selected had high qualifications in both leadership and endurance. Theirs was a loss that can never be evaluated; it compares only to that of the infantry officers in the First War. A true if chilling reminder is that for Bomber Command the war was far from over at Christmas 1944. Over 50% of a Pathfinder unit despatched could be lost and we still had our third VC, Captain Swales of the South African Air Force to lose his life in the course of duty. We cannot assess how much better off our country would have been had the 55,000 men of Bomber Command survived. We do know however that their sacrifice contributed largely to the defeat of Germany and to the liberation of Europe and for this we and our Allies throughout the world, should be eternally grateful.

'They will not be forgotten.'

Notes

1. Including 1 flown by *Gruppekommandeur*, *Hptm* Hecking (301348 L1+GK) and 1 flown by *Oblt* Huber, *Staffelführer* 6./LG 1, in 331294 L1+NP. P/O M.G. Kent-P/O Simpson of 409 'Nighthawk' Sqn RCAF in NFXIII MM466 shot down a Ju 88 of LG 1 over the mouth of the Scheldt. On 3/4 February Kent-Simpson downed a Ju 88 and F/L B.E. Plumer DFC-F/L Hargrove of 410 Sqn RCAF in a NFXXX despatched a He 219 *Uhu*.

2. In NFXIII MM456.

3. Ju 188E-1 260542 A3+QD was Somerville's 7th and final victory. Hauck, *Gfr* Kurt Wuttge, observer, *Uffz* Max Grossman, *Bordfunker* and *Fw* Heinrich Hoppe, despatcher, baled out and became PoWs.

4. Mellows fired 72 rounds of SAPI (Semi Armor Piercing Incendiary) and 68 rounds of HEI (Heavy Explosive Incendiary) to down the Bf 110. Mellows and Drew's victim probably Bf 110G-4 730370 2Z+EL of 3./NJG 6, which cr. 25 km S of Stuttgart. *Oblt* Willy Rathmann, with no victories, pilot, *Fw* Erich Berndt, *Bordfunker* and *Ogefr* Alfred Obry, *Bordschütze* KIA.

5. Who had been shot down by an 85 Sqn Mosquito flown by F/L W. House-F/Sgt R.D. MacKinnon on 13/14 September 1944.

6. In Bf 110G-4 730262 G9+CN.

7. Hanneck's adversary was either a 157 or 239 Sqn Mosquito. S/L Ryall-P/O Mulroy of 157 Sqn claimed a Bf 110 'probable' at Oberolm, while W/C Walter Gibb DSO DFC 239 Sqn CO-F/O R.C. Kendall DFC destroyed a Bf 110 at Mannheim.

8. *Stab* and I./NJG 6 crews flying Ju 88s claimed 9 Lancasters destroyed over and around Karlsruhe 2320-2340 hrs.

9. 5 Lancasters cr in the same area around the town of Bruchsal, NE of Karlsruhe on 2/3 February 1945 (3 of 189 Sqn – PB848 flown by F/L N.B. Blain cr in a wood near Heidelsheim S of Bruchsal. All except rear gunner KIA. F/Sgt Don Clement RCAF had a similar escape to Sgt Dyson, being blown from his turret by an explosion, which was possibly caused when the Lancaster was hit by Flak making a 2nd bomb run over the target with its bomb load still aboard. PB743 flown by F/L J.D. Davies, exploded on its bombing run over Weingarten, SW of Heidelsheim after dropping the 4000 pounder and part of the load of incendiaries may have been hit by a Schräge Musik equipped night-fighter. F/Sgt Les Cromarty DFM, crew tail gunner on his 2nd tour, was again the sole survivor when he was blown out of his turret and he landed by parachute. ME298/B of 463 Sqn came down at Unterowisheim nearby after being attacked by a night-fighter and possibly being hit by Flak over Karlsruhe. F/O R.K. Oliver RAAF and 4 crew KIA. They were buried in the British and Commonwealth war cemetery at Durnbach, as were the 6 crew of PB840, the remains of which fell into a wood near Oberowisheim, NE of Bruchsal. It is believed that PB840 was shot down by *Ofw* Heinrich Schmidt of 2./NJG 6 at 2321 hrs; it was Schmidt's 9th *Abschuss*. 5th Lancaster was PB306 of 467 RAAF Sqn (shot down by *Hptm* Friedrich at Karlsdorf at 2330) piloted by F/L N.S.C. Colley. All 8 crew, average age 21 KIA.

10. Bf 110G-4 730322 G9+HR of 7./NJG 1, which cr. W of Soest in the Ruhr. *Fw* Heinz Amsberg, pilot with four night victories and *Uffz* Matthias Dengs, *Bordfunker* KIA. *Gefr* Karl Kopperberg, *Bordschütze* (WIA), baled out.

11. Possibly Ju 88G-6 R4+UB of 9./NJG 5, which cr. at Stirnberg/Detmold/Germany. *Uffzs* Richard Rückert, replacement pilot with no victories, Hans Meiller, *Bordfunker* and Herbert Hoffmann, *Bordschütze*, KIA.

12. 12 Lancasters FTR, probably all to *Nachtjäger* of NJG 2, NJG 3 and NJG 5. *Lt* Herbert Altner of 8./NJG 5 claimed 3 Lancasters over Stettin.

13. The other cities were Berlin, Chemnitz and Leipzig, which like Dresden, were vital communications and supply centers for the Eastern Front. Thunderclap had been under consideration for several months and was to be implemented only when the military situation in Germany was critical.

14. In addition the U.S. 8th Air Force despatched 450 B-17s of which 316 attacked Dresden shortly after 12 noon on 14 February. Another force of 368 RAF aircraft of 4, 6 and 8 Groups went to Böhlen but the weather was bad and the bombing scattered. 1 Halifax FTR.

15. F/Sgt Base had witnessed the demise of the only Lancaster claimed shot down by night fighters. Just 6 Lancasters were lost from the 796 Lancasters and 9 Mosquitoes despatched. *Major* Hans Leickhardt, *Kommandeur* of II./NJG 5 was probably the only *Nachtjäger* to make contact with the Dresden force, he shot down 2 Lancasters.

16. *"Nachtjaeger gegen Bomberpulks: Ein Tatsachen-bericht ueber die Deutsche Nachjagd im Zweiten Weltkrieg,* Pabel Rastatt, 1960/*Duell unter den Sternen (Duel Under the Stars")* 1956/Kimber Pocket Edition 1958.

17. Bomber Support Development Unit. Howard joined 239 Sqn on 2 May 1944 and completed 32 operational sorties by 9 November 1944, during which he destroyed 3 e/a and damaged 8 trains. During 4 other sorties he damaged 8 trains in Holland Germany. Awarded DFC 9 November 1944.

18. One Bf 110 G-4 of 11./NJG 1 was reportedly shot down SW Lippstadt near Benninghausen – *Uffz* Gerhard Bauer and *Uffz* Rudolf Seratin KIA. This was probably the victim of the BSDU Mosquito.

19. Leslie 'Dutch' Holland had flown 5 hrs short of 1000 when he first joined 515 Sqn on offensive operations. This late baptism of fire came nearly 2 yrs after having spent about 6 months on home defense night-fighters. In the period between, a year spent instructing pilots destined for night-fighters and on a refresher course at an OTU, had nurtured a gradual build-up of confidence, capability and a certain amount of fatalism. Young had been an infantryman in the 'Ox and Bucks, the famous 43rd and 52nd of Foot, before transferring to the RAF.

20. On 15/16 April 1945 Holland and Young destroyed a Ju 52/3M nr. Schleissheim in FBVI PZ398/C.

21. Including diversionary and minor operations aircraft, 1283 sorties were flown.

22. The *Nachtjagd* claimed 25 kills.

23. WSW of Mönchengladbach-SW of Roermond.

24. 14 Lancasters were lost on Dortmund. Düsseldorf cost 4 Halifaxes and 1 Lancaster. Monheim resulted in the loss of 2 Halifaxes. Mittelland Canal was w/o loss. In total 22 aircraft FTR.

25. On 21/22 February German ground control identified the course and height of the bomber stream heading for Worms and before the heavies reached their target and succeeded in infiltrating 15 *Spitzenbesatzungen* of NJG 6 into the bomber stream in the area of Mannheim-Worms. No jamming of their *SN-2* sets was experienced and neither were any Mosquitoes encountered. 2030-2058 hrs 8 *Nachtjagd* crews claimed 21 bombers destroyed in the target area. *Hptm* Breves claimed 2 more *Viermots* in a 50-minute sortie in the Ruhr area as his 17th and 18th and final victories of the war. *Ofw* Günther Bahr of 1./NJG 6 flying Bf 110G 2Z+IH with *Fw* Rehmer as *Bordfunker* and *Uffz* Riediger as *Bordschütze* shot down 7 Lancasters of the Worms force in quick succession 2034-2050 hrs, all on their bombing run to the target with their bomb loads still on board. *Hptm* Johannes Hager's 6 *Viermots* were his 40th-45th *Abschüsse* (all but 6 of his 45 claims were later confirmed) and he was awarded the *Ritterkreuz. Hptm* Heinz Rökker, *Ritterkreuzträger* and *St. Kpt* of 2./NJG 2 also destroyed 6 (56th-61st kills) 2046-2119 hrs; 5 of his *Abschüsse* were of the Mittelland Canal force. Rökker ended the war with 63 *Nachtjagd Abschüsse* (including 55 *Viermots* and 1 Mosquito) + 1 day victory in 161 sorties with NJG 2.

26. Gänsler, an experienced *Bordschütze* who had formidable night-vision, had previously flown with *Oblt* Ludwig Becker and had shared in 17 kills with him. He was awarded the *Ritterkreuz*.

27. Lancaster I NG329 JO-Z of 463 Sqn was MIA at Gravenhorst. Schnaufer's final score was 121 bombers in 130 sorties (114 of his kills were four-engined Stirlings, Halifaxes and Lancasters) and he was decorated with the *Ritterkreuz* with Oak Leaves, Swords and Diamonds. *Lt* Fritz Rumpelhardt took part in 100 of these successful attacks and *Ofw* Gänsler in 98. Rumpelhardt was the most successful *Bordfunker* in *Nachtjagd* being credited with 100 *abschussbeteiligungen*, or 'contributions to claims'. Schnaufer died in a motor car accident in France on 31 July 1950.

28. Bf 110G-4 of 9./NJG 1, *Fhr* Hans Apel and his inexperienced replacement crew KIA.

29. Probably Ju 88G-6 of 2./NJG 2 (*Uffz* Rudolf Kursawe KIA, 2 crew WIA). S of Duisburg a He 219 crew (He 219A-0 190211 G9+TH) of *Hptm* Schirrmacher and *Fw* Franz Waldmann were attacked by a Mosquito, Badly damaged and unable to maintain altitude, Schirrmacher made a forced landing in which Waldmann was injured. Three nights later on 24/25 February W/C Peter Green DSO DFC -F/L D. Oxby DFC DFM** of 219 Sqn flying NFXXX MM792 shot down a *Stuka* and on the 28th S/L Don MacFadyen DFC in NFXXX NT325 claimed a UEA 'probably destroyed' at Hailfingen.

30. XIth *Luftgau Kommando* (covering the greater Hamburg area) reported 17 Mosquitoes shot down. These included FBVI RS569/V of 418 Sqn RCAF. N. Drope a/f, 13 km NE Lingen F/L H.E. Miller-F/Sgt W. Hooper. (Both KIA). FBVI PZ397/X of 418 Sqn RCAF at Altharen, 12 km NW Meppen (W/C I.C. Wickett-P/O W. Jessop both PoW, set on fire after emergency landing); HP832 hit by rail flak at Huttenbusch nr. Worpswede, 21 km NNE Bremen and exploded in mid-air (2 KIA); NS981 hit by *flak* at Barchel 6 km SW Bremervörde (1 PoW, 1 Esc); HR188 hit by *flak* at Meyenburg, 24 km NW Bremen (2 PoW); HR150 railway *flak* nr. Lemförde (2 KIA). SM-F was hit by rail *flak* 1 km W. Holm/9 km W. Rendsburg and exploded in mid-air (2 KIA). Other losses were: 125 Sqn NFXVII HK262 evening interception. W/O M.

Woodthorpe-F/Sgt D.J. Long (both KIA); 418 Sqn RCAF FBVI RS604/M patrol, Osnabrück, pm. F/L C. Hackett-F/O W S Brittain (both safe); 418 Sqn RCAF FBVI PZ388/R Patrol, Osnabrück, pm. F/L H.M. Hope-F/O L A Thorpe (Both KIA); 605 Sqn FBVI PZ406/O Day Ranger. F/L R.L. Jones-F/O C. Phillips (both KIA); 605 Sqn FBVI PZ416/H Day Ranger NW Germany, F/O R.J.R. Owen-P/O C. Thirwell (both KIA); 605 Sqn FBVI PZ409/Q Day Ranger over NW Germany, hit by flak, F/L J.C. Enticott (KIA)-F/Sgt D.C. Hinton (PoW) cr. nr Eelde; 605 Sqn FBVI HR355/K Day Ranger over NW Germany. S/L I. McCall (PoW/WIA)-P/O T Caulfield (PoW). Hit by *flak* and crashed into telegraph poles.

31. 5 crews of NJG 6 claimed 13 Lancaster kills.

32. *"Nachtjaeger gegen Bomberpulks: Ein Tatsachen-bericht ueber die Deutsche Nachjagd im Zweiten Weltkrieg,* Pabel Rastatt, 1960/*Duell unter den Sternen (Duel Under the Stars"),* 1956/Kimber Pocket Edition 1958.

33. From these 2 raids, 7 Lancasters were lost.

34. The Dornier Do 335A-1 *Pfeil* (Arrow) was potentially the fastest piston-engined fighter ever built. It was powered by a conventionally mounted Daimler Benz DB 603 engine in the nose with a 2nd engine buried in the rear fuselage driving an airscrew behind the tail via an extension shaft. Production deliveries were increasing rapidly when the war drew to a close and its is doubtful that any were delivered to an operational unit. In the Do 335A 2-seat night-fighter version with FuG 220 *Lichtenstein* SN-2 and FuG 350 *Naxos* radar the 2nd crewmember was seated above and behind the pilot. 37 Do 335As were built, including prototypes.

35. A special procedure was adopted for abandoning the a/c in emergency. The rear propeller and upper tail fin were jettisoned, followed by the cockpit cover and the pilot then left the cockpit by conventional means but at least 1 a/c was fitted with an ejection seat.

36. FuG 280 *Kiel Z* a passive infrared detector developed by Zeiss. Range 2.5 miles (4 km). Produced in limited numbers for trials.

37. 3C+BC (Wrke Nr. 622056).

38. 64 Mosquitoes of the LNSF bombed Berlin, 32 bombed Würzburg, 29 Mosquito fighters/fighter-bombers carried out patrols over the *Reich*, 12 Mosquito bombers took part in the attack on Kamen and 10 the Dortmund-Ems Canal raid but none were lost. Krause's adversary has not been identified.

39. Ju 88G-6 D5+AX 620028 of 12./NJG 3, which cr. at Elvington nr. Pocklington aerodrome, Yorkshire at 0151 hrs after hitting trees at low level was the last German aircraft to be brought down on British soil. Three people in one family died, as did *Ritterkreuzträger Hptm* Johann Dreher, *St.Kpt*, 12./NJG 3 and his crew. Dreher had been a bomber pilot on the Eastern Front and had been awarded the *Ritterkreuz*. *Maj* Bertold Ney, *Kommandeur, Stab* IV./NJG 3, was partially paralysed when he was forced to abandon his Ju 88G-6 D5+AE over the continent on return.

40. 13 Halifaxes, 9 Lancasters, Mosquito NFXIX MM640/H of 169 Sqn, which cr. at Buxton nr. Coltishall killing S/L V.J. Fenwick-F/O J.W. Pierce and Fortress III HB815/J of 214 Sqn. Fortress II KH114/B of 214 Sqn was damaged on return and landed at RAF Woodbridge, Suffolk. F/Sgt R.V. Kingdon and crew safe. Fortress II HB802/O of 214 Sqn was attacked over Peterborough and landed at Brawdy.

41. Fortress III HB815/J of 214 Sqn piloted by P/O H. Bennett was shot down in the landing circuit at Oulton, Norfolk at 0016 hrs and cr. at Lodge Farm, Oulton. Only Sgt Alastair McDermid and W/O R.W. Church, the 2 waist gunners survived. Döring's 'Lancaster' *Abschuss*, in fact, was Halifax HX332 of 10 Sqn, which cr. at Spellow Hill, Stavely, SE Ripon with 5 crew KIA. All 3 survivors critically injured.

42. After flying operations in support of the *Maquis* in France from Tempsford and attending 1651 CU at Woolfox Lodge and 1668 CU at Bottesford.

43. Ju 88G-6 622319 C9+GA of *Stab*/NJG 5 flown by *Obstlt* Walter Borchers, which cr. nr Altenburg, 25 km NW of Chemnitz. Borchers, *Ritterkreuzträger* (29 October 1944), *Kommodore*, NJG 5, a 59 victory *Experte* of which 16 had been scored by day and 43 by night and his radar operator *Lt* Friedrich Reul, KIA. The 2nd Ju 88 to fall to Gibb's guns was Ju 88G-6 622318 C9+NL of 3./NJG 5, which also cr. nr. Chemnitz. *Uffzs* Hans Dorminger, replacement pilot with no victories, Max Bartsch, Friedrich Rullman and *Ogefr* Franz Wohlschlöegel KIA. Initially, Gibb claimed 1 and 1 damaged but the latter was subsequently confirmed.

44. *Nachtjäger* claims were for 15 Lancasters and a Bomber Support B-17 Fortress.

45. Becker's score at the end of the war was 58 night victories.

46. F/L G. 'Tubby' Pow, 2nd navigator, who had broken his ankle, was hospitalised. 1st navigator, F/O Dudley Heal DFM one of the most accomplished low-level navigators in Bomber Command, landed on the roof of a tall building in the center of Buhl and became a PoW. (As a Sgt navigator on 617 Sqn, he flew the famous Dam Buster raid on 16/17 May 1943, for which he was awarded an immediate DFM by King George VI). F/O Tom Tate, Special Operator, F/Sgt Norman J. Bradley DFM, one of the waist gunners, 40-year old F/O James W. Vinall DFM, co-pilot, twice Mentioned in Dispatches, F/O Harold Frost DFM, top turret gunner, F/O Gordon Hall, radio operator, F/L Sidney C. Matthews DFC, Gunnery Leader and F/Sgt Edward A Percival DFM, the other waist gunner were rounded up. All were put in a school basement at Huchenfeld. Hans Christian Knab, the *Nazi Kreisleiter* (District Leader) of Pforzheim instructed the commander of the local *Hitler Jugend, Sturmabteilung* or SA and the *Volkssturm* to assemble with their men in civilian clothes and incite a crowd to murder the RAF airmen as a reprisal for the civilian losses in Pforzheim on 23/24 February. Wynne's crew were hauled into the street and were confronted by a lynch mob. Tate, in bare feet, managed to get away, was later apprehended by the Wehrmacht and taken into custody by 2 Luftwaffe soldiers who escorted him to PoW camp in Ludwigsburg. Bradley and Vinall got away from their captors but Matthews, Frost, Percival and Hall were murdered in cold blood. Vinall was free for a day and then he gave himself up to Wehrmacht soldiers. He was handed over to the police at Dillstein, whose station was a few yards from a *Hitler Youth* barracks. Vinall was beaten up by a mob before being murdered by Gert Biedermann a 15 year old *Hitler Youth,* who shot him in the head. Biedermann, who had dug the bodies of his mother and five brothers and sisters from the rubble after the bombing of Pforzheim, was later tried, found guilty and sentenced to 15 years imprisonment. Bradley evaded re-capture and reached the village of Grunbach SW of Pforzheim. The 5 men of HB799 are buried in the Dürnbach RAF Cemetery. In 1946 Knab was hanged following War Crimes Proceedings in Essen-Steele.

47. 4 *Experte* crews of NJG 2 and NJG 5 claimed 13 victories. *Hptm* Gerhard Raht *Gruppenkommandeur* of I./NJG 2 claimed 5 heavies for his 54th-58th kills and *Hptm* Heinz Rökker *St.Kpt* of 2./NJG 2 claimed 2 heavies nr. Düsseldorf and a Mosquito (and a B-25) at St. Trond for his 61-64th kills.

48. Werke Nr. 620045 4R+AN.

49. Some by Jung with his *Schräge Musik*, some with his forward-firing guns. Heidenreich, who had taken part in 12 kills with *Oblt* Günter Köberich who had been killed in an American raid on the a/f at Quakenbrück in April 1944, shot down the 3rd victim.

50. At 2118 hrs Hoffmann had destroyed a Lancaster SW of Schwabish Hall for his 49th victory, a Halifax at Ansbach at 2126 hrs for his 50th and a Lancaster E of Ansbach at 2130 hrs for his 51st. Hoffmann and all his crew baled out uninjured.

51. Welter claimed 10 Mosquitoes destroyed March-April. Officially his final wartime score was 56 night victories including 33 Mosquitoes, making him the most successful 'Mosquito-Jäger' (he claimed 59 and 36 respectively). Claims made by Wild Boar pilots in single-seat fighters were hard to corroborate and it is doubtful that Welter achieved anywhere near these figures. (Even Welter's pilots were known to describe him as a 'braggart' and that he had no particular gift for air-to-air firing – *The Other Battle* by Peter Hinchliffe, Airlife 1996).

52. NFXXX NT254/N of 85 Sqn on an *Intruder* to the Dutch Islands. P/O S.J. Harrop DFC and W/O G.C. Redmond (both KIA). FBVI PZ343/B of 605 Sqn on evening *Intruder* to Germany. W/C R.A. Mitchell DFC* and F/L S.H. Hatsell DFC (both KIA).

53. Baake scored his 42nd and final victory, a Lancaster 20km NW of Boxmeer, on 7/8 March 1945.

54. 3 crews of NJG 1 and NJG 2 claimed 1 Halifax each destroyed.

55. 2 crews from NJG 6 each claimed 1 Lancaster shot down.

56. Ju 88 G flown by *Oblt* Engelbert Heiner reported shot down by a RAF *Intruder* nr Gelnhausen. Heiner had seen action with the *Kondor Legion* in the Spanish Civil War as a bomber pilot and flew with 9./KG 27 in the French, British and Russian campaigns before joining *Nachtjagd*. 11 victories. Awarded the *Ritterkreuz*. Heiner joined IV./NJG 6 in 1944, becoming *Kapitän* of 12./NJG 6, gaining 4 further kills.

57. Benzol plants in Germany were attacked on successive days and nights, 17, 17/18 and 18 March.

58. An American development of the *Mandrel IV* device. Known as *Dina II*, when used against the FuG 220 *Lichtenstein SN-2* radar, the device was known as *Piperack*.

59. His 40-42nd and final victories of the war. (Hager never receivied official confirmation of 6 more victory claims; he had a total score of 48 Abschüsse).

60. The He 219 V14 *Uhu* carried a BMW 109-003 turbojet, used in the He 162 *Salamander* program, below the fuselage.

61. The He 219V-14 190014, of 3./NJG 1 was flown by *Oblt* Heinz Oloff, *Staffelkapitän*, 3./NJG 1, who had been shot down flying a He 219A-2 on New Year's Eve by F/L A. Paul Mellows-F/L S.L. 'Dickie' Drew. Oloff and his crew survived both the 1st and the 2nd time they were shot down by Mosquitoes.

62. 1 a/c was lost from the Bremen raid: Lancaster B.I (Special) PD117 of 617 Sqn was hit by flak from the railway-mounted flak battery 2./902, the aircraft exploding with tremendous force with its full bomb load on hitting the ground at Okel, S of Bremen, leaving a crater 40 meters wide. Only small fragments were found of the a/c and its 5-man crew, all of whom are commemorated on the Runnymede Memorial for the Missing of the RAF. The B.1 Special Lancaster had a crew of 5 instead of the usual 7.

63. *Hptm* Dieter Schmidt, commander of the 7th *Staffel* of NJG 1 scored his 40th and final kill; a Lancaster nr. Cologne at 0431 hrs (probably NG466 AR-Y of 460 Sqn RAAF, which had left Binbrook at 0111 hrs. 5 of the crew KIA and rest in Rheinberg War Cemetery). Only one other *Nachtjäger* (*Hptm* Kraft of 12./NJG 1) claimed a Lancaster nr. Bochum, for his 51st Abschuss. Fortress III HB803 (B-17G-40-VE 42-98033) BU-L of 214 Sqn flown by F/O P.J. Anderson was attacked by a Ju 88 and severely damaged by *Schräge Musik* cannon fire, which started fires in the fuselage and port wing. The rear gunner drove off their attacker and Anderson headed for friendly territory west of the Rhine but they were fired on again, this time by American anti aircraft gunners who opened up thinking the Fortress was a Me 262 before the crew abandoned the Fortress. Two men died. RAF Mosquitoes claimed 3 Bf 110s – to a 604 Sqn crew in NFXIII MM466/G in the Dhunn area; F/O R.I.E. Britten DFC RCAF-F/O L.E. Fownes DFC of 409 Sqn in a NFXIII and F/O K. Fleming-F/O K.L. Nagle of 488 Sqn in a NFXXX.

64. BXVI of 692 Sqn. W/O I.M. Macphee and Sgt A.V. Sullivan both KIA. NFXXX MM792 of 219 Sqn was shot down by *flak* over Venlo. F/L W.J. Henri and F/O H.P.F. Huyman, both Belgian, were KIA.

65. 195 Lancasters and 12 Mosquitoes of 5 and 8 Groups carried out the last raid on Wesel without loss.

66. F/L A.D. Wagner DFC-F/L E. T. Orringe of 605 Sqn a Ju 88 at Erfurt; F/L L.J. Leppard-F/L Houghton of 604 Sqn a Bf 109 at Haltern. F/L G.R. Leask-F/L J.W. Rolf of 410 Sqn a Bf 110 and S/L Maclavish-F/O Grant of 410 Sqn a Ju 88G.

67. F/O T.R. Wood-F/O R. Leafe of 604 Sqn, a Ju 88; F/L K.W. Stewart-F/O H.E. Brumby of 488 Sqn a Bf 110 8m NW Bocholt; F/L J.A.S. Hall DFC-P/O Taylor of 488 Sqn a Ju 88 20m N Emmerich (Mos Cr landed); F/O Reed-F/O Bricker of 219 Sqn a Ju 188; F/L B.E. Plumer DFC-F/L Bradford of 410 Sqn a Bf 110.

68. FBVI HR206/M. F/O R. Wilson and F/O F. Thompson were KIA.

69. An unusually high loss percentage, as the average losses usually only amounted to 0.99 % of the fast Berlin raiders.

70. Hudson, born in Kaponga, New Zealand on 16 November 1915, suffered from polio in early childhood which affected both his legs but he overcame this and in High School played 1st Class cricket and rugby and participated in cross-country runs to build up his stamina. (*571 Mosquito Sqn History* by Barry Blunt).

71. Becker's victim was FBVI MM131 XD-J of 139 Sqn, which had taken off from Upwood at 1912 hrs for Berlin. S/L H.A. Forbes DFC, the navigator/bomb aimer escaped and was taken prisoner but no trace has ever been found of his pilot, F/L André A.J. van Amsterdam, a Dutch escapee decorated with the DFC and the Dutch AFC. He is commemorated on panel 266 of the Runnymede Memorial.

72. Who after having served in 5./JG 301 as a Wild Boar pilot during the autumn and winter of 1943-44 flew daylight sorties against the American combat boxes in the summer of 1944. He destroyed a B-24 Liberator and was shot down by return fire and severely wounded. In February 1945 Lamm was fit for flying duties again and *Oblt* Kurt Welter asked him to join '*Kommando Welter*'.

73. On 30/31 March 4 Mosquitoes were claimed by II./NJG II: 2 by *Oblt* Welter. *Fw* Karl-Heinz Becker claimed a Mosquito at 2152 hrs and *Fw* Reichenbach claimed a Mosquito kill also. BXVI RV341 of 692 Sqn FTR (F/Sgt W. Campey and F/Sgt J. Rabiner RCAF lost w/o trace) from a raid on Berlin by 43 aircraft. On 31 March/1 April 1945 *Fw* Karl-Heinz Becker claimed a Mosquito at Tegel (Berlin). Only Mosquito lost this night was FBVI PZ394/C of 418 Sqn on patrol in the Zwolle area and MIA nr. Osnabrück. F/L G.K. Graham and F/O R.T. Styles KIA and were buried at Hoogeveen, Holland. A BXX of 139 Sqn FTR from Berlin on 2/3 April; F/L G.A. Nicholls DFC and F/L J.E. Dawes DFC both KIA.

74. BXX KB349. S/L T.R.A. Dow DFC (who was on his 90th op) and F/L J.S. Endersby both KIA.

75. Turner and Honeyman were 'new boys' who had joined the sqn in November when they were somewhat dazzled by the arrays of 'gongs' worn by aces such as Burbridge and Skelton and 'Ginger' Owen and McAllister (teams who finished the war with 21 and 15 victories respectively). They flew their *Freshman* op on the night of 29 December 1944 and would fly 17 ops together on the Mosquito. It was Turner's first tour as a pilot. He had been a gunner on Hampdens and had been shot down twice.

76. This was Kelsey and Smith's 4th victory in 100 Group and their 7th overall + 4 a/c destroyed on the ground and 1 'probable'. 3 Halifaxes and 3 Lancasters FTR from the Hamburg raid. Little damage resulted.

77. 3 *Experten* of NJG 5 each dispatched 1 Lancaster of the Lützkendorf force.

78. ML963 was abandoned after an engine fire en route to Berlin. F/O Richard D. Oliver and F/Sgt L. Max Young RAAF who were on their 6th op, baled out and landed on the west and east sides respectively of the River Elbe. Both crew evaded and returned to England. Oliver was a M/T driver in the RASC (Royal Army Service Corps) in France in 1940 and was evacuated from Dunkirk. He remustered in the RAF and completed pilot training in Tuscaloosa, Alabama in the Arnold Scheme. (*571 Mosquito Sqn History* by Barry Blunt).

79. BXXV KB502. F/O W. Hughton and F/Sgt L.A. Stegman RAAF both KIA.

80. Welter also made a claim for a Mosquito on 15 April when there were no RAF losses. On 17/18 April Welter made his final victory claim, a Mosquito, on a night when BXVI PF505 of 608 Sqn FTR from Berlin and another cr on t/o in England. (PF505 force-landed at Strassfeld a/f WSW of Bonn after the port engine failed after bombing. On touch down the u/c gave way and the a/c was wrecked. F/L G.C. Dixon RNZAF and F/O Smith safe).

81. LJ638 of 570 Sqn.

82. No records of German nightfighter claims on 12/13 April survives that could point to the identity of the claimant of LJ638.

83. Bomber Command carried out a raid on the *U-boat* yards at Kiel this night, 2 Lancasters were lost to *flak*. KB866 of 419 'Moose' Sqn RCAF cr. at 2315 hrs in a swamp, the Prinzenmoor, 20 km. SW of Rendsburg, exploding with its full bomb load on impact, the remains being swallowed by the swamp. The 7 Canadian crewmembers are still MIA.

84. 515 and 23 Sqns flew the first Mosquito Master Bomber sorties in 100 Group, dropping green TIs and orchestrating attacks by 18 Mosquitoes of 141 and 169 Sqns. Mosquitoes carrying Napalmgel bombs in the first of a series of operations code-named *Firebash*, attacked night-fighter airfields at Neuruppin nr Potsdam and Jüterborg nr Berlin. (Napalmgel is petrol thickened with a compound made from aluminium, naphthenic and palmitie acids hence 'napalm'. White phosphorous is added for ignition). The idea was borrowed from the U.S. 8th AF following a chance conversation in a 1st Class compartment of an English locomotive between W/C Charles V. 'Winnie' Winn DFC, 141 Sqn CO, en route to his station at West Raynham and a USAAF officer returning to his base in Norfolk. Winn was excited at the prospect of using this lethal weapon on enemy airfields. Before the day was out Winn had obtained permission to use his sqn to drop the gel in Mosquito 100-gallon drop tanks, providing he could obtain his own supplies. He made a call to the 8th AF and 40-gallon and 50-gallon drums of napalmgel soon began arriving at West Raynham, courtesy of the Americans. At first armorers, pumped it into drop tanks using hand pumps but then the Americans obliged with petrol-driven mechanical pumps and the operation became much easier.

85. Halifax III MZ467 Z5-C of 462 Sqn RAAF at Nordendorf, 12 km N of Gablingen at 0344 hrs. F/O A.M. Lodder RAAF was thrown clear and he and 2 of his crew were PoW. 5 KIA. *Oblt* Witzleb of III./NJG 1 claimed a Mosquito but none were lost.

86. Podge Howard fired 200 rounds (50 each gun) of 20mm on the sortie.

87. RS575/C.

88. The first was in 141 Sqn Beaufighter VIF V8744 on 23/24 December 1943 when they destroyed a Ju 88 near Düren.

89. JP299 of 58 Sqn, flown by F/L Arthur T.C. Wilmot-Dear DFC (21) off Skagen, Denmark at 0121 hrs during a search for the German vessel *Tübingen*. There were no survivors.

90. Bomber Support Development Unit.

91. *Mandrel* was an American jamming device and was used ahead of RAF night raids and U.S. 8th Air Force daylight raids.

92. During the napalmgel attack on Jägel F/O Robert Catterall DFC-F/Sgt Donald Joshua Beadle died when their Mosquito was shot down by *Flak.* During a run on Westerland, a Mosquito in 515 Sqn flown by F/L Johnson and F/O Thomason was hit but the pilot landed safely at Woodbridge on one engine. The two Halifaxes each with 8 men on board and carrying 4 500-lb bombs and large quantities of *Window* cr. at Meimersdorf, S of Kiel. Only P/O Les H. Currell, pilot of RG375/R who baled out with slight leg injuries and his rear gunner F/Sgt R. 'Jock' Hunter, survived while aboard RG373/T piloted by F/L William E. Brooks, only P/O K.N. Crane, rear gunner, survived.

93. Writing in *THE MARKER*, the journal of the Pathfinders.

APPENDICES

APPENDIX 1

BOMBER COMMAND BATTLE ORDER 5 JUNE 1944

Sqn	Station	Aircraft	Command
7	Oakington	Lancaster BI/III	Bomber
9	Bardney	Lancaster BI/III	Bomber
10	Leeming	Halifax	Bomber
12	Wickenby	Lancaster BI/III	Bomber
15	Mildenhall	Lancaster BI/III	Bomber
21	Gravesend	Mosquito FBVI	2nd TAF
35 'Madras Presidency'	Graveley	Lancaster BI/III	Bomber
44 'Rhodesia'	Dunholme Lodge	Lancaster BI/III	Bomber
49	Fiskerton	Lancaster BI/III	Bomber
50	Skellingthorpe	Lancaster BI/III	Bomber
51	Snaith	Halifax BIII	Bomber
57	East Kirkby	Lancaster BI/III	Bomber
61	Skellingthorpe	Lancaster BI/III	Bomber
69	Northolt	Wellington XIII	2nd TAF
75 RNZAF	Mepal	Lancaster BI/III	Bomber
76	Holme-on-Spalding Moor	Halifax BIII	Bomber
77	Full Sutton	Halifax BIII/IV	Bomber
78	Breighton	Halifax BIII/IV	Bomber
83	Coningsby	Lancaster BI/III	Bomber
85	Swannington	Mosquito NFXII/XVII	100 Group Bomber Cmd
88 'Hong Kong'	Hartford Bridge	Boston III/IIIa	Bomber
90	Tuddenham	Stirling III/Lancaster BI/III	Bomber
97 'Straits Settlements'	Coningsby	Lancaster BI/III	Bomber
98	Dunsfold	Mitchell II	2nd TAF
100	Grimsby	Lancaster BI/III	Bomber
101	Ludford Magna	Lancaster BI/III	Bomber
102 'Ceylon'	Pocklington	Halifax BIII/IIIa	Bomber
103	Elsham Wolds	Lancaster BI/III	Bomber
105	Bourn	Mosquito BIX/XVI	Bomber
106	Metheringham	Lancaster BI/III	Bomber
107	Lasham	Mosquito FBVI	Bomber

109	Little Staughton	Mosquito BIV/IX/XVI	Bomber
115	Witchford	Lancaster BI/III	Bomber
138	Tempsford	Halifax BII	Special Duties
139 'Jamaica'	Upwood	Mosquito BIV/IX/XVI/XX	Bomber
141	England	Mosquito NFII/FBVI/NFXXX	100 Group Bomber Cmd
156	Upwood	Lancaster BI/III	Bomber
157	Swannington	Mosquito NFXIX/NFXXX	100 Group Bomber Cmd
158	Lissett	Halifax BIII	Bomber
166	Kirmington	Lancaster BI/III	Bomber
419 'Moose' RCAF	Middleton St. George	Lancaster BX	6 Group Bomber Command
420 'Snowy Owl' RCAF	Tholthorpe	Halifax BIII	6 Group Bomber Command
424 'Tiger' RCAF	Skipton-on-Swale	Halifax BIII	6 Group Bomber Command
425 'Alouette' RCAF	Tholthorpe	Halifax BIII	6 Group Bomber Command
426 'Thunderbird' RCAF	Linton-on-Ouse	Halifax BIII	6 Group Bomber Command
427 'Lion' RCAF	Leeming	Halifax BV	6 Group Bomber Command
428 'Ghost' RCAF	Middleton St. George	Lancaster BX	6 Group Bomber Command
429 'Bison' RCAF	Leeming	Halifax BIII	6 Group Bomber Command
431 'Iroquois' RCAF	Croft	Halifax BIII/V	6 Group Bomber Command
432 'Leaside' RCAF	East Moor	Halifax BIII/V	6 Group Bomber Command
433 'Porcupine' RCAF	Skipton-on-Swale	Halifax BIII	6 Group Bomber Command
434 'Bluenose' RCAF	Croft	Halifax BIII/V	6 Group Bomber Command
460 RAAF	Binbrook	Lancaster BI/III	Bomber
463 RAAF	Waddington	Lancaster BI/III	Bomber
464 RAAF	Thorney Island	Mosquito FBVI	2nd TAF
466 RAAF	Leconfield	Halifax BIII	Bomber
467 RAAF	Waddington	Lancaster BIII	Bomber
487 RNZAF	Thorney Island	Mosquito FBVI	2nd TAF
514	Waterbeach	Lancaster BI/III	Bomber
515	Little Snoring	Mosquito FBVI	100 Group Bomber Cmd
550	North Killingholme	Lancaster BI/III	Bomber
571	Oakington	Mosquito BXVI	Bomber
576	Elsham Wolds	Lancaster BI/III	Bomber
578	Burn	Halifax B.III	Bomber
582	Little Staughton	Lancaster BI/III	Bomber
608 North Riding	Downham Market	Mosquito BXX	Bomber (formed Aug 1 44)
617	Woodhall Spa	Lancaster BI/III	Bomber
618	Skitten	Mosquito BIV	Bomber
619	Dunholme Lodge	Lancaster BI/III	Bomber
620	Fairford	Stirling IV	38 Group
622	Mildenhall	Lancaster BI/III	Bomber
625	Kelstern	Lancaster BI/III	Bomber
626	Wickenby	Lancaster BI/III	Bomber
627	Woodhall Spa	Mosquito BIV	Bomber
630	East Kirkby	Lancaster BI/III	Bomber
635	Downham Market	Lancaster BI/III	Bomber
640	Leconfield	Halifax BIII	Bomber
644	Tarrant Rushton	Halifax BV	ADGB
692 Fellowship of the Bellows	Graveley	Mosquito BIV/XVI	Bomber
1409 Met Flight	Oakington	Mosquito	Bomber Cmd

APPENDIX 2

INDIVIDUAL MOSQUITO FIGHTER/FIGHTER-BOMBER/BOMBER/PR SQUADRONS AND THE CONTINENT 1944-45

4	England	XVI/Spitfire XI	2nd TAF
21	England/Continent	FBVI	ADGB/2nd TAF
23	England	FBVI	To 100 Group May 44
25	England	FBVI/NFXVII	ADGB
29	England/Continent	NFXIII	ADGB/2nd TAF/ADGB
85	England	NFII/XII/FBVI/NFXV/XVII/XIX	Ftr Cmd. To 100 Group May 44
96	England	NFXIII	ADGB
105	England	BIX/XVI	8 (PFF)
109	England	BIV/IX/XVI	8 (PFF)
107	England/Continent	FBVI	138 Wing, 2 Group, 2nd TAF
125	England	NFXVII	ADGB
139	England	BIV/IX/XVI/XX	8 (PFF)
141	England	NFII	Ftr Cmd. To 100 Group 11.43
151	England	NFXIII	ADGB
157	England	NFII/FBVI/NFXIX/NFXXX	Ftr Cmd. To 100 Group May 1 44
169	England	NFII/FBVI/NFXIX	Ftr Cmd. To 100 Group 7 Dec 43
192	England	BIV/BXVI/Wellington X	100 Group
219	England/Continent	NFXVII	ADGB/2nd TAF
239	England	NFII	Ftr Cmd. To 100 Group Dec 43
264	England/Continent	NFXIII	ADGB/2nd TAF
305 *Ziemia Wielkopolska*	England/Continent	FBVI	138 Wing, 2 Group, 2nd TAF
307 City of Lvov' (Polish)	England	NFII/XII	ADGB
400 'City of Toronto'	England/Continent	XVI	39 (R) Wing, 83 Group, 2nd TAF
406 'Lynx' RCAF	England	NFXII/NFXXX	ADGB
409 'Nighthawk' RCAF	England/Continent	NFXIII	Ftr Cmd/148 Wing, 2nd TAF
410 'Cougar' RCAF	England/Continent	NFXIII/NFXXX	141 & 147 Wings, 2nd TAF
418 'City of Edmonton' RCAF	England/Continent	FBVI	136 Wing 2nd TAF

456 RAAF	England	NFII/FBVI/NFXVII/NFXXX	10 & 11 Groups Ftr Cmd
464 RAAF	England/Continent	FBVI	140 Wing 2 Group 2nd TAF
487 RNZAF	England/Continent	FBVI	140 Wing 2 Group 2nd TAF
488	England/Continent	NFXII/XIII/NFXXX	Ftr Cmd/ADGB/147 Wing 2nd TAF
515	England	FBVI	To 100 Group 15 Dec 43
540	England	BIX/XVI	106 PR Group
544	England	BIX/XVI	106 PR Group
571	England	BXVI	8 (PFF)
605	England/Continent	FBVI	ADGB/136 Wing, 2nd TAF
613	England/Continent	FBVI	138 Wing, 2 Group, 2nd TAF
604	England/Continent	NFXII/XIII	ADGB/141 Wing 2nd TAF
617	England	FBVI	5 Group
627	England	BIV	5 Group
692	England	BIV/XVI	8 (PFF)
8 OTU	Scotland	PRI/NFII/IV/VI/PRVIII	106 PR Group
1692 Flt	England	NFII	100 Group

APPENDIX 3

100 GROUP RAF (SPECIAL DUTIES LATER BOMBER SUPPORT) BATTLE ORDER

Sqn	Base	Aircraft	1st Op in 100 Group
141	West Raynham	Beaufighter VI Mosquito NFII/FBVI/NFXXX	December 1943
192	Foulsham	Mosquito NFII/BIV/BXVI/ Wellington BIII, Halifax III/V	December 1943
239	West Raynham	Mosquito NFII/FBVI/NFXXX	20 January 1944
515	Little Snoring/Great Massingham	Mosquito NFII/FBVI	3 March 1944
169	Little Snoring	Mosquito NFII/FBVI/NFXIX	20 January 1944
214	Sculthorpe/Oulton	Fortress II/III	20/21 April 1944
199	North Creake	Stirling III/ Halifax III	1 May 1944
157	Swannington	Mosquito NFXIX/NFXXX	May1944
85	Swannington	Mosquito NFXII/NFXVII	5/6 June 1944
23	Little Snoring	Mosquito FBVI	5/6 July 1944
223	Oulton	Liberator VI/Fortress II/III	cSept 1944
171	North Creake	Stirling II/ Halifax III	Sept 15 1944
462 RAAF	Foulsham	Halifax III	13 March 1945

APPENDIX 4

DISPOSITION OF NACHTJAGD JUNE 1944

Stab NJG 1	*Maj* Hans-Joachim Jabs	Bönninghardt	Bf 110/He 219
I./NJG 1	*Maj* Paul Förster	Venlo	Bf 110/He 219
II./NJG 1	*Hptm* Eckart-Wilhelm von Bonin	St. Trond	Bf 110
III./NJG 1	*Hptm* Martin Drewes	Twente/Leeuwarden	Bf 110/Ju 88G
IV./NJG 1	*Hptm* Heinz-Wolfgang Schnaufer	St. Trond	Bf 110
Stab NJG 2	*Obstlt* Günter Radusch	Coulommiers	Ju 88C
I./NJG 2	*Hptm* Ernst Zechlin	Eindhoven	Ju 88C/G
II./NJG 2	*Maj* Paul Semrau	Coulommiers	Ju 88C
III./NJG 2	*Maj* Bertold Ney	Langendiebach/Twente	Ju 88C/G
Stab NJG 3	*Obstlt* Helmut Lent	Stade	Ju 88C
I./NJG 3	*Maj* Werner Husemann	Vechta	Bf 110/Ju 88C
II./NJG 3	*Hptm* Klaus Havenstein	Plantlunne	Ju 88G
III./NJG 3	*Maj* Walter Barte	Stade	Bf 110
IV./NJG 3	*Hptm* Franz Buschmann	Westerland	Ju 88C/G?
Stab NJG 4	*Maj* Wolfgang Thimmig	Chenay	Bf 110/Ju 88C
I./NJG 4	*Maj* Wilhelm Herget	Florennes	Bf 110/Do 2l7/Ju 88
II./NJG 4	*Hptm* Gerhard Raht	Dijon	Bf 110
III./NJG 4	*Hptm* Hans-Karl Kamp	Juvincourt	Bf 110/Do 217/Ju 88
Stab NJG 5	*Obstlt* Walter Borchers	Laon-Athies	Bf 110
I./NJG 5	*Maj* Werner Hoffmann	St. Dizier	Bf 110
II./NJG 5	*Hptm* Hans Leickhardt	Gütersloh	Bf 110
III./NJG 5	*Maj* Paul Zorner	Laon-Athies	Bf 110
IV./NJG 5	*Hptm* Rudolf Altendorf	Mainz-Finthen	Bf 110
Stab NJG 6	*Maj* Heinrich Griese	Schleissheim	Bf 110
I./NJG 6	*Hptm* Heinz-Martin Hadeball	Neubiberg	Bf 110/Ju 88G
II./NJG 6	*Maj* Rolf Leuchs	Echterdingen	Bf 110
III./NJG 6	*Hptm* Leopold Fellerer	Hagenau	Bf 110
IV./NJG 6	*Maj* Herbert Lütje	Otopeni, Zilistea	Bf 110
I./NJG 7	*Maj* Bengsch	Handorf	Ju 88G
I./NJG 11	*Maj* Friedrich-Karl Müller	Lippstadt & Kothen	Bf 109G/Fw 190A *Wilde Sau**
I./NJG 100	*Hptm* Theodor Bellinghausen	various (Russia)	Ju 88
Stab NJG 101	*Maj* Herbert Sewing	Ingolstadt-Manching	Bf 110/Ju 88/Do 217
II./NJG 101	*Hptm* Schwab	Parndorf	Bf 110/Do 217

III./NJG 101	*Maj* Rolf Jung	Kitzingen	Bf 110/Do 2I7
Stab NJG 102	*Obstlt* Karl Theodor Hülshoff	Kitzingen	Bf 110
I./NJG 102	*Maj* Fehling	Powunden	Bf 110
II/NJG 102	*Hptm* Karl Floitgraf	Echterdingen	Bf 110
NJG 200	U/k	Various (Russia)	Bf 110/Ju 88/Fw 190
NJGr. 10	*Maj* Rudolf Schoenert	Werneuchen/Hangelar	Fw 190A

* Formed on 25 August and with Bonn-Hangelar as a forward base.
Note: *Wilde Sau Jagdgeschwadern* JG 300, 301 and 302 were by this time being employed mainly as day fighter/all weather units.

APPENDIX 5

BOMBER COMMAND VICTORIA CROSS RECIPIENTS

	Sqdn	A/c	Action/Award
Learoyd, Act Flight Lieutenant Roderick Alastair Brook, pilot.	49	Hampden	12.8.40 20.8.40
Hannah, Flight Sergeant John, WOP-AG	83	Hampden	15/16.9.40 1.10.40
Edwards, Acting Wing Commander Hughie Idwal DFC	105	Blenheim	4.7.41 22.7.41
Ward, Sergeant James Allen RNZAF, 2nd pilot	75	Wellington	7.7.41 5.8.41
Nettleton, Acting Squadron Leader John Dering, pilot	44	Lancaster	17.4.42 28,4.42
Manser, Flying Officer Leslie Thomas RAFVR pilot	50	Manchester	30/31.5.420.10.42*
Middleton, Flight Sergeant Rawdon Hume RAAF pilot	149	Stirling	28/29.11.42. 15.1.43*
Newton, Flight Lieutenant William Ellis RAAF			16.3.43
Gibson, Acting Wing Commander Guy Penrose DSO* DFC* pilot	617	Lancaster	16/17.5.43 28.5.43
Aaron, Flight Sergeant Arthur Louis DFM pilot	218	Stirling	12/13.8.43 5.1143*
Reid, Acting Flight Lieutenant William RAFVR pilot	61	Lancaster	3/4.11.43 14.12.43
Barton, Pilot Officer Cyril Joe RAFVR, pilot	578	Halifax	30/31.5.44 27.6.44*
Cheshire, Wing Commander Geoffrey Leonard DSO* DFC RAFVR pilot	617	Lancaster	8.9.44
Thompson, Flight Sergeant George RAFVR, WOp	9	Lancaster	1.1.45 20.2.45*
Palmer, Act Squadron Leader Robert Anthony Maurice DFC RAFVR pilot	109	Lancaster	23.12.44 23.4.45*
Swales, Capt Edwin DFC SAAF, 'master bomber'	582	Lancaster	23/24.2.45 24.4.45*
Bazalgette, Acting Squadron Leader Ian Willoughby DFC RAFVR 'master bomber'	635	Lancaster	4.8.44 17.8.45*
Jackson, Sergeant (later Warrant Officer) Norman Cyril RAFVR flight engineer	106	Lancaster	26/27.4.44 26.10.45
Trent, Squadron Leader Leonard Henry DFC RNZAF pilot	487	Ventura	3.5.43 1.3.46
Scarf, Squadron Leader Arthur Stewart King pilot	62	Blenheim	9.12.41 21.6.46*
Mynarski, Pilot Off Andrew Charles RCAF mid-upper gunner	419	Lancaster	12/13.6.44 11.10.46*

*Posthumous award

APPENDIX 6

THE 100 HIGHEST SCORING NACHTJAGD NIGHTFIGHTER ACES OF WORLD WAR II

1. *Major* Heinz-Wolfgang Schnaufer, 121 *Nachtjagd* victories (including 114 *Viermots*) in 164 sorties with NJG 1 and 4. *Ritterkreuz* with *Eichenlaub, Schwerter* and *Brillanten*. Died in car accident 13 July 1950.

2. *Oberst* Helmut Lent, 102 *Nachtjagd* victories (including 61 *Viermots* and 1 Mosquito) in 396 sorties with NJG 1, 2 and 3, plus 8 as *Zerstörer* in 3./ZG 76. *Ritterkreuz* with *Eichenlaub, Schwerter* and *Brillanten*. Died after landing accident at Paderborn 7 October 1944.

3. *Major* Heinrich Prinz *zu* Sayn-Wittgenstein, 83 *Nachtjagd* victories (including 23 on the Eastern Front) in 170 sorties with NJG 2, 3 and 5. *Ritterkreuz* with *Eichenlaub* and *Schwerter*. KIA 21/22 January 1944 by Lancaster return fire or by Mosquito E of Magdeburg.

4. *Oberst* Werner Streib, 67 *Nachtjagd* victories (including 30 *Viermots*) in 150 sorties with NJG 1, plus 1 as *Zerstörer* in I./ZG 1. *Ritterkreuz* with *Eichenlaub* and *Schwerter*. Died 15 June 1986 in Munich.

5. *Hptm* Manfred Meurer, 65 *Nachtjagd* victories (including 40 *Viermots* and two Mosquitoes) in 130 sorties with NJG 1 and 5. *Ritterkreuz* with *Eichenlaub*. KIA 21/22 January 1944 by debris from his final Lancaster victim 20 km E of Magdeburg.

6. *Oberst* Günter Radusch, 64 *Nachtjagd* victories (including 57 *Viermots*) in over 140 sorties with NJG 1, 2, 3 and 5, plus one victory in Spain with 2./Jgr.88. Another 14 of his *Nachtjagd* victories were allotted to other pilots. *Ritterkreuz* with *Eichenlaub*. Survived war, died 29 July 1988.

7. *Major* Rudolf Schoenert, 64 *Nachtjagd* victories (including 36 on the Eastern Front) in 376 sorties with NJG 1, 2, 5 and 100. *Ritterkreuz* with *Eichenlaub*. Survived war, died 30 November 1985 in Canada.

8. *Hptm* Heinz Rökker, 63 *Nachtjagd* victories (including 55 *Viermots* and one Mosquito), plus one in daylight in 161 sorties with NJG 2. *Ritterkreuz* with *Eichenlaub*. Survived war.

9. *Obstlt* Walter Borchers, 43 night and 16 day victories in NJG 1, 3 and 5, and ZG 76, KIA 5/6 March 1945, shot down by 239 Sqn Mosquito N of Altenburg.

10. *Major* Paul Zorner, 59 *Nachtjagd* victories in 110 sorties with NJG 2, 3, 5 and 100. Decorated with the *Ritterkreuz* with *Eichenlaub*. Survived war.

11. *Hptm* Martin Becker, 58 *Nachtjagd* victories (all *Viermots*) in 83 sorties with NJG 3, 4 and 6. *Ritterkreuz* with *Eichenlaub*. Survived war.

12. *Hptm* Gerhard Raht, 58 *Nachtjagd* victories (all but one *Viermots*) in 171 sorties with NJG 2 and 3. *Ritterkreuz* with *Eichenlaub*. Survived war, died 11 January 1977 in Rheinfeld/Holstein.

13. *Major* Wilhelm Herget, 58 *Nachtjagd* victories in NJG 3 and 4, plus 15 day victories in over 700 sorties. *Ritterkreuz* with *Eichenlaub*. Survived war, died 27 March 1974 in Munich.

14. *Oblt* Kurt Welter, 56 *Nachtjagd* victories in JG 301, 300, NJG 10 and NJG 11 (including 33 Mosquitoes), plus 7 day victories in 93 sorties. *Ritterkreuz* with *Eichenlaub*. Survived war, died in car crash 7 March 1949 at Leck/Schleswig-Holstein.

15. *Hptm* Heinz Strüning, 56 *Nachtjagd* victories in NJG 1 and 2 in 250 sorties, shot down by Mosquito of 157 Sqn and killed hitting tail unit of his Bf 110G-4 on baling out on 24/25 December 1944 near Bergisch-Gladbach. *Ritterkreuz* with *Eichenlaub*.

16. *Oblt* Gustav Eduard Francsi, 56 *Nachtjagd* victories in NJG 100 (including 49 on Eastern Front) in 150 sorties. *Ritterkreuz*. Survived war, drowned in Spain 6 October 1961.

17. *Major* Hans-Dieter Frank, 55 *Nachtjagd* victories in NJG 1. *Ritterkreuz* with *Eichenlaub*. KIA after colliding with other night fighter of *Stab* I./NJG 1 on landing NW of Celle 27/28 September 1943.

18. *Ofw* Heinz Vinke, 54 victories in NJG 1, *Ritterkreuz* with *Eichenlaub*, KIA 26 February 1944, shot down by 198 Sqn Typhoons.

19. *Hauptmann* August Geiger, 53 victories in NJG 1, *Ritterkreuz* with *Eichenlaub*, KIA 29 September 1943, shot down by Beaufighter of 141 Sqn in Ijsselmeer NW of Harderwijk.

20. *Major* Werner Hoffmann, 51 victories in NJG 3 and 5, plus 1 *Zerstörer* victories in ZG 2, *Ritterkreuz*, survived war.

21. *Major* Egmont Prinz *zur* Lippe-Weissenfeld, 51 victories in NJG 1 and 5, *Ritterkreuz* with *Eichenlaub*, KIA 12 March 1944 in flying accident near St. Hubert, Ardennes.

22. *Oberstleutnant* Herbert Lütje, 47 night and 3 day victories in NJG 1 and 6, *Ritterkreuz* with *Eichenlaub*, survived war.

23. *Hptm* Josef Kraft, 56 victories in NJG 1, 4, 5 and 6, *Ritterkreuz* with *Eichenlaub*, survived war.

24. *Hptm* Hermann Greiner, 47 day and 4 night victories in NJG 1 and 2, *Ritterkreuz* with *Eichenlaub*, survived war.

25. *Major* Martin Drewes, 43 night and 6 day victories in ZG 76, NJG 3 and NJG 1, *Ritterkreuz* with *Eichenlaub*, survived war.

26. *Obstlt* Hans-Joachim Jabs, 28 night and 22 day victories in ZG 76, NJG 3 and NJG 1, *Ritterkreuz* with *Eichenlaub*, survived war.

27. *Stfw* Reinhard Kollak, 49 night victories in NJG 1 and NJG 4, *Ritterkreuz*, survived war.

28. *Hptm* Ernst-Georg Drünkler, 45 night and 2 day victories in NJG 5, NJG 1, and NJG 3, *Ritterkreuz*, survived war.

29. *Hptm* Hans-Heinz Augenstein, 46 night victories in NJG 1, *Ritterkreuz*, KIA 6/7 December 1944, shot down by 85 Sqn Mosquito near Münster-Handorf.

30. *Hptm* Alois Lechner, 45 or 46 night victories in NJG 2, NJG 5 and NJG 100, MIA 23 February 1944, shot down by Russian Ack-ack, force-landed Brigade Leonow airfield.

31. *Major* Paul Semrau, 46 night victories in NJG 2 and NJG 6, *Ritterkreuz* with *Eichenlab*, KIA 8 February 1945, shot down by 402 Sqn Spitfire on landing at Twente airfield.

32. *Lt* Rudolf Frank, 45 night victories in NJG 3, *Ritterkreuz* with *Eichenlaub*, KIA 26/27 April 1944, crashed after being hit by debris from a 12 Sqn Lancaster.

33. *Oblt* Paul Gildner, 43 night and 2 day victories in ZG 1, NJG 1 and NJG 2, *Ritterkreuz* with *Eichenlaub*, KIA 24/25 February 1943 in failed forced landing near Gilze-Rijen airfield after engine failure.

34. *Hptm* Reinhold Knacke, 44 night victories in NJG 1, *Ritterkreuz* with *Eichenlaub*, KIA 3/4 February 1943 by return fire from 75 Sqn Stirling.

35. *Hptm* Ludwig Becker, 44 night victories in NJG 1 and NJG 2, *Ritterkreuz* with *Eichenlaub*, MIA 26 February 1943 N of Schiermonnikoog during daylight sortie.

36. *Hptm* Johannes Hager, 42 night victories in NJG 1, *Ritterkreuz*, survived war.

37. *Hptm* Werner Baake, 41 night victories in NJG 1, *Ritterkreuz*, survived war.

38. *Hptm* Leopold Fellerer, 39 night and 2 day victories in NJG 2, 1, 5 and NJG 6, *Ritterkreuz*, survived war.

39. *Oblt* Wilhelm Beier, 37 to 40 night victories in NJG 2 and NJG 1, *Ritterkreuz*, survived war.

40. *Hptm* Dietrich Schmidt, 40 night victories in NJG 1, *Ritterkreuz*, survived war.

41. *Major* Walter Ehle, 35 night and 4 day victories in ZG 1 and NJG 1, *Ritterkreuz*, KIA 17/18 November 1943 in crash at Horpmoel near St. Trond airfield.

42. Hptm Ludwig Meister, 38 night and 1 day victories in NJG 1 and NJG 4, *Ritterkreuz*, survived war.

43. *Hptm* Helmut Bergmann, 36 night victories in NJG 4, *Ritterkreuz*, KIA 6/7 August 1944 in area Avranches-Mortain, shot down by 604 Sqn Mosquito.

44. *Ofw* Günther Bahr, 35 night and 2 day victories in SKG 210, NJG 1, NJG 4 and NJG 6, *Ritterkreuz*, survived war.

45. *Ofw* Karl-Heinz Scherfling, 33 to 35 night victories in NJG 1 and NJG 2, *Ritterkreuz*, KIA 20/21 July 1944 near Mol, shot down by 169 Sqn Mosquito.

46. *Oblt* Günther Bertram, 35 night victories in *Nachtjagd Schwarm Luftflotte* 6 and NJG 100, *Deutsches Kreuz*, survived war.

47. *Major* Werner Husemann, 34 night victories in NJG 1 and NJG 3, *Ritterkreuz*, survived war.

48. *Hptm* Wilhelm Johnen, 34 night victories in NJG 1, 5 and 6, *Ritterkreuz*, survived war.

49. *Hptm* Ernst-Wilhelm Modrow, 34 night victories in NJG 1, *Ritterkreuz*, survived war.

50. *Hptm* Heinz-Horst Hissbach, 29 night and 5 day victories in KG 40 and NJG 2, *Ritterkreuz*, KIA 14/15 April 1945 near Gelnhausen, shot down by American ack-ack.

51. *Oblt* Klaus Bretschneider, 14 night and 20 day victories in JG 300, *Ritterkreuz*, KIA 24 December 1944 near Oberaula, Kassel area, in air combat with P-51 Mustangs.

52. *Hptm* Heinz-Martin Hadeball, 33 night victories in NJG 1, 4, 6 and NJG 10, *Ritterkreuz*, survived war.

53. *Major* Eckart-Wilhelm von Bonin, 32 night victories in NJG 1, *Ritterkreuz*, survived war.

54. *Major* Hubert Rauh, 31 night victories in NJG 1 and NJG 4, *Ritterkreuz*, survived war.

55. *Hptm* Hans Schmidt, 16 night and 15 day victories in ZG, NJG 3 and NJG 100, survived war.

56. *Lt* Josef Kociok, estimated to have scored 21 to 24 night victories and 9 to 12 night victories in SKG 210, ZG 1 and NJG 200, *Ritterkreuz*, KIA 26/27 September 1943 in collision with Russian DB-3.

57. *Hptm* Heinz Ferger, estimated to have scored 30 night victories in NJG 3 and NJG 2, KIA 13/14 or 14/15 April 1945, shot down near Lübeck airfield by Mosquito.

58. *Major* Friedrich-Karl Müller, 30 night victories in JG 300, NJGr 10 and NJG 11, *Ritterkreuz*, survived war.

59. *Major* Gerhard Friedrich, 30 night victories in NJG 1, 4 and NJG 6, *Ritterkreuz*, KIA 16/17 March 1945 near Bonlanen (nr. Stuttgart) in collision with 576 Sqn Lancaster.

60. *Major* Hans-Karl Kamp, estimated to have scored 28 night and 2 day victories in ZG 76, NJG 1, 4 and JG 300, KIA 31 December 1944 north of Hamburg.

61. *Hptm* Otto-Karl Klemenz, estimated to have scored 29 night victories in NJG 1 and NJG 5, survived war.

62. *Major* Heinrich Wohlers, 29 night victories in NJG 2, 1, 4 and NJG 6, *Ritterkreuz*, KIA 15 March 1944 in crash near Echterdingen airfield.

63. *Hptm* Eduard Schröder, 24 night and 5 day victories in NJG 3, survived war.

64. *Oblt* Erich Jung, 28 night victories in NJG 2, survived war.

65. *Hptm* Hans Krause, 28 night victories in NJG 3, NJG 101, *Ritterkreuz*, survived war.

66. *Ofw* Karl Maisch, estimated to have scored 28 night victories in NJG 5 and NJG 100, survived war.

67. *Hptm* Paul Szameitat, 28 night and 1 day victories in NJG 3, *Ritterkreuz*, KIA 1/2 January 1944 at Obernkirchen in air combat.

68. *Hptm* Fritz Lau, 28 night victories in NJG 1, *Ritterkreuz*, survived war.

69. *Hptm* Rudolf Altendorf, 24 night and 4 day victories in NJG 3, 4 and 5, *Deutsches Kreuz*, survived war.

70. *Lt* Heinz Grimm, 26 night and 1 day victories in NJG 1 and NJG 2, *Ritterkreuz*, died 13 October 1943 after being shot down by *flak* over Bremen four nights previously.

71. *Oblt* Lothar Linke, 24 night and 3 day victories in ZG 76, NJG 1 and NJG 2, *Ritterkreuz*, KIA 13/14 May 1943 near Lemmer due to engine failure.

72. *Hptm* Rudolf Sigmund, 25 night and 2 day victories in NJG 1, NJG 2 and NJG 3, *Ritterkreuz*, KIA 3/4 October 1943 at Fassberg SW Göttingen, probably shot down by *flak*.

73. *Oblt* Hans Gref, 24 or 25 night and 2 day victories in NJG 3, 5, 100 and NJG 1, *Deutsches Kreuz*, KIA January 1944, or 26 March 1944.

74. *Oblt* Josef Pützkuhl, 26 night victories in NJG 5 and NJG 100, survived war.

75. *Hptm* Alfons Köster, 25 night and 1 day victories in NJG 2, NJG 1 and NJG 3, *Ritterkreuz*, KIA 6/7 January 1945 near Varel in landing accident.

76. *Oblt* Walter Briegleb, 25 night victories in NJG 3 and NJG 2, *Deutsches Kreuz*, survived war.

77. *Hptm* Helmut Schulte, 25 night victories in NJG 5 and NJG 6, *Ritterkreuz*, survived war.

78. *Lt* Herbert Altner, 24 night and 1 day victories in NJG 3, NJG 5 and NJG 11, *Deutsches Kreuz*, survived war.

79. *Hptm* Rolf Bussmann, 24 night and 1 day victories in NJG 2, 3, 1 and NJG 5, *Deutsches Kreuz*, survived war.

80. *Oblt* Peter Erhardt, 24 night and 1 day victories in NJG 1, NJG 5 and NJG 11, survived war.

81. *Hptm* Fritz Söthe, 24 night and 1 day victories in NJG 4, KIA 28/29 September at Lambrecht-Neustadt, shot down by Mosquito.

82. *Hptm* Peter Spoden, 24 night and 1 day victories in NJG 5 and NJG 6, *Deutsches Kreuz*, survived war.

83. *Oblt* Reinhold Eckardt, 22 night and 3 day victories in ZG 76, NJG 1 and NJG 3, *Ritterkreuz*, KIA 29/30 July 1942 near Melsbroek in air combat with Lancaster.

84. *Ofw* Helmut Dahms, 24 night victories in NJG 100, survived war.

85. *Oblt* Klaus Scheer, 24 night victories in NJG 100, survived war.

86. *Ofw* Karl Strohecker, 24 night victories in NJG 5 and NJG 100, survived war.

87. *Ofw* Hermann Wischnewski, 16 or 17 night victories and 8 day victories in JG 300, *Ritterkreuz*, WIA 29 July 1944 in air combat at Gelbstadt.

88. *Hptm* Erhard Peters, 22 night & 2 day victories in NJG 3, KIA 19/20 February 1944 at Brandenburg-Briest, shot down by Wild Boar night fighter.

89. *Ofw* Wilhelm Glitz, estimated to have scored 23 night victories in NJG 2, *Deutsches Kreuz*, survived war.

90. *Hptm* Dr. Horst Patuschka, 23 night victories in NJG 2, *Ritterkreuz*, KIA 6/7 March 1943 near Bizerta/Tunesia in flying accident.

91. *Ofw* Ernst Reitmeyer, 23 night victories in NJG 5, survived war.

92. *Ofw* Hans Schadowski, 23 night victories in NJG 3, survived war.

93. *Ofw* Rudolf Mangelsdorf, 19 night and 4 day victories in NJG 3 and NJG 2, survived war.

94. *Oblt* Helmut Woltersdorf, 15 night and 8 day victories in ZG 76 and NJG 1, KIA 1/2 June 1942 in crash at Twente airfield, shot down by 3 Sqn Hurricane.

95. *Major* Wolfgang Thimmig, 22 night and 1 day victories in NJG 1, 2, 3, 4 and NJG 101, survived war.

96. *Oblt* Jakob Schaus, 21 night and 2 day victories in NJG 4, WIA 2/3 February 1945 at Rockenhausen/Pfalz, shot down by intruder.

97. *Hptm* Herman Leube, 22 night victories in NJG 3, KIA 27/28 or 28/29 December in crash-landing at Reeuwijk near Gouda.

98. *Hptm* Franz Brinkhaus, 21 night victories in NJG 1 and NJG 2, survived war.

99. *Hptm* Werner Hopf, 21 night victories in NJG 1 and NJG 5, survived war.

100. *Hptm* Hans Autenrieth, 22 night victories in NJG 1 and NJG 4, PoW 6 August 1944 N.E. Rennes.

APPENDIX 7

GERMAN RANKS AND THEIR EQUIVALENTS

German Ranks	U.S. equivalent	RAF Equivalent
Reichsmarschall	no equivalent	no equivalent
Generalfeldmarschall	General (5-Star)	
Generaloberst	General (4-Star)	
General der Flieger	Lieutenant General	
Generalleutnant	Major General	
Generalmajor	Brigadier General	
Oberst	Colonel	Group Captain (G/C)
Oberstleutnant (Obstlt)	Lieutenant Colonel	Wing Commander (W/C)
Major	Major	Squadron Leader (S/L)
Hauptmann (Hptm)	Captain	Flight Lieutenant (F/L)
Oberleutnant (Oblt)	1st Lieutenant	Flying Officer (F/O)
Leutnant (Lt)	2nd Lieutenant	Pilot Officer (P/O)
Stabsfeldwebel (StFw)	Flight Officer	Warrant Officer (W/O)
Oberfähnrich (Ofhr)	no equivalent	no equivalent
Oberfeldwebel (Ofw)	Master Sergeant	Flight Sergeant
Fähnrich (Fhr)	Officer candidate	no equivalent
Feldwebel (Fw)	Sergeant	Sergeant
Unteroffizier (Uffz)	Staff Sergeant	Corporal
Obergefreiter (Ogfr)	Corporal	Leading Aircraftsman (LAC)
Gefreiter (Gefr)	Private First Class	Aircraftsman 1 (AC1)
Flieger (Flg)	Private Second Class	Aircraftsman 2 (AC)

APPENDIX 8

RAF SLANG TEMS IN COMMON USE

A 48: A 48-hour leave of absence.
Adj: Adjutant.
Bang-on: Something very good or very accurate.
Battle Bloomers: WAAF Issue Knickers – name originally given to them by the WAAFs themselves.
Best Blue: Best uniform.
Big City, The: Berlin.
Binding: Moaning, Complaining.
Bird Sanctuary: WAAF quarters – usually well away from the rough airmen!
Blood Wagon: Ambulance.
Bods: People, Bodies.
Bought it: Killed, failed to return.
Cheese Cutter: Peaked Cap.
Cheesed or Cheesed Off: Fed up, bored.
Chiefy: Head of Aircraft Ground Crew – generally well respected.
Clapped Out: Worn out, well past its best
Cookie: 4000lb Bomb.
Crate: Aircraft.
Dicey: Dangerous. A dicey do. An op when there was heavy opposition.
Dicing (Dicing with death): Mainly operational flying but sometimes, just flying. Are we dicing tonight? Are we on the Battle Order?
Ditch: To land in the Drink.
Drink: The sea.
Duff Gen: Bad information.
Erks: Aircraftsmen – usually reserved for the lowest.
Fans: Propeller on aircraft. No fans – no engines.
On a Fizzer: On a charge in front of senior.
Flight: A Flight Sergeant.
Flight Offices: usually occupied by the CO, Flight Commanders and their slaves.
Flights: Where aircrew collected particularly on operational squadrons while waiting for the 'gen'. Cards and other games of chance were played here. More generally, any place around hangers where matters connected with flying took place.
Flying orifice: Observers Brevet – the polite versions.
Fruit Salad: Lots of medal ribbons particularly on Americans.
Get weaving: Get a move on – from aircraft taking avoiding action from fighters.
Getting finger out: extracting the digit. Originally RAF slang term now in common use. In RAF it implied sitting on ones hands – politely.
Going like the Clappers: moving very fast indeed.
Gone for a Burton: these terms were always used when anyone failed to return. Killed. Failed to return. It was never said that 'old so and so was killed last night'.
Gong: Medal.
Good Show: did well.
Got the chop: killed.
Got the Gen: have got the true information.
Gremlin: A mythical mischievous creature invented by the RAF, to whom is attributed the blame for anything that goes wrong in the air or on the ground. There are different sorts of gremlins skilled in different sorts and grades of evil. The origin of the term is obscure, but has been stated variously to go hack as far as the Royal Naval Air Service; to have some connection with the RAF in Russia and the Kremlin; and to have come from India, where, it is alleged, in the early 1920s an officer was opening a bottle of Fremlin's Ale when the overheated gas blew out the cork, taking him by surprise. Meaning to say, 'A goblin has jumped out of my Fremlin's', he spoonerised and said: 'A gremlin has jumped out of my Foblin's'. In his book *It's a Piece of Cake! RAF Slang Made Easy* (Sylvan Press, c.1942).
Had it: something coming to its end. For a person – 'He's had it' – he's died or is likely to.
Hairy: dangerous or very exiting.
Happy Valley: the Ruhr.
Kite: Aircraft.
Meat Wagon: Ambulance.
Milk Run: Regular run (USAAF equivalent – 'easy mission').
Passion Bafflers: WAAF Issue Knickers – name originally given to them by the WAAFs themselves.
Penguin: Non aircrew – often used for someone not popular.
A Piece of Cake: Very Easy.
Poor Show: Bad behaviour. Not done well.

Prang: a crash, usually of aircraft. To prang – to crash or to prang a target – to hit it well. A wizard prang – a good raid.
Queen Bee: WAAF Commanding Officer.
Scrambled Egg: Gold on caps of Senior Officers.
Second Dickey: Second Pilot.
Shaky do: Near miss or lucky escape.
Shoot a line: to brag, enlarge, blow ones own trumpet.
Sky Pilot: padre.
Snappers: Enemy Fighters.
Spot On: Something very good or very accurate.
Sprogs: New recruits.
A stooge: A boring flight.
Stooge Around: Loiter. Hang around, fly around waiting for happening.
Stores Basher: Someone who worked in Stores.
Suffering from the Twitch: (particularly pilots), – To be avoided at all costs.
10/10ths: complete cloud cover.
Twitch: Nervy. Bags of twitch' – suffered when in danger particularly from fighters.
Waafery: WAAF quarters – usually well away from the rough airmen!
Winco: Wing Commander usually Squadron Commanding Officer.
Wingless Wonder: Usually very unpopular non-aircrew.

GLOSSARY

*: (Medal) and Bar (second award of the medal specified)
A/c: abbreviation for aircraft
AA: Anti-Aircraft
AAA: Anti-Aircraft Artillery
Abschuss: Claim for a victory in air combat
Abschüsse: Claims for victories in air combat
Abschussbeteiligung: Contribution to a claim for a victory in air-combat
AF: Air Force
AFC: Air Force Cross
AI: Airborne Interception (radar)
Alarmstart: 'Scramble'
AM: Air Marshal
Anerkannter Abschuss: Officially confirmed air-combat victory claim
AOC: Air Officer Commanding
ASH: AI Mk.XV narrow-beam radar used for low-level operations
ASR: Air-Sea Rescue
ATS: Air Training Squadron
AVM: Air Vice-Marshal

BBC: British Broadcasting Corporation
BEM: British Empire Medal
BG: Bomb Group (USAAF)
Blip: Radar echo or response
BM: *Bordmechaniker* (flight engineer) (German)
Bogey: Unidentified aircraft
Bordfunker* or *Funker: German Radar/radio operator
BS: Bomb Squadron (USAAF)
BSDU: Bomber Support Development Unit (RAF)

Capt: Captain
CCU: Combat Crew Unit
Chaff: American *Window*
CO: Commanding Officer
CoG: Centre of Gravity
Col: Colonel
cr.: abbreviation for crashed
CRT: Cathode Ray Tube
C-scope: CRT showing frontal elevation of target

Day Ranger: Operation to engage air and ground targets within a wide but specified area, by day
DCM: Distinguished Conduct Medal
Deutsches Kreuz (DK): German Cross
'Dicke Autos': 'Fat Cars' (Four engined heavy bombers)
DFC: Distinguished Flying Cross
DFM: Distinguished Flying Medal
Diver: V-1 flying bomb operation
Drem lighting: System of outer markers and runway approach lights
DSC: Distinguished Service Cross
DSO: Distinguished Service Order
Düppel: German codename for *Window* after a town near the Danish border where RAF metal foil strips were first found.

e/a: Enemy Aircraft
Eichenlaub (El): (Knight's Cross with) Oak Leaves
Einsatz: Operational flight
Eisernes Kreuz I, II (EK I, EK II): Iron Cross (1st and 2nd Class)
Emil Emil: German codename for AI
Ergänzungsgruppe (EGr): Replacement or complement wing
ETA: Estimated Time of Arrival
Experte(n): Expert. An ace/aces (five or more confirmed victories)
Express-Express: German R/T code for 'hurry up'

FF: *Flugzeugführer* (pilot)
F/L: Flight Lieutenant
F/O: Flying Officer
F/Sgt: Flight Sergeant
Fähnrich (Fhr): Flight Sergeant
Feindberührung: Contact with an enemy aircraft
Feldwebel (Fw): Sergeant
FIDO: Fog Investigation and Dispersal Operation
Firebash: 100 Group Mosquito sorties using incendiaries/napalm against German airfields
Flak (*Flieger Abwehr Kanone(n)*: Anti-Aircraft Artillery
Flensburg: German device to enable their night fighters to homeon to *Monica*
FNSF: Fast Night Striking Force
Freelance: Patrol with the object of picking up a chance contact or visual of the enemy

FTR: abbreviation for failed to return
Führer: Leader

G/C: Group Captain
GCI: Ground Control Interception (radar)
Gee: British medium-range navigational aid using ground transmitters and an airborne receiver
Gen: General
General der Flieger: Air Marshal
Generalfeldmarschall: Marshal of the Air Force
Generalleutnant: Air Vice-Marshal
Generalmajor: Air Commodore
Generaloberst: Air Chief Marshal
Geschwader: Roughly equivalent to three RAF wings. Comprises three or four *Gruppen* Gruppe containing three or four *Staffeln*, eg: *IV./NJG1* (the fourth *Gruppe* in *Nachtjagd Geschwader* 1), *12./NJG1* (the *12th Staffel* (in the fourth *Gruppe*) of *Nachtjagd Geschwader* 1)
GP: General Purpose bomb
Gruppenkommandeur: Commander or Captain, a Gruppe command position rather than a rank

H2S: British 10-cm experimental airborne radar navigational and target location aid
Hauptmann (Hptm): Flight Lieutenant
HE: High Explosive (bomb)
HEI: High Explosive Incendiary
'Heavies': RAF/USAAF four-engined bombers
Helle Nachtjagd: illuminated night fighting
Herausschuss: Claim for a bomber shot out of formation
HMS: His Majesty's Ship
Horrido!: German for 'Tallyho'
HRH: His Royal Highness

IAS: Indicated Air Speed
IFF: Identification Friend or Foe
Intruder: Offensive night operation to fixed point or specified target
IO: Intelligence Officer

***Jagdbomber** (Jabo)*: Fighter-bomber
Jagdgeschwader (JO): Fighter wing, includes three or four *Gruppen*
Jagdwaffe: Fighter Arm or Fighter Force
Jager: Fighter
Jägerleitoffizier: JLO, or GCI-controller

***Kampfgeschwader** (KG)*: Bomber Group
Kommandeur: Commanding officer of a *Gruppe*
Kommodore: Commodore or Captain, a *Geschwader* command position rather than a rank
KüFlGr: *Küstenfliegergruppe*: Coastal Flying Wing (German)
Kurier: R/T code for 'Allied heavy bomber'

LAC: Leading Aircraftsman
***Leutnant** (Lt)*: Pilot Officer
Lichtenstein: Early form of German Al radar
LMF: Lack of Moral Fibre
LNSF: Light Night Striking Force
LORAN: Long-Range Navigation
Lt Cmdr: Lieutenant Commander
Lt Col: Lieutenant Colonel
Lt: Lieutenant
Luftflotte: Air Fleet (German)
***Luftwaffe** (LW)*: Air Force

M/T*:* Motor Transport
Mahmoud: (British) High-level bomber support sortie
Maj Gen: Major General
Maj: Major
Major: (German) Squadron Leader
Mandrel: American airborne radar jamming device
***Maschinen Gewehr** (MG)*: Machine gun
***Maschinen Kanone** (MK)*: Machine cannon
MC: Medium Capacity bomb
MCU: Mosquito Conversion Unit
Met.: Meteorological
MiD: Mention In Dispatches
Monica: British active tail warning radar device
MTU: Mosquito Training Unit

Nachtjagdgeschwader: *(NJG)* Night fighter Group
Nachtjäger: Nightfighter
NCO: Non-Commissioned Officer
NFS: Night Fighter Squadron
Night Ranger: Operation to engage air and ground targets within a wide but specified area, by night
Noball: Flying bomb (V-1) or rocket (V-2) site
nr.: Abbreviation for near

OBE: Order of the British Empire
***Oberfähnrich** (Ofhr)*: Warrant Officer
***Oberfeldwebel** (Ofw)*: Flight Sergeant
***Oberleutnant** (Oblt)*: Flying Officer
***Oberst** (Obst)*: Group Captain
***Oberstleutnant** (Obstlt)*: Wing Commander
Objektnachtjagd: Target Area Night Fighting
Oboe: Ground-controlled radar system of blind bombing in which one station indicated track to be followed and another the bomb release point
Op: Operation (mission)
OSS: Office of Strategic Services. The US intelligence service activated during the Second World War and disbanded on 1 October 1945
OT: Operational Training
OTU: Operational Training Unit

P/O*:* Pilot Officer
Pauke! Pauke!: *'Kettledrum! Kettledrum!'* (R/T code for 'Going into attack!')
PFF: Path Finder Force
PoW: Prisoner of War
PR: Photographic Reconnaissance
PRU: Photographic Reconnaissance Unit
R/T: Radio Telephony

RAAF: Royal Australian Air Force
RAE: Royal Aircraft Establishment
RAFVR: Royal Air Force Volunteer Reserve
RCAF: Royal Canadian Air Force
RCM: Radio CounterMeasures

***Reflex Visier** (Revi)*: Gunsight
***Reichsluftfahrtministerium** (RLM)*: German Air Ministry
Reichs(luft)verteidigung: Air Defence of Germany
***Ritterkreuz** (träger) (RK/RKT)*: Knight's Cross (holder)
RN: Royal Navy
RNorAF: Royal Norwegian Air Force
RNVR: Royal Naval Volunteer Reserve
Rotte: Tactical element of two aircraft
Rottenflieger: Wingman, the second man in the *Rotte*
RP: Rocket Projectile

S/L: Squadron Leader
SAAF: South African Air Force
SAS: Special Air Service
SASO: Senior Air Staff Officer
***Schlachtgeschwader** (SG)*: Ground attack Group
Schräge Musik: 'Slanting Music'; night fighters' guns firing upwards
Schwarm: Flight of four aircraft
Schwarmführer: Flight leader
***Schwerten** (S)*: (Knight's Cross with Oak Leaves and) Swords
SD: Special Duties
Serrate: British equipment designed to home in on Lichtenstejn AI radar.
***SKG**: Schnelles Kampfgeschwader*: Fast Bomber Group (German)
SOE: Special Operations Executive
Stab: Staff flight
Staffel: Roughly equivalent to a squadron, designated sequentially within the *Geschwader* by Arabic figures, eg: *4./NJG1*
***Staffelkapitän** (St.Kpt)*: Captain, a *Staffel* command position rather than a rank
Sub/Lt: Sub-Lieutenant

TIs: Target Indicators
TNT: TriNitroToluene
***Transportgeschwader** (TO)*: Transport Group

UEA: Unidentified Enemy Aircraft
U/S: Unserviceable
UHF: Ultra-High Frequency
***Uhu**: 'Owl'* Heinkel He 219 night fighter aircraft
Unteroffizier: (Uffz) Corporal
USAAF: United Sates Army Air Force

VC: Victoria Cross
VHF: Very High Frequency
***Viermot** (4-mot)*: Four-engined bomber abbreviation of *viermotorig* – four engined.
Viktor: R/T code for 'have received and understood message'

W/C: Wing Commander
W/O: Warrant Officer
WAAF: Women's Auxiliary Air Force
***Wilde Sau**: 'Wild Boar'*: Free-lance night fighting, originally by single-engined aircraft, mainly over the RAF's target, relying on freelance interceptions from a running commentary aided by the lights from fires and from searchlights
***Window**:* Metal foil strips dropped by bombers to confuse German radar

Y-Service: *Ypsilon*, *Y-Verfahren*, ***Ypsilonverfahren***: *Luftwaffe* ground-controlled navigation by means of VHF

***Zahme Sau**: 'Tame Boar'*: Tactic of feeding German twin-engined fighters into the bomber stream as soon as its track was properly established on the way to or from the target, and by means of broadcast running commentary on situation in the air
Zerstörer: 'Destroyer', heavy twin-engined fighter-bomber aircraft (Bf 110/210/410)
***Zerstörergeschwader** (ZG)*: Bf 110 unit roughly equivalent to four RAF squadrons (*Geschwader* consisted of 100-120 a/c; each *Geschwader* had a *Geschwader Stab* and three or four *Gruppen*, with 25 to 35 a/c each; each *Gruppe* had three *Staffeln* of ten a/c each).
Zweimot: Twin-engined aircraft

BIBLIOGRAPHY

Gebhard Aders, *Geschichte der deutschen Nachtjagd 1917-1945* (Stuttgart 1978)

Anonymous, Extract from *I. Jagdkorps War Diary, 15.9.43 to 20.5.44* (ADIK Report No. 416/1945, at National Archives, Washington DC, USA)

Michael Balss, *Deutsche Nachtjagd. Personalverluste in Ausbildung und Einsatz -fliegendes Personal* (Eich 1997)

Jack Bennett, *Jack's Wartime RAF. Exploits* (privately published Biggleswade 1997)

Herbert Bethke & Friedhelm Henning, *Jagdgeschwader 300. The Wild Huntsman* (Volume 1, 2000)

Theo Boiten, *Nachtjagd. The night fighter versus bomber war over the Third Reich 1939-1945* (Crowood Press Ramsbury, Marlborough 1997)

Theo Boiten, *Bristol Blenheim* (Crowood Press Ramsbury, Marlborough 1998)

Theo Boiten, *Night Airwar. Personal recollections of the conflict over Europe, 1939-1945* (Crowood Press Ramsbury, Marlborough 1999)

Martin W. Bowman & Theo Boiten, *Raiders of the Reich. Air Battle Western Europe: 1942-1945* (Shrewsbury 1996)

Martin W. Bowman, *The Men Who Flew The Mosquito* (Pen & Sword 2003)

Martin W. Bowman *Moskitopanik!* (Pen & Sword 2004)

Martin W. Bowman *Wellington The Geodetic Giant.* (Airlife 1998)

Martin W. Bowman *Confounding the Reich* (Pen & Sword 2004)

Martin W. Bowman *Mosquito Fighter.Fighter-Bomber Units of WW2.* (Osprey 1998)

Martin W. Bowman *Mosquito Bomber/Fighter-Bomber Units of WW2.* (Osprey 1998)

Martin W. Bowman *RAF Bomber Stories.* (PSL 1998)

Chaz Bowyer, *The Wellington Bomber* (London 1986)

Chaz Bowyer, *For Valour. The Air VCs* (London 1992)

W. R. Chorley, *To see the dawn breaking. 76 Squadron operations* (Ottery St. Mary 1981)

W. R. Chorley, *In Brave Company. 158 Squadron operations* (Salisbury 1990)

W. R. Chorley, *Royal Air Force Bomber Command Losses of the Second World War* (six vol, Midland Counties Leicester 1992-1998)

Coen Cornelissen, *Van Grasmat tot Fliegerhorst* (Oldenzaal 1998).

Alan W. Cooper, *Bombers over Berlin. The RAF offensive, November 1943-March 1944* (PSL Wellingborough 1989)

Wolfgang Dierich, *Die Verbände der Luftwaffe 1935-1945* (Stuttgart 1976)

Jonathan Falconer, *Stirling at War* (London 1991)

John Foreman, Johannes Matthews, Simon Parry, *Luftwaffe Night-Fighter Combat Claims 1939-45* (Red Kite. 2004)

Norman L. R. Franks, *Forever Strong. The Story of 75 Squadron RNZAF 1916-1990* (Auckland 1991)

Norman L. R. Franks, *Claims To Fame: The Lancaster.* (Arms And Armour. London, 1994)

Norman L. R. Franks, *RAF Fighter Command Losses of the Second World War.* Vol.3. 1944-45. (Midland Publishing 2000)

Roger A. Freeman, *Raiding the Reich. The Allied Strategic Bombing Offensive in Europe* (London 1997)

Mike Garbett and Brian Goulding, *The Lancaster at War* (Ian Allan London 1971)

Bryce B. Gomersall, *The Stirling File* (Tonbridge 1987)

Alex H. Gould DFC, *Tales from the Sagan Woods* (Bundanoon 1994)

J. J. Halley, *The Lancaster File* (Tonbridge 1985)

Werner Held and Holger Nauroth, *Die deutsche Nachtjagd. Bildchonik der deutschen Nachtjäger bis 1945* (Stuttgart 1982)

Georg Hentschel, *Die geheimen Konferenzen des General-Luftzeugmeisters* (Koblenz 1989)

Peter Hinchliffe, *The Other Battle. Luftwaffe night aces versus Bomber Command.* (Airlife Shrewsbury 1996)

Harry Holmes, *Avro Lancaster, The Definitive Record.* (Airlife Shrewsbury 2001)

Ab A. Jansen, *Wespennest Leeuwarden* (3 Vols) (Baarn 1976-1978)

Werner Kock, *Das Kriegstagebuch des Nachtjagdgeschwaders 6* (Wittmund 1996)

Michel Marszalek, *L'Odyssée du Halifax DT 775.* Anoux - 11/04/43 (private publication, Woippy 1995)

Merrick, K. A. *The Handley Page Halifax* (Aston 1990)

Martin Middlebrook, *The Nuremberg Raid* (London 1973)

Martin Middlebrook & Chris Everitt, *The Bomber Command War Diaries.* An operational reference book, 1939-1945 (Harmondsworth 1985)

Martin Middlebrook, *The Berlin Raids* (London 1988)

Harry Moyle, *The Hampden File* (Tonbridge 1989)

Holger Nauroth & Werner Held, *Messerschmitt Bf 110 Zerstörer an allen Fronten 1939-1945* (Stuttgart 1978)

Heinz J. Nowarra, *'Uhu' He 219, best night fighter of World War II* (West Chester 1989)

Simon W. Parry, *Intruders over Britain. The Luftwaffe Night Fighter Offensive 1940-45* (Surbiton 1987)

Richard Pape, *Boldness Be My Friend.* (Elek 1953)

Brian Philpott, *RAF Bomber Units 1939-1945* (2 Vols) (London 1977-1978)

Mark Postlethwaite *Lancaster Squadrons In Focus.* (Red Kite 2002)

Ron Pütz, Duel in de Wolken. *De luchtoorlog in de gevarendriehoek Roermond-Luik-Aken* (Amsterdam 1994)

Rapier, Brian J. *Halifax At War* (Ian Allan Ltd, 1987)

John D. Rawlings, *Fighter Squadrons of the RAF. and their aircraft* (Macdonald & Janes London 1978)

Robert S. Raymond, *A Yank in Bomber Command.* (Pacifica Press 1998)

Ron Read DFC *'If You can't take a joke' An Every night story of bomber folk.'* (Snell Print 1995)

Roland Remp, *Heinkel He 219: An Illustrated History of Germany's Premier Nightfighter.* (Schiffer2000)

Hans Ring & Werner Girbig, *Jagdgeschwader 27. Die Dokumentation über den Einsatz an allen Fronten 1939-1945* (Stuttgart 1994)

Anthony Robinson, *Night Fighter. A concise history of nightfighting since 1914* (London 1988)

Heinz Rökker, *Chronik I. Gruppe Nachtjagdgeschwader 2* (Zweibrücken 1997)

Major Heinz-Wolfgang Schnaufer, *Nachtjagd Leistungsbuch* (book of night-fighting achievements, unpublished)

Jerry Scutts, *Luftwaffe Night Fighter Units 1939-1945* (London 1978)

C. Martin Sharp & Michael J.F. Bowyer, *Mosquito* (London 1971)

J. R. Smith & Antony L. Kay, *German aircraft of the Second World War* (London 1972)

Martin Streetly, *Confound and Destroy.* (Macdonald and Jane's, London, 1978)

Christiaan Vanhee and Peter Celis, *Vinnige Valken, Vlammende Bliksems. De Vliegbasis van Sint-Truiden 1941-1945* (Luxembourg 2000)

Edwin Wheeler DFC *Just to Get a Bed* (privately published 1990)

Dennis A. Wiltshire, *Per Ardua Ad Infinitum* (unpublished autobiography, Filton 1999)

INDEX